KEY TO WORLD MAP PAGES

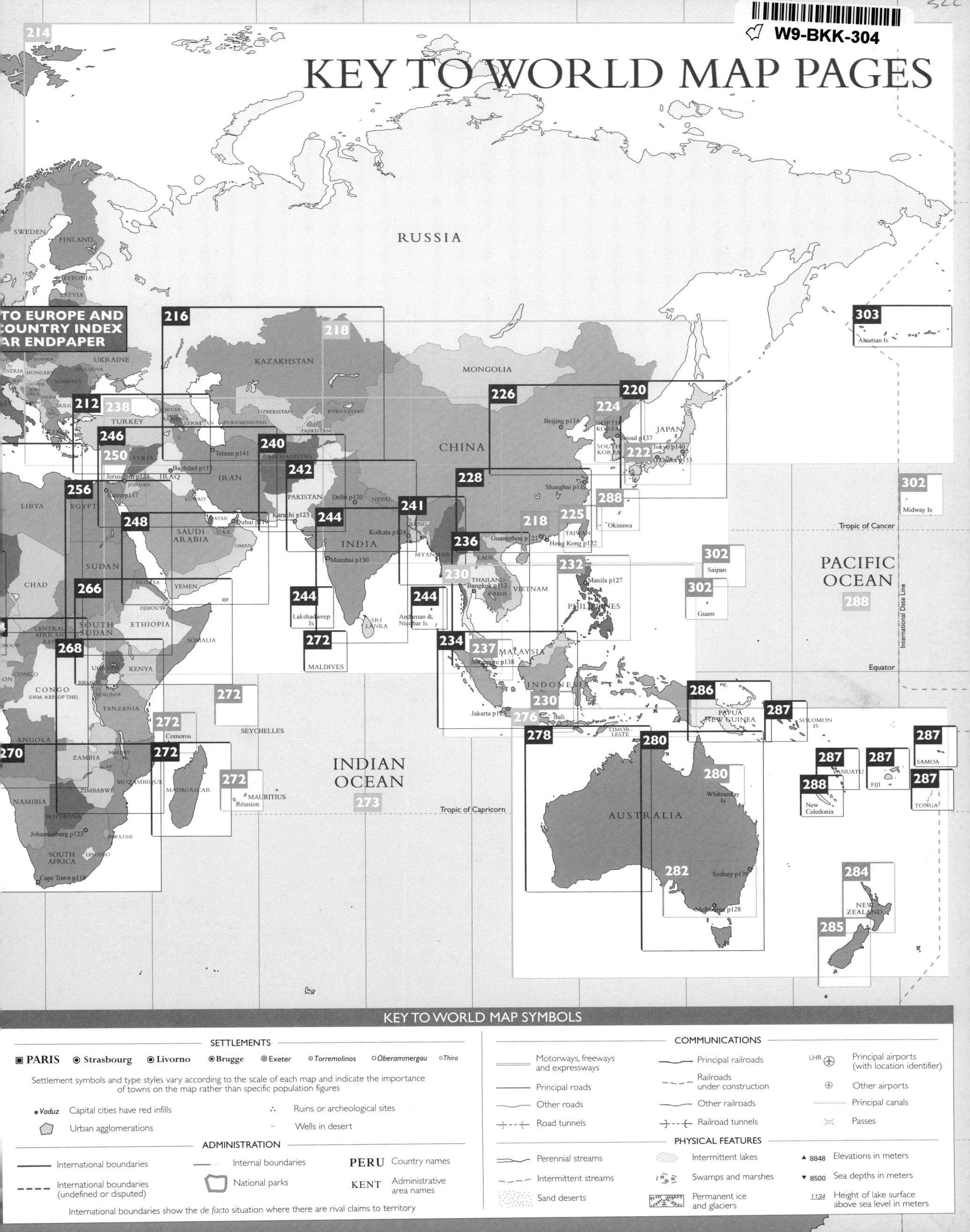

W9-BKK-304

214

303 Aleutian Is

216

218

**TO EUROPE AND
COUNTRY INDEX
AR ENDPAPER**

SWEDEN

FINLAND

ESTONIA

LATVIA

RUSSIA

KAZAKHSTAN

MONGOLIA

226

220

224

NORTH KOREA

JAPAN

222

Beijing p114

Seoul p137

Tokyo p140

Osaka p133

212

238

UKRAINE

TURKEY

GEORGIA

ARMENIA

AZERBAIJAN

TURKMENISTAN

UZBEKISTAN

KYRGYZSTAN

TAJIKISTAN

CHINA

302 Midway Is

246

250

240

242

SYRIA

Tehran p141

AFGHANISTAN

228

288

Shanghai p133

302 Saipan

PACIFIC OCEAN

288

256

Jerusalem p123

IRAQ

Baghdad p113

IRAN

JORDAN

KUWAIT

PAKISTAN

Delhi p120

NEPAL

244

241

Kolkata p124

BANG.

225

218

TAIWAN

Guangzhou p 21

Hong Kong p122

Okinawa

Tropic of Cancer

LIBYA

EGYPT

Cairo p117

248

SAUDI ARABIA

QATAR

U.A.E.

Dubai p119

Karachi p123

OMAN

INDIA

Mumbai p130

MYANMAR

236

LAOS

232

Manila p127

302 Guam

266

SUDAN

CHAD

YEMEN

DJIBOUTI

ERITREA

244

Lakshadweep Is

SRI LANKA

230

THAILAND

Bangkok p113

CAMB.

VIETNAM

244

Andaman & Nicobar Is

PHILIPPINES

CENTRAL AFRICAN REP.

SOUTH SUDAN

ETHIOPIA

SOMALIA

272 MALDIVES

234

237

MALAYSIA

Singapore p138

268

UGANDA

KENYA

RWANDA

BURUNDI

286

287

CONGO (DEM. REP. OF THE)

TANZANIA

272

SEYCHELLES

INDONESIA

230

276

Jakarta p122

Bali

TIMOR-LESTE

PAPUA NEW GUINEA

SOLOMON IS

287 SAMOA

ANGOLA

ZAMBIA

MALAWI

272

Comoros

278

280

287 VANUATU

287 FIJI

270

272

MOZAMBIQUE

MADAGASCAR

272

MAURITIUS

Réunion

INDIAN OCEAN

273

AUSTRALIA

280

Whitsunday Is

288 New Caledonia

287 TONGA

NAMIBIA

ZIMBABWE

BOTSWANA

ESWATINI

Tropic of Capricorn

282

Sydney p139

Johannesburg p123

LESOTHO

SOUTH AFRICA

Cape Town p118

Melbourne p128

284 NEW ZEALAND

285

KEY TO WORLD MAP SYMBOLS

SETTLEMENTS

■ **PARIS**   ◉ **Strasbourg**   ◉ **Livorno**   ◉ **Brugge**   ⊕ **Exeter**   ◦ *Torremolinos*   ◦ *Oberammergau*   ◦ *Thira*

Settlement symbols and type styles vary according to the scale of each map and indicate the importance of towns on the map rather than specific population figures

● *Vaduz*   Capital cities have red infills

⬠   Urban agglomerations

∴   Ruins or archeological sites

˅   Wells in desert

ADMINISTRATION

──   International boundaries

- - -   International boundaries (undefined or disputed)

·····   Internal boundaries

⬡   National parks

PERU   Country names

KENT   Administrative area names

International boundaries show the *de facto* situation where there are rival claims to territory

COMMUNICATIONS

═══   Motorways, freeways and expressways

───   Principal roads

───   Other roads

─┼───   Road tunnels

───   Principal railroads

─ ─ ─   Railroads under construction

───   Other railroads

─┼───   Railroad tunnels

LHR ✈   Principal airports (with location identifier)

⊕   Other airports

- - -   Principal canals

⤨   Passes

PHYSICAL FEATURES

⌇   Perennial streams

- - -   Intermittent streams

⠿   Sand deserts

▨   Intermittent lakes

⧬   Swamps and marshes

⬚   Permanent ice and glaciers

▲ 8848   Elevations in meters

▼ 8500   Sea depths in meters

1134   Height of lake surface above sea level in meters

OXFORD
ATLAS
OF THE
WORLD

TWENTY-SEVENTH EDITION

GAZETTEER OF NATIONS
TEXT Keith Lye/Philip's

PHOTOGRAPHIC ACKNOWLEDGEMENTS
Alamy /*AlamyCelebrity* 82, /*Jon Arnold Images Ltd* 91, /*B.A.E. Inc.* 79, /*Jens Benninghofen* 11 (center), /*Chessocampo* 8, 9, /*Mark Conlin* 85 (bottom), /*Ashley Cooper pics* 11, /*Cultura RM* 13 (bottom), /*David R. Frazier Photolibrary, Inc.* 98, /*Søren Lund Hviid* 101, /*Images and Stories* 94, /*Imaginechina Limited* 12, /*Galen Rowell/Mountain Light* 11 (bottom), /*Kevin Schafer* 85 (top), /*surasak suwanmake* 8,9, /*Travel Pix* 13 (top), /*Xinhua* 107 /*ZUMA Press Inc.* 93 (left & right);
Copernicus Sentinel data 2017 / NPA Satellite Mapping, CGG Satellite Mapping 11 (top);
Corbis /*Jay Dickman* 109 (top), /*Gideon Mendel* 89 (top), /*Liba Taylor* 104, /*David Turnley* 109 (bottom);
© Crown copyright 2007. Published by the Met Office, UK 80;
Dreamstime.com /*Maxim Blinkov* 13 (top), *Tsvibrav* 13 (middle right);
Galaxy Picture Library /*Robin Scagell* 73;
Getty Images /*Alexis Huguet/AFP* 94, /*Hannele Lahti* 85 (center);
Garrett Nagle 87;
iStock /*Ian Dyball* 13 (middle centre)s;
NASA 13 (bottom), /*ESA, HFF team (STScl)* 68, /*GSFC* 81 (bottom);
NSIDC courtesy J. Maslanik and M. Tschudi, University of Colorado 81 (top);
NPA Satellite Mapping, CGG Services (UK) Ltd 14–33, 66-67, 110–111, 144–145, 156–157, 208–209, 252–253, 274–275, 290–291, 324–325;
Science Photo Library /*Sputnik* 97;
Shutterstock /*testing* 11 (left), /*Canetti* 11 (right), /*Rich Carey* 13 (top left, top right, middle left).

EDITORIAL ACKNOWLEDGEMENTS
© OpenStreetMap contributors (openstreetmap.org);
Plastic Pollution 8-13: OurWorldInData.org (Andrady, A., … & Law, K. L. (2015); Eriksen, M. et al. (2014); Eiksen, M. et al. (2014); Jambeck, J. R., Geyer, R., Wilcox, C., Siegler, T. R., Perryman, M.; Lebreton, L., Egger, M., & Slat, B. (2019); Hannah Ritchie and Max Roser (2018)); United Nations Environment Programme; World Bank; World Wide Fund for Nature.

STAR CHARTS (PAGE 69)
Wil Tirion

CARTOGRAPHY BY PHILIP'S

WORLD CITIES
 PAGE 121, EDINBURGH, AND PAGE 125, LONDON: This product includes mapping data licensed from Ordnance Survey® with the permission of the Controller of Her Majesty's Stationery Office. © Crown copyright 2020. All rights reserved. Licence number 100011710.

Copyright © 2020 Philip's
www.philips-maps.co.uk

Philip's, a division of Octopus Publishing Group Limited (www.octopusbooks.co.uk)
Carmelite House, 50 Victoria Embankment, London EC4Y 0DZ
An Hachette UK Company (www.hachette.co.uk)

Published in North America by
Oxford University Press USA
198 Madison Avenue
New York, NY 10016

www.oup.com/us

OXFORD
UNIVERSITY PRESS
Oxford is a registered trademark of Oxford University Press

Library of Congress Cataloging-in-Publication Data available

ISBN 978-0-19-752280-6

Printing (last digit): 9 8 7 6 5 4 3 2 1

Printed in Malaysia

FOREWORD

A͟N AUTHORITATIVE AND SERIOUS REFERENCE WORK, the Oxford *Atlas of the World* is one of the finest atlases available anywhere in the world. The atlas incorporates computer-derived maps that have been produced using the very latest in digital cartographic techniques. Country names are shown in conventional English form and are those that are in common usage. They are the forms used by publications such as *Newsweek* and *The Washington Post*, and by the BBC and the British Foreign Office. Alternative country names appear in parentheses on the maps where space permits – for example, Myanmar (Burma) – and are cross-referenced in the index, for example, Ivory Coast = Côte d'Ivoire.

HOW TO USE THE ATLAS
The atlas is divided into a number of sections which are explained below.

WORLD STATISTICS AND "PLASTIC POLLUTION"
World statistics on topics such as area and population for every country in the world. Also included in this section is a listing of the world's largest cities by population, arranged in country alphabetical order. This section is followed by the highly topical "*Plastic Pollution*" feature, which examines some of the major issues concerning this threat to the natural environment.

IMAGES OF EARTH
A beautifully illustrated satellite imagery section showing 17 of the world's major cities and regions in the Americas, Europe, Africa, Asia, and Australasia.

GAZETTEER OF NATIONS
A comprehensive A–Z reference providing concise profiles of every country's geography, climate, history, politics, and economy, together with ready-reference tables, and illustrated with flags and locator maps.

WORLD GEOGRAPHY
A richly informative section comprising 42 pages of maps, charts, graphs, and diagrams that explain key themes about the world in which we live. The topics covered include the Solar System, climate, the natural world, population, energy, and trade. Explanatory text on each spread describes the patterns shown by the data.

WORLD CITIES
A detailed selection of maps for 70 urban areas around the world. These are useful for planning trips abroad as well as for comparative studies of cities worldwide.

WORLD MAPS
An outstanding collection of 179 pages of distinctive Philip's cartography. The highly acclaimed physical world maps combine relief shading with layer-colored contours to give a striking visual picture of the Earth's surface. Roads, railroads, canals, and airports are accurately depicted on the maps, and towns and cities are clearly marked. More information on the key features employed in the construction and presentation of the maps is given on the facing page.

GEOGRAPHICAL GLOSSARY AND INDEX
The 86,000-name index to the world maps includes geographical features as well as towns and cities, with both latitude/longitude and letter/figure grid references. Preceding the index is a list of geographical terms from various foreign languages that may be found in the place names on the maps and also in the index, together with their meanings.

SPECIALIST GEOGRAPHY CONSULTANTS

THE EDITORS are grateful to the following for their contributions to the '*World Geography*' section in this atlas:

Dr Dibyesh Anand	Keith Lye	Robin Scagell
John Burden	Garrett Nagle	John Woodruff
Peter Grego	Ross Reynolds	

THE EDITORS would also like to thank **Richard Chiles** and the staff at CGG Satellite Mapping, CGG Services (UK) Ltd, Edenbridge, Kent, UK (www.cgg.com/satellite) for sourcing and processing the satellite imagery that appears in the atlas.

USER GUIDE

The reference maps which form the main body of this atlas have been prepared in accordance with the highest standards of international cartography to provide an accurate and detailed representation of the Earth. The scales and projections used have been carefully chosen to give balanced coverage of the world, while emphasizing the most densely populated and economically significant regions. A hallmark of Philip's mapping is the use of hill shading and relief coloring to create a graphic impression of landforms: this makes the maps exceptionally easy to read. However, knowledge of the key features employed in the construction and presentation of the maps will enable the reader to derive the fullest benefit from the atlas.

MAP SEQUENCE

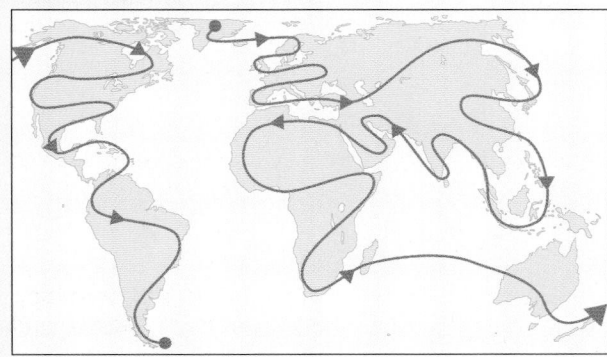

The atlas covers the Earth continent by continent: first Europe; then its land neighbor Asia (mapped north before south, in a clockwise sequence), then Africa, Australia and Oceania, North America, and South America. This is the classic arrangement adopted by most cartographers since the 16th century. For each continent, there are maps at a variety of scales. First, physical relief and political maps of the whole continent; then a series of larger-scale maps of the regions within the continent, each followed, where required, by still larger-scale maps of the most important or densely populated areas. The governing principle is that by turning the pages of the atlas, the reader moves steadily from north to south through each continent, with each map overlapping its neighbors.

MAP PRESENTATION

With very few exceptions (for example, for the Arctic and Antarctica), the maps are drawn with north at the top, regardless of whether they are presented upright or sideways on the page. In the borders will be found the map title; a locator diagram showing the area covered; continuation arrows showing the page numbers for maps of adjacent areas; the scale; the projection used; the degrees of latitude and longitude; and the letters and figures used in the index for locating place names and geographical features. Physical relief maps also have a height reference panel identifying the colors used for each layer of contouring.

MAP SYMBOLS

Each map contains a vast amount of detail which can only be conveyed clearly and accurately by the use of symbols. Points and circles of varying sizes locate and identify the relative importance of towns and cities; different styles of type are employed for administrative, geographical, and regional place names to aid identification. A variety of pictorial symbols denote landforms such as glaciers, marshes, and coral reefs, and man-made structures including roads, railroads, airports, and canals. International borders are shown by red lines. Where neighboring countries are in dispute, for example in parts of the Middle East, the maps show the *de facto* boundary between nations, regardless of the legal or historical situation.

The symbols are explained on the front endpapers of the atlas.

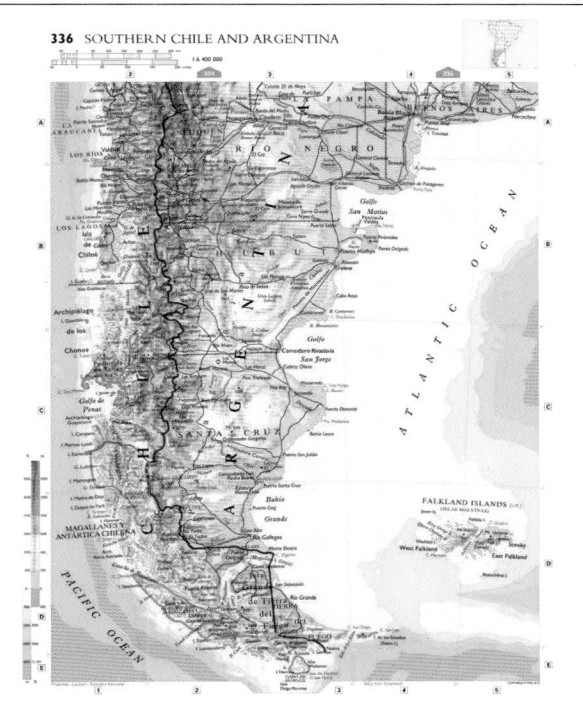

MAP SCALES

1:16 000 000
1 inch = 252 statute miles

The scale of each map is given in the numerical form known as the "representative fraction." The first figure is always one, signifying one unit of distance on the map; the second figure, usually in millions, is the number by which the map unit must be multiplied to give the equivalent distance on the Earth's surface. Calculations can easily be made in centimeters and kilometers, by dividing the Earth units figure by 100 000 (i.e. deleting the last five 0s). Thus 1:1 000 000 means 1 cm = 10 km. The calculation for inches and miles is more laborious, but 1 000 000 divided by 63 360 (the number of inches in a mile) shows that 1:1 000 000 means approximately 1 inch = 16 miles. The table below provides distance equivalents for scales down to 1:50 000 000.

LARGE SCALE		
1:1 000 000	1 cm = 10 km	1 inch = 16 miles
1:2 500 000	1 cm = 25 km	1 inch = 39.5 miles
1:5 000 000	1 cm = 50 km	1 inch = 79 miles
1:6 000 000	1 cm = 60 km	1 inch = 95 miles
1:8 000 000	1 cm = 80 km	1 inch = 126 miles
1:10 000 000	1 cm = 100 km	1 inch = 158 miles
1:15 000 000	1 cm = 150 km	1 inch = 237 miles
1:20 000 000	1 cm = 200 km	1 inch = 316 miles
1:50 000 000	1 cm = 500 km	1 inch = 790 miles
SMALL SCALE		

MEASURING DISTANCES

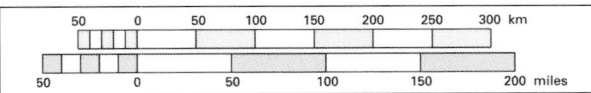

Although each map is accompanied by a scale bar, distances cannot always be measured with confidence because of the distortions involved in portraying the curved surface of the Earth on a flat page. As a general rule, the larger the map scale, the more accurate and reliable will be the distance measured. On small-scale maps such as those of the world and of entire continents, measurement may only be accurate along the "standard parallels," or central axes, and should not be attempted without considering the map projection.

MAP PROJECTIONS

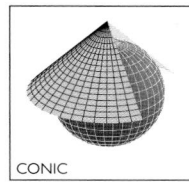  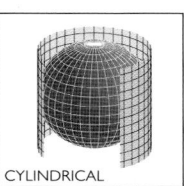

Unlike a globe, no flat map can give a true scale representation of the world in terms of area, shape, and position of every region. Each of the numerous systems that have been devised for projecting the curved surface of the Earth on to a flat page involves the sacrifice of accuracy in one or more of these elements. The variations in shape and position of land masses such as Alaska, Greenland, and Australia, for example, can be quite dramatic when different projections are compared.

For this atlas, the guiding principle has been to select projections that involve the least distortion of size and distance. The projection used for each map is noted in the border. Most fall into one of three categories – conic, azimuthal, or cylindrical – whose basic concepts are shown above. Each involves plotting the forms of the Earth's surface on a grid of latitude and longitude lines, which may be shown as parallels, curves, or radiating spokes.

LATITUDE AND LONGITUDE

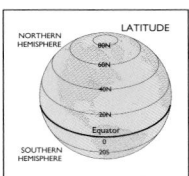 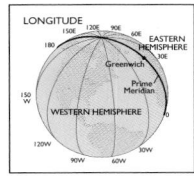 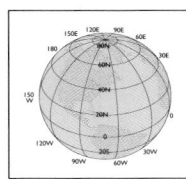

Accurate positioning of individual points on the Earth's surface is made possible by reference to the geometrical system of latitude and longitude. Latitude *parallels* are drawn west–east around the Earth and numbered by degrees north and south of the Equator, which is designated 0° of latitude. Longitude *meridians* are drawn north–south and numbered by degrees east and west of the *prime meridian*, 0° of longitude, which passes through Greenwich in England. By referring to these coordinates and their subdivisions of minutes (1/60th of a degree) and seconds (1/60th of a minute), any place on Earth can be located to within a few hundred meters. Latitude and longitude are indicated by blue lines on the maps; they are straight or curved according to the projection employed. Reference to these lines is the easiest way of determining the relative positions of places on different maps, and for plotting compass directions.

NAME FORMS

For ease of reference, both English and local name forms appear in the atlas. Oceans, seas, and countries are shown in English throughout the atlas; country names may be abbreviated to their commonly accepted form (for example, Germany, not The Federal Republic of Germany). Conventional English forms are also used for place names on the smaller-scale maps of the continents. However, local name forms are used on all large-scale and regional maps, with the English form given in brackets only for important cities – the large-scale map of Russia and Northern Asia thus shows Moskva (Moscow). For countries which do not use a Roman script, place names have been transcribed according to the systems adopted by the British and US Geographic Names Authorities. For China, the Pin Yin system has been used, with some more widely known forms appearing in brackets, as with Beijing (Peking). Both English and local names appear in the index, the English form being cross-referenced to the local form.

CONTENTS

CONTENTS

WORLD STATISTICS: COUNTRIES

This alphabetical list includes the principal countries and territories of the world. If a territory is not completely independent, the country it is associated with is named. The area figures give the total area of land, inland water, and ice. The population figures are 2020 estimates where available. The annual income is the Gross Domestic Product per capita (PPP) in US dollars; the figures are the latest available, usually 2020 estimates.

Country/Territory	Area km² *Thousands*	Area miles² *Thousands*	Population *Thousands*	Capital	Annual Income US $
Afghanistan	652	252	36,644	Kabul	2,200
Albania	28.7	11.1	3,075	Tirana	14,900
Algeria	2,382	920	42,973	Algiers	16,100
American Samoa (US)	0.20	0.08	49	Pago Pago	13,000
Andorra	0.47	0.18	77	Andorra La Vella	49,900
Angola	1,247	481	32,522	Luanda	6,800
Anguilla (UK)	0.10	0.04	18	The Valley	12,200
Antigua & Barbuda	0.44	0.17	98	St John's	30,600
Argentina	2,780	1,074	45,479	Buenos Aires	20,000
Armenia	29.8	11.5	3,021	Yerevan	11,800
Aruba (Netherlands)	0.19	0.07	119	Oranjestad	25,300
Australia	7,741	2,989	25,466	Canberra	54,800
Austria	83.9	32.4	8,859	Vienna	55,200
Azerbaijan	86.6	33.4	10,206	Baku	19,200
Azores (Portugal)	2.2	0.86	246	Ponta Delgada	15,200
Bahamas, The	13.9	5.4	338	Nassau	33,400
Bahrain	0.69	0.27	1,505	Manama	52,000
Bangladesh	144	55.6	162,651	Dhaka	5,500
Barbados	0.43	0.17	295	Bridgetown	19,400
Belarus	208	80.2	9,478	Minsk	21,200
Belgium	30.5	11.8	11,721	Brussels	50,900
Belize	23.0	8.9	400	Belmopan	8,800
Benin	113	43.5	12,865	Porto-Novo	3,600
Bermuda (UK)	0.05	0.02	72	Hamilton	85,700
Bhutan	47.0	18.1	782	Thimphu	10,600
Bolivia	1,099	424	11,640	La Paz/Sucre	8,500
Bosnia-Herzegovina	51.2	19.8	3,836	Sarajevo	14,900
Botswana	582	225	2,317	Gaborone	19,400
Brazil	8,514	3,287	211,716	Brasília	17,100
Brunei	5.8	2.2	464	Bandar Seri Begawan	85,000
Bulgaria	111	42.8	6,967	Sofia	26,000
Burkina Faso	274	106	20,835	Ouagadougou	2,200
Burundi	27.8	10.7	11,866	Bujumbura	700
Cabo Verde	4.0	1.6	583	Praia	8,700
Cambodia	181	69.9	16,927	Phnom Penh	5,000
Cameroon	475	184	27,745	Yaoundé	4,100
Canada	9,971	3,850	37,694	Ottawa	52,100
Canary Is. (Spain)	7.2	2.8	2,105	Las Palmas/Santa Cruz	19,900
Cayman Is. (UK)	0.26	0.10	62	George Town	43,800
Central African Republic	623	241	5,991	Bangui	900
Chad	1,284	496	16,877	Ndjaména	2,600
Chile	757	292	18,187	Santiago	27,200
China	9,597	3,705	1,394,016	Beijing	21,000
Colombia	1,139	440	49,085	Bogotá	16,300
Comoros	2.2	0.86	846	Moroni	2,900
Congo	342	132	5,293	Brazzaville	7,300
Congo (Dem. Rep. of the)	2,345	905	101,780	Kinshasa	900
Cook Is. (NZ)	0.24	0.09	9	Avarua	12,300
Costa Rica	51.1	19.7	5,098	San José	18,700
Côte d'Ivoire (Ivory Coast)	322	125	27,481	Yamoussoukro	4,800
Croatia	56.5	21.8	4,228	Zagreb	29,200
Cuba	111	42.8	11,059	Havana	11,900
Curaçao (Netherlands)	0.44	0.17	151	Willemstad	15,000
Cyprus	9.3	3.6	1,267	Nicosia	43,000
Czechia	78.9	30.5	10,702	Prague	40,600
Denmark	43.1	16.6	5,869	Copenhagen	55,700
Djibouti	23.2	9.0	922	Djibouti	5,900
Dominica	0.75	0.29	74	Roseau	12,900
Dominican Republic	48.5	18.7	10,500	Santo Domingo	20,600
Ecuador	284	109	16,905	Quito	11,900
Egypt	1,001	387	104,124	Cairo	14,800
El Salvador	21.0	8.1	6,481	San Salvador	8,600
Equatorial Guinea	28.1	10.8	836	Malabo	20,000
Eritrea	118	45.4	6,081	Asmara	1,100
Estonia	45.1	17.4	1,229	Tallinn	37,600
Eswatini (Swaziland)	17.4	6.7	1,104	Mbabane	11,100
Ethiopia	1,104	426	108,113	Addis Ababa	2,700
Falkland Is. (UK)	12.2	4.7	3	Stanley	96,200
Faroe Is. (Denmark)	1.4	0.54	52	Tórshavn	40,000
Fiji	18.3	7.1	936	Suva	12,700
Finland	338	131	5,572	Helsinki	49,500
France	552	213	67,848	Paris	48,600
French Guiana (France)	90.0	34.7	250	Cayenne	8,300
French Polynesia (France)	4.0	1.5	295	Papeete	17,000
Gabon	268	103	2,231	Libreville	19,800
Gambia, The	11.3	4.4	2,174	Banjul	2,900
Georgia	69.7	26.9	3,997	Tbilisi	13,200
Germany	357	138	80,160	Berlin	55,300
Ghana	239	92.1	29,340	Accra	7,300
Gibraltar (UK)	0.006	0.002	30	Gibraltar Town	61,700
Greece	132	50.9	10,607	Athens	31,600
Greenland (Denmark)	2,176	840	58	Nuuk	37,600
Grenada	0.34	0.13	113	St George's	17,400
Guadeloupe (France)	1.7	0.66	402	Basse-Terre	7,900
Guam (US)	0.55	0.21	168	Agana	30,500
Guatemala	109	42.0	17,153	Guatemala City	9,000
Guinea	246	94.9	12,527	Conakry	2,600
Guinea-Bissau	36.1	13.9	1,927	Bissau	2,100
Guyana	215	83.0	750	Georgetown	17,200
Haiti	27.8	10.7	11,068	Port-au-Prince	1,900
Honduras	112	43.3	9,235	Tegucigalpa	5,600
Hungary	93.0	35.9	9,772	Budapest	35,900
Iceland	103	39.8	351	Reykjavik	57,000
India	3,287	1,269	1,326,093	New Delhi	9,000
Indonesia	1,905	735	267,026	Jakarta	14,800
Iran	1,648	636	84,923	Tehran	17,800
Iraq	438	169	38,873	Baghdad	18,800
Ireland	70.3	27.1	5,177	Dublin	87,000
Israel	20.6	8.0	8,675	Jerusalem	40,300
Italy	301	116	62,403	Rome	41,600
Jamaica	11.0	4.2	2,809	Kingston	9,900
Japan	378	146	125,507	Tokyo	46,800
Jordan	89.3	34.5	10,821	Amman	9,900
Kazakhstan	2,725	1,052	19,092	Nur-Sultan	30,200
Kenya	580	224	53,528	Nairobi	4,100
Kiribati	0.73	0.28	112	Tarawa	2,200
Korea, North	121	46.5	25,643	Pyŏngyang	1,700
Korea, South	99.3	38.3	51,835	Seoul	46,500
Kosovo	10.9	4.2	1,933	Pristina	13,000
Kuwait	17.8	6.9	2,994	Kuwait City	67,900
Kyrgyzstan	200	77.2	5,965	Bishkek	4,200
Laos	237	91.4	7,447	Vientiane	8,700
Latvia	64.6	24.9	1,881	Riga	33,000
Lebanon	10.4	4.0	5,470	Beirut	15,600
Lesotho	30.4	11.7	1,969	Maseru	3,700
Liberia	111	43.0	5,073	Monrovia	1,400
Libya	1,760	679	6,891	Tripoli	9,400
Liechtenstein	0.16	0.06	39	Vaduz	139,100
Lithuania	65.2	25.2	2,731	Vilnius	38,800
Luxembourg	2.6	1.0	628	Luxembourg	112,000
Macedonia, North	25.7	9.9	2,126	Skopje	17,400
Madagascar	587	227	26,956	Antananarivo	1,800
Madeira (Portugal)	0.78	0.30	289	Funchal	25,800
Malawi	118	45.7	21,197	Lilongwe	1,300
Malaysia	330	127	32,652	Kuala Lumpur/Putrajaya	34,600
Maldives	0.30	0.12	392	Malé	24,800
Mali	1,240	479	19,553	Bamako	2,600
Malta	0.32	0.12	457	Valletta	49,600
Marshall Is.	0.18	0.07	78	Majuro	4,000
Martinique (France)	1.1	0.43	386	Fort-de-France	14,400
Mauritania	1,026	396	4,005	Nouakchott	5,200
Mauritius	2.0	0.79	1,379	Port Louis	26,500
Mayotte (France)	0.37	0.14	213	Mamoudzou	4,900
Mexico	1,958	756	128,650	Mexico City	21,400
Micronesia, Fed. States of	0.70	0.27	102	Palikir	3,700
Moldova	33.9	13.1	3,364	Kishinev	8,200
Monaco	0.002	0.0008	39	Monaco	115,700
Mongolia	1,567	605	3,168	Ulan Bator	15,100
Montenegro	14.0	5.4	610	Podgorica	22,000
Montserrat (UK)	0.10	0.39	5	Brades	8,500
Morocco	447	172	35,562	Rabat	9,700
Mozambique	802	309	30,098	Maputo	1,400
Myanmar (Burma)	677	261	56,590	Yangôn/Naypyidaw	7,200
Namibia	824	318	2,630	Windhoek	11,500
Nauru	0.02	0.008	11	Yaren	9,000
Nepal	147	56.8	30,328	Katmandu	3,600
Netherlands	41.5	16.0	17,280	Amsterdam/The Hague	60,300
New Caledonia (France)	18.6	7.2	290	Nouméa	31,100
New Zealand	271	104	4,925	Wellington	42,000
Nicaragua	130	50.2	6,085	Managua	5,300
Niger	1,267	489	22,772	Niamey	1,200
Nigeria	924	357	214,028	Abuja	6,200
Northern Mariana Is. (US)	0.46	0.18	51	Saipan	13,300
Norway	324	125	5,467	Oslo	79,600
Oman	310	119	4,665	Muscat	48,600
Pakistan	796	307	233,501	Islamabad	6,000
Palau	0.46	0.18	22	Melekeok	16,900
Panama	75.5	29.2	3,894	Panamá	28,500
Papua New Guinea	463	179	7,259	Port Moresby	4,100
Paraguay	407	157	7,192	Asunción	13,200
Peru	1,285	496	31,915	Lima	15,400
Philippines	300	116	109,181	Manila	10,100
Poland	323	125	38,282	Warsaw	35,700
Portugal	88.8	34.3	10,303	Lisbon	34,900
Puerto Rico (US)	8.9	3.4	3,189	San Juan	41,200
Qatar	11.0	4.2	2,444	Doha	138,900
Réunion (France)	2.5	0.97	846	St-Denis	6,200
Romania	238	92.0	21,303	Bucharest	29,600
Russia	17,075	6,593	141,722	Moscow	30,800
Rwanda	26.3	10.2	12,712	Kigali	2,600
St Kitts & Nevis	0.26	0.10	54	Basseterre	32,000
St Lucia	0.54	0.21	166	Castries	15,200
St Vincent & Grenadines	0.39	0.15	101	Kingstown	13,000
Samoa	2.8	1.1	204	Apia	6,500
San Marino	0.06	0.02	34	San Marino	62,900
São Tomé & Príncipe	0.96	0.37	211	São Tomé	3,500
Saudi Arabia	2,150	830	34,173	Riyadh	56,900
Senegal	197	76.0	15,736	Dakar	4,100
Serbia	77.5	29.9	7,012	Belgrade	19,800
Seychelles	0.46	0.18	96	Victoria	33,100
Sierra Leone	71.7	27.7	6,625	Freetown	1,800
Singapore	0.68	0.26	6,210	Singapore City	105,700
Slovakia	49.0	18.9	5,441	Bratislava	38,300
Slovenia	20.3	7.8	2,103	Ljubljana	40,300
Solomon Is.	28.9	11.2	685	Honiara	2,400
Somalia	638	246	11,757	Mogadishu	400
South Africa	1,221	471	56,464	Cape Town/Pretoria	14,000
Spain	498	192	50,016	Madrid	43,000
Sri Lanka	65.6	25.3	22,889	Colombo	14,500
Sudan	1,886	728	45,562	Khartoum	4,000
Sudan, South	620	239	10,561	Juba	1,700
Suriname	163	63.0	610	Paramaribo	16,000
Sweden	450	174	10,202	Stockholm	56,000
Switzerland	41.3	15.9	8,404	Bern	67,600
Syria	185	71.5	19,398	Damascus	-
Taiwan	36.0	13.9	23,603	Taipei	57,200
Tajikistan	143	55.3	8,874	Dushanbe	3,800
Tanzania	945	365	58,553	Dodoma	3,700
Thailand	513	198	68,977	Bangkok	21,400
Timor-Leste (East Timor)	14.9	5.7	1,384	Dili	5,300
Togo	56.8	21.9	8,608	Lomé	1,900
Tonga	0.65	0.25	106	Nuku'alofa	6,900
Trinidad & Tobago	5.1	2.0	1,209	Port of Spain	33,700
Tunisia	164	63.2	11,721	Tunis	13,100
Turkey	775	299	82,018	Ankara	29,300
Turkmenistan	488	188	5,529	Ashkhabad	21,900
Turks & Caicos Is. (UK)	0.43	0.17	56	Cockburn Town	29,100
Tuvalu	0.03	0.01	11	Fongafale	4,500
Uganda	241	93.1	43,253	Kampala	2,800
Ukraine	604	233	43,923	Kiev	10,100
United Arab Emirates	83.6	32.3	9,992	Abu Dhabi	70,400
United Kingdom	242	93.4	65,761	London	48,200
United States of America	9,629	3,718	332,639	Washington, DC	67,400
Uruguay	175	67.6	3,388	Montevideo	24,500
Uzbekistan	447	173	30,565	Tashkent	9,600
Vanuatu	12.2	4.7	298	Port-Vila	3,000
Vatican City	0.0004	0.0002	1	Vatican City	-
Venezuela	912	352	28,645	Caracas	12,400
Vietnam	332	128	98,721	Hanoi	8,700
Virgin Is. (UK)	0.15	0.06	36	Road Town	42,300
Virgin Is. (US)	0.35	0.13	106	Charlotte Amalie	36,100
Yemen	528	204	29,884	Sana'	2,300
Zambia	753	291	17,427	Lusaka	4,200
Zimbabwe	391	151	14,546	Harare	2,800

This list shows the principal cities with more than 975,000 inhabitants. The figures are taken from the most recent census or estimate available and as far as possible are the population of the metropolitan area or urban agglomeration. The list includes Metropolitan Statistical Areas from the United States Census Bureau. All the figures are in thousands. Local name forms have been used for the smaller cities (for example, Antwerpen).

AFGHANISTAN
Kabul	4,114

ALGERIA
Algiers	2,729

ANGOLA
Luanda	8,045

ARGENTINA
Buenos Aires	15,057
Córdoba	1,560
Rosario	1,510
Mendoza	1,153

ARMENIA
Yerevan	1,083

AUSTRALIA
Sydney	4,859
Melbourne	4,870
Brisbane	2,372
Perth	2,016
Adelaide	1,328

AUSTRIA
Vienna	1,915

AZERBAIJAN
Baku	2,313

BANGLADESH
Dhaka	20,284
Chittagong	4,951

BELARUS
Minsk	2,017

BENIN
Abomey-Calavi	991

BELGIUM
Brussels	2,065
Antwerpen	1,037

BOLIVIA
La Paz	1,835
Santa Cruz	1,677
Cochabamba	1,271

BRAZIL
São Paulo	21,847
Rio de Janeiro	13,374
Belo Horizonte	6,028
Brasília	4,559
Pôrto Alegre	4,115
Recife	4,078
Fortaleza	4,026
Salvador	3,797
Curitiba	3,629
Campinas	3,256
Goiânia	2,628
Belém	2,308
Manaus	2,217
Vitória	2,040
Baixada Santista	1,873
São Luís	1,473
Natal	1,427
João Pessoa	1,363
Maceió	1,309
Joinville	1,287
Florianópolis	1,218
Teresina	1,011
Aracaju	991

BULGARIA
Sofia	1,277

BURKINA FASO
Ouagadougou	2,635

CAMBODIA
Phnom Penh	2,014

CAMEROON
Yaoundé	3,822
Douala	3,536

CANADA
Toronto	6,139
Montréal	4,196
Vancouver	2,556
Calgary	1,513
Edmonton	1,430
Ottawa	1,378

CHAD
Ndjamena	1,372

CHILE
Santiago	6,724
Valparaiso	975

CHINA
Shanghai	26,317
Beijing	20,035
Chongqing	15,354
Tianjin	13,396
Guangzhou, Guangdong	12,968
Shenzhen	12,129
Chengdu	8,972
Nanjing, Jiangsu	8,546
Wuhan	8,266
Xi'an, Shaanxi	7,722
Hong Kong	7,491
Hangzhou	7,438
Dongguan, Guangdong	7,378
Foshan	7,257
Shenyang	7,069
Suzhou, Jiangsu	6,703
Harbin	6,250
Qingdao	5,499
Dalian	5,459
Jinan, Shandong	5,205
Zhengzhou	5,131
Changsha	4,461
Kunming	4,336
Changchun	4,332
Shantou	4,249
Ürümqi	4,190
Hefei	4,110
Shijiazhuang	4,031
Ningbo	3,966
Taiyuan, Shanxi	3,807
Nanning	3,744
Xiamen	3,652
Fuzhou, Fujian	3,608
Wenzhou	3,521
Nanchang	3,485
Changzhou, Jiangsu	3,449
Tangshan	3,285
Guiyang	3,226
Wuxi, Jiangsu	3,199
Lanzhou	3,008
Zhongshan	2,891
Handan	2,627
Zibo	2,596
Weifang	2,560
Huai'an	2,538
Shaoxing	2,445
Yantai	2,443
Huizhou	2,442
Luoyang	2,311
Nantong	2,199
Baotou	2,143
Liuzhou	2,104
Xuzhou	2,099
Hohhot	2,086
Yangzhou	1,946
Baoding	1,932
Linyi	1,890
Taizhou, Zhejiang	1,876
Haikou	1,847
Yancheng	1,821
Daqing	1,811
Datong	1,811
Putian	1,809
Wuhu	1,778
Lianyungang	1,762
Zhuhai	1,715
Jaingmen	1,663
Xiangyang	1,632
Quanzhou	1,631
Anshan	1,614
Jilin	1,585
Cixi	1,545
Qiqihar	1,537
Yinchuan	1,531
Xining	1,495
Yichang	1,490
Qinhuangdao	1,484
Hengyang	1,480
Huainan	1,415
Jining, Shandong	1,415
Chaozhou	1,408
Zhangjiakou	1,401
Anyang	1,394
Suqian	1,358
Tai'an	1,314
Taizhou, Jiangsu	1,314
Fushun	1,286
Yiwu	1,281
Weihai	1,260
Zhanjiang	1,259
Mianyang	1,252
Dongying	1,240
Rizhao	1,228
Ganzhou	1,221
Nanchong	1,215
Shiyan	1,202
Jiaxing	1,200
Yingkou	1,176
Zhuzhou	1,165
Chifeng	1,153
Zhenjiang	1,148
Tengzhou	1,142
Benxi	1,139
Baoji	1,131
Liuan	1,129
Ruian	1,129
Puning	1,128
Pingdingshan	1,126
Jinzhou	1,123
Suzhou	1,119
Xiangtan	1,116
Guilin	1,115
Nanyang	1,115
Huaibei	1,109
Jieyang	1,098
Liuyang	1,094
Zaozhuang	1,075
Jinhua	1,073
Xinxiang	1,062
Jingzhou	1,023
Yueqing	1,022
Liupanshui	1,021
Pizhou	1,011
Fuyang	1,007
Wenling	1,004
Yueyang	999
Ma'anshan	987
Luohe	982

COLOMBIA
Bogotá	10,779
Medellín	3,967
Cali	2,754
Barranquilla	2,246
Bucaramanga	1,313
Cartagena	1,055

CONGO
Brazzaville	2,308
Pointe-Noire	1,176

CONGO (DEM. REP. OF THE)
Kinshasa	13,734
Mbuji-Mayi	2,413
Lubumbashi	2,377
Kananga	1,395
Kisangani	1,213
Bukavu	1,025

COSTA RICA
San José	1,379

CÔTE D'IVOIRE (IVORY COAST)
Abidjan	5,059

CUBA
Havana	2,138

CZECHIA
Prague	1,299

DENMARK
Copenhagen	1,334

DOMINICAN REPUBLIC
Santo Domingo	3,245

ECUADOR
Guayaquil	2,946
Quito	1,848

EGYPT
Cairo	20,485
Alexandria	5,182

EL SALVADOR
San Salvador	1,106

ETHIOPIA
Addis Ababa	4,592

FINLAND
Helsinki	1,292

FRANCE
Paris	10,958
Lyon	1,705
Marseilles	1,603
Lille	1,058
Toulouse	1,011

GEORGIA
Tbilisi	1,077

GERMANY
Berlin	3,557
Hamburg	1,791
Munich	1,521
Cologne	1,108

GHANA
Kumasi	3,206
Accra	2,475

GREECE
Athens	3,154

GUATEMALA
Guatemala City	2,891

GUINEA
Conakry	1,889

HAITI
Port-au-Prince	2,704

HONDURAS
Tegucigalpa	1,403

HUNGARY
Budapest	1,764

INDIA
Delhi	29,399
Mumbai	20,185
Kolkata	14,755
Bengaluru	11,883
Chennai	10,711
Hyderabad	9,741
Ahmedabad	7,869
Surat	6,874
Pune	6,452
Jaipur	3,812
Lucknow	3,590
Calicut	3,365
Malappuram	3,169
Kanpur	3,100
Kochi	2,970
Thrissur	2,921
Indore	2,919
Nagpur	2,850
Coimbatore	2,713
Thiruvananthapuram	2,477
Patna	2,393
Bhopal	2,333
Agra	2,160
Vadodara	2,149
Vishakhapatnam	2,125
Kannur	2,107
Nashik	2,009
Vijayawada	1,975
Ludhiana	1,830
Rajkot	1,822
Kollam	1,761
Madurai	1,704
Meerut	1,666
Varanasi	1,639
Raipur	1,581
Jamshedpur	1,571
Srinagar	1,550
Aurangabad	1,517
Jodhpur	1,434
Tiruppur	1,433
Jabalpur	1,430
Asansol	1,410
Ranchi	1,404
Allahabad	1,374
Amritsar	1,356
Gwalior	1,348
Kota	1,343
Dhanbad	1,316
Bareilly	1,225
Bhilainagar-Durg	1,192
Mysore	1,185
Aligarh	1,177
Moradabad	1,162
Tiruchchirapalli	1,149
Bhubaneswar	1,131
Chandigarh	1,129
Guwahati	1,100
Hubli-Dharwad	1,098
Salem	1,082
Jalandhar	1,034
Solapur	1,022
Saharanpur	1,013
Siliguri	984

INDONESIA
Jakarta	10,639
Bekasi	3,277
Surabaya	2,922
Depok	2,615
Bandung	2,558
Medan	2,311
Tangerang	2,280
Semarang	1,833
Palembang	1,693
Makassar	1,556
Batam	1,473
Pekanbaru	1,171
Bogor	1,137
Bandar Lampung	1,069
Tasikmalaya	1,000
Samarinda	979

IRAN
Tehran	9,014
Mashhad	3,152
Esfahan	2,086
Shiraz	1,628
Tabriz	1,596
Karaj	1,581
Qom	1,265
Ahvaz	1,228
Kermanshah	1,005

IRAQ
Baghdad	6,974
Mosul	1,578
Basra	1,325
Kirkuk	996

IRELAND
Dublin	1,215

ISRAEL
Tel Aviv-Yafo	4,079
Haifa	1,141

ITALY
Rome	4,234
Milan	3,136
Naples	2,192
Turin	1,789

JAPAN
Tokyo–Yokohama	37,435
Osaka–Kobe	19,223
Nagoya	9,532
Fukuoka–Kitakyushu	5,540
Shizuoka–Hamamatsu	2,912
Sapporo	2,668
Sendai	2,318
Hiroshima	2,089
Kyoto	1,470

JORDAN
Amman	2,109

KAZAKHSTAN
Almaty	1,863
Nur-Sultan	1,118
Shimkent	1,021

KENYA
Nairobi	4,556
Mombasa	1,254

KOREA, NORTH
Pyŏngyang	3,061

KOREA, SOUTH
Seoul	9,962
Busan	3,466
Incheon	2,783
Daegu	2,209
Daejeon	1,562
Gwangju	1,519
Suwon	1,289
Yongin	1,062
Changwon	1,058
Goyang	1,054

KUWAIT
Kuwait City	3,052

KYRGYZSTAN
Bishkek	1,017

LEBANON
Beirut	2,407

LIBERIA
Monrovia	1,467

LIBYA
Tripoli	1,161

MADAGASCAR
Antananarivo	3,210

MALAWI
Lilongwe	1,075

MALAYSIA
Kuala Lumpur	7,780
Johor Bahru	1,003

MALI
Bamako	2,529

MAURITANIA
Nouakchott	1,259

MEXICO
Mexico City	21,672
Guadalajara	5,101
Monterrey	4,793
Puebla	3,145
Toluca	2,411
Tijuana	2,099
León	1,802
La Laguna	1,553
Ciudad Juárez	1,499
Torreón	1,498
Querétaro	1,314
San Luis Potosí	1,198
Mérida	1,142
Mexicali	1,101
Aguascalientes	1,088
Cuernavaca	1,059
Chihuahua	1,033
Tampico	986

MONGOLIA
Ulan Bator	1,553

MOROCCO
Casablanca	3,716
Rabat	1,865
Fès	1,204
Tangier	1,157
Marrakesh	989

MOZAMBIQUE
Matola	1,669
Maputo	1,104

MYANMAR (BURMA)
Rangoon	5,244
Mandalay	1,406

NEPAL
Katmandu	1,376

NETHERLANDS
Amsterdam	1,140
Rotterdam	1,009

NEW ZEALAND
Auckland	1,582

NICARAGUA
Managua	1,055

NIGER
Niamey	1,252

NIGERIA
Lagos	13,904
Kano	3,906
Ibadan	3,474
Abuja	3,095
Port Harcourt	2,873
Benin City	1,676
Onitsha	1,349
Kaduna	1,097
Uyo	1,073
Aba	1,051
Nnewi	989

NORWAY
Oslo	1,027

OMAN
Muscat	1,502

PAKISTAN
Karachi	15,741
Lahore	12,188
Faisalabad	3,385
Rawalpindi	2,196
Gujranwala	2,169
Peshawar	2,133
Multan	1,972
Hyderabad	1,815
Islamabad	1,095
Quetta	1,070

PANAMA
Panamá	1,822

PARAGUAY
Asunción	3,279

PERU
Lima	10,555

PHILIPPINES
Manila	13,699
Davao	1,785

POLAND
Warsaw	1,776

PORTUGAL
Lisbon	2,942
Porto	1,310

PUERTO RICO
San Juan	2,451

ROMANIA
Bucharest	1,812

RUSSIA
Moscow	12,476
St Petersburg	5,427
Novosibirsk	1,650
Yekaterinburg	1,493
Kazan	1,263
Nizhniy Novgorod	1,261
Chelyabinsk	1,222
Omsk	1,183
Samara	1,167
Rostov	1,135
Ufa	1,133
Krasnoyarsk	1,125
Perm	1,067
Voronezh	1,062
Volgograd	1,009

RWANDA
Kigali	1,095

SAUDI ARABIA
Riyadh	7,071
Jedda	4,522
Mecca	2,005
Medina	1,459
Dammam	1,225

SENEGAL
Dakar	3,057

SERBIA
Belgrade	1,394

SIERRA LEONE
Freetown	1,168

SINGAPORE
Singapore City	5,868

SOMALIA
Mogadishu	2,180

SOUTH AFRICA
Johannesburg	5,635
Cape Town	4,524
Ekurhuleni	3,818
Durban	3,145
Pretoria	2,473
Port Elizabeth	1,242

SPAIN
Madrid	6,559
Barcelona	5,541

SUDAN
Khartoum	5,678

SWEDEN
Stockholm	1,608

SWITZERLAND
Zürich	1,383

SYRIA
Damascus	2,354
Aleppo	1,834
Homs	1,314

TAIWAN
Xinbei	4,361
Taipei	2,713
Taoyuan	2,218
Kaohsiung	1,534
T'aichung	1,302

TANZANIA
Dar es Salaam	6,702
Mwanza	1,120

THAILAND
Bangkok	10,350
Chon Buri	1,380
Samut Prakan	1,289
Chiang Mai	1,151

TOGO
Lomé	1,785

TUNISIA
Tunis	2,328

TURKEY
Istanbul	14,968
Ankara	5,018
Izmir	2,964
Bursa	1,951
Adana	1,750
Gaziantep	1,668
Konya	1,229
Antalya	1,219
Diyarbakir	1,019
Mersin	997

UGANDA
Kampala	3,138

UKRAINE
Kiev	2,973
Kharkov	1,432
Odessa	1,010

UNITED ARAB EMIRATES
Dubai	2,833
Sharjah	1,629
Abu Dhabi	1,452

UNITED KINGDOM
London	9,177
Manchester	2,710
Birmingham	2,589
Glasgow	1,667

UNITED STATES OF AMERICA
New York	18,805
Los Angeles	12,448
Chicago	8,862
Houston	6,245
Dallas–Fort Worth	6,201
Miami	6,079
Philadelphia	5,705
Atlanta	5,689
Washington, DC	5,264
Phoenix–Mesa	4,436
Boston	4,307
Detroit	3,571
Seattle	3,406
San Francisco	3,318
San Diego	3,231
Minneapolis–St Paul	2,907
Tampa–St Petersburg	2,842
Denver	2,790
Las Vegas	2,621
Riverside–San Bernardino	2,422
Baltimore	2,319
San Antonio	2,269
St Louis	2,212
Portland	2,127
Sacramento	2,089
Austin	1,985
Charlotte	1,971
Orlando	1,923
Cleveland	1,796
San Jose	1,783
Indianapolis	1,781
Cincinnati	1,729
Pittsburgh	1,710
Kansas City	1,675
Columbus	1,621
Virginia Beach–Norfolk	1,477
Milwaukee	1,436
Raleigh	1,386
Jacksonville	1,263
Nashville	1,224
Providence	1,202
Salt Lake City	1,158
Memphis	1,144
Richmond	1,093
Louisville	1,081
Hartford	994
Buffalo	986
McAllen	986
New Orleans	985
Oklahoma	979

URUGUAY
Montevideo	1,745

UZBEKISTAN
Tashkent	2,490

VENEZUELA
Caracas	2,936
Maracaibo	2,219
Valencia	1,885
Barquisimeto	1,201
Maracay	1,190

VIETNAM
Ho Chi Minh City	8,371
Hanoi	4,480
Can Tho	1,531
Haiphong	1,259
Da Nang	1,095
Bien Hoa	981

YEMEN
Sana'	2,874

ZAMBIA
Lusaka	2,647

ZIMBABWE
Harare	1,521

PLASTIC POLLUTION

Plastics pervade every environment on Earth. Plastic waste can be found in the remotest areas, far from its place of origin. Not only found on land and sea, plastic breaks down and can be ingested by living creatures. Items that we take for granted, then discard, are left as waste that can take hundreds of years to degrade. In the years since the end of the Second World War, the rate of plastic production has grown faster than that of any other material. Recently, the problems of inadequately managed plastic waste have started to be acknowledged and some countries are now taking action to curb use and improve recycling. However, individual countries acting alone will not be enough as this is truly a global issue and effective outcomes will require international cooperation.

For more information:

107 UN Sustainable
    Development
    Goals

Plastics have become an integral part of modern life. There is no denying their usefulness and living without them is hard to contemplate. Cheap to manufacture, they can be molded into myriad forms from simple plastic bags to aircraft parts. Most are produced from non-renewable resources – oil, natural gas, and coal. It has been estimated that 8.3 billion tonnes of plastic have been produced since the early 1950s. That in itself may not be a problem, providing any waste is carefully managed. However, it has become clear that waste in many cases is not managed adequately. Many plastic items lend themselves to being used once then thrown away. Again, if managed properly, and discarded items are collected and recycled, there may not be an issue. However, it is estimated that around 60% of plastics end up in either landfill or the environment. Carelessly thrown away on land and into water, plastics can be unsightly and cause great harm to wildlife.

According to the World Bank, the world generated 242 million tonnes of plastic waste in 2016. This equated to 12% of all solid waste produced and the majority originated in three regions: East Asia and the Pacific (57 million tonnes), Europe and Central Asia (45 million tonnes), and North America (35 million tonnes). It has been predicted that the amount of plastics produced will double in the next 20 years. The map below gives a picture of which countries generate the most plastic waste per head of population. But, as stated earlier, it is inadequately managed waste that is the root cause of problems of pollution. Unfortunately, it does appear that the majority of plastic waste is not currently managed in a responsible way. According to the Ellen MacArthur Foundation, up to 32% of all plastic packaging does not enter a collection system and is not recycled.

Any attempts to eliminate plastics entirely would be unrealistic and undesirable. The material is light, pliable, durable, and cheap to manufacture. Used to wrap food, it acts as a protective barrier and extends shelf-life which subsequently helps to prevent food waste. However, reducing the amount of plastics used by substituting them with biodegradable materials is one part of strategies to manage waste. Many countries are taking steps to reduce the use of lightweight plastic shopping bags by introducing bans or charges (see map on page 11). The other necessity is to introduce effective waste management systems to recycle plastic material. This is best done close to the country of origin, rather than shipping long distances to other countries for processing.

▲ A now familiar sight – garbage left unsorted in a landfill dump. In this case, it is on the Greek island of Lesbos, but it is typical of many places where there is no, or inadequate, waste management or recycling. More developed, high-income countries have the resources, and an increasing public will, to invest in schemes to manage waste, and in particular plastic waste, more effectively. Good solutions require cooperation between commerce, government, and individuals.

PLASTIC WASTE

Plastic waste generated per capita (kg per person per day)

- Over 0.5 kg
- 0.4 – 0.5
- 0.3 – 0.4
- 0.2 – 0.3
- 0.1 – 0.2
- Under 0.1
- No data available

Source: Jambeck et al.

Highest plastic waste per capita (kg per day)	
Kuwait	0.69
Antigua & Barbuda	0.67
St Kitts & Nevis	0.65
Guyana	0.59
Barbados	0.57
St Lucia	0.52
Germany	0.49
Ireland	0.43

Lowest plastic waste per capita (kg per day)	
India	0.010
Mozambique	0.015
Madagascar	0.016
Tanzania	0.023
Brunei	0.026
Kenya	0.027
Guinea	0.030
Bangladesh	0.034

INADEQUATELY MANAGED PLASTIC WASTE

Share of a country's plastic waste inadequately managed

- 80 – 100%
- 60 – 80%
- 40 – 60%
- 20 – 40%
- 10 – 20%
- Under 10%
- No data available

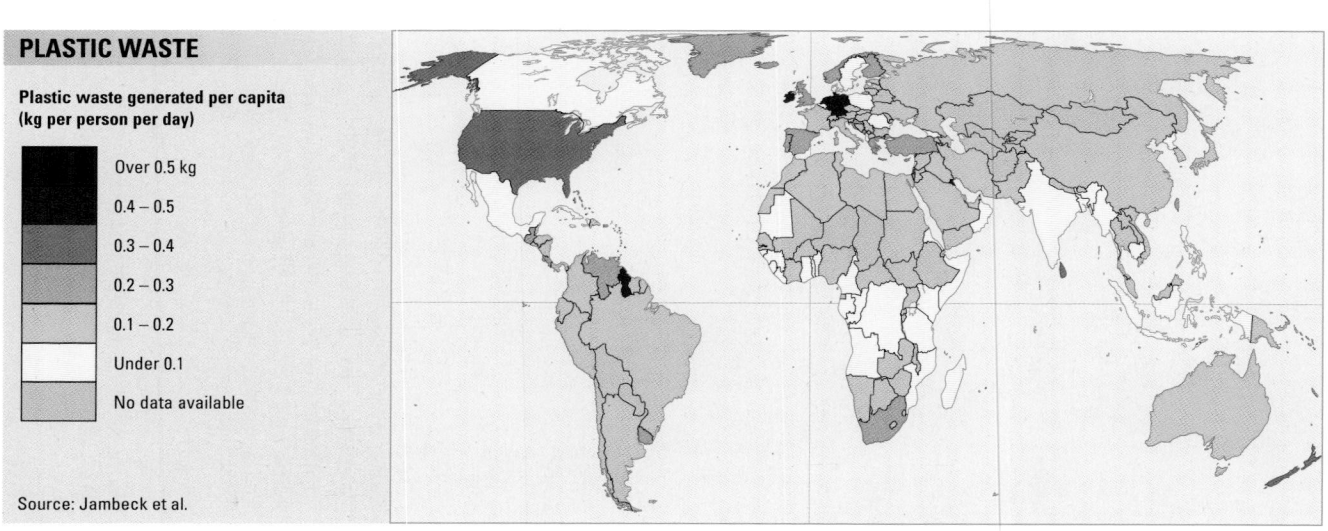

Source: Jambeck et al.

SCALE OF PLASTIC WASTE

Plastic waste as a percentage of total waste

- Over 20%
- 15 – 20%
- 10 – 15%
- 5 – 10%
- Under 5%
- No data available

Highest rates of plastic waste

Palau	32%
Micronesia, Fed. States of.	26%
Kazakhstan	25%

Lowest rates of plastic waste

Monaco	1.0%
Finland	1.5%
Denmark	1.6%

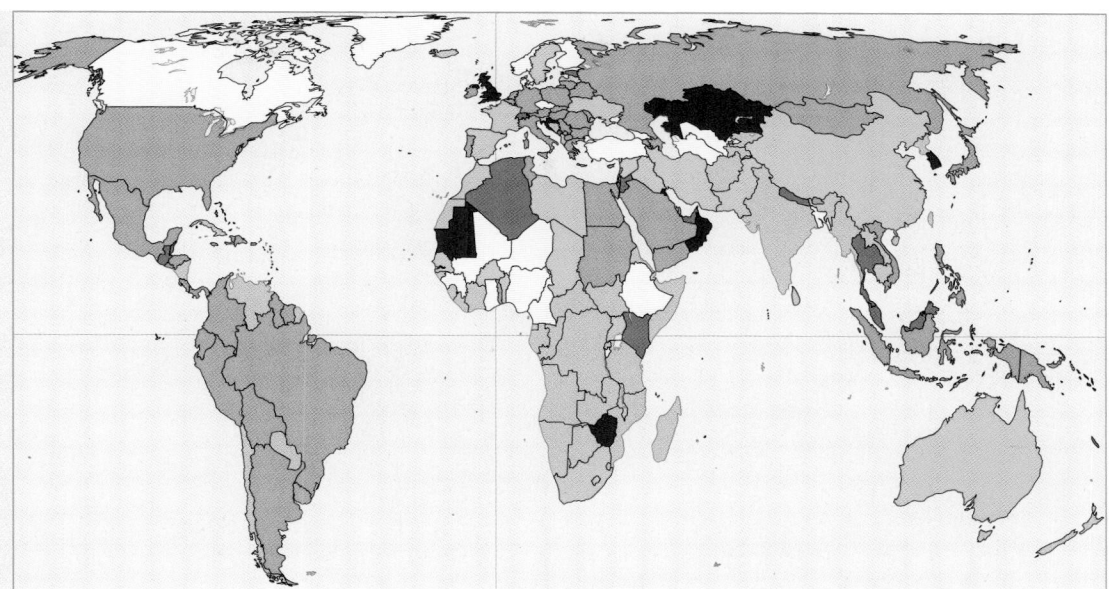

MANAGING PLASTIC WASTE

A ubiquitous sight is that of lightweight plastic bags blowing around city streets and the countryside. Until recently, such bags have been given freely to shoppers but, in many countries, legislation is being adopted to curb their use. Convenient and cheap to manufacture, they are often used once and discarded. However, many governments are now taxing the stores that provide them, suggesting or enforcing a charge paid by the consumer, and even introducing total prohibition. In 2002, Bangladesh was the first country to institute a complete ban on lightweight plastic bags. Similar steps rapidly followed elsewhere and, by 2020, 74 countries had introduced bans (see map right). Some 37 countries have introduced a charge per bag. In some countries, such as the US and Canada, legislation differs between individual states and provinces.

Countries taking steps to control the use of plastic shopping bags

- Bags banned
- Charge for bags
- Voluntary ban
- Charge or ban at regional level
- No data available

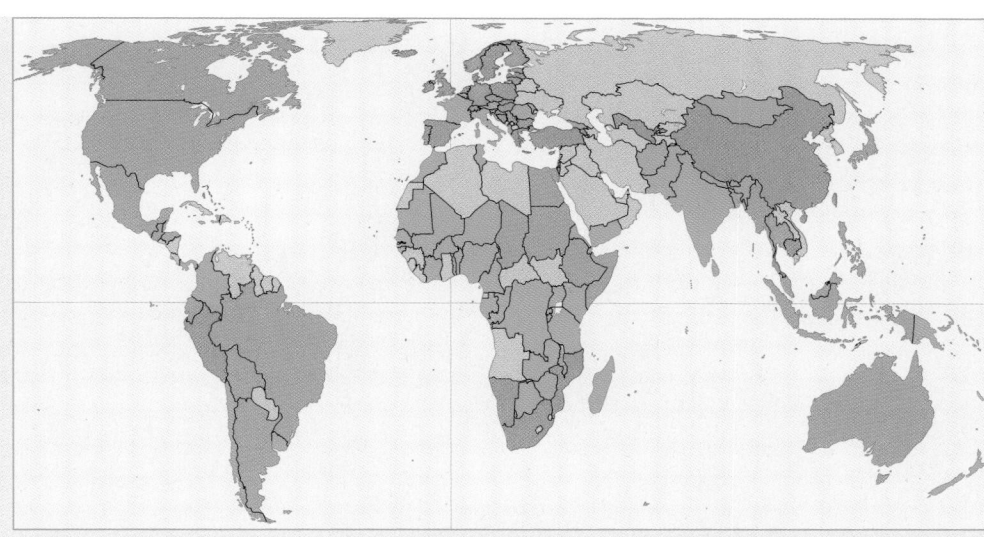

TOP TEN EXPORTERS OF PLASTICS
Cumulative exports of plastics by top ten exporting countries (1988-2016)
Source: Brooks et al. (2018)

Top 10 exporters: Hong Kong, USA, Japan, Germany, Mexico, UK, Netherlands, France, Belgium, Canada (Million Tonnes)

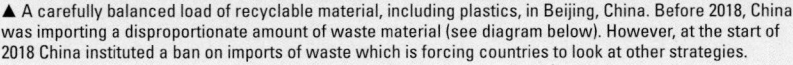
▲ A carefully balanced load of recyclable material, including plastics, in Beijing, China. Before 2018, China was importing a disproportionate amount of waste material (see diagram below). However, at the start of 2018 China instituted a ban on imports of waste which is forcing countries to look at other strategies.

MAJOR EXPORTERS OF PLASTIC WASTE TO CHINA
Million tonnes per annum (2016)

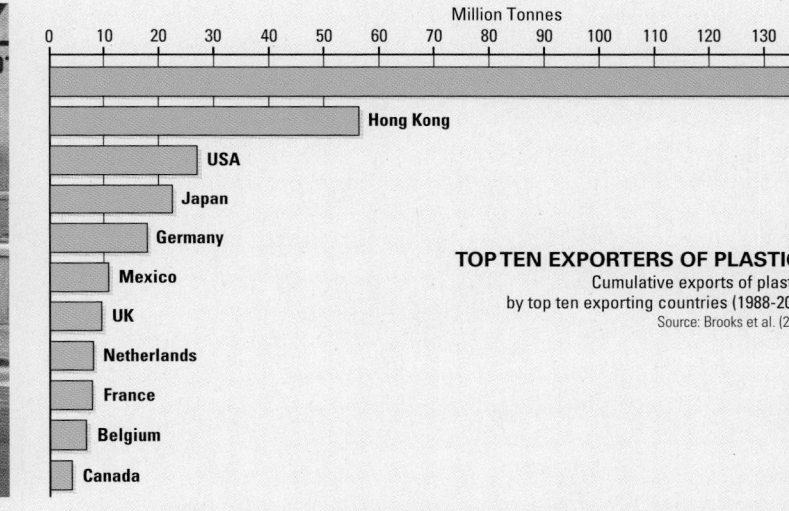

Exports to China & Hong Kong
Exports to other countries

Source: UN COMTRADE (2018)

◄ Environmental problems with plastics stem from the fact that the majority are non-biodegradable. Whereas recycling metal and glass is often financially attractive, recycled plastic is often of low value. Further complications arise from the fact that plastics are not homogeneous in their composition, which causes complications from recycling plastics that are not easily sorted. Recycling commonly leads to a degradation of the resultant material thus decreasing its monetary value. In all, recycling rates remain low at about 10-15% of the total amount produced.

For more information:

84 Ocean Currents

107 UN Sustainable
   Development
   Goals

Plastic waste, without careful manage-ment, can find its way into rivers and ultimately the ocean. The UN Environment Programme estimates that 8 million tonnes of plastic ends up in the oceans every year. A large part of this is transported by rivers, taking garbage from cities to the seas. Ten rivers alone carry over 90% of the plastic waste that ends up in the oceans. The UN also makes the alarming prediction that, by 2050, without concerted action, it is possible that the oceans could contain more plastic than fish. About 50% of all plastic waste in the oceans comes from just five countries – China, Indonesia, Thailand,

the Philippines, and Vietnam. For these countries, experiencing rapid economic growth, increased consumption of goods is producing more waste that is being adequately managed.

The phenomena of waste being swept up in ocean gyres has been recorded (see map below). Around half of the plastics contained in these oceanic areas are large items such as ropes, fishing lines, and nets. The remainder are small pieces and particles.

The effects of plastics in the oceans on wildlife are evident to see. Mammals and birds can become entangled in fishing nets and larger plastic items. Larger species such

as marine turtles, seals, and whales are more prone to injury, or death, in this way. Birds in particular are susceptible to taking in small particles and it has been estimated that over 90% of all seabirds have ingested plastic. Broken down into microscopic particles, plastic is held in suspension in water and can be ingested by fish and ultimately humans.

Plastic waste is undeniably unsightly. Globally three-quarters of beach litter is plastics, with drinks bottles being one of the largest components. Countries are beginning to control, collect, and recycle plastic waste, but much remains to be done.

MOST POLLUTING RIVERS

Rivers act as conduits to transport plastic waste to the marine environment. They are thought to be responsible for around 80% of the plastics found in the oceans. The remainder enters from coastal settlements or is discharged from ships. Estimates have been made of the amount of plastic that rivers have disgorged into the oceans (see graph right). The 20 rivers listed are responsible for two-thirds of the total input. The majority are located in Asia, with the Yangtze being responsible for 4% of the total. It is in Southeast Asia where the problems are especially acute. The fast-growing economies are struggling to keep pace with effective waste management.

The waste can consist of large items or microscopic particles held in suspension. Larger items are easier to collect and remove but once plastics have broken down, they will enter the ocean unhindered.

▼ The Yantze (Chang Jiang) is the longest river in Asia but it also has the dubious accolade of carrying the largest load of plastics to the ocean. Flowing generally eastward, it empties into the East China Sea near Shanghai.

Estimated annual plastic input to the oceans (thousand tonnes)

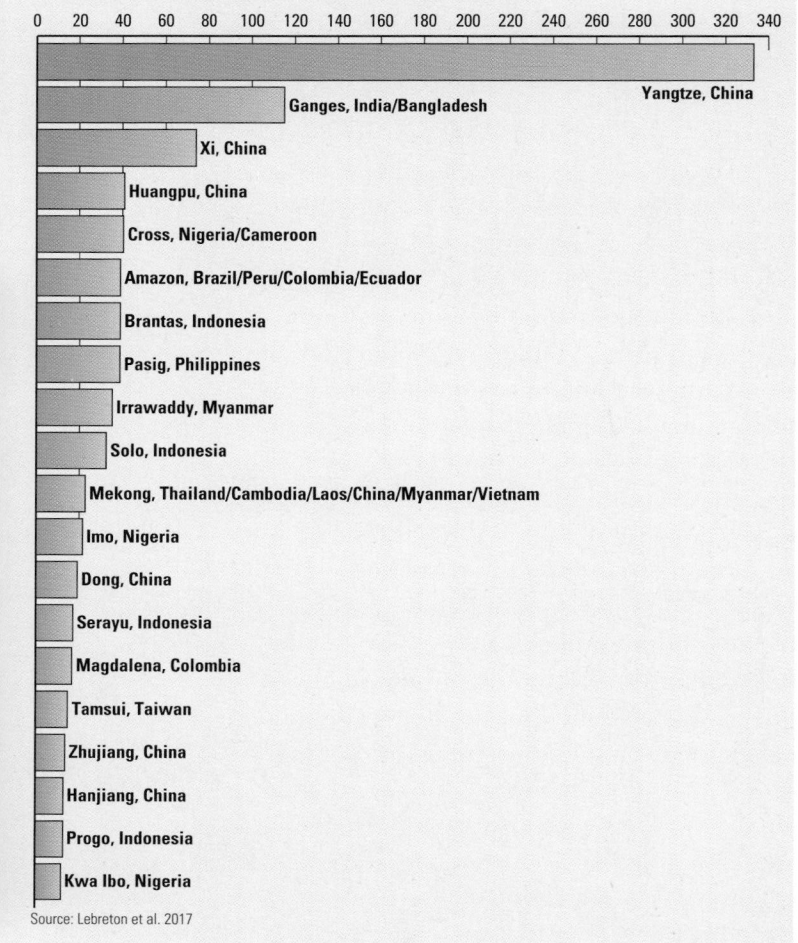

Yangtze, China
Ganges, India/Bangladesh
Xi, China
Huangpu, China
Cross, Nigeria/Cameroon
Amazon, Brazil/Peru/Colombia/Ecuador
Brantas, Indonesia
Pasig, Philippines
Irrawaddy, Myanmar
Solo, Indonesia
Mekong, Thailand/Cambodia/Laos/China/Myanmar/Vietnam
Imo, Nigeria
Dong, China
Serayu, Indonesia
Magdalena, Colombia
Tamsui, Taiwan
Zhujiang, China
Hanjiang, China
Progo, Indonesia
Kwa Ibo, Nigeria

Source: Lebreton et al. 2017

PLASTIC POLLUTION IN OCEANS

Not even the remotest parts of the world's oceans are free of the 8 million tonnes of plastic that enter the seas annually – particles have even been found in Arctic sea ice. Often discarded large items of plastic enter the oceans from rivers as a result of storm-water runoff. Coastal communities also contribute to the total, although estimates of the volume differ greatly. Once in the oceans, marine animals can be entangled in items such as netting. In time, plastics break down into small pieces called microplastics. Once ingested by fish they can be consumed by humans.

OCEANS WITH MOST PLASTIC WASTE

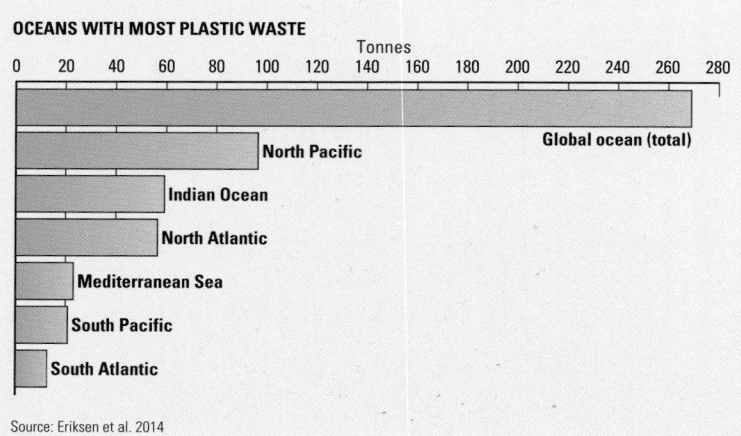

Tonnes

Global ocean (total)
North Pacific
Indian Ocean
North Atlantic
Mediterranean Sea
South Pacific
South Atlantic

Source: Eriksen et al. 2014

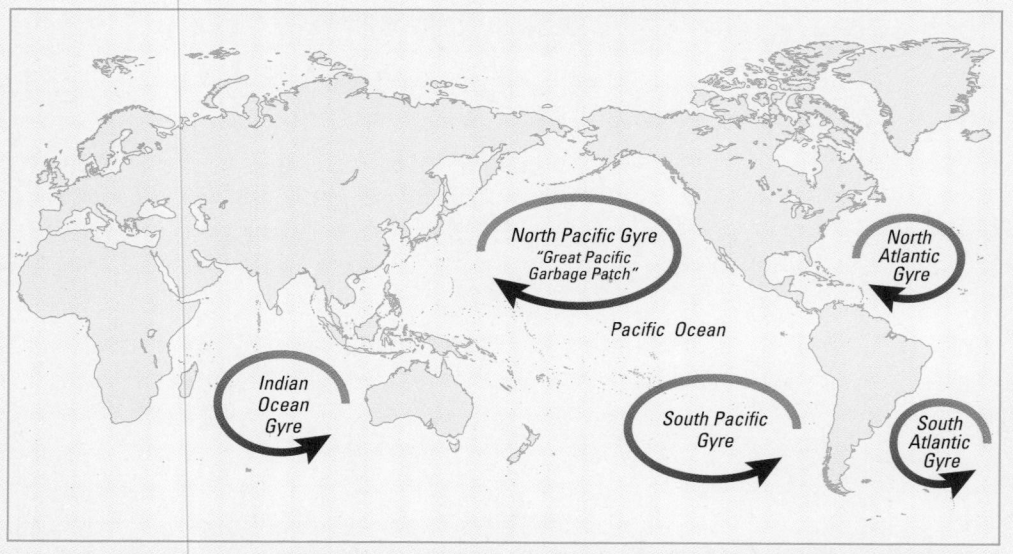

Ocean gyres are circular ocean currents formed by a combination of the Earth's rotation, global wind patterns, and the position of the continents. There are five major ocean gyres as can be seen in the map above. Wind drags on the surface waters causing the water to mirror the wind direction. The circular movement of the gyre traps plastic debris and other waste – most notably in the Great Pacific Garbage Patch. Most of the waste consists of items smaller than one centimeter.

PLASTIC BOTTLES

Human behaviour has to change to avoid scenes such as the one on the right. Plastic bottles make up a large part of discarded waste. The introduction of disposable plastic bottles, once seen as a great convenience, has turned into a major problem. Before their inception, drinks came in glass bottles and cans. It was the switch to using PET (polyethylene terephthalate) in the 1970s that provided lightweight plastic bottles that could be used successfully for carbonated drinks. Governments are now looking at ways to restrict the use of plastic bottles in the same way as they tackled the issue of lightweight plastic bags (see page 11). In some cities, facilities are being provided to allow people to refill reusable containers with safe drinking water. However, current global recycling rates remain low. Some manufacturers of drinks are now setting targets to ensure the materials they use are capable of being recycled and incorporating more recycled plastics into the manufacturing process. Efforts are being made to incorporate the cost of waste management strategies in the initial purchase price.

◄ This not the type of image normally found in tourism brochures. Photographed in 2017, this is Kuta beach, Bali, Indonesia. The results of excessive numbers of visitors coupled with a lack of adequate waste management can be seen clearly.

MARINE SPECIES THREATENED BY PLASTIC POLLUTION

It is only in recent years that the threat to the marine environment, and its wildlife, has been fully realised. A report by the World Wide Fund for Nature (WWF) estimates that more than 1,400 marine species, including sea mammals and birds, are affected by plastic pollution. Danger not only comes from large items, such as bags and discarded fishing nets, but from microscopic particles that enter the food chain. They also predict that by 2050, 99% of all seabirds will have ingested plastic. Some of the most threatened species, and their associated threats, can be grouped under the headings shown here.

Fish, animals, and birds can confuse plastics with food. When they die, their stomachs have been found to be full of plastic. Sometimes the results are not readily visible, such as with baleen whales, that filter huge amounts of seawater with the result that microplastics, and chemicals, build up within their bodies. Humans are also threatened – microplastics work their way up the food chain. The geographical focus for this problem is again Southeast Asia with its fast-growing economies and pressures from burgeoning populations.

FISH
The smallest particles of plastic can enter the bodies of fish through their gills. Lodging in the body of fish, the particles will then be transferred to humans if the fish is eaten.

SEA TURTLES
Turtles can swallow plastic in mistake for food or cvan become entangled in netting. A study found that 50% of sea turtles had swallowed plastics that contributed to their deaths.

DOLPHINS/WHALES/SHARKS
Large sea mammals and sharks can accidenty swallow large pieces of plastic in mistake for prey when hunting for food. Once entangled in their guts, they can starve to death.

SEALS/SEALIONS
Curious seals can be become dangerously entwined in discarded fishing lines and nets. If wrapped around their bodies, injuries and infections, or death, may follow.

SEA BIRDS
This penguin has become entrapped in plastic waste. Birds can swoop and take plastics from the ocean surface or dive deep into the water and mistake plastic for food.

THE FUTURE

The production of plastic has increased exponentially in the seventy years since the 1950s. To date, only a small part of this material has been recycled or incinerated. Can we collectively manage the 80% of material ever produced that is still in the environment? Given the global nature of pollution, international cooperation on an unprecedented scale is needed.

According to the WWF, effectively managing the situation requires a three-pronged attack: eliminate unnecessary plastics, vastly increase global plastic recovery, and move to sustainable plant-based sources for the remaining plastic.

Steps are now being taken in many places to reduce the use of single-use plastics – be it bottles or shopping bags. In some countries, fines are punitive with Kenya setting the highest, with the alternative of four years in jail for using, producing, or selling a plastic bag. Other countries are taking more measured steps, but the movement is spreading.

There is a growing intolerance from the public toward single-use plastics, often as the result of graphic publicity of the environmental consequences.

Plastic pollution is a complex problem that will require complex solutions. Its presence in the environment is rarely benign. The future will need commercial companies, governments, and individuals to cooperate. Improvements to waste management systems, government policies, and public engagement are the key to solutions.

◄ Single-use plastics, in particular bottles, are a major component of plastic pollution. In the US, 50 billion plastic bottles are produced per year – but only one quarter are recycled. Where facilities exist, bottles can be pressed, shredded, and recycled into new bottles.

Uluru rises dramatically from the surrounding desert plains of Central Australia. It is an immense sandstone rock, standing 1,142 feet (348 meters) tall with a base circumference of 5.8 miles (9.4 km). It is not only a great natural wonder but also a site of immense cultural and spiritual significance to the local Aboriginal people, the Anangu, who have lived in the region for at least 10,000 years. In late 2019 the rock was closed to climbers after many years of protest in order to respect its sacred nature. The characteristic red color of Uluru is caused by oxidation of iron-bearing minerals within the rock. It appears to change color according to the position of the sun, glowing a particularly fiery red at sunrise and sunset. Uluru lies within the Uluru–Kata Tjuta National Park, more than 200 miles (320 km) southwest from the nearest large town, Alice Springs.

IMAGES
OF
EARTH

In the center of this image lies Berlin. Its large inner city park, the Tiergarten, can just be seen below the undulating route of the Landwehr Canal. After World War II, Berlin was divided between the Federal Republic of Germany (West Germany) and the Democratic Republic (East Germany), and from 1961 until 1989, the Berlin Wall snaked from north to south, separating the western part of the city from the communist east. On the reunification of Germany in 1990, Berlin regained its status as capital. The River Havel is visible toward the left in this image, as are the lakes which are characteristic of the river at this point in its course. At bottom right is the new Berlin Brandenburg Airport. Its 2011 completion date has been pushed back by an array of financial and construction difficulties, and it is not now due to open until late 2020.

[Map page 115] *CGG Satellite Mapping*

The UNESCO World Heritage Site of Dubrovnik perches on a rocky promontory jutting out into the Adriatic Sea. With the barren Dinaric Alps as a background, and fortifications rising straight up from the water's edge, it is not hard to see why the city is referred to as "the pearl of the Adriatic". Dubrovnik flourished from the 14th century until its fall to Napoleon in 1806 as the city-state of Ragusa – a major maritime and mercantile power. The old town's palaces and fortresses, enclosed by medieval city walls, are a testament to the splendor and wealth of Ragusa. The Dalmatian region is famous for its clear seas and beautiful coastline dotted with bays and islands. Lokrum, the island to the south of Dubrovnik, is an uninhabited nature reserve, and – along with Dubrovnik itself – was used as a location for the filming of *Game of Thrones*.

[Map page 202] *CGG Satellite Mapping*

The center of Madrid lies slightly toward the left in this image, flanked to the west by the hilly Casa de Campo, a former royal hunting estate, and to the east by El Retiro, one of Madrid's largest public parks. Despite the city's strategic location in the heart of the Iberian Peninsula, Madrid was not a major city until Philip II moved the Spanish court there from Toledo in 1561, and it was not until the 17th and 18th centuries that it began to look like a national capital, with the building of palaces, churches and grand public buildings. The city lies on Spain's high meseta, or plateau, and the red soil typical of this semi-arid region can be seen toward the right hand side of the image. Clearly visible toward the top left is the Embalse del Pardo, a reservoir.

[Map page 127] *CGG Satellite Mapping*

The British overseas territory of Gibraltar occupies the tip of the peninsula on the eastern side of the Bay of Gibraltar, on the southern Mediterranean coast of Spain. It can be seen here on the right of the image, with the famous "Rock of Gibraltar" clearly visible as an elongated green patch. The Spanish city on the opposite side of the bay, to the left in this picture, is Algeciras. Gibraltar's strategic position at the entrance to the Mediterranean Sea from the Atlantic Ocean has long made it a desirable territory. It was captured from the Spanish by an Anglo–Dutch fleet in 1704 and formally ceded to Britain by the Treaty of Utrecht in 1713. Gibraltar has been a source of tension with Spain ever since; the population, however, has voted overwhelmingly to remain under British control.
[Map page 195] *CGG Satellite Mapping*

The Dead Sea is a salt lake in the Jordan Rift Valley, fed from the north by the River Jordan, whose muddy waters can just be seen entering the lake near the top of this image. The Dead Sea's water level is the lowest point on the Earth's land surface. The lake is famous for its high salt content, which makes the water dense enough to support bathers. Photographs of tourists floating on the surface while reading newspapers are a familiar sight. Over the last 50 years or so, the water level has fallen dramatically as the amount of water entering from the River Jordan has decreased, mainly due to dams upstream. The lower water level has caused the Dead Sea to split in two. As can clearly be seen in the image, the shallower southern portion has been divided into evaporation pools for the extraction of salt.

[Map page 251] *CGG Satellite Mapping*

The city of Tehran, in north central Iran, stretches from the center to the left of this image. It lies between the snow-covered Elburz Mountains in the north and the Dasht-e Kavir desert to the south. The Elburz Mountains contain Iran's highest peak, Damavand, and its three major ski resorts. Tehran's climate is hot and dry, with the mountains keeping the humidity of the Caspian Sea away from the city. They also, however, along with the low rainfall, serve to trap air pollution, which has become an increasing problem. From the 13th century Tehran was a wealthy trading center, famous for its pomegranates. It expanded under the Safavid dynasty in the 16th century, but did not replace Esfahan as capital of Persia, as it was then known, until the late 18th century. It is now a major metropolis, by far the most populous city in Iran, and contains one-tenth of the country's population.

[Map page 141] *CGG Satellite Mapping*

The capital of the Central Asian republic Kazakhstan was moved from Almaty in the southeast of the country to what was then known as Aqmola in 1997. Its name changed to Astana, and in 2019 to Nur-Sultan, in honor of the long-term president Nursultan Nazarbayev, who had recently resigned. Since becoming capital, the city has been expanded and reconstructed to create an astonishingly modern metropolis, complete with futuristic skyscrapers. Some features can be made out in the image. The semi-circular park protruding into the river on the left bank is the site of the Presidential Palace. Heading west from there is a wide boulevard, whose monumental buildings include the striking Bayterek Tower, which represents a sacred tree of life, topped with a golden egg. The River Ishim broadly divides Nur-Sultan between the old city, which retains hints of its Soviet past, on the right bank, and the new on the left.

[Map page 217] *CGG Satellite Mapping*

Shanghai is the most populous city in China, and one of the most populous cities in the world. Already an important commercial center, it grew rapidly with the economic reforms of the 1990s to become an international hub for trade and finance, and one of the world's busiest container ports. It also has a rich cultural history, and its blend of old and new draws tourists from around the world. The Yangtse River flows across the top of the image, joining the Yellow Sea just to the east. The Huangpu winds through the city, dividing the historic center to the left from the ultra-modern Pudong Area on the right bank. Part of Changxing Island can be seen at the top of the image, a green contrast to the built-up city. Hongqiao – one of Shanghai's two international airports – is clearly visible at the bottom left.

[Map page 138] *CGG Satellite Mapping*

The largest of Spain's Canary Islands, Tenerife lies in the Atlantic Ocean off northwest Africa. Its striking volcanic landscape together with its beaches and pleasant climate have made it a popular tourist destination, particularly for European visitors. The south central part of the island has been a National Park since 1954 and has the large Caldera de las Canadas crater at its heart. The summit of Mount Teide, Spain's highest peak, can be glimpsed in the image as a small white dot, its color coming from the dust deposited by sulfurous fumes. Tenerife's oldest city, San Cristobal de la Laguna, lies in the east of the island. It was founded in the late 15th century and contains many buildings of historical significance, reflecting its past as a center of cultural, artistic and religious significance.

[Map page 153]   *CGG Satellite Mapping*

Kampala lies on the northern shores of
Lake Victoria, which occupies a shallow
depression in a plateau that stretches
between two branches of the Great Rift
Valley. It is by the far the largest lake in Africa
and is shared between Uganda, Tanzania and
Kenya. The lake's characteristically indented
shoreline can be seen in this image, as can
some of the rivers that wind sluggishly
downhill toward the lake. Kampala is one
of Africa's fastest growing cities, with a
population that has more than doubled since
the beginning of the century. It was originally
built on seven hills but has since expanded
over many more. It became the capital of
Uganda in 1963 after the country gained
independence from the United Kingdom.
Kampala had long been an important
settlement, however, serving as the center of
power for the former kingdom of Buganda.
[Map page 268] *CGG Satellite Mapping*

Perth lies on the Indian Ocean in southwestern Australia. It is one of the world's most remote cities, with the ocean to the west and the deserts that make up the vast Australian outback to the east. It serves as the state capital of Western Australia. The two islands visible in this image are Rottnest Island and Garden Island. Rottnest, further offshore, is a nature reserve, popular for its sandy beaches, sheltered coves, salt lakes and wildlife, including the quokka, a small marsupial famous for being appealingly photogenic. Perth was founded in 1829, on the estuary of the Swan River, when the British expanded their settlement in the region. After the discovery of gold, it grew rapidly – the population of Western Australia as a whole more than trebled between 1890 and 1900. These days, the Swan River is well known for its vineyards, which line the banks upstream from Perth.

[Map page 279] *CGG Satellite Mapping*

Toronto lies on the shores of Lake Ontario,
one of the five Great Lakes of North
America. It is Canada's most populous
city, although not its capital, which is
Ottawa, roughly 220 miles (350 km) to
the northeast. Toronto's most famous
landmark is the CN Tower, which lies
slightly inland from the Harbour Front.
It was built by the Canada National
Railways and opened in 1976. With a
height of 1,815 ft (553 m), it provides
wonderful views over the surrounding
area, sometimes as far as Niagara
Falls. Toronto Island lies just offshore.
It is actually a chain of 15 small
interconnected islands, which, as can
be seen in this image, shelter Toronto
Harbour. Ferries travel to the islands
and they are a popular spot for swimming
and water sports. In the west of the
image, below center, the five runways
of Toronto's International Airport can
just be made out.
[Map page 141] *CGG Satellite Mapping*

The Niagara River and the North American Great Lakes were created about 10,000 years ago at the end of the last ice age. The Niagara River drains Lake Erie into Lake Ontario, and it was the uneven erosion of different rock strata on the river's course that eventually carved out the spectacular waterfalls. The Niagara Falls have long been a popular tourist destination, and were well known in the past for such daredevil exploits as going over them in a barrel, or crossing on a tightrope. Goat Island separates the two main waterfalls, with the slightly larger Horseshoe (or Canadian) Falls lying to the east, and the American Falls to the west. The Falls are constantly being eroded, but the rate of erosion has been considerably reduced by the diversion of water above the Falls to hydroelectric power generating facilities.

[Map page 312]   *USDA / CGG Satellite Mapping*

The city of Orlando in Florida is a popular
tourist destination, best known for its
many theme parks. Below center in the
southwestern corner of the image is the
most famous of them all, Disney World,
which opened in 1971. Its success was
a major contributing factor in Orlando's
economic growth and increase in
population over the following decades.
Other theme parks soon followed, and
Orlando is now one of the leading tourist
centers in the world. Its large international
airport can be seen on the right of the
image, below center. The terrain of Orlando
and the surrounding area is generally low
and wet, and the city itself is dotted with
numerous lakes and swamps, most of
which are home to alligators. Top left is the
southeastern corner of Orlando's largest
lake, Apopka. Bottom right is the circular
East Lake Tohopekaliga.

[Map page 133] *CGG Satellite Mapping*

The city of Kingston lies on the southeast coast of Jamaica, backed by the Blue Mountains. The narrow Palisadoes peninsula protects the fine natural harbor and is the location of the Norman Manley airport, named for the prime minister who negotiated Jamaica's full independence in 1962. Kingston itself was founded in 1692 after an earthquake destroyed Port Royal, which was situated at the tip of the peninsula. It became a trading center for raw cane sugar, bananas and rum. The mountains form a verdant backdrop to the city, rising steeply from the coastal plain. The famous Blue Mountain Coffee is grown on the lower slopes, while the higher slopes are preserved as forest. In the 1970s Kingston was a significant force in popular culture, when Bob Marley became the first reggae artist to gain international success.
[Map page 320] *CGG Satellite Mapping*

The historic city of La Paz and its younger neighbor, El Alto, are in the center of this image. La Paz, Bolivia's seat of government and de facto capital, is right of center in a deep bowl-shaped canyon, with the snowcapped peaks of the Andes looming over it from the east. El Alto – and the airport that is visible in the image – lies immediately to the west of La Paz on the flatter land of the high Altiplano. This dry plateau region contrasts with the mountainous landscape seen to the north and east. The cities are home to one of the world's largest, urban cable-car networks. Opened in 2014, it is not only a practical form of public transport for La Paz's steep and overcrowded streets, it also connects the two city centers despite a difference in altitude of more than 1,300 feet (400 meters).

[Map page 330]   *CGG Satellite Mapping*

GAZETTEER
OF
NATIONS

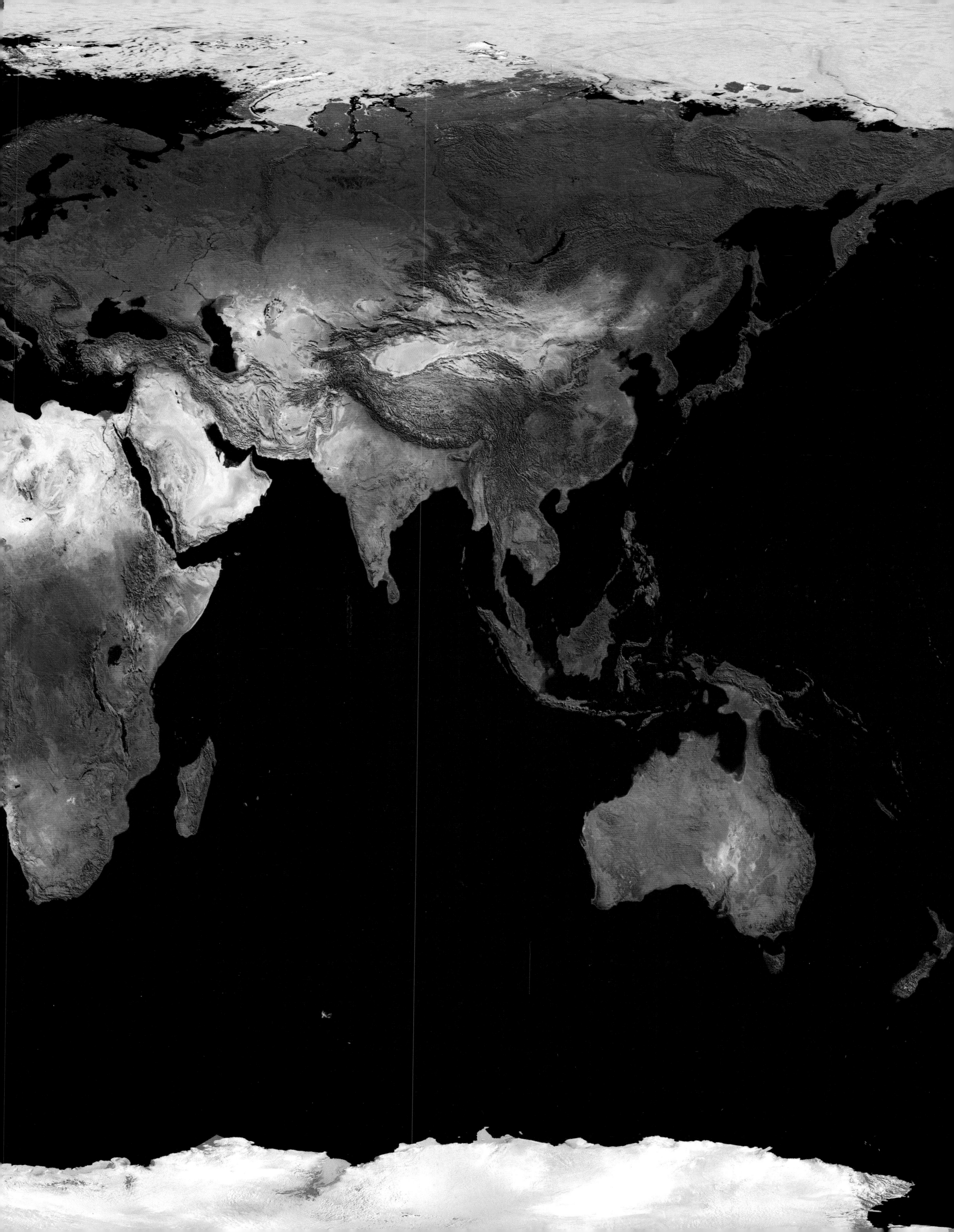

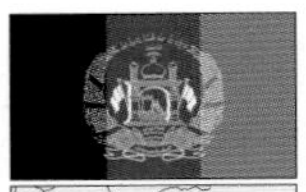
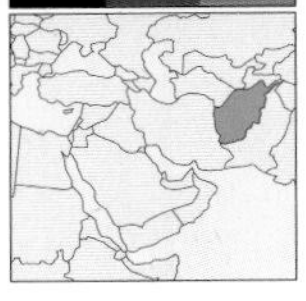

AFGHANISTAN

GEOGRAPHY The Republic of Afghanistan is a landlocked, mountainous country in southern Asia. The central highlands reach a height of more than 22,966 ft [7,000 m] in the east. The main range is the Hindu Kush. In winter, northerly winds bring cold, snowy weather to the mountains, but summers are hot and dry.

POLITICS & ECONOMY The modern history of Afghanistan began in 1747, with the unification of local tribes. In the 19th century, Russia and Britain struggled for control of the country. Following Britain's withdrawal in 1919, Afghanistan became fully independent. Soviet troops invaded in 1979 to support a socialist regime in Kabul, but they withdrew in 1989. By 2001, a group called the Taliban ("Islamic students") controlled 90% of the country. In 2001 an international force invaded Afghanistan, following the September 11 attacks on the US. This NATO-led military force failed to defeat the extremists, and its combat troops were withdrawn in 2014. Presidential elections in the same year saw Ashraf Ghani elected president, with his former rival Abdullah Abdullah becoming chief executive officer. In 2015 Islamic State emerged in the east. The Taliban insurgency continued to grow in strength and many areas remain under constant threat of attack. Despite President Ghani's offer of peace talks in 2018, the Taliban refused to negotiate with his administration. US–Taliban peace talks in 2019 broke down late in the year.

AREA 251,772 SQ MI [652,090 SQ KM] **POPULATION** 36,644,000
CAPITAL KABUL **GOVERNMENT** ISLAMIC REPUBLIC
ETHNIC GROUPS PASHTUN (PATHAN) 42%, TAJIK 27%, HAZARA 9%, UZBEK 9%, OTHERS 13%
LANGUAGES PASHTU, DARI/PERSIAN (BOTH OFFICIAL), UZBEK
RELIGIONS ISLAM (SUNNI MUSLIM 80%, SHI'ITE MUSLIM 19%), OTHERS 1%
CURRENCY AFGHANI = 100 PULS

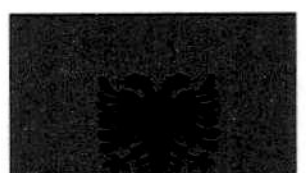
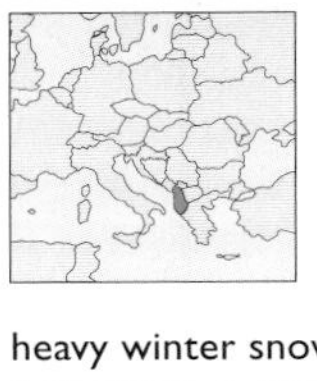

ALBANIA

GEOGRAPHY The Republic of Albania lies in the Balkan peninsula, facing the Adriatic Sea. About 70% of the land is mountainous, with most Albanians living on the western coastal lowlands.

The coastal areas of Albania experience a typical Mediterranean climate, with fairly dry, sunny summers and cool, moist winters. The mountains have a severe climate, with heavy winter snowfalls.

POLITICS & ECONOMY Albania is one of Europe's poorest nations. A former Communist country, ruled for nearly 50 years by the Stalinist dictator Enver Hoxha, Albania adopted a multiparty system in the early 1990s. The transition to democracy has been hindered by poor infrastructure and widespread corruption. A center-right government was defeated in 2013 by a Socialist-led coalition, which has pledged to fight organised crime and crack down on the trafficking and production of illegal drugs.

Albania has been a member of NATO since 2009 and was granted EU candidate status in 2014. In 2017, agriculture employed about 42% of the people. Albania has some oil, gas, and minerals; exports include footwear, chromite, copper, and nickel.

AREA 11,100 SQ MI [28,748 SQ KM] **POPULATION** 3,075,000
CAPITAL TIRANA **GOVERNMENT** MULTIPARTY REPUBLIC
ETHNIC GROUPS ALBANIAN 83%, GREEK 1%, MACEDONIAN, VLACH, ROMA
LANGUAGES ALBANIAN (OFFICIAL)
RELIGIONS ISLAM 57%, CHRISTIANITY 17% (ROMAN CATHOLIC 10%, ORTHODOX 7%)
CURRENCY LEK = 100 QINDARS

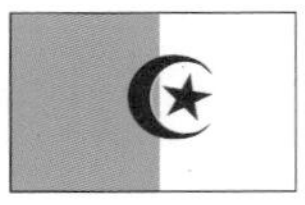
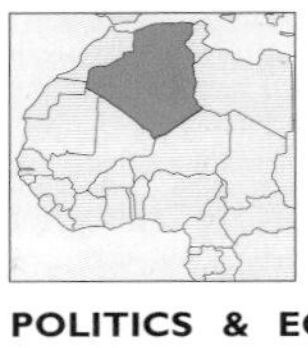

ALGERIA

GEOGRAPHY The People's Democratic Republic of Algeria is Africa's largest country. Most Algerians live in the north, on the fertile coastal plains and hill country bordering the Mediterranean Sea. Four-fifths of Algeria is in the Sahara, the world's largest desert. The coast has a Mediterranean climate but the arid Sahara is hot by day and cold at night.

POLITICS & ECONOMY France ruled Algeria from 1830 until 1962, when the socialist FLN (National Liberation Front) formed a one-party government. Following the recognition of opposition parties in 1989, a Muslim group, the FIS (Islamic Salvation Front), won an election in 1991. The FLN canceled the elections and civil conflict broke out. About 100,000 people were killed in the 1990s. Abdelaziz Bouteflika began four terms as president in 1999. Despite constitutional changes in 2016 limiting presidents to two terms, Bouteflika announced that he would stand in 2019 elections, and the resulting street protests led to his resignation. A presidential election in December of that year, boycotted by opposition parties, was won by Bouteflika's associate Abdelmadjid Tebboune.

Algeria's chief resources are oil and natural gas, which account for about 95% of export revenue. Its gas reserves are the largest in Africa. The challenge for the future is to diversify the economy. Cement, iron and steel, textiles, and vehicles are manufactured.

AREA 919,590 SQ MI [2,381,741 SQ KM] **POPULATION** 42,973,000
CAPITAL ALGIERS **GOVERNMENT** SOCIALIST REPUBLIC
ETHNIC GROUPS ARAB-BERBER 99%
LANGUAGES ARABIC AND BERBER (OFFICIAL), FRENCH **RELIGIONS** SUNNI MUSLIM 99% **CURRENCY** ALGERIAN DINAR = 100 SANTEEM

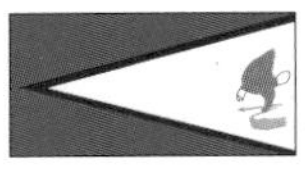
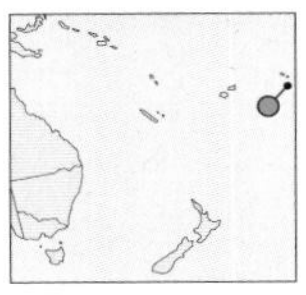

AMERICAN SAMOA

An "unincorporated territory" of the United States, American Samoa lies in the south-central Pacific Ocean.

AREA 77 SQ MI [199 SQ KM]
POPULATION 49,000 **CAPITAL** PAGO PAGO

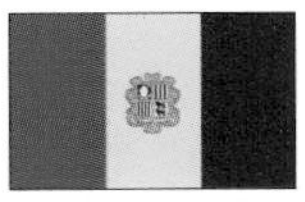
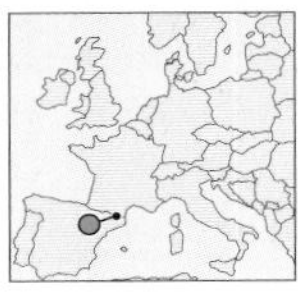

ANDORRA

In this prosperous mini-state, situated in the Pyrenees Mountains, tourism (especially winter sports) accounts for almost 80% of GDP. Most Andorrans live in the six valleys (the Valls) that drain into the River Valira.

AREA 181 SQ MI [468 SQ KM]
POPULATION 77,000 **CAPITAL** ANDORRA LA VELLA

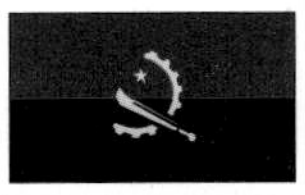
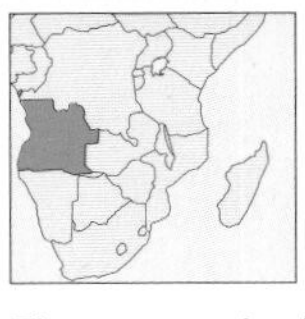

ANGOLA

GEOGRAPHY Situated in southwestern Africa, the Republic of Angola is the seventh largest country on the continent. Much of Angola lies on the South African plateau, with only a narrow coastal plain in the west.

Angola has a tropical climate, with temperatures of over 68°F [20°C] throughout the year, though the highest areas are cooler. The coast is dry, but the rainfall increases to the north and east.

POLITICS & ECONOMY Portugal controlled the coastal slave trade from the 17th century and extended its control inland in the 19th century. Independence, gained in 1975, was followed by 27 years of civil war which only finally ended when the rebel leader, Jonas Savimbi, was killed in 2002. Elections in 2008 began a transition toward a more democratic system. In 2017, after 38 years in power, Jose Eduardo dos Santos stood down as president and was replaced by former defence minister, Joao Lourenco.

Angola is a developing country, where 85% of the people are poor farmers. The main food crops are cassava and maize with coffee being exported. Angola has important oil reserves. Angola also mines diamonds and has reserves of copper, manganese, and phosphates. From 2005, foreign loans and oil revenue fueled a building boom, although growth slowed with lower oil prices worldwide.

AREA 481,351 SQ MI [1,246,700 SQ KM] **POPULATION** 32,522,000
CAPITAL LUANDA **GOVERNMENT** MULTIPARTY REPUBLIC
ETHNIC GROUPS OVIMBUNDU 37%, KIMBUNDU 25%, BAKONGO 13%, OTHERS 25%
LANGUAGES PORTUGUESE (OFFICIAL), MANY OTHERS
RELIGIONS ROMAN CATHOLIC 41%, PROTESTANT 38%, OTHERS 9%, NONE 12%
CURRENCY KWANZA = 100 CÊNTIMOS

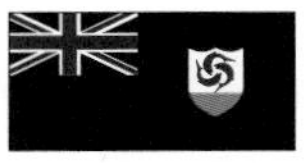
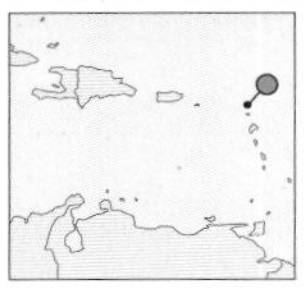

ANGUILLA

Formerly part of St Kitts and Nevis, Anguilla, the most northerly of the Leeward Islands, became a British dependency (now a British overseas territory) in 1980. The main sources of revenue are tourism and offshore banking, with lobster accounting for half of exports.

AREA 37 SQ MI [96 SQ KM]
POPULATION 18,000 **CAPITAL** THE VALLEY

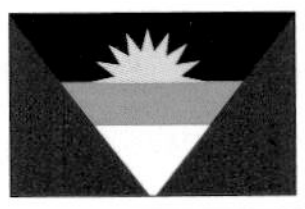
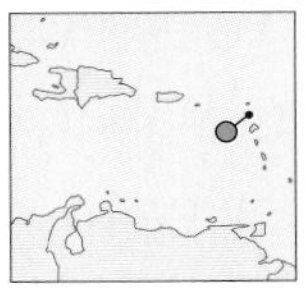

ANTIGUA & BARBUDA

This former British dependency became independent in 1981. Tourism and offshore banking are vital to its service-based economy. In 2017 Hurricane Irma devastated Barbuda.

AREA 171 SQ MI [442 SQ KM]
POPULATION 98,000 **CAPITAL** ST JOHN'S

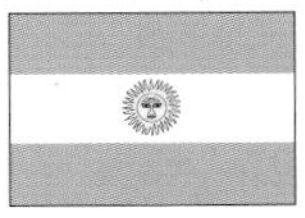
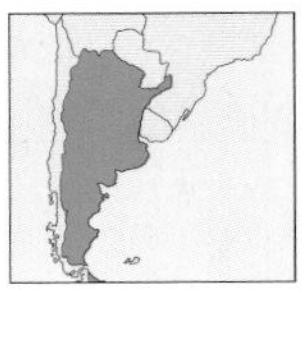

ARGENTINA

GEOGRAPHY The Argentine Republic is South America's second largest and the world's eighth largest country. In the west, the high Andes range contains Mount Aconcagua, the highest peak in the Americas. In southern Argentina, the Andes Mountains overlook Patagonia, a plateau region. The fertile plain of the Pampas occupies the east-central area.

The climate varies from subtropical in the north to temperate in the south. Rainfall is abundant in the north-east but lower to the west and south. Patagonia is largely desert.

POLITICS & ECONOMY The earliest people were American Indians, but 86% of the people are now of European ancestry. After Spanish rule ended in 1816, Argentina experienced periods of regional instability and military rule. In 1982, Argentina's military regime invaded the Falkland (Malvinas) Islands, but Britain regained the islands later that year. In 1983 civilian rule was restored.

In 1991, Argentina was a founding member of the South American trade bloc Mercosur, but it has suffered from recurring economic crises. Government policies in response to an economic, social, and political crisis in 2001 barely allowed fitful recovery, and the country defaulted on repayment of its international debt in 2002 and 2014. Despite major market reforms following the election of Conservative Mauricio Macri in 2015, the World Bank downgraded Argentina's economy to "upper-middle-income" in 2019. In presidential elections that year, Macri was defeated by the center-left Peronist candidate Alberto Fernandez. Manufactures include food products, cars, and textiles. Oil is the main resource and the chief farm products are beef, soybeans, maize, and wheat. Exports include oil, meat, soybeans, wheat, maize, hides and skins, and wool.

AREA 1,073,512 SQ MI [2,780,400 SQ KM] **POPULATION** 45,479,000
CAPITAL BUENOS AIRES **GOVERNMENT** FEDERAL REPUBLIC
ETHNIC GROUPS EUROPEAN 97%, MESTIZO, AMERINDIAN
LANGUAGES SPANISH (OFFICIAL)
RELIGIONS ROMAN CATHOLIC 92%, PROTESTANT 2%, JEWISH 2%, OTHERS
CURRENCY ARGENTINE PESO = 100 CENTAVOS

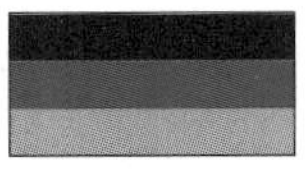
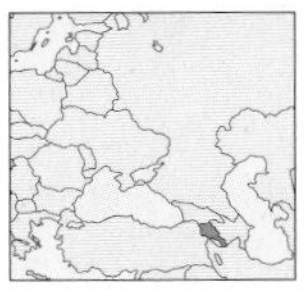

ARMENIA

GEOGRAPHY The Republic of Armenia is a landlocked country in southwestern Asia. Most of Armenia consists of a rugged plateau, crisscrossed by long faultlines which make the area prone to earthquakes. The highest point is Mount Aragats, at 13,419 ft [4,090 m] above sea level. The height of the land gives rise to severe winters and cool summers. The highest peaks are snow-capped, but the total yearly rainfall is generally low.

POLITICS & ECONOMY In 1920, Armenia became a Communist republic and, in 1922, it became, with Azerbaijan and Georgia, part of the Transcaucasian Republic within the Soviet Union. But the three territories became separate Soviet Socialist Republics in 1936. After the breakup of the Soviet Union in 1991, Armenia became an independent republic. The ongoing dispute over Nagorno-Karabakh, an area enclosed by Azerbaijan where most people are Armenians, has caused conflict and instability which has hampered economic development. The issue also sours relations with Turkey.

Armenia's economy has suffered because of its former dependency on a centrally planned Soviet system. In 2015, the country joined the Russian-led Eurasian Customs Union, and in 2017 it signed a Comprehensive and Enhanced Partnership Agreement (CEPA) with the EU. In April 2018 unprecedented street protests led to the appointment of Nikol Pashinyan as prime minister. His My Step Alliance later won a majority in parliamentary elections.

AREA 11,506 SQ MI [29,800 SQ KM] **POPULATION** 3,021,000
CAPITAL YEREVAN **GOVERNMENT** MULTIPARTY REPUBLIC
ETHNIC GROUPS ARMENIAN 98%, YEZIDI 1%
LANGUAGES ARMENIAN (OFFICIAL)
RELIGIONS ARMENIAN APOSTOLIC 95%
CURRENCY DRAM = 100 LUMA

NOTE: This alphabetical list includes the principal countries and territories of the world. The area figures give the total area of land, inland water, and ice. The population figures are 2020 estimates where available.

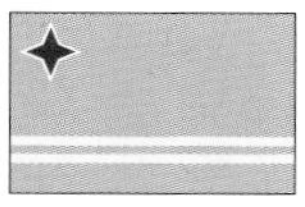
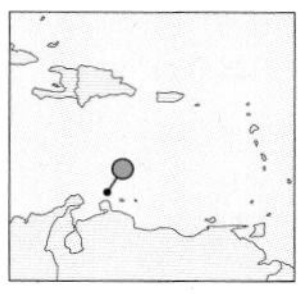

ARUBA

Formerly part of the Netherlands Antilles, Aruba (the most westerly of the Lesser Antilles) became a separate self-governing Dutch territory in 1986.

AREA 75 sq mi [193 sq km]
POPULATION 119,000 **CAPITAL** Oranjestad

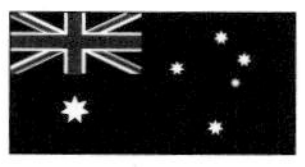
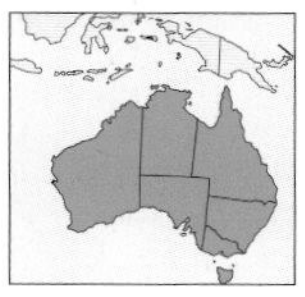

AUSTRALIA

GEOGRAPHY The Commonwealth of Australia, the world's sixth largest country, is also a continent. Australia is the flattest of the continents with its main highlands lying in the east. Here the Great Dividing Range separates the eastern coastal plains from the Central Plains. This range extends from Cape York Peninsula to Victoria in the far south. The longest rivers, the Murray and Darling, drain the southeastern part of the Central Plains. The Western Plateau makes up two-thirds of Australia. A few mountain ranges break the monotony of the generally flat landscape. Only 10% of Australia, notably the tropical north, the northeast coast and the southeast, has an average annual rainfall of more than 39 inches [1,000 mm]. But extreme weather events, including a prolonged drought in the Murray–Darling basin in the early 21st century and severe flooding in Queensland in 2010–12, cause periodic problems. Record-breaking temperatures in 2019 to 2020 led to devastating bush fires in southeast Australia.

POLITICS & ECONOMY The Aboriginal people of Australia entered the continent from Southeast Asia more than 50,000 years ago. The first European explorers were Dutch in the 17th century, but they did not settle. In 1770, the British Captain Cook explored the east coast and, in 1788, the first British settlement was established for convicts on the site of what is now Sydney. Whilst maintaining links with the British Isles, the last 50 years have seen people from other parts of Europe and, most recently, from Asia settling in the country. Ties with Britain were also weakened by Britain's membership of the European Union, and Australia has now forged stronger links with the nations of eastern Asia, especially China, Indonesia, and Japan. The issue of retaining the monarch of the UK as the head of state is a recurring theme but, in a referendum in 1999, the majority of Australians voted to remain a constitutional monarchy. The conservative Liberal–National coalition swept into power in 2013, ending six years of Labor Party rule.

Australia is a prosperous country. Crops can be grown on only 6% of the land, with dry pasture covering another 58%. Yet the country remains a major producer and exporter of farm products, particularly cattle, wheat, and wool. Grapes grown for wine-making are also important. The country is rich in a wide range of minerals, and Australia also produces oil and natural gas. Metals, minerals and farm products account for the bulk of exports. Australia's imports are mostly manufactured goods, though its own manufacturing industry is growing. The service sector contributes over 70% of total GDP.

AREA 2,988,885 sq mi [7,741,220 sq km] **POPULATION** 25,466,000
CAPITAL Canberra **GOVERNMENT** Federal constitutional monarchy
ETHNIC GROUPS Caucasian 92%, Asian 7%, Aboriginal 1%
LANGUAGES English (official) **RELIGIONS** Non-Christian 30%, Roman Catholic 23%, Protestant 23%, other Christian 6%
CURRENCY Australian dollar = 100 cents

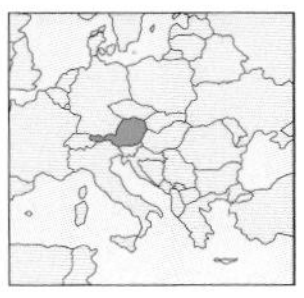

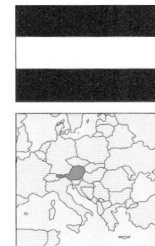

AUSTRIA

GEOGRAPHY Austria is a landlocked country at the heart of Europe. The River Danube flows across northern Austria on its way from Germany to the Black Sea. Southern Austria contains ranges of the Alps, reaching their highest point at Grossglockner, 12,457 ft [3,797 m] above sea level.

The climate is temperate in the west and more continental in the east. Winters are cold and snowy. Summers are warm and dry in the east.

POLITICS & ECONOMY Formerly part of the Austro-Hungarian Empire, Austria was annexed by Germany in 1938. In 1955, Austria became a neutral federal republic, later joining the European Union in 1995. In recent years, Austria has been governed by coalitions. In 2017 new chancellor Sebastian Kurz of the right-wing People's Party formed a coalition with the far-right Freedom Party. Following elections in 2019, he remained in power, now in coalition with the Green Party. Alexander Van der Bellen, allied with the Green Party, has been president since 2016.

Austria has a highly developed economy, with plenty of hydroelectric power and some oil, gas, and coal reserves. Although manufacturing, metals, and metal products are important to the economy, banking, insurance services, and tourism predominate. Dairy and livestock farming are the leading agricultural activities. Major crops include barley, potatoes, rye, sugar beet, and wheat.

AREA 32,378 sq mi [83,859 sq km] **POPULATION** 8,859,000
CAPITAL Vienna **GOVERNMENT** Federal republic
ETHNIC GROUPS Austrian 81%, German, Bosnian, Turkish, others
LANGUAGES German (official) **RELIGIONS** Roman Catholic 57%, Eastern Orthodox 9%, Islam 8% **CURRENCY** Euro = 100 cents

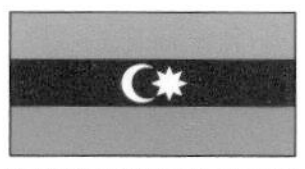
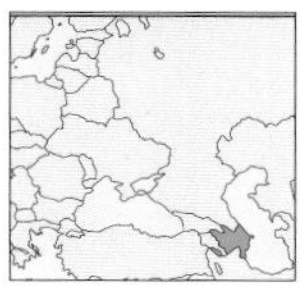

AZERBAIJAN

GEOGRAPHY The Azerbaijani Republic is a country in the southwest of Asia, facing the Caspian Sea to the east. It includes the area of the Naxçivan Autonomous Republic, which is completely cut off from the rest of Azerbaijan by Armenian territory. The Caucasus Mountains border Russia in the north.

Azerbaijan has hot summers and cool winters. The plains are fairly dry, but the mountains are rainy.

POLITICS & ECONOMY For a short period after the Russian Revolution of 1917, Azerbaijanis set up an independent state before the area was occupied by Russian forces in 1920. In 1922, the Communists set up a Transcaucasian Republic consisting of Armenia, Azerbaijan, and Georgia under Russian control. In 1936, the three areas became separate Soviet Socialist Republics within the Soviet Union. In 1991, following the breakup of the Soviet Union, Azerbaijan became an independent nation again. After independence, Azerbaijan clashed with Armenia over the enclave of Nagorno-Karabakh. A ceasefire in 1994 left Armenia in control of 20% of Azerbaijan's area, including Nagorno-Karabakh.

Azerbaijan has huge oil reserves. Oil extraction and manufacturing, including oil refining, and the production of chemicals, are vital for the export earnings which are funding investment in the country's infrastructure. Problems remain with corruption, and the government, which has been led by members of the Aliyev family since 1993, has been accused of authoritarianism.

AREA 33,436 sq mi [86,600 sq km] **POPULATION** 10,206,000
CAPITAL Baku **GOVERNMENT** Federal multiparty republic
ETHNIC GROUPS Azeri 91%, Dagestani 2%, Russian 2%, Armenian, others **LANGUAGES** Azerbaijani (official), Lezgi, Russian, Armenian
RELIGIONS Islam 93%, Russian Orthodox 2%, Armenian Orthodox 2%
CURRENCY Azerbaijani manat = 100 qapik

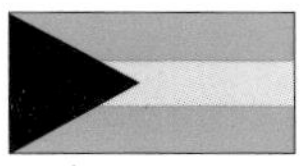
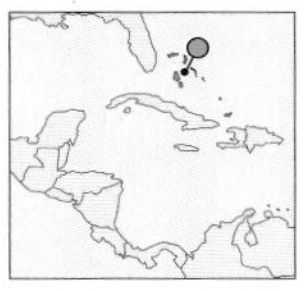

BAHAMAS, THE

A coral-limestone archipelago off the coast of Florida, The Bahamas became independent from Britain in 1973, and has since developed strong ties with the United States. Tourism and banking are major activities.

AREA 5,358 sq mi [13,878 sq km]
POPULATION 338,000 **CAPITAL** Nassau

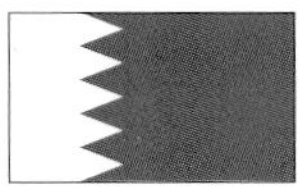
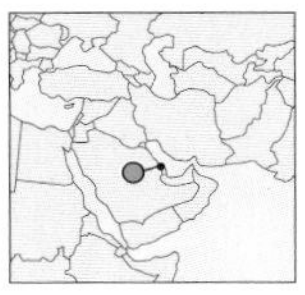

BAHRAIN

The Kingdom of Bahrain, an island nation in the Persian Gulf, became independent from the UK in 1971. An important financial services center, it is less dependent on oil than other Gulf states. Oil accounts for 60% of its exports. There have been protests by the Shia majority of the population claiming discrimination by the ruling Sunni minority.

AREA 268 sq mi [694 sq km]
POPULATION 1,505,000 **CAPITAL** Manama

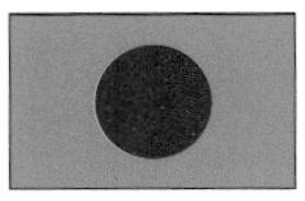
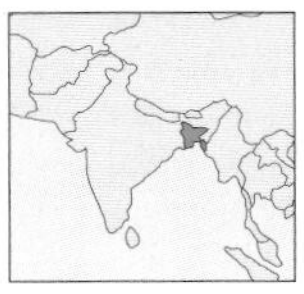

BANGLADESH

GEOGRAPHY The People's Republic of Bangladesh is one of the world's most densely populated countries. Apart from hilly regions in the far northeast and southeast, most of the land is flat and covered by fertile alluvium spread over the land by the Ganges, Brahmaputra, and Meghna rivers. These rivers overflow when they are swollen by the annual monsoon rains. Dry northerly winds blow in winter, but moist southerly winds bring heavy rain in summer. Bangladesh is likely to be badly affected by global rises in sea levels.

POLITICS & ECONOMY In 1947, British India was partitioned between the mainly Hindu India and the Muslim Pakistan. Pakistan consisted of two parts, West and East Pakistan, which were separated by about 1,000 mi [1,600 km] of Indian territory. Differences developed between West and East Pakistan and after a nine-month civil war, East Pakistan declared itself to be the new nation of Bangladesh in 1971. A famine in 1974 and military coup in 1975 were followed by political upheavals until a democratic parliamentary system of government was restored in 1991. The army briefly took control in 2007, but elections in 2008 returned Sheikh Hasina's Awami League to power. There has been a rise in Islamic extremism in recent years.

Bangladesh is one of the world's poorest countries. Its economy depends mainly on agriculture, and garment production.

AREA 55,598 sq mi [143,998 sq km] **POPULATION** 162,651,000
CAPITAL Dhaka **GOVERNMENT** Multiparty republic
ETHNIC GROUPS Bengali 98%, tribal groups
LANGUAGES Bengali (official), English **RELIGIONS** Islam 89%, Hinduism 10% **CURRENCY** Taka = 100 paisas

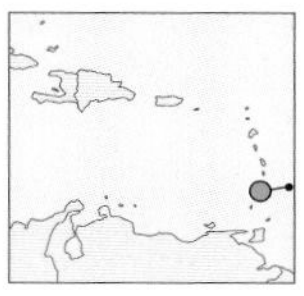

BARBADOS

The most easterly Caribbean country, Barbados became independent from the UK in 1966. A densely populated island, Barbados is prosperous by comparison with most Caribbean countries.

AREA 166 sq mi [430 sq km]
POPULATION 295,000 **CAPITAL** Bridgetown

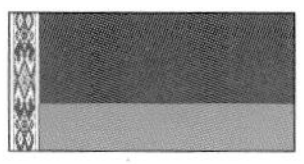
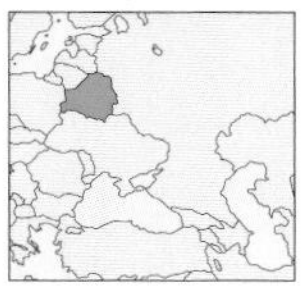

BELARUS

GEOGRAPHY The Republic of Belarus is a landlocked country in Eastern Europe. The land is low-lying and mostly flat. In the south, much of it is marshy and this area contains Europe's largest marsh and peat bog, the Pripet Marshes. The climate is affected by both the moderating influence of the Baltic Sea and continental conditions to the east. The winters are cold and the summers warm.

POLITICS & ECONOMY In 1918, Belarus (White Russia) became an independent republic, but Russia invaded the country and, in 1919, a Communist state was set up. In 1922, Belarus became a founder republic of the Soviet Union. In 1991, Belarus again became an independent republic, and though Belarus continued to support reunification with Russia, any surrender of sovereignty was not expected. President Alexander Lukashenko, who has been re-elected five times between 1994 and 2015, has been criticized for his autocratic rule, his poor record on human rights, and his disregard for freedom of speech.

According to the World Bank, Belarus has an "upper-middle-income" economy. Most economic activities remain under government control. From the 1990s, the economy stagnated, but 2017 onward saw signs of modest economic recovery. Mining and manufacturing are the most valuable activities.

AREA 80,154 sq mi [207,600 sq km] **POPULATION** 9,478,000
CAPITAL Minsk **GOVERNMENT** Multiparty republic
ETHNIC GROUPS Belarusian 84%, Russian 8%, Polish, Ukrainian, others
LANGUAGES Belarusian, Russian (both official)
RELIGIONS Eastern Orthodox 80%, others 20%
CURRENCY Belarusian ruble = 100 kapyeyka

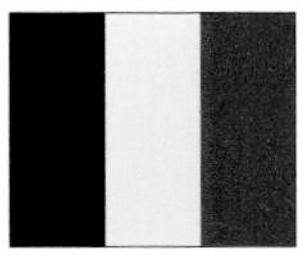
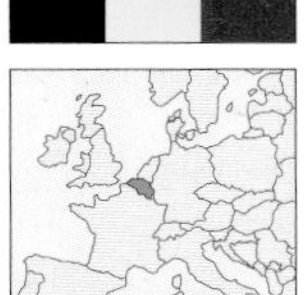

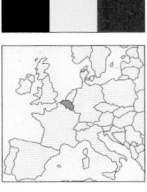

BELGIUM

GEOGRAPHY The Kingdom of Belgium is a densely populated country in Western Europe. Behind the coastline on the North Sea, which is 39 mi [63 km] long, lie its coastal plains. Central Belgium consists of low plateaux and the only highland region is the Ardennes in the southeast.

Belgium has a cool, temperate climate. Moist winds from the Atlantic Ocean bring fairly heavy rain, especially in the Ardennes.

POLITICS & ECONOMY In 1815, Belgium and the Netherlands united as the "low countries," but Belgium became independent in 1830. Belgium's economy was weakened by the two World Wars, but, from 1945, the country recovered quickly, first through

collaboration with the Netherlands and Luxembourg, which formed a customs union called Benelux, and later through its membership of the European Union.

Tension between the Dutch-speaking Flemings in the north and the French-speaking Walloons in the south is an ongoing political problem. In the 1970s, the government divided the country into three economic regions: Flanders, Wallonia, and bilingual Brussels. In 1993, Belgium adopted a federal constitution, giving each region its own parliament. Since 2014, Charles Michel has led a four-party coalition. King Philippe succeeded to the throne in 2013. In March 2016, Islamic State terrorists targeted Brussels' Zaventem Airport and Maalbeek station.

Belgium is a major trading nation, though, with few natural resources, most materials used in manufacturing are imported. Major products include chemicals, processed food, and steel. Flanders has a long history of textile production. Agriculture employs less than 2% of the people, but farmers produce most of the country's food. Barley and wheat are major crops, followed by flax, hops, potatoes, and sugar beet. But the most valuable agricultural activities are dairy farming and livestock rearing. Brussels is a major center for diplomacy.

AREA 11,787 sq mi [30,528 sq km] **POPULATION** 11,721,000
CAPITAL Brussels **GOVERNMENT** Federal constitutional monarchy
ETHNIC GROUPS Belgian 89% (Fleming 58%, Walloon 31%), others 11%
LANGUAGES Dutch, French, German (all official)
RELIGIONS Roman Catholic 75%, others 25%
CURRENCY Euro = 100 cents

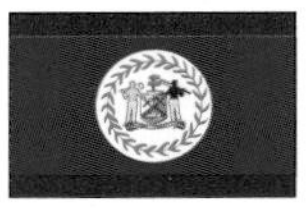
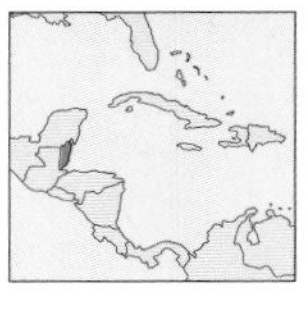

BELIZE

GEOGRAPHY Behind the southern coastal plain, the land rises to the Maya Mountains, which reach 3,674 ft [1,120 m] at Victoria Peak. The north is mostly low-lying and swampy. Temperatures are high all year round, while the average annual rainfall ranges from 51 inches [1,300 mm] in the north to over 150 inches [3,800 mm] in the south. Hurricanes caused much damage in the 1990s and 2000s, but tourist numbers have continued to increase.

POLITICS & ECONOMY From 1862, Belize (then called British Honduras) was a British colony. Full independence was achieved in 1981, but Guatemala, which had claimed the area since the early 19th century, opposed this. Relations improved in the 1990s, when Guatemala recognized Belize's independence although there are still tensions over a boundary dispute. In 2011, the United States added Belize and El Salvador to its list of illegal drug producers.

The World Bank classifies Belize as an "upper-middle-income" developing country. Its economy is based on agriculture, and sugarcane is the chief commercial crop. Other crops include bananas, citrus fruits, maize, and rice. Forestry, fishing, and tourism are other important economic activities, with the last being Belize's chief foreign earner.

AREA 8,867 sq mi [22,966 sq km] **POPULATION** 400,000
CAPITAL Belmopan **GOVERNMENT** Constitutional monarchy
ETHNIC GROUPS Mestizo 49%, Creole 25%, Mayan Indian 11%, Garifuna 6%, others 9%
LANGUAGES English (official), Spanish, Creole, Maya
RELIGIONS Roman Catholic 39%, Protestant 27%, others
CURRENCY Belizean dollar = 100 cents

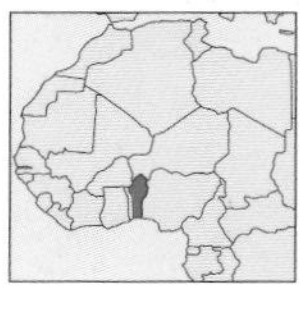

BENIN

GEOGRAPHY The Republic of Benin is one of Africa's smallest countries. It extends north–south for about 390 mi [620 km]. Lagoons line the short coastline, and the country has no natural harbors.

Benin has a hot, wet climate. The average annual temperature on the coast is about 77°F [25°C], and the average rainfall is around 52 inches [1,330 mm]. The inland plains are wetter than the coast.

POLITICS & ECONOMY After slavery was ended in the 19th century, the French gained influence in the area. Benin became self-governing in 1958 and fully independent as Dahomey in 1960. After much instability and many changes of government, a military group took over in 1972. The country, renamed Benin in 1975, became a one-party socialist state. Socialism was abandoned in 1989 and former coup leader Mathieu Kérékou served as president until 2006, when a former banker, Thomas Yayi Boni, was elected president. In 2016 elections, businessman Patrice Talon defeated the ruling party candidate.

Benin is classified by the World Bank as "low income". Exports include cotton, petroleum, and palm products. Cocoa, nuts, and shea butter are also grown for export. The Port of Cotonou is vital to Benin's economy.

AREA 43,483 sq mi [112,622 sq km] **POPULATION** 12,865,000
CAPITAL Porto-Novo **GOVERNMENT** Multiparty republic
ETHNIC GROUPS Fon, Adja, Bariba, Yoruba, Fulani
LANGUAGES French (official), Fon, Adja, Yoruba
RELIGIONS Christianity 43%, traditional beliefs 30%, Islam 27%
CURRENCY CFA franc = 100 centimes

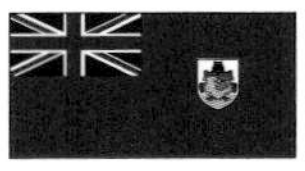
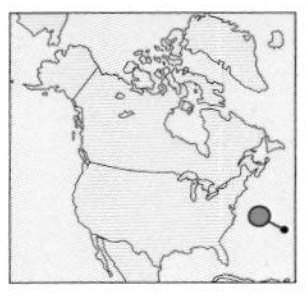

BERMUDA

A group of about 150 small islands situated 570 mi [920 km] east of the USA. Its main sources of revenue are tourism, international business, and offshore finance.

AREA 21 sq mi [53 sq km]
POPULATION 72,000 **CAPITAL** Hamilton

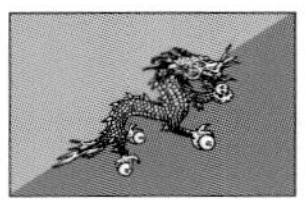
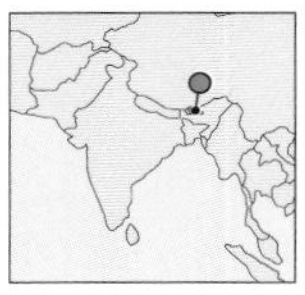

BHUTAN

GEOGRAPHY A mountainous, isolated Himalayan country located between India and Tibet. The climate is similar to that of Nepal, being dependent on altitude and affected by monsoonal winds.

POLITICS & ECONOMY The monarch of Bhutan is head of both state and government, and this predominantly Buddhist country remains, even in the Asian context, both conservative and poor, with an economy based mainly on hydropower. In 2008, Bhutan held its first ever democratic elections, turning it into a constitutional monarchy.

AREA 18,147 sq mi [47,000 sq km] **POPULATION** 782,000
CAPITAL Thimphu **GOVERNMENT** Constitutional monarchy
ETHNIC GROUPS Bhutanese 50%, Nepalese 35%
LANGUAGES Dzongkha (official) **RELIGIONS** Buddhism 75%, Hinduism 25% **CURRENCY** Ngultrum = 100 chhertum

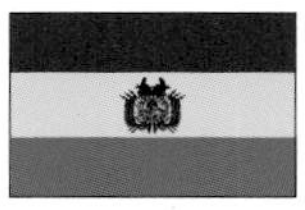
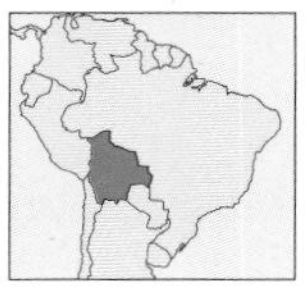

BOLIVIA

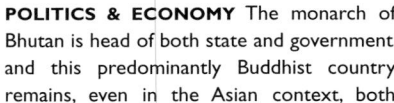

GEOGRAPHY The Plurinational State of Bolivia, as the country is officially called, is an isolated and landlocked South American country which straddles the Andes Mountains. The highest point is 21,391 ft [6,520 m] at Nevado Sajama in the west. About 40% of Bolivians live on the Altiplano, a high plateau in the Andes. The sparsely populated east consists of a vast lowland plain.

The Bolivian climate is greatly affected by altitude, with the Andean peaks permanently snow-covered and the eastern plains remaining hot and humid.

POLITICS & ECONOMY American Indians have lived in Bolivia for at least 10,000 years. The main groups today are the Aymara and Quechua people.

In the last 50 years, Bolivia has been ruled by a succession of civilian and military governments. Economic problems have led to a widening of the gap between rich and poor and, in 2005, Evo Morales, an Aymara farmer, was elected president. His policies of nationalization and redistributing wealth to peasants aroused opposition. Re-elected in 2009 and 2014, Morales advocated state control and nationalized energy production. In 2019, following a disputed election, Morales resigned, and in the constitutional crisis that followed, opposition senator Jeanine Áñez declared herself interim president. Elections are scheduled for 2020.

Although one of South America's poorest countries, it has its second largest reserves of natural gas. Other resources include silver, tin, zinc, and lithium, but the main activity is agriculture.

AREA 424,162 sq mi [1,098,581 sq km] **POPULATION** 11,640,000
CAPITAL La Paz (seat of government); Sucre (legal capital/seat of judiciary) **GOVERNMENT** Multiparty republic
ETHNIC GROUPS Mestizo 30%, Quechua 30%, Aymara 25%, White 15%
LANGUAGES Spanish, Aymara, Quechua (all official)
RELIGIONS Roman Catholic 95%
CURRENCY Boliviano = 100 centavos

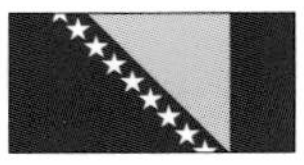
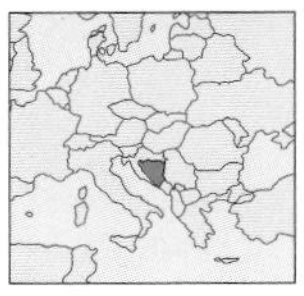

BOSNIA-HERZEGOVINA

GEOGRAPHY The Republic of Bosnia-Herzegovina is one of the seven republics to emerge from the former Federal People's Republic of Yugoslavia. Much of the country is mountainous or hilly, with an arid limestone plateau in the southwest. The River Sava, which forms most of the northern border with Croatia, is a tributary of the River Danube. Because of the country's odd shape, the coastline is limited to a short stretch of 13 mi [20 km] on the Adriatic coast. A Mediterranean climate, with dry, sunny summers and moist, mild winters, prevails only near the coast. Inland, the weather is more severe, with hot, dry summers and bitterly cold, snowy winters.

POLITICS & ECONOMY In 1918, Bosnia-Herzegovina became part of the Kingdom of the Serbs, Croats, and Slovenes, which was renamed Yugoslavia in 1929. Germany occupied the area during World War II (1939–45). From 1945, Communist governments ruled Yugoslavia as a federation containing six republics, one of which was Bosnia-Herzegovina. In the 1980s, the country faced problems as Communist policies proved unsuccessful.

In 1990, free elections were held in Bosnia-Herzegovina and the non-Communists won a majority. A Muslim, Alija Izetbegovic, was elected president. In 1991, Croatia and Slovenia, other parts of the former Yugoslavia, declared themselves independent. In 1992, Bosnia-Herzegovina held a vote on independence. Most Bosnian Serbs boycotted the vote, while the Muslims and Bosnian Croats voted in favor. Many Bosnian Serbs, opposed to independence, started a war against the non-Serbs. They soon occupied more than two-thirds of the land. The war spread when Croat forces seized other parts of the country.

In 1995, the country retained its external boundaries, but it was divided into two self-governing provinces – one Bosnian Serb and the other Muslim Croat. Stability was restored with the help of NATO, but the country remained divided. In December 2011, after 14 months of political crisis, Muslim Croat and Serb leaders agreed on the formation of a central government, with a federal presidency that rotates between a Serb, a Muslim, and a Croat. In 2016, the country formally requested membership of the European Union.

The infrastructure and economy were shattered by the war in the early 1990s. Although some stability has been regained it is still considered one of the most corrupt European states. The economy relies on exporting metals and receiving foreign aid. Farm products include fruits, maize, tobacco, vegetables, and wheat, but food has to be imported.

AREA 19,767 sq mi [51,197 sq km] **POPULATION** 3,836,000
CAPITAL Sarajevo **GOVERNMENT** Federal republic
ETHNIC GROUPS Bosnian 48%, Serb 37%, Croat 14%
LANGUAGES Bosnian, Serbian, Croatian
RELIGIONS Islam 40%, Serbian Orthodox 31%, Roman Catholic 15%, others 14% **CURRENCY** Convertible marka = 100 convertible pfenniga

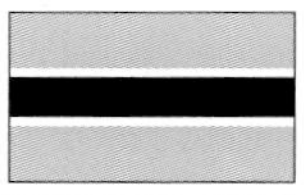
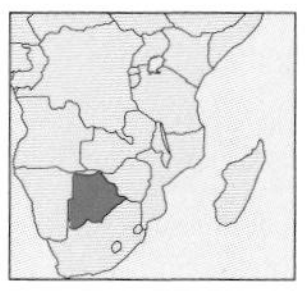

BOTSWANA

GEOGRAPHY The Republic of Botswana is a landlocked country in southern Africa. The Kalahari, a semidesert area covered mostly by grasses and thorn scrub, covers much of the country. Most of the south has no permanent streams but large depressions in the north form inland drainage basins. In one of them, the Okavango River, which rises in Angola, forms a large, swampy delta.

Temperatures are high in the summer months (October to April), but the winter months are much cooler. In winter, nighttime temperatures sometimes drop below freezing point. The average annual rainfall ranges from over 16 inches [400 mm] in the east to less than 8 inches [200 mm] in the southwest.

POLITICS & ECONOMY The earliest inhabitants of the region were the San, sometimes known as Bushmen. They had a nomadic way of life, hunting wild animals and collecting wild plant foods.

Britain ruled the area as the Bechuanaland Protectorate between 1885 and 1966. When the country became independent, it was renamed Botswana. Since then, the country has been a stable, multiparty democracy. In March 2018 Mokgweetsi Masisi was elected as the fifth president since independence. However, in a setback to development, the UN has said that around 25% of the adult population are infected with HIV/AIDS.

Since the 1960s Botswana's economy has grown quickly, and it is now classified by the World Bank as "upper-middle-income." It is the world's largest producer of diamonds. About 25% of the people depend on agriculture. Safari-based tourism is important.

AREA 224,606 sq mi [581,730 sq km] **POPULATION** 2,317,000
CAPITAL Gaborone **GOVERNMENT** Multiparty republic
ETHNIC GROUPS Tswana (or Setswana) 79%, Kalanga 11%, Basarwa 3%, others **LANGUAGES** English (official), Setswana
RELIGIONS Christianity 72%, Badimo 6%, others 2%
CURRENCY Pula = 100 thebe

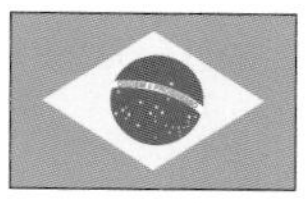
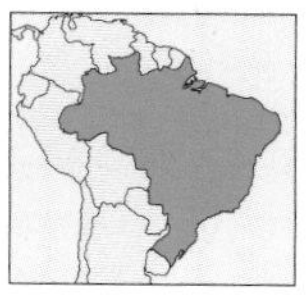

BRAZIL

GEOGRAPHY The Federative Republic of Brazil is the world's fifth largest country. It contains three main regions. The Amazon basin in the north covers more than half of Brazil. The Amazon, the world's second longest river, has a far greater volume than any other river. The second region, the north-east, consists of a coastal plain and the sertão, which is the name for the inland plateaux and hill country. The main river in this region is the São Francisco.

The third region is made up of the plateaux in the southeast. This area, which covers about a quarter of the country, is the most developed and densely populated part of Brazil. Its main river is the Paraná, which flows south through Argentina.

Manaus, on the Amazon, has high temperatures all through the year. Rainfall is heavy, though the period from June to September is drier than the rest of the year. The capital, Brasília, and the city Rio de Janeiro in the south also have tropical climates, with much more marked dry seasons than Manaus. The far south has a temperate climate. The northeastern interior is the driest region, with an average annual rainfall of only 10 inches [250 mm] in places. Rainfall is also unreliable and severe droughts are common in this region.

POLITICS & ECONOMY The Portuguese explorer Pedro Alvarez Cabral claimed Brazil for Portugal in 1500. The Portuguese developed their colony by enslaving many local Amerindian people and introducing about 4 million African slaves. Brazil declared itself an independent empire in 1822 and a republic in 1889. From the 1930s, Brazil faced periods of military rule and widespread corruption. However, civilian rule was restored in 1985.

After two unpopular presidencies, financial stability was established under President Itamar Franco. One of the "BRICS" nations (Brazil, Russia, India, China, and South Africa), Brazil has a rapidly industrializing economy. But many people, including poor farmers and residents of the favelas (city slums), do not share in the country's economic boom. Poverty led to the election of President Luíz Inácío Lula da Silva (generally called "Lula") in 2002. In 2010, he was succeeded by Dilma Roussef. She was re-elected for a second term in 2014, but was impeached in 2016 over financial irregularities and convicted of fraud in early 2018. In October 2018 Jair Bolsonaro, a polarizing figure from the far-right of Brazilian politics, was elected president.

Brazil is Latin America's leading economy, with services and industry as the most important economic sectors. It is among the world's top producers of bauxite, chrome, diamonds, gold, iron ore, manganese, and tin. It is also a major manufacturing country, and it is self-sufficient in oil.

Brazil is a major farming nation. Coffee is a leading export. Other products include bananas, citrus fruits, cocoa, maize, rice, soybeans, and sugarcane. Brazil is also South America's top producer of eggs, meat, and milk. The rate of deforestation remains a global concern, with the potential to accelerate global warming.

AREA 3,287,338 sq mi [8,514,215 sq km] **POPULATION** 211,716,000
CAPITAL Brasília **GOVERNMENT** Federal republic
ETHNIC GROUPS White 54%, Mixed 38%, Black 6%, others 2%
LANGUAGES Portuguese (official)
RELIGIONS Roman Catholic 80%
CURRENCY Real = 100 centavos

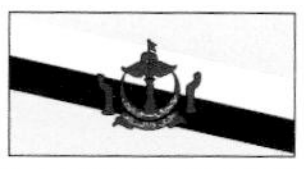
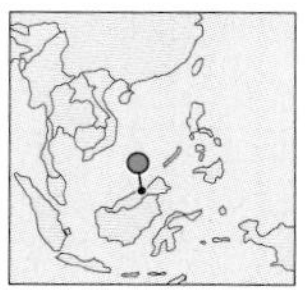

BRUNEI

The Islamic Sultanate of Brunei, a British protectorate until 1984, lies on the north coast of Borneo. The climate is tropical and rain forests cover large areas. Brunei is a prosperous country because of its oil and natural gas production, and the Sultan is said to be among the world's richest men. He has faced international criticism for his introduction of strict Islamic Sharia law in 2014.

AREA 2,226 sq mi [5,765 sq km]
POPULATION 464,000 **CAPITAL** Bandar Seri Begawan

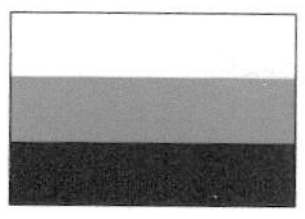
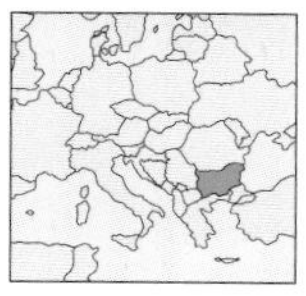

BULGARIA

GEOGRAPHY The Republic of Bulgaria is a country in the Balkan peninsula, facing the Black Sea in the east. The heart of Bulgaria is mountainous. The main ranges are the Balkan Mountains in the center and the Rhodope (or Rhodopi) Mountains in the south.

Summers are hot and winters are cold, though seldom severe. The rainfall is moderate.

POLITICS & ECONOMY Ottoman Turks ruled Bulgaria from 1396 and ethnic Turks still form a sizable minority in the country. In 1879, Bulgaria became a monarchy, and in 1908 it became fully independent. Bulgaria was an ally of Germany in World War I (1914–18) and again in World War II (1939–45). In 1944, Soviet troops invaded Bulgaria and, after the war, the monarchy was abolished and the country became a Communist ally of the Soviet Union. Reforms in the Soviet Union in the late 1980s led Bulgaria's government to introduce a multi-party system in 1990. A non-Communist government was elected in 1991, in the first free elections in 44 years. Throughout the 1990s, Bulgaria faced many problems and it sought to become aligned to the West. Bulgaria became a member of NATO in 2004 and a member of the European Union in 2007. Presidential elections in 2016 were won by Socialist-backed independent Ruman Radev, prompting early parliamentary elections and a coalition government.

Bulgaria has some mineral deposits, including brown coal, gold, and iron ore. Services and manufacturing are leading activities. Principal products include chemicals, processed foods, metal products, machinery, and textiles. Corruption and the prevalence of organized crime still hinder economic growth.

AREA 42,823 sq mi [110,912 sq km] **POPULATION** 6,967,000
CAPITAL Sofia **GOVERNMENT** Multiparty republic
ETHNIC GROUPS Bulgarian 77%, Turkish 8%, Roma 4%, Macedonian, Armenian, others **LANGUAGES** Bulgarian (official), Turkish
RELIGIONS Eastern Orthodox 59%, Islam 8%, others
CURRENCY Lev = 100 stotinki

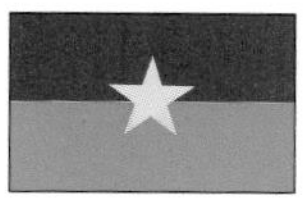
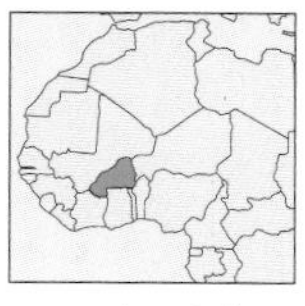

BURKINA FASO

GEOGRAPHY The Democratic People's Republic of Burkina Faso is a landlocked country, a little larger than the United Kingdom, in West Africa. However, Burkina Faso has only a quarter of the population of the UK. The country consists of a plateau, between about 650 ft and 2,300 ft [200 m to 700 m] above sea level. The plateau is cut by several, mainly seasonal, rivers.

The capital city, Ouagadougou, in central Burkina Faso, has high temperatures throughout the year. Most of the rain falls between May and September, but the rainfall is erratic and droughts are common.

POLITICS & ECONOMY The people of Burkina Faso are divided into two main groups: the Voltaic group which includes the Mossi, who form the largest single group, and the Bobo. The French conquered the Mossi capital of Ouagadougou in 1897 and they made the area a protectorate. In 1919, the area became a French colony called Upper Volta. After independence in 1960, Upper Volta became a, sometimes violent and unstable, one-party state. Following a coup in 1983, Thomas Sankara took power and, in 1984, renamed the country Burkina Faso. Long-term president Blaise Compaoré was ousted in 2014. Former PM Marc Kabore won the ensuing election. Terrorism is an increasing problem.

Burkina Faso is one of the world's poorest countries and has become very dependent on foreign aid. Most of the land is dry with thin soils. The country's main food crops are beans, maize, millet, rice, and sorghum. Cotton, groundnuts (peanuts), and shea nuts, whose seeds produce a fat used to make cooking oil and soap, are grown for sale abroad.

The country has few resources and manufacturing is on a small scale. There are deposits of gold, manganese, zinc, lead, and nickel, but lack of infrastructure hinders development. The country's key exports are cotton, gold and livestock. Many young men seek jobs abroad in Ghana and Côte d'Ivoire and the money they send home to their families is important to the country's economy.

AREA 105,791 sq mi [274,000 sq km] **POPULATION** 20,835,000
CAPITAL Ouagadougou **GOVERNMENT** Multiparty republic
ETHNIC GROUPS Mossi 40%, Gurunsi, Senufo, Lobi, Bobo, Mande, Fulani
LANGUAGES French (official), Mossi, Fulani
RELIGIONS Islam 61%, Christianity 23%, traditional beliefs 16%
CURRENCY CFA franc = 100 centimes

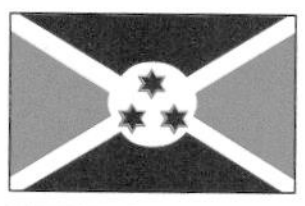
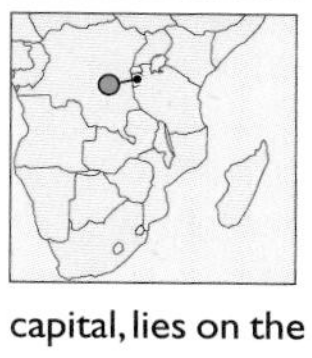

BURUNDI

GEOGRAPHY The Republic of Burundi is the fifth smallest country in mainland Africa. It is also the second most densely populated after its northern neighbor, Rwanda. Part of the Great African Rift Valley, which runs throughout eastern Africa into southwestern Asia, lies in western Burundi. It includes part of Lake Tanganyika. Bujumbura, the commercial capital, lies on the shore of Lake Tanganyika and has a warm climate. A dry season occurs from June to September, but the other months are fairly rainy. The mountains and plateaux to the east are cooler and wetter.

POLITICS & ECONOMY The Twa, a pygmy people, were the first known inhabitants of Burundi. About 1,000 years ago, the Hutu, a people who speak a Bantu language, gradually began to settle the area, pushing the Twa into remote areas.

From the 15th century, the Tutsi, a cattle-owning people from the northeast, gradually took over the country. The Hutu, though greatly outnumbering the Tutsi, were forced to serve the Tutsi overlords.

Germany conquered the area that is now Burundi and Rwanda in the late 1890s. This was followed by Belgian control during World War I (1914–18). Full independence was achieved in 1962. Since this time rivalry between the Hutu and Tutsi has led to periodic outbreaks of appalling violence, most notably in 1972 and 1993. Many thousands of civilians have been massacred. A ceasefire and power-sharing agreement was reached in 2001. Pierre Nkurunziza, a Hutu, led Burundi from 2005, although violent political unrest followed his election to a third term in 2015. Constitutional reforms in 2018 paved the way for him to continue in power until 2034, but he announced he would step down in 2020. In 2017 the International Criminal Court opened an investigation into human rights abuses in the country.

Burundi is one of the world's poorest countries. About 94% of the people live by farming, mostly at subsistence level. Livestock are raised and fishing is important. A lack of basic infrastructure and a poorly educated population are hindering development.

AREA 10,747 sq mi [27,834 sq km] **POPULATION** 11,866,000
CAPITAL Gitega (political); Bujumbura (commercial)
GOVERNMENT Republic **ETHNIC GROUPS** Hutu 85%, Tutsi 14%, Twa (Pygmy) 1% **LANGUAGES** French and Kirundi (both official)
RELIGIONS Roman Catholic 62%, traditional beliefs 23%, Islam 10%, Protestant 5% **CURRENCY** Burundi franc = 100 centimes

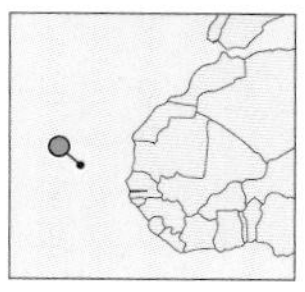

CABO VERDE

Cabo Verde consists of ten large and five small islands, and is situated 350 mi [560 km] west of Dakar in Senegal. The islands have a tropical climate, with high temperatures all year round. Cabo Verde became independent from Portugal in 1975 and is rated as a "lower-middle-income" country by the World Bank.

AREA 1,557 sq mi [4,033 sq km]
POPULATION 583,000 **CAPITAL** Praia

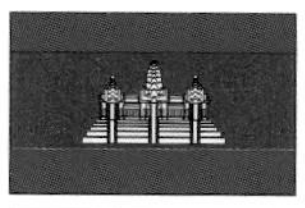
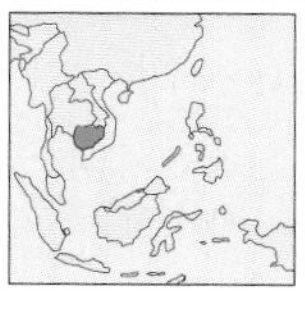

CAMBODIA

GEOGRAPHY The Kingdom of Cambodia is a country in Southeast Asia. Low mountains border the country except in the southeast. Most of Cambodia consists of plains drained by the River Mekong, which enters Cambodia from Laos in the north and exits through Vietnam in the southeast. The northwest contains Tonlé Sap (or Great Lake). In the dry season, this lake drains into the River Mekong. But in the wet season, the level of the Mekong rises and water flows in the opposite direction from the river into Tonlé Sap.

Cambodia has a tropical monsoon climate, with high temperatures throughout the year. The dry season, when winds blow from the north or northeast, runs from November to April. During the rainy season (May to October), moist winds blow from the south or southeast. The high humidity and heat often make conditions unpleasant. Rainfall is heaviest near the coast, and rather lower inland.

POLITICS & ECONOMY From 802 to 1432, the Khmer people ruled a great empire, which reached its peak in the 12th century. The Khmer capital was at Angkor. The Hindu stone temples built there and at nearby Angkor Wat form the world's largest group of religious buildings. France ruled the country between 1863 and 1954, when the country became an independent monarchy. The monarchy was abolished in 1970 and Cambodia became a republic.

In 1970, the Communists under Prime Minister Lon Nol staged a military coup and proclaimed the Khmer Republic, which plunged the country into a civil war. The Khmer Rouge under Pol Pot took control in 1975, renaming the country Kampuchea, and launched a reign of terror in which between 1 million and 2.5 million people were killed. In 1979, Vietnamese and Cambodian troops overthrew the Khmer Rouge government. Vietnam withdrew in 1989, and in 1991 Prince Sihanouk was recognized as head of state. In 1993 the monarchy was restored. In 2004, King Sihanouk abdicated and his son, Prince Norodom Sihamoni, became king. Hun Sen's Cambodian People's Party has been in power since 1998, and he has been prime minister since 1985. In 2017, the Supreme Court dissolved the only credible opposition party, leading to a predictable but controversial victory for Hun Sen's party in 2018 parliamentary elections.

Cambodia's economy, although devastated by war, has now had over 20 years of relative stability and growth. Garment manufacture, tourism, and construction are the main activities. In 2005 offshore oil reserves were discovered and there is potential to mine bauxite, iron, and gold. There are, however, still many obstacles to development.

AREA 69,898 SQ MI [181,035 SQ KM] **POPULATION** 16,927,000
CAPITAL PHNOM PENH **GOVERNMENT** CONSTITUTIONAL MONARCHY
ETHNIC GROUPS KHMER 90%, VIETNAMESE 5%, CHINESE 1%, OTHERS
LANGUAGES KHMER (OFFICIAL), FRENCH, ENGLISH
RELIGIONS BUDDHISM 96%, OTHERS 4% **CURRENCY** RIEL = 10 KAK

CAMEROON

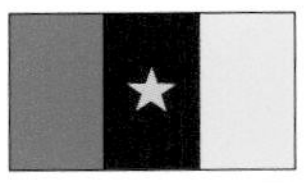

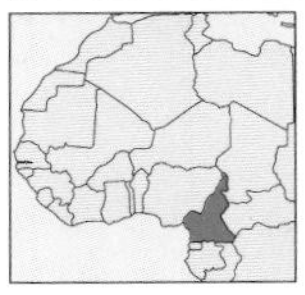

GEOGRAPHY The Republic of Cameroon in West Africa derived its name from the Portuguese word camarões, or prawns. This name was used by Portuguese explorers who fished for prawns along the coast.

Behind the narrow coastal plains on the Gulf of Guinea, the land rises to a series of plateaux, with a mountainous region in the southwest where the volcano Mount Cameroun is situated.

The rainfall is heavy, especially in the highlands, but it becomes drier to the north. Temperatures are high on the coast, while the inland plateaux are cooler.

POLITICS & ECONOMY Germany lost Cameroon after World War I (1914–18). The country was then divided into two parts, one ruled by Britain and the other by France. In 1960, French Cameroon became the independent Cameroon Republic. In 1961, after a vote in British Cameroon, part of the territory joined the Cameroon Republic to become the Federal Republic of Cameroon – the other part joined Nigeria. It adopted the name Republic of Cameroon in 1984, but the country had two official languages. In 1995, partly to placate the English-speaking people, Cameroon became the 52nd member of the Commonwealth. A controversial amendment passed by parliament in 2008 has enabled President Paul Biya to run successfully for third and fourth terms in office in 2011 and 2018 respectively. The country has faced insurgency from Boko Haram since 2014, and increased unrest in the English-speaking provinces.

Cameroon's economy is based on agriculture, which employs 70% of the work force. The chief food crops include cassava, maize, millet, sweet potatoes, and yams. Cocoa and coffee are exported, along with oil and bauxite. In 2002, Cameroon's claim over the disputed oil-rich Bakassi peninsula was upheld and the handover by Nigeria completed in 2008. Cameroon has few manufacturing industries, but it is self-sufficient in food. Despite a high literacy rate, economic development is marred by endemic corruption.

AREA 183,568 SQ MI [475,442 SQ KM] **POPULATION** 27,745,000
CAPITAL YAOUNDÉ **GOVERNMENT** MULTIPARTY REPUBLIC
ETHNIC GROUPS CAMEROON HIGHLANDERS 31%, BANTU 27%, KIRDI 11%, FULANI 10%, OTHERS **LANGUAGES** FRENCH AND ENGLISH (BOTH OFFICIAL)
RELIGIONS CHRISTIANITY 40%, TRADITIONAL BELIEFS 40%, ISLAM 20%
CURRENCY CFA FRANC = 100 CENTIMES

CANADA

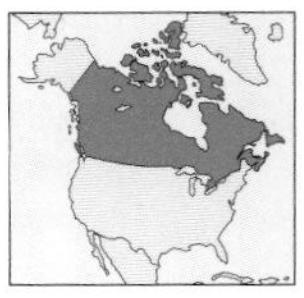

GEOGRAPHY Canada is the world's second largest country after Russia but with only 15% of its population. Much of the land is too cold or too mountainous for human settlement. Around 90% of Canadians live within 124 mi [200 km] of the southern border.

Western Canada is rugged: it includes the Pacific ranges and the mighty Rocky Mountains. East of the Rockies are the interior plains. In the north lie the bleak Arctic islands, while to the south lie the densely populated lowlands around lakes Erie and Ontario and in the St Lawrence River valley. The melting of Arctic ice, attributed to global warming, has led to concern about international rights over the Arctic waters off northern Canada.

Canada has a cold climate. In winter, temperatures fall below freezing point throughout most of Canada. But the southwestern coast has a relatively mild climate. Along the Arctic Circle, mean temperatures are below freezing for seven months a year. The west and southeast have high rainfall, but the prairies are dry with 10 inches to 20 inches [250 mm to 500 mm] of rain every year.

POLITICS & ECONOMY Canada's first people, the ancestors of the Native Americans, or Indians, arrived in North America from Asia around 40,000 years ago. The Inuit (Eskimos) were later arrivals from Asia. Europeans first reached Canada in 1497 and soon Britain and France began to compete for control.

France gained an initial advantage, and the French founded Québec in 1608. The British later occupied eastern Canada and, in 1867, they passed the British North America Act, which set up the Dominion of Canada, which was made up of Québec, Ontario, Nova Scotia, and New Brunswick. Other areas were added, the last being Newfoundland in 1949. Canada is a constitutional monarchy, and the British monarch is Canada's head of state. The provinces have a high level of autonomy.

In 1995, the people of Québec voted narrowly against a move to make Québec a sovereign state. In 2006, the national parliament voted to recognize Québec as a nation within a united Canada – a symbolic act of reconciliation. Another major issue concerns the rights of Aboriginal minorities. In 1999, Canada created the territory of Nunavut for the Inuit population. Nunavut covers 64% of what was formerly the eastern part of the Northwest Territories. Nine years of Conservative party rule were ended in late 2015 with an emphatic election victory by the Liberal Party under Justin Trudeau.

Canada is a highly developed and prosperous country. Although farmland covers only 8% of the country, high levels of productivity mean that Canada is one of the world's leading producers of barley, wheat, meat, and milk. Forestry and fishing are also important. Canada is rich in natural resources, especially oil and natural gas, and is a major exporter of minerals. The country also produces copper, gold, iron ore, uranium, and zinc. Manufacturing is important in the urban areas, where over 80% of the people live. Manufactures include processed mineral and farm products, cars, chemicals, electronic goods, paper, and timber products. Although the USA is Canada's largest trading partner, increased levels of business involve Asian countries.

AREA 3,849,653 SQ MI [9,970,610 SQ KM] **POPULATION** 37,694,000
CAPITAL OTTAWA **GOVERNMENT** FEDERAL MULTIPARTY CONSTITUTIONAL MONARCHY **ETHNIC GROUPS** BRITISH ORIGIN 28%, FRENCH ORIGIN 23%, OTHER EUROPEAN 15%, AMERINDIAN/INUIT 2%, OTHERS
LANGUAGES ENGLISH AND FRENCH (BOTH OFFICIAL)
RELIGIONS ROMAN CATHOLIC 43%, PROTESTANT 23%, JUDAISM, ISLAM, HINDUISM **CURRENCY** CANADIAN DOLLAR = 100 CENTS

CAYMAN ISLANDS

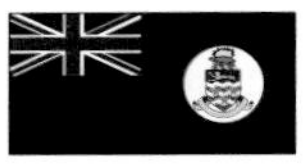

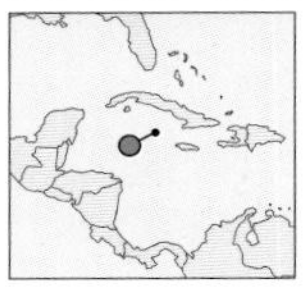

The Cayman Islands are an overseas territory of the UK, consisting of three low-lying islands. Financial services are the main economic activity and the islands offer a secret tax haven to many companies and banks.

AREA 102 SQ MI [264 SQ KM]
POPULATION 62,000 **CAPITAL** GEORGE TOWN

CENTRAL AFRICAN REPUBLIC

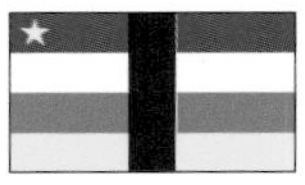

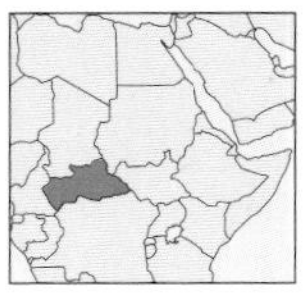

GEOGRAPHY The Central African Republic is a remote, landlocked country in the heart of Africa. It consists mostly of a plateau lying between 1,970 ft and 2,620 ft [600 m to 800 m] above sea level. The Oubangi drains the south, while the Chari (or Shari) River flows from the north to the Lake Chad basin. The climate is warm throughout the year, while the annual average rainfall in the capital Bangui totals 62 inches [1,574 mm]. The north is drier, with an average annual rainfall of about 31 inches [800 mm].

POLITICS & ECONOMY France set up an outpost at Bangui in 1889 and ruled the country as a colony from 1894. Known as Ubangi-Shari, the country was ruled by France as part of French Equatorial Africa until it gained independence in 1960.

Central African Republic became a one-party state in 1962, but army officers seized power in 1966. The head of the army, Jean-Bedel Bokassa, made himself emperor in 1976. The country was renamed the Central African Empire, but Bokassa was removed in 1979. The country again became a republic.

The election in 1993 ended 12 years of military rule. In 2003 General François Bozizé seized power; he was deposed in 2013 by rebel leader Michel Djotodia, who in turn resigned in 2014 following international pressure. The era was marked by frequent violent clashes between the government and rebel groups, and between Christian and Muslim fighters, which led to a breakdown in law and order and a refugee crisis. Faustin-Archange Touadera was elected president in February 2016 in largely peaceful elections, but the violent unrest continues.

The World Bank classifies Central African Republic as a "low-income" developing country. Over 80% of the people are farmers. The main crops are bananas, maize, manioc, millet, and yams. Coffee, cotton, timber, and tobacco are produced for export. The country has significant natural resources including uranium and diamonds. Development has been impeded by the country's remote position, its poor transport system, and its untrained work force. The country depends heavily on aid.

AREA 240,534 SQ MI [622,984 SQ KM] **POPULATION** 5,991,000
CAPITAL BANGUI **GOVERNMENT** MULTIPARTY REPUBLIC
ETHNIC GROUPS BAYA 33%, BANDA 27%, MANDJIA 13%, SARA 10%, MBOUM 7%, MBAKA 4%, OTHERS **LANGUAGES** FRENCH (OFFICIAL), SANGHO
RELIGIONS TRADITIONAL BELIEFS 35%, PROTESTANT 25%, ROMAN CATHOLIC 25%, ISLAM 15% **CURRENCY** CFA FRANC = 100 CENTIMES

CHAD

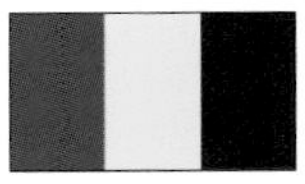

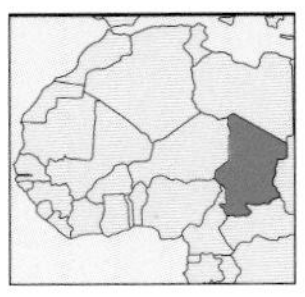

GEOGRAPHY The Republic of Chad is a landlocked country in north-central Africa. It is Africa's fifth largest country and is over twice the size of France, the country which once ruled it as a colony.

Ndjamena in central Chad has a hot, tropical climate, with a marked dry season from November to April. The south of the country is wetter, with an average yearly rainfall of around 39 inches [1,000 mm]. The burning-hot desert in the north has an average yearly rainfall of less than 5 inches [130 mm].

POLITICS & ECONOMY Chad straddles two worlds. The north is populated by Muslim Arab and Berber peoples, while black Africans live in the south. Chad became independent from France in 1960, but the 1970s were marked by ethnic strife that led to conflict with Libya. Chad and Libya agreed a truce in 1987, and in 1994 the International Court of Justice ruled against Libya's claim to the Aozou Strip. From 2004 to 2010, Chadian forces clashed with pro-Sudanese militias as the conflict in Sudan's Darfur province spilled over the border. In 2011 elections Idriss Deby retained the presidency. He won a fifth term in 2016, and a new constitution of 2018 expanded his powers. The security situation is perilous with the militant Islamist groups Boko Haram and Islamic State both active in the region.

One of the world's poorest countries, Chad has a large refugee population. Agriculture employs 80% of the population. Cotton is the chief export crop. Chad has few manufacturing industries, but it has had a recent economic boost from oil exports via a pipeline connecting its oilfields to the coast in Cameroon.

AREA 495,752 SQ MI [1,284,000 SQ KM] **POPULATION** 16,877,000
CAPITAL NDJAMENA **GOVERNMENT** MULTIPARTY REPUBLIC
ETHNIC GROUPS 200 DISTINCT GROUPS: MOSTLY MUSLIM IN THE NORTH AND CENTER; MOSTLY CHRISTIAN OR ANIMIST IN THE SOUTH
LANGUAGES FRENCH AND ARABIC (BOTH OFFICIAL), MANY OTHERS
RELIGIONS ISLAM 53%, CHRISTIANITY 34%, ANIMIST 7%
CURRENCY CFA FRANC = 100 CENTIMES

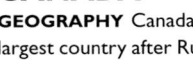

CHILE

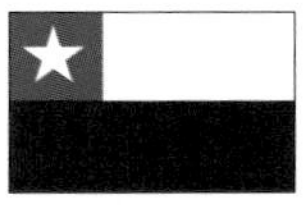

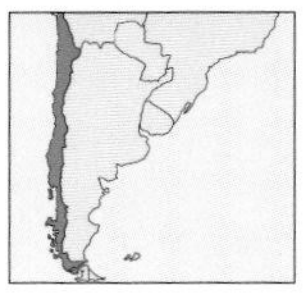

GEOGRAPHY The Republic of Chile stretches about 2,650 mi [4,260 km] from north to south, although the maximum east–west distance is only about 267 mi [430 km]. The high Andes Mountains form Chile's eastern borders with Argentina and Bolivia. To the west are basins and valleys, with coastal uplands overlooking the shore. Most people live in the central valley, where the capital, Santiago, is situated. Earthquakes are common. In February 2010, an earthquake with a magnitude of 8.8 (the biggest in 50 years) struck central Chile, killing more than 400 people.

Santiago has a Mediterranean climate with hot, dry summers and mild, moist winters. The Atacama Desert in the north is extremely arid, while the south is cold and stormy.

POLITICS & ECONOMY Amerindian people reached the southern tip of South America 8,000 years ago. In 1520, Portuguese navigator Ferdinand Magellan was the first European to sight Chile and the country became a Spanish colony in the 1540s. Independent from 1818, Chile won mineral-rich areas from Peru and Bolivia during the War of the Pacific (1879–83).

In 1970, Salvador Allende became the first Communist leader to be elected democratically. He was overthrown in 1973 by army officers, who were supported by the CIA. General Augusto Pinochet then ruled as a dictator until 1989. Since then, government leaders have been democratically elected which has contributed to the country's prosperity and stability. Presidential elections in late 2017 saw a return to office for Sebastian Pinera.

According to the World Bank classifications, Chile has a "high-income" economy, one of the strongest in Latin America. Mining, especially copper, is important and minerals dominate exports. Manufacturing and services are the most valuable activities. Products include processed foods, metals, iron and steel, transport equipment, and textiles. The chief crop is wheat, while beans, fruits, maize, and livestock products are also important. Chile's fishing industry is one of the world's largest.

AREA 292,133 SQ MI [756,626 SQ KM] **POPULATION** 18,187,000
CAPITAL SANTIAGO **GOVERNMENT** MULTIPARTY REPUBLIC
ETHNIC GROUPS MESTIZO 95%, AMERINDIAN 4%
LANGUAGES SPANISH (OFFICIAL), ENGLISH, OTHERS **RELIGIONS** ROMAN CATHOLIC 70%, PROTESTANT 17% **CURRENCY** CHILEAN PESO = 100 CENTAVOS

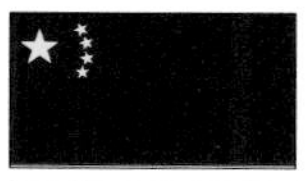
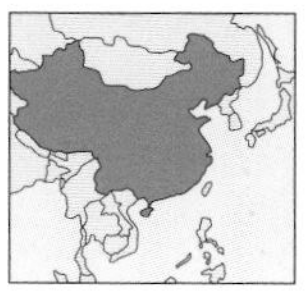

CHINA

GEOGRAPHY The People's Republic of China is the world's fourth largest country. Most people live in the east – on the coastal plains or in the fertile valleys of the Huang He (Hwang Ho or Yellow River), the Chang Jiang (Yangtse Kiang), which is Asia's longest river at 3,960 mi [6,380 km], and the Xi Jiang (Si Kiang). Western China is thinly populated. It includes the bleak Tibetan plateau, which is bounded by the Himalaya, the world's highest mountain range. Deserts include the Gobi along the Mongolian border and the Takla Makan in the far west. Earthquakes are common. Beijing has cold winters and warm summers with moderate rainfall. To the south, Shanghai has milder winters and more rain. The southeast has a wet, subtropical climate, but the west has a severe climate. Lhasa has very cold winters and a low rainfall.

POLITICS & ECONOMY China is one of the world's oldest civilizations, going back 3,500 years. Mongols conquered China in the 13th century, but Chinese rule was restored in 1368. The Manchu people of Mongolia ruled the country from 1644 to 1912, when the country became a republic.

War with Japan (1937–45) was followed by civil war between the nationalists and the Communists. The Communists triumphed in 1949, setting up the People's Republic of China. In the 1980s, following the death of the revolutionary leader Mao Zedong (Mao Tse-tung) in 1976, China encouraged formerly forbidden policies, namely private enterprise and foreign investment. But the Communist leaders have not permitted political freedom. Opponents are still harshly treated, with repressive measures in both Tibet and the Xinjiang Uighur Autonomous Region. Central control over Hong Kong has been increased, leading to widespread pro-democracy protests in 2019. Tensions remain between China and its neighbors over territorial disputes in the East and South China seas. In 2018 the Communist Party abolished the two-term presidential limit, opening the way for Xi Jinping, president since 2013, to remain in power indefinitely.

China's economy expanded from the 1970s and many new industries were set up in the east. From 1989 the economy grew by over 9% per year. The global financial crisis in 2008 slowed economic growth rate, though China's grew faster than any other major economy. In 2014 it became the world's largest economy. Since then, however, the economic growth rate has fallen. In 2020 an outbreak of the coronavirus, originating in China, caused a global health emergency and threatened to damage the economy.

Agriculture employs around 35% of the work force, although only 10% of the land is farmed. More than half the population lives in urban areas. Farm products include rice, sweet potatoes, tea, and wheat. Livestock farming is important, and China has the world's largest pig population. Resources include coal, iron ore, and other metals. Manufactures include cement, chemicals, fertilizers, machinery, cars, ships, and textiles. China is now a major producer of consumer goods, including computers, electrical machinery, and television sets. It is classified by the World Bank as an "upper-middle-income" economy but problems remain, such as pollution, inequality, and an inefficient state sector.

AREA 3,705,387 SQ MI [9,596,961 SQ KM] **POPULATION** 1,394,016,000
CAPITAL BEIJING **GOVERNMENT** SINGLE-PARTY COMMUNIST REPUBLIC
ETHNIC GROUPS HAN CHINESE 92%, MANY OTHERS
LANGUAGES MANDARIN CHINESE (OFFICIAL) **RELIGIONS** ATHEIST (OFFICIAL)
CURRENCY RENMINBI YUAN = 10 JIAO = 100 FEN

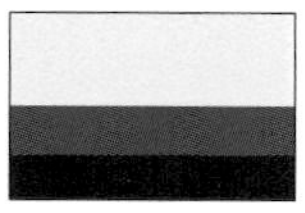
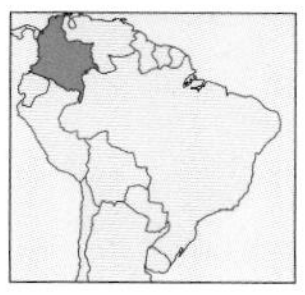

COLOMBIA

GEOGRAPHY The Republic of Colombia, in northeastern South America, is the only country in the continent to have coastlines on both the Pacific Ocean and the Caribbean Sea. Colombia also contains the northernmost ranges of the Andes Mountains.

There is a tropical climate in the lowlands, but the altitude greatly affects the climate in the Andes. The capital, Bogotá, which stands on a plateau in the eastern Andes at about 9,200 ft [2,800 m] above sea level, has mild temperatures throughout the year. Rainfall is heavy, especially on the Pacific coast.

POLITICS & ECONOMY Amerindian people have lived in Colombia for thousands of years. But today, only a small proportion of the people are of unmixed Amerindian ancestry. Colombia emerged as a republic in 1886.

The 20th century was marred by civil war and violent conflict involving drug cartels and armed rebel groups. Andrés Pastrana, president in 1998–2002, tried to end the guerrilla war, but peace talks collapsed and conflict resumed. In 2016 the government and FARC (Revolutionary Armed Forces of Colombia) signed a peace agreement, with FARC formally dissolving itself as an armed group the following year. In 2018 Ivan Duque was elected president. The peace remains fragile.

Steps have been taken to develop the country's infrastructure to boost employment, and the economy was improving strongly until 2015 when the growth of GDP fell back to 2.5% from a high of nearly 5%. Petroleum, coffee, coal, gold, emeralds, cut flowers, and chemicals are exported.

AREA 439,735 SQ MI [1,138,914 SQ KM] **POPULATION** 49,085,000
CAPITAL BOGOTÁ **GOVERNMENT** MULTIPARTY REPUBLIC
ETHNIC GROUPS MESTIZO 58%, WHITE 20%, MIXED 14%, BLACK 4%
LANGUAGES SPANISH (OFFICIAL) **RELIGIONS** ROMAN CATHOLIC 90%
CURRENCY COLOMBIAN PESO = 100 CENTAVOS

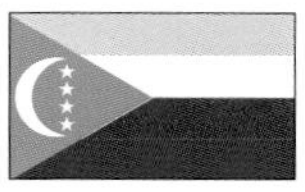
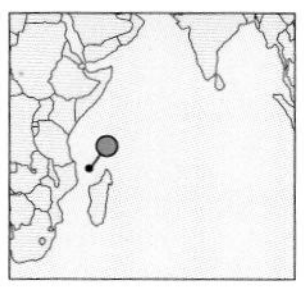

COMOROS

The Union of the Comoros consists of three large volcanic islands and some smaller ones lying at the north end of the Mozambique Channel in the Indian Ocean. France took over one of the islands, Mayotte, in 1843, and in 1886 the other islands came under French protection. They became independent in 1974, but Mayotte has remained French. Relations between the three remaining islands have been rocky. The constitution of 2001 granted greater autonomy to each island, with a rotating presidency. Changes to the constitution in 2018 undermined this system, and President Azali Assoumani, elected in 2016, was re-elected in 2019. Very dependent on foreign aid, Comoros is one of Africa's poorest nations. Exports include cloves, perfume oil, and vanilla.

AREA 863 SQ MI [2,235 SQ KM]
POPULATION 846,000 **CAPITAL** MORONI

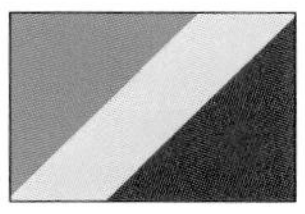
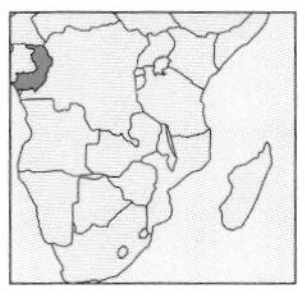

CONGO

GEOGRAPHY The Republic of the Congo is a country on the River Congo in west-central Africa. The equator runs through the center of the country. Congo has a narrow coastal plain on which its main port, Pointe Noire, stands. Behind the plain are uplands through which the River Kouilou-Niari has carved a fertile valley. Central Congo consists of high plains with the north comprising large swampy areas in the valleys of the tributaries of the River Congo.

Congo has a hot, wet equatorial climate. Brazzaville has a dry season between June and September. The coast is drier and cooler because of the cold offshore Benguela ocean current.

POLITICS & ECONOMY Part of the huge Kongo kingdom between the 15th and 18th centuries, the coast of the Congo later became a center of the European slave trade. The area came under French protection in 1880 and it was later governed as part of the larger region of French Equatorial Africa. The country remained under French control until 1960.

Congo became a one-party state in 1964 and a military group took over the government in 1968. In 1970, Congo declared itself a Communist country, though it continued to seek aid from Western countries. Multiparty elections were held in 1992, but the elected president, Pascal Lissouba, was overthrown in 1997 by former president Denis Sassou-Nguesso. Civil war broke out with a fragile peace being restored in 2002. Sassou-Nguesso, president for over 30 years, despite accusations of corruption and unfair elections, is one of Africa's longest serving leaders.

Despite being one of Africa's largest petroleum producers, around 70% of the population live in poverty. Agriculture is an important activity, employing about 32% of the people, but many farmers produce little more than they need to feed their families. Major food crops include bananas, cassava, maize, and rice, while the leading cash crops are coffee and cocoa. Congo's main exports are oil (making up more than 90% of the total), timber, sugar, and diamonds. Manufacturing is still relatively unimportant, hampered by poor transport links, but it is gradually being developed.

AREA 132,046 SQ MI [342,000 SQ KM] **POPULATION** 5,293,000
CAPITAL BRAZZAVILLE **GOVERNMENT** REPUBLIC
ETHNIC GROUPS KONGO 48%, SANGHA 20%, TEKE 17%, M'BOCHI 12%
LANGUAGES FRENCH (OFFICIAL), MANY OTHERS **RELIGIONS** CHRISTIANITY 50%, ANIMIST 48%, ISLAM 2% **CURRENCY** CFA FRANC = 100 CENTIMES

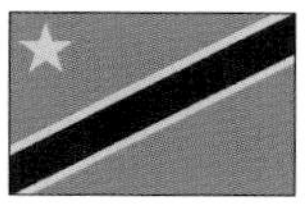
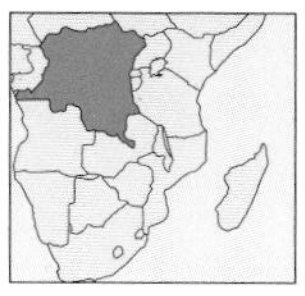

CONGO (DEMOCRATIC REPUBLIC OF THE)

GEOGRAPHY The Democratic Republic of the Congo, formerly known as Zaïre, is the world's 11th largest country. Much of the country lies within the drainage basin of the huge River Congo. The river reaches the sea at the country's short coastline, which is only 25 mi [40 km] long. Mountains rise in the east, where the country's borders run through lakes Tanganyika, Kivu, Edward, and Albert.

POLITICS & ECONOMY Portuguese navigators reached the coast in 1482, but the interior was not explored until the late 19th century. In 1885, the country, known as the Congo Free State, became the personal property of King Léopold II of Belgium and was then administered as a Belgian colony from 1908 until 1960.

The country, riven by ethnic rivalries, became a one-party state after a coup by President Mobutu in 1965. He renamed it Zaïre and held on to power for over 30 years. He was ousted in 1997 by Laurent Kabila, a rebel leader backed by Rwanda and Uganda, who gave the country its present name. Further rifts and violence continued until Kabila was assassinated in 2001. The presidency was taken over by his son Joseph, who negotiated the Pretoria Accord with Rwanda which called for an end to fighting and the establishment of a unity government. The country remains beset by violence. According to aid agencies more than 1.5 million people were internally displaced during 2017. Elections at the end of Kabila's term as president were twice delayed, but in 2019 opposition candidate Felix Tshisekedi became president.

The Democratic Republic of the Congo is one of the world's poorest countries. Decades of insurrection and instability have devastated what was once a relatively industrialized economy. It has a vast wealth of natural resources, much of it still to be exploited and, with foreign help, some reform is under way. The economy relies on mining: the country is the world's largest producer of cobalt and a major producer of copper and diamonds. However, the industry is plagued by financial irregularities. Agriculture, at subsistence level, employs 60% of the work force.

AREA 905,350 SQ MI [2,344,858 SQ KM] **POPULATION** 101,780,000
CAPITAL KINSHASA **GOVERNMENT** REPUBLIC
ETHNIC GROUPS OVER 200; THE LARGEST ARE MONGO, LUBA, KONGO, MANGBETU-AZANDE **LANGUAGES** FRENCH (OFFICIAL), TRIBAL LANGUAGES
RELIGIONS ROMAN CATHOLIC 50%, PROTESTANT 20%, ISLAM 10%, OTHERS
CURRENCY CONGOLESE FRANC = 100 CENTIMES

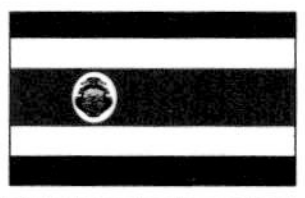
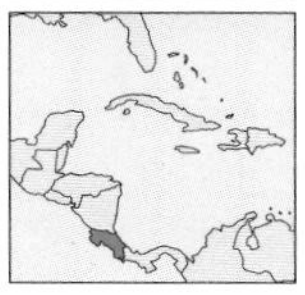

COSTA RICA

GEOGRAPHY The Republic of Costa Rica in Central America has coastlines on both the Pacific Ocean and the Caribbean Sea. Central Costa Rica consists of mountain ranges and plateaux with many volcanoes.

The coolest months of the year are December and January. The northeast trade winds bring heavy rain to the Caribbean coast,

while there are lower amounts of rainfall in the highlands and on the Pacific coastlands.

POLITICS & ECONOMY Christopher Columbus reached the Caribbean coast in 1502 and was followed by Spanish settlers. Spain ruled the country until 1821, when the Central American colonies broke away to join Mexico. In 1823, these states then split from Mexico and set up the Central American Federation. Later, this union broke up and Costa Rica became independent in 1838.

From the late 19th century onward, Costa Rica experienced a number of revolutions, with periods of dictatorship alternating with spells of democracy. In 1948, following a revolt, the armed forces were completely abolished and it remains without a standing army today. Since that year, Costa Rica has enjoyed a long period of consistent stable democracy. Center-left candidate and former Minister of Labor and Social Security, Carlos Alvarado, won the presidential elections of March 2018.

Costa Rica is one of the most prosperous countries in Central America. There are high educational standards, a high average life expectancy (about 76 years for men and 81 years for women), and the most developed welfare system in Central America. Agriculture employs 14% of the people. Costa Rica's natural resources include its forests, but it lacks minerals apart from some bauxite and manganese. Manufacturing is increasing, with the USA being Costa Rica's main trading partner. Tourism is a fast-growing industry. There are concerns, however, that the country is acting as a conduit for drugs and associated corruption.

AREA 19,730 SQ MI [51,100 SQ KM] **POPULATION** 5,098,000
CAPITAL San José **GOVERNMENT** Multiparty republic
ETHNIC GROUPS White (including Mestizo) 94%, Black 3%, Amerindian 1%, Chinese 1%, others **LANGUAGES** Spanish (official), English **RELIGIONS** Roman Catholic 76%, Evangelical Protestant 14%
CURRENCY Costa Rican colón = 100 céntimos

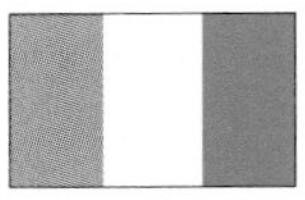

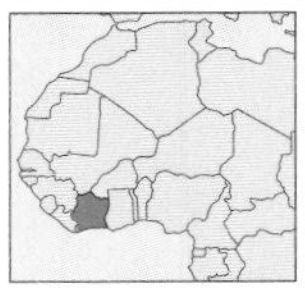

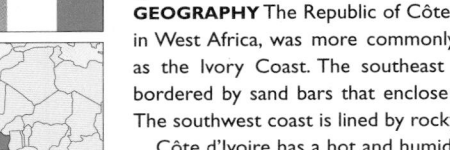

CÔTE D'IVOIRE (IVORY COAST)

GEOGRAPHY The Republic of Côte d'Ivoire, in West Africa, was more commonly known as the Ivory Coast. The southeast coast is bordered by sand bars that enclose lagoons. The southwest coast is lined by rocky cliffs.

Côte d'Ivoire has a hot and humid tropical climate, with high temperatures all year. The south has two rainy seasons: between May and July, and from October to November. Inland, the rainfall decreases and the north has one dry and one rainy season.

POLITICS & ECONOMY From 1895, the Ivory Coast, as it was known, was governed as part of French West Africa.

Côte d'Ivoire became fully independent in 1960. Its first president, Félix Houphouët-Boigny, became the longest serving head of state in Africa with an uninterrupted period in office which ended with his death in 1993. Houphouët-Boigny, a pro-Western leader, made Côte d'Ivoire a one-party state. In 1983, the National Assembly voted to make Yamoussoukro, the president's birthplace, the new capital. In 1999, a military coup occurred, but civilian rule was restored in 2000, when Laurent Gbagbo was elected president. By 2004, after an army rebellion, the government held the south, while mainly Muslim rebels held the north. Elections in 2010 were won by Alassane Outtara, but Gbagbo refused to stand down and was finally deposed in 2011. Outtara won an overwhelming 84% of the vote in 2015's elections.

Agriculture employs 68% of the population and the country is the world's largest producer of cocoa beans. Coffee and palm oil are also important exports. Political instability and the lack of modern infrastructure are impeding economic growth.

AREA 124,503 SQ MI [322,463 SQ KM] **POPULATION** 27,481,000
CAPITAL Yamoussoukro **GOVERNMENT** Multiparty republic
ETHNIC GROUPS Akan 42%, Voltaiques 18%, Northern Mandes 16%, Krous 11%, Southern Mandes 10% **LANGUAGES** French (official), many native dialects **RELIGIONS** Islam 39%, Christianity 33%, traditional beliefs 12% **CURRENCY** CFA franc = 100 centimes

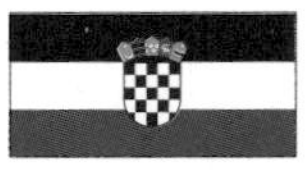

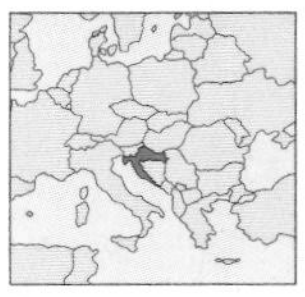

CROATIA

GEOGRAPHY The Republic of Croatia was one of the six republics that made up the former Communist country of Yugoslavia until it became independent in 1991. The region of Dalmatia borders the Adriatic Sea and here are found the coastal ranges of mountains, comprising large tracts of bare limestone. Most of the rest of the country consists of the fertile Pannonian plains.

The coastal area has a typical Mediterranean climate, with hot, dry summers and mild, moist winters. Inland, the climate becomes more continental. Winters are cold, while temperatures often soar to 100°F [38°C] in the summer months.

POLITICS & ECONOMY Once part of the Holy Roman empire, Croatia was an independent kingdom in the 10th and 11th centuries. In 1102, the crowns of Hungary and Croatia were joined, creating a union that lasted 800 years. In 1526, part of Croatia came under the Turkish Ottoman empire, while the rest fell under the control of the Austrian Habsburgs.

After Austria–Hungary was defeated in World War I (1914–18), Croatia became part of the new Kingdom of the Serbs, Croats, and Slovenes. This kingdom was renamed Yugoslavia in 1929. Germany occupied Yugoslavia during World War II (1939–45).

After the war, Communists took power with Josip Broz Tito as the country's leader. Despite ethnic differences between the people, Tito held Yugoslavia together until his death in 1980. In the 1980s, economic and ethnic problems, including a deterioration in relations with Serbia, threatened stability. In the 1990s, Yugoslavia split into five nations, one of which was Croatia, which declared itself independent in 1991.

After Serbia supplied arms to Serbs living in Croatia, war broke out between the two republics, causing great damage. Croatia lost more than 30% of its territory. But in 1992, the United Nations sent a peacekeeping force to Croatia, which effectively ended the war with Serbia. In the same year, when war broke out in Bosnia-Herzegovina, Bosnian Croats occupied parts of the country. But in 1994, Croatia helped to end Croat–Muslim conflict in Bosnia-Herzegovina and, in 1995, after retaking some areas occupied by Serbs, it helped to draw up the Dayton Peace Accord, ending the civil war.

The conflict in the early 1990s badly disrupted the economy. Slow but steady economic growth in the early 2000s was thwarted by the recession of 2008, but picked up again from 2014 onward. Croatia acceded to membership of the EU in 2013. Problems remain with high unemployment and uneven regional development. Its intricate coastline and islands on the Adriatic Sea are a gift to the tourist industry. Croatia's main exports are manufactures, especially shipbuilding.

AREA 21,829 SQ MI [56,538 SQ KM] **POPULATION** 4,228,000
CAPITAL Zagreb **GOVERNMENT** Multiparty republic
ETHNIC GROUPS Croat 90%, Serb 5%, others
LANGUAGES Croatian 96% **RELIGIONS** Roman Catholic 88%, Orthodox 4%, Islam 1%, others **CURRENCY** Kuna = 100 lipas

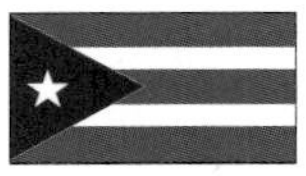

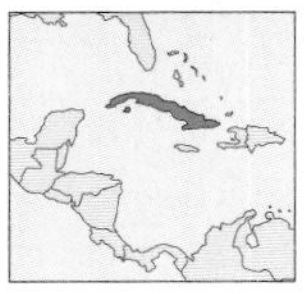

CUBA

GEOGRAPHY The Republic of Cuba is the largest island country in the Caribbean Sea. It consists of one large island, Cuba, the Isle of Youth (Isla de la Juventud), and about 1,600 small islets. Mountains and hills cover about a quarter of Cuba. The highest mountain range, the Sierra Maestra in the southeast, reaches 6,562 ft [2,000 m]. The rest of the land consists of gently rolling country or coastal plains, crossed by fertile valleys carved by the short, mostly shallow and narrow rivers.

POLITICS & ECONOMY Christopher Columbus discovered the island in 1492 and Spaniards began to settle there from 1511. Spanish rule ended in 1898, when the United States defeated Spain in the Spanish–American War. American influence in Cuba remained strong until 1959, when revolutionary forces under the leadership of Fidel Castro overthrew the dictatorship of Fulgencio Batista.

The United States opposed Castro's policies, when he turned to the Soviet Union for assistance. In 1962, a world crisis was averted when, under intense US pressure, the Soviet Union withdrew missile sites that could have been used to launch nuclear strikes against the United States. The breakup of the Soviet Union in 1991 damaged Cuba's economy and it worked to increase its trade with Latin America and China. Fidel Castro's brother, Raul, took over the leadership in 2008. He introduced reforms in 2009–12. In 2011, a new law allowed people to buy and sell private property. December 2014 saw the start of moves to normalize relations between Cuba and the US. During 2015, banking and diplomatic ties were re-established. The following year, some trade ties with the US were opened, as were diplomatic links with the EU. Fidel Castro died in April 2016. In 2017, the US government introduced new sanctions and travel restrictions. In April 2018 Raul Castro stood down and Miguel Díaz-Canel was named as president.

Sugar cane accounts for more than 60% of the country's exports. The other main crop is tobacco, and citrus fruits, rice, cattle, and milk production all make a contribution to the economy. Nickel oxide is exported and tourism is also important. Cuba has signed an agreement with Russia to exploit off-shore oil deposits.

AREA 42,803 SQ MI [110,861 SQ KM] **POPULATION** 11,059,000
CAPITAL Havana **GOVERNMENT** Socialist republic
ETHNIC GROUPS White 65%, Mestizo 25%, Black 10%
LANGUAGES Spanish (official) **RELIGIONS** Roman Catholic 27%, Santeria 13% **CURRENCY** Cuban peso = 100 centavos

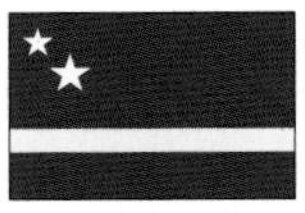

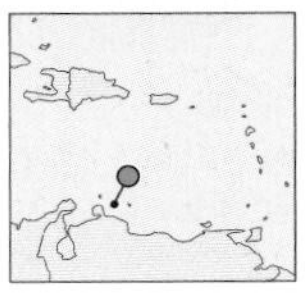

CURAÇAO

Part of the Netherlands Antilles until 2010, Curaçao is a self-governing territory within the Kingdom of the Netherlands. Oil refining, tourism and trade are important.

AREA 171 SQ MI [444 SQ KM]
POPULATION 151,000 **CAPITAL** Willemstad

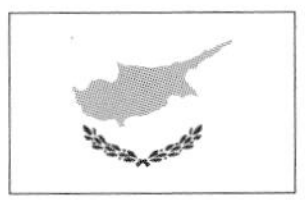

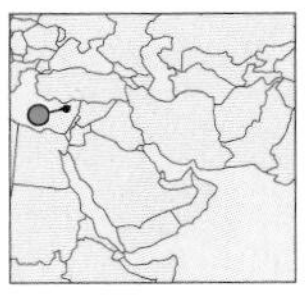

CYPRUS

GEOGRAPHY The Republic of Cyprus is an island nation in the northeastern Mediterranean Sea. Geographers regard it as part of Asia, but it resembles southern Europe in many ways. Its scenic mountain ranges include the southern Troodos Mountains, which reach 6,401 ft [1,951 m] at Mount Olympus, and the Kyrenia range in the north. Between them lies the Mesaoria plain. The climate is Mediterranean, with hot, dry summers and mild, moist winters.

POLITICS & ECONOMY Greeks settled on Cyprus around 3,200 years ago. From AD 330, the island was part of the Byzantine empire until, in the 1570s, Cyprus became part of the Turkish Ottoman empire. Turkish rule continued until 1878 when Cyprus was leased to Britain then went on to be proclaimed a colony in 1925. In the 1950s, Greek Cypriots, who made up four-fifths of the population, began a campaign for enosis (union) with Greece. Their leader was the Greek Orthodox Archbishop Makarios. A secret guerrilla force called EOKA attacked the British, who exiled Makarios in 1956; he returned to Cyprus in 1959.

Cyprus became an independent country in 1960, although Britain retained two military bases. Independent Cyprus had a constitution which provided for power-sharing between the Greek and Turkish Cypriots. But the constitution proved unworkable and fighting broke out between the two communities.

In 1974, Makarios was overthrown by Greek officers and Turkey invaded northern Cyprus. In 1979, the north was proclaimed the Turkish Republic of Northern Cyprus. The only country to recognize this state remains Turkey. In 2002, the European Union invited Cyprus to become a member in 2004. In 2004, the people voted on a UN plan to reunify Cyprus. The Turkish-Cypriots voted in favor, but the Greek-Cypriots voted against, unhappy at limits on their right to return to property located in the north. As a result, only the south was admitted to EU membership on May 1, 2004. Talks on reunification continue, but progress is slow.

Cyprus got its name from the Greek word kypros, meaning copper. But little copper remains and the chief minerals today are asbestos and chromium. However, the most valuable activity in Cyprus is tourism. Manufactures include cement, clothes, and pharmaceuticals. Only around 4% of the population are involved in agriculture but 80% are employed in the service industry.

Problems due to the global financial crisis, and the south joining the euro in 2008, resulted in a contraction of the economy and a bailout from the EU at the beginning of 2013. Cypriot banks' substantial exposure to Greek debt is a cause for concern.

AREA 3,572 SQ MI [9,251 SQ KM] **POPULATION** 1,267,000
CAPITAL Nicosia **GOVERNMENT** Multiparty republic
ETHNIC GROUPS Greek Cypriot 77%, Turkish Cypriot 18%, others
LANGUAGES Greek and Turkish (both official), English
RELIGIONS Greek Orthodox 78%, Islam 18%
CURRENCY Euro = 100 cents

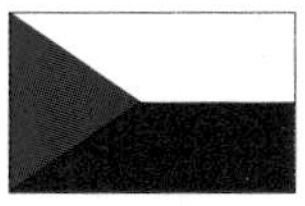

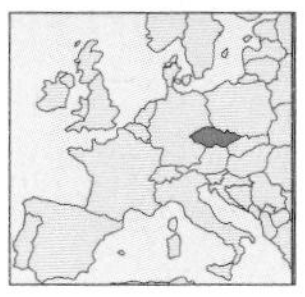

CZECHIA

GEOGRAPHY Until recently known as the Czech Republic, Czechia is the western three-fifths of the former country of Czechoslovakia. It contains two regions: Bohemia in the west and Moravia in the east. Mountains border much of the country in the west. The Bohemian basin in the north-center is a fertile lowland region, with Prague, the capital city, at its heart. Highlands cover much of the center of the country, with lowlands in the southeast.

The climate is influenced by the country's landlocked position in east-central Europe. Summers are warm and winters cold.

POLITICS & ECONOMY Czechoslovakia was born out of World War I (1914–18) and then occupied by Germany during World War II (1939–45). In 1948, Communist leaders took power and Czechoslovakia was allied to the Soviet Union. In the late 1980s, when democratic reforms were introduced in the Soviet Union, the Czechs also demanded change. Free elections were held in 1990, but differences between the Czechs and Slovaks led to the partitioning of the country (the "velvet divorce") on January 1, 1993. A former dissident, Vaclav Havel, became the first president. Czechia became a member of NATO in 1999 and a member of the European Union in 2004. In 2016, Parliament approved a new short form for the country's name, and the Czech Republic became Czechia. Milos Zeman won a second term as president in January 2018, campaigning on an anti-immigration stance.

Under Communist rule, Czechia became one of the most industrialized parts of Eastern Europe, and it remains a major producer of cars and machinery. It is classified by the World Bank as a "high-income" economy showing strong economic growth since the mid-2010s. The country has deposits of coal, uranium, and kaolin. Manufacturing employs about 38% of the work force.

AREA 30,450 SQ MI [78,866 SQ KM] **POPULATION** 10,702,000
CAPITAL PRAGUE **GOVERNMENT** MULTIPARTY REPUBLIC
ETHNIC GROUPS CZECH 64%, MORAVIAN 5%, SLOVAK 1%, POLISH, GERMAN, SILESIAN, GYPSY, HUNGARIAN, UKRAINIAN
LANGUAGES CZECH (OFFICIAL)
RELIGIONS ATHEIST 40%, ROMAN CATHOLIC 39%, PROTESTANT 4%, ORTHODOX 3%, OTHERS **CURRENCY** CZECH KORUNA = 100 HALER

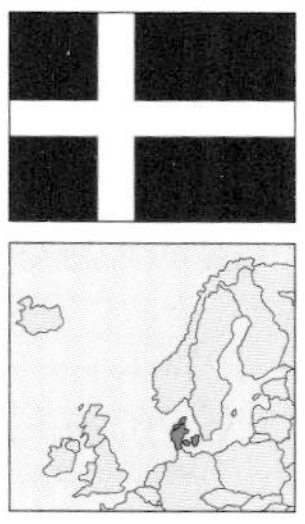

DENMARK

GEOGRAPHY The Kingdom of Denmark is the smallest country in Scandinavia. It consists of a peninsula, called Jutland (or Jylland), which is joined to Germany, and more than 400 islands, 89 of which are inhabited. The land is flat and mostly covered by rocks deposited by huge ice sheets during the last Ice Age. The highest point in Denmark is on Jutland. It is only 561 ft [171 m] above sea level. Denmark has a mild, moist climate, except during cold spells in winter when the Sound (Øresund) between Sjælland and Sweden may freeze over.

POLITICS & ECONOMY Once a Viking stronghold, Denmark formed a union with Norway and Sweden (which included Finland) in the 14th century. Sweden broke away in 1523, while Denmark lost Norway to Sweden in 1814. After 1945, Denmark joined NATO and became a member of the European Economic Community (now the European Union) in 1973. However, the country decided not to join the eurozone in a referendum in 2000. In 2009, Greenland joined the Færoe Islands in becoming a self-governing territory within the Danish realm.

Denmark is a prosperous country with a generous welfare system. Resources include oil and gas. Manufacturing employs around 12% of the work force. Products include furniture, processed food, machinery, and wind turbines. Meat and dairy farming, using intensively scientific methods, employs 3% of the people.

AREA 16,639 SQ MI [43,094 SQ KM] **POPULATION** 5,869,000
CAPITAL COPENHAGEN **GOVERNMENT** PARLIAMENTARY MONARCHY
ETHNIC GROUPS SCANDINAVIAN, INUIT, FÆROESE **LANGUAGES** DANISH (OFFICIAL), GREENLANDIC, ENGLISH, FÆROESE **RELIGIONS** EVANGELICAL LUTHERAN 75%, ISLAM 6% **CURRENCY** DANISH KRONE = 100 ØRE

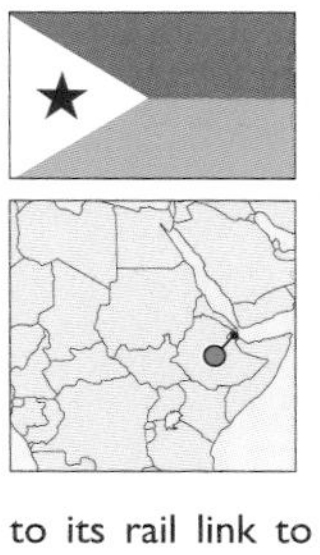

DJIBOUTI

GEOGRAPHY The Republic of Djibouti in eastern Africa occupies a strategic position where the Red Sea meets the Gulf of Aden. Djibouti has one of the world's hottest and driest climates.

POLITICS & ECONOMY Known as the French Territory of the Afars and Issas until 1977, Djibouti owes much of its importance to its rail link to Addis Ababa which allows it to function as a port for Ethiopia and other landlocked African states. It acts as a regional military base for the USA, France, China, Japan, and Italy, and is negotiating with Saudi Arabia and India. The current president, Ismail Omar Guelleh, has been in office since 1999. Djibouti is dominated by one political party, the People's Rally for Progress, with opposition parties having only limited freedom.

Djibouti is a poor country with few natural resources and the climate is unable to support much agriculture. Its economy is based largely on the revenue it gets from its port facilities and it relies heavily on foreign assistance. Unemployment is high at 40%.

AREA 8,958 SQ MI [23,200 SQ KM] **POPULATION** 922,000
CAPITAL DJIBOUTI **GOVERNMENT** MULTIPARTY REPUBLIC
ETHNIC GROUPS SOMALI 60%, AFAR 35% **LANGUAGES** ARABIC AND FRENCH (BOTH OFFICIAL) **RELIGIONS** ISLAM 94%, CHRISTIANITY 6%
CURRENCY DJIBOUTIAN FRANC = 100 CENTIMES

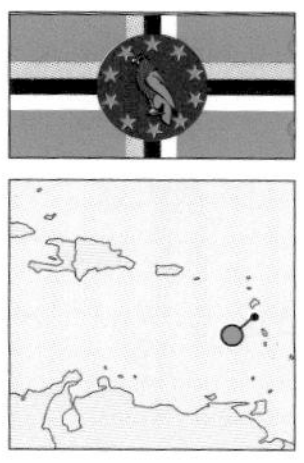

DOMINICA

The Commonwealth of Dominica, a former British colony, became independent in 1978. The island has a mountainous spine and, although less than 10% of the land is cultivated, agriculture employs 40% of the population. The economy has been over-reliant on growing bananas and Dominica is trying to develop its ecotourism business.

AREA 290 SQ MI [751 SQ KM] **POPULATION** 74,000 **CAPITAL** ROSEAU

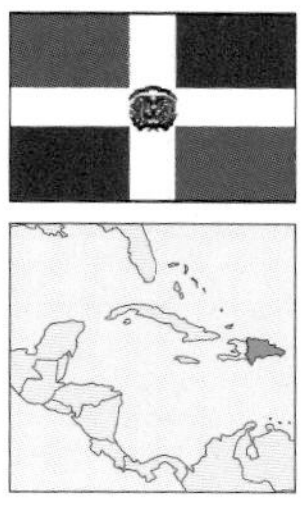

DOMINICAN REPUBLIC

GEOGRAPHY Second largest of the Caribbean nations in both area and population, the Dominican Republic shares the island of Hispaniola with Haiti, with the Dominican Republic occupying the eastern two-thirds. The country is mountainous, and the hot and humid climate eases with altitude.

POLITICS & ECONOMY In 1492, Christopher Columbus landed on Hispaniola and Spaniards soon settled the island, followed by the French, who occupied the western third of the island (which is now Haiti). From 1930 to 1961, the country was ruled by the brutal dictator Rafael Trujillo. Political upheavals in the years that followed his assassination prompted the intervention of thousands of US troops. Faltering democracies and frequent natural disasters, primarily hurricanes, hampered the Dominican Republic's development in the late 20th century, but its economy has since grown rapidly. Tourism and the service industry are the mainstays of the economy. Sugarcane, coffee, rice, bananas, and cocoa are leading crops. Gold is mined.

AREA 18,730 SQ MI [48,511 SQ KM] **POPULATION** 10,500,000
CAPITAL SANTO DOMINGO **GOVERNMENT** MULTIPARTY REPUBLIC
ETHNIC GROUPS MULATTO 73%, WHITE 16%, BLACK 11%
LANGUAGES SPANISH (OFFICIAL) **RELIGIONS** ROMAN CATHOLIC 95%
CURRENCY DOMINICAN PESO = 100 CENTAVOS

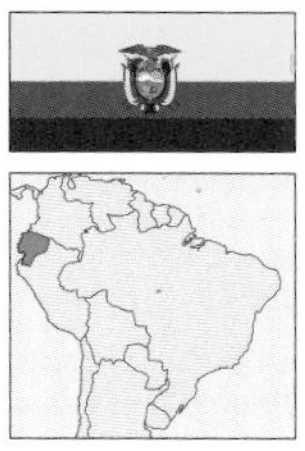

ECUADOR

GEOGRAPHY The Republic of Ecuador straddles the equator on the west coast of South America. Three ranges of the high Andes Mountains form the backbone of the country. Between the towering, snow-capped peaks of the mountains, some of which are volcanoes, lie a series of high plateaux, or basins. Nearly half of Ecuador's population live on these plateaux. The coast has a warm tropical climate, despite the cold offshore Peruvian Current. Inland, the altitude gives the plateaux spring-like weather throughout the year.

POLITICS & ECONOMY The Inca people of Peru conquered much of what is now Ecuador in the late 15th century and their language, Quechua, is still widely spoken today. Spanish forces defeated the Incas in 1533 and took control of Ecuador until 1822.

In the 19th and 20th centuries, Ecuador suffered from political instability, while successive governments failed to tackle the country's social and economic problems. A war with Peru in 1941 led to a loss of territory. Economic crises in the early 21st century led to the adoption of the US dollar as the official currency. Rafael Correa, president since 2006, was succeeded by fellow left-winger Lenin Moreno in 2017. His attempts to stabilize the economy by introducing austerity measures, with support from the IMF, provoked large-scale protests in 2019.

The World Bank classifies Ecuador as an "upper-middle-income" developing country. Much dependent on its oil resources and the fluctuating world price of petrol, Ecuador has tried to diversify its economy. There is a wide disparity in the degree to which some stratas of society benefit from oil revenue: many live in poverty. Agriculture employs 28% of the people, and bananas, cocoa, and coffee are all important crops. Fishing, forestry, mining, and manufacturing play a significant part in the economy.

AREA 109,483 SQ MI [283,561 SQ KM] **POPULATION** 16,905,000
CAPITAL QUITO **GOVERNMENT** MULTIPARTY REPUBLIC
ETHNIC GROUPS MESTIZO (MIXED WHITE/AMERINDIAN) 72%, MONTUBIO 7%, AFROECUADORIAN 7%, AMERINDIAN 7%, WHITE 6%
LANGUAGES SPANISH (OFFICIAL), QUECHUA, SHUAR
RELIGIONS ROMAN CATHOLIC 95% **CURRENCY** US DOLLAR = 100 CENTS

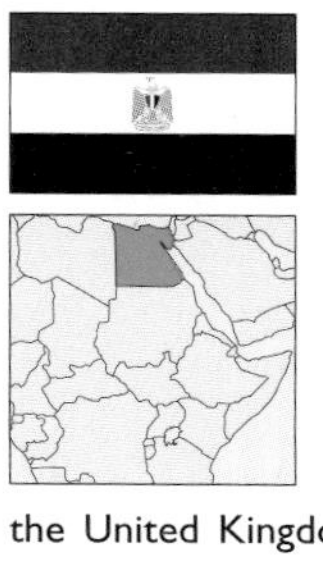

EGYPT

GEOGRAPHY The Arab Republic of Egypt is Africa's third largest country by population after Nigeria and Ethiopia, though it ranks 12th in area. Most of Egypt is desert. Almost all the people live either in the Nile Valley and its fertile delta or along the Suez Canal. This waterway, between the Mediterranean and Red seas, shortens the sea journey between the United Kingdom and India by 6,027 mi [9,700 km]. Recent attempts have been made to irrigate parts of the western desert.

Apart from the Nile Valley, Egypt can be divided into three other main regions. The Western and Eastern deserts are parts of the Sahara. The Sinai peninsula (Es Sina), to the east of the Suez Canal, is a mountainous desert region, falling geographically within Asia. It contains Egypt's highest peak, Gebel Katherîna (8,650 ft [2,637 m]); few people live in this area.

Egypt is a dry country. The low rainfall occurs, if at all, in winter and the country is one of the sunniest places on Earth.

POLITICS & ECONOMY Ancient Egypt, dating from around 5,000 years ago, was one of the great early civilizations. Throughout the country, pyramids, temples, and richly decorated tombs are memorials to its great achievements.

After Ancient Egypt declined, the country came under successive foreign rulers. The Arabs, who first occupied Egypt in the 7th century introducing their language and Islam, had a profound and lasting effect. Their influence was so great that most Egyptians now regard themselves as Arabs.

Egypt came under British rule in 1882, but it gained partial independence in 1922, becoming a monarchy. The monarchy was abolished in 1952, when Egypt became a republic, led by Gamal Abdel Nasser from 1954 to 1970. The creation of Israel in 1948 led Egypt into a series of wars. In 1979, it signed a peace treaty with Israel and regained the Sinai region, which it had lost in a war of 1967. Extremists opposed contacts with Israel and, in 1981, President Sadat, who had signed the treaty, was assassinated.

In February 2011, Hosni Mubarak, Egypt's president since 1981, was ousted following huge popular demonstrations. A Supreme Military Council took power and organized elections in 2011–12. President Muhammed Mursi from the formerly banned Muslim Brotherhood was elected in June 2012. Mursi was removed from power by the military in July 2013 and Abdel Fattah al-Sisi was elected in 2014. He was re-elected in March 2018, after credible opposing candidates withdrew or were arrested.

Egypt plays a major role in Arab affairs and is one of Africa's most industrialized countries, yet most of its people are poor. Oil and textiles are the country's main exports. Tourism is vitally important to the economy but is threatened by the rise in attacks by Islamic extremists. The country is struggling to support its rapidly growing population, and in an attempt to alleviate congestion in Cairo, a new Administrative Capital is being built to the east, although the project faces financial challenges.

AREA 386,659 SQ MI [1,001,449 SQ KM] **POPULATION** 104,124,000
CAPITAL CAIRO **GOVERNMENT** REPUBLIC
ETHNIC GROUPS EGYPTIANS/BEDOUINS/BERBERS 99%
LANGUAGES ARABIC (OFFICIAL), FRENCH, ENGLISH **RELIGIONS** ISLAM (MAINLY SUNNI MUSLIM) 90%, CHRISTIANITY (MAINLY COPTIC CHRISTIAN) AND OTHERS 10% **CURRENCY** EGYPTIAN POUND = 100 PIASTRES

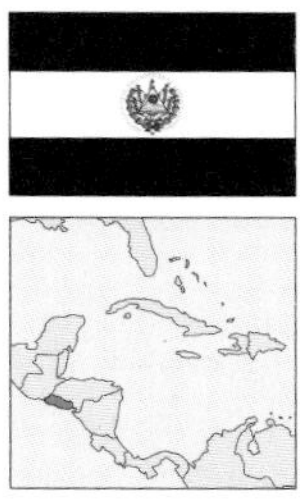

EL SALVADOR

GEOGRAPHY The Republic of El Salvador is the only country in Central America not to have a coast on the Caribbean Sea. El Salvador has a narrow coastal plain along the Pacific Ocean. Behind the coastal plain, the coastal range is a zone of rugged mountains, including volcanoes, which overlooks a densely populated inland plateau. Beyond the plateau, the land rises to the sparsely populated interior highlands. The coast has a hot tropical climate, but inland this is moderated by the altitude. Rain is heavy between May and October.

POLITICS & ECONOMY Amerindians have lived in El Salvador for thousands of years. The ruins of Mayan pyramids, built between AD 100 and 1000, are still found in the western part of the country.

Spain first conquered the area in 1524, and ruled until 1821. In 1823, all the Central American countries, except for Panama, set up the Central American Federation, with El Salvador withdrawing in 1840 and declaring its independence in 1841. It suffered from instability throughout the 19th century. The 20th century saw more stable government, although from 1931 military dictatorships alternated with elected governments.

The country remained poor and in the 1970s protesters demanded that the government introduce reforms. Kidnappings and murders committed by left- and right-wing groups were common. A civil war broke out in 1979 between the US-backed government forces and left-wing guerrillas. A ceasefire was agreed in 1992. In 2011, the United States added El Salvador and Belize to its list of countries considered to be major producers or transit routes of illegal drugs. Its murder rate is one of the world's highest.

The World Bank classifies El Salvador as a "lower-middle-income" economy. Often hit by natural disasters, the country relies heavily on remittances from abroad, especially the USA. About three-quarters of the country is farmed. Coffee, grown in the highlands, is the main export, followed by sugar and cotton, which grow on the coastal lowlands. Fishing for lobsters and shrimps is important, but manufacturing is on a small scale.

AREA 8,124 SQ MI [21,041 SQ KM] **POPULATION** 6,481,000
CAPITAL SAN SALVADOR **GOVERNMENT** REPUBLIC
ETHNIC GROUPS MESTIZO (MIXED WHITE AND AMERINDIAN) 86%, WHITE 13%, AMERINDIAN 1% **LANGUAGES** SPANISH (OFFICIAL) **RELIGIONS** ROMAN CATHOLIC 57%, PROTESTANT 21% **CURRENCY** US DOLLAR = 100 CENTS

EQUATORIAL GUINEA

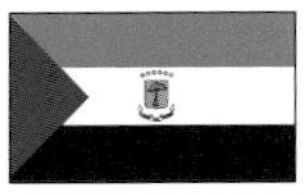

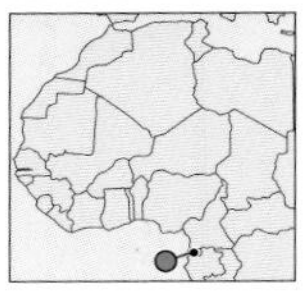

GEOGRAPHY The Republic of Equatorial Guinea is a small republic in west-central Africa. It consists of a mainland territory which makes up 90% of the land area, called Rio Muni, between Cameroon and Gabon, and five offshore islands in the Bight of Bonny, the largest of which is Bioko. The island of Annobon lies 350 mi [560 km] southwest of Rio Muni. Rio Muni consists mainly of hills and plateaux behind the coastal plains.

The climate is hot and humid. Bioko is mountainous, with the land rising to 9,869 ft [3,008 m], and hence it is particularly rainy. However, there is a marked dry season between the months of December and February. Mainland Rio Muni has a similar climate, though the rainfall diminishes inland.

POLITICS & ECONOMY Portuguese navigators reached the area in 1471. In 1778, Portugal granted Bioko, together with rights over Rio Muni, to Spain. In 1959, Spain made Bioko and Rio Muni provinces of overseas Spain and, in 1963, it gave them a degree of self-government. Equatorial Guinea became independent in 1968.

The first president of Equatorial Guinea, Francisco Macias Nguema, proved to be a tyrant. Overthrown in 1979, a Supreme Military Council then took control, led by Obiang Nguema. In 1991, a nominally democratic system was restored, with Obiang as president. He has been re-elected several times, most recently in 2016, in a series of flawed elections. Equatorial Guinea is widely recognized as one of Africa's worst abusers of human rights.

Agriculture employs two-thirds of the people. The most valuable crop is coffee. Substantial reserves of oil were discovered in 1996. It fueled rapid economic growth and accounts for most of the country's export revenue. It is one of the largest oil producers in sub-Saharan Africa.

AREA 10,830 SQ MI [28,051 SQ KM] **POPULATION** 836,000
CAPITAL MALABO **GOVERNMENT** REPUBLIC
ETHNIC GROUPS BUBI (ON BIOKO), FANG (IN RIO MUNI)
LANGUAGES SPANISH AND FRENCH (BOTH OFFICIAL)
RELIGIONS CHRISTIANITY **CURRENCY** CFA FRANC = 100 CENTIMES

ERITREA

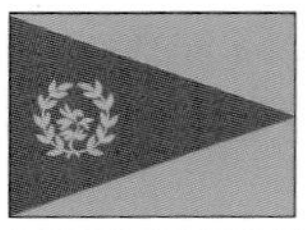

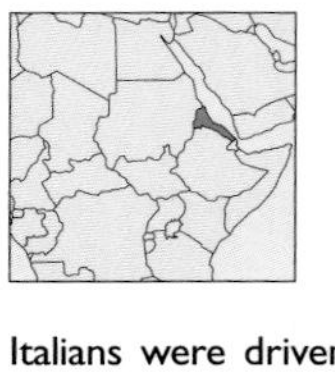

GEOGRAPHY The State of Eritrea consists of a hot, dry coastal plain facing the Red Sea, with a fairly mountainous area in the center. Most people live in the cooler highland area.

POLITICS & ECONOMY From the 1st century AD, Eritrea was part of the ancient Kingdom of Axum. The Ottoman Turks took over the area in the 16th century and it became an Italian colony in the 1880s. The Italians were driven out in 1941 and, in 1952, it became part of Ethiopia. A guerrilla struggle launched in 1961 ended in 1993, when Eritrea became independent. Economic recovery was hampered by conflict first with Yemen, over three islands in the Red Sea, and then with Ethiopia. A fragile peace has been negotiated and a treaty signed with Ethiopia in 2018. The country faces the huge task of reconstruction. The UN has repeatedly accused the country's leaders of human rights violations and hundreds of thousands of people have fled.

Eritrea's main economic activities are farming and livestock rearing, both badly affected by chronic drought, with some manufacturing based around Asmara. Exploitation of the country's copper and gold resources may drive future economic growth.

AREA 45,405 SQ MI [117,600 SQ KM] **POPULATION** 6,081,000
CAPITAL ASMARA **GOVERNMENT** TRANSITIONAL GOVERNMENT
ETHNIC GROUPS TIGRINYA 55%, TIGRE 30%, SAHO 4%, KUNAMA 2%, OTHERS 9% **LANGUAGES** TIGRINYA, ARABIC, ENGLISH (ALL OFFICIAL), OTHERS
RELIGIONS ISLAM, COPTIC CHRISTIAN, ROMAN CATHOLIC
CURRENCY NAKFA = 100 CENTS

ESTONIA

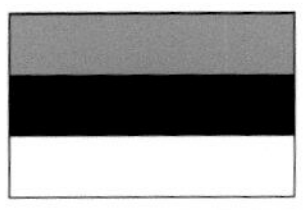

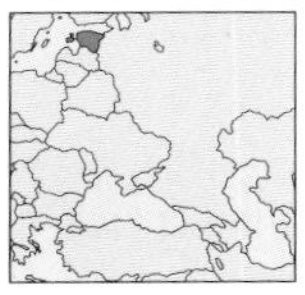

GEOGRAPHY The Republic of Estonia is the smallest of the three states on the Baltic Sea. Estonia consists of a generally flat plain which was covered by ice sheets during the Ice Age. The land is strewn with moraine (rocks deposited by the ice).

The country is dotted with more than 1,500 small lakes. The large Lake Peipus (Ozero Chudskoye) and the River Narva together make up much of Estonia's eastern border with Russia. The largest of the islands is Saaremaa (Ösel). The climate is fairly mild because of the moderating effects of the sea.

POLITICS & ECONOMY The ancestors of the Estonians, who are related to the Finns, settled in the area several thousand years ago. German crusaders, known as the Teutonic Knights, introduced Christianity in the early 13th century. By the 16th century, German noblemen owned much of the land in Estonia. In 1561, Sweden took the northern part of the country and Poland the south. From 1625, Sweden controlled the entire country until handing it over to Russia in 1721. Estonian nationalists campaigned for their independence from around the mid-19th century. Finally, Estonia was proclaimed independent in 1918.

In 1939, Germany and the Soviet Union agreed to take over parts of Eastern Europe. In 1940, Soviet forces occupied Estonia, but they were driven out by the Germans in 1941. Soviet troops returned in 1944 and Estonia became one of the 15 Soviet Socialist Republics of the Soviet Union. The Estonians strongly opposed Soviet rule and many of them were deported to Siberia.

Political changes in the Soviet Union in the late 1980s led to renewed demands for freedom. In 1990, the Estonian government declared the country independent and, finally, the Soviet Union recognized this act in September 1991.

Under Soviet rule, Estonia was the most prosperous of the three Baltic states. Turning increasingly to the West, it became a member of both the North Atlantic Treaty Organization and the European Union in 2004. In 2011, it became the 17th member of the eurozone. From March 2017 NATO made a major deployment of armed forces to Estonia amid reports of a Russian troop build-up across the border. Estonia's resources include oil shale and its forests. Industries produce fertilizers, processed food, machinery, petrochemical products, wood products, and textiles. Agriculture and fishing are also important activities. Around a quarter of the population are of Russian origin and, due to offcial language requirements, they can be subject to discrimination.

AREA 17,413 SQ MI [45,100 SQ KM] **POPULATION** 1,229,000
CAPITAL TALLINN **GOVERNMENT** MULTIPARTY REPUBLIC
ETHNIC GROUPS ESTONIAN 69%, RUSSIAN 26%, UKRAINIAN 2%, BELARUSIAN 1%, FINNISH 1% **LANGUAGES** ESTONIAN (OFFICIAL), RUSSIAN
RELIGIONS LUTHERAN, RUSSIAN AND ESTONIAN ORTHODOX, METHODIST, BAPTIST, ROMAN CATHOLIC **CURRENCY** EURO = 100 CENTS

ESWATINI

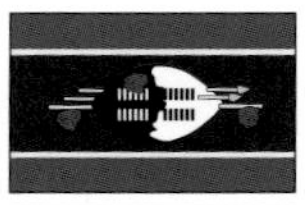

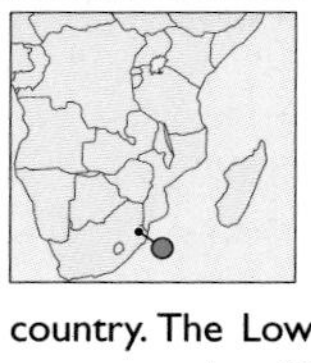

GEOGRAPHY Offically renamed in 2018 as the Kingdom of Eswatini, this is a small, landlocked country in southern Africa. The country has four regions which run north–south. In the west, the Highveld, with an average height of 3,950 ft [1,200 m], makes up 30% of Eswatini. The Middleveld, between 1,150 ft and 3,280 ft [350 m to 1,000 m], covers 28% of the country. The Lowveld, with an average height of 886 ft [270 m], covers another 33%. Finally, the Lebombo Mountains reach 2,600 ft [800 m] along the eastern border. The Lowveld is almost tropical, with average temperatures of 72°F [22°C] and low rainfall.

POLITICS & ECONOMY In 1894, Britain and the Boers of South Africa agreed to put Swaziland, as it was then known, under the control of the South African Republic (the Transvaal). But at the end of the Anglo–Boer War (1899–1902), Britain took control of the country. In 1968, when it became fully independent as a constitutional monarchy, the head of state was King Sobhuza II. Sobhuza died in 1982 and was succeeded by his son, who, in 1986, became King Mswati III. Political parties were banned in elections in 1993 and 1998 and Mswati ruled by decree. In 2005, Mswati signed a new constitution, but Eswatini remains an absolute monarchy.

This is a developing country. Farm products and processed food and drink, sugar, wood pulp, citrus fruits, and canned fruit are the leading exports. It is heavily dependent on South Africa and it shares two problems with its large neighbor – widespread poverty and the world's highest incidence of HIV/AIDS.

AREA 6,704 SQ MI [17,364 SQ KM] **POPULATION** 1,104,000
CAPITAL MBABANE **GOVERNMENT** MONARCHY
ETHNIC GROUPS AFRICAN 97%, EUROPEAN 3%
LANGUAGES SISWATI AND ENGLISH (BOTH OFFICIAL)
RELIGIONS ZIONIST (A MIX OF CHRISTIANITY AND TRADITIONAL BELIEFS) 40%, ROMAN CATHOLIC 20%, ISLAM 10% **CURRENCY** LILANGENI = 100 CENTS

ETHIOPIA

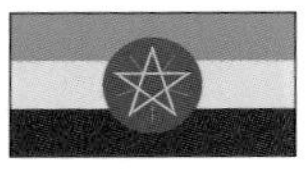

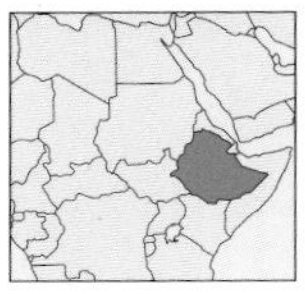

GEOGRAPHY Ethiopia is a landlocked country in northeastern Africa. The land is mainly mountainous, though there are extensive plains in the east, bordering southern Eritrea, and in the south, bordering Somalia. The highlands are divided into two blocks by an arm of the Great Rift Valley which runs throughout eastern Africa. North of the Rift Valley, the land is especially rugged, rising to 14,872 ft [4,533 m] at Ras Dashen. Southeast of Ras Dashen is Lake Tana, source of the River Abay (Blue Nile). The climate is affected by the altitude. The rainfall in the highlands is generally more than 39 inches [1,000 mm]. The lowlands are hot and arid.

POLITICS & ECONOMY Ethiopia was the home of an ancient monarchy, which became Christian in the 4th century. In the 7th century, Muslims gained control of the lowlands, but Christianity survived in the highlands. Ethiopia resisted attempts to colonize it, until Italy invaded the country in 1935. With help from the UK, the Italians were driven out in 1941 and the Emperor Haile Selassie was put back on the throne.

In 1952, Eritrea was federated with Ethiopia. But in 1961, Eritrean nationalists demanded their freedom and began a struggle that ended in their independence in 1993. Devastation caused by drought, famine, and war led to the overthrow of Haile Selassie in 1974. In 1995, because of Ethiopia's great ethnic diversity, the country was divided into nine provinces. In 1998, boundary disputes with Eritrea led to conflict. A peace agreement was reached in 2001, but border incursions by both sides continued. In 2016, human rights protests broke out across the country, leading to the resignation of PM Hailemariam Desalegn and his replacement by Abiy Ahmed in 2018. In July 2018 he signed a peace agreement with Eritrea and reopened the border.

Ethiopia's agriculture-based economy is at the mercy of a fickle climate. Coffee and the drug "khat" are leading exports. Although still heavily dependent on foreign aid, Ethiopia has one of the fastest growing non-oil economies in Africa.

AREA 426,370 SQ MI [1,104,300 SQ KM] **POPULATION** 108,113,000
CAPITAL ADDIS ABABA **GOVERNMENT** FEDERATION OF NINE PROVINCES
ETHNIC GROUPS OROMO 34%, AMHARA 27%, SOMALI 6%, TIGRAWAY 6%, SIDAMA 4%
LANGUAGES AMHARIC (OFFICIAL), OROMO, MANY OTHERS
RELIGIONS ETHIOPIAN ORTHODOX 43%, ISLAM 34%, PROTESTANT 19%
CURRENCY BIRR = 100 SANTIM

FALKLAND ISLANDS

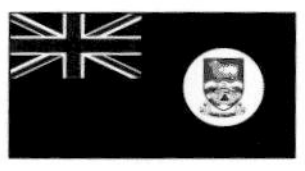

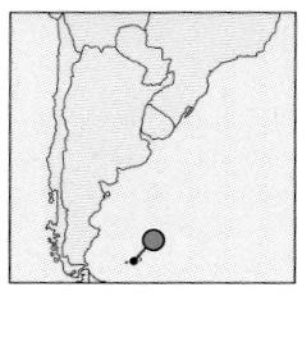

Comprising two main islands and over 200 small ones, the Falkland Islands lie 300 mi [480 km] from South America. Sheep farming and fishing are the main activities, though oil and diamonds are being sought. Argentina disputes Britain's sovereignty of the islands, but a referendum in 2013 resulted in an overwhelming vote to stay British.

AREA 4,700 SQ MI [12,173 SQ KM]
POPULATION 3,000 **CAPITAL** STANLEY

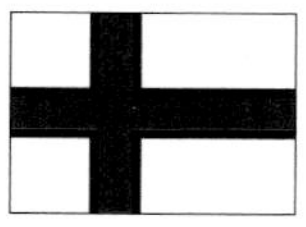
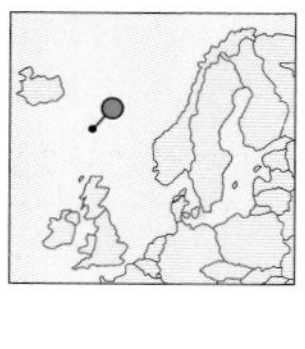

FÆROE ISLANDS

The Færoe Islands are a group of 18 volcanic islands and some reefs in the North Atlantic Ocean. The islands have been Danish since the 1380s, but they became largely self-governing in 1948. The islands are heavily reliant on fishing although the discovery of some oil may allow diversification in the future. Denmark still provides a subsidy.

AREA 540 SQ MI [1,399 SQ KM]
POPULATION 52,000 **CAPITAL** TÓRSHAVN

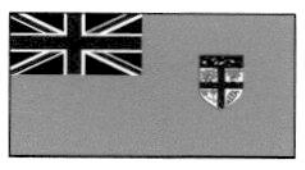
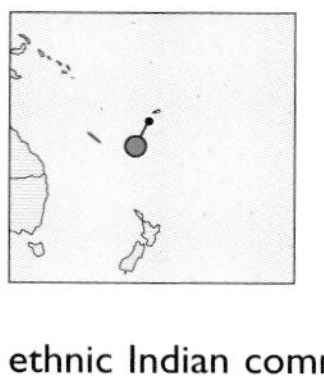

FIJI

The Republic of Fiji (the official name of Fiji since February 2011) consists of more than 800 Melanesian islands, the biggest being Viti Levu and Vanua Levu. The climate is tropical. A former British colony, Fiji became independent in 1970. Its recent history has been marred by efforts of indigenous Fijians to impose their rule, stopping members of the ethnic Indian community from holding senior cabinet posts. Such political instability has harmed the economy.

AREA 7,056 SQ MI [18,274 SQ KM] **POPULATION** 936,000 **CAPITAL** SUVA

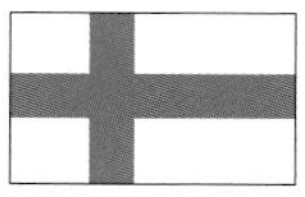
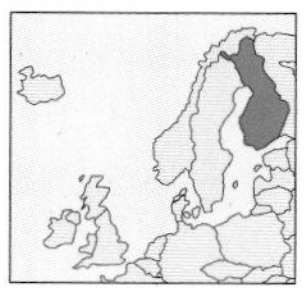

FINLAND

GEOGRAPHY The Republic of Finland is a beautiful country in northern Europe. In the south, behind the coastal lowlands where most Finns live, lies a region of sparkling lakes carved out by ice sheets in the Ice Age. The thinly populated northern uplands cover about two-fifths of the country.

Helsinki, the capital city, has warm summers, but the average temperatures between the months of December and March are below freezing. Snow covers the land in winter. The north has less precipitation than the south, but it is much colder.

POLITICS & ECONOMY Between 1150 and 1809, Finland was under Swedish rule and close links between the countries continue today. Swedish remains an official language in Finland and many towns have Swedish as well as Finnish names.

In 1809, Finland became a grand duchy of the Russian empire. It finally declared itself independent in 1917, following the Russian Revolution. But during World War II (1939–45), the Soviet Union declared war on Finland and took part of Finland's territory. Finland allied itself with Germany, but it lost more land to the Soviet Union at the end of the war.

After World War II, Finland became a neutral country and negotiated peace treaties with the Soviet Union. Finland also strengthened its relations with other northern European countries and became an associate member of the European Free Trade Association (EFTA) in 1961 and a full member in 1986. It then joined the European Union on January 1, 1995, adopting the euro as its currency in 2002.

Forests are the chief resource and wood, wood products, and paper once dominated the economy. They still make up about a quarter of exports, but, since World War II, Finland has set up many new industries, which employ around a quarter of the people. One of Finland's main advantages is a well-qualified work force who enjoy one of the highest rates of per capita income in Western Europe. Major exports include electrical equipment, machinery, and paper products. However, dealing with a growing aging population is a challenge to be met.

AREA 130,558 SQ MI [338,145 SQ KM] **POPULATION** 5,572,000
CAPITAL HELSINKI **GOVERNMENT** MULTIPARTY REPUBLIC
ETHNIC GROUPS FINNISH 93%, SWEDISH 6%
LANGUAGES FINNISH AND SWEDISH (BOTH OFFICIAL)
RELIGIONS EVANGELICAL LUTHERAN 71% **CURRENCY** EURO = 100 CENTS

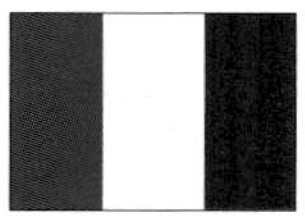
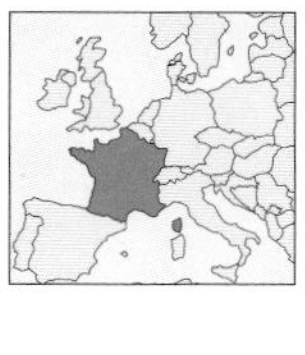

FRANCE

GEOGRAPHY The Republic of France is the largest country in Western Europe. The scenery is extremely varied. The Vosges Mountains overlook the Rhine valley in the northeast, the Jura Mountains and the Alps form the borders with Switzerland and Italy in the southeast, while the Pyrenees straddle France's border with Spain. The only large highland area entirely within France is the Massif Central between the Rhône–Saône valley and the basin of Aquitaine in southern France.

Brittany (Bretagne) and Normandy (Normande) form a scenic region. Fertile lowlands cover most of northern France, including the densely populated Paris basin. Another major lowland area, the Aquitanian basin, is in the southwest, while the Rhône–Saône valley and the Mediterranean lowlands are in the southeast.

The climate of France varies from west to east and from north to south. The west comes under the moderating influence of the Atlantic Ocean, giving generally mild weather. To the east, summers are warmer and winters colder. The climate also becomes warmer as one travels from north to south. The Mediterranean Sea coast has hot, dry summers and mild, moist winters. The Alps, Jura, and Pyrenees mountains have snowy winters. Winter sports centers are found in all three areas.

POLITICS & ECONOMY The Romans conquered France (then called Gaul) in the 50s BC. Roman rule began to decline in the 5th century AD and, in 486, the Frankish realm (as France was known) became independent under a Christian king, Clovis. In 800, Charlemagne, who had been king since 768, became emperor of the Romans. He extended France's boundaries, but in 843 his empire was divided into three parts and the area of France contracted. After the Norman invasion of England in 1066, large areas of France came under English rule, but this was all but ended in 1453.

France later became a powerful monarchy. But the French Revolution (1789–99) ended absolute rule by French kings. In 1799, Napoleon Bonaparte took power and fought a series of brilliant military campaigns before his final defeat in 1815. The monarchy was restored until 1848, when the Second Republic was founded. In 1852, Napoleon's nephew became Napoleon III, but the Third Republic was established in 1875. France was the scene of much fighting during World War I (1914–18) and World War II (1939–45), causing great loss of life and much damage to the economy.

In 1946, France adopted a new constitution, establishing the Fourth Republic. But political instability and costly colonial wars slowed France's post-war recovery. In 1958, Charles de Gaulle was elected president and he introduced a new constitution, giving the president extra powers and inaugurating the Fifth Republic.

Since the 1960s, France has made rapid economic progress, becoming one of the most prosperous nations in the European Union. But France's government faced a number of problems, including unemployment, pollution, and the growing number of elderly people. France is still facing economic challenges due to low growth and high public spending. A social issue concerns the large numbers of immigrants, including Muslims from North Africa, and in 2005, France was rocked by inter-ethnic violence. It has suffered several terrorist attacks since 2015.

In 2002, the euro replaced the franc as France's currency. In 2009, the right-wing president Nicolas Sarkozy announced that France would rejoin NATO. Presidential elections in 2017 were won by Emmanuel Macron. His proposed labor reforms sparked strikes in 2018, and price increases introduced to reduce the use of fossil fuels prompted violent street demonstrations by the "yellow shirts" from 2018 to 2019.

France is one of the world's most developed countries. Its principal natural resource is its fertile soil, and fast-flowing rivers offer the potential for much hydroelectric power. France is also one of the world's top manufacturing nations, and it has often innovated in bold and imaginative ways. The TGV and hypermarkets are typical examples. Paris is a world center of fashion industries. Manufactures include aircraft, cars, chemicals, electronic and metal products, machinery, processed food, steel, and textiles.

Agriculture employs about 4% of the people, but France is the largest producer of farm products in Western Europe, producing most of the food it needs. Wheat is the leading crop and livestock farming is of major importance. Fishing and forestry are leading industries, while tourism is a major activity.

AREA 212,934 SQ MI [551,500 SQ KM] **POPULATION** 67,848,000
CAPITAL PARIS **GOVERNMENT** MULTIPARTY REPUBLIC
ETHNIC GROUPS CELTIC, LATIN, ARAB, TEUTONIC, SLAVIC
LANGUAGES FRENCH (OFFICIAL) **RELIGIONS** ROMAN CATHOLIC 85%, ISLAM 8%, OTHERS **CURRENCY** EURO = 100 CENTS

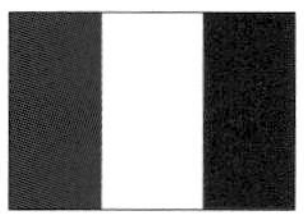
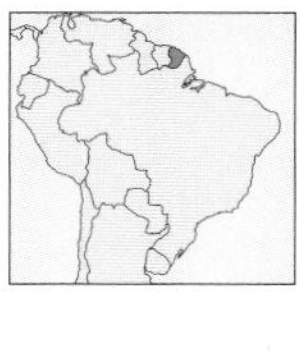

FRENCH GUIANA

GEOGRAPHY French Guiana is the smallest country in mainland South America. The coastal plain is swampy in places, but some dry areas are cultivated. Inland lies a plateau, with the low Serra Tumucumaque in the south. Most of the rivers run north toward the Atlantic Ocean.

French Guiana has a hot, equatorial climate, with high temperatures throughout the year. The rainfall is heavy, especially between December and June, but the climate is dry between August and October. The northeast trade winds blow constantly across the country.

POLITICS & ECONOMY The first people to live in what is now French Guiana were Amerindians. Today, only a few of them survive in the interior. The first Europeans to explore the coast arrived in 1500, and they were followed by adventurers seeking El Dorado, the mythical city of gold. Cayenne was founded in 1637 by a group of French merchants and the area became a French colony in the late 17th century.

France used the colony as a penal settlement for political prisoners from the times of the French Revolution in the 1790s. From the 1850s to 1945, the country became notorious as a place where prisoners were harshly treated. Many of them died, unable to survive in the tropical conditions.

In 1946, French Guiana became an overseas department of France, and in 1974 it also became an administrative region. An independence movement developed in the 1980s, but most people want to retain their links with France. In 2010, the people voted in a referendum to reject plans for increased autonomy.

Although it has rich forest and mineral resources, such as bauxite (aluminum ore), French Guiana is a developing country. It depends greatly on France for money to run its services and the government is the country's biggest employer. Since 1968, Kourou, the European Space Agency's rocket-launching site, has earned money for France by sending communications satellites into space.

AREA 34,749 SQ MI [90,000 SQ KM] **POPULATION** 250,000
CAPITAL CAYENNE **GOVERNMENT** OVERSEAS DEPARTMENT OF FRANCE
ETHNIC GROUPS BLACK OR MIXED 66%, EAST INDIAN/CHINESE AND AMERINDIAN 12%, WHITE 12%, OTHERS 10%
LANGUAGES FRENCH (OFFICIAL) **RELIGIONS** ROMAN CATHOLIC
CURRENCY EURO = 100 CENTS

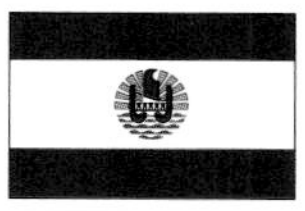
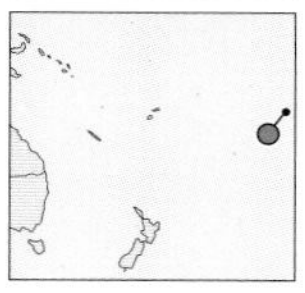

FRENCH POLYNESIA

French Polynesia consists of 130 islands, of which Tahiti is the most densely populated. A French protectorate since 1843, France has tested nuclear weapons on the uninhabited atolls. French Polynesia gained increased autonomy in 1984, but the links with France ensure a high standard of living.

AREA 1,544 SQ MI [4,000 SQ KM]
POPULATION 295,000 **CAPITAL** PAPEETE

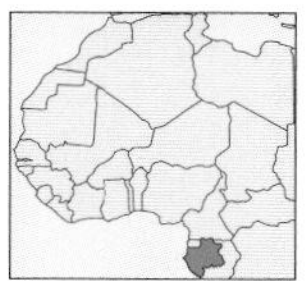

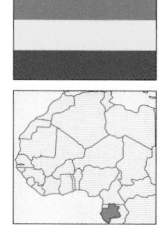

GABON

GEOGRAPHY The Gabonese Republic lies on the equator in west-central Africa. In area, it is a little larger than the United Kingdom, with a coastline 500 mi [800 km] long. Behind the narrow, partly lagoon-lined coastal plain, the land rises to hills, plateaux, and mountains divided by deep valleys carved by the River Ogooué and its tributaries.

Most of Gabon has an equatorial climate, with high temperatures and humidity throughout the year.

POLITICS & ECONOMY Gabon became a French colony in the 1880s, but it achieved full independence in 1960. In 1964, an attempted coup was put down when French troops intervened and crushed the revolt. In 1967, Bernard-Albert Bongo, who later renamed himself El Hadj Omar Bongo, became president and remained in power until his death in 2009, when he was succeeded by his son, Ali Ben Bongo Ondimba. In 2016 presidential elections, marred by violence and accusations of fraud, Ali Bongo won a second term.

Gabon's natural resources include its forests, oil and gas deposits, manganese, and uranium. Its economy is heavily dependent on oil, but falling oil revenue means that it has to diversify. One growth sector is ecotourism, but agriculture still employs about 30% of the people and many farmers produce little more than they need to support their families.

AREA 103,347 SQ MI [267,668 SQ KM] **POPULATION** 2,231,000
CAPITAL LIBREVILLE **GOVERNMENT** MULTIPARTY REPUBLIC
ETHNIC GROUPS FOUR MAJOR BANTU TRIBES: FANG, BAPOUNOU, NZEBI AND OBAMBA **LANGUAGES** FRENCH (OFFICIAL), FANG, MYENE, NZEBI, BAPOUNOU/ESCHIRA, BANDJABI
RELIGIONS CHRISTIANITY 65%, ANIMIST, ISLAM
CURRENCY CFA FRANC = 100 CENTIMES

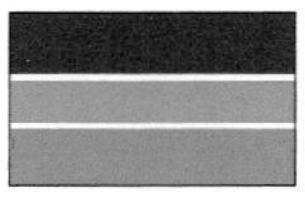
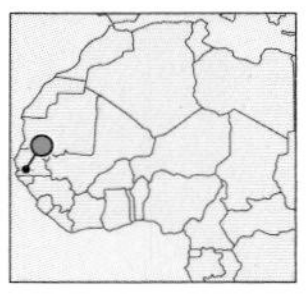

GAMBIA, THE

GEOGRAPHY The Republic of The Gambia is the smallest country in mainland Africa. It consists of a narrow strip of land bordering the River Gambia. The Gambia is almost entirely enclosed by Senegal, except along the short Atlantic coastline.

The Gambia has hot and humid summers, but winter temperatures (November to May) drop to around 61°F [16°C]. In the summer, moist southwesterlies bring rain, which is heaviest on the coast.

POLITICS & ECONOMY English traders established themselves on the River Gambia in the late 16th century and the country was a British colony from 1888 until independence in 1965.

In 1981, an attempted coup in The Gambia was put down with the help of Senegalese troops. Following this, in 1982, The Gambia and Senegal set up a defense alliance, called the Confederation of Senegambia, which was dissolved in 1989. In 1994, a military group led by Captain Yahya Jammeh overthrew the government of Sir Dawda Jawara. Jammeh remained in power until 2016, when he was defeated by Adama Barrow. Jammeh refused to accept the result and left only after neighboring countries undertook mediation and threatened armed intervention. Barrow's United Democratic Party won a landslide victory at parliamentary elections in 2017.

Agriculture is the chief activity, employing three-quarters of the population and accounting for around 30% of GDP. Food crops include cassava, millet, and sorghum, but groundnuts (peanuts) and groundnut products are the main exports. About one-third of the population live below the poverty line. Tourism is important to the economy, as are remittances sent back from overseas workers. Offshore oilfields were discovered in 2004 but this resource has yet to be developed.

AREA 4,361 sq mi [11,295 sq km] **POPULATION** 2,174,000
CAPITAL Banjul **GOVERNMENT** Republic
ETHNIC GROUPS Mandinka 42%, Fula 18%, Wolof 16%, Jola 10%, Serahuli 9%, others
LANGUAGES English (official), Mandinka, Wolof, Fula
RELIGIONS Islam 90%, Christianity 8%, traditional beliefs 2%
CURRENCY Dalasi = 100 bututs

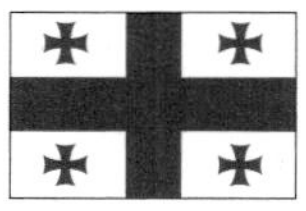
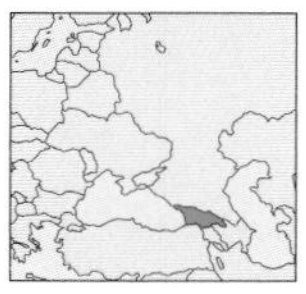

GEORGIA

GEOGRAPHY Georgia is a country on the borders of Europe and Asia, facing the Black Sea. The land is rugged with the Caucasus Mountains forming its northern border.

The highest mountain in this range, Mount Elbrus (18,510 ft [5,642 m]), lies over the border in Russia. The Black Sea plains have hot summers and mild winters. The rainfall is heavy, though inland areas are drier.

POLITICS & ECONOMY The first Georgian state was set up nearly 2,500 years ago but has been overrun by a variety of conquering armies. From the 16th to the 18th centuries, Persia and the Turkish Ottoman empire struggled for control of the area, and in the late 18th century Georgia sought the protection of Russia. By the early 19th century, it was part of the Russian empire. After the Russian Revolution of 1917, Georgia declared its independence, but Russia invaded, making it part of the Soviet regime. Georgia declared itself independent in 1991 and it became a separate country when the Soviet Union was dissolved in 1991.

Georgia contains three regions populated by minority peoples: Abkhazia in the northwest, South Ossetia in north-central Georgia, and Ajaria in the southwest. Civil war broke out in South Ossetia in the early 1990s, while fierce fighting continued in Abkhazia until the late 1990s. In 2000, Georgia agreed to recognize Ajaria's autonomy in the country's constitution. In 2003, the pro-Western Mikhail Saakashvili was elected president following the "Rose Revolution." Following Saakashvili's re-election in 2008, relations with Russia deteriorated. In August 2008, Georgia tried to retake South Ossetia by force. Russian troops counterattacked and drove Georgian troops out of South Ossetia and Abkhazia. Saakashvili resigned after parliamentary elections in 2012 were won by the opposition Georgian Dream coalition. They changed the presidency to a mainly ceremonial role and won a majority in 2016 elections. In 2019 Giorgi Gakharia became prime minister.

The World Bank classifies Georgia as an "upper-middle-income" economy. Agriculture and food processing are important activities. Products include barley, citrus fruits, grapes for winemaking, maize, tea, and vegetables. Sheep and cattle are reared. Hydroelectricity provides most of Georgia's power needs but gas and oil have to be imported. Unemployment remains high.

AREA 26,911 sq mi [69,700 sq km] **POPULATION** 3,997,000
CAPITAL Tbilisi **GOVERNMENT** Multiparty republic
ETHNIC GROUPS Georgian 84%, Azeri 7%, Armenian 6%, Russian 1%, others 2%
LANGUAGES Georgian (official), Russian, Armenian, Azeri; Abkhaz (official in Abkhazia) **RELIGIONS** Georgian Orthodox 84%, Islam 10%, Armenian Gregorian 4% **CURRENCY** Lari = 100 tetri

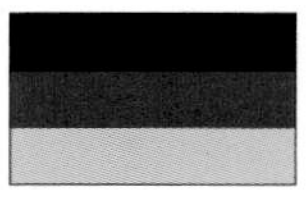
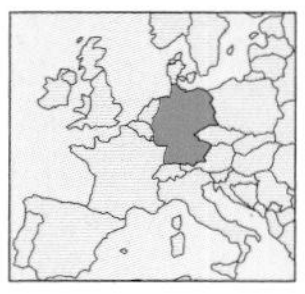

GERMANY

GEOGRAPHY The Federal Republic of Germany is the fourth largest country in Western Europe, after France, Spain, and Sweden. The North German Plain borders the North Sea in the northwest and the Baltic Sea in the northeast. Major rivers draining the plain include the Weser, Elbe, and Oder.

The central highlands include the Harz Mountains, the Thuringian Forest (Thüringer Wald), the Ore Mountains (Erzgebirge), and the Bohemian Forest (Böhmerwald) on the Czech border. The Bavarian Alps in the south contain Germany's highest peak, Zugspitze, at 9,718 ft [2,962 m] above sea level. The Black Forest (Schwarzwald) in the southwest overlooks the River Rhine. Northwestern Germany has a mild climate, but the Baltic coasts are cooler. To the south, the climate becomes more continental, especially in the highlands.

POLITICS & ECONOMY Germany and its allies were defeated in World War I (1914–18) and the country became a republic. Adolf Hitler came to power in 1933 and ruled as a dictator. His order to invade Poland led to the start of World War II (1939–45), which ended with Germany in ruins.

In 1945, Germany was divided into four military zones. In 1949, the American, British, and French zones were amalgamated to form the Federal Republic of Germany (West Germany), while the Soviet zone became the German Democratic Republic (East Germany), a Communist state. Berlin, which had also been partitioned, became a divided city. West Berlin was part of West Germany, while East Berlin became the capital of East Germany. Bonn was the capital of West Germany.

Tension between East and West mounted during the Cold War, but West Germany rebuilt its economy quickly. In East Germany, the recovery was less rapid. In the late 1980s, reforms in the Soviet Union led to unrest in East Germany. Free elections were held in East Germany in 1990 and, on October 3, 1990, Germany was reunited.

In the 1990s, the government faced many problems, especially those arising from reunification. In 1999, the parliament moved from Bonn to the reconstructed Reichstag building in Berlin. In 2005, Angela Merkel became Germany's first female Chancellor. Merkel's unpopular policy of welcoming asylum seekers adversely affected her party's showing in 2017 elections and boosted the vote of the far-right.

West Germany's "economic miracle" after World War II was greatly helped by foreign aid. Today, Germany is one of the world's major economic powers. It is a leading member of the European Union and the 19-member eurozone. Since 2011, it has helped to maintain the eurozone by supporting debt-ridden countries, such as Greece. The mainstay of its export-led economy is manufacturing. Exports include machinery, metals, chemicals, and vehicles. Germany has some coal, potash, and rock salt deposits, but it imports many industrial raw materials. Germany also imports food. Leading agricultural products include fruits, grapes for winemaking, potatoes, sugar beet, and vegetables. Livestock include beef cattle and pigs.

AREA 137,846 sq mi [357,022 sq km] **POPULATION** 80,160,000
CAPITAL Berlin **GOVERNMENT** Federal multiparty republic
ETHNIC GROUPS German 92%, Turkish 2%, Serbo-Croatian, Italian, Greek, Polish, Spanish **LANGUAGES** German (official)
RELIGIONS Protestant (mainly Lutheran) 34%, Roman Catholic 34%, Islam 4%, others **CURRENCY** Euro = 100 cents

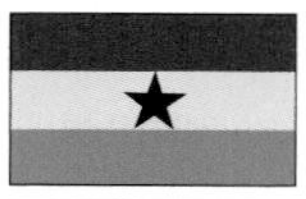
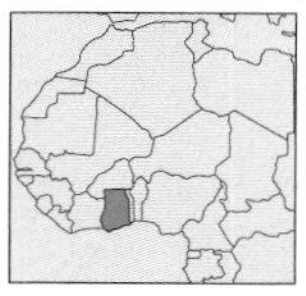

GHANA

GEOGRAPHY The Republic of Ghana faces the Gulf of Guinea in West Africa, just north of the equator. In the southwest, behind the thickly populated southern coastal plains, which are lined with lagoons, lies a plateau region. Accra has a hot, tropical climate. Rain occurs all through the year, though Accra is drier than areas inland.

POLITICS & ECONOMY Portuguese explorers reached the area in 1471 and named it the Gold Coast. The area became a center of the slave trade in the 17th century until it was ended in the 1860s and, gradually, the British took control of the area. After independence in 1957 the country was renamed Ghana. Attempts were made to develop the economy by creating large state-owned manufacturing industries, but debt and corruption, together with falls in the price of cocoa, caused economic problems. Instability and frequent coups followed. In 1981, power was invested in a Provisional National Defense Council, led by Flight-Lieutenant Jerry Rawlings. The government steadied the economy and introduced reforms. Incumbent John Dramani Mahama lost to human rights lawyer Nana Akufo-Addo in the 2016 presidential elections.

The World Bank classifies Ghana as a "lower-middle-income" developing country, although the majority of the people are poor and farming employs 56% of the population. Ghana is benefiting from years of stable government and efficient administration and has one of Africa's fastest growing economies. It is exploiting recently discovered offshore oil reserves. Its other major exports are gold and cocoa.

AREA 92,098 sq mi [238,533 sq km] **POPULATION** 29,340,000
CAPITAL Accra **GOVERNMENT** Republic
ETHNIC GROUPS Akan 47%, Mole-Dagbon 17%, Ewe 14%, Ga-Dangme 7%, Gurma 6% **LANGUAGES** English (official), Asante, Ewe, Fante, Boron, Dagomba **RELIGIONS** Christianity 71%, Islam 18%, traditional beliefs 5% **CURRENCY** Cedi = 100 pesewas

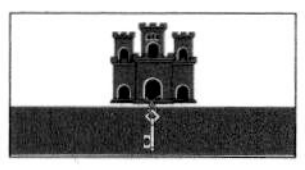
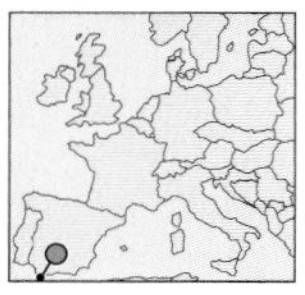

GIBRALTAR

Gibraltar occupies a strategic position on the south coast of Spain where the Mediterranean meets the Atlantic. It was recognized as a British possession in 1713 and, despite Spanish claims, its population has consistently voted to retain its contacts with Britain.

AREA 2.3 sq mi [6 sq km]
POPULATION 30,000 **CAPITAL** Gibraltar Town

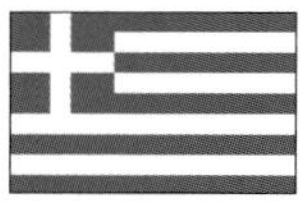
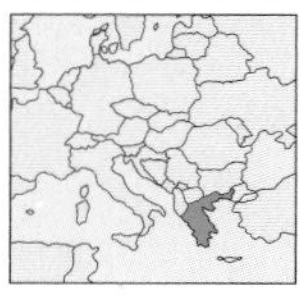

GREECE

GEOGRAPHY The Hellenic Republic, as Greece is officially called, is a rugged country situated at the southern end of the Balkan peninsula. Olympus, at 9,570 ft [2,917 m], is the highest peak. Islands make up about a fifth of the land area. Low-lying areas in Greece have mild, moist winters and hot, dry summers. The east coast has more than 2,700 hours of sunshine a year and only about half of the rainfall of the west. The mountains have a much more severe climate, with snow on the higher slopes in winter.

POLITICS & ECONOMY Around 2,500 years ago, Greece became the birthplace of Western civilization, and Ancient Greek ruins and art still attract millions of tourists to the country. The first civilization, the Minoan, was centered on Crete. It flourished between about 3000 and 1400 BC. Following the end of the related Mycaenean period on the mainland (1580–1100 BC), a "dark age" lasted until about 800 BC. But from 750 BC, Greeks became rich traders and the city-state of Athens reached its peak in 461–431 BC. Greece became a Roman province in 146 BC and, in 365, it became part of the Byzantine empire.

The Byzantine empire fell to the Turks in 1453. But Greece became an independent monarchy in 1830. After World War II (1939–45), when Germany ruled Greece, a civil war broke out between Greek Communists and nationalists. It ended in 1949 and a military dictatorship seized power in 1967. The monarchy was abolished in 1973 and democracy was restored in 1974. Greece joined the European Community (now the European Union) in 1981 and, on January 1, 2002, the euro became the sole unit of currency. Greece suffered hugely following the international financial crisis of 2008, entering into three international bailout agreements. From 2018 there were signs of economic recovery.

Greece is one of the EU's less economically developed members. Manufactured products include processed food, cement, chemicals, metal products, textiles, and tobacco. Greece also mines lignite (brown coal), bauxite, and chromite. Crops include barley, grapes, dried fruits, olives, potatoes, sugar beet, and wheat. Livestock farming is important and tourism is a major industry.

AREA 50,949 sq mi [131,957 sq km] **POPULATION** 10,607,000
CAPITAL Athens **GOVERNMENT** Multiparty republic
ETHNIC GROUPS Greek 93% **LANGUAGES** Greek (official)
RELIGIONS Greek Orthodox 98%
CURRENCY Euro = 100 cents

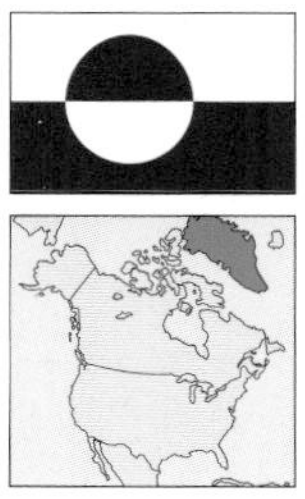

GREENLAND

Greenland is the world's largest island. With an ice sheet covering four-fifths of the land, settlements are confined to the coast. Greenland became a Danish possession in 1380. Full internal self-government was granted in 1981 and, in 2009, Greenland became a self-governing territory, though it remains dependent on Danish subsidies.

AREA 838,999 SQ MI [2,175,600 SQ KM]
POPULATION 58,000 **CAPITAL** NUUK

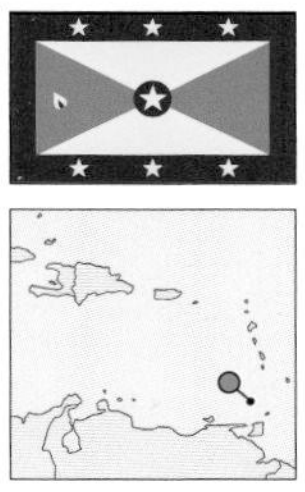

GRENADA

The most southerly of the Windward Islands in the Caribbean Sea, Grenada became independent from the UK in 1974. A military group seized power in 1983, when the prime minister was killed. US troops intervened and restored order and constitutional government.

AREA 133 SQ MI [344 SQ KM]
POPULATION 113,000 **CAPITAL** ST GEORGE'S

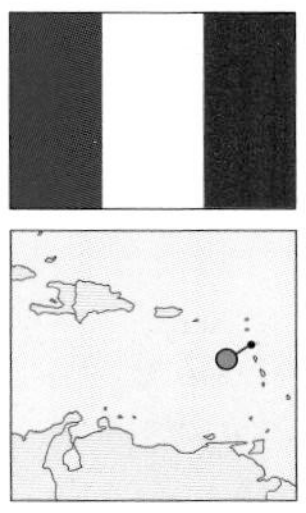

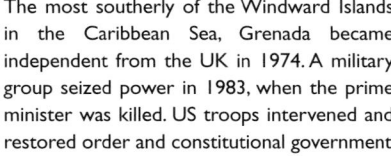

GUADELOUPE

Guadeloupe is a French overseas department which includes seven Caribbean islands, the largest of which is Basse-Terre. French aid has helped to maintain a reasonable standard of living for the people.

AREA 658 SQ MI [1,705 SQ KM]
POPULATION 402,000 **CAPITAL** BASSE-TERRE

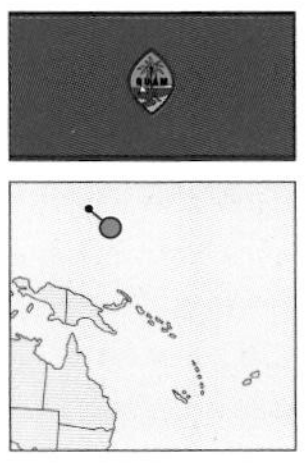

GUAM

Guam, a strategically important "unincorporated territory" of the USA, is the largest of the Mariana Islands in the Pacific Ocean. Its economy depends on US military spending.

AREA 212 SQ MI [549 SQ KM]
POPULATION 168,000 **CAPITAL** HAGATNA

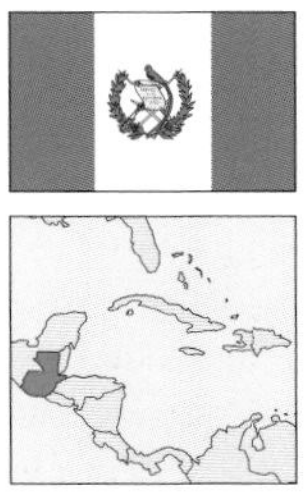

GUATEMALA

GEOGRAPHY The Republic of Guatemala in Central America contains a densely populated mountain region, with fertile soils. There are many volcanoes, some active. South of the mountains lie the thinly populated Pacific coastlands, while a large inland plain occupies the north. The lowlands of Guatemala are hot and rainy, but the central highlands are cooler and drier. Guatemala City has a pleasant, warm climate with a dry season between November and April.

POLITICS & ECONOMY Much of what is now Guatemala was part of the Maya empire which thrived between AD 300 and 900. Spain ruled the area from the 1520s until 1821, with Guatemala achieving full independence in 1839. Instability and periodic violence have marred its progress. Guatemala has a long-standing claim over Belize, but this was reduced in 1983 to the southern fifth of the country. Between 1960 and 1996, civil war occurred between left-wing groups, including many Amerindians, and government forces. Jimmy Morales served as president from 2015 till 2020, when conservative Alejandro Giammattei took office, amid voter discontent over corruption and unemployment.

Guatemala is ranked as an "upper-middle-income" economy with agriculture employing 38% of the population. Coffee, sugar, bananas, and beef are exported, and cardamom and cotton are also important. Maize is the main food crop. Poverty is endemic in the countryside, with high rates of malnutrition, infant mortality, and illiteracy, as well as violence associated with drug trafficking.

AREA 42,042 SQ MI [108,889 SQ KM] **POPULATION** 17,153,000
CAPITAL GUATEMALA CITY **GOVERNMENT** REPUBLIC
ETHNIC GROUPS LADINO (MIXED HISPANIC AND AMERINDIAN) 55%, AMERINDIAN 43%, OTHERS 2%
LANGUAGES SPANISH (OFFICIAL), AMERINDIAN LANGUAGES
RELIGIONS ROMAN CATHOLIC, INDIGENOUS MAYAN BELIEFS
CURRENCY QUETZAL = 100 CENTAVOS

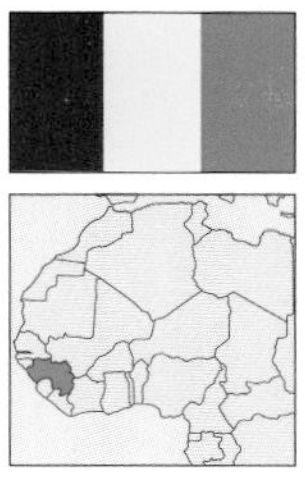

GUINEA

GEOGRAPHY The Republic of Guinea faces the Atlantic Ocean in West Africa. A flat, swampy plain borders the coast. Behind this plain, the land rises to a plateau region called Fouta Djallon. The Upper Niger Plains in the northeast are where the Niger, one of Africa's longest rivers, rises.

Guinea has a tropical climate and Conakry has its rainy period between May and November, the coolest season. In the dry season, hot harmattan winds blow from the Sahara.

POLITICS & ECONOMY Guinea came under the influence of several medieval African states, including Ancient Ghana and Ancient Mali. France began to control the area in the late 19th century with Guinea becoming independent in 1958. Its leaders pursued socialist policies but resorted to repressive measures to hold on to power. A military regime under Lansana Conté took over in 1984, but a multiparty system was restored in 1992. Following Conté's death in 2008, an army group led by Captain Mousa Dadis Camara seized power. But in 2010, Alpha Condé was elected president in Guinea's first democratic election since independence. He was re-elected in 2015.

Guinea is a "low-income" developing country. Its resources include bauxite (aluminum ore), diamonds, gold, iron ore, and uranium. Bauxite and alumina (processed bauxite) account for more than half of the country's exports. Agriculture employs more than 75% of the people, but most farmers are poor. Manufactures include alumina, processed food, and textiles.

AREA 94,925 SQ MI [245,857 SQ KM] **POPULATION** 12,527,000
CAPITAL CONAKRY **GOVERNMENT** MULTIPARTY REPUBLIC
ETHNIC GROUPS PEUHL 40%, MALINKE 30%, SOUSSOU 20%, OTHERS 10%
LANGUAGES FRENCH (OFFICIAL)
RELIGIONS ISLAM 85%, CHRISTIANITY 8%, TRADITIONAL BELIEFS 7%
CURRENCY GUINEAN FRANC = 100 CENTIMES

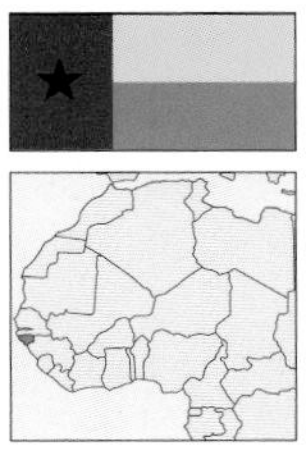

GUINEA-BISSAU

GEOGRAPHY The Republic of Guinea-Bissau, formerly known as Portuguese Guinea, is a small country in West Africa. The land is mostly low-lying, with a broad, swampy coastal plain and many flat offshore islands. The country has a tropical climate, with a dry season (December to May) and a wet season (June to November).

POLITICS & ECONOMY Portuguese explorers reached Guinea-Bissau in 1446 and the area became a center of the slave trade. From 1836, Portugal administered Guinea-Bissau with the Cape Verde Islands, but in 1879 the territories were separated.

In 1956, African nationalists in Portuguese Guinea (as Guinea-Bissau was then known) and Cape Verde founded the African Party for the Independence of Guinea and Cape Verde (PAIGC). The PAIGC began a guerrilla war in 1963 and, by 1968, it held two-thirds of the country. In 1972, a rebel National Assembly, elected by the people in the PAIGC-controlled area, voted to make the country independent as Guinea-Bissau.

The newly independent Guinea-Bissau faced many problems arising from its underdeveloped economy and its lack of trained people to work in the administration. One objective of the leaders of Guinea-Bissau was to unite their country with Cape Verde. But, in 1980, army leaders overthrew Guinea-Bissau's government. The Revolutionary Council, which took over, opposed unification with Cape Verde. Guinea-Bissau ceased to be a one-party state in 1991 and multiparty elections were held in 1994. Civil war and military coups followed until a civilian government was restored in 2004. Following another military coup in 2012, a government by Transitional National Council was established. Jose Mario Vaz was elected president in 2014, but political infighting continued. Umaro Sissoco Embalo was declared president in 2020 after a run-off vote.

The economy is massively in debt and relies on foreign aid: Guinea-Bissau is one of the world's poorest countries. Agriculture employs 82% of the people. Crops include cashew nuts, coconuts, groundnuts (peanuts), maize, and rice. The country is a major hub for drug trafficking between Latin America and Europe.

AREA 13,948 SQ MI [36,125 SQ KM] **POPULATION** 1,927,000
CAPITAL BISSAU **GOVERNMENT** REPUBLIC
ETHNIC GROUPS BALANTA 30%, FULA 20%, MANJACA 14%, MANDINGA 13%, PAPEL 7% **LANGUAGES** PORTUGUESE (OFFICIAL), CRIOULO
RELIGIONS ISLAM 50%, TRADITIONAL BELIEFS 40%, CHRISTIANITY 10%
CURRENCY CFA FRANC = 100 CENTIMES

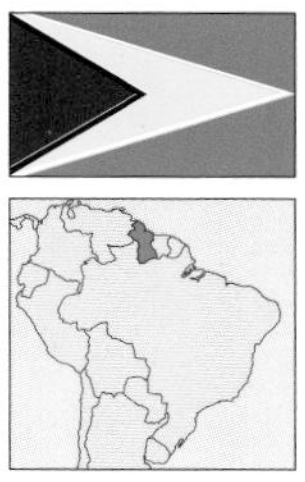

GUYANA

GEOGRAPHY The Cooperative Republic of Guyana faces the Atlantic Ocean in northeastern South America. The coastal plain is flat and much of it is below sea level. The climate is hot and humid, though the interior highlands are cooler than the coast. Rainfall is heavy, occurring on more than 200 days a year.

POLITICS & ECONOMY Britain gained control of the area in 1814 and ruled British Guiana until it became independent as Guyana in 1966. A black lawyer, Forbes Burnham, was the first prime minister. He served as president under a new constitution adopted in 1980, until his death in 1985. Ethnic tensions and political rivalries persisted between the descendants of African slaves and those descended from Indians brought in by the British. In 2015 David Granger was elected president, ending 23 years of rule by the Indian-dominated People's Progressive Party. He was re-elected in 2020 in an election tainted by accusations of fraud.

The discovery of substantial oil deposits has sparked interest from international oil companies. Oil revenue looks set to transform Guyana's economy. Other resources include gold, bauxite, forests, and fertile soils. Sugarcane and rice are leading crops.

AREA 83,000 SQ MI [214,969 SQ KM] **POPULATION** 750,000
CAPITAL GEORGETOWN **GOVERNMENT** MULTIPARTY REPUBLIC
ETHNIC GROUPS EAST INDIAN 43%, BLACK 30%, AMERINDIAN 9%, OTHERS 18%
LANGUAGES ENGLISH (OFFICIAL), CREOLE, HINDI, URDU
RELIGIONS CHRISTIANITY 57%, HINDUISM 28%, ISLAM 7%, OTHERS 8%
CURRENCY GUYANESE DOLLAR = 100 CENTS

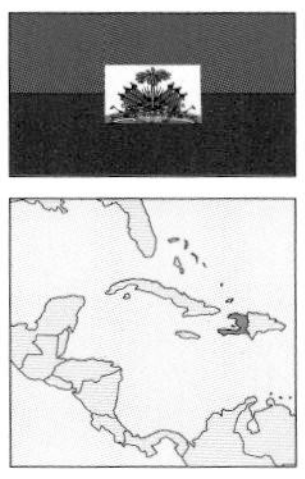

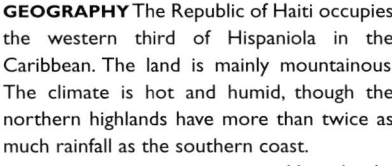

HAITI

GEOGRAPHY The Republic of Haiti occupies the western third of Hispaniola in the Caribbean. The land is mainly mountainous. The climate is hot and humid, though the northern highlands have more than twice as much rainfall as the southern coast.

POLITICS & ECONOMY Visited by Christopher Columbus in 1492, Haiti was later developed by the French. The country became independent in 1804. Haiti subsequently suffered from instability and violence, and under the dictatorial rule of "Papa Doc" and "Baby Doc" Duvalier from 1957 to 1986. The political landscape in the following decades was dominated by Jean-Bertrand Aristide. Elections in 2016 were won by Jovenel Moise, but the political situation remained unstable.

In January 2010, an earthquake hit Port-au-Prince, killing up to 230,000 people and devastating the economy. As many as 60% of the people live below the poverty line.

AREA 10,714 SQ MI [27,750 SQ KM] **POPULATION** 11,068,000
CAPITAL PORT-AU-PRINCE **GOVERNMENT** MULTIPARTY REPUBLIC
ETHNIC GROUPS BLACK 95%, MIXED/WHITE 5%
LANGUAGES FRENCH AND CREOLE (BOTH OFFICIAL)
RELIGIONS ROMAN CATHOLIC 80%, PROTESTANT 16%, VOODOO
CURRENCY GOURDE = 100 CENTIMES

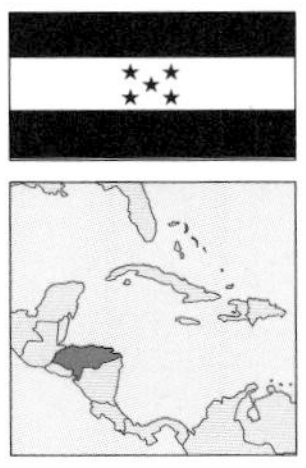

HONDURAS

GEOGRAPHY The Republic of Honduras is the second largest country in Central America. The northern coast, on the Caribbean Sea, extends for more than 373 mi [600 km], but the Pacific coast in the southeast is only about 50 mi [80 km] long. Honduras has a tropical climate, but the highlands are cooler. The rainiest months are between May and November. Hurricanes often hit the north coast. Hurricane Mitch in 1998 caused the worst destruction in modern times.

POLITICS & ECONOMY Once part of the Maya empire, the area was claimed for Spain by Christopher Columbus in 1502, and Spain ruled from 1625 until 1821. Honduras became part of the Central American Federation but withdrew in 1838.

In the 1890s, American companies developed plantations to grow bananas. But instability slowed economic progress. Since 1980, civilian governments friendly toward the United States have ruled Honduras, but in 2008 it joined the "Bolivarian Alternative to the Americas," a left-wing alliance then headed by Venezuelan President Chavez. In 2014 Juan Orlando Hernández became president and was re-elected in a disputed election in 2017. He pledged to reduce the levels of drug-related gang violence.

Honduras is one of Central America's least industrialized countries with around 50% of its economy linked to the USA and very high levels of inequality. Its few resources include silver, lead, and zinc. Agriculture is the main activity. Bananas and coffee are exported and maize is the chief food crop. Products include processed food and textiles. Violent crime makes the country one of the least secure in Central America. It has one of the world's highest murder rates.

AREA 43,277 SQ MI [112,088 SQ KM] **POPULATION** 9,235,000
CAPITAL TEGUCIGALPA **GOVERNMENT** REPUBLIC
ETHNIC GROUPS MESTIZO 90%, AMERINDIAN 7%, BLACK (INCLUDING BLACK CARIB) 2%, WHITE 1%
LANGUAGES SPANISH (OFFICIAL), AMERINDIAN DIALECTS
RELIGIONS ROMAN CATHOLIC 97%
CURRENCY HONDURAN LEMPIRA = 100 CENTAVOS

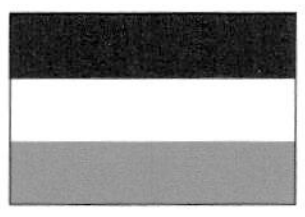
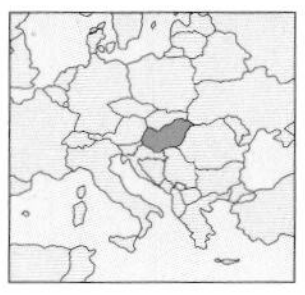

HUNGARY

GEOGRAPHY Hungary is a landlocked country in central Europe. The land is mostly low-lying and drained by the Danube (Duna) and its tributary, the Tisza. Most of the land east of the Danube belongs to the region of the Great Plain (Nagy Alföld), which covers about half of Hungary.

Hungary lies far from the moderating influence of the sea, but it does contain Lake Balaton, the largest lake in central Europe. As a result of its position in the European landmass, summers are warmer and sunnier, and the winters colder than in Western Europe.

POLITICS & ECONOMY Following first an alliance, then occupation by Germany during World War II, Hungary was gradually taken over by a Communist government. From 1949, Hungary was an ally of the Soviet Union with Soviet troops crushing an anti-Communist revolt in 1956. But in the 1980s, reforms in the Soviet Union led to the growth of anti-Communist groups and, in 1989, Hungary adopted a new constitution making it a multiparty state and made moves toward a more free market economy. In 2004, Hungary became a member of both the North Atlantic Treaty Organization and the European Union. Right-wing prime minister Viktor Orban won a third term in power in April 2018 campaigning on an anti-immigrant, anti-Muslim ticket. Widespread protests followed.

Before World War II, Hungary's economy was based mainly on agriculture but the Communist era saw the introduction of many manufacturing industries. From the late 1980s, the increase in private ownership of businesses caused problems, including high rates of unemployment and inflation. High levels of government borrowing left the country vulnerable to the recession of 2008 when the country had to ask for outside financial help. Leading manufactures include vehicles, chemicals, electrical and electronic goods.

AREA 35,920 SQ MI [93,032 SQ KM] **POPULATION** 9,772,000
CAPITAL BUDAPEST **GOVERNMENT** MULTIPARTY REPUBLIC
ETHNIC GROUPS MAGYAR 92%, ROMA, GERMAN, SERB, ROMANIAN, SLOVAK
LANGUAGES HUNGARIAN (OFFICIAL)
RELIGIONS ROMAN CATHOLIC 52%, CALVINIST 16%, LUTHERAN 3%, OTHERS
CURRENCY FORINT = 100 FILLÉR

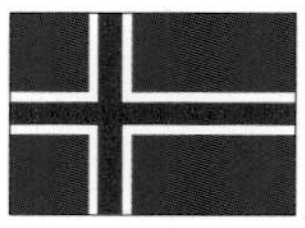
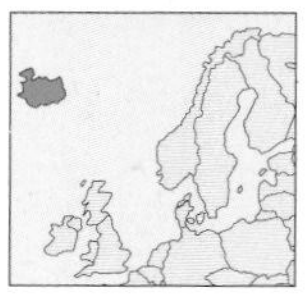

ICELAND

GEOGRAPHY The Republic of Iceland, in the North Atlantic Ocean, is closer to Greenland than Scotland. Iceland sits astride the Mid-Atlantic Ridge and it is slowly getting wider as the ocean is being stretched apart by continental drift.

Iceland has around 200 volcanoes, and eruptions are frequent. An eruption under the Vatnajökull ice cap in 1996 created a subglacial lake which subsequently burst, causing severe flooding. Geysers and hot springs are common, and in 2010 a volcanic eruption and its resulting ash cloud disrupted international air services. Ice caps and glaciers cover about an eighth of the land. The only habitable regions are the coastal lowlands. Despite its northerly position, Iceland's climate is moderated by the warm waters of the North Atlantic Drift. The port of Reykjavik is ice-free all year round.

POLITICS & ECONOMY Norwegian Vikings colonized Iceland in AD 874, and in 930 the settlers founded the world's oldest parliament, the Althing.

Iceland joined forces with Norway in 1262. But when Norway united with Denmark in 1380, Iceland came under Danish rule. Iceland became a self-governing kingdom, still with links to Denmark, in 1918, and a fully independent republic in 1944. Elections in the fall of 2017, after the collapse of the previous government, led to Katrin Jakobsdottir of the Left-Green movement heading a broad coalition.

Iceland has few resources besides its fishing grounds, and fishing and fish processing dominate overseas trade. To protect this vital part of its economy, it has been involved in several fishing and whaling disputes. In 2013 it suspended its application to join the EU citing potential difficulties with fishing agreements. Barely 1% of the land is used to grow crops, but 23% of the country can be used for grazing sheep and cattle. Vegetables and fruit are grown in greenhouses, heated by water from the hot springs. Iceland's economy was particularly hard hit by the global financial crisis of 2008, but recovered steadily from the mid-2010s, helped by a growth in tourism.

AREA 39,768 SQ MI [103,000 SQ KM] **POPULATION** 351,000
CAPITAL REYKJAVIK **GOVERNMENT** MULTIPARTY REPUBLIC
ETHNIC GROUPS ICELANDIC 97%, DANISH 1%
LANGUAGES ICELANDIC (OFFICIAL) **RELIGIONS** EVANGELICAL LUTHERAN 87%, OTHER PROTESTANT 4%, ROMAN CATHOLIC 2%, OTHERS
CURRENCY ICELANDIC KRÓNA

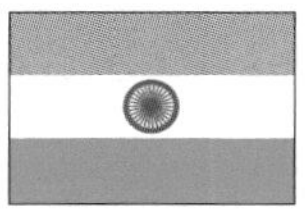
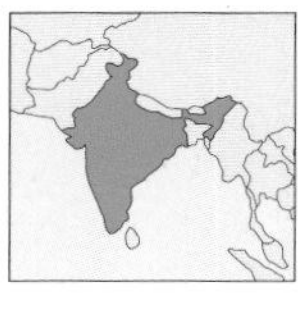

INDIA

GEOGRAPHY The Republic of India is the world's seventh largest country. In population, it ranks second only to China. The north is mountainous, with mountains and foothills of the Himalayan range. Rivers, such as the Brahmaputra and Ganges (Ganga), rise in the Himalaya and flow across the fertile northern plains. Southern India consists of the Deccan, an extensive plateau. The Deccan is bordered by two mountain ranges, the Western Ghats and the Eastern Ghats.

India has three main seasons. The cool season runs from October to February. The hot season runs from March to June. The rainy monsoon season starts in the middle of June and continues into September. Delhi has moderate rainfall, with about 25 inches [640 mm] a year. The southwestern coast and the northeast have far more rain. Darjeeling in the northeast has an average annual rainfall of 120 inches [3,040 mm]. But parts of the Thar Desert in the northwest have only 2 inches [50 mm] of rain.

POLITICS & ECONOMY In southern India, most of the people are descendants of the dark-skinned Dravidians, who were among India's earliest people. Most northerners are descendants of lighter-skinned Aryans who arrived around 3,500 years ago.

India was the birthplace of several major religions, including Hinduism, Buddhism, and Sikhism. Islam was introduced from about AD 1000. The Muslim Mughal empire was founded in 1526. From the 17th century, Britain began to gain influence and, from 1858 to 1947, India was ruled as part of the British empire. An independence movement began after the Sepoy Rebellion (1857–59), and in 1885 the Indian National Congress was formed. In 1920, Mohandas K. Gandhi became its leader. When independence was finally achieved in 1947, British India was divided into modern India and Muslim Pakistan. Partition was marred by mass slaughter as Hindus and Sikhs fled from Pakistan, and Indian Muslims poured into Pakistan. In the ensuing disputes, some 1 million people were killed.

India has 15 major languages and hundreds of minor ones, together with many religions. The country remains the world's largest democracy. It has faced many problems, especially with Pakistan, over the disputed territory of Jammu and Kashmir. Two wars in 1965 and 1972 failed to alter greatly the 1948 cease-fire lines. In the late 1980s, Kashmiri nationalists in the Indian-controlled area waged a campaign, demanding either integration into Pakistan or independence. India sent in troops and accused Pakistan of intervention. In the 1990s, Pakistani-backed guerrillas fought to break India's hold on the Srinagar valley, Kashmir's most populous region. Tension mounted following the testing of nuclear devices by both countries in 1998. Relations improved, but an attack on buildings in Mumbai in 2008, allegedly by Pakistanis, caused further tension. In 2009–11, the dispute with Maoists in central and eastern India flared up again. In May 2014, a landslide election was won by the Hindu nationalist Bharatiya Janata Party, led by Narendra Modi, who promised to revitalize the economy.

Classified by the World Bank as "lower-middle-income," India's economy has fluctuated in the 21st century. It benefits from a young population, but challenges include poor power generation, inadequate infrastructure, and discrimination against women.

Agriculture employs about 53% of the people, and services 31%. Crops include rice, wheat, millet, sorghum, peas, and beans. India has more cattle than any other country. Resources include coal, iron ore, and oil. Manufacturing has expanded greatly since 1947. Iron and steel, machinery, refined petroleum, textiles, transport equipment, and information technology are major products.

AREA 1,269,212 SQ MI [3,287,263 SQ KM] **POPULATION** 1,326,093,000
CAPITAL NEW DELHI **GOVERNMENT** MULTIPARTY FEDERAL REPUBLIC
ETHNIC GROUPS INDO-ARYAN (CAUCASOID) 72%, DRAVIDIAN 25%, OTHERS (MAINLY MONGOLOID) 3%
LANGUAGES HINDI, ENGLISH, TELUGU, BENGALI, MARATHI, TAMIL, URDU, GUJARATI, MALAYALAM, KANNADA, ORIYA, PUNJABI, ASSAMESE, KASHMIRI, SINDHI, AND SANSKRIT ARE ALL OFFICIAL LANGUAGES
RELIGIONS HINDUISM 80%, ISLAM 13%, CHRISTIANITY 2%, SIKHISM 2%, BUDDHISM, AND OTHERS **CURRENCY** INDIAN RUPEE = 100 PAISE

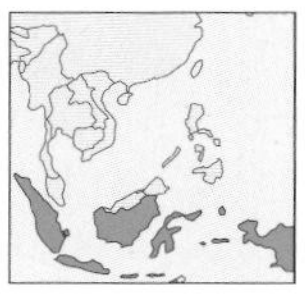

INDONESIA

GEOGRAPHY The Republic of Indonesia is an island nation in Southeast Asia. In all, Indonesia contains about 13,600 islands, fewer than 6,000 of which are inhabited. Three-quarters of the country is made up of five main areas: the islands of Sumatra, Java and Sulawesi (Celebes), together with Kalimantan (southern Borneo), and western New Guinea. The islands are generally mountainous and volcanic. The larger islands have extensive coastal lowlands. The climate is hot and humid, with a high rainfall. Only Java and the Sunda Islands have relatively dry seasons.

POLITICS & ECONOMY Indonesia is the world's most populous Muslim nation, though Islam was introduced as recently as the 15th century. It became a Dutch colony in 1799. After a long struggle, the Netherlands recognized Indonesia's independence in 1949. The economy has expanded, but ethnic and religious conflict has slowed down economic progress.

In the early 21st century, Indonesia was facing many problems, arising from widespread corruption in the government and the army. Separatists were operating in Aceh province in northern Sumatra and in West Papua, Christian–Muslim clashes led to loss of life in the Moluccas, and East (formerly Portuguese) Timor became an independent country. In December 2004, a tsunami killed more than 100,000 people. Aceh province was granted autonomy in 2006, but separatists in the Papua region continue to agitate for independence. Indonesia has suffered an increasing number of terrorist attacks from Islamist groups in recent years. In 2019 it was announced that Indonesia's capital would move to a yet-to-be-built city on Kalimantan. Its current capital, Jakarta, is the one of the fastest sinking cities in the world and under threat from rising sea levels, as well as suffering from chronic traffic congestion.

Indonesia, a developing country, has a growing industrial sector hampered by inadequate infrastructure. It exports oil and natural gas, and mines tin and other minerals. Timber, textiles, rubber, coffee, and tea are also exported. Rice is the main food crop.

AREA 735,354 SQ MI [1,904,569 SQ KM] **POPULATION** 267,026,000
CAPITAL JAKARTA **GOVERNMENT** MULTIPARTY REPUBLIC
ETHNIC GROUPS JAVANESE 41%, SUNDANESE 15%, MADURESE 3%, MINANGKABAU 3%, BETAWI 2%, BUGIS 2%, BANTEN 2%, OTHERS 32%
LANGUAGES BAHASA INDONESIAN (OFFICIAL), MANY OTHERS
RELIGIONS ISLAM 86%, PROTESTANT 6%, ROMAN CATHOLIC 3%, HINDUISM 2%, BUDDHISM 1%
CURRENCY INDONESIAN RUPIAH

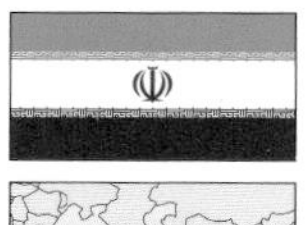
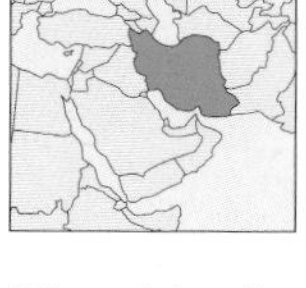

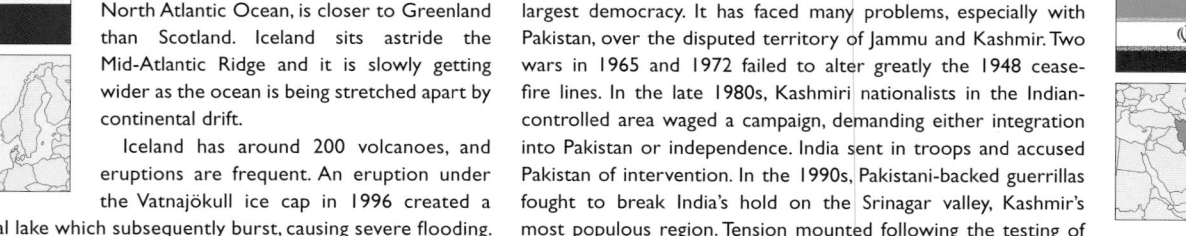

IRAN

GEOGRAPHY The Republic of Iran contains a barren central plateau which covers about half of the country. It includes the Dasht-e Kavir (Great Salt Desert) and the Dasht-e Lut (Great Sand Desert). The Elburz Mountains north of the plateau contain Iran's highest peak, Damavand, while narrow lowlands lie between the mountains and the Caspian Sea. West of the plateau are the Zagros Mountains, beyond which the land descends to the plains bordering the Persian Gulf.

Much of Iran has a severe, dry climate, with hot summers and cold winters. In Tehran, rain falls on only about 30 days in the year and the annual temperature range is more than 45°F [25°C]. The climate in the lowlands, however, is generally milder.

POLITICS & ECONOMY Iran was called Persia until 1935. The empire of Ancient Persia flourished between 550 and 350 BC. Islam was introduced in AD 641.

Britain and Russia competed for influence in the area in the 19th century, and in the early 20th century the British began to

develop the country's oil resources. In 1925, the Pahlavi family took power. Reza Khan became shah (king) and worked to modernize the country. The Pahlavi dynasty ended in 1979 when a religious leader, Ayatollah Ruhollah Khomeini, made Iran an Islamic republic. In 1980–88, Iran and Iraq fought a war over disputed borders. Khomeini died in 1989. In 2005, a hardliner, Mahmoud Ahmadinejad, was elected president. Iran's nuclear policies led to the application of international sanctions against it in 2009–12. The more moderate Hassan Rouhani was elected president in 2013 and re-elected in 2017. In 2015, after years of negotiations, a deal was agreed allowing for some economic sanctions to be lifted if Iran limited its nuclear activity. The following year UN inspectors reported satisfactory progress. In 2018, however, the US administration accused Iran of non-compliance and withdrew from the deal and renewed sanctions. Iran's prosperity is based on its oil production and oil accounts for more than 80% of the country's exports. Agriculture is important and the main crops are wheat and barley. Livestock farming and fishing are other important activities, although Iran has to import much of the food it needs.

AREA 636,368 sq mi [1,648,195 sq km] **POPULATION** 84,923,000
CAPITAL Tehran **GOVERNMENT** Islamic republic
ETHNIC GROUPS Persian 53%, Azeri 16%, Kurd 10%, Lur 6%, Arab 2%, Baloch 2%, Turkmen 2% **LANGUAGES** Persian, Turkic, Kurdish
RELIGIONS Islam 98% (Shi'ite Muslim 89%)
CURRENCY Iranian rial = 100 dinars

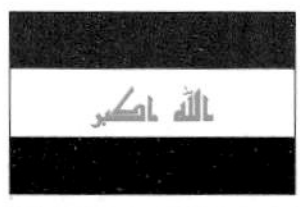

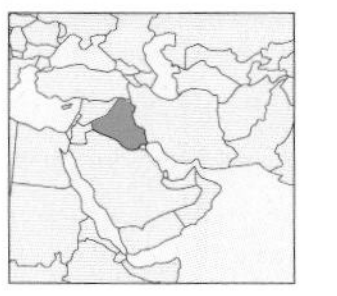

IRAQ

GEOGRAPHY The Republic of Iraq lies at the head of the Persian Gulf. Rolling deserts cover western and southwestern Iraq, with part of the Zagros Mountains in the northeast. The northern plains, across which flow the rivers Euphrates (Nahr al Furat) and Tigris (Nahr Dijlah), are dry. But the southern plains, including Mesopotamia and the delta of the Shatt al Arab, contain irrigated farmland, together with marshland.

The climate of Iraq ranges from temperate in the north to subtropical in the south. Baghdad, in central Iraq, has cool winters, with occasional frosts, and hot summers. The rainfall is generally low.

POLITICS & ECONOMY Mesopotamia was the home of several great civilizations, including Sumer, Babylon, and Assyria. It later became part of the Persian empire. Islam was introduced in AD 637 and Baghdad became the brilliant capital of the powerful Arab empire. But Mesopotamia declined after the Mongols invaded it in 1258. From 1534, Mesopotamia became part of the Turkish Ottoman empire. Britain invaded the area in 1916 and, in 1921, renamed the country Iraq and set up an Arab monarchy. Iraq finally became independent in 1932.

By the 1950s, oil dominated Iraq's economy. In 1952, Iraq agreed to take 50% of the profits of the foreign oil companies. This revenue enabled the government to pay for welfare services and development projects. Since 1958, when army officers killed the king and made Iraq a republic, Iraq has undergone turbulent times. In the 1960s, the Kurds, who live in northern Iraq and also in Iran, Turkey, Syria, and Armenia, pressed for self-rule. The government rejected their demands and war broke out. A peace treaty was signed in 1975, but conflict has continued.

In 1979, Saddam Hussein became Iraq's president. Under his leadership, Iraq invaded Iran in 1980, starting an eight-year war. Iraqi Kurds supported Iran and the Iraqi government attacked Kurdish villages with poison gas. In 1990, Iraqi troops occupied Kuwait, but an international force drove them out in 1991. From 1991, Iraqi troops attacked Shi'ite Marsh Arabs and Kurds. In 1998, Iraq's failure to permit UN inspectors, charged with disposing of Iraq's deadliest weapons, access to suspect sites led to the Western bombardment of Iraqi military sites. Another major offensive occurred in 2001. In March–April 2003, a coalition force headed by the United States invaded Iraq, overthrowing Saddam Hussein's regime. Despite ongoing sectarian violence, regular elections have been held since 2005. From 2013 Islamic State militants seized control of large parts of the country, with the loss of thousands of lives. By late 2017 they had largely been driven out by government troops with Kurdish and other allies. In 2019 large-scale protests over corruption and high unemployment led to the resignation of the prime minister and the appointment of Mohammed Tawfiq Allawi in 2020. The government continues to block any Kurdish ambitions toward independence.

Civil war, war damage, mismanagement, and UN sanctions have damaged the economy. Oil remains the main resource. Farmland covers about a fifth of the land. Products include barley, cotton, dates, fruit, livestock, wheat, and wool. But Iraq still has to import food. Manufactures include refined oil, petrochemicals, and consumer goods.

AREA 169,235 sq mi [438,317 sq km] **POPULATION** 38,873,000
CAPITAL Baghdad **GOVERNMENT** Parliamentary Democracy
ETHNIC GROUPS Arab 77%, Kurdish 19%, Assyrian and others
LANGUAGES Arabic (official), Kurdish (official in Kurdish areas), Assyrian, Armenian **RELIGIONS** Islam 97% (Shi'ite Muslim 63%)
CURRENCY Iraqi dinar = 1,000 fils

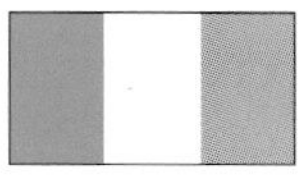

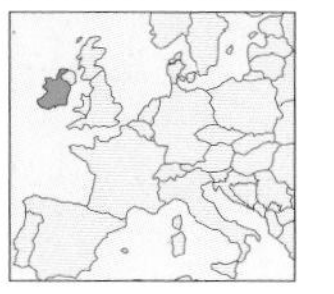

IRELAND

GEOGRAPHY Ireland occupies five-sixths of the island which is also called Ireland. The country consists of a large lowland region surrounded by a broken rim of low mountains. The uplands include the Mountains of Kerry where Carrauntoohill, Ireland's highest peak at 3,415 ft [1,041 m], is situated. The River Shannon is the longest in Ireland, flowing through three large lakes, loughs Allen, Ree, and Derg.

Ireland has a mild, rainy climate influenced by the warm North Atlantic Drift, whose effects are greatest in the west. However, Dublin in the east is cooler than places on the west coast.

POLITICS & ECONOMY In 1801, the Act of Union created the United Kingdom of Great Britain and Ireland. But Irish discontent intensified in the 1840s when a potato blight caused a famine in which a million people died and nearly a million emigrated. Britain was blamed for not having done enough to help. In 1916, an uprising in Dublin was crushed, but between 1919 and 1922 civil war broke out. In 1922, the Irish Free State was created as a Dominion in the British Commonwealth, but Northern Ireland remained part of the UK.

Ireland became a republic in 1949. In 1973, it became a member of the European Community (now the European Union) and, until the global financial crisis of 2008–9, it prospered. In 1998, Ireland took part in the negotiations to produce a constitutional settlement in Northern Ireland. Ireland agreed to give up its claim on Northern Ireland and, in 2007, a power-sharing government was set up in the north. From 2008–14 Irish politics was dominated by the fallout from the financial crisis. Questions now remain over the implications for Ireland, its economy, and its borders following the departure of the UK from the EU in 2020.

Major farm products include barley, cattle and dairy products, pigs, potatoes, poultry, sheep, sugar beet, and wheat. Fishing is important. Manufacturing and services are the main activities.

AREA 27,132 sq mi [70,273 sq km] **POPULATION** 5,177,000
CAPITAL Dublin **GOVERNMENT** Multiparty republic
ETHNIC GROUPS Irish 94% **LANGUAGES** Irish (Gaelic) and English (both official) **RELIGIONS** Roman Catholic 92%, Protestant 3%
CURRENCY Euro = 100 cents

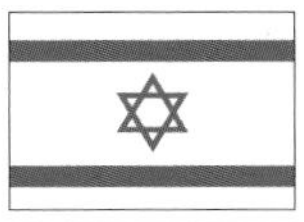

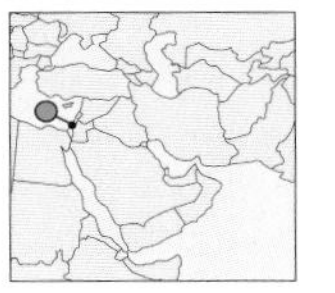

ISRAEL

GEOGRAPHY The State of Israel is a small country in the eastern Mediterranean. It includes a fertile coastal plain, where Israel's main industrial cities, Haifa (Hefa) and Tel Aviv-Jaffa, are situated. Inland lie the Judaeo-Galilean highlands, which run from northern Israel to the northern tip of the Negev Desert. To the east lies part of the Great Rift Valley, which contains the River Jordan, the Sea of Galilee, and the Dead Sea. Summers are hot and dry. Winters on the coast are mild and moist, but rainfall decreases from west to east and from north to south.

POLITICS & ECONOMY Israel is part of a region called Palestine. Some Jews have always lived in the area, though most modern Israelis are descendants of immigrants who began to settle there from the 1880s. Britain ruled Palestine from 1917. Large numbers of Jews escaping Nazi persecution arrived in the 1930s, provoking an Arab uprising against British rule. In 1947, the UN agreed to partition Palestine into an Arab and a Jewish state with the State of Israel coming into being in May 1948. Other Arab–Israeli wars in 1956, 1967, and 1973 led to land gains for Israel.

In 1978, Israel signed a treaty with Egypt which led to the return of the occupied Sinai peninsula to Egypt in 1979. But conflict continued between Israel and the PLO (Palestine Liberation Organization). In 1993, the PLO and Israel agreed to establish Palestinian self-rule in two areas: the occupied Gaza Strip, and in the town of Jericho in the occupied West Bank. The agreement was extended in 1995 to include more than 30% of the West Bank. Israel's prime minister, Yitzhak Rabin, was assassinated in 1995. In 1996, Benjamin Netanyahu was elected prime minister. The peace process stalled until Ehud Barak defeated Netanyahu in 1999. In 2001, Ariel Sharon became prime minister and, in 2005, he handed over the Gaza Strip to the Palestinian Authority. Israeli forces clashed with Palestinians in Gaza and southern Lebanon in 2005–9. Talks in 2010 and 2013 between Israel and the Palestinian Authority collapsed. Further violence along the Gaza border in 2018 led to attempts by the UN and Egypt to broker a long-term ceasefire. Benjamin Netanyahu was re-elected for a record-breaking fifth time in 2019.

Israel has developed a very diverse economy. Manufactures include chemicals, electronic equipment, plastics, processed food, scientific instruments, and textiles. Fruit and vegetables are major exports. Lacking natural resources, Israel has to import raw materials, crude oil, and grain. Offshore gas fields are being exploited.

AREA 7,954 sq mi [20,600 sq km] **POPULATION** 8,675,000
CAPITAL Jerusalem **GOVERNMENT** Multiparty republic
ETHNIC GROUPS Jewish 76%, Arab and others 24%
LANGUAGES Hebrew and Arabic (both official)
RELIGIONS Judaism 76%, Islam (mostly Sunni) 17%, Christianity 2%, Druze and others 5% **CURRENCY** New Israeli shekel = 100 agorot

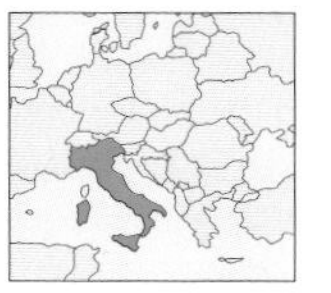

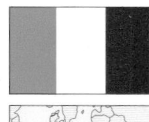

ITALY

GEOGRAPHY The Republic of Italy is famous for its history and traditions, its art and culture, and its beautiful scenery. Northern Italy is bordered in the north by the high Alps, with their many climbing and skiing resorts. The Alps overlook the northern plains – Italy's most fertile and densely populated region – drained by the River Po. The rugged Apennines form the backbone of southern Italy. Bordering the range are scenic hilly areas and coastal plains. Southern Italy contains a string of volcanoes, stretching from Vesuvius, through the Lipari Islands, to Etna on Sicily, the largest Mediterranean island. Northern Italy has cold, often snowy, winters, but the summer months are warm and sunny, with brief summer thunderstorms. Rainfall is abundant. The south has mild, moist winters and warm, dry summers.

POLITICS & ECONOMY Magnificent ruins throughout Italy testify to the glories of the ancient Roman empire, which was founded, according to legend, in 753 BC. Reaching its peak in the AD 100s, it finally collapsed in the 400s, although the Eastern Roman empire, also called the Byzantine empire, survived for another 1,000 years.

In the Middle Ages, Italy was split into many tiny states. These states made a great contribution to the Renaissance, the revival of art and learning, in the 14th to 16th centuries. Beautiful cities, such as Florence (Firenze) and Venice (Venézia), testify to the artistic achievements of this period.

Italy finally became a united kingdom in 1861, although the Papal Territories (a large area ruled by the Roman Catholic Church) were not added until 1870. The Pope and his successors disputed this takeover and it was not finally resolved until 1929, when the Vatican City was set up in Rome as a fully independent state.

Italy fought in World War I (1914–18) alongside the Allies – Britain, France, and Russia. In 1922, the dictator Benito Mussolini, leader of the Fascist Party, took power. Under Mussolini, Italy conquered Ethiopia. During World War II (1939–45), Italy at first fought on Germany's side against the Allies until late in 1943 it declared war on Germany. Italy became a republic in 1946. Playing an important part in European affairs, it was a founder member of the North Atlantic Treaty Organization (NATO) in 1949 and also, in 1958, of what has since become the European Union.

After the setting up of the European Union, Italy's economy developed quickly, despite problems such as greater prosperity in the north compared to the south. The greater economic development in the north forced many people to leave the poor south to find jobs in the north or abroad. Social problems, corruption at high levels of society, and a succession of weak coalition governments all contributed to instability. Between 1998 and 2011, power shifted between center-left and center-right coalitions. In 2016, constitutional changes aimed at creating more stable governments were rejected in a referendum, leading to prime minister Matteo Renzi's resignation. A populist coalition government took office in 2018.

Only 50 years ago, Italy was a mainly agricultural society, but it is now a leading industrial power. It lacks mineral resources, and imports most of the raw materials used in industry. Manufactures include textiles and clothing, processed food, machinery, cars, and chemicals. The chief industrial region is in the northwest.

Farmland covers around 42% of the land, pasture 17%, and forest and woodland 22%. Major crops include citrus fruits, grapes which are used to make wine, olive oil, sugar beet, and vegetables. Livestock farming is important, though meat is imported.

AREA 116,339 SQ MI [301,318 SQ KM] **POPULATION** 62,403,000
CAPITAL ROME **GOVERNMENT** MULTIPARTY REPUBLIC
ETHNIC GROUPS ITALIAN 94%, GERMAN, FRENCH, ALBANIAN, SLOVENE, GREEK
LANGUAGES ITALIAN (OFFICIAL), GERMAN, FRENCH, SLOVENE
RELIGIONS PREDOMINANTLY ROMAN CATHOLIC
CURRENCY EURO = 100 CENTS

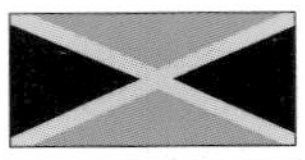

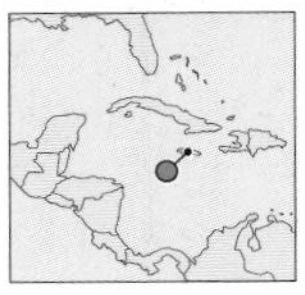

JAMAICA

GEOGRAPHY Jamaica is the third largest of the Caribbean islands. Half the country lies above 1,000 ft [300 m] and moist southeast trade winds bring rain to the central mountain range.

The "cockpit country" in the northwest of the island is an inaccessible limestone area of steep broken ridges and isolated basins.

POLITICS & ECONOMY Jamaica gained independence from Britain in 1962. Since then, power has alternated between the People's National Party and the Jamaica Labor Party and, despite some violence, there has been relative political stability. There is some support for becoming a republic. Problems arise from the drug trade, and the marked polarization of society between rich and poor. The murder rate is high. Tourism and sugarcane farming are important, with alumina and bauxite being exported.

AREA 4,244 SQ MI [10,991 SQ KM] **POPULATION** 2,809,000
CAPITAL KINGSTON **GOVERNMENT** CONSTITUTIONAL MONARCHY
ETHNIC GROUPS BLACK 91%, MIXED 7%, EAST INDIAN 1%
LANGUAGES ENGLISH (OFFICIAL), PATOIS ENGLISH
RELIGIONS PROTESTANT 65%, ROMAN CATHOLIC 3%
CURRENCY JAMAICAN DOLLAR = 100 CENTS

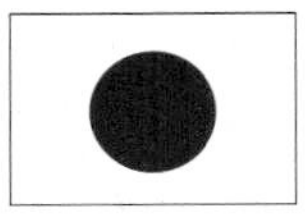

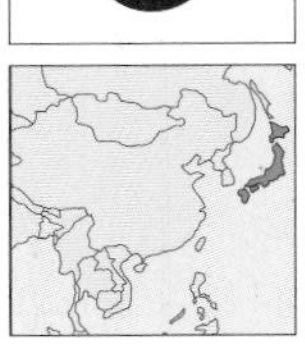

JAPAN

GEOGRAPHY Japan's four largest islands – Honshu, Hokkaido, Kyushu, and Shikoku – make up 98% of the country. But Japan contains thousands of small islands. The four largest islands are mainly mountainous, while many of the small islands are the tips of volcanoes. Japan has more than 150 volcanoes, about 60 of which are active. Volcanic eruptions, earthquakes and tsunamis (powerful sea waves) are common. In March 2011, a massive earthquake, the most powerful recorded in Japan (magnitude 9.0), struck Honshu in the northeast. The tremors and a tsunami caused great loss of life and severe damage to nuclear reactors at Fukushima, shutting down all nuclear power generation at that time.

The climate of Japan varies greatly from north to south. Hokkaido in the north has cold, snowy winters. At Sapporo, temperatures below 4°F [–20°C] have been recorded between December and March. But summers are warm, with temperatures sometimes exceeding 86°F [30°C]. Rain falls throughout the year, though Hokkaido is one of the driest parts of Japan. Tokyo has higher rainfall and temperatures, while the southern islands of Shikoku and Kyushu have warm temperate climates. Summers are long and hot; winters are cold.

POLITICS & ECONOMY In the late 19th century, Japan began a program of modernization. Under its new imperial leaders, it began to look for lands to conquer. In 1894–95, it fought a war with China and, in 1904–5, it defeated Russia. Soon its overseas empire included Korea and Taiwan. In 1930, Japan invaded Manchuria (northeast China), and in 1937 it began a war against China. In 1941, Japan launched an attack on the US base at Pearl Harbor in Hawai'i. This drew both Japan and the United States into World War II.

Japan surrendered in 1945 when the Americans dropped atomic bombs on two cities, Hiroshima and Nagasaki. The United States occupied Japan until 1952, during which time Japan adopted a democratic constitution. The emperor, who had previously been regarded as a god, became a constitutional monarch. In 2017, parliament passed a bill allowing the emperor to abdicate. Akihito stood down in favor of his son, Naruhito, in 2019.

From the 1960s, Japan rapidly built up new industries, but economic success brought problems, including housing shortages and pollution due to the rapid growth of cities. Other problems arise from an aging population.

The leading activities are manufacturing and services. Lacking natural resources, Japan imports most of the materials and fuels it needs, and its success has been based on its use of the latest technology, its skilled work force, its vigorous export policies, and the relatively low expenditure on defense. Exports include vehicles, machinery, electrical and electronic equipment, iron and steel, chemicals, textiles, and ships. Japan's economy suffered a stagnation in the 1990s. Signs of recovery from 2005 were shattered by the global financial crisis in 2008–9, and again by the 2011 earthquake and tsunami. The economy has largely recovered with Prime Minister Shinzo Abe's economic reforms, becoming the world's third largest.

Japan is one of the world's top fishing nations and fish is an important source of protein for the Japanese. Because the land is so rugged, only 15% of the country can be farmed. Yet Japan produces about 70% of the food it needs. Rice is the chief crop, taking up about half of the total farmland.

AREA 145,880 SQ MI [377,829 SQ KM] **POPULATION** 125,507,000
CAPITAL TOKYO **GOVERNMENT** CONSTITUTIONAL MONARCHY
ETHNIC GROUPS JAPANESE 99%, CHINESE, KOREAN, BRAZILIAN, AND OTHERS
LANGUAGES JAPANESE (OFFICIAL)
RELIGIONS SHINTOISM AND BUDDHISM 84% (MOST JAPANESE CONSIDER THEMSELVES TO BE BOTH SHINTO AND BUDDHIST), OTHERS
CURRENCY YEN = 100 SEN

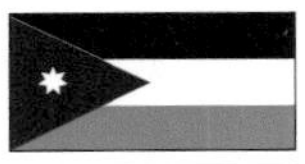

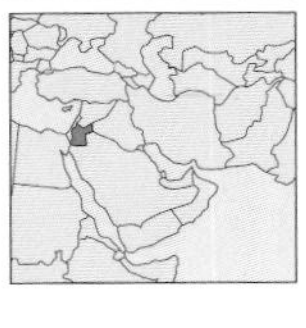

JORDAN

GEOGRAPHY The Hashemite Kingdom of Jordan is an Arab country in southwestern Asia. The Great Rift Valley in the west contains the River Jordan and the Dead Sea, which Jordan shares with Israel. East of the Rift Valley is the Transjordan plateau, where most Jordanians live. To the east and south lie vast areas of desert.

Amman has a much lower rainfall and longer dry season than the Mediterranean lands to the west. The Transjordan plateau, on which Amman stands, is a transition zone between the Mediterranean climate zone and the desert climate to the east.

POLITICS & ECONOMY In 1921, Britain created the territory of Transjordan east of the River Jordan. In 1923, Transjordan became self-governing, but Britain retained control of its defenses, finances, and foreign affairs. This territory became fully independent as Jordan in 1946. Jordan has suffered from instability arising from the Arab–Israeli conflict since the creation of the State of Israel in 1948. After the first Arab–Israeli War in 1948–49, Jordan acquired East Jerusalem and the fertile area of the West Bank. In 1967, Israel occupied this area. In Jordan, the presence of Palestinian refugees led to civil war in 1970–71.

In 1974, Arab leaders declared that the PLO (Palestine Liberation Organization) was the sole representative of the Palestinian people. In 1988, King Hussein of Jordan renounced Jordan's claims to the West Bank and passed responsibility for it to the PLO. Opposition parties were legalized in 1991 and elections were held in 1993. In October 1994, Jordan and Israel signed a peace treaty, ending a state of war that had lasted more than 40 years. Jordan's King Hussein commanded respect for his role in Middle Eastern affairs until his death in 1999. He was succeeded by his eldest son, who became Abdullah II. In 2005, suicide bombings on hotels in Amman damaged Jordan's reputation as a stable country. The king has the power to dissolve parliament and appoint governments. Prime Minister Hani Al-Mulki resigned in 2018 after street protests over his economic reforms, and was replaced by Omar al-Razzaz.

Jordan has an "upper-middle-income" economy. It lacks natural resources, apart from phosphates and potash, and depends on substantial aid. The country is facing economic challenges caused by the arrival of hundreds of thousands of refugees from the civil war in Syria.

AREA 34,495 SQ MI [89,342 SQ KM] **POPULATION** 10,821,000
CAPITAL AMMAN **GOVERNMENT** CONSTITUTIONAL MONARCHY
ETHNIC GROUPS ARAB 98%, OF WHICH PALESTINIANS MAKE UP ROUGHLY HALF
LANGUAGES ARABIC (OFFICIAL)
RELIGIONS ISLAM (MOSTLY SUNNI) 92%, CHRISTIANITY (MOSTLY GREEK ORTHODOX) 6%
CURRENCY JORDANIAN DINAR = 100 PIASTRE

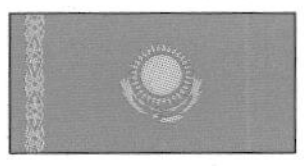

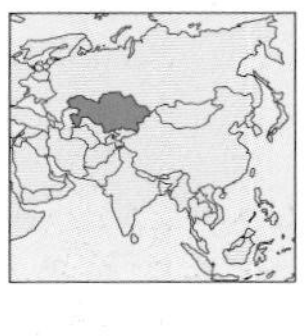

KAZAKHSTAN

GEOGRAPHY Kazakhstan is a large country in west-central Asia. In the west, the Caspian Sea lowlands include the Karagiye depression, which reaches 433 ft [132 m] below sea level. The lowlands extend eastward through the Aral Sea area. The north contains high plains, but the highest land is along the eastern and southern borders. These areas include parts of the Altai and Tian Shan mountain ranges. Eastern Kazakhstan contains several freshwater lakes, the largest of which is Lake Balkhash. The water in the rivers has been used for irrigation, causing ecological problems. For example, the Aral Sea, deprived of water, shrank from 25,830 sq mi [66,900 sq km] in 1960 to 6,630 sq mi [17,160 sq km] in 2004. Large areas are now barren desert, although a dam built in 2005 is reviving the north section.

Kazakhstan has an extreme climate. Winters are cold and snowy. The rainfall is generally low.

POLITICS & ECONOMY After the Russian Revolution of 1917, many Kazakhs wanted to make their country independent. But the Communists prevailed and in 1936 Kazakhstan became a republic of the Soviet Union, called the Kazakh Soviet Socialist Republic. During World War II and also after the war, the Soviet government moved many people from the west into Kazakhstan. From the 1950s, people were encouraged to work on a "Virgin Lands" project, which involved bringing large areas of grassland under cultivation.

Reforms in the Soviet Union in the 1980s led to its breakup in December 1991. Kazakhstan maintained contacts with Russia through the Commonwealth of Independent States (CIS). In 1997, the government moved its capital from Almaty to Aqmola (later renamed Astana), a town in the north. By the mid-2000s, the economy was in better shape than the other ex-Soviet republics in Central Asia, although President Nazarbayev, first elected in 1991, was criticized for his authoritarian rule. In 2007, constitutional changes enabled Nazarbayev to stand for the presidency as many times as he wished, and he was re-elected, virtually unopposed, in 2011 and 2015. After his unexpected resignation in 2019, the capital was renamed Nur-Sultan in his honor. Snap elections were won by his long-standing colleague Kassym-Jomart Tokayev.

The World Bank classifies Kazakhstan as an "upper-middle-income" developing country. Livestock farming, especially sheep and cattle, is an important activity, and major crops include barley, cotton, rice, and wheat. The country is rich in mineral resources, including coal and oil reserves, together with uranium, bauxite, copper, lead, tungsten, and zinc. Manufactures include chemicals, food products, machinery, and textiles. Oil is exported to Europe via a pipeline through Russia, and directly to China.

AREA 1,052,084 SQ MI [2,724,900 SQ KM] **POPULATION** 19,092,000
CAPITAL NUR-SULTAN **GOVERNMENT** MULTIPARTY REPUBLIC
ETHNIC GROUPS KAZAKH 63%, RUSSIAN 24%, UZBEK 3%, UKRAINIAN 2%, OTHERS 8%
LANGUAGES KAZAKH (OFFICIAL); RUSSIAN, THE FORMER OFFICIAL LANGUAGE, IS WIDELY SPOKEN
RELIGIONS ISLAM 70%, RUSSIAN ORTHODOX 24%
CURRENCY TENGE = 100 TIYN

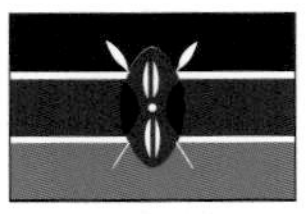

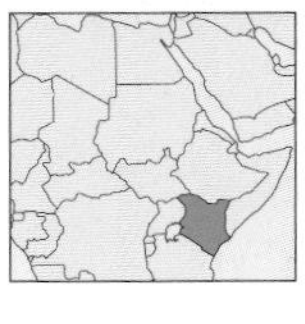

KENYA

GEOGRAPHY The Republic of Kenya is a country in East Africa which straddles the equator. Behind the narrow coastal plain on the Indian Ocean, the land rises to high plains and highlands, broken by volcanic mountains, including Mount Kenya, the country's highest peak at 17,057 ft [5,199 m]. Crossing the country is an arm of the Great Rift Valley, on the floor of which are several lakes, including Baringo, Magadi, Naivasha, Nakuru, and, on the northern frontier, Lake Turkana (formerly Lake Rudolf). Nairobi, in the southwestern highlands, has summer temperatures which are about 10°F [18°C] lower than humid Mombasa. Only about 15% of Kenya has a reliable annual rainfall of 31 inches [800 mm].

POLITICS & ECONOMY The Kenyan coast has been a trading center for more than 2,000 years. Britain took over the coast in 1895 and soon extended its influence inland. In the 1950s, a secret movement, called Mau Mau, launched an armed struggle against British rule. Although Mau Mau was eventually defeated, Kenya became independent in 1963.

Kenya was a one-party state for much of the time after 1963, with democracy restored in 1992. Elections in 2007 led to interethnic violence when the opposition refused to accept the declared results. A deal was agreed by President Mwai Kibaki and Raila Odinga, who became prime minister. In 2011, Somali attacks and kidnappings in northern Kenya provoked Kenya to send forces into Somalia to try to combat the Islamist al-Shabab group, who nevertheless remain active in the country. Elections in August 2017 were declared void because of irregularities. The opposition boycotted the re-run and Uhuru Kenyatta won.

Many Kenyans are subsistence farmers. The chief food crop is maize. The main cash crops and the leading exports are coffee and tea. Manufactures include chemicals, leather and footwear, petroleum products, and textiles. Oil was discovered in 2012.

AREA 224,080 sq mi [580,367 sq km] **POPULATION** 53,528,000
CAPITAL Nairobi **GOVERNMENT** Multiparty republic
ETHNIC GROUPS Kikuyu 22%, Luhya 14%, Luo 13%, Kalenjin 12%, Kamba 11%, others
LANGUAGES Kiswahili and English (both official)
RELIGIONS Protestant 47%, Roman Catholic 23%, Islam 11%, others 19%
CURRENCY Kenyan shilling = 100 cents

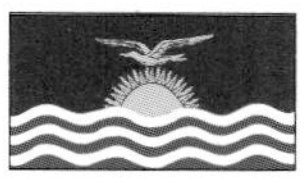

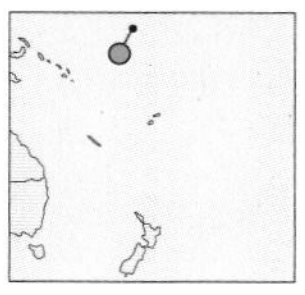

KIRIBATI

The Republic of Kiribati comprises three groups of coral atolls scattered over about 2 million sq mi [5 million sq km]. Kiribati straddles the equator and temperatures are high and the rainfall is abundant.

Formerly part of the British Gilbert and Ellice Islands, Kiribati became independent in 1979. The main export is copra and the country depends heavily on foreign aid. It is at risk from rising sea levels.

AREA 280 sq mi [726 sq km] **POPULATION** 112,000 **CAPITAL** Tarawa

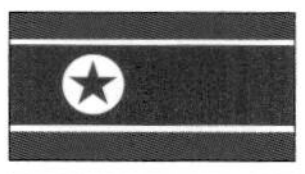

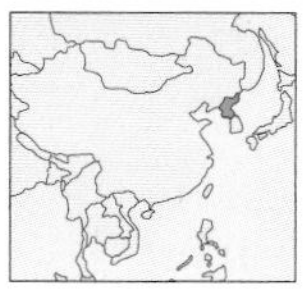

KOREA, NORTH

GEOGRAPHY The Democratic People's Republic of Korea occupies the northern part of the Korean peninsula. Mountains form the heart of the country, with the highest peak, Paektu-san, reaching 9,003 ft [2,744 m]. North Korea has a severe climate, with cold, snowy winters. In summer, winds from the oceans bring rain.

POLITICS & ECONOMY North Korea was created in 1945, when the peninsula, which had been a Japanese colony since 1910, was divided into two parts. Soviet forces occupied the north, with US forces in the south. Soviet occupation led to a Communist government being established in 1948 under the leadership of Kim Il Sung, who became a dictator, effectively founding the Kim dynasty.

The Korean War began in June 1950 when North Korean troops invaded the South. North Korea, aided by China and the Soviet Union, fought with South Korea, which was supported by troops from the United States and other UN members. The war ended in July 1953. An armistice was signed but no permanent peace treaty was agreed. The end of the Cold War in the late 1990s eased the situation. North and South Korea joined the United Nations in 1991, though North Korea remained isolated from most other countries. In 1993, North Korea withdrew from the Nuclear Non-Proliferation Treaty, arousing suspicions that it was developing nuclear weapons. Kim Il Sung died in 1994 and was succeeded by his son, Kim Jong Il. From 2003, the United States accused North Korea of developing nuclear weapons, and it has since then carried out several tests, resulting in increased international isolation and tension. Kim Jong Il died in 2011, and his son, Kim Jong-Un, succeeded him. He expanded the nuclear program, but also appeared willing to negotiate with the US, although with no concrete results. In 2018 he became the first North Korean leader to enter South Korea.

North Korea's resources include coal, copper, iron ore, lead, tin, tungsten, and zinc. Manufactures include chemicals, iron and steel, machinery, processed food, and textiles. Rice is the chief food crop, but food shortages have occurred in recent years.

AREA 46,540 sq mi [120,538 sq km] **POPULATION** 25,643,000
CAPITAL Pyŏngyang **GOVERNMENT** Single-party people's republic
ETHNIC GROUPS Korean 99% **LANGUAGES** Korean (official)
RELIGIONS Buddhism and Confucianism
CURRENCY North Korean won = 100 chon

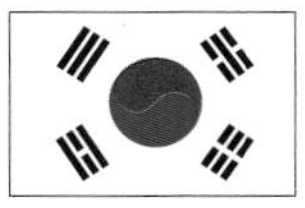

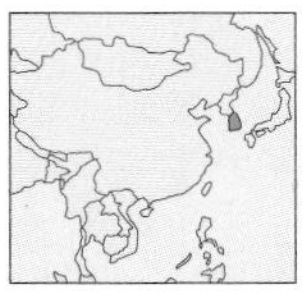

KOREA, SOUTH

GEOGRAPHY The Republic of Korea, as South Korea is officially known, occupies the southern part of the Korean peninsula. Mountains cover much of the country.

The southern and western coasts are major farming regions. Many islands are found along the west and south coasts. The largest of these is Jeju-do, which contains South Korea's highest peak, Hallasan, which rises to 6,398 ft [1,950 m].

Like North Korea, South Korea is chilled in winter by cold, dry winds from central Asia. Summers are hot and wet, especially in July and August.

POLITICS & ECONOMY After Japan's defeat in World War II (1939–45), North Korea was occupied by troops from the Soviet Union, while South Korea was occupied by United States forces. A National Assembly elected in 1948 in South Korea created the Republic of Korea, while North Korea became a Communist state. North Korea invaded the South in June 1950, sparking off the Korean War (1950–53). Despite the destruction caused by the war, South Korea under a series of rather authoritarian governments began to industrialize the economy between the 1960s and 1980s. In 1987, a new constitution permitted the election of presidents every five years. Tensions between South and North Korea continue, but at an historic meeting in 2018, South Korea's President Moon and North Korea's Kim Jon-Un agreed to work toward peace and reducing nuclear arms on the Korean peninsula.

Until the onset of the global financial crisis in 2008, South Korea had one of the world's fastest growing economies. Heavy industries produce chemicals, fertilizers, iron and steel, and ships, together with a wide range of consumer products, such as mobile phones, computers, cars, and television sets. The economy relies heavily on exports. Farming and fishing remain important. Rice is the chief crop, together with fruits, grains, and vegetables.

AREA 38,327 sq mi [99,268 sq km] **POPULATION** 51,835,000
CAPITAL Seoul **GOVERNMENT** Multiparty republic
ETHNIC GROUPS Korean 99% **LANGUAGES** Korean (official)
RELIGIONS No affiliation 43%, Christianity 32%, Buddhism 24%, others 1% **CURRENCY** South Korean won = 100 jeon

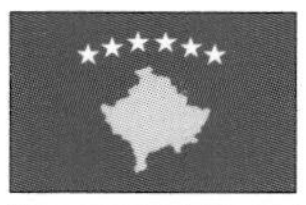

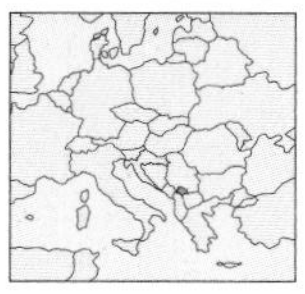

KOSOVO

GEOGRAPHY The Republic of Kosovo in the central Balkans, formerly part of Serbia, declared its independence in February 2008. Its independence was recognized by the United States and major EU countries, but Serbia, and its ally Russia, refused recognition. It is a landlocked country, consisting of a river basin bounded by uplands in the north and southwest. It has cold, snowy winters and hot, dry summers.

POLITICS & ECONOMY Most people are Albanian-speakers who are Muslims, but there is an important Christian Serb minority. In the early 13th century, Kosovo was part of the Serbian empire but, after 1389, it came under Muslim Turkish Ottoman rule.

Serbia regained control of Kosovo in 1912 and, in 1918, it became part of the Kingdom of Serbia. In 1946, it became part of the Socialist Federal Republic of Yugoslavia, becoming an autonomous province within the Republic of Serbia. In 1989, Serbia curtailed Kosovo's autonomy, while Albanian speakers declared their province independent. In 1995, the Albanian speakers set up the Kosovo Liberation Army, which launched an uprising against Serbia. In 1998, Serbia began repressive measures against Kosovo, resulting in massacres and ethnic cleansing of Albanian-speaking Kosovars. In 1999, NATO forces bombed Serbia and placed Kosovo under a temporary administration. Finally, the Kosovo Assembly declared its independence on February 17, 2008. Whilst Serbia still does not recognize Kosovo as an independent state, the two countries are engaged in diplomatic talks.

Kosovo is a poor country, with one of the lowest per capita incomes in Europe, although its economy is slowly improving. Many people are subsistence farmers and its industries suffer from lack of investment. The economy is highly dependent on international aid.

AREA 4,203 sq mi [10,887 sq km] **POPULATION** 1,933,000
CAPITAL Pristina **GOVERNMENT** Republic **ETHNIC GROUPS** Albanian 92%, others 8% **LANGUAGES** Albanian and Serbian (both official), Turkish **RELIGIONS** Islam, Serbian Orthodox, Roman Catholic
CURRENCY Euro = 100 cents

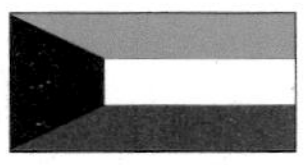

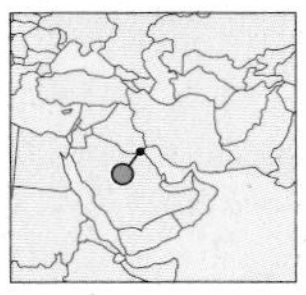

KUWAIT

GEOGRAPHY The State of Kuwait, at the northern end of the Persian Gulf, is an emirate. The land is low-lying and largely desert in nature. Summer temperatures are high but winters are cooler. Rainfall is low.

POLITICS & ECONOMY British influence began in 1775 and, in 1899, the local ruler concluded a treaty with Britain, agreeing to support British interests in return for protection. Kuwait became independent in 1961. Prosperity came from oil exports. Iraq invaded Kuwait in 1990, but it was liberated in 1991 by a coalition force. In 2004, the government announced legislation for women to vote and stand for parliament. In recent years there has been increasing unrest caused by militant Islamists, as well as tension between parliament and the ruling Al-Sabah family.

AREA 6,880 sq mi [17,818 sq km]
POPULATION 2,994,000 **CAPITAL** Kuwait City

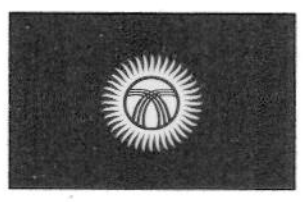

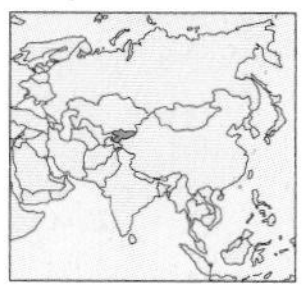

KYRGYZSTAN

GEOGRAPHY The Republic of Kyrgyzstan is a landlocked country between China, Tajikistan, Uzbekistan, and Kazakhstan. The country is mountainous, with spectacular scenery. The highest mountain, Pik Pobedy in the Tian Shan range, reaches 24,406 ft [7,439 m] in the east. The lowlands have warm summers and cold winters. But January temperatures in the mountains plummet to –18°F [–28°C]. Kyrgyzstan has a low annual rainfall.

POLITICS & ECONOMY In 1876, Kyrgyzstan became a province of Russia. In 1916, Russia crushed a rebellion among the Kyrgyz, and many subsequently fled to China. In 1922, the area became a self-governing region of the newly formed Soviet Union, but in 1936 it became one of the Soviet Socialist Republics. Under Communist rule, local customs and religious worship were suppressed, but education and health services were greatly improved.

In 1991, Kyrgyzstan became an independent country following the breakup of the Soviet Union. The Communist Party was dissolved, but the country maintained links with Russia. The first two elections as an independent state produced unpopular presidents who were swept from power and had to flee the country. Sooronbay Jeenbekov won more than 54% of votes in the presidential elections of October 2017.

As one of the poorest countries of the former Soviet Union, Kyrgyzstan sought to reform its Soviet-style economy in the 1990s. Classified as a "lower-middle income" economy by the World Bank, agriculture and mining – mainly gold – are the principal activities. Major products include cotton, eggs, fruits, grain, tobacco, vegetables, and wool, but food is imported. Attracting foreign investment and legitimizing business practices will be vital to economic growth.

AREA 77,181 sq mi [199,900 sq km] **POPULATION** 5,965,000
CAPITAL Bishkek **GOVERNMENT** Multiparty republic
ETHNIC GROUPS Kyrgyz 65%, Uzbek 14%, Russian 13%
LANGUAGES Kyrgyz and Russian (both official) **RELIGIONS** Islam 75%, Russian Orthodox 20% **CURRENCY** Kyrgyzstani som = 100 tyiyn

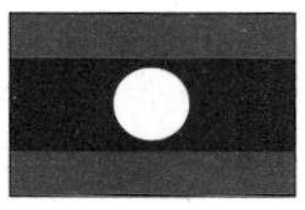

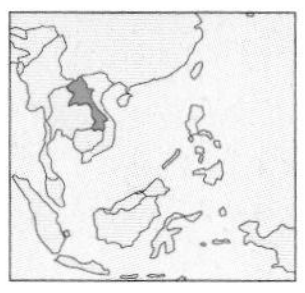

LAOS

GEOGRAPHY The Lao People's Democratic Republic is a landlocked country in Southeast Asia. Mountains and plateaux cover much of the country. Most people live on the plains bordering the River Mekong and its tributaries. This river, one of Asia's longest, forms much of the country's northwestern and southwestern borders.

Laos has a tropical monsoon climate. Winters are dry and sunny with winds blowing from the northeast. From April, the monsoon season starts with the arrival of moist southwesterly winds.

POLITICS & ECONOMY France made Laos a protectorate in the late 19th century and ruled it, with Cambodia and Vietnam, as part of French Indochina. Laos became an independent kingdom in 1954. After independence, a power struggle between royalist government forces and a pro-Communist group called Pathet Lao caused instability. A civil war broke out and continued into the 1970s. The Pathet Lao took control in 1975 and the king abdicated. In the 1990s, Laos started to open to the world and began tentative reforms. In 2011, a stock exchange was opened in Vientiane, as part of a gradual move toward capitalism.

Laos relies heavily on foreign aid. Agriculture employs nearly 73% of the population and accounts for about 20% of the gross domestic product. Rice is the main crop. Timber and coffee are exported. The most valuable export is electricity, which is produced at hydroelectric power stations on the Mekong, although the environmental impact of the dams is a cause for concern. Laos also produces opium.

AREA 91,428 sq mi [236,800 sq km] **POPULATION** 7,447,000
CAPITAL Vientiane **GOVERNMENT** Single-party republic
ETHNIC GROUPS Lao 55%, Khmou 11%, Hmong 8%, others 26%
LANGUAGES Lao (official), French, English **RELIGIONS** Buddhism 67%, traditional beliefs and others 33% **CURRENCY** Kip = 100 att

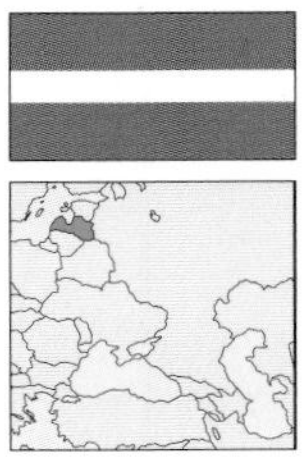

LATVIA

GEOGRAPHY The Republic of Latvia is one of three states on the southeastern corner of the Baltic Sea which were ruled as parts of the Soviet Union between 1940 and 1991. Latvia consists mainly of flat plains separated by low hills, composed of glacial moraine.

Riga has warm summers, but the winter months are sub-zero. The rainfall is moderate.

POLITICS & ECONOMY In 1800, Russia was in control of Latvia, but Latvians declared their independence after World War I. In 1940, under a German–Soviet pact, Soviet troops occupied Latvia, but they were driven out by the Germans in 1941. Soviet troops returned in 1944 and Latvia became part of the Soviet Union. Under Soviet rule, many Russian immigrants settled in Latvia and many Latvians feared that the Russians would become the dominant ethnic group.

In the late 1980s, when reforms were being introduced in the Soviet Union, Latvia's government ended absolute Communist rule and made Latvian the official language. In 1990, it declared the country to be independent, an act which was finally recognized by the Soviet Union in September 1991.

Latvia held the first free elections to its parliament (the Saeima) in 1993. Voting was limited only to citizens of Latvia on June 17, 1940, and their descendants. This meant that about 34% of Latvian residents were unable to vote. In 1994, Latvia restricted the naturalization of non-Latvians, including many Russian settlers, who were not allowed to vote or own land. However, in 1998, the government agreed that all children born since independence should have automatic citizenship. In 2004, Latvia became a member of the North Atlantic Treaty Organization and the European Union. Latvia was hit hard by the global financial crisis in 2009. It adopted the euro in January 2014.

The World Bank classifies Latvia as a "high-income" country. Manufactures include electronic goods, machinery, wood and wood products, processed food, and vehicles. Latvia produces only about a tenth of the electricity it needs; it imports the rest from Belarus, Russia, and Ukraine.

AREA 24,942 sq mi [64,600 sq km] **POPULATION** 1,881,000
CAPITAL Riga **GOVERNMENT** Multiparty republic
ETHNIC GROUPS Latvian 59%, Russian 28%, Belarusian, Ukrainian, Polish, Lithuanian **LANGUAGES** Latvian (official), Russian, Lithuanian **RELIGIONS** Lutheran, Russian Orthodox, Roman Catholic
CURRENCY Euro = 100 cents

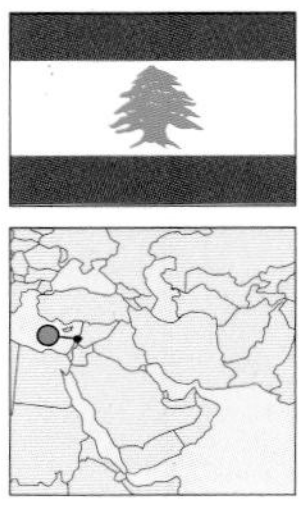

LEBANON

GEOGRAPHY The Republic of Lebanon is a country on the eastern shores of the Mediterranean Sea. Behind the coastal plain are the rugged Lebanon Mountains (Jabal Lubnan), which rise to 10,131 ft [3,088 m]. Another range, the Anti-Lebanon Mountains (Al Jabal Ash Sharqi), forms the eastern border with Syria. Between the two ranges is the Bekaa (Biqa) Valley, a fertile farming region. The coast has hot, dry summers and mild, wet winters. Heavy rain falls on the mountains, with snow at high altitudes.

POLITICS & ECONOMY Lebanon was ruled by Turkey from 1516 until World War I. France then took control from 1923 until independence in 1946. Muslims and Christians then agreed to share power, and Lebanon made rapid economic progress until the late 1950s, when development was slowed by periodic conflict between Sunni and Shia Muslims, Druze, and Christians. The situation was further complicated by the presence of Palestinian refugees, who used bases in Lebanon to attack Israel.

In 1975, civil war broke out as private armies representing the many factions struggled for power. This led to intervention by Israel in the south and Syria in the north. UN peacekeeping forces arrived in 1978, but violence continued in the 1980s. Peace was restored in the 1990s, but, in 2005, the assassination of Rafik Hariri, former prime minister, was blamed on Syria. Under pressure, Syria withdrew its forces from Lebanon. In 2006, a 34-day conflict between Israeli troops and Hezbollah guerrillas caused devastation in southern Lebanon. The civil war in Syria had a destabilizing effect on Lebanon, with some violence. Refugees from Syria now make up one-third of the population.

Lebanon's civil war almost destroyed the valuable trade and financial services that had been Lebanon's chief source of income, together with tourism and manufacturing. The years 2011–17 were marked by slow economic growth. In 2018 Lebanon announced plans to explore potential offshore gas and oil reserves.

AREA 4,015 sq mi [10,400 sq km] **POPULATION** 5,470,000
CAPITAL Beirut **GOVERNMENT** Multiparty republic
ETHNIC GROUPS Arab 95%, Armenian 4%, others
LANGUAGES Arabic (official), French, English, Armenian
RELIGIONS Islam 60%, Christianity 39%
CURRENCY Lebanese pound = 100 piastres

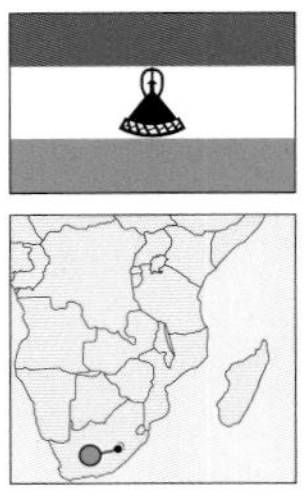

LESOTHO

GEOGRAPHY The Kingdom of Lesotho is a landlocked country, completely enclosed by South Africa. The land is mountainous, rising to 11,424 ft [3,482 m] on the northeastern border. The Drakensberg range covers most of the country.

The climate of Lesotho is greatly affected by the altitude, because most of the country lies above 4,920 ft [1,500 m]. Summers are warm but winters are cold. The rainfall averages about 28 inches [700 mm].

POLITICS & ECONOMY The political entity that eventually became Lesotho coalesced under King Moshoeshoe I in the 1820s who united various groups fleeing from tribal wars in southern Africa. Britain made the area a protectorate in 1868 and, in 1871, placed it under the British Cape Colony in South Africa. In 1884, Basutoland, as the area was called, was reconstituted as a British protectorate, where whites were not allowed to own land.

The country became independent in 1966 as the Kingdom of Lesotho, with Moshoeshoe II, great-grandson of Moshoeshoe I, as its king. Since independence, times have been turbulent with various factions, including the military, vying for power. Since 2012, a coalition government has been in place, under Thomas Thabane (2012–15) and then Pakalitha Mosisili (2015–17). Thabane returned to power in 2017 after Mosisili lost a vote of no confidence.

Lesotho faces many problems: agriculture is vulnerable to vagaries of the weather and the population has one of the highest rates of HIV/AIDS infection in the world. The UN has classified 40% of the people as "ultra-poor."

Lesotho lacks natural resources with agriculture employing 86% of the people, mostly at subsistence level. Remittances sent home by Basotho working abroad, mainly in South Africa, are important to the economy. Lesotho's main exports are textiles and diamonds.

AREA 11,720 sq mi [30,355 sq km] **POPULATION** 1,969,000
CAPITAL Maseru **GOVERNMENT** Constitutional monarchy
ETHNIC GROUPS Sotho 99% **LANGUAGES** Sesotho and English (both official) **RELIGIONS** Christianity 80%, traditional beliefs 20%
CURRENCY Loti = 100 lisente

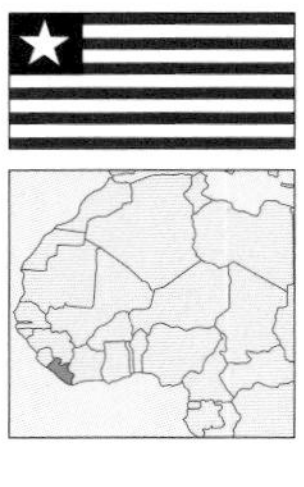

LIBERIA

GEOGRAPHY The Republic of Liberia is a country in West Africa. Behind the coastline, 311 mi [500 km] long, lies a narrow coastal plain. Beyond, the land rises to a plateau region, with the highest land along the border with Guinea. Liberia has a tropical climate with high temperatures and high humidity all through the year. Rainfall is abundant all year round, but there is a particularly wet period from June to November. Rainfall generally increases from east to west.

POLITICS & ECONOMY In the late 18th century, some white Americans in the United States wanted to help freed black slaves return to Africa. In 1816, they set up the American Colonization Society, which bought land in what is now Liberia.

In 1822, the Society landed former slaves at a settlement which they named Monrovia after US president Monroe. In 1847, Liberia became a fully independent republic with a constitution much like that of the United States. For many years, Americo-Liberians controlled the country's government with the American Firestone Company, which ran the rubber plantations, being especially influential. Other foreign companies readily exploited Liberia's mineral resources, including its huge iron-ore deposits.

In 1980, a military group composed of people from the local population killed the Americo-Liberian president, William R. Tolbert. An army sergeant, Samuel K. Doe, was made president. Elections held in 1985 resulted in victory for Doe. From 1989, the country was plunged into civil war between various ethnic groups. Doe was assassinated in 1990 and the struggle with rebel groups continued. West African peacekeeping forces arrived in Liberia and, in 1995, a ceasefire was agreed. A council of state was set up in 1997 and Charles Taylor became president. Taylor fled the country in 2003, and in 2006 he was extradited and faced war crimes charges, on several of which he was convicted in 2012. Following elections in 2005, Ellen Johnson-Sirleaf became Africa's first woman president. She was re-elected in 2011. Elections in 2017 were won by former soccer player George Weah.

Liberia's economy was devastated by the civil war and, more recently, by the regional outbreak of Ebola. Agriculture is important, but mostly at subsistence level. Food crops include cassava, rice, and sugarcane, while rubber, cocoa, and coffee are exported. The most valuable exports are rubber, iron ore, and gold. Liberia also obtains revenue from its "flag of convenience" which is used by about one-sixth of the world's commercial shipping.

AREA 43,000 sq mi [111,369 sq km] **POPULATION** 5,073,000
CAPITAL Monrovia **GOVERNMENT** Multiparty republic
ETHNIC GROUPS Indigenous African tribes 95% (including Kpelle, Bassa, Grebo, Gio, Kru, Mano)
LANGUAGES English (official), ethnic languages
RELIGIONS Christianity 86%, Islam 12%, traditional beliefs and others 2% **CURRENCY** Liberian dollar = 100 cents

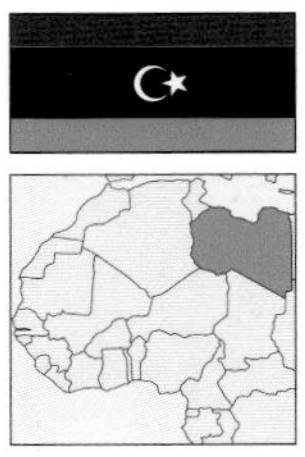

LIBYA

GEOGRAPHY Bordering the Mediterranean Sea, the State of Libya is the fourth largest country in Africa. Most people live on the coastal plains in the northeast and northwest. The Sahara, the world's largest desert, which occupies 95% of Libya, reaches the Mediterranean coast along the Gulf of Sidra (Khalij Surt).

The coastal plains in the northeast and northwest have Mediterranean climates, with hot, dry summers and mild, sometimes wet winters. Hot desert conditions prevail inland.

POLITICS & ECONOMY Italy took possession of Libya in 1911, but lost it during World War II. Britain and France jointly ruled Libya until 1951, when the country became independent.

In 1969, a military group headed by Colonel Muammar Gaddafi deposed the king and set up a military government. Under Gaddafi, the government took control of the economy and used money from oil exports to finance welfare services and development projects. Gaddafi was criticized for supporting terrorist groups around the world, and Libya became isolated from the mid-1980s.

From 2004, relations with the West improved and diplomatic links were restored with many nations, including the United States. However, in February 2011, the arrest of a human rights campaigner sparked off protests in Benghazi which rapidly spread. In October of that year, Gaddafi was killed and a National Transition Council was set up as the de facto government. Libya has struggled to find political stability and the elections held in 2014 produced rival governments, backed by secular and Islamist militias, which are fighting for control. Libya is a major route for migrants from Africa to Europe.

The discovery of oil and natural gas in 1959 led to a transformation of Libya's economy. This formerly poor country soon became Africa's richest in terms of its per capita income. But it remains a developing country, because oil accounts for nearly all of its export revenues. Agriculture is important, although Libya imports about 80% of its food. Crops include barley, citrus fruits, dates, olives, potatoes, and wheat, while cattle, sheep, and poultry are raised. Libya has oil refineries and petrochemical plants. Development and foreign investment await political stability.

AREA 679,358 sq mi [1,759,540 sq km] **POPULATION** 6,891,000
CAPITAL Tripoli **GOVERNMENT** Transitional
ETHNIC GROUPS Libyan Arab and Berber 97% **LANGUAGES** Arabic (official), Berber **RELIGIONS** Islam (Sunni Muslim) 97%
CURRENCY Libyan dinar = 1,000 dirhams

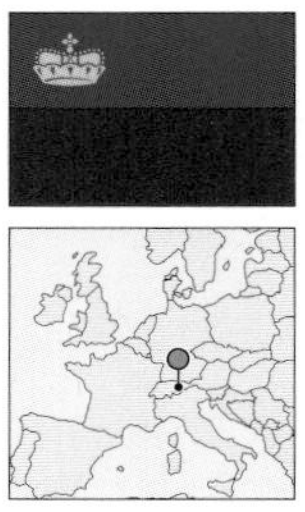

LIECHTENSTEIN

The tiny Principality of Liechtenstein is sandwiched between Switzerland and Austria. The River Rhine flows along its western border, while Alpine peaks rise in the east and south. The climate is relatively mild. Since 1924, Liechtenstein has been in a customs union with Switzerland. Taxation is low and the country is a haven for foreign companies. In 2004, the head of state Prince Hans-Adam II handed over the running of the country to his son, Prince Alois, though he remains titular head of state. In 2009, Liechtenstein agreed to share tax information with a number of countries in order to improve its reputation as a legitimate financial center.

AREA 62 sq mi [160 sq km] **POPULATION** 39,000 **CAPITAL** Vaduz

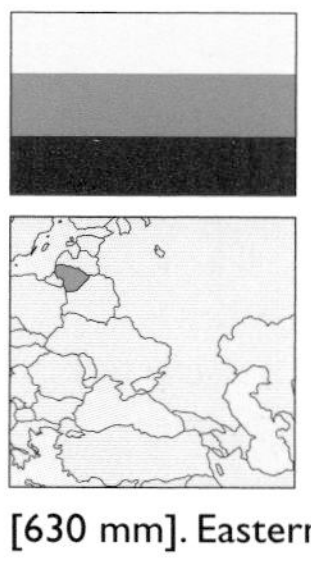

LITHUANIA

GEOGRAPHY The Republic of Lithuania is the southernmost of the three Baltic states which were ruled as part of the Soviet Union between 1940 and 1991. Much of the land is flat or gently rolling, with the highest land in the southeast.

Winters are cold and summers warm. The annual rainfall in the west is about 25 in [630 mm]. Eastern areas are drier.

POLITICS & ECONOMY The Lithuanian people were united into a single nation in the 12th century, and later joined a union with Poland. In 1795, Lithuania came under Russian rule. After World War I (1914–18), Lithuania declared itself independent, and in 1920 it signed a peace treaty with the Russians. In 1940, the Soviet Union occupied Lithuania, but was ousted by Germany a year later. After Soviet forces returned in 1944, Lithuania was integrated into the Soviet Union. However, Lithuanians resisted attempts to suppress their culture and steadfastly clung on to their language and staunch Catholic faith. In 1988, when the Soviet Union was introducing reforms, the Lithuanians demanded independence which was recognized by the Soviet Union in 1991.

Since 1991, Lithuania has sought to reform its economy and introduce a private enterprise system. Lithuania has also drawn closer to the West and, in 2004, it became a member of both the North Atlantic Treaty Organization and the European Union. Its first attempt to join the eurozone in 2007 was rejected due to high inflation but it adopted the euro in 2015.

The World Bank now classifies Lithuania as a "high-income" economy and it is growing faster than most other EU economies. Lithuania lacks natural resources. Manufacturing, based on imported materials, and services are the most valuable activities.

AREA 25,174 sq mi [65,200 sq km] **POPULATION** 2,731,000
CAPITAL Vilnius **GOVERNMENT** Multiparty republic
ETHNIC GROUPS Lithuanian 84%, Polish 6%, Russian 5%, Belarusian 1% **LANGUAGES** Lithuanian (official), Russian, Polish
RELIGIONS Mainly Roman Catholic **CURRENCY** Euro = 100 cents

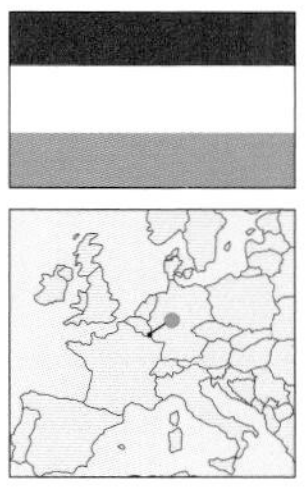

LUXEMBOURG

GEOGRAPHY The Grand Duchy of Luxembourg is one of the smallest and oldest countries in Europe. Luxembourg has a temperate climate. The south has warm summers and falls, when grapes ripen in sheltered southeastern valleys. Winters are sometimes severe, especially in upland areas.

POLITICS & ECONOMY Germany occupied Luxembourg in World Wars I and II. In 1944–45, northern Luxembourg was the scene of the Battle of the Bulge. In 1948, Luxembourg joined Belgium and the Netherlands in "Benelux," a customs union, and in the 1950s, it was one of the six founders of what is now the European Union. Its capital is a major financial center and contains several international agencies. In 2008, parliament restricted the monarch to a ceremonial role following the grand duke's refusal to sign a law allowing euthanasia.

Luxembourg has iron-ore reserves and has traditionally been a major steel producer. A decline in the industry prompted Luxembourg to diversify, particularly into financial services. Steel and other manufactures, including chemicals, rubber products, glass, and aluminum, continue to dominate the country's exports. The "LuxLeaks" scandal in 2009, which revealed advantageous tax arrangements for several multi-national companies, temporarily damaged Luxembourg's reputation.

AREA 998 sq mi [2,586 sq km] **POPULATION** 628,000
CAPITAL Luxembourg **GOVERNMENT** Constitutional monarchy (Grand Duchy) **ETHNIC GROUPS** Luxembourger 63%, Portuguese 13%, Italian, French, Belgian, Slavs **LANGUAGES** Luxembourgish (official), Portuguese, French, German **RELIGIONS** Roman Catholic 87%, others 13% **CURRENCY** Euro = 100 cents

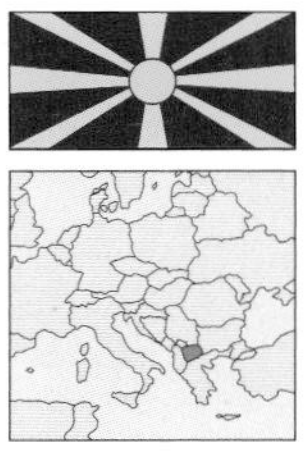

MACEDONIA, NORTH

GEOGRAPHY The Republic of North Macedonia is a country in southeastern Europe, which was once one of the six republics that made up the former Yugoslavia. This landlocked country is largely mountainous or hilly. North Macedonia has hot summers, though highland areas are cooler. Winters are cold and snowfalls are often heavy. The climate is fairly continental in character and rain occurs throughout the year.

POLITICS & ECONOMY Until the 20th century, North Macedonia's history was closely tied to the larger area of Macedonia, which included parts of northern Greece and southwestern Bulgaria. This region reached its peak in power at the time of Philip II (382–336 BC) and his son Alexander the Great (336–323 BC). After Alexander's death, his empire was split up and it gradually declined. The area became a Roman province in the 140s BC and part of the Byzantine empire from AD 395. In the 6th century, Slavs from eastern Europe settled in the area, followed by Bulgars from central Asia in the 9th century. The Byzantine empire regained control in 1018, but Serbia took Macedonia in the early 14th century. In 1371, the Ottoman Turks conquered the area and ruled it for more than 500 years.

In 1913, at the end of the Balkan Wars, the area was divided between Serbia, Bulgaria, and Greece. At the end of World War I, Serbian Macedonia became part of the Kingdom of the Serbs, Croats, and Slovenes, which was renamed Yugoslavia in 1929.

In the early 1990s, the country broke up into five separate republics with Macedonia declaring its independence in 1991. Greece objected to the use of the name Macedonia, which it considered to be a Greek name. It also objected to a symbol on Macedonia's flag and a reference in the constitution to the desire to reunite the three parts of the old Macedonia.

Macedonia adopted a new clause in its constitution rejecting any Macedonian claims on Greek territory and, in 1993, the United Nations accepted the new republic as a member under the name of the Former Yugoslav Republic of Macedonia (FYROM). By the end of 1993, all the countries of the EU, except Greece, were establishing diplomatic relations with the FYROM. In 1995, Greece lifted its trade ban when Macedonia agreed to redesign its flag. The issue over its name remained unresolved until 2018, when Macedonia and Greece agreed on the new name of the Republic of North Macedonia, paving the way for North Macedonia to apply for membership of the EU and NATO.

The World Bank describes North Macedonia as an "upper-middle-income" economy showing steady growth since independence due to conservative government financial policies working toward a more open economy. Manufactures dominate the country's exports. Coal is mined, but oil and natural gas are imported. The country is self-sufficient in its basic food needs and has a low rate of inflation, although it remains one of Europe's poorest economies and unemployment is high.

AREA 9,928 sq mi [25,713 sq km] **POPULATION** 2,126,000
CAPITAL Skopje **GOVERNMENT** Multiparty republic
ETHNIC GROUPS Macedonian 64%, Albanian 25%, Turkish 4%, Romanian 3%, Serb 2% **LANGUAGES** Macedonian and Albanian (official) **RELIGIONS** Macedonian Orthodox 65%, Islam 33%
CURRENCY Macedonian denar = 100 deni

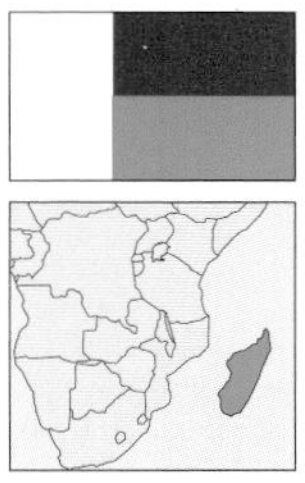

MADAGASCAR

GEOGRAPHY The Democratic Republic of Madagascar, in southeastern Africa, is an island nation, which has an area larger than France. Behind the narrow coastal plains in the east lies a highland zone, mostly between 2,000 ft and 4,000 ft [610 m to 1,220 m] above sea level. Broad plains border the Mozambique Channel in the west.

Temperatures in the highlands are moderated by the altitude. The winters (from April to September) are dry, but heavy rains occur in summer. The eastern coastlands are warm and humid. The west is drier, and the south and southwest are hot and dry. It has a unique fauna and flora.

POLITICS & ECONOMY People from Southeast Asia began to settle on Madagascar around 2,000 years ago. Subsequent influxes from Africa and Arabia added to the island's diverse heritage, culture, and language.

The island was a French colony from 1895 until it achieved independence as the Malagasy Republic in 1960. In 1972, army officers seized control and, in 1975, under the leadership of Lieutenant-Commander Didier Ratsiraka, the country was renamed Madagascar. In 2002, the country came close to civil war when Ratsiraka and his opponent, Marc Ravalomanana, both claimed victory in presidential elections. Ravalomanana became president, but he was deposed in 2009, in a move backed by the military and condemned internationally; Andry Rajoelina assumed power. Elections in 2013 were won by Hery Rajaonarimampiana, but Rajoelina returned to power after elections in 2018.

Madagascar is a poor country. Poverty and population growth impose pressure on the dwindling forests and the unique wildlife, as well as causing severe soil erosion. Farming, fishing, and forestry employ about 80% of the people. Food crops include bananas, cassava, rice, and sweet potatoes. Coffee and vanilla are exported.

AREA 226,657 sq mi [587,041 sq km] **POPULATION** 26,956,000
CAPITAL Antananarivo **GOVERNMENT** Republic
ETHNIC GROUPS Merina, Betsimisaraka, Betsileo, Tsimihety, Sakalava and others
LANGUAGES Malagasy and French (both official)
RELIGIONS Traditional beliefs 52%, Christianity 41%, Islam 7%
CURRENCY Malagasy ariary = 5 iraimbilanja

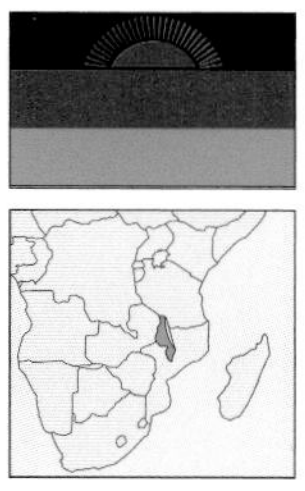

MALAWI

GEOGRAPHY The Republic of Malawi includes part of Lake Malawi, which is drained by the River Shire, a tributary of the River Zambezi. The land is mostly mountainous. The highest peak, Mulanje, reaches 9,849 ft [3,002 m] in the southeast.

While the low-lying areas of Malawi are hot and humid all year round, the uplands have more pleasant weather. Lilongwe has a warm and sunny climate. Frosts sometimes occur in July and August, in the middle of the long dry season.

POLITICS & ECONOMY Malawi, then called Nyasaland, became a British protectorate in 1891. In 1953, Britain established the Federation of Rhodesia and Nyasaland, which also included what are now Zambia and Zimbabwe. Black African opposition, led in Nyasaland by Dr Hastings Kamuzu Banda, led to the dissolution of the federation in 1963. In 1964, Nyasaland became independent as Malawi, with Banda as prime minister. Banda was an autocrat who maintained his control of the country by operating a one-party system and being made "president for life" in 1971 until he retired after elections in 1994. Bakili Muluzi became the first president after Banda and, despite Malawi aspiring toward more open government, subsequent administrations have been mired in accusations of corruption and treason.

Malawi is one of the world's poorest countries with more than half the population living below the poverty line. About 80% of the people are farmers, but many grow little more than they need to feed their families. Malawi is starting to exploit its uranium resources, but development is hampered by lack of infrastructure and the country's very high rates of HIV/AIDS infection.

AREA 45,747 sq mi [118,484 sq km] **POPULATION** 21,197,000
CAPITAL Lilongwe **GOVERNMENT** Multiparty republic
ETHNIC GROUPS Chewa, Lomwe, Yao, Ngoni, Tumbuka, Nyanja, Sena, Tonga, Ngonde and others
LANGUAGES Chichewa and English (both official)
RELIGIONS Christianity 68%, Islam 25%
CURRENCY Malawian kwacha = 100 tambala

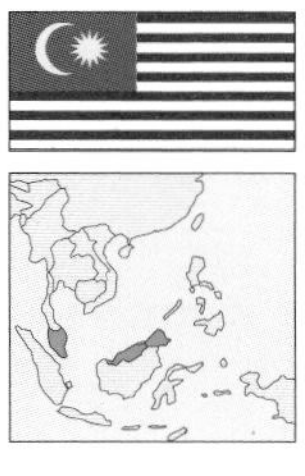

MALAYSIA

GEOGRAPHY The Federation of Malaysia consists of two main parts. Peninsular Malaysia, which is joined to mainland Asia, contains about 80% of the population. The other main regions, Sabah and Sarawak, are in northern Borneo, an island which Malaysia shares with Indonesia. Behind the coastal lowlands, the interior is mountainous.

Malaysia has a hot equatorial climate. The temperatures are high all through the year, though the mountains are much cooler than the lowland areas. Rainfall is heavy throughout the year.

POLITICS & ECONOMY Around 1,200 years ago, Indian traders introduced Hinduism and Buddhism into the Malay peninsula, while Arabs introduced Islam in the 15th century. Portuguese traders reached Melaka in 1509, but the Dutch took over in 1641. Britain became established in this region in 1786.

Japan occupied the area during World War II (1939–45), but it reverted to British rule in 1945. Malaya (Peninsular Malaysia) became independent in 1957. Malaysia was created in 1963, when Malaya, Singapore, Sabah, and Sarawak agreed to unite, but Singapore withdrew in 1965.

From 1981, Malaysia experienced rapid economic progress under the 22-year term of Prime Minister Mahathir bin Mohamad. Although not unaffected by global financial crises, the succeeding governments continued to develop a broad-based economy with an emphasis on manufacturing, tourism, and the service industry. In 2018 Mahathir was again elected prime minister, at the age of 92.

The World Bank classifies Malaysia as an "upper-middle-income" developing country. Palm oil, rubber, and tin are major products. Manufactures include cars, chemicals, a wide range of electronic goods, plastics, textiles, rubber, and wood products.

AREA 127,320 sq mi [329,758 sq km] **POPULATION** 32,652,000
CAPITAL Kuala Lumpur; Putrajaya (administrative capital)
GOVERNMENT Federal constitutional monarchy
ETHNIC GROUPS Malay and other indigenous groups 61%, Chinese 24%, Indian 7%, others
LANGUAGES Malay (official), Chinese, English
RELIGIONS Islam, Buddhism, Daoism, Hinduism, Christianity, Sikhism
CURRENCY Ringgit = 100 sen

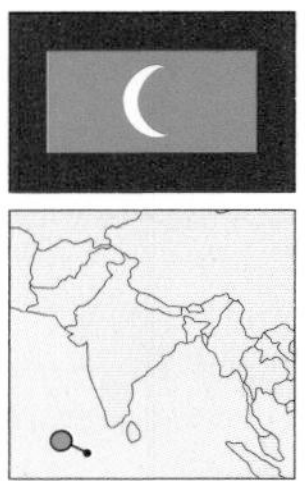

MALDIVES

The Republic of the Maldives consists of about 1,200 low-lying coral islands, south of India. The highest point is 79 ft [24 m], but most of the land is only 6 ft [1.8 m] above sea level, making it vulnerable to the effects of climate change. It became a British territory in 1887 and independent in 1965. It left the Commonwealth of Nations in 2016. Tourism and fishing are the main industries.

AREA 115 sq mi [298 sq km] **POPULATION** 392,000 **CAPITAL** Malé

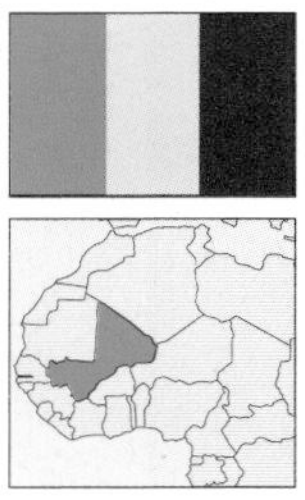

MALI

GEOGRAPHY The Republic of Mali is a landlocked country in northwestern Africa. The land is generally flat, with the highest land in the north. Northern Mali is hot and practically rainless. The south has enough rain for farming.

POLITICS & ECONOMY Between the 4th and 16th centuries, Mali was part of three African empires – Ancient Ghana, Ancient Mali and Songhay. However, after 1591, when Songhay was defeated by Morocco, the area was divided into small kingdoms. France ruled the area, then known as French Sudan, from 1893 until the country became independent as Mali in 1960.

The first socialist government was overthrown in 1968 by an army group led by Moussa Traoré, who was not ousted until 1991. Multiparty democracy was restored in 1992 and Alpha Oumar Konaré was elected president. Konaré stood down in 2002 and Ahmadou Touré, who had restored democracy in 1992, was elected president. In 2012, an army coup overthrew Touré; three successive "unity cabinets" followed. The coup leaders said that the government was failing to give them enough arms to tackle a rebellion by ethnic Tuaregs in northern Mali. A fragile peace prevails, although there has been an increase in terrorist attacks by Islamist groups in recent years.

Mali is a very poor country and 70% of the land is desert or semi-desert. Only about 2% of the land is used for growing crops, while 25% is used for grazing animals. Agriculture employs about 80% of the people, many of whom subsist by nomadic livestock rearing. Mali's chief exports are cotton and gold.

AREA 478,838 sq mi [1,240,192 sq km] **POPULATION** 19,553,000
CAPITAL Bamako **GOVERNMENT** Multiparty republic
ETHNIC GROUPS Mande 50% (Bambara, Malinke, Soninke), Peul 17%, Voltaic 12%, Songhai 6%, Tuareg and Moor 10%, others
LANGUAGES French (official), many African languages
RELIGIONS Islam 95%, traditional beliefs 3%, Christianity 2%
CURRENCY CFA franc = 100 centimes

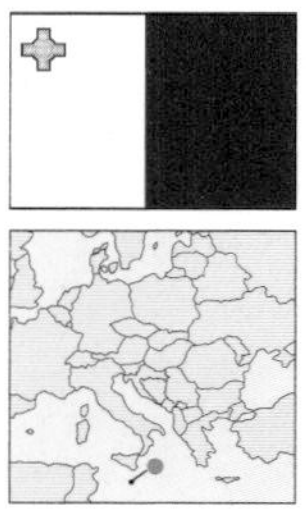

MALTA

GEOGRAPHY The Republic of Malta consists of two main islands, Malta and Gozo, with a third, much smaller island called Comino lying between the two large islands, and two islets. The climate is typically Mediterranean, with hot, dry summers and mild, moist winters.

POLITICS & ECONOMY Malta has fascinating Stone Age and Bronze Age remains. The islands later came under Phoenician, Greek, Carthaginian, Roman, and Arab rule. In about 1090, Malta fell under the Norman kings of Sicily and, from 1530, the Knights Hospitallers (also called the Knights of St John of Jerusalem). France took the islands in 1798, but the British drove them out in 1800. British rule was officially recognized in 1815.

During World War I (1914–18), Malta was an important naval base. In World War II (1939–45), Italian and German aircraft bombed the islands. In recognition of the islanders' bravery, the British King George VI awarded the George Cross to Malta in 1942: the emblem is incorporated into its flag. Malta became independent in 1964 and a republic in 1974. Since the 1980s Malta has pursued a policy of neutrality whilst maintaining links with Europe and the United States. It became a member of the European Union in May 2004, and adopted the euro as its official currency in 2008.

The World Bank classifies Malta as a "high-income" developing country. It lacks natural resources, and most people work in the former naval dockyards, which are now used for commercial shipbuilding and repair, in manufacturing industries, notably electronics, and in tourism and financial services.

Manufactures include processed food and chemicals. Farming is difficult, because of the rocky soils. Crops include barley, fruits, potatoes, and wheat. Malta also has a small fishing industry.

AREA 122 sq mi [316 sq km] **POPULATION** 457,000
CAPITAL Valletta **GOVERNMENT** Multiparty republic
ETHNIC GROUPS Maltese 96%, British 2%
LANGUAGES Maltese and English (both official)
RELIGIONS Roman Catholic 98%
CURRENCY Euro = 100 cents

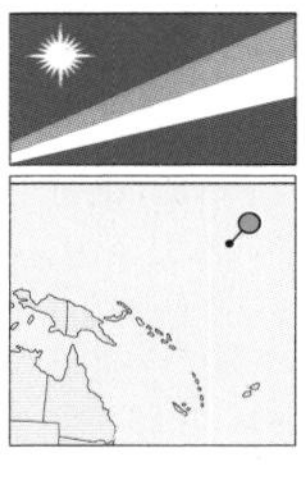

MARSHALL ISLANDS

The Republic of the Marshall Islands, a former US territory, became fully independent in 1991. This island nation, lying north of Kiribati in a region known as Micronesia, is heavily dependent on US aid. The main activities are agriculture and tourism.

AREA 70 sq mi [181 sq km]
POPULATION 78,000 **CAPITAL** Majuro

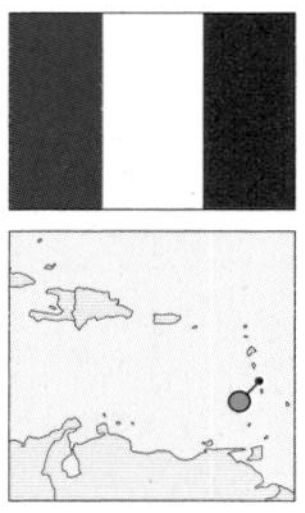

MARTINIQUE

Martinique, a volcanic island nation in the Caribbean, was colonized by France in 1635. It became a French overseas department in 1946. Tourism and agriculture are major activities. About 70% of Martinique's gross domestic product is provided by the French government, allowing for a good standard of living.

AREA 425 sq mi [1,102 sq km]
POPULATION 386,000 **CAPITAL** Fort-de-France

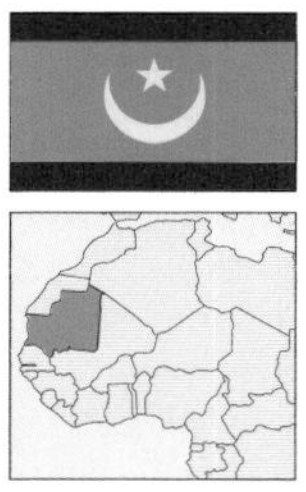

MAURITANIA

GEOGRAPHY The Islamic Republic of Mauritania in northwestern Africa is nearly twice the size of France. But France has almost 20 times as many people. Part of the world's largest desert, the Sahara, covers northern Mauritania and most Mauritanians live in the southwest. The amount of rainfall and the length of the rainy season increase from north to south. Much of the land is desert, but southwesterly winds bring summer rain to the south.

POLITICS & ECONOMY Originally part of the great African empires of Ghana and Mali, Mauritania became a French protectorate in 1903. In 1920, the country became a territory of French West Africa and a French colony. Mauritania finally became independent in 1960.

In 1976, Spain withdrew from Spanish (now Western) Sahara, a territory bordering Mauritania to the north. Morocco occupied the northern two-thirds of this territory, while Mauritania took the rest. Following this, Saharan guerrillas belonging to POLISARIO (the Popular Front for the Liberation of Saharan Territories) began an armed struggle for independence. In 1979, Mauritania withdrew from the southern part of Western Sahara, which was then occupied by Morocco. Democracy was restored after a new constitution was adopted in 1991. A military group seized power in 2005, but democratic elections were held in 2007. The military again seized control in 2008, and in 2009 its leader, Mohamad Ould Abdel Aziz, was elected president. He was re-elected in 2014. In 2010–11, al Qaeda militants committed terrorist attacks in Mauritania, and they remain a threat.

Mauritania is a "lower-middle-income" developing country. Nearly half of the population are engaged in agriculture and at the mercy of frequent droughts. The coastal waters provide good fishing grounds. In 2006, Mauritania became Africa's newest oil producer, when an offshore platform came online for the first time. Mauritania has extensive mineral deposits.

AREA 395,953 sq mi [1,025,520 sq km] **POPULATION** 4,005,000
CAPITAL Nouakchott **GOVERNMENT** Multiparty Islamic republic
ETHNIC GROUPS Mixed Moor/Black 40%, Moor 30%, Black 30%
LANGUAGES Arabic (official), Pulaar, Soninke, Wolof, French
RELIGIONS Islam **CURRENCY** Ouguiya = 5 khoums

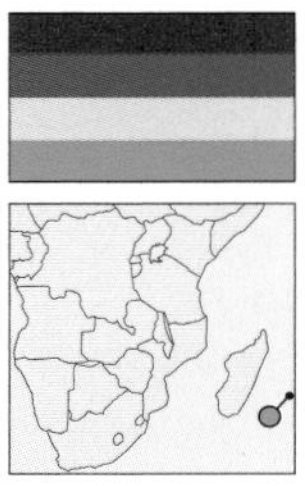

MAURITIUS

The Republic of Mauritius lies in the Indian Ocean east of Madagascar. It was previously ruled by France and Britain until it achieved independence in 1968. It became a republic in 1992. Sugar production is in decline with tourism and textiles vital to the economy. It has few natural resources.

AREA 788 sq mi [2,040 sq km]
POPULATION 1,379,000 **CAPITAL** Port Louis

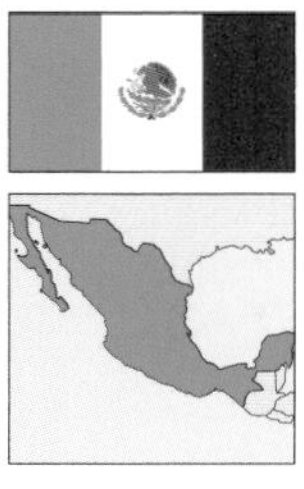

MEXICO

GEOGRAPHY The United Mexican States, as Mexico is officially named, is the world's most populous Spanish-speaking country. Much of the land is mountainous, although most people live on the central plateau. Mexico contains two large peninsulas: Lower (or Baja) California in the northwest, and the flat Yucatán peninsula in the southeast.

The climate varies according to the altitude. The resort of Acapulco on the southwest coast has a dry and sunny climate. Mexico City, at about 7,546 ft [2,300 m] above sea level, is much cooler. Most rain occurs between June and September.

POLITICS & ECONOMY In the mid-19th century, Mexico lost land to the United States, and between 1910 and 1921 violent revolutions created chaos. Reforms were introduced in the 1920s and, in 1929, the Institutional Revolutionary Party (PRI) was formed. The PRI ruled Mexico effectively as a one-party state until 2001. The new president, Vicente Fox, faced many problems. He was succeeded by Felipe Calderón in 2006, who prioritized a crackdown on the increasing gang violence related to drug trafficking. The left-winger Andres Manuel López Obrado was elected president in 2018.

The World Bank classifies Mexico as an "upper-middle-income" developing country. Agriculture is important. Food crops include beans, maize, rice, and wheat, while cash crops include coffee, cotton, fruits, and vegetables. However, oil and oil products are the chief exports, while manufacturing is the most valuable activity. Mexico is the world's leading silver producer, and it also mines copper, gold, lead, zinc, and other minerals. Factories near the northern border assemble goods, such as car parts and electrical products, for US companies.

Hopes for the future lie in increasing cooperation with the US and Canada. The election of Donald Trump as US President in 2016 led to the renegotiation of the North American Free-Trade Agreement (NAFTA). In October 2018 a new trade deal – United States-Mexico-Canada Agreement (USMCA) – was negotiated.

AREA 756,061 sq mi [1,958,201 sq km] **POPULATION** 128,650,000
CAPITAL Mexico City **GOVERNMENT** Federal republic
ETHNIC GROUPS Mestizo 60%, Amerindian 30%, White 9%
LANGUAGES Spanish (official) **RELIGIONS** Roman Catholic 83%, Protestant 2%, others 15% **CURRENCY** Mexican peso = 100 centavos

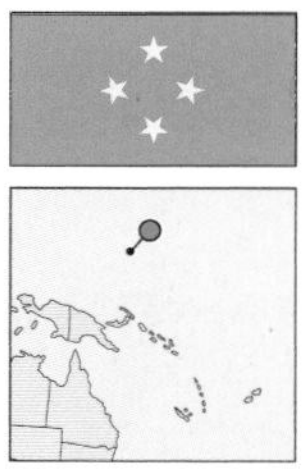

MICRONESIA

The Federated States of Micronesia, a former US territory in the western Pacific Ocean, became fully independent in 1991. The main exports are fish and agricultural products. Tourism is important.

AREA 271 sq mi [702 sq km]
POPULATION 102,000 **CAPITAL** Palikir

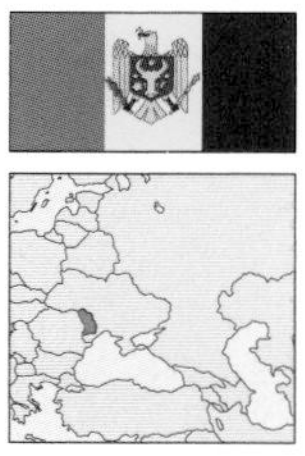

MOLDOVA

GEOGRAPHY The Republic of Moldova is a small country sandwiched between Ukraine and Romania. It was formerly one of the 15 republics that made up the Soviet Union.

Much of the land is hilly and the highest areas are located near the center of the country.

Moldova has a moderately continental climate, with warm summers and fairly cold winters when temperatures dip below freezing point. Most of the rain comes in the warmer months.

POLITICS & ECONOMY In the 14th century, the Moldavian people formed a state that comprised part of Romania and the historic region of Bessarabia. Following rule by the Ottoman Turks, Russia took control of Bessarabia in 1812. After World War I (1914–18), Bessarabia declared independence and voted to unite with Romania. This move was not recognized by Russia and in 1940 the area was annexed by the USSR. From 1944, the Moldovan Soviet Socialist Republic became part of the Soviet Union.

In 1989, the Moldovans asserted their independence and ethnicity by making Romanian the official language and, at the end of 1991, Moldova became an independent nation. But Trans-Dniester, an area east of the River Dniester inhabited by mainly Russian and Ukrainian speakers, has sought autonomy. In 2006, its people voted for independence and union with Russia, but this vote was not recognized internationally.

From 2001 to 2009 the Communist Party was in power, but pro-Western coalitions have ruled since 2010. In 2014, Moldova signed its Association Agreement with the EU. Russia restricted some agricultural imports in response. In 2016, in the first direct presidential elections in some years, pro-Russian Igor Dodon was elected with 55% of the vote.

In terms of its GNP per capita, Moldova is one of Europe's poorest countries. Agriculture is the leading activity and products include fruits, maize, tobacco, and wine. Moldova has few natural resources and it imports materials and fuels for its industries.

AREA 13,070 sq mi [33,851 sq km] **POPULATION** 3,364,000
CAPITAL Chisinau **GOVERNMENT** Multiparty republic
ETHNIC GROUPS Moldovan/Romanian 78%, Ukrainian 8%, Russian 6%, Gagauz 4%, others **LANGUAGES** Moldovan/Romanian (official), Gagauz, Russian **RELIGIONS** Eastern Orthodox 98%
CURRENCY Moldovan leu = 100 bani

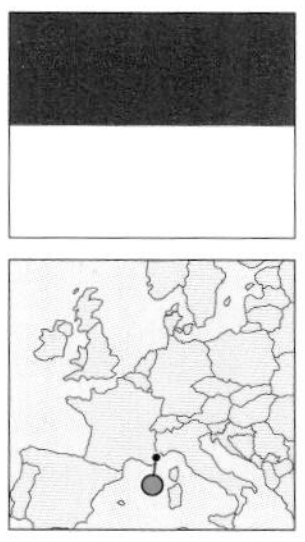

MONACO

The tiny Principality of Monaco consists of a narrow strip of coastline and a rocky peninsula on the French Riviera. Its considerable wealth is derived largely from banking, finance, gambling, recreation, and tourism. Monaco's citizens do not pay any income tax. The Grimaldi family have ruled the country for over 720 years with Prince Albert II as the current reigning monarch.

AREA 0.8 sq mi [2 sq km] **POPULATION** 39,000 **CAPITAL** Monaco

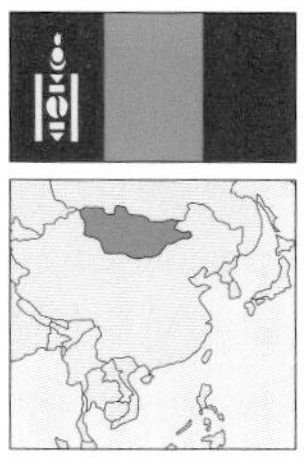

MONGOLIA

GEOGRAPHY The State of Mongolia is the world's largest landlocked country. It consists mainly of high plateaux, with a cold desert, the Gobi, in the southeast.

Ulan Bator lies on the northern edge of the desert plateau. It has bitterly cold winters. Summer temperatures are moderated by the altitude.

POLITICS & ECONOMY In the 13th century, Genghis Khan united the Mongolian peoples and built up a great empire. Under his grandson, Kublai Khan, the Mongol empire extended from Korea and China to eastern Europe and present-day Iraq.

The Mongol empire broke up in the late 14th century. In the early 17th century, Inner Mongolia came under Chinese control, and by the late 17th century Outer Mongolia had become a Chinese province. In 1911, the Mongolians drove the Chinese out of Outer Mongolia and made the area a Buddhist kingdom. But in 1924, under Russian influence, the Communist Mongolian People's Republic was set up. In 1990, the people demonstrated for more freedom, and free elections in June 1990 were won by the Communist Mongolian People's Revolutionary Party (MPRP). The Democratic Party coalition won in 1996, but the MPRP regained control in 2000. In 2009, the Democratic Party candidate, Tsakhiagiin Elbegdorj, was elected president. He was re-elected in 2013. In 2016 parliamentary elections, the Mongolian People's Party won a landslide. Presidential elections in 2017 were won by former martial arts star Khaltmaa Battulga of the Democratic Party.

The majority of the population were once nomads but, under Communist rule, most people were moved into permanent homes on government-owned farms. Livestock and animal products remain important, but minerals and fuels now account for more than three-fifths of Mongolia's exports. There is much mineral wealth yet to be exploited.

AREA 604,826 sq mi [1,566,500 sq km] **POPULATION** 3,168,000
CAPITAL Ulan Bator **GOVERNMENT** Multiparty republic
ETHNIC GROUPS Khalkha Mongol 95%, Kazakh 5%
LANGUAGES Khalkha Mongolian (official), Turkic, Russian
RELIGIONS Tibetan Buddhist Lamaism 53%
CURRENCY Mongolian tögrög = 100 möngös

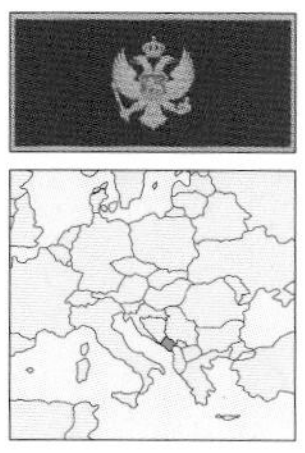

MONTENEGRO

The Republic of Montenegro, on the shores of the Adriatic Sea, became independent in 2006.

The coastal region has a Mediterranean climate. However, inland, the Dinaric Alps, which reach a height of 8,274 ft [2,522 m], have a more severe climate.

Serbia fell under Turkish rule in the 14th century, but Montenegro remained Christian. Montenegro was absorbed into Serbia in 1918 and it later became part of the Kingdom of the Serbs, Croats, and Slovenes, renamed as Yugoslavia in 1929. After World War II, Montenegro was recognized as one of the six republics of Yugoslavia. In the 1990s, as the other republics became independent, Montenegro remained with Serbia as the Federal Republic of Yugoslavia. It became independent in 2006.

In 2016, long-term prime minister Milo Djukanovich was replaced by Dusko Markovic. Two years later, Djukanovich, a pro-European, was elected president, a post he had also held from 1997–2002. Montenegro is a candidate for EU membership and joined NATO in 2017.

Manufacturing is the main activity, and steel and aluminum are major products. Farming also remains important. Montenegro became a member of the World Trade Organization in 2012.

AREA 5,415 sq mi [14,026 sq km] **POPULATION** 610,000
CAPITAL Podgorica **GOVERNMENT** Republic
ETHNIC GROUPS Montenegrin 43%, Serb 32%, Bosnian 8%, Albanian 5%, others **LANGUAGES** Serbian and Montenegrin (both official), Bosnian, Albanian **RELIGIONS** Orthodox, Islam, Roman Catholic **CURRENCY** Euro = 100 cents

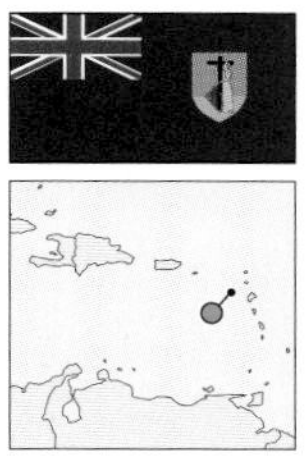

MONTSERRAT

Montserrat is a British overseas territory in the Caribbean Sea. The climate is tropical and hurricanes often cause much damage. Intermittent eruptions of the Soufrière Hills volcano between 1995 and 1998, and again in 2003, led to the emigration of many people and the virtual destruction of Plymouth, the then capital. A new airport was opened in 2005.

AREA 39 sq mi [102 sq km] **POPULATION** 5,000 **CAPITAL** Brades

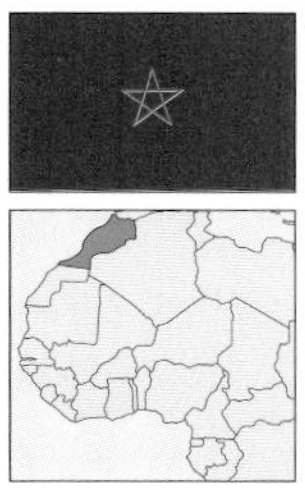

MOROCCO

GEOGRAPHY The Kingdom of Morocco lies in northwestern Africa. Behind the western coastal plain the land rises to a broad plateau and ranges of the Atlas Mountains. The High (Haut) Atlas contains the highest peak, Djebel Toubkal, at 13,665 ft [4,165 m]. East of the mountains, the land descends to the Sahara. The Canaries Current cools the Atlantic coast. Inland, summers are hot and dry. Winters are mild, with moderate rainfall. Snow often falls on the High Atlas Mountains.

POLITICS & ECONOMY The original people of Morocco were the Berbers, but, in the 680s, Arab invaders introduced Islam and the Arabic language. By the early 20th century, France and Spain controlled Morocco, which became an independent kingdom in 1956. Although Morocco is a constitutional monarchy, King Hassan II ruled the country in a generally authoritarian way, from his accession in 1961 to his death in 1999. His successor, Mohamed VI, faced several problems, including that of Western Sahara, which he claimed for Morocco (partly for its phosphate reserves), and the activities of Islamist extremists. After pro-democracy protests in 2011, a new constitution was introduced, granting the prime minister more power. A moderate Islamist party won a majority in parliamentary elections in 2011 and 2017.

Morocco is classified as a "lower-middle-income" developing country. It is the world's third largest producer of phosphate rock, which is used to make fertilizer. Farming employs about 40% of Moroccans. Chief crops include barley, beans, citrus fruits, maize, olives, sugar beet, and wheat. Processed phosphates are exported, but most of Morocco's manufactures are for home consumption. Fishing and tourism are also important.

AREA 172,413 sq mi [446,550 sq km] **POPULATION** 35,562,000
CAPITAL Rabat **GOVERNMENT** Constitutional monarchy
ETHNIC GROUPS Arab-Berber 99% **LANGUAGES** Arabic (official), Berber dialects, French **RELIGIONS** Islam 99%
CURRENCY Moroccan dirham = 100 santeem

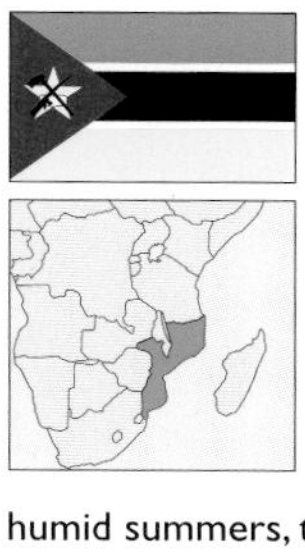

MOZAMBIQUE

GEOGRAPHY The Republic of Mozambique borders the Indian Ocean in southeastern Africa. The coastal plains are narrow in the north but broaden in the south. Inland lie plateaux and hills, which make up another two-fifths of the country. Mozambique has a mostly tropical climate. The capital, Maputo, which lies outside the tropics, has hot and humid summers, though the winters are mild and fairly dry.

POLITICS & ECONOMY In 1885, when the European powers divided Africa, Mozambique was recognized as a Portuguese colony. But black African opposition to European rule gradually increased. In 1961, the Front for the Liberation of Mozambique (FRELIMO) was founded to oppose Portuguese rule. In 1964, FRELIMO launched a guerrilla war, which continued for ten years, until Mozambique became independent in 1975.

After independence, Mozambique became a one-party state. Its government aided African nationalists in Rhodesia (now Zimbabwe) and South Africa. But the white governments of these countries helped an opposition group, the Mozambique National Resistance Movement (RENAMO), to lead an armed struggle against Mozambique's government. Civil war, combined with droughts, caused much suffering in the 1980s. In 1989, FRELIMO ended one-party rule and multiparty elections were held in 1994. In 1995 Mozambique became the 53rd member of the Commonwealth. In January 2015, Filipe Nyusi became the country's 4th president.

In the early 1990s, the UN rated Mozambique as one of the world's poorest countries, but from the second half of the 1990s there has been economic growth, although hampered by cycles of drought and flood, most recently the hugely destructive Cyclone Idai in 2019. About 80% of the people are poor farmers. Mozambique is set to become a major exporter of natural gas.

AREA 309,494 sq mi [801,590 sq km] **POPULATION** 30,098,000
CAPITAL Maputo **GOVERNMENT** Multiparty republic
ETHNIC GROUPS Indigenous tribal groups (Shangaan, Chokwe, Manyika, Sena, Makua, others) 99% **LANGUAGES** Portuguese (official), many others **RELIGIONS** Roman Catholic 28%, Protestant 28%, Islam 18% **CURRENCY** Metical = 100 centavos

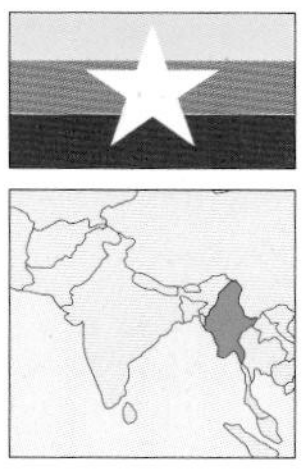

MYANMAR (BURMA)

GEOGRAPHY The Union of Burma has been officially known as the Union of Myanmar since 1989. Mountains border the country in the east and west, with the highest mountains in the north. Myanmar's highest mountain is Hkakabo Razi, which is 19,294 ft [5,881 m] high. Between these ranges are the fertile valleys of the Irrawaddy and Sittang rivers. The Irrawaddy delta is a leading rice-growing area.

Myanmar has a tropical monsoon climate with three seasons. The rainy season runs from late May to mid-October. A cool, dry season follows, between late October and the middle part of February. The hot season lasts from late February to mid-May. In May 2008, cyclone Nargis devastated the south, including the Irrawaddy delta, killing more than 80,000 people.

POLITICS & ECONOMY The ancestors of the country's main ethnic group today, the Burmese, arrived in the 9th century AD. They encroached on areas occupied since ancient times by a variety of indigenous tribes. Britain conquered Burma in the 19th century making it a province of British India until, in 1937, they granted Burma limited self-government. Japan then invaded and occupied Burma from 1942 until the end of World War II in 1945. Burma became a fully independent country in 1948.

Revolts by Communists and various hill people led to instability in the 1950s. In 1962, Burma became a military dictatorship and, in 1974, a one-party state. The National League for Democracy led by Aung San Suu Kyi won the elections in 1990, but the military continued their repressive rule by ignoring the results.

In 2010, Aung San Suu Kyi was released from house arrest. A military-backed party was victorious in elections in 2010, and in 2011 a civilian government, backed by the military, took power. In 2012, Aung San Suu Kyi won a parliamentary seat, while her party, the National League for Democracy (NLD), won 43 of the 44 contested seats. The general elections held in 2015 were a victory for

the NLD, although constitutional rules have barred Aung San Suu Kyi from officially becoming president. In 2017 a crackdown by the military after conflict between the Buddhist majority and minority ethnic groups, notably the Muslim Rohingya, led to the flight of up to a million Rohingya to Bangladesh. The UN has since termed the violence ethnic cleansing.

Agriculture is the main activity, employing 70% of the people. The chief crop is rice with maize, pulses, oilseeds, and sugarcane also important. Myanmar's chief exports are natural gas, wood products and rice. Myanmar has many mineral resources including oil and gas. Tourism is set to become increasingly important.

AREA 261,227 SQ MI [676,578 SQ KM] **POPULATION** 56,590,000
CAPITAL RANGOON (YANGON); NAYPYIDAW (ADMINISTRATIVE CAPITAL)
GOVERNMENT MULTIPARTY REPUBLIC **ETHNIC GROUPS** BURMAN 68%, SHAN 9%, KAREN 7%, RAKHINE 4%, CHINESE, INDIAN, MON
LANGUAGES BURMESE (OFFICIAL); MINORITY ETHNIC GROUPS HAVE THEIR OWN LANGUAGES **RELIGIONS** BUDDHISM 89%, CHRISTIANITY, ISLAM
CURRENCY KYAT = 100 PYAS

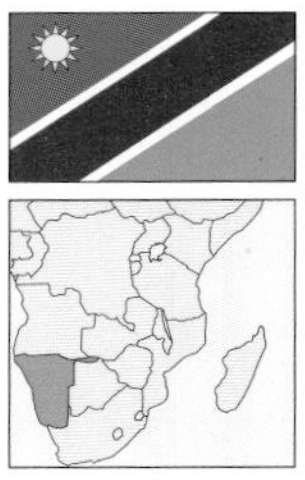

NAMIBIA

GEOGRAPHY When it was ruled by South Africa, the Republic of Namibia was known as South West Africa. The coastal region contains the arid Namib Desert, which is virtually uninhabited. Inland is a central plateau, bordered by a rugged spine of mountains stretching north–south. Eastern Namibia contains part of the Kalahari, a semi-desert area extending into Botswana. Namibia has a warm and arid climate. Windhoek has an average annual rainfall of 15 inches [370 mm], which often occurs in thunderstorms during the hot summer.

POLITICS & ECONOMY During World War I, South African troops defeated the Germans who ruled what is now Namibia. After World War II, many people challenged South Africa's right to govern the territory, and a civil war began in the 1960s between African guerrillas and South African troops. A ceasefire was agreed in 1989 and Namibia became independent in 1990. In the 1990s, the government pursued a policy of "national reconciliation." An enclave on the coast, Walvis Bay (Walvisbaai), remained part of South Africa until 1994, when it was transferred to Namibia. In 2004, the nationalist leader, Sam Nujoma, president since 1990, retired. He was succeeded by Hifikepunye Pohamba, who in turn was followed by Hage Geingob after elections in 2014.

Namibia has reserves of diamonds, uranium, zinc, and copper. Agriculture employs around 19% of the people and much is at subsistence level. Fishing is important. Namibia has few industries and unemployment is high at around 34%. Potential offshore oil reserves are being explored. Tourism is expanding.

AREA 318,259 SQ MI [824,292 SQ KM] **POPULATION** 2,630,000
CAPITAL WINDHOEK **GOVERNMENT** MULTIPARTY REPUBLIC
ETHNIC GROUPS OVAMBO 50%, KAVANGO 9%, HERERO 7%, DAMARA 7%, WHITE 6%, NAMA 5%
LANGUAGES ENGLISH (OFFICIAL), AFRIKAANS, GERMAN, INDIGENOUS DIALECTS
RELIGIONS CHRISTIANITY 90% (LUTHERAN 51%)
CURRENCY NAMIBIAN DOLLAR = 100 CENTS

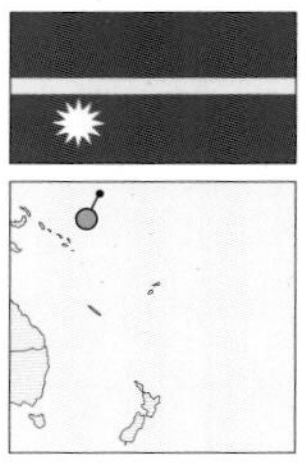

NAURU

Nauru is the world's smallest republic, located in the western Pacific Ocean. Independent since 1968, Nauru's prosperity is based on the mining of increasingly depleted reserves of phosphate. Since 2013, Australia has detained asylum-seekers on the island.

AREA 8 SQ MI [21 SQ KM]
POPULATION 11,000 **CAPITAL** YAREN

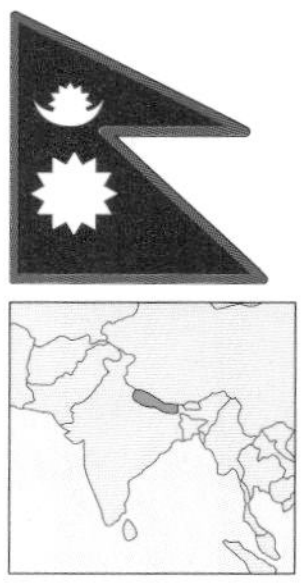

NEPAL

GEOGRAPHY Over three-quarters of Nepal lies in the Himalayan region, culminating in the world's highest peak (Mount Everest, or Chomolongma in Nepali) at 29,035 ft [8,850 m]. As a result, climatic conditions vary widely according to the altitude.

POLITICS & ECONOMY Nepal was united in the late 18th century, although it remains a diverse patchwork of peoples. From the mid-19th century to 1951, power was held by the royal Rana family. The first democratic elections in 32 years were held in 1991, but, by the early 21st century, Nepal faced many problems, including an uprising of Maoist guerrillas. In 2005, King Gyanendra seized power but failed to stop the conflict. In 2006, the Maoists joined a provisional coalition government. In elections in April 2008, the Maoists became the largest single party. In May, Nepal became a republic after the abolition of the monarchy. A new constitution was adopted in 2015. Parliamentary elections in 2017 were won by a coalition of Communist and Maoist parties, and Khadga Prasad Sharma Oli became prime minister in 2018.

Agriculture is the main activity and poverty is rife in this overwhelmingly rural country. Nepal is heavily dependent on aid and remittances sent from abroad. Tourism is growing in importance. There are also ambitious plans to exploit the hydroelectric potential offered by the ferocious Himalayan rivers.

AREA 56,827 SQ MI [147,181 SQ KM] **POPULATION** 30,328,000
CAPITAL KATMANDU **GOVERNMENT** MULTIPARTY REPUBLIC
ETHNIC GROUPS BRAHMAN, CHHETRI, NEWAR, GURUNG, MAGAR, TAMANG, SHERPA, AND OTHERS
LANGUAGES NEPALI (OFFICIAL), LOCAL LANGUAGES
RELIGIONS HINDUISM 81%, BUDDHISM 11%, ISLAM 4%
CURRENCY NEPALESE RUPEE = 100 PAISA

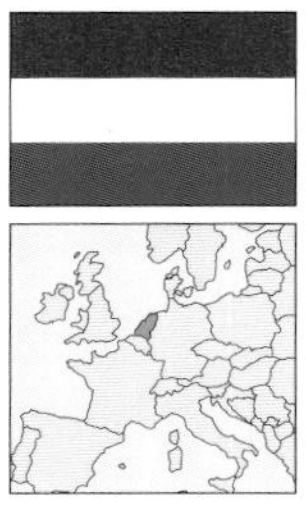

NETHERLANDS

GEOGRAPHY The Netherlands lies at the western end of the North European Plain, which extends to the Ural Mountains in Russia. Except for the far southeastern corner, the Netherlands is flat and about 40% lies below sea level at high tide. To prevent flooding, the Dutch have built dykes (sea walls) to hold back the waves. Large areas which were once under the sea, but which have been reclaimed, are known as polders. Because of its position on the North Sea, the Netherlands has a temperate climate, with mild, rainy winters.

POLITICS & ECONOMY Before the 16th century, the area that is now the Netherlands was under a succession of foreign rulers, including the Romans, the Germanic Franks, the French, and the Spanish. The Dutch declared their independence from Spain in 1581 and their status was finally recognized by Spain in 1648. In the 17th century, the Dutch built up a great overseas empire, especially in Southeast Asia. But in the early 18th century, the Dutch lost control of the seas to England.

France controlled the Netherlands from 1795 to 1813. In 1815, the Netherlands, then containing Belgium and Luxembourg, became an independent kingdom. Belgium broke away in 1830 and Luxembourg followed in 1890.

The Netherlands was neutral in World War I (1914–18), but was occupied by Germany in World War II (1939–45). After the war, the Netherlands Indies became independent as Indonesia. The Netherlands became active in West European affairs and, with Belgium and Luxembourg, it formed the customs union of Benelux in 1948. In 1949, it joined NATO (the North Atlantic Treaty Organization), and the European Coal and Steel Community (ECSC) in 1953. In 1957, it became a founder member of the European Economic Community (now the European Union), and, in 2002, it adopted the euro as its sole unit of currency. After a series of short-lived governments, Mark Rutte's VVD has led a stable coalition since 2012, and remained the largest party after elections in 2017. The right-wing Freedom Party did not make the expected gains. In 2013, after a 33-year reign, Queen Beatrix abdicated in favor of her son, Prince Willem Alexander.

2010 saw the dissolution of the Netherlands Antilles, an island territory in the Caribbean. Curaçao and St Maarten became nations in the Kingdom of the Netherlands. The small islands of Bonaire, St Eustatius, and Saba became special municipalities.

The Netherlands is a highly industrialized country, and industry and commerce are the most valuable activities. Its resources include natural gas, some oil, salt, and china clay. But the Netherlands imports many of the materials needed by its industries and it is, therefore, a major trading country. Industrial products are wide-ranging, including aircraft, chemicals, electronic equipment, machinery, textiles, and vehicles. Farming is scientific and yields are high. Dairy farming is the leading farming activity. Major products include barley, flowers and bulbs, potatoes, sugar beet, and wheat.

AREA 16,033 SQ MI [41,526 SQ KM] **POPULATION** 17,280,000
CAPITAL AMSTERDAM; THE HAGUE (SEAT OF GOVERNMENT)
GOVERNMENT CONSTITUTIONAL MONARCHY
ETHNIC GROUPS DUTCH 81%, INDONESIAN, TURKISH, MOROCCAN, AND OTHERS **LANGUAGES** DUTCH AND FRISIAN (BOTH OFFICIAL)
RELIGIONS ROMAN CATHOLIC 30%, PROTESTANT 20%, ISLAM 6%, OTHERS
CURRENCY EURO = 100 CENTS

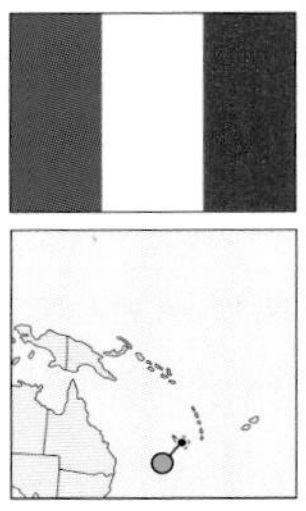

NEW CALEDONIA

New Caledonia is the most southerly of the Melanesian countries in the Pacific. It has been a French possession since 1853 and an Overseas Territory since 1958. In a referendum in 2018 the population voted against becoming independent. The country is rich in mineral resources, especially nickel.

AREA 7,172 SQ MI [18,575 SQ KM] **POPULATION** 290,000 **CAPITAL** NOUMÉA

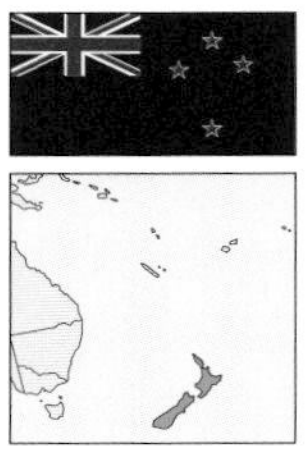

NEW ZEALAND

GEOGRAPHY New Zealand lies about 994 mi [1,600 km] southeast of Australia. It consists of two main islands and several other small ones. Much of North Island is volcanic. Active volcanoes include Ngauruhoe and Ruapehu. Hot springs and geysers are common, and steam from the ground is used to produce electricity. The Southern Alps, which contain the country's highest peak, Aoraki Mount Cook, at 12,217 ft [3,724 m], form the backbone of South Island. This island also has some large, fertile plains.

New Zealand lies on the geologically active "Pacific ring of fire." Most of the 14,000 earthquakes that occur every year have a magnitude of less than 5.0. But, in 2010 and 2011, two earthquakes, with magnitudes of 7.0 and 6.3 respectively, struck Christchurch on South Island, causing great damage. The 2011 earthquake resulted in a death toll of more than 180.

Auckland in the north has a warm, humid climate throughout the year. Wellington has cooler summers, while in Dunedin, in the southeast, temperatures sometimes dip below freezing in winter. The rainfall is heaviest on the western highlands.

POLITICS & ECONOMY Evidence suggests that early Maori settlers arrived in New Zealand more than 1,000 years ago. The Dutch navigator Abel Tasman reached New Zealand in 1642, but his discovery was not followed up. In 1769, the British Captain James Cook rediscovered the islands. During the early 19th century, British settlers arrived and, in 1840, under the Treaty of Waitangi, Britain took possession of the islands. From the 1870s, the Maoris were slowly integrated into colonial society.

In 1907, New Zealand became a self-governing dominion in the British Commonwealth. The country's economy developed quickly and the people became increasingly prosperous. However, after Britain joined the European Economic Community in 1973, New Zealand's exports to Britain shrank and the country had to reassess its economic and defense strategies and seek new markets. The world recession led the government to cut back on welfare spending in the 1990s. The preservation of Maori culture and rights are major issues as the Maoris, a Polynesian people, make up about 15% of the population. Other mainly Polynesian Pacific people make up another 7%. Ties with Britain have been reduced. In November 2008, the center-right National Party defeated the Labor Party in elections. John Key was Prime Minister from 2008–16, when he resigned and was replaced by the socially conservative Bill English. Elections in 2017 resulted in a coalition between Jacinda Adern's National Party, the Greens and New Zealand First. In 2019 the country was shocked by an anti-Islamic terrorist attack in Christchurch.

The economy once depended on agriculture, but manufacturing now employs twice as many people as farming. Meat and dairy products are leading commodities. Sheep rearing has declined as the area under cattle, deer, and vines has expanded. In 2008–9, New Zealand's economy entered a period of recession. The economy is now growing but is still fragile.

AREA 104,453 SQ MI [270,534 SQ KM] **POPULATION** 4,925,000
CAPITAL WELLINGTON **GOVERNMENT** CONSTITUTIONAL MONARCHY
ETHNIC GROUPS EUROPEAN 68%, MAORI 15%, ASIAN 9%, POLYNESIAN 7%
LANGUAGES ENGLISH AND MAORI (BOTH OFFICIAL)
RELIGIONS ANGLICAN 24%, PRESBYTERIAN 18%, ROMAN CATHOLIC 15%, OTHERS **CURRENCY** NEW ZEALAND DOLLAR = 100 CENTS

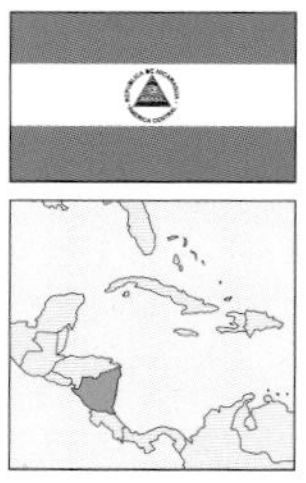

NICARAGUA

GEOGRAPHY The Republic of Nicaragua is a large country in Central America. In the east is a broad plain bordering the Caribbean Sea. The plain is drained by rivers that flow from the Central Highlands. The fertile western Pacific region contains about 40 volcanoes, many of which are active, and earthquakes are common.

Nicaragua has a tropical climate. Managua is hot throughout the year and there is a marked rainy season from May to October. In October 1998, Hurricane Mitch caused great devastation in Nicaragua. The Central Highlands and Caribbean region are cooler and wetter. The wettest region is the humid Caribbean plain.

POLITICS & ECONOMY In 1502, Christopher Columbus claimed the area for Spain, which ruled Nicaragua until 1821. By the early 20th century, the United States had considerable influence in the country and, in 1912, US forces entered Nicaragua. From 1927 to 1933, rebels under General Augusto César Sandino tried to drive US forces out of the country. In 1933, US marines set up a Nicaraguan army, the National Guard, to help to defeat the rebels. Its leader, Anastasio Somoza Garcia, had Sandino murdered in 1934, and from 1937 Somoza ruled as a dictator.

In the mid-1970s, many people began to protest against Somoza's rule and joined a guerrilla force, called the Sandinista National Liberation Front, named after General Sandino. The rebels defeated the Somoza regime in 1979. In the 1980s, US-supported forces, called the "Contras," launched a campaign against the Sandinista government. The US government opposed the Sandinista regime, under Daniel José Ortega Saavedra, claiming that it was a Communist dictatorship. A coalition, the National Opposition Union, defeated the Sandinistas in 1990. In 2001, the Sandinista candidate, Ortega, was defeated in presidential elections, but he was re-elected in 2006, 2011, and 2016. In 2018 he backed down from proposed reforms to the social security system after widespread and violent protests.

In the early 1990s, Nicaragua faced many problems in rebuilding its shattered economy. Agriculture employs about 28% of the people with coffee, cotton, sugar and bananas being grown for export, while rice is the main food crop. Attempts are being made to develop the tourist industry.

AREA 50,193 sq mi [130,000 sq km] **POPULATION** 6,203,000
CAPITAL Managua **GOVERNMENT** Multiparty republic
ETHNIC GROUPS Mestizo 69%, White 17%, Black 9%, Amerindian 5%
LANGUAGES Spanish (official)
RELIGIONS Roman Catholic 59%, Protestant 23%, others
CURRENCY Nicaraguan córdoba = 100 centavos

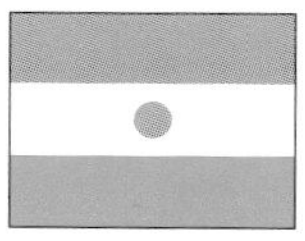

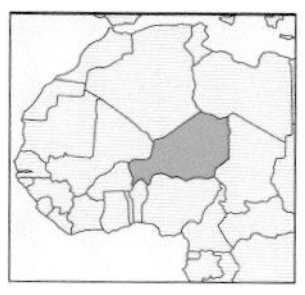

NIGER

GEOGRAPHY The Republic of Niger is a landlocked nation in north-central Africa. The northern plateaux lie in the desert area of the Sahara, while central Niger contains the rugged Aïr Mountains. The most fertile, densely populated region is the Niger valley.

Niger has a tropical climate and the south has a rainy season between June and September. The north is practically rainless.

POLITICS & ECONOMY Since independence in 1960, Niger, a French territory from 1900, has suffered severe droughts. Food shortages and the collapse of the traditional nomadic way of life of some of Niger's people have caused political instability. After a period of military rule, a multiparty constitution was adopted in 1992, but the military again seized power in 1996. Later that year, the coup leader, Colonel Ibrahim Barre Mainassara, was elected president. He was assassinated in 1999, but parliamentary rule was restored. After a coup in 2010, Mahamadou Issoufou was elected president in 2011. He gained a second term in a largely uncontested election in 2016. Islamist militants are an increasing problem.

Niger's chief resource is uranium and the country is one of the world's largest producers. The export of minerals accounts for 40% of total exports although there is much more to be exploited. Despite its considerable resources, Niger remains one of the world's poorest countries. Only 13% of the land can be used for crops but agriculture supports around 90% of the people.

AREA 489,189 sq mi [1,267,000 sq km] **POPULATION** 22,772,000
CAPITAL Niamey **GOVERNMENT** Multiparty republic
ETHNIC GROUPS Hausa 55%, Djerma 21%, Tuareg 9%, Fula 8%, others **LANGUAGES** French (official), Hausa, Djerma
RELIGIONS Islam 80%, indigenous beliefs, Christianity
CURRENCY CFA franc = 100 centimes

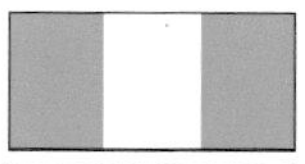

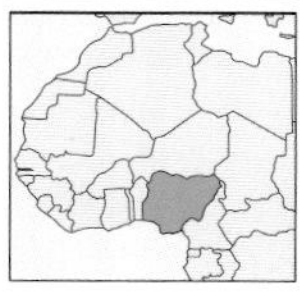

NIGERIA

GEOGRAPHY The Federal Republic of Nigeria is the most populous nation in Africa. The country's main rivers are the Niger and Benue, which meet in central Nigeria. North of the two river valleys are high plains and plateaux. The Lake Chad basin is in the north-east, with the Sokoto plains in the northwest. The south contains hilly uplands and plains, and has a hot, rainy climate. The north is drier and often hotter than the south.

POLITICS & ECONOMY Nigeria has a long artistic tradition. Major cultures include the Nok (500 BC to AD 200), the Ife, a major Yoruba culture which developed about 1,000 years ago, and the Benin (15th to 17th centuries). Britain gradually extended its influence over the area in the second half of the 19th century.

Nigeria became an independent nation in 1960 and a federal republic in 1963. A federal constitution dividing the country into regions was necessary because Nigeria contains more than 250 ethnic and linguistic groups, as well as several religious ones. Local rivalries have long been a threat to national unity, and six new states were created in 1996 in an attempt to overcome this. Civil war occurred between 1967 and 1970, when the people of the southeast attempted unsuccessfully to secede during the Biafran War. Between 1960 and 1998, Nigeria had only nine years of civilian government.

In 1998–99, civilian rule was restored but Nigeria faced many problems, including violence in the Niger delta region and religious conflict. From 2009 onward, northern Nigeria has been hit by violent attacks from the Islamist organization Boko Haram. 2015 saw the first ever democratic change of power in Nigeria when Muhammadu Buhari was elected president. He was re-elected in 2019.

Nigeria is a developing country with great potential although most of the population currently live in poverty. Its chief natural resource is oil, which accounts for most of its exports. Agriculture employs 70% of the people and the country is a major producer of cocoa, palm oil and palm kernels, groundnuts (peanuts), and rubber. Industry is increasing and manufactures include cement, chemicals, fertilizers, textiles, and timber.

AREA 356,667 sq mi [923,768 sq km] **POPULATION** 214,028,000
CAPITAL Abuja **GOVERNMENT** Federal multiparty republic
ETHNIC GROUPS Hausa and Fulani 29%, Yoruba 21%, Ibo (or Igbo) 18%, Ijaw 10%, Kanuri 4%, many others
LANGUAGES English (official), Hausa, Yoruba, Ibo
RELIGIONS Islam 50%, Christianity 40%, traditional beliefs 10%
CURRENCY Naira = 100 kobo

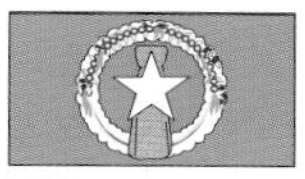

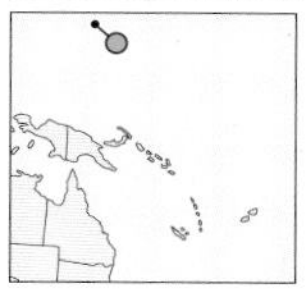

NORTHERN MARIANA ISLANDS

The Commonwealth of the Northern Mariana Islands contains 16 mountainous islands north of Guam in the western Pacific Ocean. In a 1975 plebiscite, the islanders voted for Commonwealth status in union with the United States, and in 1986 they were granted US citizenship.

AREA 179 sq mi [464 sq km] **POPULATION** 51,000 **CAPITAL** Saipan

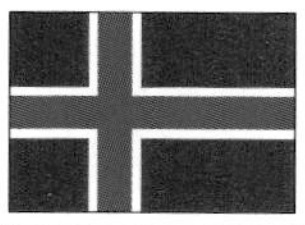

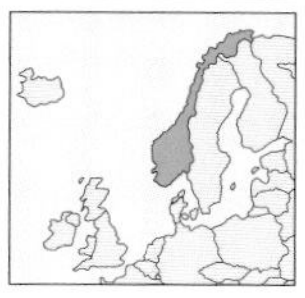

NORWAY

GEOGRAPHY The Kingdom of Norway forms the western part of the rugged Scandinavian peninsula. The deep inlets along the highly indented coastline were gouged out by glaciers during the Ice Age. The warm North Atlantic Drift off the coast of Norway moderates the climate, with mild winters and cool summers. Nearly all the ports are ice-free throughout the year. Inland, winters are colder and snow cover lasts for at least three months a year.

POLITICS & ECONOMY Norway was united with Denmark for over 400 years from the 14th century until 1814 when Denmark handed Norway over to Sweden. Denmark retained control of Norway's colonies – Greenland, Iceland and the Færoe Islands. The union with Sweden ended in 1903 and Norway became independent. Although Germany occupied Norway during World War II (1939–45), the country recovered quickly afterward and it now has one of the world's highest standards of living. In 1960, Norway and six other countries formed the European Free Trade Association (EFTA), but, in 1994, it voted against joining the European Union. Erna Solberg has been prime minister since 2013, heading a center-right coalition government. Harald V came to the throne in 1991.

Norway's chief resources and exports are offshore oil and natural gas, which are exploited via tightly regulated companies. To guard against the future decline of oil and gas production, a large sovereign wealth fund has been built up. Farmland covers only 3% of the land. Dairy farming, meat production, and fishing are important, but Norway has to import food. Norway has many industries powered by cheap hydroelectricity.

AREA 125,049 sq mi [323,877 sq km] **POPULATION** 5,467,000
CAPITAL Oslo **GOVERNMENT** Constitutional monarchy
ETHNIC GROUPS Norwegian 94% **LANGUAGES** Norwegian (official)
RELIGIONS Evangelical Lutheran 86%
CURRENCY Norwegian krone = 100 øre

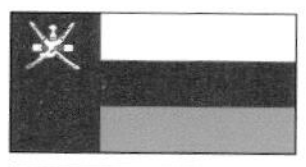

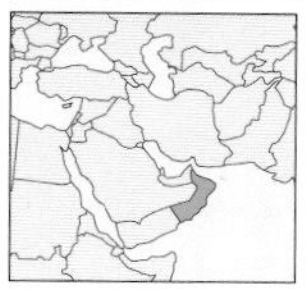

OMAN

GEOGRAPHY The Sultanate of Oman occupies the southeastern corner of the Arabian peninsula. It also includes the tip of the Musandam peninsula, overlooking the strategic Strait of Hormuz. Oman has a hot tropical climate. In Muscat, temperatures may reach 117°F [47°C] in the summer months.

POLITICS & ECONOMY Although strongly influenced by Britain since the end of the 18th century, Oman never became a colony. From 1970 when Qaboos ibn Said, the absolute ruler, overthrew his father in a bloodless coup, Oman followed a path of modernization. In 2000, Oman held elections to its consultative parliament and, in 2004, the Sultan appointed Oman's first woman minister. Anti-government demonstrations in 2011 led to the promise of more reforms. In 2020 Haitham bin Tariq Al Said succeeded to the throne on the death of Qaboos.

Oil and natural gas make up about 80% of Oman's exports; reserves are declining, and Oman is actively seeking to diversify its economy. Agriculture and fishing remain important. Crops include alfalfa, bananas, coconuts, dates, limes, tobacco, vegetables, and wheat, but Oman still has to import food. The tourist industry has grown rapidly in recent years.

AREA 119,498 sq mi [309,500 sq km] **POPULATION** 4,665,000
CAPITAL Muscat **GOVERNMENT** Monarchy with consultative council
ETHNIC GROUPS Arab, Baluchi, Indian, Pakistani
LANGUAGES Arabic (official), Baluchi, English **RELIGIONS** Islam (mainly Ibadhi), Christian 5%, Hinduism 5% **CURRENCY** Omani rial = 1,000 baisa

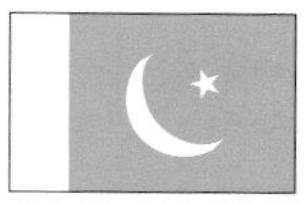

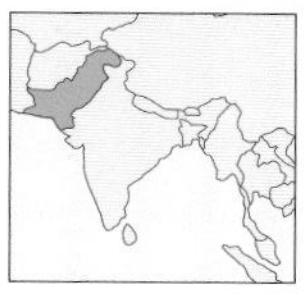

PAKISTAN

GEOGRAPHY The Islamic Republic of Pakistan contains high mountains, fertile plains, and rocky deserts. The Karakoram range, which contains K2, the world's second highest peak, lies in the northern part of Jammu and Kashmir, which is occupied by Pakistan but claimed by India. Other mountains rise in the west. Plains, drained by the River Indus and its tributaries, occupy much of eastern Pakistan. Arid areas include the Thar Desert and the Baluchistan plateau. Most of Pakistan has hot summers and mild winters, though the mountains are cold in winter. The rainfall is generally sparse.

POLITICS & ECONOMY Pakistan was the site of the Indus Valley civilization which developed about 4,500 years ago. However, Pakistan's modern history dates from 1947, when British India was divided into India and Pakistan. Muslim Pakistan was divided into two parts: East and West Pakistan, but East Pakistan broke away in 1971 to become Bangladesh. In 1948–49, 1965, and 1971, Pakistan and India clashed over Kashmir. In 1998, Pakistan responded in kind to India's nuclear weapons tests, but, in 2003–7, Pakistan and India launched a series of initiatives aimed at achieving peace.

Pakistan has been subject to alternating periods of military and civilian rule: the latter often characterized by inefficiency and corruption. The country's leaders have experienced turbulent times: Benazir Bhutto (daughter of the hanged prime minister, Zulfiqar Ali Bhutto) was twice dismissed as prime minister on charges of corruption in 1990 and 1996, and subsequently assassinated during an election campaign in 2007. Nawaz Sharif, prime minister from 2013 to 2017, resigned after corruption charges, and in 2018 former international cricketer Imran Khan became prime minister.

Both government and military struggle to control the Afghan border region where Taliban-linked extremists are active. Terrorist activity emanating from this region has hit targets elsewhere in the country. The Christian minority has also been targeted.

Lack of political stability has hindered economic development and discouraged foreign investment. The economy is agrarian, employing nearly half the population. Textiles are the main export and remittances from overseas workers are crucial.

AREA 307,372 sq mi [796,095 sq km] **POPULATION** 233,501,000
CAPITAL Islamabad **GOVERNMENT** Federal republic
ETHNIC GROUPS Punjabi, Sindhi, Pashtun (Pathan), Baluchi, Muhajir
LANGUAGES English and Urdu (both official), many others
RELIGIONS Islam 97%, Christianity, Hinduism
CURRENCY Pakistani rupee = 100 paisa

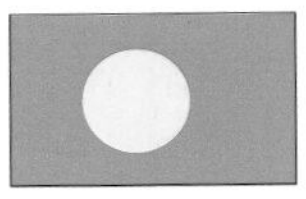
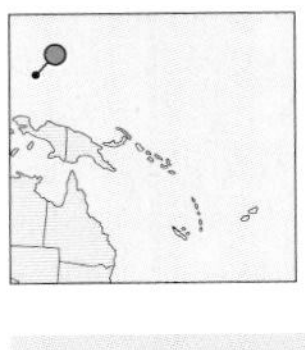

PALAU

The Republic of Palau became independent in 1994, after 47 years as a US-administered UN Trust Territory. The economy relies heavily on aid from the USA and Taiwan, tourism, fishing, and subsistence agriculture. The main crops include cassava, coconuts, and copra. Palau's low-lying islands are vulnerable to rising sea levels.

AREA 177 sq mi [459 sq km] **POPULATION** 22,000 **CAPITAL** Ngerulmud

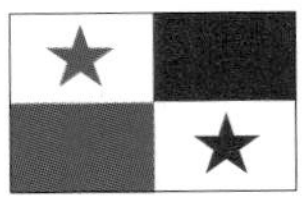
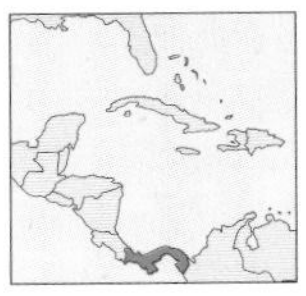

PANAMA

GEOGRAPHY The Republic of Panama forms an isthmus linking Central America to South America. The Panama Canal, which is 50.7 mi [81.6 km] long, cuts across the isthmus. It has made the country a major transport hub.

Panama has a tropical climate. Temperatures are high, though the mountains are much cooler than the coastal plains. The main rainy season is between May and December.

POLITICS & ECONOMY Christopher Columbus landed in Panama in 1502 and Spain soon took the area. In 1821, Panama became independent from Spain and a province of Colombia.

In 1903, Colombia refused a request by the United States to build a canal. Panama revolted against Colombian rule, and became an independent state. The United States then began to build the canal, which was opened in 1914. The United States administered the Panama Canal Zone, a strip of land along the canal. But many Panamanians resented US influence and, in 1979, the Canal Zone was returned to Panama. Control of the canal itself was handed over by the USA to Panama on December 31, 1999.

Panama's government has changed many times since independence, and there have been periods of military dictatorships, including that of General Manuel Antonio Noriega in the 1980s. He was finally convicted of drug offences in the United States in 1992. In 2019 Laurentino Cortizo was elected president, promising to work to reduce corruption and inequality. The Panama Canal is an important source of revenue and, since 2016, new locks and channels have increased capacity and the size of ships that can be accommodated. The other main activity is agriculture, which employs 17% of the work force. The service industry accounts for nearly 80% of GDP. In 2011, the US Congress approved a long-stalled free-trade agreement with Panama.

AREA 29,157 sq mi [75,517 sq km] **POPULATION** 3,894,000
CAPITAL Panamá City **GOVERNMENT** Multiparty republic
ETHNIC GROUPS Mestizo 70%, Black and Mixed 14%, White 10%, Amerindian 6% **LANGUAGES** Spanish (official), English
RELIGIONS Roman Catholic 85%, Protestant 15%
CURRENCY US dollar; Balboa = 100 centésimos

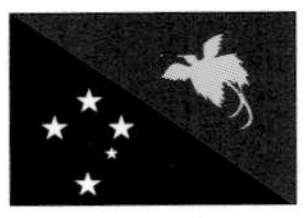
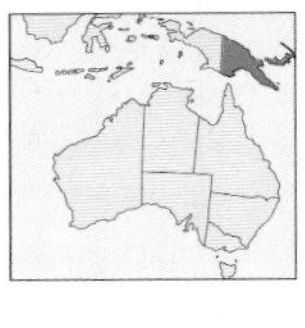

PAPUA NEW GUINEA

GEOGRAPHY Papua New Guinea is an independent country in the Pacific Ocean, north of Australia. Papua New Guinea includes the eastern part of New Guinea, the Bismarck Archipelago, the northern Solomon Islands, the D'Entrecasteaux Islands, and the Louisiade Archipelago. The land is largely mountainous.

Papua New Guinea has a tropical climate, with high temperatures. Most of the rain occurs during the monsoon season (December–April). In the dry season, winds blow from the southeast.

POLITICS & ECONOMY The Dutch colonized western New Guinea (now part of Indonesia) in 1828, but it was not until 1884 that Germany appropriated northeastern New Guinea and Britain took the southeast. In 1906, Britain handed the southeast over to Australia when it became known as the Territory of Papua. When World War I broke out in 1914, Australia took German New Guinea, and in 1921 the League of Nations gave Australia a mandate to rule the area, which was named the Territory of New Guinea. In 1949, Papua and New Guinea were combined as one entity, becoming fully independent in 1975.

In the 1990s there was a secessionist revolt on the island of Bougainville, at the eastern end of the territory. A peace agreement in 2001 granted a degree of autonomy and in a non-binding referendum in 2019, the island voted in favor of independence.

There was political turmoil in 2011–12, when Prime Minister Michael Somare was replaced by Peter O'Neill, who was formally elected prime minister in August 2012. In 2019 O'Neill resigned amid accusations of corruption and was replaced by James Marape.

Agriculture employs 85% of the people, mostly at subsistence level. Mining is important with copper a major export. There are large reserves of natural gas and the development of production facilities to convert this to liquefied form for export could have a profound effect on the economy.

AREA 178,703 sq mi [462,840 sq km] **POPULATION** 7,259,000
CAPITAL Port Moresby **GOVERNMENT** Constitutional monarchy
ETHNIC GROUPS Papuan, Melanesian, Micronesian
LANGUAGES English, Tok Pisin, Hiri Motu (all official); more than 800 indigenous languages **RELIGIONS** Traditional beliefs 34%, Roman Catholic 22%, Lutheran 16% **CURRENCY** Kina = 100 toea

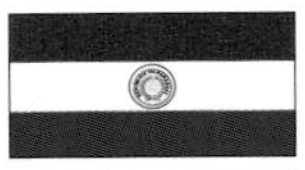
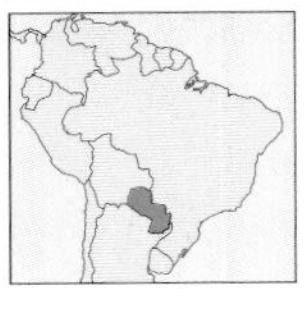

PARAGUAY

GEOGRAPHY The Republic of Paraguay is a landlocked country, and rivers, notably the Paraná, Pilcomayo (Brazo Sur), and Paraguay, form most of its borders. The flat region of the Gran Chaco lies in the northwest, while the southeast contains plains, hills and plateaux. Northern Paraguay lies in the tropics, while the south is subtropical. Most of the country has a warm, humid climate.

POLITICS & ECONOMY Paraguayans achieved independence in 1811 after being part of a wider Spanish colonial possession since 1776. For many years, Paraguay was torn by internal strife and conflict with its neighbors. A war against Brazil, Argentina, and Uruguay (1865–70) led to the deaths of more than half of Paraguay's population, and a great loss of territory.

General Alfredo Stroessner took power in 1954 and ruled as a dictator until he was overthrown in 1989 (he died in exile in Brazil in 2006). The return of democracy in the years that followed often seemed precarious, because of rivalries between politicians and army leaders, together with economic problems arising partly from the financial crises experienced in neighboring Argentina and Brazil in 1999. In 2008, a former Roman Catholic bishop, Fernando Lugo, who was regarded as a champion of the poor, was elected president, ending more than six decades of rule by the Colorado Party. They returned to power, however, in the 2013 presidential election, which was won by Horacio Cartes, and in 2018, with the election of Mario Abdo Benítez.

Agriculture and forestry, employing about a fifth of the population, are important, and Paraguay is major exporter of soybeans. It produces hydroelectricity and exports power to its neighbors although it has few other natural resources. Paraguay remains a conduit for smuggling drugs.

AREA 157,047 sq mi [406,752 sq km] **POPULATION** 7,192,000
CAPITAL Asunción **GOVERNMENT** Multiparty republic
ETHNIC GROUPS Mestizo 95% **LANGUAGES** Spanish and Guaraní (both official) **RELIGIONS** Roman Catholic 90%, Protestant 6%
CURRENCY Guaraní = 100 céntimos

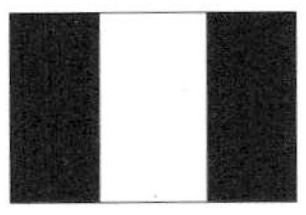
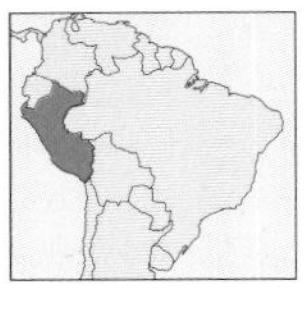

PERU

GEOGRAPHY The Republic of Peru lies in the tropics in western South America. A narrow coastal plain borders the Pacific Ocean in the west. Inland are ranges of the Andes Mountains, which rise to 22,205 ft [6,768 m] at Nevado Huascarán, an extinct volcano. East of the Andes lies the Amazon basin.

Lima, on the coastal plain, has an arid climate. The coastal region is chilled by the cold, offshore Humboldt Current. Rainfall increases inland and many mountains in the high Andes are snow-capped.

POLITICS & ECONOMY Spanish conquistadores conquered the Inca empire in Peru in the 1530s. In 1820, an Argentinian, José de San Martín, led an army into Peru and declared it independent although Spain still held large areas. In 1823, the Venezuelan Simon Bolívar led another army into Peru which resulted in surrender by the Spanish in 1826. Peru suffered much instability throughout the 19th century.

Political turmoil continued in the 20th century. In 1980, when civilian rule was restored, a left-wing group called the Sendero Luminoso, or the "Shining Path," instigated guerrilla warfare against the government. From 1990 to 2000 Alberto Fujimori was president. His increasingly authoritarian rule saw, in 1992, the suspension of the constitution and dismissal of the legislature. Fujimori left Peru in 2000, but was later extradited, and in 2009 he was found guilty of ordering killings and kidnappings and was sentenced to 25 years in jail. President Padro Pablo Kuczynski resigned over allegations of corruption in 2018 and was replaced by Vice-President Martin Vizcarra.

Peru's economy benefits from a wide range of mineral resources, with copper, lead, and silver among the most valuable exports, but the environmental effect of mining is concerning. Fish products are exported. Although recent economic growth has been strong, lack of basic infrastructure prevents the spread of prosperity inland.

AREA 496,222 sq mi [1,285,216 sq km] **POPULATION** 31,915,000
CAPITAL Lima **GOVERNMENT** Constitutional republic
ETHNIC GROUPS Amerindian 45%, Mestizo 37%, White 15%
LANGUAGES Spanish and Quechua (both official), Aymara, other Amazonian languages **RELIGIONS** Roman Catholic 81%
CURRENCY Nuevo sol = 100 céntimos

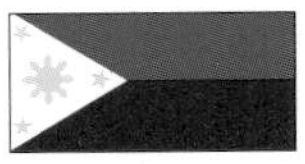
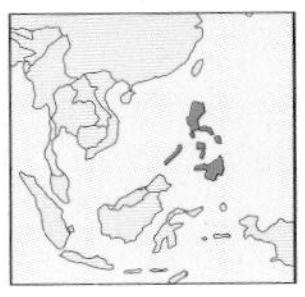

PHILIPPINES

GEOGRAPHY The Republic of the Philippines is an island nation in southeastern Asia. It includes about 7,100 islands, of which 2,770 are named and about 1,000 are inhabited. Luzon and Mindanao, the two largest islands, make up more than two-thirds of the country. The land is mainly mountainous.

The country has a hot tropical climate. The dry season runs from December to April. The rest of the year is wet. Much of the rainfall comes from the typhoons which periodically strike the east coast with devastating effect. In November 2013, Typhoon Haiyan, one of the strongest typhoons ever recorded, resulted in the deaths of over 6,000 people.

POLITICS & ECONOMY The first European to reach the Philippines was the Portuguese navigator Ferdinand Magellan in 1521. Spanish explorers claimed the region in 1565 when they established a settlement on Cebu. The Spaniards ruled the country until 1898, when the United States took over at the end of the Spanish–American War. Japan invaded the Philippines in 1941, but US forces returned in 1944. The country became fully independent as the Republic of the Philippines in 1946.

Since independence, the country's problems have included armed uprisings by left-wing guerrillas, Muslim separatist groups, crime, corruption, and unemployment. An outline peace plan was agreed in 2012 between the government and the Muslim rebel Moro Islamic Liberation Front, but other rebel groups persist, and Islamic State militants are an increasing problem in the south.

The dominant political figure in recent times was Ferdinand Marcos, who ruled in a dictatorial manner from 1965 to 1986. His most recent successor, elected in 2016, is the populist Rodrigo Duterte, whose harsh crackdown on drug dealers and users is popular domestically but has led to international claims of human rights abuses.

The Philippines is a developing country and is recovering steadily from the 2008 global financial crisis. Agriculture employs roughly 25% of the population. The main foods are rice and maize, while bananas, cocoa, coffee, sugarcane, and tobacco are grown commercially. Shellfish and sea fishing are also important, while manufacturing plays an increasingly significant part in the economy. Remittances from overseas workers make a large contribution and attempts are being made to encourage foreign investment.

AREA 115,830 sq mi [300,000 sq km] **POPULATION** 109,181,000
CAPITAL Manila **GOVERNMENT** Multiparty republic
ETHNIC GROUPS Tagalog 28%, Cebuano 13%, Ilocano 9%, Bisaya 8%, and others **LANGUAGES** Filipino (Tagalog) and English (both official), and eight major dialects
RELIGIONS Roman Catholic 83%, Protestant 9%, Islam 5%
CURRENCY Philippine peso = 100 centavos

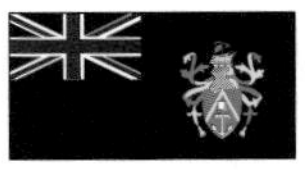
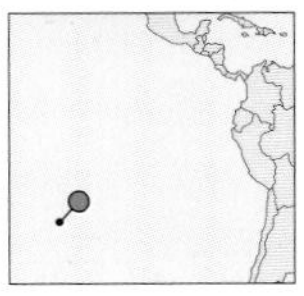

PITCAIRN

Pitcairn Island is a British overseas territory in the Pacific Ocean. Its inhabitants are descendants of the original settlers – nine mutineers from HMS Bounty and 18 Tahitians who arrived in 1790.

AREA 21 sq mi [55 sq km]
POPULATION 50 **CAPITAL** Adamstown

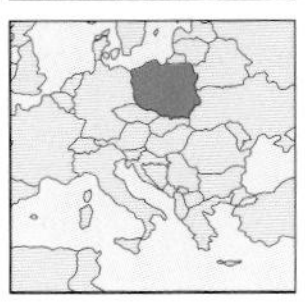

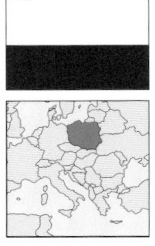

POLAND

GEOGRAPHY The Republic of Poland faces the Baltic Sea and behind its lagoon-fringed coast lies a broad plain. A plateau lies in the southeast, while the Sudeten Highlands straddle part of the border with Czechia. Part of the Carpathian Range (the Tatra) lies in the southeast.

Poland's climate is influenced by its position in Europe. Warm, moist air masses come from

the west, while cold air masses come from the north and east. Summers are warm, but winters are cold and snowy.

POLITICS & ECONOMY Poland's boundaries have changed several times in the last 200 years, partly as a result of its geographical location between the powers of Germany and Russia. It disappeared from the map in the late 18th century, when the Polish state of the Grand Duchy of Warsaw was established. But in 1815, the country was partitioned between Austria, Prussia, and Russia. Poland became independent in 1918, but in 1939 it was divided between Germany and the Soviet Union. The country again became independent in 1945, when it lost land to Russia but gained some from Germany. Communists took power in 1948, but opposition mounted and eventually became focused through an organization called Solidarity.

A coalition government was formed between Solidarity and the Communists in 1989. In 1990, the Communist Party was dissolved and Lech Walesa, a trade unionist, became president. Facing many problems in developing a market economy, he was defeated in presidential elections in 1995. Poland joined NATO in 1999 and the European Union in 2004. In 2017 Mateusz Morawiecki of the conservative Law and Justice Party became prime minister. There were demonstrations by people fearing that new laws would curb democracy.

Poland's economy has grown strongly since the fall of Communism and especially since accession to the EU. It has large reserves of coal. Manufactures include chemicals, food, machinery, ships, steel, and textiles. Farming, although important, lacks investment and needs modernization.

AREA 124,807 SQ MI [323,250 SQ KM] **POPULATION** 38,282,000
CAPITAL WARSAW **GOVERNMENT** MULTIPARTY REPUBLIC
ETHNIC GROUPS POLISH 97%, GERMAN, BELARUSIAN, UKRAINIAN
LANGUAGES POLISH (OFFICIAL) **RELIGIONS** ROMAN CATHOLIC 90%, EASTERN ORTHODOX **CURRENCY** ZLOTY = 100 GROSZY

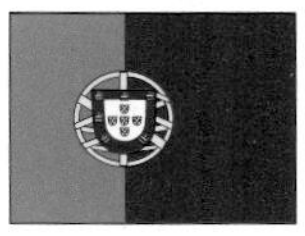
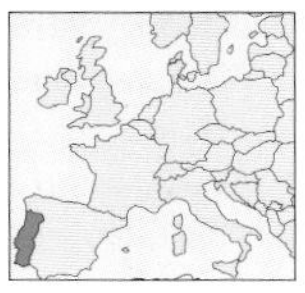

PORTUGAL

GEOGRAPHY The Republic of Portugal is the most westerly of Europe's mainland countries. The land rises from the coastal plains on the Atlantic Ocean to the western edge of the huge plateau, or Meseta, which occupies most of the Iberian peninsula. The climate is moderated by winds blowing from the Atlantic. Summers are cooler and winters are milder than in other Mediterranean lands. Portugal also contains two autonomous regions: the Azores and Madeira island groups.

POLITICS & ECONOMY Portugal became a separate country, independent of Spain, in 1143. In the 15th century, Portugal led the "Age of European Exploration" resulting in the growth of a large Portuguese empire. Portuguese power began to decline in the 16th century and, between 1580 and 1640, Portugal was ruled by Spain. In 1910 Portugal became a republic. Instability hampered progress and army officers seized power in 1926. In 1928, they chose Antonio de Salazar to be minister of finance.

Salazar became prime minister in 1932 and ruled as a dictator from 1933 until 1968. In 1974, army officers mounted a coup which led to free elections in 1978. Portugal joined the European Community (now the European Union) in 1986, and in 2002 joined the eurozone. In 2011–12, there was public unrest when the government introduced austerity measures in order to obtain an international financial bailout to help its weak economy. In 2014 Portugal was able to exit the international bailout, and from 2015 the center-left government has relaxed some of the measures.

Agriculture and fishing were the economic mainstays until the mid-20th century, when the economy started to diversify. Services and manufacturing are now the most valuable activities. Lagging behind the economies of other Western European countries, Portugal faces increasing competition from central Europe and Asia.

AREA 34,285 SQ MI [88,797 SQ KM] **POPULATION** 10,303,000
CAPITAL LISBON **GOVERNMENT** MULTIPARTY REPUBLIC
ETHNIC GROUPS PORTUGUESE 99% **LANGUAGES** PORTUGUESE (OFFICIAL)
RELIGIONS ROMAN CATHOLIC 85%, PROTESTANT
CURRENCY EURO = 100 CENTS

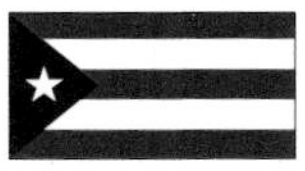
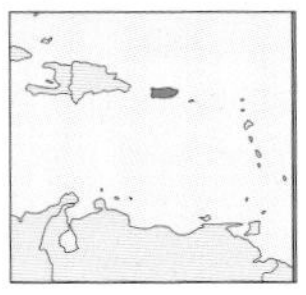

PUERTO RICO

The Commonwealth of Puerto Rico, a mainly mountainous island, is the easternmost of the Greater Antilles chain. The climate is hot and wet. Puerto Rico is a dependent territory of the United States and the people are US citizens. 2017's non-binding referendum resulted in a vote to become a US state, but the turnout was only 23%. Puerto Rico is the most industrialized country in the Caribbean. Tax exemptions attract US companies to the island and manufacturing is expanding. The chief exports are chemicals, machinery, and food.

AREA 3,427 SQ MI [8,875 SQ KM]
POPULATION 3,189,000 **CAPITAL** SAN JUAN

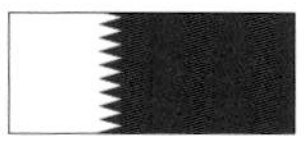
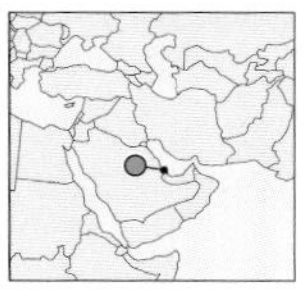

QATAR

The prosperous State of Qatar occupies a low, barren peninsula on the Persian Gulf. A British protectorate from 1916, Qatar became independent in 1971. Oil is the mainstay of the economy. In 2017 Saudi Arabia, the UAE, Egypt, and Bahrain implemented a blockade on Qatar over its alleged connections to radical Islamist groups. In 2019 Qatar withdrew from OPEC.

AREA 4,247 SQ MI [11,000 SQ KM] **POPULATION** 2,444,000 **CAPITAL** DOHA

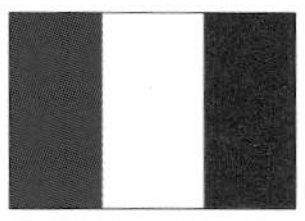
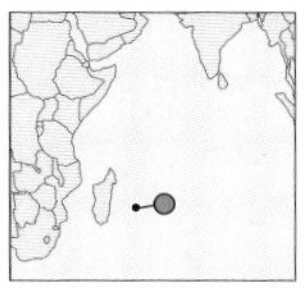

RÉUNION

Réunion is a French overseas department in the Indian Ocean. The land is mainly mountainous, though the lowlands are intensely cultivated. Sugar and sugar products are the main exports, but French aid, given to the island in return for its use as a military base, is important to the economy.

AREA 969 SQ MI [2,510 SQ KM]
POPULATION 846,000 **CAPITAL** ST-DENIS

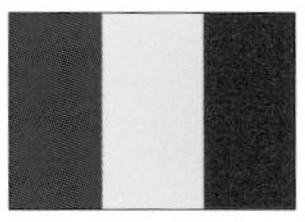
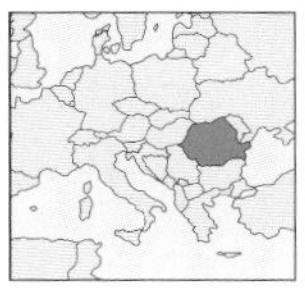

ROMANIA

GEOGRAPHY Romania is a country on the Black Sea in Eastern Europe. Eastern and southern Romania form part of the Danube river basin. The delta region, near the mouth of the Danube, where the river flows into the Black Sea, is one of Europe's finest wetlands. The southern part of the coast contains several resorts. At the heart of the country is the region of Transylvania, ringed in the east, south, and west by scenic mountains which are part of the Carpathian mountain system. Romania has hot summers and cold winters. Rainfall is heaviest in spring and early summer.

POLITICS & ECONOMY The entity that eventually coalesced into modern Romania was born out of the breakup of the Turkish empire in the late 18th century. In 1862 the regions of Wallachia and Moldavia were united under the new heading of Romania. After World War I (1914–18), Romania, which had fought on the side of the Allies, gained territory, including Transylvania, where most people were Romanians. This almost doubled the country's size and population. In 1939, Romania lost territory to Hungary, Bulgaria, and the Soviet Union. Occupied by Soviet troops in 1944, Romania regained northern Transylvania from Hungary in 1945. In 1947, Romania officially became a Communist country. It was ruled for decades by the dictator Ceausescu.

In 1990, Romania held its first free elections since the end of World War II. Initially the government was dominated by former Communists, led by Ion Iliescu, but there was a move toward the center-right at the elections in 1996. Iliescu again served as president from 2000 until 2004. Romania joined NATO in 2004 and the European Union in 2007. Klaus Iohannis of the center-right became president in December 2014.

Romania has an "upper-middle-income" economy but growth has been hindered by political instability, lack of reform, corruption, and the international financial crisis of 2008. Following the global downturn, the government was forced to implement austerity measures which led to civil unrest. Exports are increasing and include cars, industrial machinery, metals, textiles, and chemicals. Trade is mainly with other EU states especially Germany and Italy.

AREA 92,043 SQ MI [238,391 SQ KM] **POPULATION** 21,303,000
CAPITAL BUCHAREST **GOVERNMENT** MULTIPARTY REPUBLIC
ETHNIC GROUPS ROMANIAN 89%, HUNGARIAN 7%, ROMA 2%, UKRAINIAN **LANGUAGES** ROMANIAN (OFFICIAL), HUNGARIAN, ROMANY **RELIGIONS** EASTERN ORTHODOX 87%, PROTESTANT 7%, ROMAN CATHOLIC 5% **CURRENCY** LEU = 100 BANI

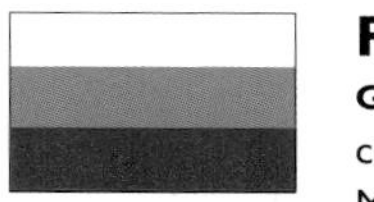
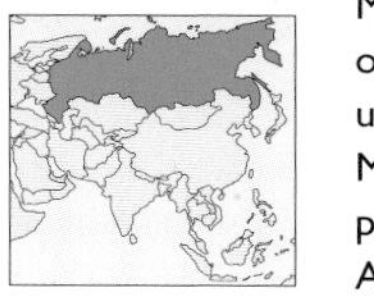

RUSSIA

GEOGRAPHY Russia is the world's largest country. About 25% lies west of the Ural Mountains in European Russia, where 80% of the population lives. It is mostly flat or undulating, but the land rises to the Caucasus Mountains in the south, where Russia's highest peak, Elbrus, at 18,510 ft [5,642 m], is found. Asian Russia, or Siberia, contains vast plains and plateaux, with mountains in the east and south. The Kamchatka peninsula in the far east has many active volcanoes. Russia contains several of the world's longest rivers. It also includes part of the world's largest inland body of water, the Caspian Sea, and Lake Baikal, the world's deepest lake.

Moscow has a continental climate, with cold, snowy winters and hot summers. Siberia has a harsher, drier climate.

POLITICS & ECONOMY In the 9th century AD, a state called Kievan Rus was founded by people known as the East Slavs. Kiev, now capital of Ukraine, became a major trading center, but, in 1237, Mongol armies conquered Russia and destroyed Kiev. Russia was part of the Mongol empire until the late 15th century with Moscow becoming the most important Russian city.

In the 16th century, Moscow's grand prince was retitled "tsar," and the first one, Ivan the Terrible, expanded the Russian territory. In 1613, Michael Romanov became tsar, founding a dynasty which ruled until 1917. In the 18th century, Tsar Peter the Great began to westernize Russia and, by 1812, when Napoleon failed to conquer the country, Russia was a major European power. However, in the 19th century demands for reform were growing.

In World War I (1914–18), the Russian people suffered great hardships and, in 1917, Tsar Nicholas II was forced to abdicate. In November 1917, the Bolsheviks seized power under Vladimir Lenin and set up the Union of Soviet Socialist Republics (also called the USSR or the Soviet Union).

From 1924, Joseph Stalin introduced a socialist economic program, suppressing all opposition. In 1939, the Soviet Union and Germany signed a non-aggression pact, but Germany invaded the Soviet Union in 1941. Soviet forces pushed the Germans back, occupying Eastern Europe. They reached Berlin in May 1945. From the late 1940s, tension between the Soviet Union and its allies and Western nations developed into a "Cold War." This continued until 1991, when the Soviet Union was dissolved.

The Soviet Union collapsed due to the failure of its economic policies. From 1991, Boris Yeltsin, as president of the newly independent Russia, introduced democratic and economic reforms. Yeltsin retired in 1999 and, in 2000, was succeeded by Vladimir Putin. Putin, who was re-elected in 2004, sought to develop contacts with the West. Russia's size and diversity make national unity hard to achieve with secessionist movements instigating violent, sometimes fatal, incidents in Chechenia, Dagestan, Ingushetia, and Kabardino-Balkaria. From 2006, relations with the West appeared to deteriorate, with Russia criticizing the expansion of NATO in Eastern Europe.

In 2008, Putin was replaced by Dmitry Medvedev, but was re-elected in 2012 and 2018. In August 2008, Russia fought a short war against Georgia, which had attacked the secessionist region of South Ossetia. In early 2014, political unrest in Ukraine allowed pro-Russian forces to bring Crimea under Russian control. Further tensions with the West have arisen over Russia's support for the regime of Syria's President Assad, accusations that Russia interfered in the 2016 US presidential election, and Putin's increasingly tight control over political opposition and the media.

Russia's economy was thrown into disarray after the collapse of the Soviet Union, but is now classified as an "upper-middle-income" economy. It is underpinned by a wealth of natural resources: in particular, natural gas and coal. Gazprom, the state-run gas corporation, is a major supplier to Europe. Reliance on exporting such commodities makes the economy vulnerable to fluctuations in global prices. Future prosperity needs economic reform and investment in infrastructure.

Russia is a major producer of farm products. Crops include barley, flax, fruits, oats, rye, potatoes, sugar beet, sunflower seeds, vegetables, and wheat.

AREA 6,592,812 SQ MI [17,075,400 SQ KM] **POPULATION** 141,722,000
CAPITAL MOSCOW **GOVERNMENT** FEDERAL MULTIPARTY REPUBLIC
ETHNIC GROUPS RUSSIAN 80%, TATAR 4%, UKRAINIAN 2%, CHUVASH 1%, MORE THAN 100 OTHERS
LANGUAGES RUSSIAN (OFFICIAL), MANY OTHERS
RELIGIONS MAINLY RUSSIAN ORTHODOX, ISLAM, JUDAISM
CURRENCY RUSSIAN RUBLE = 100 KOPEKS

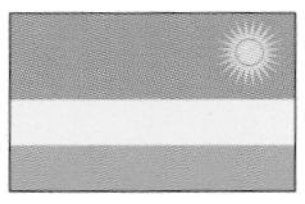

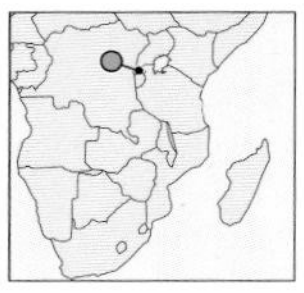

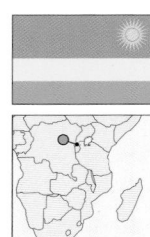

RWANDA

GEOGRAPHY The Republic of Rwanda is a small, landlocked country in east-central Africa. Lake Kivu and the River Ruzizi in the Great African Rift Valley form the country's western border.

Kigali stands on the central plateau of Rwanda. Here, temperatures are moderated by the altitude. Rainfall is abundant, but much heavier rain falls on the western uplands, while the Rift Valley floor is drier and warmer than the rest of Rwanda.

POLITICS & ECONOMY Germany conquered the area, called Ruanda-Urundi, in the 1890s. However, Belgium occupied the region during World War I (1914–18) and ruled it until 1961 when it became independent as a republic. This decision followed a rebellion by the majority Hutu people against the Tutsi monarchy which resulted in about 150,000 deaths. Many Tutsis fled to Uganda, where they formed a rebel army. Relations between Hutus and Tutsis deteriorated and, in 1994, between 500,000 and 800,000 people were massacred in Rwanda. After the Tutsis had restored order, Hutu rebels fled into the Democratic Republic of the Congo. In 2009, Rwanda became the 54th member of the Commonwealth. Paul Kagame has been president since 2000.

According to the World Bank, Rwanda is a "low-income" developing country with economic growth driven by exporting tea and coffee. Most people are poor farmers. Food crops include bananas, beans, cassava, and sorghum. Some cattle are raised.

AREA 10,169 sq mi [26,338 sq km] **POPULATION** 12,712,000
CAPITAL Kigali **GOVERNMENT** Republic
ETHNIC GROUPS Hutu 84%, Tutsi 15%, Twa 1%
LANGUAGES French, English and Kinyarwanda (all official)
RELIGIONS Roman Catholic 57%, Protestant 26%, Adventist 11%, Islam 5% **CURRENCY** Rwandan franc = 100 centimes

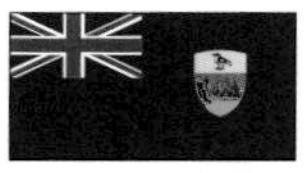

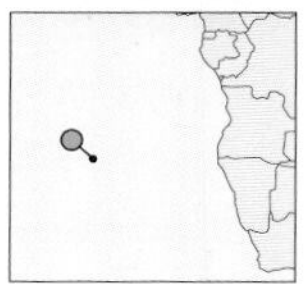

ST HELENA

St Helena, which became a British colony in 1834, is an isolated volcanic island in the South Atlantic Ocean. Now a British overseas territory, it is also the administrative center of Ascension and Tristan da Cunha.

AREA 47 sq mi [122 sq km]
POPULATION 5,000 **CAPITAL** Jamestown

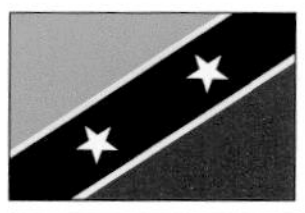

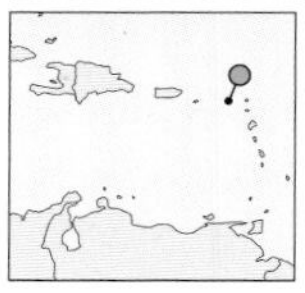

ST KITTS AND NEVIS

The Federation of St Kitts and Nevis comprises two well-watered volcanic islands, whose highest mountain rises to 3,793 ft [1,156 m]. The islands were the first in the Caribbean to be colonized by Britain (in 1623 and 1628), and they became an independent country in 1983. In 1998, a vote for the secession of Nevis fell short of the two-thirds majority required. Tourism, offshore finance, and service industries have replaced sugar as the principal earner.

AREA 101 sq mi [261 sq km]
POPULATION 54,000 **CAPITAL** Basseterre

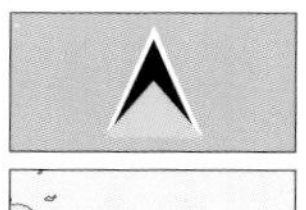

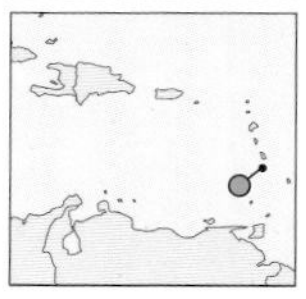

ST LUCIA

St Lucia, which became independent from Britain in 1979, is a mountainous, forested island of extinct volcanoes. It exports bananas and coconuts, and now attracts many tourists.

AREA 208 sq mi [539 sq km]
POPULATION 166,000 **CAPITAL** Castries

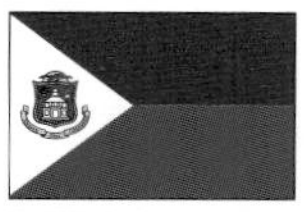

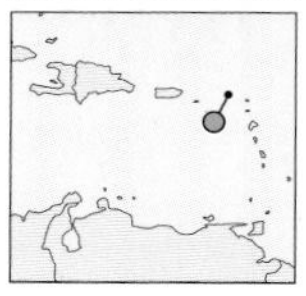

ST MAARTEN

Part of the Netherlands Antilles until 2010, the southern part of the island of St Maarten is a self-governing territory within the Kingdom of the Netherlands. In 2017, Hurricane Irma caused extensive damage.

AREA 13 sq mi [34 sq km]
POPULATION 44,000 **CAPITAL** Philipsburg

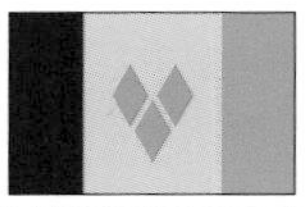

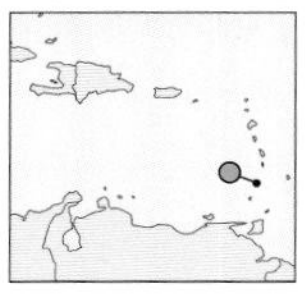

ST VINCENT AND THE GRENADINES

St Vincent and the Grenadines achieved its independence from Britain in 1979. Tourism is growing, but the territory is less prosperous than its neighbors. Its main export is bananas.

AREA 150 sq mi [388 sq km]
POPULATION 101,000 **CAPITAL** Kingstown

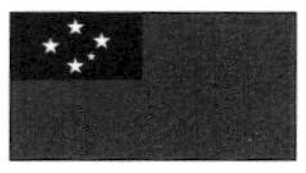

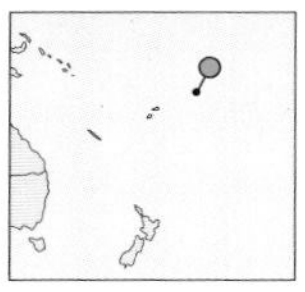

SAMOA

The Independent State of Samoa (formerly Western Samoa) comprises two islands in the south Pacific Ocean. Governed by New Zealand from 1920, the territory became independent in 1962. Exports include coconut cream and beer.

AREA 1,093 sq mi [2,831 sq km]
POPULATION 204,000 **CAPITAL** Apia

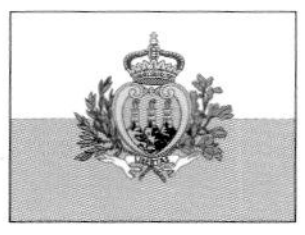

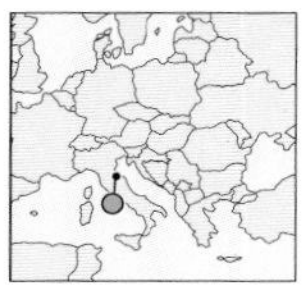

SAN MARINO

San Marino in northern Italy has been independent since 885 and a republic since the 14th century. It is the world's oldest republic. It has a friendship and cooperation treaty with Italy dating back to 1862. The state is governed by an elected council and has its own legal system. It has no armed forces and the police are "hired" from the Italian constabulary. The chief occupations are tourism, limestone quarrying, textiles, and wine-making.

AREA 24 sq mi [61 sq km] **POPULATION** 34,000 **CAPITAL** San Marino

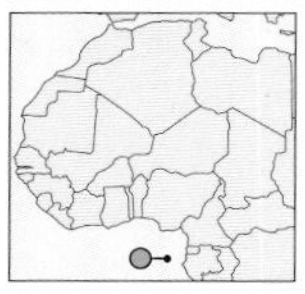

SÃO TOMÉ AND PRÍNCIPE

The Democratic Republic of São Tomé and Príncipe is a mountainous island territory west of Gabon. It became a colony of Portugal in 1522 and independent in 1975. The economy relies heavily on cocoa and foreign aid. Future growth depends on offshore oil.

AREA 372 sq mi [964 sq km] **POPULATION** 211,000 **CAPITAL** São Tomé

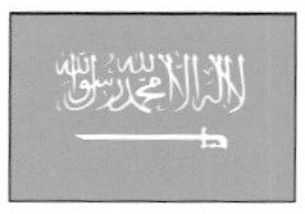

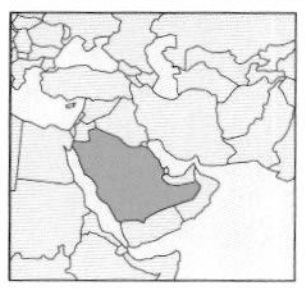

SAUDI ARABIA

GEOGRAPHY The Kingdom of Saudi Arabia occupies about three-quarters of the Arabian peninsula in southwest Asia. Deserts cover most of the land with mountains bordering the Red Sea plains in the west. In the north is the sandy Nafud Desert (An Nafud). In the south is the Rub' al Khali (the "Empty Quarter"), one of the world's bleakest deserts. Saudi Arabia has a hot dry climate. Summer temperatures in Riyadh often exceed 104°F [40°C].

POLITICS & ECONOMY Saudi Arabia contains the two holiest places in Islam – Mecca (or Makka), the birthplace of the Prophet Muhammad in AD 570, and Medina (Al Madinah), where he died in 632. These places are visited by huge numbers of pilgrims.

The monarch, King Salman, has supreme authority in this ultra-conservative country. In March 2015 Saudi Arabia began its controversial military involvement in Yemen, launching airstrikes against Houthi rebels. In 2017, Saudi Arabia, the UAE, Bahrain, and Egypt imposed a blockade on Qatar. The Crown Prince Muhammad bin Salman has introduced a few small reforms, including the re-opening of cinemas and overturning the ban on women driving.

Since 1933, oil has been the mainstay of the economy: the country has more than 18% of the world's known reserves. Oil products make up about 90% of exports. Irrigation and desalination projects have increased crop production. Problems have arisen from increasing unemployment, especially among the young, and moves are being made to diversify the economy.

AREA 829,995 sq mi [2,149,690 sq km] **POPULATION** 34,173,000
CAPITAL Riyadh **GOVERNMENT** Absolute monarchy with consultative assembly **ETHNIC GROUPS** Arab 90%, Afro-Asian 10%
LANGUAGES Arabic (official) **RELIGIONS** Islam 100%
CURRENCY Saudi riyal = 100 halalas

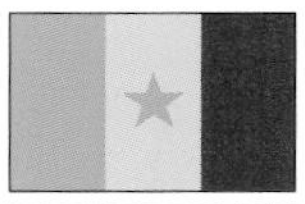

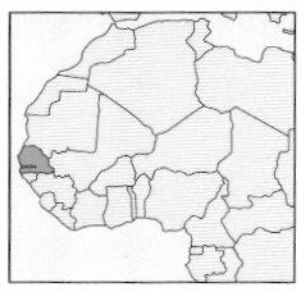

SENEGAL

GEOGRAPHY The Republic of Senegal is on the west coast of Africa. The volcanic Cape Verde (Cap Vert), on which Dakar stands, is the most westerly point in Africa. Plains cover most of Senegal, though the land rises gently in the southeast.

Dakar has a tropical climate, with a short rainy season between July and October.

POLITICS & ECONOMY In 1882, Senegal became a French colony, and from 1895 it was ruled as part of French West Africa, the capital of which, Dakar, developed as a major port and city.

In 1959, Senegal joined French Sudan (now Mali) to form the Federation of Mali. But Senegal withdrew in 1960 and became the separate Republic of Senegal. Its first president, Léopold Sédar Senghor, served until 1981, when he was succeeded by Abdou Diouf. However, in 2000, Diouf was defeated in elections by Abdoulaye Wade which peacefully ended the 40-year rule of the Socialist Party. The current president is Macky Sall.

Classified by the World Bank as a "lower-middle-income" country, Senegal is dependent on foreign aid and remittances from abroad. It was badly hit in the 1960s and 1970s by droughts. Agriculture still employs 77% of the population, though many farmers produce little more than they need to feed their families. Food crops include groundnuts (peanuts), millet, and rice. Phosphates are the country's chief resource, but there are plans to develop its offshore oil reserves. Dakar is a busy port. Tourism is growing. Economic growth will depend on modernizing infrastructure and guaranteeing reliable power supplies.

AREA 75,954 sq mi [196,722 sq km] **POPULATION** 15,736,000
CAPITAL Dakar **GOVERNMENT** Multiparty republic
ETHNIC GROUPS Wolof 43%, Pular 24%, Serer 15%
LANGUAGES French (official), tribal languages
RELIGIONS Islam 94%, Christianity (mainly Roman Catholic) 5%, traditional beliefs 1%
CURRENCY CFA franc = 100 centimes

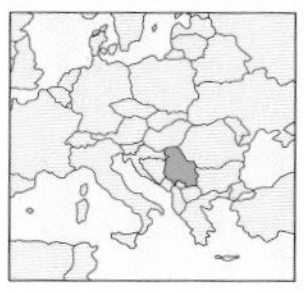

SERBIA

GEOGRAPHY The Republic of Serbia lies in the central Balkan peninsula. A landlocked country, it contains large, fertile lowlands drained by the River Danube and its tributaries, with uplands in the south. Most of Serbia has a continental climate, with cold, snowy winters and hot, dry summers. Heavy rains occur in the spring and the fall.

POLITICS & ECONOMY Around 1,500 years ago, South Slavs moved into the Balkan peninsula, and each group founded its own state. Serbia came under the Turkish Ottoman empire in the 15th century. In 1918, the South Slavs united as the Kingdom of the Serbs, Croats, and Slovenes, which was renamed Yugoslavia in 1929. Germany invaded in 1941, but Communist partisans, led by Josip Broz Tito, took power in 1945.

From 1945, the country became the Federal People's Republic of Yugoslavia. In 1991–92, the country split apart, with Bosnia-Herzegovina, Croatia, Macedonia and Slovenia proclaiming their independence. The remaining republics, Serbia and Montenegro, retained the name Yugoslavia. In 2003, these two republics agreed to form the loose Union of Serbia and Montenegro. In 2006, the Montenegrins voted for full independence, and Serbia and Montenegro became separate republics. In 2008, the province of Kosovo declared itself independent, an act which Serbia refused to recognize. In 2011, the European Commission recommended Serbia for European Union candidate status, but said talks could start only after it normalized ties with Kosovo. Accession talks started in January 2014 although Serbia still falls short of acknowledging Kosovo as fully independent.

Serbia's resources include bauxite, coal, copper, and other metals, together with oil and natural gas. The country relies on exports and manufacturing, with aluminum, machinery, plastics, steel, textiles, and vehicles being important. Agriculture employs around one-fifth of the work force with crops including fruits, maize, potatoes, and wheat. There are serious challenges to development including unemployment and an aging population.

AREA 29,913 sq mi [77,474 sq km] **POPULATION** 7,012,000
CAPITAL Belgrade **GOVERNMENT** Republic
ETHNIC GROUPS Serb 83%, Hungarian 4%, others
LANGUAGES Serbian (official), Hungarian
RELIGIONS Serbian Orthodox, Roman Catholic, Islam, Protestant
CURRENCY New dinar = 100 paras

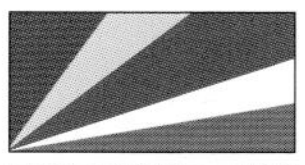
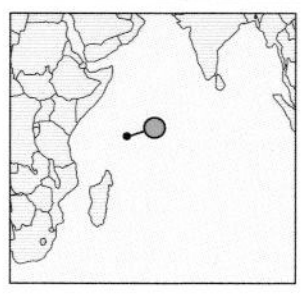

SEYCHELLES

The Republic of Seychelles in the western Indian Ocean achieved independence from Britain in 1976. Coconuts are the main cash crop, and fishing and tourism are important to the country's economy.

AREA 176 SQ MI [455 SQ KM]
POPULATION 96,000 **CAPITAL** VICTORIA

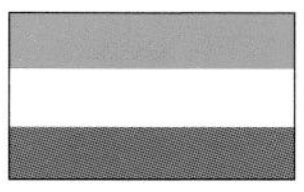
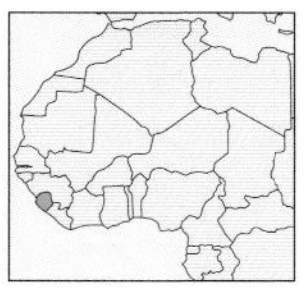

SIERRA LEONE

GEOGRAPHY The Republic of Sierra Leone in West Africa is about the same size as the country of Ireland. The coast contains several estuaries in the north, and extensive mangrove swamps. The most prominent feature is the mountainous Freetown (or Sierra Leone) peninsula.

Sierra Leone has a tropical climate, with heavy rainfall between April and November.

POLITICS & ECONOMY In the early 19th century, Freetown was established by British abolitionists as a destination for freed slaves. In 1961 it became independent from Britain, and a republic in 1971. The military seized power in 1992 and the following years of civil war resulted in tens of thousands of deaths and mutilations. The war ceased in 2002 with the intervention of the UK and a UN peacekeeping force. The last of the UN troops left the country in 2005, and elections were held in 2007. In 2010, the UN Security Council lifted the last remaining sanctions against Sierra Leone. In 2018 Julius Maada Bio of the People's Party was elected president.

Sierra Leone has a "low-income" economy, which, although showing signs of reasonable growth, has been hampered by the legacy of destruction left by the war, and by the outbreak of the Ebola virus in 2014–16. About 59% of the people live by subsistence farming. The leading exports are minerals, including iron ore and rutile (titanium ore), and diamonds. The trade in the latter as "blood diamonds" helped perpetuate the civil war and much diamond mining is still unlicensed.

AREA 27,699 SQ MI [71,740 SQ KM] **POPULATION** 6,625,000
CAPITAL FREETOWN **GOVERNMENT** MULTIPARTY REPUBLIC **ETHNIC GROUPS** NATIVE AFRICAN TRIBES 90% **LANGUAGES** ENGLISH (OFFICIAL), MENDE, TEMNE, LIMBA **RELIGIONS** ISLAM 60%, TRADITIONAL BELIEFS 30%, CHRISTIANITY 10%
CURRENCY LEONE = 100 CENTS

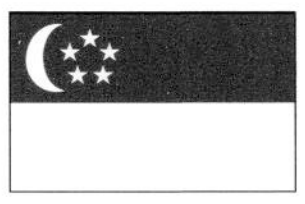
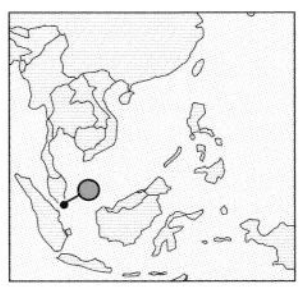

SINGAPORE

GEOGRAPHY The Republic of Singapore is an island country at the southern tip of the Malay peninsula. It consists of the large Singapore Island and 58 small islands, 20 of which are inhabited. The climate is hot and humid. Temperatures are high and rainfall is heavy throughout the year.

POLITICS & ECONOMY In 1819, Sir Thomas Stamford Raffles, agent of the British East India Company, made a treaty with the Sultan of Johor allowing the British to build a settlement on Singapore Island. Singapore soon became the leading British trading center in Southeast Asia and it later became a naval base. Japanese forces seized the island in 1942, but British rule was restored in 1945.

In 1963, Singapore became part of the Federation of Malaysia, which also included Malaya and the territories of Sabah and Sarawak on Borneo. In 1965, Singapore broke away and became independent.

The People's Action Party (PAP) has ruled Singapore since 1959. Its leader, Lee Kuan Yew, served as prime minister from 1959 until 1990, when he was succeeded by Goh Chok Tong. In 2004, Lee Hsien Loong, son of Lee Kuan Yew, became prime minister and has since been re-elected three times, in 2006, 2011, and 2015.

The World Bank classifies Singapore as a "high-income" economy, where a skilled work force has created a fast-growing economy. Trade and finance are major activities. The global financial crisis in 2008–9 caused great concern, but recovery was rapid. Manufactures include electronic products, machinery, scientific instruments, textiles, and ships. Petroleum products and manufactures are the main exports.

AREA 264 SQ MI [683 SQ KM] **POPULATION** 6,210,000
CAPITAL SINGAPORE CITY **GOVERNMENT** MULTIPARTY REPUBLIC
ETHNIC GROUPS CHINESE 77%, MALAY 14%, INDIAN 8%
LANGUAGES CHINESE, MALAY, TAMIL AND ENGLISH (ALL OFFICIAL)
RELIGIONS BUDDHISM, ISLAM, CHRISTIANITY, HINDUISM
CURRENCY SINGAPORE DOLLAR = 100 CENTS

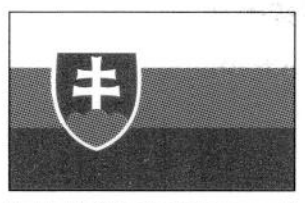
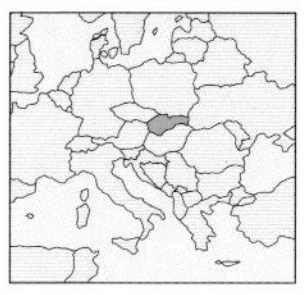

SLOVAKIA

GEOGRAPHY Slovakia is a predominantly mountainous country, consisting of part of the Carpathian range. The highest peak is Gerlachovsky in the Tatra Mountains, which reaches 8,711 ft [2,655 m]. The south is comprised of a fertile lowland. Slovakia has cold winters and warm summers. Kosice, in the east, has average temperatures ranging from 27°F [–3°C] in January to 68°F [20°C] in July. The highland areas are much colder. Snow or rain falls throughout the year. Kosice has an average annual rainfall of 24 inches [600 mm], the wettest months being July and August.

POLITICS & ECONOMY Slavic peoples settled here in the 5th century AD. They were subsequently conquered by Hungary, beginning a millennium of Hungarian rule and suppression of Slovak culture.

In 1867, Hungary and Austria united to form Austria–Hungary, of which the present-day Slovakia was a part. Austria–Hungary collapsed at the end of World War I (1914–18) and the Czech and Slovak people then united to form a new nation, Czechoslovakia. But Czech domination led to resentment by many Slovaks. In 1939, Slovakia declared itself independent, before Germany occupied the country. At the end of World War II, Slovakia again became part of Czechoslovakia.

The Communist Party took control in 1948 and although many people sought reform in the 1960s, they were crushed by the Russians. In the late 1980s, demands for democracy mounted and a non-Communist government took office in 1990. Elections in 1992 led to victory for the Movement for a Democratic Slovakia headed by a former Communist and nationalist, Vladimir Meciar, and Slovakia became independent in 1993.

Independence raised national aspirations among Slovakia's Magyar-speaking community which makes up about 10% of the population. Issues about the status of this minority group have soured relations with Hungary, and were not helped by the government making Slovak the only official language. Slovakia became a member of NATO and the European Union in 2004. On January 1, 2009, it became the 16th country to adopt the euro. In 2012, the opposition party Smer, led by former prime minister Robert Fico, won a landslide election. Fico stood down in the aftermath of the murder of an investigative journalist. He was replaced by Peter Pellegrini.

Before 1948, Slovakia's economy was based on farming, but Communist governments developed manufacturing industries. Economic and social reform, following membership of the eurozone, has resulted in strong economic growth, driven by the export of cars and electronic goods. Since the late 1980s, many state-run businesses have been handed over to private owners.

AREA 18,924 SQ MI [49,012 SQ KM] **POPULATION** 5,441,000
CAPITAL BRATISLAVA **GOVERNMENT** MULTIPARTY REPUBLIC
ETHNIC GROUPS SLOVAK 86%, HUNGARIAN 10%
LANGUAGES SLOVAK (OFFICIAL), HUNGARIAN
RELIGIONS ROMAN CATHOLIC 69%, PROTESTANT 11%, OTHERS
CURRENCY EURO = 100 CENTS

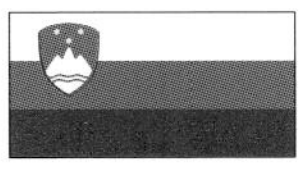
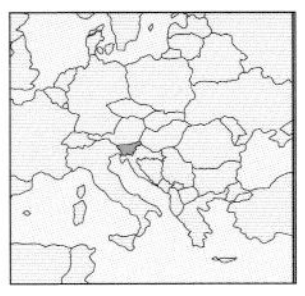

SLOVENIA

GEOGRAPHY The Republic of Slovenia was one of the six republics which made up the former Yugoslavia. Much of the land is mountainous, rising to 9,396 ft [2,864 m] at Mount Triglav in the Julian Alps (Julijske Alpe) in the northwest. Central Slovenia contains the limestone Karst region. The Postojna caves near Ljubljana are among the largest in Europe.

The coast has a mild Mediterranean climate, but inland the climate is more continental.

POLITICS & ECONOMY In the last 2,000 years, the Slovene people have been independent as a nation for less than 50 years. The Austrian Habsburgs ruled over the region from the 13th century until World War I when, in 1918, Slovenia became part of the Kingdom of the Serbs, Croats, and Slovenes (later called Yugoslavia). During World War II, Slovenia was invaded and partitioned between Italy, Germany, and Hungary, but, after the war, Slovenia again became part of Yugoslavia.

From the late 1960s, some Slovenes demanded independence, but the central government opposed the breakup of the country. In 1990, when Communist governments had collapsed throughout Eastern Europe, elections were held and a non-Communist coalition government was set up. Slovenia then declared itself independent. This led to fighting between Slovenes and the federal army, but Slovenia did not become a battlefield. Slovenia's independence was recognized in 1992 and a coalition led by the Liberal Democrats was elected. In 2004, Slovenia became a member of the North Atlantic Treaty Organization and the European Union. In 2013, the coalition government of Janez Jansa collapsed amidst criticisms of its austerity measures and allegations of corruption. In 2018 elections, despite big gains for the anti-immigration SDS party, Marjan Sarec became prime minister, heading a center-left minority government.

The reform of the formerly state-run economy caused problems for Slovenia. However, from 1993, the country made considerable economic progress although this stumbled in the European financial crisis of 2012 when tough austerity measures were unpopular.

Manufacturing and services are the strongest parts of the economy, and exports include chemicals, machinery and transport equipment, metal goods, and textiles. Slovenia mines some iron ore, lead, lignite, and mercury. Fruits, maize, potatoes, and wheat are major crops, and livestock are also raised.

AREA 7,821 SQ MI [20,256 SQ KM] **POPULATION** 2,103,000
CAPITAL LJUBLJANA **GOVERNMENT** MULTIPARTY REPUBLIC
ETHNIC GROUPS SLOVENE 83%, CROAT 2%, SERB 2%, HUNGARIAN, BOSNIAN **LANGUAGES** SLOVENIAN (OFFICIAL), SERBO-CROATIAN
RELIGIONS ROMAN CATHOLIC 58%
CURRENCY EURO = 100 CENTS

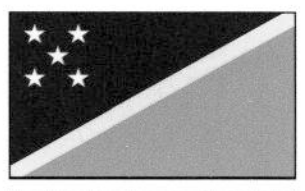
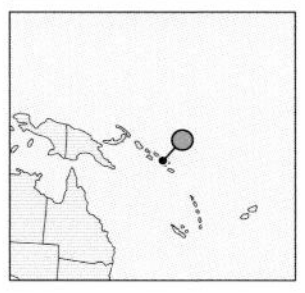

SOLOMON ISLANDS

The Solomon Islands, a chain of mainly volcanic islands in the Pacific Ocean extending for some 1,400 mi [2,250 km], were a British territory between 1893 and 1978. Most people are Melanesians, and the islands have a young population profile, with about 35% of the people aged under 15. The country is struggling to recover from five years of civil conflict and poverty is rife. Fish, coconuts, cocoa, and forestry products underpin the economy.

AREA 11,157 SQ MI [28,896 SQ KM]
POPULATION 685,000 **CAPITAL** HONIARA

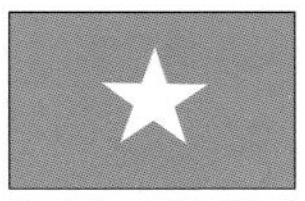
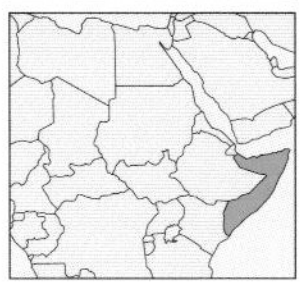

SOMALIA

GEOGRAPHY The Federal Republic of Somalia is in a region known as the "Horn of Africa." It is more than twice the size of Italy, the country which once ruled the southern part of Somalia. The most mountainous part of the country is in the north, behind the narrow coastal plains that border the Gulf of Aden. Rainfall is sparse, with the wettest regions in the south and northern mountains. Droughts are common and temperatures are generally high.

POLITICS & ECONOMY European powers became interested in the Horn of Africa in the 19th century. In 1884, Britain made the northern part of what is now Somalia a protectorate, while Italy took the south in 1905. The new boundaries divided the Somalis into five areas: the two Somalilands, Djibouti (which was taken by France in the 1880s), Ethiopia, and Kenya. Since then, many Somalis have wanted to create a Greater Somalia. Italy invaded British Somaliland in 1940, but was defeated in 1941. Britain ruled both Somalilands until 1950, when the United Nations asked Italy to take over the former Italian Somaliland for ten years. In 1960, the two Somalilands united to become Somalia.

Somalia has faced many problems. Economic difficulties led a military group to seize power in 1969. In the 1970s, Somalia supported an uprising of Somali-speaking people in the Ogaden region of Ethiopia. But, in 1988, Somalia and Ethiopia signed a peace treaty. In the 1990s, Somalia gradually broke apart. In 1991, the people in what was once British Somaliland set up the "Somaliland Republic," but it failed to get international recognition. The northeast, called Puntland, also seceded, while the south was riven by clan warfare. In 2004–5, a Somali parliament was set up in Kenya, moving to Baidoa, in Somalia, in 2006 (Mogadishu was regarded as unsafe). In 2006, Mogadishu was taken over by the Islamist Union of Islamic Courts, but government forces backed by Ethiopian troops defeated the Islamists. Ethiopia finally withdrew all its troops in January 2009. In 2012, the militant group al-Shabab was driven out of central Somalia, but continues to carry out attacks. President Mohamed Abdullahi Mohamed, elected in 2017, has indicated that he is willing to talk to the militants.

Somalia's economy has been shattered by war, droughts, and periodic floods. Many Somalis are nomads, who raise livestock.

Live animals, meat, and hides and skins are exported. Crops include bananas, citrus fruits, cotton, maize, and sugarcane.

AREA 246,199 SQ MI [637,657 SQ KM] **POPULATION** 11,757,000
CAPITAL Mogadishu **GOVERNMENT** Single-party republic, military dominated **ETHNIC GROUPS** Somali 85%, Bantu, Arab
LANGUAGES Somali (official), Arabic **RELIGIONS** Islam (Sunni Muslim)
CURRENCY Somali shilling = 100 cents

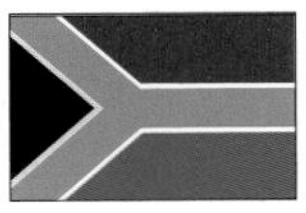
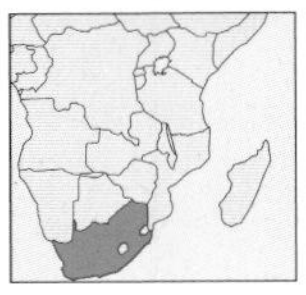

SOUTH AFRICA

GEOGRAPHY The Republic of South Africa comprises mainly of the southern part of the huge plateau which makes up most of southern Africa. The highest peaks are in the Drakensberg range. Part of the Namib Desert lies in the northwest. The area around Cape Town has a sunny climate with mild, rainy winters. Inland, large areas of the plateau are arid.

POLITICS & ECONOMY Early inhabitants in South Africa were the Khoisa, followed in the last 2,000 years by Bantu-speaking people. Their descendants include the Zulu, Xhosa, Sotho, and Tswana. The Dutch founded a settlement at the Cape in 1652, but Britain colonized the area in the early 19th century. The Dutch, called Boers or Afrikaners, resented British rule and moved inland. Rivalry between the groups led to Anglo–Boer Wars in 1880–81 and 1899–1902.

In 1910, the country was united as the Union of South Africa. In 1948, the National Party won power and introduced the policy of apartheid, under which non-whites could not vote and their human rights were strictly limited. Multiracial elections were held in 1994 and Nelson Mandela, leader of the African National Congress (ANC), became president following 27 years in prison. After Mandela retired, the ANC won elections in 1999 and 2004, led by Thabo Mbeki, and in 2009 when Jacob Zuma became president. Zuma resigned in 2018 over allegations of corruption, which he denies. He was replaced by Cyril Ramaphosa.

South Africa is Africa's most developed country and is one of the "BRICS" group of emerging global economic powers. However, most of the black people are poor, with farms still white-owned. Unemployment is high at 26% and it has nurtured an associated high crime rate. Natural resources include diamonds and gold; services, mining and manufacturing are valuable activities. Crops include maize, wheat, and sugarcane.

AREA 471,442 SQ MI [1,221,037 SQ KM] **POPULATION** 56,464,000
CAPITAL Cape Town (legislative); Pretoria/Tshwane (administrative); Bloemfontein (judiciary) **GOVERNMENT** Multiparty republic
ETHNIC GROUPS Black 79%, White 10%, Colored 9%, Asian 2%
LANGUAGES Afrikaans, English, Ndebele, Pedi, Sotho, Swazi, Tsonga, Tswana, Venda, Xhosa and Zulu (all official)
RELIGIONS Christianity 68%, Islam 2%, Hinduism 1%
CURRENCY Rand = 100 cents

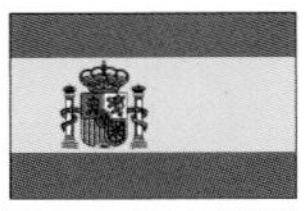
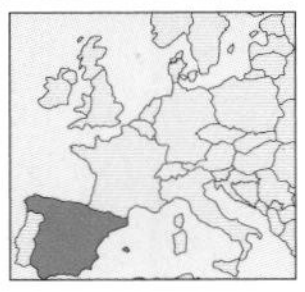

SPAIN

GEOGRAPHY The Kingdom of Spain is the second largest country in Western Europe after France. It shares the Iberian peninsula with the much smaller Portugal. The Meseta, an extensive plateau, covers most of Spain. It is mainly flat, but is crossed by the sierras, a series of mountain ranges.

The northern highlands include the Cantabrian Mountains (Cordillera Cantabrica) and the high Pyrenees, which form Spain's border with France. But Mulhacén, the highest peak on the Spanish mainland, is in the Sierra Nevada in the southeast. Spain also has fertile coastal plains. Other major lowlands include the Ebro river basin in the northeast and the Guadalquivir river basin in the southwest. Spain also encompasses the Balearic Islands in the Mediterranean Sea and the Canary Islands off the northwest coast of Africa.

The Meseta has a continental climate, with hot summers and cold winters, when temperatures often fall below freezing point. Snow frequently covers the mountain ranges on the Meseta. The Mediterranean coasts have hot, dry summers and mild winters.

POLITICS & ECONOMY In the early 16th century, Spain rose to be a world power. At its peak, it controlled much of Central and South America, parts of Africa, and the Philippines in Asia. Spain's influence began to decline in the late 16th century. Its sea power was destroyed by a British fleet in the Battle of Trafalgar (1805), and by the 20th century it was a poor country.

Spain became a republic in 1931, but the republicans were defeated in the Spanish Civil War (1936–39). General Francisco Franco became the country's dictator, though technically Spain remained a monarchy. On Franco's death in 1975, there was a peaceful transition to democracy, with Juan Carlos as king. In 2014 he abdicated in favor of his son Felipe.

Within Spain there are several groups, with their own languages and cultures, who have been vocal in their aim to run their own affairs. In the northern Basque region, the separatist group, ETA, waged a long-running terrorist campaign, finally announcing its complete disarmament in 2017.

Spain's regional makeup is complicated and the powers devolved to the regional parliaments since the 1970s are unevenly distributed. There are 17 regions, with Catalonia, the Basque Country, and Galicia having gained special status. A referendum in Catalonia in October 2017 led the regional government to declare independence. The central government swiftly cracked down and imposed direct rule.

Spain was badly affected by the global recession of 2008; sluggish economic growth and an unemployment rate of 26% in 2013 forced the country to undertake drastic austerity measures.

Agriculture employs only 4% of the population, as compared with 19% in industry and 76% in the service sector. Farmland occupies two-thirds of the land area. Manufactures include cars, chemicals, electronic goods, food, metal goods, and textiles. Spain lacks natural resources apart from some iron ore.

AREA 192,103 SQ MI [497,548 SQ KM] **POPULATION** 50,016,000
CAPITAL Madrid **GOVERNMENT** Constitutional monarchy
ETHNIC GROUPS Composite of Mediterranean and Nordic types
LANGUAGES Castilian Spanish (official) 74%, Catalan 17%, Galician 7%, Basque 2% **RELIGIONS** Roman Catholic 94%, others 6% **CURRENCY** Euro = 100 cents

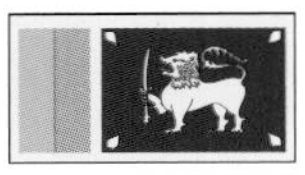
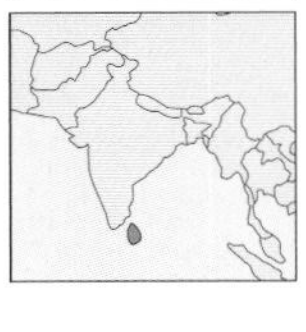

SRI LANKA

GEOGRAPHY The Democratic Socialist Republic of Sri Lanka is an island nation, separated from the southeast coast of India by the Palk Strait. The land is mostly low-lying, but a mountain region dominates the south-central part of the country.

The western part of Sri Lanka has a wet equatorial climate. Temperatures are high and the rainfall is heavy.

POLITICS & ECONOMY From the early 16th century, Ceylon (as Sri Lanka was then known) was ruled successively by the Portuguese, Dutch, and British. Independence was achieved in 1948 and the country was renamed Sri Lanka in 1972.

After independence, rivalries between the two main ethnic groups, the Buddhist Sinhalese and the minority Hindu Tamils, marred progress. In 1956 Solomon Bandaranaike was elected prime minister on a wave of Sinhalese nationalism, but he was assassinated in 1959 by an extremist Buddhist monk. He was succeeded by his wife, Sirimavo Bandaranaike, the world's first woman prime minister.

Conflict between Tamils and Sinhalese continued in the 1970s and 1980s. In 1987, India helped to engineer a ceasefire but withdrew its troops in 1990 after failing to subdue the main guerrilla group, the Tamil Tigers, who wanted to set up an independent Tamil homeland in the northeast. The Tamil Tigers were finally defeated in May 2009. In 2019, Islamist terrorists killed several hundred people in a series of suicide bombings.

In late 2004, a tsunami, caused by a sudden movement of the plates underlying the eastern Indian Ocean, struck parts of the coast of Sri Lanka, killing more than 30,000 people.

Economic growth has been strong since the end of the conflict with the Tamil Tigers, and Sri Lanka is now classified as an "upper-middle-income" economy. Agriculture employs about 30% of the people. Coconuts, rubber, and tea are exported. Rice is the main food crop. Factories process farm products and manufacture textiles.

AREA 25,332 SQ MI [65,610 SQ KM] **POPULATION** 22,889,000
CAPITAL Colombo **GOVERNMENT** Multiparty republic
ETHNIC GROUPS Sinhalese 74%, Tamil 9%, Moor 7%
LANGUAGES Sinhala and Tamil (both official)
RELIGIONS Buddhism 69%, Islam 8%, Hinduism 7%, Christianity 6%
CURRENCY Sri Lankan rupee = 100 cents

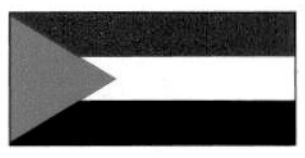
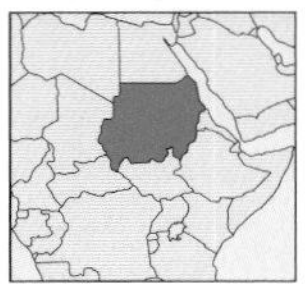

SUDAN

GEOGRAPHY The Republic of Sudan was Africa's largest country until 2011, when the people in the south voted to secede and form the new nation of South Sudan. Sudan is mainly arid, with part of the vast Sahara in the north. The main feature is the fertile River Nile valley, where most people live.

POLITICS & ECONOMY In the 19th century, Egypt gradually took control of Sudan. In 1881, a Muslim religious teacher, the Mahdi ("divinely appointed guide"), led a rebellion which was quashed, in 1898, by Britain and Egypt. In 1899, these two countries agreed to rule Sudan jointly as a condominium. After independence in 1952, the black Africans in the south feared domination by the Muslim north. They objected to Arabic becoming the sole official language and, in 1964, civil war broke out. The war ended in 1972, when the south was granted regional self-government.

In 1983, the announcement that Islamic law would apply throughout Sudan sparked off further resistance from the rebel Sudan People's Liberation Army (SPLA) in the south. In 1998, Sudan's government announced that it accepted the idea of a referendum. In 2005, a peace agreement was signed, and the referendum took place in 2011, when around 99% of the people in the south voted to set up their own country, South Sudan.

From 2003, conflict raged in the western province of Darfur, where government-backed militias battled with local rebel forces. A peace accord was agreed in 2010 but some conflict continues. In 2008, the International Criminal Court charged President al-Bashir with war crimes. In 2019 he was ousted and arrested by the military. A civilian-military transitional government was set up.

The majority of the population are poor and live by subsistence agriculture. Cotton (the main crop), gum arabic, and sesame seeds are exported, but the most valuable exports are gold and oil products. More than 80% of the oil is produced in South Sudan, but Sudan has the infrastructure to exploit and export it.

AREA 728,222 SQ MI [1,886,086 SQ KM] **POPULATION** 45,562,000
CAPITAL Khartoum **GOVERNMENT** Transitional
ETHNIC GROUPS Arab, Black, Beja, others **LANGUAGES** Arabic and English (both official), Nubian, Beja **RELIGIONS** Islam, traditional beliefs
CURRENCY Sudanese pound = 100 piastres

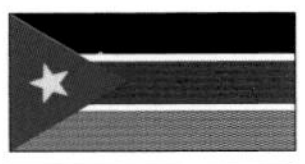
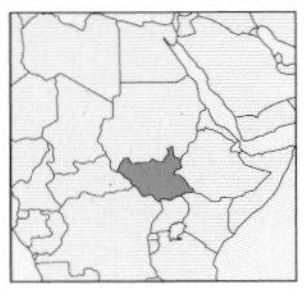

SUDAN, SOUTH

GEOGRAPHY The Republic of South Sudan is a landlocked country in east-central Africa. Much of the land is low-lying and drained by the White Nile and its tributaries. Mountains lie in the far south. The country has a wet tropical climate. Forests, swamps, and grasslands cover large areas.

POLITICS & ECONOMY South Sudan has about 200 ethnic groups. The South's deep cultural differences with the mainly Arab-Muslim north led to civil war (1964–1972 and 1983–2005). In January 2011, as part of the peace agreement, a referendum was held in which the vast majority of the people in the south voted for independence. Civil war broke out in 2013, displacing millions. Fighting was reduced after the president signed a power-sharing agreement in 2018. A transitional coalition government was formed in 2020, with Salva Kiir remaining as president and his former rival Riek Machar as vice president.

South Sudan has many mineral resources, including oil, but the country's infrastructure is undeveloped and poverty is widespread. Much of the population depends on subsistence agriculture.

AREA 239,285 SQ MI [619,745 SQ KM] **POPULATION** 10,561,000
CAPITAL Juba **GOVERNMENT** Transitional Coalition
ETHNIC GROUPS Dinka, Kakwa, Bari, Azande, Shilluk, others
LANGUAGES English and Arabic (both official), local languages
RELIGIONS Traditional beliefs, Christianity
CURRENCY South Sudanese pound = 100 piastres

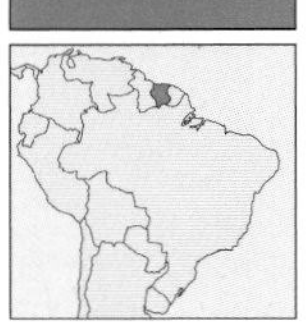

SURINAME

GEOGRAPHY The Republic of Suriname is sandwiched between French Guiana and Guyana in northeastern South America. The narrow coastal plain was once swampy, but it has been drained and now consists mainly of farmland. Inland lie hills and low mountains, which rise to 4,035 ft [1,230 m].

Suriname has a hot, wet and humid climate. Temperatures are high throughout the year.

POLITICS & ECONOMY In 1667, the British handed Suriname to the Dutch in return for New Amsterdam, an area that is now the state of New York. Slave revolts and Dutch neglect hampered development. In the early 19th century, Britain and the Netherlands disputed the ownership of the area with Britain relinquishing its claim in 1813. Slavery was abolished in 1863 and Indian and Indonesian laborers were introduced to work on the plantations.

Suriname became fully independent in 1975, but the economy was weakened when thousands of skilled people emigrated from

Suriname to the Netherlands. Following a coup in 1980, Suriname was ruled by a military dictator, Desiré ("Dési") Bouterse. The adoption of a new constitution led to the restoration of democracy in 1988. In 2010, however, the Mega Combination coalition, led by former military leader Bouterse, won parliamentary elections and Bouterse became president.

Suriname's economy is based on gold mining and oil. It was a leading producer of bauxite, but this has declined. Tourism has potential. The guilder was replaced by the Surinamese dollar in 2004.

AREA 63,037 SQ MI [163,265 SQ KM] **POPULATION** 610,000
CAPITAL PARAMARIBO **GOVERNMENT** MULTIPARTY REPUBLIC
ETHNIC GROUPS HINDUSTANI/EAST INDIAN 37%, CREOLE (MIXED WHITE AND BLACK) 31%, JAVANESE 15%, BLACK 10%, AMERINDIAN 2%, CHINESE 2%, OTHERS
LANGUAGES DUTCH (OFFICIAL), SRANANG TONGO
RELIGIONS HINDUISM 27%, PROTESTANT 25%, ROMAN CATHOLIC 23%, ISLAM 20% **CURRENCY** SURINAMESE DOLLAR= 100 CENTS

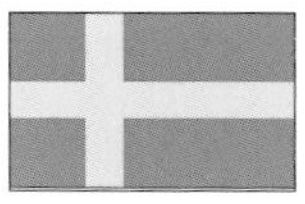
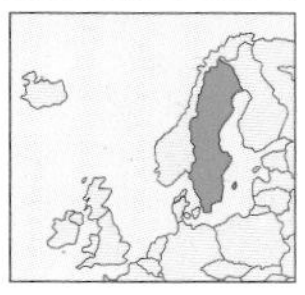

SWEDEN

GEOGRAPHY The Kingdom of Sweden is the largest of the countries of Scandinavia in both area and population. It shares the Scandinavian peninsula with Norway. The western part of the country, along the border with Norway, is mountainous. The highest point is Kebnekaise, which reaches 6,936 ft [2,114 m] in the northwest. The climate becomes increasingly severe from south to north.

POLITICS & ECONOMY Swedish Vikings plundered areas to the south and east between the 9th and 11th centuries. Sweden, Denmark, and Norway were united in 1397, but Sweden regained its independence in 1523. In 1809, Sweden lost Finland to Russia, but, in 1814, it gained Norway from Denmark. The union between Sweden and Norway was dissolved in 1905. Sweden remained neutral in World Wars I and II. Since 1945, Sweden has become a prosperous country and, in 1995, it joined the European Union. However, it did not adopt the euro, nor has it joined NATO.

Sweden has wide-ranging welfare provision but it comes at a high cost to the taxpayer. In 2006, a center-right alliance defeated the Social Democrats, who had governed for 65 of the previous 74 years. Stefan Löfven has been prime minister since 2014, heading a center-left minority government, and was re-elected in 2019 after losing a vote of no confidence the previous year.

Sweden is a highly developed industrial country: the economy is strong and unemployment low. Major products include steel and steel goods. Steel is used in the country's engineering industry to manufacture aircraft, cars, and machinery. Sweden has some of the world's richest iron ore deposits which are found near Kiruna in the far north. Most of this ore is exported, and Sweden has to import most of the materials needed by its own industries. Forestry is also important and hydroelectricity is a major source of energy.

AREA 173,731 SQ MI [449,964 SQ KM] **POPULATION** 10,202,000
CAPITAL STOCKHOLM **GOVERNMENT** CONSTITUTIONAL MONARCHY
ETHNIC GROUPS SWEDISH 91%, FINNISH, SAMI **LANGUAGES** SWEDISH (OFFICIAL), FINNISH, SAMI
RELIGIONS LUTHERAN 87%, ROMAN CATHOLIC, ORTHODOX
CURRENCY SWEDISH KRONA = 100 ÖRE

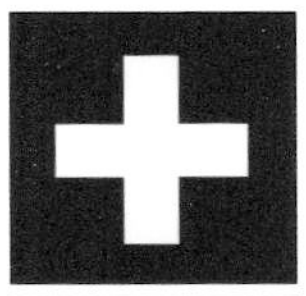
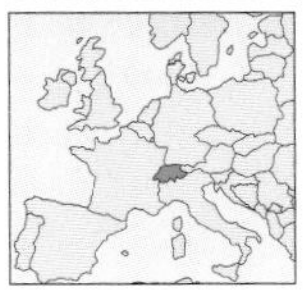

SWITZERLAND

GEOGRAPHY The Swiss Confederation is a landlocked country in Western Europe. Much of the land is mountainous. The Jura Mountains lie along Switzerland's western border with France, while the Swiss Alps make up about 60% of the country in the south and east. Four-fifths of the population live on the fertile Swiss plateau, which contains most of Switzerland's large cities.

The climate of Switzerland is generally temperate but varies greatly according to the altitude. The plateau has warm summers and cold, snowy winters. Rain occurs throughout the year.

POLITICS & ECONOMY In 1291, three small cantons (states) united to defend their freedom against the Habsburg rulers of the Holy Roman empire. They were Schwyz, Uri, and Unterwalden, and they called the confederation they formed "Switzerland." Switzerland expanded and, in the 14th century, defeated Austria in three wars of independence. After a defeat by the French in 1515, the Swiss adopted a policy of neutrality, which they still follow. In 1815, the Congress of Vienna expanded Switzerland to 22 cantons and guaranteed its neutrality. Switzerland's 23rd canton, Jura, was created in 1979 from part of Bern.

Neutrality combined with the vigor and independence of its people have made Switzerland prosperous. In 2002, it became a member of the United Nations, although it has remained outside the EU.

Switzerland's neutrality has helped it to become prosperous. Although lacking in natural resources, it is a wealthy, industrialized country. Products include chemicals, electrical equipment, machinery, precision instruments, processed food, watches, and textiles. Farmers produce about three-fifths of the country's food – the rest is imported. Crops include fruits, potatoes, and wheat. Tourism and banking are important. Swiss banks attract investors from all over the world.

AREA 15,940 SQ MI [41,284 SQ KM] **POPULATION** 8,404,000
CAPITAL BERN **GOVERNMENT** FEDERAL REPUBLIC
ETHNIC GROUPS GERMAN 65%, FRENCH 18%, ITALIAN 10%, ROMANSCH 1%, OTHERS **LANGUAGES** GERMAN, FRENCH, ITALIAN AND ROMANSCH (ALL OFFICIAL) **RELIGIONS** ROMAN CATHOLIC 42%, PROTESTANT 35% **CURRENCY** SWISS FRANC = 100 CENTIMES

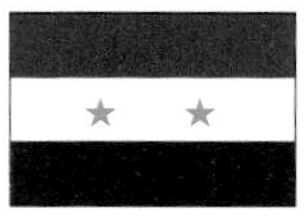
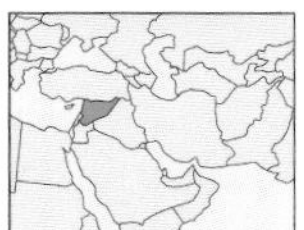

SYRIA

GEOGRAPHY The Syrian Arab Republic has a narrow coastal plain and is overlooked by a low mountain range which runs north–south. Another range, the Jabal ash Sharqi, runs along the border with Lebanon.

The coast has a Mediterranean climate, with dry, warm summers and wet, mild winters. The low mountains cut off Damascus from the sea. It has less rainfall than the coastal areas. To the east, the land becomes drier.

POLITICS & ECONOMY After the collapse of the Turkish Ottoman empire in World War I, Syria was governed by France until independence in 1946. In 1967 Syria lost the strategic Golan Heights to Israel. In 1970, Lieutenant-General Hafez al-Assad took power, establishing a stable but repressive regime. Hafez al-Assad died in 2000 and was succeeded by his son, Bashar al-Assad. From 2011, civil war, and the occupation of Syrian territory by jihadist militants, devastated the country with the number of deaths of civilians, rebels and government forces estimated at over half a million. Millions of people were internally displaced or sought refuge elsewhere. By 2019, the government, with the help of Russian forces, had regained control of most of Syria's biggest cities, and the Islamic State had been reduced to a small enclave on the Iraqi border. Parts of the countryside remain under the control of rebels and Kurds. The government has repeatedly been accused of using chemical warfare on its own citizens. Syria remains in a state of crisis.

Syria's main resources are oil, hydroelectricity, and fertile land. However, the economy has been crippled by the civil war.

AREA 71,498 SQ MI [185,180 SQ KM] **POPULATION** 19,398,000
CAPITAL DAMASCUS **GOVERNMENT** MULTIPARTY REPUBLIC
ETHNIC GROUPS ARAB 90%, KURDISH, ARMENIAN, OTHERS
LANGUAGES ARABIC (OFFICIAL), KURDISH, ARMENIAN
RELIGIONS SUNNI MUSLIM 74%, OTHER ISLAM 16%
CURRENCY SYRIAN POUND = 100 PIASTRES

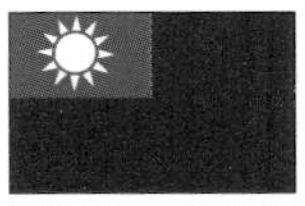
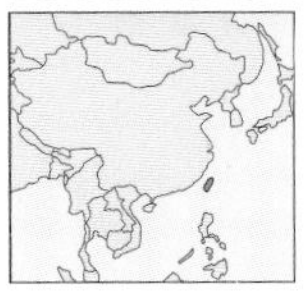

TAIWAN

GEOGRAPHY High mountain ranges run down the length of the island, with dense forest in many areas. The climate is warm, moist, and suitable for agriculture.

POLITICS & ECONOMY Chinese settlers occupied Taiwan from the 7th century. In 1895, Japan seized the territory from the Portuguese, who had named it Isla Formosa, or "beautiful island." China regained the island after World War II and, in 1949, it became the refuge of the Nationalists who had been driven out of China by the Communists. They set up the Republic of China, which, with US help, began to widen its economic base and develop manufacturing industries.

In the early 21st century, the Taiwanese declared full nationhood; however, China has never relinquished its claim of sovereignty over the island. Relations have improved since Taiwan and China signed a free-trade pact in 2010 although tensions still surface periodically. China is now Taiwan's main export market. Its major exports are electronic goods and petrochemicals.

AREA 13,900 SQ MI [36,000 SQ KM] **POPULATION** 23,603,000
CAPITAL TAIPEI **GOVERNMENT** UNITARY MULTIPARTY REPUBLIC
ETHNIC GROUPS TAIWANESE 84%, MAINLAND CHINESE 14%
LANGUAGES MANDARIN CHINESE (OFFICIAL), MIN, HAKKA
RELIGIONS BUDDHISM, TAOISM, CHRISTIANITY
CURRENCY NEW TAIWAN DOLLAR = 100 CENTS

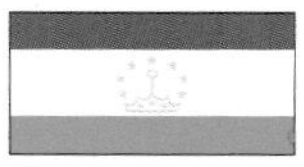
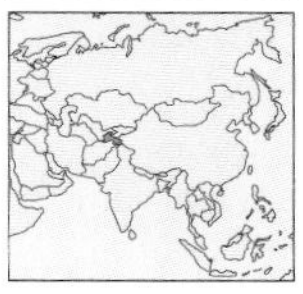

TAJIKISTAN

GEOGRAPHY The Republic of Tajikistan is one of the five central Asian republics that formed part of the former Soviet Union. Only 7% of the land is below 3,280 ft [1,000 m], while almost all of eastern Tajikistan is above 9,840 ft [3,000 m]. The highest point is Pik Imeni Ismail Samani (formerly known as Communism Peak or Pik Kommunizma), which reaches 24,590 ft [7,495 m]. The main ranges are the westward extension of the Tian Shan Range in the north and the snow-capped Pamirs in the southeast. Earthquakes are common throughout the country. The climate is continental, with hot, dry summers in the lower valleys and bitterly cold winters, especially in the mountains.

POLITICS & ECONOMY Russia conquered parts of Tajikistan in the late 19th century, and by 1920 Russia took complete control. In 1924, Tajikistan became part of the Uzbek Soviet Socialist Republic, but, in 1929, it was expanded, taking in some areas populated by Uzbeks, becoming the Tajik Soviet Socialist Republic.

While the Soviet Union began to introduce reforms during the 1980s, many Tajiks demanded freedom. In 1989, the Tajik government made Tajik the official language instead of Russian and, in 1990, it stated that its local laws overruled Soviet ones. Tajikistan became fully independent in 1991, following the breakup of the Soviet Union. In 1992, civil war broke out between the government, which was run by former Communists, and an alliance of democrats and Islamic forces. A ceasefire was agreed in 1996. In 2013, Emomali Rahmon, president since 1994, was re-elected for a 4th term. Elections have been tainted by accusations of fraud and his rule has become increasingly autocratic.

Tajikistan is the poorest country in Central Asia and many people have left to work in Russia. Economic hardship has fueled interest in radical Islam. The country relies on Russia both economically and for security, but is fostering links with China. It struggles with its position on the drug transit route from neighboring Afghanistan. Cotton, grains and fruits are the main crops. It produces aluminum, and has mineral resources and hydroelectric potential.

AREA 55,521 SQ MI [143,100 SQ KM] **POPULATION** 8,874,000
CAPITAL DUSHANBE **GOVERNMENT** REPUBLIC
ETHNIC GROUPS TAJIK 80%, UZBEK 15%, RUSSIAN 1%, KYRGYZ 1%
LANGUAGES TAJIK (OFFICIAL), RUSSIAN
RELIGIONS ISLAM (SUNNI MUSLIM 95%, SHIA MUSLIM 3%)
CURRENCY SOMONI = 100 DIRAMS

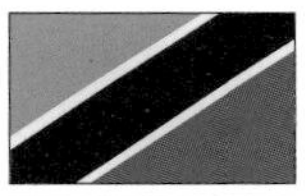
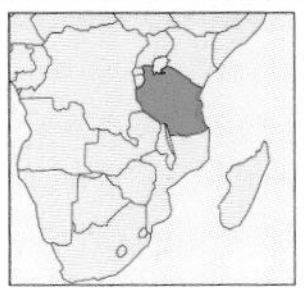

TANZANIA

GEOGRAPHY The United Republic of Tanzania consists of the former mainland country of Tanganyika and the island nation of Zanzibar, which also includes the island of Pemba. Behind a narrow coastal plain, most of Tanzania is a plateau, which is broken by arms of the Great African Rift Valley. In the west, this valley contains lakes Nyasa and Tanganyika. The highest peak is Kilimanjaro, Africa's highest mountain at 19,340 ft [5,895 m].

The coast has a hot and humid climate, with the greatest rainfall in April and May. The inland plateaux and mountains are cooler and less humid.

POLITICS & ECONOMY Mainland Tanganyika became a German territory in the 1880s, while Zanzibar and Pemba became a British protectorate in 1890. Following Germany's defeat in World War I, Britain took over Tanganyika, which remained a British territory until its independence in 1961. In 1964, Tanganyika and Zanzibar united to form the United Republic of Tanzania. The country's president, Julius Nyerere, pursued socialist policies of self-help (ujamaa) and egalitarianism. Many of his social reforms were successful, though the country failed to make economic progress. Nyerere resigned as president in 1985. His successors followed more liberal economic policies.

Crops are grown on only 4% of the land, yet agriculture employs about 65% of the people and provides 65% of exports.

Food crops include bananas, cassava, and maize. Gold, coffee, tea, tobacco, and cashews are exported. Offshore gas fields have been discovered.

AREA 364,899 SQ MI [945,090 SQ KM] **POPULATION** 58,553,000
CAPITAL DODOMA **GOVERNMENT** MULTIPARTY REPUBLIC
ETHNIC GROUPS NATIVE AFRICAN 99% (OF WHICH 95% ARE BANTU CONSISTING OF MORE THAN 130 TRIBES)
LANGUAGES SWAHILI (KISWAHILI) AND ENGLISH (BOTH OFFICIAL)
RELIGIONS ISLAM 35% (99% IN ZANZIBAR), TRADITIONAL BELIEFS 35%, CHRISTIANITY 30%
CURRENCY TANZANIAN SHILLING = 100 CENTS

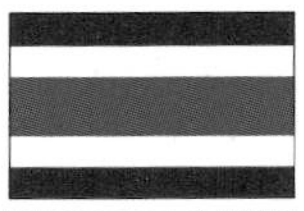
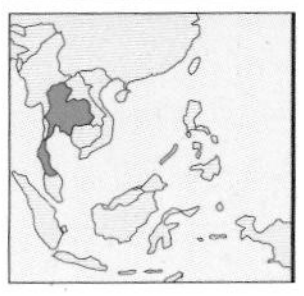

THAILAND

GEOGRAPHY The Kingdom of Thailand is one of the ten countries in Southeast Asia. The highest land is in the north, where Doi Inthanon, the highest peak, reaches 8,415 ft [2,565 m]. The Khorat plateau, in the north-east, makes up about 30% of the country and is the most heavily populated part of Thailand. In the south, Thailand shares the finger-like Malay peninsula with Burma and Malaysia.

Thailand has a tropical climate. Monsoon winds from the south-west bring heavy rains in May to October. Mountains shelter the central plains from the rain-bearing winds.

POLITICS & ECONOMY The first Thai state was set up in the 13th century and, by 1350, it included most of what is now Thailand. European contact began in the early 16th century, but their interference was unwelcome and, by the late 17th century, all Europeans were forced to leave. In 1782, a Thai General, Chao Phraya Chakkri, became king, founding a dynasty which continues today. The country became known as Siam. From the mid-19th century, contacts with the West were restored. In World War I, Siam supported the Allies against Germany and Austria–Hungary although in 1941 it was aligned with Japan against the UK and US.

After 1967, when Thailand became a member of ASEAN (Association of Southeast Asian Nations), its economy expanded rapidly. In 1997, with other eastern Asian economies, it suffered an economic recession. Thailand has also faced conflict in the south, where the government has clashed with minority Muslim groups. In 2001, Thaksin Shinawatra, a businessman, became prime minister. In 2006, his party won a majority, the result of a boycott of opposition parties. Following mass protests, a military junta took power until civilian rule was restored in 2007. In 2011, Thaksin's sister, Yingluck Shinawatra, was elected prime minister. Elections held in early 2014 were later declared invalid and the military took control, with General Prayuth Chan-ocha appointed prime minister. In disputed elections in 2019 his position was formally confirmed.

Classified as an "upper-middle-income country," Thailand has a well-developed infrastructure and an export-led economy. Agriculture employs 32% of the people and rice is the chief crop. Cassava, cotton, maize, rubber, sugarcane, and tobacco are also grown. Tin is mined, but the chief exports are manufactures and food products. Tourism plays a significant part in the economy.

AREA 198,114 SQ MI [513,115 SQ KM] **POPULATION** 68,977,000
CAPITAL BANGKOK **GOVERNMENT** CONSTITUTIONAL MONARCHY
ETHNIC GROUPS THAI 75%, CHINESE 14%, OTHERS 11%
LANGUAGES THAI (OFFICIAL), ENGLISH, ETHNIC AND REGIONAL DIALECTS
RELIGIONS BUDDHISM 95%, ISLAM, CHRISTIANITY
CURRENCY THAI BAHT = 100 SATANG

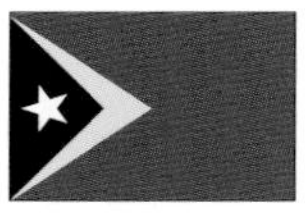
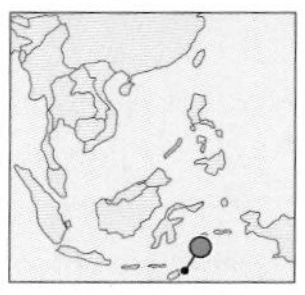

TIMOR-LESTE

The Republic of Timor-Leste (East Timor) is mainly rugged. Temperatures are generally high and the rainfall is moderate. Portugal, the ruling colonial power, withdrew in 1975 and Indonesia seized control. Brutal suppression by Indonesia led to a vote for independence in 1999, which came into force in 2002. Support from the UN and Australia was crucial in bringing stability and allowing reconstruction. In 2006, Timor-Leste and Australia signed a deal to share the revenue from oil and natural gas deposits under the Timor Sea. Its economy is now dominated by oil, and the challenge is to diversify. Agriculture employs 40% of the work force. Crops include rice, maize, cassava, and sweet potatoes.

AREA 5,743 SQ MI [14,874 SQ KM] **POPULATION** 1,384,000 **CAPITAL** DILI

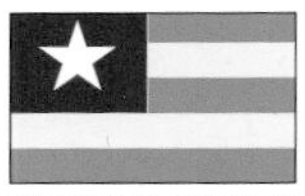
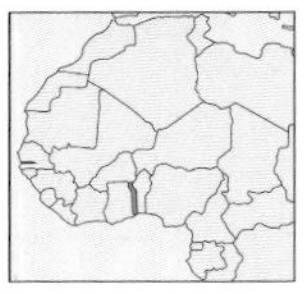

TOGO

GEOGRAPHY The Republic of Togo is a long, narrow country in West Africa. From north to south, it extends about 311 mi [500 km]. Its coastline on the Gulf of Guinea is only 40 mi [64 km] long and it is only 90 mi [145 km] at its widest point.

Togo's climate is generally tropical, and it has high temperatures all through the year. The main wet season is from March to July, with a minor wet season in October and November.

POLITICS & ECONOMY Togo became a German protectorate in 1884, but, in 1919, Britain took over the western third of the territory, while France took over the eastern two-thirds. In 1956, the people of British Togoland voted to join Ghana, while French Togoland became an independent republic in 1960.

A military regime took power in 1963. In 1967, General Gnassingbé Eyadéma became head of state, a position he maintained until his death in 2005. Elections held during this period were deemed unfair and were boycotted by opposition parties. His son, Faure Gnassingbé, took over as president, but international pressure forced him to step down. He was, however, re-elected in 2005, 2010, and 2015. Serious challenges to the stranglehold of this family will have to await future elections.

Togo is a poor, developing country dependent on agriculture. Major food crops include cassava, maize, millet, and yams. Togo is one of the world's largest producers and exporters of phosphates. Economic growth will depend on reforms and foreign assistance.

AREA 21,925 SQ MI [56,785 SQ KM] **POPULATION** 8,608,000
CAPITAL LOMÉ **GOVERNMENT** MULTIPARTY REPUBLIC
ETHNIC GROUPS NATIVE AFRICAN 99% (LARGEST TRIBES ARE EWE, MINA AND KABRE) **LANGUAGES** FRENCH (OFFICIAL), AFRICAN LANGUAGES
RELIGIONS TRADITIONAL BELIEFS 51%, CHRISTIANITY 29%, ISLAM 20%
CURRENCY CFA FRANC = 100 CENTIMES

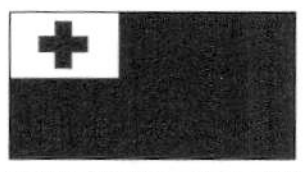
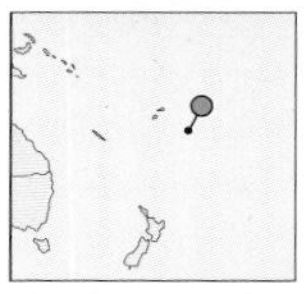

TONGA

The Kingdom of Tonga, a former British protectorate, became independent in 1970. Situated in the south Pacific Ocean, it contains more than 170 islands, 36 of which are inhabited. In 2010, Tonga held its first election for a popularly elected parliament. Agriculture is the main activity and unemployment is high.

AREA 251 SQ MI [650 SQ KM] **POPULATION** 106,000 **CAPITAL** NUKU'ALOFA

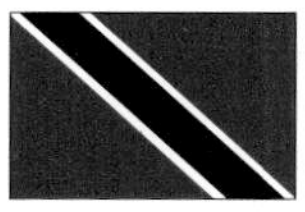
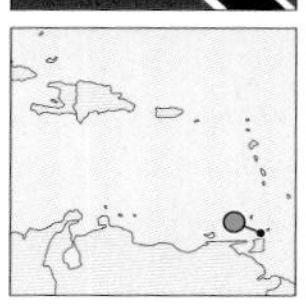

TRINIDAD AND TOBAGO

The Republic of Trinidad and Tobago became independent from Britain in 1962. These tropical islands, populated by people of African, Asian (mainly Indian) and European origin, are hilly and forested, though there are some fertile plains. Oil and natural gas production is the mainstay of the economy

AREA 1,981 SQ MI [5,130 SQ KM]
POPULATION 1,209,000 **CAPITAL** PORT OF SPAIN

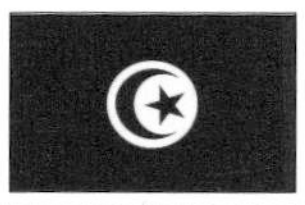
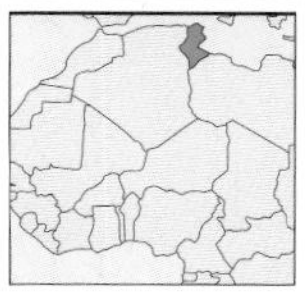

TUNISIA

GEOGRAPHY The Republic of Tunisia is the smallest country in North Africa. The mountains in the north are an eastward and comparatively low extension of the Atlas Mountains. To the north and east of the mountains lie fertile plains, especially between Sfax, Tunis, and Bizerte. In the south, low-lying regions contain the Chott Djerid, a vast salt pan, part of the Sahara.

Northern Tunisia has a Mediterranean climate, with dry, sunny summers, and mild winters with a moderate rainfall. The average yearly rainfall decreases toward the south.

POLITICS & ECONOMY Phoenicians first settled in what is now Tunisia in about 1100 BC. It later became of strategic importance to Romans, Arabs and Ottoman Turks, and was ruled by France from 1881 to 1956. The monarchy was abolished and Tunisia declared a republic in 1957, with the nationalist leader, Habib Bourguiba, as president. His government introduced reforms, including votes for women, but problems included unemployment among the middle class and fears that the ideas of Western visitors might undermine Muslim values. In 1987, the prime minister, Zine el Abidine Ben Ali, removed Bourguiba, and became president. He was re-elected five times until, in 2011, anti-government demonstrations forced him to flee the country. Kais Saied assumed the presidency in 2019.

The World Bank classifies Tunisia as a "lower-middle-income" developing country. The main resources and chief exports are phosphates and oil. Most industries are concerned with food processing. Fishing is important. The tourist industry has been hit hard by the fallout from Islamist State terrorist attacks in 2015.

AREA 63,170 SQ MI [163,610 SQ KM] **POPULATION** 11,721,000
CAPITAL TUNIS **GOVERNMENT** MULTIPARTY REPUBLIC
ETHNIC GROUPS ARAB 98%, EUROPEAN 1% **LANGUAGES** ARABIC (OFFICIAL), FRENCH **RELIGIONS** ISLAM 98%, CHRISTIANITY 1%, OTHERS
CURRENCY TUNISIAN DINAR = 1,000 MILLIMES

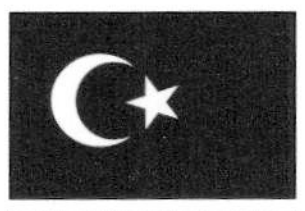
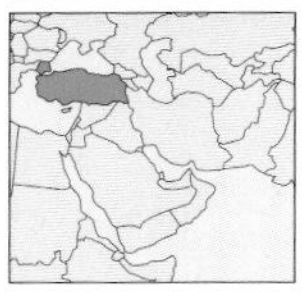

TURKEY

GEOGRAPHY The Republic of Turkey lies in two continents. European Turkey, also called Thrace, lies west of a waterway linking the Mediterranean and Black seas. Most of Asian Turkey consists of plateaux and mountains, which rise to 16,945 ft [5,165 m] at Mount Ararat, near the border with Armenia. Earthquakes are common. Central Turkey has a dry climate, with hot, sunny summers and cold winters. The west has a Mediterranean climate, but the Black Sea coast has cooler summers.

POLITICS & ECONOMY In AD 330, the Roman empire moved its capital to Byzantium, which it renamed Constantinople. Muslim Seljuk Turks from central Asia invaded Anatolia (Asian Turkey) in the 11th century. In the 14th century, another group of Turks, the Ottomans, conquered the area and, in 1453, they took Constantinople, renaming it Istanbul. The Ottomans built up a vast empire which collapsed during World War I (1914–18). Turkey became a republic in 1923 and Mustafa Kemal, or Atatürk ("father of the Turks"), began to modernize and secularize the country.

Since the 1940s, Turkey has sought to strengthen its ties with Western powers. It joined NATO in 1951 and it applied to join the European Economic Community in 1987. But Turkey's conflict with Greece, together with its invasion of northern Cyprus in 1974, have led many Europeans to treat Turkey's aspirations to full EU membership with caution. Political instability, military coups, ongoing conflict with Kurdish nationalists in eastern Turkey, and concern about the country's record on human rights are problems still to be solved.

Turkey has enjoyed democracy since 1983. In 1999, the Muslim Virtue Party (successor to the Islamist Welfare Party) lost ground. The largest numbers of parliamentary seats were won by the ruling Democratic Left Party and the far-right National Action Party. However, in the elections in 2002, the moderate Islamic Justice and Development Party (AKP) won 362 of the 500 seats in parliament. Despite concerns about its Islamist roots, the AKP was re-elected in 2007 and 2011. In 2014, Recep Tayyip Erdogan was elected president after serving as prime minister since 2003. The conflict in Syria has increased tensions along the border, and Turkey has carried out several attacks on Kurdish areas of Syria and Iraq. A failed coup in 2016 was followed in 2017 by a referendum on giving the president more powers. The result was a disputed narrow victory for Erdogan, who went on to win a further term as president in 2018.

Turkey came close to economic collapse in 2002, but its recovery enabled it to withstand the global financial crisis in 2008, and bounce back by 2010–11. However, the economy is vulnerable to political instability in the region and investor confidence. Agriculture employs 20% of the people, with barley, cotton, fruits, nuts, maize, tobacco, and wheat being the major crops.

AREA 299,156 SQ MI [774,815 SQ KM] **POPULATION** 82,018,000
CAPITAL ANKARA **GOVERNMENT** MULTIPARTY REPUBLIC
ETHNIC GROUPS TURKISH 73%, KURDISH 18%
LANGUAGES TURKISH (OFFICIAL), KURDISH, ARABIC
RELIGIONS ISLAM (MAINLY SUNNI MUSLIM) 99%
CURRENCY TURKISH LIRA = 100 KURUS

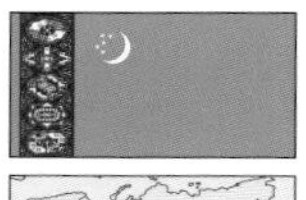
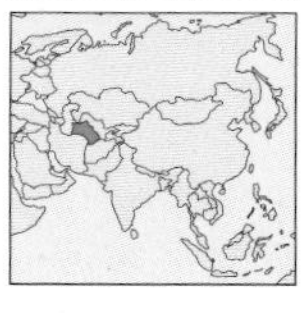

TURKMENISTAN

GEOGRAPHY The Republic of Turkmenistan is one of the five central Asian republics which once formed part of the former Soviet Union. Most of the land is low-lying, with mountains stretching along the southern and south-western borders. In the west lies the salty Caspian Sea. Most of Turkmenistan is arid and the Garagum (Kara Kum), Asia's largest sand

desert, covers about 80% of the country. Turkmenistan has a continental climate, with average annual rainfall varying from 3 inches [80 mm] in the desert to 12 inches [300 mm] in the mountains. Summer months are hot, but winter temperatures drop well below freezing point.

POLITICS & ECONOMY Just over 1,000 years ago, Turkic people settled in the lands east of the Caspian Sea and the name "Turkmen" dates from this time. Mongol armies conquered the area in the 13th century and Islam was introduced in the 14th century. Russia took over the area in the 1870s and 1880s. The area came under Communist rule in 1917 and, in 1924, it became the Turkmen Soviet Socialist Republic.

In the 1980s, when the Soviet Union began to introduce reforms, the Turkmen began to demand more freedom and, in 1991, asserted that their own laws held sway over those of Soviet Russia. In late 1991, Turkmenistan became fully independent although the country maintained ties with Russia through the Commonwealth of Independent States (CIS).

In 1992, Turkmenistan adopted a new constitution, allowing for the setting up of political parties, providing that they were not ethnic or religious in character. But, effectively, Turkmenistan remained a one-party state and, in 1992, Saparmurad Niyazov, the former Communist and at that time Democratic Party leader, was the only presidential candidate. In 1999, parliament declared Niyazov president for life. Niyazov died in 2006 and was succeeded by Gurbanguly Berdymukhamedov. He was returned to power in undemocratic elections in 2012 and 2017.

Faced with many economic problems, Turkmenistan began to look south rather than to the CIS for support. In 1992, it joined the Economic Cooperation Organization, which had been set up in 1985 by Iran, Pakistan, and Turkey. In 1996, a rail link from Turkmenistan to the Iranian coast was completed. Oil and natural gas are the chief resources, and gas pipelines to China and Iran were opened in 2009 and 2010 respectively. A pipeline to India, via Afghanistan and Pakistan, is under construction. Agriculture remains important, with cotton as the main commercial crop. Manufactures include cement, glass, petrochemicals, and textiles.

AREA 188,455 sq mi [488,100 sq km] **POPULATION** 5,529,000
CAPITAL Ashkhabad **GOVERNMENT** Single-party republic
ETHNIC GROUPS Turkmen 85%, Uzbek 5%, Russian 4%
LANGUAGES Turkmen (official), Russian, Uzbek
RELIGIONS Islam 89%, Eastern Orthodox 9%
CURRENCY Turkmen manat = 100 tenge

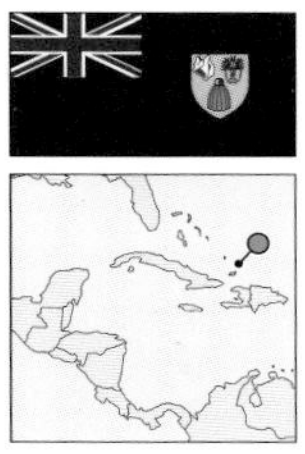

TURKS AND CAICOS ISLANDS

The Turks and Caicos Islands, a British territory since 1776, are a group of about 30 islands. Fishing, tourism, and offshore finance are the major economic activities.

AREA 166 sq mi [430 sq km]
POPULATION 56,000 **CAPITAL** Cockburn Town

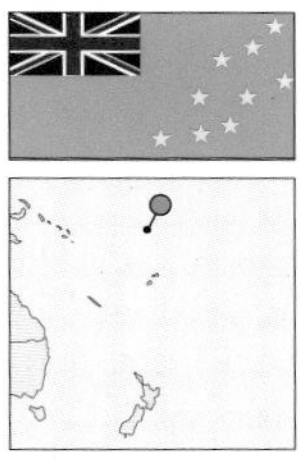

TUVALU

Tuvalu, formerly called the Ellice Islands, was a British territory from the 1890s until it became independent in 1978. It consists of nine low-lying coral atolls in the southern Pacific Ocean. Copra is the only significant export. It is vulnerable to rising sea levels.

AREA 10 sq mi [26 sq km]
POPULATION 11,000 **CAPITAL** Funafuti

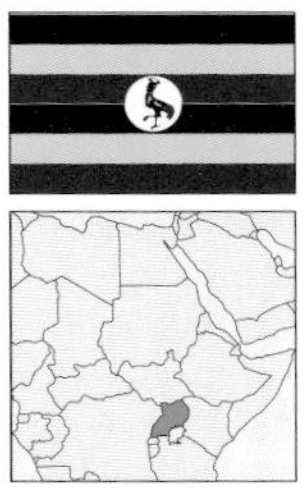

UGANDA

GEOGRAPHY The Republic of Uganda is a landlocked country on the East African plateau. It contains part of Lake Victoria, Africa's largest lake and a source of the River Nile, which occupies a shallow depression in the plateau. The equator runs through Uganda, and the country is warm throughout the year, though the high altitude moderates the temperature. The wettest regions are the lands to the north of Lake Victoria, where the capital, Kampala, is situated, and the western mountains, especially the high Ruwenzori range.

POLITICS & ECONOMY Little is known of the early history of Uganda. When Europeans first reached the area in the 19th century, many of the people were organized in kingdoms, the most powerful of which was Buganda, the home of the Baganda people. Britain took control of the country between 1894 and 1914, and administered it until independence in 1962.

In 1967, Uganda became a republic and Buganda's Kabaka (king), Sir Edward Mutesa II, was made president. But tensions between the Kabaka and the prime minister, Apollo Milton Obote, led to the dismissal of the Kabaka in 1966. Obote also abolished the traditional kingdoms, including Buganda. Obote was overthrown in 1971 by an army group led by General Idi Amin Dada. Amin ruled as adictator: he forced most of the Asians who lived in Uganda to leave the country and had many of his opponents killed.

In 1978, a border dispute between Uganda and Tanzania led Tanzanian troops to enter Uganda. With help from Ugandan opponents of Amin, they overthrew Amin's government. In 1980, Obote led his party to victory in the elections, but following charges of fraud, Obote's opponents instigated a guerrilla war. A military group overthrew Obote in 1985, though strife continued until 1986, when Yoweri Museveni's National Resistance Movement seized power. In 1993, Museveni restored the traditional kingdoms. Elections were held in 1994, but political parties were forbidden. Museveni was re-elected five times between 1996 and 2016. From the late 1980s, Uganda faced the rebel Lord's Resistance Army in the north. Their brutal activities extended into the Central African Republic, the Democratic Republic of the Congo, and Sudan, but were substantially reduced by the mid-2010s. By 2017, more than a million South Sudanese fleeing civil war had sought refuge in Uganda.

Agriculture dominates the economy, employing over 70% of the work force. The chief exports are coffee and gold. Economic reforms and some investment in infrastructure have resulted in a strengthening of the economy. Newly discovered oil will be a valuable asset.

AREA 93,065 sq mi [241,038 sq km] **POPULATION** 43,253,000
CAPITAL Kampala **GOVERNMENT** Republic
ETHNIC GROUPS Baganda 17%, Ankole 8%, Basogo 8%, Iteso 8%, Bakiga 7%, Langi 6%, Rwanda 6%, Bagisu 5%, Acholi 4%, Lugbara 4%, and others
LANGUAGES English and Swahili (both official), Ganda
RELIGIONS Roman Catholic 42%, Protestant 42%, Islam 12%, traditional beliefs 4%
CURRENCY Ugandan shilling

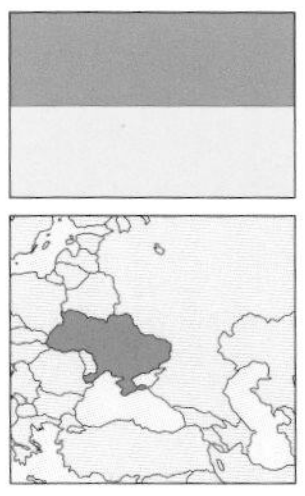

UKRAINE

GEOGRAPHY Ukraine is the second largest country in Europe after Russia. It was formerly part of the Soviet Union, which split apart in 1991. This mostly flat country faces the Black Sea in the south. The Crimean peninsula includes a highland region overlooking Yalta. Ukraine has warm summers, but the winters are cold, becoming more severe from west to east. In the summer, the east is often warmer than the west. Most rain falls in the summer months.

POLITICS & ECONOMY Kiev was the original capital of the early Slavic civilization known as Kievan Rus. In the 17th and 18th centuries, parts of Ukraine came under Polish and Russian rule, but, by the late 18th century, Russia had gained most of Ukraine. In 1918, Ukraine gained independence, but only until 1922 when it became part of the Soviet Union.

In the 1980s, Ukrainian people demanded more say over their affairs and regained their independence in 1991. In the early 21st century, Ukraine has been pulled in two directions – either closer integration with Russia or with the EU. In 2005, the pro-Western leader Viktor Yushchenko was elected president. Economic problems, and political infighting, led to a Russian-leaning party, led by Viktor Yanukovych, winning most seats in parliament in 2006. An election in 2007 resulted in a pro-Western coalition government led by Yulia Tymoshenko. In 2010, the pro-Russian Viktor Yanukovych was declared winner of the presidential election, but in 2013–14 mass protests over his backtracking on a cooperation agreement with the EU forced him from power. Russia subsequently invaded, seized Crimea, and sent troops into other parts of eastern Ukraine, where unrest continues. The annexation of Crimea has not been recognized by Ukraine or the wider world. A pro-Western government has been in power since 2014. The actor Volodymyr Zelensky became president in 2019.

Manufacturing is the chief economic activity including iron and steel, machinery, and vehicles. Ukraine has large coalfields and its own hydroelectric and nuclear power plants, but the country imports oil and natural gas (much of it from Russia). Agriculture contributes 13% of GDP and wheat and sugar are exported.

AREA 233,089 sq mi [603,700 sq km] **POPULATION** 43,923,000
CAPITAL Kiev **GOVERNMENT** Multiparty republic
ETHNIC GROUPS Ukrainian 78%, Russian 17%, Belarusian, Moldovan, Bulgarian, Hungarian, Polish
LANGUAGES Ukrainian (official), Russian
RELIGIONS Mostly Ukrainian Orthodox
CURRENCY Hryvnia = 100 kopiykas

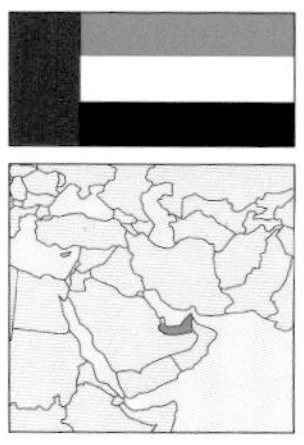

UNITED ARAB EMIRATES

The United Arab Emirates (UAE) were formed in 1971 when the seven Trucial States of the Persian Gulf (Abu Dhabi, Dubai, Sharjah, Ajman, Umm al Qawayn, Ra's al Khaymah, and Al Fujayrah) joined together. The economy of this hot and dry state depends on oil production, and the resulting revenues give the UAE one of the highest per capita GDPs in Asia. Tourism and finance are important sources of revenue.

AREA 32,278 sq mi [83,600 sq km]
POPULATION 9,992,000 **CAPITAL** Abu Dhabi

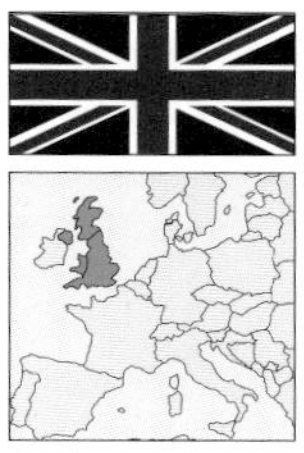

UNITED KINGDOM

GEOGRAPHY The United Kingdom (or UK) is a union of four countries. Three of them – England, Scotland, and Wales – make up Great Britain. The fourth country is Northern Ireland. The Isle of Man and the Channel Islands are not part of the UK. They are self-governing British dependencies.

The land is highly varied. Much of Scotland and Wales is mountainous, and the highest peak is Scotland's Ben Nevis at 4,411 ft [1,345 m]. England has some highland areas, including the Cumbrian Mountains (or Lake District) and the Pennine range in the north, but it also has extensive areas of fertile lowland. Northern Ireland is also a mixture of lowlands and uplands and it contains the UK's largest lake, Lough Neagh.

The UK has a mild climate, influenced by the warm North Atlantic Drift which is a continuation of the Gulf Stream originating from the Gulf of Mexico. Moist winds from the south-west bring rain, but the rainfall decreases from west to east. Winds from the east and north bring cold weather in winter.

POLITICS & ECONOMY In ancient times, Britain was invaded by many peoples, including Iberians, Celts, Romans, Angles, Saxons, Jutes, Norsemen, Danes, and the Normans, who arrived in 1066. King Edward I annexed Wales in 1282 and united it with England. Union with Scotland was achieved in 1707 and this created a country known as the United Kingdom of Great Britain.

Ireland came under Norman rule in the 11th century, and much of its later history was concerned with a struggle against English domination. In 1801, Ireland became part of the United Kingdom of Great Britain and Ireland. But in 1921, southern Ireland, where most of the people were Roman Catholics, broke away to become the Irish Free State. In Northern Ireland, where the majority of the people were Protestants, most people wanted to remain citizens of the United Kingdom. The country now became the United Kingdom of Great Britain and Northern Ireland.

The modern history of the UK began in the 18th century with the expansion of the British empire, despite the loss in 1783 of its 13 North American colonies. The other significant milestone occurred in the late 18th century, when the UK became the first country to industrialize its economy.

The British empire broke up after World War II (1939–45), though the UK still administers many small, mainly island, territories around the world. The empire was transformed into the Commonwealth of Nations, a free association of independent countries which numbered 54 in 2020.

The UK has retained an important world role. In 2001, it played a prominent role in creating a broad alliance to counter international terrorism following attacks on the United States. It was also a member of the coalition force which invaded Iraq in 2003. It became a member of the European Economic Community (now the European Union) in 1973. Membership of the EU has been important to the British economy, but some have feared a loss of British sovereignty and identity. A referendum in June 2016 on the UK's future in the EU resulted in a narrow vote to leave. The process of leaving was triggered in March 2017 and following long negotiations and a change in prime minister, the UK left at the end of January 2020. Many details, notably around trade and border issues, remain unresolved.

Since the late 1990s some powers have been devolved to Scotland, Wales, and Northern Ireland. The Northern Ireland Assembly has followed a fitful path since its establishment in 1998. The National Assembly for Wales and the Scottish Parliament both opened in 1999. In a referendum on Scottish independence held in 2014, 55% of voters elected to stay within the UK.

The UK is a major industrial and trading nation. Natural resources include coal and iron ore, as well as dwindling reserves of oil and natural gas. It imports most of the materials for its industries. The UK also has to import food, because it produces only about two-thirds of the food it needs. In the first half of the 20th century, Britain was a major exporter of cars, ships, steel, and textiles. But many industries have suffered from competition from other countries, with lower labor costs. From 2008, Britain's economy was hit by a global financial crisis, which led the country into recession. Severe austerity measures were introduced.

The UK is one of the world's most urbanized countries, and agriculture employs only 1% of the work force. Production is high because of the use of scientific methods and modern machinery. However, in the early 21st century, especially following the outbreak of foot-and-mouth disease in 2001, questions were raised about the future of rural industries. Major crops include barley, potatoes, sugar beet, and wheat. Sheep are the leading livestock, but beef and dairy cattle, pigs, and poultry are also important. Fishing is a major activity. It remains to be seen how the UK's economy will be affected by its departure from the EU.

Service industries play a major part in the UK's economy. Financial and insurance services bring in much-needed foreign exchange, while tourism has long been a major earner.

AREA 93,381 SQ MI [241,857 SQ KM] **POPULATION** 65,761,000
CAPITAL LONDON **GOVERNMENT** CONSTITUTIONAL MONARCHY
ETHNIC GROUPS ENGLISH 84%, SCOTTISH 9%, WELSH 5%, N. IRISH 3%, WEST INDIAN, INDIAN, PAKISTANI AND OTHERS
LANGUAGES ENGLISH (OFFICIAL), WELSH, GAELIC
RELIGIONS CHRISTIANITY (ANGLICAN, ROMAN CATHOLIC, PRESBYTERIAN, METHODIST), ISLAM, SIKHISM, HINDUISM, JUDAISM
CURRENCY POUND STERLING = 100 PENCE

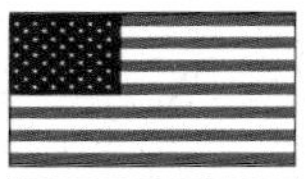
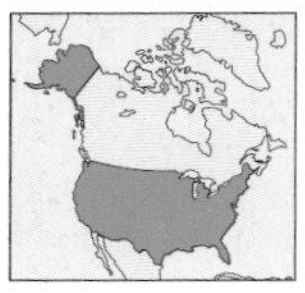

UNITED STATES OF AMERICA

GEOGRAPHY The United States of America is the world's third largest country in area and the third largest in population. It contains 50 states, 48 of which lie between Canada and Mexico, plus Alaska in northwestern North America, and Hawai'i, a group of volcanic islands in the north Pacific Ocean. Densely populated coastal plains lie to the east and south of the Appalachian Mountains. The central lowlands, drained by the Mississippi–Missouri rivers, stretch from the Appalachians to the Rocky Mountains in the west. The Pacific region contains fertile valleys, separated by mountain ranges.

The climate varies greatly, ranging from the Arctic cold of Alaska to the intense heat of Death Valley, a bleak desert in California. Of the 48 states between Canada and Mexico, winters are cold and snowy in the north, but mild in the south.

POLITICS & ECONOMY The first people in North America, the ancestors of the Native Americans (or American Indians), arrived perhaps 40,000 years ago from Asia. Although Vikings probably reached North America 1,000 years ago, European exploration proper did not begin until the late 15th century.

The first Europeans to settle in large numbers were the British, who founded settlements on the eastern coast in the early 17th century. British rule ended in the War of Independence (1775–83). The country expanded in 1803 when a vast territory in the south and west was acquired through the Louisiana Purchase, while the border with Mexico was fixed in the mid-19th century. The Civil War (1861–65) ended slavery and the serious threat that the nation might split into two parts. In the late 19th century, the West was opened up, while immigrants flooded in from Europe and elsewhere.

During the late 19th and early 20th centuries, industrialization led to the United States becoming the world's leading economic superpower and a pioneer in science and technology. It took on the mantle of the champion of Western democracy and, following the breakup of the former Soviet Union, it became the world's only superpower. But the attacks on the country on September 11, 2001, revealed its vulnerability to terrorists and rogue states. The response was vigorous. In 2001, it attacked the Taliban government in Afghanistan, which was protecting al Qaeda terrorists. Then, in 2003, it led a coalition force to invade Iraq and overthrow Saddam Hussein.

From 2008–16, Democrat Barack Obama was president. Bitterly fought elections in 2016 resulted in a win for Republican businessman Donald Trump, on a ticket of protectionism, removing Obama's changes to health care and a crackdown on immigration. Policy announcements included major tax cuts, and the imposition of high import tariffs on such products as steel. In 2020 Trump was impeached on charges of abuse of power and obstruction of Congress, relating to his election. He was found not guilty by a Republican-dominated Senate. Tension with Iran increased in 2020 when a prominent Iranian military commander was killed in US drone strikes.

The US economy has long been one of the world's largest, but some authorities now see it being challenged by China. Recovery from the global financial crisis of 2008 has been slow. There is a wide disparity between rich and poor, and as many as 30 million Americans live below the poverty line. The US has been badly affected by the global outbreak of coronavirus in 2020, and the long-term effects on the economy are likely to be severe.

Natural resources include oil, natural gas, coal, metal ores, and timber. Manufacturing employs around 10% of the work force; major products include vehicles, food products, chemicals, machinery, printed goods, metal products, and scientific instruments. California, with its many high-tech electronics industries, is the top manufacturing state.

AREA 3,717,792 SQ MI [9,629,091 SQ KM] **POPULATION** 332,639,000
CAPITAL WASHINGTON, DC **GOVERNMENT** FEDERAL REPUBLIC
ETHNIC GROUPS WHITE 80%, AFRICAN AMERICAN 13%, ASIAN 4%, AMERINDIAN 1%, OTHERS
LANGUAGES ENGLISH, SPANISH, MORE THAN 30 OTHERS
RELIGIONS PROTESTANT 51%, ROMAN CATHOLIC 24%, JUDAISM 2%, MORMON 2%, ISLAM 1% **CURRENCY** US DOLLAR = 100 CENTS

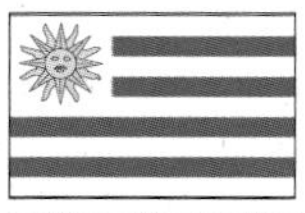
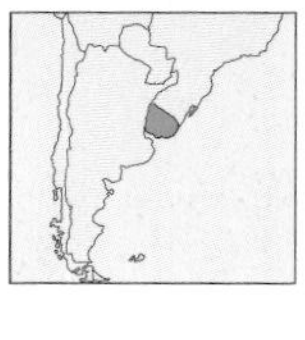

URUGUAY

GEOGRAPHY Uruguay is South America's second smallest independent country after Suriname. The land consists mainly of flat plains and hills. The River Uruguay, which forms the country's western border, flows into the Río de la Plata, a large estuary which leads into the South Atlantic Ocean.

Uruguay has a mild climate, with rain in every month, though droughts sometimes can occur. Summers are pleasantly warm and winters relatively mild.

POLITICS & ECONOMY In 1726, Spanish settlers founded Montevideo in order to halt the Portuguese gaining influence in the area. By the late 18th century, Spaniards had settled in most of the country and Uruguay became part of a colony called the Viceroyalty of La Plata, which also included Argentina, Paraguay, and parts of Bolivia, Brazil, and Chile. In 1820 Brazil annexed Uruguay, ending Spanish rule. In 1825, Uruguayans, supported by Argentina, began a struggle for independence.

Finally, in 1828, Brazil and Argentina recognized Uruguay as an independent republic. Social and economic developments were slow, but, from 1903, Uruguay became stable and democratic.

From the 1950s, economic problems incited unrest from terrorist groups, notably the Tupumaros, until the army took over the government in 1973. Military rule continued until elections were held in 1984. In the early 21st century, Uruguay faced many economic problems, many of which were the result of the economic crisis in Argentina. Tabaré Vázquez replaced Jose Mujica as president in March 2015. Vázquez had previously been president in 2005–10.

The World Bank now classifies Uruguay as a "high-income" economy but, although it is one of the more prosperous countries in South America, there is still a minority underclass living in poverty. Agriculture employs 13% of the work force, and farm products, notably hides and leather goods, beef, and wool, are the main exports, while many manufacturing industries process farm products. Crops include maize, potatoes, wheat, and sugar beet. Uruguay depends largely on renewable power for energy, notably hydropower, wind and solar. In 2008, Uruguay announced the discovery of an offshore natural gas field, which is being explored.

AREA 67,574 SQ MI [175,016 SQ KM] **POPULATION** 3,388,000
CAPITAL MONTEVIDEO **GOVERNMENT** MULTIPARTY REPUBLIC
ETHNIC GROUPS WHITE 88%, MESTIZO 8%, MULATTO OR BLACK 4%
LANGUAGES SPANISH (OFFICIAL)
RELIGIONS CHRISTIANITY 58% (ROMAN CATHOLIC 47%), OTHERS
CURRENCY URUGUAYAN PESO = 100 CENTÉSIMOS

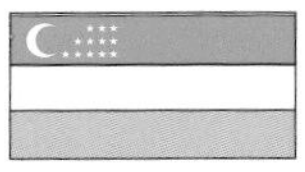
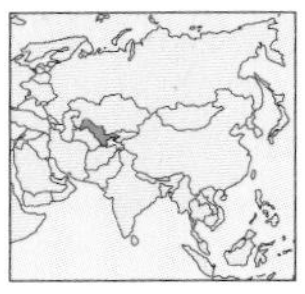

UZBEKISTAN

GEOGRAPHY The Republic of Uzbekistan is one of the five republics in Central Asia which were once part of the Soviet Union. Plains cover most of western Uzbekistan, with highlands in the east. The main rivers, the Amudarya and Syrdarya, drain into the Aral Sea. So much water has been taken from these rivers to irrigate the land to grow cotton that the Aral Sea has now shrunk to about a quarter of its size in 1960. The former lake area is now desert. Uzbekistan has cold winters and hot summers. The largely uninhabited Kyzyl Kum desert lies in central Uzbekistan.

POLITICS & ECONOMY Russia took the area in the 19th century. After the Russian Revolution of 1917, the Communists took over and, in 1924, they set up the Uzbek Soviet Socialist Republic. Under Communism, all aspects of Uzbek life were controlled and religious worship was discouraged, but education, health, housing, and transport were improved. In the late 1980s, the people demanded more autonomy, leading to independence in 1991 with the breakup of the Soviet Union.

Islam Karimov, leader of the People's Democratic Party (formerly the Communist Party), was first elected president in December 1991. Dissent was not tolerated and opposition leaders were arrested and accused of threatening national stability. Initially, Karimov's government allowed the US to use Uzbekistan as a base for its military campaign in Afghanistan, but relations cooled in 2005 and the US was asked to remove its troops. In an about-face in 2009, ties with Russia deteriorated and those with the US improved and they were again able to transport supplies through Uzbekistan to their troops. The United Nations has condemned the country's human rights record. Karimov remained in power until his death in 2016, when Prime Minister Shavjat Mirziyoyev was elected to replace him. Mirziyoyev has improved relations with neighboring countries and made moves to open up the economy.

The World Bank classifies Uzbekistan as a "lower-middle-income" developing country. Uzbekistan is one of the world's largest cotton exporters, although this has declined in recent years. The country produces coal, copper, gold, oil, and natural gas.

AREA 172,741 SQ MI [447,400 SQ KM] **POPULATION** 30,565,000
CAPITAL TASHKENT **GOVERNMENT** SOCIALIST REPUBLIC
ETHNIC GROUPS UZBEK 80%, RUSSIAN 5%, TAJIK 5%, KAZAKH 3%, TATAR 2%, KARA-KALPAK 2%
LANGUAGES UZBEK (OFFICIAL), RUSSIAN **RELIGIONS** ISLAM 88%, EASTERN ORTHODOX 9% **CURRENCY** UZBEKISTANI SUM = 100 TIYIN

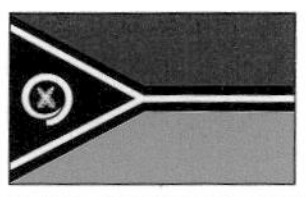
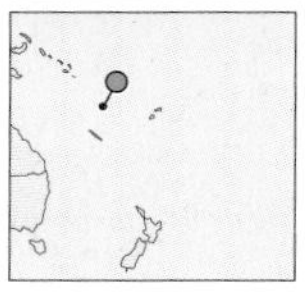

VANUATU

The Republic of Vanuatu, formerly the Anglo-French Condominium of the New Hebrides, became independent in 1980. It consists of a chain of 80 islands in the south Pacific Ocean. Its economy is based on agriculture, and it exports copra, beef and veal, timber, and cocoa.

AREA 4,706 SQ MI [12,189 SQ KM]
POPULATION 298,000 **CAPITAL** PORT-VILA

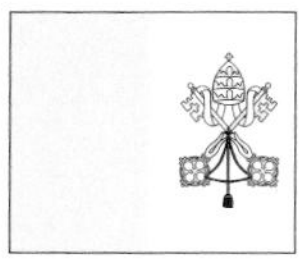
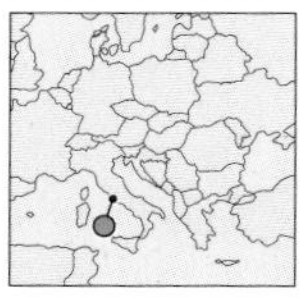

VATICAN CITY

Vatican City State, the world's smallest independent nation, is an enclave on the west bank of the River Tiber in Rome. It forms an independent base for the Holy See, the governing body of the Roman Catholic Church.

AREA 0.17 SQ MI [0.44 SQ KM]
POPULATION 1,000

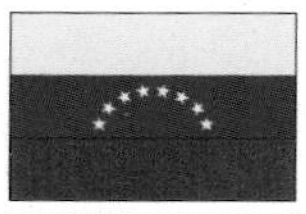
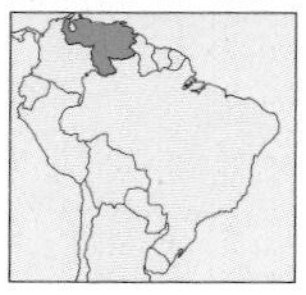

VENEZUELA

GEOGRAPHY The Bolivarian Republic of Venezuela, in northern South America, contains the Maracaibo lowlands around the oil-rich Lake Maracaibo in the west. Andean ranges enclose the lowlands and extend across most of the northern part of the country. The Orinoco river basin, containing tropical grasslands called llanos, lies between the northern highlands and the Guiana Highlands in the southeast. The Orinoco is Venezuela's longest

river. Venezuela has a tropical climate. Rainfall is heaviest in the mountains, but much of the country has a dry season between December and April.

POLITICS & ECONOMY In the early 19th century, Venezuelans such as Simón Bolívar and Francisco de Miranda rebeled against Spanish colonial rule, leading to full independence in 1821.

The country has greatly benefited from its oil resources (first exploited in 1917) which are some of the world's largest In 1960, Venezuela helped to form OPEC (the Organization of Petroleum Exporting Countries) and, in 1976, the government of Venezuela took control of the country's oil industry. In 1999, Hugo Chavez, who had staged an unsuccessful coup in 1992, was elected president. Chavez remained in office until his death in 2013 when he was succeeded by the socialist Nicolás Maduro. A severe economic downturn followed and Maduro's rule became increasingly autocratic. In 2018 he was re-elected, but the election was widely regarded as fraudulent. The result was declared invalid by the National Assembly, whose leader, Juan Guaidó, declared himself interim president in 2019. He is recognized as such by the EU, US and much of Latin America. Maduro, supported by the security forces, has refused to step down. The ongoing crisis has led to hyperinflation and shortages of food, medicines and electricity.

The political crisis has devastated Venezuela's economy, which has long been dependent on petroleum refining and oil exports. The majority of the people live in poverty and unemployment is high. Other exports include bauxite and aluminum, iron ore, and farm products. Beef cattle, dairy cattle, and poultry are raised. Crops include bananas, citrus fruits, coffee, and rice. Cement and steel are also produced.

AREA 352,143 SQ MI [912,050 SQ KM] **POPULATION** 28,645,000
CAPITAL Caracas **GOVERNMENT** Federal republic
ETHNIC GROUPS Spanish, Italian, Portuguese, Arab, German, African, indigenous people **LANGUAGES** Spanish (official), indigenous dialects **RELIGIONS** Roman Catholic 96%
CURRENCY Bolívar = 100 céntimos

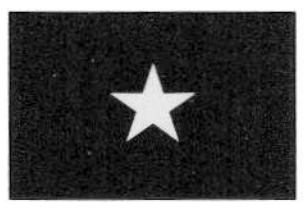
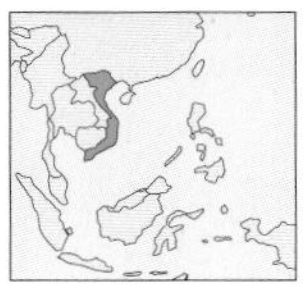

VIETNAM

GEOGRAPHY The Socialist Republic of Vietnam occupies an S-shaped strip of land facing the South China Sea in Southeast Asia. The coastal plains include two densely populated, fertile delta regions: the Red (Hong) delta facing the Gulf of Tonkin in the north, and the Mekong delta in the south.

Vietnam has a tropical climate, though the driest months of January to March are a little cooler than the wet, hot summer months, when monsoon winds blow from the southwest. Typhoons (cyclones or hurricanes) sometimes hit the coast, causing extensive flooding and much damage.

POLITICS & ECONOMY China dominated Vietnam for a thousand years before AD 939, when a Vietnamese state was founded. The French took over the area between the 1850s and 1880s, and they ruled Vietnam as part of French Indochina, which also included Cambodia and Laos.

Japan conquered Vietnam during World War II (1939–45). In 1946, war broke out between the Vietminh, a nationalist group, and the French colonial government. France withdrew in 1954 and Vietnam was divided into a Communist North Vietnam, led by the Vietminh leader, Ho Chi Minh, and a non-Communist South.

In 1957, a Communist insurgency, led by the Viet Cong, rebeled against South Vietnam's government provoking a war that gradually escalated. The United States aided the South, but after it withdrew in 1975, South Vietnam surrendered. In 1976, the united Vietnam became a socialist republic. From the mid-1990s, diplomatic and trade relations were restored between the US and Vietnam, and the US is now its main trading partner. In 2007, Vietnam became a member of the World Trade Organization after 12 years of negotiations. The benefits of moves to modernize the economy have not been enjoyed by all groups in society: there is poverty in rural areas. Human rights issues remain a concern. Political power remains entirely in the hands of the ruling Communist Party.

Agriculture is the main activity although its share of economic output is diminishing. Rice and coffee are the main crops. Vietnam produces electronic goods, textiles, chromium, tin, and phosphates.

AREA 128,065 SQ MI [331,689 SQ KM] **POPULATION** 98,721,000
CAPITAL Hanoi **GOVERNMENT** Socialist republic
ETHNIC GROUPS Vietnamese 87%, Chinese, Hmong, Thai, Khmer, Cham, mountain groups
LANGUAGES Vietnamese (official), English, Chinese
RELIGIONS Buddhism, Christianity, indigenous beliefs
CURRENCY Dong = 10 hao = 100 xu

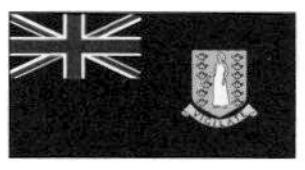
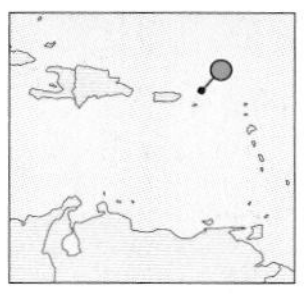

VIRGIN ISLANDS, BRITISH

The British Virgin Islands, the most northerly of the Lesser Antilles, are a British overseas territory, with a substantial measure of self-government.

AREA 58 SQ MI [151 SQ KM]
POPULATION 35,000 **CAPITAL** Road Town

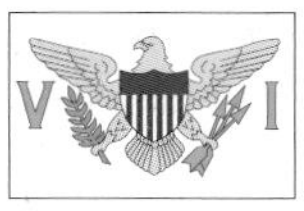
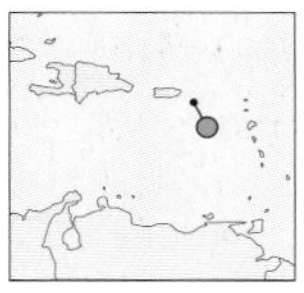

VIRGIN ISLANDS, US

The Virgin Islands of the United States, a group of three islands and 65 small islets, are a self-governing US territory, which was purchased from Denmark in 1917. Its residents are US citizens and they elect a non-voting delegate to the US House of Representatives.

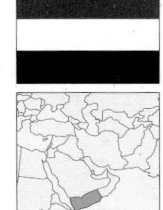

AREA 134 SQ MI [347 SQ KM]
POPULATION 106,000 **CAPITAL** Charlotte Amalie

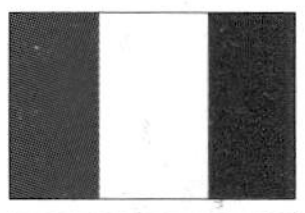
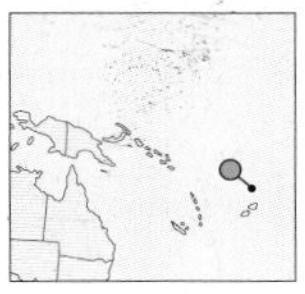

WALLIS AND FUTUNA

Wallis and Futuna, in the south Pacific Ocean, is the smallest and the poorest of France's overseas "collectivities." French aid is vital to an economy based on subsistence agriculture.

AREA 77 SQ MI [200 SQ KM]
POPULATION 16,000 **CAPITAL** Mata-Utu

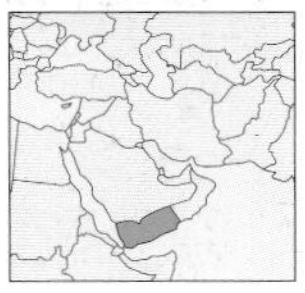

YEMEN

GEOGRAPHY The Republic of Yemen faces the Red Sea and the Gulf of Aden in the southwestern corner of the Arabian peninsula. Behind the narrow coastal plain along the Red Sea, the land rises to the mountains of the High Yemen. The climate ranges from hot and often humid conditions on the coast to the cooler highlands. Most of the country is arid. The south coasts are particularly hot and humid.

POLITICS & ECONOMY After World War I, northern Yemen, which had been ruled by Turkey, began to evolve into a separate state from the south, where Britain was in control. Britain withdrew in 1967 and a left-wing government took power in the south. In North Yemen, the monarchy was abolished in 1962 and the country became a republic.

Clashes occurred between the two factions but, in 1990, the two Yemens merged to form a single country. In the 2000s, the government faced conflict with Shi'ite northern rebels, called Houthis, al Qaeda supporters, and southern separatists. Protests in 2011 resulted in the resignation of President Ali Abdullah Saleh and a transfer of power to Abdrabbuh Mansour Hadi. The instability allowed the Houthi rebels to seize territory in the north. Civil war had taken hold by 2014. A Saudi-led coalition attacked the Houthi, while US drone strikes targeted Islamic State and al-Qaeda bases. However, the Houthi remain in control of much of the north-west of the country, including Sana'. The government is based in the city of Aden, where separatist unrest continues. The world's largest humanitarian crisis is unfolding, with a huge refugee crisis, thousands of civilian deaths, famine, and a major cholera outbreak.

Yemen is the poorest country in the Middle East, and its economy has been devastated by the civil war. Sheep are reared and crops such as barley, fruits, wheat, and vegetables are grown. Cash crops include coffee and cotton. Petroleum extraction is important to the economy. Remittances from Yemenis abroad are a major source of revenue.

AREA 203,848 SQ MI [527,968 SQ KM] **POPULATION** 29,884,000
CAPITAL Sana' **GOVERNMENT** Multiparty republic
ETHNIC GROUPS Predominantly Arab **LANGUAGES** Arabic (official)
RELIGIONS Islam **CURRENCY** Yemeni rial = 100 fils

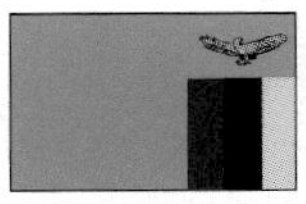
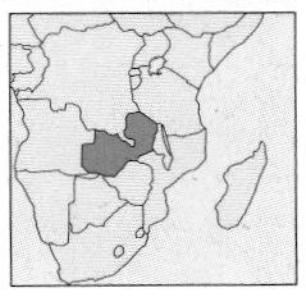

ZAMBIA

GEOGRAPHY The Republic of Zambia is a landlocked country in southern Africa. Zambia lies on the plateau that makes up most of the southern part of the continent. Much of the land is between 2,950 ft and 4,920 ft [900 m to 1,500 m] above sea level. The Muchinga Mountains in the northeast rise above this flat land. Lakes include Bangweulu, which is entirely within Zambia, together with parts of lakes Mweru and Tanganyika in the north. Zambia lies in the tropics, but temperatures are moderated by the altitude.

POLITICS & ECONOMY European contact with Zambia began in the 19th century, when the explorer David Livingstone crossed the River Zambezi. In the 1890s, the British South Africa Company, set up by Cecil Rhodes, the British financier and statesman, made treaties with local chiefs and gradually took over the area. In 1911, the Company named the area Northern Rhodesia and, in 1924, Britain took control of the country.

In 1953, Britain formed a federation of Northern Rhodesia, Southern Rhodesia (now Zimbabwe), and Nyasaland (now Malawi). Due to African opposition, the federation was dissolved in 1963 and Northern Rhodesia gained independence as Zambia in 1964. Kenneth Kaunda became president and remained in office for 27 years until Frederick Chiluba was elected in 1996. The current president, Edgar Lungu, took office in 2015.

At nearly 7% per annum, Zambia's economy grew strongly in the early years of this century, until copper prices began to fall in 2015. Copper, however, remains the main resource, and accounts for about 60% of the country's exports. Zambia also produces cobalt, lead, zinc, and gemstones. Agriculture employs about 55% of the people. Food crops include cassava, fruits and vegetables, maize, millet, and sorghum. Cash crops include coffee, sugarcane, and tobacco.

AREA 290,586 SQ MI [752,618 SQ KM] **POPULATION** 17,427,000
CAPITAL Lusaka **GOVERNMENT** Multiparty republic
ETHNIC GROUPS Native African (Bemba, Tonga, Maravi/Nyanja)
LANGUAGES English, Bemba, Kaonda, Nyanja and about 70 others
RELIGIONS Christianity 62%, Islam, Hinduism
CURRENCY Zambian kwacha = 100 ngwee

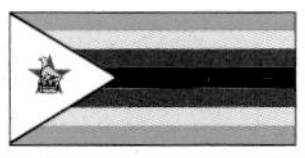
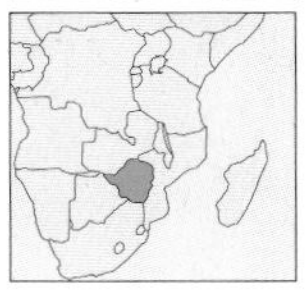

ZIMBABWE

GEOGRAPHY The Republic of Zimbabwe is a landlocked country in southern Africa. Most of the country lies on a high plateau between the Zambezi and Limpopo rivers, ranging from 2,950 ft to 4,920 ft [900 m to 1,500 m] above sea level. From October to March, the weather is hot and wet, but in the winter, daily temperatures can vary greatly.

POLITICS & ECONOMY The Shona people became dominant in the region about 1,000 years ago. The British South Africa Company, under the statesman Cecil Rhodes, occupied the area in the 1890s, after obtaining mineral rights from local chiefs. The area was named Rhodesia, and later Southern Rhodesia, becoming a self-governing British colony in 1923. Between 1953 and 1963, Southern and Northern Rhodesia (now Zambia) were united with Nyasaland (Malawi) in the Central African Federation.

In 1965, the European government of Southern Rhodesia (then called Rhodesia) declared their country independent, but Britain refused to accept this. After a civil war, the country became legally independent in 1980. Order was restored when the Shona prime minister, Robert Mugabe, brought his Ndebele rivals into his government. In 1987, Mugabe became the country's executive president.

From the late 1990s, Mugabe's government supported a violent campaign of land redistribution, seizing white-owned farms to be occupied by landless "war veterans." In elections in 2008, Mugabe lost to Morgan Tsvangirai, but intimidation of opposition supporters led Tsvangirai to withdraw from a run-off. In September 2008, a power-sharing government was set up, with Mugabe as president and Tsvangirai as prime minister. The election in 2013 saw Mugabe returned as president for the seventh time. He was finally forced out by military intervention in late 2017 and replaced by his former vice-president Emmerson Mnangagwa, who went on to win a narrow victory in presidential elections in 2018.

In the 2000s, the economy collapsed and many people starved as a result of food shortages. The breakdown of public services led to a cholera epidemic. In 2009 the government allowed the use of foreign currencies in an effort to stem hyperinflation. Zimbabwe has valuable mineral reserves. Agriculture employs 66% of the work force. Maize is the main food crop. Cash crops include cotton, sugar, and tobacco. Cattle ranching is also important.

AREA 150,871 SQ MI [390,757 SQ KM] **POPULATION** 14,546,000
CAPITAL Harare **GOVERNMENT** Multiparty republic
ETHNIC GROUPS Shona 82%, Ndebele 14%, other African groups 2%, mixed and Asian 1% **LANGUAGES** English, Shona, Ndebele
RELIGIONS Christianity, traditional beliefs
CURRENCY Multiple currencies

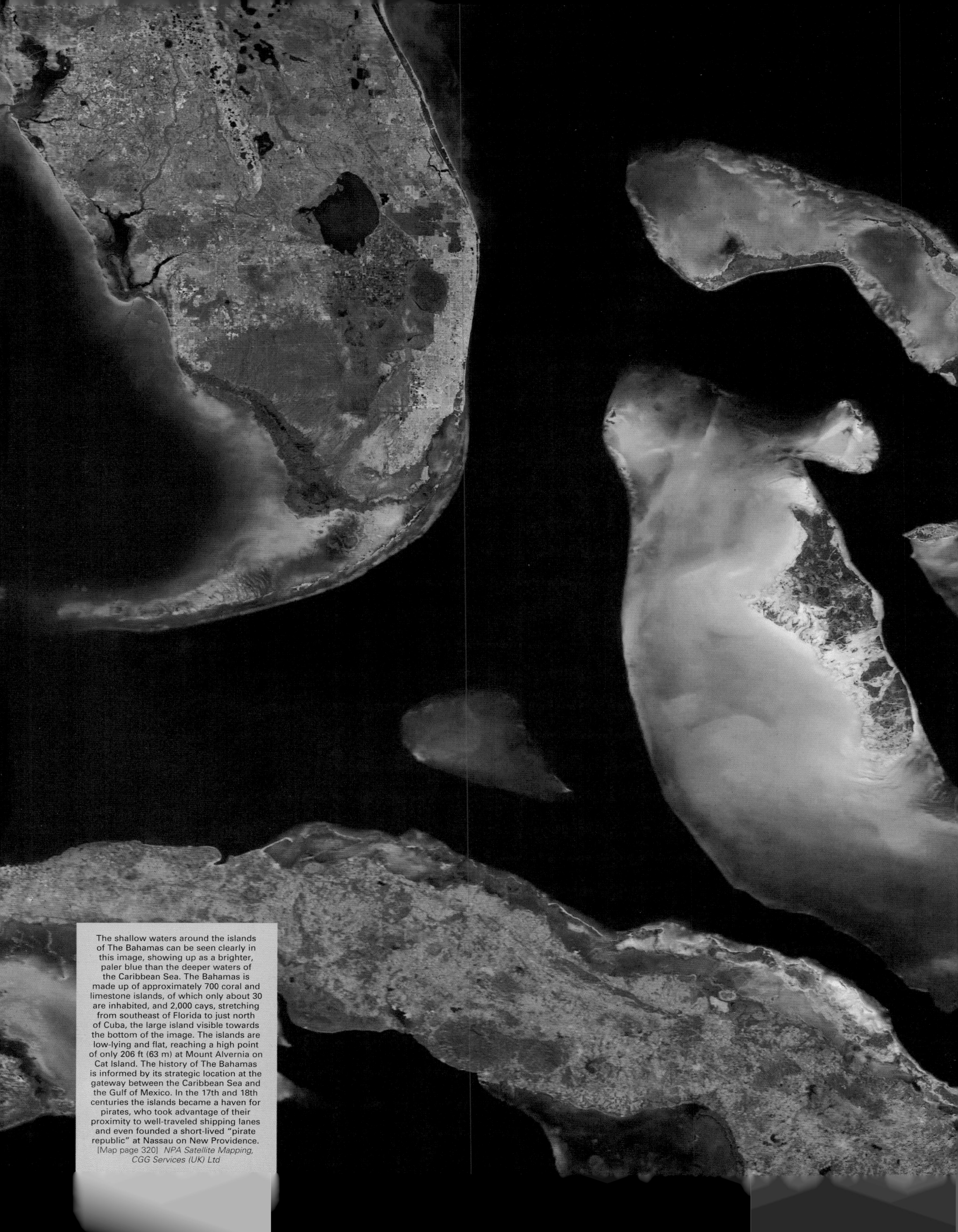

The shallow waters around the islands of The Bahamas can be seen clearly in this image, showing up as a brighter, paler blue than the deeper waters of the Caribbean Sea. The Bahamas is made up of approximately 700 coral and limestone islands, of which only about 30 are inhabited, and 2,000 cays, stretching from southeast of Florida to just north of Cuba, the large island visible towards the bottom of the image. The islands are low-lying and flat, reaching a high point of only 206 ft (63 m) at Mount Alvernia on Cat Island. The history of The Bahamas is informed by its strategic location at the gateway between the Caribbean Sea and the Gulf of Mexico. In the 17th and 18th centuries the islands became a haven for pirates, who took advantage of their proximity to well-traveled shipping lanes and even founded a short-lived "pirate republic" at Nassau on New Providence.

[Map page 320] *NPA Satellite Mapping, CGG Services (UK) Ltd*

WORLD GEOGRAPHY

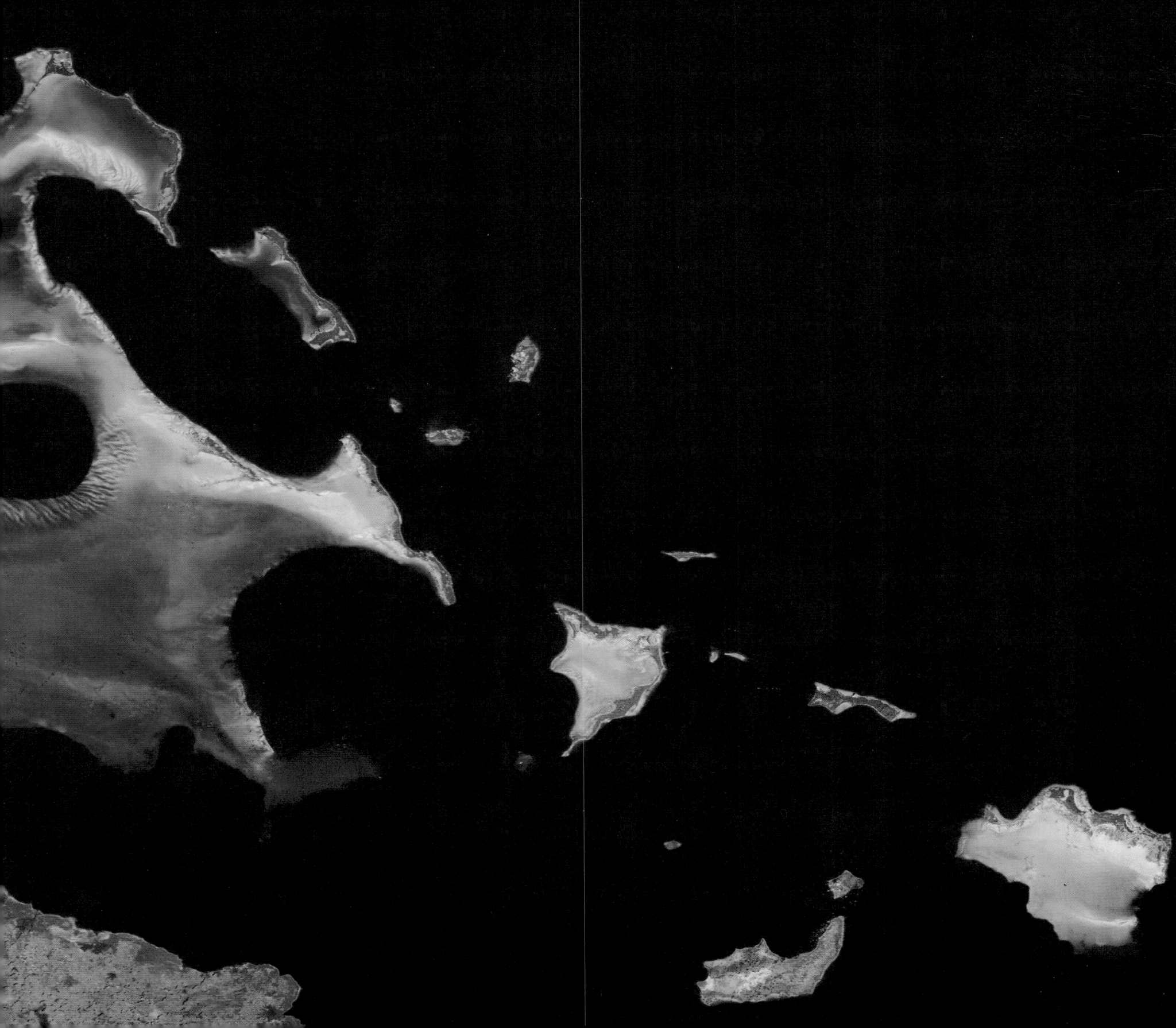

About 13.8 billion years ago, time and space began with the most colossal explosion in cosmic history: the so-called Big Bang that is believed to have initiated the Universe. According to current theory, in the first millionth of a second of its existence it expanded from a dimensionless point of infinite mass and density into a fireball about the size of our present Solar System – and it has been expanding ever since.

It took about 380,000 years for the primal fireball to cool enough for atoms to form. They were mostly hydrogen which is still the most abundant material in the Universe. The radiation from this era still pervades the Universe, though its subsequent expansion means that we see it at about 3° above absolute zero instead of its original 3,000°C. Observations of this faint background glow reveal slight fluctuations. It is these which appear to have become, over the next billion years or so, the large-scale structures in the present Universe. As well as the matter which we can see, there is evidence of a much greater quantity of dark matter whose nature remains unknown. Within knots of this dark matter, the first stars and galaxies formed, probably within the first billion years of the life of the Universe. Our own Galaxy was among them.

There were several generations of stars, each feeding on the wreckage of its extinct predecessors as well as the original galactic gas swirls. With each new generation, pro-gressively larger atoms were forged in stellar furnaces, and the Galaxy's range of elements, once restricted to hydrogen and helium, grew larger. About 9 billion years after the Big Bang, a star formed on the outskirts of our Galaxy with enough matter left over to create a retinue of planets. Nearly 5 billion years after that, human beings evolved.

The Sun is one of more than 100 billion stars in the home galaxy alone. Our Galaxy, in turn, forms part of a local group consisting of approximately 50 similar structures, mostly small "dwarf" galaxies but a few large ones, and one – the Andromeda Galaxy – similar in size to our own. There are at least 100 billion galaxies in the Universe, many of which are members of huge galaxy clusters.

LIFE OF A STAR

For most of its existence, a star produces energy by the nuclear fusion of hydrogen into helium at its core. The duration of this hydrogen-burning period – known as the *main sequence* – depends on the star's mass; the greater the mass, the higher the core temperatures and the sooner the star's supply of hydrogen is exhausted. Dim, dwarf stars consume their hydrogen slowly, eking it out over billions of years. The Sun, like other stars of its mass, should spend about 10 billion years on the main sequence; since it was formed less than 5 billion years ago, it still has half its life left.

Once all of a star's core hydrogen has been fused into helium, nuclear activity moves outward into layers of unconsumed hydrogen. For a time, energy production sharply increases: the star grows hotter and expands enormously, turning into a so-called red giant. Its energy output will increase a thousandfold, and it will swell to a hundred times its former diameter.

After a few hundred million years, helium in the core will become sufficiently compressed to initiate a new cycle of nuclear fusion: from helium to carbon. The star will contract somewhat, before beginning its last expansion, in the Sun's case engulfing the Earth and perhaps Mars. In this bloated condition, the Sun's outer layers will break off into space, leaving a tiny inner core, mainly of carbon, that shrinks progressively under its own gravity. The white dwarf star thus formed can attain a density more than 10,000 times that of normal matter, with crushing surface gravity to match. Gradually, the nuclear fires will die down, and the Sun will reach its terminal stage: a black dwarf, emitting insignificant amounts of energy.

Black holes

However, stars more massive than the Sun may undergo a different transformation. The additional mass allows gravitational collapse to continue indefinitely: eventually, all the star's remaining matter shrinks to a point, and its density approaches infinity – a state that will not permit even subatomic structures to survive.

The star has become a *black hole*: an anomalous "singularity" in the fabric of space and time. Although vast coruscations of radiation will be emitted by any matter falling into its grasp, the singularity itself has an escape velocity that exceeds the speed of light, and nothing can ever be released from it. Within the boundaries of the black hole, the laws of physics are suspended.

GALACTIC STRUCTURES

Many of the Universe's 100 billion galaxies show clear structural patterns, originally classified by the American astronomer Edwin Hubble in 1925. Spiral galaxies like our own have a central, almost spherical bulge and a surrounding disk composed of spiral arms. Barred spirals have a central bar of stars across the nucleus, with spiral arms trailing from the ends of the bar. Elliptical galaxies have a more uniform appearance, ranging from a flattened disk to a near sphere.

▲ The galaxy cluster Abell 2744, nicknamed Pandora's Cluster for the wide range of galaxy phenomena within it. The brightest galaxies are ellipticals of various shapes, but spiral and barred spiral galaxies are also visible. The cross-shaped features on the star images are optical effects in the Hubble Space Telescope.

Most galaxies, however, have no obvious structure at all. Galaxies also vary enormously in size, from dwarf galaxies only 2,000 light years across to great assemblies of stars 80 or more times larger.

THE HOME GALAXY

The Sun and its planets are located in one of the spiral arms of the Galaxy, about 26,000 light years from the galactic center and orbiting around it in a period of about 220 million years. The center is invisible from the Earth, masked by vast, light-absorbing clouds of interstellar dust.

The Galaxy is probably around 12 billion years old and, like other spiral galaxies, has three distinct regions. The central bulge is about 30,000 light years in diameter. The disk in which the Sun is located is not much more than 1,000 light years thick, but approximately 130,000 light years from end to end. Around the Galaxy is the halo, a spherical zone 300,000 light years across, studded with globular star clusters and sprinkled with individual suns.

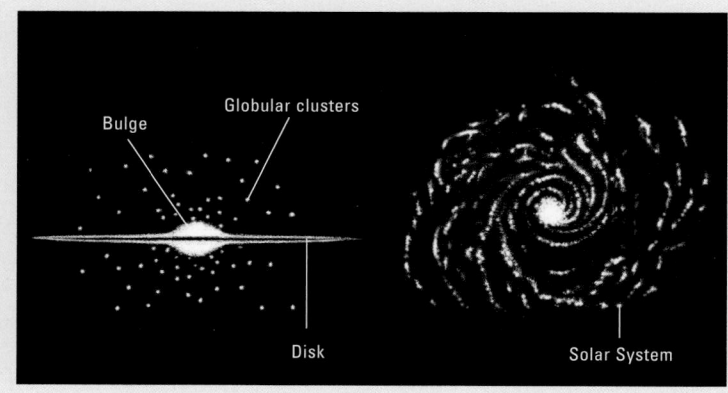

Bulge   Globular clusters   Disk   Solar System

THE END OF THE UNIVERSE

The likely fate of the Universe is disputed. According to one theory (*top of diagram, below*), the expansion begun at the time of the Big Bang will continue "indefinitely," with aging galaxies moving farther and farther apart in an immense, dark graveyard.

Alternatively, gravity may overcome the expansion (*bottom of diagram*). Galaxies will fall back together until everything is again concentrated at a single point, followed by a new Big Bang and a new expansion, in an endlessly repeated cycle.

Observations of distant galaxies suggest that the expansion of the Universe is accelerating. This is attributed to a hypothetical dark energy filling the Universe, so continued expansion is considered likely.

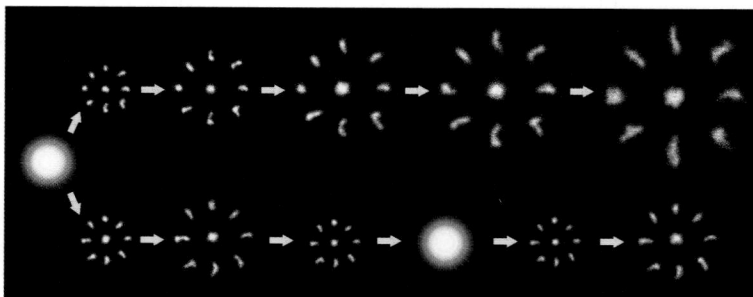

THE NEAREST STARS

The nearest stars, excluding the Sun, with their distance from Earth in light years*

Star	ly	Star	ly	Star	ly
Proxima Centauri	4.2	UV Ceti A & B	8.8	Procyon A & B	11.4
Alpha Centauri A & B	4.4	Ross 154	9.7	Struve 2398 A & B	11.5
Barnard's Star	6.0	Ross 248	10.3	Groombridge 34 A & B	11.6
Luhman 16 A & B	6.5	Epsilon Eridani	10.4	DX Cancri	11.7
WISE 0855-0714	7.3	HD 217987	10.7	Tau Ceti	11.8
Wolf 359	7.9	Ross 128	11.0	Epsilon Indi A & B	11.9
Lalande 21185	8.3	L789-6 A, B & C	11.1	* A light year is about 5,900
Sirius A & B	8.7	61 Cygni A & B	11.4	billion miles [9,500 billion km]

Many of the nearest stars, like Alpha Centauri A and B, are double stars, orbiting about their common center of gravity and to all intents and purposes equidistant from Earth. Many of them are dim objects including brown dwarfs: self-luminous objects which are intermediate in mass between planets and stars.

However, they include Sirius, the brightest star in the sky, and Procyon, the seventh brightest. Both are larger than the Sun; of the nearest stars, only Epsilon Eridani is similar in size and luminosity. Most of the other bright stars in the sky are within 500 light years of the Sun – a small fraction of the diameter of our Galaxy.

STAR CHARTS

**NORTHERN
HEMISPHERE SKY**

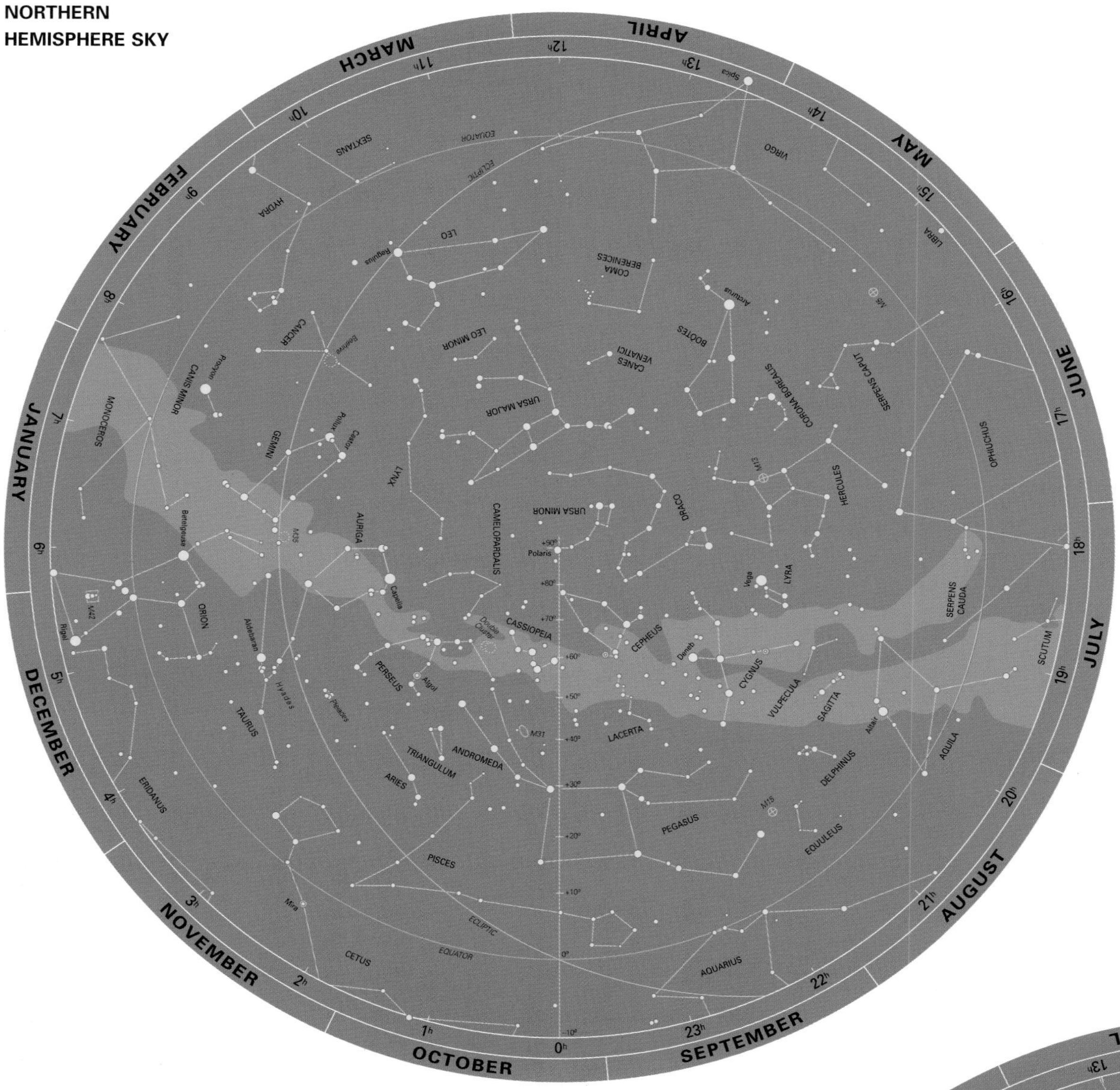

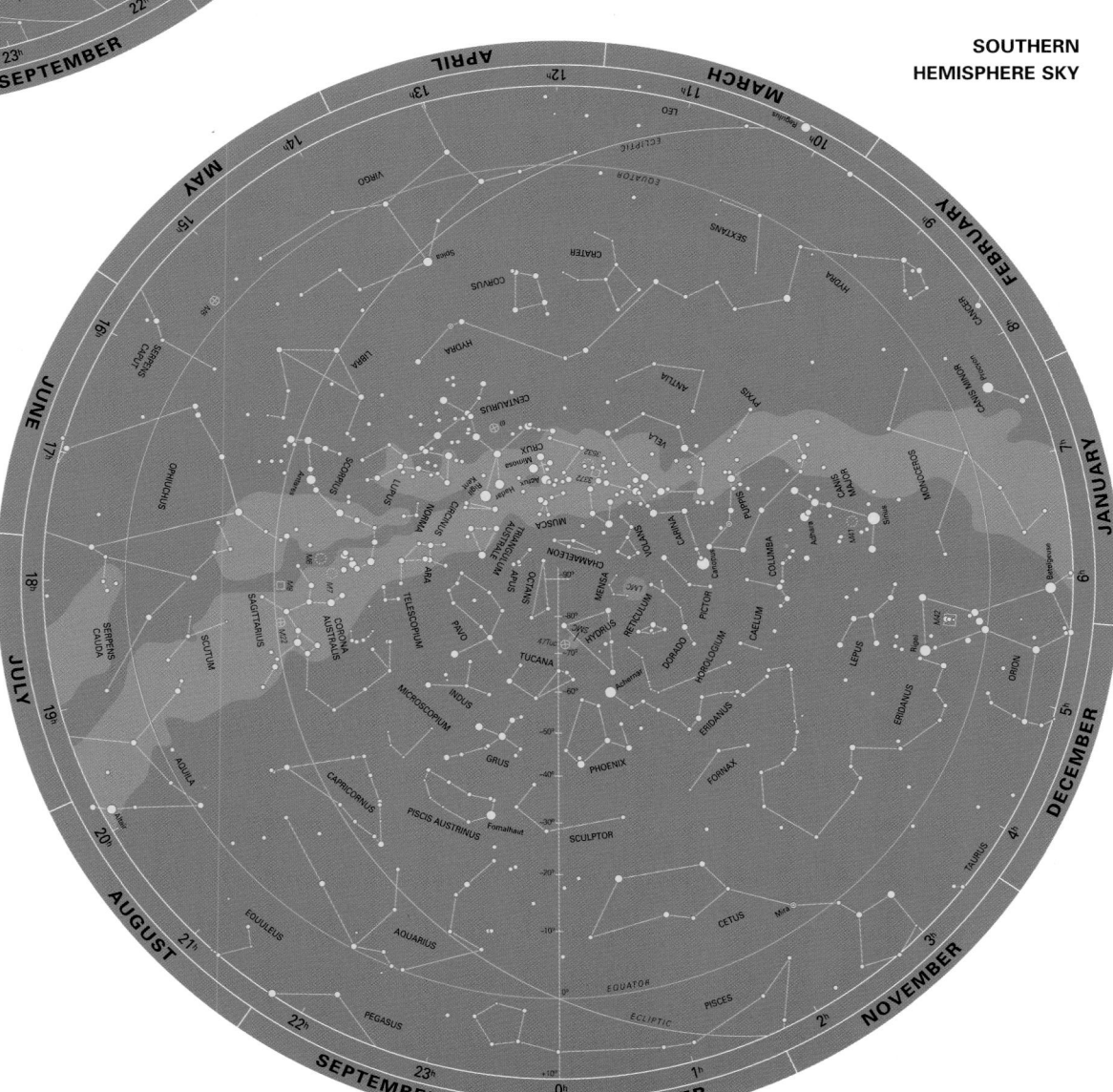

THE CONSTELLATIONS
The constellations and their English names

Andromeda	Andromeda	Lacerta	Lizard
Antlia	Air Pump	Leo	Lion
Apus	Bird of Paradise	Leo Minor	Little Lion
Aquarius	Water Carrier	Lepus	Hare
Aquila	Eagle	Libra	Scales
Ara	Altar	Lupus	Wolf
Aries	Ram	Lynx	Lynx
Auriga	Charioteer	Lyra	Lyre
Boötes	Herdsman	Mensa	Table Mountain
Caelum	Chisel	Microscopium	Microscope
Camelopardalis	Giraffe	Monoceros	Unicorn
Cancer	Crab	Musca	Fly
Canes Venatici	Hunting Dogs	Norma	Level
Canis Major	Great Dog	Octans	Octant
Canis Minor	Little Dog	Ophiuchus	Serpent Bearer
Capricornus	Sea Goat	Orion	Orion
Carina	Ship's Keel	Pavo	Peacock
Cassiopeia	Cassiopeia	Pegasus	Winged Horse
Centaurus	Centaur	Perseus	Perseus
Cepheus	Cepheus	Phoenix	Phoenix
Cetus	Whale	Pictor	Easel
Chamaeleon	Chameleon	Pisces	Fishes
Circinus	Compasses	Piscis Austrinus	Southern Fish
Columba	Dove	Puppis	Ship's Stern
Coma Berenices	Berenice's Hair	Pyxis	Mariner's Compass
Corona Australis	Southern Crown	Reticulum	Net
Corona Borealis	Northern Crown	Sagitta	Arrow
Corvus	Crow	Sagittarius	Archer
Crater	Cup	Scorpius	Scorpion
Crux	Southern Cross	Sculptor	Sculptor
Cygnus	Swan	Scutum	Shield
Delphinus	Dolphin	Serpens	Serpent
Dorado	Swordfish	Sextans	Sextant
Draco	Dragon	Taurus	Bull
Equuleus	Little Horse	Telescopium	Telescope
Eridanus	River Eridanus	Triangulum	Triangle
Fornax	Furnace	Triangulum Australe	Southern Triangle
Gemini	Twins	Tucana	Toucan
Grus	Crane	Ursa Major	Great Bear
Hercules	Hercules	Ursa Minor	Little Bear
Horologium	Clock	Vela	Ship's Sails
Hydra	Water Snake	Virgo	Virgin
Hydrus	Sea Serpent	Volans	Flying Fish
Indus	Indian	Vulpecula	Fox

**SOUTHERN
HEMISPHERE SKY**

The charts on this page show the entire heavens divided into northern and southern hemispheres, with 10° of overlap between them around the perimeter of each one. However, the view from any particular location on Earth will be different, and will change both hourly as the Earth turns, and throughout the year as the Earth goes around the Sun.

The Sun's annual path through the heavens is known as the "ecliptic," and is shown here by an orange line. When the Sun is in the sky its light drowns out our view of the stars, so only that part of the heavens opposite the Sun is visible at a particular time. The sky's equivalent of longitude is known as "right ascension." As the stars appear to rotate around the Earth once every 24 hours, right ascension is measured eastward in hours and minutes, and is marked around the edge of the maps. The equivalent of latitude is "declination," measured in degrees north or south of the celestial equator, and shown by the vertical line on each chart.

Using the charts

At any place and time you can see half of the whole sky, assuming a flat horizon. If you were at one of the poles your view would be shown as a circle centered on the middle of the map for the appropriate hemisphere, with the horizon marked by the celestial equator. From all other locations the center of your view (your overhead point) will be at some other point on the map whose location changes with time. The closer you are to Earth's equator, the closer the center will be to the edge of the map and more stars in the opposite hemisphere will be visible.

So first choose the appropriate chart for your hemisphere and hold it with the month at the bottom. At 11 p.m., not allowing for Daylight Saving Time (Summer Time), your overhead point will be at the same declination as your geographical latitude and stars lower on the map will be due south (or north in the southern hemisphere). From latitude 50° in mid August, for example, your overhead point will be close to the star Deneb in the constellation of Cygnus. Stars on the opposite side of the map will be below your northern horizon, while stars below Deneb will be due south.

STAR MAGNITUDES
Apparent visual magnitudes

The magnitude scale of star brightnesses is developed from the system used by the Ancient Greeks in which the brightest stars were first magnitude and the faintest visible to the naked eye were sixth. Today the scale has a mathematical basis and extends, at the brightest end, through to negative magnitudes.

The Milky Way is shown in light blue on these charts.

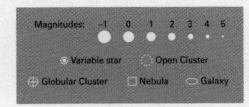

Lying about halfway from the center of one of billions of galaxies that populate the observable Universe, our Solar System contains eight planets and their moons, at least five dwarf planets, innumerable asteroids, comets and other icy bodies, and a miscellany of dust and gas, all tethered by the immense gravitational field of the Sun, the star whose thermonuclear furnaces provide them all with heat and light.

The Solar System was formed about 5 billion years ago, when a spinning cloud of gas, mostly hydrogen but seeded with other heavier elements, condensed enough to ignite a nuclear reaction and create a star. The Sun still accounts for almost 99.9% of the system's total mass.

By composition as well as distance, the planetary array divides quite neatly in two: an inner system of four small, solid planets, including the Earth, and an outer system, from Jupiter to Neptune, of four much larger planets composed of lighter materials, such as gas, liquid, and ice. Lying mostly between the two groups is a scattering of rocky asteroids, numbering perhaps a million or more. They may be debris left over from the formation of the inner Solar System. In 2006, Pluto was demoted from its former status as a planet and is now regarded as a member of the Kuiper Belt of icy bodies at the fringes of the Solar System.

Much of the early history of science is the story of people trying to make sense of the wandering points of light that were all they knew of the planets. Now, men have stood on the Earth's Moon, space probes have landed on several bodies, and distant landscapes have been mapped with astonishing accuracy, transforming our knowledge of our celestial environment.

In the 1980s, the Voyager space probes skimmed all four major planets of the outer Solar System, bringing new revelations with each close approach. The Magellan (Venus), Galileo (Jupiter) and Cassini–Huygens (Saturn) missions have transformed our knowledge of those planets and the giants' moons, and a host of orbiters and landers have shown us Mars in a new light. A spacecraft also reached Pluto in 2015.

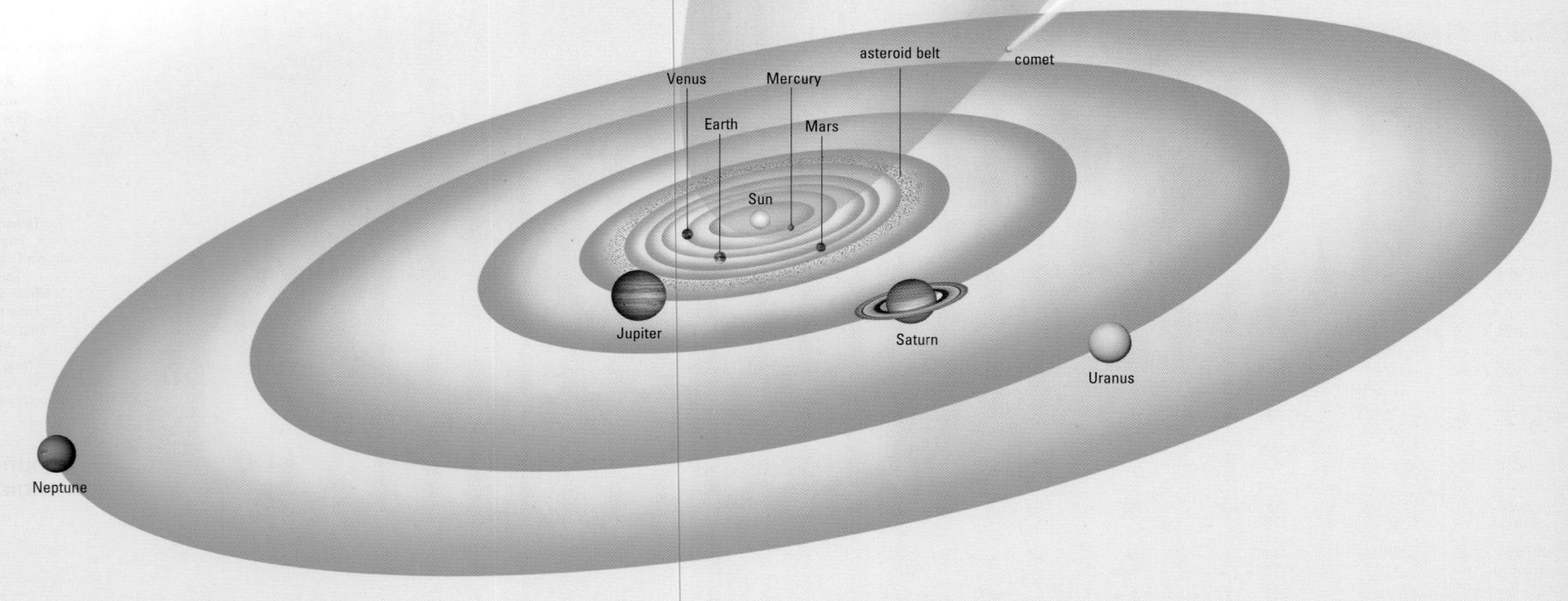

Diagram not drawn to scale

ORBITS OF THE PLANETS

The diagram above shows the Solar System as it might appear to an observer a few light-hours away in the direction of the constellation Hercules. Seen from such a position, above the plane of the ecliptic, all the planets revolve about the Sun in a counterclockwise direction. The perspective view exaggerates the elliptical form of all the planetary orbits: only Mercury follows a path that deviates noticeably from circularity.

The diagram also portrays the main asteroid belt between Mars and Jupiter, and the orbit of a comet. Comets reside in a vast spherical halo beyond the Solar System, and are occasionally diverted toward the Sun on highly elliptical orbits which may take many thousands of years to complete. Most, therefore, still await discovery, though there are a number of shorter-period comets which return regularly, such as Halley's Comet.

PLANETARY DATA

	Mean distance from Sun (million miles)	Mass (Earth = 1)	Period of orbit (Earth days/years)	Period of rotation (Earth days)	Equatorial diameter (miles)	Average density (water = 1)	Surface gravity (Earth = 1)	Number of known satellites*
Sun	–	332,946	–	25.38	865,000	1.41	27.9	–
Mercury	36.0	0.06	87.97d	58.65	3,032	5.43	0.38	0
Venus	67.2	0.82	224.7d	243.02	7,521	5.24	0.91	0
Earth	93.0	1.00	365.3d	1.00	7,926	5.51	1.00	1
Mars	141.6	0.11	687.0d	1.029	4,220	3.94	0.38	2
Jupiter	484.0	317.8	11.86y	0.411	88,848	1.33	2.36	79
Saturn	891.0	95.2	29.45y	0.428	74,900	0.69	0.91	82
Uranus	1,785.2	14.5	84.02y	0.720	31,764	1.27	0.89	27
Neptune	2,793.1	17.2	164.8y	0.673	30,776	1.64	1.13	14

Planetary days are given in sidereal days – that is, with respect to the stars rather than the Sun. The difference is caused by the movement of the planet in its orbit, so the interval between successive noons is slightly different from that between the rising of a particular star. The Earth's own sidereal day is 23h 56m in solar time. The equatorial diameters of most planets differ from their polar diameters as a consequence of their rotation, which is most marked in the case of Jupiter and Saturn, which are very noticeably flattened at the poles. Strictly speaking, the figures for surface gravity apply to the four inner planets only, as the outer planets have no solid surfaces. In their case, the figure is given for an arbitrary point in the atmosphere where the pressure is 1 bar.

* Number of known satellites at mid-2020

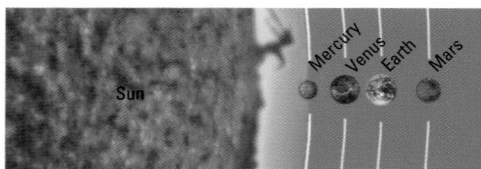

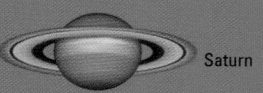

THE PLANETS

Mercury is the closest planet to the Sun and hence the fastest-moving. It is very hot, with a cratered, wrinkled surface very similar to that of Earth's Moon. It is small and has low gravity, so there is no significant atmosphere.

Venus has much the same physical dimensions as Earth. Its dense atmosphere is composed of 97% carbon dioxide resulting in a runaway greenhouse effect that makes the surface, at 890°F, the hottest of all the planets in the Solar System. Radar mapping revealed a terrain consisting of highland regions and vast, rolling plains crossed by volcanic flows and dotted with craters. Discharges from volcanic regions could explain the sulfuric-acid rain detected by spacecraft. Soft-landers last less than an hour in Venus's fierce climate.

Earth seen from space is easily the most beautiful of the inner planets; it is also, and more objectively, the largest, as well as the only known home of life. Living things are the main reason why the Earth is able to retain a substantial proportion of reactive oxygen in its atmosphere; the oxygen in turn supports the life that constantly regenerates it. The Earth's natural satellite, the Moon, is believed to have been created when an asteroid struck our planet in its infancy.

Mars, smaller and cooler than the Earth, is nevertheless the most likely planet other than Earth where life may have formed. The planet was, at some stage in the distant past, a geologically active world with water on its surface: rivers, lakes, and even an ocean. Liquid water may well exist today, but trapped beneath its dusty, boulder-strewn surface. The Martian landscape features huge extinct volcanoes, a giant canyon system, craters, and sand dunes. Its thin atmosphere is mostly carbon dioxide, and its polar caps are of frozen carbon dioxide and water ice. It has two tiny moons, probably captured asteroids.

Jupiter has about three times the mass of all the other planets combined. The planet is mostly gas, under intense pressure in the lower atmosphere above a core of fiercely compressed hydrogen and helium. The upper layers form strikingly colored rotating belts, the outward sign of the intense storms created by Jupiter's rapid rotation. The Great Red Spot is a storm feature that has persisted for at least 130 years. Jupiter has at least 79 moons. Most are very small, but the four largest – Io, Europa, Ganymede, and Callisto – are fascinating worlds in their own right. Io is the most volcanically active world known, and Europa possesses an ocean deep below its icy surface. The planet also has a system of rings, though nowhere near as prominent as Saturn's.

Saturn is structurally similar to Jupiter, rotating fast enough to produce an obvious bulge at its equator. It is composed of 89% hydrogen and 11% helium, and has wind velocities in the outer atmosphere of 1,600 ft/sec. Ever since the invention of the telescope, Saturn's rings have been the feature that has most attracted observers. The rings consist of thousands of individual ringlets, composed of icy particles ranging in size from 30 feet down to microscopic. Titan, the largest of Saturn's 82 known moons, has a dense atmosphere.

Uranus was unknown to the ancients. Although it is faintly visible to the naked eye, it was not established as a planet until 1781. In its interior is probably a rocky core surrounded by frozen methane, water, and ammonia; the atmosphere is of hydrogen, helium, and some methane, which gives the planet its greenish-blue color. There is a system of thin, dark rings and a retinue of 27 moons, all but five of which are small.

Neptune is always more than 2.5 billion miles from Earth, and despite its diameter of over 31,000 miles, it can only be seen by telescope. Its discovery in 1846 was the result of mathematical predictions by astronomers seeking to explain irregularities in the orbit of Uranus. Like Uranus, it has a ring system; recent observations have revealed a total of 14 moons.

In 2006, following an increasing number of discoveries of objects orbiting the Sun of similar size to Pluto but at a greater distance, the International Astronomical Union issued for the first time a definition of a planet. A planet is defined as "a body orbiting the Sun, which is essentially round as a consequence of its gravity, and which does not share its orbital neighborhood with similar bodies." On this definition, Pluto is no longer classified as a planet, but is instead a member of a new category of "dwarf planet," which relaxes the last criterion but excludes bodies in orbit around another one.

Mean distance from the
Sun in millions of miles

Mercury · 36.0 Mercury

Venus · 67.2 Venus

Earth · 93.0 Earth

Mars · 141.6 Mars

Jupiter · 483.7 Jupiter

Saturn · 886.6 Saturn

Uranus · 1,784.0 Uranus

Neptune · 2,795.2 Neptune

Diagrams not drawn to scale

 Uranus

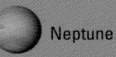 Neptune

The basic units of time measurement are the day and the year. The day is one rotation of the Earth on its axis. Our present calendar is based on the solar year of 365.24 days, the time taken by the Earth to orbit the Sun. Calendars based on the movements of the Sun and Moon have been used since ancient times. The length of the year, reckoned by the Julian Calendar introduced by Julius Caesar, was about 11 minutes too long. The cumulative error was rectified in 1582 by the Gregorian

Calendar, when Pope Gregory XIII decreed that the day following October 4 was October 15, and that century years did not count as leap years unless they were divisible by 400. England finally adopted the reformed calendar in 1752, when it was 11 days behind the European mainland.

The rotation of the Earth on its axis causes day and night. The Earth rotates through 360° every 24 hours, and the world is divided into 24 time zones centered on lines of longitude at 15° intervals.

The tilt of the Earth's axis, which is also called the "obliquity of the ecliptic," accounts for the seasons which are so familiar in the middle latitudes. However, geological evidence shows that, over long periods of time, climates change, and the advances and retreats of the ice during the Pleistocene Ice Age may have been caused by regular variations in the Earth's tilt, its orbit around the Sun, and changes in the season when it is closest to the Sun (perihelion).

THE SEASONS

Seasons occur because the Earth's axis is tilted at an angle of approximately 23½°. When the northern hemisphere is tilted to a maximum extent toward the Sun, on June 20 or 21, the Sun is overhead at the Tropic of Cancer (latitude 23½° North). This is midsummer, or the summer solstice, in the northern hemisphere.

On September 22 or 23, the Sun is overhead at the equator, and day and night are of equal length throughout the world. This is the autumnal equinox in the northern hemisphere.

On December 21 or 22, the Sun is overhead at the Tropic of Capricorn (23½° South), the winter solstice in the northern hemisphere. The overhead Sun then tracks north until, on March 20 or 21, it is overhead at the equator. This is the spring (vernal) equinox in the northern hemisphere.

In the southern hemisphere, the seasons are the reverse of those in the north.

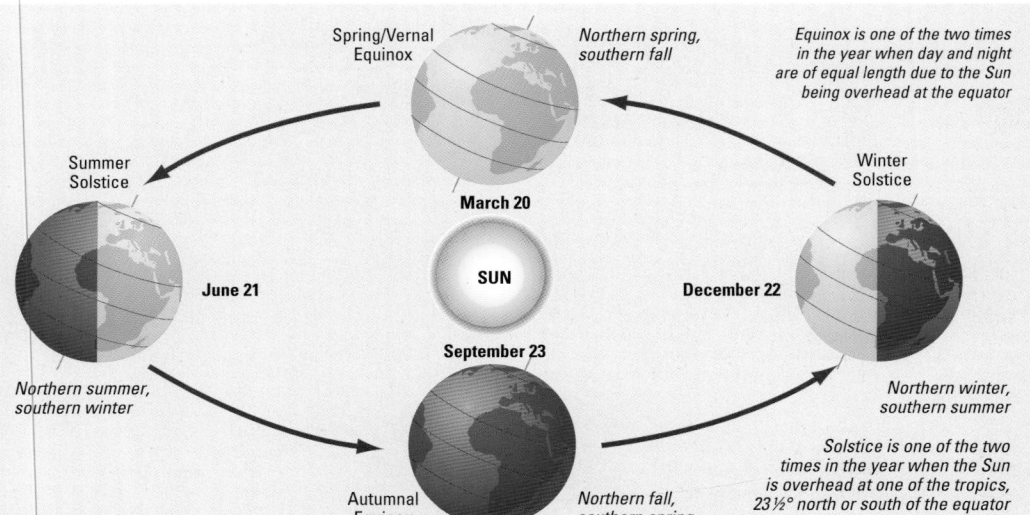

DAY AND NIGHT

The Sun appears to rise in the east, reach its highest point at noon, and then set in the west, to be followed by night. In reality, it is not the Sun that is moving but the Earth rotating from west to east. The moment when the Sun's upper limb first appears above the horizon is termed sunrise; the moment when the Sun's upper limb disappears below the horizon is sunset.

At the summer solstice in the northern hemisphere (June 21), the Arctic has total daylight and the Antarctic total darkness. The opposite occurs at the winter solstice (December 21 or 22). At the equator, the length of day and night are almost equal all year.

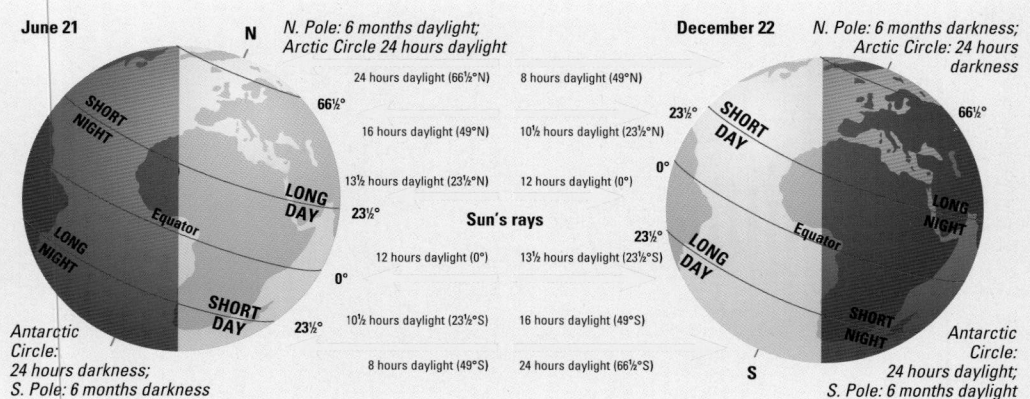

EARTH DATA

Aphelion (maximum distance from Sun):	94,500,000 miles	Length of year:	365 days, 5 hours, 48 minutes, 45 seconds of mean solar time	Polar circumference:	24,860 miles
Perihelion (minimum distance from Sun):	91,400,000 miles			Equatorial diameter:	7,926 miles
		Superficial area:	197,000,000 sq miles	Polar diameter:	7,900 miles
Angle of tilt (obliquity of the ecliptic):	23° 26′	Land surface:	57,500,000 sq miles (29.2%)	Equatorial radius:	3,963 miles
				Polar radius:	3,950 miles
Length of year – solar tropical (equinox to equinox):	365.24 days	Water surface:	139,500,000 sq miles (70.8%)	Volume of the Earth:	259,880 × 10⁶ cu miles
		Equatorial circumference:	24,901 miles	Mass of the Earth:	5.97 × 10²⁴ kg

SUNRISE AND SUNSET

The term "equinox" comes from the Latin for "equal night." At the spring and autumnal equinoxes, the Sun is vertically overhead at midday at the equator and all places on Earth have 12 hours of darkness and 12 hours of daylight. The graphs of sunrise and sunset show that these occasions occur on March 21 and on September 22 or 23. The graphs also show that, because the Sun remains high in the sky at the equator throughout the year, the length of day and night there remains roughly the same throughout the year, with sunrise around 6 a.m. and sunset around 6 p.m.

The further north or south one travels, the greater the difference between the number of hours of daylight and darkness. For example, the graph (*right*) shows that at latitude 60°N sunrise varies from just after 9 a.m. in midwinter (on December 22 or 23) to about 2.30 a.m. in midsummer (around the summer solstice on June 21). By contrast, the second graph (*far right*) shows that sunset at latitude 60°N occurs at about 2.45 p.m. in midwinter and 9.20 p.m. in midsummer.

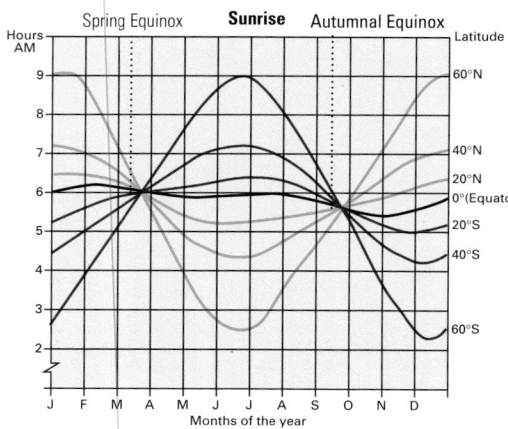

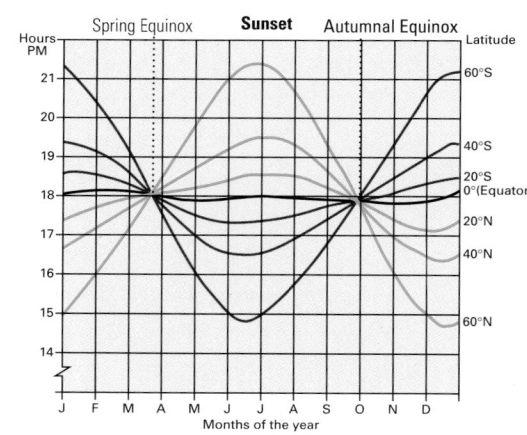

THE MOON

The Moon rotates more slowly than the Earth, taking just over 27 days to make one complete rotation on its axis. This corresponds to the Moon's orbital period around the Earth, and therefore the Moon always presents the same hemisphere toward us; some 41% of the Moon's far side is never visible from the Earth. The interval between one New Moon and the next is 29½ days – this is called a lunation, or lunar month. The Moon shines only by reflected sunlight, and emits no light of its own. During each lunation the Moon displays a complete cycle of phases, caused by the changing angle of illumination from the Sun.

PHASES OF THE MOON

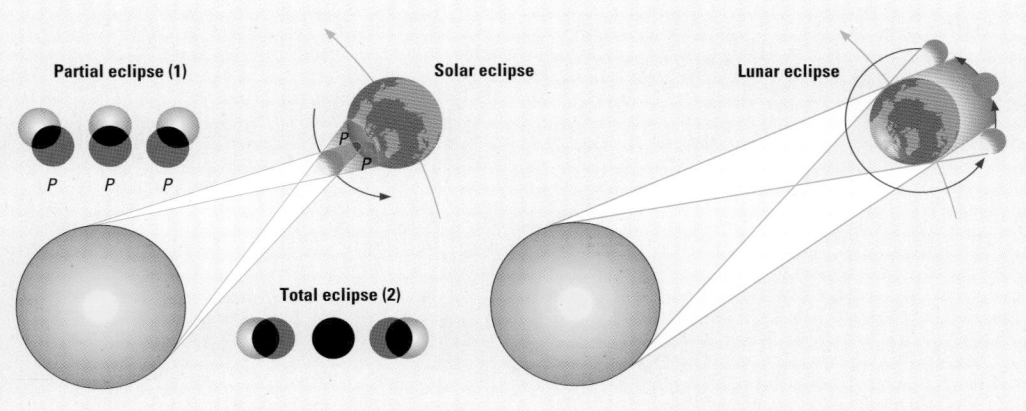

Mean distance from Earth: 238,856 miles; Mean diameter: 2,159 miles;
Mass: approximately 1/80 that of Earth; Surface gravity: one-sixth of Earth's;
Daily range of temperature at lunar equator: 504°F; Average orbital speed: 2,287 mph

| New Moon | Waxing Crescent | First Quarter | Waxing Gibbous | Full Moon | Waning Gibbous | Last Quarter | Waning Crescent | New Moon |

MOON DATA

Distance from Earth

The Moon orbits at a mean distance of 238,856 miles, at an average speed of 2,287 mph in relation to the Earth.

Size and mass

The average diameter of the Moon is 2,159 miles. It is 400 times smaller than the Sun but is about 400 times closer to the Earth, so we see them as the same size. The Moon has a mass of 7.35×10^{22} kg, with a density 3.344 times that of water.

Visibility

Only 59% of the Moon's surface is visible from the Earth over time. Sunlight reflected from the Moon takes 1.3 seconds to reach the Earth (the Sun itself is around 8½ light-minutes away).

Temperature

With the Sun overhead, the temperature on the lunar equator can reach 243°F [117°C]. At night it can sink to −261°F [−163°C].

ECLIPSES

When the Moon passes between the Sun and the Earth, the Sun becomes partially eclipsed (1). A partial eclipse becomes a total eclipse if the Moon proceeds to cover the Sun completely (2) and the dark central part of the lunar shadow touches the Earth. The broad geographical zone covered by the Moon's outer shadow (P) has only a very small central area (often less than 62 miles wide) that experiences totality. Totality can never last for more than 7½ minutes at maximum, but is usually much briefer than this. Lunar eclipses take place when the Moon moves through the shadow of the Earth, and can be partial or total. Any single location on Earth can experience a maximum of four solar and three lunar eclipses in any single year, while a total solar eclipse occurs an average of once every 360 years for any given location.

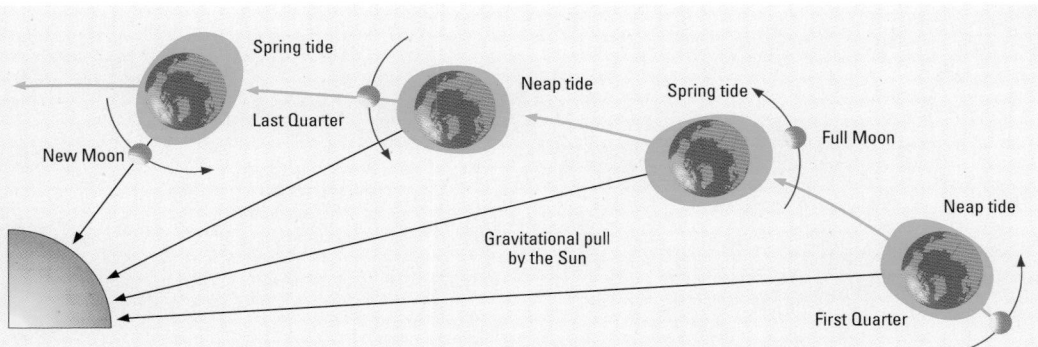

Partial eclipse (1)

Solar eclipse

Lunar eclipse

P P P

Total eclipse (2)

TIDES

The daily rise and fall of the ocean's tides are the result of the gravitational pull of the Moon and that of the Sun, though the effect of the latter is not as strong as that of the Moon. This effect is greatest on the hemisphere facing the Moon and causes a tidal "bulge." Spring tides occur when the Sun, Earth, and Moon are aligned; high tides are at their highest, and low tides fall to their lowest. When the Moon and Sun are farthest out of line (near the Moon's First and Last Quarters), neap tides occur, producing the smallest range between high and low tides.

Spring tide

Neap tide

Spring tide

Last Quarter

New Moon

Full Moon

Gravitational pull by the Sun

Neap tide

First Quarter

TIME ZONES

The Earth rotates through 360° in 24 hours, and so moves 15° every hour. The world is divided into 24 standard time zones, each centered on lines of longitude at 15° intervals. At the center of the first zone lie the prime meridian, or Greenwich meridian. All places to the west of Greenwich are one hour behind for every 15° of longitude; places to the east are ahead by one hour for every 15°.

International Date Line

When it is 12 noon on the Greenwich meridian, 180° east it is midnight of the same day – while 180° west the day is just beginning. To overcome this, the International Date Line was established, approximately following the 180° meridian. Thus, if you were to travel eastward from Japan (140°E) to Hawai'i (160°W), you would pass from Sunday night into Sunday morning.

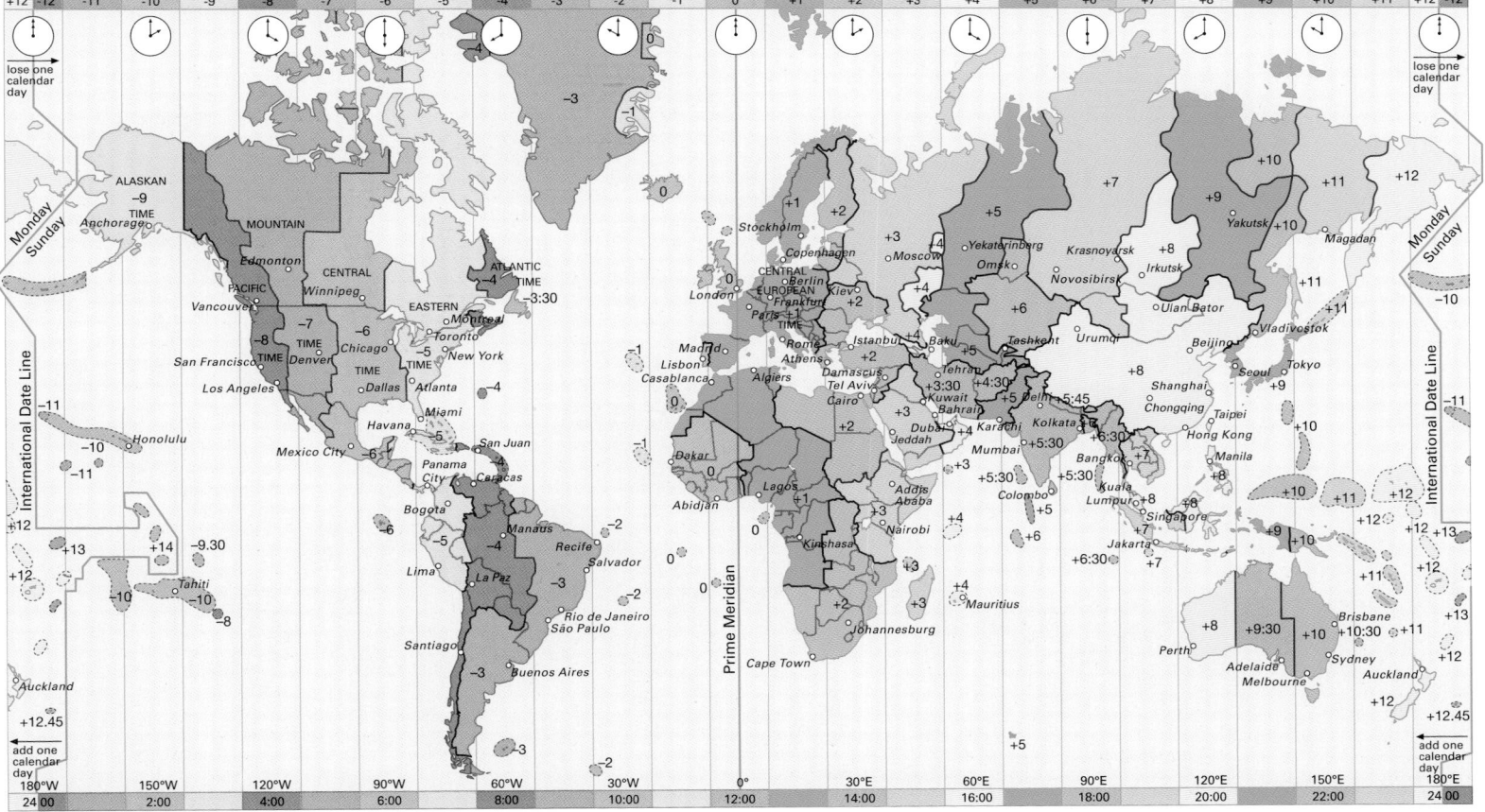

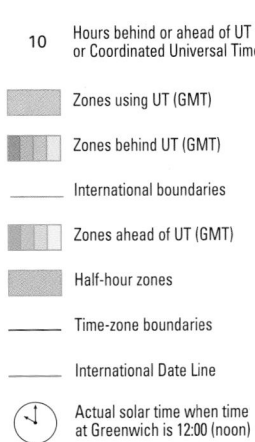

| 10 | Hours behind or ahead of UT or Coordinated Universal Time |

Zones using UT (GMT)

Zones behind UT (GMT)

International boundaries

Zones ahead of UT (GMT)

Half-hour zones

Time-zone boundaries

International Date Line

Actual solar time when time at Greenwich is 12:00 (noon)

Note: Some of the above time zones are affected by the incidence of Daylight Saving Time in countries where it is adopted.

Projection: *Mercator*

For more information:
98 Minerals

Every year, earthquakes and volcanic eruptions cause much destruction throughout the world. Such phenomena were once thought to be unconnected, but since the late 1960s, scientists have understood that these events are surface manifestations of the tremendous forces operating in the Earth's interior that are slowly but constantly changing the face of our planet.

The Earth is divided into three zones. The crust, a brittle, low-density zone, overlies the dense mantle. Separating the crust from the mantle is a distinct boundary called the Mohorovičić (or Moho) discontinuity. Enclosed by the mantle is the Earth's core, which consists mainly of iron and nickel.

Temperatures inside the Earth range from about 1,600°F in the upper mantle to perhaps 9,000°F in the core. Heat creates convection currents in a semimolten part of the mantle called the asthenosphere. Above the asthenosphere is the lithosphere, a solid layer about 40 miles thick, consisting of the crust and part of the mantle. The lithosphere is divided into rigid plates, moved around by the currents in the asthenosphere, a process named plate tectonics.

The Earth was formed around 4.6 billion years ago. Lighter elements floated toward the surface, where they formed crustal rocks. The oldest rocks so far discovered are about 4 billion years old, while the oldest fossils occur in rocks formed around 3.5 billion years ago. An explosion of life occurred at the start of the Cambrian period, 570 million years ago. The fossil record since the start of the Cambrian has enabled scientists to piece together the story of life on Earth.

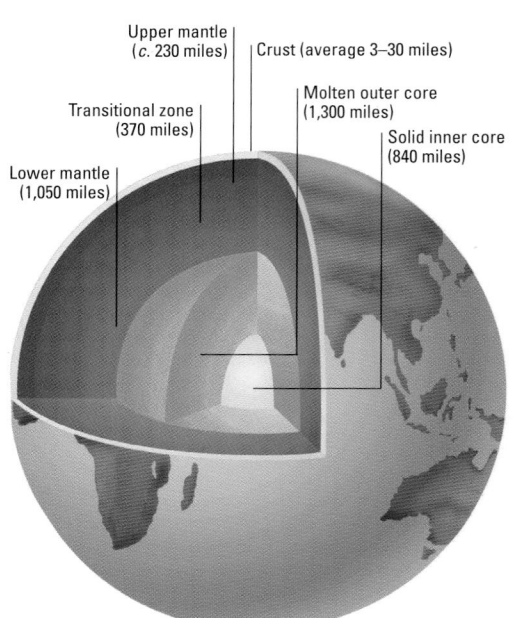

Upper mantle (c. 230 miles)
Crust (average 3–30 miles)
Transitional zone (370 miles)
Molten outer core (1,300 miles)
Solid inner core (840 miles)
Lower mantle (1,050 miles)

CONTINENTAL DRIFT

— Trench
— Rift
▨ New ocean floor
— Zones of slippage

In 1915, Alfred Wegener produced a series of world maps proposing that, around 200 million years ago, the continents had been joined together in a supercontinent that he called Pangaea. This land mass started to break up about 180 million years ago and the parts drifted to their present positions. In the 1950s and 1960s, evidence from studies of the ocean floor suggested that the low-density continents rest on huge slow-moving plates. The arrows on the present-day world map (*below*) show that the continents are still on the move.

Laurasia
Tethys Sea
Gondwanaland

180 million years ago

135 million years ago

Present day

DISTRIBUTION OF VOLCANOES

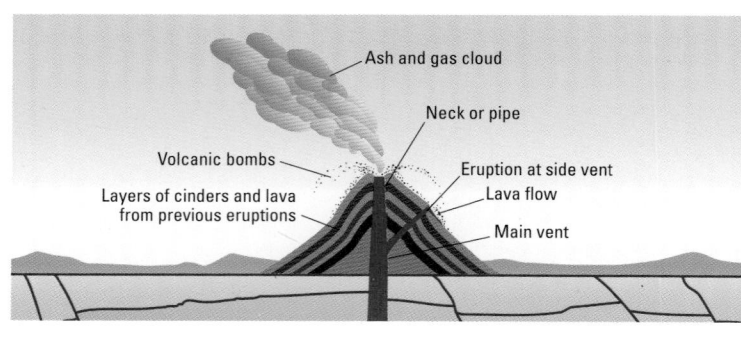

Ash and gas cloud
Neck or pipe
Volcanic bombs
Eruption at side vent
Lava flow
Layers of cinders and lava from previous eruptions
Main vent

Volcanoes occur when hot liquefied rock beneath the Earth's crust is pushed up by pressure to the surface as molten lava. There are some 550 known active volcanoes, around 20 of which are erupting at any one time.

∘ Submarine volcanoes
▲ Land volcanoes active since 1700
— Boundaries of tectonic plates

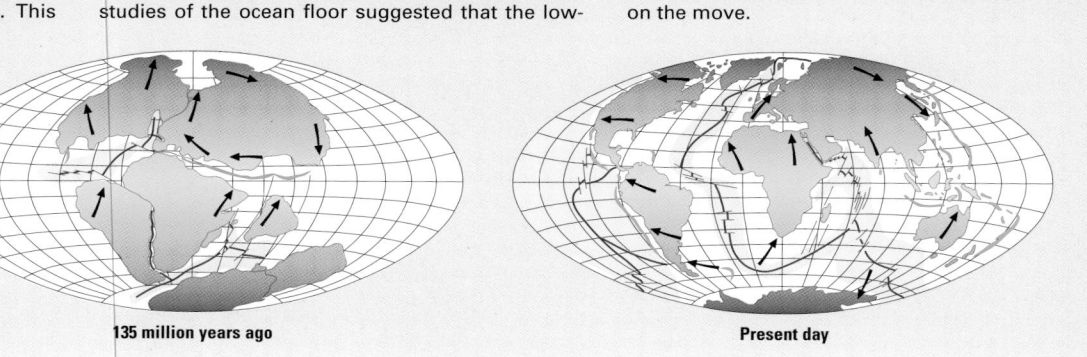

PLATE TECTONICS

The huge ridges that run through the oceans represent boundaries between plates. Here plates are diverging and molten magma from the mantle rises along a central rift valley to form new crustal rock. These ocean ridges, which are active zones where earthquakes and volcanic eruptions are common, are called constructive plate margins. Destructive plate margins, which occur when two contrasting plates converge, are marked by deep-ocean trenches as one plate is forced under the other. The descending plate is melted to produce the magma that fuels volcanoes alongside the trenches. Movements of descending plates are often sudden, triggering earthquakes in overlying continental areas.

Sea-floor spreading in the Atlantic Ocean and plate collision

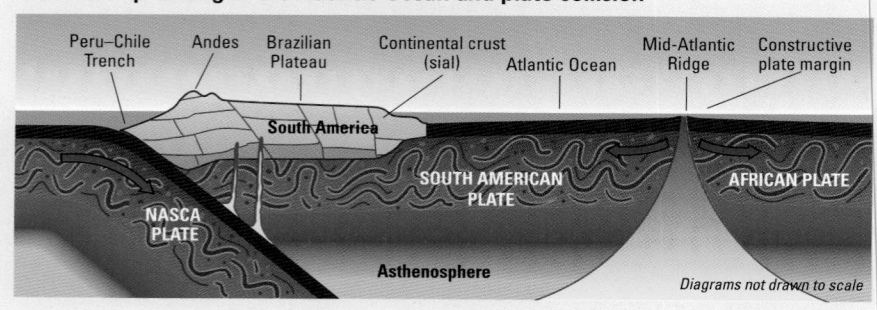

Peru–Chile Trench
Andes
Brazilian Plateau
Continental crust (sial)
Atlantic Ocean
Mid-Atlantic Ridge
Constructive plate margin
South America
NASCA PLATE
SOUTH AMERICAN PLATE
AFRICAN PLATE
Asthenosphere
Diagrams not drawn to scale

Sea-floor spreading in the Indian Ocean and continental plate collision

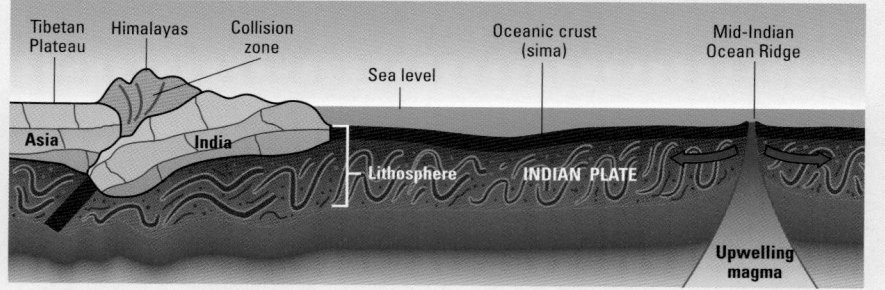

Tibetan Plateau
Himalayas
Collision zone
Oceanic crust (sima)
Mid-Indian Ocean Ridge
Sea level
Asia
India
Lithosphere
INDIAN PLATE
Upwelling magma

GEOLOGICAL TIME

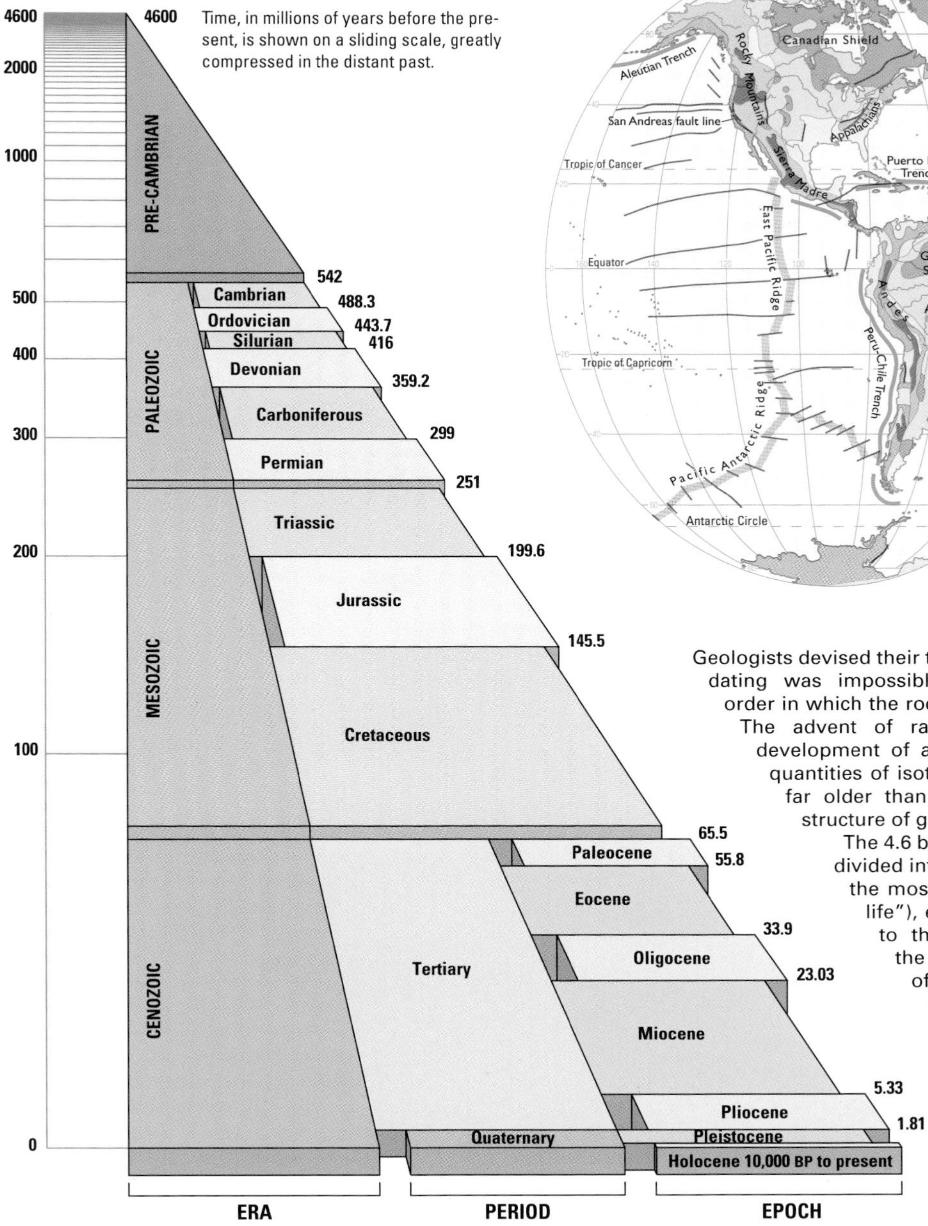

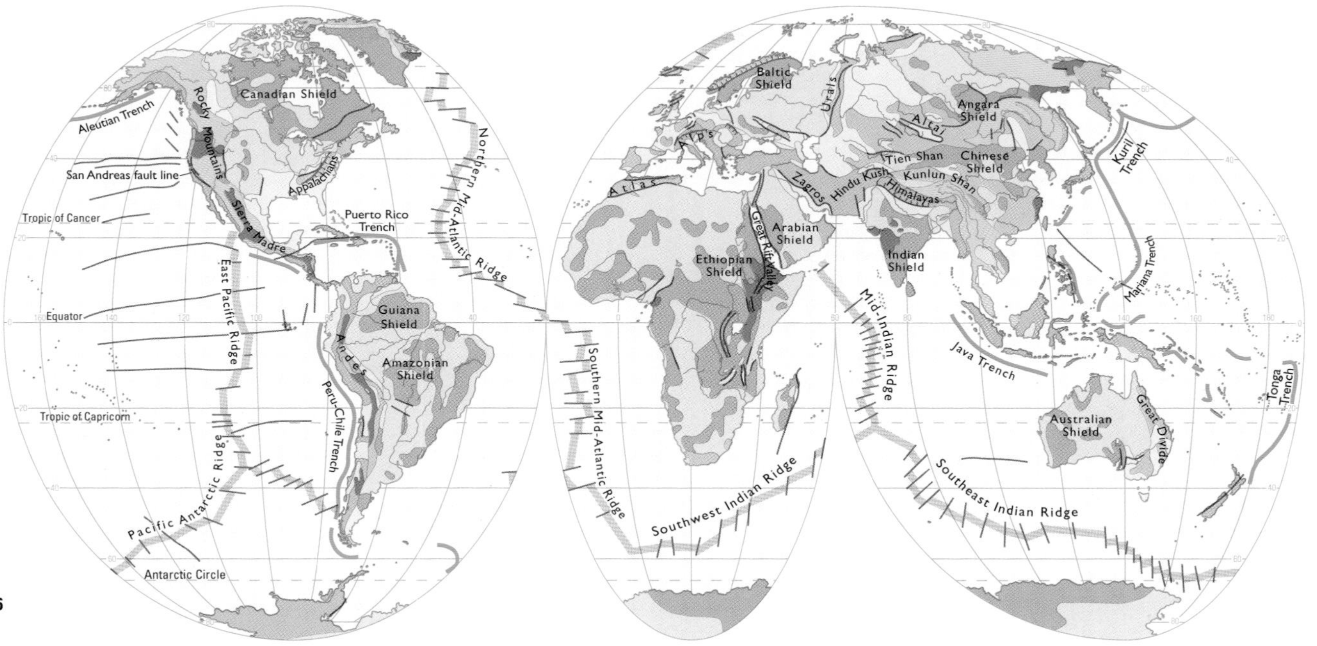

Time, in millions of years before the present, is shown on a sliding scale, greatly compressed in the distant past.

ERA	PERIOD	EPOCH	Ma
PRE-CAMBRIAN			4600
PALEOZOIC	Cambrian		542
	Ordovician		488.3
	Silurian		443.7
	Devonian		416
	Carboniferous		359.2
	Permian		299
MESOZOIC	Triassic		251
	Jurassic		199.6
	Cretaceous		145.5
CENOZOIC	Tertiary	Paleocene	65.5
		Eocene	55.8
		Oligocene	33.9
		Miocene	23.03
		Pliocene	5.33
	Quaternary	Pleistocene	1.81
		Holocene 10,000 BP to present	

Geologists devised their timescale on the basis of relative, not calendar, ages. Accurate dating was impossible and estimates were often bitterly disputed, but the order in which the rocks were formed could be deduced from careful observation. The advent of radioactive dating – culminating in the 1950s with the development of a mass spectrometer capable of accurately measuring tiny quantities of isotopes – appears to have settled the arguments. The Earth is far older than geologists first imagined, but their painstakingly-created structure of geological time has withstood the advent of high technology.

The 4.6 billion (4,600 million) years since the formation of the Earth are divided into four great eras, further split into periods and, in the case of the most recent era, epochs. The present era is the Cenozoic ("new life"), extending backward through "middle life" and "ancient life" to the Pre-Cambrian, named after the Latin word for Wales, the location of some of the earliest known fossils. Most of the Earth's geological history is encompassed by the Pre-Cambrian: though traces of ancient life have since been found, it was largely the proliferation of fossils from the beginning of the Paleozoic era onward, some 570 million years ago, which first allowed precise subdivisions to be made.

Like the Cambrian, most are named after regions exemplifying a period's geology. Others – such as the Carboniferous ("coal-bearing") or the Cretaceous ("chalk-bearing") – are more directly descriptive.

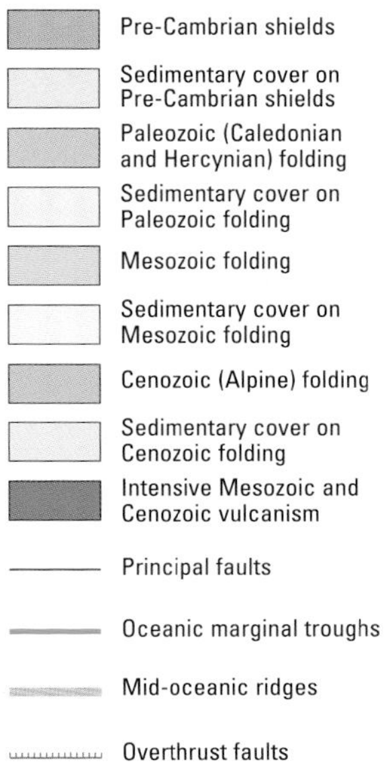

Pre-Cambrian shields
Sedimentary cover on Pre-Cambrian shields
Paleozoic (Caledonian and Hercynian) folding
Sedimentary cover on Paleozoic folding
Mesozoic folding
Sedimentary cover on Mesozoic folding
Cenozoic (Alpine) folding
Sedimentary cover on Cenozoic folding
Intensive Mesozoic and Cenozoic vulcanism
Principal faults
Oceanic marginal troughs
Mid-oceanic ridges
Overthrust faults

EARTHQUAKES

Earthquake magnitude is usually rated according to either the Richter scale or the Modified Mercalli scale, both devised by seismologists in the 1930s. The Richter scale measures absolute earthquake power with mathematical precision: each step upward represents a tenfold increase in the amplitude of the shockwave. Theoretically, there is no upper limit, but most of the largest earthquakes measured have been rated at between 8.8 and 8.9. The 12-point Mercalli scale, based on observed effects, is often more meaningful, ranging from I (earthquakes noticed only by seismographs) to XII (total destruction); intermediate points include V (people awakened at night; unstable objects overturned), VII (collapse of ordinary buildings; chimneys and monuments fall), and IX (conspicuous cracks in ground; serious damage to reservoirs).

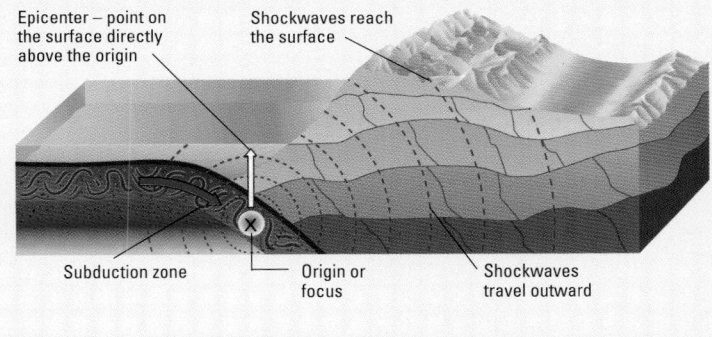

Epicenter – point on the surface directly above the origin
Shockwaves reach the surface
Subduction zone
Origin or focus
Shockwaves travel outward

Mobile land areas
Submarine zones of mobile land areas
Stable land platforms
Submarine extensions of land platforms
Mid-oceanic volcanic ridges
Oceanic platforms

1976 Principal earthquakes and dates (since 1900)

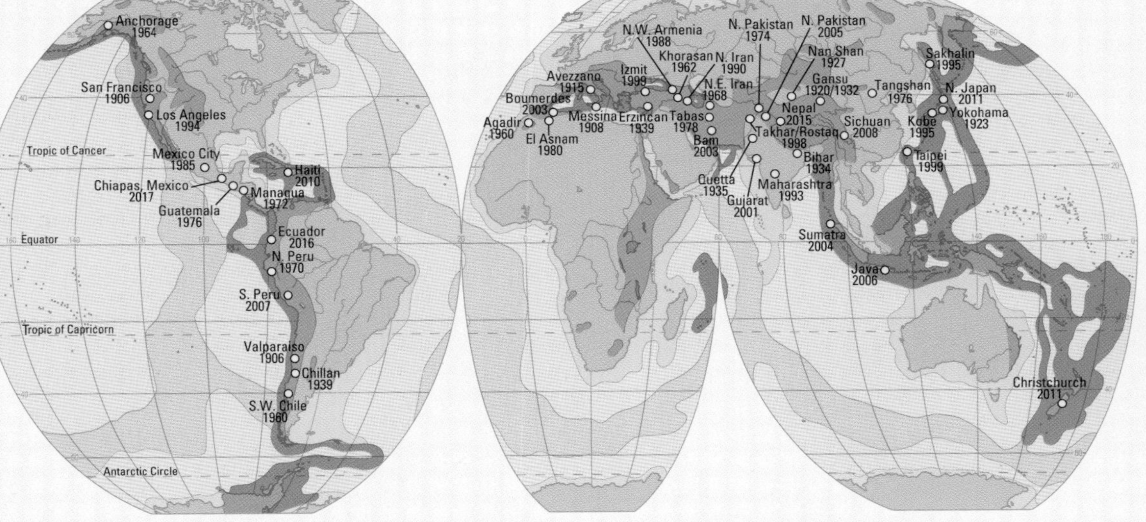

Earthquakes are a series of rapid vibrations originating from the slipping or faulting of parts of the Earth's crust when stresses within build up to breaking point. They usually happen at depths varying from 5 to 20 miles. Severe earthquakes cause extensive damage when they take place in populated areas, destroying structures and severing communications. Most initial loss of life occurs due to secondary causes such as falling masonry, fires, and flooding.

Notable Earthquakes Since 1900

Year	Location	Mag.	Deaths
1906	San Francisco, USA	8.3	3,000
1906	Valparaiso, Chile	8.6	22,000
1908	Messina, Italy	7.5	83,000
1915	Avezzano, Italy	7.5	30,000
1920	Gansu (Kansu), China	8.6	180,000
1923	Yokohama, Japan	8.3	143,000
1927	Nan Shan, China	8.3	200,000
1932	Gansu (Kansu), China	7.6	70,000
1934	Bihar, India/Nepal	8.4	10,700
1935	Quetta, India*	7.5	60,000
1939	Chillan, Chile	8.3	28,000
1939	Erzincan, Turkey	7.9	30,000
1960	S. W. Chile	9.5	2,200
1960	Agadir, Morocco	5.8	12,000
1962	Khorasan, Iran	7.1	12,230
1964	Anchorage, USA	9.2	125
1968	N. E. Iran	7.4	12,000
1970	N. Peru	7.8	70,000
1972	Managua, Nicaragua	6.2	5,000
1974	N. Pakistan	6.3	5,200
1976	Guatemala	7.5	22,500
1976	Tangshan, China	8.2	255,000
1978	Tabas, Iran	7.7	25,000
1980	El Asnam, Algeria	7.3	20,000
1985	Mexico City, Mexico	8.1	4,200
1988	N.W. Armenia	6.8	55,000
1990	N. Iran	7.7	36,000
1993	Maharashtra, India	6.4	30,000
1994	Los Angeles, USA	6.6	51
1995	Kobe, Japan	7.2	5,000
1995	Sakhalin, Russia	7.5	2,000
1998	Takhar, Afghanistan	6.1	4,200
1998	Rostaq, Afghanistan	7.0	5,000
1999	Izmit, Turkey	7.4	15,000
2001	Gujarat, India	7.7	14,000
2003	Bam, Iran	6.6	30,000
2004	Sumatra, Indonesia	9.0	250,000
2005	N. Pakistan	7.6	74,000
2006	Java, Indonesia	6.4	6,200
2007	S. Peru	8.0	600
2008	Sichuan, China	7.9	70,000
2010	Haiti	7.0	230,000
2011	Christchurch, NZ	6.3	182
2011	N. Japan	9.0	20,000
2015	Nepal	7.8	8,500
2016	Ecuador	7.8	668
2017	Chiapas, Mexico	8.2	98

* now Pakistan

The atmosphere is a meteor shield, a radiation deflector, a thermal blanket, and a source of chemical energy for the Earth's diverse life forms. Five-sixths of its mass is in the lowest layer, the troposphere, which ranges in thickness from 11–6 miles between the equator and the poles. Powered by the Sun, the air is always on the move, flowing generally from high- to low-pressure areas. The troposphere is the layer where virtually all weather phenomena, including clouds, precipitation, and winds, occur. Above the troposphere is the stratosphere, which contains the important ozone layer and extends to about 30 miles above the Earth's surface. Beyond 60 miles, atmospheric density is lower than most laboratory vacuums.

STRUCTURE OF THE ATMOSPHERE

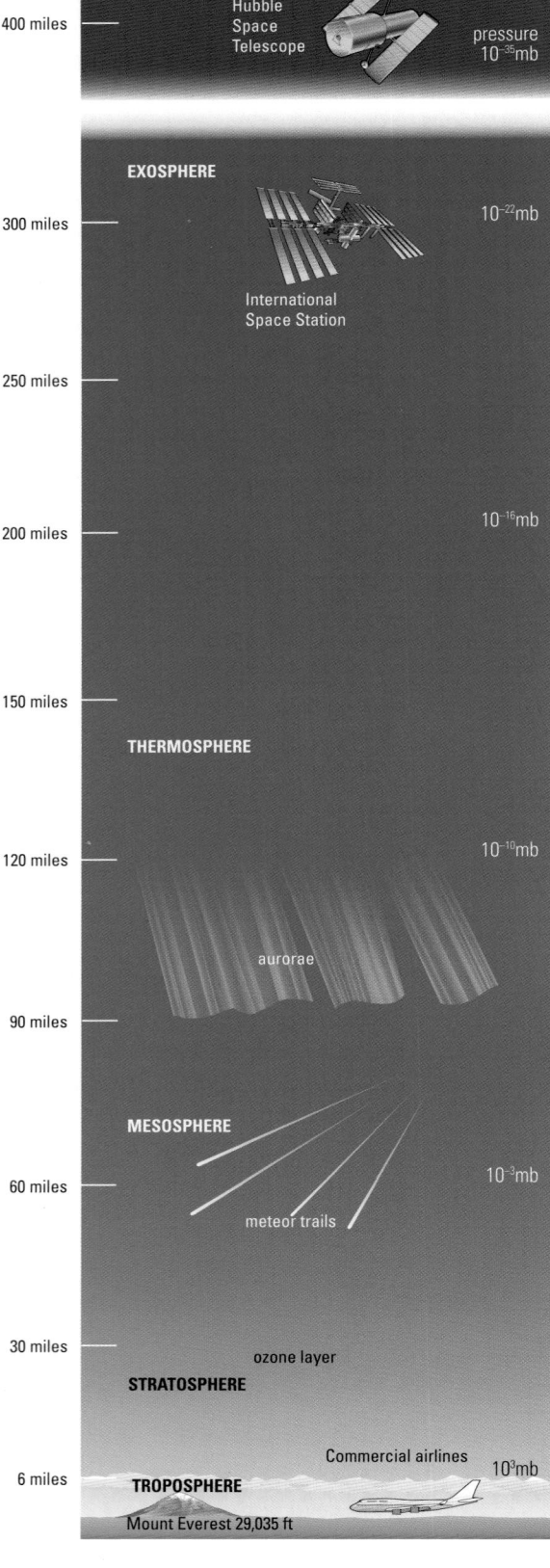

CIRCULATION OF THE AIR

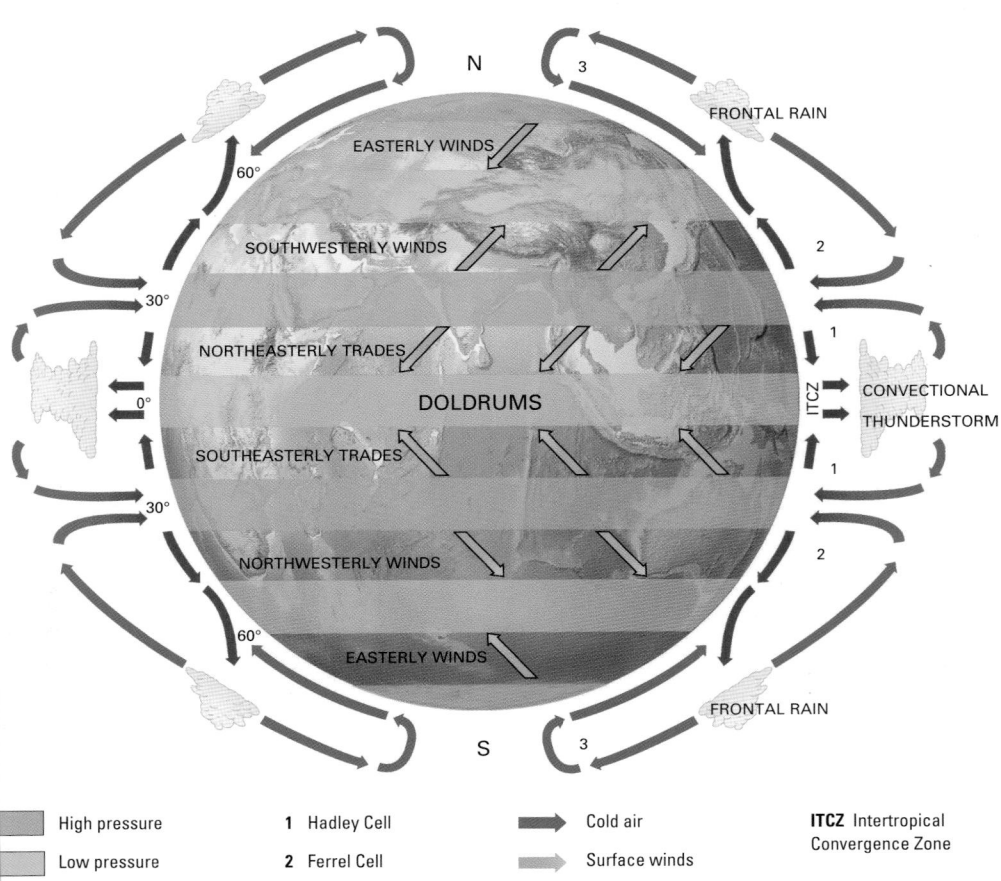

High pressure	**1** Hadley Cell	Cold air
Low pressure	**2** Ferrel Cell	Surface winds
Warm air	**3** Polar Cell	Clouds

ITCZ Intertropical Convergence Zone

FRONTAL SYSTEMS

Depressions, also known as cyclones or lows, form on the polar front where relatively cold and dry polar air flows alongside warmer, moister subtropical air. They occur when the flow high above the polar front generates a surface inward-swirling circulation that moves along the polar front as a wave.

The warm front is the leading edge of the subtropical air that glides up and over the cooler air ahead of it. This gently ascending flow produces a characteristic sequence of clouds ahead of the warm front and a band of precipitation a few hundred miles wide immediately in advance it. Conditions within the warm sector are often overcast with layer cloud and generally light rain or drizzle. The cloud sometimes breaks up downwind of hills.

Another band of precipitation often occurs just ahead of the cold front that is the leading edge of the cooler polar air. Cumulus clouds tend to occur in the air behind the cold front, producing scattered showers. The changes of temperature, wind direction, and cloud, etc, are illustrated by the diagram below.

CHEMICAL COMPOSITION

Gaseous composition of the principal atmospheric layers

Helium vanishes with increasing altitude. Above 1,500 miles the exosphere is almost entirely composed of hydrogen.

The high energy of mesospheric gas gives it a notional temperature of more than 3,600°F, although its density is negligible.

Stratospheric air contains enough ozone to make it poisonous, although it is in any case too rarified to breathe.

The narrowest of all the layers, this thin region contains about 85% of the atmosphere's total mass and almost all of its water vapor. It is also the realm of the Earth's weather.

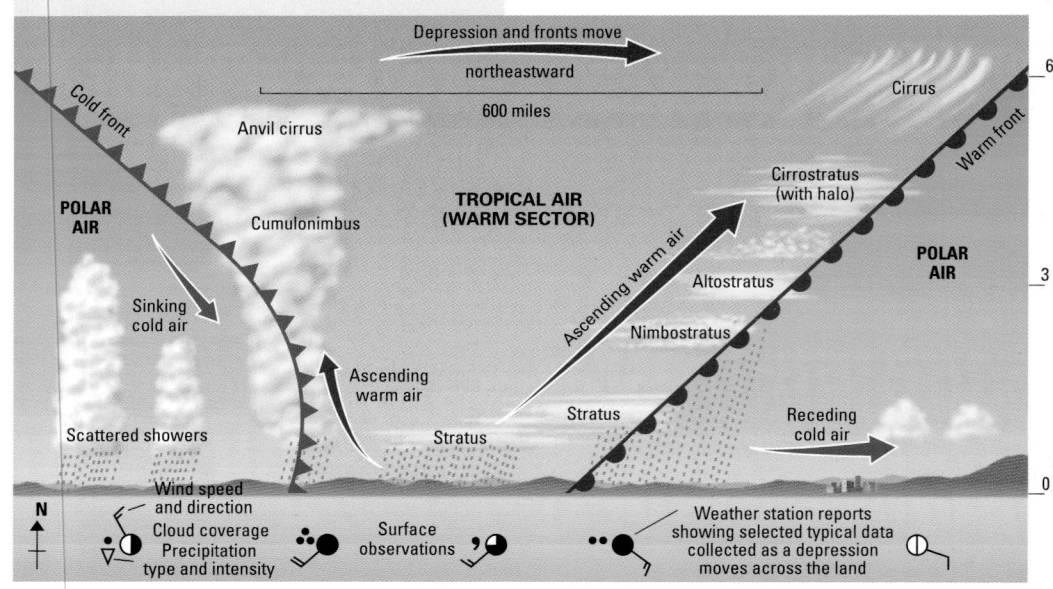

AIR MASSES

Air masses are large bodies of air where the variations of the main physical properties (that is, temperature and humidity) are relatively gentle. The term is generally applied only to the lower layers of the atmosphere, although air masses can cover areas of tens of thousands of square miles.

Air masses derive their temperature and humidity from the regions over which they lie. These regions are known as "source regions." The principal ones are:

• areas of relative calm, such as semipermanent high-pressure areas;
• areas where the surface is relatively uniform, including deserts, oceans, and ice-fields.

These are the "highs" marked on the map below.

As air masses move from their source regions, they may be changed due to the effects of the surface over which they move. These changes create "secondary air masses." For example, a warm air mass that travels over a cold surface is cooled and becomes more stable. Hence, it may form low cloud or fog, but is unlikely to produce much rain. By contrast, a cold air mass that passes over a warm surface is warmed and becomes less stable. The rising air is likely to produce more rain.

When two contrasting air masses meet, they form a "front." As warm air is lighter than cold, dense air, it begins to rise over it, condensing as it rises to form cloud and rain.

CLASSIFICATION OF CLOUDS

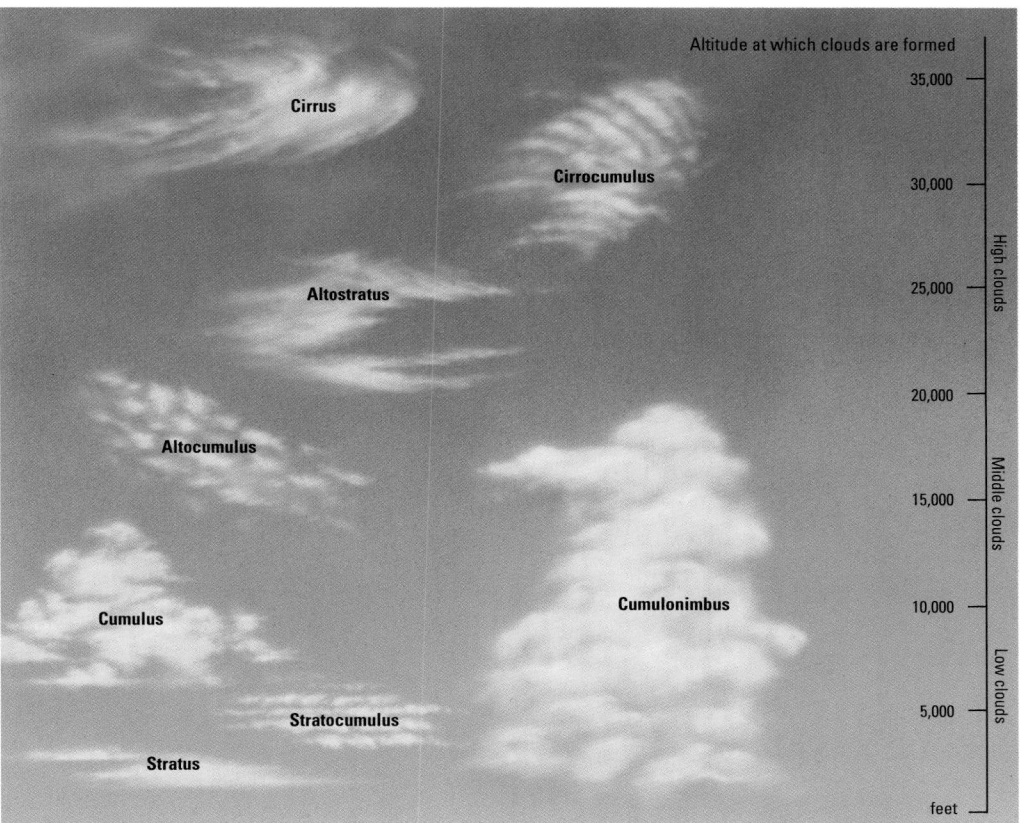

Clouds form when damp, usually rising, air is cooled. Thus they form when a wind rises to cross hills or mountains; when a mass of air rises over, or is pushed up by, another mass of denser air; or when local heating of the ground causes convection currents.

The first classification of clouds was developed by a London chemist, Luke Howard, in 1803, and it was later modified by the World Meteorological Organization. The types of clouds are classified according to altitude as high, middle, or low. The high ones, composed of ice crystals, are cirrus, cirrostratus, and cirrocumulus.

The middle clouds are altostratus — a gray or bluish striated, fibrous or uniform sheet producing light drizzle — and altocumulus, a thicker and fluffier version of cirrocumulus.

Low clouds include nimbostratus, a dark gray layer that brings rain or snow; cumulus, a detached heap, dark at the base; stratus, which forms dull, overcast skies at low levels; and stratocumulus, which consists of fluffy grayish-white layers.

Cumulonimbus, associated with storms and rains, heavy and dense with a flat base and a high, fluffy outline, can be tall enough to occupy middle as well as low altitudes.

PRESSURE AND SURFACE WINDS

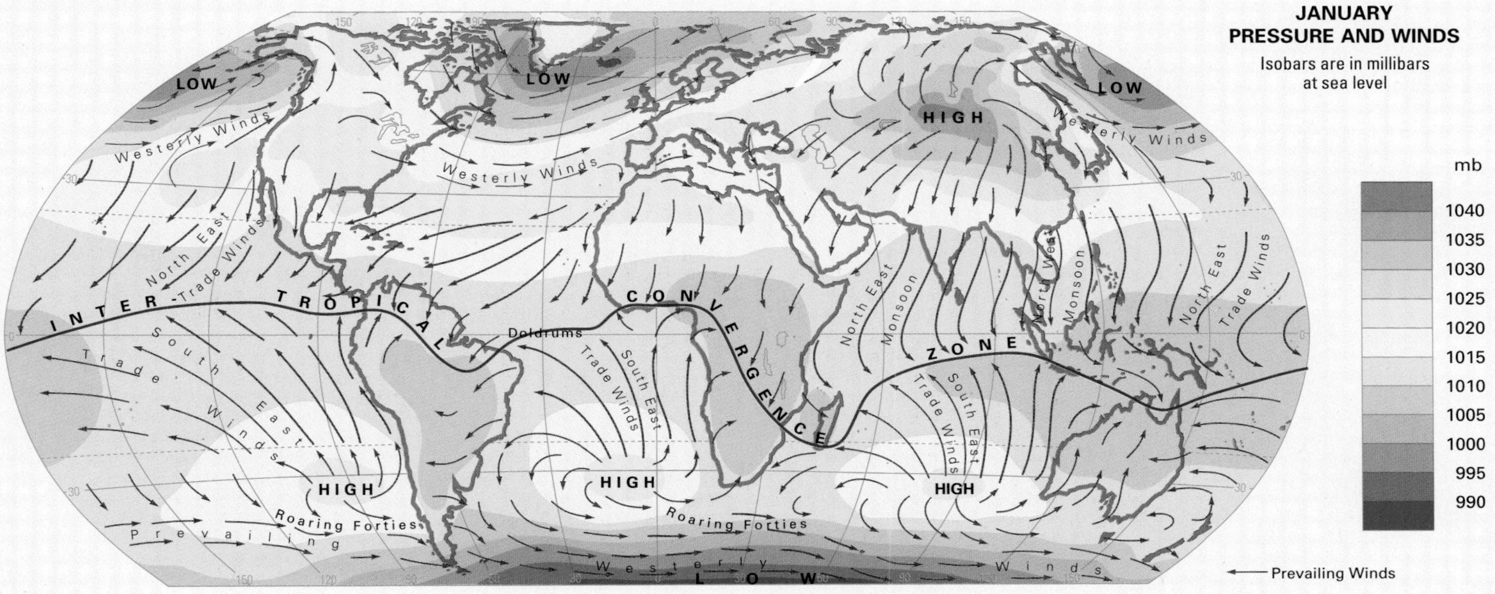

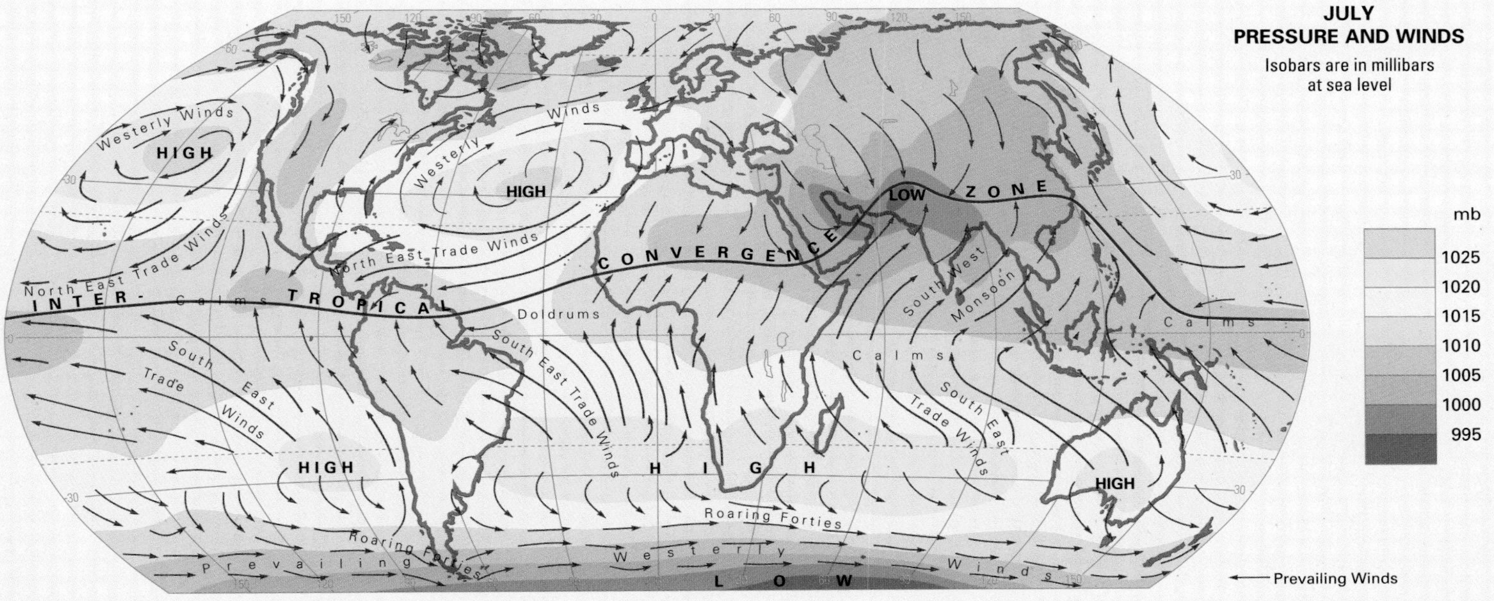

JANUARY PRESSURE AND WINDS
Isobars are in millibars at sea level

mb
| 1040 |
| 1035 |
| 1030 |
| 1025 |
| 1020 |
| 1015 |
| 1010 |
| 1005 |
| 1000 |
| 995 |
| 990 |

← Prevailing Winds

JULY PRESSURE AND WINDS
Isobars are in millibars at sea level

mb
| 1025 |
| 1020 |
| 1015 |
| 1010 |
| 1005 |
| 1000 |
| 995 |

← Prevailing Winds

WEATHER RECORDS

Pressure and winds

Highest barometric pressure:
Agata, Siberia, 1,083.8 mb at altitude 862 ft [262 m], December 31, 1968.

Lowest barometric pressure:
Typhoon Tip, 300 mi [480 km] west of Guam, Pacific Ocean, 870 mb, October 12, 1979.

Highest recorded wind speed:
Bridge Creek, Oklahoma, USA, 318 mph [512 km/h], May 3, 1999. Measured by Doppler radar monitoring a tornado.

Windiest place:
Port Martin, Antarctica, where winds of more than 40 mph [64 km/h] occur for not less than 100 days a year.

Worst recorded storm:
Bangladesh (then East Pakistan) cyclone, November 13, 1970 — over 300,000 dead or missing. The 1991 cyclone, Bangladesh's and the world's second worst in terms of loss of life, killed an estimated 138,000 people.

Worst recorded tornado:
Tri-state tornado — Missouri/Illinois/Indiana, USA, March 18, 1925 — 695 deaths, lasted 3 hours with 219 mi [352 km] path length. A suspected tornado in Bangladesh on April 26, 1989, killed approximately 1,300 people.

Weather is the day-to-day or hour-to-hour condition of the air, while climate is weather in the long term – the seasonal pattern of hot and cold, wet and dry, averaged over a long period.

Most classifications of climate are based on a system developed in the early 19th century by Vladimir Köppen, a Russian meteorologist. Using a code based on letters and a classification centered on two main features, temperature and precipitation, he identified five main climatic types: tropical (A), dry (B), warm temperate (C), cold temperate (D), and polar (E). A highland mountain climate (H) was added later to account for the variety of altitudinal climatic zones on high mountains. Each

of these main regions was then further subdivided.

Latitude is a major factor in determining climate, but other factors add to the complexity. These include the differential heating of land and sea, the distance from the sea, the effect of mountains on winds, and the influence of ocean currents. For example, New York City, Naples, and the Gobi Desert share almost the same latitude, but their climates are very different.

During the last Ice Age, the Earth underwent alternating cold periods, called glacials, separated by warm interglacials. The Milankovich theory suggests such cycles may be caused by variations in the Earth's path around the Sun, changing

from almost circular to elliptical every 95,000 years, and variations in the Earth's tilt from 21.5° to 24.5° every 42,000 years. Another factor is that the Earth is now closest to the Sun in the middle of winter in the northern hemisphere and furthest away in summer. But 12,000 years ago, at the height of the last glacial period, the northern winter fell with the Sun at its most distant.

Studies of these cycles suggest that we are now in an interglacial with a new glacial period on the way. However, scientists believe that global warming, largely a result of burning fossil fuels and deforestation, may be occurring much faster than the great, slow cycles of the Solar System.

Tropical rainy climates
All mean monthly temperatures above 64°F [18°C].

Af	Rain forest climate
Am	Monsoon climate
Aw	Savanna climate

Dry climates
Low rainfall combined with a wide range of temperatures.

| BS | Steppe climate |
| BW | Desert climate |

Warm temperate rainy climates
The mean temperature is below 64°F [18°C] but above 26°F [–3°C] and that of the warmest month is over 50°F [10°C].

Cw	Dry winter climate
Cs	Dry summer climate
Cf	Climate with no dry season

Cold temperate rainy climates
The mean temperature of the coldest month is below 26°F [–3°C] but that of the warmest month is still over 50°F [10°C].

| Dw | Dry winter climate |
| Df | Climate with no dry season |

Polar climates
The mean temperature of the warmest month is below 50°F [10°C], giving permanently frozen subsoil.

| ET | Tundra climate |

The mean temperature of the warmest month is below 32°F [0°C], giving permanent ice and snow.

| EF | Polar climate |

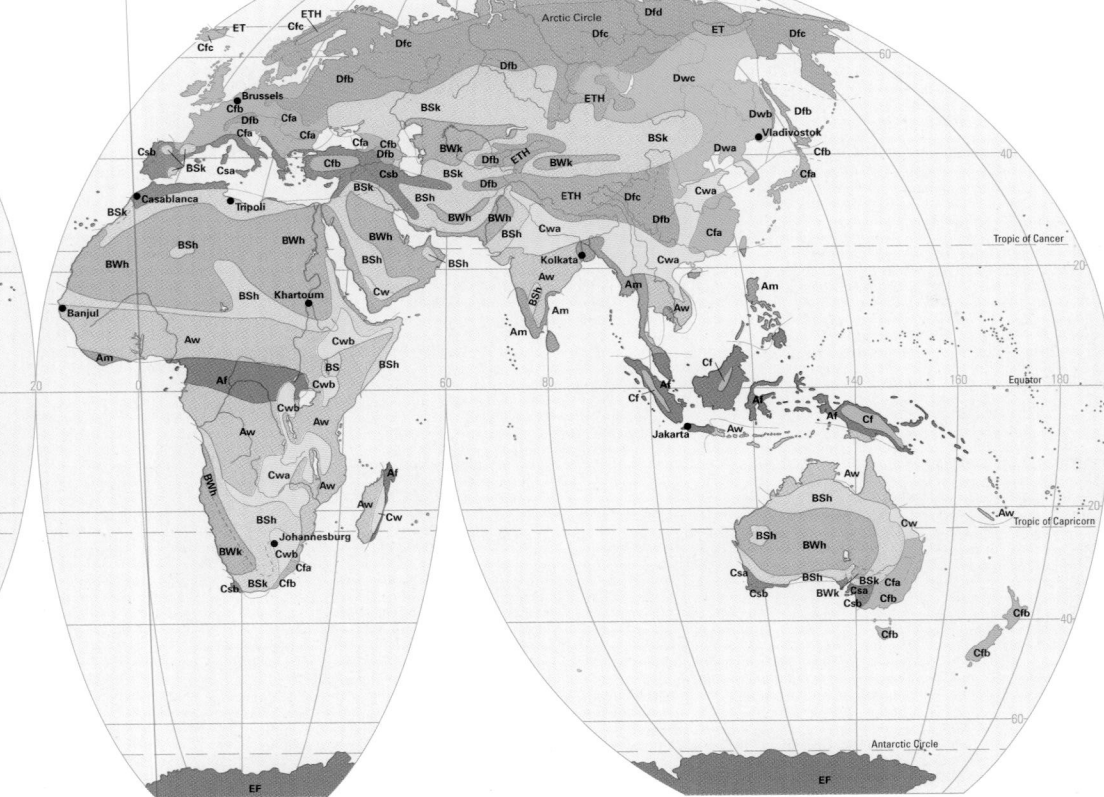

CLIMATE REGIONS

Vladimir Köppen divided the world's land areas into five main climatic regions, designated **A**, **B**, **C**, **D**, and **E**, which correspond broadly to the five vegetation types. Each of the five climatic regions is further subdivided using other letter codes. For example, dry climates are subdivided into deserts (**W**) and dry, semiarid steppe (**S**), while polar climates contain areas permanently covered by ice sheets and ice caps (**F**) and tundra areas (**T**).

Other letters cover particular features of precipitation, namely **f** for places with precipitation throughout the year; **m** for tropical areas with a marked monsoon season; **s** for places with a dry summer season; and **w** for places with a dry winter.

Another group of letters is concerned primarily with temperature, namely **a** for places with a hot summer; **b** for places with a warm summer; **c** for places with a cool, short summer; **d** for places with a cool, short summer and a cold winter; **h** for a hot, dry climate; and **k** for a cool, dry climate.

The classification **H** is sometimes used for mountain climates, which may, in the tropics, range from Af or Aw at the base, with ET and EF climates at the top.

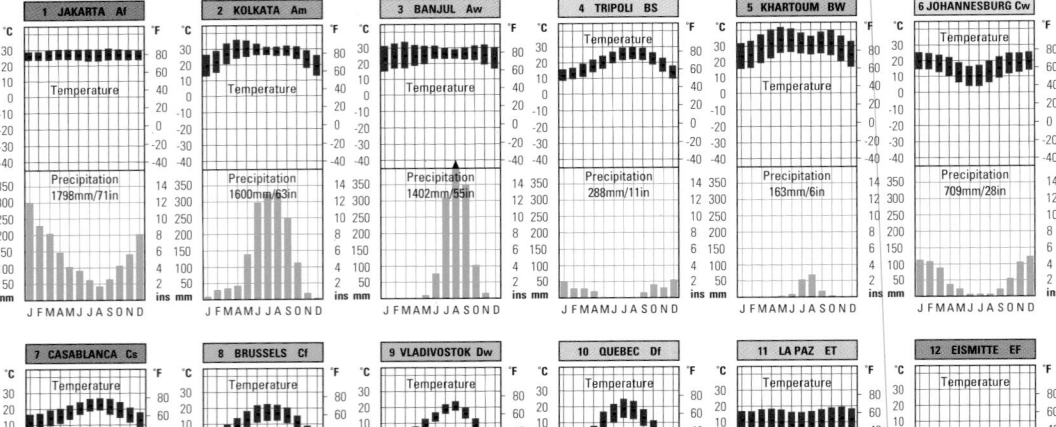

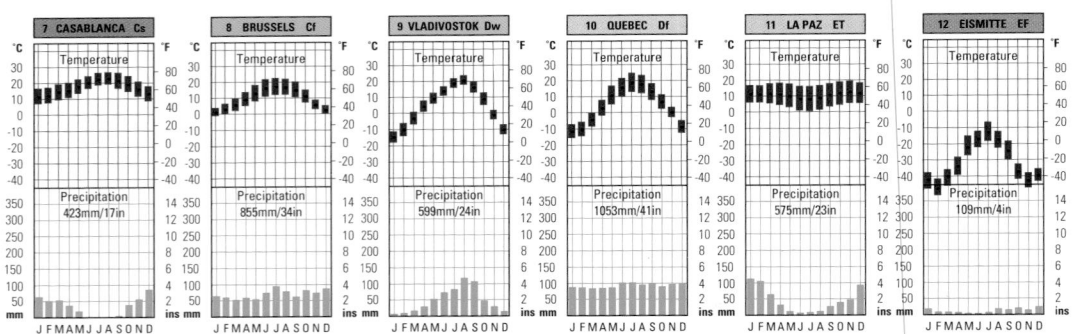

CLIMATE AND WEATHER TERMS

Anticyclone: area of high pressure with light winds and generally quiet weather.

Absolute humidity: mass of water vapor contained in a given volume of air.

Cloud cover: amount of cloud in the sky; measured in oktas (from 0–9), with 0 clear, and 9 "sky obscured."

Condensation: the conversion of water vapor into liquid.

Cyclone: violent storm resulting from counterclockwise rotation of winds in the northern hemisphere and clockwise in the southern: called hurricane in North America, typhoon in the Far East.

Depression: large area of low barometric pressure, a few thousand miles across.

Dew: deposition of small water droplets on the Earth's surface by direct condensation of water vapor.

Dew point: the temperature at which air becomes saturated by cooling at constant barometric pressure and absolute humidity

Drizzle: precipitation drops between 0.01–0.02 inches [0.2 and 0.5 mm] in diameter.

Evaporation: conversion of water from liquid into vapor or moisture in the air.

Front: the dividing line between two air masses.

Frost: the surface deposition of water vapor as minute ice crystals, when temperature reaches the frost point.

Hail: variably-sized pieces of ice that fall in downdrafts from cumulonimbus clouds.

Humidity: amount of water vapor in the air.

Isobar: line joining places with the same barometric pressure.

Isotherm: line connecting places of equal temperature.

Lightning: massive electrical discharge released in thunderstorm from cloud to cloud or cloud to ground, the result of the top becoming positively charged and the bottom negatively charged.

Precipitation: measurable rain, snow, sleet, or hail.

Prevailing wind: most common direction of wind at a given location.

Rain: precipitation of liquid particles with diameter larger than 0.02 inches [0.5 mm].

Relative humidity: observed quantity of water vapor in a mass of air over the saturation value at a given temperature (as a percentage).

Snow: flake-like coagulations of ice crystals that fall from clouds in subzero temperatures.

Thunder: sound produced by the rapid expansion of air heated by lightning.

Tornado: rapidly-rotating funnel-shaped cloud or debris column that must reach the surface and be attached to a parent cumulonimbus cloud.

BEAUFORT WIND SCALE

Named after Admiral Sir Francis Beaufort, the 19th-century British naval officer who devised it, the Beaufort Scale assesses wind speed according to its effects. It was originally designed as an aid for sailors, but has since been adapted for use on the land. It is used internationally.

Scale	Wind speed mph	km/h	Effect
0	0–1	0–1	**Calm** Smoke rises vertically
1	1–3	1–5	**Light air** Wind direction shown only by smoke drift
2	4–7	6–11	**Light breeze** Wind felt on face; leaves rustle; vanes moved by wind
3	8–12	12–19	**Gentle breeze** Leaves and small twigs in constant motion; wind extends small flag
4	13–18	20–28	**Moderate** Raises dust and loose paper; small branches move
5	19–24	29–38	**Fresh** Small trees in leaf sway; crested wavelets on inland waters
6	25–31	39–49	**Strong** Large branches move; difficult to use umbrellas; overhead wires whistle
7	32–38	50–61	**Near gale** Whole trees in motion; difficult to walk against wind
8	39–46	62–74	**Gale** Twigs break from trees; walking very difficult
9	47–54	75–88	**Strong gale** Slight structural damage
10	55–63	89–102	**Storm** Trees uprooted; serious structural damage
11	64–72	103–117	**Violent storm** Widespread damage
12	73+	118+	**Hurricane**

▲ In the Pacific Ocean, off south-east Asia, Typhoon Haiyan developed into a Category 5 storm during November 2013. Moving westwards, wind speeds of 170 mph (275 km/h) were recorded before it hit the Philippines. This makes it the strongest typhoon to make landfall, and over 6,000 people lost their lives.

THE MONSOON

Monsoon is the term given to the seasonal reversal of wind direction, most noticeably in Southeast Asia. It results from a combination of factors: the extreme heating and cooling of large land masses in relation to the less marked changes in temperature of the adjacent seas; the northward movement of the Intertropical Convergence Zone (ITCZ); and the effect of the Himalayas on the circulation of the air.

In March, winds blow outward from the mainland. But as the Sun and the ITCZ move northward, the land is intensely heated, and a low-pressure system develops. The southeast trade winds change direction and are sucked into the interior to become southwesterlies, bringing heavy rain. By November, the Sun and the ITCZ have again moved south and the wind directions are again reversed. Cool winds blow from the Asian interior to the sea, losing any moisture on the Himalayas before descending to the coast.

TEMPERATURE

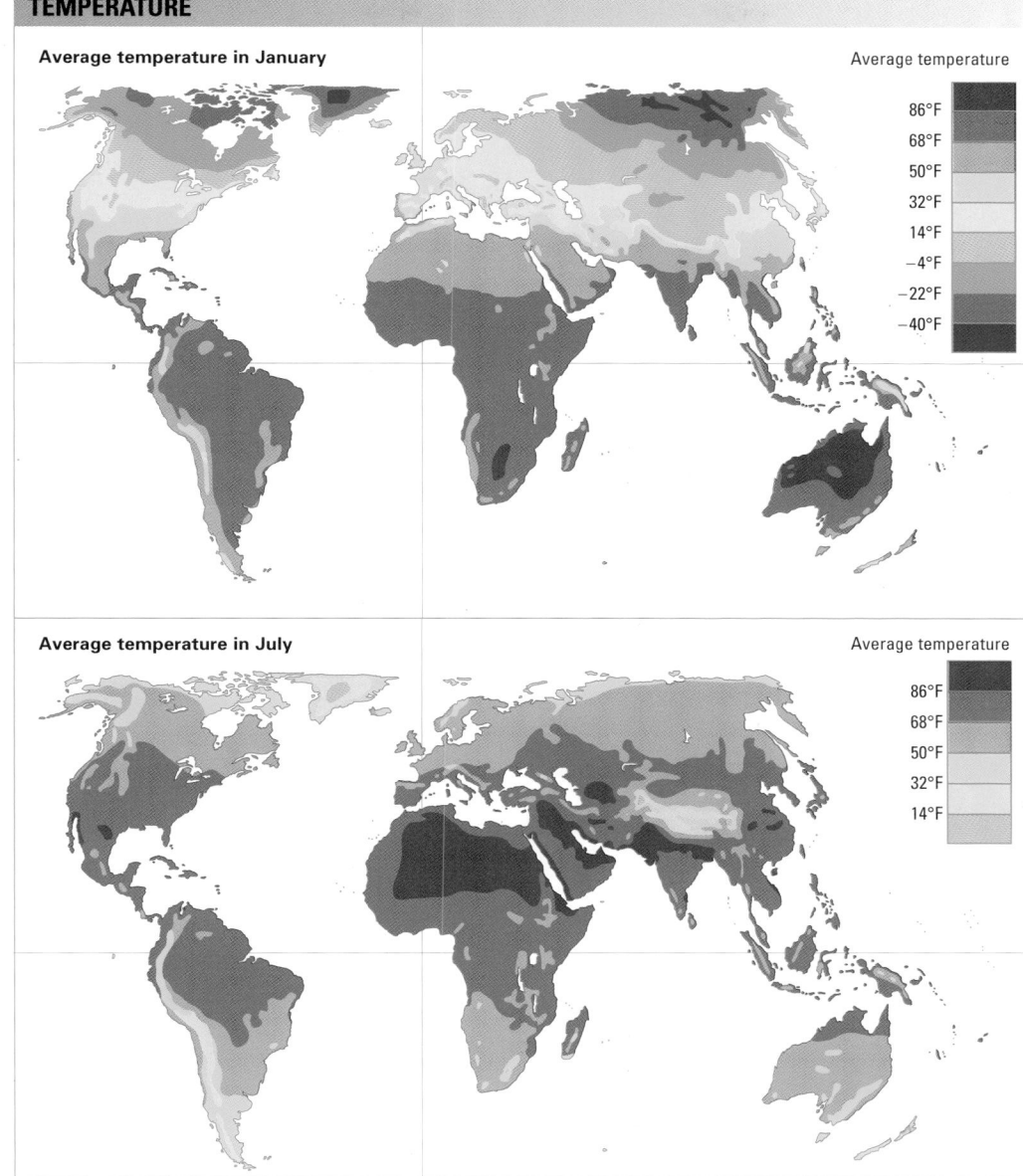

PRECIPITATION (RAINFALL AND SNOW)

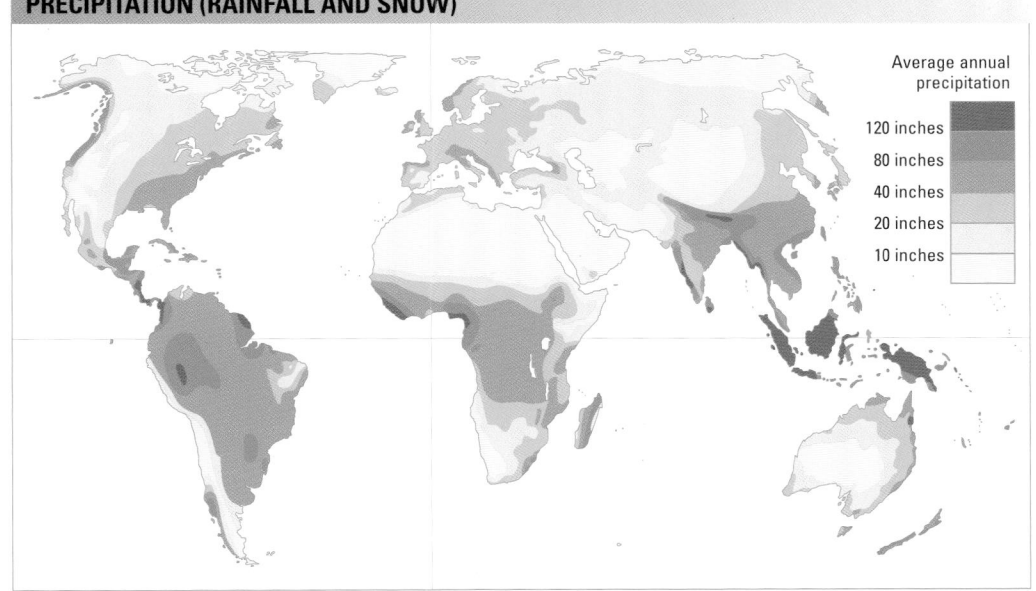

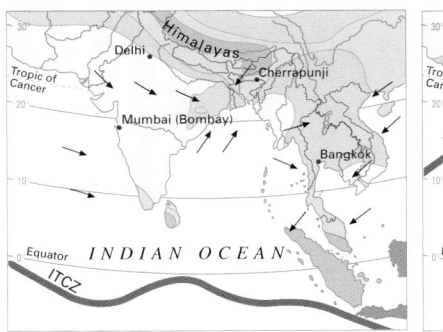
March – Start of the hot, dry season. The ITCZ is over the southern Indian Ocean.

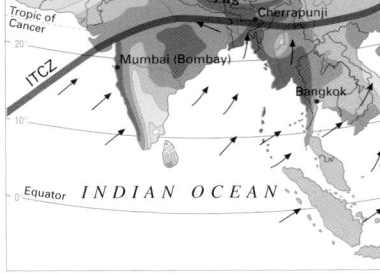
July – The rainy season. The ITCZ has migrated northward; winds blow onshore.

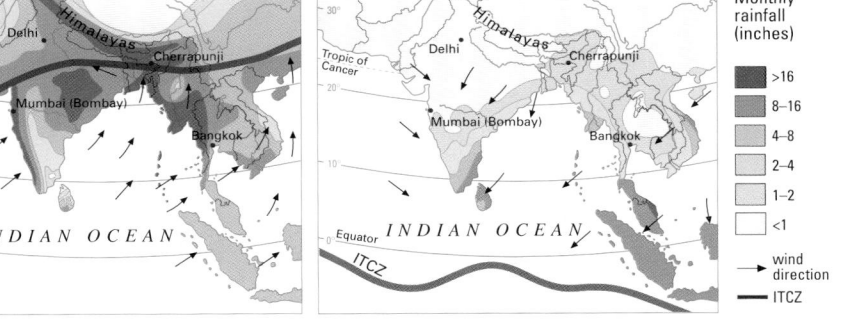
November – The ITCZ has returned south. The offshore winds are cool and dry.

CLIMATE RECORDS

TEMPERATURE

Highest recorded temperature: Death Valley, California, USA, 134°F [56.7°C], 10 July 1913.

Highest mean annual temperature: Dallol, Ethiopia, 94°F [34.4°C], 1960–6.

Longest heatwave: Marble Bar, W. Australia, 162 days over 100°F [38°C], October 23, 1923, to April 7, 1924.

Lowest recorded temperature (outside poles): Verkhoyansk, Siberia, −93.6°F [−69.8°C], February 7, 1982. Verkhoyansk also registered the greatest annual range of temperature: −90°F to 98°F [−68°C to 37°C].

Lowest mean annual temperature: Polus Nedostupnosti, Pole of Cold, Antarctica, −72°F [−57.8°C].

PRECIPITATION

Driest place: Quillagua, N. Chile, mean annual rainfall 0.02 inches [0.5 mm], 1964–2001.

Wettest place (average): Mt Wai'ale'ale, Hawai'i, USA, mean annual rainfall 459.8 inches [11,680 mm].

Wettest place (12 months): Cherrapunji, Meghalaya, N.E. India, 1,042 inches [26,461 mm], August 1860 to August 1861. Cherrapunji also holds the record for rainfall in one month: 115 inches [2,930 mm], July 1861. (See Monsoon maps below.)

Wettest place (24 hours): Fac Fac, Réunion, Indian Ocean, 71.9 inches [1,825 mm], March 15–16, 1952.

Heaviest hailstones: Gopalganj, Bangladesh, up to 2.25 lb [1.02 kg], April 14, 1986 (killed 92 people).

Heaviest snowfall (continuous): Bessans, Savoie, France, 68 inches [1,730 mm] in 19 hours, April 5–6, 1969.

Heaviest snowfall (season/year): Mt Baker, Washington, USA, 1,140 inches [28,956 mm], June 1998 to June 1999.

Ever since the Industrial Revolution began, the amount of carbon dioxide in the atmosphere has steadily increased. It is the result of burning fossil fuels, and the destruction of forests which absorb carbon dioxide. In the late 18th century, carbon dioxide made up about 280 parts per million by volume (ppmv). It has risen to over 410 ppmv in 2020.

Carbon dioxide is one of the "greenhouse gases" which also include CFCs (which also cause ozone depletion in the upper atmosphere), methane, and nitrous oxides. Another greenhouse gas is water vapor. The quantity of vapor in the atmosphere has increased during recent decades as an expression of increased evaporation. This enhances the greenhouse effect as a positive feedback.

Greenhouse gases are so-called because they absorb part of the Earth's radiation going out to space and re-radiate a proportion of it back down. This critically important natural process acts to insulate the Earth and is essential to life. Without it, our planet would be some 54°F [30°C] colder than it is. But the increase in the volume of carbon dioxide in particular has caused global temperatures to rise. These changes were detailed by the Intergovernmental Panel on Climate Change (IPCC) report in 2013. While computer projections are difficult to make, the IPCC report concluded that a rise in temperatures of between 2.7°F [1.5°C] (compared to the 1850–1900 global mean) and at least 3.6°F [2.0°C] is likely by 2100. Global warming will almost certainly alter weather patterns, causing food and water shortages in vulnerable parts of the world, massive floods, and a rise in sea levels of between 1.71 ft [0.52 m] and 3.22 ft [0.98 m].

While an international ban has been imposed on some greenhouse gases, their residence time in the atmosphere may have long-lasting consequences.

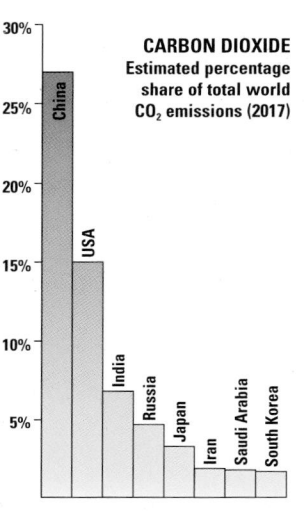

CARBON DIOXIDE
Estimated percentage share of total world CO_2 emissions (2017)

In 2017, the total world CO_2 emmissions had reached over 36 billion tonnes. China remains the world's largest CO_2 emitter - accounting for more than one-quarter of all emmissions.

GLOBAL WARMING

High atmospheric concentrations of heat-absorbing gases are a major cause in the rise of average surface temperatures worldwide – up by 1.78°F [0.99°C] between 1880 and 2016. Global warming is also likely to bring about a rise in sea levels that may flood some of the world's densely populated coastal areas (see panel at foot of page 81).

Evidence of global warming is attributed mainly to the "greenhouse effect," caused by the emission of certain gases, notably carbon dioxide, into the atmosphere. Despite international action to control emissions of some greenhouse gases, carbon dioxide levels are still rising.

Carbon dioxide emissions in tonnes per capita (2017)

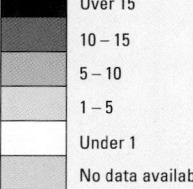

	Over 15
	10 – 15
	5 – 10
	1 – 5
	Under 1
	No data available

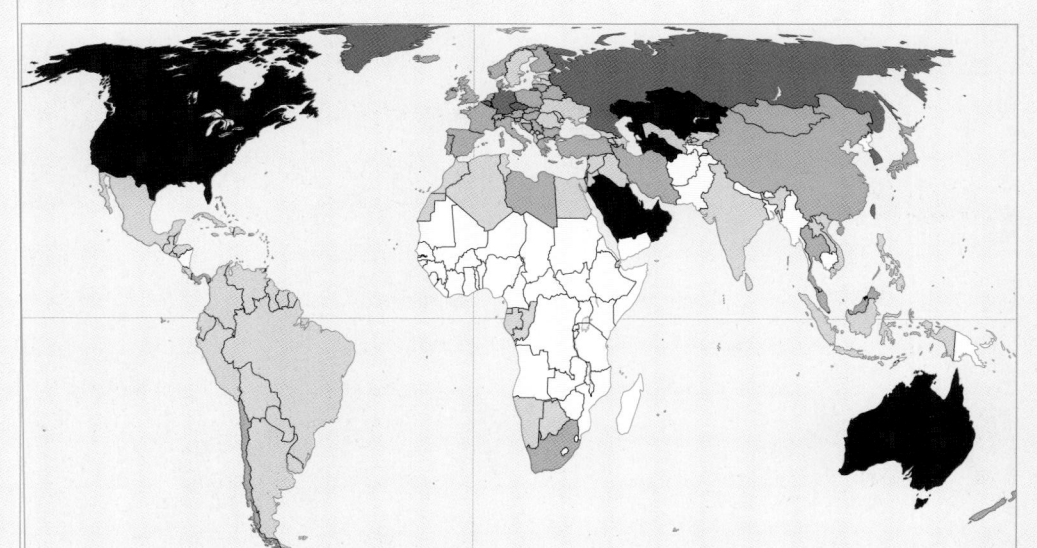

CLIMATE CHANGE

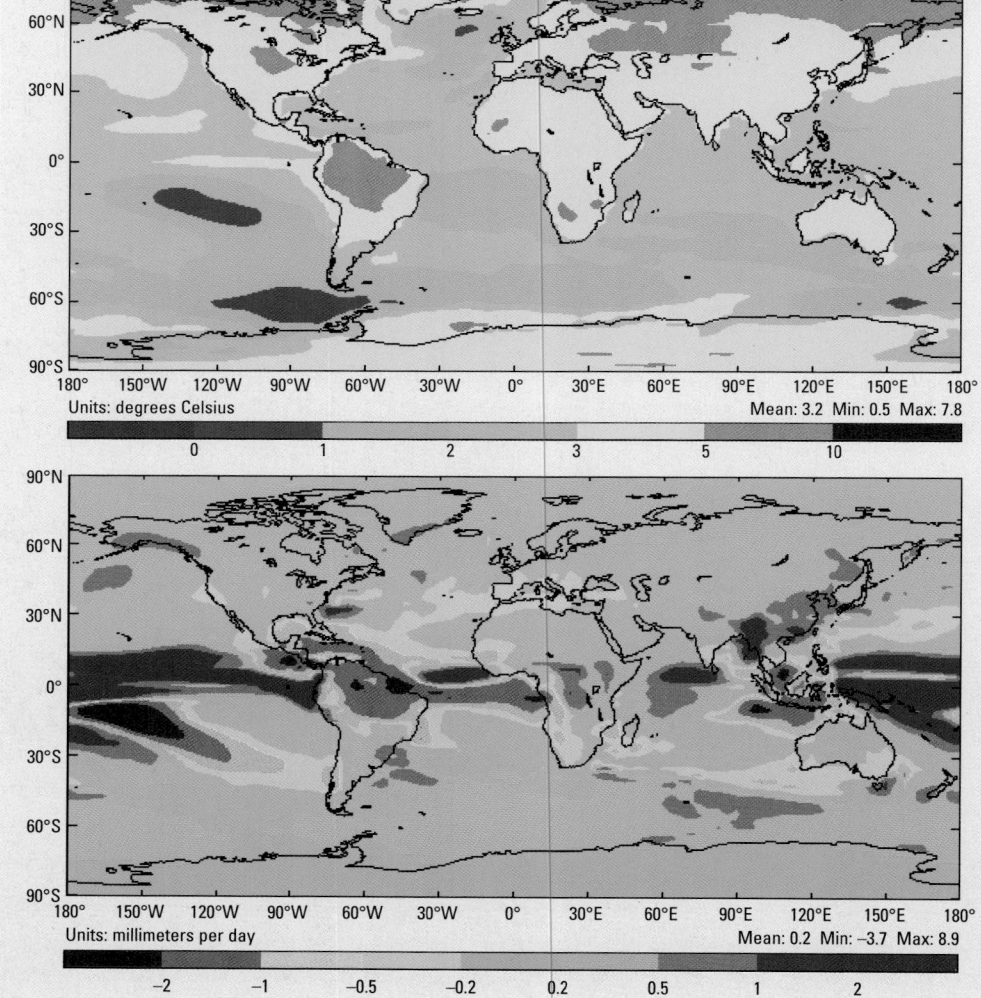

Units: degrees Celsius   Mean: 3.2 Min: 0.5 Max: 7.8

0   1   2   3   5   10

Units: millimeters per day   Mean: 0.2 Min: –3.7 Max: 8.9

–2   –1   –0.5   –0.2   0.2   0.5   1   2

Annual average surface air temperature

The map summarizes the change in long-term mean values between the predicted average for the period from 2070 to 2100, and the observed average for 1960 to 1990. The predictions are from a long-term "run" of a "coupled" atmosphere-ocean computer model that represents the complex processes in the Earth's climate system. It assumes that the atmospheric concentration of carbon dioxide will increase more than twofold during the 21st century, assuming "medium growth" of the global economy, and that no measures to combat the emission of greenhouse gases are taken. Note that the predicted increase in average surface temperature suggests a warming across Britain and Ireland of between 2°C [3.6°F] in the north and west to possibly 4°C [7.2°F] in the southeast. Very broadly, the oceans and some adjacent continental areas are likely to see the smaller increases.

Annual average precipitation

Predictions from climate models always involve some degree of uncertainty. This is because our understanding of the climate system and its complex workings are imperfect, as are the model representations of the physical system. Additionally, we are unsure quite how the world will evolve economically and politically over the coming decades – although different scenarios are used in this regard. The map of predicted precipitation change indicates broadly, for example, an increase across Britain and Ireland. The largest increases of some 0.01–0.02 inches [0.2–0.5 mm] a day are anticipated to be over northern and western areas. This equates to some 3–7 inches [75–180 mm] a year.

It should be noted that both these maps mask quite significant seasonal detail, which is also predicted by the models.

ARCTIC SEA ICE

The fact that the Arctic sea ice is disappearing has been known for decades. The underlying cause is believed by all but a handful of climatologists to be global warming, brought about by greenhouse-gas emissions. At current rates of shrinkage, this looks likely to happen some time between 2020 and 2050.

The reason is that Arctic air is warming twice as fast as the atmosphere as a whole. While some of the causes of this are understood, others are not. The darkness of land and water compared to the reflectiveness of snow and ice means that when the snow and ice melt to reveal land or water, the area exposed absorbs more heat from the Sun and reflects less of it back into space. The result is a feedback loop that accelerates local warming.

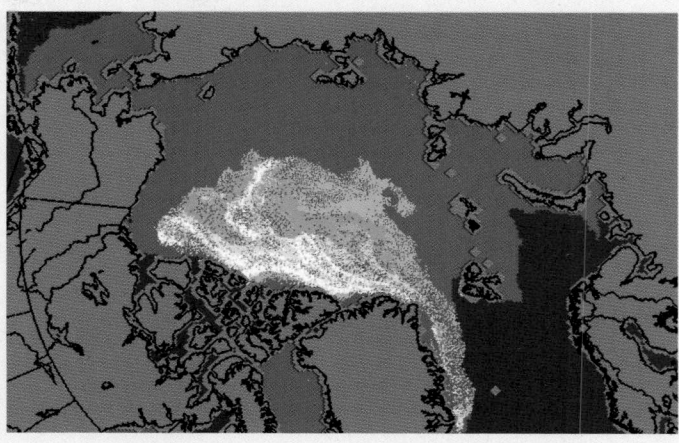

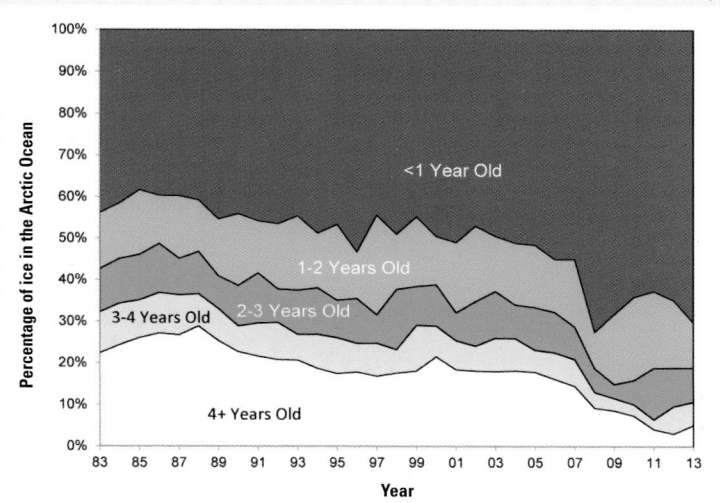

The diagram and map show that ice older than 1 year, which used to cover up to 60% of the Arctic Ocean, now covers only 30%. The oldest ice, over 4 years old, now comprises only 5% of the ice in the Arctic Ocean, whereas during the 1980s it covered roughly 25% of the region.

NSIDC courtesy J. Maslanik and M. Tschudi, University of Colorado

REGIONAL CLIMATE CHANGE

Climate modelers have produced simulations of global and continental surface temperature changes over the last century. This is done using only "natural forcing" by modeling the impact on atmospheric temperatures from known solar variability and volcanic eruptions. In addition, the same period of time is simulated by adding to natural forcing the impact of anthropogenic (human) influence due to measured changes in the concentration of greenhouse gases, particulate matter, etc.

The separate model "runs" are then compared with the observed temperature changes to illustrate which of the simulations matches the observations best.

This is a powerful means of verifying the relative roles of natural and human induced changes in atmospheric composition, and known solar output fluctuations on climate change.

▶ Climate model simulations for 1906 to 2009 using "natural forcings only" (blue bands) and "natural plus anthropogenic forcings" (pink bands). Regional decadal averages of observed temperature (black lines) are plotted as anomalies with respect to the 1880 to 1919 average. Blue and pink bands define the 5% to 95% range of possibilities for multiple runs for just natural forcings and natural plus anthropogenic forcings of the Coupled Model Intercomparison Project Phase 5.

Models using only natural forcings

Models using both natural and anthropogenic forcings

Observations (dashed when spatial coverage is less than 50%)

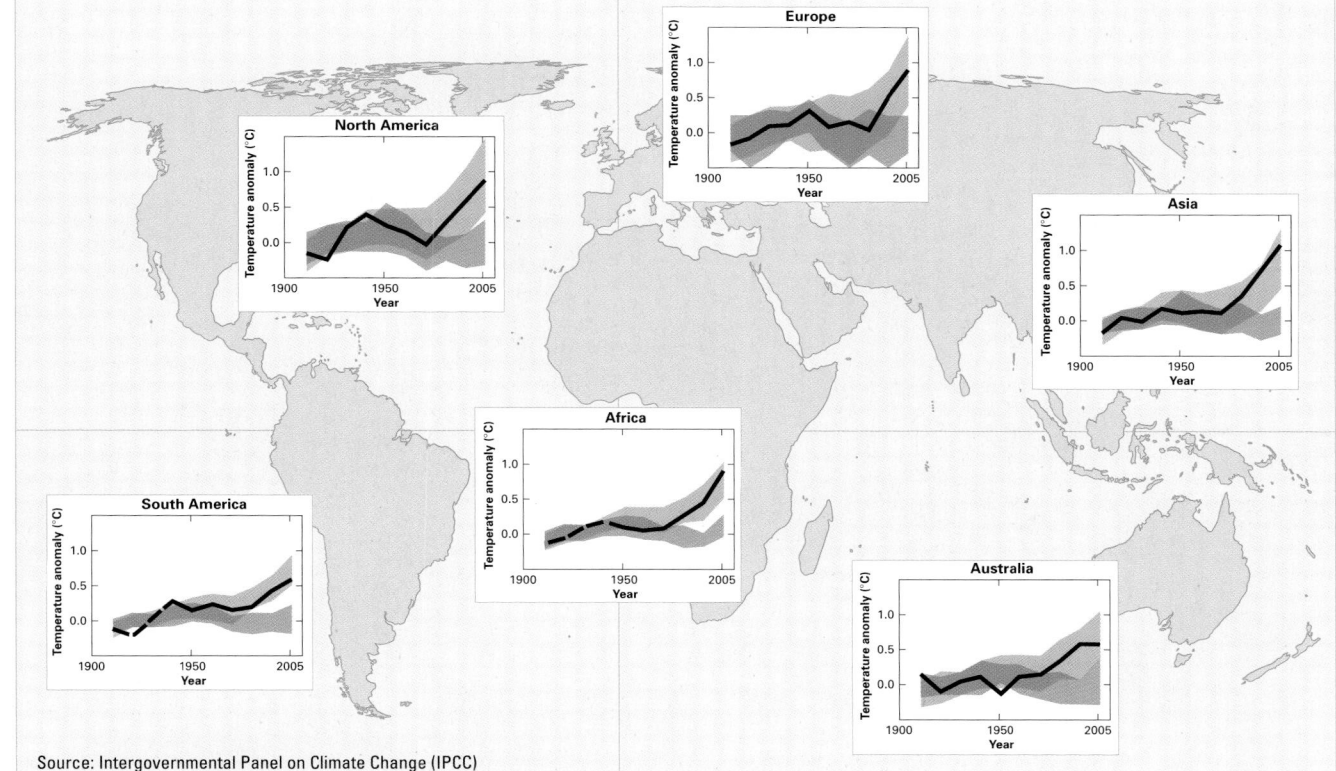

Source: Intergovernmental Panel on Climate Change (IPCC)

PROJECTED CHANGE IN GLOBAL WARMING

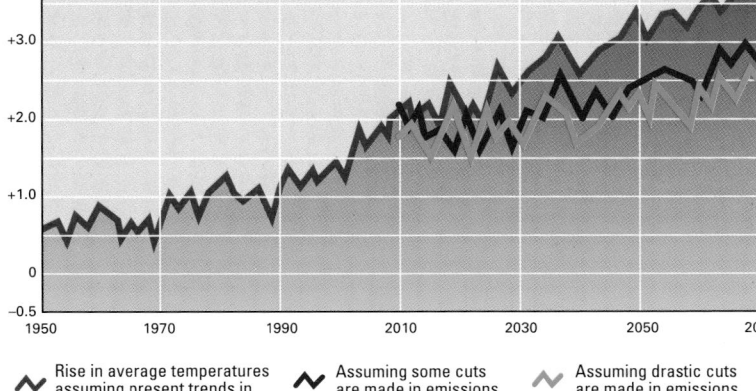

Rise in average temperatures assuming present trends in CO₂ emissions continue

Assuming some cuts are made in emissions

Assuming drastic cuts are made in emissions

Climate models are used to provide the best scientifically-based estimates of the future global climate. A typical method is to run the models for some decades ahead and then to compare the predicted average with a past 30-year period. A range of climate models are used, run with different scenarios that express the breadth of possibilities of, for example, industrial development and the degree of atmospheric pollution "clean-up" by industrial nations.

The diagram above shows global observed and predicted surface mean temperature change from 1950 to 2070 with three prediction scenarios. The first (red) assumes rapid economic growth and continued population increases. The second (blue) assumes some attempts are made to cut greenhouse gas emissions, while the green line involves the greater use of cleaner technologies, with global population peaking mid-century then declining.

REGIONAL CLIMATE CHANGE

The rate at which global sea level has increased since about the middle of the 19th century exceeds the increase estimated over the last two thousand years. The recent change is one expression of the impact of global warming through a combination of glacier melt and thermal expansion of the ocean; it is estimated that these count for 75% of the total observed rise since the 1970s. A combination of tide-gauge records and, more recently, altimeter observations from satellites, indicate that the global average increase of sea-level from 1901 to 2010 was 7.5 inches [190 mm] with an averaged global annual rise of 0.07 inches [1.7 mm] per year. This value has increased in recent periods from 0.08 inches [2.0 mm] per year (1971–2010) to 0.13 inches [3.2 mm] per year (1993–2010).

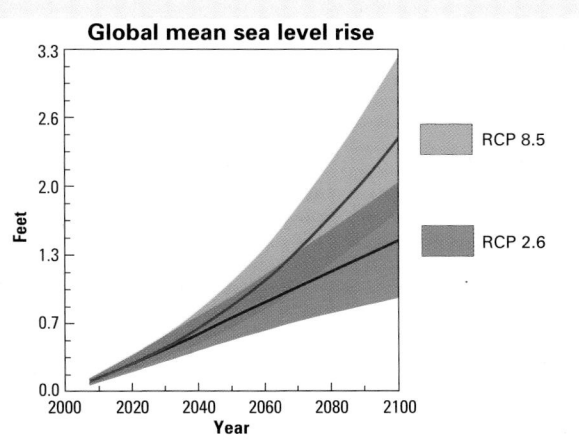

Source: Intergovernmental Panel on Climate Change (IPCC)

A combination of advanced global climate prediction models run through to 2100 produce an averaged forecast of the likely range of global mean sea level increase for two extreme CO₂, and other greenhouse gas, scenarios. The values on the graph are relative to the global mean conditions for the period 1986–2005. These "Representative Concentration Scenarios" (RCPs) vary from the lowest impact future (RCP 2.6) for which CO₂ concentration reaches 421 ppm by 2100, to the strongest

impact (RCP 8.5) for which CO₂ increases to 936 ppm by 2100.

The upper and lower boundaries of the two bands of color on the graph show the predicted upper and lower possibilities of future sea level increase. The solid colored line is the median value that has 50% of estimates above it and 50% below. The low impact future indicates a median value of a 1.31 ft [0.4 m] increase by 2100 while the highest impact future is about double that at 2.46 ft [0.75 m].

Without the hydrological cycle, by which water is constantly recycled between the oceans, the atmosphere and the land, the continents would be barren. Precipitation enables plants to grow and soils to form, creating the world's natural vegetation regions and the ecosystems that support animal life.

Running water also plays a major role in shaping landforms. Yet in many parts of the world, people do not have safe water to drink and suffer from diseases caused by water-borne organisms and pollution. It is estimated that 770 million people lack access to safe water and more people have a mobile phone than a toilet.

Experts argue that world demand for water is increasing at about twice the rate of population growth. It is predicted that, by 2025, half the world's population will face water shortages. This could lead to conflict and even boundary wars – 300 major rivers cross national frontiers and access to their water is likely to be disputed.

THE HYDROLOGICAL CYCLE

The world's water balance is regulated by the constant recycling of water between the oceans, the atmosphere and the land. The movement of water between these three reservoirs is known as the "hydrological cycle." The oceans play a vital role in the hydrological cycle: 74% of the total precipitation falls over the oceans and 84% of the total evaporation comes from the oceans. Water vapor in the atmosphere circulates around the planet, transporting energy as well as the water itself. When the vapor cools, it falls as rain or snow. The whole cycle is driven by the Sun.

Transfer of water vapor
10% of the balance of precipitation/
evaporation over oceans

Evaporation from oceans
84% of total
evaporation

Evapotranspiration
16% of total evaporation

Precipitation
74% of total
precipitation

Precipitation
26% of total
precipitation

Surface runoff

Runoff
10% of the balance of
precipitation/evaporation
over land

Surface storage

Infiltration

Groundwater flow

WATER DISTRIBUTION

The distribution of planetary water is shown by percentage. Oceans and ice caps together account for more than 99% of the total; the breakdown of the remainder is estimated.

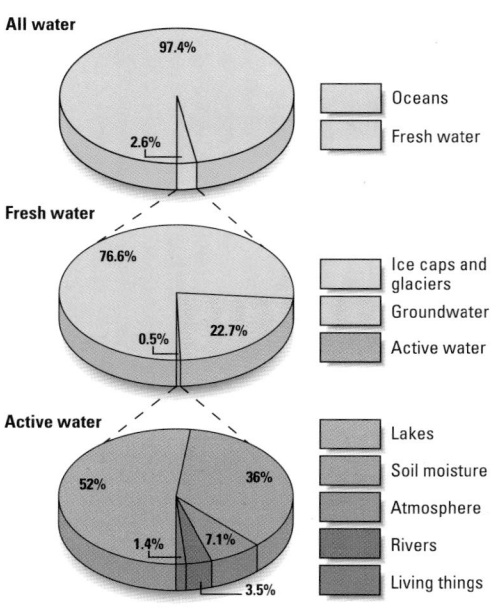

All water
97.4%
2.6%
- Oceans
- Fresh water

Fresh water
76.6%
0.5%
22.7%
- Ice caps and glaciers
- Groundwater
- Active water

Active water
52%
36%
1.4%
7.1%
3.5%
- Lakes
- Soil moisture
- Atmosphere
- Rivers
- Living things

Almost all the world's water is 3,000 million years old, and all of it cycles endlessly through the hydrosphere, though at different rates. Water vapor circulates over days, even hours; deep-ocean water circulates over millennia; and ice-cap water remains solid for millions of years.

ANNUAL SEDIMENT YIELD

tonnes/sq miles/year

0 250 500 750 1,000 1,250 1,500 1,750 2,000 2,250 2,500 2,750 3,000 3,250 3,500

- Hwang Ho
- Brahmaputra
- Ganges
- Indus
- Mekong
- Colorado
- Amazon
- Orinoco
- Mississippi
- Orange
- Danube
- Nile
- Murray
- Lena
- Dnepr

Around 20% of all land-derived sediment is carried by three Asian rivers: the Hwang Ho (Yellow River), the Brahmaputra, and the Ganges. Together, these three rivers carry around 3,000 million tonnes of sediment each year into the oceans. Sediment yield is affected by runoff and vegetation cover, and is steadily increasing due to large-scale deforestation, most notably in South-east Asia and the Amazon basin. In these regions, deforesting the slopes allows the heavy tropical rains to wash away whatever thin and fragile soil there is, leading to severe erosion of the land.

▼ To prevent as excess of sediment building up and slowing the flow of the Hwang Ho (Yellow River), the river's mud, silt and sand is blasted downstream at an annual event at the Xiaolangdi Reservoir, near Jiyuan, in Henan province.

LONGEST RIVERS

		miles	km
Nile	Africa	4,160	6,695
Amazon	South America	4,010	6,450
Yangtse	Asia	3,960	6,380
Mississippi-Missouri	North America	3,710	5,971
Yenisey-Angara	Asia	3,445	5,550
Hwang Ho	Asia	3,395	5,464
Ob-Irtysh	Asia	3,360	5,410
Congo	Africa	2,900	4,670
Paraná-Plate	South America	2,796	4,500
Mekong	Asia	2,796	4,500
Amur	Asia	2,760	4,442
Lena	Asia	2,735	4,402
Irtysh	Asia	2,640	4,250
Mackenzie	North America	2,630	4,240
Niger	Africa	2,595	4,180
Yenisey	Asia	2,540	4,090
Missouri	North America	2,540	4,088
Mississippi	North America	2,350	3,782
Murray-Darling	Australia	2,330	3,750
Volga	Europe	2,300	3,700
Ob	Asia	2,285	3,680
Zambezi	Africa	2,200	3,540
Purus	South America	2,080	3,350
Madeira	South America	1,990	3,200
Yukon	North America	1,980	3,185
Indus	Asia	1,925	3,100
Darling	Australia	1,905	3,070
Rio Grande	North America	1,880	3,030
Brahmaputra	Asia	1,800	2,900
São Francisco	South America	1,800	2,900
Syrdarya	Asia	1,775	2,860
Danube	Europe	1,770	2,850
Salween	Asia	1,740	2,800
Paraná	South America	1,740	1,740
Tocantins	South America	1,710	2,750
Orinoco	South America	1,700	2,740
Euphrates	Asia	1,675	2,700
Murray	Australia	1,600	2,575
Paraguay	South America	1,580	2,550
Amudarya	Asia	1,575	2,540

WATER SCARCITY

Human populations require fresh water for many purposes – drinking, cooking, washing, farming, industry, recreation and energy production. Given population growth and rising standards of living in some areas, there will inevitably be increased pressure on this resource in certain places. Water scarcity can be physical and/or economic.

Areas with little or no water scarcity – less than 25% of water from rivers is withdrawn for agriculture, industry and domestic purposes

Areas with physical water scarcity – more than 75% of water from rivers is withdrawn for agriculture, industry and domestic purposes

Areas approaching physical water scarcity – more than 60% of water from rivers is withdrawn and scarcity is expected in the near future

Areas with economic water scarcity – less than 25% of water from rivers is withdrawn but human, institutional and financial problems limit access to water

No data available

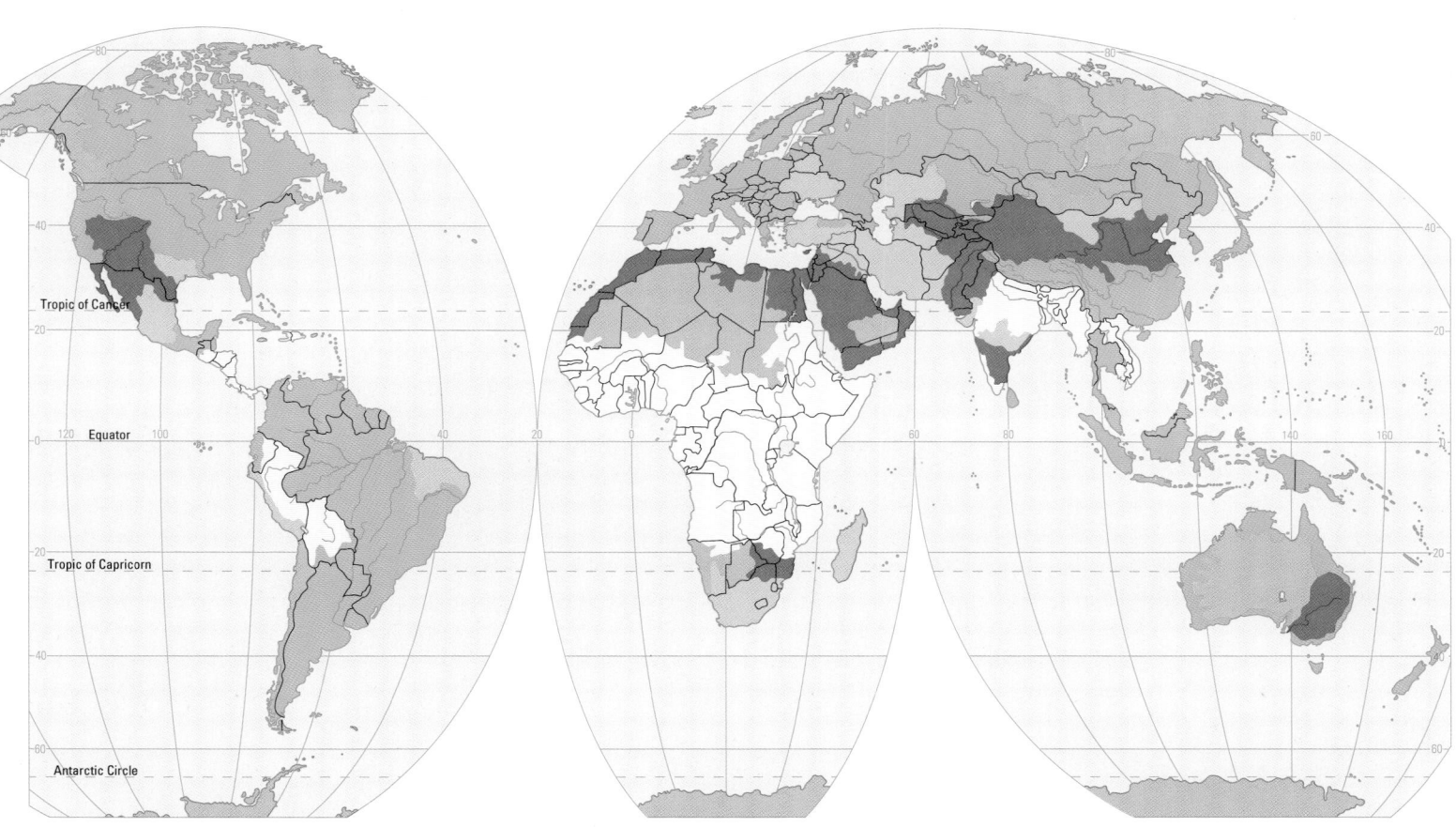

NATURAL VEGETATION

The map below illustrates the natural "climax vegetation" of a region, as dictated by its climate and topography. In most cases, human agricultural activity has drastically altered the pattern of the vegetation. The various vegetation regions support different kinds of animals and wildlife, and, in an undisturbed state, they are highly developed biological communities, or "biomes."

The blue line on the map represents the northern limit of tree growth, and the red lines indicate the northern and southern limits of palm growth. The majority of the numerous species are tropical or subtropical. Some, such as the coconut, date, sago, and oil palms, are important economically.

Tropical rain forest

Subtropical and temperate rain forest

Monsoon woodland and open jungle

Subtropical and temperate woodland, scrub, and bush

Tropical savanna, with low trees and bush

Tropical savanna and grasslands

Dry semidesert, with shrub and grass

Desert shrub

Desert

Dry steppe and shrub

Temperate grasslands, prairie, and steppe

Mediterranean hard-wood forest and scrub

Temperate deciduous forest and meadow

Temperate deciduous and coniferous forest

Northern coniferous forest (taïga)

Mountainous forest, mainly coniferous

High plateau steppe and tundra

Arctic tundra

Polar and mountain-ous ice desert

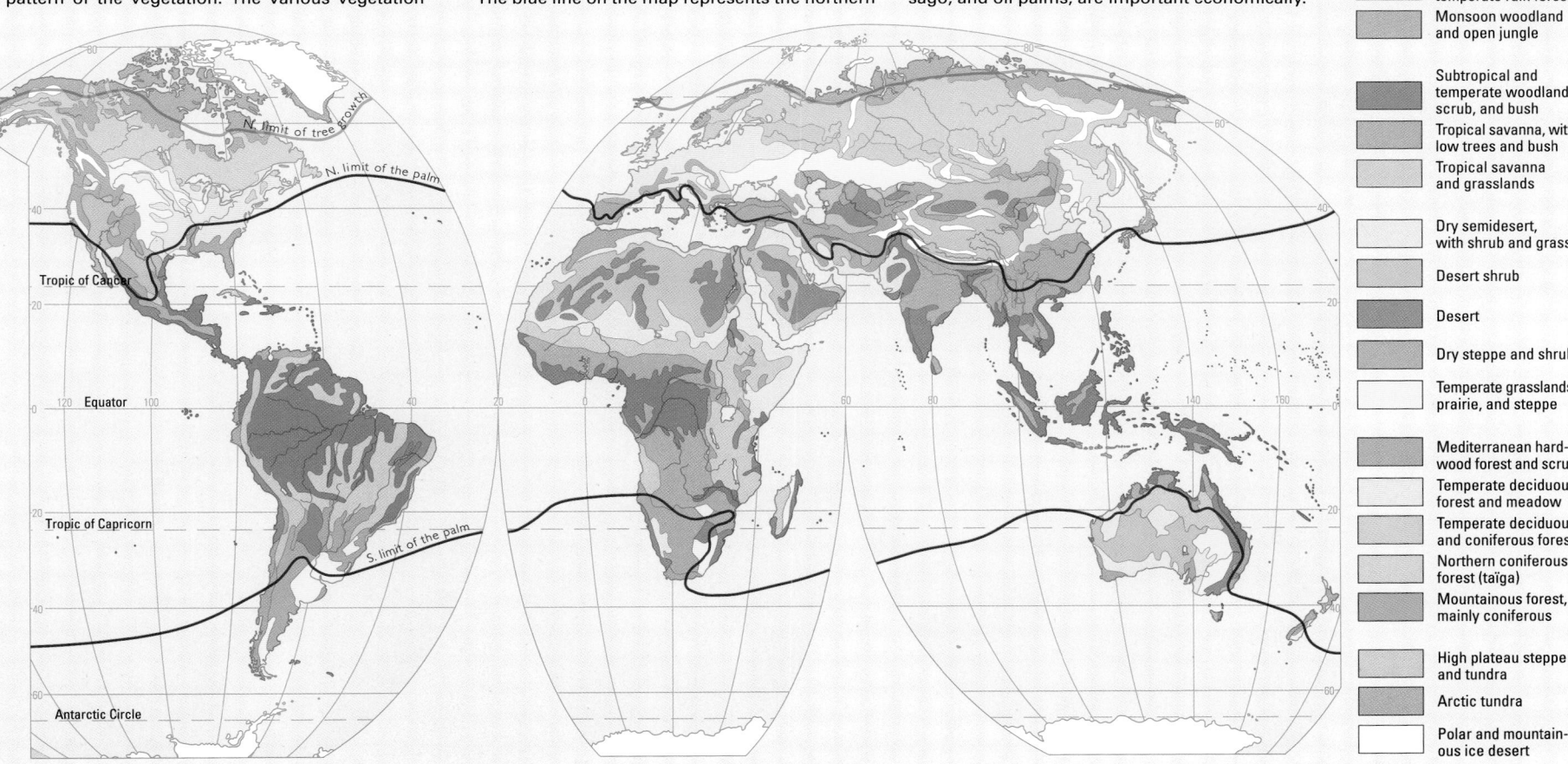

Oceans cover about 70% of the Earth's surface and are of great importance to humans in a number of ways. These include regulating global climates and providing a source of economic materials, such as food resources. In addition, oceans are important for leisure and recreation. They have also been described as the "highways in the globalized world." However, anthropogenic (man-made) stresses are changing the oceans faster than at almost any time in our planet's history.

Increasingly larger fishing fleets are now catching fewer large predatory fish but greater quantities of the smaller fish that are further down the food chain. The most prized food fish, such as cod and salmon, which tend to be top-level predators, are declining in numbers, leaving smaller, less desirable fish to be caught. Not only does this affect the type of fish available for human consumption, but it could also change marine ecosystems forever.

There are a number of possible strategies

for the future, but there are clearly no simple solutions to the problems associated with such a politically, economically, and environmentally sensitive global industry. Fish resources could be conserved in a number of ways – for example, the protection of juveniles as well as policies to encourage breeding and discourage the marketing of illegal catches would help boost stocks. Catches could be restricted in order to match supply with demand and to protect sensitive species.

OCEANIC CONVEYOR BELTS

Oceanic convection occurs where cold, salty water from polar regions sinks into the depths and makes its way toward the Equator. The densest water is found in the Antarctic area. This cold, dense water sweeps round Antarctica at a depth of about 2.5 miles [4 km]. It then spreads into the deep basins of the Atlantic Ocean, the Pacific Ocean, and the Indian Ocean. Surface currents bring warm water to the North Atlantic from the Indian and Pacific Oceans. These waters give up their heat to cold winds, which blow from Canada across the North Atlantic. This water then sinks and starts the reverse convection of the deep ocean current. The amount of heat given up is about a third of the energy that is received from the Sun. Because the conveyor operates in this way, the North Atlantic is warmer than the North Pacific, so there is proportionally more evaporation there. The water left behind by evaporation contains more salt and it is therefore much denser, which causes it to sink. Eventually, this water is transported into the Pacific Ocean where it picks up more warm water, and thus its salinity and therefore its density is reduced.

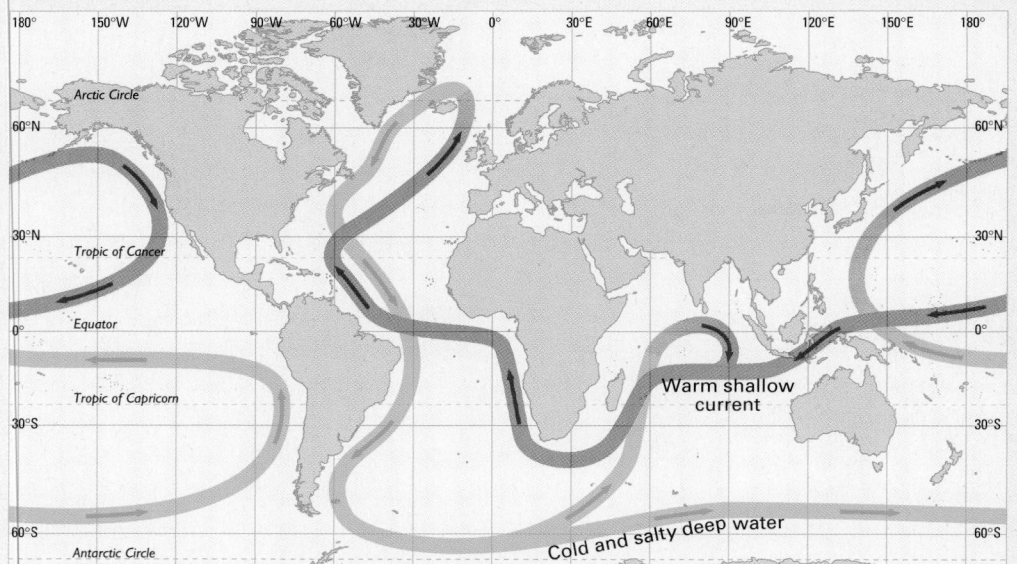

OCEAN CURRENTS

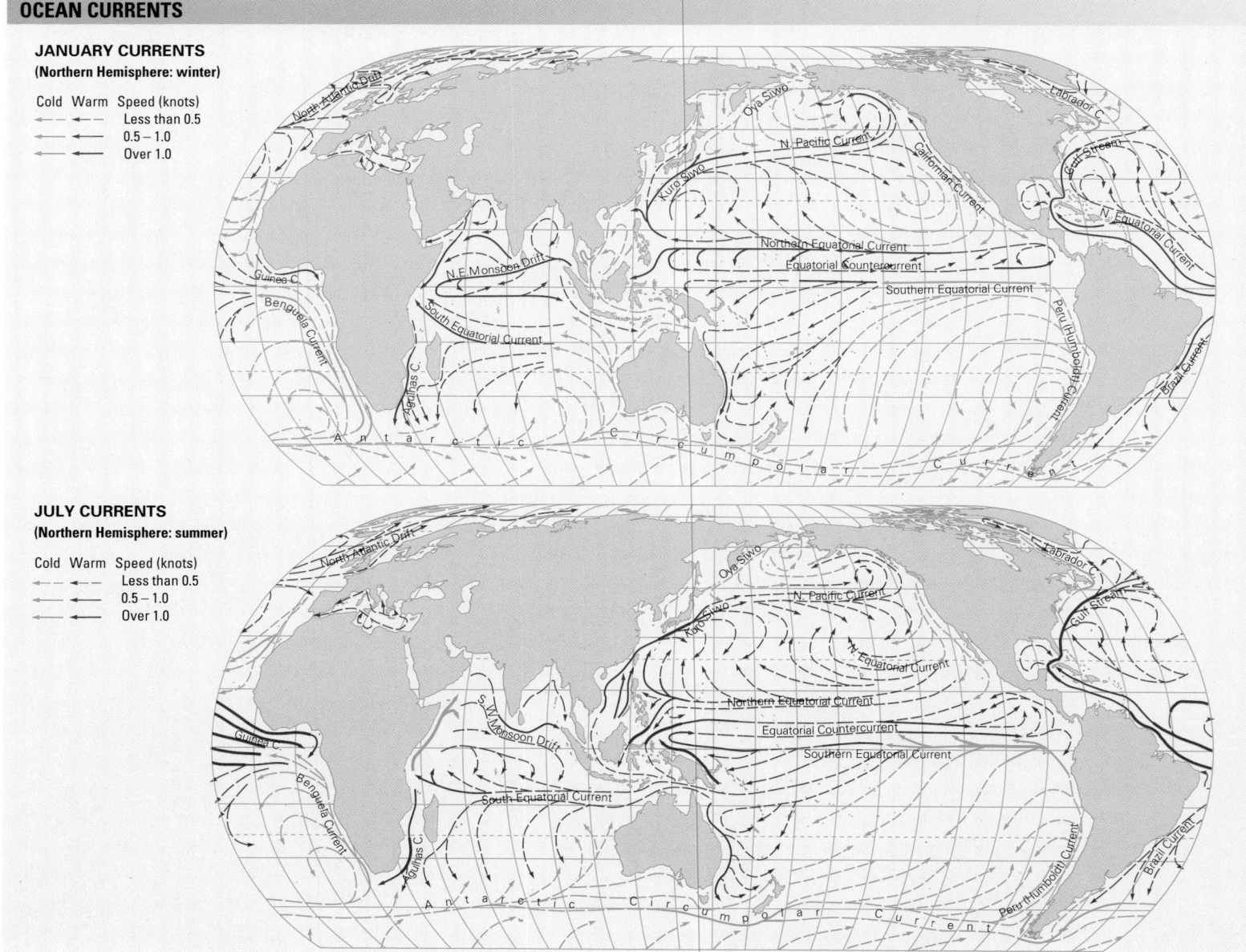

JANUARY CURRENTS
(Northern Hemisphere: winter)

Cold Warm Speed (knots)
              Less than 0.5
              0.5 – 1.0
              Over 1.0

JULY CURRENTS
(Northern Hemisphere: summer)

Cold Warm Speed (knots)
              Less than 0.5
              0.5 – 1.0
              Over 1.0

Moving immense quantities of energy as well as billions of tonnes of water every hour, the ocean currents are a vital part of the great heat engine that drives the Earth's climate. They themselves are produced by a twofold mechanism. At the surface, winds push huge masses of water before them; in the deep ocean below, an abrupt temperature gradient separates the churning surface waters from the still depths (*see the ocean conveyor belt diagram above*).

Coriolis effect
The pattern of circulation of the great surface currents is determined by the displacement known as the "Coriolis effect." As the Earth turns, the vast mass of ocean water is deflected to one side. The deflection is most obvious near the Equator, where the Earth's surface is spinning eastward at 1,000 mph; currents moving poleward are curved clockwise in the northern hemisphere and counterclockwise in the southern hemisphere.

Ocean currents
The result is a system of spinning circles known as "gyres." Warm currents move constantly from the Equator toward the poles, while cold water moves in the reverse direction. In this way, ocean currents act like a thermostat, helping to regulate temperatures around the world.

Depending on the annual movements of the prevailing wind belts, some currents on or near the Equator may reverse their direction in the course of the year, a variation on which Asia's monsoon rains depend and whose occasional failure has brought disaster to millions of people.

FISHING

As stocks are overfished and dwindle, it is important to manage them carefully so that there are sufficient resources for future generations. The Marine Stewardship Council (MSC) is an international, non-profit organization set up to help make the seafood market sustainable. It oversees and manages the distinctive blue labeling system that tells consumers which species of fish they can buy without destroying stocks. This system is popular with large food retailers who wish to be seen supporting sustainable fish catches. It is estimated that over 30% of shoppers worldwide recognize the MSC ecolabel. However, only 8% of the world's fisheries are MSC certified.

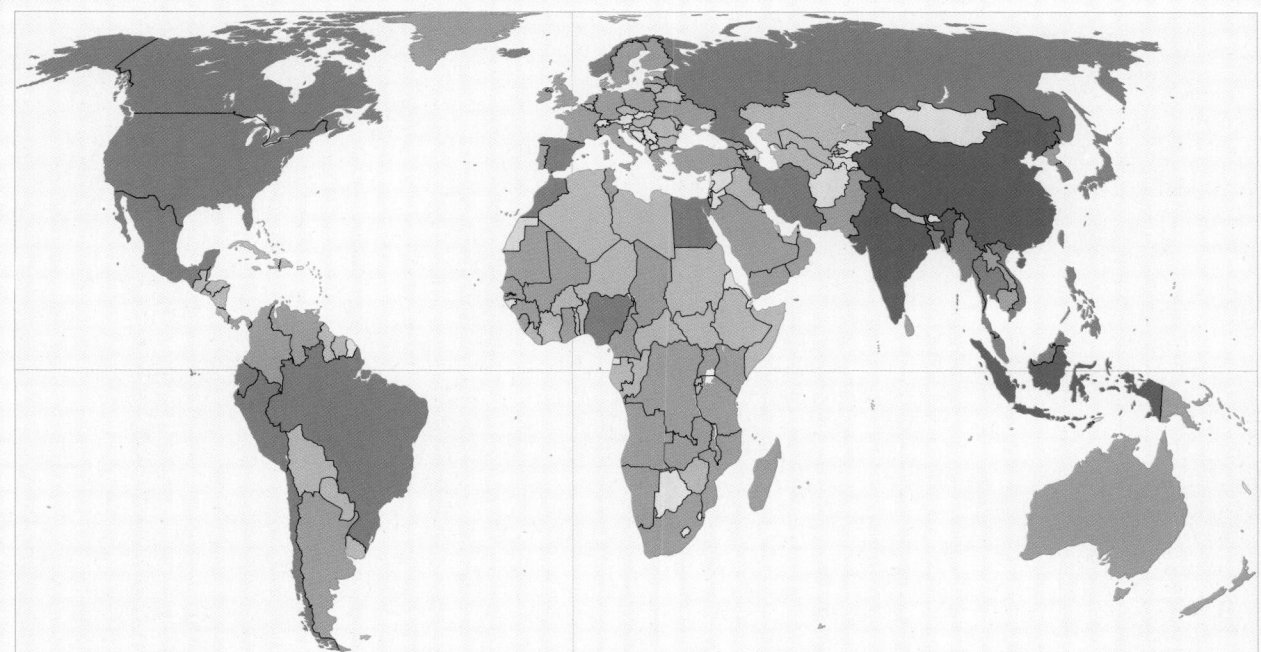

There has been a dramatic rise in world wild fish catches, from under 20 million tonnes in 1950 to an estimated 90.9 million tonnes in 2016, but this is now leveling off as the stocks become depleted and protection of fish stocks increases. Farmed fish totals rose from almost nothing in 1950 to 2019 where farmed fish will overtake the wild catch. Currently, about 3 billion people get 20% of their animal protein from fishery products.

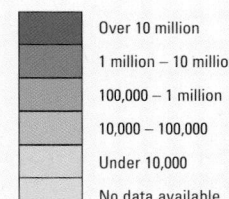

Total world fish catch in metric tonnes, inland and marine fishing (2017)

- Over 10 million
- 1 million – 10 million
- 100,000 – 1 million
- 10,000 – 100,000
- Under 10,000
- No data available

AQUACULTURE

▲ This aerial photo shows shrimp farms, near Mahajanga, in northwestern Madagascar. Shrimp farming is being used to stimulate the country's economy.

Aquaculture involves raising fish commercially, usually for food. In contrast, a fish hatchery releases juvenile fish into the wild for recreational fishing or to supplement a species' natural numbers. The most important fish species raised by fish farms are salmon, carp, tilapia, catfish, and cod. Salmon makes up 85% of the total sale of Norwegian fish farming. Farming was introduced when populations of wild Atlantic salmon in the North Atlantic and Baltic Sea crashed due to overfishing.

Technological costs are high, and include using drugs, such as antibiotics to keep fish healthy and steroids to improve growth. Breeding programs are also expensive. Outputs are high per hectare and per farmer, and efficiency is high also. However, environmental effects can be damaging. Salmon are carnivores and so need to be fed pellets made from other fish. It is possible that farmed salmon actually represent a net loss of protein in the global food supply, as it takes between 4–11 lbs [2–5 kg] of wild fish to grow 2 lbs [1 kg] of salmon. In contrast, most global aquaculture production (c. 85%) uses non-carnivorous fish species, such as tilapia and catfish, for domestic markets. Fish like herring, mackerel, sardine, and anchovy are used to produce the feed for farmed salmon, and so the production of salmon leads to the depletion of other fish species on a global scale.

Other environmental costs include the sea lice and disease that spread from farmed salmon into wild stocks, and pollution (created by uneaten food, faeces, and chemicals used to treat them) contaminating surrounding waters. Organic debris of this type, with steroids and other chemical waste, can contaminate coastal waters. In addition, the accidental escape of fish can affect local wild fish gene pools, when escaped fish interbreed with wild populations, reducing their genetic diversity, and potentially introducing non-natural genetic variation. In some parts of the world, escapees of farmed fish threaten native wild fish, as salmon is an alien species (for example, the salmon farming industry in British Columbia, Canada, has inadvertently introduced a non-native species – Atlantic salmon – into the Pacific Ocean).

However, the positive environmental benefits of not removing fish from wild stocks, but of growing them in farms, are great. Wild populations are allowed to breed and maintain stocks, whilst the farmed variety provides food.

▲ These floating aquaculture pens contain northern bluefin tuna in Baja California, Mexico. Small tuna are caught off-shore and moved to large enclosures.

PLASTIC

Yet more alarming for the health of the oceans and their wildlife is the plague of plastic. The UN Environment Program estimated in 2006 that every square kilometer of sea held nearly 18,000 pieces of floating plastic. Much of it was, and is, in the central Pacific, where scientists believe as much as 100 million tonnes of plastic jetsam are suspended in two separate "gyres" of garbage over an area twice the size of the USA. This has been referred to as the Great Pacific Garbage Patch – about 90% of the plastic in the sea has been carried there by wind or water from land. It takes decades to sink or decompose.

▲ In the main, the plastic in the oceans comes from food and drink packaging. The larger pieces can be mistakenly eaten by animals such as seals, and turtles, which can choke them. Smaller pieces are swallowed by fish which can then work their way up through the food chain to humans. Harm is also caused by the chemicals contained within plastics.

RESPONSES TO THE THREATS

In the case of the oceans, a conservative estimate of the cost of climate change is that by the year 2100 it will amount to nearly US $2 trillion annually, or about 0.4% of global GDP. Economists at the Stockholm Environment Institute arrived at the figure by looking at five measures: how much fisheries and tourism stood to lose, and what the economic impact would be of rising sea levels, more storms, and less carbon being absorbed by the oceans.

If the world continues to warm at its present rate and temperatures rise by 7.2°F [4°C] by 2100, the total will come to US $1.98 trillion. However, if drastic measures are taken to cut emissions and they rise by only 4°F [2.2°C], this figure will be US $612 billion. Governments worldwide were urged by the 1972 Stockholm Convention to control the dumping of waste in their oceans by implementing new laws. The United Nations met in London after this recommendation to begin the Convention on the Prevention of Marine Pollution by Dumping of Wastes and Other Matter, which was implemented in 1975. The International Maritime Organization was given responsibility for this convention and a Protocol was finally adopted in 1996, a major step in the regulation of ocean dumping.

The United Nations Convention on the Law of the Sea, signed in 1982 but only entering into force in 1994, established a framework of law for the oceans, including rules for deep-sea mining and economic exclusion zones extending 200 nautical miles around nation states.

Biodiversity refers to the variety of living material. It includes the variety of species, the variety within the same species, and the variety of ecosystems within which species operate. Estimates of the number of species in the world vary from between 7 million and 80 million. The currently accepted total is about 14 million, yet only 2 million species have been formally identified.

Biodiversity is vital for human survival. It remains the basis for our food and most of our medicine. In less economically developed countries (LEDCs), over 20% of the food consumed is gathered from natural sources. At a global level, over 15% of animal protein consumed is from sea fish. More than 60% of the world's population rely on traditional medicines for their health care. In Mexico, the Popoluca Indians "farm" over 250 species of plant. Many medicines come from natural sources.

Aspirin, for example, comes from an acid taken from the bark of willow trees. The anti-cancer drug "taxol" originates from the wild Pacific yew tree. It is estimated that the pharmaceuticals industry gains US $32 billion per year in profits from traditional remedies.

However, the loss of biodiversity is increasing at an accelerating rate. Up to 27,000 species a year may be lost, and the United Nations Environment Programme (UNEP) suggests that the current rate of extinction is 50–100 times greater than "normal", and believes that up to 25% of all the world's species may be lost by 2025. The main reasons for the decline are the introduction of alien species and habitat destruction. Human impact on biodiversity has brought about more extinctions than any other single factor since the extinction of the dinosaurs (65 million years ago).

Since 1600, 39% of animal extinctions have been due to the introduction of alien species, 36% from habitat destruction, and 23% from hunting or deliberate extermination. The introduction of rats, cats and other species has led to the extinction of many flightless birds in Polynesia. Plantation crops, such as rubber, often thrive best when taken away from their natural homes, since in the new lands there may not be the pests to control them. One noted example of extinction was caused by the introduction of the Nile perch into Lake Victoria, East Africa: introduced in the 1960s, it led to the extinction of some 50 species of cichlid fish within 20 years.

In 2020, over 31,000 species out of approximately 116,000 species on the IUCN (International Union for Conservation of Nature and Natural Resources) Red List of Threatened Species, were in danger of extinction. This included one in four mammals, two in five amphibians, one in three coral and one in eight birds.

THREATENED SPECIES
Total number of threatened species for selected countries in each continent

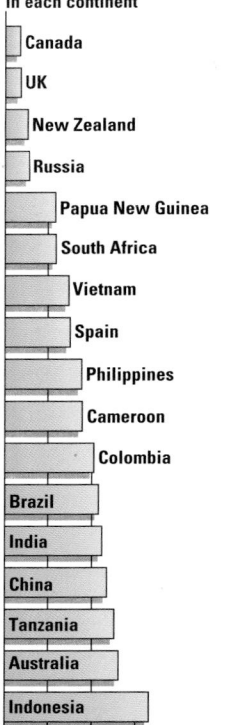

Canada
UK
New Zealand
Russia
Papua New Guinea
South Africa
Vietnam
Spain
Philippines
Cameroon
Colombia
Brazil
India
China
Tanzania
Australia
Indonesia
USA
Mexico
Malaysia
Ecuador
Madagascar

500 1000 1500 2000 2500 3000

Source: IUCN Red List 2020

THREATENED MAMMAL SPECIES

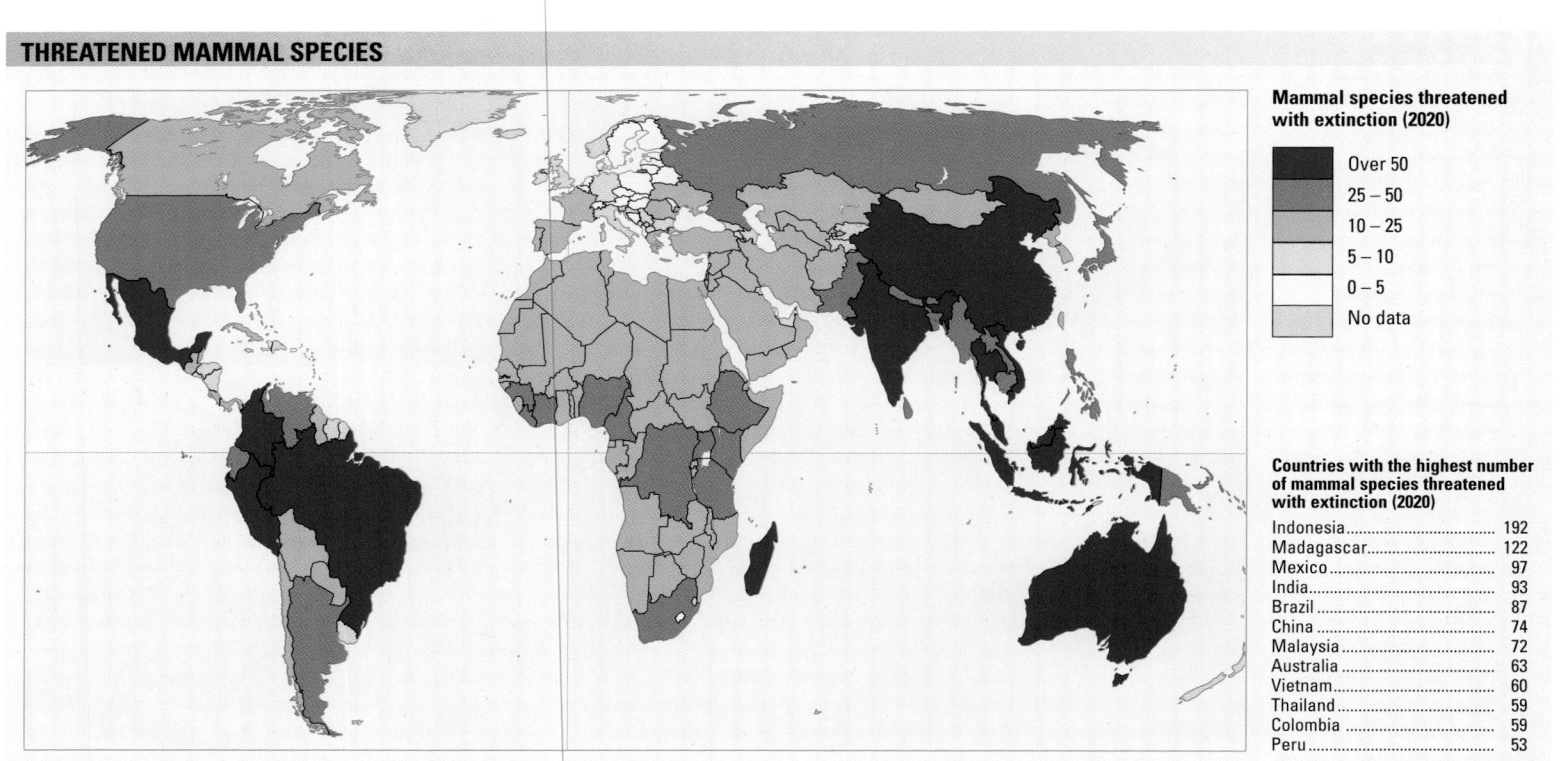

Mammal species threatened with extinction (2020)

- Over 50
- 25 – 50
- 10 – 25
- 5 – 10
- 0 – 5
- No data

Countries with the highest number of mammal species threatened with extinction (2020)

Indonesia	192
Madagascar	122
Mexico	97
India	93
Brazil	87
China	74
Malaysia	72
Australia	63
Vietnam	60
Thailand	59
Colombia	59
Peru	53

BIODIVERSITY HOTSPOTS

Up to 75% of the world's most threatened mammals, birds and amphibians live in an area covering just 2.3% of the Earth's surface, and roughly half of all flowering plant species and 42% of land-based vertebrates exist in 36 biological hotspots.

Scientists argue that, with limited financial resources, governments and conservationists should prioritize by protecting the small total land areas that account for a very high percentage of global biodiversity. In 1999, scientists identified 25 such areas, mostly in the tropics, which were the centre of global biodiversity.

The number of hotspots has risen to 36. These include the mountains of central Asia, the whole of Japan, the Horn of Africa including the Ethiopian highlands, and the Himalayas region. The hotspots once covered 15.7% of the Earth's surface, an area roughly the size of Russia and Australia combined – now they cover only 2.3% of the Earth's surface, an area slightly larger than India.

Over 70% of all mammals, 86% of all birds, and 92% of all amphibians are crammed into this small area of the world's total land mass. Madagascar and the Indian Ocean Islands hotspot was found to have very high concentrations of plant and vertebrate families that are found nowhere else on the globe.

Global warming could have a devastating effect on biodiversity hotspots such as the Amazonian and Indonesian rainforests. By 2100, between 12% and 39% of the land surface of the Earth will have a new climate. There are numerous species that will be unable to move in order to stay within their preferred climate range. These species will either have to evolve rapidly or die out.

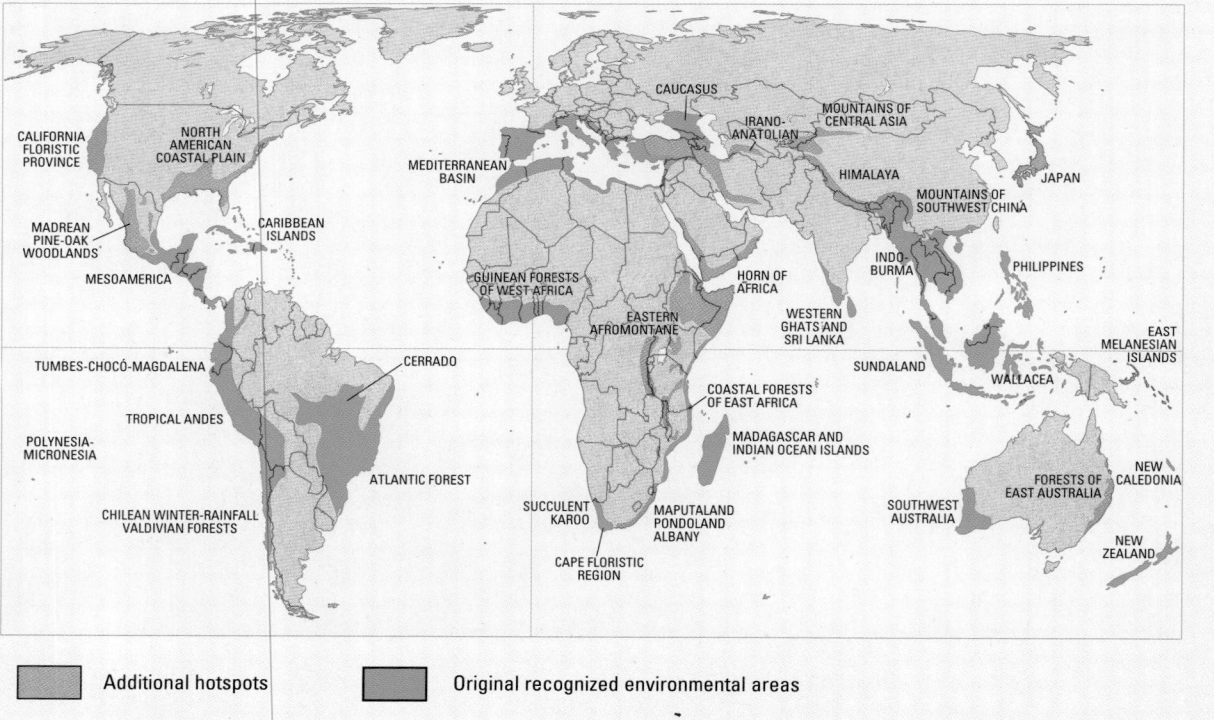

Additional hotspots   Original recognized environmental areas

AUSTRALIA'S INTRODUCED SPECIES

Australia's native plants and animals adapted to life on an isolated continent over millions of years. Since European settlement in the 18th century they have had to compete with a range of species introduced by the settlers, which impact on the native species by predation, competition for food and shelter, destroying habitat, and by spreading diseases. Introduced species typically have few predators or fatal diseases, and some have very high reproductive rates.

Management and the prevention of the introduction of new invasive species are key environmental and agricultural policy issues for the Australian federal and state governments.

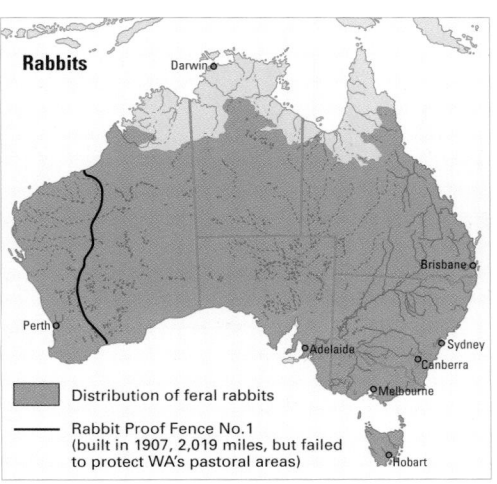

Rabbits

☐ Distribution of feral rabbits

— Rabbit Proof Fence No.1 (built in 1907, 2,019 miles, but failed to protect WA's pastoral areas)

▲ Rabbits were introduced to Australia from England in 1859 for hunting, and quickly spread throughout the country. They are one of the most destructive introduced species in Australia, competing with native wildlife, damaging vegetation, and degrading the land.

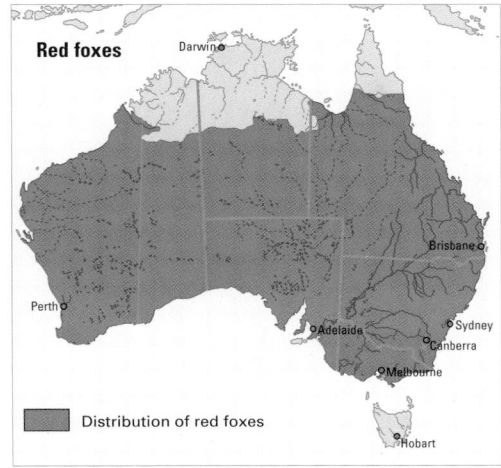

Red foxes

☐ Distribution of red foxes

▲ The red fox was introduced from Europe for recreational hunting in 1855 and populations became established in the wild within 15 years. They prey on newborn lambs and have also been responsible for the decline of a number of native species.

Cane toads

☐ Distribution of cane toads

▲ Cane toads were introduced in 1935 to control beetles which were threatening the sugar-cane industry. However, this failed as both the toad and the beetle are still thriving. They adapted well to the Australian environment and with no natural predators they quickly spread. They eat small native wildlife and poison any predators.

THE VALUE OF NATURE

According to the National Ecosystem Assessment (NEA), lakes, forests, parks, and wildlife are a huge financial asset. Moreover, it is claimed that the natural world is vital for human existence, not only in providing food, water, and air, but also for the cultural and spiritual benefits that it provides.

Economic benefits include food production, which utilizes insects for pollination, earthworms for mixing the soil, and soil microbes for recycling nutrients. In the UK, for example, the value of pollinating insects has been calculated to be $727 million, and the value of wetlands, which help to provide clean water, at $2.5 billion. Globally, bees are believed to provide $368 billion worth of services, or about 9.5% of the total economic value of agriculture. One third of the food the world produces is dependent on bees for pollination.

Although the natural world provides many benefits including food supply, water supply, climate regulation, and breakdown of waste products, these are under-valued. Some of the benefits are non-quantifiable but include recreation and long-term health. Moreover, the way in which ecosystems have been used has changed over the last sixty years or so. Population increase and rising standards of living have contributed to a huge growth in agricultural production. It has also, however, contributed to the decline in ecosystem services, such as air, water, and soil quality.

Although some ecosystems are delivering services well, there are others which are showing long-term decline. Those that are in decline include marine fisheries, wild species diversity, and soil quality.

Ecosystems, and ecosystems services, constantly change as a result of demographic, economic, social, and cultural factors. For example, since the 1940s there has been intensification of agriculture at the expense of many habitats, including wetlands, forests, and grasslands.

Types of ecosystem service

Provisioning services
These are the services obtained from ecosystems such as food, fibre, fuel, and water from aquifers, rivers, and lakes. Goods can come from heavily managed ecosystems (intensive farms and fish farms) or from semi-natural ones (such as by hunting and fishing). Most of these food producing ecosystems are land-based but some are water-based (aquaculture). Ecosystems also provide a variety of materials for construction and fuel including wood, charcoal, biofuels, and plant oils. They are also an important source of raw materials for the pharmaceuticals industry.

Supporting services
These are the essentials for life and include primary productivity, soil formation, and the cycling of nutrients. Ecosystems provide the conditions for growing food. Habitats provide all that an individual plant or animal needs to survive: food; water; nutrients; and shelter. Every habitat provides a variety of niches that can be essential for a species' lifecycle. For example, migratory birds depend on different habitats at different times of the year.

Ecosystems also help maintain genetic diversity (biodiversity) which is the variety of genetic materials between ecosystems, niches, and populations.

Regulating services
These are a diverse set of services and include pollination, regulation of pests and diseases, and production of goods. Other services include climate and climatic hazard regulation, and water quality regulation. For example, trees provide shade and influence water availability and, by removing air pollutants from the atmosphere, they improve air quality. Ecosystems influence global climate by storing and sequestering greenhouse gases such

as carbon dioxide. As vegetation grows, it removes carbon dioxide and locks it in its tissue.

Ecosystems moderate extreme events: they act as buffers against natural disasters. Mangrove forests can help protect a shoreline against hurricane damage, and wetlands can help absorb flood waters. Vegetation can help reduce soil erosion.

Insects and the wind help pollinate plants. Around 90 out of 115 leading food crops, such as cocoa and coffee, depend upon animal pollination.

Ecosystems are also important for the control of pests and vector borne diseases. Birds, bats, wasps, frogs, and fungi are all examples of natural controls.

Cultural services
These occur when people interact with the environment and this provides cultural goods and benefits. Open spaces provide the opportunity for outdoor recreation, learning, and spiritual well-being. Recreation can lead to major improvements in physical and mental health. Also, tourism provides a major source of income to many countries.

▲ The wide variety of provisions on display in this Malaysian market are testament to the value of ecosystems for the supply of food.

▲ The destruction of large areas of vegetation can lessen the value of ecosystems. The deforested and drowned rain forest at Batang Ai, Sarawak, Malaysia, above, is the result of land being cleared for a hydroelectric power station.

The goods and services derived from mountains, moorlands, and heaths, and those from woodlands are shown in the table.

	Mountains, moorlands, and heaths	Woodlands
Provisioning	Food*	Timber*
	Fibre*	Species diversity*
	Fuel*	Fuelwood*
	Freshwater*	Freshwater*
Regulating	Climate regulation†	Climate regulation†
	Flood regulation†	Flood regulation†
	Wildfire regulation†	Erosion control†
	Water quality regulation†	Disease and pest control†
	Erosion control†	Wildfire regulation†
		Air and water quality regulation†
		Soil quality regulation†
		Noise regulation†
Cultural	Recreation and tourism*	Recreation and tourism*
	Aesthetic values*	Aesthetic values*
	Cultural heritage*	Cultural heritage*
	Spiritual values*	Employment*
	Education*	Education*
	Sense of place*	Sense of place*
	Health benefits*	Health benefits*

Key
Items marked * denote goods
Items marked † denote services

For more information:

90 Urbanization of the Earth

Urban population

91 Largest cities

In 8000 BC, following the development of agriculture, the world had an estimated population of 8 million and by AD 1000 it was about 300 million. The onset of the Industrial Revolution in the late 18th century led to a population explosion. The 1,000 million mark was passed by 1850, it doubled by the 1920s, and doubled again to 4,000 million by 1975.

In the 1990s, demographers estimated that the world's population, which passed the 7 billion mark in 2012, would reach 9.3 billion by 2050 and only level out in 2200, at a peak of around 11 billion. However, in the early 21st century, after the rate of population growth had shown signs of decline, the Institute for Applied Systems Analysis suggested that the world's population might peak at about 9 billion in 2070. Whatever the global projections, everyone agreed that the greatest population growth would be in the developing countries.

The developing world includes what the World Bank (2020) describes as low-income economies (per capita GNI of US $1,025 or less), lower-middle-income economies (per capita GNI of US $1,025 to US $3,995), and upper-middle-income economies (per capita GNI of US $3,995 to US $12,235). Most developing countries are in Africa, Asia, and Latin America. The developed world, made up of high-income, industrialized economies (per capita GNI of US $12,235 or more), contains Australasia, most of Europe and North America, and Japan.

In developing countries, a high proportion of the population is young and so these countries face high expenditure on health and education. In developed countries, the population pyramids are becoming top-heavy, with increasingly aging populations.

LARGEST NATIONS

The world's most populous nations, in millions (2020)

1.	China	1,394
2.	India	1,326
3.	USA	333
4.	Indonesia	267
5.	Pakistan	234
6.	Nigeria	214
7.	Brazil	212
8.	Bangladesh	163
9.	Russia	142
10.	Mexico	129
11.	Japan	126
12.	Philippines	109
13.	Ethiopia	108
14.	Egypt	104
15.	Congo (Dem. Rep.)	102
16.	Vietnam	99
17.	Iran	85
18.	Turkey	82
19.	Germany	80
20.	Thailand	69
21.	France	68
22.	UK	66
23.	Italy	62
24.	Tanzania	59
25.	Myanmar (Burma)	57

MOST CROWDED NATIONS

Population per square mile (2020)

1.	Monaco	45,882
2.	Singapore	23,883
3.	Bahrain	5,574
4.	Vatican City	5,000
5.	Malta	3,811
6.	Maldives	3,266
7.	Bangladesh	2,925
8.	Mauritius	1,746
9.	San Marino	1,712
10.	Barbados	1,704

LEAST CROWDED

Population per square mile (2020)

1.	Mongolia	5.2
2.	Namibia	8.3
3.	Australia	8.5
4.	Iceland	8.8
5.	Guyana	9.0
6.	Suriname	9.7
7.	Canada	9.8
8.	Mauritania	10.1
9.	Libya	10.1
10.	Botswana	10.3

POPULATION DENSITY

The places marked on the map reflect the size of the urban agglomerations and conurbations, rather than the actual city limits. San Francisco itself, for example, has an official population of less than a million people. All cities with more than 5 million inhabitants are named on the map.

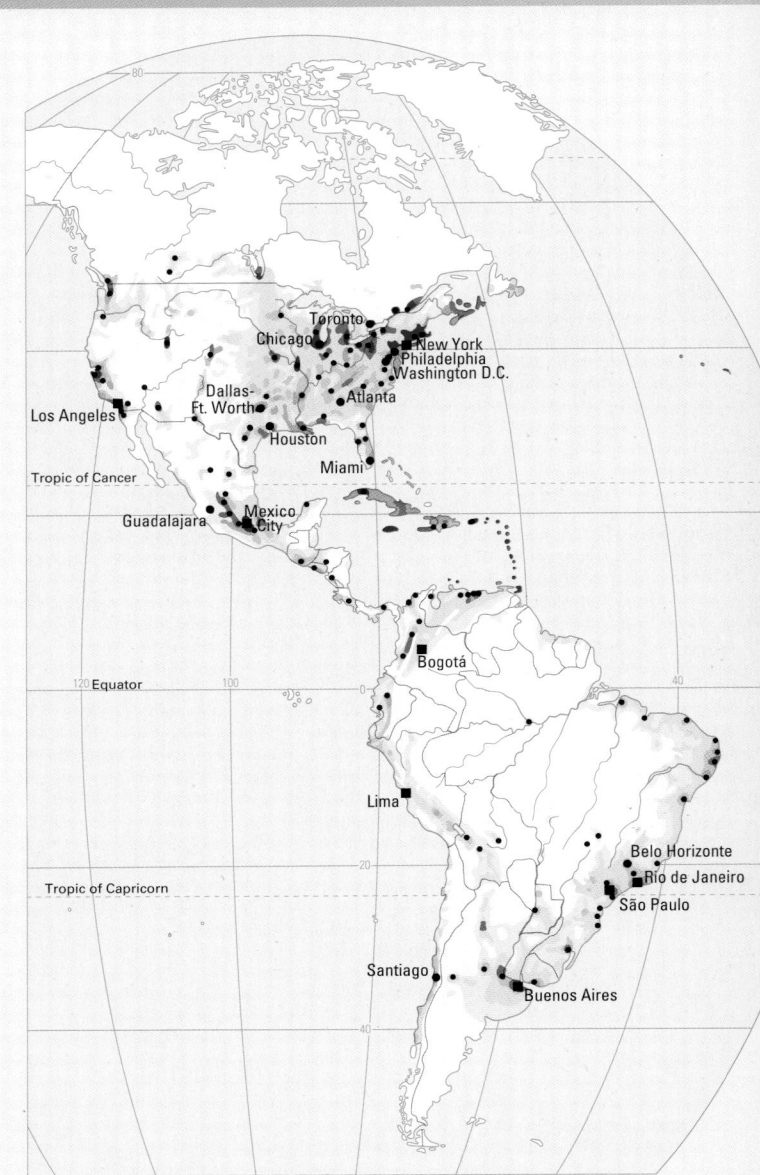

Inhabitants per square mile

- Over 500
- 250 – 500
- 125 – 250
- 65 – 125
- 15 – 65
- 8 – 15
- 3 – 8
- Under 3

Urban population

- ■ Over 10,000,000
- ● 5,000,000 – 10,000,000
- • 1,000,000 – 5,000,000

POPULATION CHANGE

The projected population change for the years 2004–2050

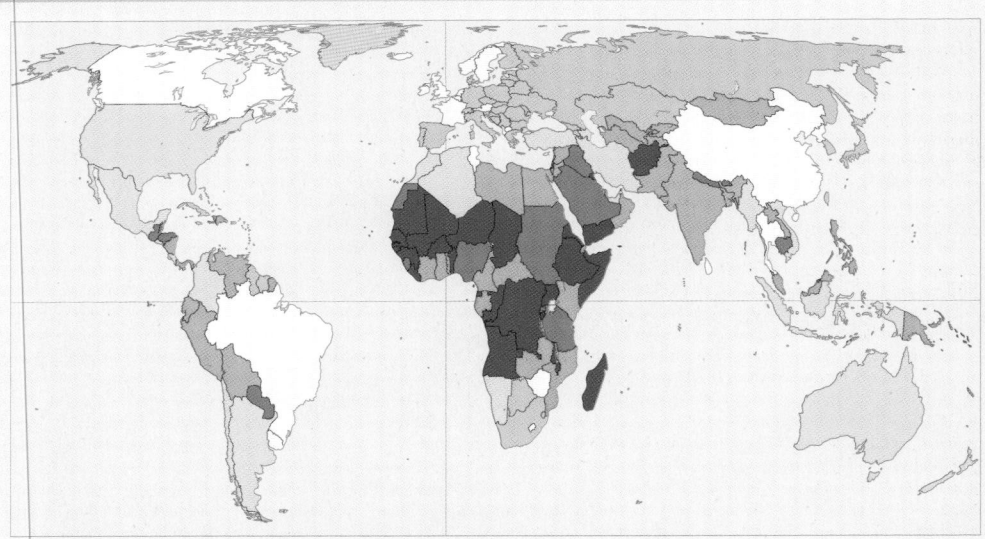

- Over 125% population gain
- 100 – 125% population gain
- 50 – 100% population gain
- 25 – 50% population gain
- 0 – 25% population gain
- No change or population loss
- No data available

Based on estimates for the year 2050, below are listed the ten most populous nations in the world, in millions:

1.	India	1,628	6.	Pakistan	295
2.	China	1,437	7.	Bangladesh	280
3.	USA	420	8.	Brazil	221
4.	Indonesia	308	9.	Congo (Dem. Rep.)	181
5.	Nigeria	307	10.	Ethiopia	173

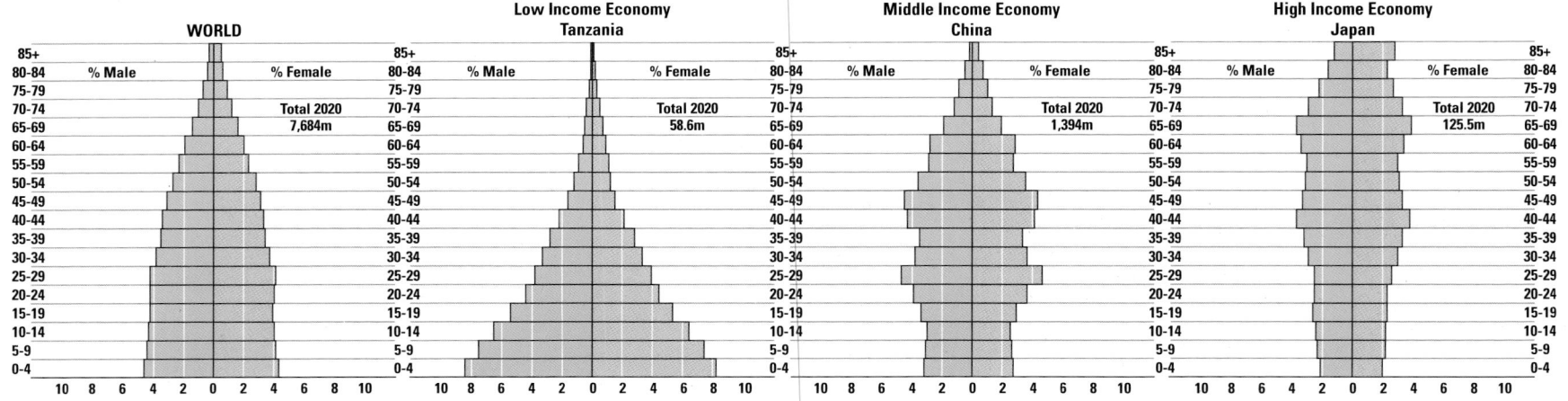

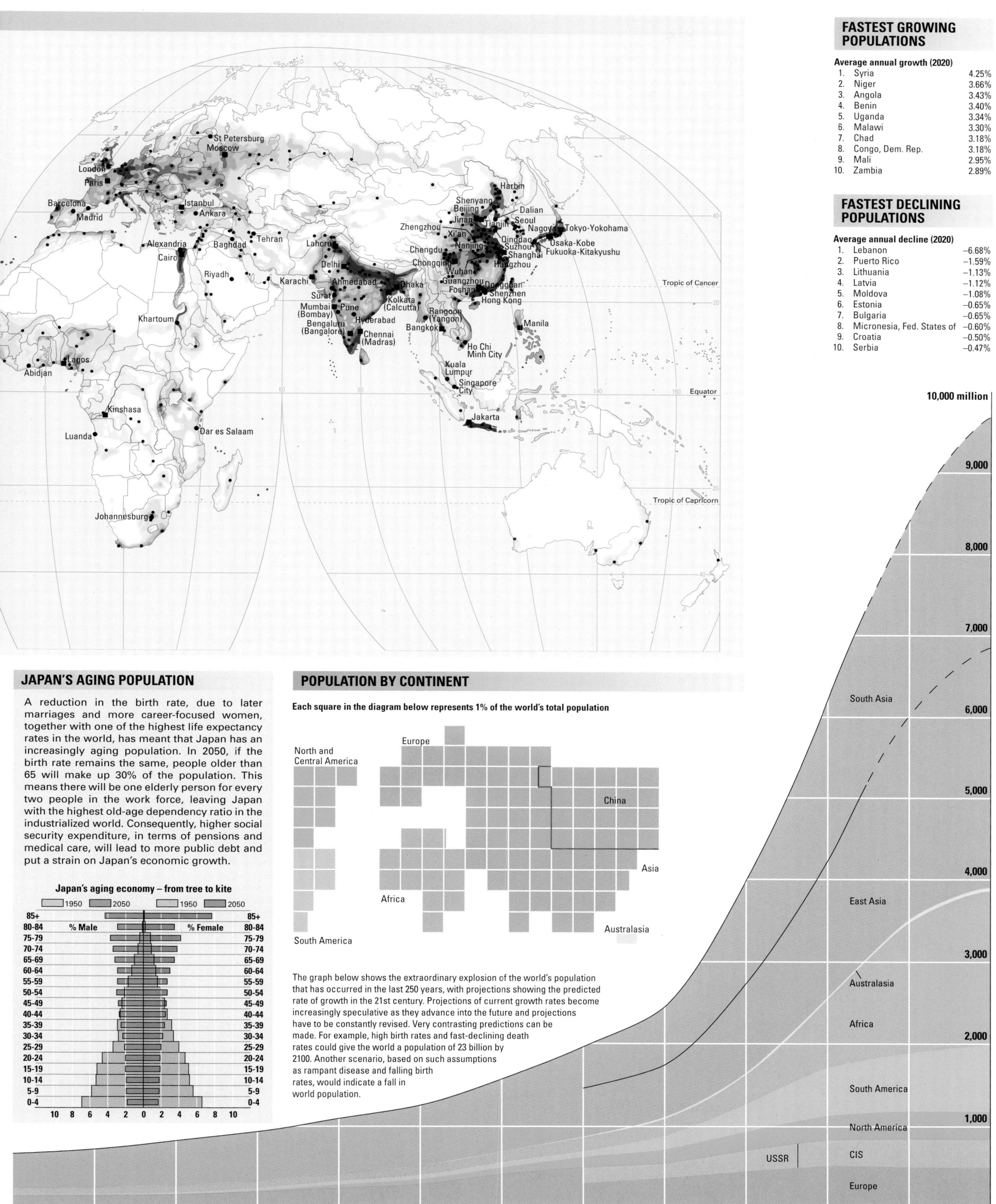

FASTEST GROWING POPULATIONS

Average annual growth (2020)

1.	Syria	4.25%
2.	Niger	3.66%
3.	Angola	3.43%
4.	Benin	3.40%
5.	Uganda	3.34%
6.	Malawi	3.30%
7.	Chad	3.18%
8.	Congo, Dem. Rep.	3.18%
9.	Mali	2.95%
10.	Zambia	2.89%

FASTEST DECLINING POPULATIONS

Average annual decline (2020)

1.	Lebanon	−6.68%
2.	Puerto Rico	−1.59%
3.	Lithuania	−1.13%
4.	Latvia	−1.12%
5.	Moldova	−1.08%
6.	Estonia	−0.65%
7.	Bulgaria	−0.65%
8.	Micronesia, Fed. States of	−0.60%
9.	Croatia	−0.50%
10.	Serbia	−0.47%

JAPAN'S AGING POPULATION

A reduction in the birth rate, due to later marriages and more career-focused women, together with one of the highest life expectancy rates in the world, has meant that Japan has an increasingly aging population. In 2050, if the birth rate remains the same, people older than 65 will make up 30% of the population. This means there will be one elderly person for every two people in the work force, leaving Japan with the highest old-age dependency ratio in the industrialized world. Consequently, higher social security expenditure, in terms of pensions and medical care, will lead to more public debt and put a strain on Japan's economic growth.

POPULATION BY CONTINENT

Each square in the diagram below represents 1% of the world's total population

The graph below shows the extraordinary explosion of the world's population that has occurred in the last 250 years, with projections showing the predicted rate of growth in the 21st century. Projections of current growth rates become increasingly speculative as they advance into the future and projections have to be constantly revised. Very contrasting predictions can be made. For example, high birth rates and fast-declining death rates could give the world a population of 23 billion by 2100. Another scenario, based on such assumptions as rampant disease and falling birth rates, would indicate a fall in world population.

In 2008, for the first time in history, more than half of the world's population lived in urban areas. By 2050, it is thought that 5.3 billion people in the developing world will be living in an urban environment, with Asia having over 60% of the world's urban population and Africa almost 25%.

Urbanization is greatest in industrialized countries. For example, in 2010, 82% of the people in the US lived in urban areas; but in low-income countries, which had nearly 40% of the world's population in the early 21st century, only 31% lived in urban areas.

A typical city in a developing country contains millions of people living, often illegally, in shanty towns (or "informal settlements"), while thousands live on the streets. Yet many of these shanty towns are healthier than the industrial cities of 19th-century Europe and North America. Indeed, surveys have shown that migrants to cities in developing countries are less likely to face poverty than they are in rural areas, while benefiting from greater access to healthcare services and education.

Modern cities face many problems today, including pollution, unemployment, and crime. Yet, with competent government, they are capable of generating the wealth they need to solve them, as well as making a major contribution to the nation's economy.

Megacities are cities with a population of over 10 million people. Megacities grow as a result of economic growth, rural to urban migration, and high rates of natural increase. As the cities grow, they swallow up rural areas and nearby towns. Some of these cities have populations that are bigger than those of entire countries – Mumbai, for example, has more people than Sweden and Norway combined.

Nevertheless, megacities contain between 4% and 7% of the world's total population, and grow at relatively slow rates, perhaps 1.5% per year. The first megacity was Tokyo, which now has a population of about 37 million (larger than Canada's population). By 2020, other megacities will include Mumbai, Delhi, Mexico City, São Paulo, New York, Dhaka, Karachi, and Lagos. Lagos has been growing at a very fast rate of 5% per annum and is expected to increase at this rate until after 2020. Usually, very large cities grow more slowly than medium-sized cities.

By 2020, all but four of the world's megacities will be in developing regions, 12 of them in Asia alone. The impact of megacities on their region is huge. For example, rapid economic growth and urbanization in China has had a negative impact on the urban environment. China contains 16 of the 20 most polluted cities in the world and is the largest producer of greenhouse gases.

Megacities are important for the generation of wealth – in more economically developed countries (MEDCs) urban areas generate over 80% of national economic output, while in less economically developed countries (LEDCs) it is over 40%. However, there are some aspects of megacities, such as crime and environmental issues, where they are less than attractive.

URBAN POPULATION

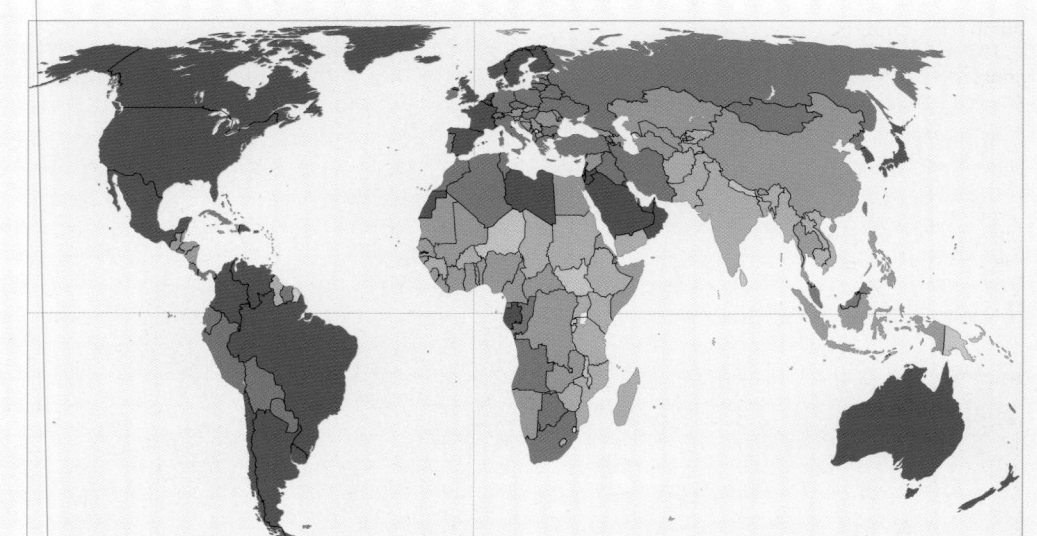

Percentage of total population living in towns and cities (2020)

- Over 80%
- 60 – 80%
- 40 – 60%
- 20 – 40%
- Under 20%
- No data available

Most urbanized		Least urbanized	
Kuwait	100%	Papua New Guinea	13%
Monaco	100%	Burundi	14%
Singapore	100%	Liechtenstein	14%
Qatar	99%	Niger	17%
Belgium	98%	Malawi	17%

THE URBANIZATION OF THE EARTH

City-building, 1900–2005; each white spot represents a city of at least 1 million inhabitants

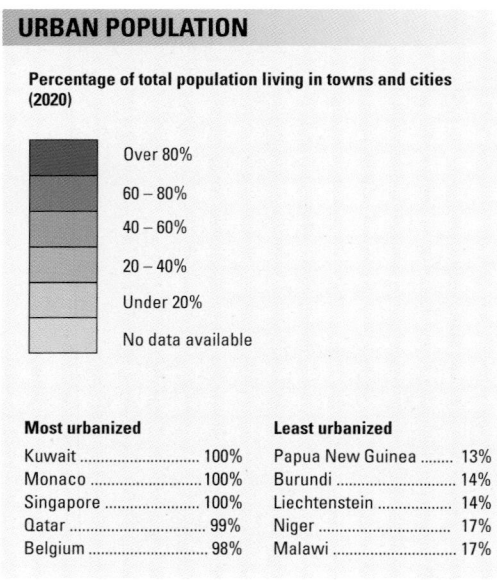

1900

1950

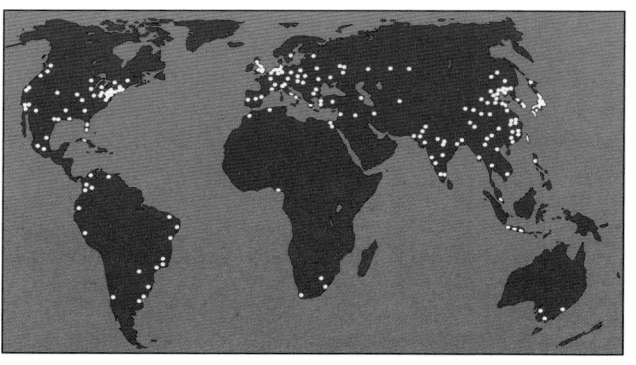

1975

2005

URBANIZATION

The urban population of 3.7 billion people in 2012 was larger than the entire global population in 1947, 65 years earlier. Cities and urban areas are gaining an estimated 60 million people per year – over 1 million every week.

Urbanization rates vary across the world; the US and UK have far lower rates of urbanization compared to less developed countries. This is because a high proportion of their populations already live in cities. The largest percentage increases in the urban population in the next decade will be in Africa and Asia. For example, Lagos in Nigeria increased from 675,000 inhabitants in 1960 to 13,463,000 in 2018.

Rapid urban growth reflects three factors:
1. Migration to cities from rural areas.
2. Natural population increases (births minus deaths).
3. Reclassification of previously rural areas as urban as they become built up and engulfed by urban sprawl.

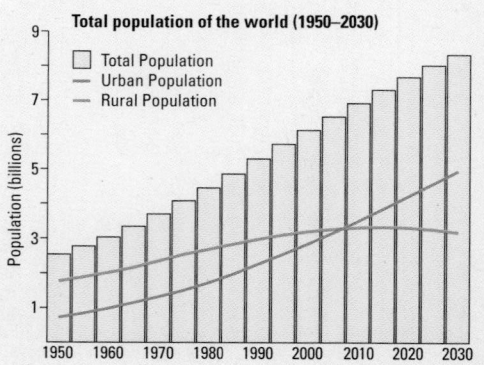

Total population of the world (1950–2030)

- ☐ Total Population
- — Urban Population
- — Rural Population

SLUM CITIES

The total number of slum dwellers in the world reached 1 billion in 2007, with one in every three city residents living in inadequate housing, with no or few basic services.

Urbanization in most developing countries has been proceeding so rapidly that local governments have been unable to provide the necessary services and housing to meet demand.

In some cities, many people make their homes in squatter settlements, or slums, which are frequently without basic services such as power, water, and sanitation. They are often on hazardous, dangerous or polluted land, and the building structures are inadequate and sometimes unsafe. Slum dwellers have limited access to credit and formal job markets due to stigmatization, discrimination, and geographical isolation.

Slums have a high concentration of poverty and social and economic deprivation, which may include broken families, unemployment, and economic, physical, and social exclusion. Yet these communities are often a dynamic part of the city's economy, keeping the wheels of the city turning in many different ways. Their inhabitants often take the initiative in setting up their own local government and self-help associations.

Some of the world's richest cities also have a homeless underclass, although calculating the numbers of people involved is problematic. Yet it is the case that homelessness and unemployment are currently affecting an increasing number of people in the developed world.

The locus of poverty is moving from the countryside to cities, in a process now recognized as the "urbanization of poverty."

Efforts to improve the living conditions of slum dwellers peaked during the 1980s. However, renewed concern about poverty has recently led governments to adopt specific targets on slums in the United Nations Millennium Declaration, which aims to improve the lives of at least 100 million slum dwellers by the year 2020.

SLUM FACTBOX

- A slum is defined by the UN as "a dilapidated area of a city characterized by substandard housing, squalor, and lacking in tenure security."
- 78% of the urban population in developing countries live in slums.
- More than 41% of Kolkata's slum households have lived there for more than 30 years.
- In most African cities between 40% and 70% of the city's population live in slums or squatter settlements.
- Slum populations in some parts of the world often include university lecturers, students, civil servants, and formal private-sector employees.
- The majority of slum households in Bangkok have a color television.
- Singapore is one of the few countries that successfully practises comprehensive public-sector housing development.
- Slums are the fastest growing human habitat in the world.

SUSTAINABLE CITIES

Large sprawling cities are often considered unsustainable because they consume huge amounts of resources and produce vast amounts of waste. The concept of "Sustainable Urban Development" is designed to meet the needs of the present generation without compromising the needs of future generations.

In the "compact" sustainable city, inputs are smaller and there is more recycling. Compact cities minimize the amount of distance traveled, use less space, require less infrastructure (pipes, cables, roads, etc), reduce urban sprawl, and the provision of public transport is easier. But if the compact city covers too large an area, it becomes congested, overcrowded, overpriced, and polluted. As a result, it then becomes unsustainable.

In order to achieve sustainability, a number of options are available:

- reducing the use of fossil fuels, e.g. by promoting public transport;
- keeping waste production to within levels that can be treated locally;
- providing sufficient green spaces;
- reusing and reclaiming land, e.g. brownfield sites;
- active involvement of the local community;
- conservation of non-renewable resources;
- using renewable resources.

LARGEST CITIES

CITY GROWTH

The growth of some of the world's largest cities in millions, 1950–2019
Comparisons of city populations over time are problematic due to changes in the definition of the city limits. These figures attempt to take such changes into consideration.

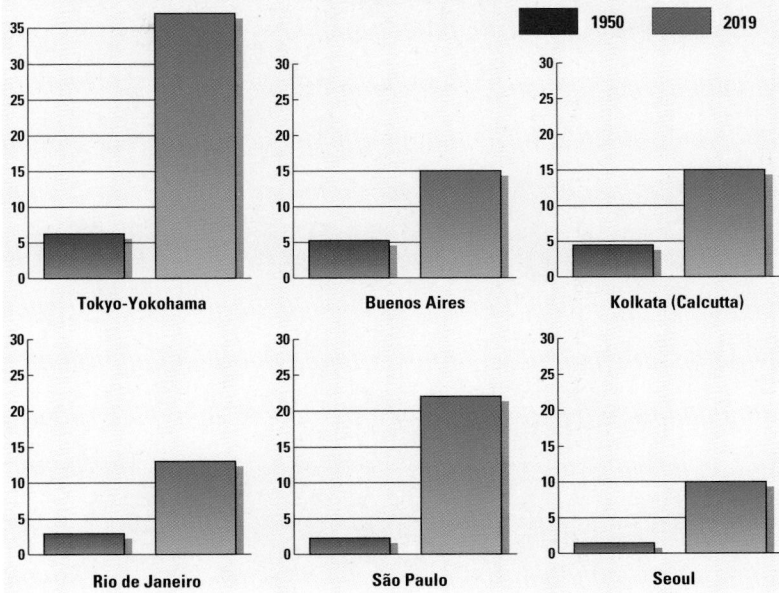

■ 1950   ■ 2019

Tokyo-Yokohama · Buenos Aires · Kolkata (Calcutta) · Rio de Janeiro · São Paulo · Seoul

◄ Mt. Fuji stands sentinel over the futuristic skyline of the Shinjuku area of Tokyo, the world's most populous city. Originally a fishing village called Edo, the greater metropolitan area of Tokyo–Yokohama is now home to over 38 million people and is the capital of Japan.

In 2008, for the first time in history, the majority of the world's population lived in cities. Below is a list of the urban areas in the world with over 10 million inhabitants in 2019

1.	Tokyo–Yokohama	37.4
2.	Delhi	29.4
3.	Shanghai	26.3
4.	São Paulo	21.8
5.	Mexico City	21.7
6.	Cairo	20.5
7.	Dhaka	20.3
8.	Mumbai	20.2
9.	Beijing	20.0
10.	Osaka-Kobe	19.2
11.	New York	18.8
12.	Karachi	15.7
13.	Chongqing	15.4
14.	Buenos Aires	15.1
15.	Istanbul	15.0
16.	Kolkata	14.8
17.	Lagos	13.9
18.	Kinshasa	13.7
19.	Manila	13.7
20.	Rio de Janeiro	13.4
21.	Tianjin	13.4
22.	Guangzhou	13.0
23.	Moscow	12.5
24.	Los Angeles	12.4
25.	Lahore	12.2
26.	Shenzhen	12.1
27.	Bengaluru	11.9
28.	Paris	11.0
29.	Bogotá	10.8
30.	Chennai	10.7
31.	Jakarta	10.6
32.	Lima	10.6
33.	Bangkok	10.4

The population figures above are based on urban agglomerations rather than legal city limits. In some cases, where two adjacent cities have merged into one concentration, such as Tokyo–Yokohama, they have been regarded as a single unit.

URBAN ADVANTAGES

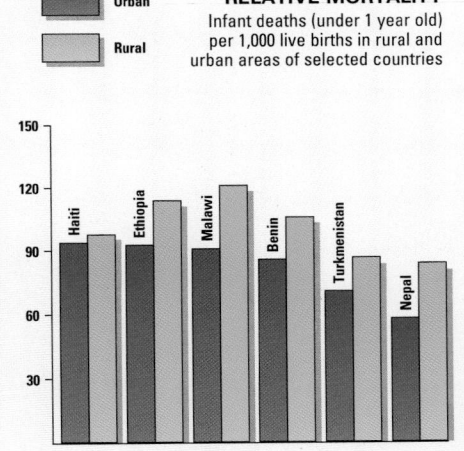

RELATIVE MORTALITY
Infant deaths (under 1 year old) per 1,000 live births in rural and urban areas of selected countries

■ Urban
■ Rural

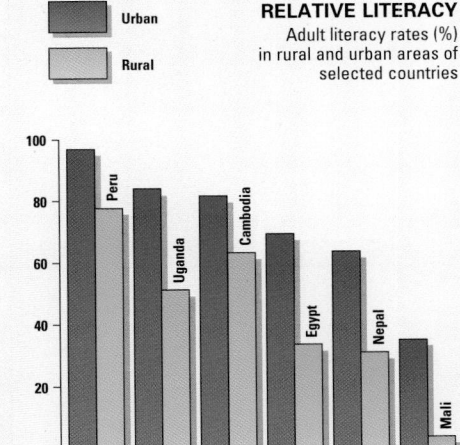

RELATIVE LITERACY
Adult literacy rates (%) in rural and urban areas of selected countries

■ Urban
■ Rural

Despite overcrowding and poor housing, living standards in the developing world's cities are almost invariably better than in the surrounding countryside. Resources – financial, material, and administrative – are concentrated in the towns, which are usually also the centers of political activity and pressure. Governments – frequently unstable, and rarely established on a solid democratic base – are usually more responsive to urban discontent than to rural misery.

In many developing countries, especially in Africa, food prices are kept artificially low, thus appeasing the underemployed urban masses at the expense of agricultural development.

This imbalance encourages further cityward migration, helping to account for the astonishing rate of post-1950 urbanization and putting great strain on the ability of many nations to provide even modest improvements for their people.

Migration is the permanent or semi-permanent change in residence. Migration can be voluntary or forced, international or internal, long- or short-distance. Most voluntary migrants are moving for work (especially for young people), to retire, or for educational or health reasons. In contrast, forced migrations may be due to civil conflict, environmental damage, or persecution.

According to the United Nations, the number of international migrants, as a percentage of the total world population, is continuing to grow. They represented 2.8% of the total population in 2000 growing to 3.5% in 2019, a total of 272 million people. Most live in Europe (82 million) with 59 million in northern America and 49 million in Africa. The fastest growth in migrant numbers has been in Africa, with many migrants heading north hoping to reach Europe. There has been substantial growth in the number of people displaced by force, up to 70.8 million at the end of 2018. It has been estimated that, on average, some 44,000 people are forced to flee their homes every day. In terms of numbers, the United States remains, by far, the top destination country for international migrants. The Mexico–United States migration corridor is the largest in the world. Mexico has been establishing a new role for itself as a country of transmigration and also of settlement. In recent years there has been a huge influx of people from Central America trying to access the United States via Mexico.

Migrants sending money home to their families, remittances, constitute a vital flow of financial aid to some economies. According to the World Bank, worldwide remittances had grown to US $715 billion in 2019, with three-quarters of this total destined for developing nations. The true size, including unrecorded flows through formal and informal channels, is believed to be significantly larger. Recorded remittances are more than twice as large as official aid and nearly two-thirds of foreign direct investment.

The definition of a refugee is someone who has been forced to flee their own country, as to remain there would be unsafe. Refugees are a sub-group of international migrants, numbering about 10% of the total in 2018, around 26 million people. The vast majority of refugees (who may also apply for the status of asylum seeker in the host country) stay in developing countries rather than richer countries. Lebanon, with 1 in 6 of its population being a refugee, has the world's highest ratio of refugees in relation to its national population. The ten leading countries of asylum took in 62% of the worldwide refugee population in 2019. The largest numbers are in Jordan (1 in 14) and Turkey (1 in 22).

DESTINATIONS AND ORIGINS OF MIGRANTS

Top destination countries for international migrants, in millions (2019)

1. USA 51
2. Saudi Arabia....................................13
3. Germany..13
4. Russia 12
5. UK 10
6. UAE 9
7. France 8
8. Canada 8
9. Australia 8
10. Spain 6

Top countries of origin of international migrants, in millions (2019)

1. India 18
2. Mexico 12
3. China 11
4. Russia 10
5. Bangladesh 8
6. Syria 8
7. Pakistan 6
8. Ukraine 6
9. Philippines 6
10. UK 5

MIGRANTS

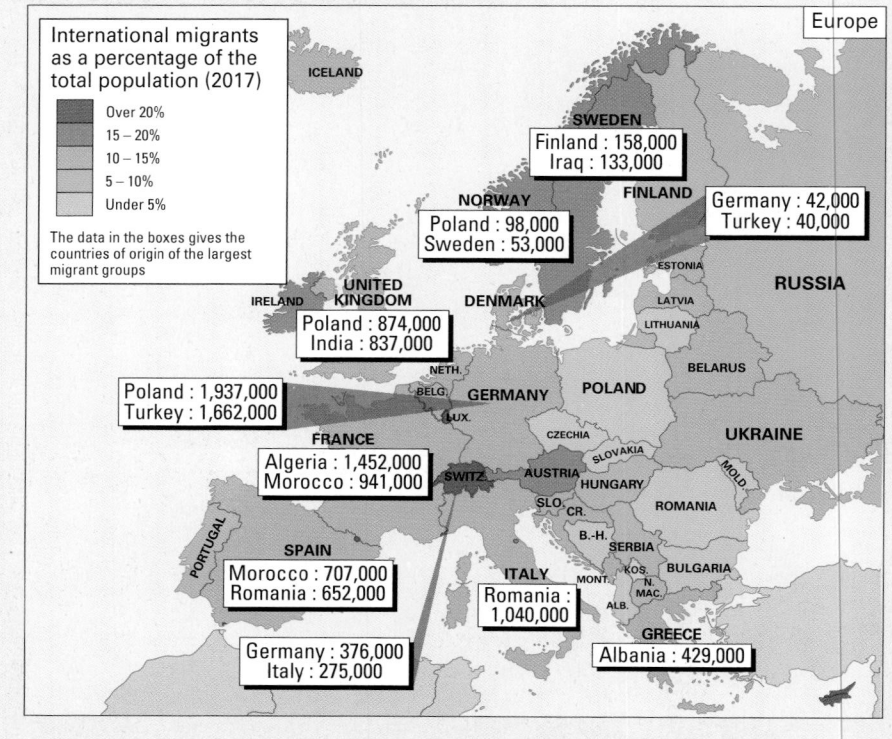

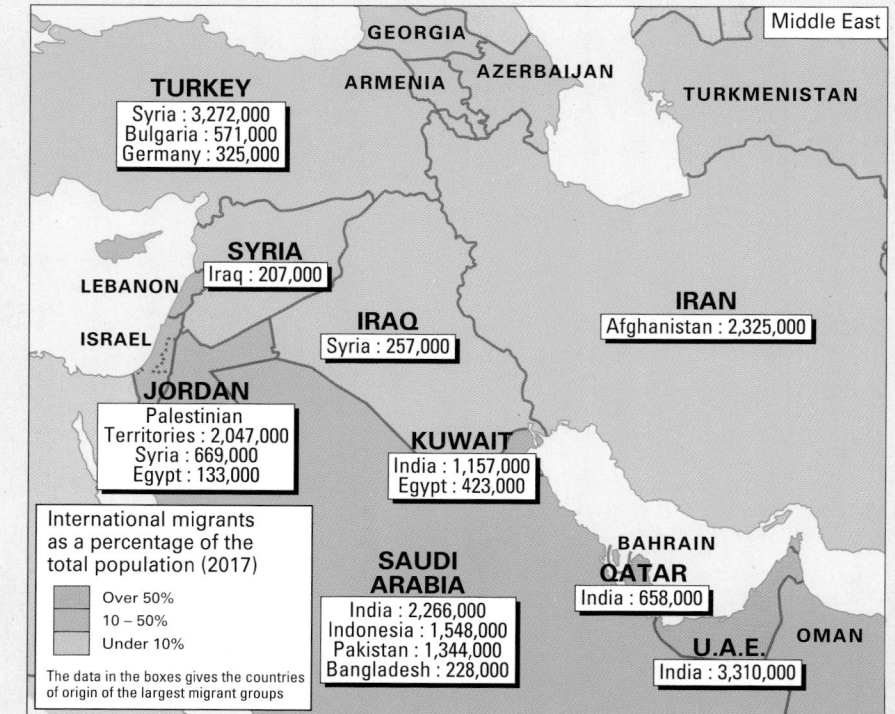

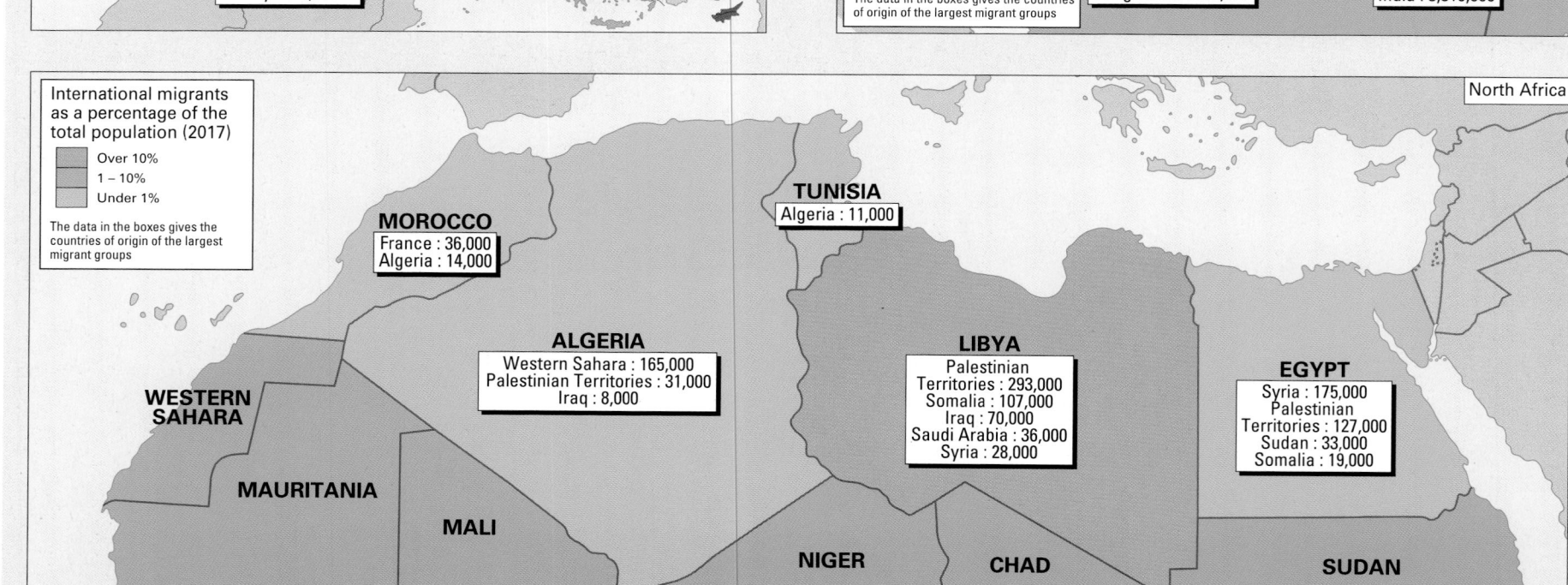

REMITTANCES

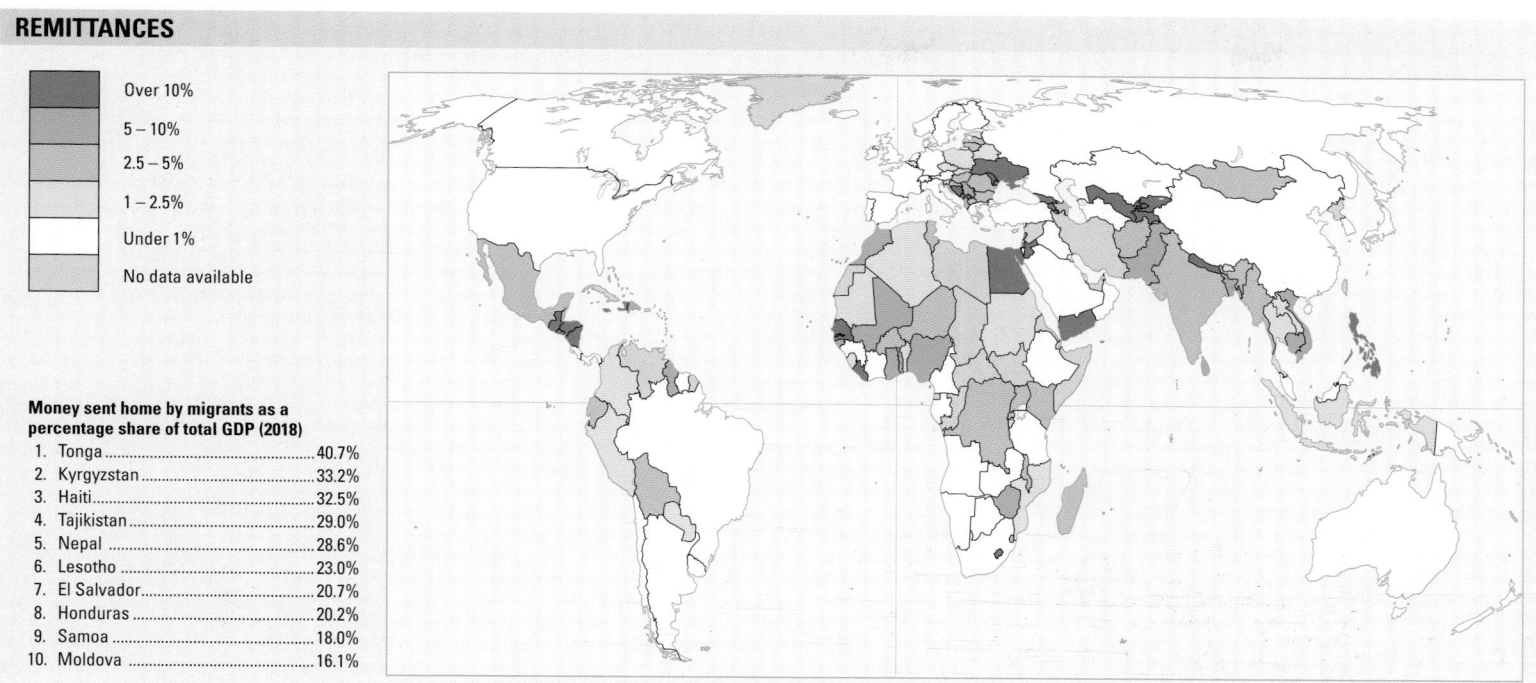

Over 10%	
5 – 10%	
2.5 – 5%	
1 – 2.5%	
Under 1%	
No data available	

Money sent home by migrants as a percentage share of total GDP (2018)

1. Tonga 40.7%
2. Kyrgyzstan 33.2%
3. Haiti....................................32.5%
4. Tajikistan 29.0%
5. Nepal 28.6%
6. Lesotho 23.0%
7. El Salvador..........................20.7%
8. Honduras 20.2%
9. Samoa 18.0%
10. Moldova 16.1%

REFUGEES

◄ Since August 2017, over 700,000 Rohingya people, from the northern Rakhine province in Myanmar, have fled to refugee camps in neighbouring Bangladesh. Fleeing persecution and the destruction of their homes in Myanmar, they are now living in difficult conditions in camps such as this one at Cox's Bazar. The United Nations have called the Rohingya's situation the "world's fastest growing refugee crisis".

REFUGEES Total refugees and people in a refugee-like situation, in millions (2019)

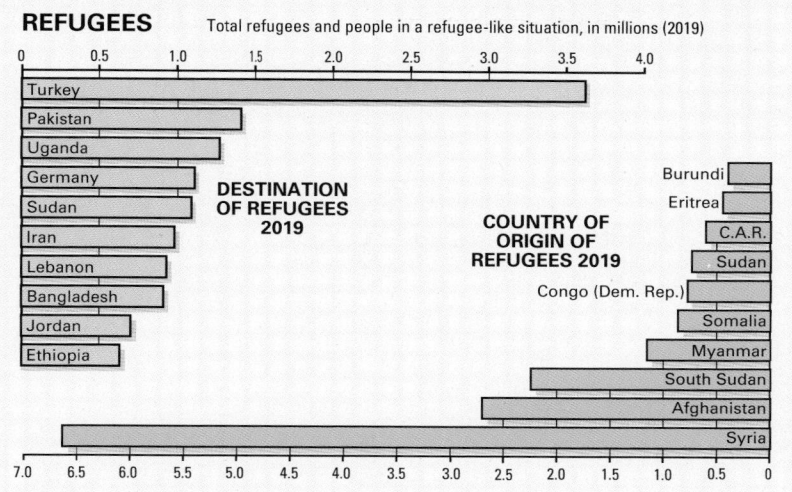

DESTINATION OF REFUGEES 2019

Turkey, Pakistan, Uganda, Germany, Sudan, Iran, Lebanon, Bangladesh, Jordan, Ethiopia

COUNTRY OF ORIGIN OF REFUGEES 2019

Burundi, Eritrea, C.A.R., Sudan, Congo (Dem. Rep.), Somalia, Myanmar, South Sudan, Afghanistan, Syria

Refugee population by region (2018)

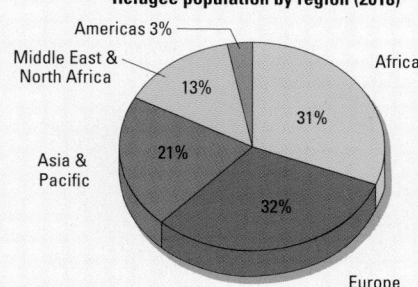

- Americas 3%
- Middle East & North Africa 13%
- Asia & Pacific 21%
- Europe 32%
- Africa 31%

Internally Displaced Persons, in millions (2018)

At the end of 2018, an estimated 41 million people were displaced within their own countries due to armed conflict, generalized violence, or human rights violations. The top ten countries with internally displaced people are (in millions):

1. Syria.........................6.1
2. Colombia 5.8
3. Congo, Dem. Rep...........3.1
4. Somalia 2.6
5. Afghanistan 2.6
6. Yemen 2.3
7. Nigeria....................2.2
8. Ethiopia 2.1
9. Sudan 2.1
10. Iraq.........................2.0

▲ It is estimated that some 41 million people worldwide have been internally displaced. Although not legally classified as refugees, they can find themselves living in similar situations whilst remaining within their own country's borders. Make shift shelters, such as this in eastern Ghouta in Syria, have become home to families fleeing fighting between rebel groups and the Syrian regime.

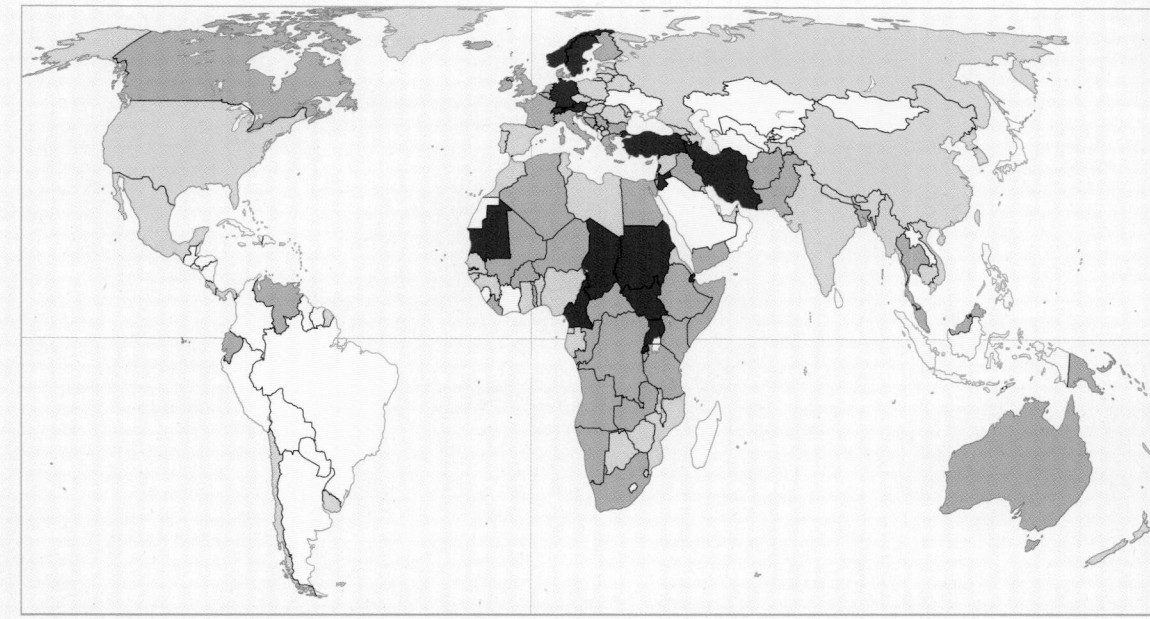

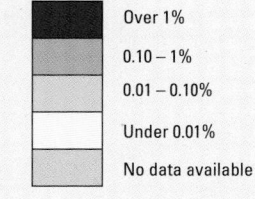

Total refugees* as a percentage of the population (2019)

Over 1%	
0.10 – 1%	
0.01 – 0.10%	
Under 0.01%	
No data available	

*includes people in a refugee-like situation

For more information:
92 Migration

In the late 1980s, many people hoped that the end of the Cold War, following the collapse of Communist regimes in the former Soviet Union and Eastern Europe, would herald a new era of international stability. Instead, ethnic and religious antagonisms surfaced in many areas. Nationalist rivalries, suppressed under Communist rule, replaced ideological factors as the major cause of conflict. Since, 2010, there has been accelerated political change, especially across North Africa and the Middle East.

Some countries are more likely to fail than others. Demographic stress is a major factor. Where there are large numbers of unemployed youths concentrated in large cities and a lack of growth, the chances of conflict escalate.

The causes of state failure and civil disintegration are multiple, but certain characteristics increase vulnerability. Extreme income and gender inequality increase the risk of discord. Corrupt governments that are widely regarded as illegitimate and ineffective are "at risk." Democracy, especially with a strong parliament, lowers the risk of state failure; autocracy increases it. Population pressure, exacerbated by internally displaced people, refugees, and food scarcity, contribute to state failure and civil unrest. Governments that fail to protect human rights are especially prone to fail.

The Arab Spring, a term given to the Arab Revolution, is a wave of demonstrations, protests, and wars that began in December 2010. A number of rulers have been forced from power in Tunisia, Egypt, Libya, and Yemen. In addition, there have been civil uprisings in Bahrain, Syria, and Ukraine. However, the major oil-rich nations (Saudi Arabia, UAE, Qatar, Kuwait, and Oman) have managed to keep their ruling families in power.

The protests have shared techniques of civil resistance in sustained campaigns involving strikes, demonstrations, marches, and rallies, but were also noticeable for their use of social media to organize and raise awareness of the situation.

Despite the words of John F. Kennedy, US President 1961–3, that "Mankind must put an end to war or war will put an end to mankind," in 2019 military conflicts are taking place around the world in countries such as Afghanistan, Somalia, Yemen, Pakistan, Mexico (the "drugs war"), South Sudan, Nigeria, Syria, Iraq, Libya, and Ukraine.

▲ UN peacekeepers in the Democratic Republic of the Congo, April 2019. The UN is currently involved in 14 operations worldwide.

ARMED CONFLICTS

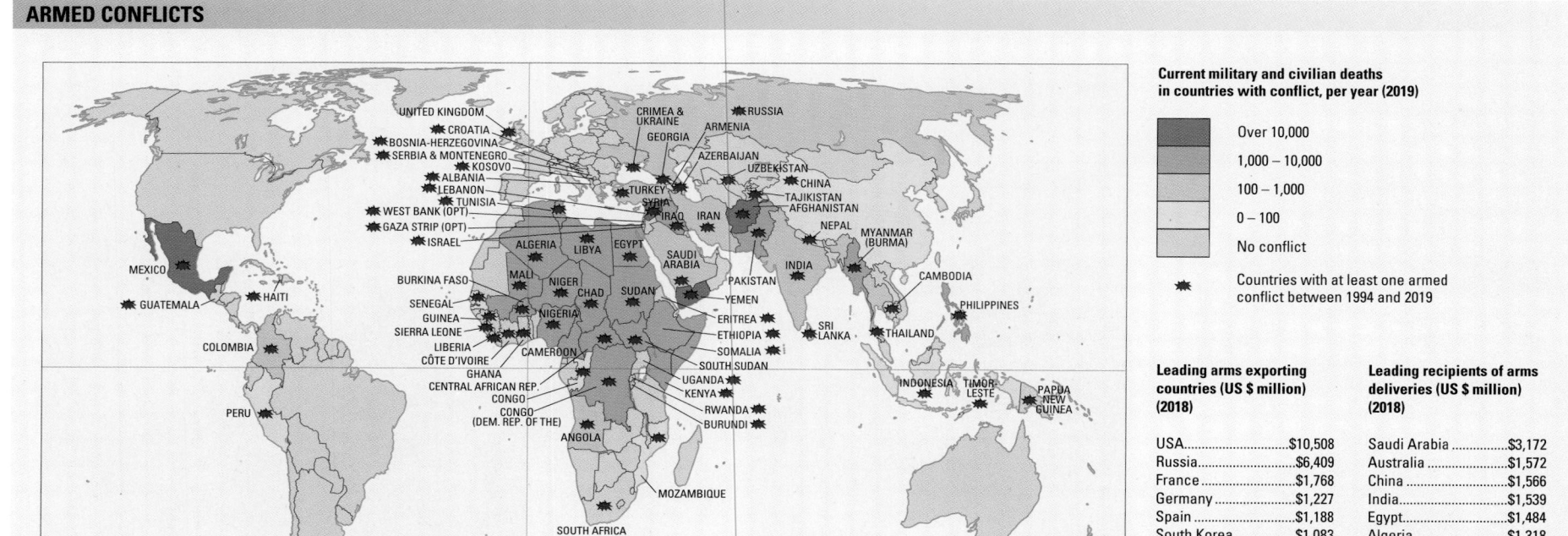

Current military and civilian deaths in countries with conflict, per year (2019)

- Over 10,000
- 1,000 – 10,000
- 100 – 1,000
- 0 – 100
- No conflict

✷ Countries with at least one armed conflict between 1994 and 2019

Leading arms exporting countries (US $ million) (2018)		Leading recipients of arms deliveries (US $ million) (2018)	
USA	$10,508	Saudi Arabia	$3,172
Russia	$6,409	Australia	$1,572
France	$1,768	China	$1,566
Germany	$1,227	India	$1,539
Spain	$1,188	Egypt	$1,484
South Korea	$1,083	Algeria	$1,318
China	$1,040	South Korea	$1,317
UK	$741	UAE	$1,101
Israel	$707	Qatar	$816
Italy	$611	Pakistan	$777

GLOBAL PEACE INDEX

The Global Peace Index (GPI) is an attempt to measure the relative position of nations' peacefulness. It quantifies: levels of security and safety; domestic and international conflict; and degree of militarization. Syria remains the least peaceful country with Libya and Ukraine showing the most deterioration.

Global Peace Index (2019)

- Under 1.500 (most peaceful)
- 1.501 – 2.000
- 2.001 – 2.500
- 2.501 – 3.000
- Over 3.001 (least peaceful)
- No data available

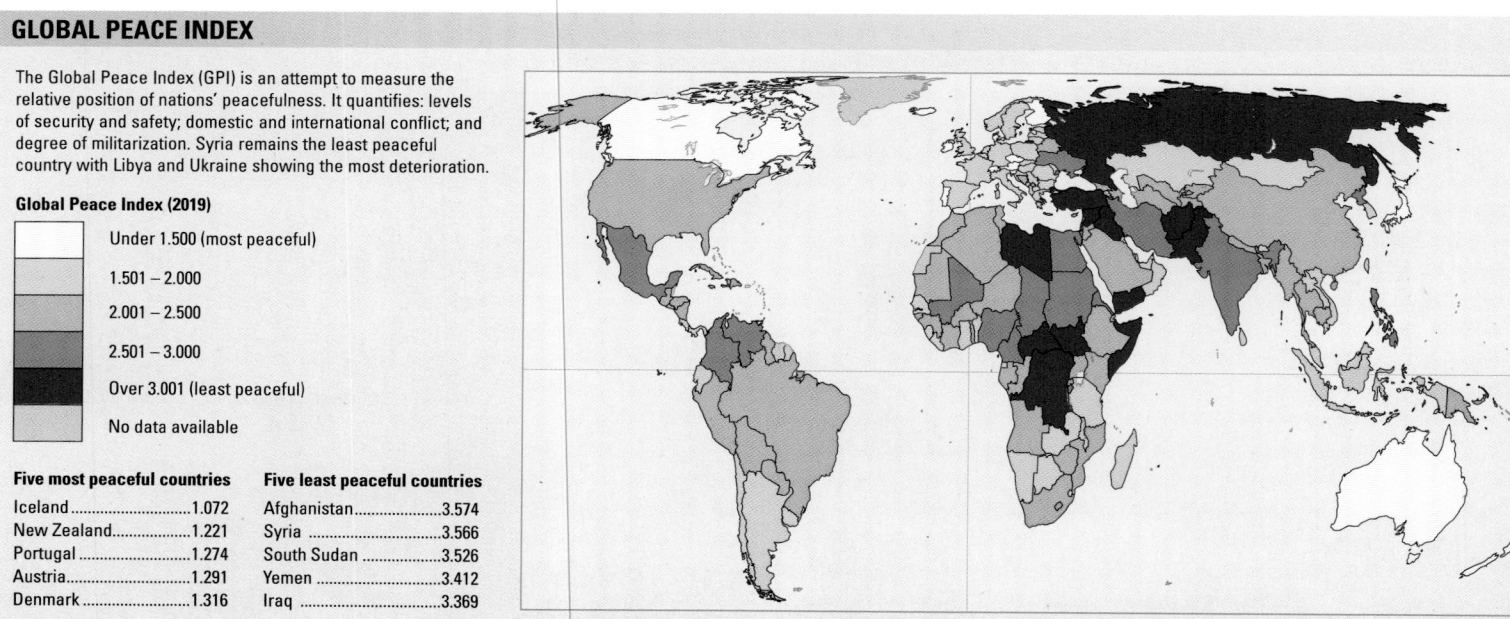

Five most peaceful countries		Five least peaceful countries	
Iceland	1.072	Afghanistan	3.574
New Zealand	1.221	Syria	3.566
Portugal	1.274	South Sudan	3.526
Austria	1.291	Yemen	3.412
Denmark	1.316	Iraq	3.369

INTERNATIONAL ORGANIZATIONS

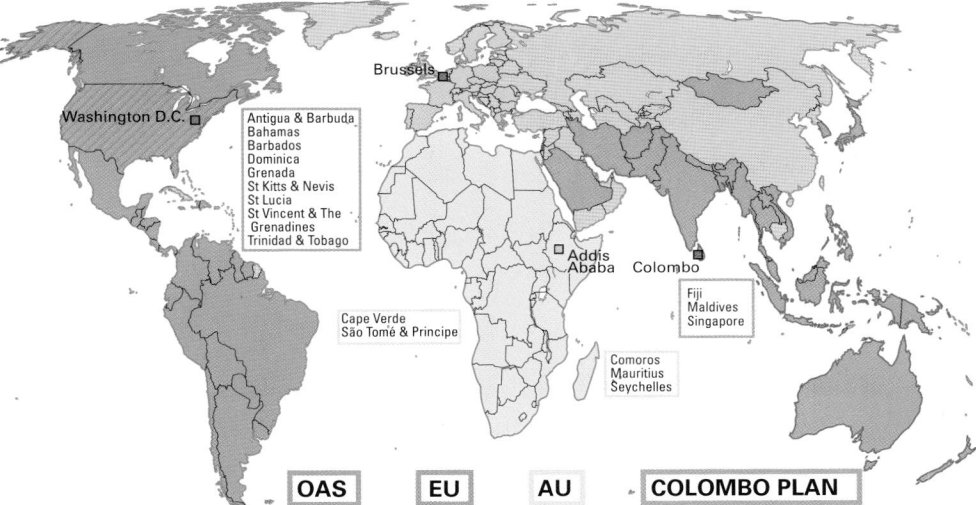

UN

Year of joining
- 1940s
- 1950s
- 1960s
- 1970s
- 1980s
- 1990s
- 2000s
- Non-members

★ 1% – 10% contribution to funding
☆ Over 10% contribution to funding

Antigua & Barbuda
Bahamas
Barbados
Dominica
Grenada
St Kitts & Nevis
St Lucia
St Vincent & The Grenadines
Trinidad & Tobago

Washington D.C.
Brussels
Addis Ababa
Colombo
Cape Verde / São Tomé & Príncipe
Fiji / Maldives / Singapore
Comoros / Mauritius / Seychelles

OAS   **EU**   **AU**   **COLOMBO PLAN**

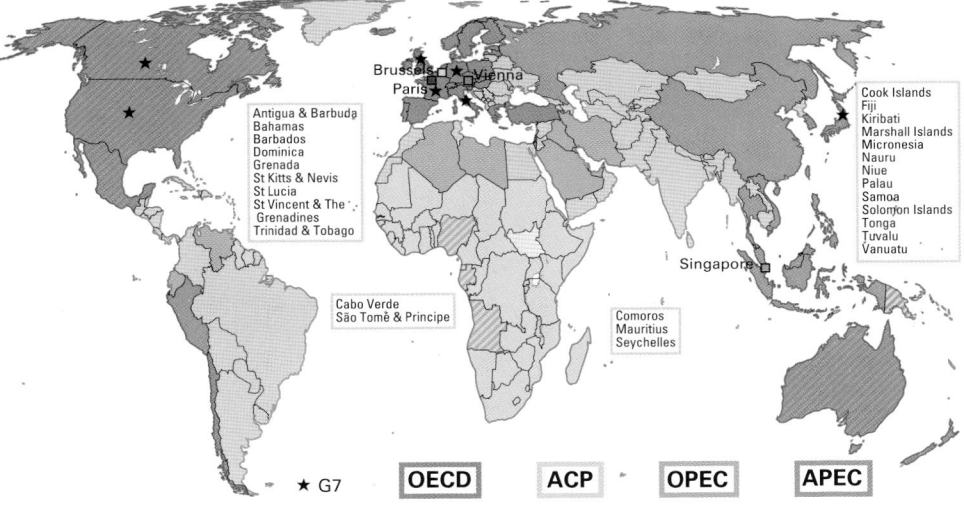

Brussels   Vienna   Paris
Antigua & Barbuda
Bahamas
Barbados
Dominica
Grenada
St Kitts & Nevis
St Lucia
St Vincent & The Grenadines
Trinidad & Tobago

Cook Islands
Fiji
Kiribati
Marshall Islands
Micronesia
Nauru
Niue
Palau
Samoa
Solomon Islands
Tonga
Tuvalu
Vanuatu

Singapore
Cabo Verde / São Tomé & Príncipe
Comoros / Mauritius / Seychelles

★ G7   **OECD**   **ACP**   **OPEC**   **APEC**

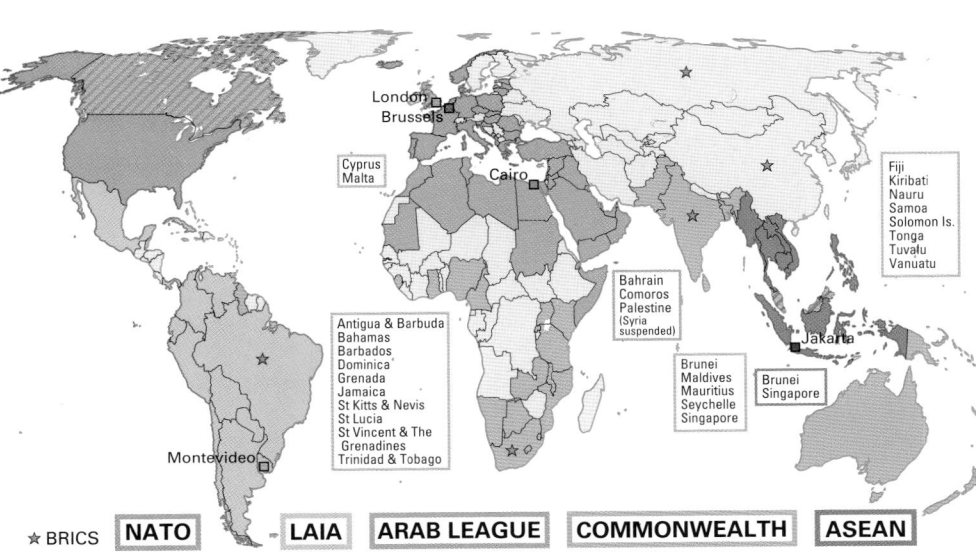

London   Brussels   Cairo
Cyprus / Malta

Fiji
Kiribati
Nauru
Samoa
Solomon Is.
Tonga
Tuvalu
Vanuatu

Bahrain
Comoros
Palestine (Syria suspended)

Jakarta

Antigua & Barbuda
Bahamas
Barbados
Dominica
Grenada
Jamaica
St Kitts & Nevis
St Lucia
St Vincent & The Grenadines
Trinidad & Tobago

Brunei / Maldives / Mauritius / Seychelle / Singapore
Brunei / Singapore

Montevideo

★ BRICS   **NATO**   **LAIA**   **ARAB LEAGUE**   **COMMONWEALTH**   **ASEAN**

UNITED NATIONS

The creation of the United Nations in 1945 held out hope that the world's nations, tired of war, would have the means to control humanity's aggressive instincts. Although the UN lacks the power to halt conflicts, it has often helped to achieve negotiation. Economic pressures have led to another kind of cooperation, resulting in the creation of common markets and economic unions, such as ASEAN in Southeast Asia, the European Union, and NAFTA in North America.

The United Nations Organization was born as World War II drew to its conclusion. That body would replace the League of Nations, which, since its inception in 1920, had failed to curb the aggression of some of its member nations. At the United Nations Conference on International Organization held in San Francisco, the United Nations Charter was drawn up. Ratified by the Security Council and signed by the 51 original members, it came into effect on October 24, 1945.

The Charter set out the aims of the organization: to maintain peace and security, and to develop friendly relations between nations; to achieve international cooperation in solving economic, social, cultural, and humanitarian problems; to promote respect for human rights and fundamental freedoms; and to harmonize the activities of nations in order to achieve these common goals.

Membership From the original 51, membership of the UN has now grown to 193. There are only two independent states that are not members – Taiwan and the Vatican City. Official languages are Chinese, English, French, Russian, Spanish, and Arabic.

Funding The UN budget, now set yearly, for 2020 was US $3 billion. Contributions are assessed by the members' ability to pay, with the maximum 22% of the total (the USA's share), and the minimum 0.001%. The 27-member EU pays approximately 35% of the budget.

Peacekeeping The UN has been involved in 67 peacekeeping operations worldwide since 1948. They are involved in 14 operations in mid 2019.

OAS The **Organization of American States** was formed in 1948. It aims to promote social and economic cooperation between countries in the developed North America and developing Latin America.
EU The **European Union** evolved from the European Community in 1993. Cyprus, Czechia, Estonia, Hungary, Latvia, Lithuania, Malta, Poland, Slovakia, and Slovenia joined the EU in May 2004; Bulgaria and Romania joined in 2007; Croatia joinded in 2013. The other 14 members of the EU are Austria, Belgium, Denmark, Finland, France, Germany, Greece, Ireland, Italy, Luxembourg, Netherlands, Portugal, Spain, and Sweden. The UK left the EU in 2020. Together, the 27 members aim to integrate economies, coordinate social developments, and bring about political union.
AU The **African Union** was set up in 2002, taking over from the Organization of African Unity (1963). It has 55 members. The main objectives of the OAU were, *inter alia*, to rid the continent of the remaining vestiges of colonization and apartheid; to promote unity and solidarity among African states; to coordinate and intensify cooperation for development; to safeguard the sovereignty and territorial integrity of member states; and to promote international cooperation within the framework of the United Nations.
COLOMBO PLAN Formed in 1951, its 27 members aim to promote economic and social development in Asia and the Pacific. Saudi Arabia joined in 2012.

G7 Group of seven leading industrialized nations, comprising Canada, France, Germany, Italy, Japan, the UK, and the USA. Periodic meetings are held to discuss major world issues, such as world recessions. The EU is also represented at meetings. Russian membership was suspended in 2014.
OECD The **Organization for Economic Cooperation and Development** (formed in 1961) comprises 36 major free-market economies. The "G7" is its "inner group" of leading industrial nations, comprising Canada, France, Germany, Italy, Japan, the UK, and the USA. The mission of the OECD is to promote policies that will improve the economic and social well-being of people around the world.
ACP The **African, Caribbean and Pacific Group of States** was formed in 1963. Members enjoy economic ties with the EU. The ACP Group´s main objectives are sustainable development of its member states and their gradual integration into the global economy, which entails making poverty reduction a matter of priority; coordination of the activities of the ACP Group in the framework of the implementation of ACP–EU Partnership Agreements; establishment and consolidation of peace and stability in a free and democratic society.
OPEC The **Organization of Petroleum Exporting Countries** was formed in 1960. It controls about three-quarters of the world's oil supply. Its mission is to coordinate and unify the petroleum policies of its member countries, and to ensure the stabilization of oil markets in order to secure an efficient, economic, and regular supply of petroleum to consumers, a steady income to producers, and a fair return on capital for those investing in the petroleum industry. Qatar left in January 2019.
APEC Formed in 1989, the **Asia–Pacific Economic Cooperation** aims to enhance economic growth and prosperity for the region and to strengthen the Asia–Pacific community. APEC is the only intergovernmental grouping in the world operating on the basis of non-binding commitments, open dialog, and equal respect for the views of all participants. There are 21 member economies.

NATO The **North Atlantic Treaty Organization** (formed in 1949) continues despite the winding-up of the Warsaw Pact in 1991. Bulgaria, Estonia, Latvia, Lithuania, Romania, Slovakia, and Slovenia became members in 2004, and Albania and Croatia in 2009. Montenegro joined in 2017. Its main aim is to provide peace and security to its North Atlantic members through collective defense – an attack on one country is seen as an attack on all of NATO.
LAIA The **Latin American Integration Association** (formed in 1980) superceded the Latin American Free Trade Association formed in 1961. Its aim is to promote freer regional trade.
ARAB LEAGUE Formed in 1945, the Arab League aims to promote economic, social, political, and military cooperation. There are 22 member nations. Syria's membership was suspended in 2011.
COMMONWEALTH The **Commonwealth of Nations** evolved from the British Empire. Pakistan was suspended in 1999, but reinstated in 2004. Zimbabwe was suspended in 2002 and, in response to its continued suspension, Zimbabwe left the Commonwealth in 2003. Fiji was suspended in 2006 following a military coup. Rwanda joined the Commonwealth in 2009, as the 54th member state, becoming only the second country that was not formerly a British colony to be admitted to the group. The Gambia left between 2013 and 2018. Their objective is to build stronger democratic institutions and processes across the Commonwealth and to support economic growth in their member countries. There are currently 53 members.
ASEAN The **Association of Southeast Asian Nations** was formed in 1967. Cambodia joined in 1999. The aims of ASEAN include: to accelerate the economic growth, social progress, and cultural development in the region; to promote regional peace and stability; and to collaborate more effectively for the greater utilization of their agriculture and industries, the expansion of their trade, including the study of the problems of international commodity trade, the improvement of their transportation and communications facilities, and the raising of the living standards of their peoples.

Every year, the world's energy consumption is about the equivalent of what would come from burning 12,000 million tonnes of oil (12,000 MtOe) – a 20-fold increase since 1850. Two-fifths of this total actually comes from burning oil and most of the rest comes from coal and natural gas.

The oil crises in the 1970s precipitated concern over dependence on finite fossil fuels as the primary source of energy, and growing environmental awareness has added impetus to the search for alternative energy resources. Fossil fuel combustion damages the environment through the release of gases and particulate matter, but two other major sources of energy, hydroelectricity and nuclear power, are also controversial. Hydroelectricity production involves flooding large areas to create reservoirs, while nuclear power stations generate dangerous radioactive wastes and can cause major disasters. Nuclear power has been a growing source of energy, but the 2011 Japanese earthquake, with the consequent serious damage to the Fukushima nuclear power station, has caused many countries to rethink their energy strategies.

Alternative energy resources may soon provide a much larger proportion of the world's energy consumption. Solar and wind energy may become important in such countries as China and India, while tidal, wave, and geothermal energy all have potential in appropriate areas. Experts calculate that solar power could, in theory, supply between five and ten times the present electricity supply of developing countries.

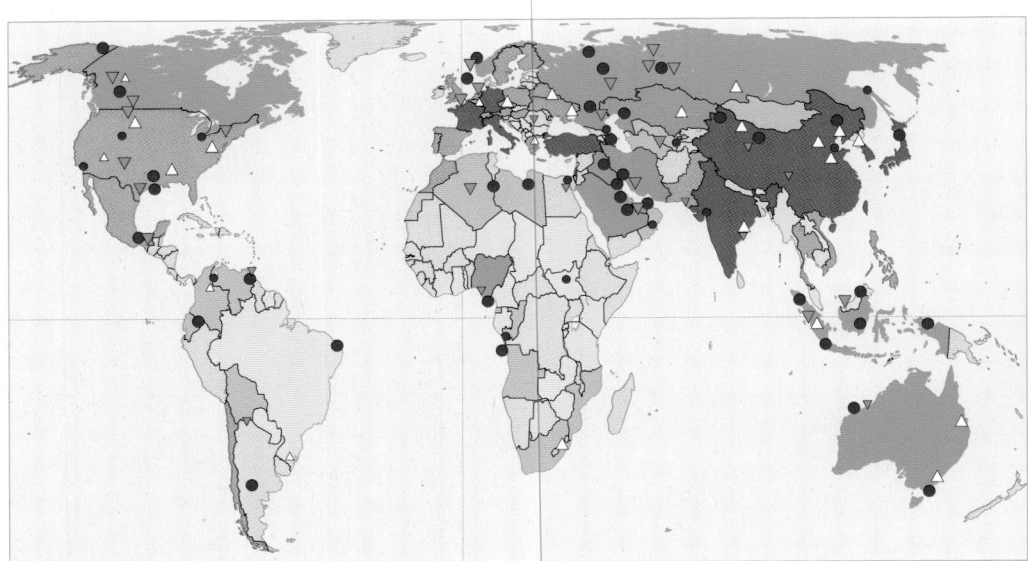

ENERGY BALANCE

Difference between energy production and consumption in millions of tonnes of oil equivalent (MtOe) (2018)

- Over 100 MtOe surplus
- 10 – 100 MtOe surplus
- 0 – 10 MtOe surplus
- 0 – 10 MtOe deficit
- 10 – 100 MtOe deficit
- Over 100 MtOe deficit
- No data available

- ● Principal oilfields
- ▼ Principal gasfields
- △ Principal coalfields
- ● Secondary oilfields
- ▼ Secondary gasfields
- △ Secondary coalfields

ENERGY CONSUMPTION

Energy consumed by world regions, measured in million tonnes of oil equivalent in 2017. Total world consumption was 13,513 MtOe. Energy from commercially traded fuels, and modern renewables used to generate electricity, are included. Excluded are biomass fuels such as wood, peat and animal waste which, though important locally in some countries, are not always reliably documented statistically.

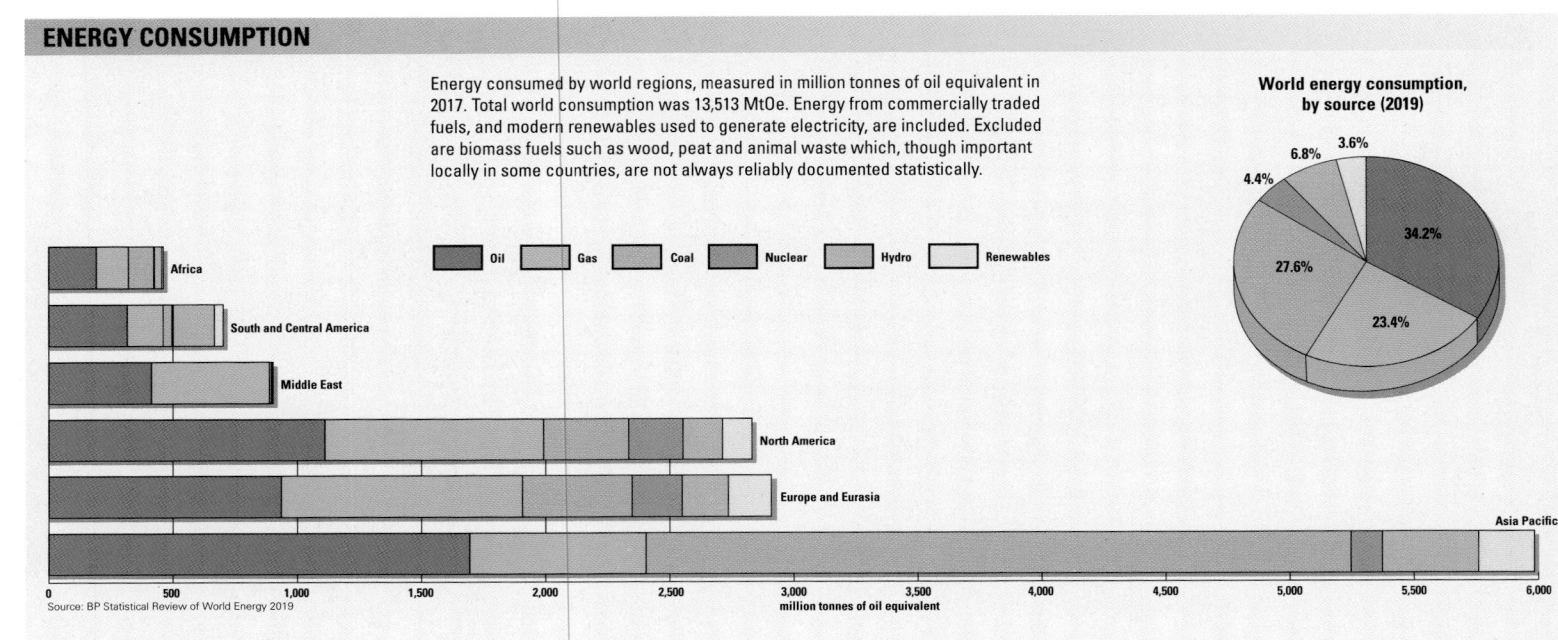

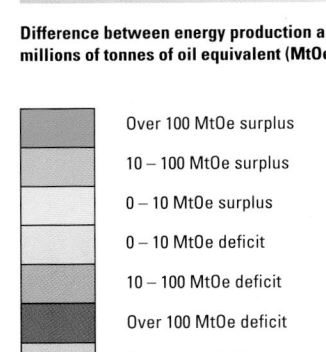

World energy consumption, by source (2019)

- Oil
- Gas
- Coal
- Nuclear
- Hydro
- Renewables

34.2%
27.6%
23.4%
6.8%
4.4%
3.6%

Source: BP Statistical Review of World Energy 2019

million tonnes of oil equivalent

ENERGY PRODUCTION

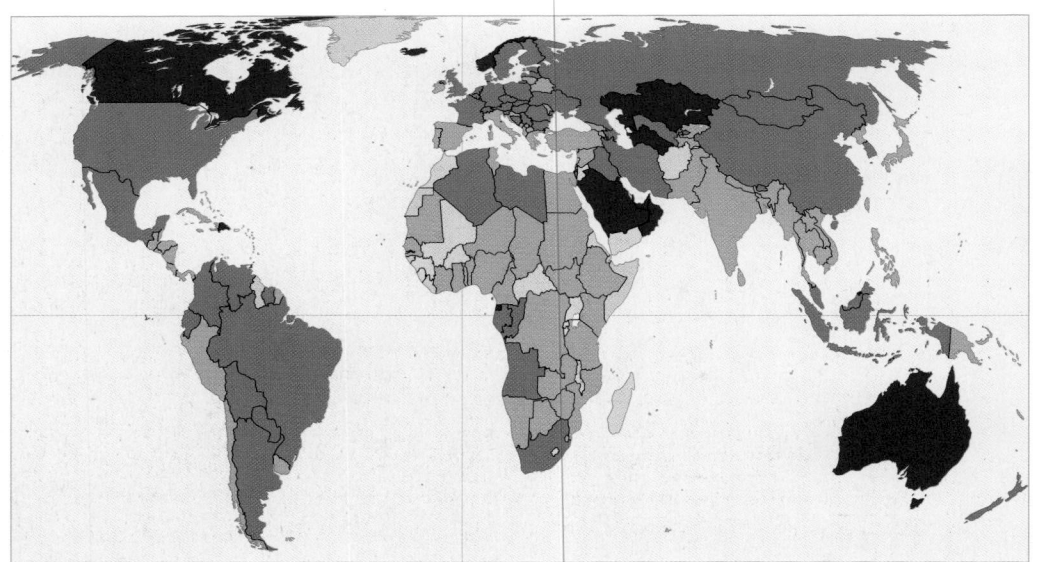

Energy production in tonnes of oil equivalent per capita (2018)

- Over 10
- 1 – 10
- 0.1 – 1
- 0 – 0.1
- No data available

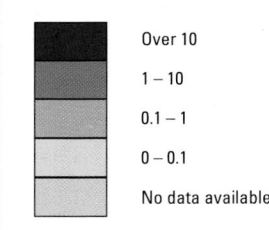

Highest energy producers, tonnes of oil equivalent per capita (2018)

Qatar	95.3
Kuwait	57.6
Brunei	34.6
Trinidad & Tobago	26.8
Equatorial Guinea	25.7

OIL MOVEMENTS

Major oil exporting regions

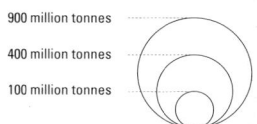

900 million tonnes
400 million tonnes
100 million tonnes

Major global oil movements (percentage of total world trade)

Over 10%
5 – 10%
2 – 5%
Under 2%

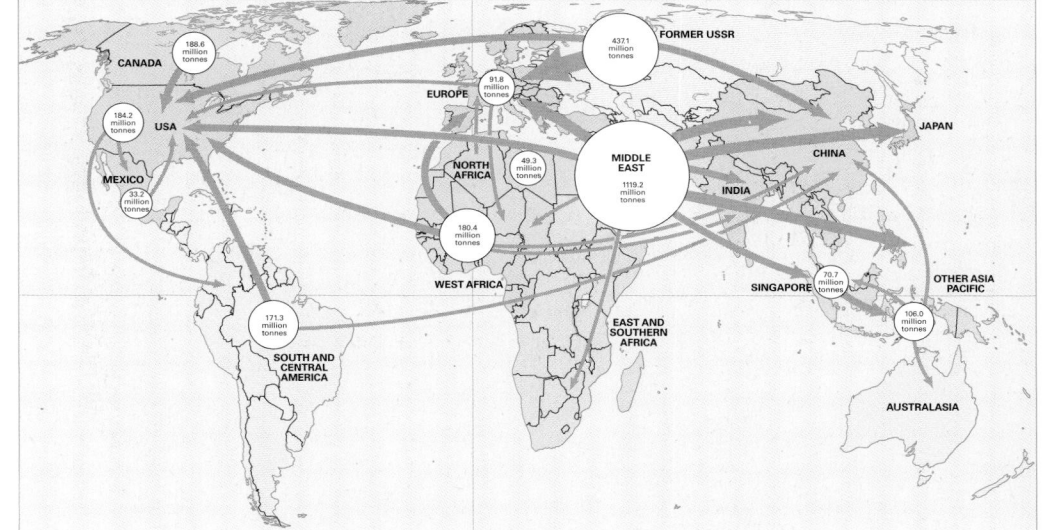

▲ A view over the tanks of the Liquefied Natural Gas (LNG) tanker Grand Aniva. LNG is natural gas that has been filtered and purified then cooled to -260°F (-162°C), which turns it into a liquid, 1/600th of its original volume, allowing it to be transported in special highly-insulated tanks on ships to markets around the world.

ENERGY RESERVES

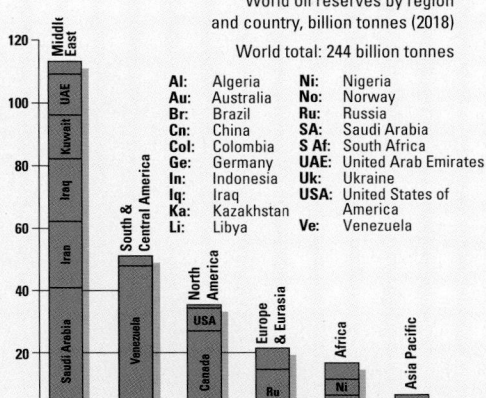

WORLD OIL RESERVES
World oil reserves by region and country, billion tonnes (2018)
World total: 244 billion tonnes

Al:	Algeria	Ni:	Nigeria
Au:	Australia	No:	Norway
Br:	Brazil	Ru:	Russia
Cn:	China	SA:	Saudi Arabia
Col:	Colombia	S Af:	South Africa
Ge:	Germany	UAE:	United Arab Emirates
In:	Indonesia	Uk:	Ukraine
Iq:	Iraq	USA:	United States of
Ka:	Kazakhstan		America
Li:	Libya	Ve:	Venezuela

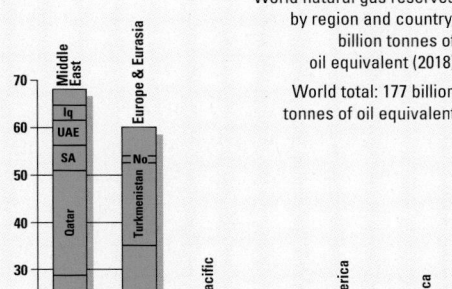

WORLD GAS RESERVES
World natural gas reserves by region and country, billion tonnes of oil equivalent (2018)
World total: 177 billion tonnes of oil equivalent

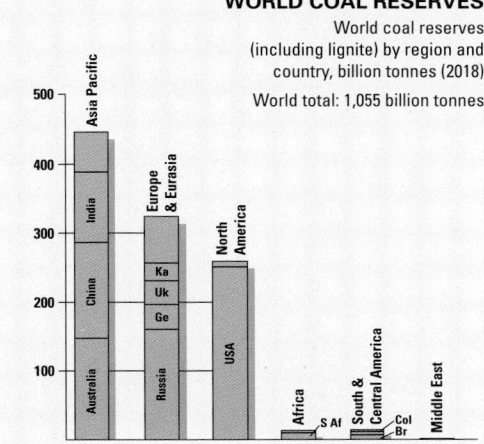

WORLD COAL RESERVES
World coal reserves (including lignite) by region and country, billion tonnes (2018)
World total: 1,055 billion tonnes

NUCLEAR POWER

Major producers by percentage of domestic electricity generation (2018)

Country	% of nuclear as proportion of domestic electricity	Country	% of nuclear as proportion of domestic electricity
1. France	72	11. Finland	32
2. Slovakia	55	12. Armenia	26
3. Ukraine	53	13. South Korea	24
4. Hungary	51	14. Spain	20
5. Sweden	40	15. USA	19
6. Belgium	39	16. Russia	18
7. Switzerland	38	17. UK	18
8. Slovenia	36	18. Romania	17
9. Bulgaria	35	19. Canada	15
10. Czechia	35	20. Taiwan	11

Although the 1980s were a bad time for the nuclear power industry, the industry picked up in the early 1990s. Despite this, growth has recently been curtailed whilst countries review their energy mix, in light of the March 2011 Japanese earthquake and tsunami that seriously damaged the Fukushima nuclear power station. Germany, for example, is phasing out its nuclear power production.

PEAK OIL

"Peak oil" refers to the peak of oil production. We depend on oil for many things: we use it for fuel, transport and heating, as a raw material in the plastics industry, and for fertilizer in food production. But as oil production decreases after peak oil, so will all of these, unless we can find new materials and alternatives.

Peak oil varies by country. The peak of oil discovery occurred in the 1960s, and by the 1980s the world was using more oil than was being discovered. Since then, the gap between use and discovery has been increasing, and many countries have now passed their peak oil production.

The International Energy Agency suggests that global peak oil will occur between 2013 and 2037. In contrast, the US Geological Survey suggests it will not occur until 2059. M. King Hubbert, who popularized the theory of peak oil, predicted that it would occur in 1995. It is claimed that in 1950 the world consumed 4 billion barrels of oil per annum, while the average discovery was 30 billion barrels per annum. Now, however, research suggests the figures are reversed: new discoveries are around 4 billion barrels per year, with an annual consumption of 30 billion barrels.

FRACKING

Hydraulic fracturing, commonly known as "fracking," releases natural gas or oil that is trapped in shale rock and is unobtainable by conventional techniques. This is accomplished by boring holes into the rock and injecting a liquid mix of chemicals under pressure, thus fracturing the rock and forcing the trapped oil or gas to the surface.

Just as nuclear scientists in the 1950s and 1960s believed that nuclear energy was going to be the answer to the world's energy needs, oil and gas producers believe that gas derived from shale could provide a plentiful supply of low-cost energy. As a result, shale gas could transform the pattern of energy trade in the world. Nevertheless, fracking has its critics and there may be problems related to the extraction of shale gas.

Shale is one of the most common forms of sedimentary rock on Earth. Significant reserves have been found in China, Argentina, the USA, and South Africa, and these are therefore having a new geopolitical influence. The world's gas trade has long been dominated by Russia, Qatar, and Algeria, but shale gas development has since taken off in the USA. In 2010, the USA replaced Russia as the world's largest gas producer and a new wave of gas producers may soon emerge.

However, as with the nuclear dawn, there are potential drawbacks with fracking. It may pollute soil and ground water, release methane, produce toxic byproducts that have to be disposed of, and it may also trigger earthquakes.

HYDROELECTRICITY

Major producers by percentage of world total and by percentage of domestic electricity generation (2018)

Country	% of world total production	Country	% of hydroelectric as proportion of domestic electricity
1. China	27.2	1. Albania	100.0
2. United States	8.0	2. Paraguay	100.0
3. Brazil	8.0	3. Congo, Dem. Rep.	99.9
4. Canada	6.3	4. Nepal	99.8
5. Japan	3.9	5. Namibia	99.1
6. India	3.9	6. Zambia	97.2
7. Russia	3.8	7. Tajikistan	97.1
8. Norway	2.5	8. Norway	96.0
9. Turkey	2.2	9. Ethiopia	95.6
10. France	2.0	10. Kyrgyzstan	91.3

Countries heavily reliant on hydroelectricity are usually small and non-industrial: a high proportion of hydroelectric power more often reflects a modest energy budget than vast hydroelectric resources. The USA, for instance, produces only 6% of its domestic power requirements from hydroelectricity; yet that 6% amounts to almost half the hydropower generated by the whole of Africa.

ALTERNATIVE ENERGY RESOURCES

Solar: Each year the Sun bestows upon the Earth almost a million times as much energy as is locked up in all the planet's oil reserves, but only an insignificant fraction is trapped and used commercially. In a few installations around the world, mirrors focus the Sun's rays on to boilers, whose steam generates electricity by spinning turbines, and the use of photovoltaic panels in sunny climates has also started to become established.

Wind: Caused by uneven heating of the Earth, winds are themselves a form of solar energy. Windmills have been long used for wind power; recent models are often arranged in banks on wind-swept high ground or situated off coastlines. Wind-power figures are given in the table (*right*). Wind power contributes over 30% of all electricity generated in Denmark.

Tidal: The energy from tides is potentially enormous, although only a few installations have so far been built to exploit it. In theory, at least, waves and currents could also provide almost unimaginable power, and the thermal differences in the ocean depths are another huge well of potential energy. But work on extracting it is still at the experimental stage.

Geothermal: The Earth's temperature rises by 1°F for every 50 feet descent, with much steeper temperature gradients in geologically active areas. El Salvador, for example, produces 25% of its electricity from geothermal power stations, whilst the USA is the world's leading producer. Some of the oldest and most successful applications are in Iceland, where 87% of all households are heated by geothermal energy.

Biomass: The oldest of human fuels ranges from animal dung, still burned in cooking fires in much of North Africa and elsewhere, to sugarcane plantations feeding high-technology distilleries to produce ethanol for motor-vehicle engines. In Brazil and South Africa, plant ethanol provides up to 25% of motor fuel. Throughout the developing world, most biomass energy comes from firewood: although accurate figures are impossible to obtain, it may yield as much as 10% of the world's total energy consumption.

WIND POWER

World wind energy generating capacity, in megawatts

Year	MW
1996	6,115
1998	9,600
2000	17,800
2002	31,000
2003	39,300
2004	47,671
2005	58,982
2006	74,151
2007	93,927
2008	121,188
2009	157,899
2010	196,653
2011	238,035
2012	282,482
2013	318,105
2014	370,000
2015	434,856
2016	486,661
2017	540,000
2018	597,000

For more information:
74 Geology
101 Globalization

The use of metals played a vital part in the evolving technologies of early peoples. Copper first came into use around 10,000 years ago, bronze about 5,000 years ago, and iron 3,300 years ago. In the early stages of the Industrial Revolution, the location of coal, iron ore, and water power usually determined the location of new industries. But due to continuing improvements in transport, including oil pipelines, industries can now be located almost anywhere.

Minerals are distributed unevenly and some industrial countries, lacking their own mineral resources, import most of the raw materials they need. Some imports come from mineral-rich countries, such as Australia, but others come from developing countries, especially in Africa and South America. Most developing countries export unprocessed ores, losing out on the higher revenues gained from exporting metals.

Most minerals come from land deposits, because undersea deposits, with the exception of oil reserves under the continental shelves, have been inaccessible. But shortages of terrestrial minerals may one day encourage exploitation of the ocean floor.

► Bingham Canyon Mine in Utah, USA, is one of the largest open-pit mines in the world. It measures over 2.5 miles [4 km] wide and 3,900 ft [1,200 m] deep. Copper-containing rocks are excavated from the surface downward in terraces. These terraces are 50–80 ft [15–25 m] high and provide access for equipment to work the rock face whilst maintaining stability of the sloping pit walls.

Today's copper market is booming due to global demands from construction, telecommunications, and electronics companies. Over 17 million tonnes of copper have been mined from Bingham Canyon Mine to date, as well as gold, silver and other minerals.

URANIUM

Uranium was first discovered by the German chemist Martin Klaproth in 1789. In its pure state, uranium is an immensely heavy, white metal. Its main use is as a fuel in nuclear reactors and in nuclear weaponry, although depleted uranium is employed as a projectile in anti-missile cannons, where its mass ensures a lethal punch.

Uranium is very scarce: the main source is the rare ore pitchblende, which itself contains only 0.2% uranium oxide. This blackish, lustrous ore occurs in quartz veins. Only a minute fraction of that is the radioactive U^{235} isotope, though so-called breeder reactors can transmute the more common U^{238} into highly radioactive plutonium.

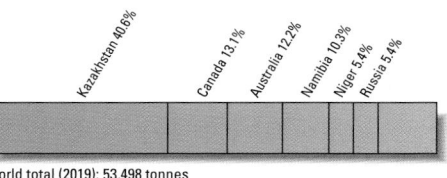

World total (2019): 53,498 tonnes

DIAMOND

Most of the world's diamond is found in kimberlite, or "blue ground," a basic igneous rock; erosion may wash the diamond from its kimberlite matrix and deposit it with sand or gravel on river beds. Only a small proportion of the world's diamond, the most flawless, is cut into gemstones – "diamonds"; most are used in industry, where the material's remarkable hardness and abrasion resistance finds a use in cutting tools, drills, and dies. In 2018, the world's major producers were Russia (30.2%), Australia (27.0%), the Democratic Republic of the Congo (23.8%), Botswana (11.1%), South Africa (3.2%), and Zimbabwe (3.2%). Natural diamonds now account for about 3% of all industrial diamond output. Synthetic diamond production in centers such as China, Ireland, Japan, Russia, and the USA far exceeds it.

BLOOD DIAMONDS

Blood Diamonds, or "Conflict Diamonds," are stones that are produced in areas controlled by rebel forces that are opposed to internationally recognized governments. The rebels sell these diamonds, using the money to purchase arms or to fund their military actions. These diamonds are often the main source of funding for the rebels – however, arms merchants, smugglers, and dishonest diamond traders facilitate their actions.

The flow of Blood Diamonds originated mainly from Sierra Leone, Angola, Democratic Republic of Congo, Liberia, and Côte d'Ivoire. In 2003, the United Nations and other groups introduced a certification procedure known as the "Kimberley Process," to try to eradicate this practice. This procedure requires each nation to certify that all rough diamond exports are produced through legitimate mining and sales activity.

Over 80 countries participate in the agreement.

Aluminum: Produced mainly from its oxide, bauxite, which yields 25% of its weight in aluminum. The cost of refining and production is often too high for producer-countries to bear, so bauxite is largely exported. Lightweight and corrosion resistant, aluminum alloys are widely used in aircraft, vehicles, cans, and packaging.

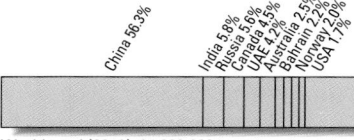

World total (2019): 64,000,000 tonnes

Lead: A soft metal, obtained mainly from galena (lead sulfide), which occurs in veins associated with iron, zinc, and silver sulfides. Its use in vehicle batteries accounts for the USA's prime consumer status; lead is also made into sheeting and piping. Its use as an additive to paints and petrol is decreasing.

World total (2019): 4,500,000 tonnes

Tin: Soft, pliable and non-toxic, used to coat "tin" (tin-plated steel) cans, in the manufacture of foils and in alloys. The principal tin-bearing mineral is cassiterite (SnO_2), found in ore formed from molten rock.

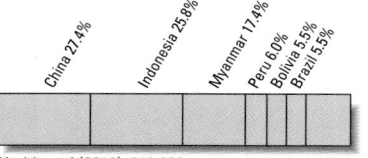

World total (2019): 310,000 tonnes

Gold: Regarded for centuries as the most valuable metal in the world and used to make coins, gold is still recognized as the monetary standard. A soft metal, it is alloyed to make jewelry; the electronics industry values its corrosion resistance and conductivity.

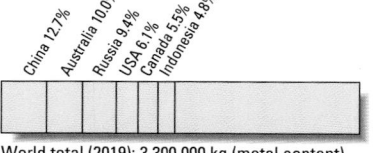

World total (2019): 3,300,000 kg (metal content)

Copper: Derived from low-yielding sulfide ores, copper is an important export for several developing countries. An excellent conductor of heat and electricity, it forms part of most electrical items, and is used in the manufacture of brass and bronze. Major importers include Japan and Germany.

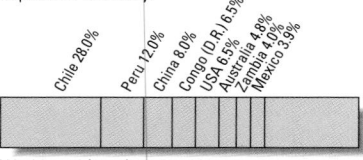

World total (2019): 20,000,000 tonnes

Mercury: The only metal that is liquid at normal temperatures, most is derived from its sulfide, cinnabar, found only in small quantities in volcanic areas. Apart from its value in thermometers and other instruments, most mercury production is used in anti-fungal and anti-fouling preparations, and to make detonators.

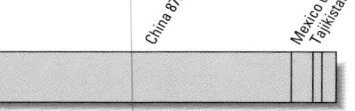

World total (2019): 4,000,000 tonnes (metal content)

Zinc: Often found in association with lead ores, zinc is highly resistant to corrosion, and about 40% of the refined metal is used to plate sheet steel, particularly vehicle bodies – a process known as galvanizing. Zinc is also used in dry batteries, paints, and dyes.

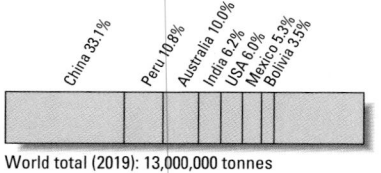

World total (2019): 13,000,000 tonnes

Silver: Most silver comes from ores mined and processed for other metals (including lead and copper). Pure or alloyed with harder metals, it is used for jewelry and ornaments. Industrial use includes dentistry, electronics, photography, and as a chemical catalyst.

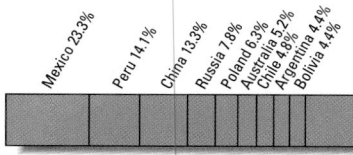

World total (2019): 27,000 tonnes (metal content)

DISTRIBUTION OF MINERALS

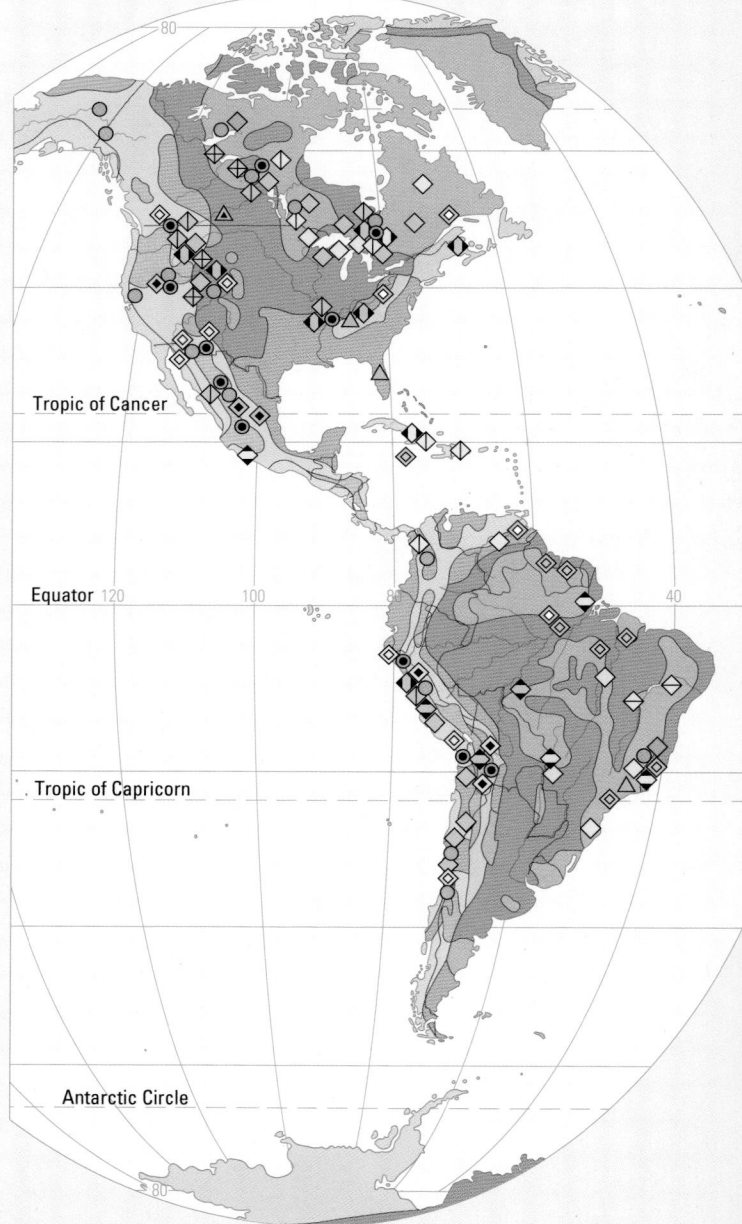

Tropic of Cancer

Equator

Tropic of Capricorn

Antarctic Circle

IRON ORE

Ever since the art of high-temperature smelting was discovered, some time in the second millennium BC, iron has been by far the most important metal known to man. The earliest iron plows transformed primitive agriculture and led to the first human population explosion, while iron weapons – or the lack of them – ensured the rise or fall of entire cultures.

Widely distributed around the world, iron ores usually contain 25–60% iron; blast furnaces process the raw product into pig-iron, which is then alloyed with carbon and other minerals to produce steels of various qualities. From the time of the Industrial Revolution, steel has been almost literally the backbone of modern civilization, the prime structural material on which all else is built.

Iron smelting usually developed close to the sources of ore and, later, to the coalfields that fueled the furnaces. Today, most ore comes from a few richly-endowed locations where large-scale mining is possible.

Iron and steel plants are generally built at coastal sites so that giant ore carriers, which account for a sizable proportion of the world's merchant fleet, can more easily discharge their cargoes.

World production of pig-iron (2019)

**Total world production:
1,300 million tonnes**

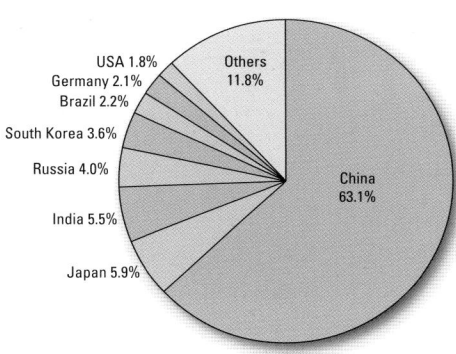

- Others 11.8%
- USA 1.8%
- Germany 2.1%
- Brazil 2.2%
- South Korea 3.6%
- Russia 4.0%
- India 5.5%
- Japan 5.9%
- China 63.1%

Iron ore

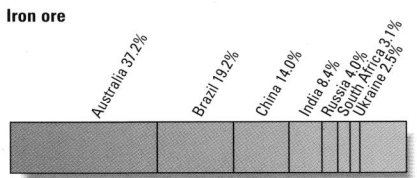

- Australia 37.7%
- Brazil 19.2%
- China 14.0%
- India 8.4%
- Russia 4.0%
- South Africa 3.1%
- Ukraine 2.5%

World total (2019): 2,500,000 tonnes

RARE EARTHS

Rare earth elements, or rare earth metals, are a set of 17 chemical elements, specifically the 15 lanthanides plus scandium and yttrium. Despite their name, rare earth elements are relatively plentiful, but are typically dispersed and not often found concentrated in economically exploitable ore deposits.

Until 1948, most of the world's rare earths were sourced from sand deposits in India and Brazil. Between the 1960s and the 1980s, the leading producer was California, USA. Today, China produces over 90% of the world's rare earth supply, although it only has less than 23% of proven reserves. The US Geological Survey is currently actively surveying southern Afghanistan for rare earth deposits under the protection of US military forces.

New demand has recently strained supply, and there is a growing concern that the world may soon face a shortage of the rare earths. In recent years, China has reduced its export quotas and halted production in some of its mines in order to conserve scarce resources and protect the environment.

A recently developed source of rare earths is electronic waste, and other wastes have rare earth components. Advances in recycling technology have made extraction of rare earths from these materials more feasible.

Rare earths are used as follows:

- **Neodymium** To make powerful magnets in loudspeakers and computer hard drives; also used in wind turbines and hybrid cars.
- **Lanthanum** In camera and telescope lenses.
- **Cerium** In catalytic converters in cars, and in the refining of oil.
- **Praseodymium** As an alloy, to create strong metals in aircraft engines.
- **Gadolinium** For X-ray machines, MRI scanning systems, and television screens.
- **Yttrium, terbium, europium** For television and computer screens, and for visual display units.

SCRAP METAL

Scrap metal has been an important source material for the manufacturing industry in domestic markets for decades, its value fluctuating according to the state of the local economy. Recently, however, with growing concern for the global environment and the rapid development of the economies in the Far East, the industry has become far more globalized. Container loads of processed-metal scrap from time-expired machinery in the Western world are now being exported to the Far East to be recycled. Processed-steel scrap accounts for almost half of the requirements for "furnace feed" for the world's steelmakers, and 40% of the world's copper requirements are derived from scrap.

Two major advantages of using scrap rather than refining mined ore are the energy and raw material savings that can be made. If 1 tonne of steel scrap is recycled, it saves 120 lb [54 kg] of limestone, 2,500 lb [1,130 kg] of iron ore and 1,400 lb [635 kg] of coal, with a consequent 86% reduction in air pollution, 40% saving in water use, and 76% reduction in water pollution. Huge energy savings, with consequent cuts in greenhouse-gas emissions, can also be made by using scrap.

As well as bulk minerals, such as those quoted above, alloys using nickel, chromium, tungsten, molybdenum, cobalt, and titanium, which are often only available in limited supplies and are expensive to produce, can also be recycled. The techniques involved to do this work are often very sophisticated, involving X-ray spectrometry and other computer-controlled methods, in order to recover high-value but low-volume metals from devices such as computers and televisions.

With companies having to take increased responsibility for their products, from manufacturing to sale and thence to their ultimate disposal at the end of their useful life, recycling scrap metals will become a much more important method of conserving the world's raw materials and preserving the environment in the future.

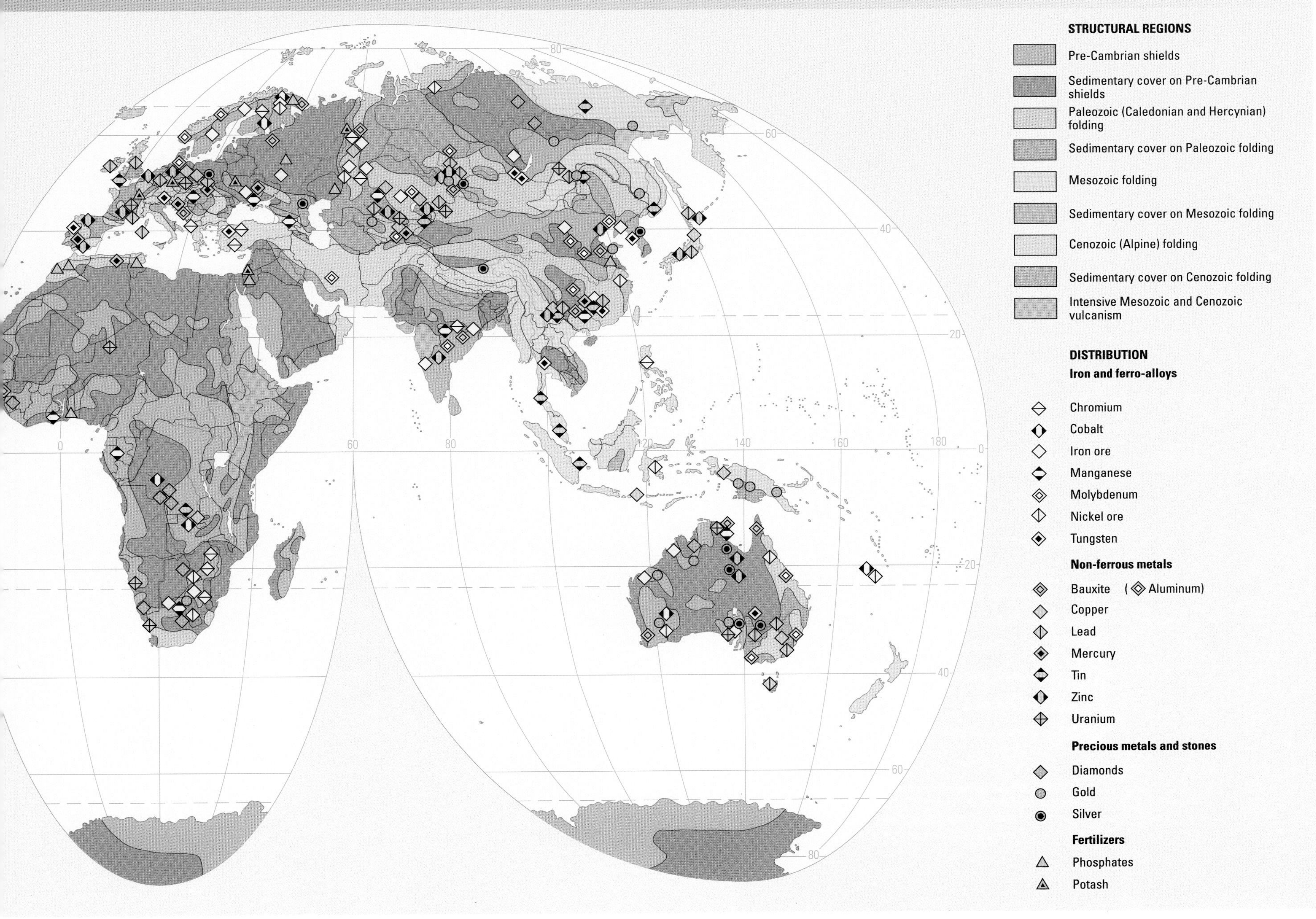

STRUCTURAL REGIONS

- Pre-Cambrian shields
- Sedimentary cover on Pre-Cambrian shields
- Paleozoic (Caledonian and Hercynian) folding
- Sedimentary cover on Paleozoic folding
- Mesozoic folding
- Sedimentary cover on Mesozoic folding
- Cenozoic (Alpine) folding
- Sedimentary cover on Cenozoic folding
- Intensive Mesozoic and Cenozoic vulcanism

DISTRIBUTION

Iron and ferro-alloys

- Chromium
- Cobalt
- Iron ore
- Manganese
- Molybdenum
- Nickel ore
- Tungsten

Non-ferrous metals

- Bauxite (Aluminum)
- Copper
- Lead
- Mercury
- Tin
- Zinc
- Uranium

Precious metals and stones

- Diamonds
- Gold
- Silver

Fertilizers

- Phosphates
- Potash

The Industrial Revolution, which began in Britain in the late 18th century, represented a major technological advance in the evolution of human society. It enabled a group of countries to become prosperous by replacing expensive human labor with increasingly sophisticated machinery. In economic terms, manufacturing is the transformation of raw materials, energy, labor, and machines into finished goods, which have a higher value than the various elements used in production.

The economies of countries can be compared by reference to their per capita Gross Domestic Products (GDPs), namely, the total value of goods and services produced within a country in a year, divided by the population. If this is calculated using Purchasing Power Parity (PPP) exchange rates, it better reflects the real state of the economy by taking into account differences in price levels in each country. The industrialized, or developed, countries accounted for 15% of the world's population in 2018 with an average per capita GDP of over US $45,000. On the other hand, low-income developing countries, with small industrial sectors, accounted for 77% of the world's population. Their per capita GDPs can be as low as $400.

Tanzania, with its low-income economy, had a per capita GDP in 2018 of US $3,200. Agriculture employs 80% of the people, while light industry together with services employs 20%. By contrast, Germany had a per capita GDP in 2018 of $53,000. Agriculture employs only 2% of the population, with 25% in industry and 74% in services. Germany's industrial sector differs greatly from Tanzania's, with its emphasis on vehicles, machinery, chemicals, and electronics.

Since the 1970s, some former developing countries in eastern Asia achieved rapid economic growth through industrialization. Despite setbacks in the late 1990s, they demonstrated that a developing industrial sector can transform an economy, which starts off with certain advantages, such as low labor costs. But economic success also depends on such factors as education to provide skills, and regulations that attract foreign investors. China, whose economy grew by more than 10% per year between 2002 and 2012, satisfies many of these criteria, though its record on human rights leaves much to be desired.

EMPLOYMENT

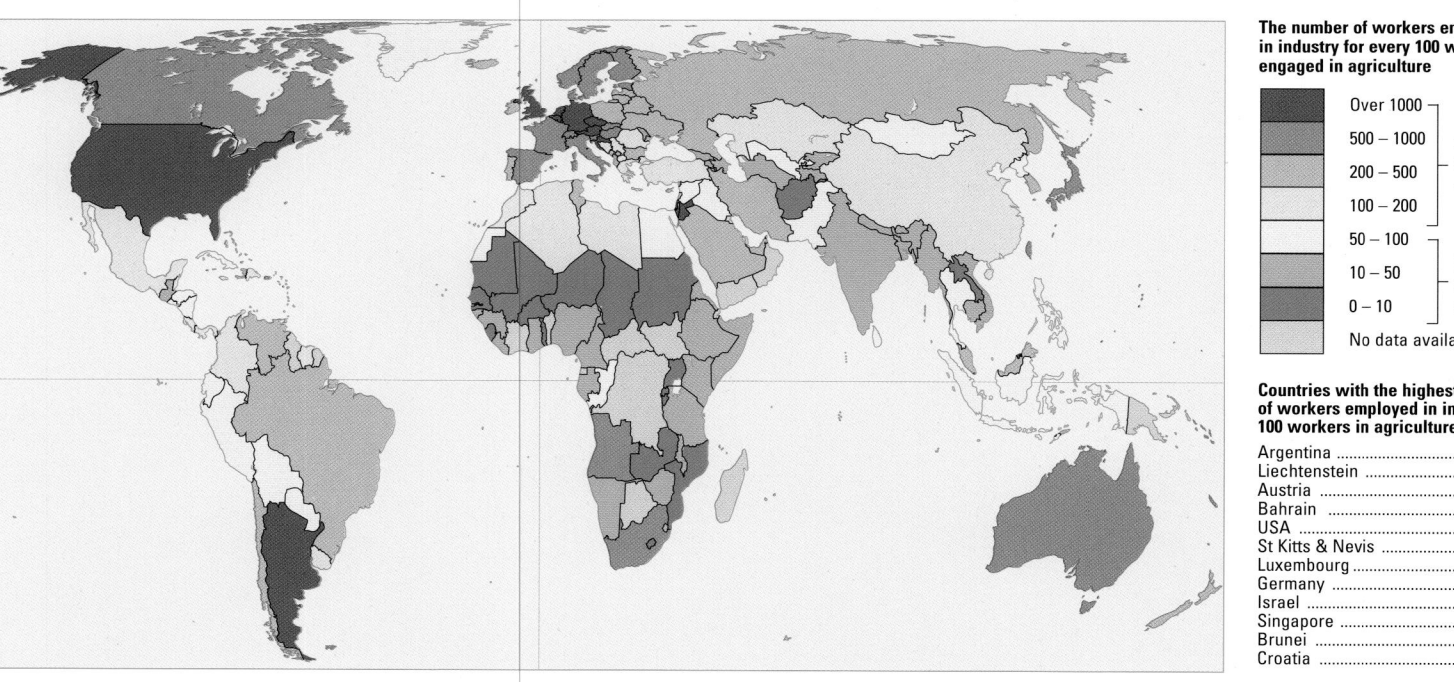

The number of workers employed in industry for every 100 workers engaged in agriculture

- Over 1000
- 500 – 1000 } Mainly industrial countries
- 200 – 500
- 100 – 200
- 50 – 100 } Mainly agricultural countries
- 10 – 50
- 0 – 10
- No data available

Countries with the highest number of workers employed in industry per 100 workers in agriculture

Argentina	4,960
Liechtenstein	4,613
Austria	3,614
Bahrain	3,200
USA	2,900
St Kitts & Nevis	2,727
Luxembourg	1,818
Germany	1,729
Israel	1,573
Singapore	1,550
Brunei	1,495
Croatia	1,453

DIVISION OF EMPLOYMENT

Distribution of workers between agriculture, industry and services, selected countries

The six countries selected illustrate the usual stages of economic development, from dependence on agriculture through industrial growth to the expansion of the service sector.

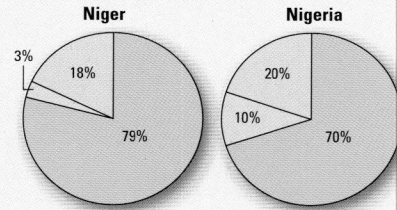
Niger
3%
18%
79%

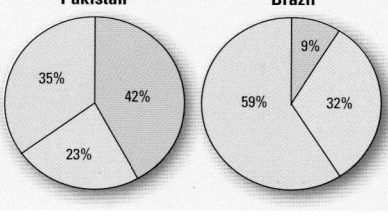
Nigeria
20%
10%
70%

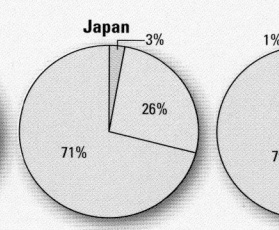
Pakistan
35%
42%
23%

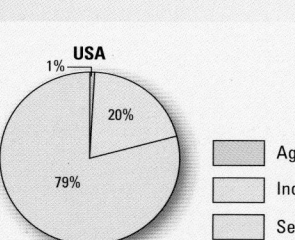
Brazil
9%
59%
32%

Japan
3%
26%
71%

USA
1%
20%
79%

- Agriculture
- Industry
- Services

WORLD TRADE

Percentage share of total world exports by value (2019)

- Over 10% of world trade
- 1 – 10% of world trade
- 0.1 – 1.0% of world trade
- 0 – 0.1% of world trade
- No world trade
- No data available

International trade is dominated by a handful of powerful maritime nations: the members of "G7" (Canada, France, Germany, Italy, Japan, UK and USA) and the "BRICS" nations (Brazil, Russia, India, China, and South Africa).

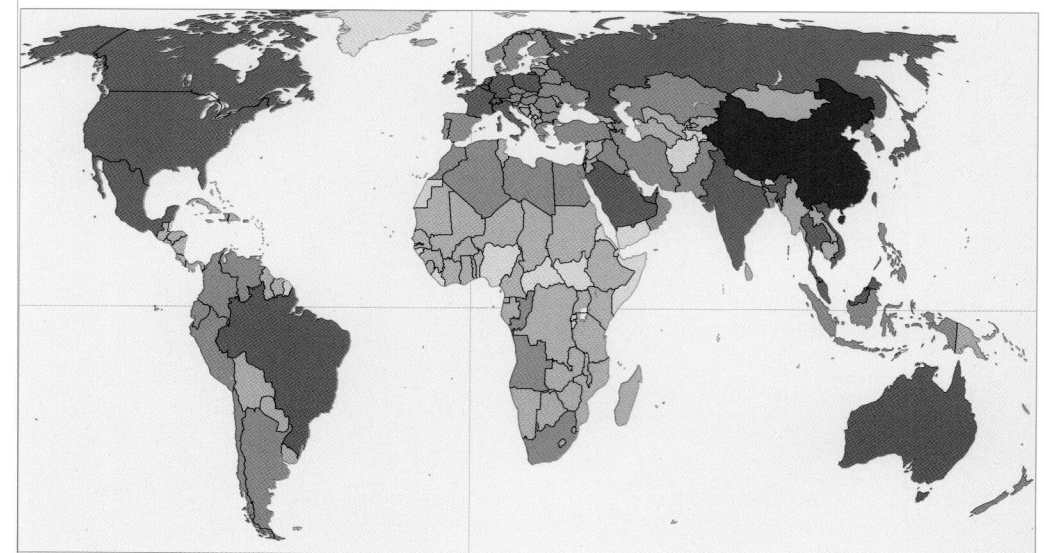

INDUSTRY AND TRADE

Manufactured goods (including machinery and transport) as a percentage of total exports (2018)

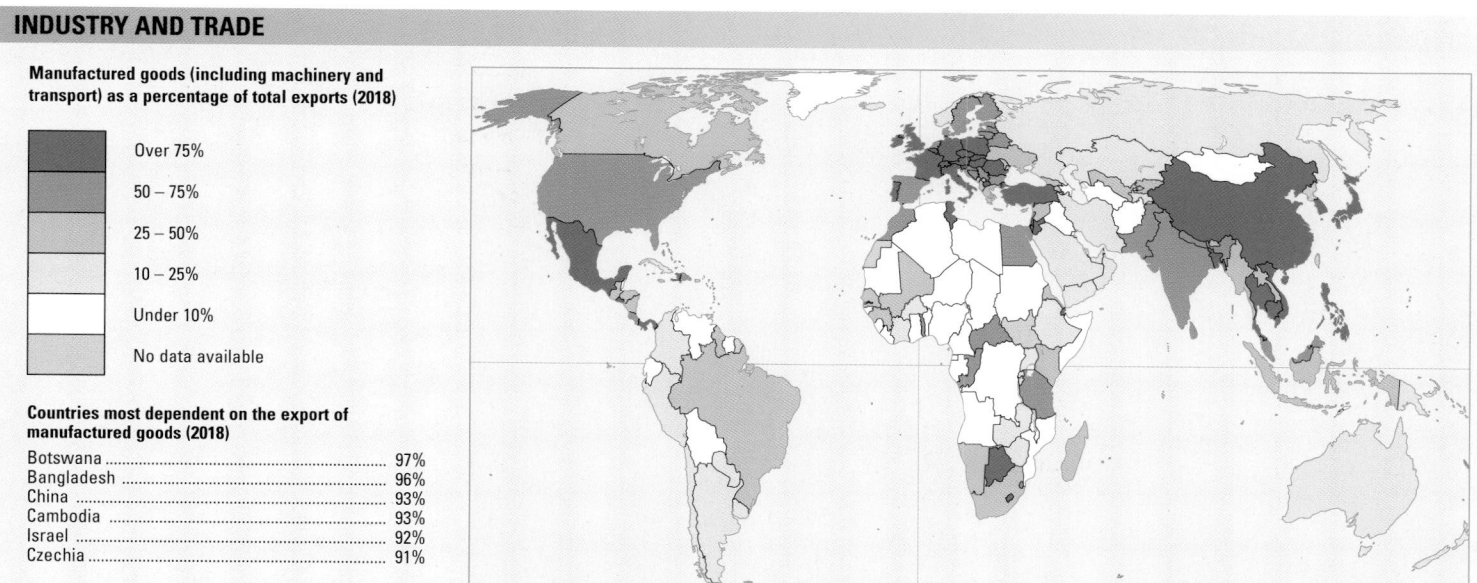

	Over 75%
	50 – 75%
	25 – 50%
	10 – 25%
	Under 10%
	No data available

Countries most dependent on the export of manufactured goods (2018)

Botswana	97%
Bangladesh	96%
China	93%
Cambodia	93%
Israel	92%
Czechia	91%

UNEMPLOYMENT

Highest rates of unemployment, percentage of the labor force (2019)

1.	Burkina Faso	77%
2.	Syria	50%
3.	Senegal	48%
4.	Haiti	41%
5.	Kenya	40%
6.	Djibouti	40%
7.	Namibia	34%
8.	Venezuela	33%
9.	Kiribati	31%
10.	Libya	30%
11.	South Africa	29%
12.	Kosovo	29%
13.	Lesotho	28%
14.	Gabon	28%
15.	Eswatini	28%
16.	Yemen	27%
17.	Mozambique	25%
18.	Grenada	24%
19.	Afghanistan	24%
20.	Nauru	23%

IMPORTANCE OF SERVICE SECTOR

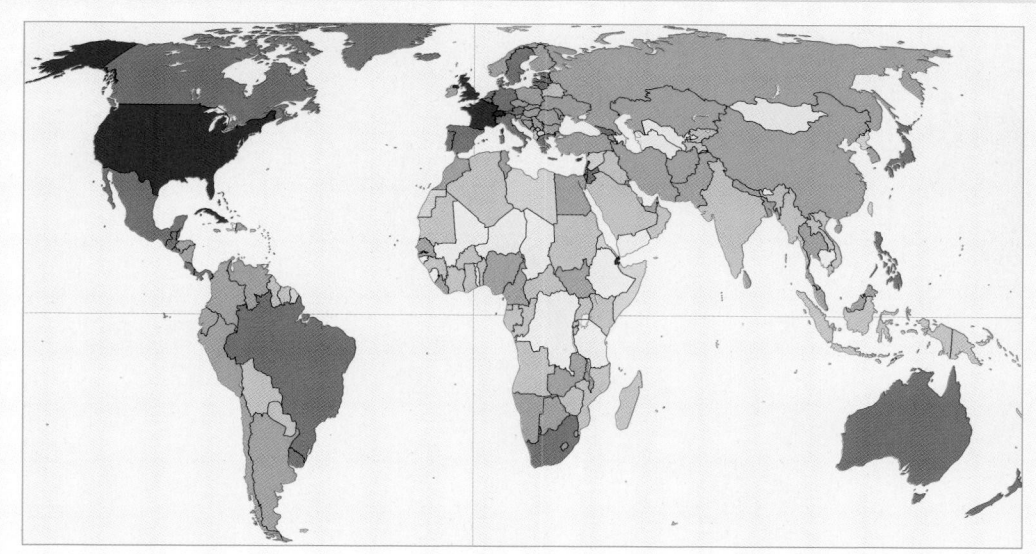

Percentage of total GDP from service sector (2019)

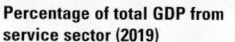
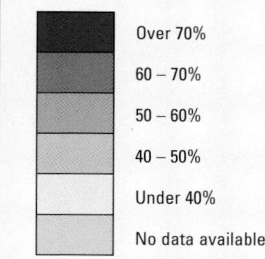

	Over 70%
	60 – 70%
	50 – 60%
	40 – 50%
	Under 40%
	No data available

The service sector involves those parts of business such as accountancy, advertising, financial services, tourism, etc. No actual goods are produced, but high levels of income may be generated.

GLOBALIZATION

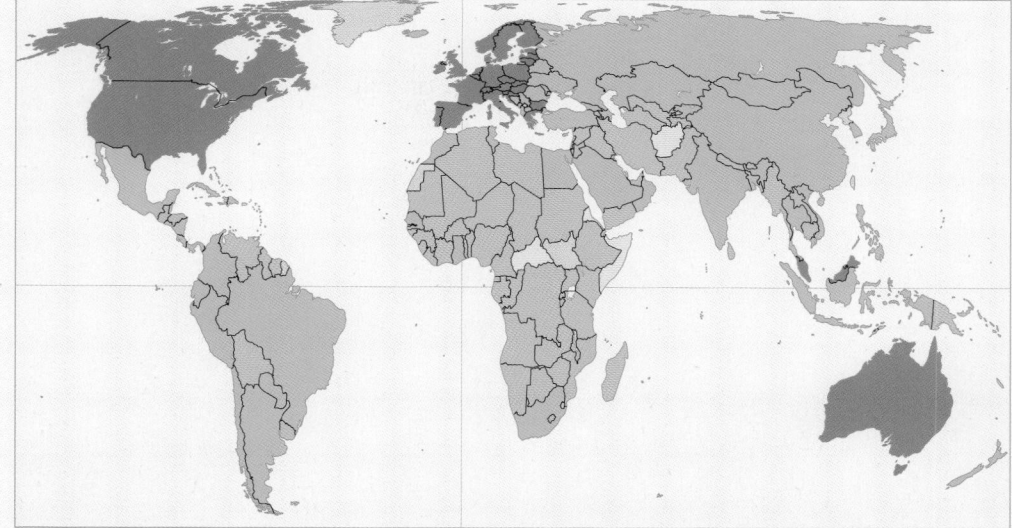

GLOBALIZATION INDEX
2019 KOF Globalization Index
(Rankings for 2017)

	Over 80
	60 – 80
	40 – 60
	20 – 40
	No data available

The KOF index of globalization is named after the Swiss Federal Institute of Technology in Zürich, Switzerland, which devised it. Countries are scored on each of the three criteria below:

- **economic globalization**, characterized as long-distance flows of goods, capital and services, as well as information and perceptions that accompany market exchanges (this accounts for 38% of the globalization index);
- **political globalization**, characterized by a diffusion of government policies (this accounts for 23% of the globalization index);
- **social globalization**, expressed as the spread of ideas, information, images, and people (this accounts for the remaining 39% of the globalization index).

The higher values denote a greater level of globalization.

The concept of globalization developed in the 1960s after the Canadian academic Marshall McLuhan used the term "global village" to describe the breakdown of spatial barriers around the world. He argued that the similarities between places were greater than the differences between them, and that much of the world had been caught up in the same economic and social processes. He suggested that economic activities operated at a global scale and that other scales were becoming less important.

Today, globalization is defined by the International Monetary Fund (IMF) as "the growing interdependence of countries worldwide through the increasing volume and variety of cross-border transactions in goods and services and of international capital flows, and through the more rapid and widespread diffusion of technology." Essentially, it means that all countries, with the possible exception of North Korea, are increasingly bound in a global network of migration, trade, products and services, investment, and the diffusion of ideas and culture.

Globalization has occurred as a result of many factors, such as:
- improvements in transport and ICT, leading to a "shrinking" world;
- the desire to reach new markets;
- the attempt to tap cheap sources of labor;
- the expansion of economic activity to use resources from a wide range of locations;
- the rise of free-market economies and the spread of democratic governments;
- the role of trading blocs, free trade, and the impact of the World Trade Organization;
- the importance of multinational companies.

Tourism and travel is one of the world's largest economic sectors in terms of revenue generated. It has the potential to create prosperity in all parts of the world. Small economies in attractive areas are often completely dominated by tourism: in some Caribbean islands, for example, tourist spending provides over 90% of the total income and is the biggest foreign-exchange earner.

In 2019, the World Trade and Tourism Council reported that this sector, directly and indirectly, provided over 330 million jobs. This equates to 1 in 10 jobs around the world and this is predicted to grow in the coming years. In terms of the economic impact, the industry contributed 10.3% to global GDP in 2019 (US$8.9 trillion).

Increasingly, attention is being paid to the development potential of tourism in less developed countries. The United Nations General Assembly declared 2017 as the International Year of Sustainable Tourism for Development. This has the aim of raising awareness of the potential for economic growth, social inclusion and the preservation of culture and the environment. It is also seen as a contributing factor towards ensuring that tourism is fundamental to the implementation of the 17 UN Sustainable Development Goals (see page 107).

Even with new initiatives, challenges lie ahead. The Coronavirus pandemic of 2020 will have significant consequences.

AIR TRAVEL

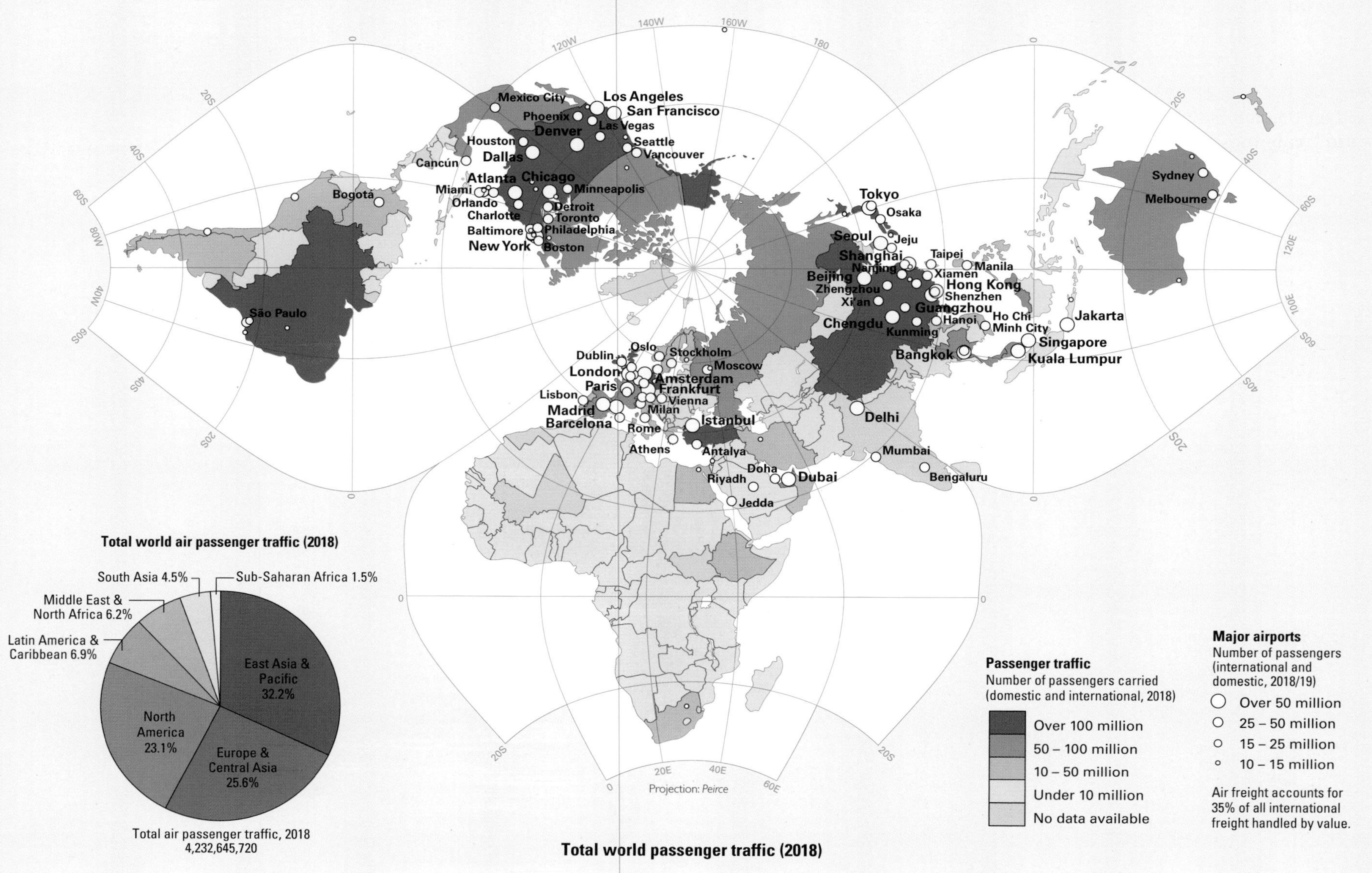

Total world air passenger traffic (2018)

- South Asia 4.5%
- Sub-Saharan Africa 1.5%
- Middle East & North Africa 6.2%
- Latin America & Caribbean 6.9%
- East Asia & Pacific 32.2%
- North America 23.1%
- Europe & Central Asia 25.6%

Total air passenger traffic, 2018
4,232,645,720

Total world passenger traffic (2018)

Projection: Peirce

Passenger traffic
Number of passengers carried (domestic and international, 2018)

- Over 100 million
- 50 – 100 million
- 10 – 50 million
- Under 10 million
- No data available

Major airports
Number of passengers (international and domestic, 2018/19)

- Over 50 million
- 25 – 50 million
- 15 – 25 million
- 10 – 15 million

Air freight accounts for 35% of all international freight handled by value.

MAJOR AIRPORTS

WORLD'S BUSIEST AIRPORTS
Total passengers in millions (2019)

1. Atlanta Hartsfield Intl. (ATL) 110.5
2. Beijing Capital Intl. (PEK) 100.0
3. Los Angeles Intl. (LAX) 88.1
4. Tokyo Haneda (HND) 87.1
5. Dubai Intl. (DXB) 86.4
6. Chicago O'Hare Intl. (ORD)..............84.4
7. London Heathrow (LHR) 80.8
8. Shanghai Pudong Intl. (PVG) 76.2
9. Paris Charles de Gaulle (CDG) 76.2
10. Dallas/Fort Worth (DFW) 75.1
11. Guangzhou Baiyun (CAN)................73.4
12. Amsterdam Schiphol (AMS)............71.7
13. Hong Kong Intl. (HKG) 71.5
14. Frankfurt (FRA) 70.6
15. Denver (DEN)....................................69.9

Dubai International handles the most international passengers (88.9 million in 2018), followed by London's Heathrow (75.3 million).

▲ Hartsfield-Jackson Atlanta International Airport, Georgia, USA, is the world's busiest airport.

IMPORTANCE OF TOURISM

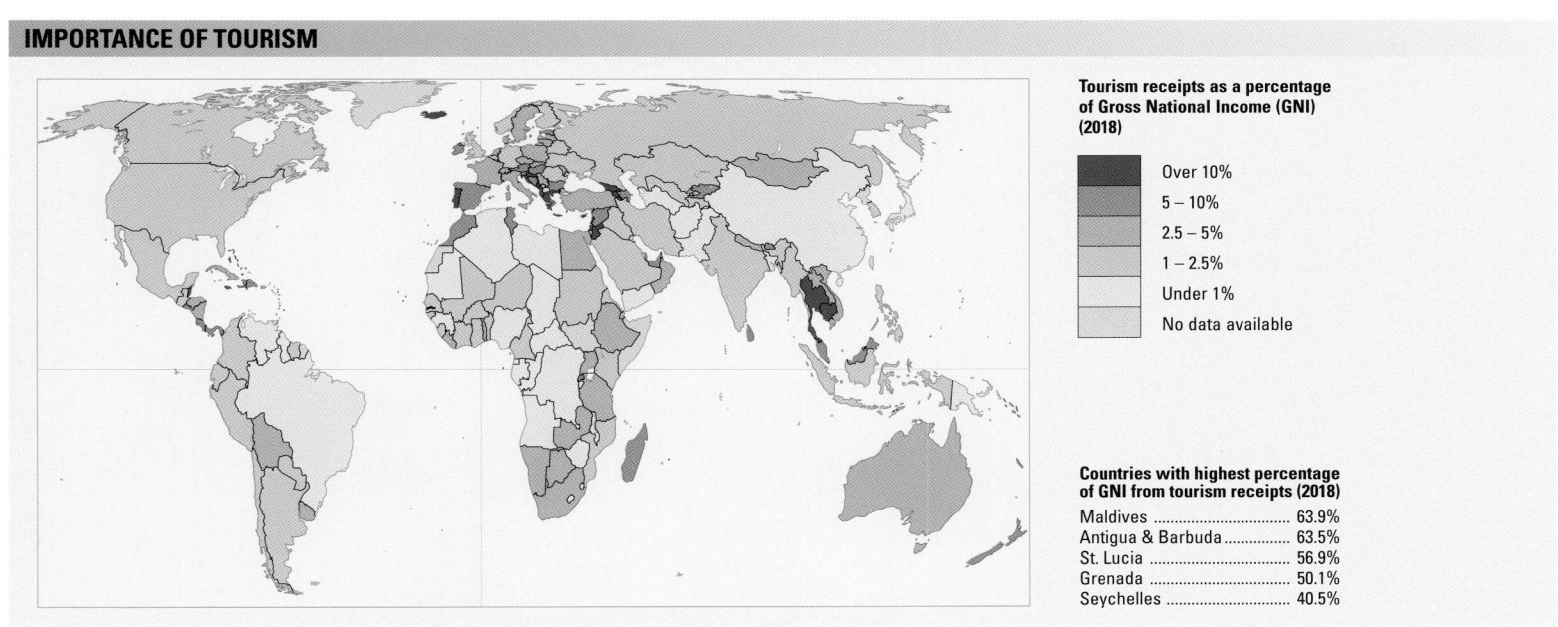

Tourism receipts as a percentage of Gross National Income (GNI) (2018)

- Over 10%
- 5 – 10%
- 2.5 – 5%
- 1 – 2.5%
- Under 1%
- No data available

Countries with highest percentage of GNI from tourism receipts (2018)

Maldives	63.9%
Antigua & Barbuda	63.5%
St. Lucia	56.9%
Grenada	50.1%
Seychelles	40.5%

TOURIST DESTINATIONS

UNESCO WORLD HERITAGE SITES 2019
Total sites = 1,121 (869 cultural, 209 natural and 39 mixed)

Region	Cultural sites	Natural sites	Mixed sites
Africa	53	38	5
Arab States	78	5	3
Asia & Pacific	189	67	12
Europe & North America	453	65	11
Latin America & Caribbean	96	38	8

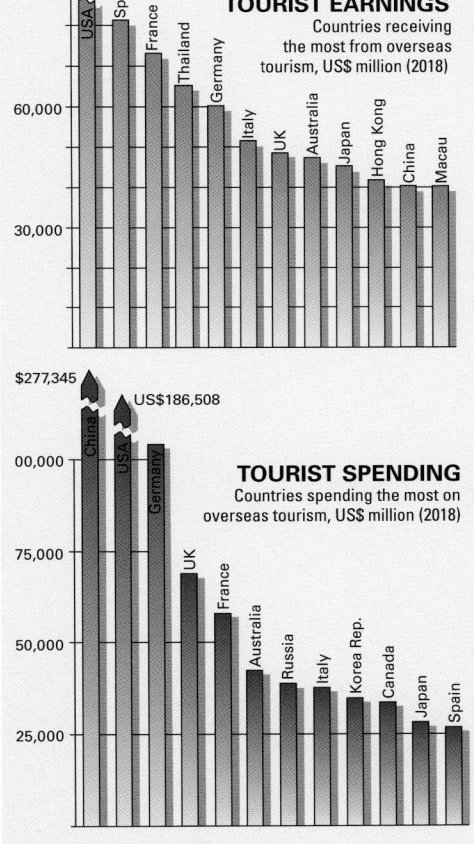

TOURIST EARNINGS
Countries receiving the most from overseas tourism, US$ million (2018)

TOURIST SPENDING
Countries spending the most on overseas tourism, US$ million (2018)

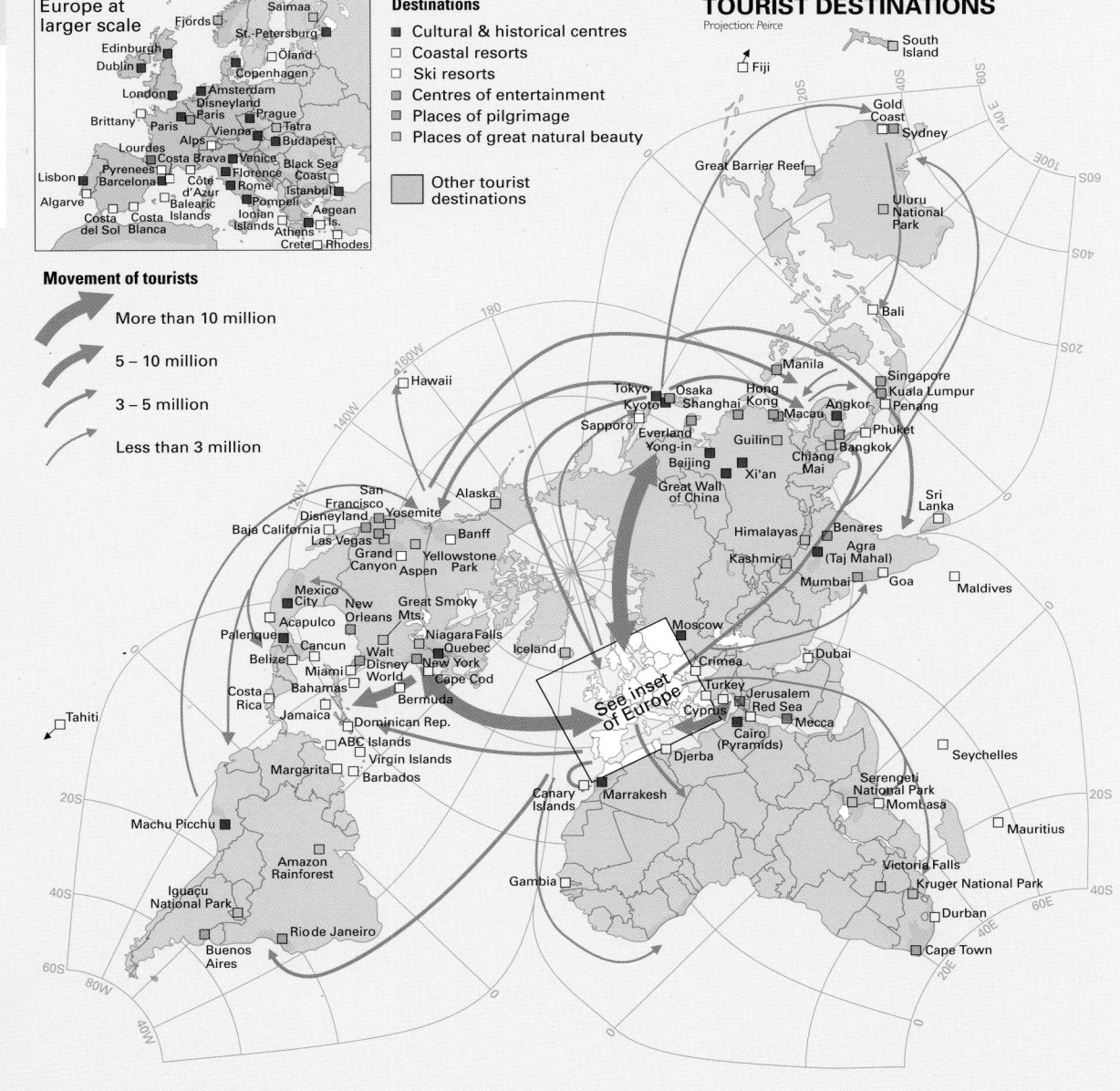

Destinations
- Cultural & historical centres
- Coastal resorts
- Ski resorts
- Centres of entertainment
- Places of pilgrimage
- Places of great natural beauty

Other tourist destinations

TOURIST DESTINATIONS
Projection: Peirce

Movement of tourists
- More than 10 million
- 5 – 10 million
- 3 – 5 million
- Less than 3 million

World's top tourism destinations
The UNWTO (United Nations World Tourism Organization) ranks countries by international tourism receipts (see top bar chart above) and international tourist arrivals (see table right). The USA continues to top the international tourism receipts ranking (214,500 million US$ in 2018) with Spain in second place. France has remained at the top of the list of main destinations for several years, with Spain rising to second place in 2017. In 2018, France recorded 89 million visitors and it is ranked third in terms of tourism earnings.

International tourist arrivals

		millions (2018)
1.	France	89.4
2.	Spain	82.8
3.	United States of America	79.6
4.	China	62.9
5.	Italy	62.1
6.	Turkey	45.8
7.	Mexico	41.4
8.	Germany	38.9
9.	Thailand	38.3
10.	United Kingdom	36.3

Visitors to the USA

		thousands (2018)
1.	Mexico	19,200
2.	Canada	12,300
3.	United Kingdom	4,900
4.	Japan	3,500
5.	China	3,000
6.	South Korea	2,200
7.	Brazil	2,200
8.	Germany	2,100
9.	France	1,800
10.	Australia	1,400

Until the late 1990s, when the full extent of the AIDS crisis emerged, average life expectancies at birth were rising almost everywhere. By 2011, they ranged from 81 years in high-income economies to 56 in sub-Saharan Africa. These figures represented an enormous advance on the situation in 1880, when citizens of Berlin had an estimated life expectancy of 30 years.

The ravages of AIDS have been greatest in southern Africa. One of the worst affected countries is Eswatini, where over 25% of the adult population were thought to be infected in 2009. Life expectancy fell from 61 years in 2000, to 32 years in 2009, but recovered to 58 years in 2020. In much of the world, average life expectancies are still increasing. The rises are attributed to improvements in agriculture and, hence, nutrition, as well as health education, improved sanitation and the quality of drinking water, together with advances in medicine.

Besides AIDS, the people of the developing world are subject to another affliction – malnutrition. The map below shows that in most of Africa, Asia, and Latin America, the average daily calorie supply per person is so low as to cause malnutrition. Malnutrition is a serious condition – among pregnant women it causes high rates of child mortality.

Deficiency diseases occur when people do not have a balanced diet. Protein deficiency causes stunting and kwashiorkor, which can be fatal, especially among young children, while vitamin deficiencies cause such illnesses as beri beri, pellagra, scurvy, and rickets. Iron deficiency causes anemia, while a lack of iodine causes mental retardation.

Infectious diseases, in association with deficient diets, continue to affect people in developing countries. Around the turn of the century, a WHO report stated that infectious diseases cause over 16 million deaths a year. Most of the victims are young and otherwise fit people in developing countries. The major killers are AIDS, cholera, dysentery, malaria, measles, pneumonia, respiratory infections, tuberculosis, and typhoid.

Infectious diseases are much less important as causes of death in developed countries, where cancer and circulatory diseases, such as atherosclerosis and hypertension, which cause strokes and heart attacks, are the most common causes of fatality. Because these diseases tend to kill older people, they are relatively less important in the developing countries where people have shorter lifespans.

Harmful habits are also generally practiced more by the rich than the poor. For example, smoking is an important cause of death in developed countries, while poor diet and high alcohol consumption can badly affect health.

▲ Almost 10% of the world's population does not have access to safe water (see map at the bottom of this page to see the results on mortality by nation). This places a huge strain on the millions of mainly women and children who have to walk, collect, and carry drinkable water in order to survive. UNICEF is dedicated to help improve this situation and to react swiftly in the case of emergencies such as civil war, as with the case of this man in Liberia.

MALNUTRITION

Prevalence of undernourishment as a percentage of the population (2017)

▰	Over 30%
▰	20 – 30%
▰	15 – 20%
▰	10 – 20%
▢	Under 10%
▰	No data available

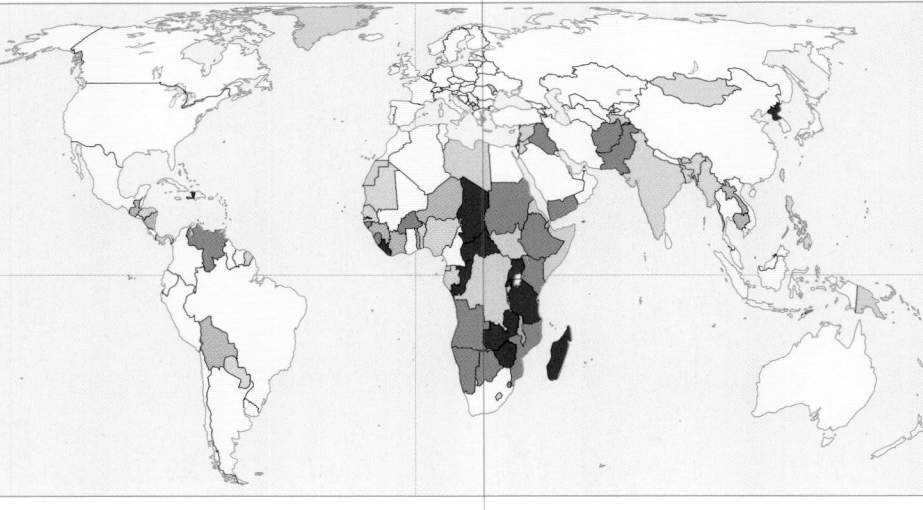

This map highlights the countries where, for a large part of the population, the food intake is insufficient to meet dietary energy requirements.

MATERNAL MORTALITY RATE

The number of mothers who died during pregnancy or childbirth per 100,000 live births (2017)

Countries with highest maternal mortality rate

South Sudan	1,150
Chad	1,140
Sierra Leone	1,120
Nigeria	917
Central African Republic	829
Somalia	829
Mauritania	766
Guinea-Bissau	667
Guyana	667
Liberia	661

The maternal mortality rate is the annual number of female deaths per 100,000 live births from any cause related to or aggravated by pregnancy or its management (excluding accidental or incidental causes).

UNSAFE DRINKING WATER

Mortality rate attributed to unsafe water, deaths per 100,000 people

▰	Over 50
▰	25 – 50
▰	10 – 25
▰	2.5 – 10
▰	1 – 2.5
▢	Under 1
▰	No data available

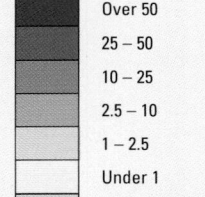

Countries with highest mortality rate (per 100,000 people)

Chad	101
Somalia	87
Central African Republic	82
Sierra Leone	81
Niger	71
Mali	71
Nigeria	69
Burundi	65
Congo (Dem. Rep.)	60
Benin	60

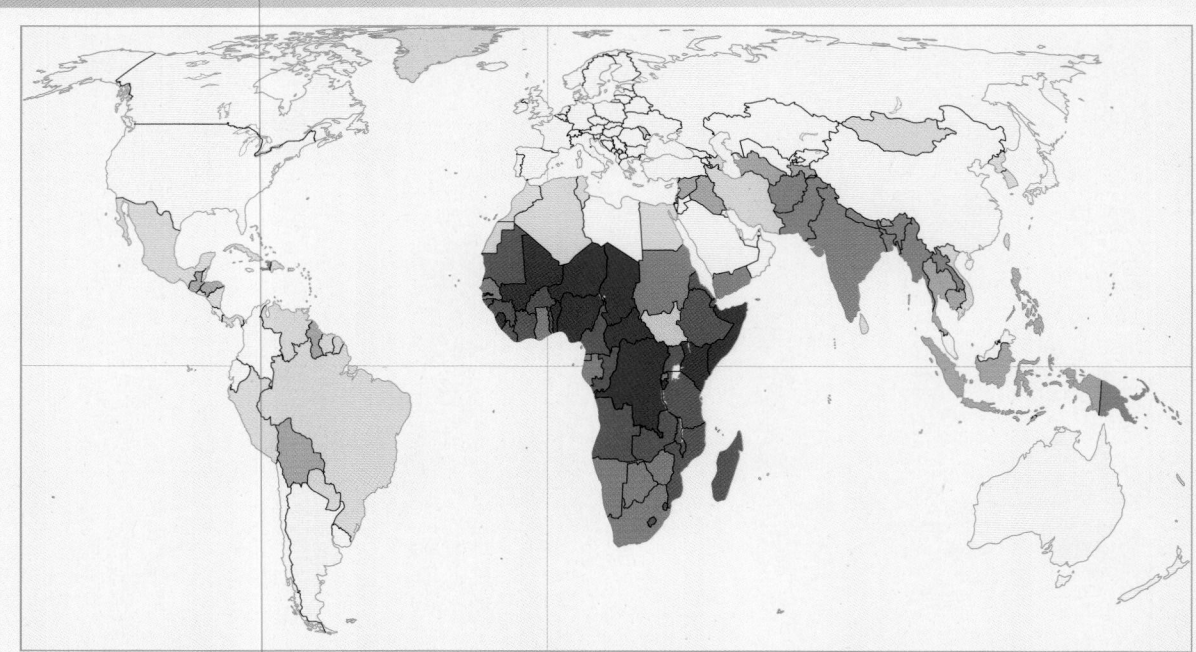

INFANT MORTALITY

Number of babies who died under the age of one, per 1,000 live births (2019)

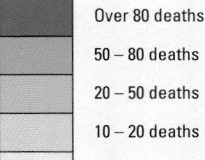

- Over 80 deaths
- 50 – 80 deaths
- 20 – 50 deaths
- 10 – 20 deaths
- Under 10 deaths
- No data available

Highest infant mortality

Afghanistan	104.3 deaths
Somalia	89.5 deaths
Central African Republic	80.6 deaths

Lowest infant mortality

Slovenia	1.7 deaths
Monaco	1.9 deaths
Japan	1.9 deaths

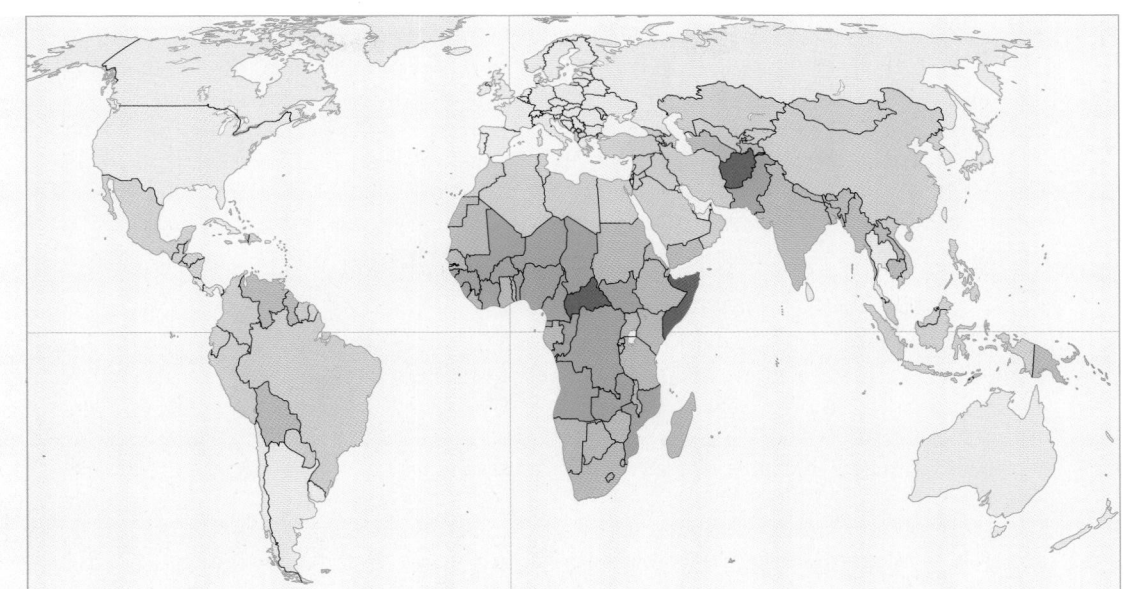

THE AIDS CRISIS

Number of children orphaned due to AIDS (2018)

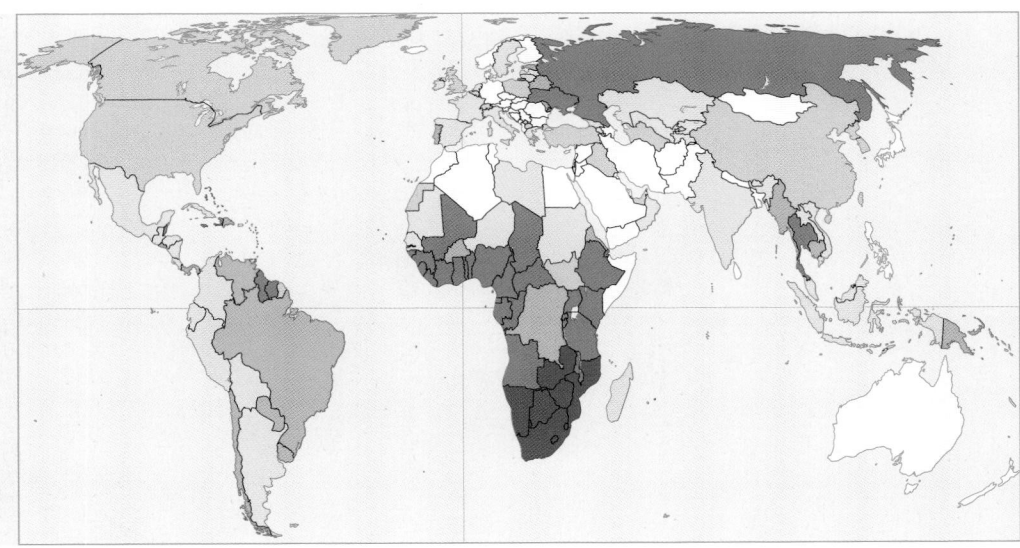

Millions of children

South Africa, Mozambique, Nigeria, Uganda, Tanzania, Kenya, Zimbabwe, Malawi, Cameroon, D. R. Congo

Percentage of adults living with HIV/AIDS (2018)

- Over 10 %
- 1 – 10 %
- 0.5 – 1 %
- 0.2 – 0.5 %
- Under 0.2 %
- No data available

EXPENDITURE ON HEALTH

Government health expenditure as a percentage of general government expenditure (2017)

- Over 20%
- 15 – 20%
- 10 – 15%
- 5 – 10%
- Under 5%
- No data available

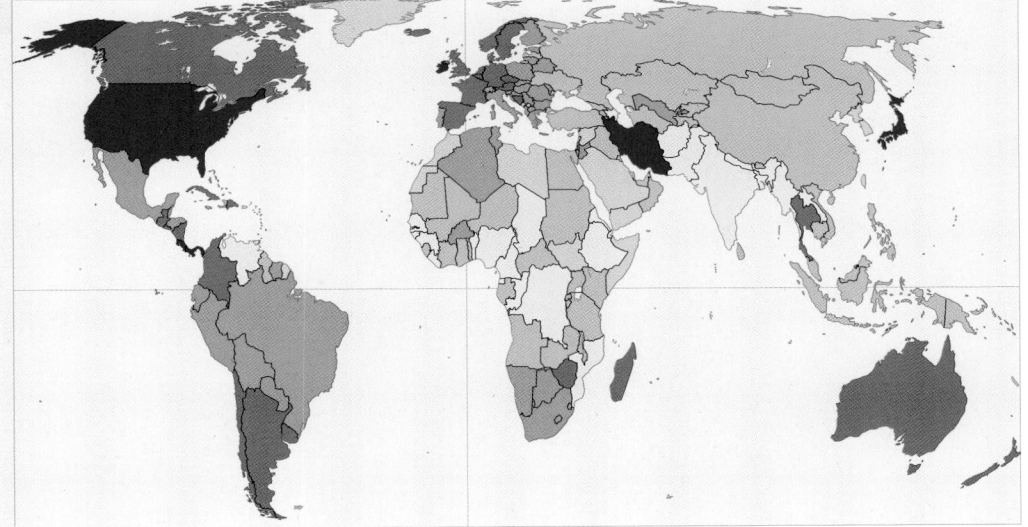

Countries with highest expenditure rate

Costa Rica	26.9%
Japan	23.6%
Iran	22.9%
USA	22.5%
Maldives	21.8%

MEDICAL PROFESSIONALS

Availability of doctors per 1,000 people (latest data available in 2020)

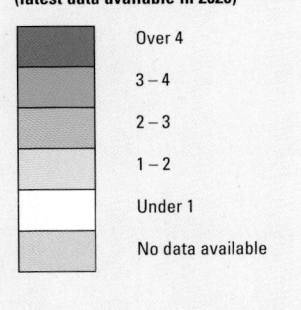

- Over 4
- 3 – 4
- 2 – 3
- 1 – 2
- Under 1
- No data available

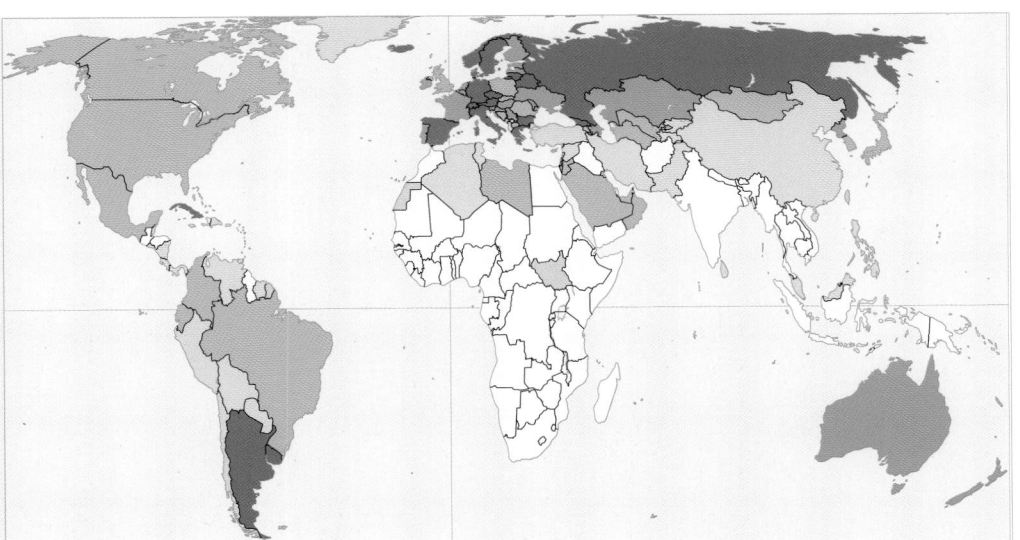

Perhaps the most glaring differences in the world today are those between the rich and the poor. The World Bank divides countries into three main groups based on average economic production expressed in terms of per capita GNI (Gross National Income). They are the low-income economies (most African countries and much of Asia), the middle-income economies (most of Latin America and most of the former USSR), and the high-income economies of Canada, the United States, Western Europe, Japan, and Australia.

Per capita GNIs are a measure of the total goods and services produced by a country divided by the population, and then converted into US dollars at official exchange rates. They are useful indicators of a country's prosperity, though, like all statistics, they must be treated with care. For example, the prices for goods and services in China are far cheaper than they are in the United States. China's per capita GNI in 2018 was $9,460 (as compared with $63,080 in the US), but the PPP (Purchasing Power Parity, which adjusts the figure for cost-of-living differences) estimate of China's per capita GNI was considerably higher at $16,121. Another problem with per capita GNIs is that they are averages, which often conceal wide internal variations.

The pattern of poverty varies from region to region. In Latin America, much progress has been made through industrialization, though startling inequalities still exist between rich and poor. China and other countries in eastern Asia, including South Korea and Taiwan, have followed Japan's example in pursuing export-led industrial policies. The success of China's Special Economic Zones, where foreign investment is encouraged, has led to a huge rise in China's per capita GNI.

In contrast to the dynamism of Asia, Africa lags behind as an impoverished continent. Corrupt governments, wasteful expenditures, civil wars, natural disasters, faulty national and international policy environments, high population growth, and the failure to break away from the neo-colonial trading patterns – all these contribute to keeping the majority of Africans impoverished. An initiative in some African countries has been to improve the infrastructure and develop tourism, creating employment and providing much-needed foreign currency. But the social and environmental cost of mass tourism needs to be taken seriously too.

The International Monetary Fund and the World Bank argue that real economic progress in Africa will be achieved only when African countries create market-friendly economies that encourage trade through export-led manufacturing, while at the same time strictly controlling public spending.

CONTINENTAL SHARES

Shares of population and of wealth (GNI) by continent

These generalized continental figures show the startling difference between rich and poor, but mask the successes or failures of individual countries. Japan, for example, with just over 3% of Asia's population, produces almost 19% of the continent's output. Within countries, the difference between rich and poor can also be startling. In Brazil, for example, the richest 20% of the population own 60% of the wealth.

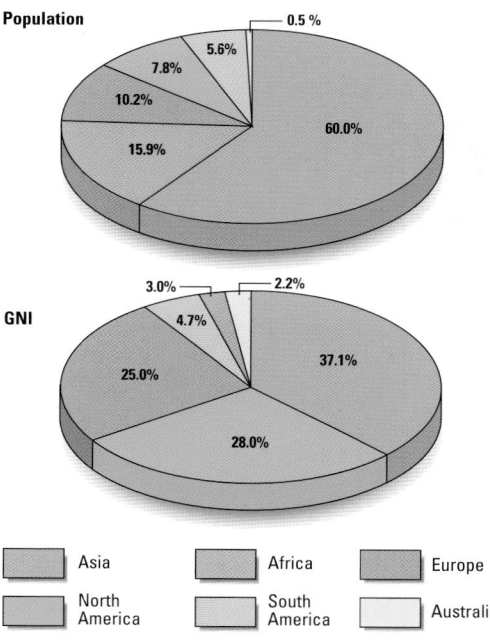

Population

GNI

Asia — Africa — Europe — North America — South America — Australia

LEVELS OF INCOME

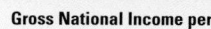

Gross National Income per capita: the value of total production divided by the population (2018)

- Over 400% of world average (US $10,552)
- 200 – 400%
- 100 – 200%
- 50 – 100%
- 25 – 50%
- 10 – 25%
- Under 10%
- No data available

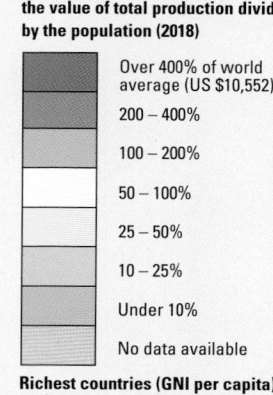

Richest countries (GNI per capita)

Switzerland	US $84,410
Norway	US $80,610
Luxembourg	US $70,870
Iceland	US $67,960
USA	US $63,080

Poorest countries (GNI per capita)

Burundi	US $280
Malawi	US $360
Niger	US $390
Mozambique	US $460
Central African Rep.	US $490

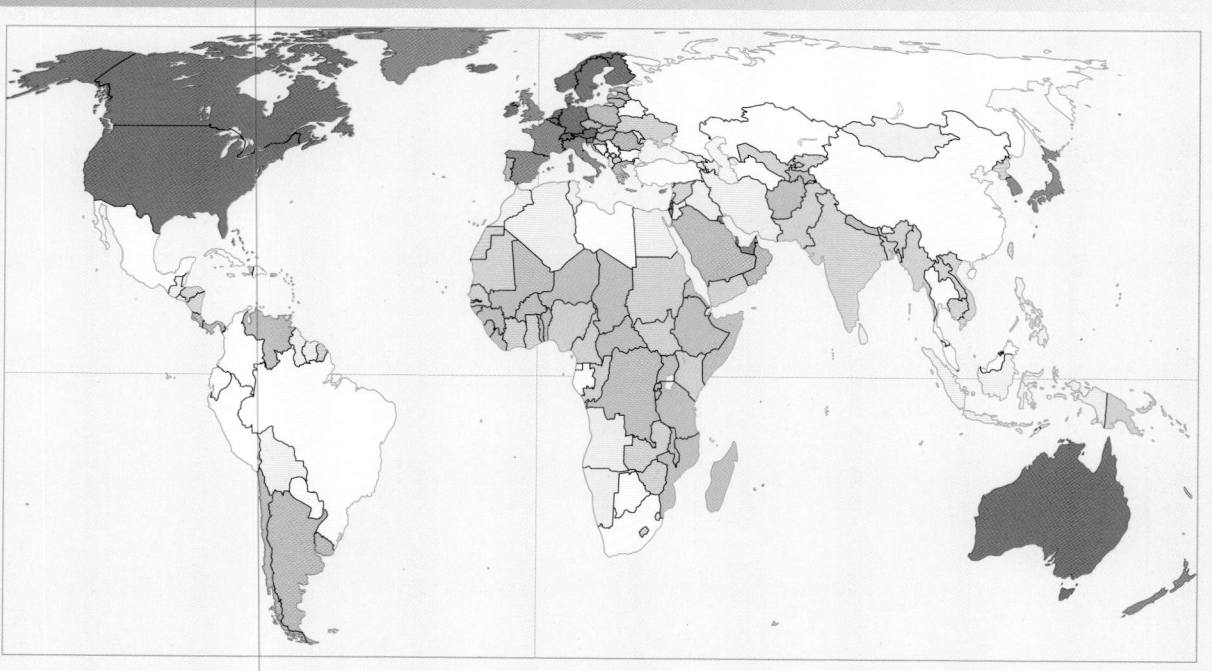

INDICATORS

The gap between the world's rich and poor is now so great that it is difficult to illustrate on a single graph. Within each income group (as defined by the World Bank), however, comparisons have some meaning. The wealth gap in many developing countries, though, is wide, with a small, rich class and a large, impoverished majority, while many high-income countries contain an underclass of unemployed and homeless people.

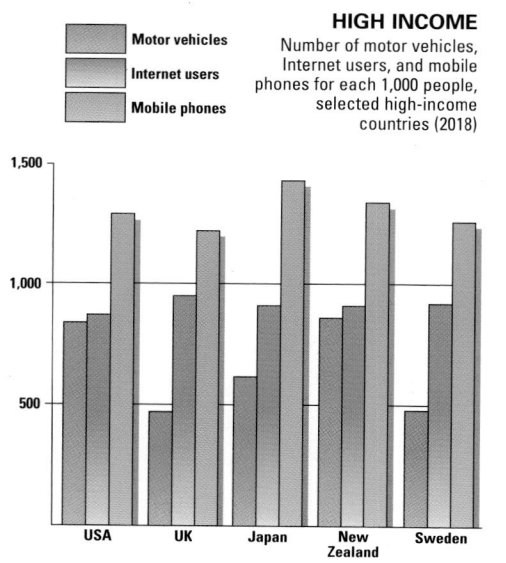

HIGH INCOME

Motor vehicles — Internet users — Mobile phones

Number of motor vehicles, Internet users, and mobile phones for each 1,000 people, selected high-income countries (2018)

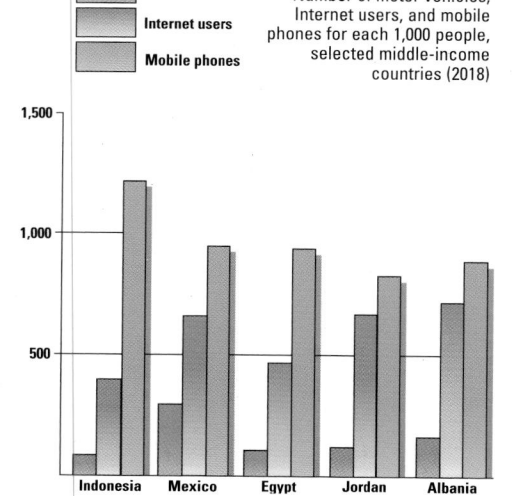

MIDDLE INCOME

Motor vehicles — Internet users — Mobile phones

Number of motor vehicles, Internet users, and mobile phones for each 1,000 people, selected middle-income countries (2018)

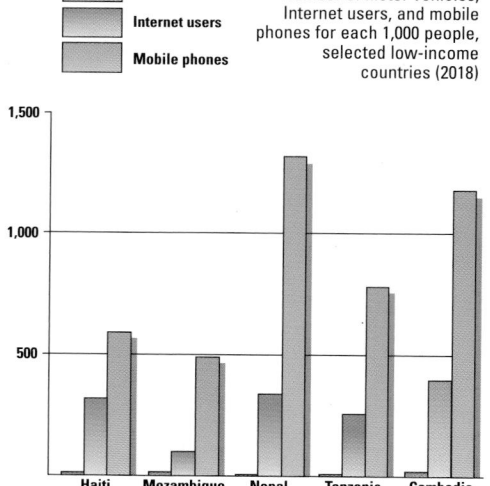

LOW INCOME

Motor vehicles — Internet users — Mobile phones

Number of motor vehicles, Internet users, and mobile phones for each 1,000 people, selected low-income countries (2018)

STATE FINANCE

Inflation rates (*shown on the map, right*) are an indication of a country's financial stability and, usually, of its prosperity. Annual inflation rates above 20% are usually marked by slow or even negative growth of the GNI. Above 50%, it becomes hyperinflation and an economy is left reeling.

In the late 1980s and early 1990s, many high-income countries had to contend with annual inflation rates of 10% or more, while Japan, the growth leader, had an average inflation rate of just 1.3% between 1985 and 1994.

Market-friendly policies, including low taxes and state spending, liberal trade policies, and a warm welcome for foreign investors, are major factors in countries that have enjoyed rapid economic growth in the decades since 1980. For example, the setting-up of Special Economic Zones in eastern China has led to a spectacular rise in that country's per capita GNI. However, an effective government remains a crucial factor in economic growth in most countries.

Other successful countries include South Korea and Singapore, although an Asian market crash in 1997 temporarily halted the dramatic economic expansion of these countries.

INFLATION

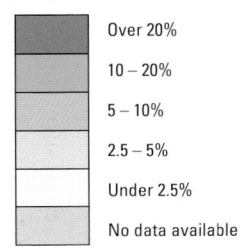

Average annual rate of inflation (2019)

	Over 20%
	10 – 20%
	5 – 10%
	2.5 – 5%
	Under 2.5%
	No data available

Highest average inflation*
Zimbabwe 176%
South Sudan 56%
Argentina 54%
* Venezuela experienced hyperinflation in 2019

Lowest average inflation
Libya .... -7.1%
Burundi .... -4.0%
Burkino Faso .... -3.9%

UNITED NATIONS SUSTAINABLE DEVELOPMENT GOALS

In 2000, the United Nations set out 8 Millennium Development Goals (MDGs) that were to be achieved by 2015. The goals were:

1. To eradicate extreme poverty and hunger.
2. To achieve universal primary education.
3. To promote gender equality and empower women.
4. To reduce child mortality.
5. To improve maternal health.
6. To combat HIV/AIDS, malaria, and other diseases.
7. To ensure environmental sustainability.
8. To develop a global partnership for development.

Progress towards achieving these goals has been uneven: some countries achieved many of the goals, whereas others achieved few, if any. However, some targets have been met such as the MDG for poverty reduction. According to the 2015 MDG Report, the poverty rates and the number of people living in extreme poverty fell in every developing region – including in Sub-Saharan Africa, where rates were highest. In the developing regions, the proportion of people living on less than $1.25 a day fell from 47% in 1990 to 14% in 2015. In 2015, about 900 million fewer people than in 1990 lived in conditions of extreme poverty.

To follow on from the MDG, the Sustainable Development Goals (SDGs) were adopted by all the world's governments at the United Nations in September 2015. The aim is that they will guide global development for the 15 years until 2030. There are 17 goals - as illustrated by the official United Nations icons below. Although the SDGs are not legally binding, governments are expected to establish national frameworks in order to achieve them.

The ultimate aim is to go further than the MDGs and end all forms of poverty. It has been recognized that defeating poverty has to be coupled with strategies to encourage economic growth, and to address a range of social needs including education, health, social protection, and job opportunites, while tackling climate change and protecting the environment.

Progress will be monitored by using a set of global indicators, and annual reports will be published. There is, of course, a cost to achieving these goals. The more developed countries will have to provide development assistance to help the countries most in need.

It is acknowledged that climate change has affected public health, food and water security, migration, peace, and security. Collective action will have to be taken to mitigate the worst effects of climate change. Goal 13 (Climate Action) reflects the importance of this issue, and the hope is that it will be possible to limit the increases in global mean temperature to no more than 3.6°F [2.0°C] above pre-industrial levels.

▲ To mark the 70th anniversary of the United Nations, and ahead of the United Nations Sustainable Development Summit in September 2015, massive projections of the icons for the 17 goals are seen on the façade of the General Assembly building in New York, United States. The aim was to raise awareness of the 2030 Agenda for Sustainable Development.

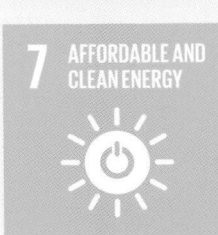

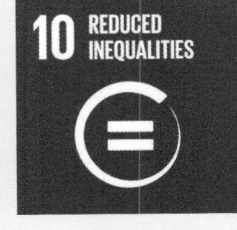

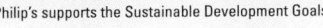
Philip's supports the Sustainable Development Goals

Wealth is a basic factor in determining standards of living. Everywhere, the rich have more of everything, including higher average life expectancies, while the poor have to spend most of their income on basic human needs, such as food and clothing. Yet poverty and wealth are relative terms: slum dwellers living on social security in an industrial society feel their poverty acutely, but have far more resources than an average African living in a rural area.

In 1990 the United Nations Development Program published its first Human Development Index (HDI), an attempt to construct a comparative scale by which a simplified form of well-being might be measured. The HDI, expressed as a value between 0 and 0.999, combines figures for life expectancy and literacy with a wealth scale, based on Purchasing Power Parity.

The world's countries are divided into three groups: those with a high HDI (0.8 and above); those with a medium HDI (0.5 to 0.799); and those with a low HDI (below 0.5). In 2019, Norway and Switzerland were top in the world rankings and Niger was bottom. In fact, 34 of the 41 countries with a low HDI were from Africa. Besides having low per capita GNIs, the average life expectancy in these countries was 59 years, while the adult literacy rate was 36%. By comparison, the average life expectancy at birth in countries in the high HDI group was 79 years, while the literacy rate was 94%.

Comparisons between countries with similar per capita GNIs reveal the effects of government actions. For example, the World Bank classifies both India and China as low-income economies, but India's HDI at 0.640 is much lower than that of China, at 0.752. This reflects not only China's economic progress in the 1980s and 1990s, but also differences in average life expectancies (69 years in India and 76 years in China), and adult literacy rates (71% in India and 96% in China).

Disparities in standards of living exist not only between countries but also between individuals, groups, and regions within countries. For example, income distribution figures show that, in the United States, the poorest 10% of households receive less than 2% of the income.

Other contrasts exist in developing countries between rural communities, where incomes are low and basic services are often in short supply, and urban areas, where even those living in slums are generally better off than their rural neighbors. Other striking differences exist between men and women. For example, while adult literacy rates for men and women living in developed countries are more or less the same, large differences exist in many developing countries. In countries in the lowest HDI category, only 36% of women were literate, as compared with 58% of men.

Female education is a factor in population control, especially as women's fertility rates appear to fall in direct proportion to the amount of secondary education they receive. This point was acknowledged in 2004 by the UN Population Fund, which defined four main objectives relating to women and population control: the reduction of maternal, infant, and child mortality; better education, especially for girls; universal access to reproductive health services; and gender equality.

Statistical analysis presents many problems of interpretation, especially when trying to define such intangible factors as a sense of well-being. For example, education helps create wealth; but are rich countries wealthy because their people are well educated, or are they well educated because they are rich?

HUMAN DEVELOPMENT INDEX

The Human Development Index (HDI), calculated by the UN Development Program (UNDP), gives a value to countries using indicators of life expectancy, education, and standards of living (2020).

	Over 0.9
	0.8 – 0.9
	0.7 – 0.8
	0.6 – 0.7
	0.5 – 0.6
	0.4 – 0.5
	Under 0.4
	No data available

Highest values
Norway 0.953
Switzerland 0.944
Australia 0.939
Ireland 0.938
Germany 0.936

Lowest values
Niger 0.354
Central African Rep. 0.367
South Sudan.................... 0.388
Chad 0.404
Burundi 0.417

EDUCATION

The developing countries made great efforts in the 1970s and 1980s to bring at least a basic education to their people. In all but the poorest nations, primary school enrolments rose above 60%. However, figures often include teenagers or young adults, and there are still 300 million children worldwide who receive no schooling at all. A lack of resources has restricted the development of secondary and higher education. Most primary school education is free in the poorer countries, but fees are often paid for secondary and higher education, thus heightening the differences between rich and poor.

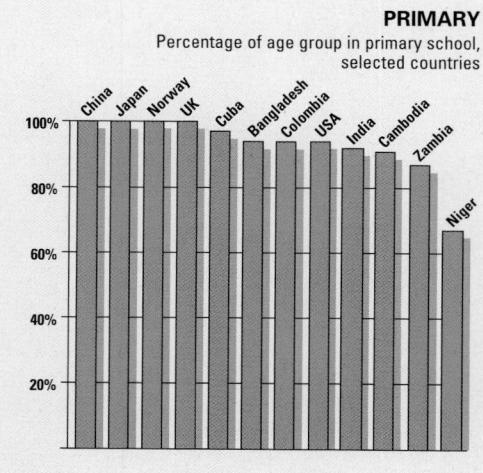

PRIMARY
Percentage of age group in primary school, selected countries

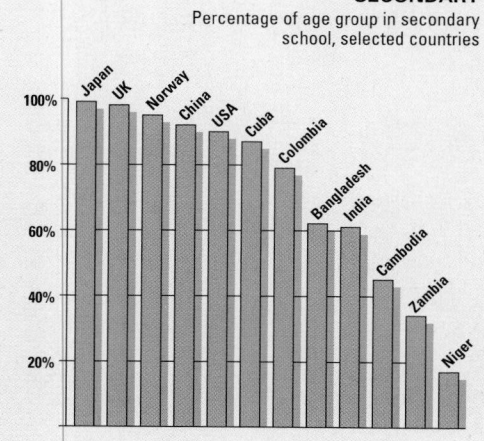

SECONDARY
Percentage of age group in secondary school, selected countries

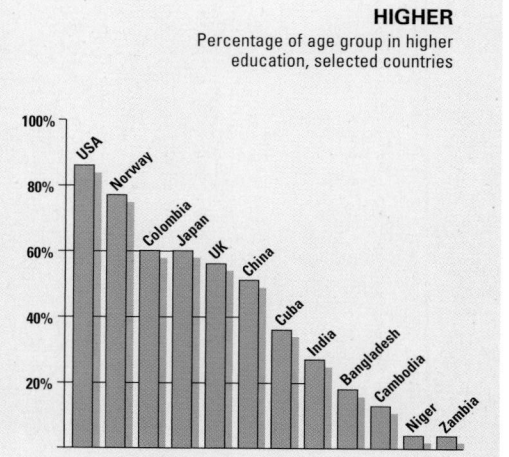

HIGHER
Percentage of age group in higher education, selected countries

DISTRIBUTION OF SPENDING

Percentage share of household spending

A high proportion of the average income of households in developing nations is spent on basic needs such as food and clothing. In most Western countries food and clothing account for less than 25% of expenditure.

☐ Food	☐ Clothing	☐ Energy & Housing
☐ Medicine & Education	☐ Transport	☐ Other

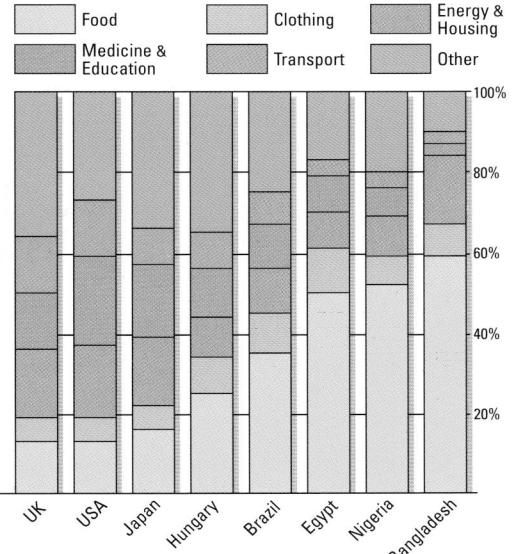

▲ These two images illustrate the reality of suburban life for people at either end of the economic scale. At the top is part of a huge area of "tract housing" in California, where large houses of a similar design are laid out by a developer, complete with gardens, drives, and swimming pools. Below, is a much more haphazard arrangement of home-built, rudimentary shelters, many without sanitation and most with no electricity, in Crossroads Township, outside Cape Town in South Africa.

FERTILITY AND EDUCATION

Fertility rates compared with female education, selected countries

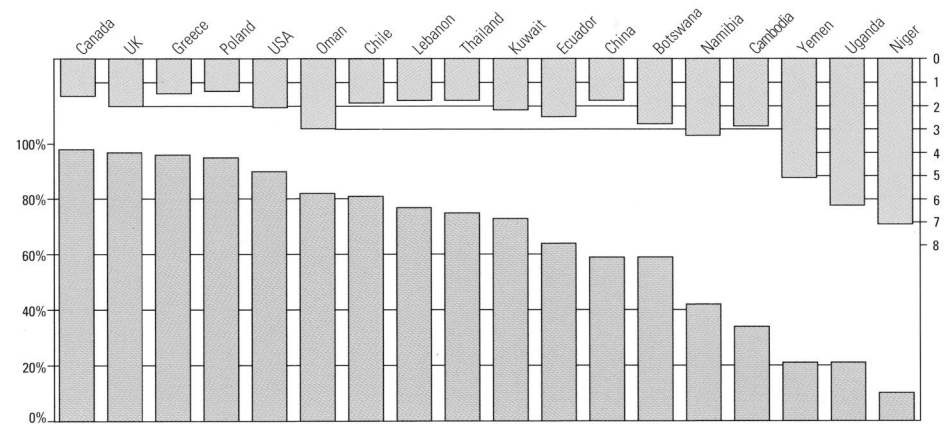

There seems to be a strong link between access to secondary education and the fertility rate. In developed countries, young girls have a high access to education and a low fertility rate. In contrast, in many developing countries women have a high fertility rate but lack access to education. This can be for a complex mix of social, economic, and cultural reasons. Despite a few high-profile examples of female politicians in different parts of the world, all evidence points to the continuing marginalization of women from the political and economic processes of decision-making. Female wages are, on average, only two-thirds of those of men.

☐ Fertility rate: average number of children borne per woman

☐ Percentage of females aged 12–17 in secondary education

GENDER INEQUALITY INDEX

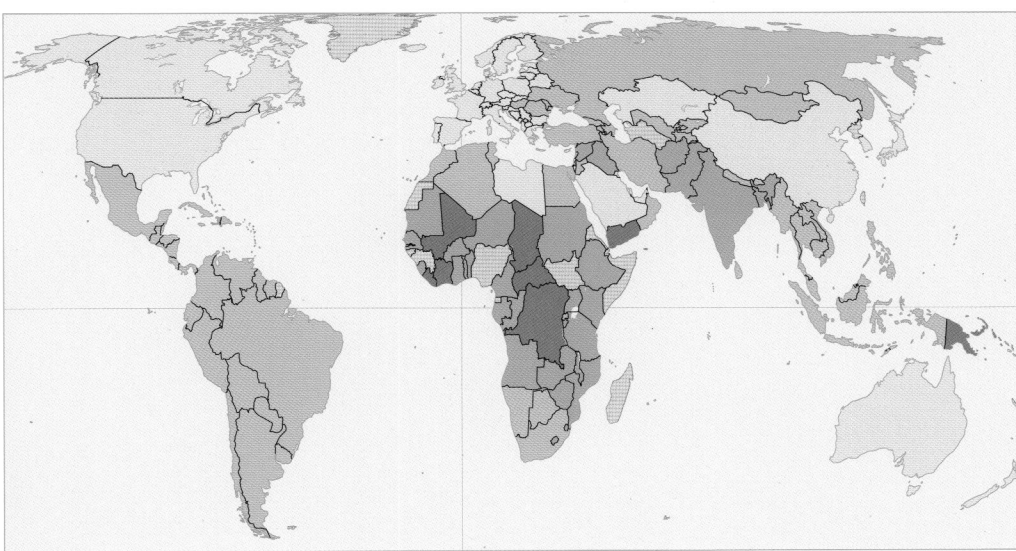

The Gender Inequality Index is a composite measure reflecting inequality in achievements between women and men in three categories: reproductive health, empowerment, and the labor market. It varies between 0, when women and men fare equally, and 1, when women or men fare poorly compared to the other in all categories (2018).

☐	Over 0.65
☐	0.5 – 0.65
☐	0.25 – 0.5
☐	Under 0.25
☐	No data available

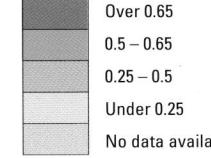

Most equal
Switzerland 0.037
Sweden 0.040
Denmark 0.040

Least equal
Yemen....................................... 0.834
Papua New Guinea.................. 0.740
Chad 0.701

GENDER EQUALITY

The UN's Millennium Development Goal 3 was to *"Eliminate gender disparity in primary and secondary education"* in all levels of education no later than 2015. According to the 2015 Millennium Development Goal Report, achieving parity in education is an important step toward equal opportunity for men and women in the social, political, and economic domains. The Gender Parity Index (GPI) shows the ratio between the enrolment rate of girls and that of boys. The GPI grew from 91% in 1999 to 98% in 2015 for the developing regions as a whole – falling within the +/- 3-point margin of 100% that is the accepted measure for parity.

While most of the developing world had reached a GPI of at least 99% at the primary level by 2015, the Index was still lagging behind in Western Asia and sub-Saharan Africa. These two regions, however, have recorded the

greatest progress. Between 1999 and 2015, girls' participation in primary education increased from 72% to 96% in sub-Saharan Africa, and from 87% to 97% in Western Asia.

Girls have shown the greatest progress at the secondary level of education. The GPI for secondary education in the developing world as a whole has risen from 78% in 1990 to 98% in 2015.

It is in tertiary education where the greatest disparities are to be found. Only one developing region, Western Asia, has achieved the target. The most extreme disparities at the expense of women are in sub-Saharan Africa and Southern Asia.

In general, countries with lower levels of national wealth tend to have more men enrolled in tertiary education than women, while the opposite occurs in countries with higher average incomes.

The GPI measures the rate of girls' school enrolment as a percentage of boys' enrolment in primary, secondary and tertiary education.

GENDER PARITY INDEX (GPI)

☐ 1999 ☐ 2015 ☐ Target for GPI is between 97% and 103% ☐ 1999 ☐ 2015

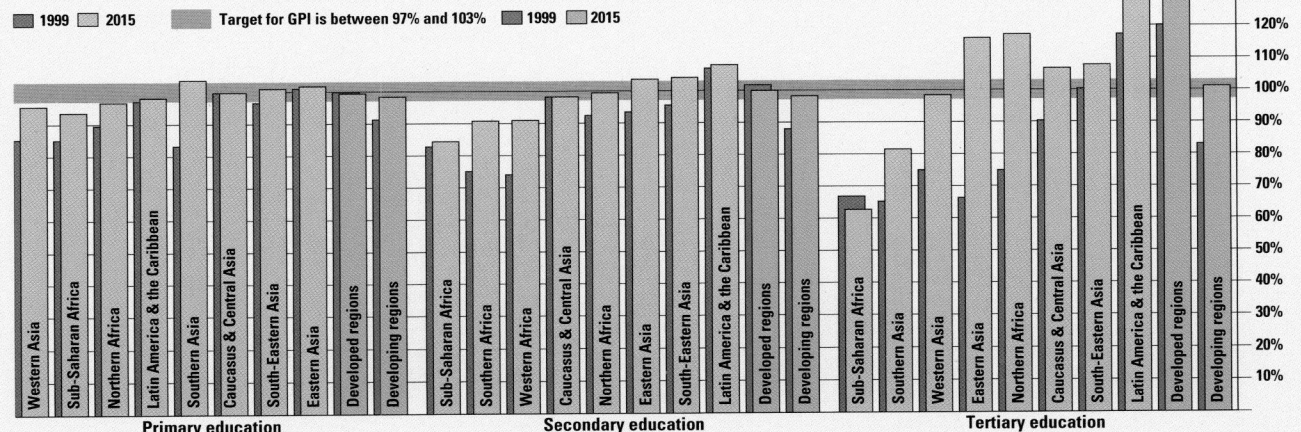

WORLD CITIES

The Venetian Lagoon is clearly visible in this image, with the mainland to the left and the sandbanks that protect the lagoon from the Adriatic Sea toward the bottom right corner. The Ponte della Libertà – the bridge connecting Venice to the mainland — can just be made out as a thin line in the center of the image. Tourists arriving by train or car can get no further than the end of this bridge. Travel within the city itself is strictly by boat or on foot. The tides that surge into the lagoon through three gaps in the sandbanks flush out the hundreds of small canals. High tides, however, have long caused flooding in the city, and with rising sea levels, and the sinking of the islands themselves, these floods have been increasingly frequent and more damaging. The city's survival depends on the success of huge flood barriers now under construction.
[Map page 199] *CGG Satellite Mapping*

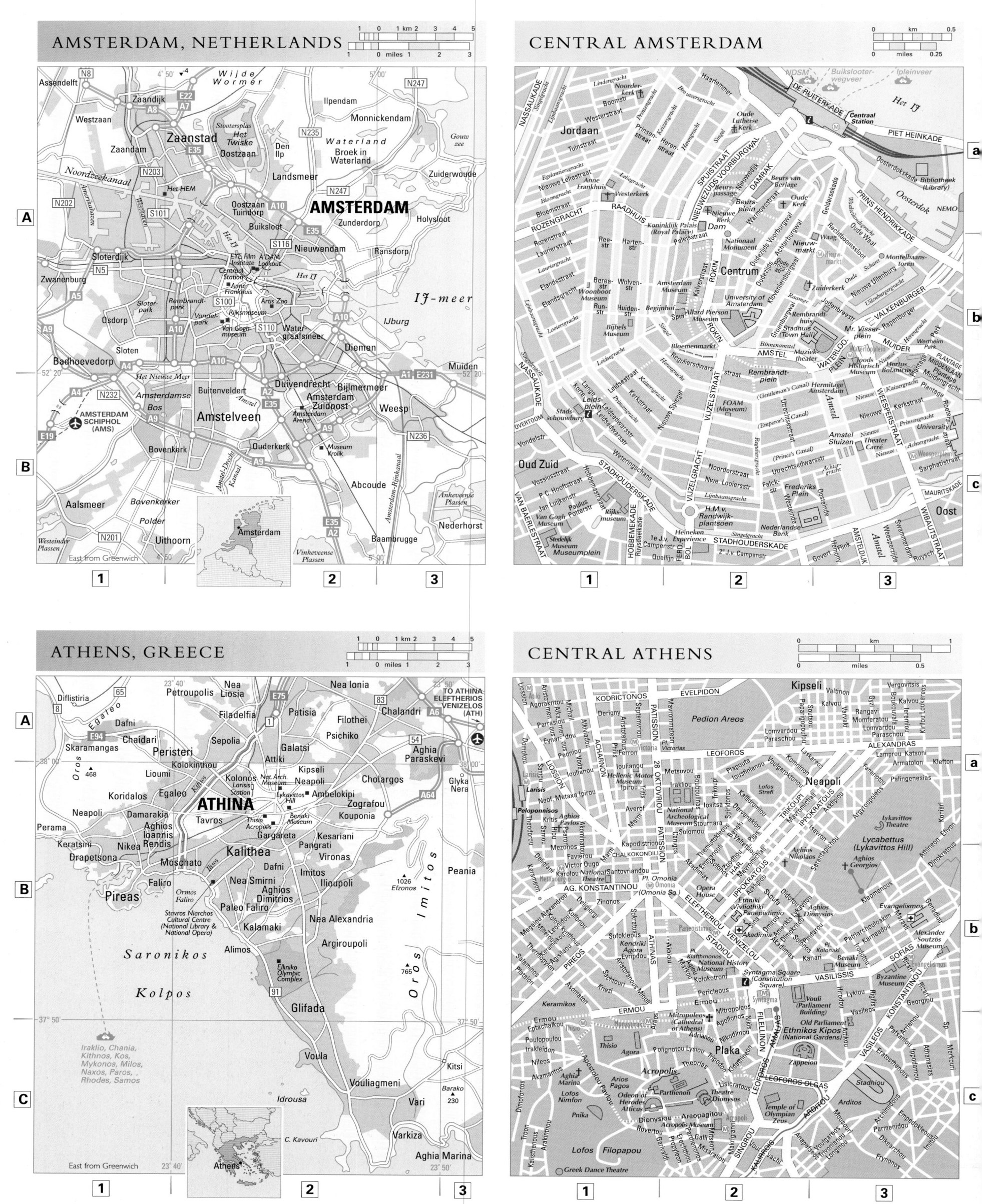

ATLANTA, GEORGIA

A B C

1 2 3

Interstate route numbers   U.S. route numbers   State route numbers

BAGHDAD, IRAQ

A B

1 2 3

International Zone (Green Zone)

BANGKOK, THAILAND

A B C

1 2

CENTRAL BANGKOK

a b c

1 2 3

Skytrain   Shrine   Temple

COPYRIGHT PHILIP'S

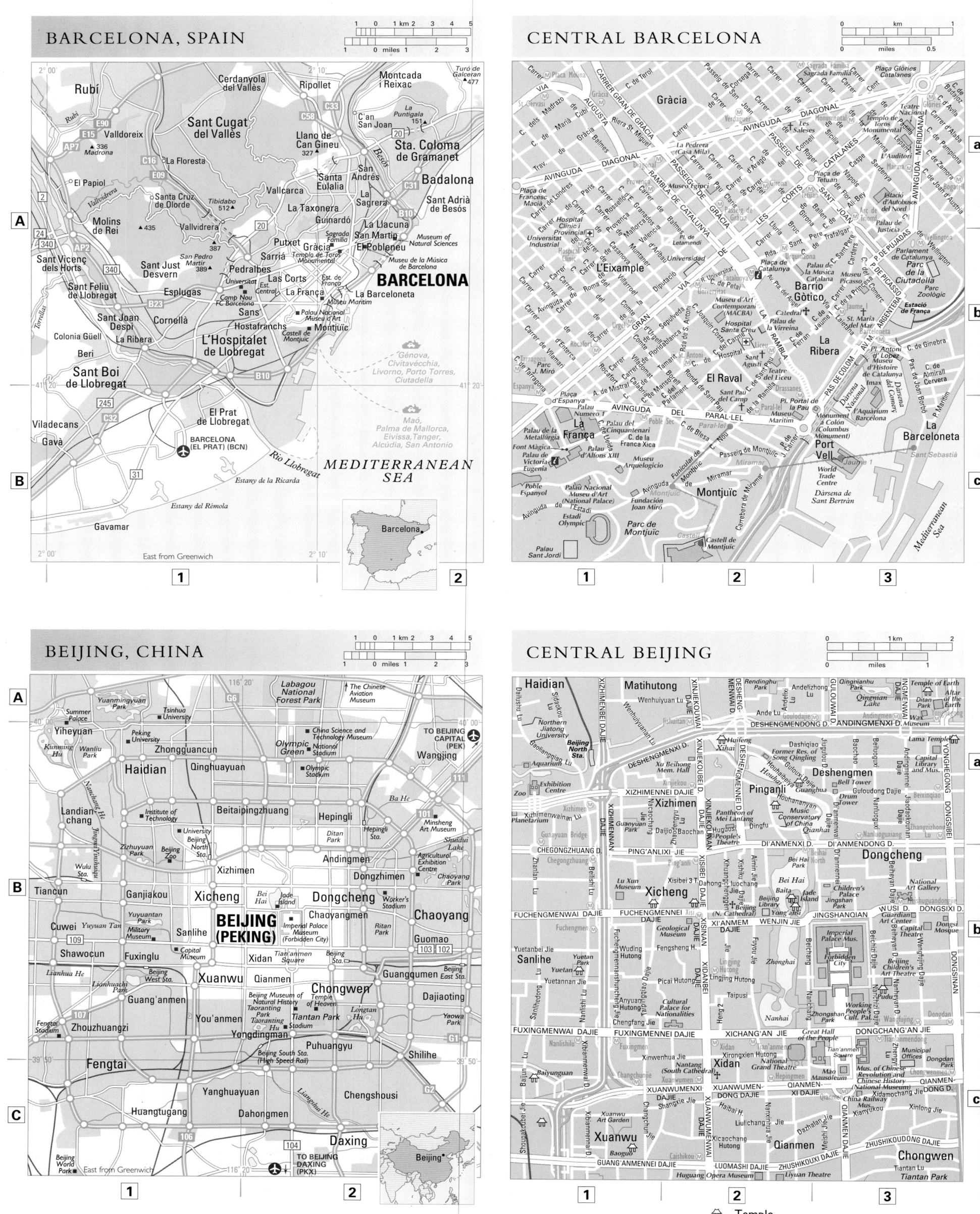

BARCELONA, SPAIN

Rubí
Cerdanyola del Vallès
Ripollet
Montcada i Reixac
Turó de Galceran ▲477
Valldoreix
E90
E15
AP7
Sant Cugat del Vallès
C'an San Joan
La Puntigala 151
C58
C33
▲336 Madrona
C16
La Floresta
Llano de Can Gineu 327
Sta. Coloma de Gramanet
El Papiol
2
C09
Santa Cruz de Olorde
Vallcarca
Santa Eulalia
San Andrés
Badalona
C31
Tibidabo 512
La Sagrera
Sant Adrià de Besòs
Molins de Rei
340
Vallvidrera
La Taxonera
Guinardó
B10
A
24
San Pedro Martir 389 ▲387
Putxet
Gràcia
Sagrada Familia
El Poblenou
20
Sant Vicenç dels Horts
AP2
340
Sant Just Desvern
Sarrià
Templo de Toros Monumental
San Martin
Museu de la Música de Barcelona
Sant Feliu de Llobregat
Pedralbes
Universitat
Est. Central
La França
BARCELONA
B23
Las Corts
Esplugas
Camp Nou FC Barcelona
Museu Marítim
Colonia Güell
Cornellà
Sans
Hostafranchs
La Barceloneta
Beri
La Ribera
Castell de Montjuïc
Palau Nacional Museo d'Art
Génova, Civitavécchia, Livorno, Porto Torres, Ciutadella
Sant Joan Despí
Montjuïc
Sant Boi de Llobregat
L'Hospitalet de Llobregat
41 20
41 20
245
Viladecans
C32
El Prat de Llobregat
Maó, Palma de Mallorca, Eivissa, Tanger, Alcúdia, San Antonio
Gavà
31
BARCELONA (EL PRAT) (BCN)
Río Llobregat
MEDITERRANEAN SEA
Estany de la Ricarda
B
Estany del Rémola
Gavamar
2° 00'
2° 10'
East from Greenwich
Barcelona
1
2

CENTRAL BARCELONA

Gràcia
Sagrada Familia
Plaça Glòries Catalanes
a
Plaça de Francesc Macià
AVINGUDA DIAGONAL
L'Auditori
Estació d'Autobuses del Nord
L'Eixample
Plaça de Catalunya
Barrio Gòtic
Parc de la Ciutadella
b
Museu d'Art Contemporani (MACBA)
Catedral
St. Maria del Mar
La Ribera
Estació de França
Hospital Santa Creu
El Raval
La Rambla
Parc Zoològic
Plaça d'Espanya
Palau Numero 1
AVINGUDA DEL PARAL·LEL
Monument a Colón (Columbus Monument)
La Barceloneta
La França
Port Vell
Poble Espanyol
Palau Nacional Museu d'Art (National Palace)
Fundació Joan Miró
Montjuïc
World Trade Centre
Dàrsena de Sant Bertràn
Parc de Montjuïc
Estadi Olympic
Castell de Montjuïc
Mediterranean Sea
Palau Sant Jordi
1
2
3

BEIJING, CHINA

Labagou National Forest Park
The Chinese Aviation Museum
G6
A
Summer Palace
Yuanmingyuan Park
Tsinghua University
China Science and Technology Museum
TO BEIJING CAPITAL (PEK)
Yiheyuan
Peking University
Olympic Green
National Stadium
Wangjing
Kunming Hu
Wanliu Park
Zhongguancun
Olympic Stadium
111
Landian chang
Haidian
Qinghuayuan
Beitaipingzhuang
Hepingli
Ba He
Institute of Technology
Ditan Park
Hepingli Sta.
101
Zizhuyuan Park
University
Beijing North Sta.
Minsheng Art Museum
B
Tiancun
Wulu Sta.
Beijing Zoo
Andingmen
Agricultural Exhibition Centre
Shudu

Ganjiakou
Xicheng
Bei Hai
Jade Island
Dongcheng
Worker's Stadium
Chaoyang Park
Chaoyang
Cuwei
Yuyuantan Tan
Military Museum
Sanlihe
BEIJING (PEKING)
Imperial Palace Museum (Forbidden City)
Chaoyangmen
Ritan Park
109
Shawocun
Capital Museum
Xidan
Tian'anmen Square
Guomao
103 102
Fuxinglu
Beijing West Sta.
Xuanwu
Qianmen
Beijing South Sta. (High Speed Rail)
Beijing East Sta.
Guang'anmen
Beijing Museum of Natural History
Taoranting Park
Chongwen
Dajiaoting
107
Zhouzhuangzi
You'anmen
Tiantan Park
Longtan Hu
Yaowa Park
Fengtai Stadium
Yongdingman
Puhuangyu
G1
Yanghuayuan
Chengshousi
39 50
39 50
Huangtugang
Dahongmen
106
104
Daxing
Fengtai
TO BEIJING DAXING (PKX)
Beijing World Park
East from Greenwich
116 20
Beijing
1
2

CENTRAL BEIJING

Haidian
Matihutong
Temple of Earth
Altar of the Earth
a
Northern Jiaotong University
Deshengmen
Lama Temple
Beijing North Sta.
Pinganli
Capital Library
Zoo
Exhibition Centre
Xizhimen
YONGHEGONG
Xicheng
Bei Hai
Dongcheng
National Art Gallery
b
Lu Xun Museum
Xisibei
Children's Palace Jingshan Park
Dongsi Mosque
Sanlihe
Geological Museum
Beijing Library (N. Cathedral)
Imperial Palace Mus.
Forbidden City
Xidan
Working People's Cult. Pal.
Cultural Palace for Nationalities
Beijing Children's Art Theatre
FUXINGMENWAI DAJIE
XICHANG'AN JIE
DONGCHANG'AN JIE
Great Hall of the People
Tian'anmen Square
Municipal Offices
Dongdan Park
c
Xuanwu
Mao Mausoleum
National Museum
China Railway Mus.
Qianmen
Tiantan Park
1
2
3

⇧ Temple

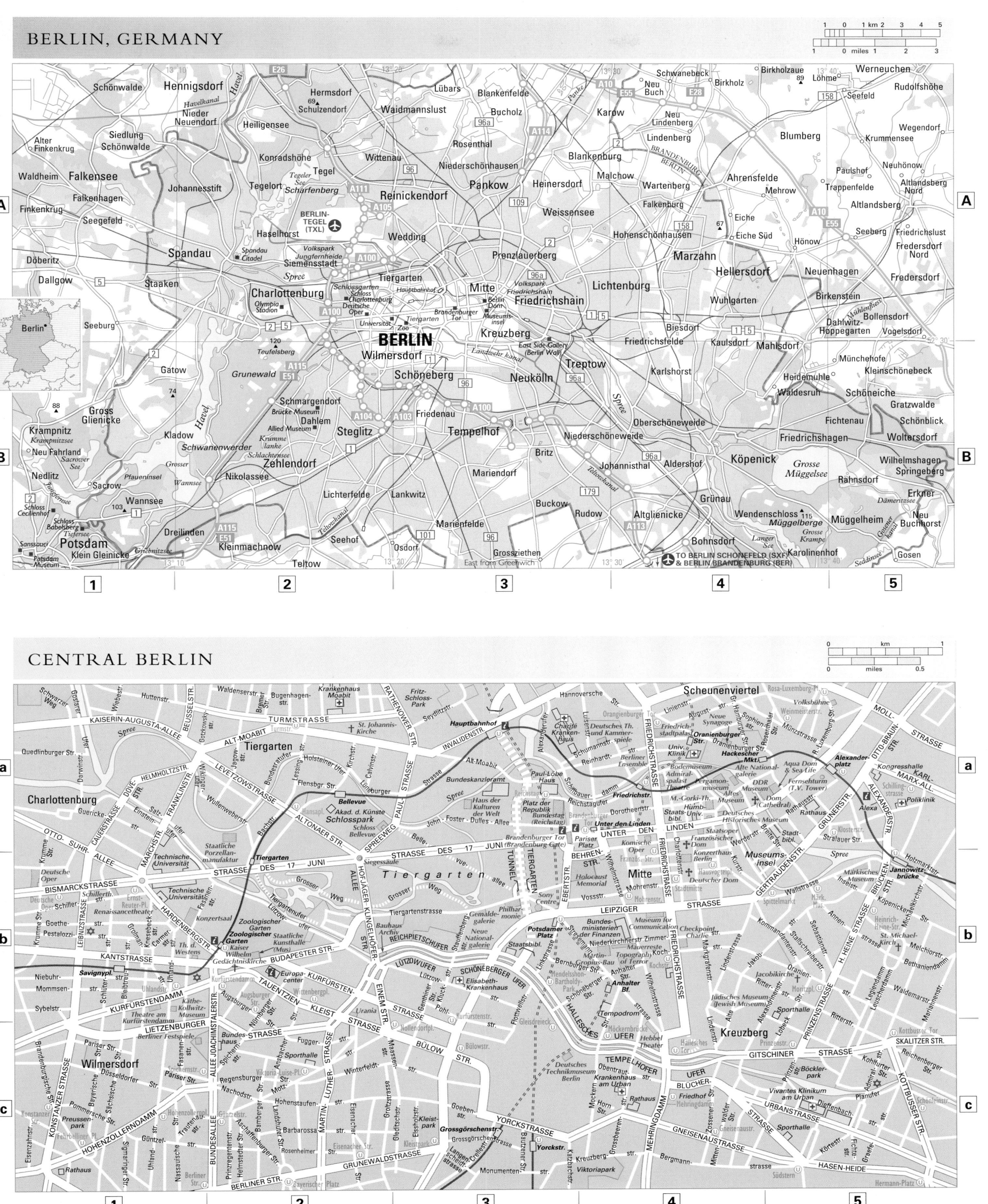

BERLIN, GERMANY

CENTRAL BERLIN

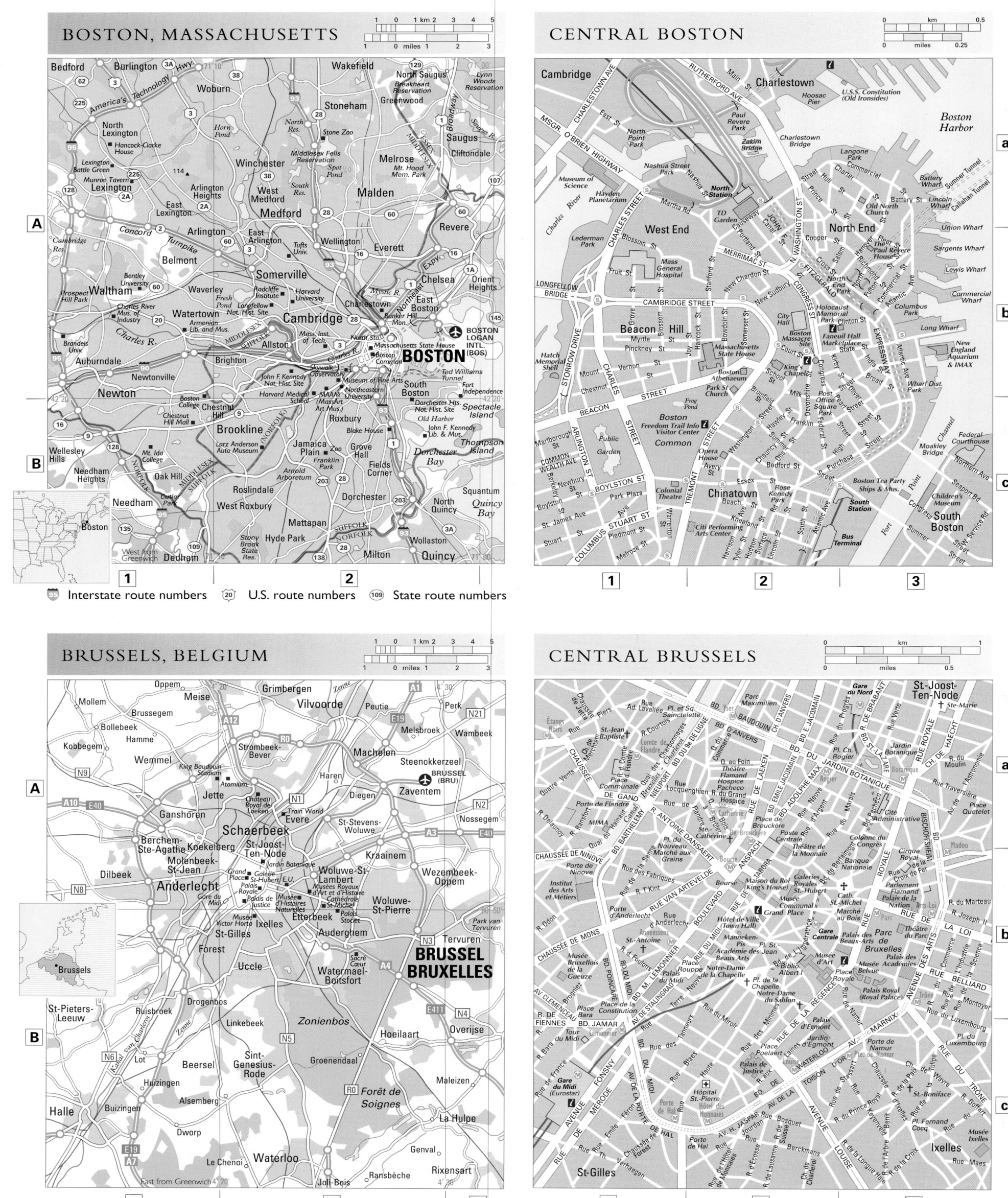

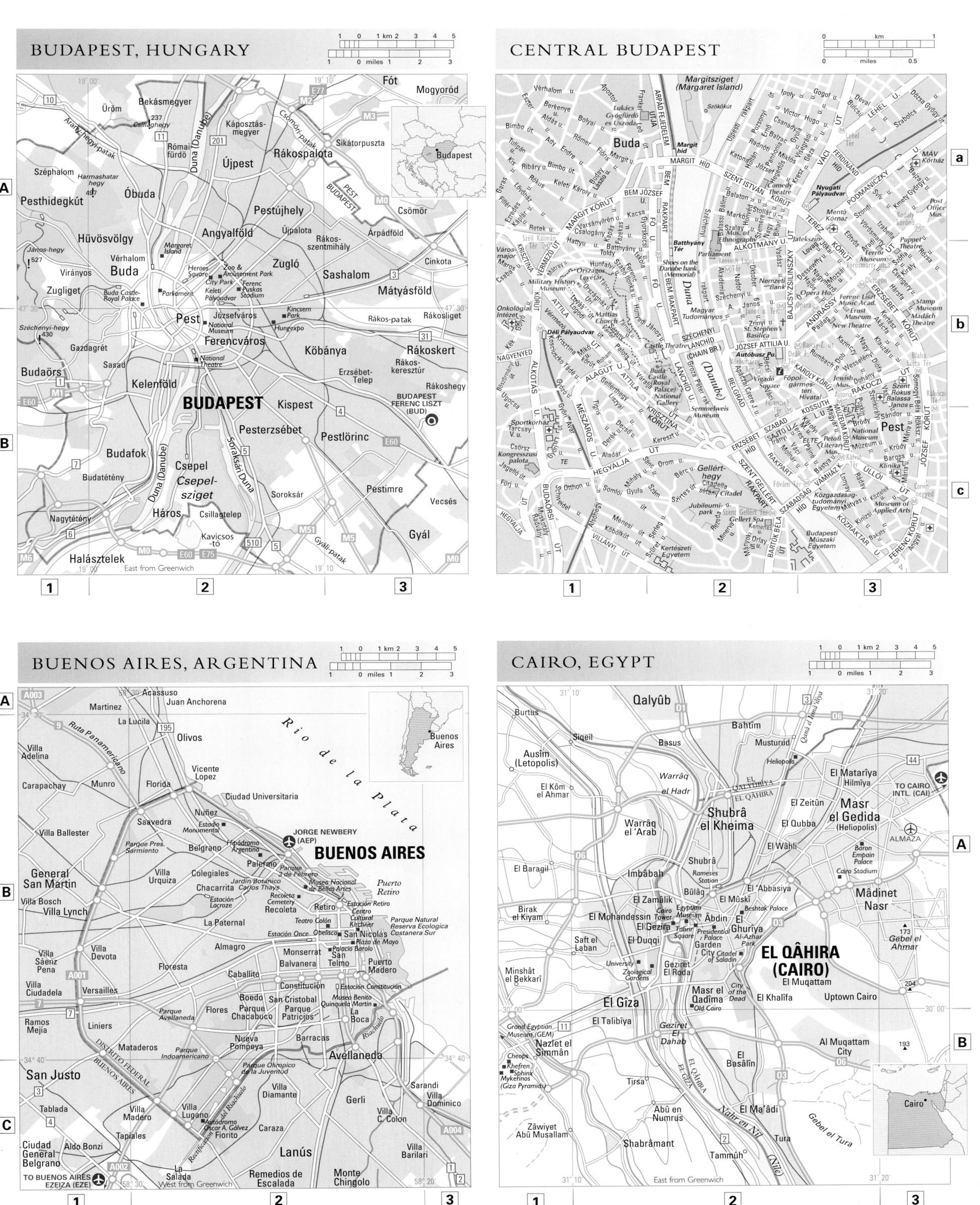

BUDAPEST, HUNGARY

CENTRAL BUDAPEST

BUENOS AIRES, ARGENTINA

CAIRO, EGYPT

COPYRIGHT PHILIP'S

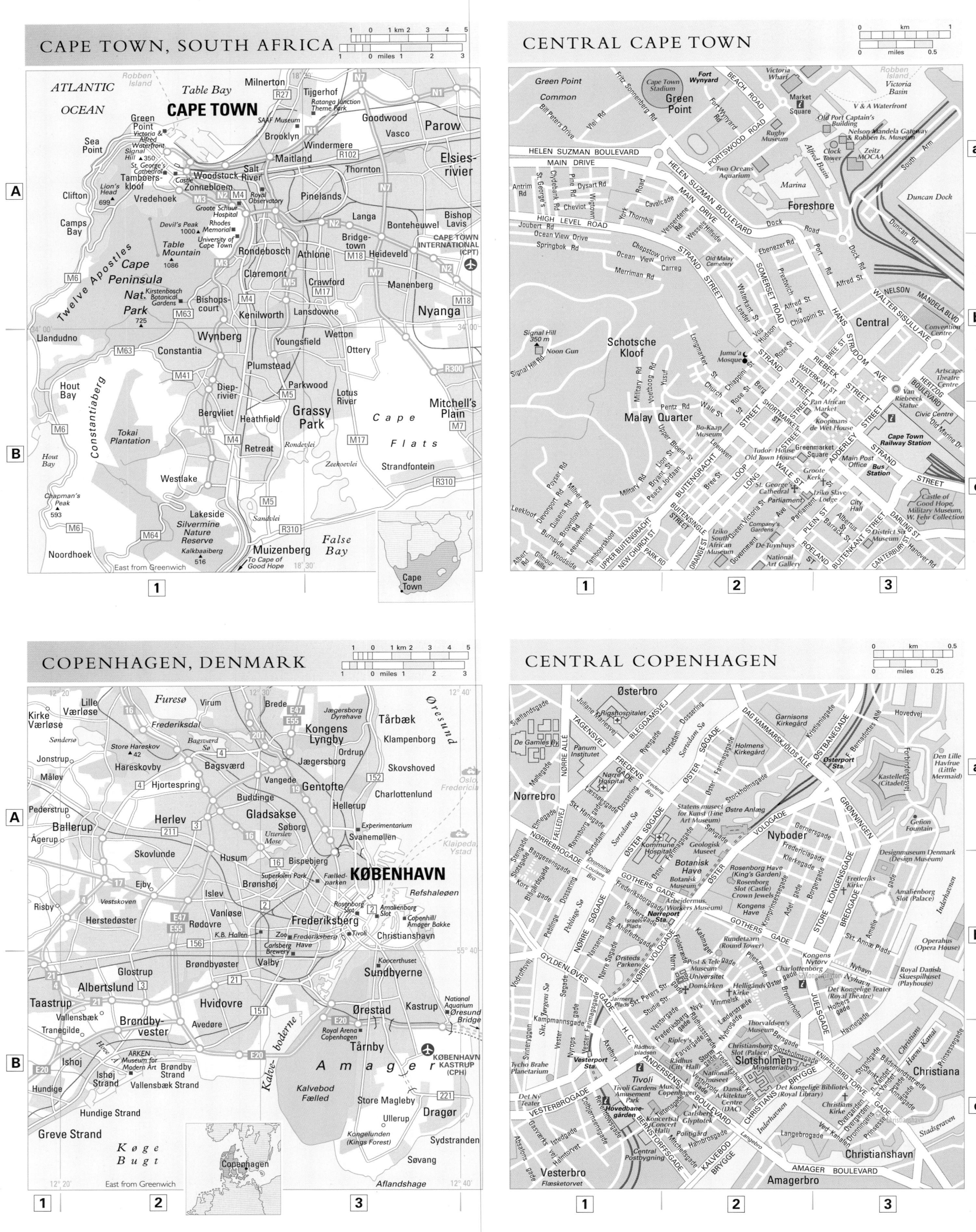

CAPE TOWN, SOUTH AFRICA

ATLANTIC OCEAN

Robben Island
Table Bay
Milnerton
Tijgerhof
Ranaga Junction Theme Park
CAPE TOWN
Goodwood
Vasco
Parow
Brooklyn
Windermere
Elsiesrivier
Green Point
Victoria & Alfred Waterfront
Signal Hill 350
Sea Point
Clifton
Lion's Head 699
St. George's Cathedral
Tamboerskloof
Woodstock
Zonnebloem
Salt River
Castle
Maitland
Thornton
Vredehoek
Camps Bay
Devil's Peak 1000
Groote Schuur Hospital
Royal Observatory
Pinelands
Langa
Bontehuwel
Bishop Lavis
Rhodes Memorial
Table Mountain 1086
University of Cape Town
Rondebosch
Bridgetown
Heideveld
CAPE TOWN INTERNATIONAL (CPT)
Twelve Apostles
Cape Peninsula Nat. Park
Kirstenbosch Botanical Gardens
Claremont
Athlone
Crawford
Manenberg
725
Bishopscourt
Kenilworth
Lansdowne
Nyanga
Llandudno
Wynberg
Youngsfield
Wetton
Ottery
Constantia
Hout Bay
Plumstead
Parkwood
Lotus River
Mitchell's Plain
Dieprivier
Constantiaberg
Bergvliet
Heathfield
Grassy Park
Cape Flats
Hout Bay
Tokai Plantation
Retreat
Rondevlei
Chapman's Peak 593
Westlake
Zeekoevlei
Strandfontein
Lakeside
Silvermine Nature Reserve
Noordhoek
Kalkbaaiberg 516
Muizenberg
False Bay
East from Greenwich
To Cape of Good Hope

Cape Town

CENTRAL CAPE TOWN

Green Point Common
Cape Town Stadium
Fort Wynyard
Green Point
BEACH ROAD
Victoria Wharf
V & A Waterfront
Victoria Basin
Market Square
Old Port Captain's Building
Nelson Mandela Gateway & Robben Is. Museum
HELEN SUZMAN BOULEVARD
MAIN DRIVE
PORTSWOOD ROAD
Rugby Museum
Clock Tower
Zeitz MOCAA
South Arm
Two Oceans Aquarium
Marina
Alfred Basin
Duncan Dock
Foreshore
HIGH LEVEL ROAD
Ocean View Drive
Springbok Rd
STRAND STREET
Old Malay Cemetery
SOMERSET ROAD
Duncan Rd
WALTER SISULU AVE
NELSON MANDELA BLVD
Signal Hill 350 m
Noon Gun
Schotsche Kloof
Jumu'a Mosque
Central
Convention Centre
Malay Quarter
Pan African Market
Koopmans de Wet House
Artscape Theatre Centre
Bo-Kaap Museum
Greenmarket Square
Van Riebeeck Statue
Civic Centre
Tudor House Old Town House
HERTZOG BOULEVARD
Old Marine Rd
Cape Town Railway Station
Main Post Office
Bus Station
St. George's Cathedral
Iziko Slave Lodge
Groote Kerk
Castle of Good Hope, Military Museum, W. Fehr Collection
Company's Gardens
Parliament
City Hall
Iziko South African Museum
De Tuynhuys
Government
National Art Gallery
District Six Museum

COPENHAGEN, DENMARK

Furesø
Lille Værløse
Virum
Brede
Jægersborg Dyrehave
Kirke Værløse
Søndersø
Frederiksdal
Tårbæk
Kongens Lyngby
Klampenborg
Jonstrup
Store Hareskov 42
Bagsværd Sø
Ordrup
Øresund
Måløv
Hareskovby
Bagsværd
Jægersborg
Skovshoved
Pederstrup
Hjortespring
Gentofte
Charlottenlund
Ballerup
Buddinge
Hellerup
Ågerup
Herlev
Søborg
Experimentarium
Skovlunde
Gladsakse
Svanemøllen
Klaipeda/Ystad
Risby
Ejby
Husum
Utslev Mose
Fælledparken
KØBENHAVN
Vestkoven
Islev
Bispebjerg
Brønshøj
Refshaleøen
Herstedøster
Vanløse
Rosenborg Slot
Amalienborg Slot
Rødovre
Frederiksberg
Christianshavn
Glostrup
K.B. Hallen
Zoo
Copenhill/Amager Bakke
Tivoli
Albertslund
Carlsberg Brewery
Frederiksberg Have
Brøndbyøster
Valby
Koncerthuset
Taastrup
Sundbyerne
Vallensbæk
Brøndbyvester
Hvidovre
National Aquarium Denmark
Øresund Bridge
Tranegilde
Avedøre
Ørestad
Kastrup
Ishøj
ARKEN Museum for Modern Art
Brøndby Strand
Tårnby
KØBENHAVN KASTRUP (CPH)
Hundige
Ishøj Strand
Vallensbæk Strand
Kalvebod Fælled
Store Magleby
Dragør
Greve Strand
Køge Bugt
Ullerup
Kongelunden (Kings Forest)
Sydstranden
Søvang
East from Greenwich
Aflandshage

Copenhagen

CENTRAL COPENHAGEN

Østerbro
Rigshospitalet
Garnisons Kirkegård
Hovedvej
De Gamles By
Panum Institutet
Holmens Kirkegård
ØSTERPORT GADE
Den Lille Havfrue (Little Mermaid)
Nørrebro
Nørre Hospital
Østerport Sta.
Kastellet (Citadel)
Statens museum for Kunst (Fine Art Museum)
Østre Anlæg
Nyboder
Gefion Fountain
Kommune Hospital
Geologisk Museet
Botanisk Have (Botanical Garden)
Rosenborg Have (King's Garden)
Designmuseum Denmark (Design Museum)
Botanisk Museum
Rosenborg Slot (Castle) Crown Jewels
Frederiks Kirke
Amalienborg Slot (Palace)
Arbejdermus. (Workers' Museum)
Kongens Have
Nørreport Sta.
Rundetårn (Round Tower)
Charlottenborg
Operahus (Opera House)
Post & Tele Museum
Universitet
Kongens Nytorv
Nyhavn
Royal Danish Skuespilhuset (Playhouse)
Domkirken
Helligånds Kirke
Det Kongelige Teater (Royal Theatre)
Thorvaldsen's Museum
Ripley's
Christiansborg Slot (Palace)
Christiania
Tycho Brahe Planetarium
Rådhus (City Hall)
Nationalmuseet
Slotsholmen
Ministerialbyg.
Det Nye Teater
Tivoli
Tivoli Gardens Amusement Park
Hovedbanegården
Carlsberg Glyptotek
Dansk Arkitektur Centre (DAC)
Det Kongelige Bibliotek (Royal Library)
Vesterport Sta.
Christians Kirke
Vesterbro
Central Postbygning
Amager Boulevard
Amagerbro
Christianshavn

COPYRIGHT PHILIP'S

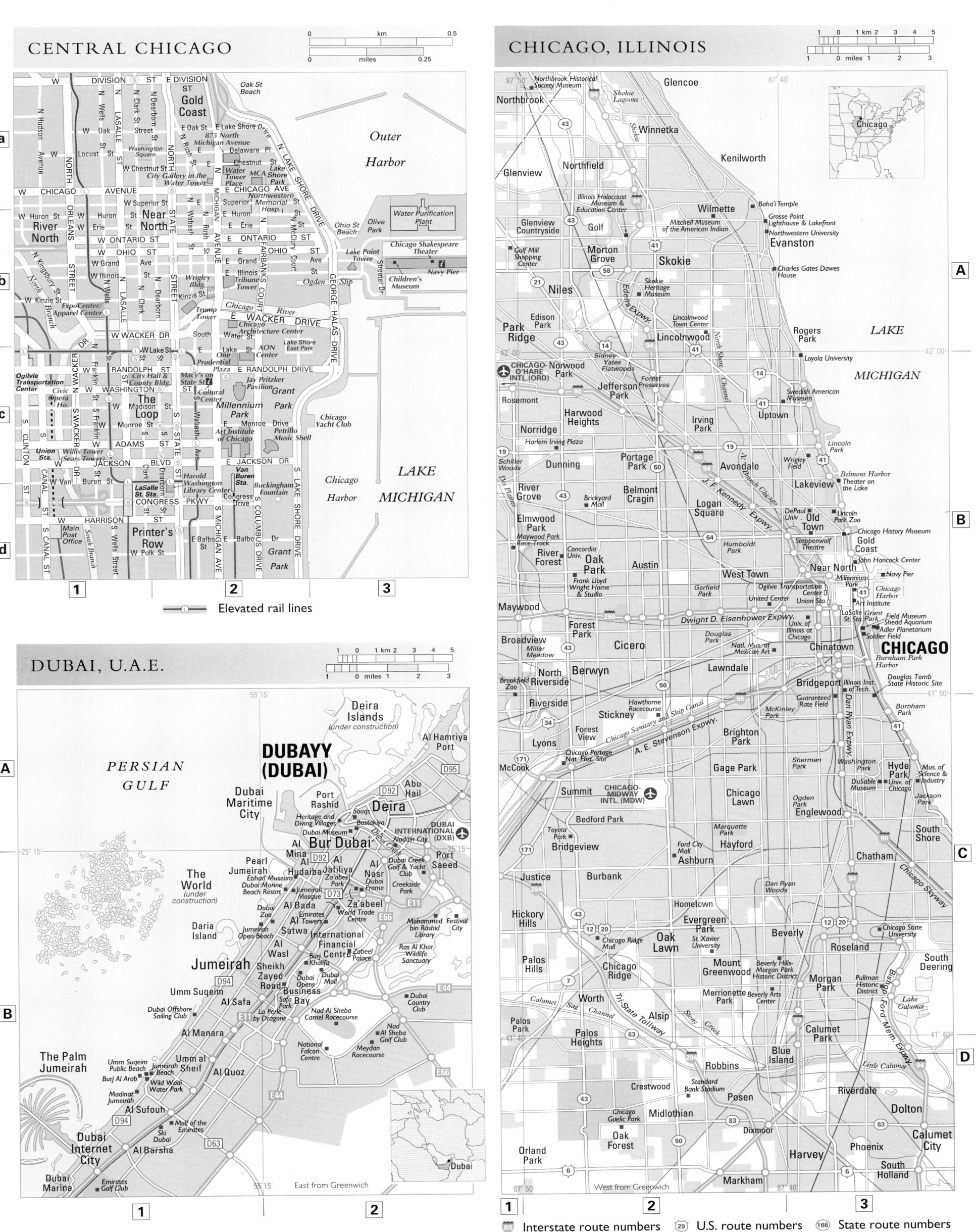

CENTRAL CHICAGO

km 0.5

miles 0.25

Outer Harbor

Oak St Beach

Gold Coast

E Oak St
875 North Michigan Avenue
Water Tower Place
City Gallery in the Water Tower
Chestnut St
MCA
Lake Shore Park

W DIVISION ST
E DIVISION ST

W Wells St
N Clark Street
N Dearborn
N Rush
N State
N Wabash
N Michigan Avenue

Washington Square
W Chestnut St
W Oak St
W Locust

Near North

River North

W CHICAGO AVENUE
E CHICAGO AVE

Northwestern Memorial Hosp.

W Superior St
W Huron St
E Superior St
E Huron St

N Orleans Street
N Kingsbury St
N Franklin
N LaSalle

W ONTARIO ST
E ONTARIO ST
W OHIO ST
E OHIO ST
W GRAND Ave
E GRAND Ave
W ILLINOIS St

Fairbanks Court
McClurg Court

Ohio St Beach
Olive Park

Water Purification Plant

Wrigley Bldg.
Chicago Tribune Tower

Kinzie St

Trump Tower

Chicago Shakespeare Theater

Navy Pier
Children's Museum

N Kinzie St
ExpoCenter/Apparel Center

Chicago River

W WACKER DR
E WACKER DRIVE

Streeter Dr

Chicago Architecture Center
Water St

Lake Point Tower

Ogden Slip

GEORGE HALAS DRIVE

WACKER DRIVE

W Lake St
E Lake St
One
AON Center

Lake Shore East Park

N LAKE SHORE DRIVE

W RANDOLPH ST
E RANDOLPH DRIVE

Ogilvie Transportation Center

Civic Opera Ho.

City Hall & County Bldg.
Prudential Plaza

Jay Pritzker Pavilion

Grant Park

W WASHINGTON
W MADISON St
W MONROE St

The Loop

Cultural Center
Millennium Park

Chicago Yacht Club

S Clinton
S Canal St
S Wacker DR
S Franklin
S LaSalle

N Wells
N Franklin
N LaSalle

Art Institute of Chicago
Petrillo Music Shell

W ADAMS ST

Union Sta.

Willis Tower (Sears Tower)

W JACKSON BLVD
E JACKSON DR

Buckingham Fountain

Chicago Harbor

W Van Buren St
Van Buren Sta.

LAKE MICHIGAN

Harold Washington Library Center

LaSalle St. Sta.
CONGRESS PKWY

W HARRISON St

Printer's Row

Main Post Office

Congress Drive

S COLUMBUS DRIVE
E BALBO Ave

Grant Park

S CANAL ST
S Wells Street

W Polk St

South Branch

Elevated rail lines

DUBAI, U.A.E.

1 0 1 km 2 3 4 5
0 miles 1 2 3

PERSIAN GULF

Deira Islands (under construction)
Al Hamriya Port

DUBAYY (DUBAI)

Dubai Maritime City
Port Rashid
Abu Hail

Heritage and Diving Villages
Souq

Deira

D95

Dubai Museum
Al Bur Dubai

D92

Mina Al
Dubai International (DXB)

Pearl Jumeirah
Al Hudaiba
Al Jafiliya
Za'abeel Park

Etihad Museum
Dubai Marine Beach Resort

The World (under construction)

Al Bada
Emirates Towers

Dubai Zoo

Al Towers

World Trade Centre

Port Saeed

Dubai Creek Golf & Yacht Club

Creekside Park

Daria Island

Jumeirah Open Beach

Satwa

International Financial Centre

Festival City

Mohammed bin Rashid Library

Jumeirah

Sheikh Zayed Road

Al Wasl

Burj Khalifa

Zabeel Palace

Ras Al Khor Wildlife Sanctuary

Dubai Mall

Umm Suqeim

Al Safa

Business Bay

Nad Al Sheba Camel Racecourse

Dubai Offshore Sailing Club

Al Manara

Safa Bay
La Perle by Dragone

Dubai Country Club

The Palm Jumeirah

Umm Suqeim Public Beach
Jumeirah Beach

Al Sufouh

Burj Al Arab

Wild Wadi Water Park

Madinat Jumeirah

Al Quoz

Meydan Racecourse

National Falcon Centre

Nad Al Sheba Golf Club

Dubai Internet City

Ski Dubai
Mall of the Emirates

Al Barsha

East from Greenwich

Dubai Marina
Emirates Golf Club

Dubai

CHICAGO, ILLINOIS

1 0 1 km 2 3 4 5
1 0 miles 1 2 3

Chicago

Northbrook Historical Society Museum
Glencoe
Skokie Lagoons

Northbrook
Winnetka
Kenilworth

Glenview
Northfield

Glenview Countryside
Illinois Holocaust Museum & Education Center
Wilmette
Baha'i Temple

Golf
Mitchell Museum of the American Indian
Grosse Point Lighthouse & Lakefront
Northwestern University

Golf Mill Shopping Center
Morton Grove
Evanston

Niles
Skokie
Skokie Heritage Museum
Charles Gates Dawes House

Park Ridge
Edison Park
Lincolnwood Town Center

LAKE MICHIGAN

Lincolnwood
Rogers Park

Loyola University

CHICAGO-O'HARE INTL. (ORD)
Norwood Park
Swedish American Museum

Rosemont
Jefferson Park
Forest Preserves

Harwood Heights
Irving Park
Uptown
Lincoln Park

Norridge
Harlem Irving Plaza

Schiller Woods
Dunning
Portage Park
Wrigley Field

River Grove
Avondale
Lakeview

Belmont Harbor Theater on the Lake

Brickyard Mall
Belmont Cragin
Logan Square
DePaul Univ.
Old Town
Lincoln Park Zoo

Elmwood Park
Humboldt Park
Steppenwolf Theatre
Chicago History Museum

Maywood Park Race Track
Concordia Univ.
Garfield Park
Ogilvie Transportation Center
Gold Coast
John Hancock Center

River Forest
Oak Park
West Town
United Center
Union Sta.
Near North
Navy Pier

Frank Lloyd Wright Home & Studio
Austin
LaSalle St. Sta.
Millennium Park
Chicago Harbor

Maywood
Dwight D. Eisenhower Expwy.
Univ. of Illinois at Chicago
Grant Park
Art Institute

Forest Park
Douglas Park
Field Museum
Shedd Aquarium
Adler Planetarium
Soldier Field

Broadview
Miller Meadow
Cicero
Lawndale
Natl. Mus. of Mexican Art
Chinatown
CHICAGO
Burnham Park Harbor

North Riverside
Berwyn
Illinois Inst. of Tech.
Bridgeport
Douglas Tomb State Historic Site

Brookfield Zoo
Riverside
Stickney
Hawthorne Racecourse
McKinley Park
Guaranteed Rate Field
Burnham Park

Lyons
Forest View
Chicago Sanitary and Ship Canal
Brighton Park
Sherman Park
Washington Park
Hyde Park
Mus. of Science & Industry

McCook
A. E. Stevenson Expwy.
Gage Park
DuSable Museum
Univ. of Chicago
Jackson Park

Summit
CHICAGO-MIDWAY INTL. (MDW)
Chicago Lawn
Ogden Park

Bedford Park
Englewood
South Shore

Toyota Park
Marquette Park
Hayford

Bridgeview
Ford City Mall
Ashburn
Chatham

Justice
Burbank
Dan Ryan Woods

Hickory Hills
Evergreen Park
Beverly
Chicago State University

Chicago Ridge Mall
St. Xavier University
Oak Lawn
Roseland

Palos Hills
Mount Greenwood
Beverly Hills-Morgan Park Historic District
Beverly Arts Center
Morgan Park
Pullman Historic District

Chicago Ridge
Merrionette Park
South Deering

Worth
Alsip
Lake Calumet

Palos Park
Palos Heights
Blue Island
Calumet Park

Robbins
Standard Bank Stadium
Little Calumet
Riverdale

Crestwood
Posen
Dolton

Chicago Gaelic Park
Midlothian
Dixmoor
Calumet City

Orland Park
Oak Forest
Harvey
Phoenix
South Holland
Markham

West from Greenwich

Interstate route numbers   U.S. route numbers   State route numbers

COPYRIGHT PHILIP'S

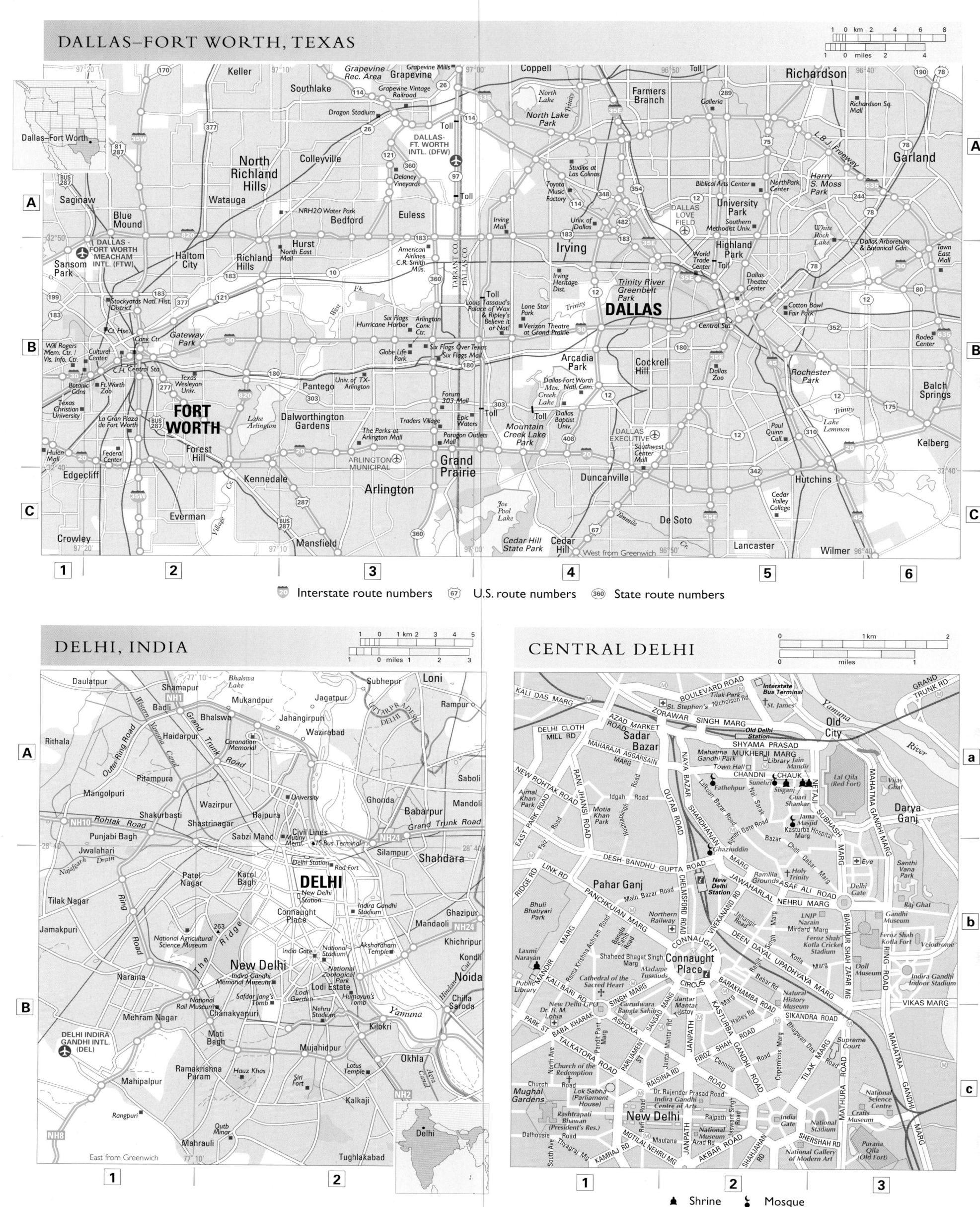

DALLAS–FORT WORTH, TEXAS

Interstate route numbers · U.S. route numbers · State route numbers

DELHI, INDIA

CENTRAL DELHI

Shrine · Mosque

COPYRIGHT PHILIP'S

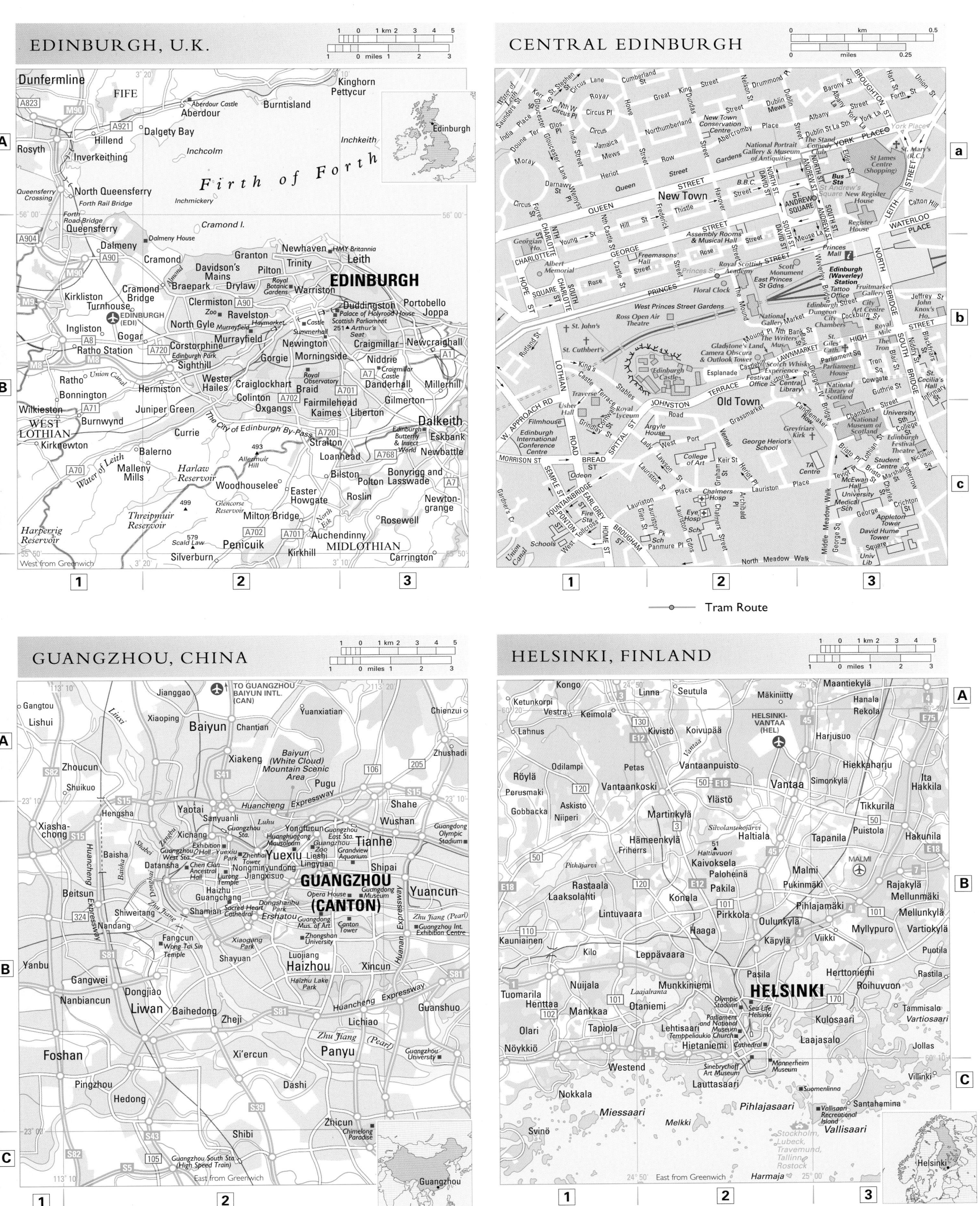

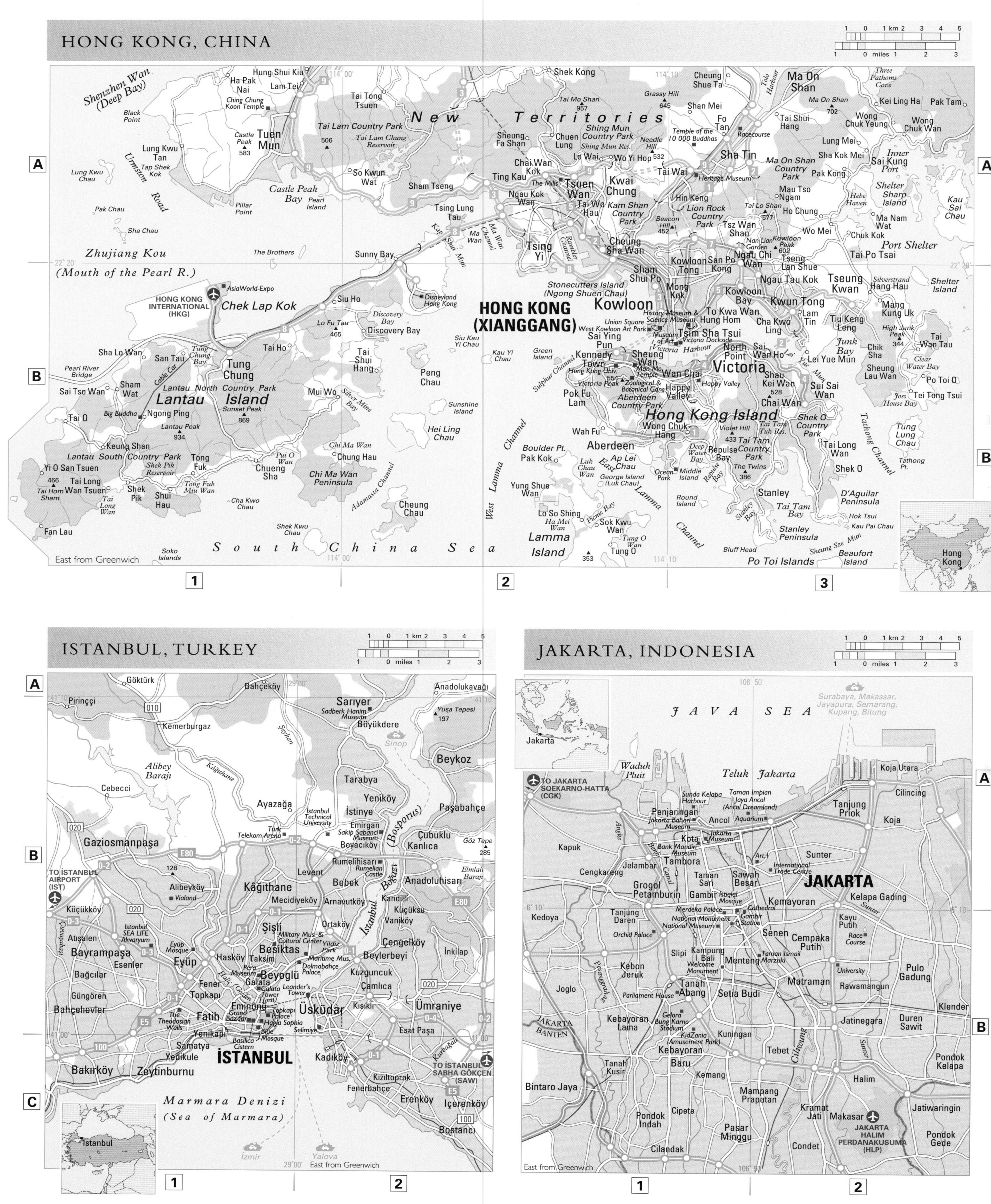

HONG KONG, CHINA

ISTANBUL, TURKEY

JAKARTA, INDONESIA

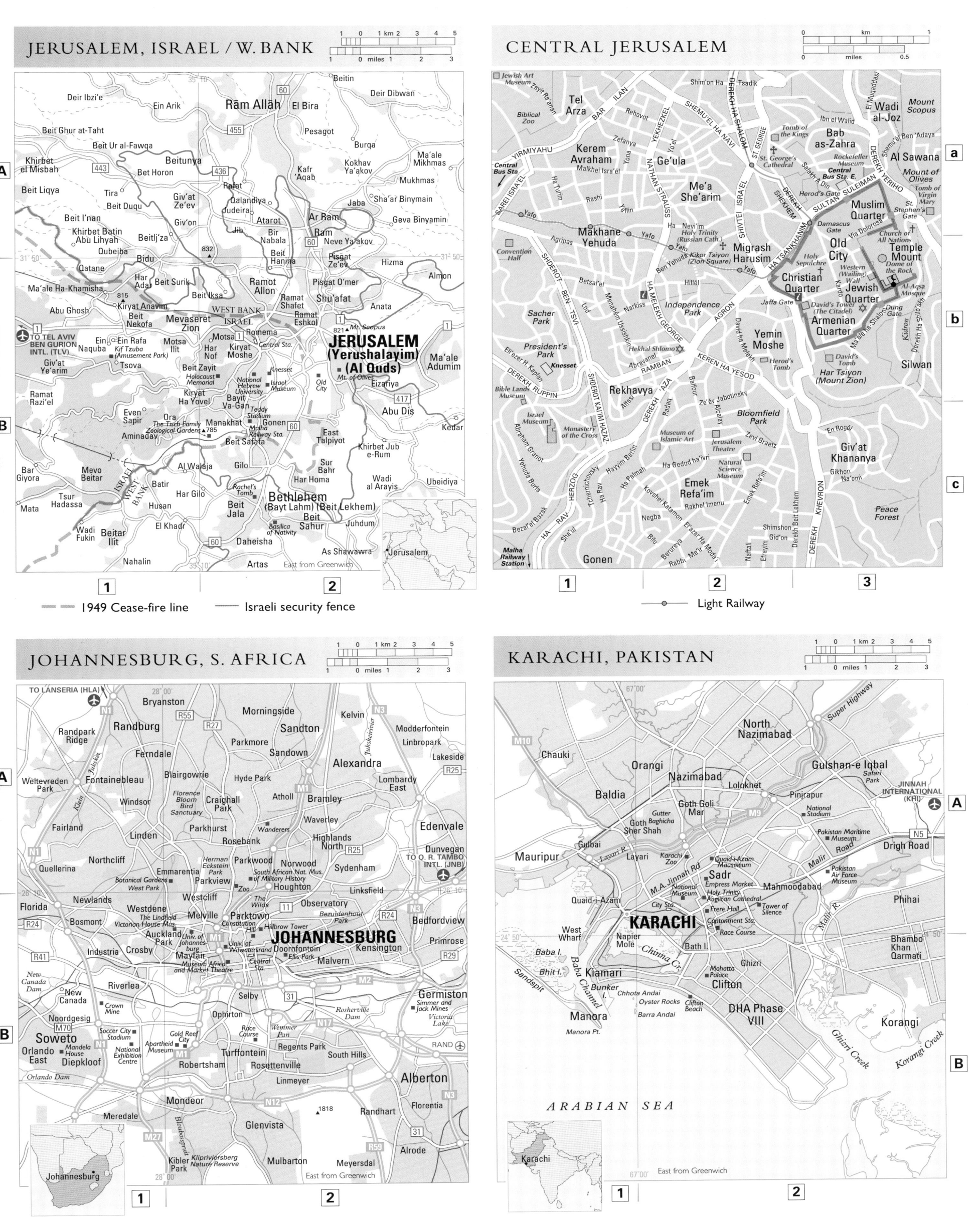

KOLKATA, INDIA

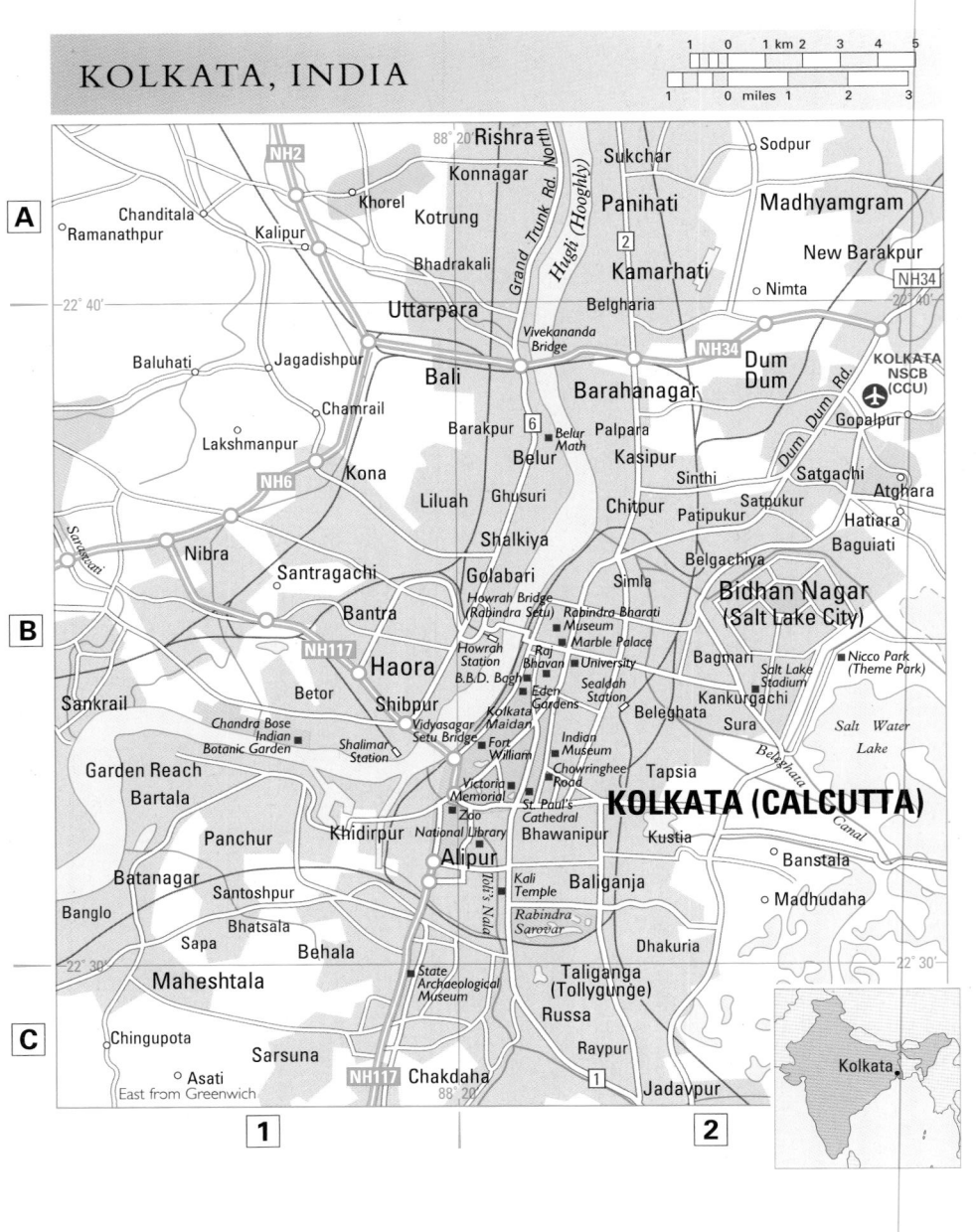

LAGOS, NIGERIA

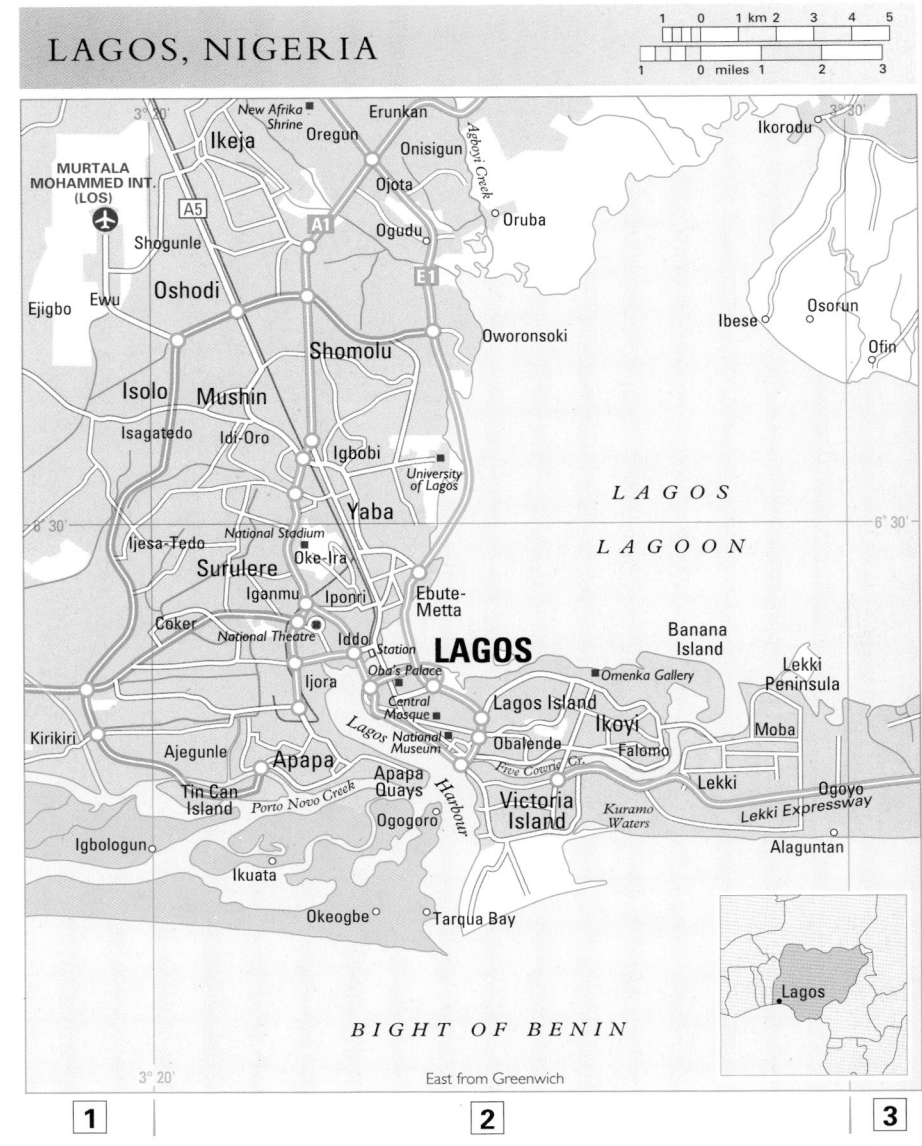

LAS VEGAS, NEVADA

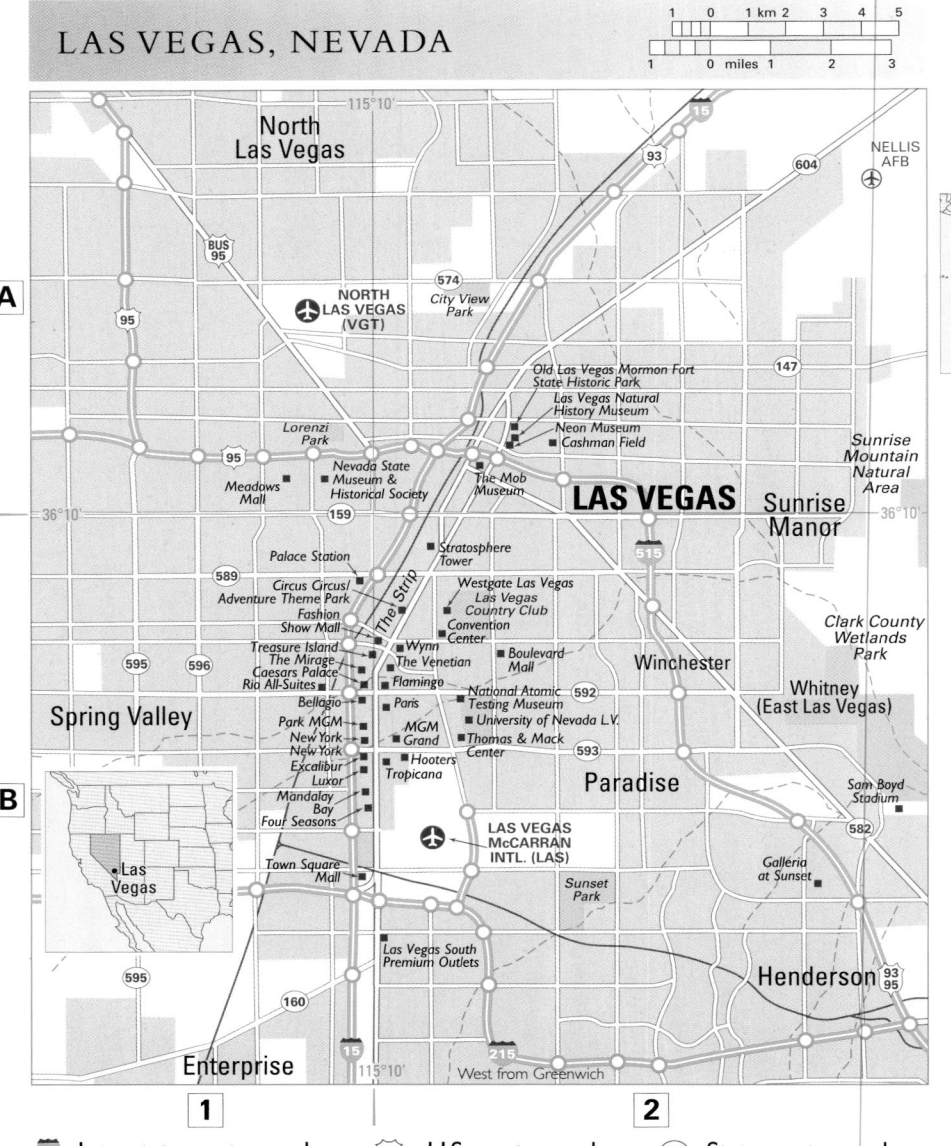

LIMA, PERU

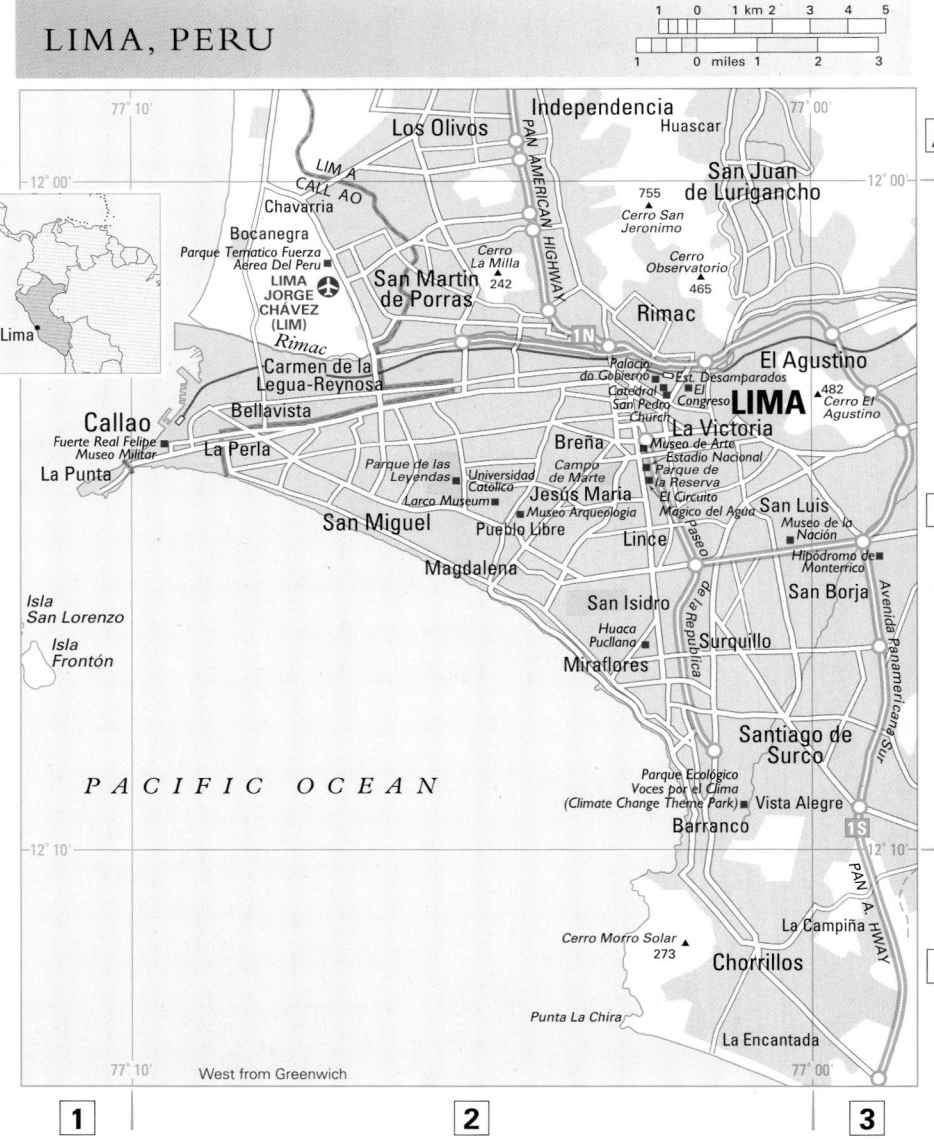

🛡 Interstate route numbers   95 U.S. route numbers   147 State route numbers

LONDON, U.K.

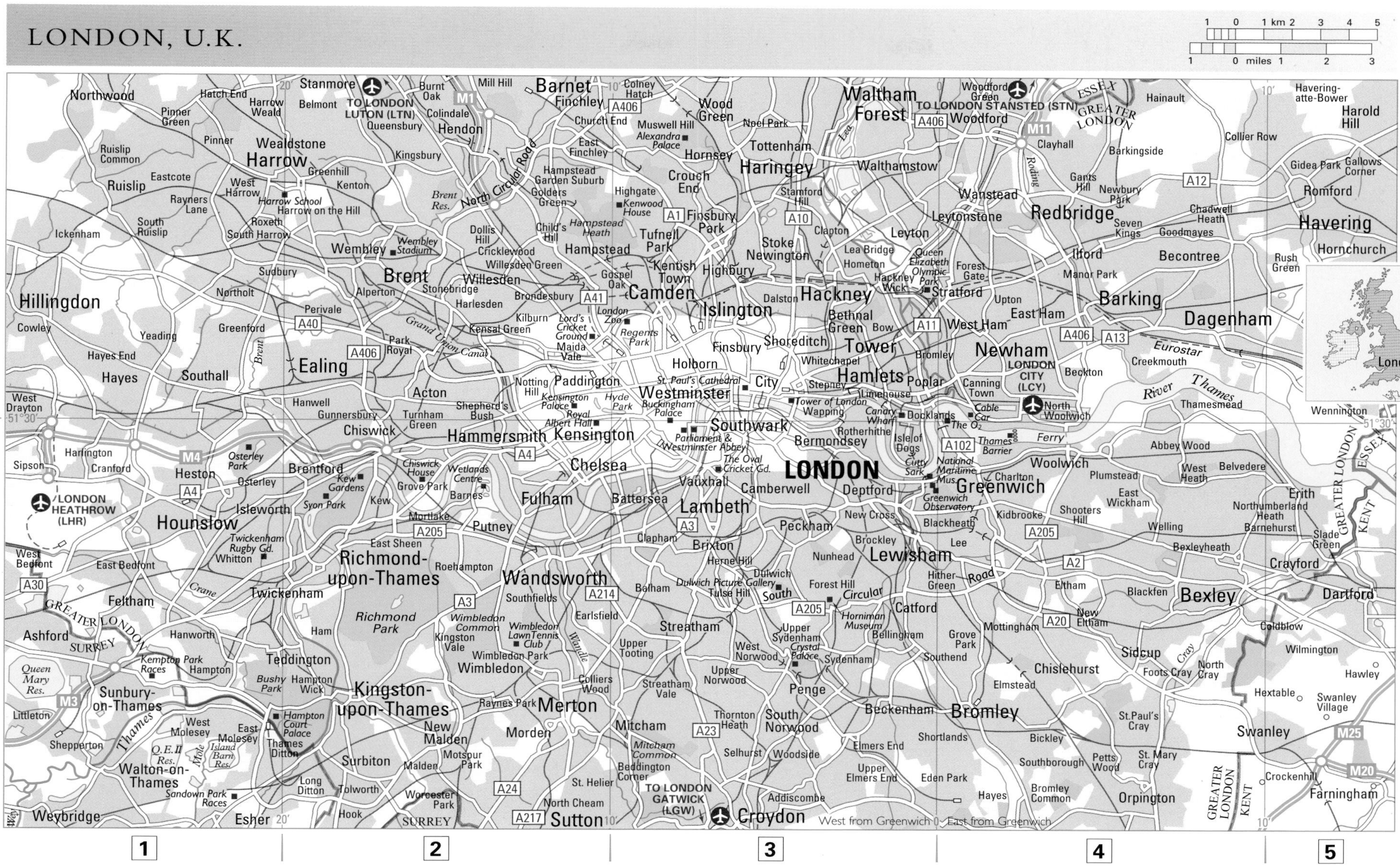

Scale bars: 1 0 1 km 2 3 4 5 / 1 0 miles 1 2 3

London (inset location map)

Grid references A–B (vertical), 1–5 (horizontal)

Northwood, Stanmore, TO LONDON LUTON (LTN), Barnet, Finchley, Colney Hatch, Wood Green, Waltham Forest, Woodford, TO LONDON STANSTED (STN), GREATER LONDON, ESSEX, Hainault, Havering-atte-Bower, Harold Hill

Pinner Green, Hatch End, Belmont, Queensbury, Hendon, Church End, Muswell Hill, Alexandra Palace, Hornsey, Tottenham, Walthamstow, Woodford, Clayhall, Barkingside, Gidea Park, Gallows Corner, Romford, Havering, Hornchurch

Ruislip Common, Pinner, Wealdstone, Kingsbury, Hampstead Garden Suburb, Goldors Green, Highgate, Crouch End, Haringey, Leyton, Leytonstone, Redbridge, Gants Hill, Newbury Park, Seven Kings, Chadwell Heath, Goodmayes

Eastcote, West Harrow, Harrow, Greenhill, Kenton, Cricklewood, Child's Hill, Hampstead Heath, Kenwood House, Finsbury Park, Stoke Newington, Highbury, Clapton, Hackney Wick, Forest Gate, Ilford, Manor Park, Becontree, Harrow Weald

Ruislip, Rayners Lane, Harrow School, Harrow on the Hill, Roxeth, South Harrow, Wembley, Willesden Green, Brondesbury, Kensal Green, Maida Vale, Regents Park, Holborn, Shoreditch, Bethnal Green, Bow, West Ham, Newham, East Ham, Barking, Dagenham

Hillingdon, Ickenham, Cowley, Hayes End, Yeading, Northolt, Perivale, Park Royal, Acton, Notting Hill, Paddington, St Paul's Cathedral, City, Stepney, Poplar, Canning Town, LONDON CITY (LCY), North Woolwich, Eurostar, Creekmouth, Wennington

Hayes, Southall, Hanwell, Ealing, Shepherd's Bush, Kensington, Hyde Park, Buckingham Palace, Westminster, Southwark, Bermondsey, Rotherhithe, Wapping, Isle of Dogs, Canary Wharf, Docklands, Cable Car, The O2, Thames Barrier, Thamesmead

West Drayton, LONDON HEATHROW (LHR), Cranford, Heston, Osterley, Brentford, Chiswick, Hammersmith, Chelsea, Fulham, Vauxhall, Lambeth, Camberwell, Deptford, Greenwich, Charlton, Woolwich, Plumstead, Abbey Wood, West Heath, Belvedere, Erith

Sipson, Harlington, Isleworth, Syon Park, Kew Gardens, Kew, Barnes, Putney, Battersea, The Oval Cricket Gd., Peckham, New Cross, Greenwich Observatory, Blackheath, Kidbrooke, Shooters Hill, Welling, Bexleyheath, Northumberland Heath

Hounslow, Twickenham, Richmond-upon-Thames, Mortlake, Wandsworth, Clapham, Brixton, Herne Hill, Nunhead, Brockley, Lewisham, Lee, Eltham, East Wickham, Barnehurst, Crayford

Feltham, Whitton, Twickenham Rugby Gd., East Sheen, Roehampton, Southfields, Dulwich Picture Gallery, Forest Hill, Hither Green, Mottingham, Blackfen, Bexley, Dartford

Ashford, East Bedfont, West Bedfont, Hanworth, Richmond Park, Ham, Wimbledon Common, Earlsfield, Balham, Dulwich, Tulse Hill, Sydenham, Catford, New Eltham, Sidcup, Foots Cray, North Cray, Coldblow, Wilmington, Hawley

Shepperton, Walton-on-Thames, Sunbury-on-Thames, Teddington, Bushy Park, Hampton Wick, Kingston-upon-Thames, New Malden, Wimbledon, Streatham, Upper Norwood, Crystal Palace, Penge, Beckenham, Bromley, Chislehurst, St. Paul's Cray, Swanley Village, Hextable

Weybridge, Esher, Hook, Tolworth, Surbiton, Worcester Park, Sutton, Mitcham, Merton, Morden, Thornton Heath, South Norwood, Elmers End, Shortlands, Bickley, Petts Wood, Orpington, St. Mary Cray, Swanley, Farningham

TO LONDON GATWICK (LGW), Croydon, Addiscombe, Eden Park, Bromley Common, GREATER LONDON, KENT, SURREY

West from Greenwich 0 · East from Greenwich

CENTRAL LONDON

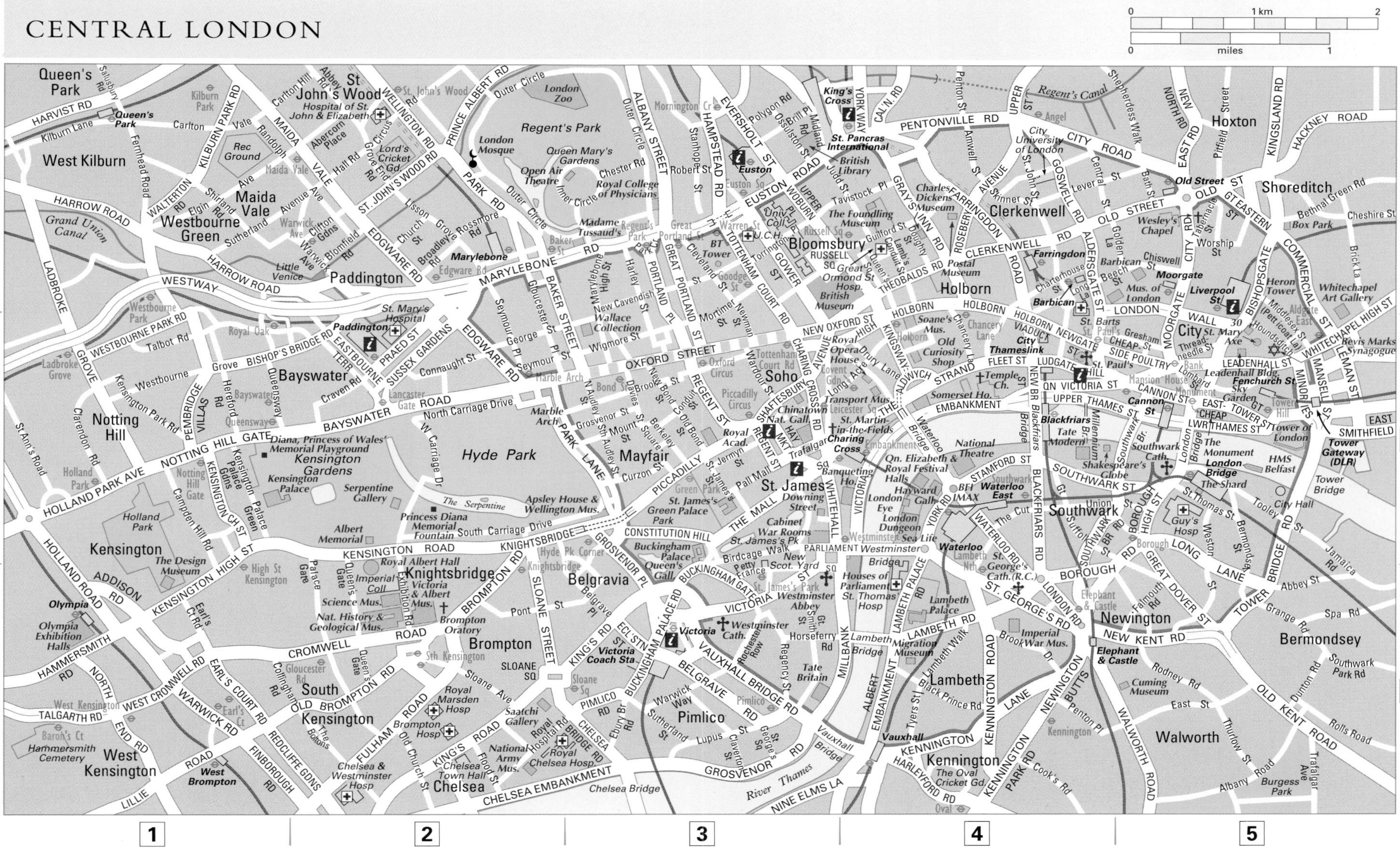

Scale bars: 0 1 km 2 / 0 miles 1

Grid references a–c (vertical), 1–5 (horizontal)

Queen's Park, West Kilburn, Kilburn, St John's Wood, Regent's Park, London Zoo, King's Cross, St. Pancras International, Euston, Hoxton, Shoreditch

Maida Vale, Westbourne Green, Paddington, Marylebone, Madame Tussaud's, Bloomsbury, Holborn, Clerkenwell, Old Street, Moorgate, Liverpool St., Whitechapel Art Gallery

Notting Hill, Bayswater, Hyde Park, Mayfair, Soho, Covent Garden, St Paul's, City, Bank, Aldgate

Kensington, Holland Park, Knightsbridge, Belgravia, St. James, Westminster, Charing Cross, Trafalgar Square, Waterloo, Southwark, London Bridge, The Shard, Tower of London, Tower Bridge

South Kensington, Brompton, Sloane Square, Pimlico, Victoria, Buckingham Palace, Houses of Parliament, Westminster Abbey, Tate Britain, Lambeth, Imperial War Mus., Elephant & Castle, Bermondsey

West Kensington, Earl's Court, West Brompton, Chelsea, Chelsea Embankment, Battersea, Vauxhall, Kennington, The Oval Cricket Gd., Walworth

Legend: ▬ Congestion Charging Zone

LISBON, PORTUGAL

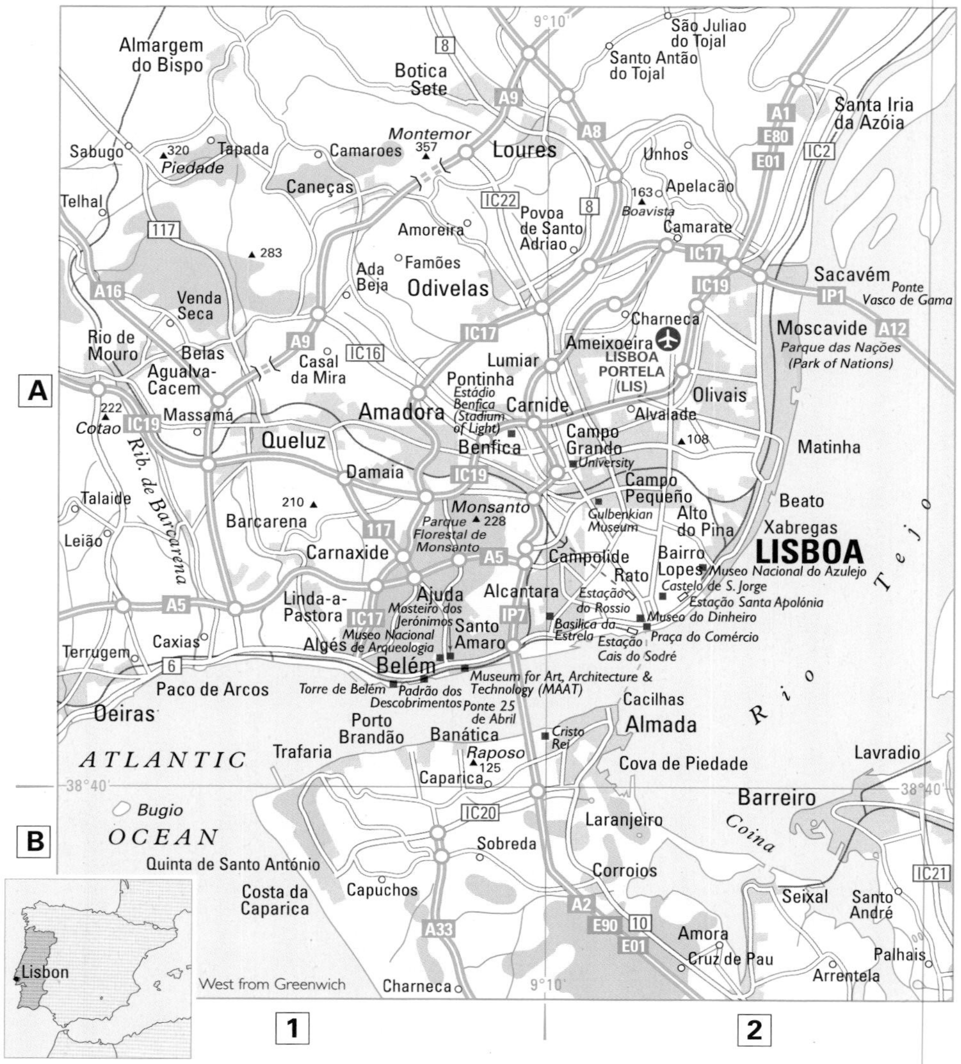

CENTRAL LISBON

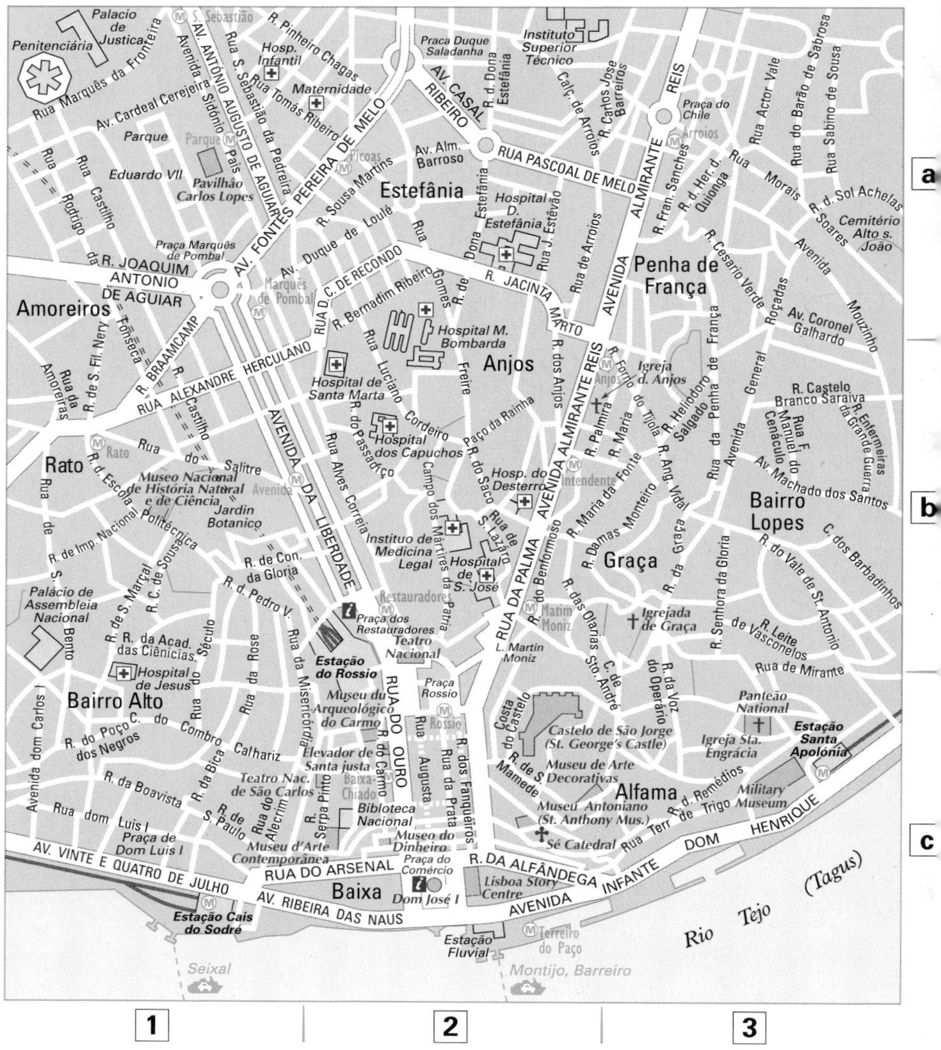

LOS ANGELES, CALIFORNIA

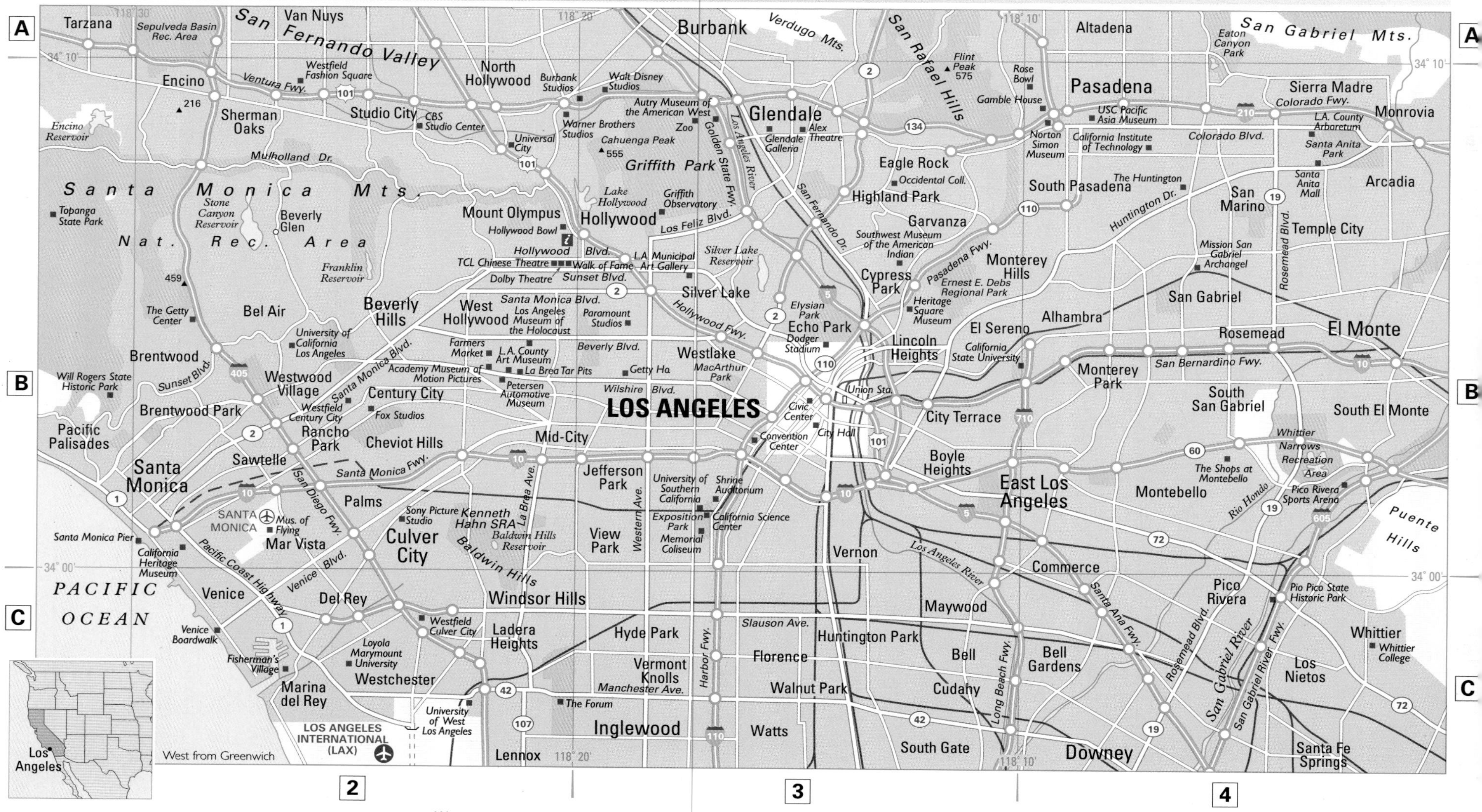

Interstate route numbers U.S. route numbers State route numbers

COPYRIGHT PHILIP'S

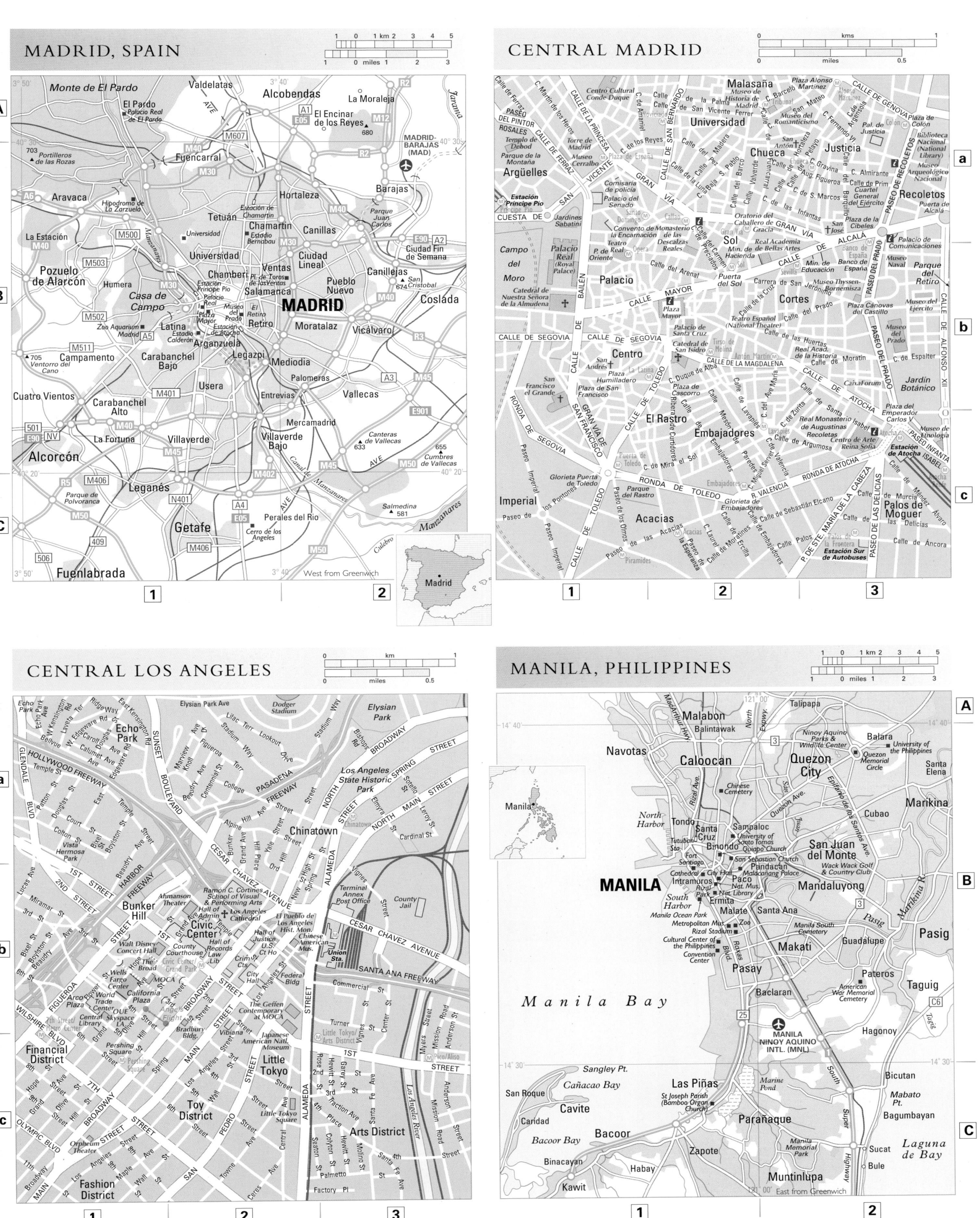

MEXICO CITY, MEXICO

CENTRAL MEXICO CITY

Federal route numbers

MELBOURNE, AUSTRALIA

MILAN, ITALY

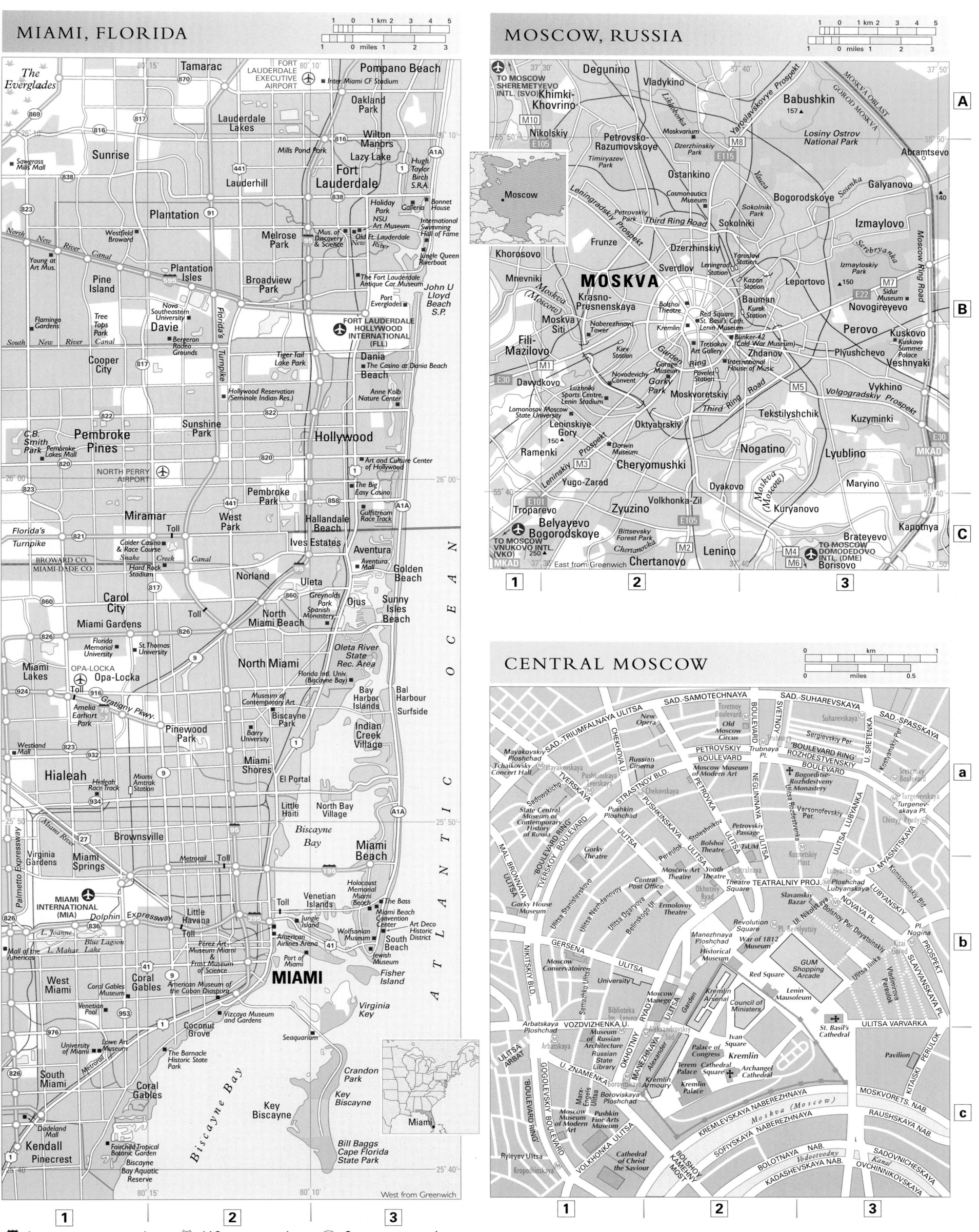

MIAMI, FLORIDA

The Everglades
Tamarac
Pompano Beach
FORT LAUDERDALE EXECUTIVE AIRPORT
Inter Miami CF Stadium
Oakland Park
Lauderdale Lakes
Wilton Manors
Lazy Lake
Fort Lauderdale
Hugh Taylor Birch S.R.A.
Sunrise
Lauderhill
Mills Pond Park
Plantation
Holiday Park
Galleria
NSU Art Museum
Bonnet House
International Swimming Hall of Fame
Melrose Park
Mus. of Discovery & Science
Old Ft. Lauderdale
Jungle Queen Riverboat
Westfield Broward
Nova Southeastern University
Broadview Park
The Fort Lauderdale Antique Car Museum
Pine Island
Plantation Isles
Port Everglades
Tree Tops Park
Davie
Bergeron Rodeo Grounds
John U Lloyd Beach S.P.
Flamingo Gardens
Young at Art Mus.
Cooper City
Tiger Tail Lake Park
Dania Beach
The Casino at Dania Beach
Hollywood Reservation (Seminole Indian Res.)
Anne Kolb Nature Center
Pembroke Pines
C.B. Smith Park
Pembroke Lakes Mall
Sunshine Park
Hollywood
Art and Culture Center of Hollywood
NORTH PERRY AIRPORT
Pembroke Park
The Big Easy Casino
Miramar
West Park
Hallandale Beach
Gulfstream Race Track
Florida's Turnpike
Calder Casino & Race Course
Hard Rock Stadium
Ives Estates
Aventura
Aventura Mall
Carol City
Norland
Uleta
Golden Beach
Miami Gardens
Greynolds Park
Ojus
Sunny Isles Beach
Spanish Monastery
Florida Memorial University
St. Thomas University
North Miami Beach
Oleta River State Rec. Area
Miami Lakes
OPA-LOCKA
Opa-Locka
North Miami
Museum of Contemporary Art
Bay Harbor Islands
Bal Harbour
Surfside
Amelia Earhart Park
Museum of Contemporary Art
Biscayne Park
Indian Creek Village
Pinewood Park
Barry University
Miami Shores
Westland Mall
El Portal
Hialeah
Hialeah Race Track
Miami Amtrak Station
Little Haiti
North Bay Village
Brownsville
Biscayne Bay
Miami Beach
Virginia Gardens
Holocaust Memorial Miami Beach
Miami Springs
Metrorail
The Bass
Miami Beach Convention Center
Wolfsonian Museum
Art Deco Historic District
MIAMI INTERNATIONAL (MIA)
Dolphin Expressway
Jungle Island
American Airlines Arena
Pérez Art Museum Miami
Phillip and Patricia Frost Museum of Science
Port of Miami
South Beach
L. Joanne
Blue Lagoon Lake
L. Mahar
Mall of the Americas
West Miami
Coral Gables
American Museum of the Cuban Diaspora
MIAMI
Fisher Island
Venetian Pool
Coral Gables Museum
American Museum of the Cuban Diaspora
Virginia Key
University of Miami
Lowe Art Museum
Coconut Grove
Vizcaya Museum and Gardens
Seaquarium
The Barnacle Historic State Park
Crandon Park
Key Biscayne
South Miami
Coral Gables
Bill Baggs Cape Florida State Park
Kendall
Pinecrest
Dadeland Mall
Fairchild Tropical Botanic Garden
Biscayne Bay Aquatic Reserve
ATLANTIC OCEAN
West from Greenwich

MOSCOW, RUSSIA

Degunino
TO MOSCOW SHEREMETYEVO INTL. (SVO)
Khimki-Khovrino
Vladykino
Babushkin
Nikolskiy
Moskvarium
Losiny Ostrov National Park
Petrovsko-Razumovskoye
Abramtsevo
Timiryazev Park
Cosmonautics Museum
Ostankino
Sokolniki Park
Galyanovo
Khorosovo
Frunze
Bogorodskoye
Izmaylovo
Sverdlov
Yaroslavl Station
Leningrad Station
Kazan Station
Leportovo
Novogireyevo
Mnevniki
MOSKVA
Krasno-Presnenskaya
Bauman
Kursk Station
Perovo
Kuskovo
Moskva Siti
Bolshoi Theatre
Red Square
St. Basil's Cath.
Lenin Museum
Zhdanov
Kremlin
Yeshnyaki
Fili-Mazilovo
Kiev Station
Tretiakov Art Gallery
International House of Music
Vykhino
Davydkovo
Novodevichy Convent
Gorky Park
Moskvoretskiy
Tekstilyshchik
Kuzminki
Lomonosov Moscow State University
Luzhniki Sports Centre, Lenin Stadium
Darwin Museum
Leninskiye Gory
Oktyabrskiy
Ramenki
Cheryomushki
Nogatino
Lyublino
Leninsky Prospekt
Yugo-Zarad
Dyakovo
Maryino
Troparevo
Zyuzino
Volkhonka-Zil
Kuryanovo
Belyayevo
Bogorodskoye
Bittsevsky Forest Park
TO MOSCOW VNUKOVO INTL. (VKO)
Chertanovo
Lenino
Brateyevo
Kapotnya
East from Greenwich
Chertanovo
Borisovo
TO MOSCOW DOMODEDOVO INTL. (DME)

CENTRAL MOSCOW

Mayakovskiy Ploshchad
SAD.-SAMOTECHNAYA
SAD.-SUHAREVSKAYA
SAD.-SPASSKAYA
Tchaikovsky Concert Hall
New Opera
Tsvetnoy Boulevard
Old Moscow Circus
BOULEVARD
Sergievsky Per.
Svetnoy
BOULEVARD RING
ROZHDESTVENSKY
U. SRETENKA
State Central Museum of Contemporary History of Russia
Pushkin Ploshchad
Moscow Museum of Modern Art
PETROVKA
Turgenevskaya Pl.
Gorky Theatre
Pushkin Ploshchad
Bolshoi Theatre
TsUM
Kuznetsky Most
Lubyanka
Moscow Art Youth Theatre
U. MYASNITSKAYA
Moscow Art Theatre
TEATRALNY PROJ.
Ploshchad Lubyanskaya
NOVAYA PL.
Central Post Office
Okhotny Ryad
Teatralnaya Square
Revolution Square
PL. Revolyutsiy
War of 1812 Museum
Moscow Conservatoires
Manezhnaya Ploshchad
Historical Museum
GUM Shopping Arcade
PL. Nogina
University
Red Square
Lenin Mausoleum
Kremlin Arsenal
Council of Ministers
St. Basil's Cathedral
ULITSA VARVARKA
Arbatskaya Ploshchad
Museum of Russian Architecture
Russian State Library
Ivan Square
Palace of Congress
Terem Palace
Kremlin
Archangel Cathedral
Pavilion
ULITSA ARBAT
Kremlin Armoury
Kremlin Palace
MOSKVORETS. NAB.
Moscow Museum of Modern Art
Pushkin Fine Arts Museum
KREMLEVSKAYA NABEREZHNAYA
Moskva (Moscow)
RAUSHSKAYA NAB.
Cathedral of Christ the Saviour
SOFIYSKAYA NABEREZHNAYA
BOLOTNAYA NAB.
SADOVNICHESKAYA

COPYRIGHT PHILIP'S

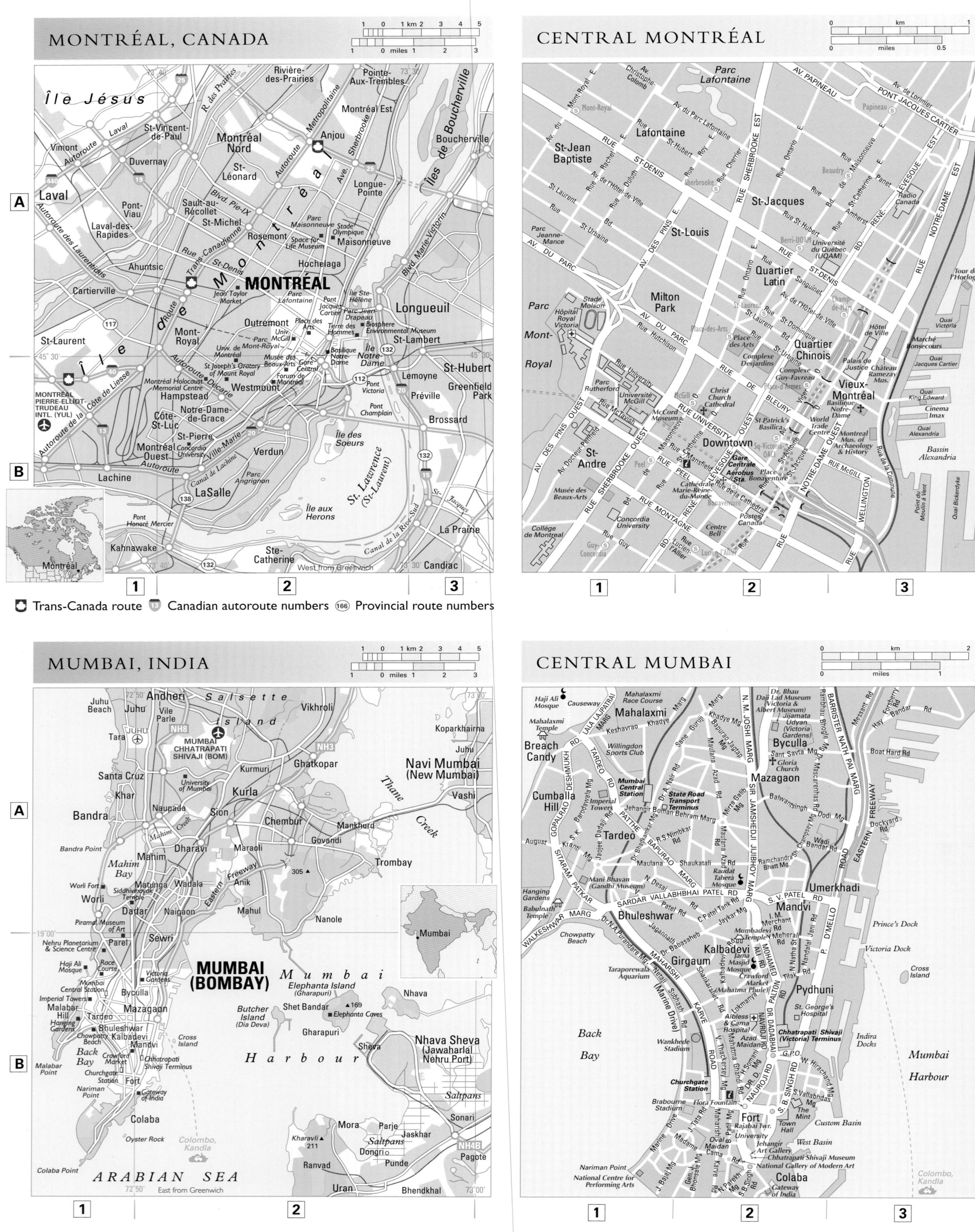

MONTRÉAL, CANADA

Île Jésus

Laval
St-Vincent-de-Paul
Vimont
Duvernay
Montréal Nord
Montréal Est
Rivière-des-Prairies
Pointe-Aux-Trembles
Anjou

Laval
Pont-Viau
Sault-au-Récollet
St-Léonard
St-Michel
Longue-Pointe
de Boucherville
Îles de Boucherville

Ahuntsic
Laval-des-Rapides
Rosemont
Hochelaga
Stade Olympique
Maisonneuve
Space for Life Museum

Cartierville
Jean Talon Market
Parc Lafontaine
Parc Jean-Drapeau
Longueuil

St-Laurent
Outremont
Mont-Royal
MONTRÉAL
Biosphere
Environmental Museum
St-Lambert

Côte de Liesse
Hampstead
Westmount
Unv. de Montréal
Musée des Beaux-Arts
Basilique Notre-Dame
Gare Central
Forum de Montréal
Île Ste-Hélène
Île Notre-Dame
St-Hubert

MONTRÉAL PIERRE-ELLIOT-TRUDEAU INTL. (YUL)
St-Joseph's Oratory of Mount Royal
Lemoyne
Greenfield Park

Côte-St-Luc
St-Pierre
Montréal Ouest
Concordia University
Ville-Marie
Notre-Dame-de-Grâce
Pont Victoria
Préville
Brossard

Lachine
Verdun
Île des Soeurs
St. Lawrence (St-Laurent)

LaSalle
Parc Angrignon
Île aux Herons

Pont Honoré Mercier
Canal de la Rive Sud
La Prairie

Kahnawake
Ste-Catherine
West from Greenwich
Candiac

🛡 Trans-Canada route   ⑬ Canadian autoroute numbers   ⑯⑥ Provincial route numbers

CENTRAL MONTRÉAL

Parc Lafontaine
PONT JACQUES CARTIER
St-Jean Baptiste
Lafontaine
Radio Canada

St-Jacques
Tour de l'Horloge
St-Louis
Université du Québec (UQAM)
Champ-de-Mars
Hôtel de Ville
Quai Victoria
Marché Bonsecours

Parc Mont-Royal
Hôpital Royal Victoria
Milton Park
Quartier Latin
Quai Jacques Cartier
Château Ramezay Mus.

Parc Rutherford
Université McGill
Place-des-Arts
Place des Arts
Complexe Desjardins
Quartier Chinois
Vieux-Montréal
Basilique Notre-Dame
Quai King Edward
Cinema Imax

St-André
Christ Church Cathedral
McCord Museum
St Patrick's Basilica
World Trade Centre
Palais de Justice
Quai Alexandria
Bassin Alexandria

Downtown
Cathédrale Marie-Reine-du-Monde
Sq-Victoria OACI
Montreal Mus. of Archaeology & History

Musée des Beaux-Arts
Gare Centrale Aerobus Sta.
Place Bonaventure
Pointe du Moulin à Vent
Quai Bickerdyke

Collège de Montréal
Concordia University
Postes Canada
Centre Bell
Guy-Concordia

MUMBAI, INDIA

Salsette Island
Andheri
Juhu Beach
Juhu
Vile Parle
Vikhroli
Tara
Koparkhairna

MUMBAI CHHATRAPATI SHIVAJI (BOM)
Ghatkopar
Juhu
Santa Cruz
Kurmuri
Navi Mumbai (New Mumbai)

University of Mumbai
Khar
Kurla
Vashi

Bandra
Naupade
Sion
Chembur
Mankhurd
Govandi

Bandra Point
Mahim
Dharavi
Maraoli
Trombay

Mahim Bay
Matunga
Wadala
Anik
305 ▲

Worli Fort
Siddhivinayak Temple
Naigaon
Mahul
Nanole

Worli
Dadar
Piramal Museum of Art

Nehru Planetarium & Science Centre
Parel
Sewri
Mumbai

Haji Ali Mosque
Race Course
MUMBAI (BOMBAY)
Elephanta Island (Gharapuri)
Nhava

Mumbai Central Station
Victoria Gardens
Butcher Island (Dia Deva)
Shet Bandar
169 ▲
Elephanta Caves
Nhava Sheva (Jawaharlal Nehru Port)

Imperial Towers
Malabar Hill
Byculla
Mazagaon
Gharapuri
Sheva

Hanging Gardens
Tardeo
Cross Island
Mumbai Harbour

Bhuleshwar
Kalbadevi
Mandvi
Chhatrapati Shivaji Terminus
Saltpans

Malabar Point
Back Bay
Crawford Market
Churchgate Station
Fort

Nariman Point
Gateway of India

Colaba
Mora
Parje
Jaskhar
Saltpans
Sonari

Oyster Rock
Kharavli
211 ▲
Dongrio
Punde

Colombo, Kandla
Colaba Point
Ranvad
Uran
Bhendkhal

ARABIAN SEA
East from Greenwich

CENTRAL MUMBAI

Haji Ali Mosque
Causeway
Mahalaxmi Race Course
Dr. Bhau Daji Lad Museum (Victoria & Albert Museum)
BARRISTER NATH PAI MARG

Mahalaxmi Temple
Mahalaxmi
Jijamata Udyan (Victoria Gardens)

Breach Candy
Willingdon Sports Club
Byculla
Gloria Church
Boat Hard Rd

Cumballa Hill
Mumbai Central Station
State Road Transport Terminus
Mazagaon
Dockyard Rd

Tardeo
Imperial Towers
Eastern Freeway

Hanging Gardens
Mani Bhavan (Gandhi Museum)
Raudat Tahera Mosque
Umerkhadi

Babulnath Temple
SARDAR VALLABHBHAI PATEL RD
Mandvi
Prince's Dock

Chowpatty Beach
Bhuleshwar
I.M. Merchant Rd

Taraporewala Aquarium
Kalbadevi
Girgaum
Mumbadevi Temple
Crawford Market
Victoria Dock
Cross Island

Pydhuni
St. George's Hospital
Indira Docks

Wankhede Stadium
Azad Maidan
Chhatrapati Shivaji (Victoria) Terminus
Mumbai Harbour

Back Bay
Albless & Cama Hospital
G.P.O.

Brabourne Stadium
Flora Fountain
Fort
Rajabai Twr.
University
Town Hall
The Mint
Custom Basin
West Basin

Nariman Point
National Centre for Performing Arts
Jehangir Art Gallery
Chhatrapati Shivaji Museum
National Gallery of Modern Art
Oval Maidan
Colaba
Gateway of India
Colombo, Kandla

COPYRIGHT PHILIP'S

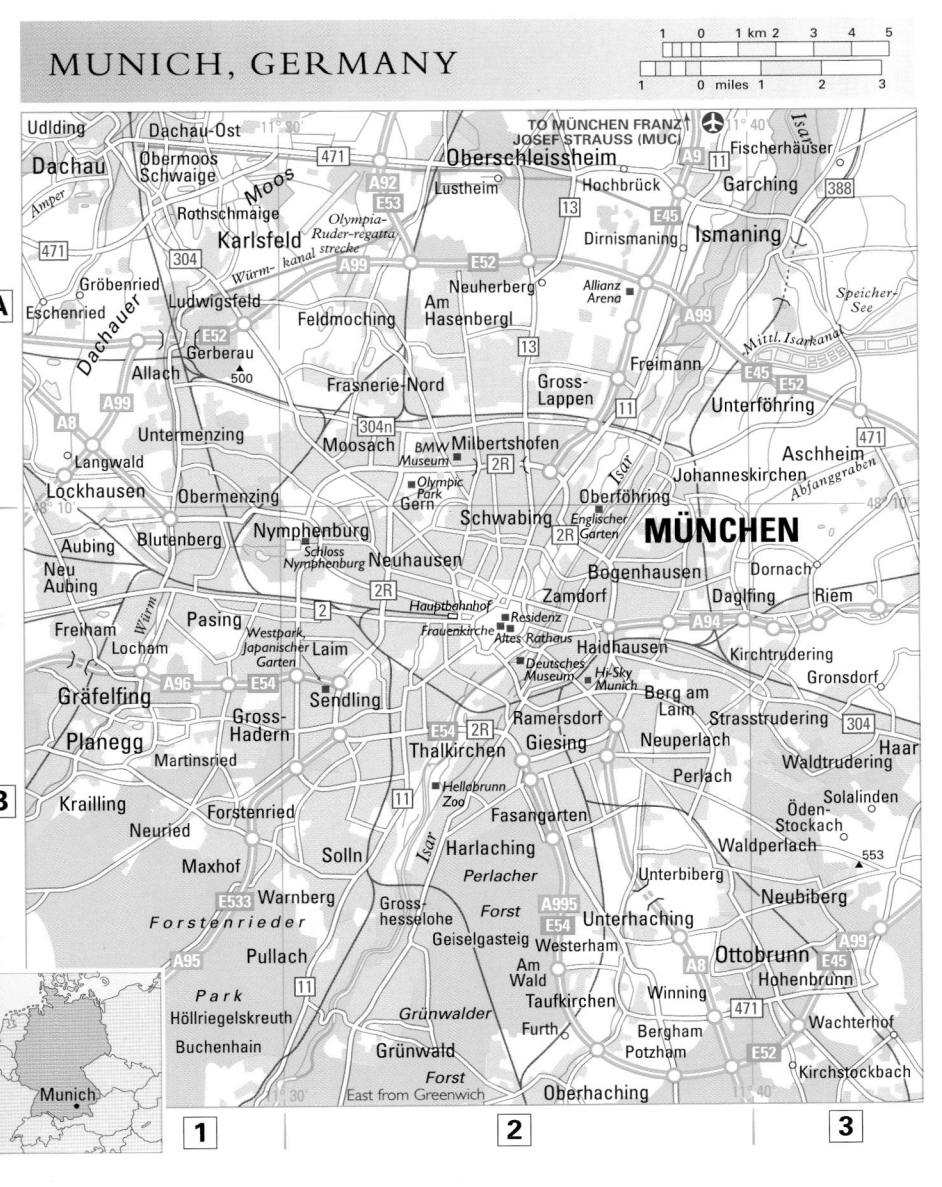

MUNICH, GERMANY

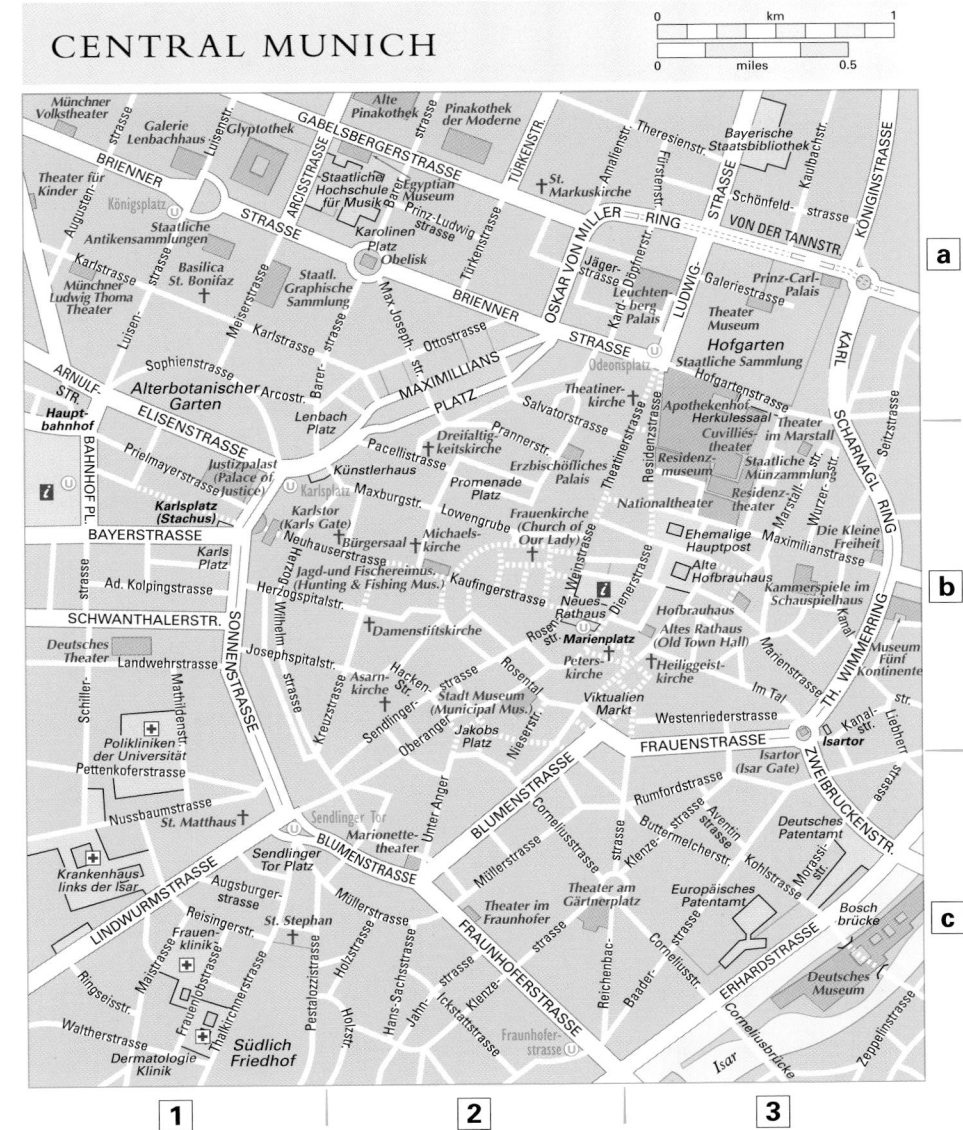

CENTRAL MUNICH

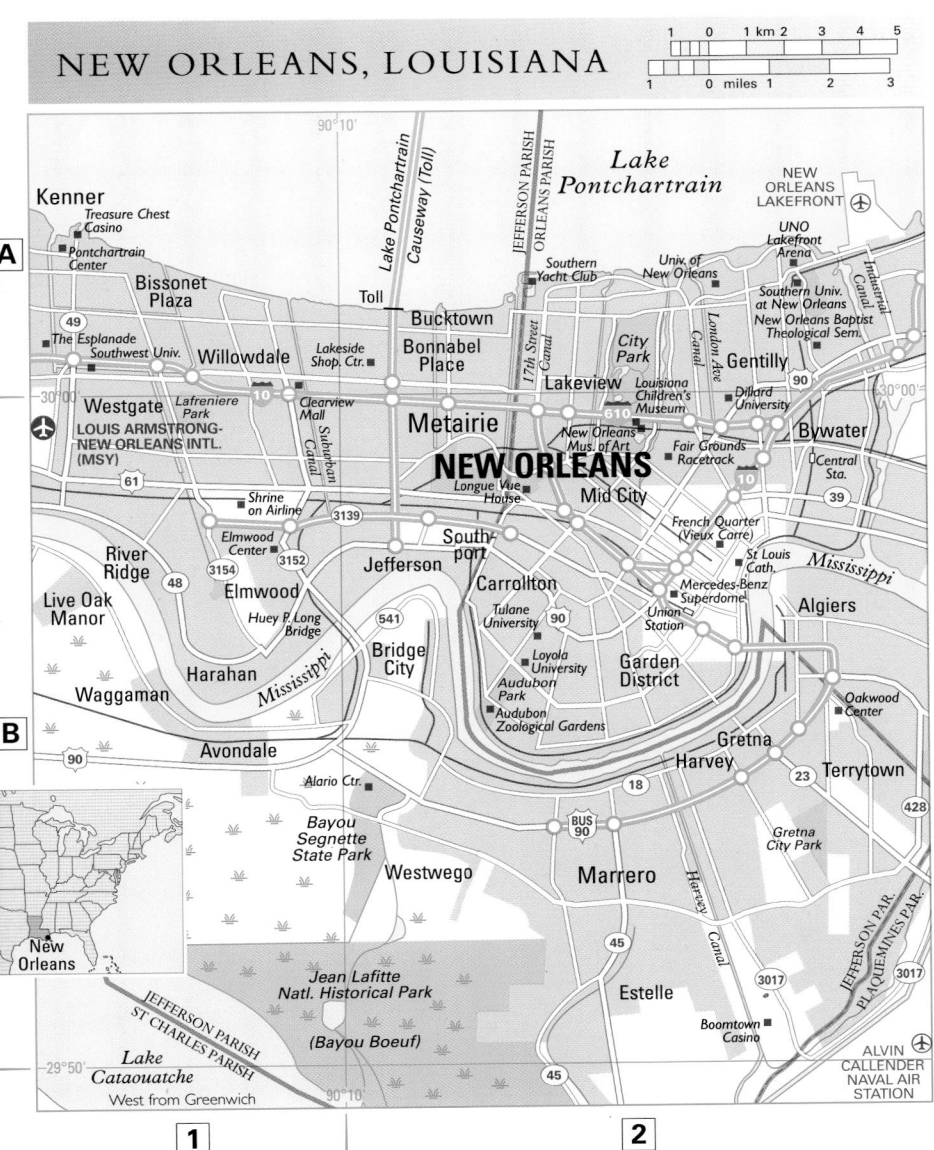

NEW ORLEANS, LOUISIANA

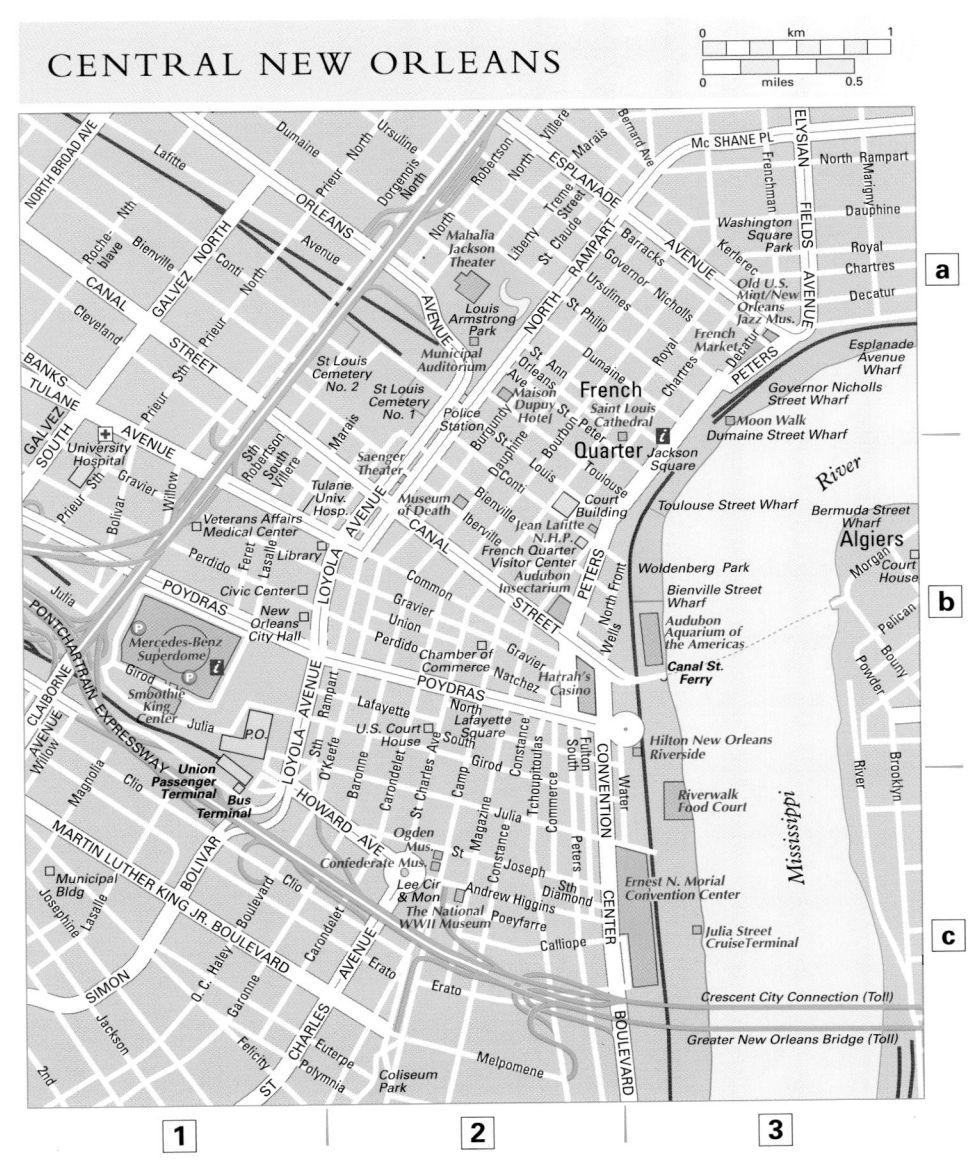

CENTRAL NEW ORLEANS

4 Interstate route numbers   17 U.S. route numbers   417 State route numbers

COPYRIGHT PHILIP'S

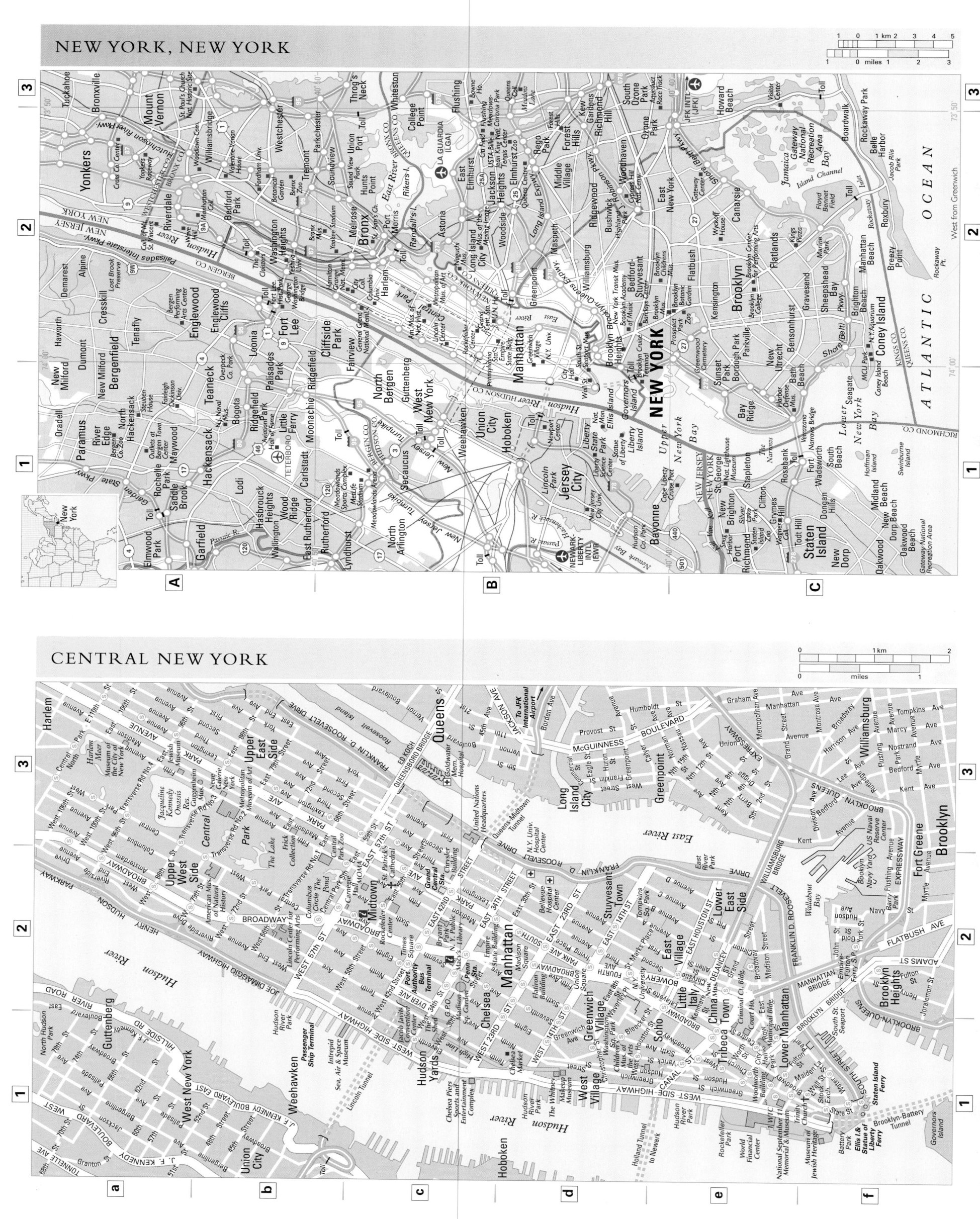

NEW YORK, NEW YORK

CENTRAL NEW YORK

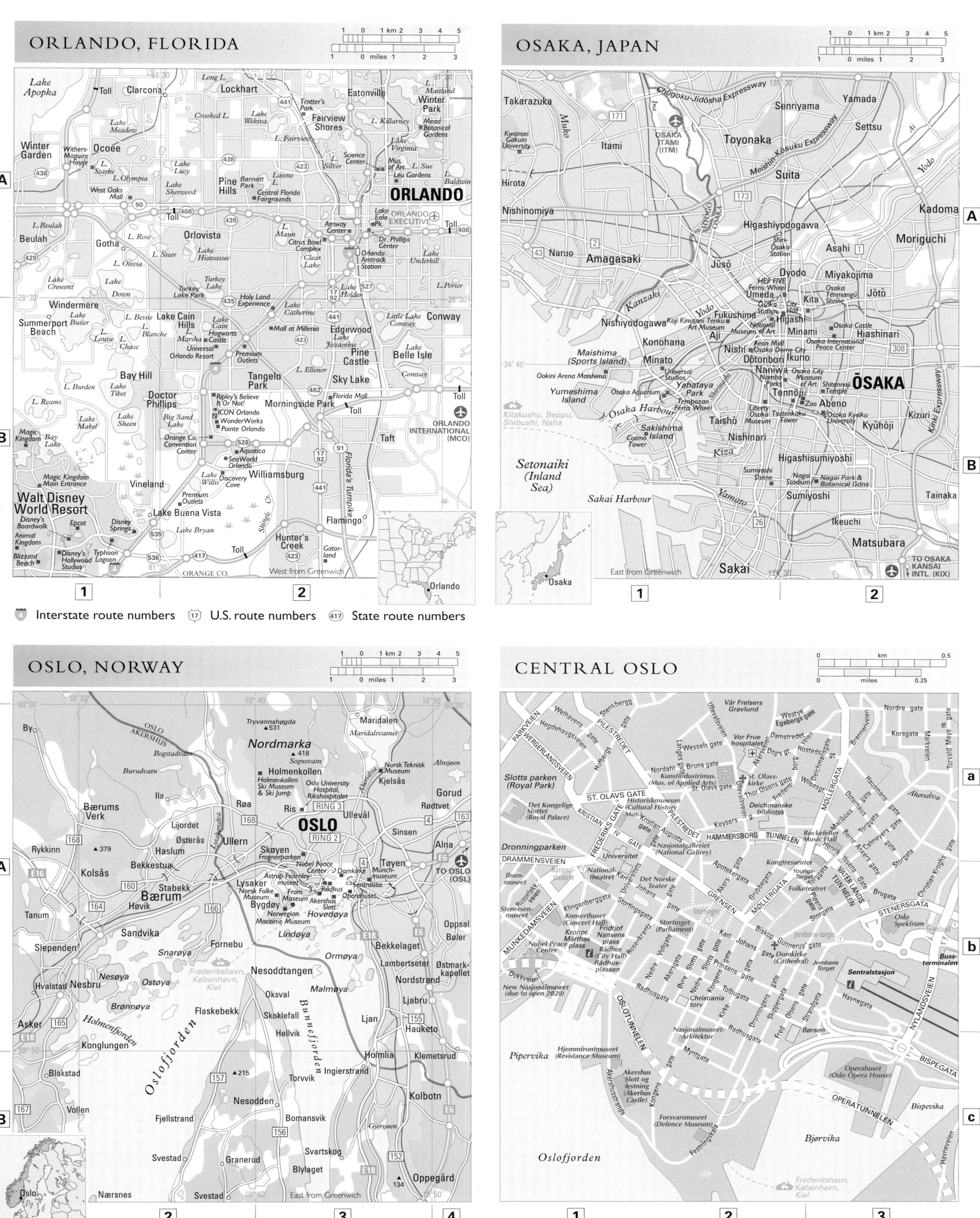

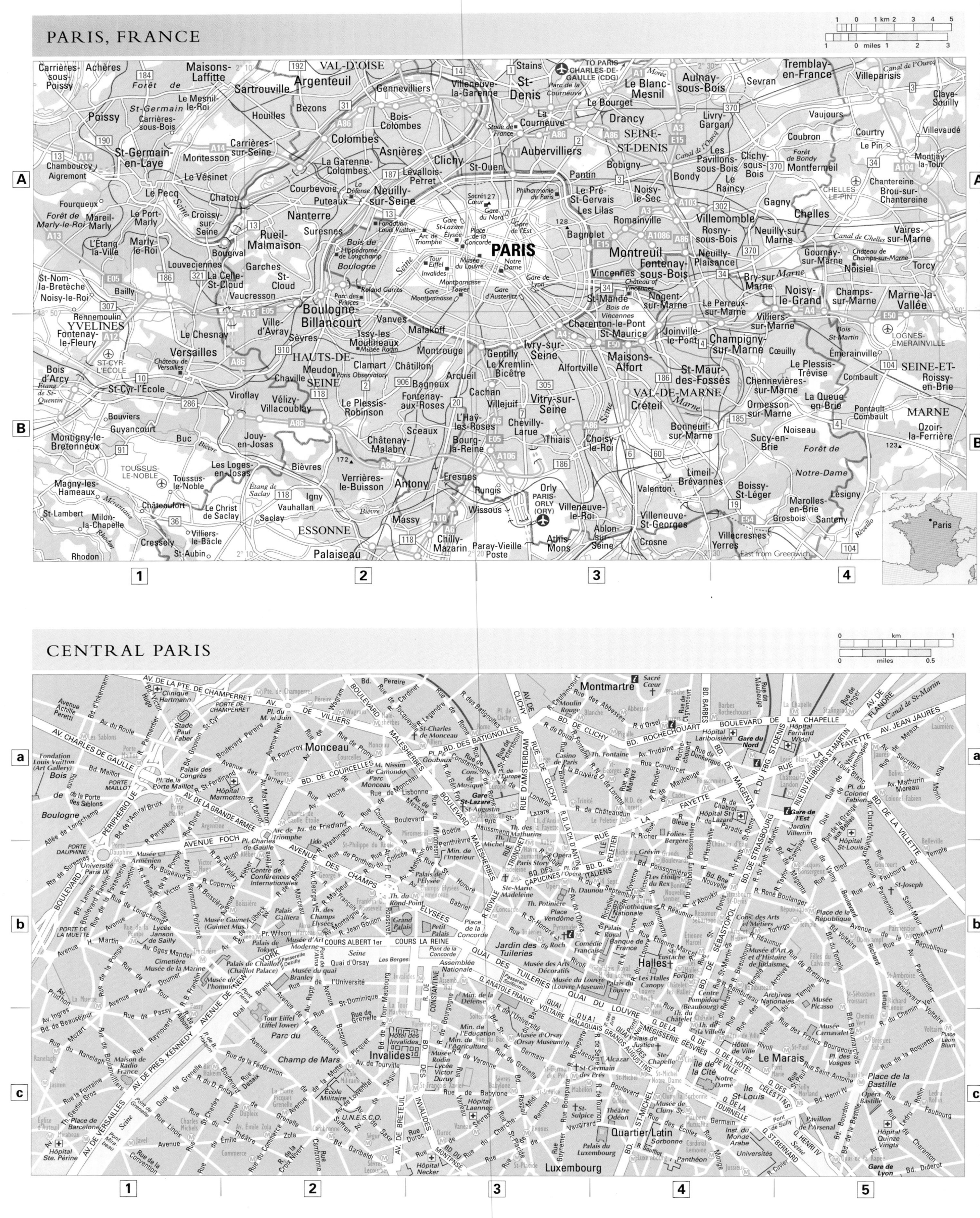

PARIS, FRANCE

CENTRAL PARIS

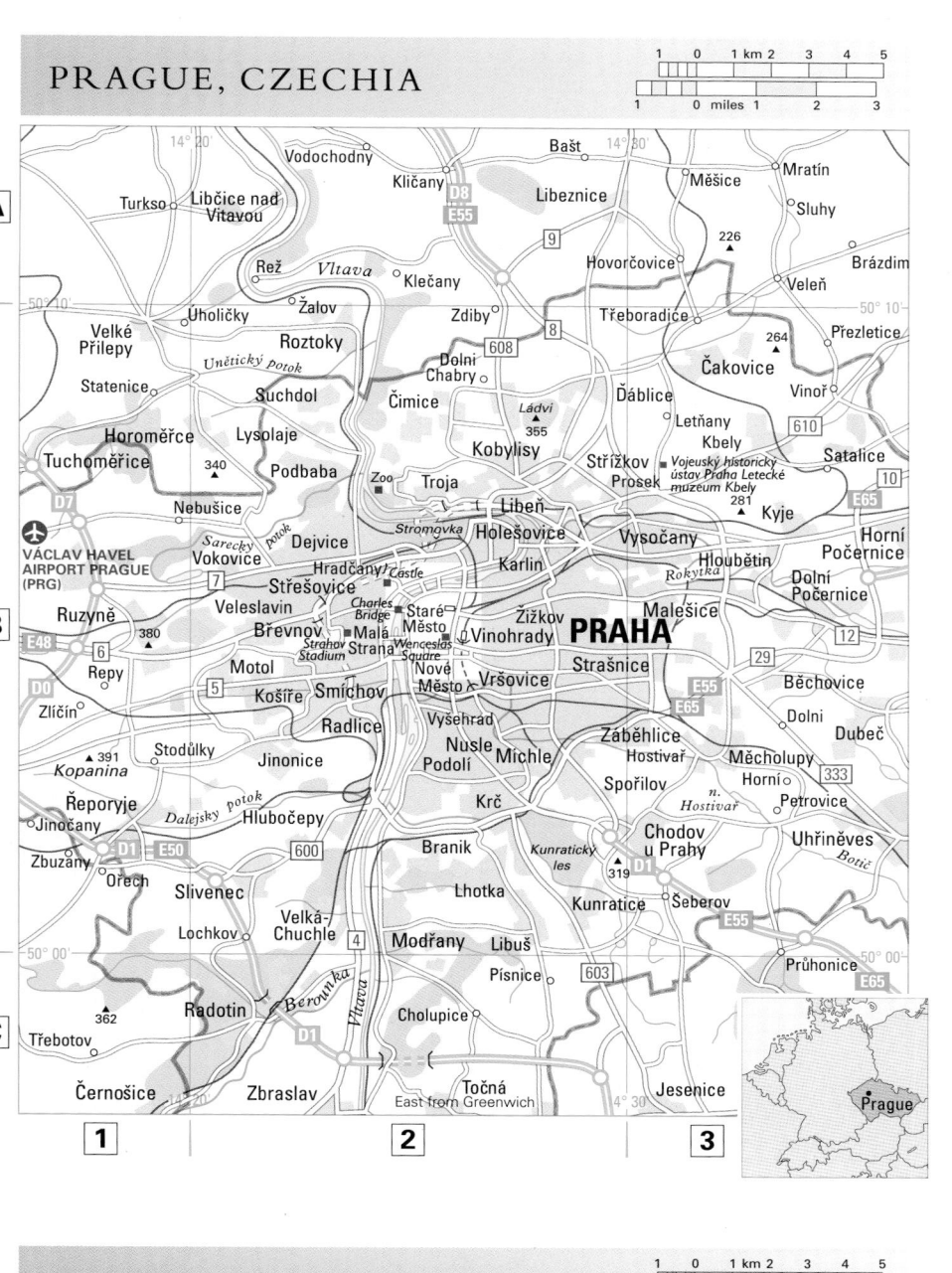

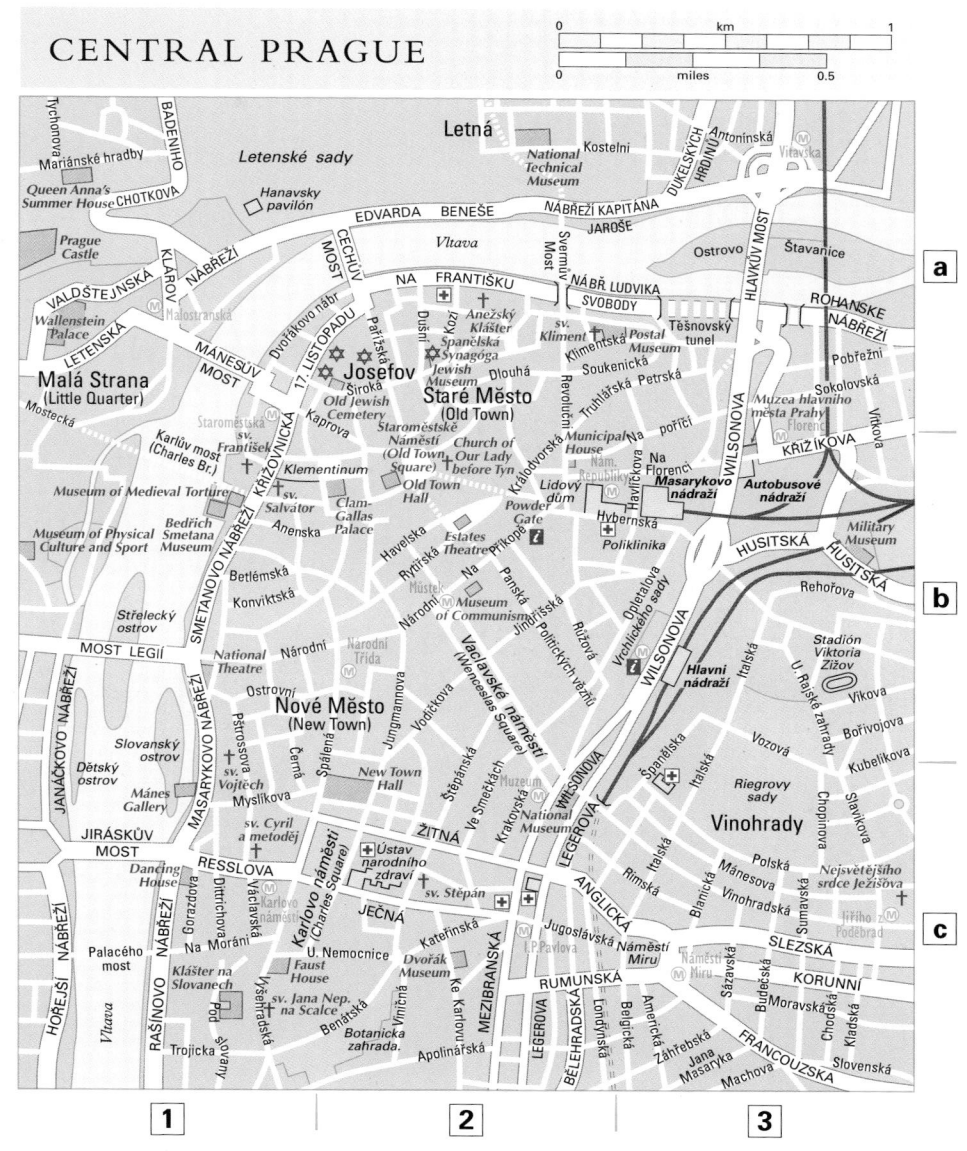

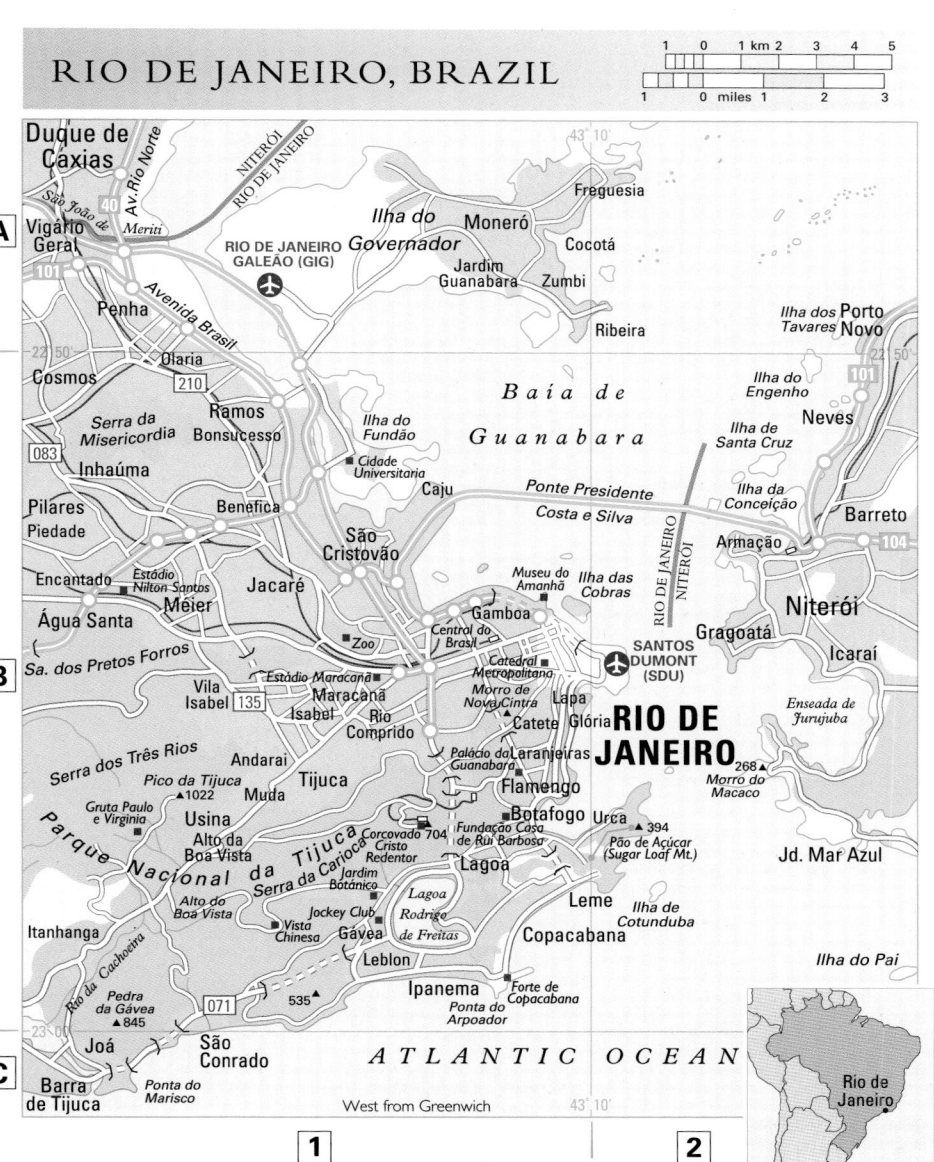

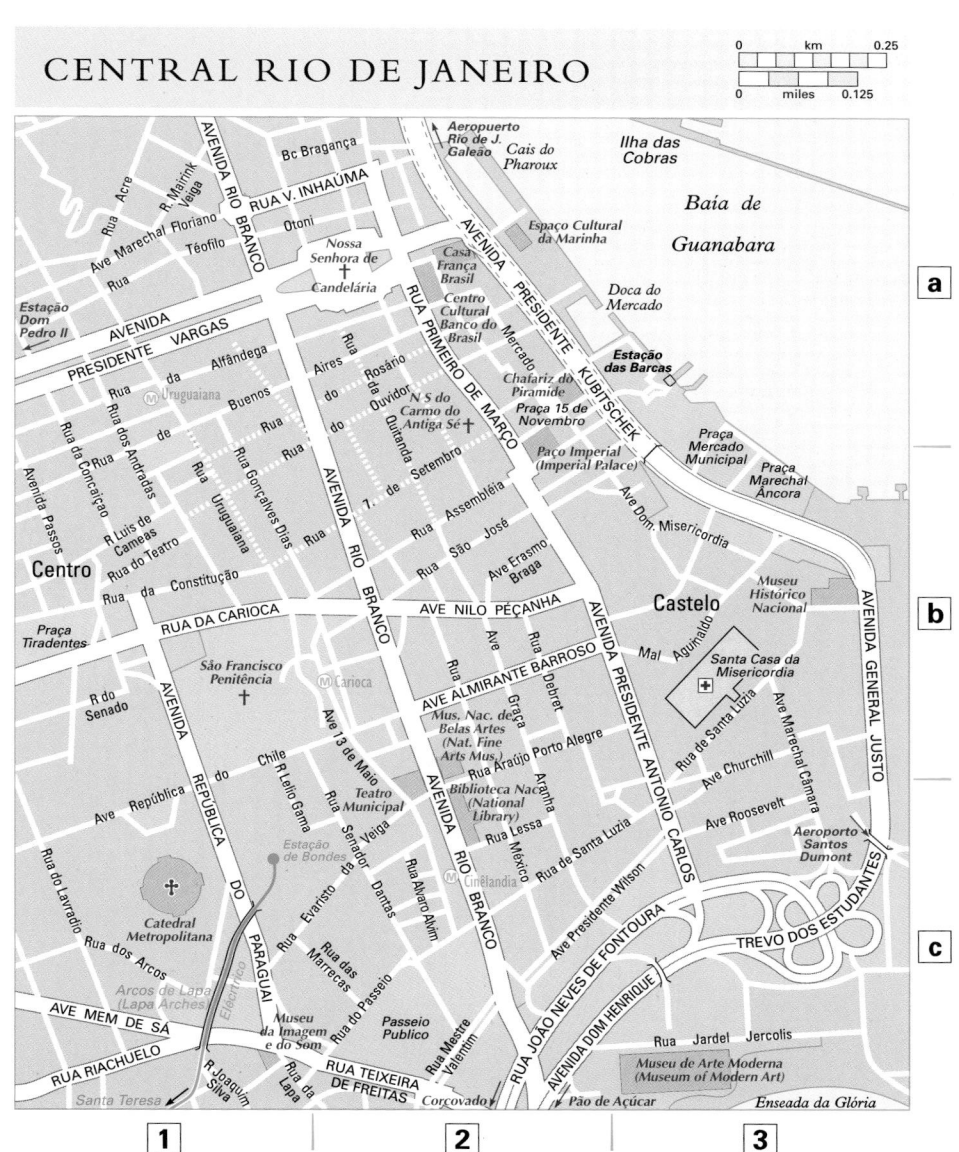

COPYRIGHT PHILIP'S

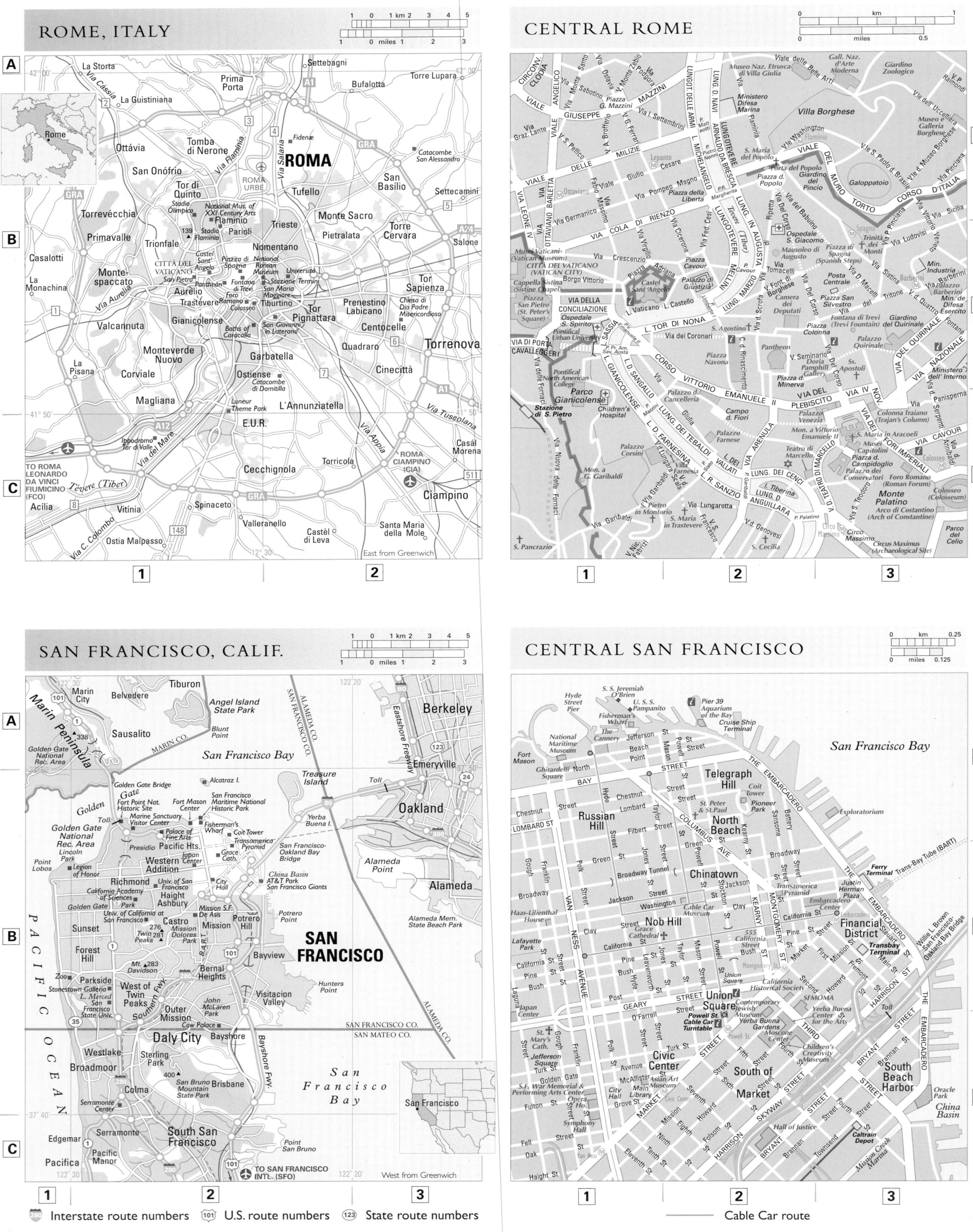

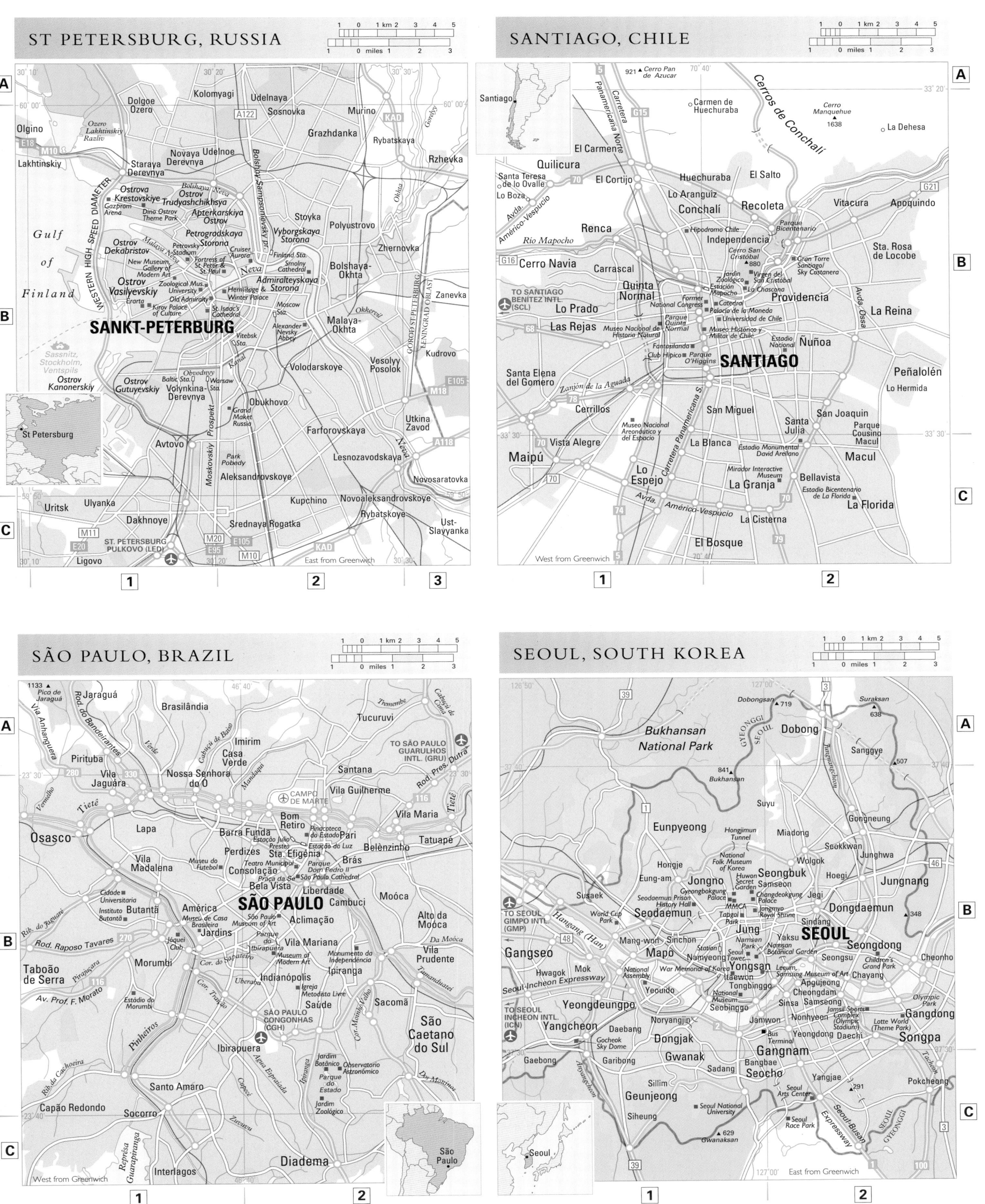

ST PETERSBURG, RUSSIA

SANTIAGO, CHILE

SÃO PAULO, BRAZIL

SEOUL, SOUTH KOREA

COPYRIGHT PHILIP'S

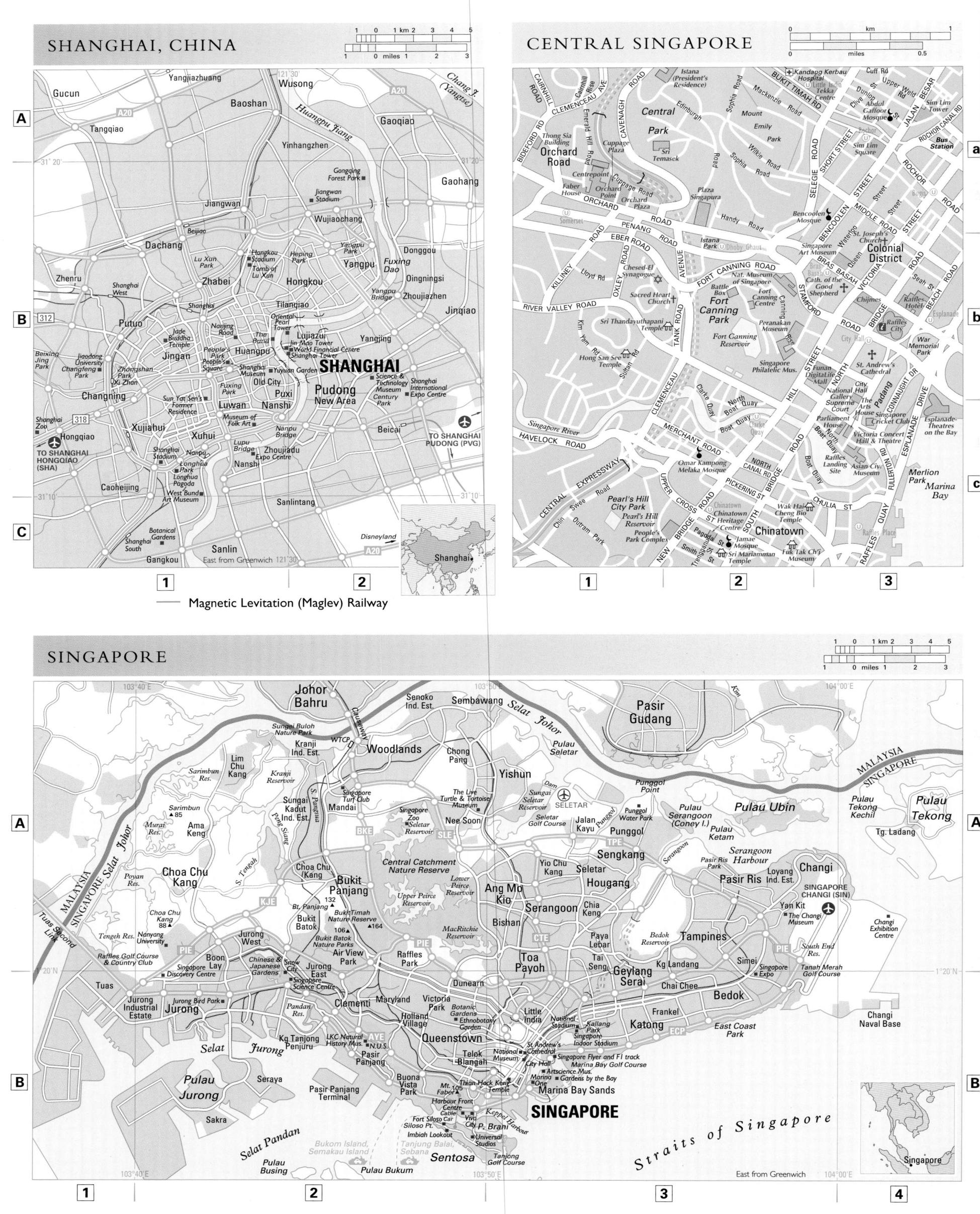

SHANGHAI, CHINA

Gucun
Tangqiao
Yangjiazhuang
Wusong
A20
Chang J. (Yangtse)
Baoshan
Gaoqiao
A20
Huangpu Jiang
Yinhangzhen
Gaohang
Gongqing Forest Park
Jiangwan Stadium
Beijiao
Jiangwan
Wujiaochang
Donggou
Qingningsi
Dachang
Lu Xun Park
Hongkou Stadium
Tomb of Lu Xun
Heping Park
Yangpu Park
Fuxing Dao
Zhenru
Shanghai West
Zhabei
Shanghai
Hongkou
Yangpu
Yangpu Bridge
Zhoujiazhen
Jinqiao
Putuo
Jade Buddha Temple
Nanjing Road
The Bund
Oriental Pearl Tower
Tilanqiao
Yangjing
Beixing Jing Park
Jiaodong University
Changfeng Park
Zhongshan Park
Xi Zhan
Jingan
People's Park
People's Square
Huangpu
Lujiazui
Jin Mao Tower
World Financial Centre
Shanghai Tower
SHANGHAI
Yangting
Changning
Huangpu
Shanghai Museum
Old City
Yuyuan Garden
Pudong New Area
Fuxing Park
Puxi
Nanshi
Science & Technology Museum
Shanghai International Expo Centre
Century Park
TO SHANGHAI PUDONG (PVG)
Shanghai Zoo
Hongqiao
318
Zhongshan Park
Xi Zhan
Xujiahui
Xuhui
Museum of Folk Art
Nanpu Bridge
Beicai
TO SHANGHAI HONGQIAO (SHA)
Shanghai Stadium
Nanpu Bridge
Lupu Bridge
Zhoujiadu
Nanshi
Zhoujiadu Expo Centre
Caoheijing
Longhua Park
Longhua Pagoda
West Bund Art Museum
Sanlintang
Botanical Gardens
Shanghai South
Sanlin
Disneyland
A20
Gangkou
Caohejing
East from Greenwich 121°30'
Shanghai

31°20'
31°10'
121°30'

A B C
1 2

Magnetic Levitation (Maglev) Railway

CENTRAL SINGAPORE

km
miles

CAIRNHILL ROAD
Istana (President's Residence)
Kandang Kerbau Hospital
Little India
Cuff Rd
Upper Weld Rd
BIDEFORD RD
CLEMENCEAU AVE
BUKIT TIMAH RD
Dunlop
Clive
Abdul Gaffoor Mosque
Sim Lim Tower
Thong Sia Building
Central Park
Edinburgh
Sophia Road
Mackenzie
Road
Tekka Centre
Jalan Besar
Orchard Road
Emily Park
Rochor Canal Rd
Bus Station
Cuppage Plaza
Sri Temasek
Mount
Sophia
Wilkie Road
SELEGIE ROAD
SHORT STREET
ROCHOR
Centrepoint
Faber House
Orchard Point
Orchard Plaza
Handy
Road
Bencoolen
MIDDLE ROAD
Street
Somerset
PENANG ROAD
Bencoolen Mosque
Waterloo
Singapore Art Museum
Queen
St. Joseph's Church
Colonial District
ORCHARD ROAD
EBER ROAD
Istana Park
Dhoby Ghaut
Cath. of the Good Shepherd
VICTORIA STREET
Chijmes
Raffles Hotel
Beach Road
KILLINEY ROAD
Lloyd Rd
Chesed-El Synagogue
FORT CANNING ROAD
Nat. Museum of Singapore
Bras Basah
STAMFORD
Peranakan Museum
Raffles City
Esplanade
OXLEY ROAD
Sacred Heart Church
Fort Canning Park
Fort Canning Centre
City Hall
St. Andrew's Cathedral
War Memorial Park
RIVER VALLEY ROAD
Sri Thandayuthapani Temple
TANK ROAD
Fort Canning Reservoir
Padang
Hong San See Temple
Sultan Rd
Singapore Philatelic Mus.
Funan DigitaLife Mall
National Gallery Supreme Court
The Arts House Singapore Cricket Club
Victoria Concert Hall & Theatre
Esplanade-Theatres on the Bay
CLEMENCEAU
Clarke Quay
North Boat Quay
Parliament House
Boat Quay
Asian Civ. Museum
HAVELOCK ROAD
Singapore River
MERCHANT ROAD
South Boat Quay
Raffles Landing Site
Merlion Park
Marina Bay
CENTRAL EXPRESSWAY
Omar Kampong Melaka Mosque
NORTH CANAL RD
UPPER CROSS
PICKERING ST
CHULIA ST
Fullerton Rd
Swee
Pearl's Hill City Park
Pearl's Hill Reservoir
Chinatown
Wak Hai Cheng Bio Temple
RAFFLES QUAY
Chin
People's Park Complex
NEW BRIDGE ROAD
SOUTH BRIDGE ROAD
Chinatown Heritage Centre
Chinatown
Papaya
Pagoda St
Smith St
Raffles Place
Jamae Mosque
Sri Mariamman Temple
Fuk Tak Ch'i Museum
Trengganu St

a b c
1 2 3

SINGAPORE

Johor Bahru
Senoko Ind. Est.
Sembawang
Selat Johor
Pasir Gudang
Sungei Buloh Nature Park
Causeway
WTCP
Kranji Ind. Est.
Chong Pang
Pulau Seletar
Kim
MALAYSIA
SINGAPORE
Lim Chu Kang
Kranji Reservoir
Woodlands
Yishun
Sungai Seletar Reservoir
Dam
Punggol Point
Sarimbun Res.
S. Pandan
Singapore Turf Club
Mandai
The Live Turtle & Tortoise Museum
SELETAR
Punggol Water Park
Pulau Ubin
Pulau Tekong Kechil
Pulau Tekong
Sarimbun △ 85
Sungai Kadut Ind. Est.
Singapore Zoo
Seletar Reservoir
Nee Soon
SLE
Punggol
Jalan Kayu
Punggol Serangon (Coney I.)
Pulau Ketam
Tg. Ladang
Murai Res.
Ama Keng
Poyan Res.
S. Tengah
Choa Chu (Kang
BKE
Central Catchment Nature Reserve
Seletar Golf Course
Yio Chu Kang
Sengkang
Seletar
Serangoon Harbour
Pasir Ris Park
Loyang Ind. Est.
Choa Chu Kang
Bukit Panjang
Upper Peirce Reservoir
Lower Peirce Reservoir
Ang Mo Kio
Hougang
Chia Keng
Pasir Ris
Changi
SINGAPORE CHANGI (SIN)
Tengeh Res.
Nanyang University
KJE
Bt. Panjang △132
Bukit Timah Nature Reserve
Serangoon
Bishan
Yan Kit
The Changi Museum
Choa Chu Kang 88 △
Bukit Batok
△164
MacRitchie Reservoir
Paya Lebar
Bedok Reservoir
Tampines
Simei
Changi Exhibition Centre
Raffles Golf Course & Country Club
PIE
Jurong West
Bukit Batok Nature Parks △106
Air View Park
Raffles Park
Toa Payoh
Tai Seng
PIE
Singapore Expo
Boon Lay
Chinese & Japanese Gardens
Snow City
Jurong East
Science Centre
PIE
Dunearn
Geylang Serai
Chai Chee
Tanah Merah Golf Course
Jurong Industrial Estate
Jurong
Jurong Bird Park
Pandan Res.
Clementi
Maryland
Victoria Park
Botanic Gardens
Ethnobotany Garden
Little India
National Stadium
Sallang Park
Singapore Indoor Stadium
Frankel
Katong
Bedok
East Coast Park
Changi Naval Base
Tuas
Selat Jurong
Kg Tanjong Penjuru
LKC Natural History Mus.
N.U.S.
Holland Village
Queenstown
St. Andrew's Cathedral
City Hall
National Museum
Marina Bay Golf Course
ECP
AYE
Pasir Panjang
Telok Blangah
Buona Vista Park
Mt. △105 Faber
Thian Hock Keng Temple
Marina One
Gardens by the Bay
Artscience Mus.
Pulau Vista
Pasir Panjang Terminal
Harbour Front
Cable Car
VivoCity
P. Brani
Marina Bay Sands
SINGAPORE
Pulau Jurong
Seraya
Fort Siloso Car
Siloso Pt.
Imbiah Lookout
Keppel Harbour
Sakra
Selat
Jurong
Pasir Panjang
Buona Vista Park
Universal Studios
Sentosa
Tanjong Golf Course
Straits of Singapore
Bukom Island, Semakau Island
Pulau Busing
Pulau Bukum
Tanjung Balai Sebana
East from Greenwich
Singapore

103°40'E
103°50'E
103°50'E
104°00'E
104°00'E
1°20'N
1°20'N

A B
1 2 3 4

STOCKHOLM, SWEDEN

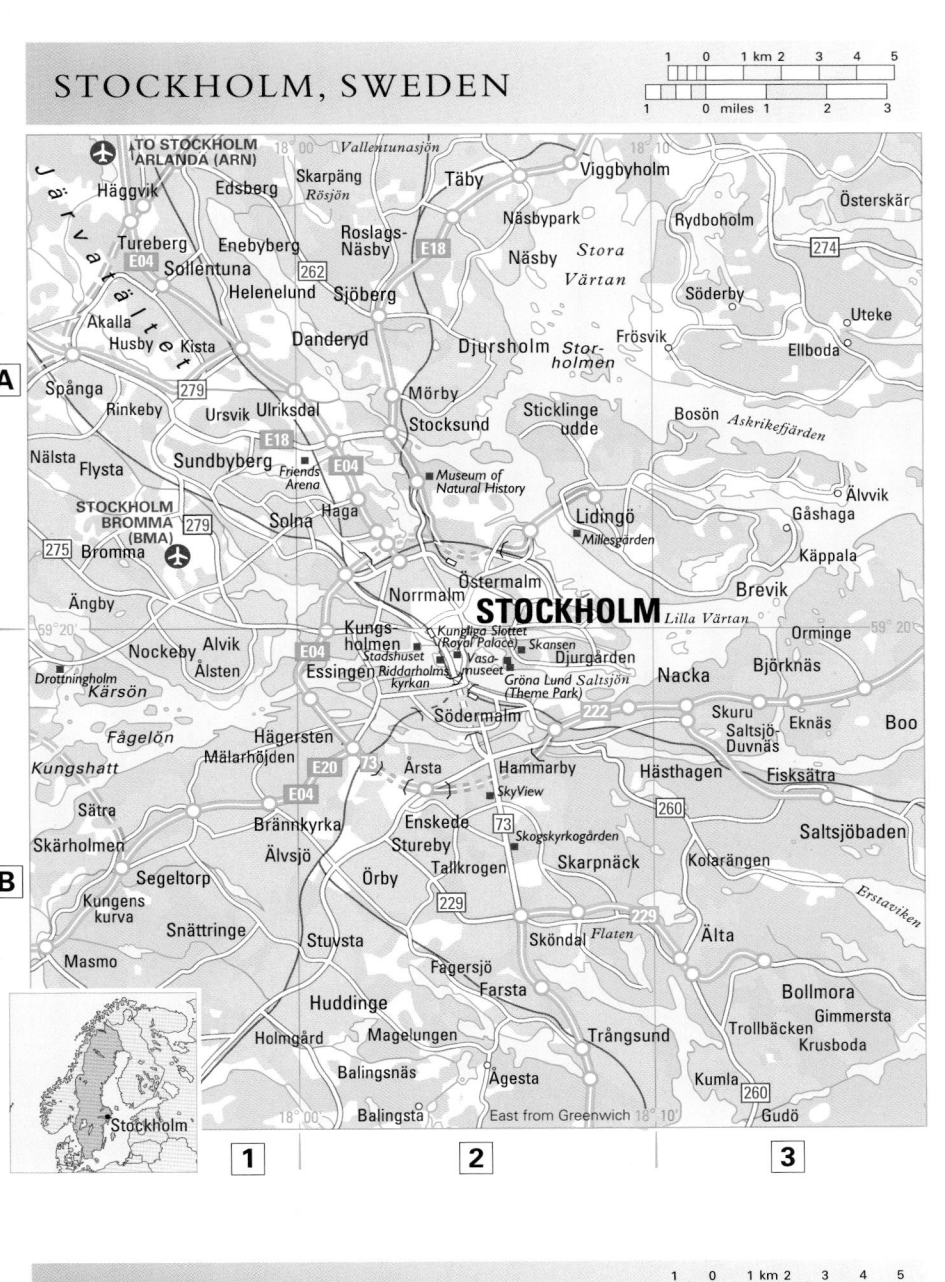

CENTRAL STOCKHOLM

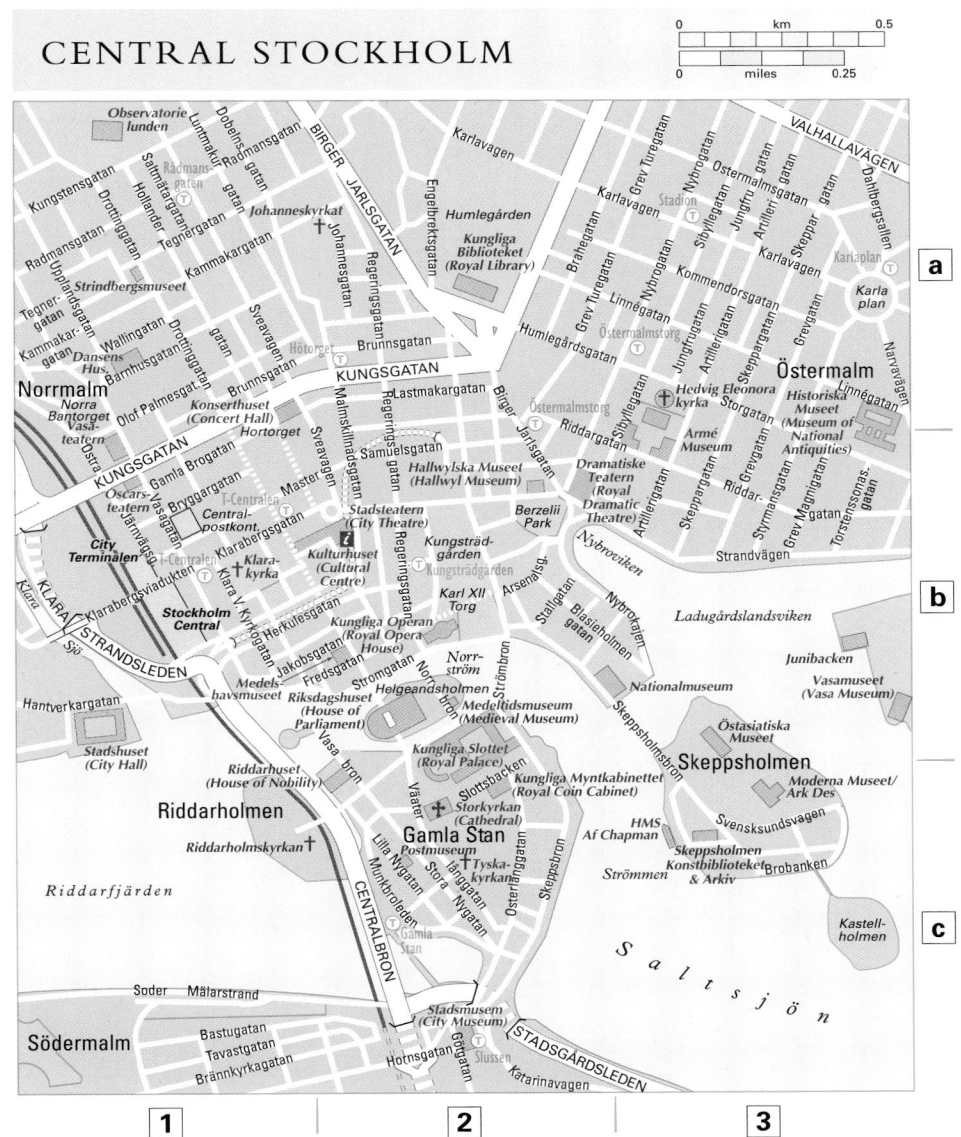

SYDNEY, AUSTRALIA

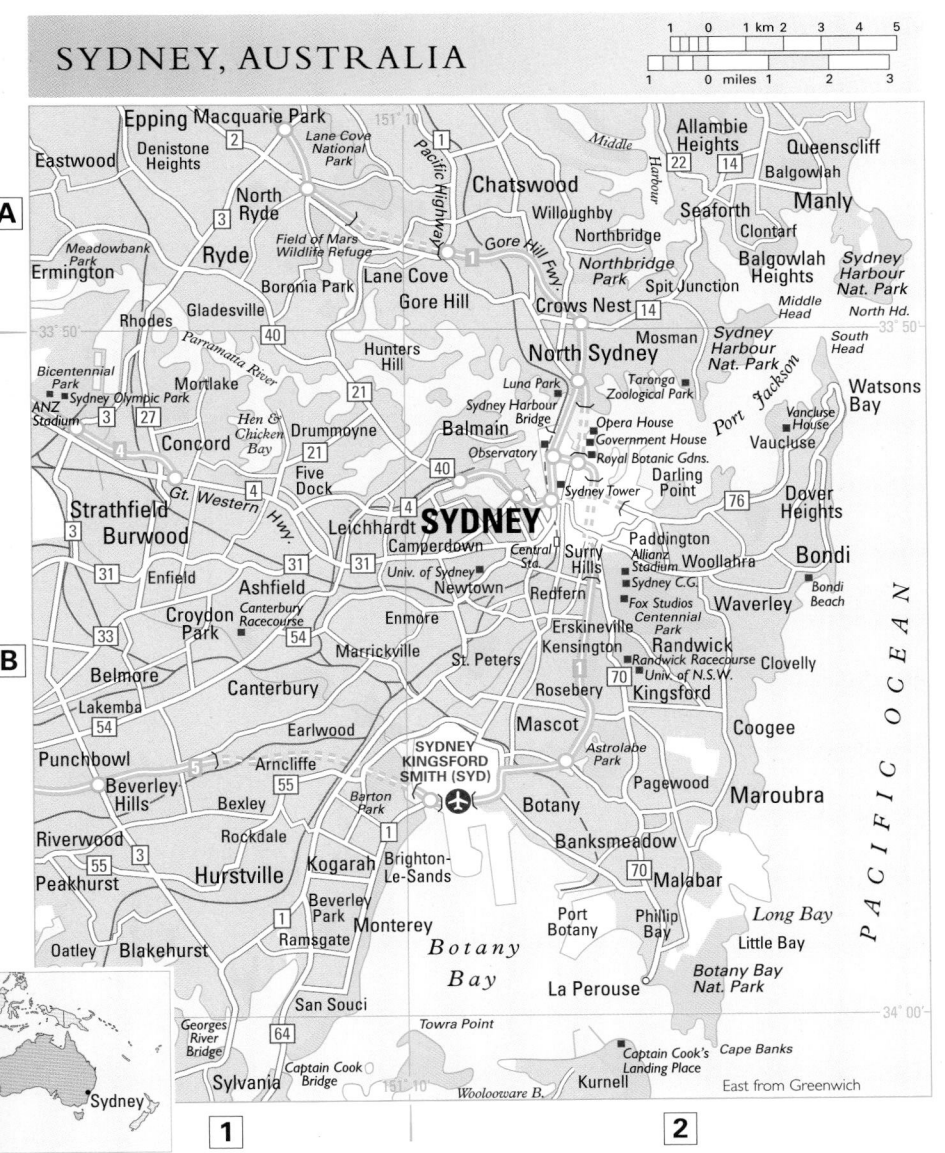

CENTRAL SYDNEY

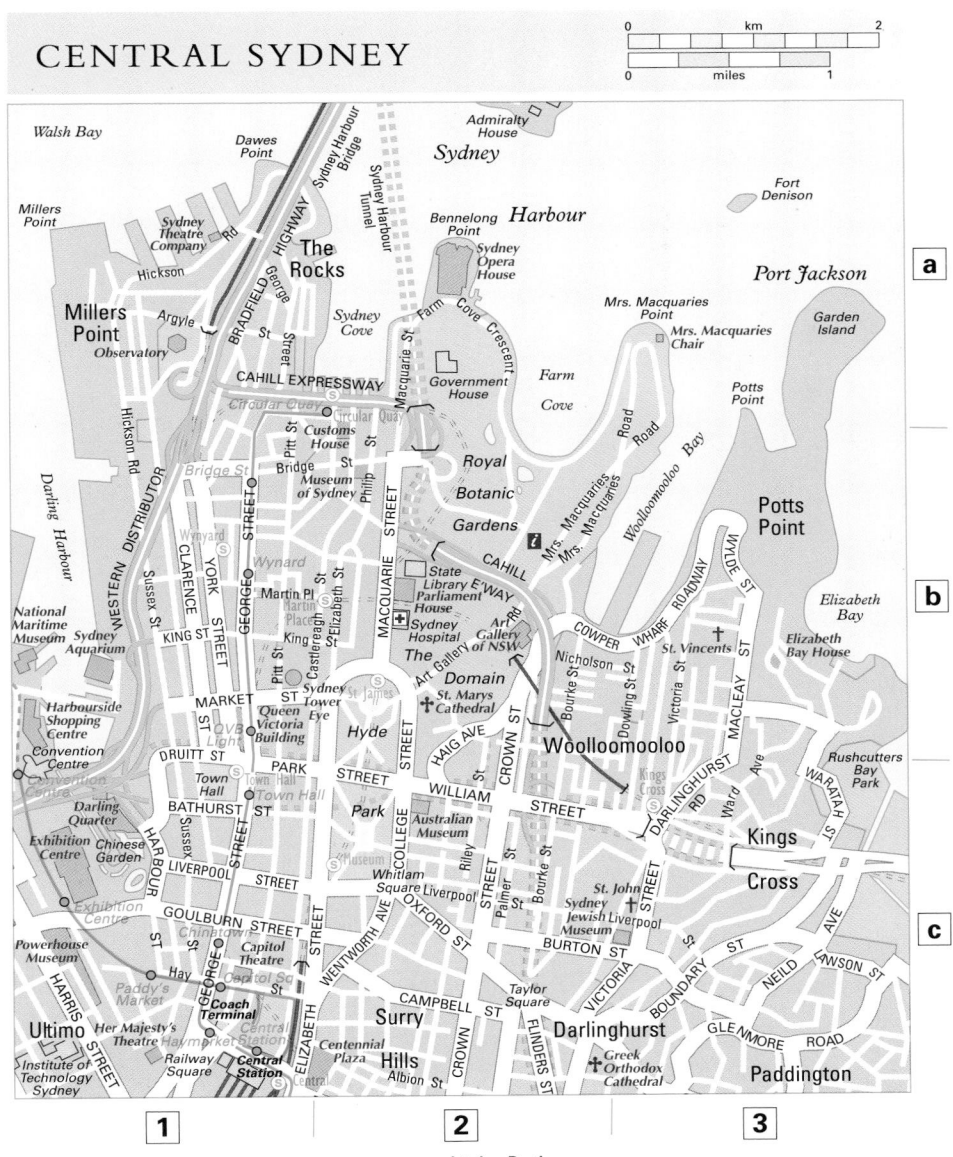

— Light Railway

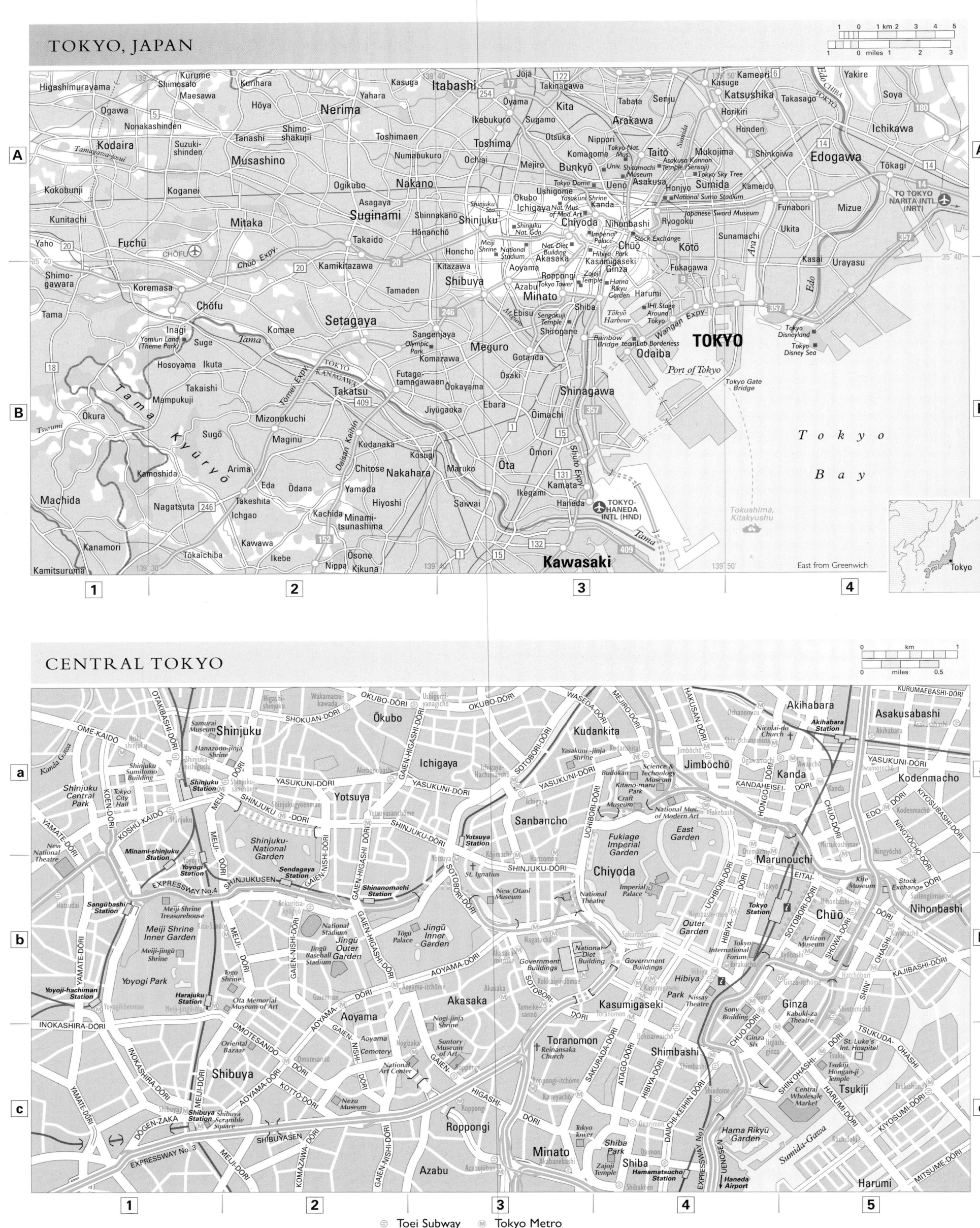

TOKYO, JAPAN

1 0 1 km 2 3 4 5

1 0 miles 1 2 3

A
Higashimurayama · Kurume · Shimosato · Kasuga · Itabashi · Jūjō · Takinagawa · Kasuge · Kameari · Yakire · Soya
Ogawa · Kurihara · Maesawa · Yahara · Oyama · Kita · Tabata · Senju · Katsushika · Takasago · Ichikawa
Hōya · Nonakashinden · Nerima · Ikebukuro · Sugamo · Arakawa · Horikiri · Honden · Edogawa
Kodaira · Tanashi · Shimo-shakujii · Toshimaen · Toshima · Otsuka · Nippori · Tokyo Nat. Mus. · Mukojima · Shinkoiwa · Tōkagi
Kokubunji · Musashino · Ogikubo · Nakano · Numabukuro · Komagome · Taitō · Asakusa Kannon Temple (Sensōji) · Honjo · Sumida · Kameido · Mizue
Koganei · Asagaya · Shinnakano · Mejiro · Bunkyō · Ushigome · Univ. Shitamachi · Tokyo Sky Tree · Sumida
Yaho · Kunitachi · Mitaka · Takaido · Suginami · Shinjuku · Okubo · Yasukuni Shrine · Ueno · Kanda · National Sumo Stadium · Funabori

139°40'

A
Koremasa · Kamikitazawa · Honcho · Nat. Mus. of Mod. Art · Chiyoda · Nihonbashi · Ryogoku · Japanese Sword Museum · TO TOKYO NARITA INTL (NRT)
Shimo-gawara · Chōfu · Kitazawa · Shibuya · Aoyama · Imperial Palace · Stock Exchange · Kasai · Urayasu
Inagi · Yomiuri Land (Theme Park) · Komae · Sangenjaya · Meguro · Roppongi · Tokyo Tower · Zōjōji Temple · Ginza · Fukagawa

CENTRAL TOKYO

0 km 1

0 miles 0.5

⊖ Toei Subway   Ⓜ Tokyo Metro

COPYRIGHT PHILIP'S

TEHRAN, IRAN

Reshteh-ye Kūhhā-ye Alborz (Elburz Mts.)

Tehran

Darakeh
Darband
Niāvarān
Towchāl Cable Car
Sa'dabad Palace
Niāvarān Palace
Sowhānak
Evin
Tehrān International Exhibition
Emāmzādeh Sāleh
Tajrīsh
Heşārak
Sa'ādatābād
Pārk-e Mellat
Lavīzān
Qolhak
Darrūs
Qāsemābād
Pūnak
Shahrak-e Qods (Gharb)
Vanak
Dāvūdīyeh
Tehrān Pārs
Bāgh-e Feyz
Pardisān Nature Park
Milād Tower
Yūsofābād
Reza Abbasi Museum
Hasanābād
Amīrābād
Nārmak
Karaj Expwy.
Tehran West Bus Terminal
Tehran Museum of Contemporary Art
Carpet Mus.
Laleh Park
Jamshīdīyeh
University
Tehran Now
TEHRAN
TEHRAN MEHRĀBĀD (THR)
Azadi Tower
City Theatre
Museum of Glass and Ceramics
Jey
National Mus. of Iran
City Park
Farahābād
Akbarābād
Razi Park
Shah Mosque
Golestan Palace (Ethnographical Mus.)
Bāzār
Dūlāb
Qasr-e Fīrūzeh
Tehran Station
Javādīyeh
Tehran South Bus Terminal
Afsarīyeh
Vasfenārd
Velayat Great Park
Yaftābād
N'ematābād
Dowlatābād
Pārk-e Azādegān
Qal'eh Morghī
Shahrak-e Golshahr
Āzādegān Expwy.
Qom Expwy.
Shahr-e Rey (Rey)
Mesgarābād
TO TEHRAN IMAM KHOMEINI INTL. (IKA)
East from Greenwich

CENTRAL TORONTO

University of Toronto
Queen's Park
College Street
Granby Street
McGill Street
Galbraith Road
St George St
Toronto General Hospital
Barbara Ann Scott Park
Gerrard Street East
Ryerson University
Glenholme Pl
COLLEGE STREET
Ross Street
Beverley Street
Orde Street
Princess Margaret Hospital
Mt Sinai Hospital
Gerrard Street West
Hospital for Sick Children
Elm St
Bond
St Michael's Cathedral
Moss Park Armoury
Moss Park
Cecil St
Henry Street
McCaul Street
Toronto Rehab Institute
Elm Street
Edward St
Victoria Street
DUNDAS STREET EAST
Baldwin Street
D Arcy Street
Edward St
Coach Terminal
DUNDAS STREET WEST
Huron Street
St Patrick's Church
DUNDAS ST WEST
Textile Museum of Canada
Foster Pl
Trinity Sq
Toronto Eaton Centre
St Michael's Church
Metro United Church
Toronto's First P.O.
The Art Gallery of Ontario
Grange Avenue
Beverley Street
McCaul Street
St Patrick Street
Simcoe Street
County Courthouse
City Hall
Nathan Phillips Square
Old City Hall
QUEEN STREET EAST
China Town
Grange Park
Osgoode Hall
Stephanie St
Campbell Ho
Downtown
RICHMOND ST EAST
St James Park
Sullivan Street
Phoebe Street
John St
Renfrew Place
Osgoode
Bank of Canada
National Bank Bldg
Richmond Adelaide Centre
ADELAIDE STREET EAST
St James Cathedral
Bulwer Street
QUEEN
RICHMOND
John
Nelson Street
STREET
Toronto Stock Exchange
Scotia Plaza
Lombard Street
Commerce Court
Colborne Street
ADELAIDE
STREET
Royal Alexandra Theatre
Pearl St
St Andrew
Roy Thomson Hall
TD Gallery of Inuit Art
King Street
KING STREET EAST
FRONT STREET EAST
KING
Mercer Street
Windsor Street
Simcoe St
Wellington
Canada Trust Tower P.O.
Hockey Hall of Fame
St Lawrence Market
Metro Hall
Wellington Street West
Simcoe Park
WEST
Canada Revenue Agency
Som Centre for the Performing Arts
SPADINA
CBC Broadcast Cen & Mus
FRONT
Metro Toronto Conv. Cen. (Nth)
Bus Terminal
Clarence Square Park
Windsor Street
STREET
Union Station
The Esplanade
Isabella Valancy Crawford Park
Convention Centre (Sth) Boulevard
Scotiabank Arena
LAKE SHORE BOULEVARD EAST
City Core Golf & Driving Range
Rogers Centre (Sky Dome)
CN Tower
Bremner Roundhouse Park
Police Station
Harbour Square Park
Redpath Sugar Museum
Bremner Boulevard West
Old Roundhouse Park
HARBOUR ST
Queen's Quay East
GARDINER EXPRESSWAY
LAKE SHORE BOULEVARD WEST
West
Harbourfront Park
Queen's Quay Terminal
Jack Layton Ferry Terminal
Lake Ontario
GARDINER EXPRESSWAY
Queen's Quay

TORONTO, CANADA

Boyd Conservation Area
East Don
Markham
Toronto Zoo
Rouge
Fairport
Rouge Hill
Vaughan
Thornhill
The Promenade
Concord
Brown
Little Rouge
West Rouge
Pine Grove
Edgeley
ETR
Newtonbrook
North Yorkzion Schoolhouse
48
Agincourt
Malvern
Highland Creek
Port Union
Woodbridge
Fisherville
Willowdale
G. Ross Lord Park
Gibson House Museum
Fairview Mall
East Don Parkland
Macdonald-Cartier Frwy.
Morningside Park
2A
Humber Summit
York University
Black Creek Pioneer Village
Lansing
Scarborough Town Centre
Bendale
Woburn
West Hill
Beaumonte Heights
Northwood Park
North York
Armour Heights
York Mills
Victoria Village
Wexford
Scarborough
Guildwood
Thistletown
Rowntree Mills Park
Downsview Park
Don Mills
Cliffside
Kipling Heights
Humberwood Park
Woodbine Centre
Downsview
Lawrence Heights
Edwards Gardens & the Toronto Botanical Garden
Aga Khan Museum
Clairville Reservoir
Rexdale
Yorkdale Shopping Centre
York Univ. Glendon
Sunnybrook Health Sciences Centre
Scarborough Junction
Malton
Woodbine Racetrack
Humberlea
Weston
Forest Hill
Ontario Science Centre
Thorncliffe
Danforth
Bluffers Park
York Museum
Cedarvale Park
Leaside
Dentonia Park
Scarborough Bluffs
Humber Valley Village
Mount Dennis
York
Casa Loma
East York
Birch Cliff
TORONTO PEARSON INTL. (YYZ)
Kew Gardens
Hanlon
Royal Ontario Museum
University of Toronto
Ontario Legislative Building
Riverdale Park
Ashbridge's Bay Park
Lambton Mills
Swansea
Old City Hall
CN Tower & Rogers Centre
Union Sta.
Lower Don Lands
Islington
Kingsway
Humber
High Park
Parkdale
Old Fort York
Gardiner Expy.
Burnhamthorpe
Markland Wood
Humber Bay
Exhibition Place
BILLY BISHOP TORONTO CITY (YTZ)
Toronto Island Airport
Tommy Thompson Park
Summerville
Ontario Place
Toronto Harbour
TORONTO
Alderwood
Mimico
Toronto Islands
Gibraltar Point
LAKE ONTARIO
Dixie Mall
New Toronto
Humber College
Samuel Smith Park
Mississauga
Long Branch
West from Greenwich
Cooksville
Square One
Toronto

(427) Provincial route numbers

COPYRIGHT PHILIP'S

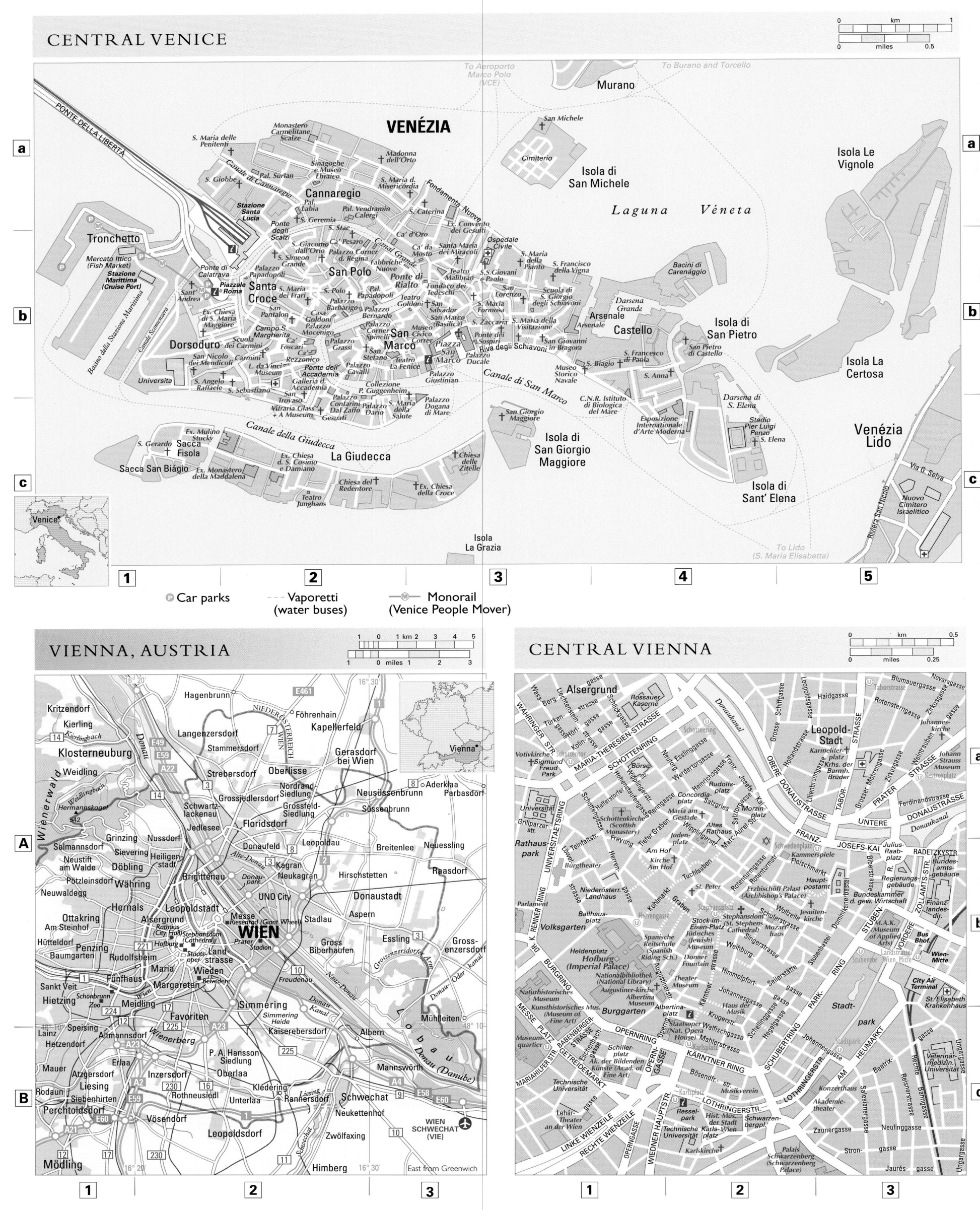

WARSAW, POLAND

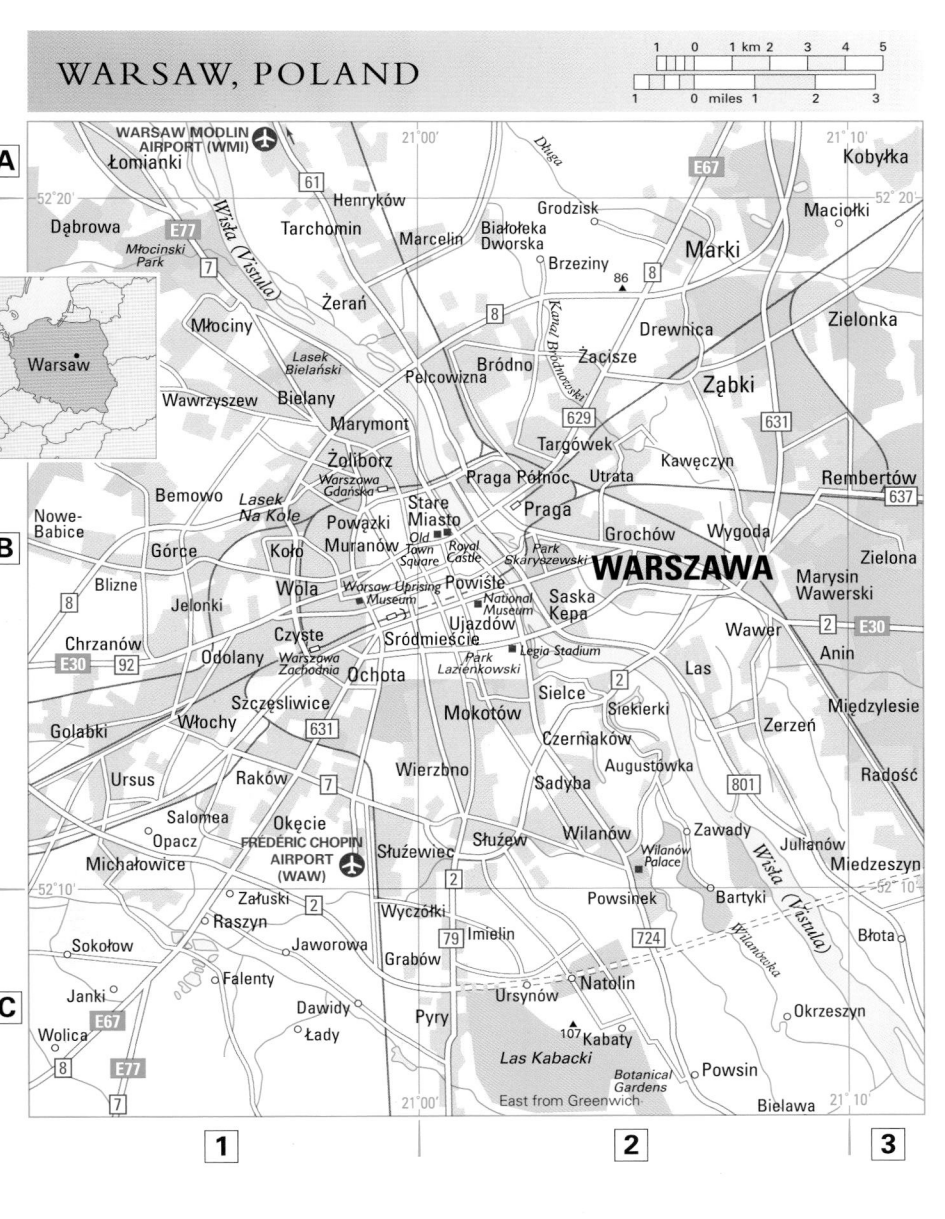

CENTRAL WARSAW

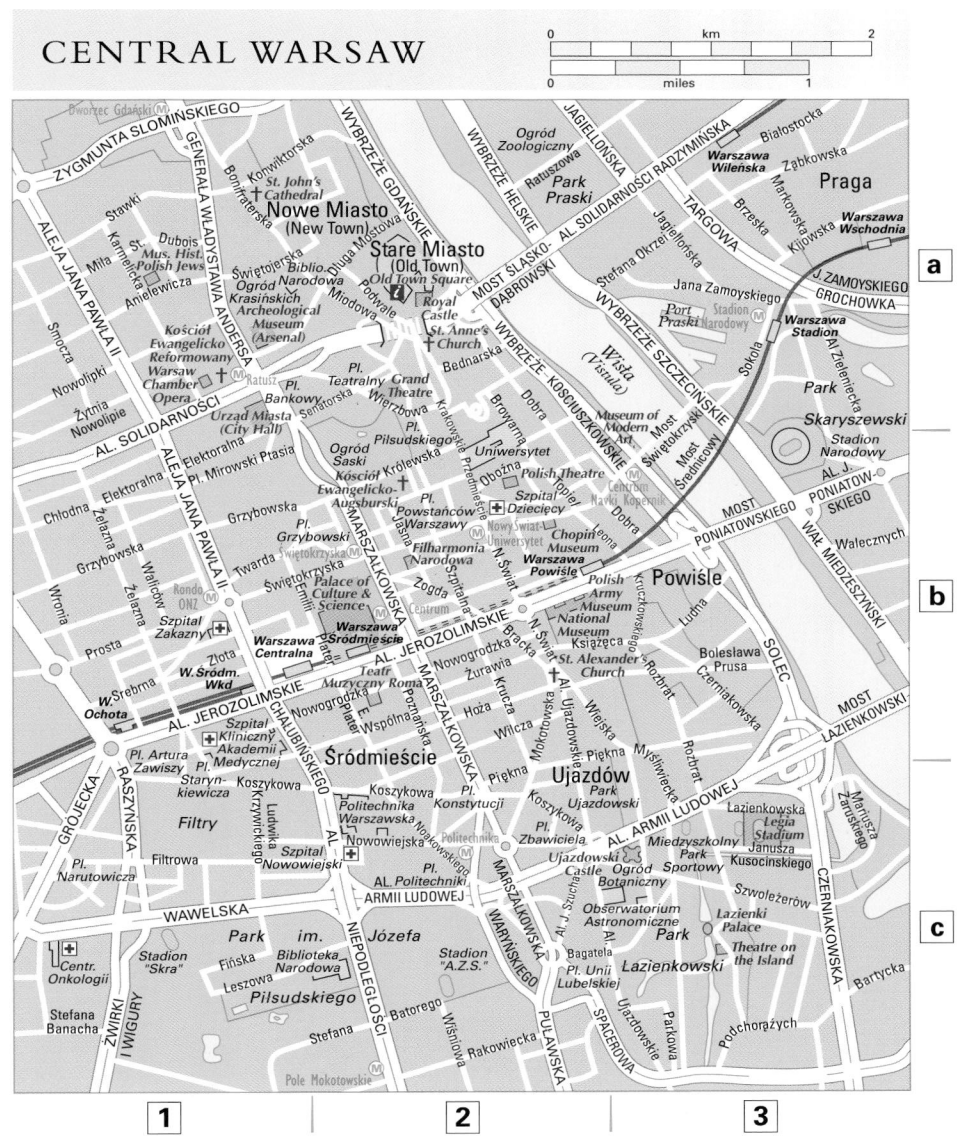

WASHINGTON D.C.

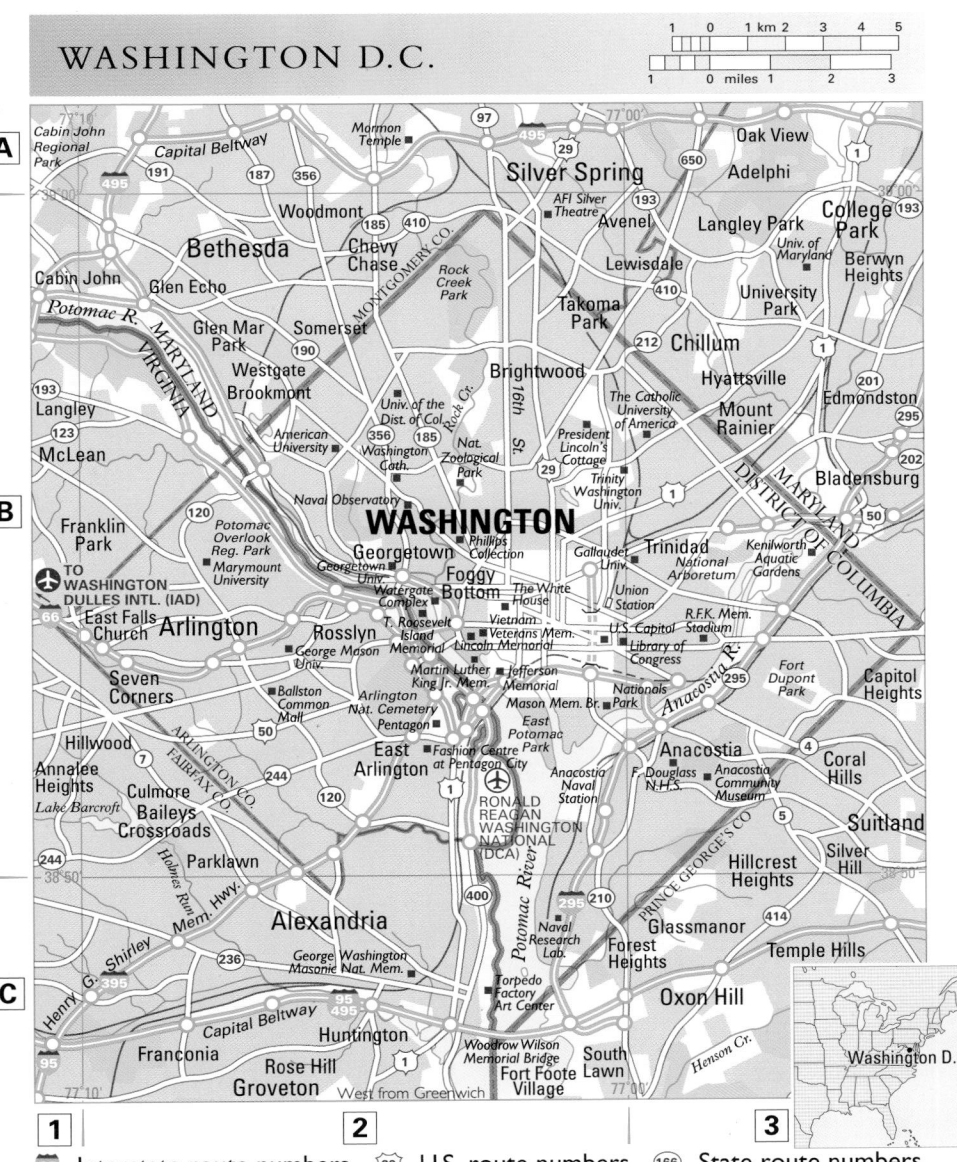

CENTRAL WASHINGTON

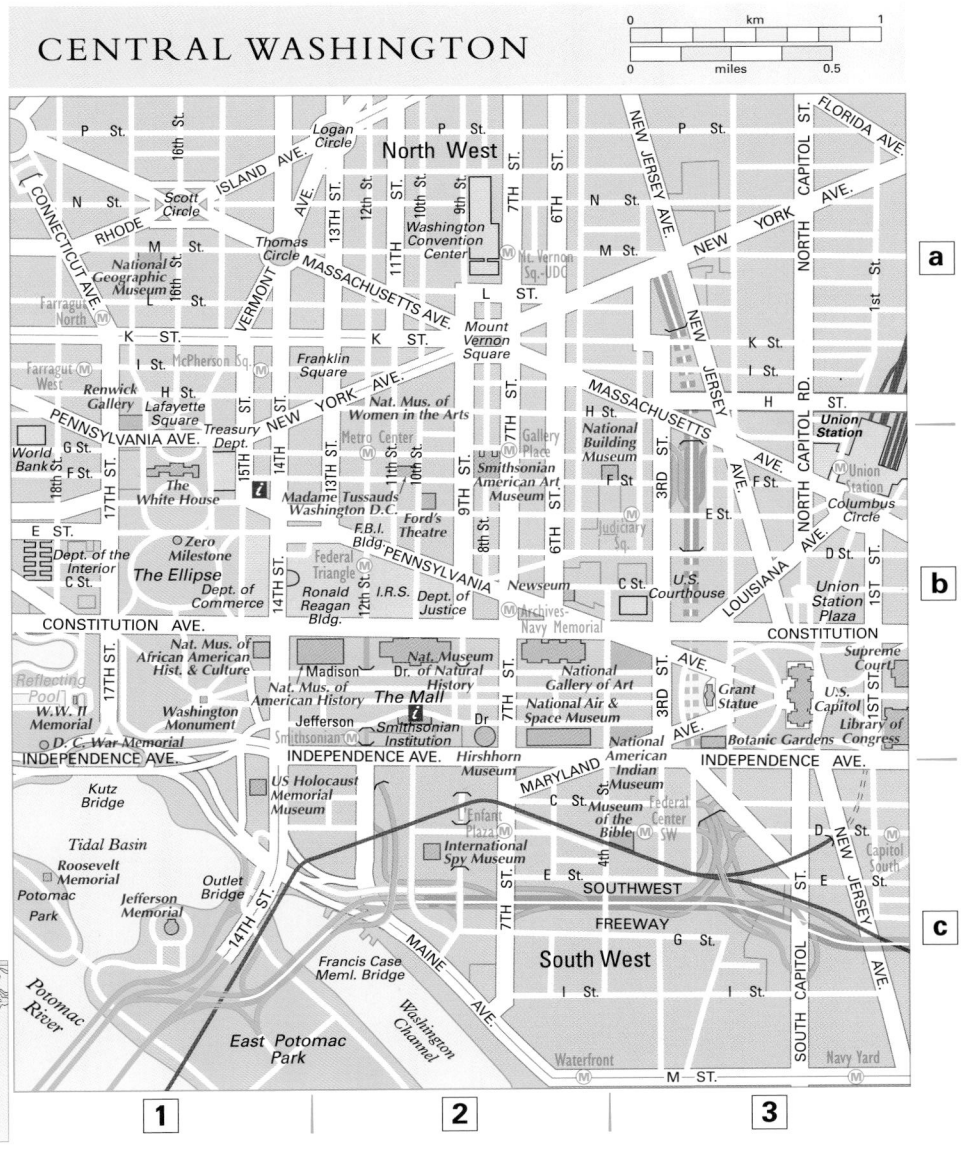

85 Interstate route numbers   29 U.S. route numbers   166 State route numbers

WORLD MAPS

Equatorial Scale 1:76 000 000

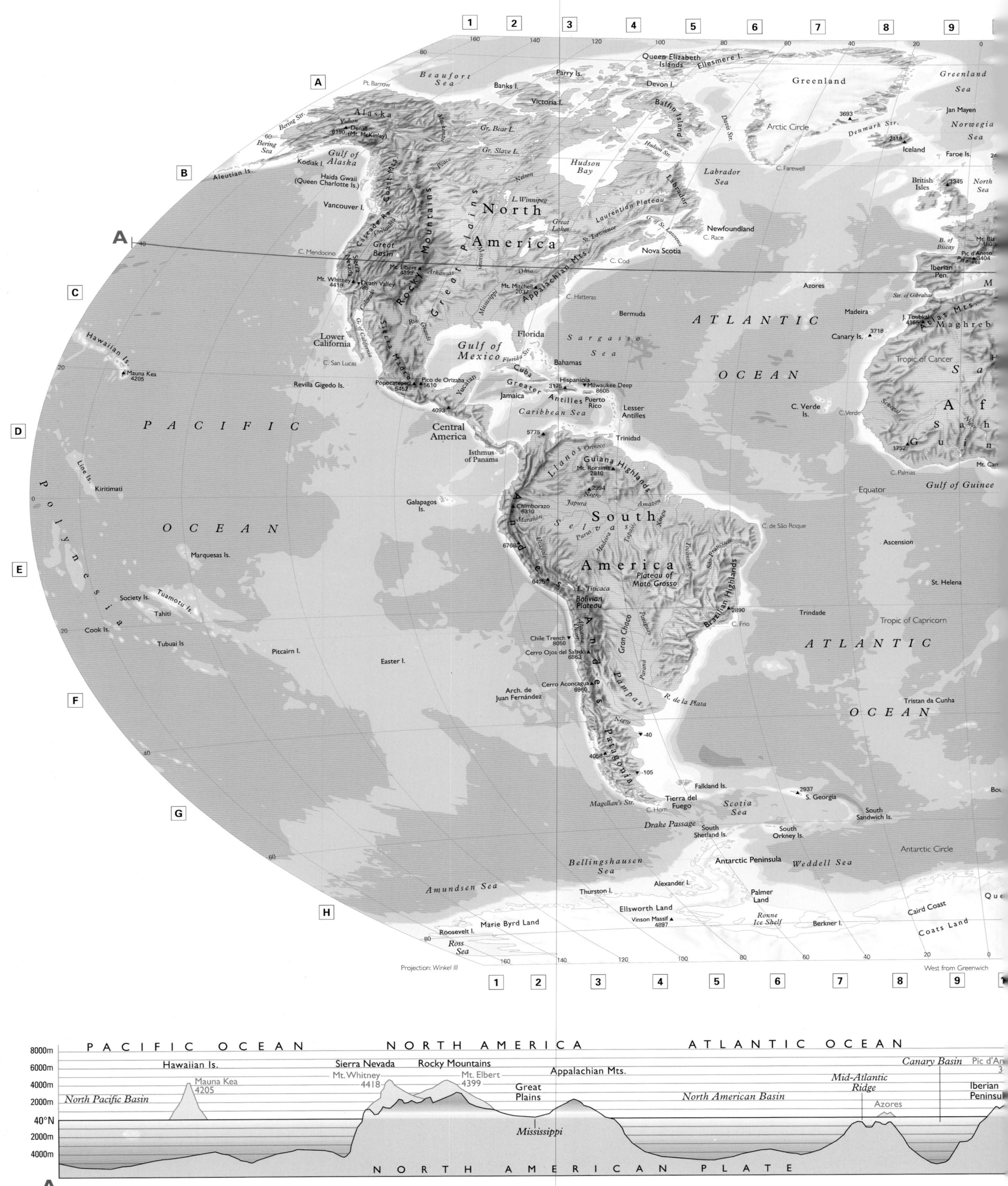

Projection: Winkel III

West from Greenwich

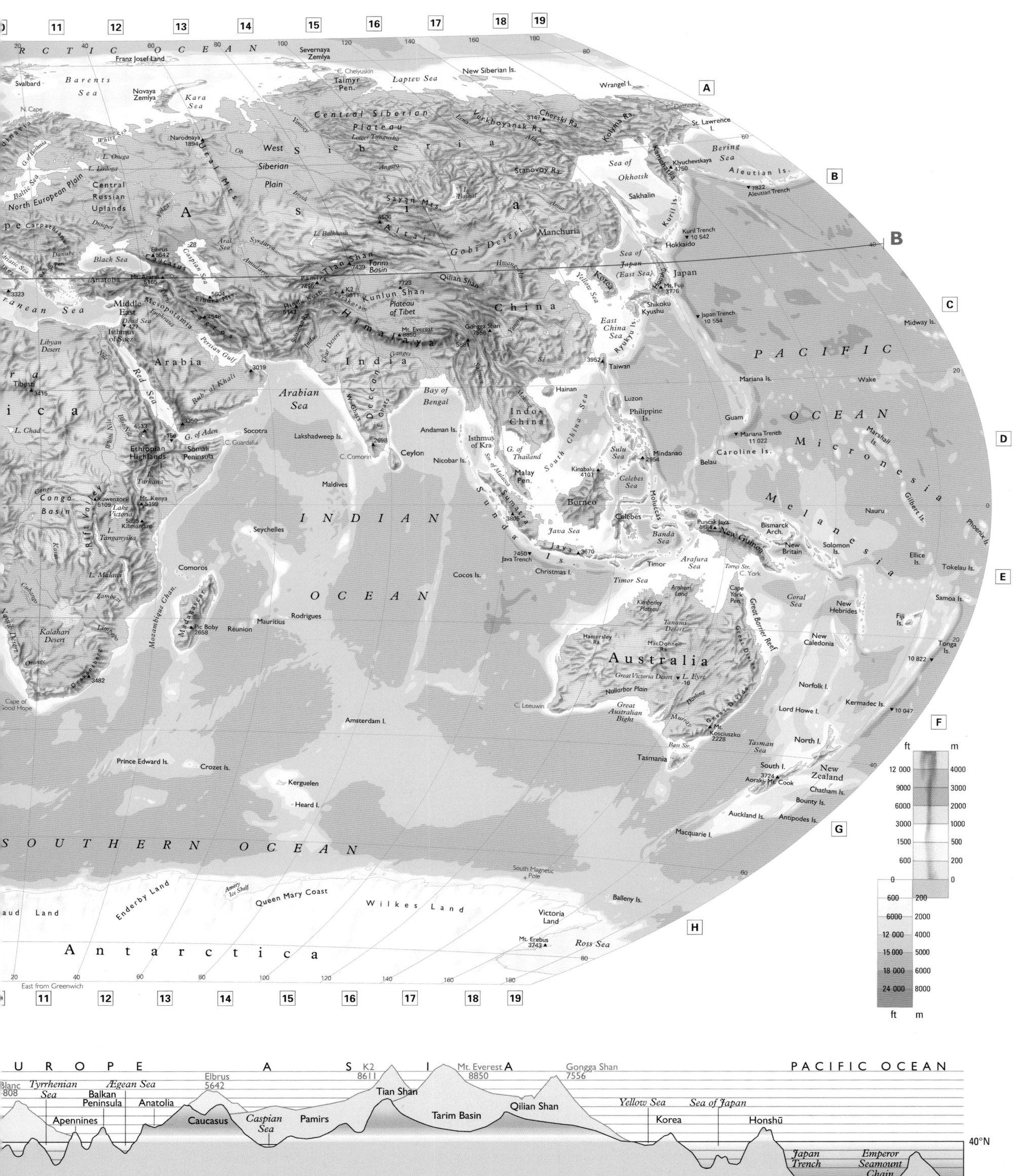

ARCTIC OCEAN

Franz Josef Land

Svalbard

N. Cape

Barents Sea

Novaya Zemlya

Severnaya Zemlya

Taimyr Pen.

C. Chelyuskin

Laptev Sea

New Siberian Is.

Wrangel I.

St. Lawrence I.

C. Dezhneva

A

Kara Sea

Central Siberian Plateau

Verkhoyansk Ra.

Cherski Ra.

Kolyma Ra.

Kamchatka

Klyuchevskaya ▲4750

Bering Sea

Aleutian Is.

B

Narodnaya 1894

Ural Mts.

West Siberian Plain

S i b e r i a

Stanovoy Ra.

Sea of Okhotsk

Sakhalin

Kuril Is.

▼7822 Aleutian Trench

L. Onega

White Sea

Ob

Yenisey

Lower Tunguska

Angara

Amur

Hokkaido

▼ Kuril Trench 10 542

B

L. Ladoga

Baltic Sea

North European Plain

Central Russian Uplands

Dnieper

Volga

Irtysh

Sayan Mts.
4506▲

Baikal

Altai

L. Balkhash

Gobi Desert

Manchuria

Sea of Japan (East Sea)

Japan

40

Carpathians

Danube

Black Sea

Elbrus 5642

Caspian Sea

28

Aral Sea

Syrdarya

Amudarya

Tian Shan 7439

Tarim Basin

Hwang-ho

Korea

Yellow Sea

Mt. Fuji 3776

C

▲3323

Adriatic Sea

Mt. Ararat 5165

Caucasus

5604 Elburz

Pamirs 7495

K2 8611

7723

Kunlun Shan

Qilian Shan

China

East China Sea

Shikoku

Kyushu

▼ Japan Trench 10 554

Midway Is.

Mediterranean Sea

Anatolia

Middle East

Mesopotamia

4548

Hindu Kush 5143

Karakoram

Plateau of Tibet

Yangtze

Ryukyu Is.

C

Dead Sea -427

Euphrates

Tigris

Himalaya

Mt. Everest ▲8850

Gongga Shan 7556

Si

20

Libyan Desert

Isthmus of Suez

Arabia

Persian Gulf

Thar Desert

Ganges

5881

3952

Taiwan

Hainan

PACIFIC

Nile

Red Sea

India

Deccan

Luzon

Mariana Is.

Wake

▲3415

Tibesti

G. of Aden

Rub' al Khali

3019

Arabian Sea

Bay of Bengal

Irrawaddy

Indo-China

Philippine Is.

OCEAN

Guam

Mariana Trench 11 022

D

L. Chad

Socotra

C. Guardafui

Somali Peninsula

Lakshadweep Is.

Andaman Is.

2698

Isthmus of Kra

G. of Thailand

Mindanao 2954

Caroline Is.

M i c r o n e s i a

Blue Nile

4533

Ethiopian Highlands

Nicobar Is.

Malay Pen.

South China Sea

Sulu Sea

Kinabalu 4101

Belau

D

3350

C. Comorin

Ceylon

Maldives

Celebes Sea

Nauru

Ruwenzori 5109

Mt. Kenya 5199

L. Victoria

Kilimanjaro 5895

Seychelles

Sumatra

Borneo

Celebes

Moluccas

Puncak Jaya 4884▲

Bismarck Arch.

New Guinea

Solomon Is.

M e l a n e s i a

Phoenix Is.

Congo Basin

Rift Valley

L. Tanganyika

L. Malawi

Zambezi

3805

Java Sea

Banda Sea

New Britain

Gilbert Is.

Ellice Is.

E

7450▼ Java Trench

3670

Java

Timor

Arafura Sea

Torres Str.

C. York

Fiji Is.

New Hebrides

Samoa Is.

Tokelau Is.

E

INDIAN

Rodrigues

Cocos Is.

Christmas I.

Timor Sea

Arnhem Land

Kimberley Plateau

Coral Sea

New Caledonia

Comoros

Madagascar

Pic Boby 2658

Réunion

Mauritius

Cape York Pen.

Tanami Desert

Hamersley Ra.

MacDonnell Ra.

Great Barrier Reef

Tonga Is.

10 822 ▼

F

Kalahari Desert

Orange

Limpopo

OCEAN

Australia

Norfolk I.

Great Dividing

Lord Howe I.

▼ 10 047

Drakensberg 3482

Great Victoria Desert

L. Eyre -16

Nullarbor Plain

Darling

Murray

Mt. Kosciuszko 2228

Tasman Sea

North I.

C. of Good Hope

C. Leeuwin

Great Australian Bight

Bass Str.

South I.

3724 Aoraki Mt. Cook

New Zealand

Chatham Is.

40

Prince Edward Is.

Crozet Is.

Amsterdam I.

Tasmania

Bounty Is.

Auckland Is.

Antipodes Is.

G

Kerguelen

Heard I.

Macquarie I.

G

SOUTHERN OCEAN

South Magnetic Pole

Balleny Is.

60

Maud Land

Enderby Land

Amery Ice Shelf

Queen Mary Coast

Wilkes Land

Victoria Land

H

Mt. Erebus 3743

Ross Sea

A n t a r c t i c a

80

ft	m
12 000	4000
9000	3000
6000	2000
3000	1000
1500	500
600	200
0	0
600	200
6000	2000
12 000	4000
15 000	5000
18 000	6000
24 000	8000

F

ft　m

E U R O P E　A S　I　A　PACIFIC OCEAN

Blanc 4808

Tyrrhenian Sea

Ægean Sea

Elbrus 5642

K2 8611

Mt. Everest 8850

Gongga Shan 7556

Apennines

Balkan Peninsula

Anatolia

Caucasus

Caspian Sea

Pamirs

Tian Shan

Tarim Basin

Qilian Shan

Yellow Sea

Sea of Japan

Korea

Honshū

Japan Trench

Emperor Seamount Chain

40°N

E U R A S I A N　P L A T E

COPYRIGHT PHILIP'S **B**

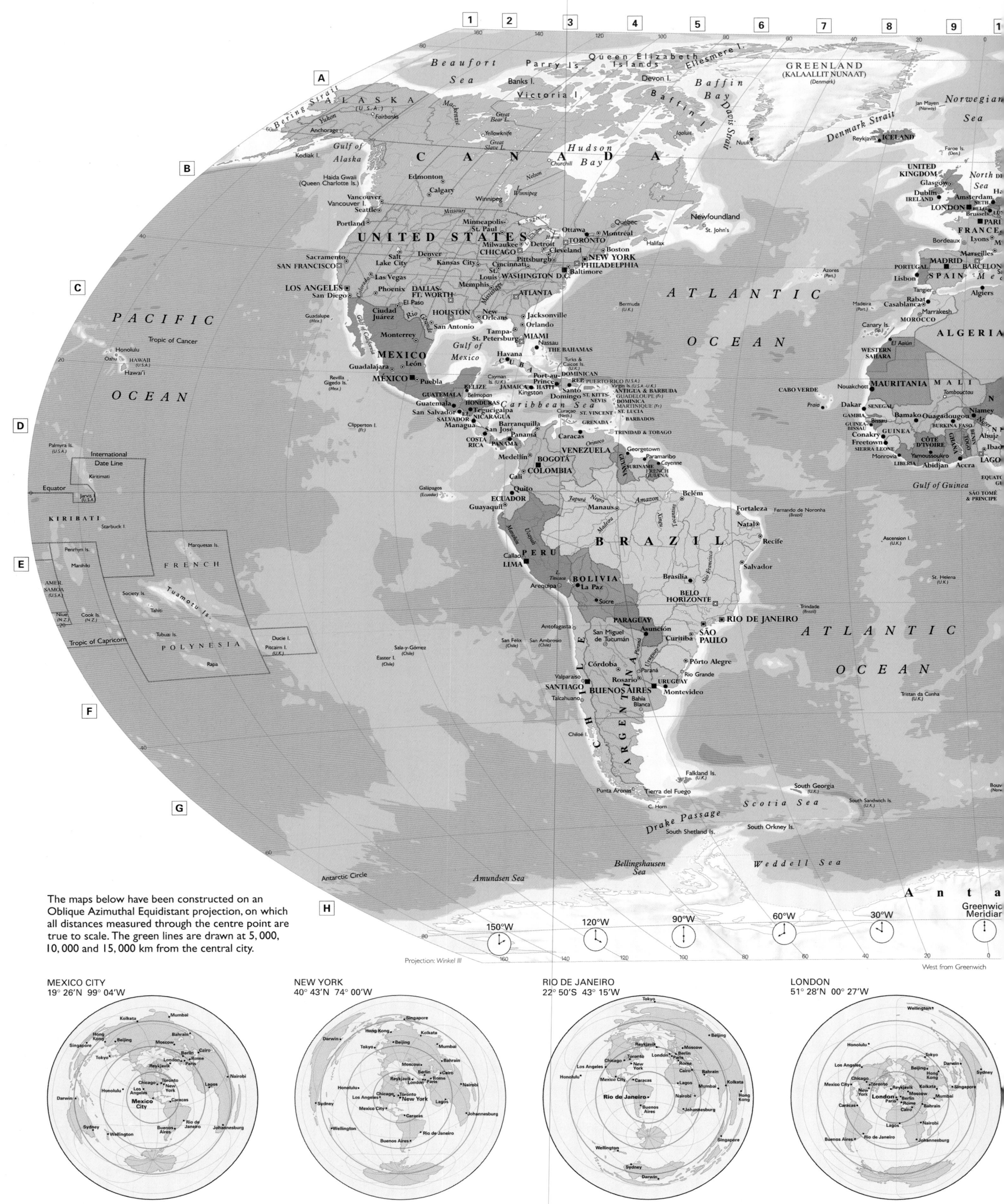

The maps below have been constructed on an Oblique Azimuthal Equidistant projection, on which all distances measured through the centre point are true to scale. The green lines are drawn at 5,000, 10,000 and 15,000 km from the central city.

Projection: Winkel III

West from Greenwich

MEXICO CITY
19° 26'N 99° 04'W

NEW YORK
40° 43'N 74° 00'W

RIO DE JANEIRO
22° 50'S 43° 15'W

LONDON
51° 28'N 00° 27'W

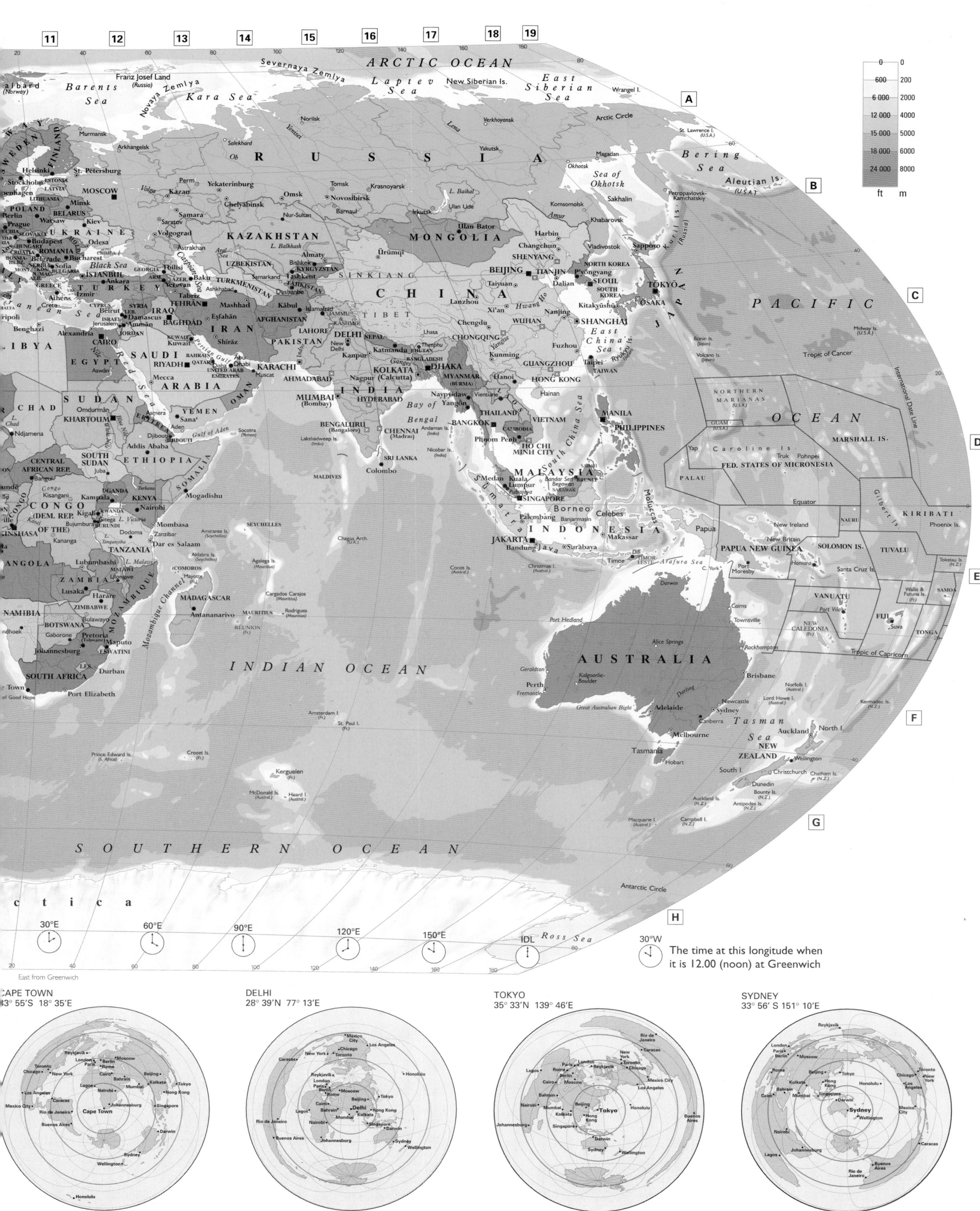

ARCTIC OCEAN

Barents Sea Franz Josef Land (Russia) Severnaya Zemlya *Laptev Sea* New Siberian Is. *East Siberian Sea* Wrangel I.

Novaya Zemlya *Kara Sea*

Norilsk Verkhoyansk Arctic Circle St. Lawrence I. (U.S.A.)

Murmansk Salekhard Yenisey Ob Yakutsk Magadan Bering Sea

Arkhangelsk R U S S I A Lena Yakutsk *Sea of Okhotsk* Petropavlovsk-Kamchatskiy Aleutian Is. (U.S.A.)

SWEDEN FINLAND Helsinki St. Petersburg Tomsk Krasnoyarsk L. Baikal Okhotsk Sakhalin

Stockholm ESTONIA Yekaterinburg Omsk Novosibirsk Komsomolsk Khabarovsk

MOSCOW Volga Kazan Perm Chelyabinsk Irkutsk Ulan Ude Amur Vladivostok Sapporo

Minsk KAZAKHSTAN L. Balkhash Almaty Ulan Bator Changchun Harbin

POLAND BELARUS Samara Saratov Nur-Sultan Barnaul MONGOLIA SHENYANG NORTH KOREA TŌKYŌ

Berlin Warsaw Kiev Volgograd Astrakhan Aral Sea Bishkek Ürümqi BEIJING TIANJIN Pyongyang ŌSAKA

Prague UKRAINE UZBEKISTAN KYRGYZSTAN SINKIANG Taiyuan Dalian SEOUL SOUTH KOREA

Budapest ROMANIA Odesa Tashkent TAJIKISTAN C H I N A Lanzhou Xi'an Kitakyūshū

ROMANIA Bucharest Black Sea GEORGIA Tbilisi TURKMENISTAN Samarkand Dushanbe TIBET Chengdu Hwang Ho

Sofia BULGARIA ARM.AZER. Baku Ashkhabad Mashhad Lhasa WUHAN Nanjing SHANGHAI

GREECE ISTANBUL Ankara Tabriz TEHRÃN Kābul JAMMU Chongqing East China Sea

Izmir T U R K E Y CYPRUS SYRIA IRAQ Esfahān AFGHANISTAN KASHMIR DELHI NEPAL Kunming Fuzhou Ryūkyū

Crete Beirut LEB. Damascus BAGHDĀD I R A N Islamabad New Delhi Thimphu GUANGZHOU TAIPEI

Tripoli Athens ISRAEL Amman Shirāz LAHORE PAKISTAN Kanpur Katmandu BHUTAN HONG KONG TAIWAN

Alexandria Jerusalem JORDAN KUWAIT Kuwait BAHRAIN Abu Dhabi Nagpur BANGLADESH Hainan

CAIRO SAUDI RIYADH QATAR UNITED ARAB EMIRATES KARACHI AHMADABAD KOLKATA (Calcutta) DHAKA Hanoi

Benghazi EGYPT A R A B I A Mecca Muscat I N D I A Nagpur MYANMAR (BURMA) Naypyidaw Vientiane South China Sea

LIBYA Aswān OMAN MUMBAI (Bombay) HYDERABAD Bay of Bengal Yangon THAILAND VIETNAM MANILA

SUDAN Omdurmān YEMEN Sana' Aden BENGALURU (Bangalore) CHENNAI (Madras) BANGKOK CAMBODIA PHILIPPINES

CHAD KHARTOUM ERITREA Gulf of Aden Socotra (Yemen) Andaman Is. (India) Phnom Penh HO CHI MINH CITY

Ndjamena L. Chad Asmera DJIBOUTI Lakshadweep (India) Nicobar Is. (India)

CENTRAL AFRICAN REP. SOUTH SUDAN ETHIOPIA SOMALIA SRI LANKA MALDIVES S Medan Kuala Lumpur MALAYSIA BRUNEI

Bangui Juba Addis Ababa Colombo Bandar Seri Begawan SARAWAK Papua

CONGO (DEM. REP. OF THE) UGANDA KENYA Mogadishu SINGAPORE Borneo Celebes

Kisangani Kampala Nairobi RWANDA L. Victoria Chagos Arch. (U.K.) Palembang Banjarmasin Makassar Moluccas

KINSHASA Kigali BURUNDI Bujumbura TANZANIA SEYCHELLES I N D O N E S I A New Ireland

ANGOLA Kananga Mombasa Amirante Is. (Seychelles) JAKARTA Surabaya New Britain PAPUA NEW GUINEA SOLOMON IS.

Lubumbashi L. Malawi Dar es Salaam Zanzibar Dodoma Aldabra Is. (Seychelles) Java Bandung Timor TIMOR-LESTE Honiara

ZAMBIA MALAWI Lilongwe COMOROS Agalega Is. (Mauritius) Darwin C. York Port Moresby Santa Cruz Is.

NAMIBIA Lusaka Harare Mayotte (Fr.) Cargados Carajos VANUATU

ZIMBABWE MADAGASCAR MAURITIUS Rodrigues (Mauritius) Cairns Port Vila FIJI

BOTSWANA Bulawayo Antananarivo RÉUNION (Fr.) Townsville NEW CALEDONIA (Fr.) Suva

Windhoek Gaborone Pretoria ESWATINI Alice Springs Rockhampton TONGA

Johannesburg Maputo LES. Geraldton A U S T R A L I A Brisbane

SOUTH AFRICA Durban Prince Edward Is. (S. Africa) Crozet Is. (Fr.) Kalgoorlie-Boulder Darling Newcastle Lord Howe I. (Austral.)

Cape of Good Hope Port Elizabeth Kerguelen (Fr.) Perth Fremantle Great Australian Bight Adelaide Sydney Canberra Norfolk I. (Austral.)

M O Z A M B I Q U E C H A N N E L Amsterdam I. (Fr.) St. Paul I. (Fr.) Port Hedland Melbourne Tasman Sea Auckland North I.

I N D I A N   O C E A N McDonald Is. (Austral.) Heard I. (Austral.) Tasmania Hobart NEW ZEALAND Wellington

Kermadec Is. (N.Z.) South I. Christchurch Chatham Is. (N.Z.)

Auckland Is. (N.Z.) Bounty Is. (N.Z.) Dunedin Antipodes Is. (N.Z.)

S O U T H E R N   O C E A N Macquarie I. (Austral.) Campbell I. (N.Z.)

Antarctic Circle Ross Sea

A n t a r c t i c a

PACIFIC OCEAN

Midway Is. (U.S.A.) Bonin Is. (Japan) Volcano Is. (Japan) Tropic of Cancer

NORTHERN MARIANAS (U.S.A.) GUAM (U.S.A.) International Date Line

Caroline Is. Yap Truk Pohnpei MARSHALL IS.

FED. STATES OF MICRONESIA PALAU Equator KIRIBATI

NAURU Gilbert Is. Phoenix Is. (Kiribati)

TUVALU Tokelau Is. (N.Z.)

Wallis & Futuna Is. (Fr.) SAMOA

Tropic of Capricorn

| 30°E | 60°E | 90°E | 120°E | 150°E | IDL | 30°W |

East from Greenwich

The time at this longitude when it is 12.00 (noon) at Greenwich

CAPE TOWN
33° 55'S 18° 35'E

DELHI
28° 39'N 77° 13'E

TOKYO
35° 33'N 139° 46'E

SYDNEY
33° 56'S 151° 10'E

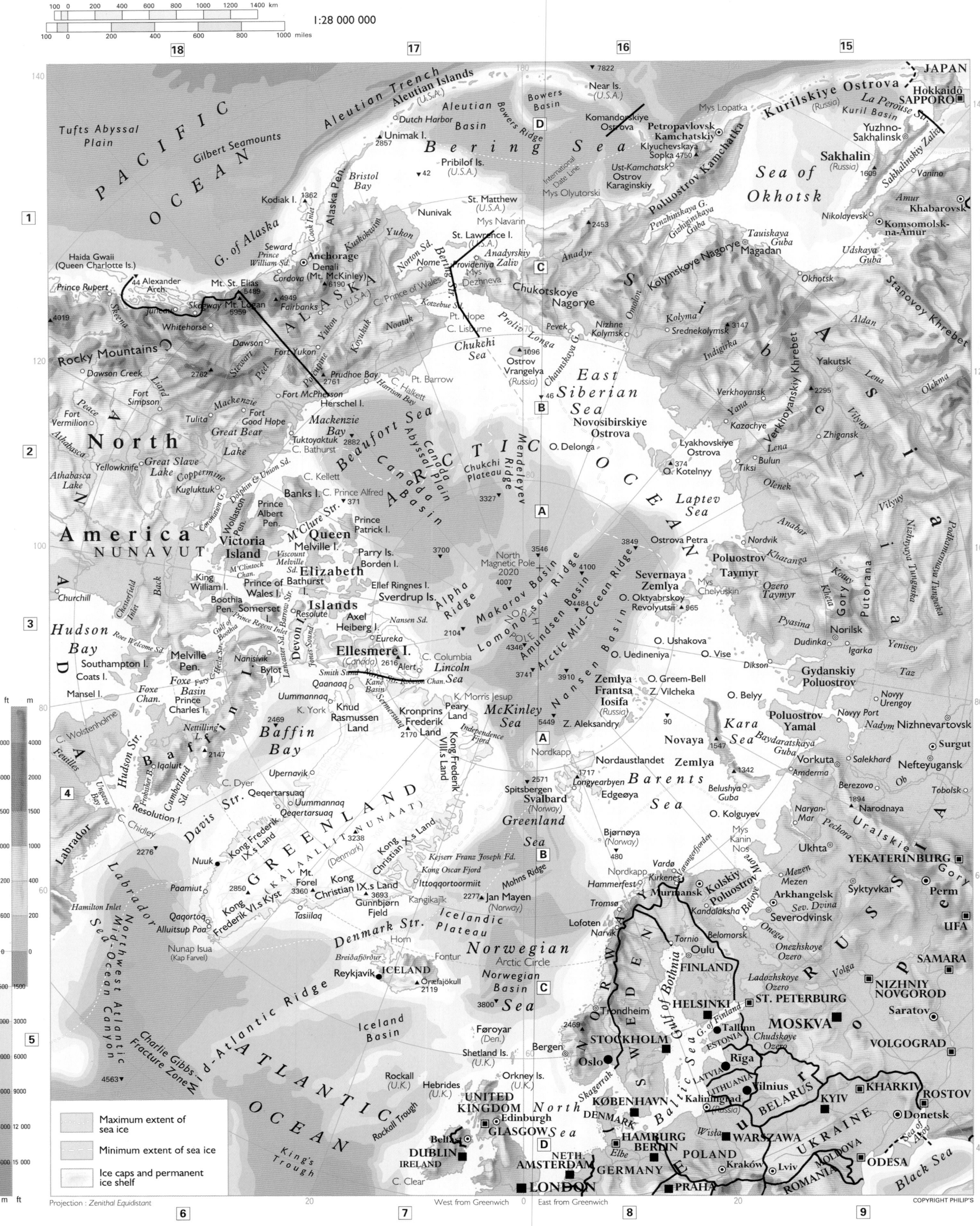

1:28 000 000

Projection : Zenithal Equidistant

West from Greenwich   East from Greenwich

COPYRIGHT PHILIP'S

Maximum extent of sea ice

Minimum extent of sea ice

Ice caps and permanent ice shelf

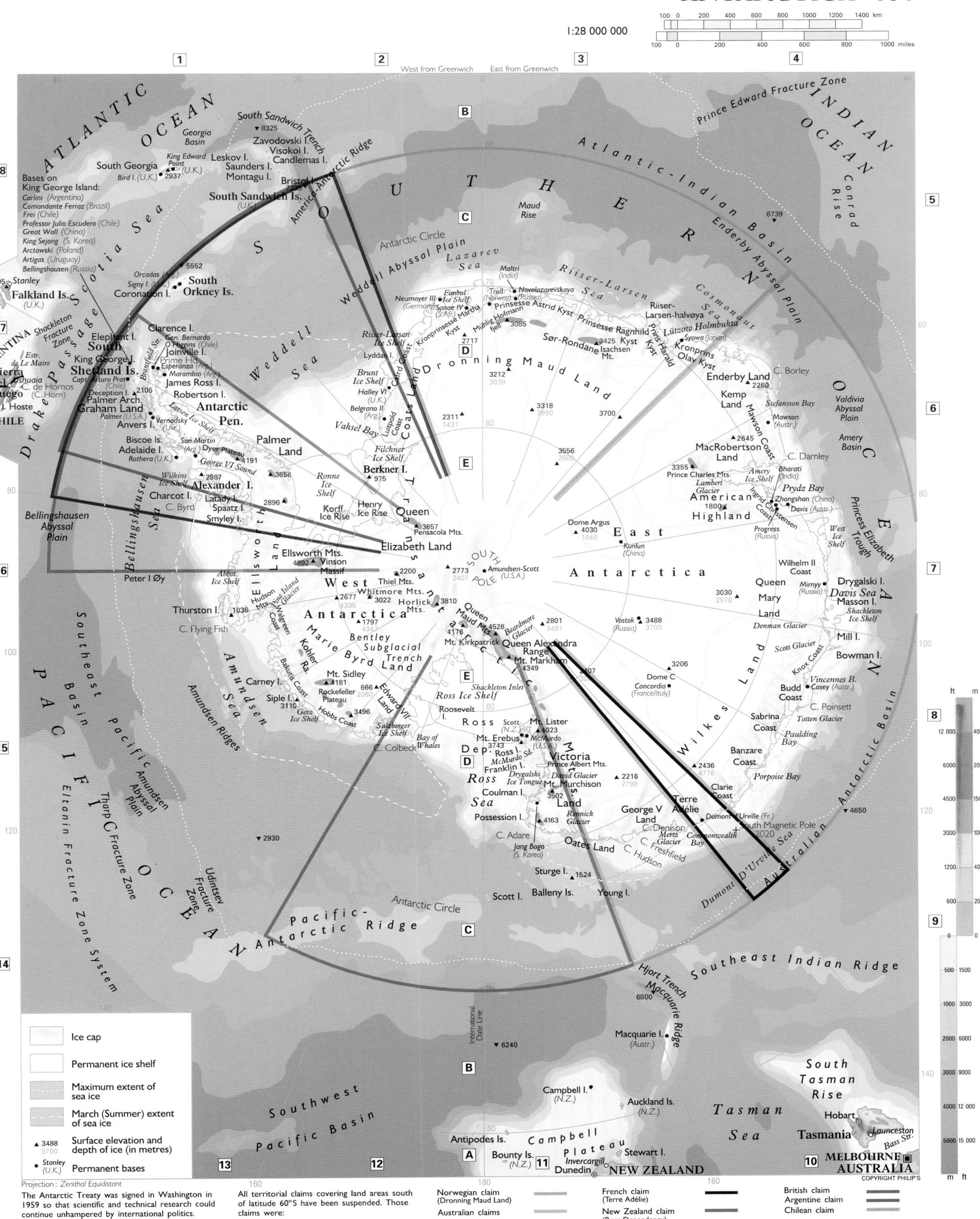

1:28 000 000

100 0   200 400 600 800 1000 1200 1400 km
100 0   200   400   600   800   1000 miles

1   2   West from Greenwich   3   4
         East from Greenwich

ATLANTIC OCEAN

SOUTHERN

Georgia Basin

South Sandwich Trench

Zavodovski I.
Visokoi I.
Candlemas I.

King Edward
Point (U.K.)
▼2937

South Georgia
Bird I. (U.K.)

Leskov I.
Saunders I.
Montagu I.

Bristol I. (U.K.)

South Sandwich Is.
(U.K.)

Bases on
King George Island:
Carlini (Argentina)
Comandante Ferraz (Brazil)
Frei (Chile)
Professor Julio Escudero (Chile)
Great Wall (China)
King Sejong (S. Korea)
Arctowski (Poland)
Artigas (Uruguay)
Bellingshausen (Russia)

05 Stanley

Falkland Is.
(U.K.)

Scotia Sea

Orcadas (Arg.)
▼5552
Signy I. (U.K.)
Coronation I.

South Orkney Is.

Antarctic Circle

Maud Rise

Prince Edward Fracture Zone

INDIAN OCEAN

Conrad Rise

Atlantic-Indian Ridge

Atlantic-Indian Basin

Enderby Abyssal Plain

6739

American-Antarctic Ridge

Weddell Abyssal Plain

Lazarev Sea

Maltri (India)

Riiser-Larsen Sea

Neumayer III (Germany)
Fimbul Ice Shelf
Sanae IV (S.Afr.)
Troll (Norway)
Novolazarevskaya (Russia)

Prinsesse Astrid Kyst
Mühlig-Hofmann fjell
2717
3085

Prinsesse Ragnhild Kyst

Riiser-Larsen-halvøya

Cosmonaut

Lützow-Holmbukta

Syowa (Japan)

Kronprins Olav Kyst

17 Argentina
Shackleton
Fracture
Zone

Elephant I.
Clarence I.
Gen. Bernardo
O'Higgins (Chile)
Joinville I.

South
Shetland Is.

Tierra
del Fuego

King George I.
Deception I. ▼2105
Robertson I.

Estr.
de le Maire
Ushuaia
C. de Hornos
(C. Horn)
I. Hoste

CHILE

Brunsfield Str.
Capt. Arturo Prat (Chile)
Esperanza (Arg.)
Prime Hd.
Marambio (Arg.)
James Ross I.

Graham Land
Palmer (U.S.A.)
Anvers I.
Vernadsky (Ukr.)
Larsen Ice Shelf

Antarctic
Pen.

Biscoe Is.
San Martin (Arg.)
Adelaide I.
Dyer Plateau
Rothera (U.K.)

Charcot I.
C. Byrd

Wilkins Ice Shelf
▼2987

Alexander I.
Latady I.
Spaatz I.
Smyley I.

Weddell
Sea

Riiser-Larsen Ice Shelf

Coats Land
Lyddan I.

Brunt Ice Shelf
Halley VI (U.K.)
Belgrano II (Arg.)

Vahsel Bay

Filchner Ice Shelf

Berkner I.

Ronne Ice Shelf

Korff Ice Rise

Henry Ice Rise

3212
3039

2311
1431

Dronning Maud Land

3318
3990

3700

3556
2608

Sør-Rondane
Isachsen Mt.
3425 Kyst

Enderby Land
2260

Kemp Land

Stefansson Bay

Mawson (Austr.)

C. Borley

Valdivia Abyssal Plain

Amery Basin

6

MacRobertson
Land
2645

3355
Prince Charles Mts.
Lambert Glacier

C. Darnley

Amery Ice Shelf

Bharati (India)

American
Highland

Prydz Bay

Ingrid Christensen Coast
Zhongshan (China)
Davis (Austr.)

Princess Elizabeth Trough

16

Bellingshausen
Sea

Bellingshausen Abyssal Plain

Adelaide I.

George VI Sound
4191
3658

Palmer Land

2896

Elizabeth Land

Dome Argus
4030
1040

Kunlun (China)

East Antarctica

West Ice Shelf

7

3030
2570

Queen Mary Land

Mirnyy (Russia)

Drygalski I.
Davis Sea
Masson I.

Denman Glacier

Scott Glacier

Pensacola Mts.
3657

Peter I Øy

Ellsworth Mts.
4892
Vinson Massif

2773
2407

Amundsen-Scott
(U.S.A.)

SOUTH POLE

Thiel Mts.
3810

Vostok (Russia)
3488
3700

3206

Knox Coast
Vincennes B.
Casey (Austr.)

Bowman I.

C. Poinsett

Mill I.

Thurston I.
1036

Abbot Ice Shelf
2200

Whitmore Mts.
3022
Horlick Mts.

Hudson Mts.
Pine Island Glacier
2677
3335

West Antarctica
1797
4342

Queen Maud Mts.
4528
4176

Beardmore Glacier
Mt. Kirkpatrick
2801

Queen Alexandra
Range
Mt. Markham
4349

Dome C
Concordia (France/Italy)

Budd Coast

Sabrina Coast

Totten Glacier

Wilkes Land

Paulding Bay

8
ft   m
12 000   4000

C. Flying Fish

Marie Byrd Land

Bentley Subglacial Trench

Carney I.

Mt. Sidley
4181
Kohler Ra.
Siple I.
3110

666
Rockefeller Plateau
2080

Edward VII Land

Amundsen Sea

Amundsen Abyssal Plain

Bakutis Coast

Getz Ice Shelf
3496

Hobbs Coast

Shackleton Inlet
3407

Ross Ice Shelf

Roosevelt I.

Bay of Whales

C. Colbeck

Ross Dep.

Scott (N.Z.)

Mt. Lister
4023

Mt. Erebus
3743
McMurdo (U.S.A.)
Ross I.
McMurdo Sd.

Franklin I.

Victoria
Prince Albert Mts.
David Glacier
Drygalski Ice Tongue

2216
2798

Banzare Coast

C. Poinsett

2436
4776

Clarie Coast

Porpoise Bay

15

PACIFIC OCEAN

Pacific Basin

Amundsen Ridges

Coulman I.

Mt. Murchison
3502

Possession I.
4163

Land

George V Land

Rennick Glacier

Terre Adélie

Dumont d'Urville (Fr.)
South Magnetic Pole
2020

Dumont D'Urville Sea

Australian
Antarctic
Basin

4650

9

Tharp Fracture Zone

2930

Ross Sea

C. Adare
Jang Bogo (S. Korea)

Oates Land

C. Denison
Mertz Glacier
C. Freshfield
C. Hudson

Commonwealth Bay

14

Eltanin Fracture Zone System

Udintsev Fracture Zone

Antarctic Circle

Sturge I.
1524

Scott I.

Balleny Is.

Young I.

Southeast Indian Ridge

Hjort Trench
Macquarie
Ridge
6800

500   1500

Pacific-Antarctic Ridge

International Date Line

6240

B

Campbell I.
(N.Z.)

Auckland Is.
(N.Z.)

South Tasman Rise

1000   3000

2000   6000

3000   9000

Southwest Pacific Basin

Tasman Sea

Hobart
Launceston
Bass Str.

Tasmania

4000   12 000

5000   15 000

A

Antipodes Is.
(N.Z.)

Bounty Is.
(N.Z.)

Campbell Plateau

Stewart I.

Invercargill
Dunedin

NEW ZEALAND

MELBOURNE
AUSTRALIA
COPYRIGHT PHILIP'S

m   ft

Legend:

Ice cap

Permanent ice shelf

Maximum extent of sea ice

March (Summer) extent of sea ice

▲3488
3700
Surface elevation and depth of ice (in metres)

• Stanley (U.K.)
Permanent bases

Projection : Zenithal Equidistant

The Antarctic Treaty was signed in Washington in 1959 so that scientific and technical research could continue unhampered by international politics.

All territorial claims covering land areas south of latitude 60°S have been suspended. Those claims were:

Norwegian claim (Dronning Maud Land)

Australian claims

French claim (Terre Adélie)

New Zealand claim (Ross Dependency)

British claim

Argentine claim

Chilean claim

Equatorial Scale 1:41 000 000

CANADA

Hudson Bay
James Bay
Labrador Sea
Davis Strait
Denmark Strait
GREENLAND (Denmark)
Nuuk
Tasilaq
Nunap Isua (K. Farvel)
Reykjavik
ICELAND
Ør*æfajökull 2119
Norwegian Sea
Norwegian Basin
Tórshavn
Føroyar (Den.)
Trondheim
NORWAY
Oslo
Bergen
Stockholm
Göteborg
DENMARK
København
Malmö
Hamburg
Berlin
GERMANY
Warszawa
POLAND
CZECHIA
SLOVAK
HUNGARY
AUSTRIA
Wien
Zagreb
Milan
Roma
ITALY
Napoli
Sardegna
Corse
Barcelona
Madrid
SPAIN
Lisboa
PORTUGAL
Porto
A Coruña
C. Fisterra
Vigo
Douro
Bordeaux
Biscay Abyssal Plain
Bay of Biscay
Mt. Blanc 4808
FRANCE
Paris
Le Havre
Loire
Brussel
London
UNITED KINGDOM
Glasgow
Dublin
IRELAND
Liverpool
Amsterdam
Celtic Sea
English Channel
North Sea
Baltic Sea
Gdansk

Winnipeg
Regina
L. Winnipeg
Churchill
Nelson
Albany
Moosonee
Belcher Is.
C. Henrietta Maria
Hudson Str.
C. Chidley
Hamilton Inlet
Str. of Belle Isle
Newfoundland
Gulf of St. Lawrence
Cape Breton I.
C. Race
St. John's
Flemish Cap
Grand Banks of Newfoundland
Halifax
Québec
Montréal
Ottawa
Toronto
L. Ontario
L. Erie
Boston
C. Cod
New York
Philadelphia
Baltimore
Washington D.C.
Chesapeake Bay
C. Hatteras
Charleston
Jacksonville
UNITED STATES
Minneapolis
St. Paul
Chicago
Detroit
Pittsburgh
St. Louis
Omaha
L. Superior
L. Michigan
L. Huron
Ohio
Missouri
Mississippi
Arkansas
Red
Tennessee
Alabama
Atlanta
Appalachian Mts.
New England Seamounts
Sohm Abyssal Plain
Corner Seamounts
Bermuda (U.K.)
6028
Bermuda Rise
Hatteras Abyssal Plain
Sargasso Sea
Nares Abyssal Plain
Charlie Gibbs Fracture Zone
Reykjanes Ridge
Rockall (U.K.)
Rockall Trough
Porcupine Abyssal Plain
King's Trough
Azores-Biscay Rise
5225
Açores (Port.)
2351
Ponta Delgada
C. de São Vicente
Tanger
Str. of Gibraltar
Rabat
Casablanca
MOROCCO
Marrakech
Madeira (Port.)
Funchal
Alger
Tunis
TUNISIA
Tarābulus
Chott Djerid
Mediterranean Sea
Sicilia
MALTA
Adriatic Sea

ATLANTIC OCEAN

Mid Atlantic Ridge

Houston
Galveston
New Orleans
Gulf of Mexico
Sigsbee Deep 3504
G. de Campeche
Veracruz
Tampico
Canal de Yucatan
La Habana
CUBA
Miami
Nassau
Florida Strait
BAHAMAS
Tropic of Cancer
West Indies
MEXICO
GUATEMALA
BELIZE
G. de Honduras
HONDURAS
EL SALVADOR
NICARAGUA
L. de Nicaragua
COSTA RICA
PANAMA
Panamá
Panama Canal
G. de Panamá
G. del Darién
Santiago de Cuba
HAITI
DOM. REP.
JAMAICA
Kingston
Santo Domingo
San Juan
PUERTO RICO (U.S.A.)
Milwaukee Deep 8605
Puerto Rico Trench
Cayman Trough
ANTIGUA
ST. KITTS
Leeward Is.
GUADELOUPE (Fr.)
DOMINICA
MARTINIQUE (Fr.)
ST. LUCIA
BARBADOS
ST. VINCENT
GRENADA
Windward Is.
Curaçao
Colombian Basin
Caribbean Sea
G. de Venezuela
Barranquilla
Sierra Nevada de Santa Marta 5775
Caracas
TRINIDAD & TOBAGO
Port of Spain
Demerara Abyssal Plain
Ceara Rise
5638
Cape Verde Abyssal Plain
Cape Verde Plateau
Ras Nouâdhibou
Is. Canarias 3718
Las Palmas
El Aaiún
Saharan Seamounts
WESTERN SAHARA
Sahara
ALGERIA
Nouadhibou
CABO VERDE
2829
Praia
Dakar
St-Louis
SENEGAL
GAMBIA
GUINEA-BISSAU
MAURITANIA
Tombouctou
Senegal
Kayes
MALI
NIGER
Bamako
Ouagadougou
BURKINA FASO
Kano
NIGERIA
Conakry
GUINEA
Freetown
SIERRA LEONE
LIBERIA
Monrovia
CÔTE D'IVOIRE
GHANA
TOGO
BENIN
Abidjan
Accra
Sekondi-Takoradi
Lagos
Port Harcourt
CAMEROON
Niger
Benue

VENEZUELA
Meta
Bogotá
COLOMBIA
Cali
Sierra Parima
Mt. Roraima 2810
Orinoco
GUYANA
Georgetown
Paramaribo
SURINAME
FRENCH GUIANA
Cayenne
C. Orange
Essequibo
Branco
Negro
Japurá
Putumayo
C. de San Francisco
Quito
Cotopaxi 5897
ECUADOR
G. de Guayaquil
Guayaquil
Chimborazo 6310
Pta. Pariñas
Trujillo
PERU
Lima
Amazonas
Manaus
Santarém
Belém
São Luís
Fortaleza
Natal
Recife
Maceió
C. de São Roque
Atol das Rocas
Fernando de Noronha (Brazil)
São Pedro & São Paulo (Brazil)
7758
Equator
Ceara Abyssal Plain
6537
Pernambuco Abyssal Plain
Gulf of Guinea
Guinea Basin
Annobón
Pointe Noire
GABON
EQUATORIAL GUINEA
SÃO TOMÉ & PRÍNCIPE
Bioko 3008
C. Lopez
Libreville
Sierra Leone Rise
Sierra Leone Basin

BRAZIL
Madeira
Purus
Juruá
Ucayali
Marañón
Iquitos
Xingu
Tapajós
Tocantins
Parnaíba
Araguaia
São Francisco
Negro
Brasília
Goiânia
Belo Horizonte
Vitória
2890
Trindade (Brazil)
Martin Vaz
Hotspur Seamount
Banco Abrolhos
Nevado Ancohuma 6550
La Paz
BOLIVIA
L. Titicaca
L. Poopó
Arica
Iquique
Antofagasta
6064
Ojos del Salado 6893
San Ambrosio (Chile)
San Félix
Nazca Ridge
Peru-Chile Trench
Gran Chaco
Pilcomayo
PARAGUAY
Asunción
Paraná
Pampas
Brazil Basin
Ascension I. (U.K.) 859
5656
Angola
ANGOLA
Luanda
Benguela
Namibe
Angola Abyssal Plain
St. Helena (U.K.) 820
Walvis Bay
NAMIBIA
Lüderitz (Namibia)
Port Nolloth
Nambia Abyssal Plain
SOUTH AFRICA
Cape Town
C. of Good Hope
Cape Basin
Walvis Ridge

São Paulo
Santos
Rio de Janeiro
Curitiba
C. Frio
Sierra da Mantiqueira
C. de São Tomé
Tropic of Capricorn
ATLANTIC OCEAN
Vitória Seamount

CHILE
Córdoba
ARGENTINA
Aconcagua 6962
Valparaíso
Santiago
Concepción
San Miguel de Tucumán
Salado
Rosario
Santa Fe
URUGUAY
Montevideo
Buenos Aires
Río de la Plata
L. dos Patos
Pôrto Alegre
638
Colorado
Bahía Blanca
Río Grande Rise
Mid Atlantic Ridge
Tristan da Cunha (U.K.) 2062
Inaccessible I. (U.K.)
Gough I. (U.K.) 910
5457
887
SOUTH AFRICA
411
Discovery Seamount
Agulhas Ridge

PACIFIC OCEAN
Chile Rise
Arch. de Juan Fernández (Chile)
Puerto Montt
I. de Chiloé
Arch de los Chonos
Pen. de Taitao
G. de Penas
8066
Chubut
Golfo San Jorge
G. San Matías
Pen. Valdés
Bahía Blanca
Argentine Basin
Patagonia
Est. de Magallanes (Magellan Str.)
705
Tierra del Fuego
I. Santa Inés
Punta Arenas
C. de Hornos
Falkland Is. (U.K.)
Stanley
Burdwood Bank
Falkland Plateau
Falkland Ridge
Argentine Abyssal Plain
5704
102
Shag Rocks
Georgia Basin
South Georgia (U.K.)
Grytviken 8325
Mt. Paget 2937
South Sandwich Trench
Bouvetøya (Norw.)

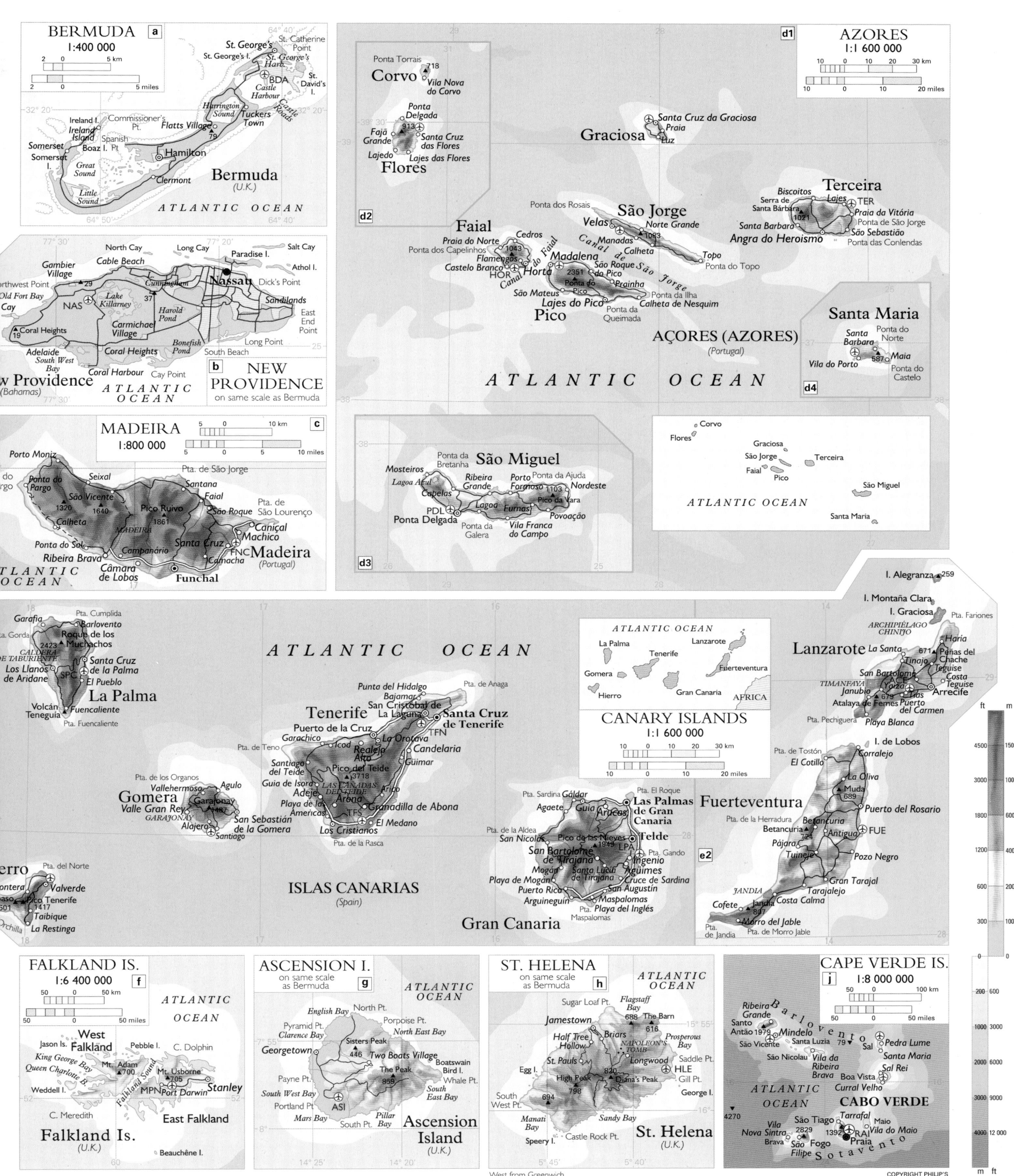

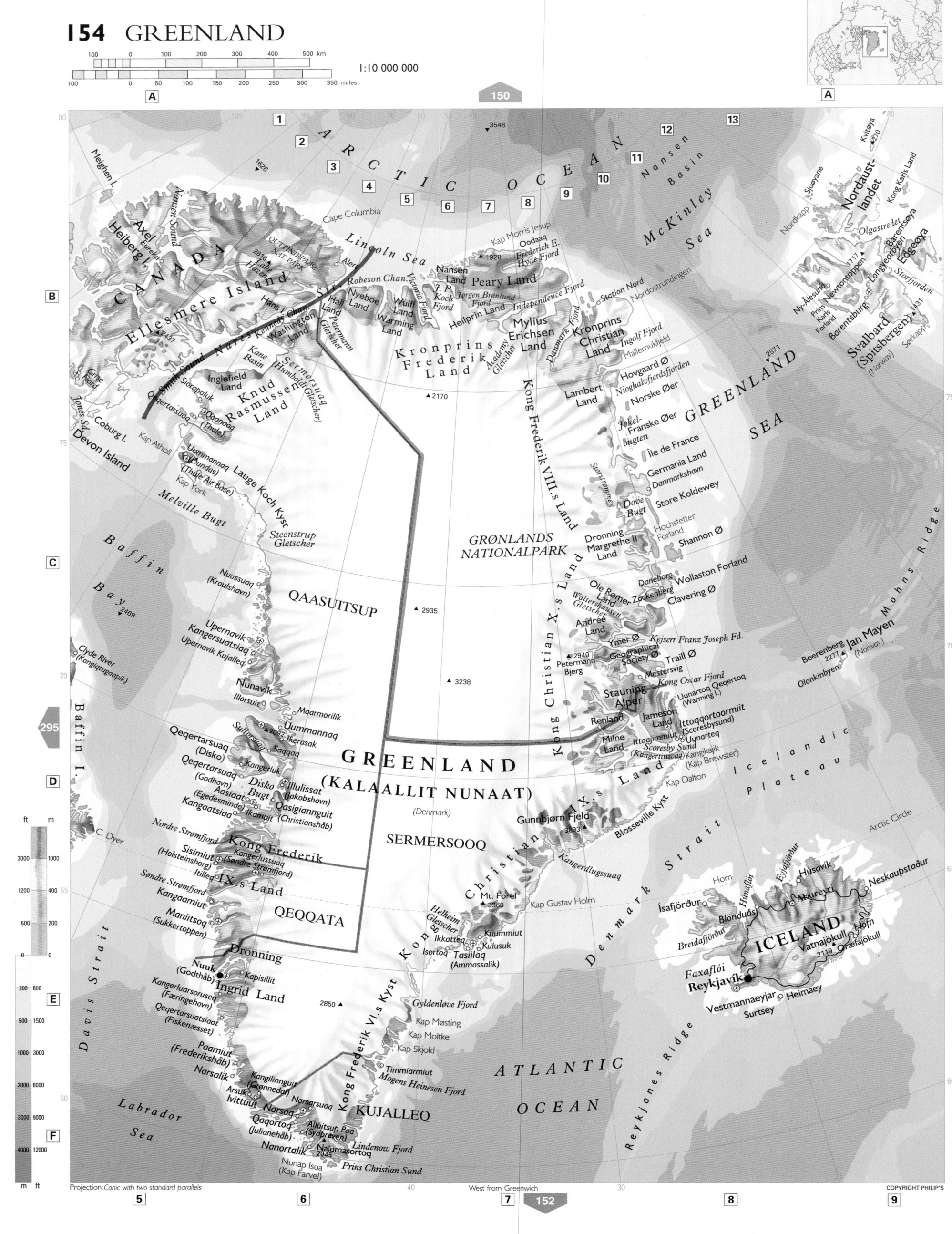

ARCTIC OCEAN

McKinley Sea

Nansen Basin

Nordaust-landet

Kong Karls Land

Svalbard
(Spitsbergen) (Norway)

CANADA

Ellesmere Island

Axel Heiberg I.

Meighen I.

Nansen Sound

QUTTINIRPAAQ NAT. PARK

Cape Columbia

Lincoln Sea

Alert

Kap Morris Jesup

Oodaaq

Nansen Land   Peary Land

Frederick E. Hyde Fjord

Robeson Chan.

Nyeboe Land

Wulff Land

Warming Land

Half Land

J.P. Koch Fjord

Jørgen Brønlund Fjord

Independence Fjord

Heilprin Land

Mylius Erichsen Land

Kronprins Christian Land

Station Nord

Nordostrundingen

Kronprins Frederik Land

Academy Gletscher

Kennedy Chan.

Hans Land

Washington Land

Petermann Gletscher

Kane Basin

Inglefield Land

Humboldt Gletscher

Knud Rasmussen Land

Sermersuaq

Denmark Fjord

Ingolf Fjord

Mallemukfjeld

Hovgaard Ø

Nioghalvfjerdsfjorden

Lambert Land

Norske Øer

GREENLAND

Jøkel-Franke Øer

Île de France

Germania Land

Danmarkshavn

Dove Bugt

Store Koldewey

GREENLAND SEA

Mohns Ridge

Jan Mayen (Norway)

Beerenberg

GRØNLANDS NATIONALPARK

Kong Frederik VIII.s Land

Dronning Margrethe II Land

Shannon Ø

Hochstetter Forland

Wollaston Forland

Daneborg

Zackenberg

Clavering Ø

Ole Romer Land

Andrée Land

Waltershausen Gletscher

Ymer Ø

Kejser Franz Joseph Fd.

Geographical Society Ø

Traill Ø

Stauning Alper

Petermann Bjerg

Renland

Milne Land

Jameson Land

Kong Oscar Fjord

Uunartoq Qeqertoq (Warming I.)

Ittoqqortoormiit (Scoresbysund)

Ittajgimmiut

Scoresby Sund (Kangertittivaq)

Uunarteq

Kangikajik (Kap Brewster)

Icelandic Plateau

QAASUITSUP

Nuussuaq (Kraulshavn)

Upernavik

Kangersuatsiaq

Upernavik Kujalleq

Nunavik

Illorsuit

Maarmorilik

Uummannaq

Baffin Bay

Clyde River (Kangiqtugaapik)

Melville Bugt

Steenstrup Gletscher

Qeqertarsuaq (Disko)

Sullorsuaq

Ikerasak

Saqqaq

Kangerluk

Qeqertarsuaq (Godhavn)

Illulissat (Jakobshavn)

Disko Bugt

Aasiaat (Egedesminde)

Kangaatsiaq

Ikamiut

Qasigiannguit (Christianshåb)

GREENLAND
(KALAALLIT NUNAAT)

(Denmark)

SERMERSOOQ

Gunnbjørn Fjeld

Blosseville Kyst

Kap Dalton

Arctic Circle

Nordre Strømfjord

Kong Frederik IX.s Land

Sisimiut (Holsteinsborg)

Kangerlussuaq (Søndre Strømfjord)

Itilleq

Søndre Strømfjord

Kangaamiut

QEQQATA

Maniitsoq (Sukkertoppen)

Kangerdlugssuaq

Mt. Forel

Kap Gustav Holm

Denmark Strait

Kong Christian IX.s Land

Helheim Gletscher

Ikkatteq

Isortoq

Kuummiut

Kulusuk

Tasiilaq (Ammassalik)

Dronning

Nuuk (Godthåb)

Kapisillit

Ingrid Land

Kangerluarsoruseq (Færingehavn)

Qeqertarsuatsiaat (Fiskenæsset)

Gyldenløve Fjord

ICELAND

Ísafjörður

Bolungarvík

Blönduós

Akureyri

Húsavik

Neskaupstaður

Hofn

Vatnajökull

Öræfajökull

Reykjavík

Faxaflói

Vestmannaeyjar

Heimaey

Surtsey

Breiðafjörður

Kap Møsting

Paamiut (Frederikshåb)

Narsalik

Kangilinnguit (Grønnedal)

Arsuk

Ivittuut

Kap Moltke

Kap Skjold

Timmiarmiut

Mogens Heinesen Fjord

ATLANTIC OCEAN

Davis Strait

Labrador Sea

Kong Frederik VI.s Kyst

Narsarsuaq

Narsaq

Qaqortoq (Julianehåb)

Alluitsup Paa (Sydprøven)

KUJALLEQ

Nanortalik

Nunap Isua (Kap Farvel)

Lindenow Fjord

Prins Christian Sund

Reykjanes Ridge

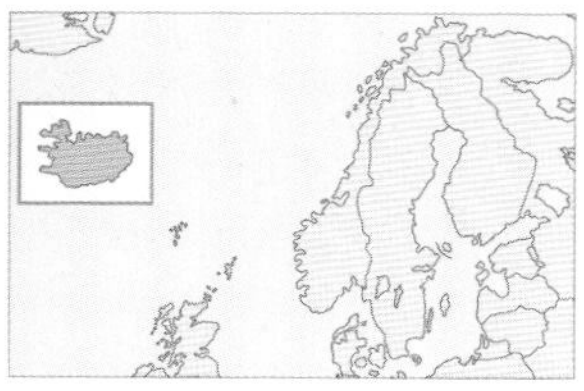

1:2 000 000

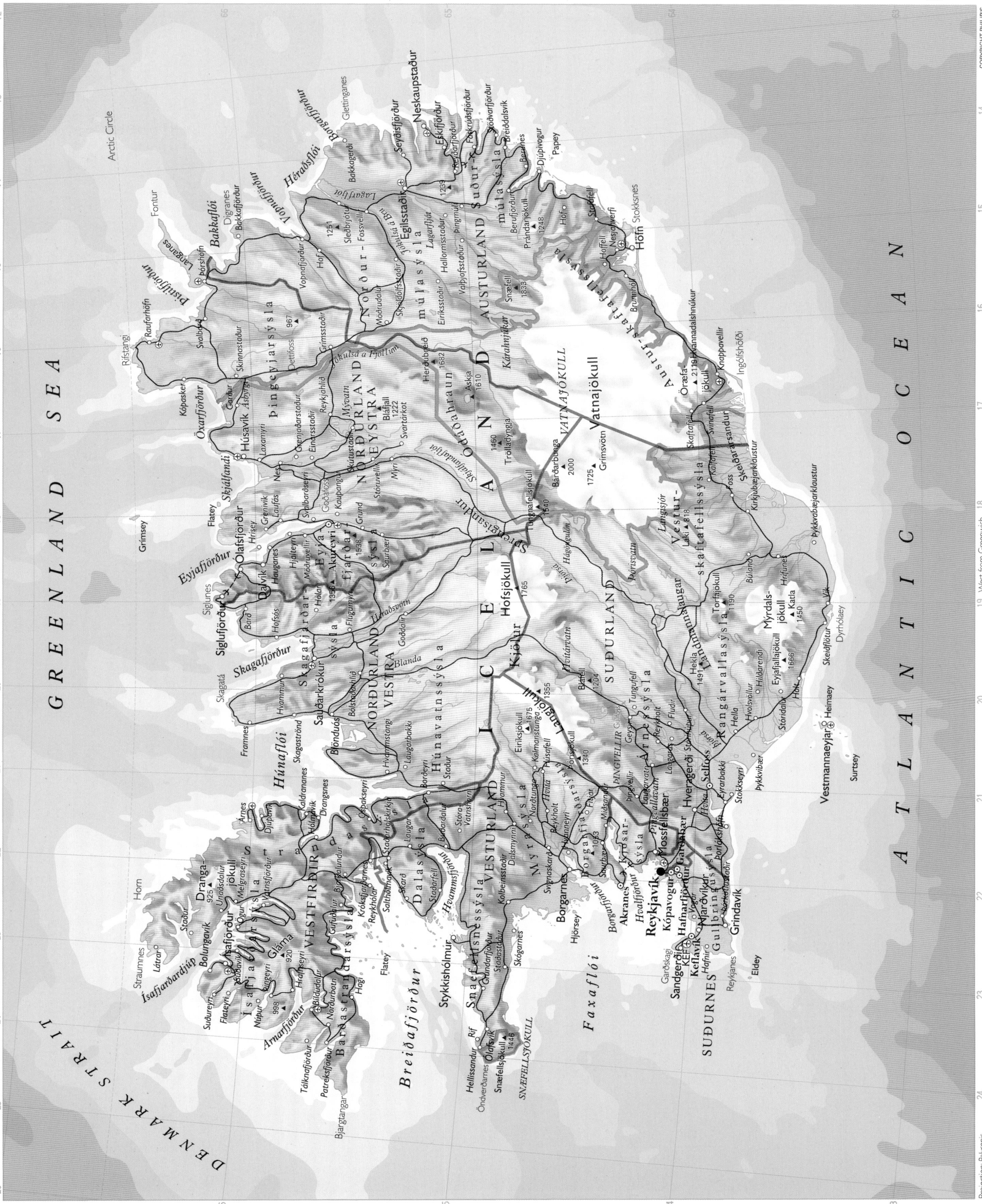

10 0 10 20 30 40 50 60 70 80 100 km
10 0 10 20 30 40 50 60 miles

COPYRIGHT PHILIP'S

GREENLAND SEA

DENMARK STRAIT

ATLANTIC OCEAN

ICELAND

Arctic Circle

West from Greenwich

Projection: Polyconic

Regions / Districts

VESTFIRÐIR
NORÐURLAND VESTRA
NORÐURLAND EYSTRA
AUSTURLAND
SUÐURLAND
VESTURLAND
SUÐURNES

Norður-Múlasýsla
Suður-Múlasýsla
Austur-Skaftafellssýsla
Vestur-Skaftafellssýsla
Rangárvallasýsla
Árnessýsla
Gullbringusýsla
Borgarfjarðarsýsla
Mýrasýsla
Snæfellsnessýsla
Dalasýsla
Barðastrandarsýsla
Ísafjarðarsýsla
Strandasýsla
Húnavatnssýsla
Skagafjarðarsýsla
Eyjafjarðarsýsla
Þingeyjarsýsla

Glaciers / Ice caps

VATNAJÖKULL
Hofsjökull
Langjökull
Mýrdalsjökull
Eyjafjallajökull
Snæfellsjökull
Drangajökull
Eiríksjökull
Tungnafellsjökull
Torfajökull
Breiðamerkurjökull

Water features

Faxaflói
Breiðafjörður
Húnaflói
Skagafjörður
Eyjafjörður
Öxarfjörður
Þistilfjörður
Héraðsflói
Vopnafjörður
Berufjörður
Ísafjarðardjúp
Arnarfjörður

Settlements

Reykjavík
Kópavogur
Hafnarfjörður
Mosfellsbær
Garðabær
Akranes
Borgarnes
Keflavík
Njarðvík
Grindavík
Sandgerði
Selfoss
Hveragerði
Eyrarbakki
Stokkseyri
Hvolsvöllur
Hella
Vík
Höfn
Djúpivogur
Breiðdalsvík
Stöðvarfjörður
Fáskrúðsfjörður
Reyðarfjörður
Eskifjörður
Neskaupstaður
Seyðisfjörður
Egilsstaðir
Vopnafjörður
Þórshöfn
Raufarhöfn
Kópasker
Húsavík
Akureyri
Dalvík
Ólafsfjörður
Siglufjörður
Sauðárkrókur
Blönduós
Hvammstangi
Ísafjörður
Bolungarvík
Patreksfjörður
Stykkishólmur
Grundarfjörður
Ólafsvík
Hellissandur
Rif
Vestmannaeyjar
Heimaey
Surtsey

Peaks / heights

2119 Hvannadalshnúkur
2000 Bárðarbunga
1833 Snæfell
1765
1725 Grímsvötn
1675
1666 Katla
1632 Herðubreið
1610 Askja
1491 Hekla
1460
1450
1446
1355
1310
1300
1239
1238
1222 Blàfjall
1204
1190
1053
998
967
925
920
818 Laki

rivers: Þjórsá, Hvítá, Jökulsá á Fjöllum, Blanda, Lagarfljót, Markarfljót, Tungnaá, Skjálfandafljót

100 0 100 200 300 400 500 600 700 800 km

1:16 000 000

100 0 100 200 300 400 500 miles

ROCKALL Sea areas named in weather forecasts

Projection: Bonne

East from Greenwich   West from Greenwich

Seas and oceans:
ATLANTIC OCEAN
Norwegian Sea
North Sea
Barents Sea
White Sea
Baltic Sea
Mediterranean Sea
Black Sea
Caspian Sea
Adriatic Sea
Tyrrhenian Sea
Ligurian Sea
Ionian Sea
Aegean Sea
Celtic Sea
Irish Sea
Sea of Azov
Sea of Marmara
Sea of Crete
Cyclades Sea
Dodecanese Sea
Kattegat
Skagerrak
G. of Bothnia
Gulf of Finland
Gulf of Riga
Gulf of Gdansk
Gulf of Venice
Gulf of Lions
Gulf of Antalya
Bay of Biscay
Onega Bay
Chesha Boy

Land regions and mountains:
Iceland
Ireland
Great Britain
British Isles
Scandinavia
Lapland
Finland
Scandinavian Mts.
Ural Mountains
Northern Urals
West Siberian Lowlands
Timan Ridge
European Plain
Central Russian Uplands
Valdai Hills
Volga Hts.
Obshchi Syrt
Kirgiziya Steppe
Caspian Depression
Transcaucasia
Caucasus
Armenia
Kurdistan
Anatolia (Asia Minor)
Taurus Mts.
Pontine Mts.
Mesopotamia
Ukraine
Wallachia
Plain of Hungary
Carpathians
Transylvanian Alps
Balkans
Rhodope
Pindus
Dinaric Alps
Peloponnese
Calabria
Apennines
Alps
Jura
Vosges
Black Forest
Bohemian Forest
Sudeten
Moravian Hts.
Harz
Erzgebirge
Massif Central
Pyrenees
Iberian Peninsula
Old Castile
New Castile
Andalusia
Sierra Nevada
Sierra Morena
Cantabrian Mts.
Picos de Europa
Brittany
Africa
Plateau of the Shotts

Rivers and lakes:
Volga
Don
Dnieper
Dniester
Danube
Kama
Pechora
Ural
Rhine
Rhône
Loire
Seine
Garonne
Ebro
Tagus
Douro
Guadiana
Guadalquivir
Elbe
Oder
Vistula
Warta
Po
Tiber
Tisza
Sava
Drava
Thames
Severn
Trent
L. Ladoga
L. Onega
L. Ilmen
L. Constance
L. Geneva
L. Garda
L. Balaton
L. Ohrid
L. Prespa
L. Shkodër

Islands:
Shetland Is.
Orkney Is.
Hebrides
Faeroes
Gotland
Öland
Bornholm
Zealand
Fyn
Lolland
Corsica
Sardinia
Sicily
Malta
Crete
Rhodes
Cyprus
Balearic Is.
Majorca
Minorca
Ibiza
Lofoten
Vesterålen
Ionian Is.

Capes and points:
North Cape
Nordkinn
C. Finisterre
C. St. Vincent
C. Trafalgar
C. da Roca
Str. of Gibraltar
Str. of Messina
Str. of Bonifacio
Str. of Otranto
English Channel
Bay of Biscay

m   ft
15 000   5000
12 000   4000
6000   2000
3000   1000
1200   400
600   200
0   0

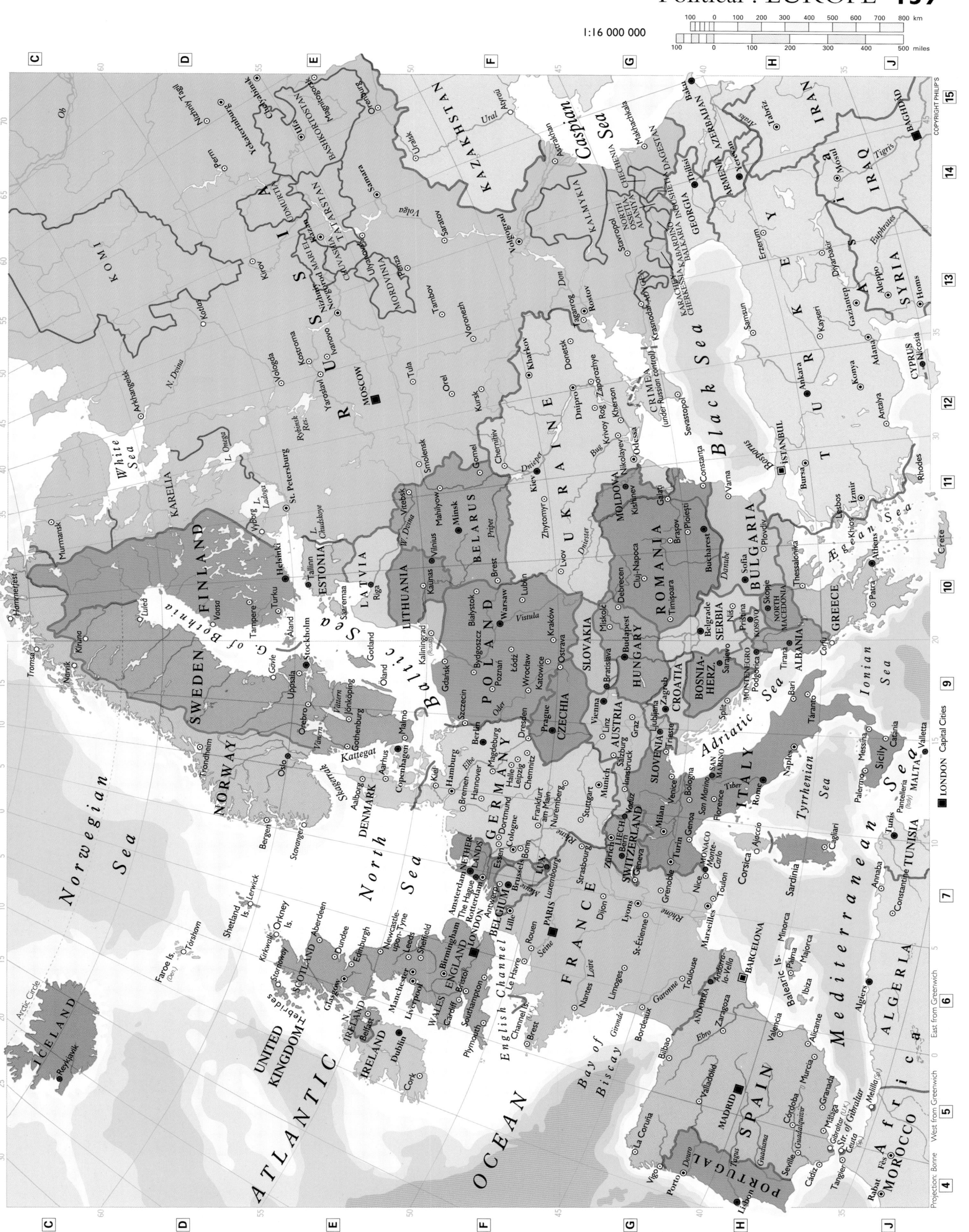

1:16 000 000

Projection: Bonne

COPYRIGHT PHILIP'S

■ LONDON Capital Cities

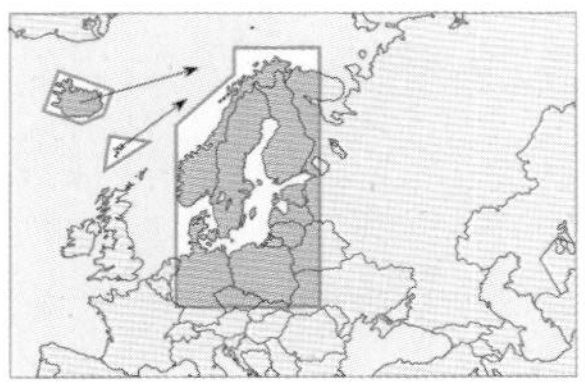

50 · 0 · 25 · 50 · 75 · 100 · 125 · 150 · 175 km

50 · 0 · 25 · 50 · 75 · 100 · 125 miles

1:4 800 000

A · B · C · D · E · F

B A R E N T S   S E A

R U S S I A

K A R E L I A

F I N L A N D

S W E D E N

N O R W A Y

L a p l a n d

Murmansk
Kolskiy Poluostrov
Varangerfjorden
Varanger-halvøya
Kirkenes
Nordkinn-halvøya
Laksefjorden
Nordkapp
Magerøya
Hammerfest
Tromsø
Narvik
Inarijärvi
Rovaniemi
Kemi
Tornio
Oulu
Kuopio
Tampere (Tammerfors)
Vaasa
Kokkola
Umeå
Luleå
Boden
Kiruna
Gällivare
Skellefteå
Piteå
Östersund
Sundsvall
Trondheim
Namsos
Bodø
Mo
Jämtland
Härjedalen
Österdalen
Gudbrandsdalen

ATLANTIC OCEAN
NORWEGIAN SEA
Gulf of Bothnia
Lofoten
Vesterålen

ICELAND
on same scale

Reykjavik
Akureyri
Vatnajökull
Faxaflói
Breiðafjörður

FÆROE
ISLANDS
on same scale

Føroyar
(Færoe Is.)
(Den.)
Tórshavn
Streymoy
Suðuroy

ICELAND

ATLANTIC OCEAN

Arctic Circle
West from Greenwich

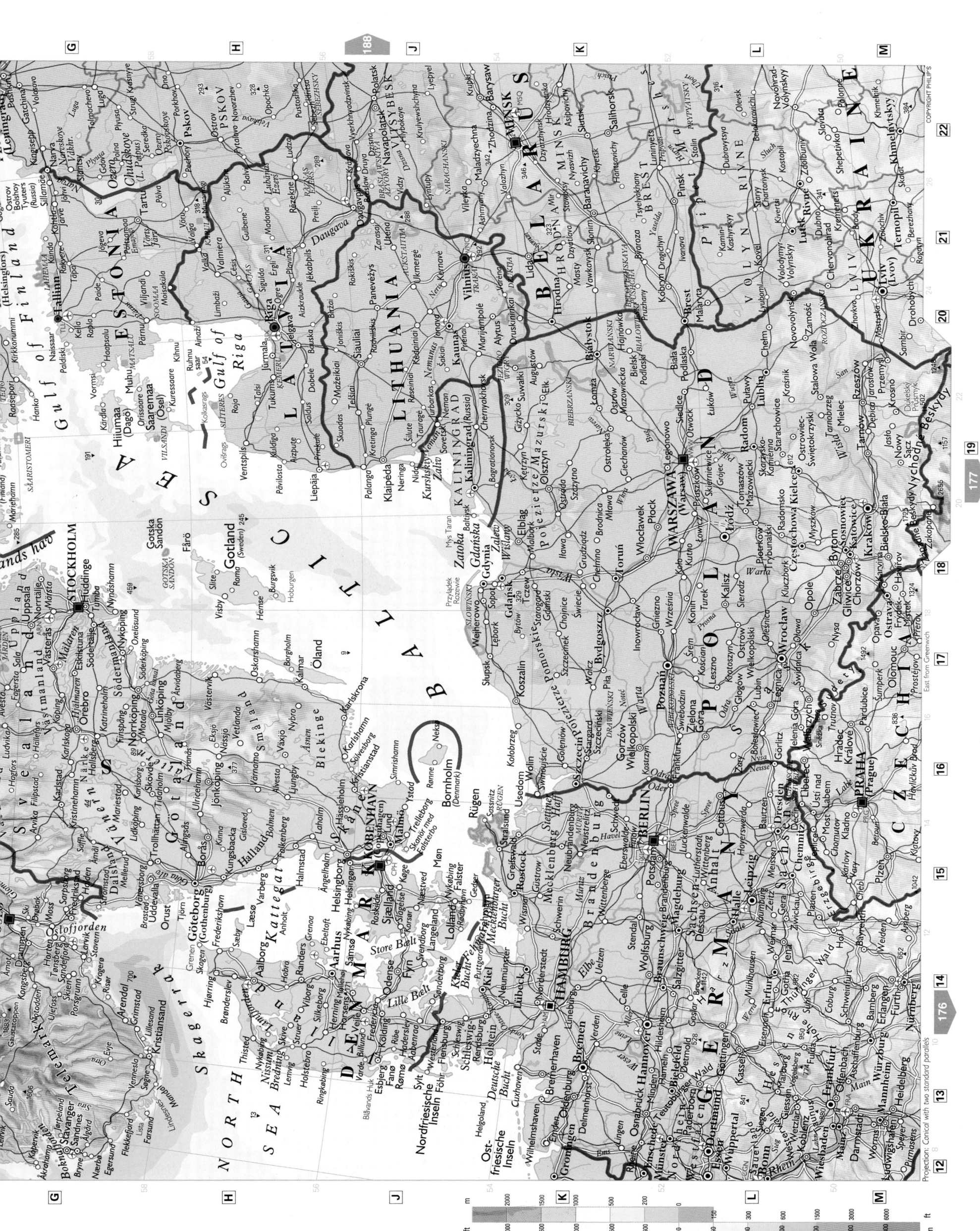

East from Greenwich

Projection: Conical with two standard parallels

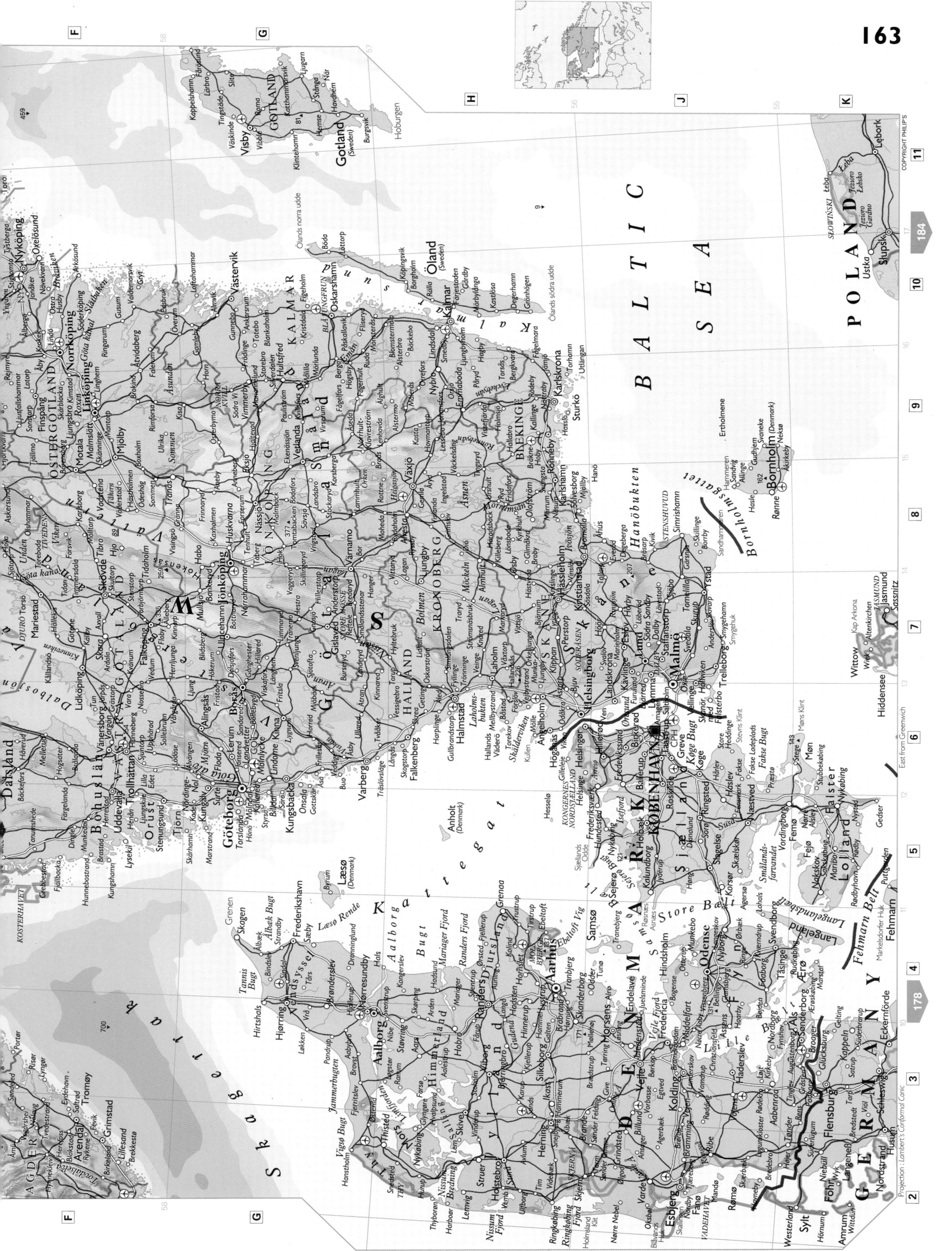

Projection: Lambert's Conformal Conic

East from Greenwich

1:2 000 000

Projection: *Lambert's Conformal Conic*

East from Greenwich

Major regions

NORWEGIAN SEA

SØR-TRØNDELAG
MØRE OG ROMSDAL
HEDMARK
OPPLAND
SOGN OG FJORDANE
HORDALAND
BUSKERUD
TELEMARK
ROGALAND
AUST-AGDER
VEST-AGDER
VESTFOLD
ØSTFOLD
AKERSHUS
SWEDEN

HARDANGERVIDDA
JOTUNHEIMEN
DOVREFJELL
REINHEIMEN
RONDANE
FEMUNDSMARKA
GUTULIA
TRESTICKLAN
SKAGERRAK
KOSTERHAVET

Selected towns and cities

Trondheim
Kristiansund
Molde
Ålesund
Bergen
Stavanger
Sandnes
Haugesund
Oslo
Drammen
Lillehammer
Hamar
Gjøvik
Elverum
Kongsvinger
Skien
Porsgrunn
Larvik
Tønsberg
Sandefjord
Horten
Moss
Sarpsborg
Fredrikstad
Halden
Arendal
Grimstad
Kristiansand
Mandal
Flekkefjord
Egersund
Lillesand
Trollhättan
Uddevalla
Strömstad

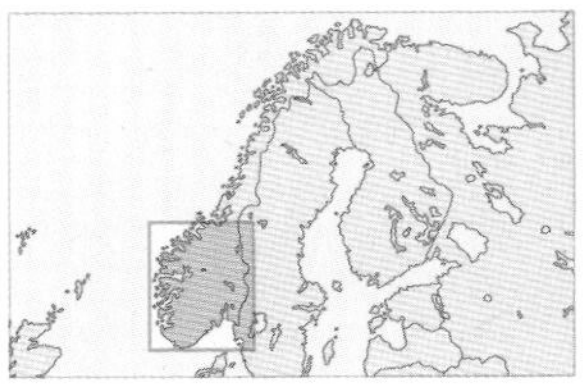

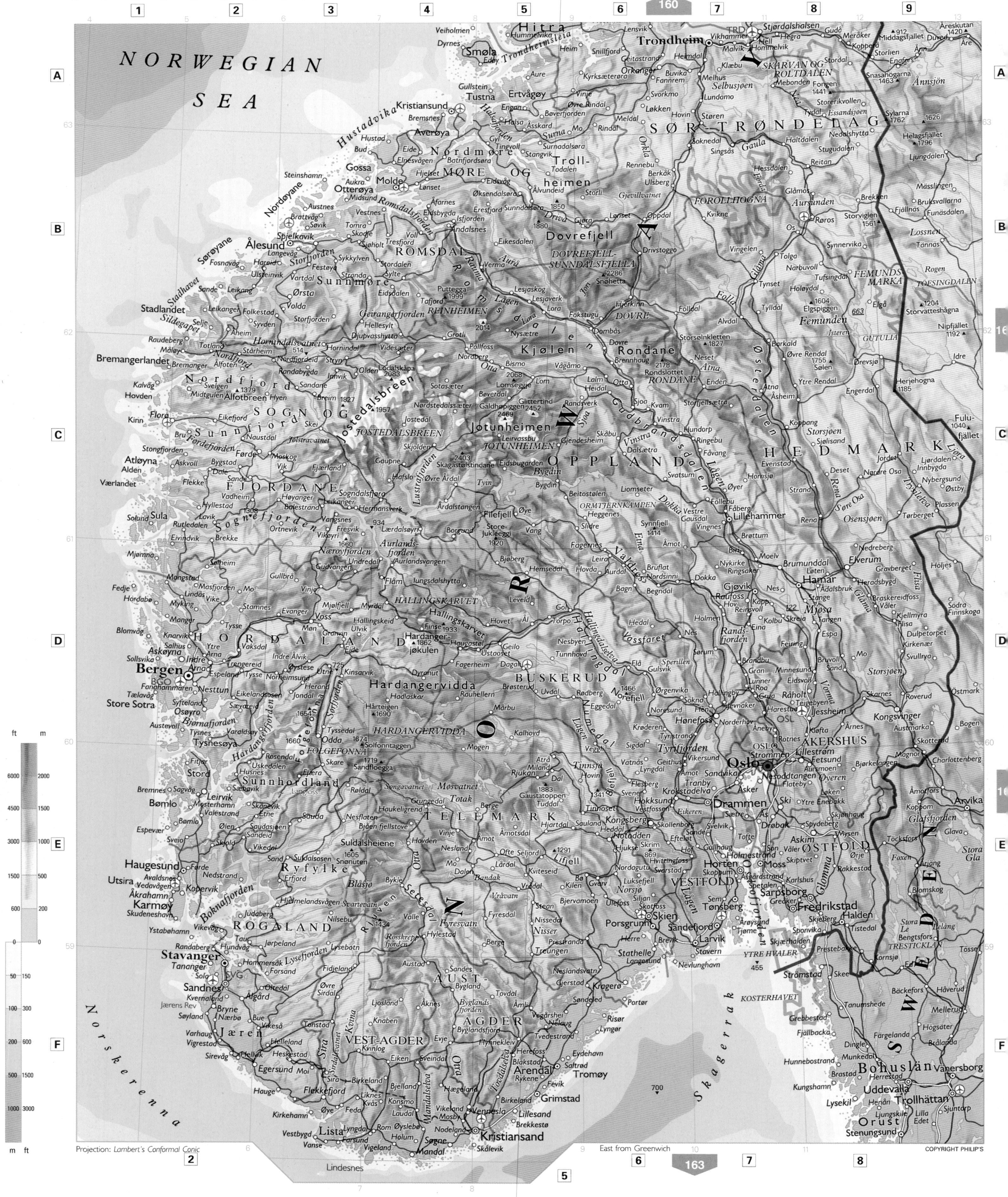

1:4 000 000

Projection: Conical with two standard parallels

West from Greenwich

East from Greenwich
COPYRIGHT PHILIP'S

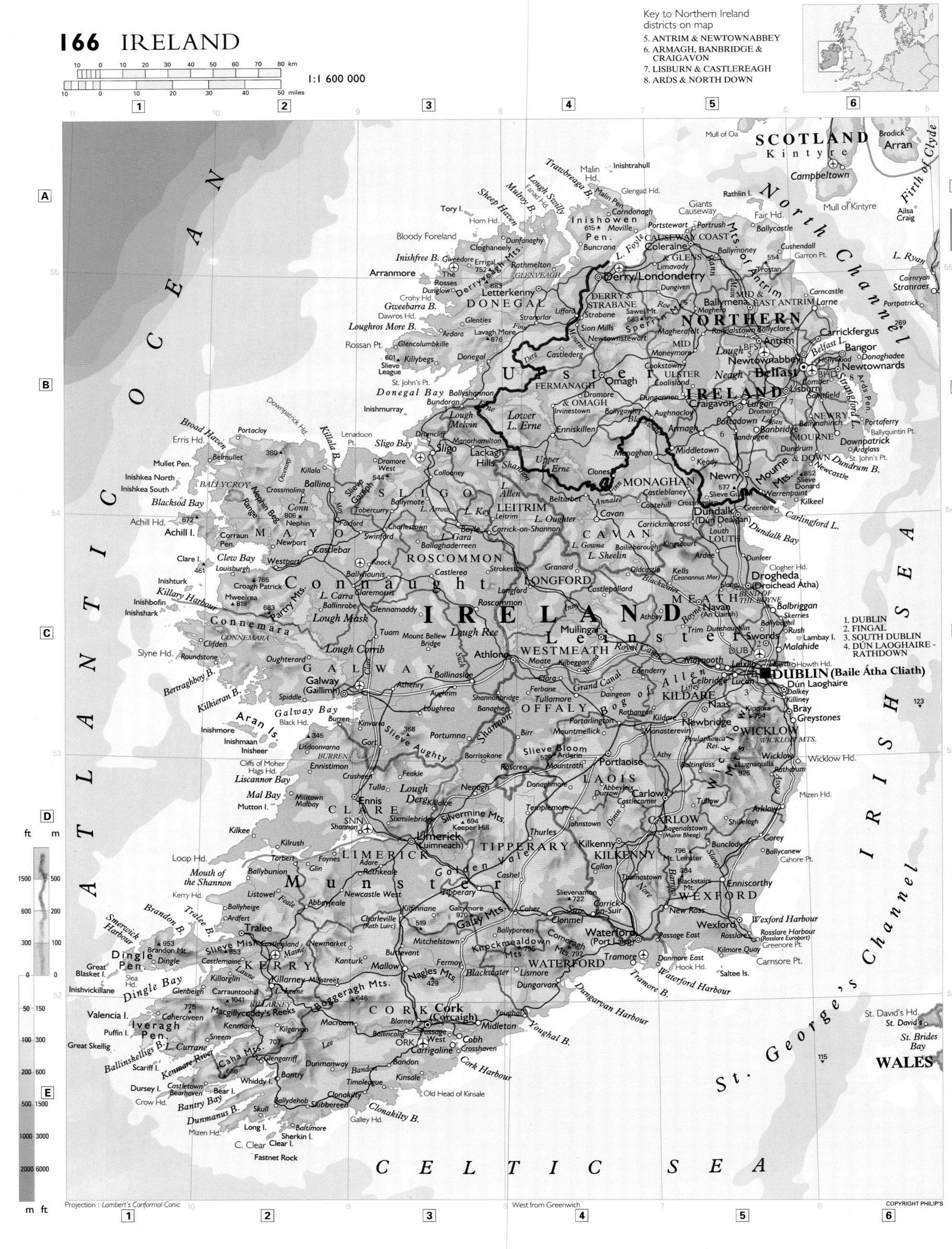

1:1 600 000

Key to Northern Ireland
districts on map
5. ANTRIM & NEWTOWNABBEY
6. ARMAGH, BANBRIDGE &
   CRAIGAVON
7. LISBURN & CASTLEREAGH
8. ARDS & NORTH DOWN

Projection : Lambert's Conformal Conic

West from Greenwich

COPYRIGHT PHILIP'S

1:1 600 000

10 0 10 20 30 40 50 60 70 80 km
10 0 10 20 30 40 50 miles

Key to Scottish unitary authorities on map

1 ABERDEEN CITY	8 EAST RENFREWSHIRE
2 DUNDEE CITY	9 NORTH LANARKSHIRE
3 WEST DUNBARTONSHIRE	10 FALKIRK
4 EAST DUNBARTONSHIRE	11 CLACKMANNANSHIRE
5 GLASGOW CITY	12 WEST LOTHIAN
6 INVERCLYDE	13 CITY OF EDINBURGH
7 RENFREWSHIRE	14 MIDLOTHIAN

ORKNEY IS. on same scale

ORKNEY

North Ronaldsay
Papa Westray
Westray
Eday
Sanday
Rousay
Shapinsay
Stronsay
Brough Hd.
Stromness
Mainland
Kirkwall
St. Mary's
Hoy
481
Scapa Flow
Burray
Burwick
South Ronaldsay
Dunnet Hd.
Stroma
Pentland Firth
Duncansby Head
John o' Groats
Sinclair's Bay
Thurso

SHETLAND IS. on same scale

SHETLAND

Muckle Flugga
Haroldswick
Unst
Fetlar
Yell
Out Skerries
Whalsay
Bressay
Lerwick
Scalloway
West Burra
Boddam
Foula
Papa Stour
Walls
St. Magnus Bay
Esha Ness
Yell Sound
Sullom Voe
Voe
Ulsta

Projection : Lambert's Conformal Conic

SCOTLAND

Hoy
Scapa Flow
Burwick
Pentland Firth
Dunnet Hd.
Stroma
John o' Groats
Thurso
Dounreay
Halkirk
Strathy Pt.
C. Wrath
Durness
L. Eriboll
Tongue
Ben Hope 927
Reay Forest
Caithness
Wick
Noss Hd.
Sinclair's Bay
Lybster
Helmsdale
Ord of Caithness
705
Brora
Golspie
Dornoch
Dornoch Firth
Tarbat Ness
Bonar Bridge
Lairg
L. Shin
Oykel
Brora
Helmsdale
961
Sutherland
Handa
Eddrachillis B.
Pt. of Stoer
Enard B.
L. Assynt
Lochinver
Ben More Assynt 998
Coigeach
Rubha
Butt of Lewis
Flannan Is.
Gallan Hd.
Stornoway
Broad Bay
Eye Peninsula
Lewis
115
Greenstone Pt.
L. Ewe
Ullapool
Grunard B.
1081
Ben Dearg
Carron
Strathpeffer
Dingwall
Muir of Ord
Beauly
Inverness
Moray Firth
Invergordon
Cromarty
Alness
Nairn
Forres
Elgin
Lossiemouth
Portknockie
Portsoy
Rosehearty
Kinnairds Hd.
Fraserburgh
Buckie
Cullen
Banff
Macduff
Peterhead
Buchan Ness
Cruden Bay
Ellon
Oldmeldrum
MORAY
BUCHAN
Huntly
Turriff
Aberchirder
Keith
Fochabers
Rothes
Dufftown
Charlestown of Aberlour
Tomintoul
ABERDEENSHIRE
Alford
Kintore
Inverurie
Westhill
Aberdeen
Girdle Ness
Peterculter
Banchory
Stonehaven
Inverbervie
Laurencekirk
Brechin
Montrose
Arbroath
Carnoustie
Monifieth
Firth of Tay
Dundee
ANGUS
Forfar
Kirriemuir
Blairgowrie
Alyth
Coupar Angus
Sidlaw Hills
Perth
Scone
Taypott
Leuchars
St. Andrews
Fife Ness
FIFE
Cupar
Ladybank
Glenrothes
Leven
Buckhaven
Anstruther
Kirkcaldy
Cowdenbeath
Dunfermline
Firth of Forth
North Berwick
Dunbar
St. Abb's Head
Eyemouth
Berwick-upon-Tweed
Coldstream
Kelso
Jedburgh
Melrose
Galashiels
Selkirk
Hawick
SCOTTISH BORDERS
Peebles
Moorfoot Hills
Lammermuir Hills
Haddington
Musselburgh
EDINBURGH
Livingston
Bonnyrigg
Dalkeith
Penicuik
Pentland Hills
Bathgate
Linlithgow
Falkirk
Grangemouth
Bo'ness
Cumbernauld
Airdrie
Coatbridge
GLASGOW
Paisley
Hamilton
East Kilbride
Motherwell
Wishaw
Carluke
Lanark
Biggar
Strathaven
SOUTH LANARKSHIRE
Broad Law 840
Moffat
Lockerbie
Langholm
Ettrick Water
The Cheviot 816
Carter Bar
NORTHUMBERLAND
Alnwick
Alnmouth
Amble
Morpeth
Newcastle-upon-Tyne
Gateshead
Blaydon
Consett
Stanley
Crook
Bishop Auckland
DURHAM
Barnard Castle
Cross Fell 893
Appleby-in-Westmorland
Penrith
Keswick
Skiddaw 931
Cockermouth
Workington
Whitehaven
St. Bees Hd.
Maryport
Wigton
Silloth
CUMBRIA
Carlisle
Gretna
Annan
Solway Firth
Kirkcudbright
Dalbeattie
Castle Douglas
Gatehouse of Fleet
Newton Stewart
Wigtown
Wigtown B.
Whithorn
Burrow Hd.
Mull of Galloway
Luce Bay
Portpatrick
Stranraer
Cairnryan
L. Ryan
Girvan
Ailsa Craig
Ballantrae
DUMFRIES & GALLOWAY
New Galloway
Sanquhar
Cumnock
Dalmellington
Maybole
Ayr
AYRSHIRE
SOUTH AYRSHIRE
EAST AYRSHIRE
Prestwick
Troon
Kilmarnock
Irvine
Saltcoats
Ardrossan
Kilwinning
Dalry
NORTH AYRSHIRE
Arran
Goat Fell 874
Brodick
Firth of Clyde
Campbeltown
Mull of Kintyre
Kintyre
Kilbrannan Sd.
NORTHERN IRELAND
Belfast
Larne
Carrickfergus
Bangor
Donaghadee
Newtownards
North Channel
Cushendall
Garron Pt.
Lochranza
Largs
Gourock
Greenock
Port Glasgow
Dumbarton
Clydebank
Helensburgh
Alexandria
L. Ryan
Rothesay
Bute
Dunoon
Tarbert
Gigha
Lochgilphead
ARGYLL AND BUTE
Loch Fyne
Inveraray
Loch Lomond
LOCH LOMOND
Luss
Aberfoyle
Callander
Doune
Dunblane
STIRLING
Bannockburn
Alloa
Stirling
Crianlarich
Killin
Ben Lawers 1214
Ben More 1174
Crieff
Auchterarder
Ochil Hills
Kinross
L. Leven
Auchtermuchty
Comrie
Aberfeldy
Pitlochry
Blair Atholl
Forest of Atholl
Kingussie
Cairngorm Mts.
Ben Macdhui 1309
Braemar
Ballater
Aboyne
Lochnagar 1154
N. Esk
S. Esk
PERTH AND KINROSS
Rannoch
L. Rannoch
Rannoch Moor
Glen Coe
Ballachulish
Kinlochleven
Fort William
Ben Nevis 1345
Spean
Glen Spean
L. Lochy
Glen Garry
L. Garry
Spean Bridge
Fort Augustus
Loch Ness
Glen Moriston
Invermoriston
Drumnadrochit
Glen Affric
Carn Eige 1182
Cairn Gorm
Aviemore
Grantown-on-Spey
Carn Ban
Newtonmore
Monadhliath Mts.
Strath Spey
Grampian Mountains
Blair Atholl 1121
CAIRNGORMS
Carrbridge
Strath Dearn
Tomatin
Cannich
Beauly
HIGHLAND
Kyle of Lochalsh
Kyleakin
Broadford
Sleat
Sd. of Sleat
Mallaig
Arisaig
L. Morar
Morar
Glenfinnan
Acharacle
L. Shiel
Sunart
L. Sunart
Strontian
Morvern
Lochaline
Sd. of Mull
Tobermory
Mull
Ben More 966
Iona
Staffa
Ulva
Dervaig
Salen
Craignure
Kerrera
Oban
Firth of Lorn
Luing
Scarba
Corryvreckan
Jura
Sd. of Jura
Islay
Port Ellen
Bowmore
Port Askaig
Rhinns Pt.
Mull of Oa
Rubh' a' Mhail
Ardnave Pt.
Colonsay
Oronsay
Coll
Tiree
Passage of Tiree
Pt. of Ardnamurchan
Canna
Rùm (Rhum)
Eigg
Muck
Barra Hd. 268
Vatersay
Sandray
Barra
Castlebay
Eriskay
Sea of the Hebrides
Lochboisdale
South Uist
Ben Mhor 620
Ardivachar Pt.
Benbecula
Balivanich
Grimsay
North Uist
Baleshare
Lochmaddy
Sound of Harris
Pabbay
Berneray
EILEAN SIAR (WESTERN ISLES)
OUTER HEBRIDES
Harris
Toe Hd.
Tarbert
Clisham 799
Scarp
Taransay
L. Seaforth
Little Minch
North Minch
Rubha Hunish
Sound of Raasay
Uig
Dunvegan
Portree
Raasay
Scalpay
Cuillin Hills 992
Cuillin Sound
Bracadale
L. Snizort
Skye
L. Gairloch
Gairloch
Torridon
L. Torridon
Applecross
Inner Sound
Stromeferry
L. Carron
Carron
Kishorn
L. Monar 1083
L. Mullardoch
Glen Cannich
Ben Wyvis 1045
Muir of Ord
Fortrose
Fort George
Cawdor
Culloden
Drynachan
L. Maree 1053
Kinlochewe
L. Fannich
Rona
ATLANTIC OCEAN
Wiay
NORTH SEA
ENGLAND
HADRIAN'S WALL
Hexham
Haltwhistle
Brampton
Haydon Bridge
Aspatria

ft m
3000 1000
1500 500
300 100
150
100
50
0
0
150 50
300 100
600 200
1500 500
3000 1000
m ft

West from Greenwich

COPYRIGHT PHILIP'S

10 0 10 20 30 40 50 60 70 80 km
10 0 10 20 30 40 50 miles

1:1 600 000

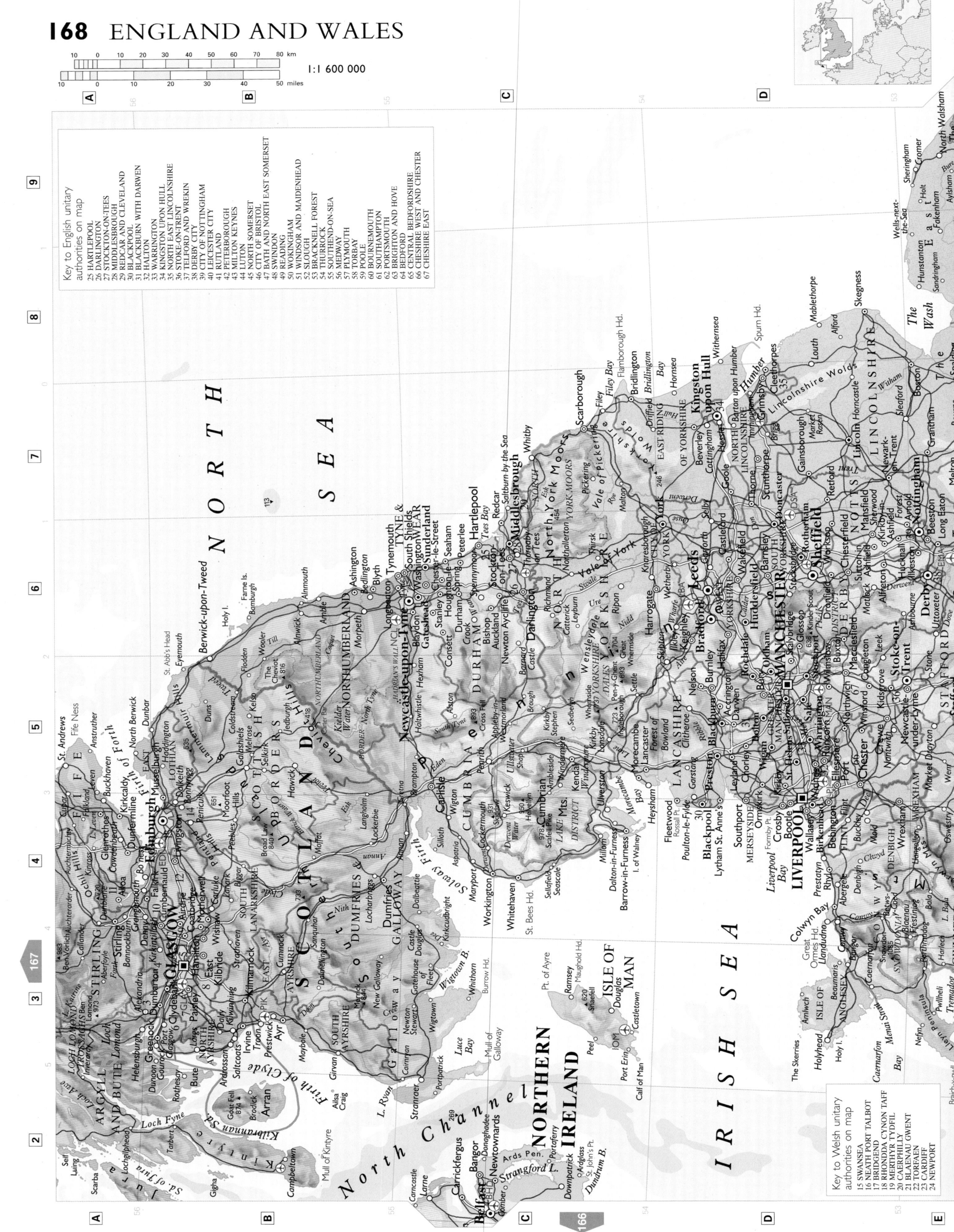

Key to English unitary
authorities on map

25 HARTLEPOOL
26 DARLINGTON
27 STOCKTON-ON-TEES
28 MIDDLESBROUGH
29 REDCAR AND CLEVELAND
30 BLACKPOOL
31 BLACKBURN WITH DARWEN
32 HALTON
33 WARRINGTON
34 KINGSTON UPON HULL
35 NORTH EAST LINCOLNSHIRE
36 STOKE-ON-TRENT
37 TELFORD AND WREKIN
38 DERBY CITY
39 CITY OF NOTTINGHAM
40 LEICESTER CITY
41 RUTLAND
42 PETERBOROUGH
43 MILTON KEYNES
44 LUTON
45 NORTH SOMERSET
46 CITY OF BRISTOL
47 BATH AND NORTH EAST SOMERSET
48 SWINDON
49 READING
50 WOKINGHAM
51 WINDSOR AND MAIDENHEAD
52 SLOUGH
53 BRACKNELL FOREST
54 THURROCK
55 SOUTHEND-ON-SEA
56 MEDWAY
57 PLYMOUTH
58 TORBAY
59 POOLE
60 BOURNEMOUTH
61 SOUTHAMPTON
62 PORTSMOUTH
63 BRIGHTON AND HOVE
64 BEDFORD
65 CENTRAL BEDFORDSHIRE
66 CHESHIRE WEST AND CHESTER
67 CHESHIRE EAST

Key to Welsh unitary
authorities on map

15 SWANSEA
16 NEATH PORT TALBOT
17 BRIDGEND
18 RHONDDA CYNON TAFF
19 MERTHYR TYDFIL
20 CAERPHILLY
21 BLAENAU GWENT
22 TORFAEN
23 CARDIFF
24 NEWPORT

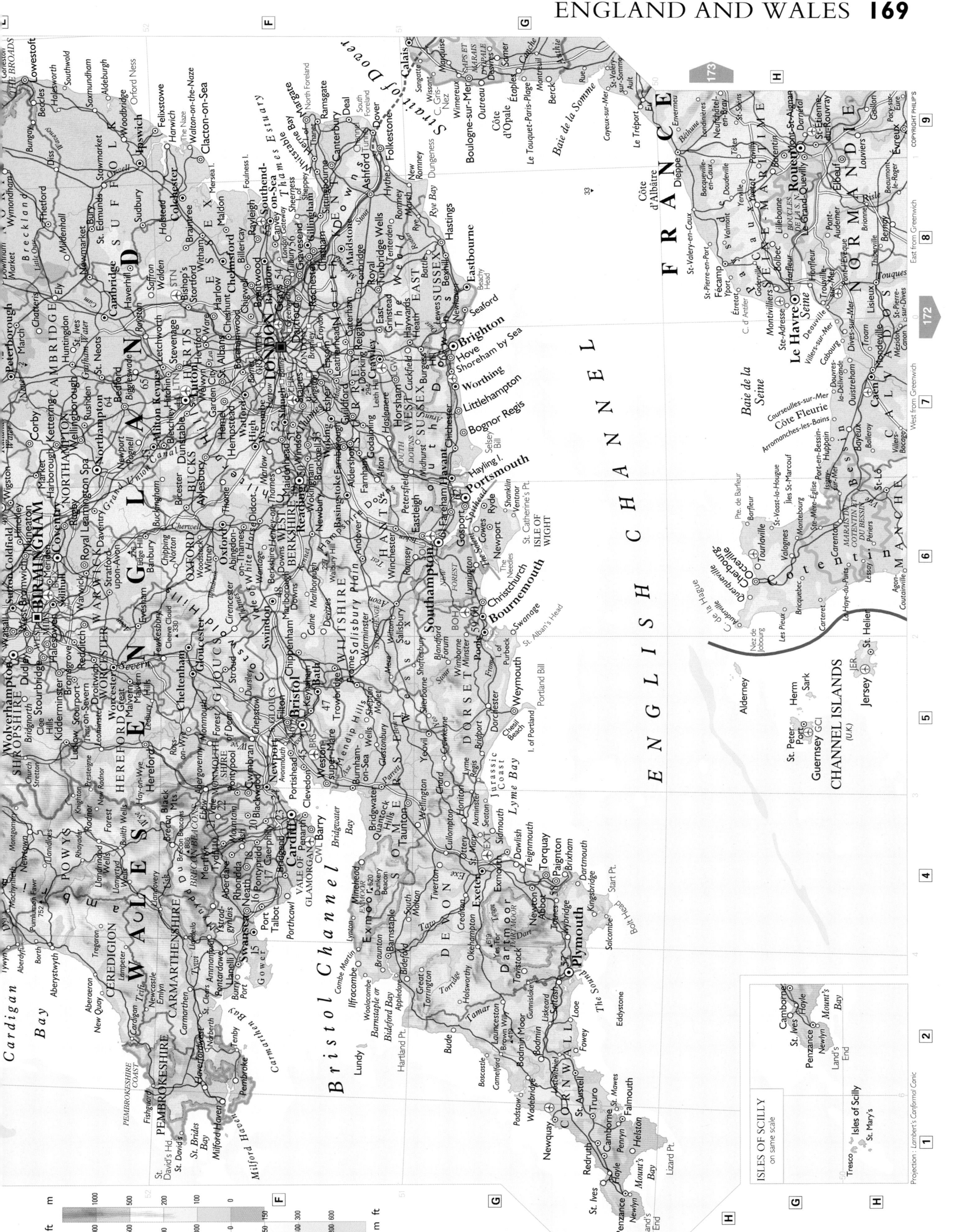

COPYRIGHT PHILIP'S

East from Greenwich   West from Greenwich

ISLES OF SCILLY
on same scale

Isles of Scilly

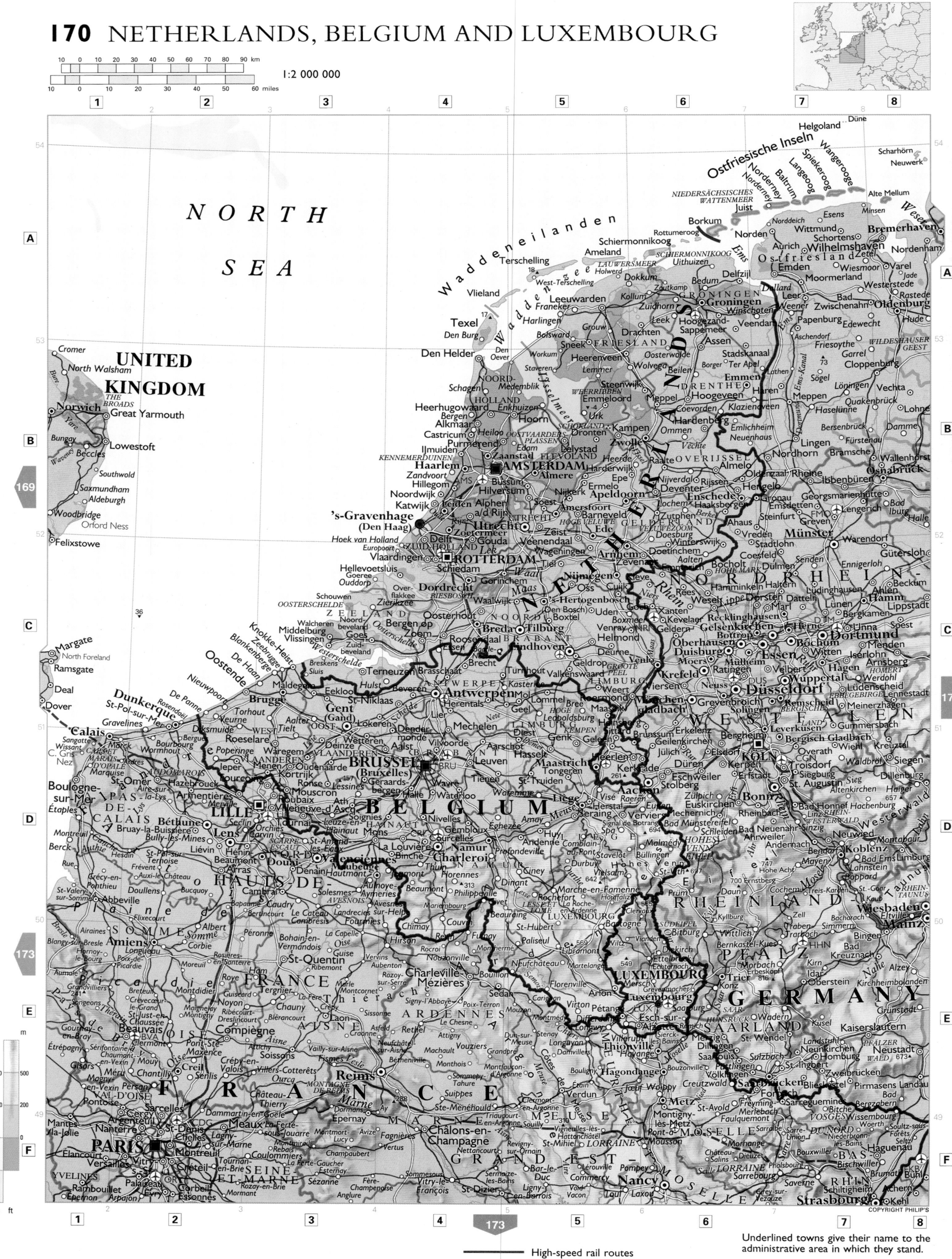

1:2 000 000

━━━ High-speed rail routes

Underlined towns give their name to the administrative area in which they stand.

COPYRIGHT PHILIP'S

1:4 000 000

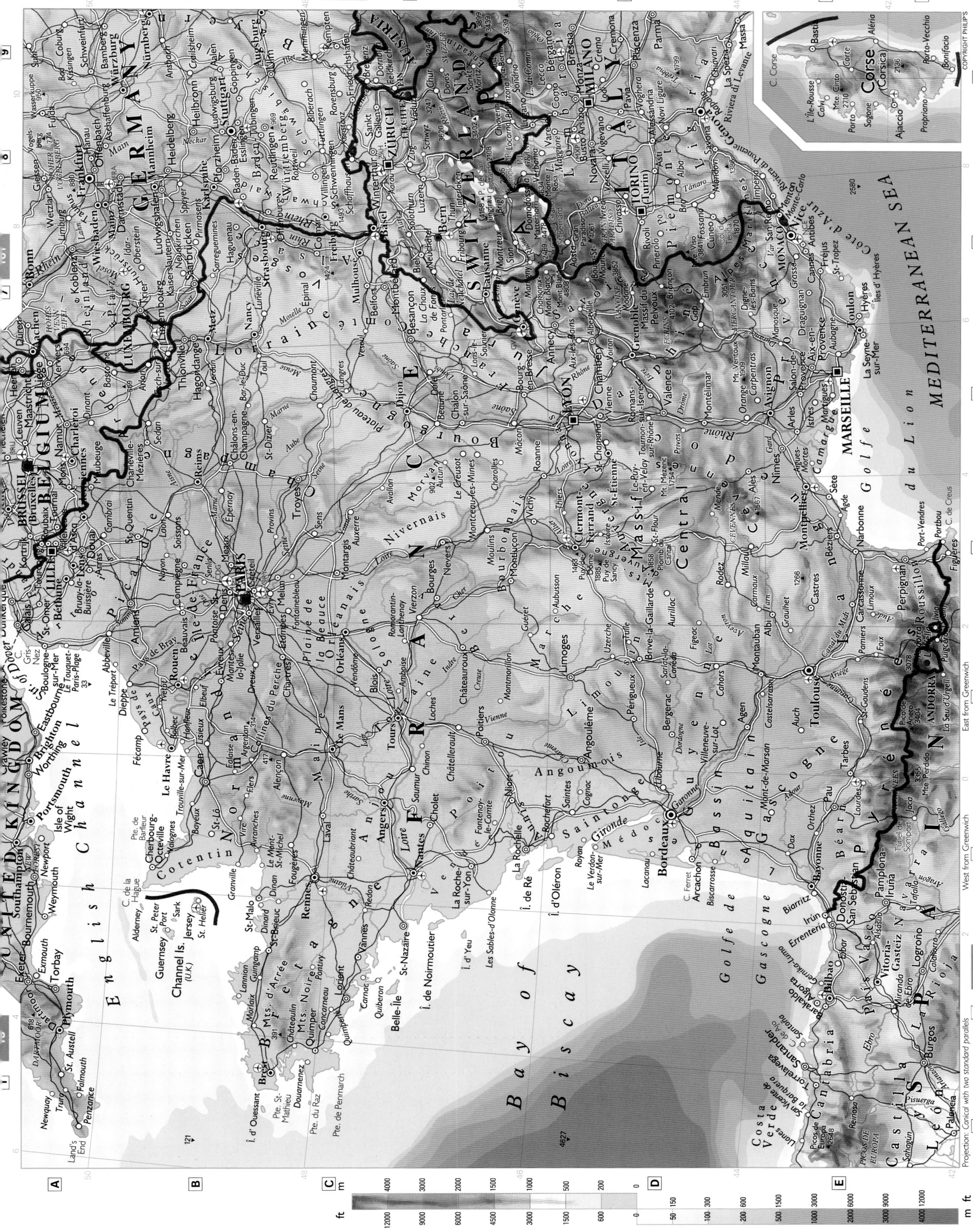

50   0   25   50   75   100   125   150   175 km

50   0   25   50   75   100   125 miles

GERMANY

SWITZERLAND

ITALY

FRANCE

BELGIUM

LUXEMBOURG

UNITED KINGDOM

SPAIN

MONACO

AUSTRIA

Corse (Corsica)

MEDITERRANEAN SEA

Golfe du Lion

Bay of Biscay

English Channel

Str. of Dover

Côte d'Azur

Golfe de Gascogne

PARIS

MARSEILLE

LYON

BRUSSEL / Bruxelles

BERN

ZÜRICH

MILANO

TORINO (Turin)

Bordeaux

Toulouse

Nantes

Lille

Strasbourg

Nancy

Metz

Rennes

Pyrénées

Massif Central

Alpes

Projection: Conical with two standard parallels

East from Greenwich   West from Greenwich

m ft

1:2 000 000

Projection : Lambert's Conformal Conic

West from Greenwich

DÉPARTEMENTS IN THE PARIS AREA
1 Ville de Paris   2 Seine-St-Denis   3 Val-de-Marne   4 Hauts-de-Seine

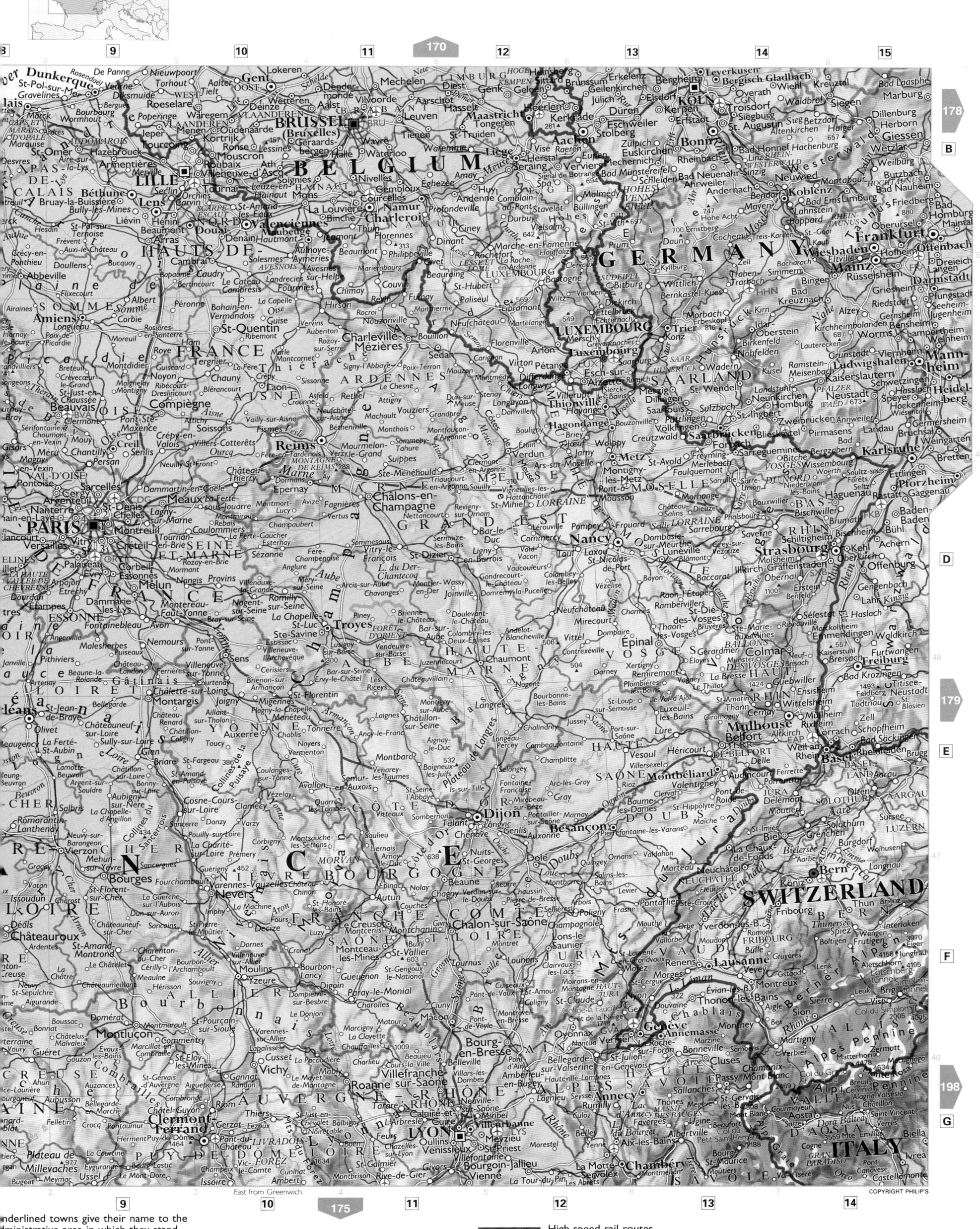

East from Greenwich

Underlined towns give their name to the
administrative area in which they stand.

—— High-speed rail routes

High-speed rail routes

1:4 000 000

50 0 25 50 75 100 125 150 175 km
50 0 25 50 75 100 125 miles

NORTH SEA

BALTIC SEA

DENMARK

UNITED KINGDOM

NETHERLANDS

BELGIUM

LUXEMBOURG

GERMANY

FRANCE

SWITZERLAND

LIECHTENSTEIN

AUSTRIA

ITALY

CZECH

SLOVENIA

HAMBURG · BERLIN · BREMEN · Hannover · Köln (Cologne) · Frankfurt · Stuttgart · München (Munich) · Düsseldorf · Dortmund · Essen · Leipzig · Dresden · Nürnberg

AMSTERDAM · 's-Gravenhage (Den Haag) · ROTTERDAM · Utrecht

BRUSSEL (Bruxelles) · Antwerpen · Gent · LILLE

LUXEMBOURG · Luxembourg

PARIS · Reims · Metz · Strasbourg · Dijon · LYON · Grenoble · MARSEILLE · MONACO · Nice

ZÜRICH · Bern · Genève · Lausanne · Basel

PRAHA (Prague) · Plzeň

MILANO · TORINO (Turin) · Venézia (Venice) · Bologna

Ljubljana

ADRIATIC SEA

Golfo di Génova

Projection: Conical with two standard parallels

161 · 165 · 171 · 192

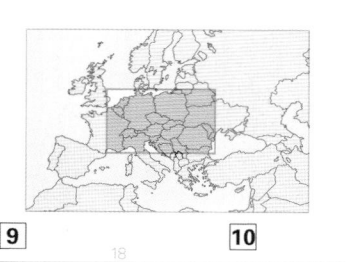

1:2 000 000

10 0 10 20 30 40 50 60 70 80 90 km
10 0 10 20 30 40 50 60 miles

NORTH SEA

BALTIC SEA

DENMARK

POLAND

NETHERLANDS

GERMANY

BERLIN

Hamburg

Bremen

Hannover

Magdeburg

Leipzig

Dresden

Rostock

Lübeck

Kiel

Flensburg

Schwerin

MECKLENBURG-VORPOMMERN

BRANDENBURG

SACHSEN-ANHALT

SACHSEN

THÜRINGEN

NORDRHEIN-WESTFALEN

NIEDERSACHSEN

SCHLESWIG-HOLSTEIN

Rügen

Usedom

Potsdam

Cottbus

Görlitz

Chemnitz

Zwickau

Gera

Jena

Weimar

Erfurt

Gotha

Kassel

Dortmund

Essen

Düsseldorf

Köln

Bonn

Münster

Osnabrück

Bielefeld

Paderborn

Braunschweig

Wolfsburg

Elbe

Weser

Rhein

Oder

Neisse

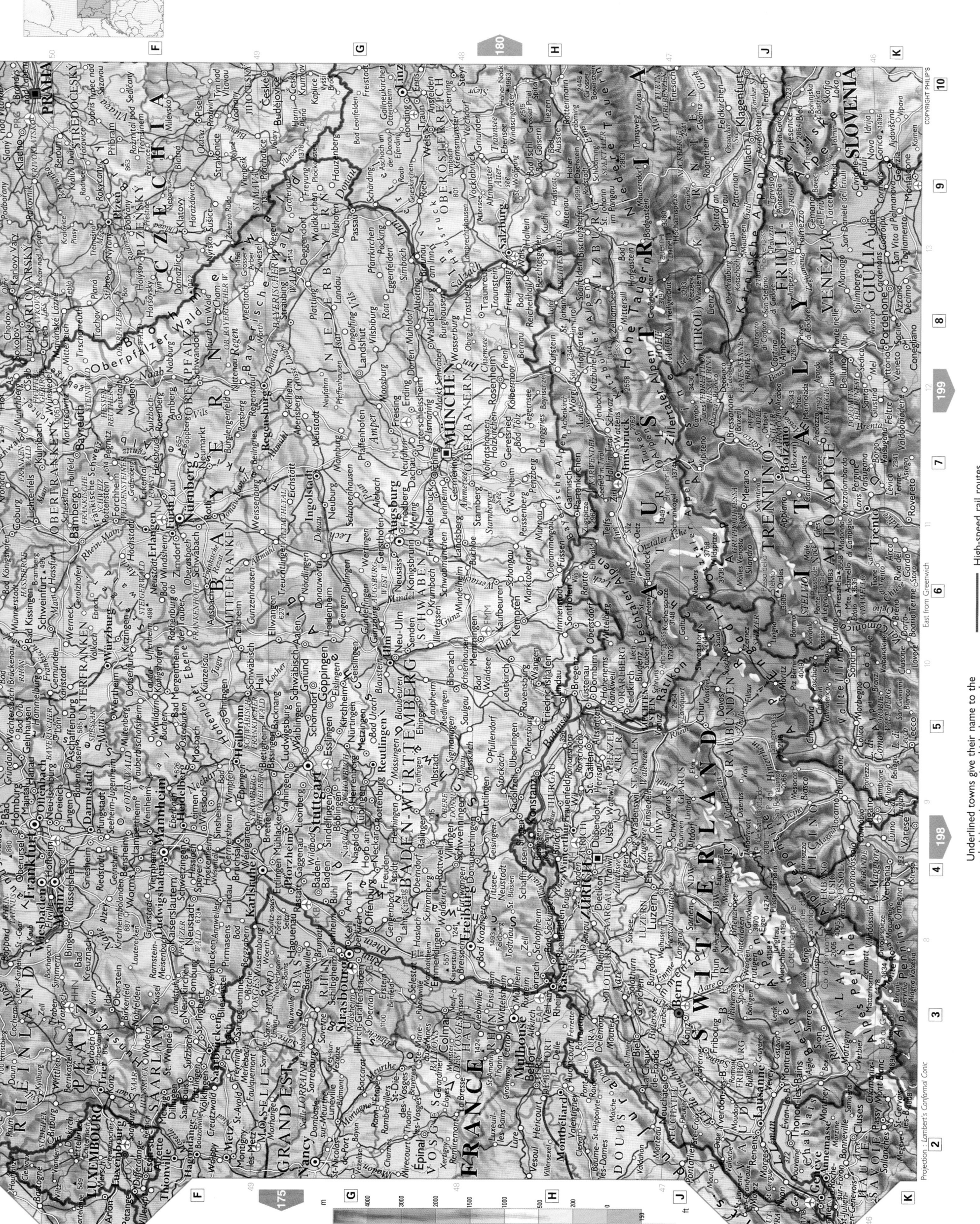

Projection : Lambert's Conformal Conic

East from Greenwich

Underlined towns give their name to the
administrative area in which they stand.

——— High-speed rail routes

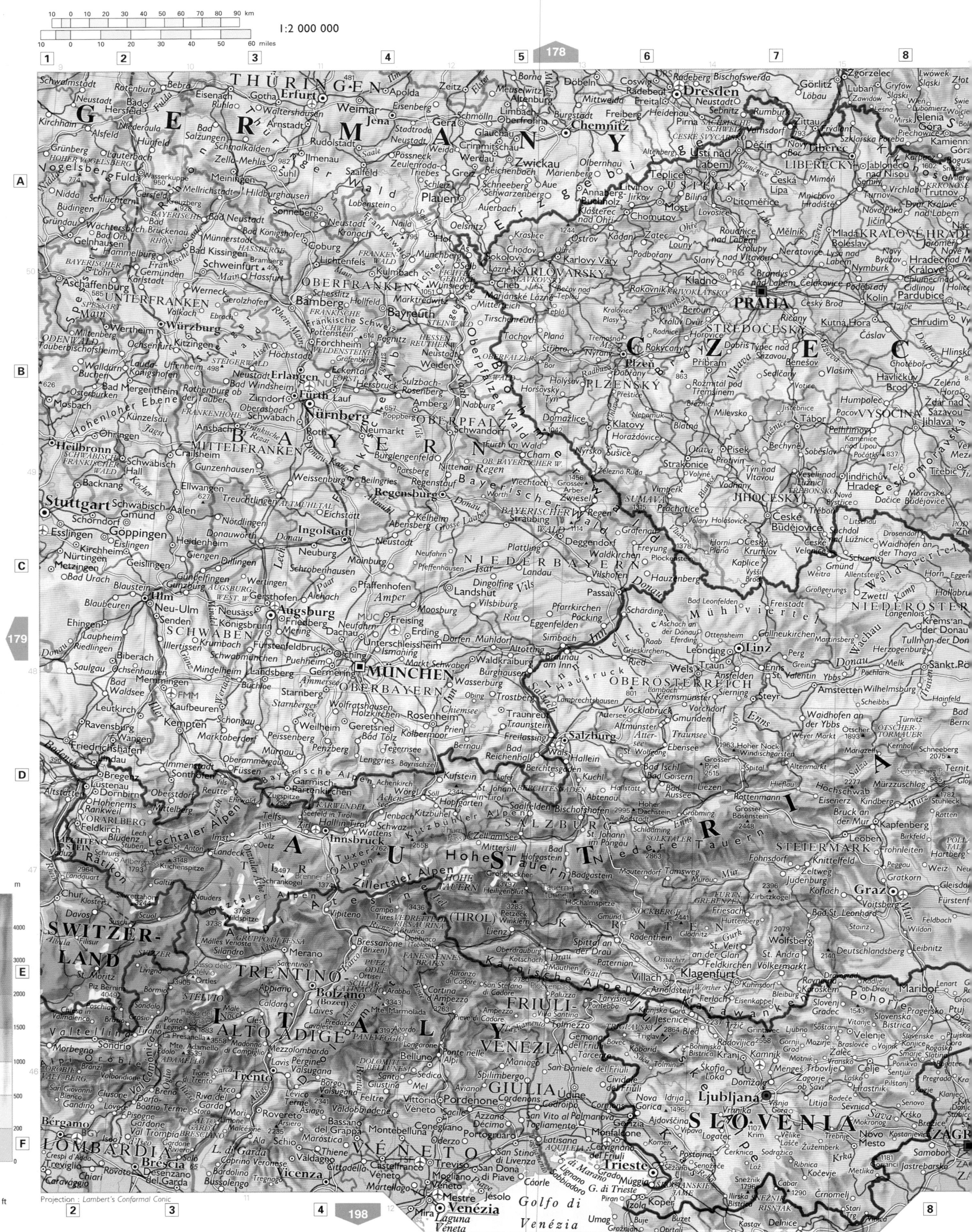

Underlined towns give their name to the administrative area in which they stand.

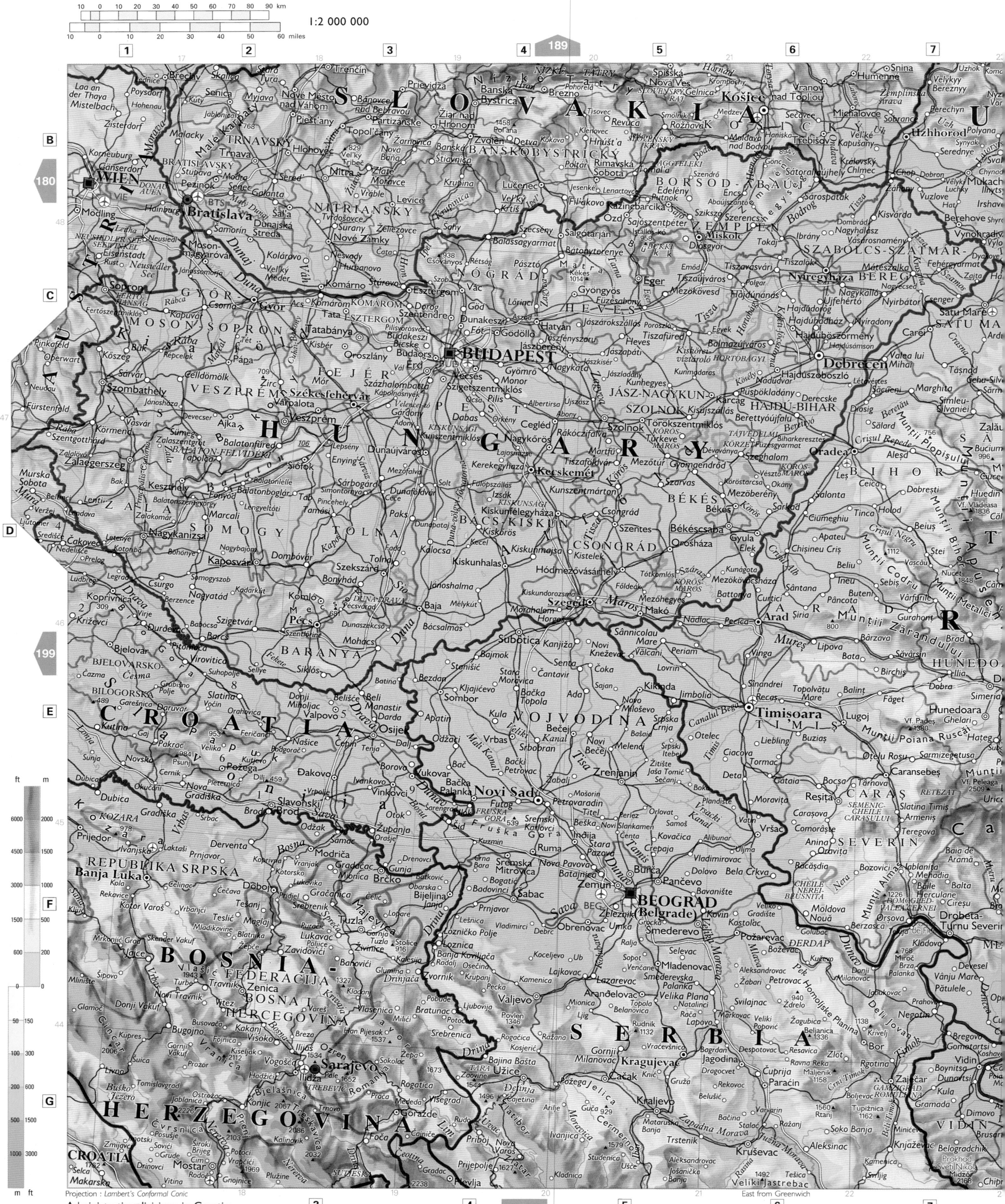

1:2 000 000

10 0 10 20 30 40 50 60 70 80 90 km

10 0 10 20 30 40 50 60 miles

SLOVAKIA

AUSTRIA

HUNGARY

CROATIA

BOSNIA-FEDERACIJA BOSNA I HERCEGOVINA

REPUBLIKA SRPSKA

HERZEGOVINA

SERBIA

VOJVODINA

BUDAPEST

WIEN

Bratislava

Beograd (Belgrade)

Sarajevo

Timişoara

Arad

Oradea

Debrecen

Miskolc

Novi Sad

Zenica

Banja Luka

Projection : Lambert's Conformal Conic

East from Greenwich

Administrative divisions in Croatia:
1 Brodsko-Posavska   4 Medimurska   6 Požeško-Slavonska
2 Koprivničko-Križevačka   5 Osječko-Baranjska   8 Virovitičko-Podravska   9 Vukovarsko-Srijemska

ft   m
6000   2000
4500   1500
3000   1000
1500   500
600   200
50   150
100   300
200   600
1000   3000
m   ft

189
189
203

Underlined towns give their name to the
administrative area in which they stand.

1:2 000 000

10 0 10 20 30 40 50 60 70 80 90 km
10 0 10 20 30 40 50 60 miles

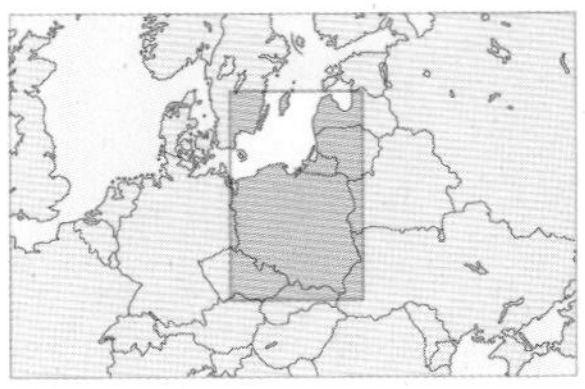

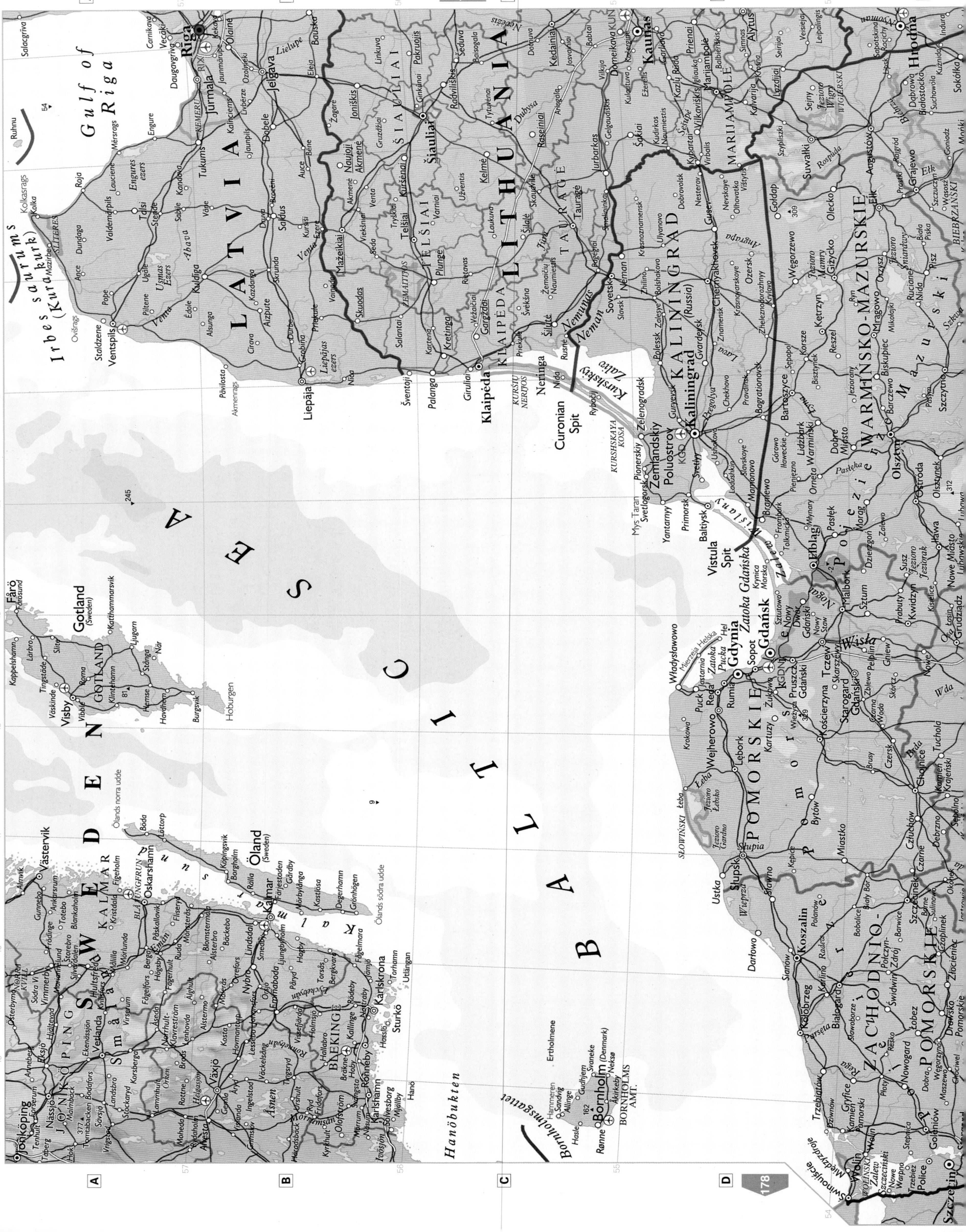

188 163 178

Gulf of Riga

LATVIA

LITHUANIA

KALININGRAD (Russia)

SWEDEN

Gotland (Sweden)

Öland (Sweden)

BALTIC SEA

Hanöbukten

Bornholm (Denmark)
BORNHOLMS AMT.

Irbes saurums (Kura kurk)

Riga Jūrmala Jelgava Šiauliai Kaunas MARIJAMPOLE

Telšiai KLAIPĖDA Klaipėda Neringa Curonian Spit Kaliningrad Zemlandskiy

Liepāja Ventspils

ZEMAITIJA TAURAGĖ

Neman *Nemunas*

WARMIŃSKO-MAZURSKIE Mazurski POJEZIERZE

Elbląg Malbork Gdańsk Zatoka Gdańska Gdynia Sopot Vistula Spit

POMORSKIE Pomorze

Słupsk Koszalin Ustka Dartowo

ZACHODNIO-POMORSKIE

Gotland GOTLAND Visby Fårö

Kalmar Öland Oskarshamn Västervik Karlskrona BLEKINGE SMÅLAND JÖNKÖPING

Wisła

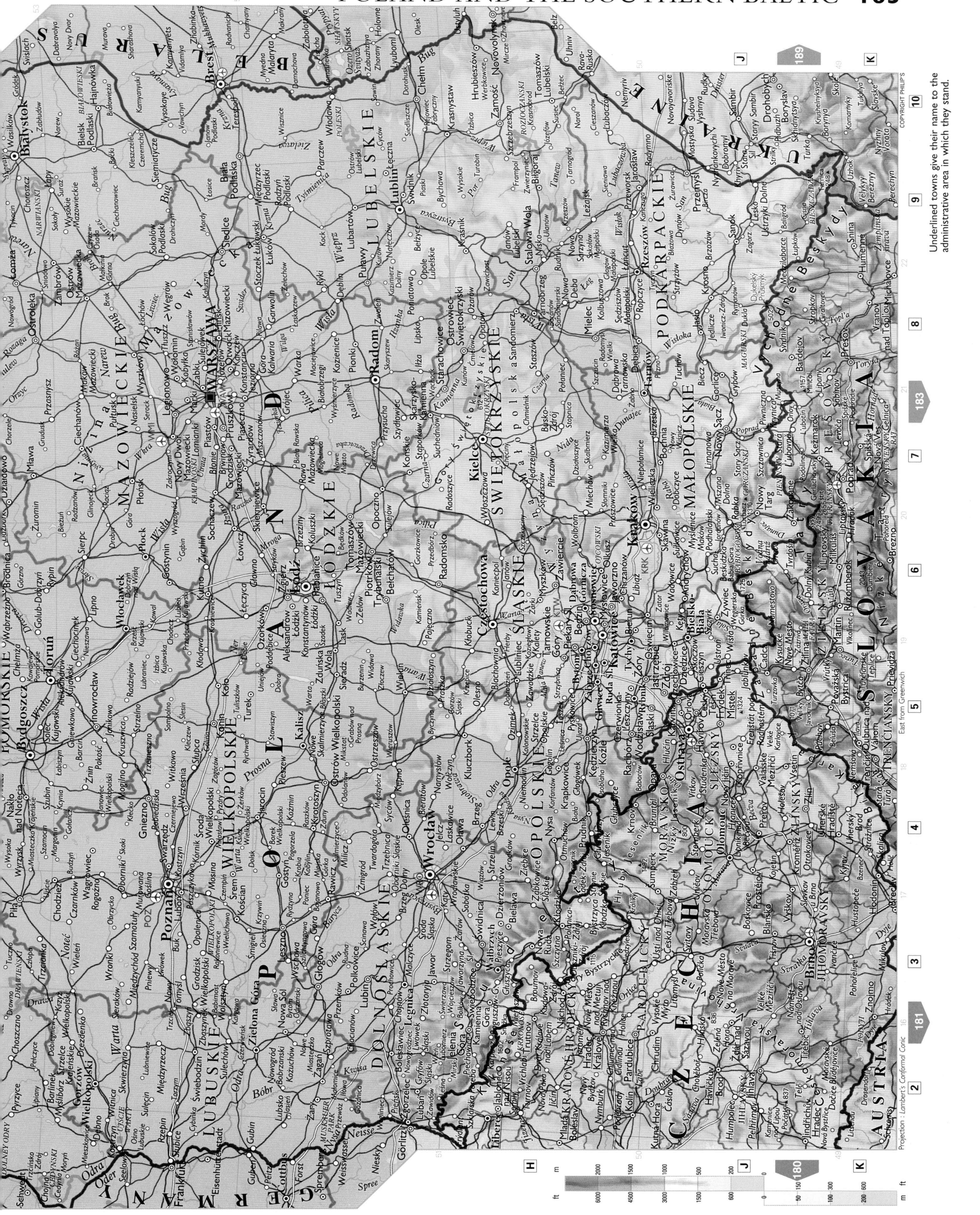

Underlined towns give their name to the
administrative area in which they stand.

COPYRIGHT PHILIPS

BELARUS

UKRAINE

SLOVAKIA

CZECH

AUSTRIA

GERMANY

POLAND

MAZOWIECKIE

WIELKOPOLSKIE

DOLNOŚLĄSKIE

LUBUSKIE

POMORSKIE

KUJAWSKO-POMORSKIE

ŁÓDZKIE

LUBELSKIE

ŚWIĘTOKRZYSKIE

ŚLĄSKIE

OPOLSKIE

MAŁOPOLSKIE

PODKARPACKIE

JIHOMORAVSKÝ

MORAVSKO-SLEZSKÝ

OLOMOUCKÝ

PARDUBICKÝ

KRÁLOVÉHRADECKÝ

LIBERECKÝ

ZLÍNSKÝ

TRENČIANSKY

ŽILINSKÝ

PREŠOVSKÝ

Białystok • Warszawa • Łódź • Poznań • Wrocław • Kraków • Lublin • Radom • Kielce • Częstochowa • Katowice • Bydgoszcz • Toruń • Brno • Olomouc • Ostrava • Rzeszów • Brest

Projection: Lambert's Conformal Conic

East from Greenwich

181   183   189   180

ft m — 6000 4500 3000 1500 600 300 150 0 — m ft

1:8 000 000

50 0 100 200 300 400 km
50 0 50 100 150 200 250 miles

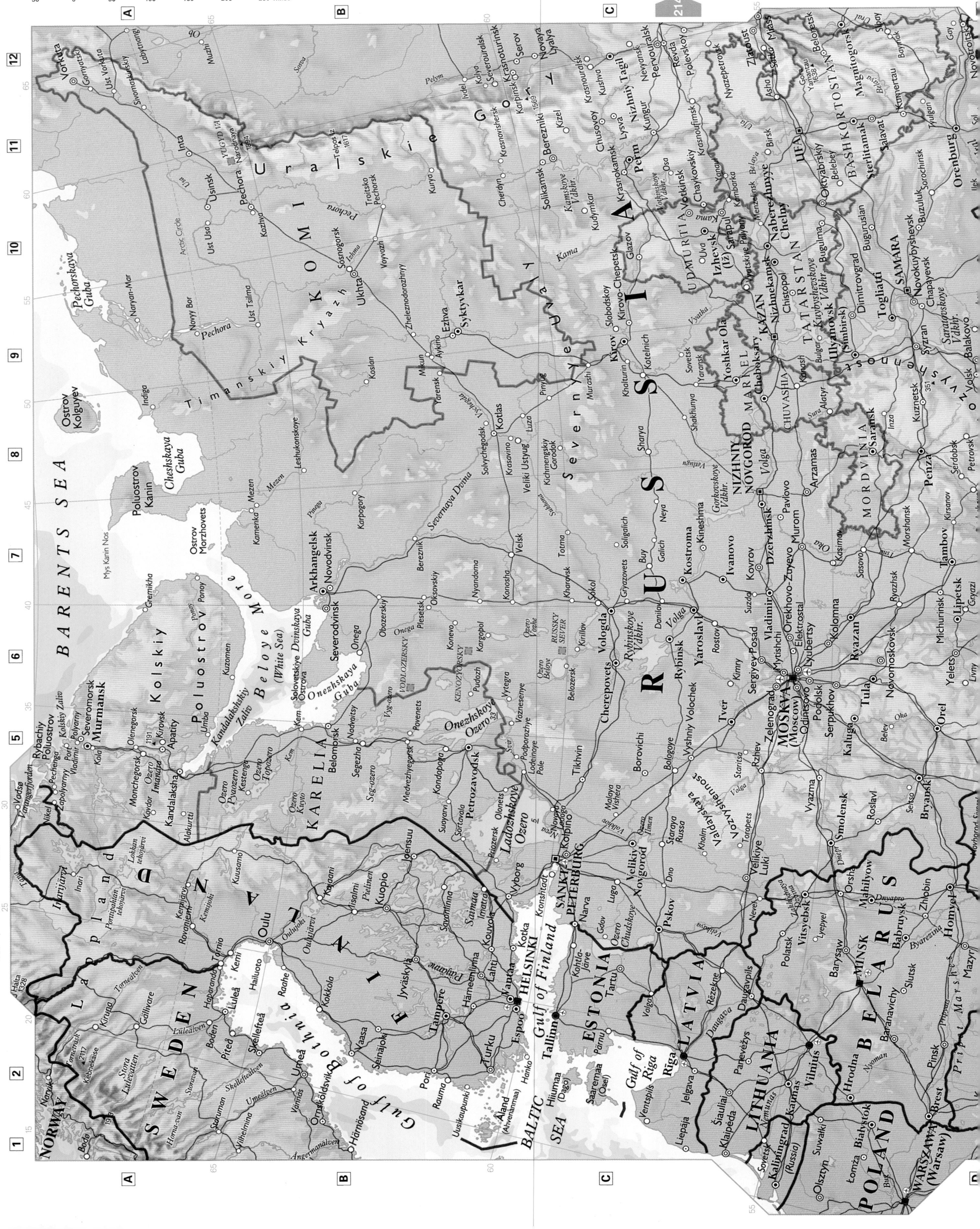

214

BARENTS SEA

NORWAY

SWEDEN

Lapland

FINLAND

Gulf of Bothnia

Gulf of Finland

BALTIC SEA

Gulf of Riga

ESTONIA

LATVIA

LITHUANIA

POLAND

BELARUS

R U S S I A

Kolskiy Poluostrov

Poluostrov Kanin

Cheshskaya Guba

Beloye More (White Sea)

Onezhskaya Guba

Ladozhskoye Ozero

Onezhskoye Ozero

KARELIA

KOMI

Uralskie Gory

Timanskiy Kryazh

Severnyye Uvaly

TATARSTAN

BASHKORTOSTAN

UDMURTIA

MARI EL

CHUVASHIA

MORDVINIA

NIZHNIY NOVGOROD

Murmansk
Arkhangelsk
Severodvinsk
Syktyvkar
Vorkuta
Ukhta
Pechora
Naryan-Mar
Vologda
MOSKVA (Moscow)
SANKT-PETERBURG
HELSINKI
Tallinn
Riga
Vilnius
MINSK
WARSZAWA (Warsaw)
Kaliningrad (Russia)
PERM
UFA
SAMARA
Orenburg
KAZAN
Izhevsk
Nizhniy Tagil
Magnitogorsk
Petrozavodsk

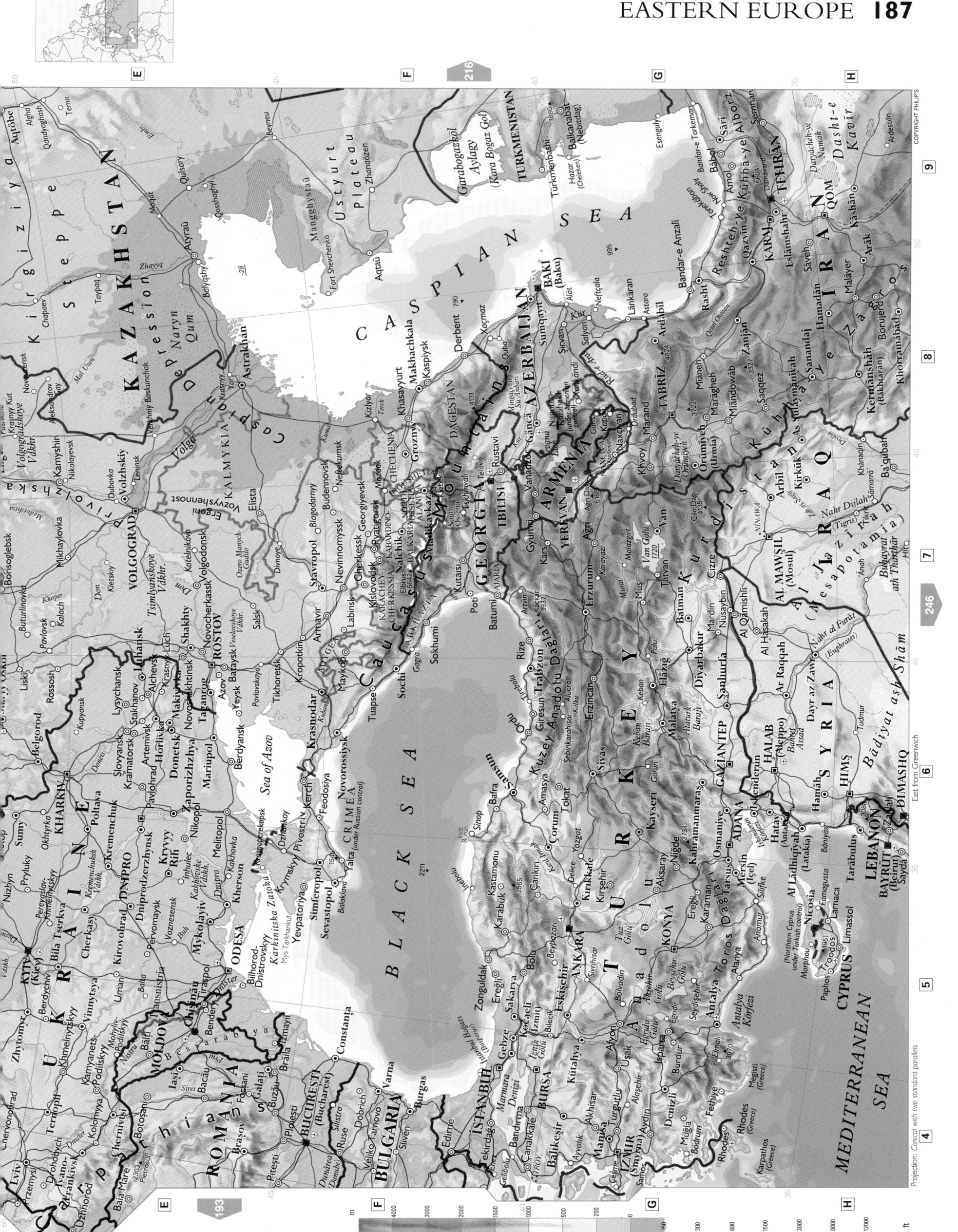

Projection: Conical with two standard parallels

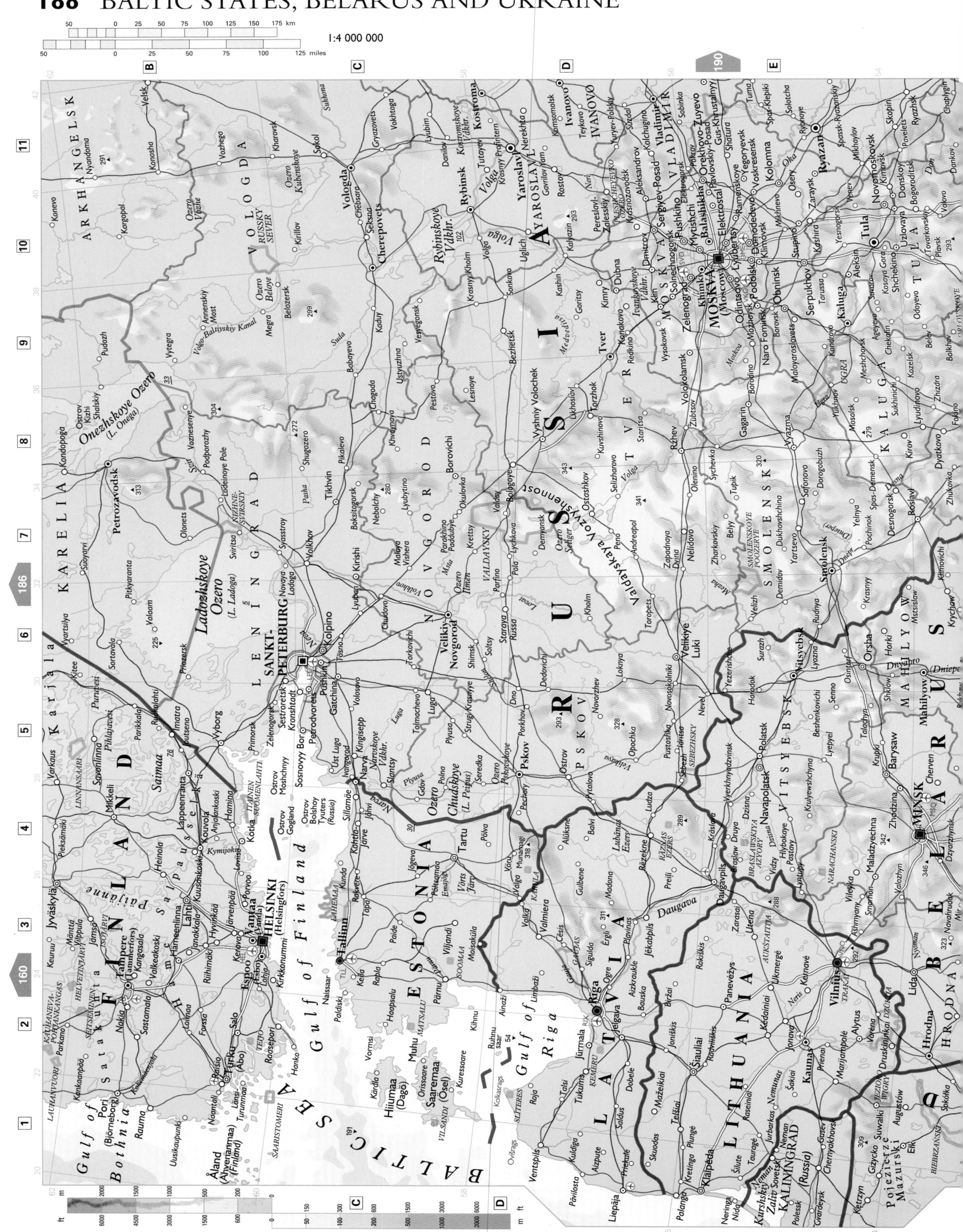

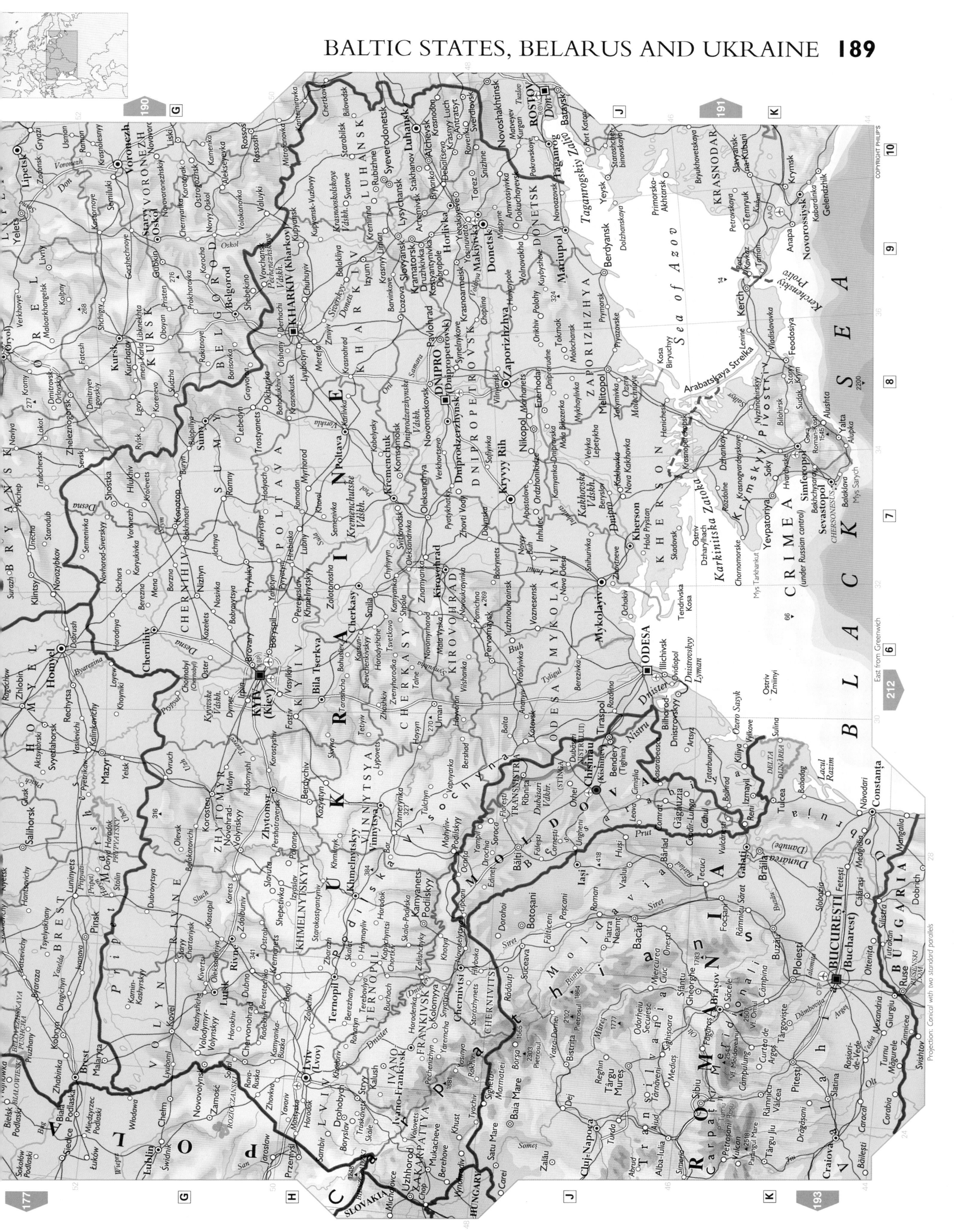

50 0 25 50 75 100 125 150 175 km

50 0 25 50 75 100 125 miles

1:4 000 000

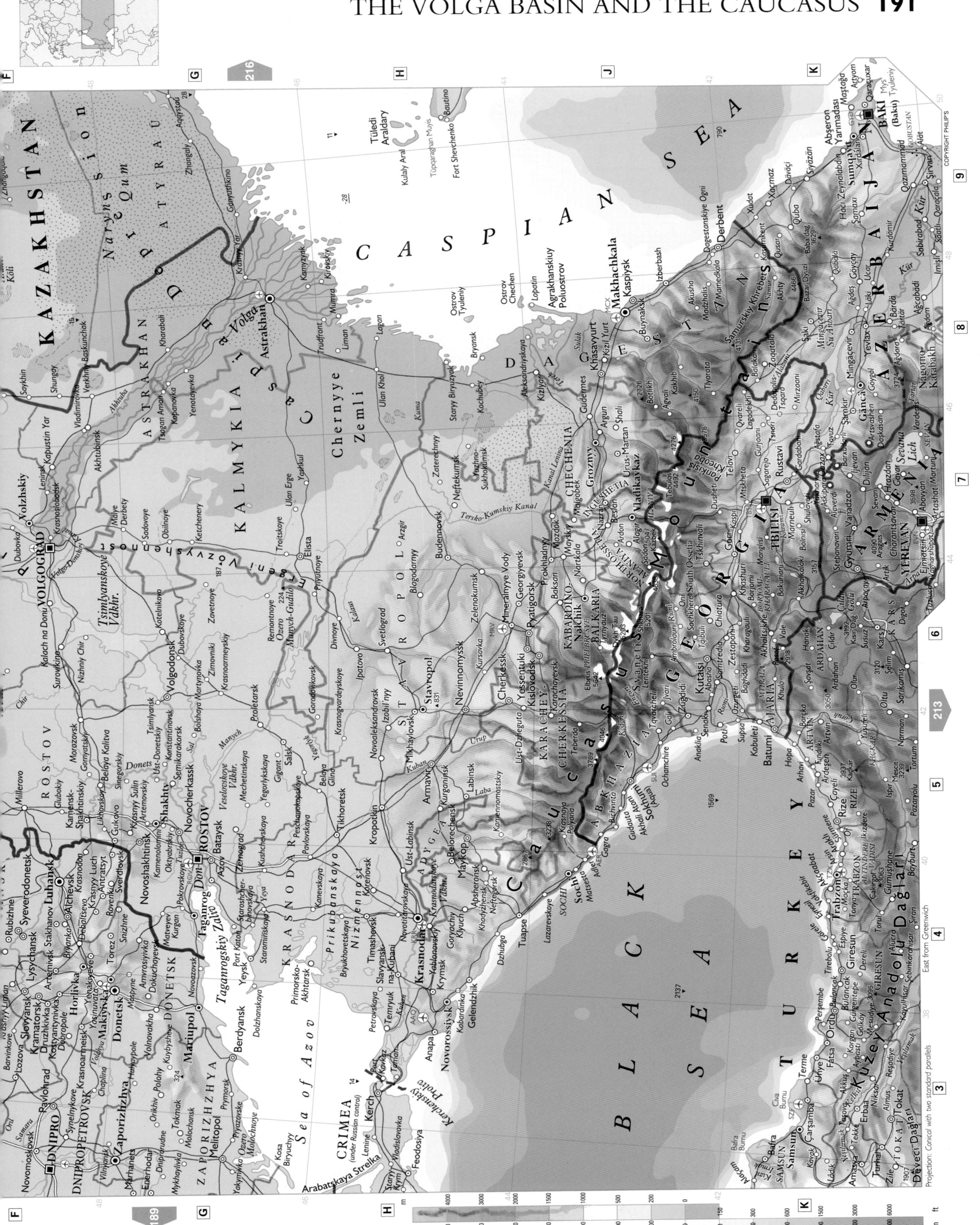

KAZAKHSTAN

CASPIAN SEA

Astrakhan

ASTRAKHAN

KALMYKIA

Chernyye Zemli

Tüledi Araldary

Fort Shevchenko

Makhachkala
Kaspiysk
Izberbash
Derbent

DAGESTAN

CHECHENIA
Grozny

INGUSHETIA
Nazran

Budennovsk

STAVROPOL

NORTH OSSETIA
Vladikavkaz

Pyatigorsk

KABARDINO-
BALKARIA
Nalchik

KARACHEY-
CHERKESSIA
Cherkessk

Caucasus

AZERBAIJAN
BAKI
(Baku)
Sumqayit

GEORGIA
TBILISI

ARMENIA
YEREVAN

ABKHAZIA

SOUTH OSSETIA
Tskhinvali

AJARIA
Batumi

KRASNODAR

ADYGEA
Maykop

Sochi

Novorossiysk

CRIMEA
(under Russian control)

Kerch

Sea of Azov

VOLGOGRAD
Volzhskiy

ROSTOV
ROSTOV
Novocherkassk
Shakhty
Taganrog
Azov

DONETSK
Donetsk
Makiyivka

Mariupol

LUHANSK
Luhansk

DNIPROPETROVSK
DNIPRO
Zaporizhzhya

ZAPORIZHZHYA

TURKEY
Trabzon
SAMSUN
Samsun

Kars

Anadolu Dağları

BLACK SEA

East from Greenwich

Projection: Conical with two standard parallels

COPYRIGHT PHILIP'S

ATLANTIC OCEAN

Bay of Biscay

Golfe de Gascogne

ENGLISH CHANNEL

U.K.

LONDON

NETHERLANDS

BELGIUM

GERMAN

FRANCE

PARIS

Massif Central

Pyrénées

PORTUGAL

SPAIN

MADRID

LISBOA

Sierra Morena

La Mancha

Islas Baleares
(Spain)

Mallorca

BARCELONA

MEDITERRANEAN SEA

MARSEILLE

SWITZERLAND

MILANO

TORINO

Génova

LIGURIAN SEA

Corse
(France)

Sardegna
(Italy)

TYRRHENIAN SEA

ROMA

SAN MARINO

NÁPOLI

MOROCCO

RABAT

Haut Atlas

Moyen Atlas

Hauts Plateaux

Atlas Saharien

ALGERIA

ALGER
(Algiers)

TUNIS

CARTHAGE

Golfe de Hammamet

Golfe de Gabès

Djerba

Sahara

Grand Erg Occidental

Grand Erg Oriental

TARĀBULUS
(Tripoli)

Sicil

Paler

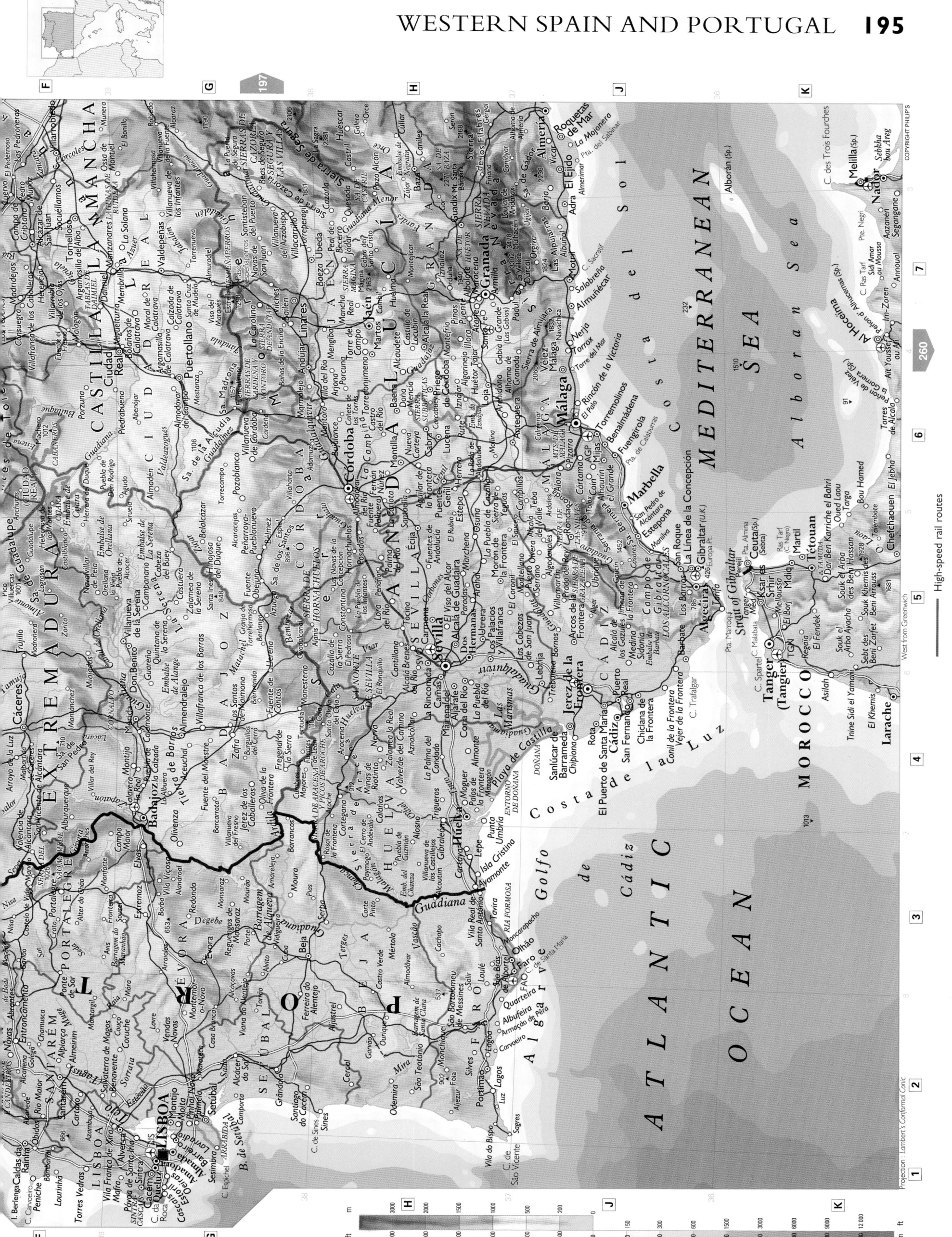

High-speed rail routes

High-speed rail routes

Projection: Lambert's Conformal Conic

1:2 000 000

Projection : Lambert's Conformal Conic

East from Greenwich

...ministrative divisions in Croatia:

...rodsko-Posavska   3 Krapinsko-Zagorska   6 Požeško-Slavonska   8 Virovitičko-Podravska

...oprivničko-Križevačka   4 Medimurska   7 Varaždinska   10 Zagrebačka

— High-speed rail routes

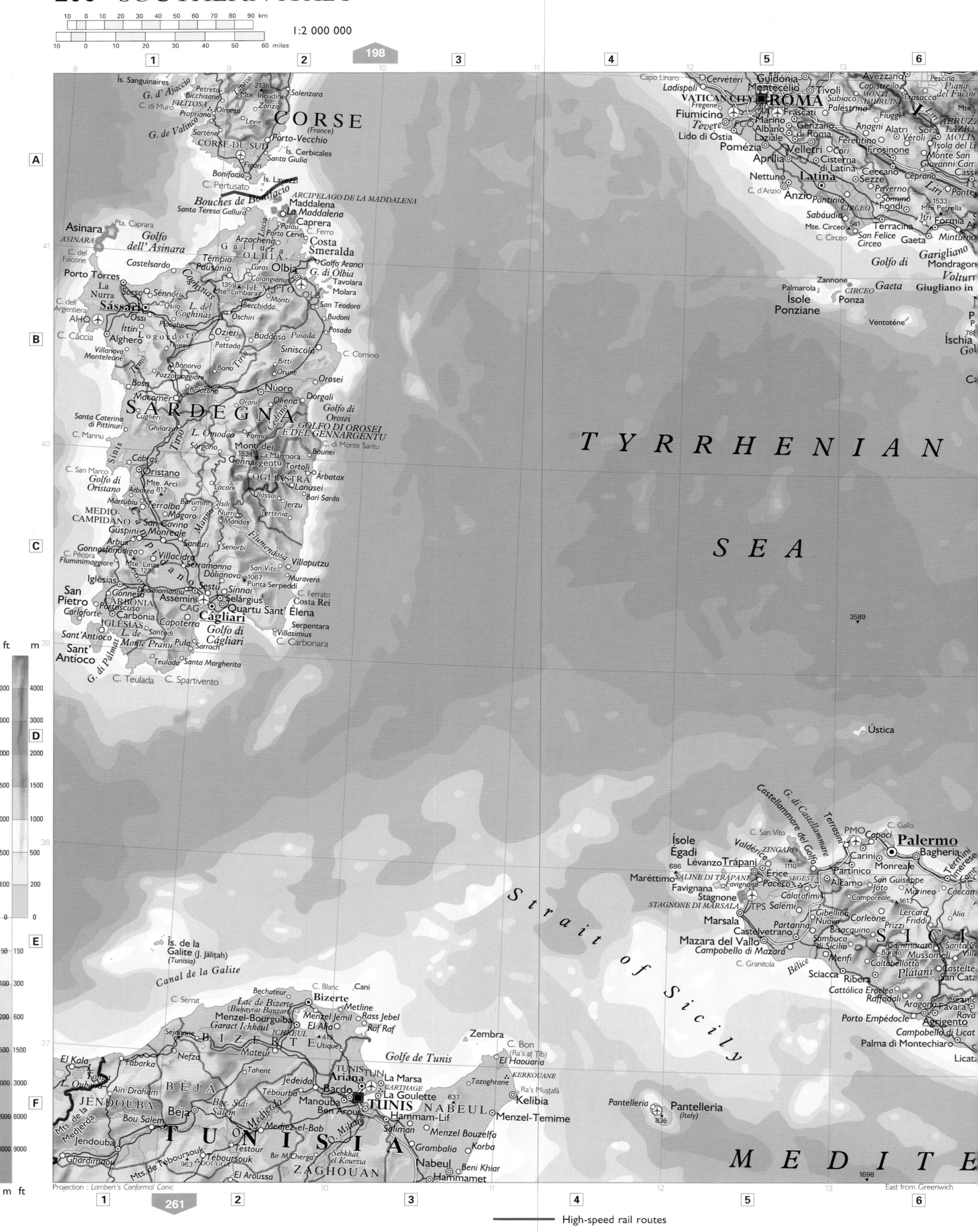

1:2 000 000

198

261

TYRRHENIAN

SEA

CORSE
(France)

SARDEGNA

Strait of Sicily

TUNISIA

MEDITE

Projection : Lambert's Conformal Conic

East from Greenwich

High-speed rail routes

ADRIATIC

SEA

ALBANIA

Durrës

Tiranë

Strait of Otranto

GREECE

Kerkyra (Corfu)

CALABRIA

BASILICATA

Golfo di Táranto

Bari

Táranto

Lecce

Brindisi

Cosenza

Crotone

Catanzaro

Golfo di Squillace

Stir. di Messina

Ísole Eólie

Messina

Réggio di Calábria

IONIAN

SEA

Catánia

Siracusa

RRANEAN SEA

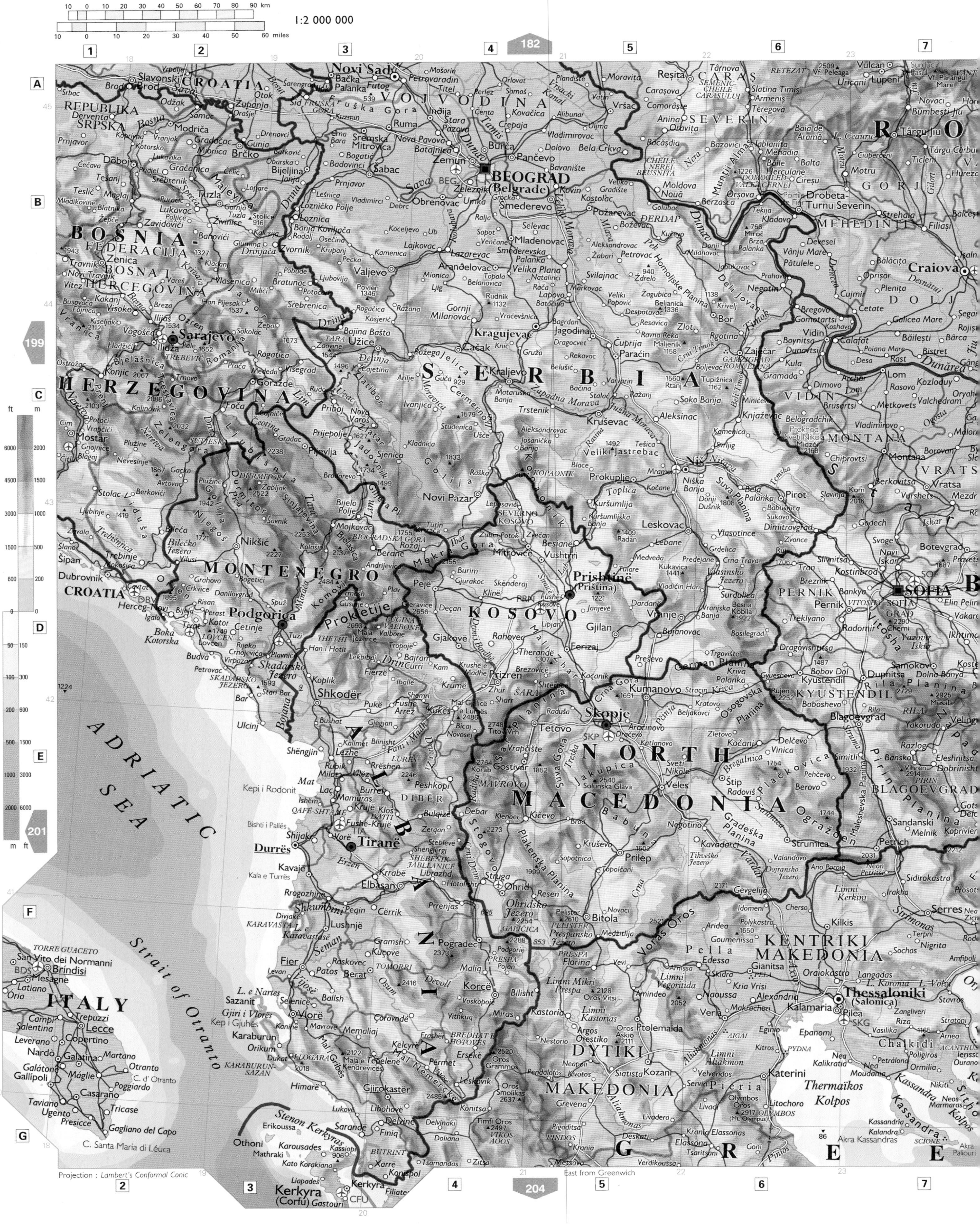

1:2 000 000

10 0 10 20 30 40 50 60 70 80 90 km
10 0 10 20 30 40 50 60 miles

Grid references: 1 2 3 4 182 5 6 7

A B C D E F G

ft m
6000 2000
4500 1500
3000 1000
1500 500
600 200
0 0
50 150
100 300
200 1500
1000 3000
2000 6000
m ft

Countries and regions:

CROATIA
REPUBLIKA SRPSKA
BOSNIA-FEDERACIJA
BOSNA I HERCEGOVINA
HERZEGOVINA
MONTENEGRO
SERBIA
VOJVODINA
KOSOVO
SEVERNO KOSOVO
NORTH MACEDONIA
ITALY
GREECE
KENTRIKI MAKEDONIA
DYTIKI MAKEDONIA
ROMANIA

Seas and waters:

ADRIATIC SEA
Strait of Otranto
Boka Kotorska
SKADARSKO JEZERO
Ohridsko Jezero
Thermaïkos Kolpos

Major cities:

Novi Sad, BEOGRAD (Belgrade), Sarajevo, Podgorica, Prishtinë (Pristina), Skopje, Tiranë, SOFIA, Craiova, Thessaloniki (Salonica), Mostar, Dubrovnik, Durrës, Brindisi, Lecce

Projection : Lambert's Conformal Conic

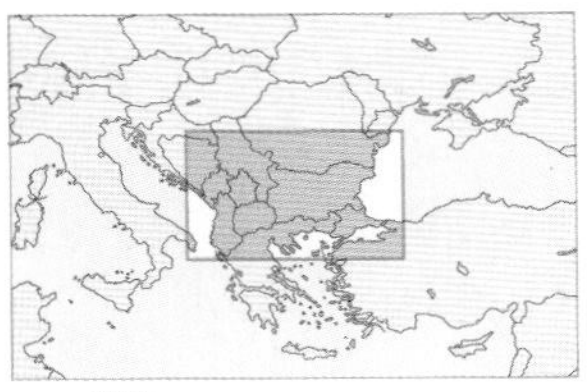

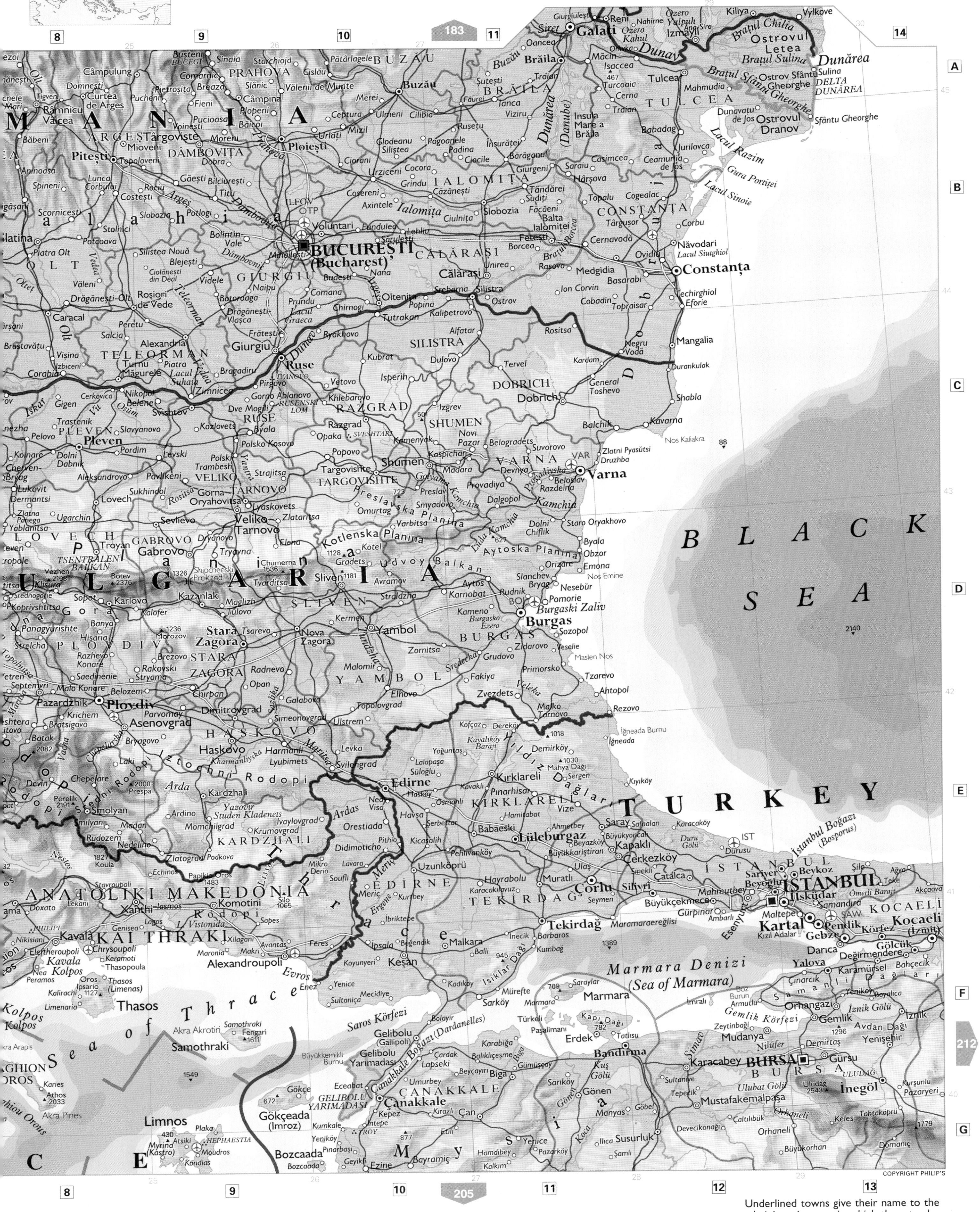

ROMANIA · **BULGARIA** · **TURKEY**

BUCUREŞTI (Bucharest)

Galaţi · Brăila · Buzău · Ploieşti · Piteşti · Târgovişte · Râmnicu Vâlcea · Câmpulung

Constanţa · Mangalia · Năvodari · Tulcea

DELTA DUNĂREA · Ostrovul Letea · Sfântu Gheorghe

Dunărea (Danube) · Dunav

Giurgiu · Ruse · Silistra · Dobrich · Varna

Pleven · Veliko Tarnovo · Gabrovo · Targovishte · Shumen

BULGARIA

Plovdiv · Pazardzhik · Asenovgrad · Haskovo · Kardzhali · Smolyan

Stara Zagora · Sliven · Yambol · Burgas

Burgaski Zaliv · Nesebŭr · Pomorie · Sozopol · Ahtopol

BLACK SEA

TURKEY

Edirne · Kırklareli · Lüleburgaz · Tekirdağ · Çorlu

İSTANBUL · Üsküdar · Kartal · Pendik · Gebze · Kocaeli (İzmit) · Gölcük

İstanbul Boğazı (Bosporus)

Marmara Denizi (Sea of Marmara)

Çanakkale Boğazı (Dardanelles) · Gelibolu (Gallipoli) · Gökçeada (İmroz)

BURSA · İnegöl · Mudanya · Bandırma · Erdek

ANATOLIKI MAKEDONIA KAI THRAKI

Kavala · Xanthi · Komotini · Alexandroupoli · Thasos · Samothraki · Limnos

Sea of Thrace

COPYRIGHT PHILIP'S

Underlined towns give their name to the administrative area in which they stand.

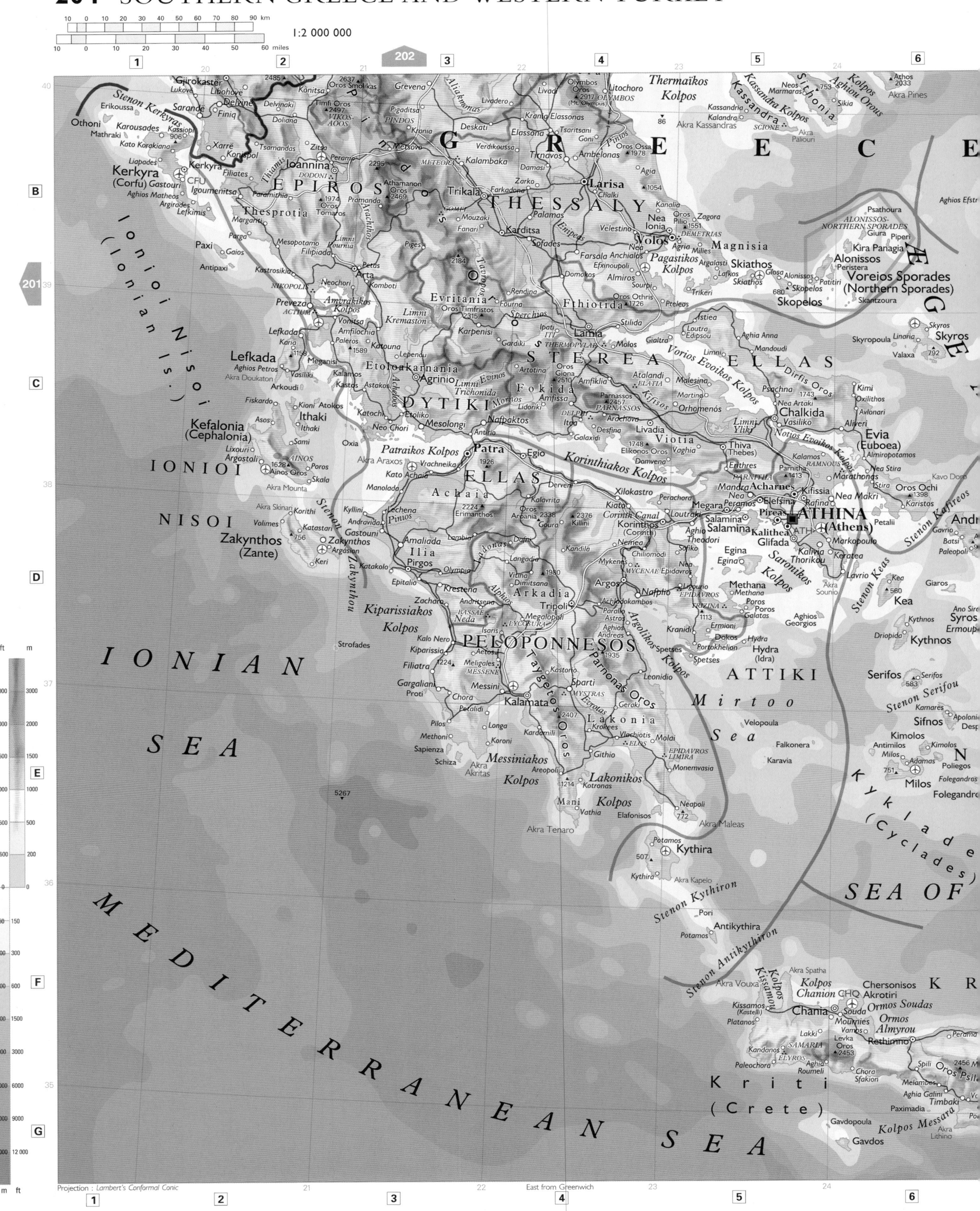

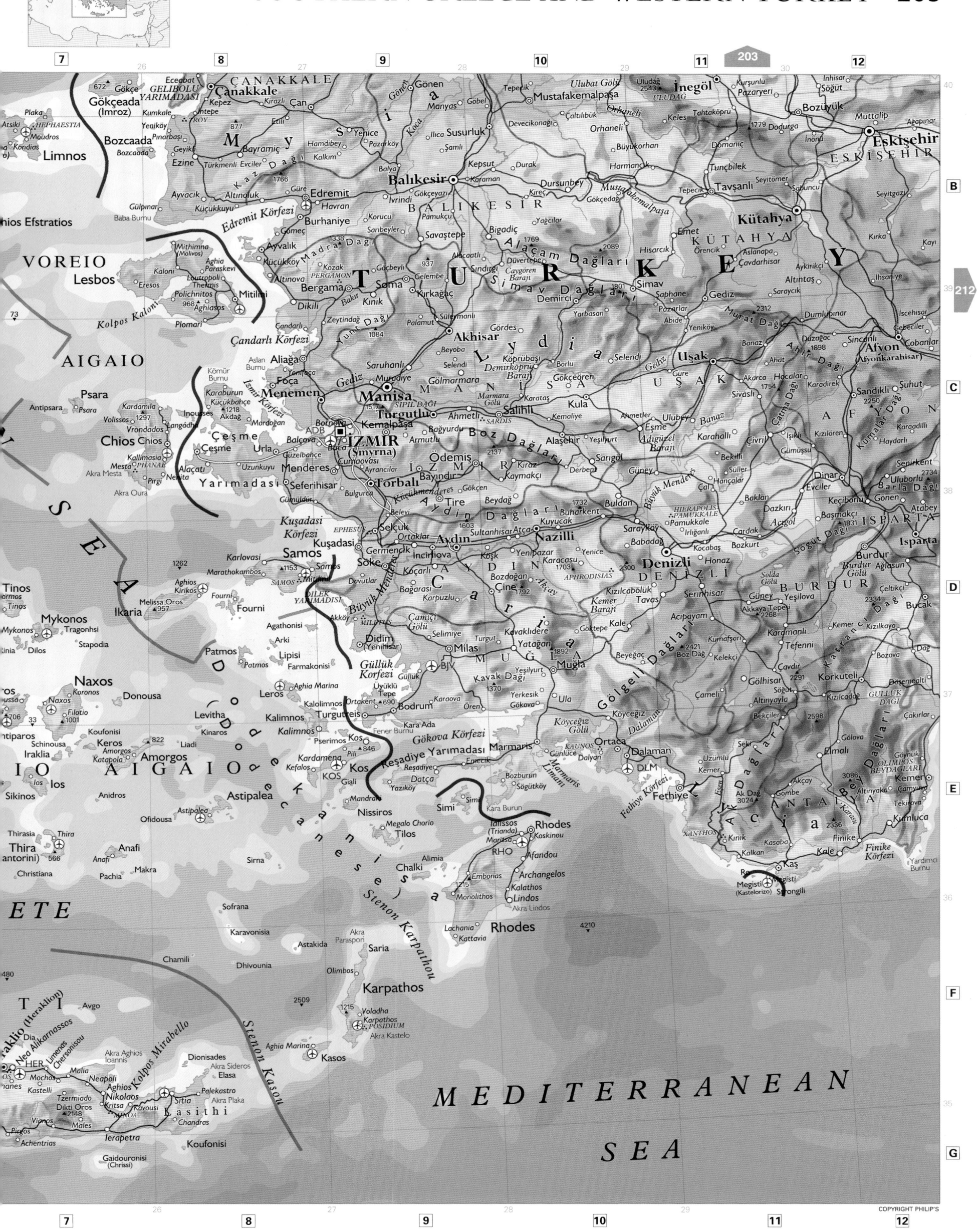

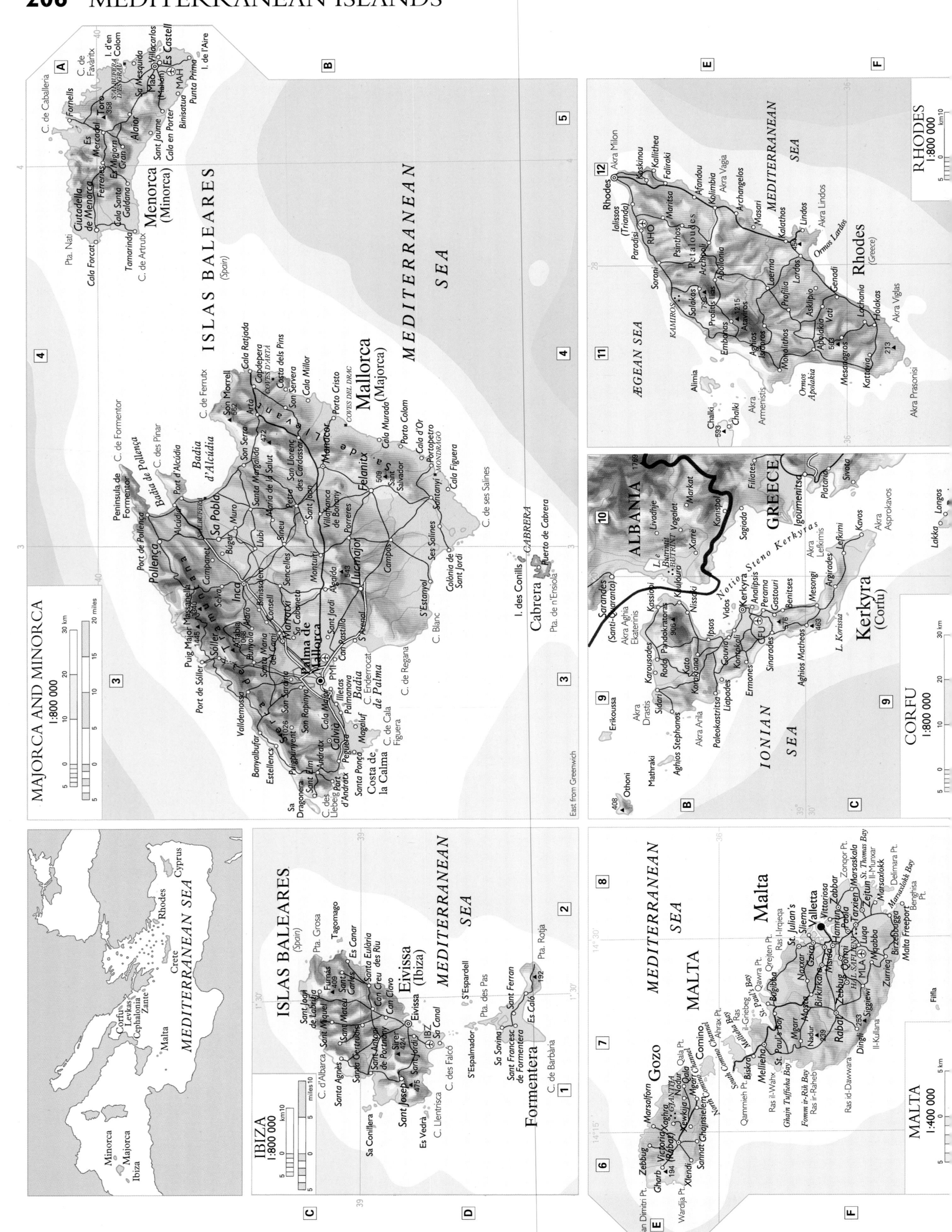

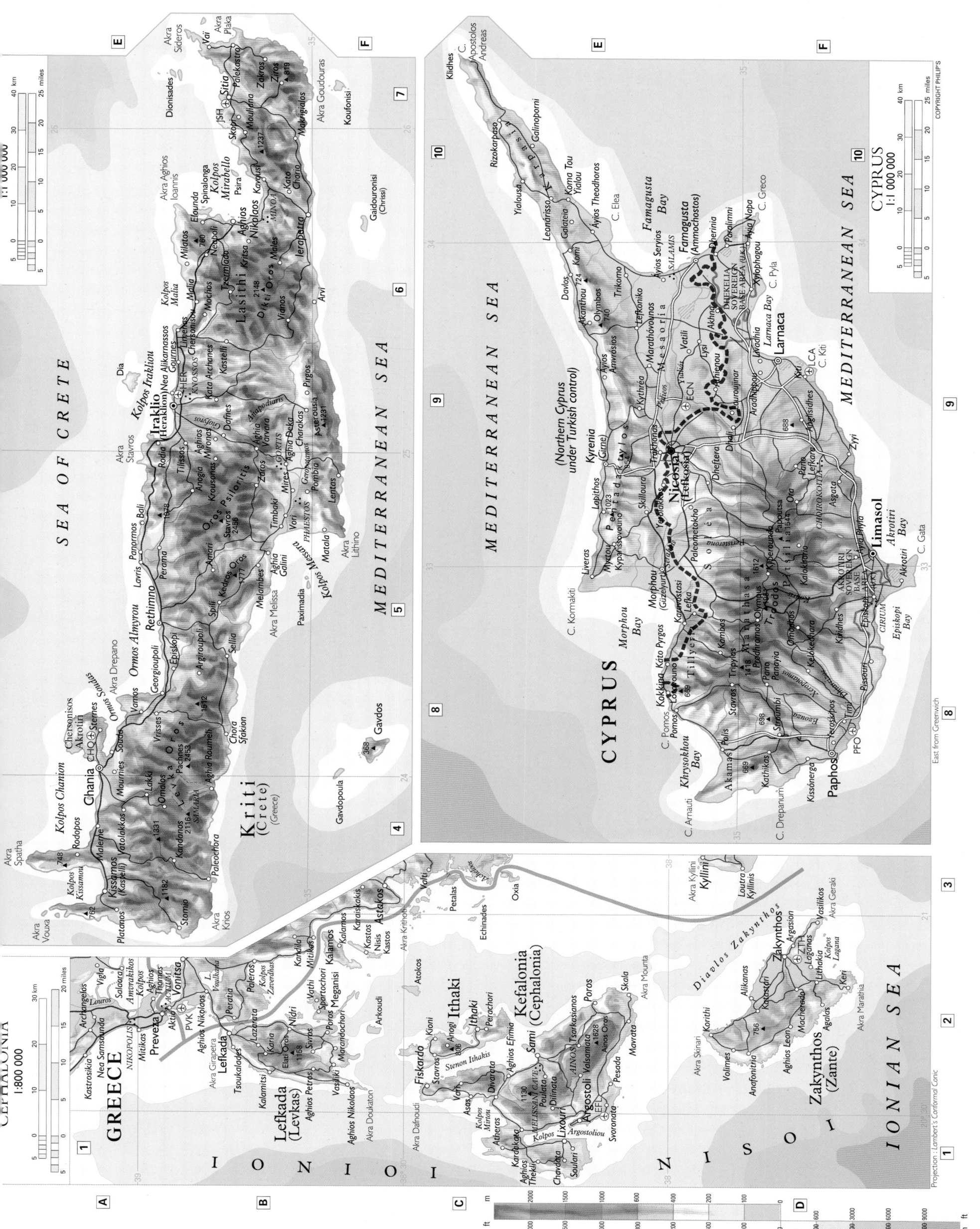

Projection : Lambert's Conformal Conic

East from Greenwich

CYPRUS
1:1 000 000

GREECE

CEPHALONIA
1:800 000

Kriti
(Crete)
(Greece)

Lefkada
(Levkas)

Kefalonia
(Cephalonia)

Zakynthos
(Zante)

CYPRUS

SEA OF CRETE

MEDITERRANEAN SEA

IONIAN SEA

IONIOI NISOI

MEDITERRANEAN SEA

(Northern Cyprus
under Turkish control)

ASIA

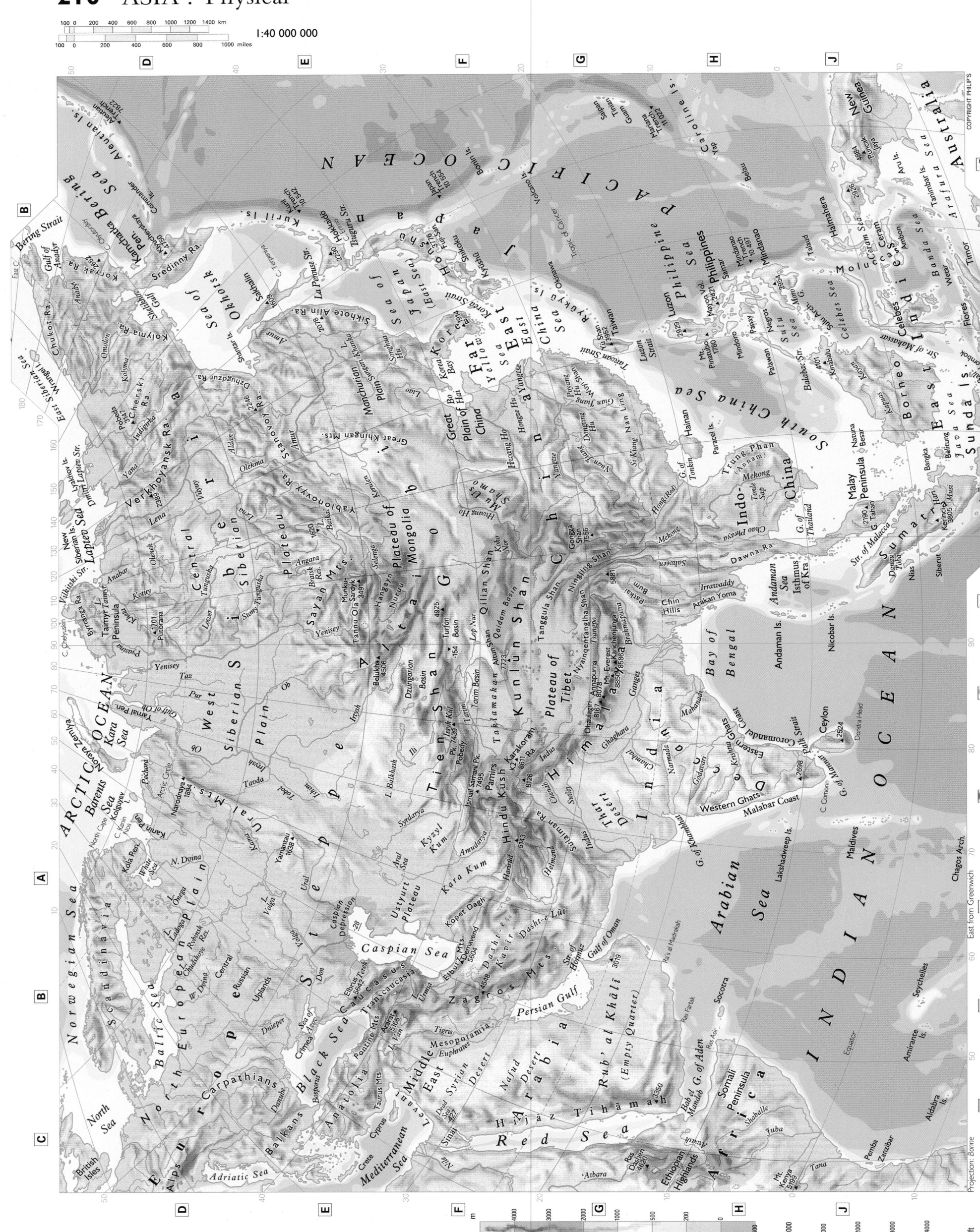

100 0 200 400 600 800 1000 1200 1400 km

1:40 000 000

100 0 200 400 600 800 1000 miles

COPYRIGHT PHILIP'S

East from Greenwich

Projection: Bonne

m 4000 3000 2000 1000 500 200 0

ft 12 000 9000 6000 3000 1500 600 0

ft 0 600 1500 3000 6000 12 000 18 000 24 000

m 0 200 600 1000 3000 6000

1:40 000 000

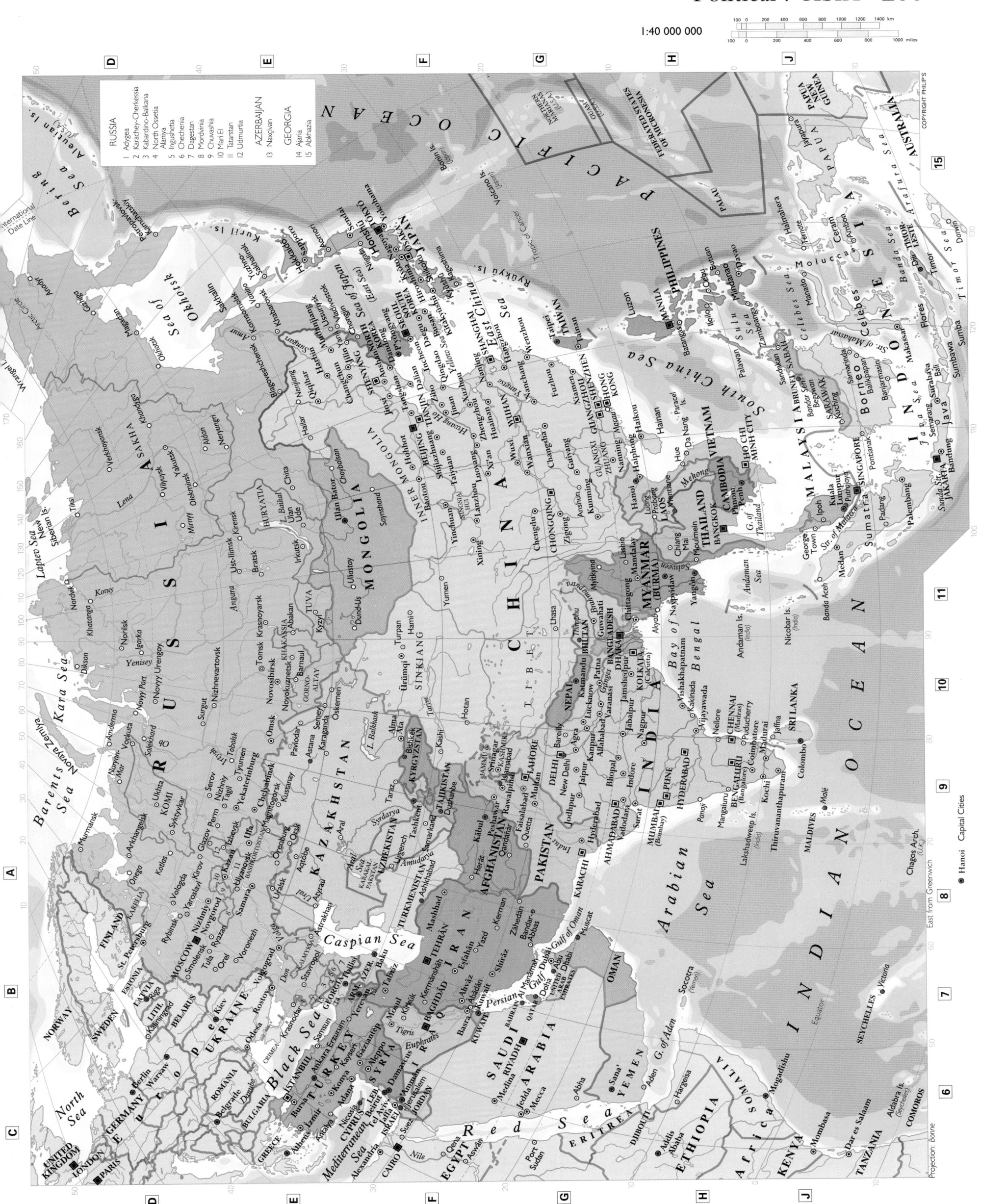

1 : 4 000 000

50   0   25   50   75   100   125   150   175 km
50   0   25   50   75   100   125 miles

189

| 1 | 2 | 3 | 4 | 5 | 6 | 7 |

BULGARIA

B L A C K   S E A

Stara Zagora Yambol Aytos Burgas Nos Emine
Elhovo Michurin Igneada Igneada Burnu
Kırklareli Demirköy Kerempe Burnu Cide İnce Burun Sinop
Edirne Pınarhisar Vize Saray Çatalzeytin Ayancık Erfelek
Arda Babaeski Lüleburgaz Çerkezköy İnebolu Abana Küre Devrekâni Gerze
Uzunköprü Muratlı Çorlu Çatalca Zonguldak Kilimli Bartın Kastamonu Boyabat Bafra SAMSUN
Hayrabolu İstanbul Boğazı Çaycuma Safranbolu Daday Kargı Vezirköprü Altınkaya Barajı Samsun
İpsala Keşan Tekirdağ Silivri (Bosporus) Ereğli Karabük Araç Tosya Osmancık Merzifon Havza Kavak Çarşamba
Enez Malkara Şarköy Büyükçekmece İSTANBUL Kozlu Devrek Gerede Çankırı Gümüşhacıköy Suluova Ünye Terme
Saros Körfezi Şile Kandıra Karasu Akçakoca Bolu Çerkeş İskilip Amasya Erbaa Niksar Fatsa
Gökçeada Gelibolu Karabiga Gebze Kocaeli Sakarya Hendek Düzce Kurşunlu Çorum Turhal Zile Reşadiye
Marmara Denizi Darıca (İzmit) Adapazarı Mudurnu Beypazarı Çubuk Kırıkkale Tokat Yeşilırmak
(Sea of Marmara) Orhangazi İznik Göynük ANKARA Elmadağ Yozgat Sungurlu Almus Deveci Dağları
Çanakkale Biga Bandırma Gemlik Gölcük Sapanca Nallıhan Kazan Keskin Yerköy Sorgun TOKAT
TROY Gönen Karacabey İnegöl Bilecik Söğüt Ayaş Polatlı Bala Çiçekdağı Kırşehir Yıldızeli SİVAS
Ezine Balya Susurluk BURSA Uludağ Bozüyük Eskişehir Haymana Kaman Kozaklı Sivas Hafik Zara
Bayramiç Edremit Balıkesir Dursunbey Kütahya Emet Seyitgazi Sivrihisar Kulu NEVŞEHİR Şarkışla Kangal
Ayvacık Bergama Soma Akhisar Manisa Simav Gediz Afyon Çay Aksaray Kayseri Gemerek Divriği
Ayvalık Kınık Demirci Uşak Banaz (Afyonkarahisar) Eber Gölü Tuz Gölü NEVŞEHİR Talas Bünyan Kangal
Mitilini Akhisar MANISA Sındırgı Murat Dağı Bolvadin Akşehir Gölü Cihanbeyli Ortaköy GÖREME Develi Gürün
Lesbos Foça Turgutlu Salihli Alaşehir Kula Şuhut Akşehir Sultan Dağları Obruk Aksaray Derinkuyu Yeşilhisar Pınarbaşı Sarız
Chios Menemen İZMİR Ödemiş Uşak Çivril Dinar Yalvaç Ilgın Kadınhanı KONYA Bor Niğde Tomarza Elbistan
Karaburun İZMİR (Smyrna) Torbalı Tire Nazilli Pamukkale Şenirkent Eğirdir KONYA Karapınar NİĞDE Çamardı Afşin KAHRAMAN MARAŞ
Çeşme Urla Boz Dağları Aydın Buldan Denizli Gelendost Beyşehir Karaman Ereğli Ulukışla Bakırdağı Feke Göksun
Samos Kuşadası Söke İncirliova Nazilli Çardak Burdur Beyşehir İçericumra Pozantı Kozan Kadirli Elbistan
Ikaria Miletus Koçarlı Aydın Çine Tavas Gölü Isparta Çumra Karaisalı İmamoğlu Kahramanmaraş
Fourni DİLEK YARIMADASI Milas Yatağan Muğla   Acıgöl Bucak Seydişehir Sugla Gölü Seyhan Barajı Osmaniye GAZİANTEP
Patmos Kalimnos Bodrum Ören Ula Göltepe Korkuteli Suğla Gölü Çamardı Seyhan Ceyhan İslahiye (Antep)
Kos KOS Gökova Körfezi Marmaris Dalaman Elmalı ANTALYA Taşkent MERSİN ADANA Dörtyol HATAY
GREECE Reşadiye Bozburun Fethiye Ak Dağ Kaş Kemer Antalya Manavgat Alanya Mut Silifke Tarsus Mersin İskenderun Kilis HALAB
Rhodes Köyceğiz Kalkan Finike Antalya Körfezi Anamur Gülnar Erdemli İskenderun Körfezi Belen (Aleppo)
Karpathos Kaş Kale Kumluca Anamur Burnu Bozyazı İnceburun Silifke Karataş Uluçınar Hatay Reyhanlı
Kasos Megisti Yardımcı Burnu Gazipaşa Anamur Samandağ Harbiye Afrin

C Y P R U S

Rizokarpaso C. Apostolos Andreas
Al Lādhiqīyah (Latakia)
Morphou Kyrenia Famagusta IDLIB
Nicosia Khān Shaykhūn
Polis Troodos Larnaca Hamāh S
Paphos Olympus Episkopi Baniyas HAMĀH
Limassol Akrotiri Tartūs As Salamīyah
CYPRUS TARTŪS HIMS
HIMS (Homs)

M E D I T E R R A N E A N   S E A

Tarābulus (Tripoli) Al Qaryatayn
LEBANON Jūniyah An Nabk
BAYRŪT (Beirut) Zahlah DIMASHQ (Damascus)
Saydā Jaramānah
Şūr Qunaytirah
Qiryat Shemona AS SUWAYDĀ'
HEFA (Haifa) As Suwaydā'
ISRAEL Nazerat Irbid JORDAN
Netanya Hadera Zarqā'
TEL AVIV-YAFO WEST BANK AMMAN
Ashdod Jerusalem Ashqelon

Projection: Conical with two standard parallels

256 3   4   5   7

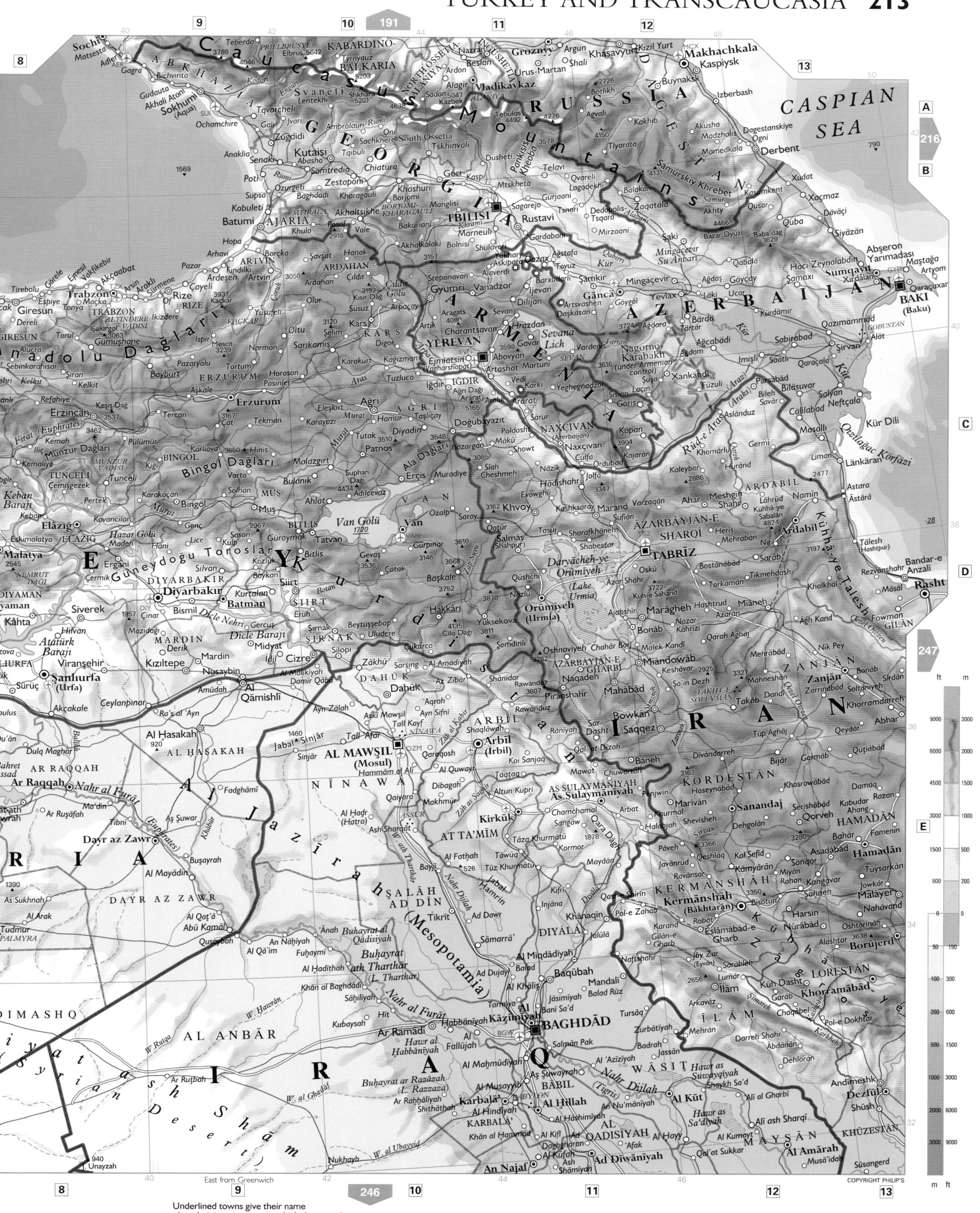

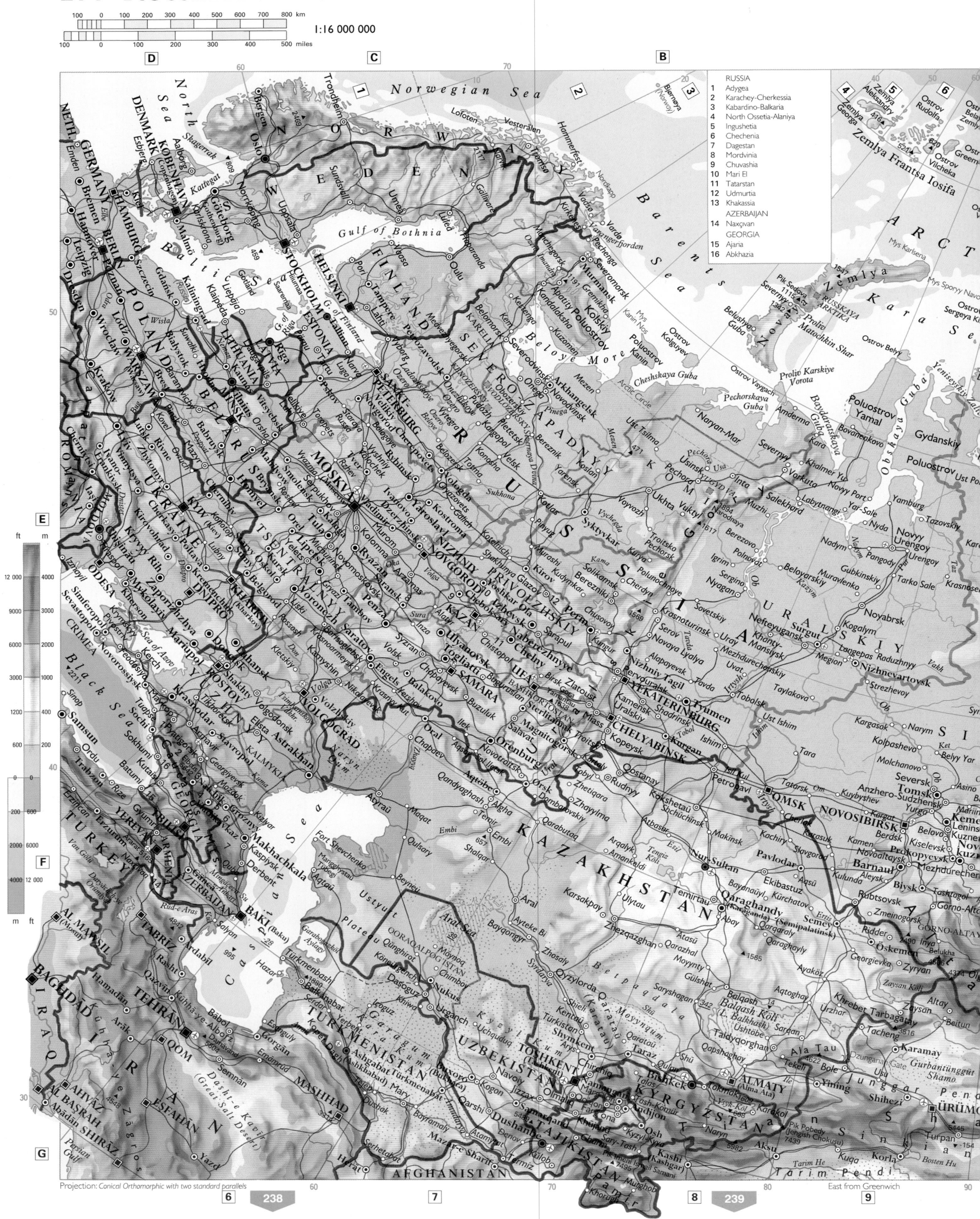

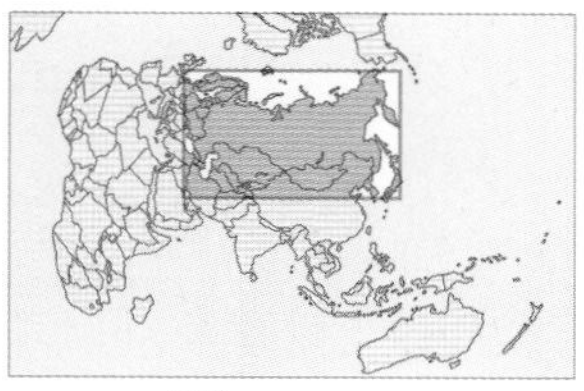

A
150
B
C
D
E
F
OCEAN
Laptev Sea
East Siberian Sea
Chukchi Sea
Bering Sea
Bering Str.
Sea of Okhotsk
Sea of Japan (East Sea)
Severnaya Zemlya
Poluostrov Taymyr
Gory Byrranga
Novosibirskiye Ostrova
Ostrov Vrangelya
Chukotskiy Poluostrov
Chukotskoye Nagorye
Koryakskoye Nagorye
Kolymskoye Nagorye
Khrebet Cherskogo
Verkhoyanskiy Khrebet
Stanovoy Khrebet
Yablonovyy Khrebet
Khrebet Dzhugdzur
Sikhote Alin
Sredinnyy Khrebet
Poluostrov Kamchatka
Kurilskiye Ostrova
Sakhalin
Hokkaido
Honshū
RUSSIA
MONGOLIA
CHINA
NORTH KOREA
SOUTH KOREA
JAPAN
Da Hinggan Ling
Dongbei (Manchuria)
Gobi
Hangayn Nuruu
Hentiyn Nuruu
Ozero Baykal
Sayan
Yakutsk
Magadan
Petropavlovsk-Kamchatskiy
Khabarovsk
Vladivostok
Irkutsk
Ulan Ude
Chita
Bratsk
Krasnoyarsk
Norilsk
Tiksi
ULAANBAATAR
HARBIN
CHANGCHUN
SHENYANG
BEIJING
PYONGYANG
SEOUL
SAPPORO
Arctic Circle

218
219

Underlined towns give their name to the
administrative area in which they stand.

COPYRIGHT PHILIP'S

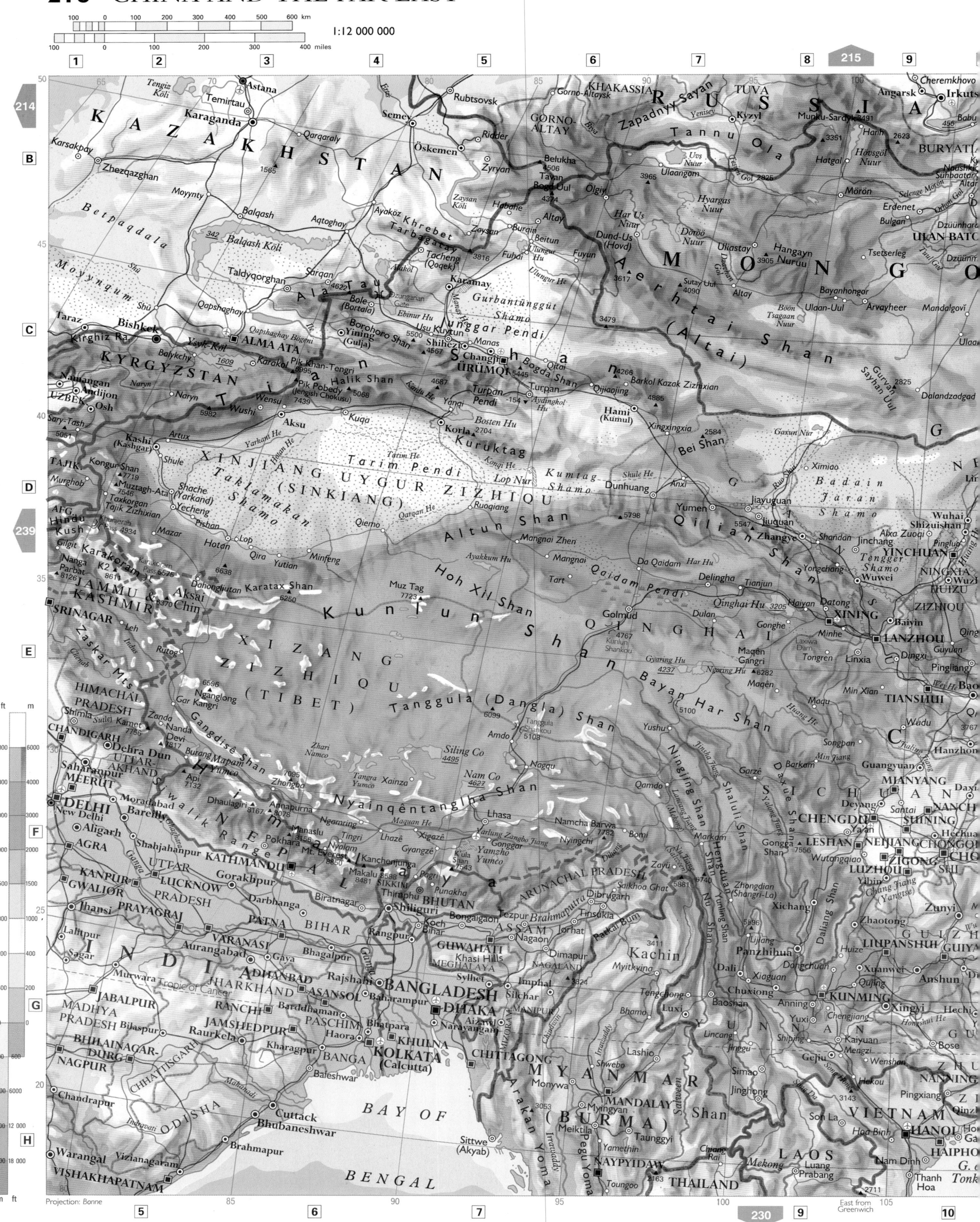

1:12 000 000

Projection: Bonne

East from Greenwich

HONG KONG, MACAU
AND SHENZHEN
1:800 000

COPYRIGHT PHILIP'S

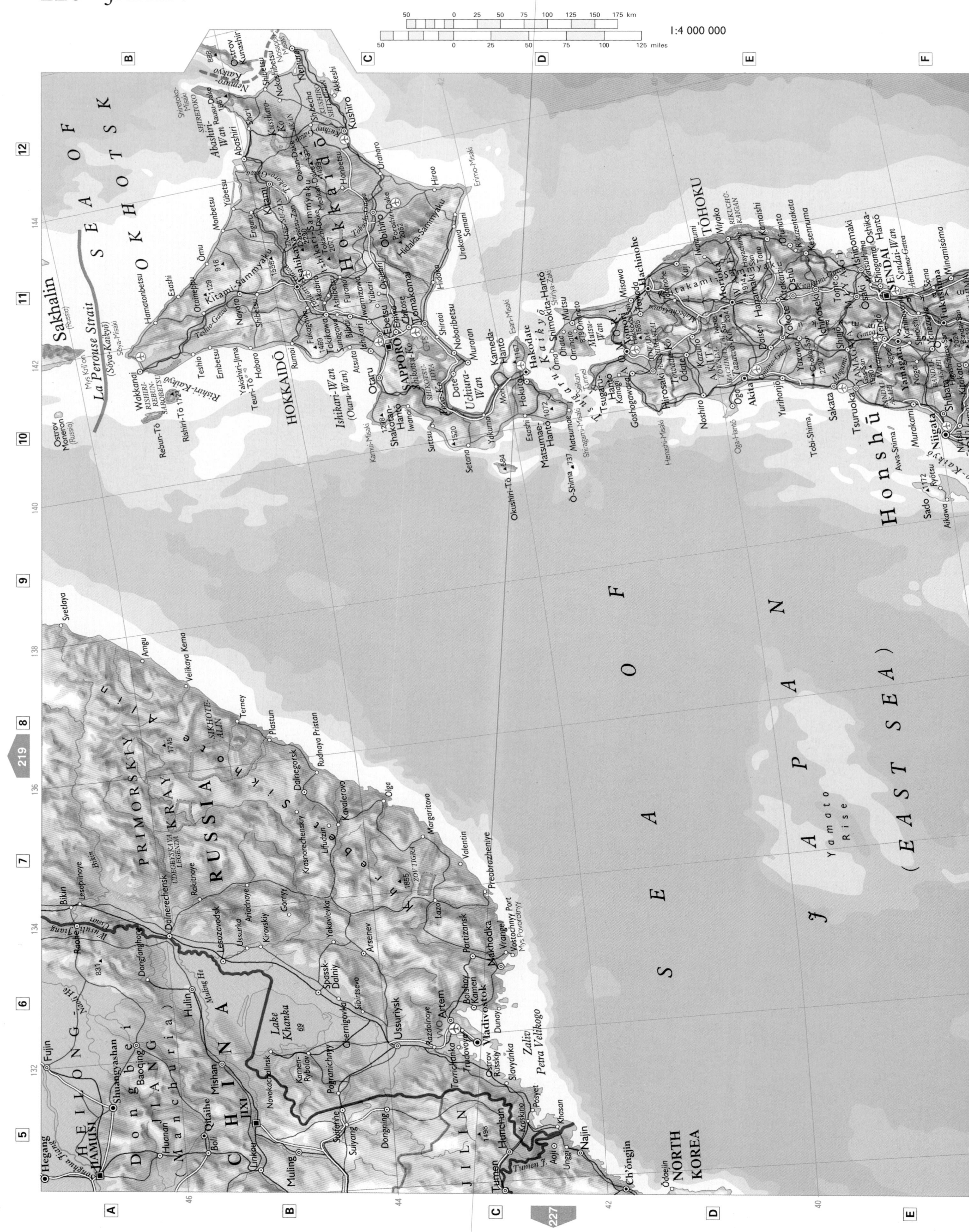

1:4 000 000

SEA OF OKHOTSK

Sakhalin

La Perouse Strait

HOKKAIDŌ

SAPPORO

TOHOKU

Honshū

SENDAI

RUSSIA

PRIMORSKY KRAY

Vladivostok

SIKHOTE ALIN'

Lake Khanka

CHINA

Manchuria

Heilongjiang

Jilin

NORTH KOREA

SEA OF JAPAN (EAST SEA)

Yamato Rise

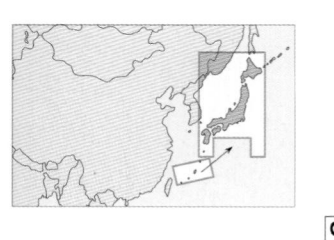

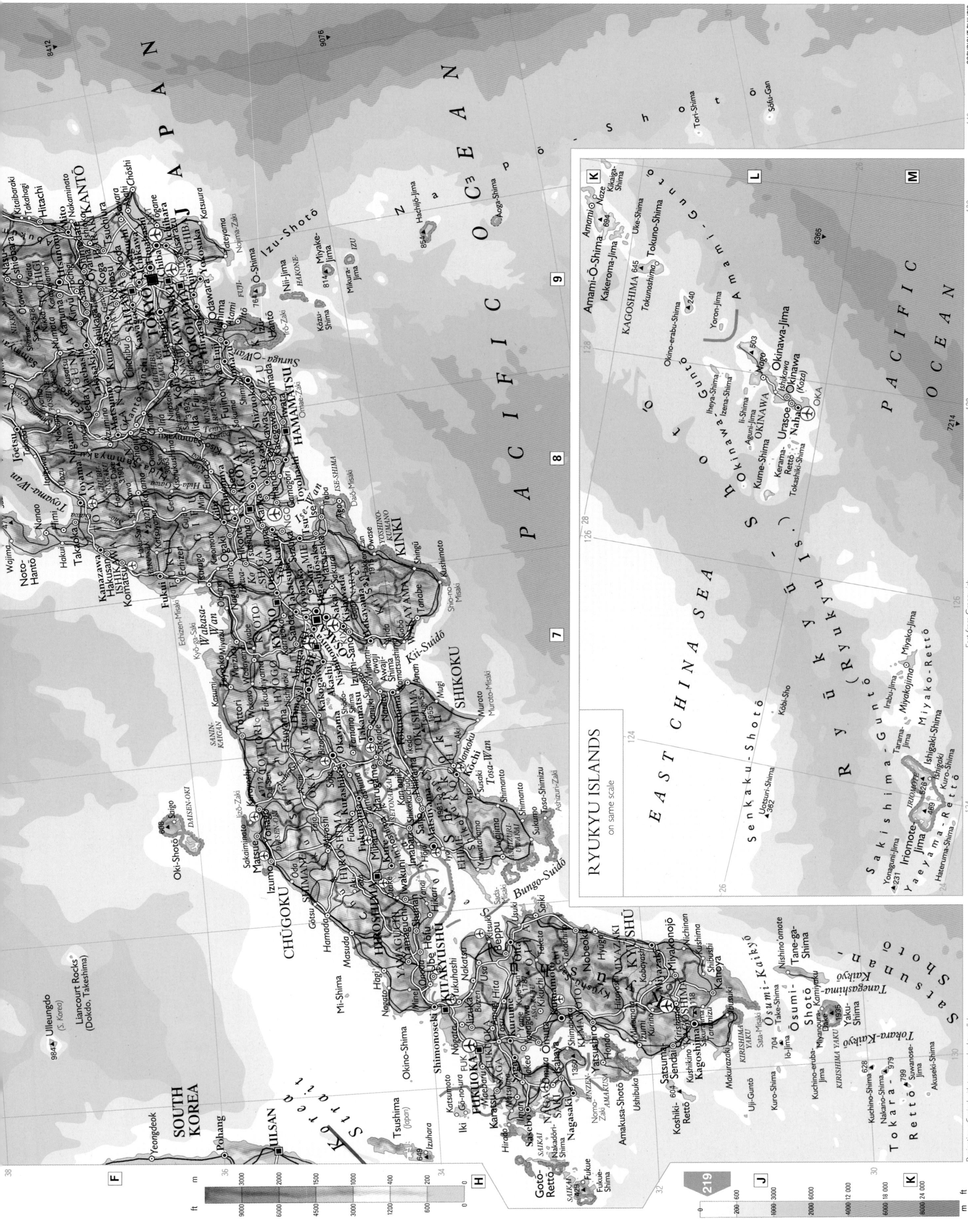

RYUKYU ISLANDS
on same scale

East from Greenwich

Projection : Conical with two standard parallels

COPYRIGHT PHILIP'S

10 0 10 20 30 40 50 60 70 80 90 km

1:2 000 000

10 0 10 20 30 40 50 60 miles

1 **2** **3** **4** **5** **6**

130 131 132 133 134

A

224

Yeongdeok

Heunghae

Pohang

SOUTH KOREA

36

S E A   O F   J A P A N

(E A S T   S E A)

Oki-Shotō

Daimanji-San
Dōgo ▲ 608
Saigō
DAISEN-OKI

Dōzen

H o n s h u

B

SANIN-KAIGAN

DAISEN-OKI
Shimane-Hantō
Hi-no-Misaki   Jizō-Zaki
Hirata Shinji Matsue Sakaiminato Yonago   Iwami   Kasumi
Taisha Shinji-Ko Yasugi   Toyooka
CHŪGOKU-DISTRICT   Izumo Daitō Dai-Sen Kurayoshi Wakasa Hidaka
                                    1729   TOTTORI   Tottori
                 Oda Sanbe-San Kisuki   Dōgo-San Katsuyama Chizu Suga-no-Sen
Gōtsu IWAMI 1126   1269   Ochiai Tsuyama Yamasaki 1510 Wadayama
      GINZAN SHIMANE S a n   i n   HYOG   Nishiya
Hamada   Miyoshi Shōbara Niimi Yonago Ikuno
                                   Takahashi OKAYAMA Sayo Kasai
35   Bingo-Ochiai Tōjō Wake Himeji
Mi-Shima   Akiōta Yakage Sōja Okayama Bizen Takasago
Ōmi-Shima Hagi Aono-Yama Kannun-Yama HIROSHIMA Fuchū Ibara Kurashiki Akō Kakogawa
Tsuno-Shima   908 1339 Oku-Gawa Higashi- Mihara Kannabe Konkō Tamano Ieshima- Akas
Katsumoto Nagato Atō Hiroshima Onomichi Kasaoka Shōdo- Shotō Harima-
Iki Gō-no-ura YAMAGUCHI HIROSHIMA Hatsukaichi Kure Takehara In'noshima Shima A Tonoshō Nada
Tsushima Yamaguchi ITSUKUSHIMA Ōtake- Ōmi- Aki-Nada Marugame Takamatsu Awaji-Shima
Mitsushima Mine Ogōri Tokuji Iwakuni Shima Kurahashi- Zentsuji Sanuki Higashi- Sumoto
Izuhara San'yō Shin-Nan'yō Jima Hōjō kagawa Naruto
649 Hōfu Shunan KAGAWA Itano Minar
Kō-Saki Onoda Ube Hikari Naga-Shima Yashiro- Matsuyama Mima awaj
Shimonoseki Kudamatsu Jima Hime-Jima Iyo Yoshino- Tokushim
Higashi-Suidō KITAKYŪSHŪ Yanai Heigun-Tō Hōjō gawa Tōyō
Ō-Shima Nakama Suō-Nada Matsuyama EHIME TOKUSHIMA
34 Genkai- Munakata Nōgata Yukuhashi Ishizuchi-Yama Ōtoyo Tsurugi-San Anan
Nada Fukuma Miyata Tagawa Nagahama 1981 SHIKOKU 1955
Koga Iizuka Kama Nakatsu Futago-Yama Ōzu Uchiko 1562 Ino KŌCHI 1423 Mugi
Iki-Kaikyō FUKUOKA Buzen 721 Kunisaki Yawatahama Sakawa Nankoku Kami Mugi
FUKUOKA Dazaifu Chikushino Usa Iyo-Nada Uwa Kōchi Noichi Tōyō
Yobuko Maebaru FUK Kasuga Hita Kitsuki Sada-Misaki-Hantō Tosa Aki
Karatsu Sefuri-yama Amagi Hiji Uwajima Kihoku Shimanto
Imari 1055 Tōsu Ogōri Kusu Beppu-Wan Tsurusaki Nishi-Tosa Saga
Matsuura SAGA Kurume Yufu-Dake Beppu Ōita Tosa-Wan Muroto
Saza Taku Ōgi 1584 ŌITA Saganoseki Tsushima Muroto-Misaki
Takeo Saga Chikugo Ōita Usuki Misho Sukumo
Arita Yanagawa Yame Kurogi ASO Bungo-Katsu Oki-no-Shima 865 Shimanto
NAGA Ōkawa Ōmuta Setaka KUJŪ 1787 Taketa Mie ASHIZURI- Tosa-Shimizu
Ōmura- Ureshino Ariake-Tara Arao Yamaga Ogumi Kuju-San Tsukumi UWAKAI Ashizuri-Zaki
Wan 1076 Tara-Dake Kikuchi Aso Saiki **Shikoku**
Ōmura Isahaya Tamana Ichinomiya Soba-Yama Kamae **SHIKOKU-DISTRICT**
Nagayo Unzen KUMAMOTO Kōshi 1592 Aso-Zan 1758
Nagasaki Dake Shimabara Ozu Takachiho
1360 KUMAMOTO Mashiki Hinokage
Obama Matsubase Kunimi-Dake Nobeoka

E
Kuchinotsu Misumi Uto 1739
Hondo Kami- Yatsushiro Shiiba
Amusa-Shotō Amakusa Itsuki Hyūga
Nada Shimo- Taragi MIYAZAKI
Ushibuka Jima Hitoyoshi
Naga-Shima Minamata **Kyūshū**
Akune Izumi Saito Takanabe **KYŪSHŪ-DISTRICT**
Ōkuchi Ebino Sadowara
Kami-Koshiki- Miyanojō Yoshimatsu Kobayashi Miyazaki
Jima Kurino 1700 KIRISHIMA
Koshiki- Satsuma- Aira YAKU Miyakonojō
Rettō Sendai Hayato Kirishima Soo Nichinan
604 Kushikino KO Aburatsu
Shimo-Koshiki- On-Take 1118 Miyakonojō
Jima Kagoshima Ijūin Sakurajima
Fukiage KAGOSHIMA
Koshiki- Fukage Tarumizu Shibushi
Kaikyō Kaseda Kanoya Kushima
Noma-Saki Kawanabe Ōsaki Shibushi-Wan

1
Makurazaki Kōyama 968
Bō-no-Misaki Ibusuki
Projection: 130 Kaimon-Dake Yamagawa
Lambert's 924 KIRISHIMA
Conformal YAKU
Conic Sata-Misaki 131

5737

Kyūshū Trench

⌐ Shinkansen lines

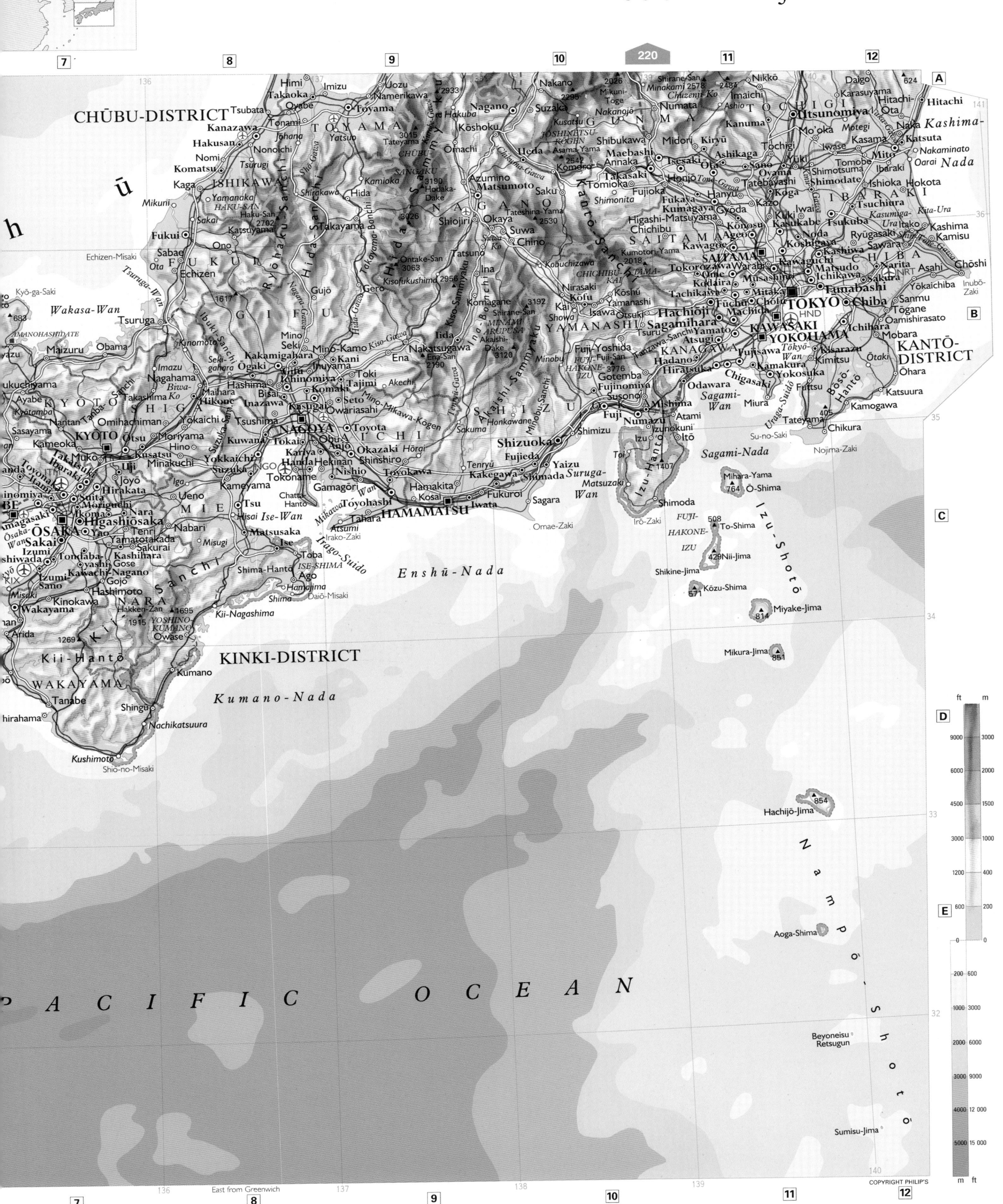

CHŪBU-DISTRICT

Tsubata
Himi
Imizu
Uozu
Namerikawa
Nakano
Mikuni-Tōge
Numata
Nikkō
Daigo
624
Karasuyama

Takaoka
Oyabe
TOYAMA
Takaoka
Hakuba
Kōshoku
Suzaka
Shirane-San
Minakami 2578
Ashio
Kanuma
Utsunomiya
Hitachi-Ota
Hitachi

Kanazawa
Tonami
Toyama
Nagano
Kusatsu
TOCHIGI
Mo'oka
Motegi
Kasama
Naka
Kashima-Nada

Hakusan
Johana
Yatsuo
Ueda
Asama Yama
Shibukawa
Midori
Kiryū
Tochigi
Iwase
Tomobe
Mito
Nakaminato
Oarai Nada

Nomi
Nonoichi
Ōmachi
Azumino
Maebashi
Annaka
Takasaki
Ōta
Sano
Oyama
Shimotsuma
Ishioka
Ibaraki
Hokota

Komatsu
ISHIKAWA
Kamioka
Hida
Matsumoto
Saku
Tomioka
Honjō
Fujioka
IBARAKI
Tsuchiura
Kashima

Kaga
Yamanaka
Takayama
Hodaka-Dake
NAGANO
Shimonita
Kumagaya
Hanyū
Kazo
Tsukuba
Kasumiga-ura
Itako

Fukui
Katsuyama
Shirakawa
Okaya
Chichibu
Higashi-Matsuyama
Gyōda
Kōnosu
Kuki
Kasukabe
Ryūgasaki
Kita-Ura
Kamisu

Sabae
Ono
Shiojiri
Suwa
SAITAMA
Tokorozawa
Ōme
Iwatsuki
Kawagoe
Kashiwa
CHIBA

Echizen
Gujō
Chino
Kōshū
Kōdaira
Warabi
Musashino
Mitaka
Matsudo
Narita NRT
Asahi
Chōshi

FUKUI
Gero
Ina
Nirasaki
Kōfu
Yamanashi
Hachiōji
Fuchū
Chōfu
Funabashi
Yōkaichiba
Inubō-Zaki

Echizen-Misaki
Mino
Komagane
Kai
Isawa
Showa
YAMANASHI
Machida
TOKYO
Chiba

Seki
Nakatsugawa
Minobu
Tsuru
HAKONE
Sagamihara
Kawasaki
YOKOHAMA
Ichihara

Mino-Kamo
Ena
Fuji-Yoshida
Fuji-San 3776
Atsugi
KANAGAWA
Fujisawa
Yokosuka
Mobara

Kakamigahara
Toki
Akechi
Gotemba
Hadano
Hiratsuka
Kamakura
Ōtaki

Gifu
Kani
Tajimi
Numazu
Odawara
Chigasaki
Sagami-Wan
Miura
Kimitsu
Ōhara

NAGOYA
Seto
Toyota
Fujinomiya
Susono
Mishima
Atami
Izunokuni
Tateyama
Katsuura

Ichinomiya
Kasugai
Okazaki
Hōrai
Fuji
Shizuoka
Shimizu
Izu
Itō
Kamogawa

Tsushima
Inazawa
Komaki
Honkawane
Fujieda
Shimoda
Kawasaki

KINKI-DISTRICT

KANTŌ-DISTRICT

Wakasa-Wan

PACIFIC OCEAN

Kumano-Nada

Enshū-Nada

Sagami-Nada

Izu-Shotō

Ō-Shima 764
Mihara-Yama

To-Shima 508

Nii-Jima 429

Shikine-Jima
Kōzu-Shima 571

Miyake-Jima 814

Mikura-Jima 851

Hachijō-Jima 854

Aoga-Shima

Beyonēsu Retsugun

Sumisu-Jima

Nampō Shotō

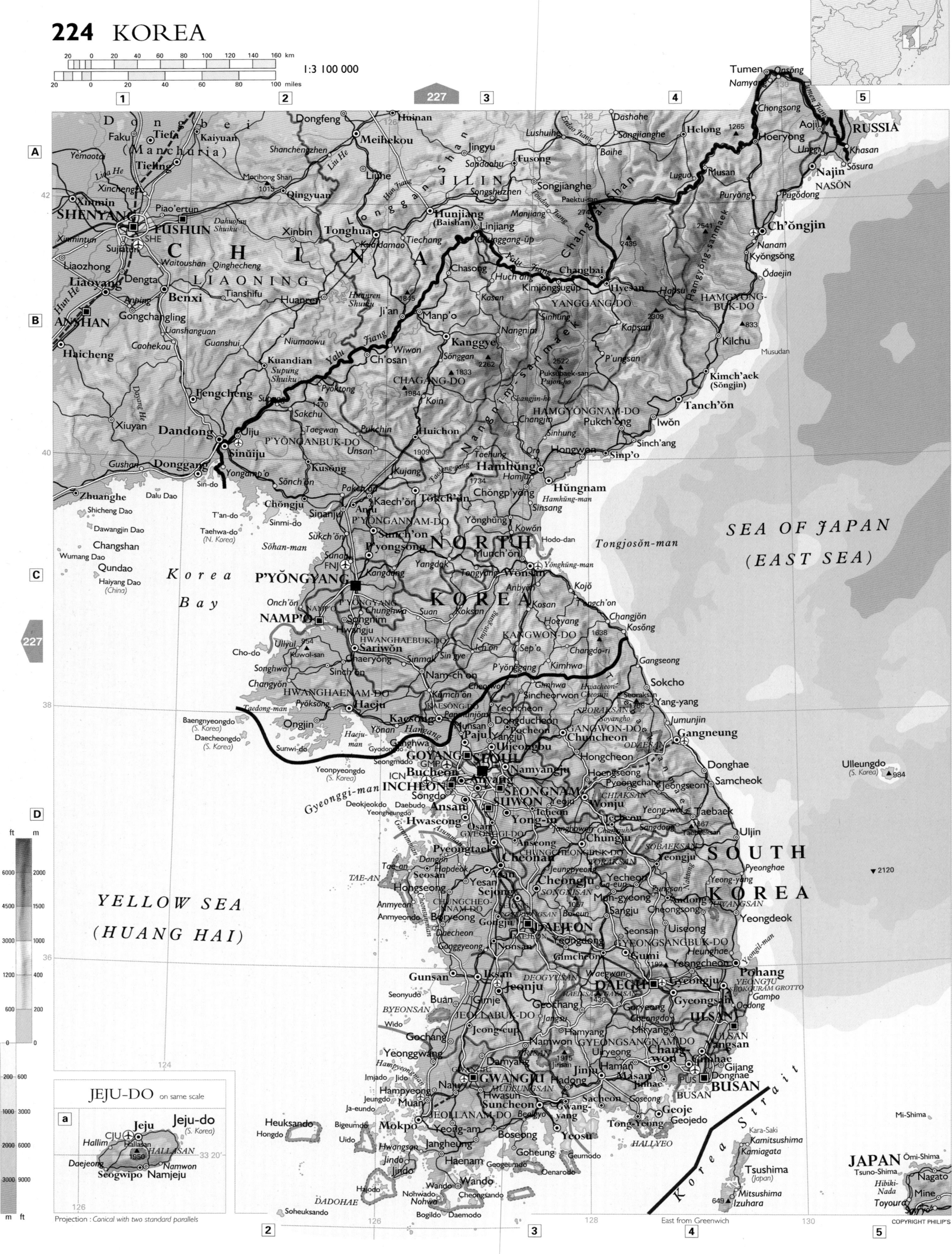

1:3 100 000

SEA OF JAPAN
(EAST SEA)

NORTH
KOREA

YELLOW SEA
(HUANG HAI)

SOUTH
KOREA

JEJU-DO on same scale

JAPAN

—— High-speed rail routes

1:1 400 000

Projection: Lambert Conformal Conic

Taiwan High Speed Rail (THSR)

Inset a — CHINMEN (on same scale)

CHINA FUJIAN
Jimei
Xinglin
Shijing
Jinjing
Wutou Wan
XMN
Kuahao
XIAMEN
Chinmen (Quemoy)
Hsiao-chinmen Tao
Chinmen Tao (Taiwan)
Zhenhai
Xiamen Gang
Taiwan Strait
CHINMEN

Inset b — MATSU (on same scale)

CHINA FUJIAN
Huangqi
Lianjiang
Liang Tao
Tungyin Tao
Langqi
Min Jiang
Peikant'ang Tao
Tongsha Tao
Matsu Tao (Taiwan)
Changle
FOC
Paichuan
Liehtao
Taiwan Strait
MATSU

STRAIT

TAIWAN STRAIT

T A I W A N   S T R A I T

P'ENGHU

Yüweng Tao
Hsiyu
Paisha
Huhsi
Makung
P'enghu
P'enghu Tao
Ch'üntou (Pescadores)
Chipei Tao
Hua Yü
Wangan
Pachao Yü
Ch'imei Yü
Ch'imei
Tungchi Yü
Waisanting

Northern Taiwan

Fukuei Chiao
Shihmen
Chinshan
NEW T'AIPEI
Tanshui
YANGMINGSHAN
Chilung (Keelung)
Tanshui Kang
Hsiafu
Pali
Wanli
Pitou Chiao
Chuwei
Peitou
Haichih
Juifang
Santiaoling
Kuanyin
Tayuan
IPE
Sanch'ung
Nankang
Maoao
Santiao Chiao
T'AOYUAN
Panch'iao
Chungho
T'AIPEI (Taibei)
Hsinchuang
Taoyuan
Kunglao
Niulantsun
Chungli
Pate
Hsintien
Talichien
Hsinfeng
Yangmei
Hukou
Lungt'an
Wulai
Waiao
Kueishan Tao
Hsinchu (Xinzhu)
Chupei
Kuanhsi
Fuhsing
Chiaohsi
T'ouch'eng
Hsiangshan
Chutung
Shihmen
Yuanshan
Ilan
Chungwei
Chunan
Toufen
T'aman Shan 2131
Sanhsing Hsi
Wuchieh
HSINCHU
Neiwan
Paleng
Chingshui
Lotung
Houlung
Sanwan
Chitan
Lanyang
Tungshan
Suao
Kungssuliao
Miaoli
Shihtan
Shihiu
T'uch'ang
Nanao
MIAOLI
Kungkuan
2573
ILAN
T'unghsiao
SHEI-PA
Tungao
Yüanli
Sani
Tahu
Tachoshui
Taan
Tachia
Innan
Houli
Hsüeh Shan
3886
Shei Shan
3740 Nanhuhan Shan
Kuanyin
Ch'ingshui
Yengtun
Cholan
Ushan
2646
Chingshui
Lungchin
Shalu
Tungshih
Tachia Hsi
TAROKO
Wuch'i
T'antzu
Peitun
Hsinche
Hoping
Tayuling
T'ailuko
Hsinch'eng
Shenkang
Hoping
Kukuan
Chilaishu Shan
Homei
T'AICHUNG (Taizhong)
Hsinche
Wujih
Wufeng
3605
Peipu
Changhua
Hsiushui
Kuohsing
Jenai
Hualien (Hualian)
Lukang
Wantou
Shihkangkeng
Taping
Nengkao Shan 3349
Chian
CHANGHUA
Peitou
Yüanlin
Ts'aot'un
Puli
Chishih
Nant'ou
Yüchih
Jenho
Puyen
Chih
NANT'OU
Mingchien
HUALIEN
Shoufeng
Fangyüan
Pitou
Shetou
Shuili
Chosheta Shan 3344
Shuilien
Ernlin
T'enchung
Chieht'ou
Chushan
Tingkan
Wulicheng
Fenglin
Tacheng
Hsilo
Chichi
3344
Chichi
Mailiao
Lunpei
Tzutung
Linnei
Luku
Hsini
Wanjung
Kuangfu
Taihsi
YÜNLIN
Huwei
Touliu
Tafu
Fengpin
Santiaolun
Tuku
Tounan
Luyeh
K'ouhu
Ssuhu
Yüanch'ang
Talin
TAIWAN
Juisui
Kanghsi
Kuk'eng
Meishan
Alishan 2480
Takangkou
Chingpu
Peikang
Minhsiung
Fenchih
3833
Tropic of Cancer
Ch'üntou
P'otzu
Chiai
Chuchi
Jade Mt.
Sanhsien
Changyuan
Tungshih
CHIAI
Fanlu
3952 YÜ SHAN
Choch'i
Yüli
Putai
Chu
Shuishang
Leyeh
1331
Ch'angpin
Peimen
Houpi
Chungpu
Kuan Shan
Antung
Hsüehchia
Yenshui
Paiho
Yunshui
Tapu
Meishan
Wulu
Shajuwan
Chiangchun
Liuying
Hsinying
Tsengwen
Shuili
Fuhsing
Fuli
Sanhsien
Chiali
Matou
Chiku
Shanhua
Shanhu
Taoyuan
Chihshang
Ch'engkung
Chengnan
Antin
Hsinshih
Yuching
TAITUNG
Hsinhua
Chiahsien
Hsinfa
TAI-JIANG
Hsikang
T'AINAN (Tainan)
Jente
Yungk'ang
Kuanmiao
Shanlin
Peinanchu Shan
Kuanshan
Hoping
Chiehting
Hune
Ch'ishan
Luikuei
KAOHSUNG
Lichia
Tungho
Luchu
Meinung
Tulan
Yungan
Kaoshu
Chianapu
T'AITUNG
Kangshan
Yenchao
Likang
Lichia
Chialulantsun
Tzukuan
Chiaot'ou
Yenpu
Santi
Chuju
Peinan
Tsoying
Chiuju
Changchih
Ch'ihpen
KAOHSIUNG (Gaoxiong)
Fengshan
Pingtung (Pingdong)
Lü Tao (Green I.)
KHH
Taliao
Neipu
Lütao
Chienchen
3090 Peitawu Shan
Wanluan
T'aimali
Hsiaokang
Wantan
Ch'aochou
Ch'inlun
Hsinchuang
Hsinpi
Hsiatahsu
Linyuan
Hsinyuan
Linpien
Tungkang
Chiatung
Liuch'iu Yü
Liuch'iu
Fangliao
P'INGTUNG
Tawu
Lan Yü (Orchid I.)
Fangshan
Tajen
Lanyü
Shouchia
Fengkang
Tanlu
Hsühsiatsun
Ch'ulin
Mutanshe
Kangtzu
Ch'ech'eng
Hengch'un
Manchou
Hsiaohungt'ou Hsü
KENTING
Nanwan
Maopi T'ou
Oluanpi
Oluan Pi

P A C I F I C   O C E A N

B a s h i   C h a n n e l

East from Greenwich

COPYRIGHT PHILIP'S

229
2
232

Elevation scale (ft / m):
9000 / 3000
6000 / 2000
4500 / 1500
3000 / 1000
1200 / 400
600 / 200
0
200 / 600
1000 / 3000
2000 / 6000
3000 / 9000
4000 / 12 000
5000 / 15 000
5391

50 0 50 100 150 200 km
1:4 800 000
50 0 50 100 150 miles

219

2 3 4 5 6 7 8

ÖVÖR HANGAY
▲3582
Arts Bogd Uul

DUNDGOVĬ
Ongi Mandalgovĭ
Ulaanjirem Böhöt Har-Ayrag Delgerhet Hongor Chonogol
Ulaan Nuur
Töhöm Buyant-Uhaa (Saynshand) Havirga Dong Ujimqin
SÜHBAATAR
Ovoot

DORNOGOVĬ
Öldziyt Dzüünbayan Ulaan-Uul

GOBI GURVAN SAYKHAN
▲2825 Hanhongor
Gurvan Sayhan Uul
Dalay Dalandzadgad
Noyon Baruunsuu Üydzin Hövsgöl Borhoyn Tal Erenhot Sonid Zuoqi Xilinhot Abagan
Nomgon Ihbulag Ergel Qagan Nur Dalai Nur
Erdenetsogt Galbïn Govĭ Sonid Youqi Habirag Duolun 1931
Bayan Obo Xianghuang Qi Taibus Qi
Darhan Muminggan Huade Shangdu Guyuan Fengning
Daqing Shan Siziwang Qi ▲2174 Qahar Youyi Zhongqi Zhongbei Chongli Chicheng
Wuyuan Dashetai Wulanbulang Guyang Wuchuan Jining Xinghe Wanquan Xuanhua Shangyi
Hanggin Houqi Linhe Ulansuhai Nur Shiguaigou HET **HOHHOT** Zhuozi **ZHANGJIAKOU** Zhangjiabu (Kalgan) Yanqing
▲2364 (Hwang Ho) 2187 **BAOTOU** BAV Bikeqi Horinger Togtoh Qingshuihe Liangcheng Fengzhen Tianzhen Zhuolu Badaling Huairou
Dengkou Urad Qianqi Huang He Tumd Youqi Shahukou Youyu **DATONG** YINYANG SHIKU Qiaocun Xiaowutai Shan Yu Xian **BEIJING (PEKING)**
Jartai Jiudengkou Ordos (Dongsheng) DSN Jungar Qi Qingshui Hequ Pinglu Shanyin Hunyuan Huairen Xiaowutai Guangling Zhuozhou Zhoukoudian Langfang
Minqin Wuhai ▲2149 Wuda Hanggin Qi Uxin Qi Shenmu Fugu Baode Wuzhai Kelan Dai Xian ▲3058 Yuanping Fanshi Laiyuan Jiuxincheng Bazhou
Tengger Shamo Shizuishan Mu Us Shamo (Ordos) Fangshan Shilou Xing Xian Lan Xian Ningwu Wutai Shan ▲2783 Shouyang Fuping Wan Xian **BAODING**
Alxa Zuoqi Pingluo Taole Huinong UYN **YULIN** Jia Xian Jingle Xinzhou Yu Xian Lingqiu Gaoyang Wangdu Daic
Helan Shan ▲3556 INC **YINCHUAN** Hengcheng Hengshan Mizhi Lin Xian Guandi Shan ▲2831 Gujiao **TAIYUAN** Yangquan Pingding SJW Quyang Li Xian Hejian Cangzh
Qingtongxia Yongning Zhongyang Fenyang Wenshui Jinzhong (Yuci) Xiyang Zhao Xian Raoyang Anping Xian X
Lingwu Wuzhong Qingjian Qingxu Taigu Heshun Zuoquan ▲2301 Lingshou **SHIJIAZHUANG** Xinji Shenze Wuji
Yanchi Dingbian Jingbian Ansai Yanchuan Yonghe Xiaoyi Jiexiu Pingyao Yushe Wuxiang **XINGTAI** Shahe Ren Xian Jize Julu Wucheng
Guangwu Jinji Honghu He Hui'anbu Zhidan Yanchang Fenxi Lingshi Xiangyuan Neiqiu Nangong
Yingpanshui Zhongning Baixu Shan Qingjian Fenxi Xi Xian Huozhou Qinyuan She Xian **HANDAN** Feixiang Qinghe Gaot
4843 WALL 1708 Zichang Suide Daning Pu Xian Huo Shan ▲2347 Tunliu Fucheng Weihe Yongnian **LINQING**
Jingtai Huang He Zhongwei **NINGXIA HUIZU ZIZHIQU** Yan'an Luo He Linzhenzhen Hongtong **Changzhi** Linzhou YIN XU Hebi **ANYANG** Liaocheng Dongp
Yongdeng Dalachi Haiyuan Huan Xian Quzi Ganquan Yichuan Linfen Yicheng Gaoping Lingchuan Qingfeng Wenshang Yanzh
LANZHOU Baiyin Jingyuan Heichengzhen Huan Jiang Yijun Luochuan Fu Xian Xiangning Fushan Huixian Linqi Puyang Fan Xian Dongp
▲3670 Dingxi ▲3011 Wating Pingliang Xifeng Heshui Huangling Hejin Houma ▲2322 Jiangxian Qinshui Xinxiang Changyuan **HEZE** Juye Jinxiang
Weiyuan ▲2609 Jingning ▲2942 Migang Shan Longde Jing He Zhenyuan Ning Xian Changwu Xunyi Yijun Jishan Wanrong Wenxi Yangcheng Jiaozuo Mengjin Xingyang Lankao Dingtao Chengwu
Longxi Tongwei Qin'an Lintai Changwu Tongchuan Yao Xian Cheng'an Yuncheng Xia Xian Yuanqu Ji Xian Qinyang Yuanyang Fengqiu
Wushan ▲3100 Li Xian Qingshui Qianyang Lingtai Bin Xian Yijun Jingchuan Yongji Anyi Bo'ai Mianchi **ZHENGZHOU** Xinmi Kaifeng Cao Xian Shan Xian Zhaox
Xihe **TIANSHUI** Fengxiang Qishan Qian Xian Jingyang Sanyuan Dali Mianchi **LUOYANG** Gongyi Dengfeng Ningling **SHANGQIU**
Liangdang Hui Xian Mei Xian Xingping **XIANYANG** XIY Huayin Tongguan LONGMEN SHIKU Yiyang Ruzhou Xuchang Fugou Huiting Zhecheng
Zhuqu Min Xian ▲3767 Taibai Shan Zhouzhi **XI'AN** Weinan Hua Xian ▲2160 Lingbao Luoning Yanshi **YUZHOU** Weichuan Sui Xian Taik
Wudu Chengu Fuping Lantian Luanan Chuankou Lushi Song Xian Ruyang Jia Xian Linying Bozhou HUA
▲3002 Wudu Foping Zhashui Shangzhou Danfeng ▲2192 Taipingzhen SPRING TEMPLE BUDDHA Nanzhao Xiangcheng Xuchang Luyi Boxu Gaoyang
Pingwu ▲5588 Hanzhong Ningqiang Chenggu Xixiang Shiquan Hanyin Shanyang Shangnan Fuhiu Shan Ye Xian **PINGDINGSHAN** Zhoukou Huaiyang Shenqiu Linquan Meng
Wen Xian Yangpingguan Hanyin Zhen'an Ningshan Jingziguan Xichuan Nanzhao Luohe Fangcheng Wuyang Xiping Shangshui Jieshou
Guangyuan Ankang Ziyang Baihe Xunyang Yun Xian Neixiang Zhenping Fangcheng Tanghe Biyang Runan Queshan Linquan FU
NANYANG Zhumadian Wuchan Han Shui Han Shui

ft m
12 000 4000
9000 3000
6000 2000
4500 1500
3000 1000
1200 400
600 200
0 0
200 600
2000 6000
m ft
ZGC

219
220
229

B

C

D

E

F

G

H

9   10   11   12   13   14   15   16

HARBIN   Bin Xian

HEILONGJIANG

HXI   Novokachalinsk

RUSSIA

Lake Khanka

MUDANJIANG

Ussuriysk

CHANGCHUN   JILIN

Vladivostok

Manchuria

Changbai Shan

CHIFENG (Ulanhad)

SHENYANG   FUSHUN

LIAONING

ANSHAN

NORTH KOREA

SEA OF JAPAN (EAST SEA)

P'YŎNGYANG

NAMP'O

BO HAI

Bo Hai Haixia

DALIAN (Lüda)

Korea Bay

SEOUL   SEONGNAM

INCHEON

SUWON

SOUTH KOREA

YANTAI

Weihai

Shandong Bandao

WEIFANG

QINGDAO

DAEJEON

DAEGU   ULSAN

YELLOW SEA (HUANG HAI)

GWANGJU

Chang-won   **BUSAN**

Korea Strait

Tsushima (Japan)

Heuksando (S. Korea)

Soheuksando (S. Korea)

Jeju Haehyop

Jeju-do (S. Korea)

JAPAN

Nagasaki

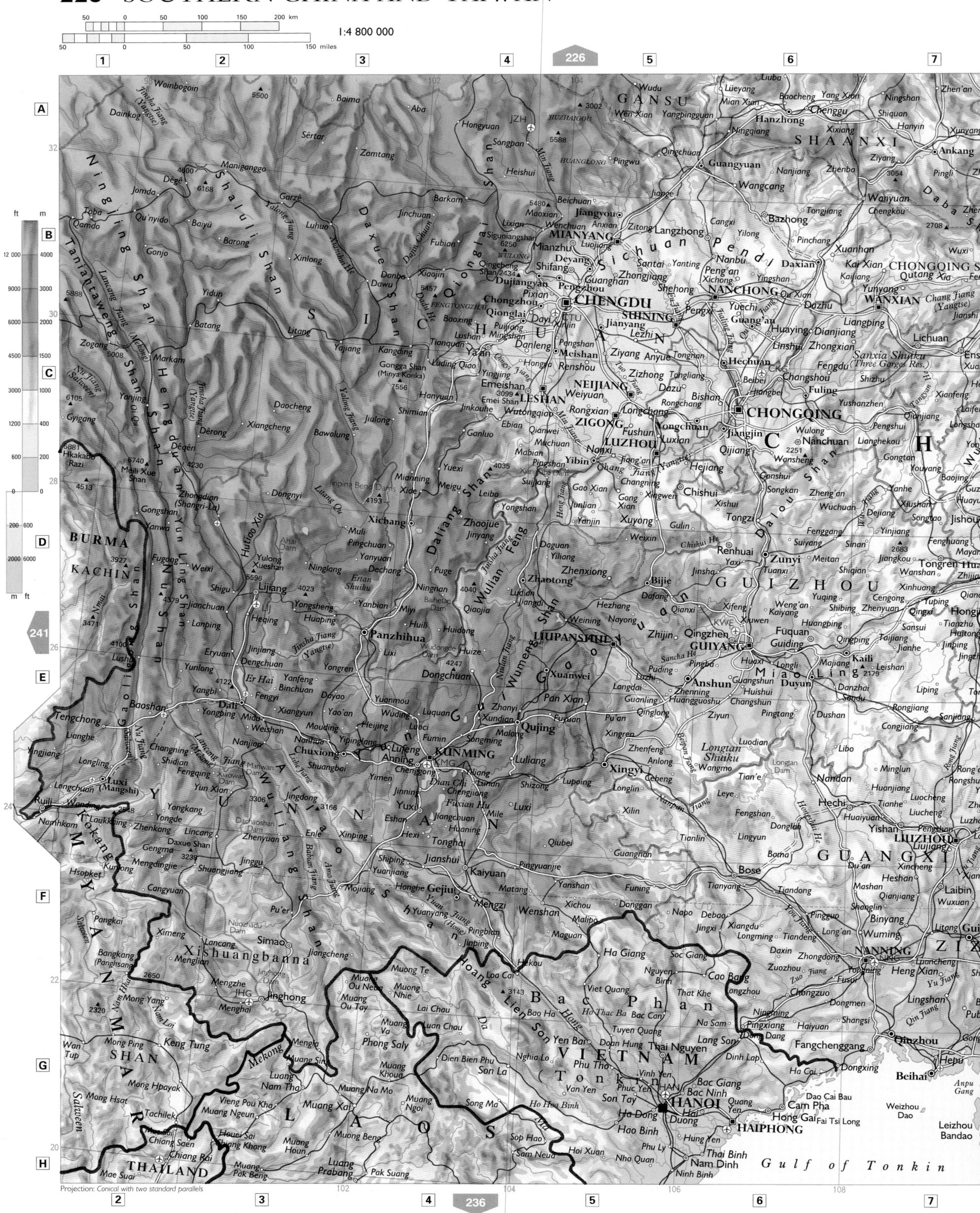

1:4 800 000

Projection: Conical with two standard parallels

Gulf of Tonkin

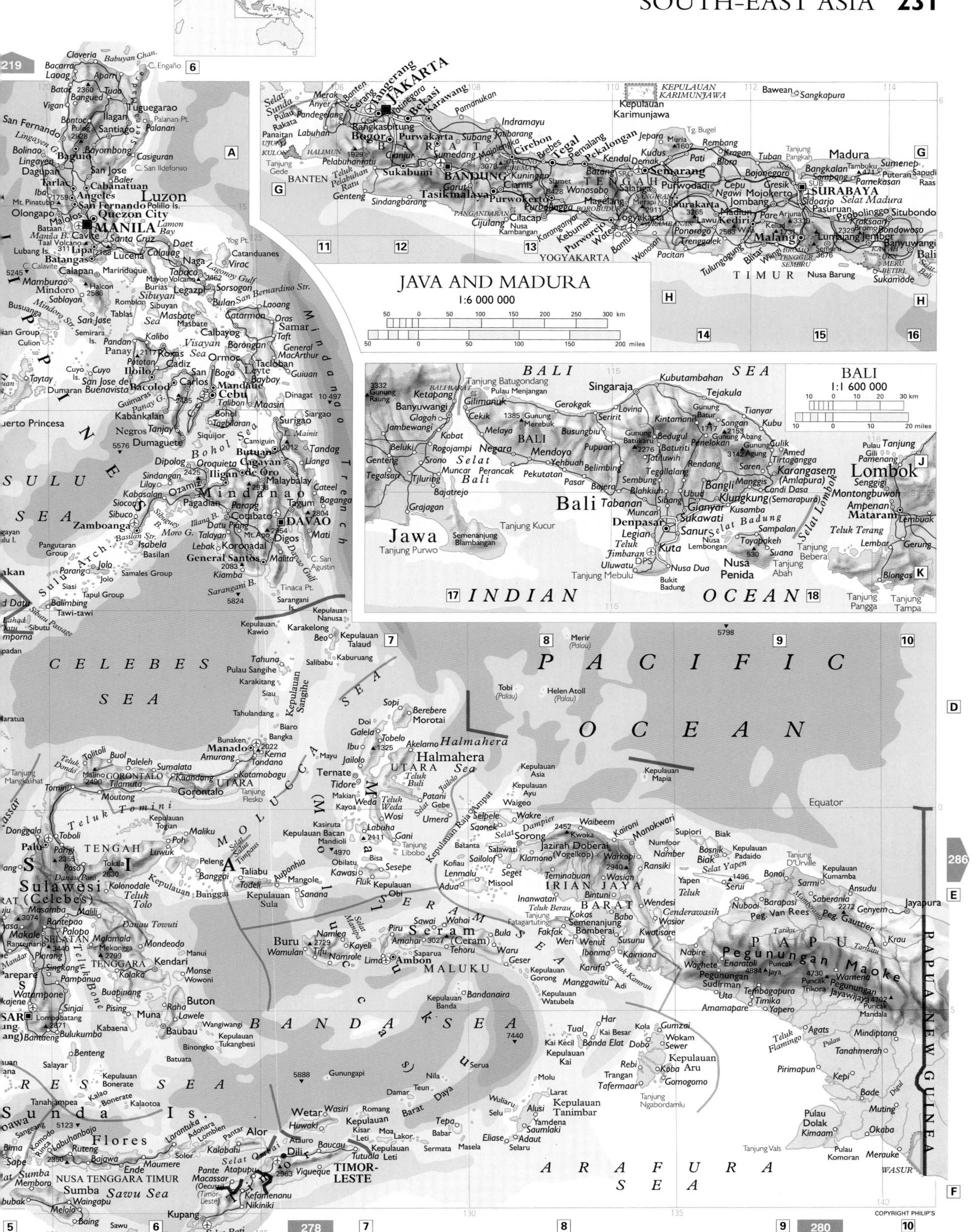

JAVA AND MADURA
1:6 000 000

50 0 50 100 150 200 250 300 km
50 0 50 100 150 200 miles

BALI
1:1 600 000
10 0 10 20 30 km
10 0 10 20 miles

INDIAN OCEAN

COPYRIGHT PHILIP'S

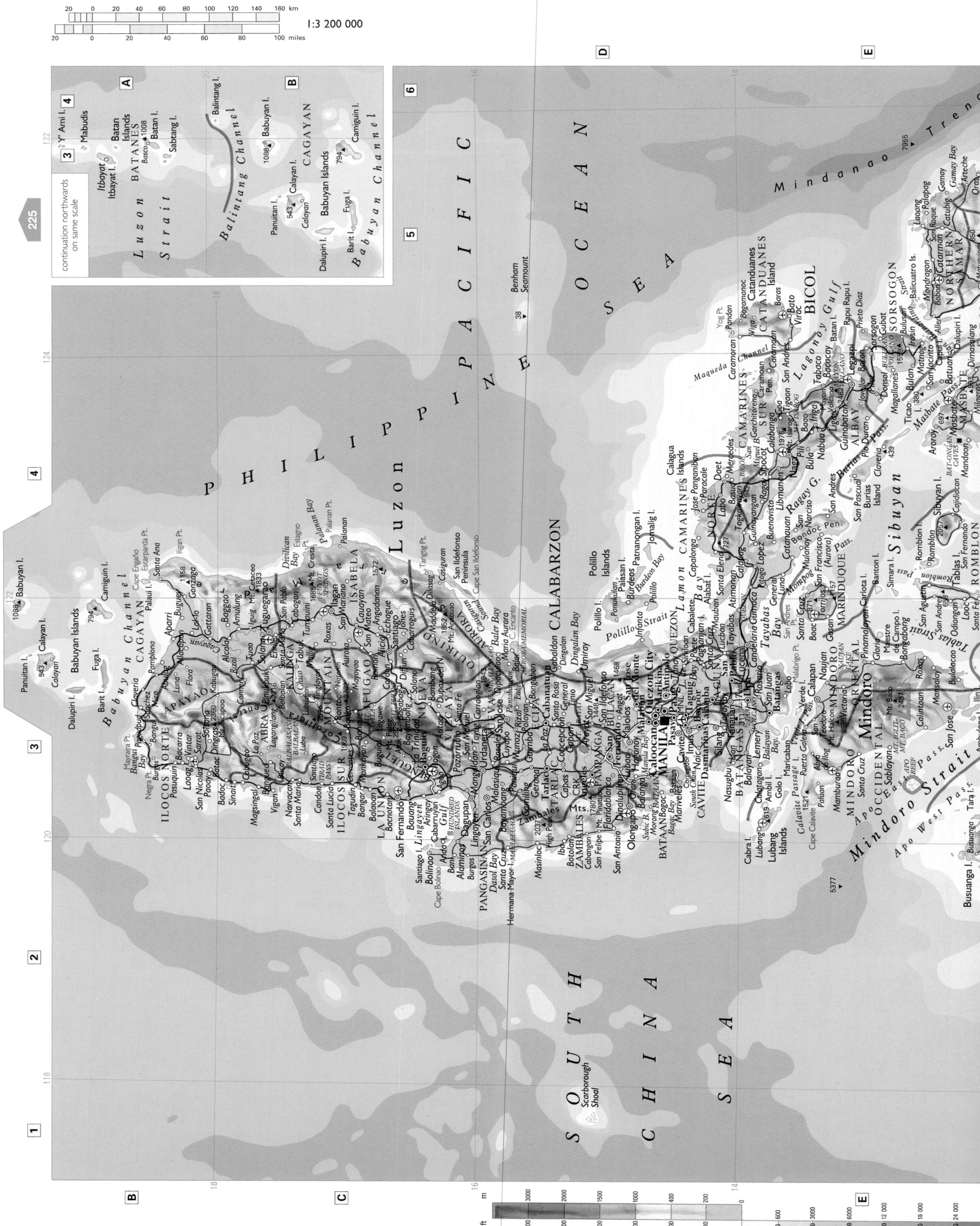

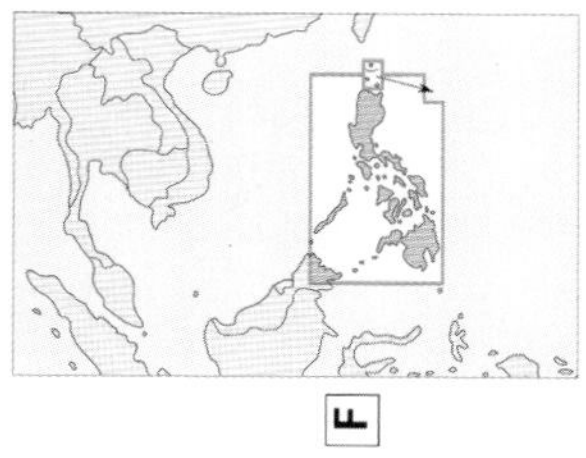

MIMAROPA

CARAGA

EASTERN SAMAR

SAMAR

NORTHERN SAMAR

Leyte Gulf

SOUTHERN LEYTE

SURIGAO DEL NORTE

SURIGAO DEL SUR

DINAGAT ISLANDS

BILIRAN

Camotes Sea

CEBU

BOHOL

Bohol Sea

AGUSAN DEL NORTE

AGUSAN DEL SUR

DAVAO ORIENTAL

DAVAO DE ORO

COMPOSTELA VALLEY

DAVAO DEL NORTE

DAVAO

DAVAO DEL SUR

DAVAO OCCIDENTAL

MISAMIS ORIENTAL

MISAMIS OCCIDENTAL

CAMIGUIN

BUKIDNON

LANAO DEL NORTE

LANAO DEL SUR

NORTH COTABATO

COTABATO

SULTAN KUDARAT

SOUTH COTABATO

SARANGANI

MAGUINDANAO

BANGSAMORO

SOCCSKSARGEN

Moro Gulf

Illana Bay

ZAMBOANGA DEL NORTE

ZAMBOANGA DEL SUR

ZAMBOANGA Peninsula

SIBUGAY

Zamboanga

BASILAN

Isabela

Pilas Group

CELEBES SEA

SULU SEA

NEGROS OCCIDENTAL

NEGROS ORIENTAL

SIQUIJOR

GUIMARAS

ILOILO

CAPIZ

AKLAN

ANTIQUE

Panay

Panay Gulf

Tañon Strait

Guimaras Strait

Visayan Sea

VISAYAS

Bacolod

Iloilo

Roxas

Mindanao

Mindanao Sea

PALAWAN

Puerto Princesa

PUERTO PRINCESA SUBTERRANEAN RIVER

Cuyo West Pass.

Cuyo Islands

Cuyo Group

Cagayan Is.

Calamian Group

Green Island

Tayabas Bay

TUBBATAHA REEFS

Balabac Str.

Palawan Passage

Templar Bank

Cagayan Sulu I.

Bancoran

San Miguel Islands

Keenapusan

SULU Group

Jolo

Jolo Group

Pata I.

Tapul Group

Pangutaran Group

Samales Group

TAWI-TAWI

Tawi-Tawi Island

Tawi-tawi Group

Sibutu Group

Sibutu Island

Sibutu Passage

Turtle Islands

SABAH

MALAYSIA

Sandakan

Borneo

Pulau Miangas (Indonesia)

1:5 600 000

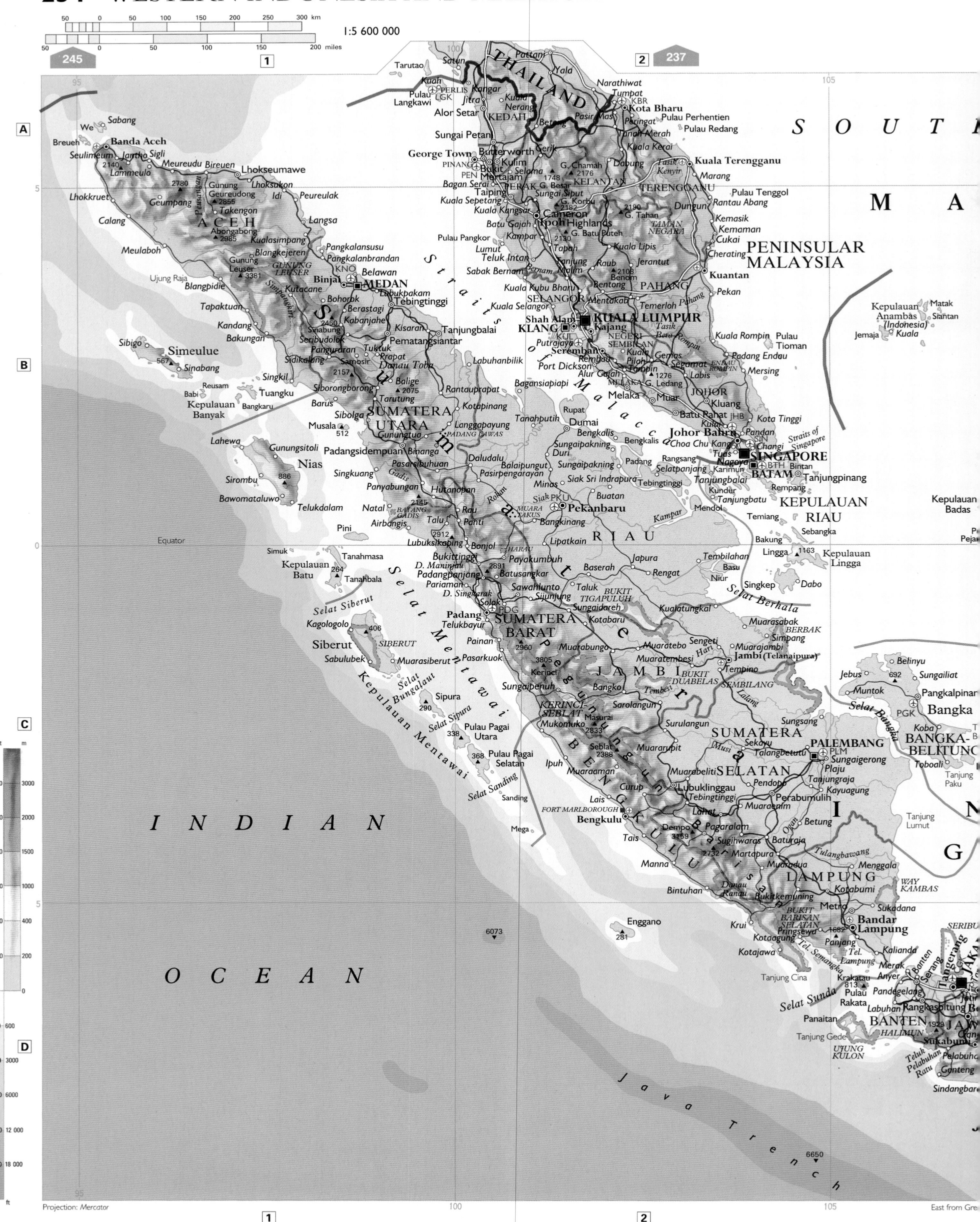

Projection: Mercator

East from Gre

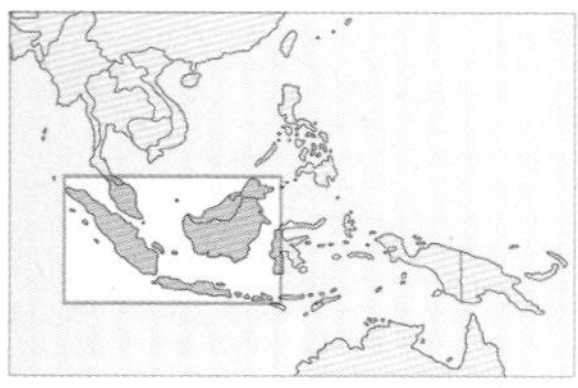

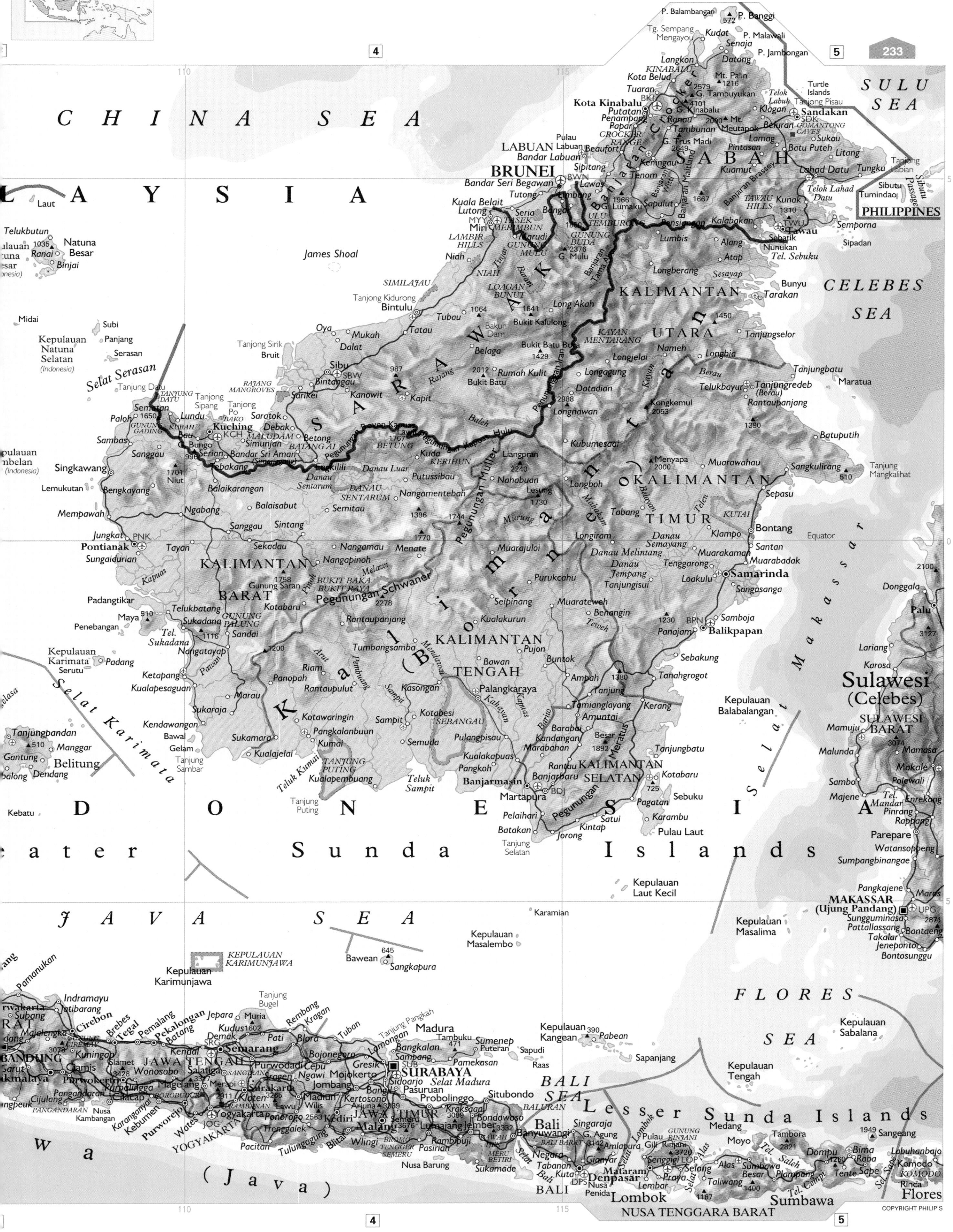

CHINA SEA

SULU SEA

CELEBES SEA

MALAYSIA

BRUNEI

Kota Kinabalu

SABAH

SARAWAK

PHILIPPINES

KALIMANTAN UTARA

KALIMANTAN TIMUR

Kalimantan (Borneo)

KALIMANTAN BARAT

KALIMANTAN TENGAH

KALIMANTAN SELATAN

Pontianak

Samarinda

Balikpapan

Banjarmasin

Sulawesi (Celebes)

SULAWESI BARAT

MAKASSAR (Ujung Pandang)

Selat Makassar

Selat Karimata

JAVA SEA

Greater Sunda Islands

INDONESIA

Java (Jawa)

JAWA TENGAH

JAWA TIMUR

JAWA BARAT

SURABAYA

BANDUNG

Semarang

Surakarta

YOGYAKARTA

Malang

Denpasar

BALI

BALI SEA

FLORES SEA

Lesser Sunda Islands

Lombok

Sumbawa

Flores

NUSA TENGGARA BARAT

Madura

Equator

COPYRIGHT PHILIP'S

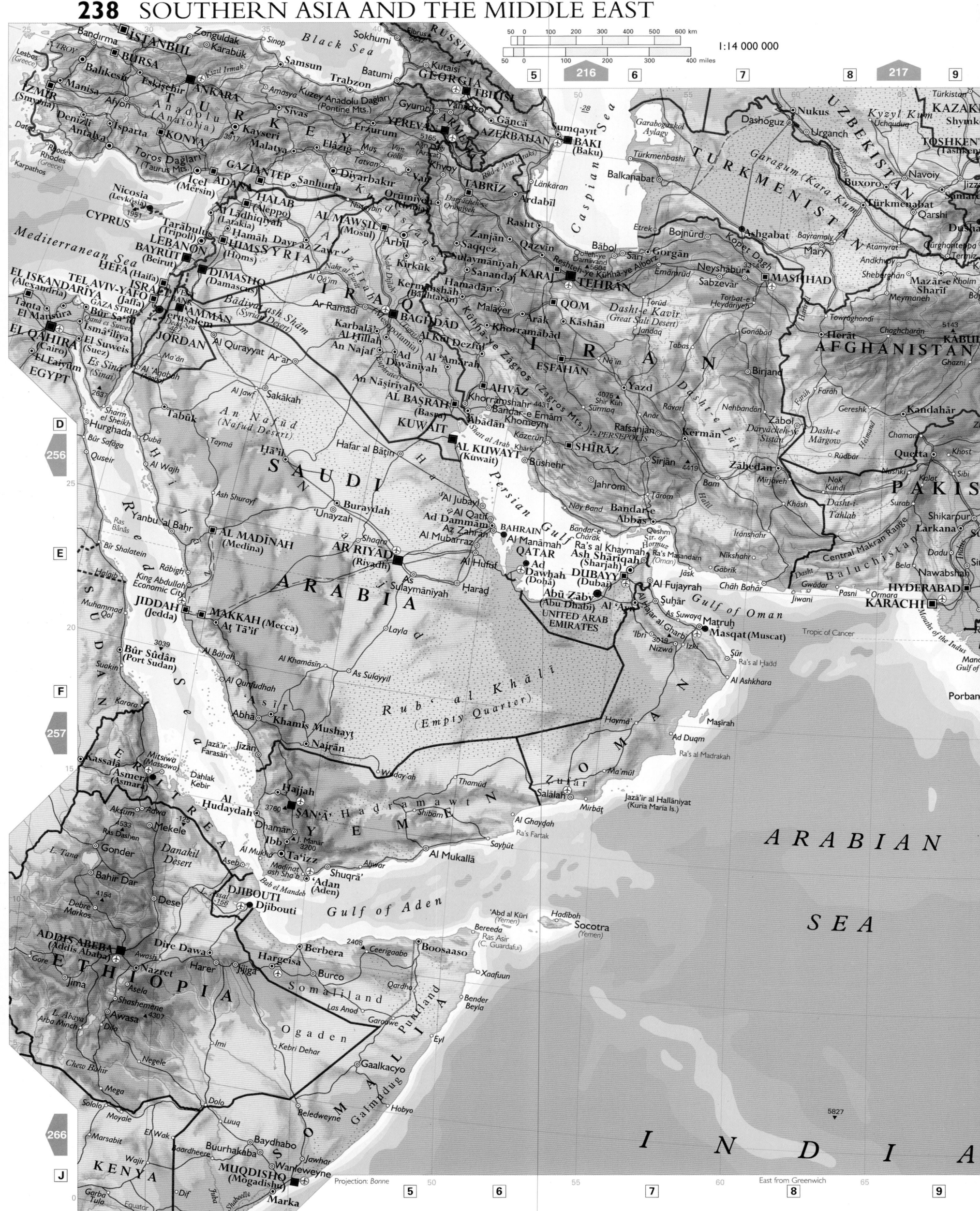

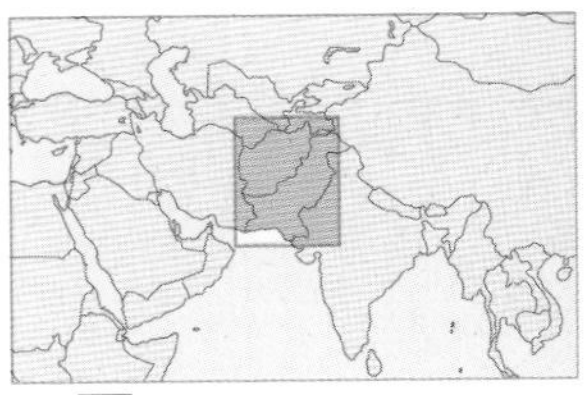

1:5 600 000

50 0 50 100 150 200 250 300 km
50 0 50 100 150 200 miles

1 **2** **217** **3** **4**

Garagum (Kara Kum)

UZBEKISTAN
TAJIKISTAN
Dushanbe
CHINA

TURKMENISTAN

MASHHAD
MHD

IRAN

Mary
Tejen
Dushak
Baýramaly
Yolöten

Beshkent
Qarshi
Shahrisabz
Hisor
Nurek
Kŭlob
Khorugh
Murghob
Bulungkol
Kongur Shan 7719
Taxkorgan

Amudarya (Oxus)
Termiz
Kondoz
Kondoz
Feyzābād
BADAKHSHĀN
Wākhān
Karakoram Ra.

Mazār-e Sharif
BALKH
SAMANGĀN
TAKHĀR
Baghlān
Narin
JAMMU
AND
KASHMIR

FĀRYĀB
SAR-E POL
Band-e Torkestan
Meymaneh
Sayghān
BAMIĀN
Chārikār
PARVĀN
PANJSHIR
Chitral
KHYBER-
PAKHTUNKHWA
Mingora
Gilgit
Skardu

BĀDGHĪS
HERĀT
GHOWR
Herāt
Chaghcharān
DAYKONDĪ
Dasht-i-Nawar
KABUL
VARDAK
NANGARHAR
Jalālābad
PESHAWAR
Attock
ISLAMABAD
SRINAGAR
RAWALPINDI
Jammu

A F G H A N I S T A N

FARĀH
Farāh
ORUZGĀN
Ghaznī
GHAZNĪ
PAKTĪĀ
PAKTĪKĀ
KHOWST
Waziristan
Mianwali
Bannu
Gujranwala
FAISALABAD
LAHORE
AMRITSAR

HELMAND
Kandahār
Lashkar Gāh
KANDAHĀR
Chaman
Khojak Pass
Toba Kakar
Hindu Bagh
Quetta
MULTAN
PUNJAB
Bahawalpur
Bikaner

NIMRŪZ
Zaranj
Rīgestān
Dera Ismail Khan
Sukkur
Khairpur
Thar Desert
INDIA
RAJASTHAN
JODHPUR
Ajmer

Sistan
IRAN
Zāhedān
Dasht-i
Ras Koh
B A L U C H I S T Ā N
Kalat
Khuzdar
Kirthar Range
Larkana
Shikarpur
Jacobabad
SIND
Nawabshah

M a k r a n
Central Makran Range
Panjgur
Turbat
Makran Coast Range
Gwadar
Karachi
HYDERABAD
Mirpur Khas
Rann of Kachchh
GUJARAT
Bhuj

A R A B I A N
S E A

Tropic of Cancer

Mouths of the Indus

Projection: Conical with two standard parallels   East from Greenwich   COPYRIGHT PHILIP'S

ft m
18 000 6000
12 000 4000
9000 3000
6000 2000
4500 1500
3000 1000
1200 400
600 200
0 0
200 600
1000 3000
2000 6000
3000 9000
m ft

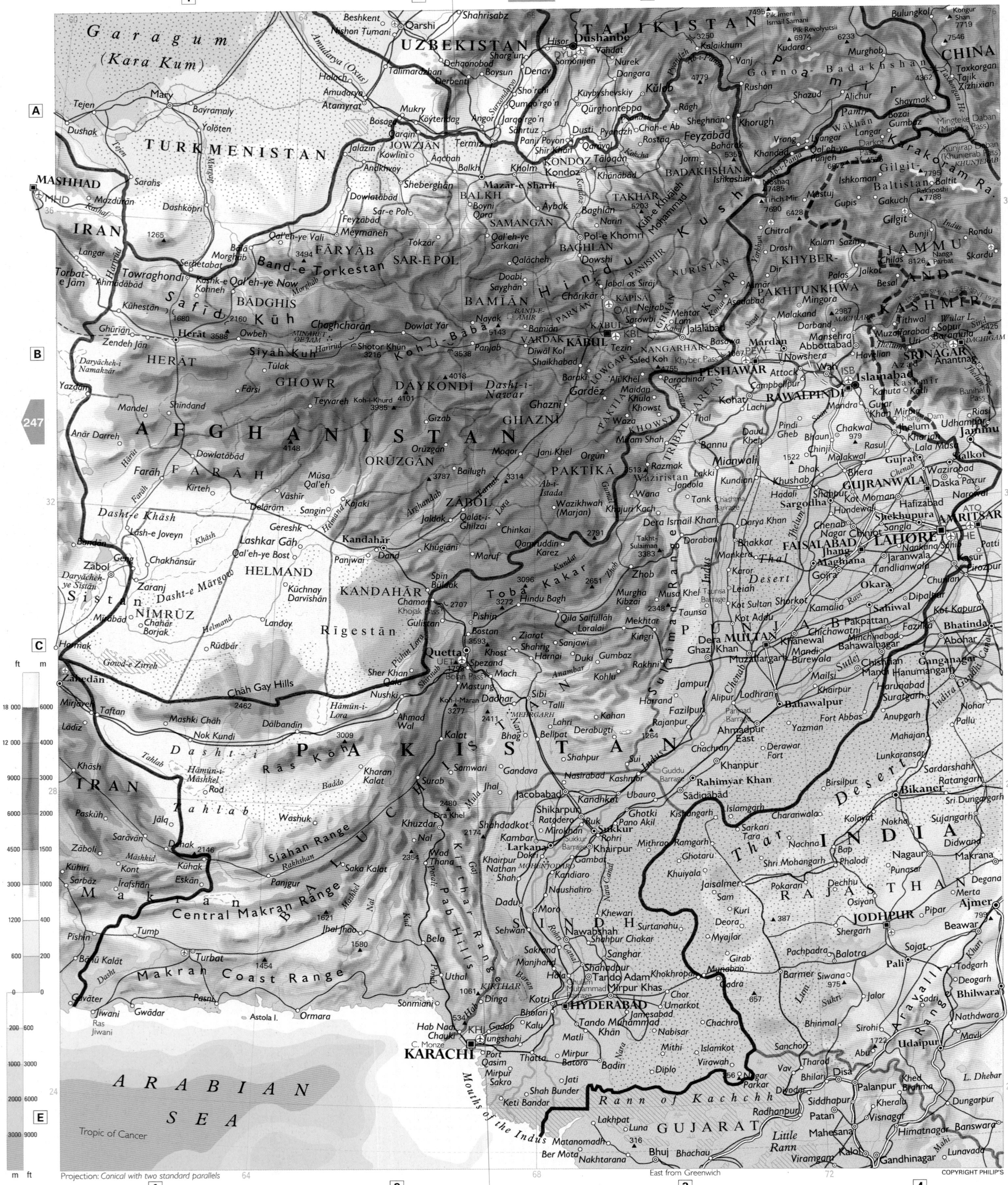

1:4 800 000

50 0 50 100 150 200 km
50 0 50 100 150 miles

CHINA

XIZANG ZIZHIQU (TIBET)

Yarlung Zangbo Jiang (Brahmaputra)

INDIA

ARUNACHAL PRADESH

Mishmi Hills

Abor Hills

NEPAL

SIKKIM

BHUTAN

ASSAM

NAGALAND

KACHIN

MANIPUR

MEGHALAYA

Khasi Hills

Garo Hills

Shillong

GUWAHATI

Tezpur

Dibrugarh

Tinsukia

YUNNAN

CHINA

SYLHET

BANGLADESH

DHAKA

DHAKA

TRIPURA

Agartala

MIZORAM

Aizawl

Tropic of Cancer

KHULNA

KOLKATA

Barisal

CHITTAGONG

Sundarbans

Mouths of the Ganges

The Sandheads

SAGAING

MANDALAY

MANDALAY

Bhamo

Lashio

SHAN

MYANMAR

(BURMA)

RAKHINE

Sittwe (Akyab)

Cox's Bazar

CHIN

MAGWAY

NAYPYIDAW

KAYAH

BAY

OF

BENGAL

Arakan Coast

Ramree I.

Cheduba I.

BAGO

THAILAND

Chiang Mai

KAYIN

MON

YANGON (RANGOON)

AYEYAWADY

Pathein (Bassein)

Bago (Pegu)

Mawlamyine

Dawna Range

INDIAN

OCEAN

G. of Mottama

Mouths of the Irrawaddy

East from Greenwich

Projection: Conical with two standard parallels

ft m
18 000 6000
12 000 4000
9000 3000
6000 2000
4500 1500
3000 1000
1200 400
600 200
0 0
600 200
3000 1000
6000 2000
9000 3000
m ft

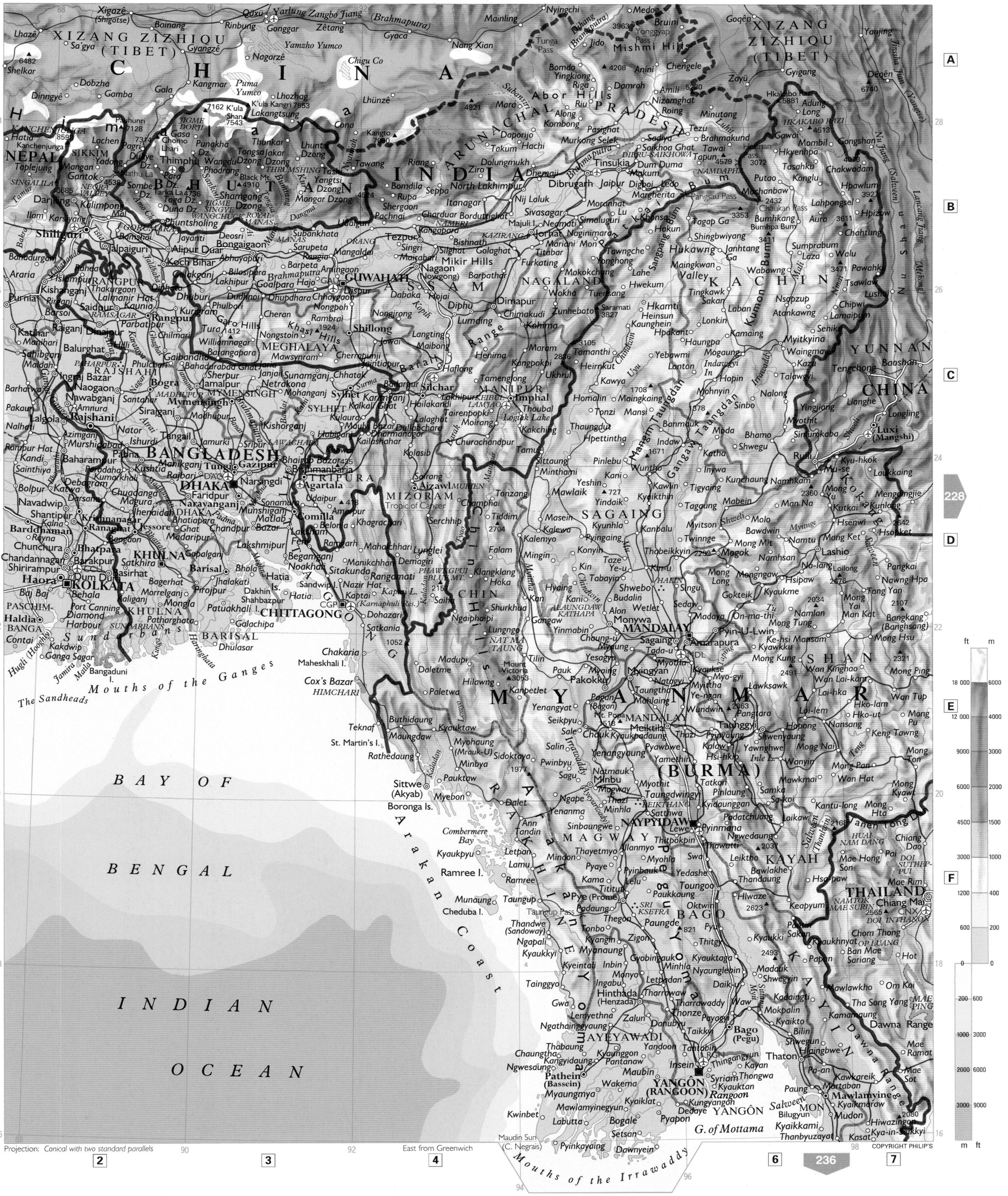

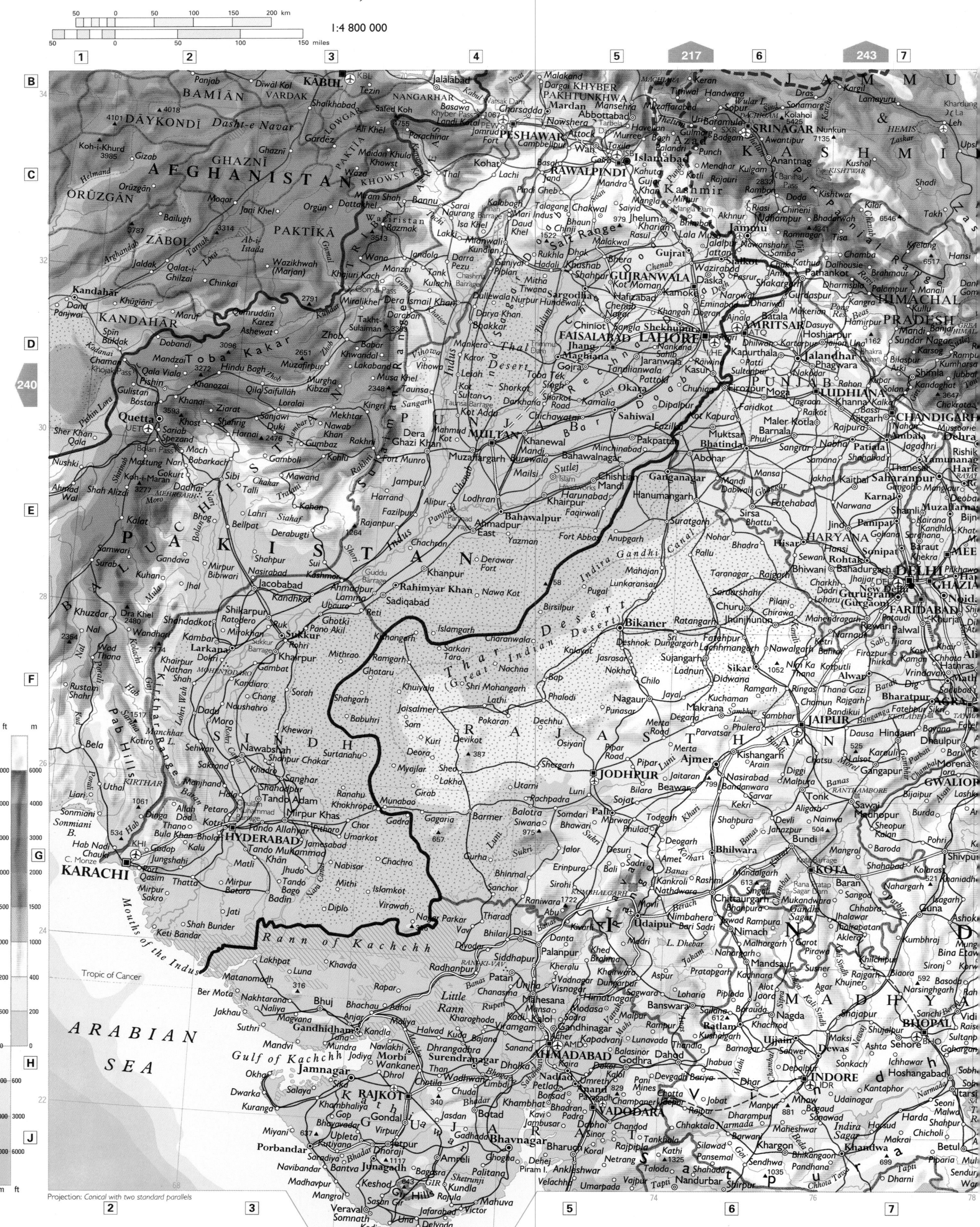

1:4 800 000

Projection: Conical with two standard parallels

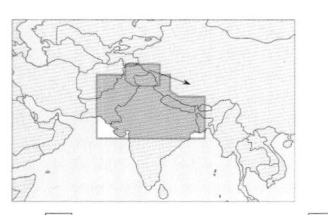

JAMMU AND KASHMIR
on same scale

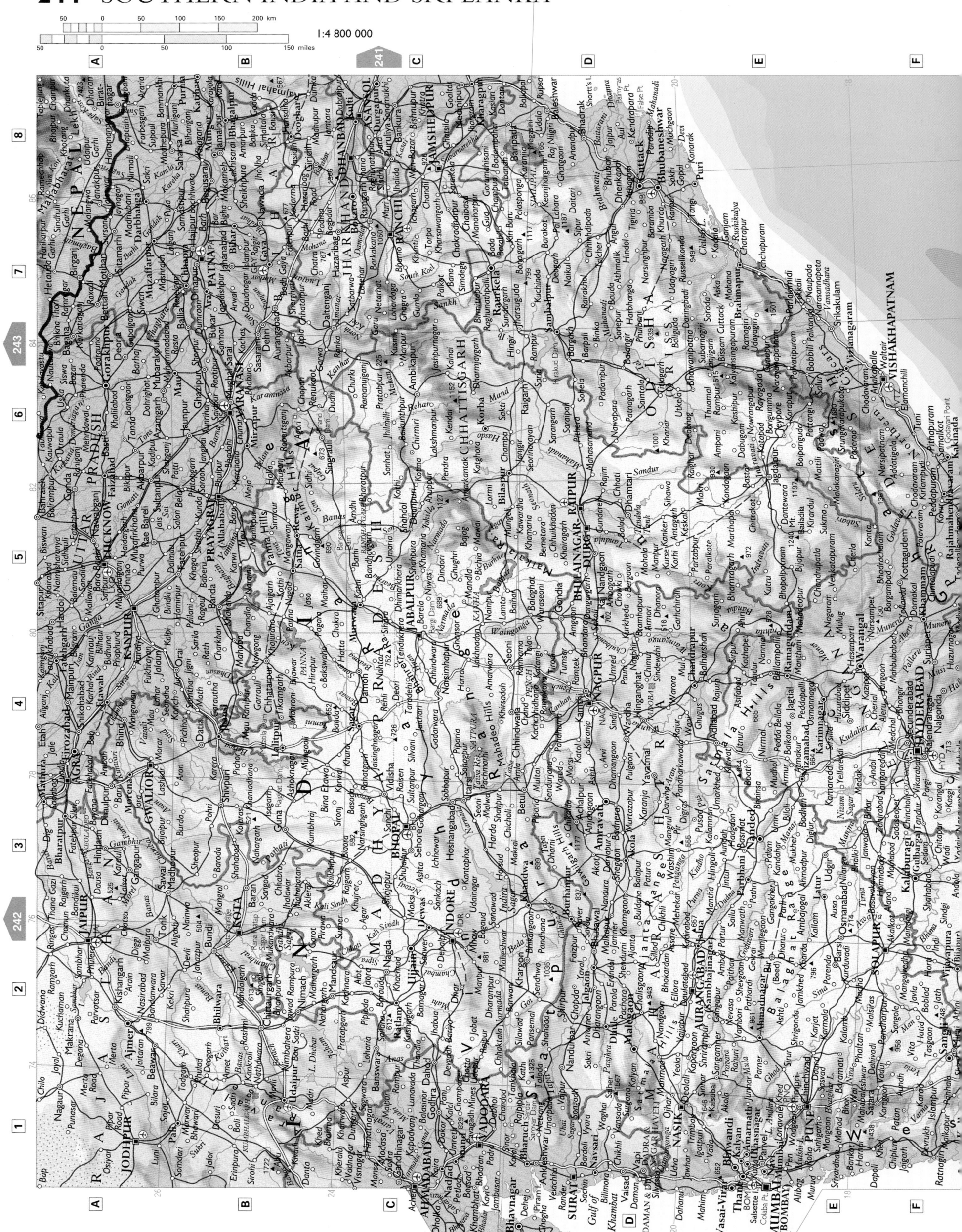

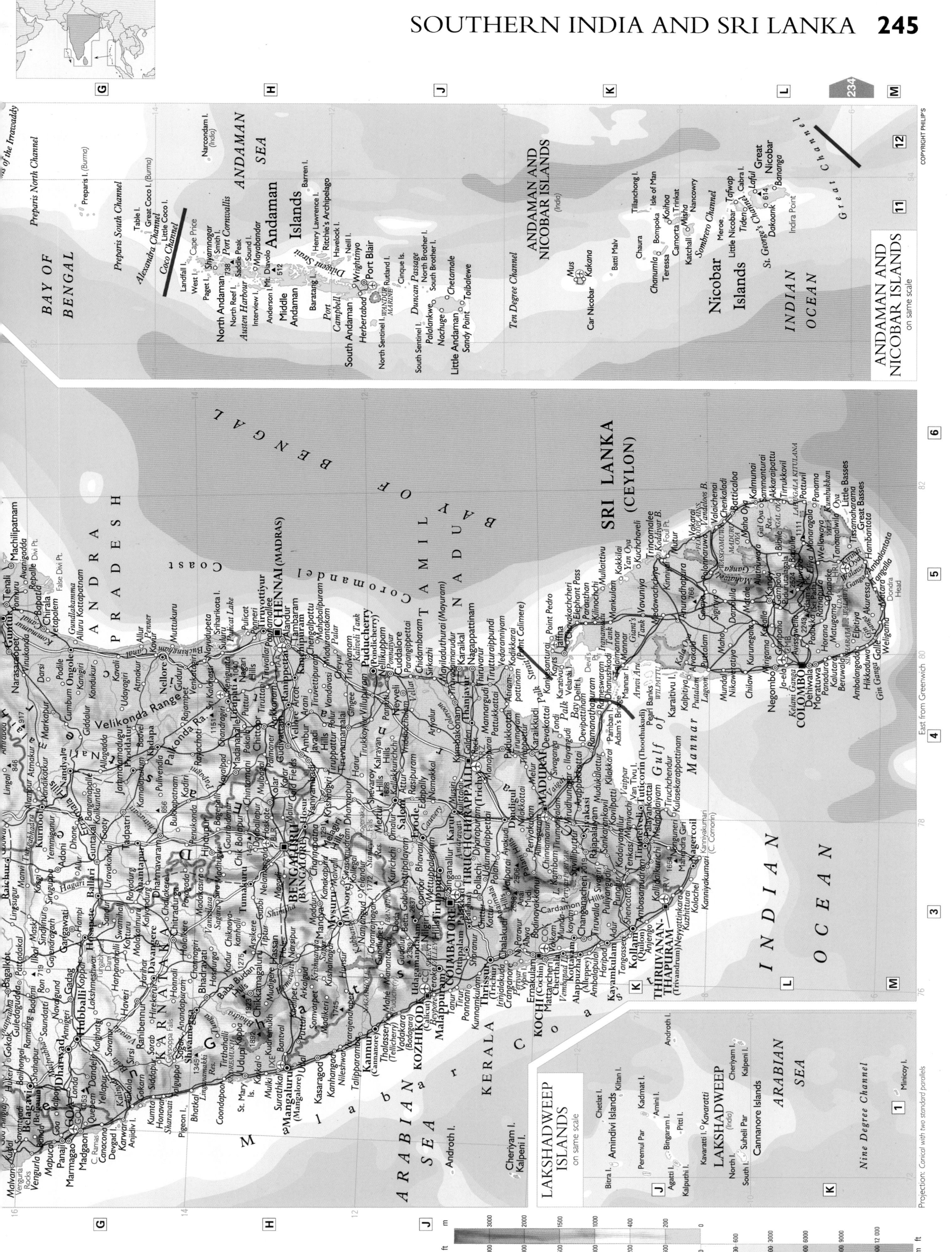

50 0 50 100 150 200 250 300 km

1:5 600 000

50 0 50 100 150 200 miles

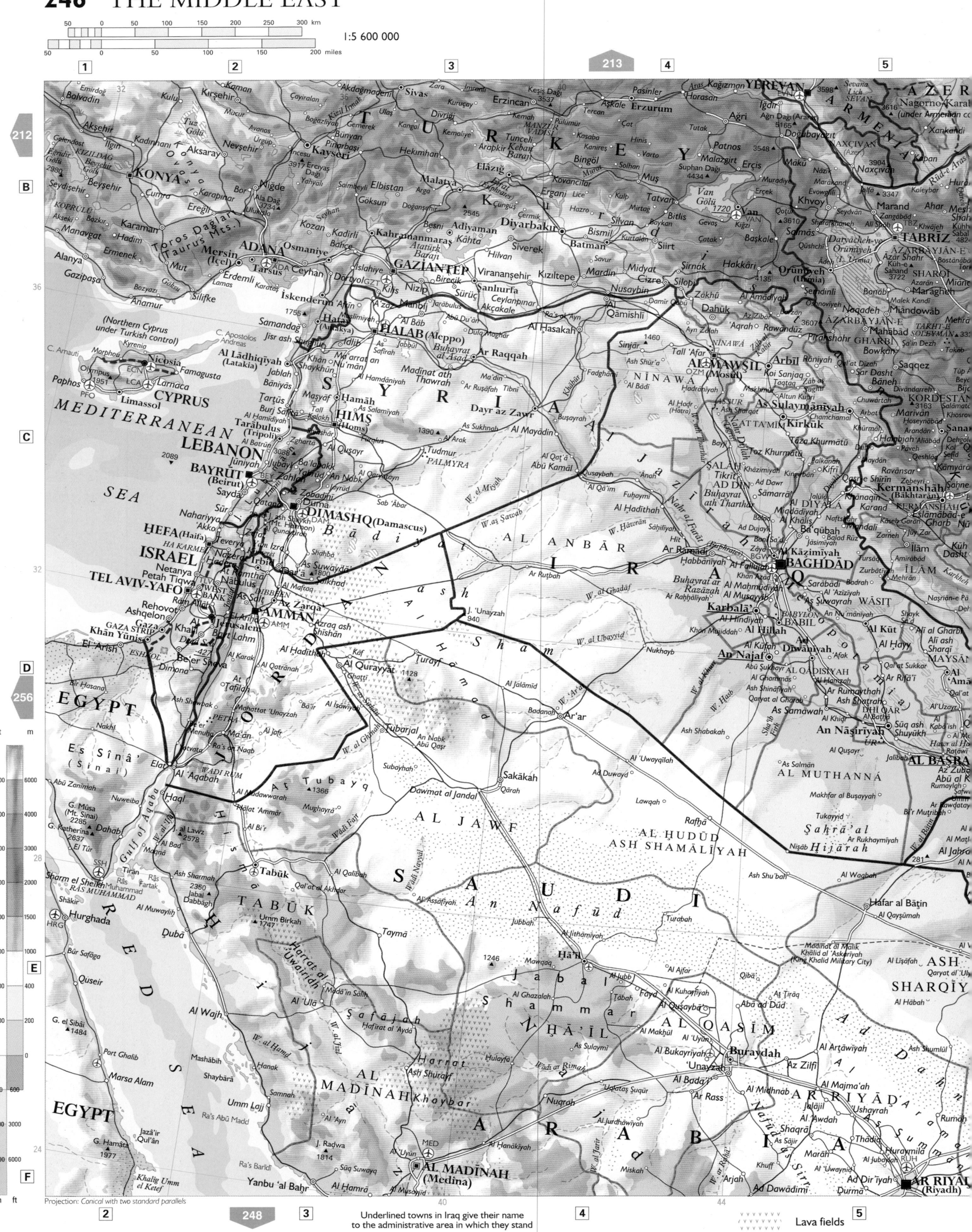

ft   m

18 000 6000

12 000 4000

9000 3000

6000 2000

4500 1500

3000 1000

1200 400

600 200

0 0

200 600

1000 3000

2000 6000

m ft

Projection: Conical with two standard parallels

Underlined towns in Iraq give their name
to the administrative area in which they stand

Lava fields

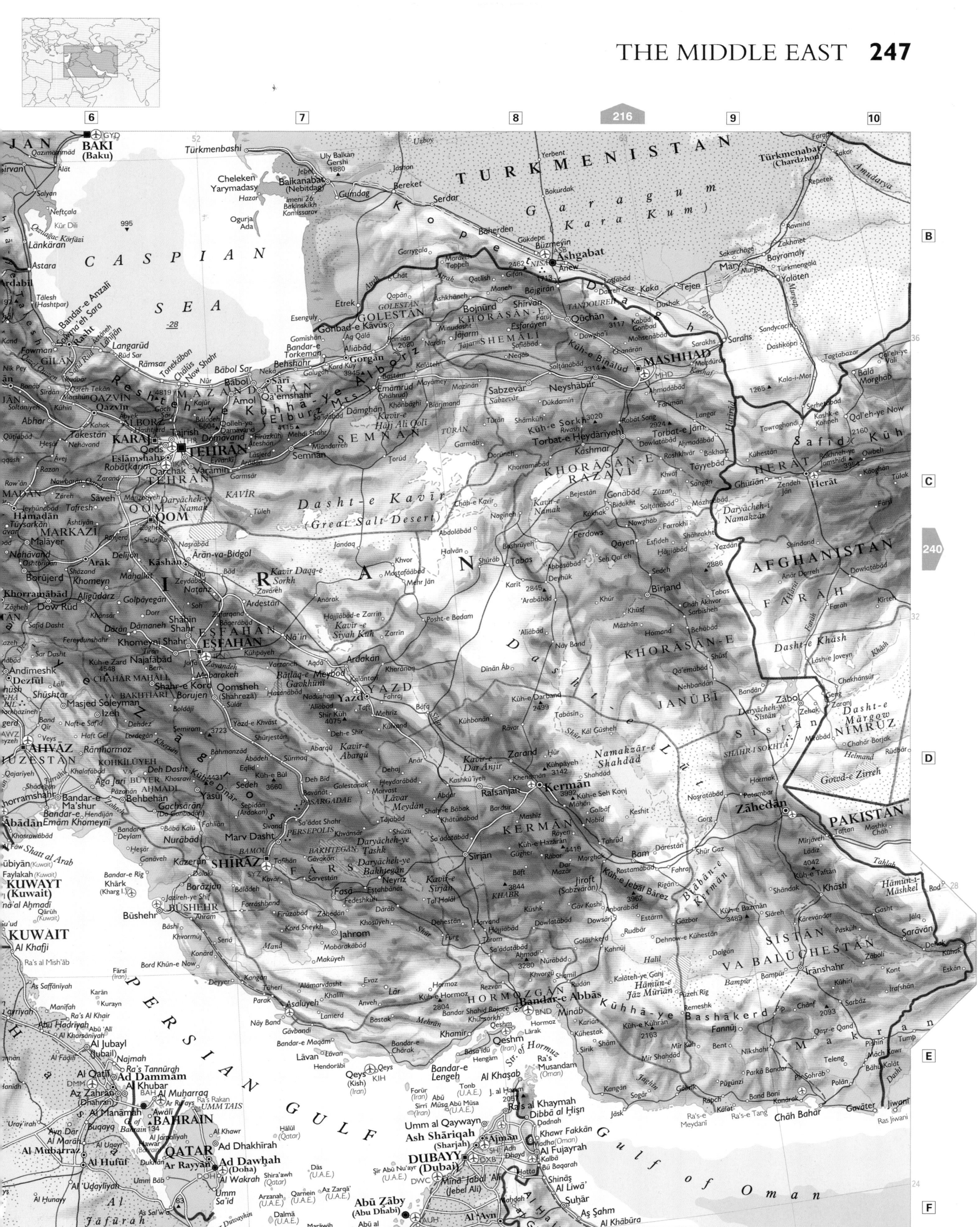

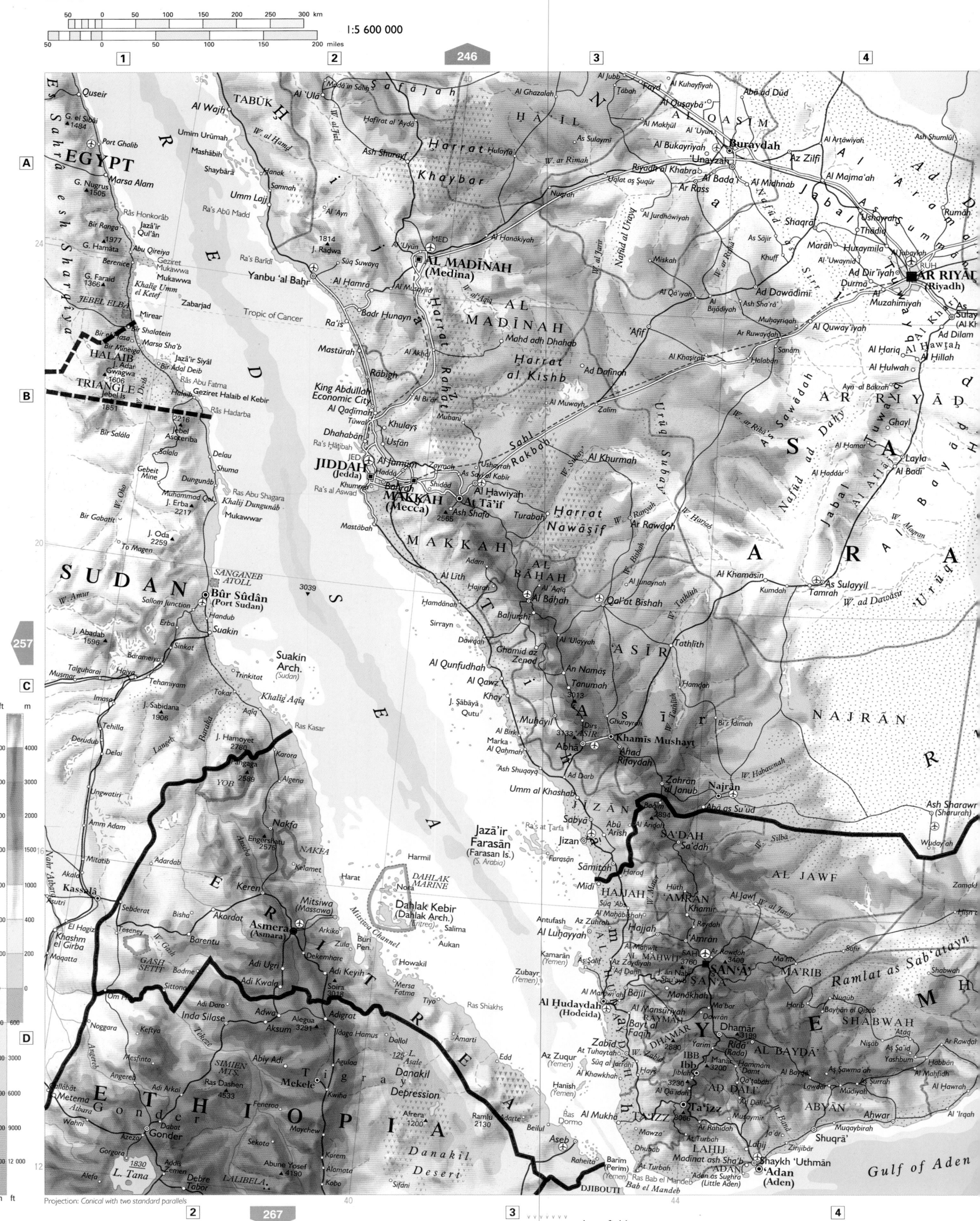

1:5 600 000

Projection: Conical with two standard parallels

Lava fields

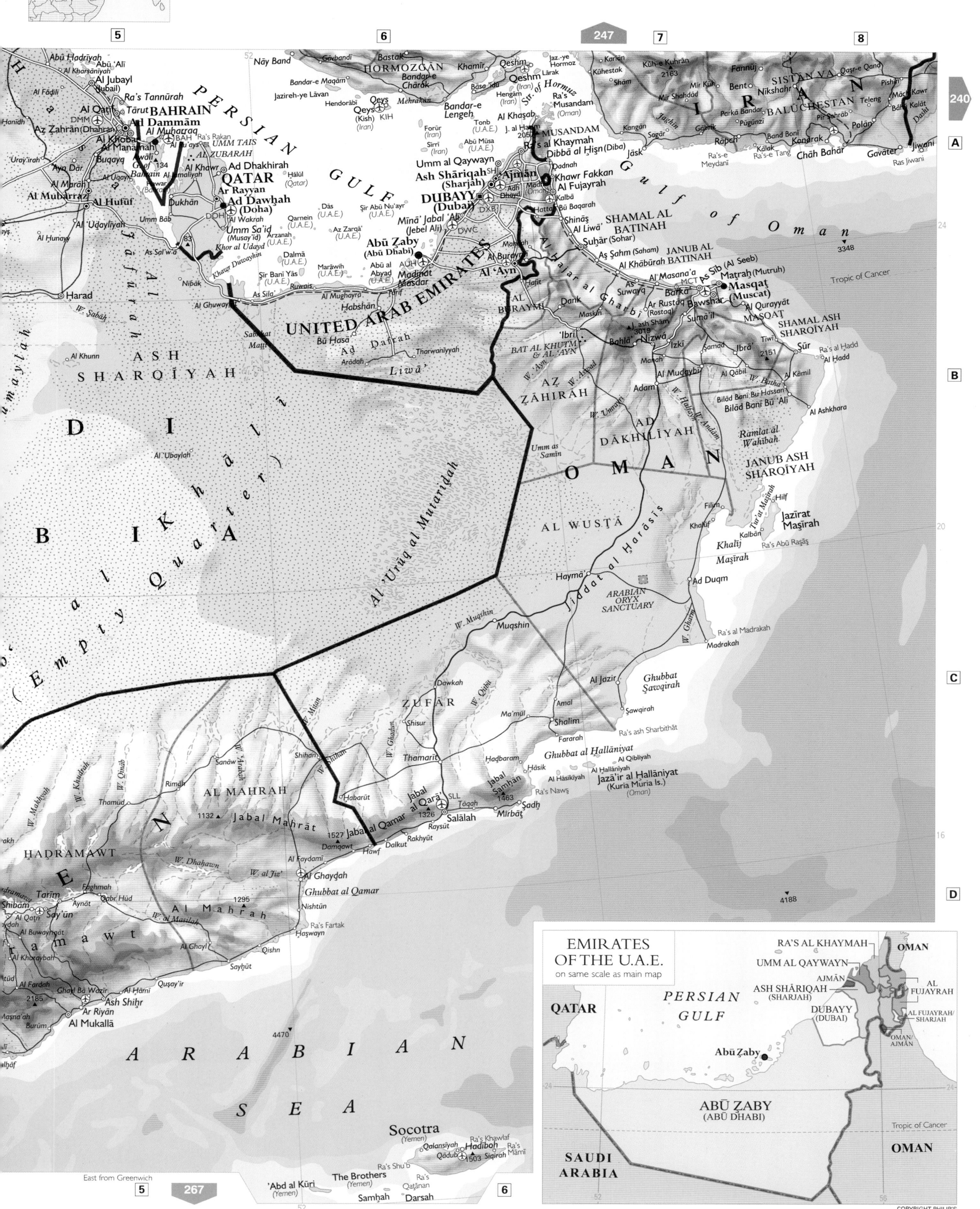

5   6   7   8

A

B

C

D

PERSIAN GULF

Nāy Band
Gavbandi
Bastak
HORMOZGĀN
Khamīr
Qeshm
Bandar-e Chārak
Jaz-ye Hormoz
Kārīn
Kūh-e Kuhrān
2163
Fannūj
SĪSTĀN VA
Qasr-e Qand
Pishīn
Mūch
Kalāt
Bāht
Kawr
Teleng

Abū Hadrīyah
Abū 'Alī
Al Kharsānīyah
Al Jubayl
Al Fāḍilī
Ra's Tannūrah
DMM
Al Khobar
Az Zahrān (Dhahran)
Al Dammām
Al Muharraq
BAH
Ra's Rakan
(Qatar)
UMM TAIS
AL ZUBARAH
BAHRAIN
Al Manāmah
QATAR
Ad Dhakhirah
Al Khawr
Ar Rayyān
Dukhān
Ad Dawḥah (Doha)
DOH
Al Wakrah
Umm Sa'id (Musay'id)
Khor al Udayd

Bandar-e Maqām
Jazireh-ye Lāvān
Hendorābī
Qeys
Qeys (Kish)
KIH
Mehrān
Forūr (Iran)
Sirrī (Iran)
Dās (U.A.E.)
Qarnein (U.A.E.)
Az Zarqā' (U.A.E.)
Arzanah (U.A.E.)
Dalmā (U.A.E.)
Sīr Abū Nu'ayr (U.A.E.)
Sīr Banī Yās (U.A.E.)
Marāwih (U.A.E.)

Bandar-e Lengeh
Tonb (U.A.E.)
Abū Mūsā (U.A.E.)
Al Khasab
Ra's Musandam (Oman)
J. al Ḥarīm 2050
MUSANDAM
Ra's al Khaymah
Dibbā al Ḥiṣn (Diba)
Dadnah
Khawr Fakkān
Al Fujayrah
Kalbā

STR. of HORMUZ
Jāsk
Gulf of Oman
Ra's-e Meydānī
Ra's-e Tang
Chāh Bahār
Gavāter
Ras Jiwani
Jiwani

Umm al Qaywayn
Ash Shāriqah (Sharjah)
Ajmān
DUBAYY (Dubai)
DXB
Mīnā' Jabal 'Ali (Jebel Ali)
DWC
Abū Ẓaby (Abu Dhabi)
AUH
Abū al Abyad (U.A.E.)
Madīnat Masdar
Ruwais

UNITED ARAB EMIRATES

Al 'Ayn
Al Burayqī
AL BURAYMĪ
Ḥafīt
Ḥabshān
Bū Ḥasā
Ad Dafrah
Liwā'
Tharwanīyah
Arādah
Sabkhat Maṭṭī
As Sila'
Al Ghuwayfāt
Al Mughayrā'

Shināṣ
Al Liwā'
Suḥār (Sohar)
Aṣ Ṣahm (Saham)
SHAMAL AL BATINAH
JANUB AL BATINAH
Al Khābūrah
Suwayq
Al Maṣna'a
As Sīb (Al Seeb)
Barkā
MCT
Ra's Sīb
Matraḥ (Mutruh)
Masqaṭ (Muscat)
Baushar
Ar Rustāq (Rostaq)
3348
Tropic of Cancer
24

Harad
Al Khunn
Al 'Ubaylah

ASH SHARQĪYAH

AR RUB' AL KHĀLĪ (Empty Quarter)

Al 'Urūq al Mutaridah

BAT AL KHUTM & AL 'AYN
'Ibrī
Maskīn
Ash Shām 3019
Bahlā
Nizwā
Izkī
Samad
Adam
Al Mudaybī
Ibrā 2151
Al Qābil
Sūr
Ra's al Ḥadd
Al Ḥadd
Al Kāmil
W. Baṭha
Bilād Banī Bū Ḥassan
Bilād Banī Bū 'Ali
Al Ashkhara

AZ ZĀHIRAH
AD DĀKHILĪYAH
W. 'Anḍam
W. Ḥalfayn
W. Andām
W. Umarrī
Umm as Samīm

MASQAT
SHAMAL ASH SHARQĪYAH
Tiwī
Ra's al Madrakah

OMAN

AL WUSTĀ
Haymā'
ARABIAN ORYX SANCTUARY
Ad Duqm
JANUB ASH SHARQĪYAH
Ramlat al Wahībah
Filim
Khalūf
Ṭur 'at Maṣīrah
Ḥilf
Kalbān
Jazirat Maṣīrah
Maṣīrah
Khalīj Maṣīrah
Ra's Abū Rasās

W. Muqshin
Muqshin
Dawkah
W. Qitbīt
Shisur

ZUFĀR
Ma'mūl
Ḥaṣīk
Thamarīt
Ḥaḍbaram
Jabal Samḥan 1463
Raysūt
Salālah
Mirbāṭ
Ṣadḥ
Ṭāqah

Ma'mūl
Shalim
Sawqirah
Al Jazir
Ghubbat Ṣawqirah
Ra's ash Sharbithāt
Al Qibliyah
Al Ḥallānīyah
Jazā'ir al Ḥallānīyah (Kuria Muria Is.) (Oman)
Ghubbat al Ḥallāniyat
Al Ḥāsikīyah
Ra's Nawṣ
4188

AL MAHRAH
Sanāw
'Arabah
Shiḥan
Shaḥan
Ḥabarūt
Jabal al Qarā 1326
Jabal Mahrāt
1132
1527
Jabal Qamar
Damqawt
Hawf
Dalkut
Rakhyūt

YEMEN
HADRAMAWT
Thamūd
Rimāh
Tarīm
Shibām
Say'ūn
Al Qatn
Ghayl Bā Wazīr
2185
Ash Shiḥr
Ar Riyān
Al Mukallā
Qabr Hūd
Al Buwayqāt
Foghmah
Aynāt
1295
W. al Jīz
AL MAHRAH
Nishtūn
Al Ghaydah
Ghubbat al Qamar
W. Masīlah
Al Ghayl
Qishn
Sayḥūt
Qusay'ir
Burūm

ARABIAN SEA

Socotra (Yemen)
Qalansīyah
Hadibōh
Siqirah
1503
Ra's Khawlaf
Ra's Mūmī
'Abd al Kūri (Yemen)
The Brothers (Yemen)
Ra's Shu'b
Qaṭanan (Yemen)
Samhah
Darsah

East from Greenwich
5
267
52
6

20

16

EMIRATES OF THE U.A.E.
on same scale as main map

QATAR

PERSIAN GULF

RA'S AL KHAYMAH
UMM AL QAYWAYN
ASH SHĀRIQAH (SHARJAH)
AJMĀN
DUBAYY (DUBAI)
OMAN
AL FUJAYRAH
AL FUJAYRAH/ SHARJAH
OMAN/ AJMĀN

Abū Ẓaby

ABŪ ẒABY (ABŪ DHABI)

SAUDI ARABIA

Tropic of Cancer

OMAN

10 0 10 20 30 40 50 60 70 80 90 km

1:2 000 000

10 0 10 20 30 40 50 60 miles

A **B** **C** 246 **D** **E**

MEDITERRANEAN SEA

CYPRUS

(Northern Cyprus under Turkish control)

Nicosia (Lefkosia)

Limassol

Larnaca

Famagusta (Ammochostos)

Paphos

Morphou Bay

Troodos 1951

Akrotiri Bay

Episkopi Bay

Famagusta Bay

Larnaca Bay

C. Greco

C. Apostolos Andreas

SYRIA

DIMASHQ (Damascus)

HALAB (Aleppo)

HIMS

HAMAH

Hamah

Tartus

Al Ladhiqiyah (Latakia)

Tarabulus (Tripoli)

LEBANON

BAYRUT (Beirut)

Sayda (Sidon)

Sur (Tyre)

Nahariyya

'Akko (Acre)

Hefa (Haifa)

TURKEY

GAZIANTEP

ADANA

Tarsus

Mersin (Içel)

Antalya

Alanya

Iskenderun

Antalya Körfezi

Iskenderun Körfezi

TAURUS Mts

KARAMAN

KONYA

ANTALYA

HATAY

As Suwayda

JABAL AD DURUZ

GOLAN

193

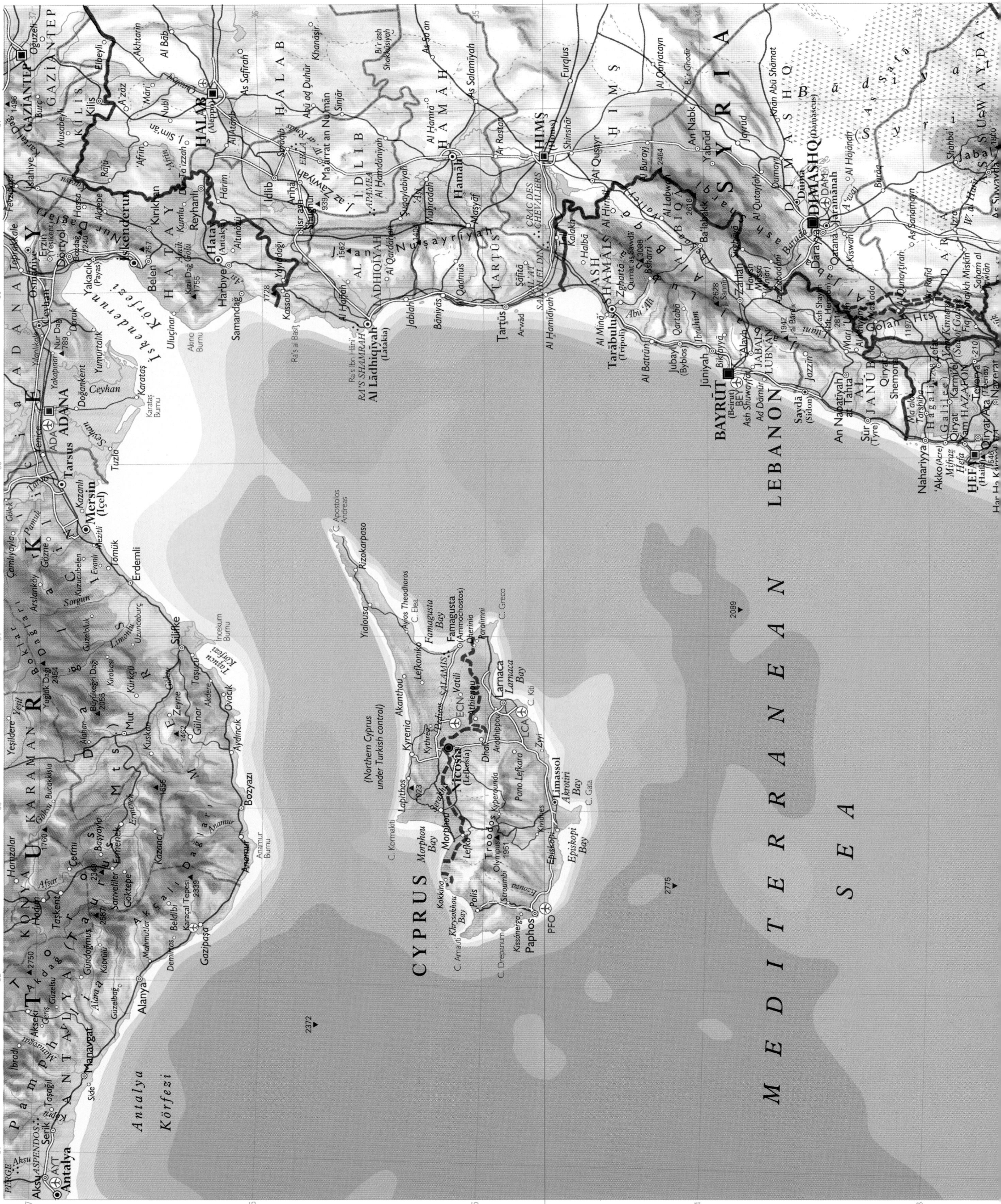

AFRICA

1:33 600 000

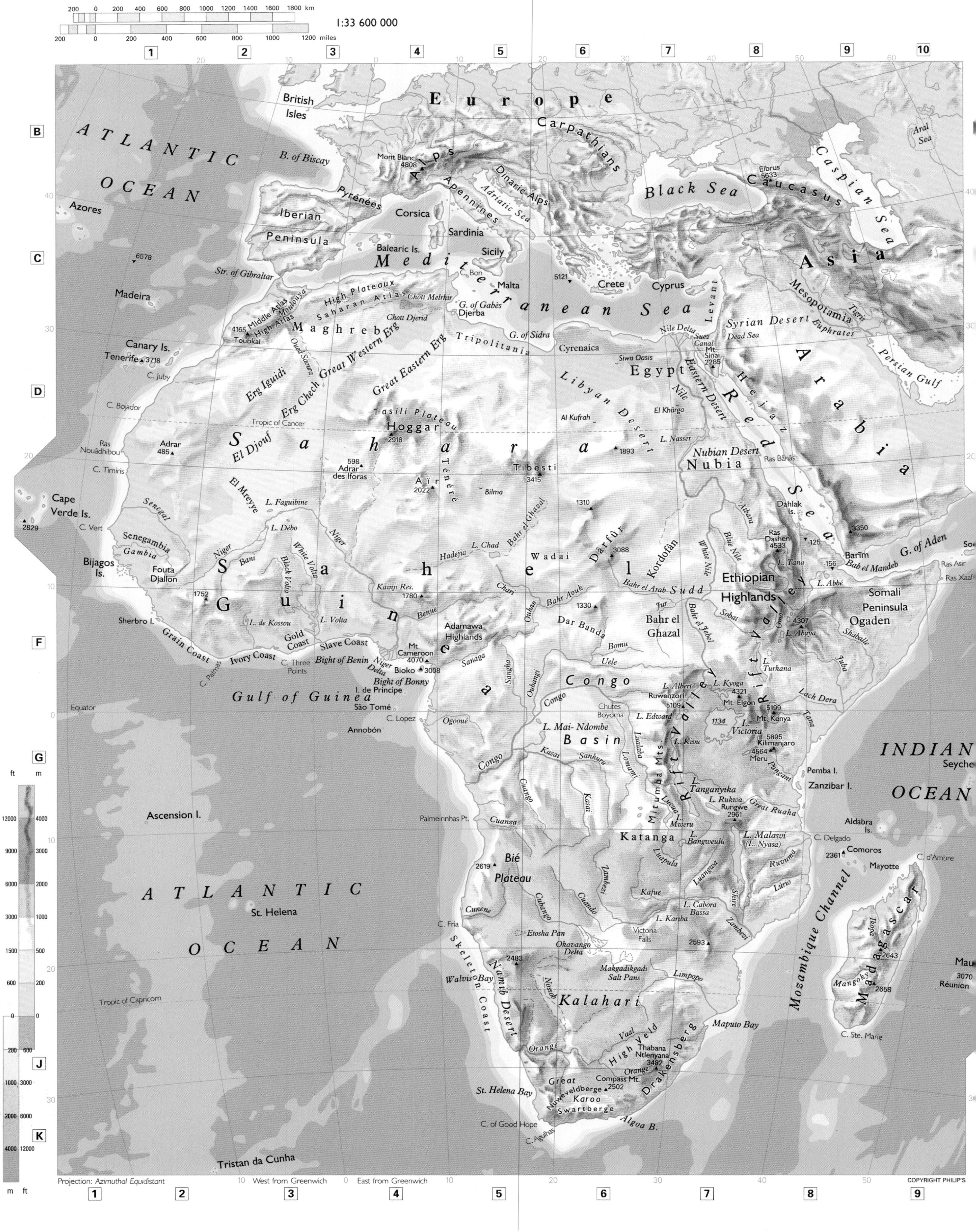

200 0 200 400 600 800 1000 1200 1400 1600 1800 km
200 0 200 400 600 800 1000 1200 miles

British Isles

E u r o p e

Carpathians

ATLANTIC OCEAN

B. of Biscay
Mont Blanc 4808
Alps
Dinaric Alps
Pyrénées
Apennines
Adriatic Sea
Corsica
Iberian Peninsula
Sardinia
Balearic Is.
Sicily
Crete
Cyprus
Black Sea
Caucasus
Elbrus 5633
Caspian Sea
Aral Sea
Asia
Azores
6578
Madeira
Str. of Gibraltar
M e d i t e r r a n e a n   S e a
Malta
C. Bon
5121
Levant
Mesopotamia
Tigris
Euphrates
Canary Is.
Tenerife 3718
C. Juby
Middle Atlas
High Atlas 4165
Toubkal
Saharan Atlas
High Plateaux
Maghreb
Chott Melrhir
Chott Djerid
Djerba
G. of Gabès
Tripolitania
G. of Sidra
Cyrenaica
Nile Delta
Suez Canal
Mt. Sinai 2285
Syrian Desert
Dead Sea
Egypt
Hejaz
Persian Gulf
Arabia
C. Bojador
Tropic of Cancer
Erg Iguidi
Erg Chech
Great Western Erg
Great Eastern Erg
Tasili Plateau
Hoggar 2918
Libyan Desert
Siwa Oasis
Al Kufrah
El Khârga
Eastern Desert
Nile
Red Sea
Ras Nouâdhibou
C. Timiris
Adrar 485
S a h a r a
El Djouf
Adrar des Iforas 598
Aïr 2022
Ténéré
Tibesti 3415
Bilma
1893
L. Nasser
Nubian Desert
Ras Bânâs
Nubia
Dahlak Is.
3350
Cape Verde Is.
2829
C. Vert
Senegal
Senegambia
Gambia
Bijagos Is.
Fouta Djallon
L. Meyye
El Meyye
L. Faguibine
Niger
White Volta
Black Volta
Bani
L. Débo
Niger
Hadejia
Bahr el Ghazal
L. Chad
1310
Wadai
Darfûr
3088
Kordofan
White Nile
Atbara
Blue Nile
Ras Dashen 4533
L. Tana
−125
Barîm
Bab el Mandeb
G. of Aden
Ras Asir
Ras Xaaf
S u d a n
S a h e l
G u i n e a
1752
Kainji Res.
1780
L. de Kossou
L. Volta
Gold Coast
Slave Coast
Bight of Benin
Niger Delta
Bioko 3008
Mt. Cameroon 4070
Adamawa Highlands
Sanaga
Benue
Chari
Oubangi
Bahr Aouk
1330
Dar Banda
Bahr el Arab
Jur
Sudd
Bahr el Ghazal
Bomu
Uele
−156
L. Abbé
Ethiopian Highlands
4307
L. Abaya
Somali Peninsula
Ogaden
Shabelle
Juba
L. Turkana
Lach Dera
Sherbro I.
Grain Coast
Ivory Coast
C. Palmas
C. Three Points
Bight of Bonny
I. de Principe
São Tomé
Gulf of Guinea
Annobón
C. Lopez
Equator
Ogooué
Congo
Congo
Sangha
Uele
Congo Basin
Lualaba
Lomami
L. Mai-Ndombe
Kasai
Sankuru
Kasai
L. Albert
Ruwenzori 5109
L. Edward
L. Kivu
Mirumba Mts.
Rift Valley
L. Kyoga 4321
Mt. Elgon 5199
1134
L. Victoria
Mt. Kenya 5895
Kilimanjaro
Meru 4564
Pangani
Pemba I.
Zanzibar I.
INDIAN OCEAN
Seychelles
Ascension I.
Cuanza
Palmeirinhas Pt.
Kwango
Kasai
Luapula
Katanga
L. Tanganyika
Luvua
Lukuga
L. Rukwa
Rungwe 2961
Great Ruaha
L. Bangweulu
L. Mweru
L. Malawi (L. Nyasa)
Ruvuma
Lúrio
2361
C. Delgado
Comoros
Aldabra Is.
Mayotte
C. d'Ambre
2619
Bié Plateau
Zambezi
Kafue
Luangwa
Cabora Bassa
L. Kariba
Shire
Mozambique Channel
Madagascar
Nosy Be
2643
Ikopa
Mangoky
2658
3070
Réunion
Mauritius
St. Helena
ATLANTIC OCEAN
Cunene
C. Fria
Etosha Pan
Okavango Delta
Makgadikgadi Salt Pans
Victoria Falls
2593
Limpopo
Skeleton Coast
2483
Namib Desert
Walvis Bay
Nossob
Kalahari
Tropic of Capricorn
Orange
Vaal
Orange
High Veld
Thabana Ntlenyana 3482
Drakensberg
Maputo Bay
Great Nuweveldberge
Compass Mt. 2502
Karoo
Swartberge
Algoa B.
St. Helena Bay
C. of Good Hope
C. Agulhas
Tristan da Cunha

ft m
12000 4000
9000 3000
6000 2000
3000 1000
1500 500
600 200
0 0
200 600
1000 3000
2000 6000
4000 12000
m ft

Projection: Azimuthal Equidistant

West from Greenwich
East from Greenwich

COPYRIGHT PHILIP'S

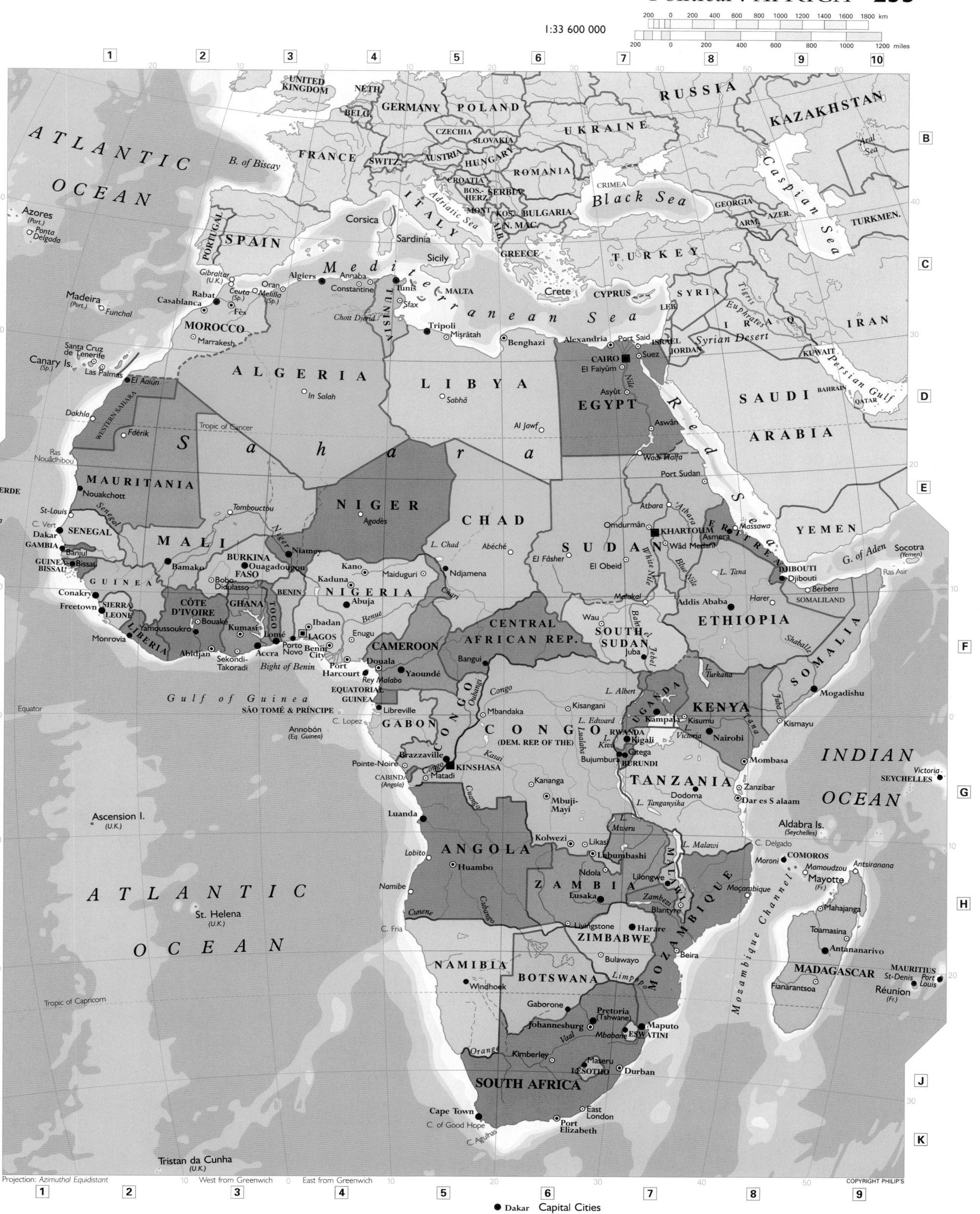

1:33 600 000

Projection: *Azimuthal Equidistant*

West from Greenwich   East from Greenwich

● Dakar Capital Cities

COPYRIGHT PHILIP'S

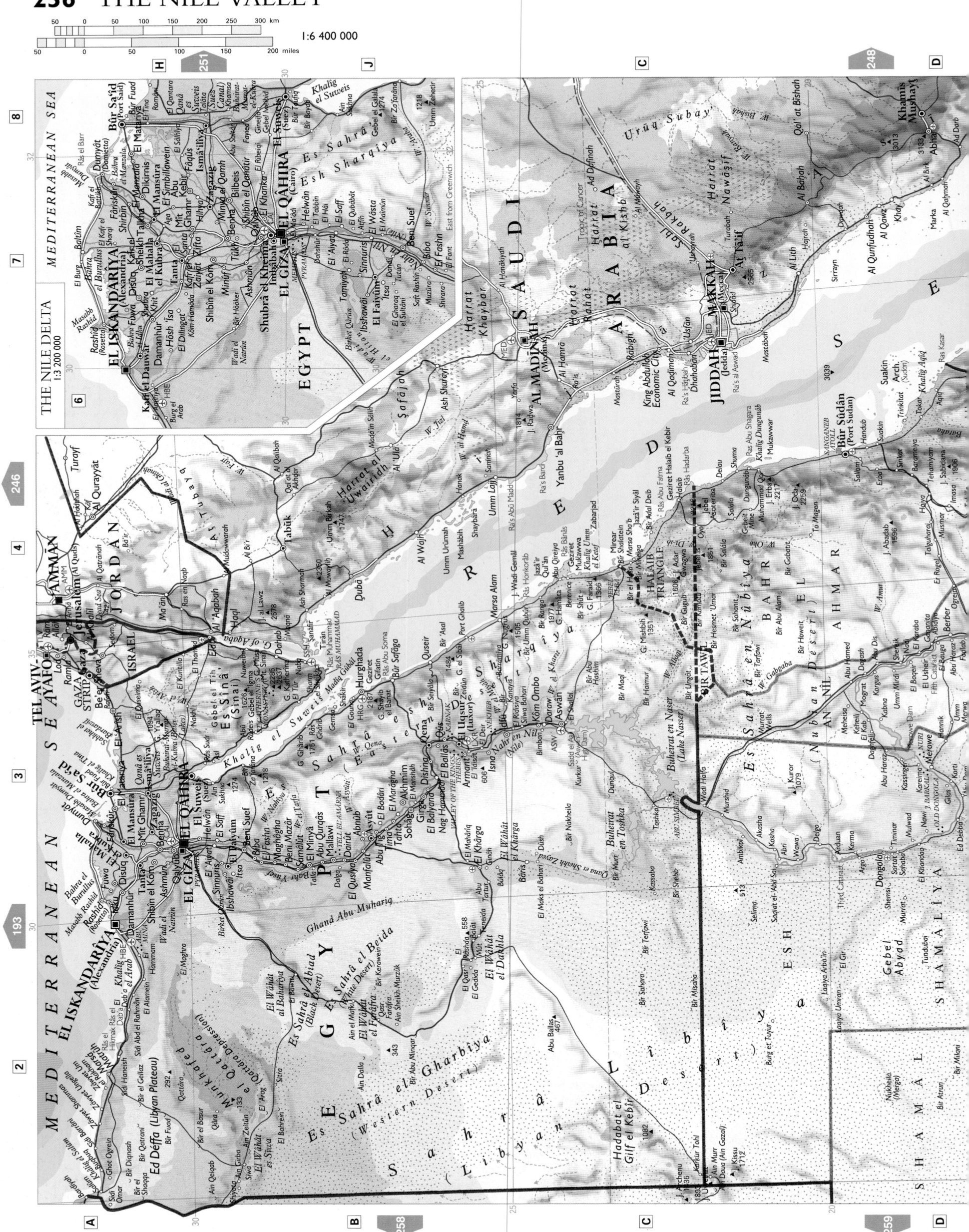

1:6 400 000

THE NILE DELTA
1:3 200 000

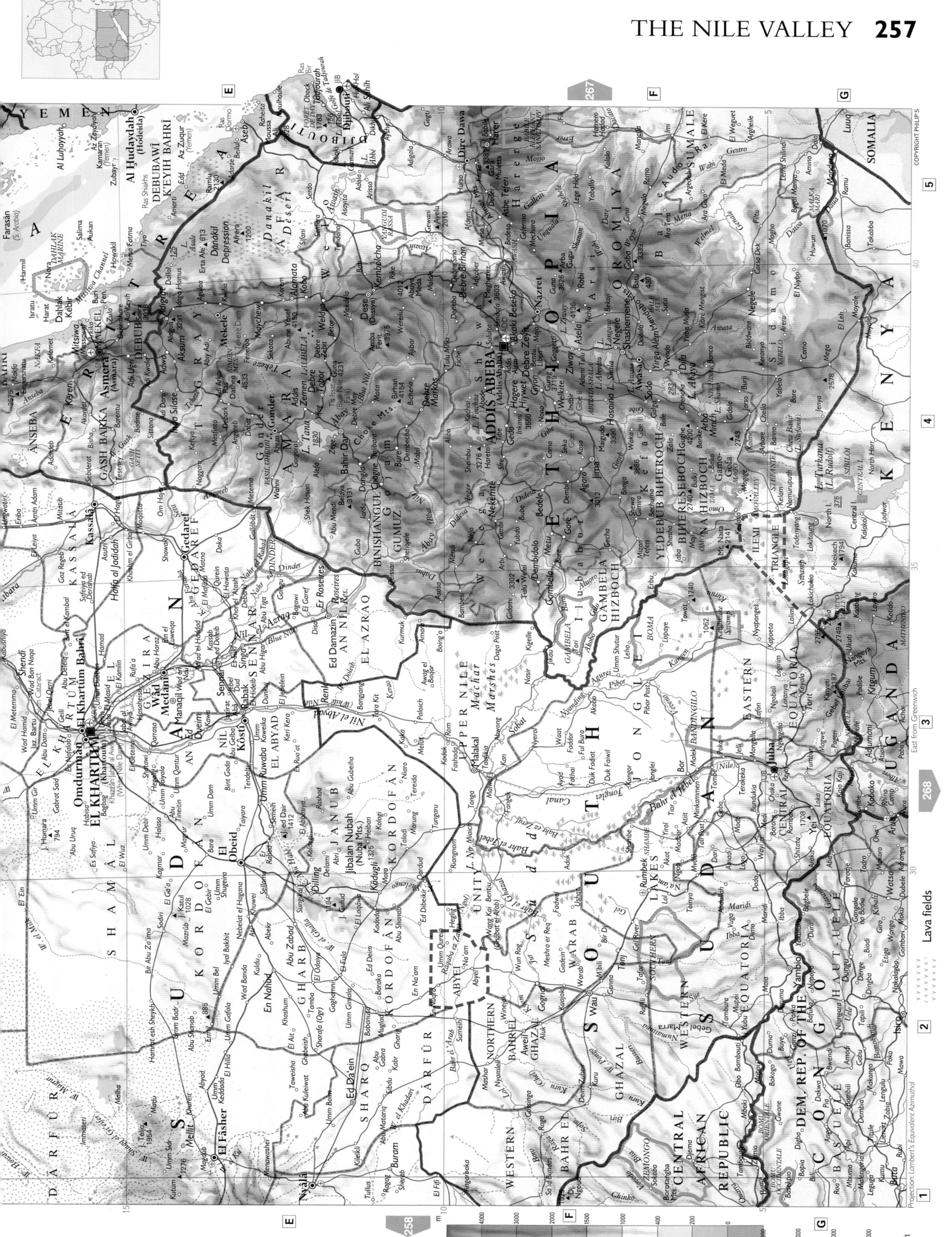

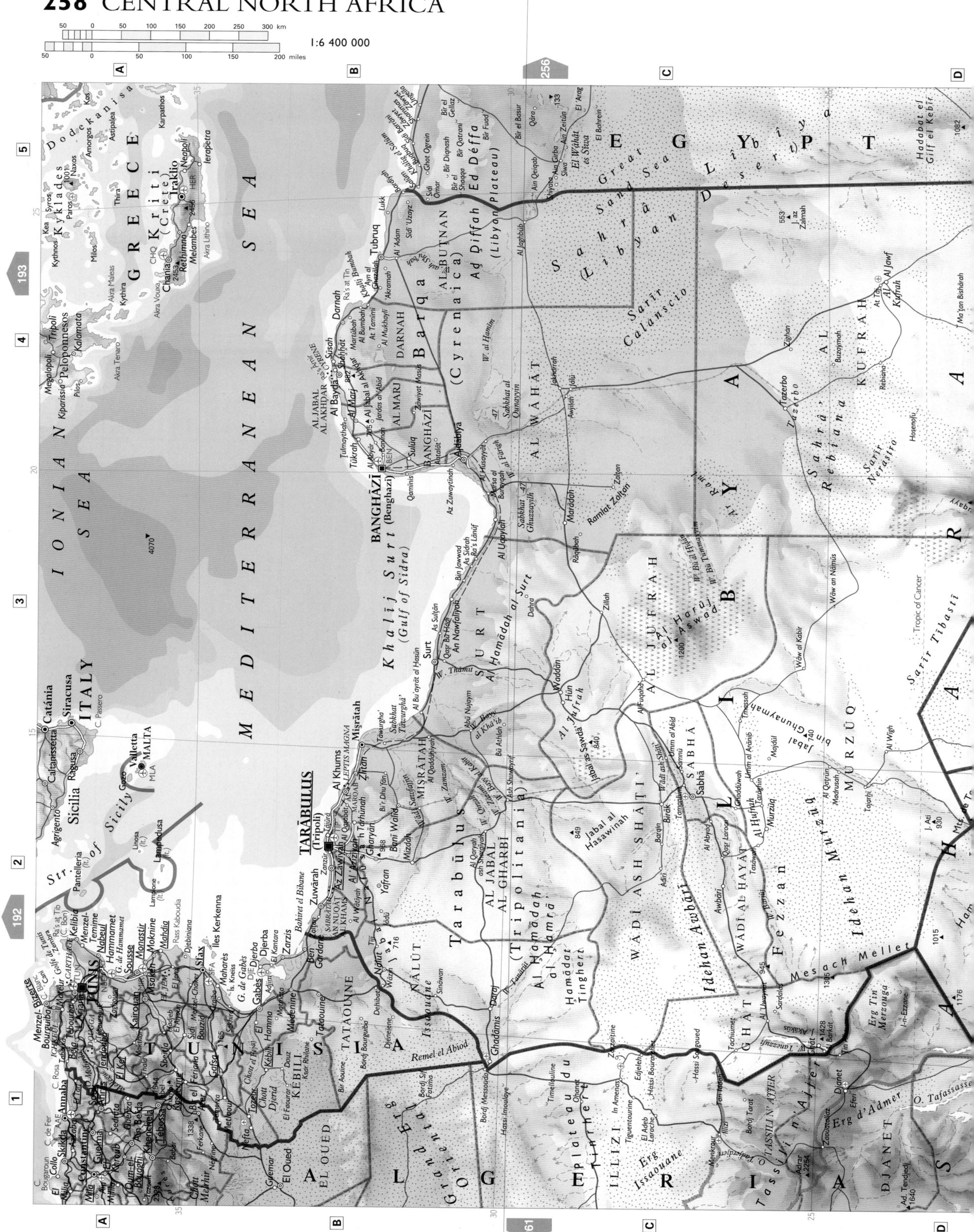

1:6 400 000

MEDITERRANEAN SEA

IONIAN SEA

GREECE

Kríti (Crete)

ITALY

Sicilia

MALTA

TUNISIA

ALGERIA

TARÀBULUS (Tripoli)

BANGHÀZÌ (Benghazi)

L I B Y A

Khalìj Surt (Gulf of Sidra)

Barqa (Cyrenaica)

Sarìr Calanscio

E G Y P T

Sahrā Lībiyā (Libyan Desert)

Great Sand Sea

AL KUFRAH

Fezzan

MURZÙQ

Idehan Murzùq

Idehan Awbàri

TASSILI-N-AJJER

DJANET

Tropic of Cancer

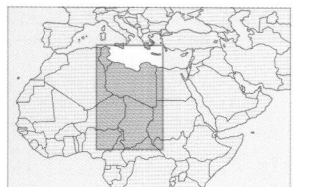

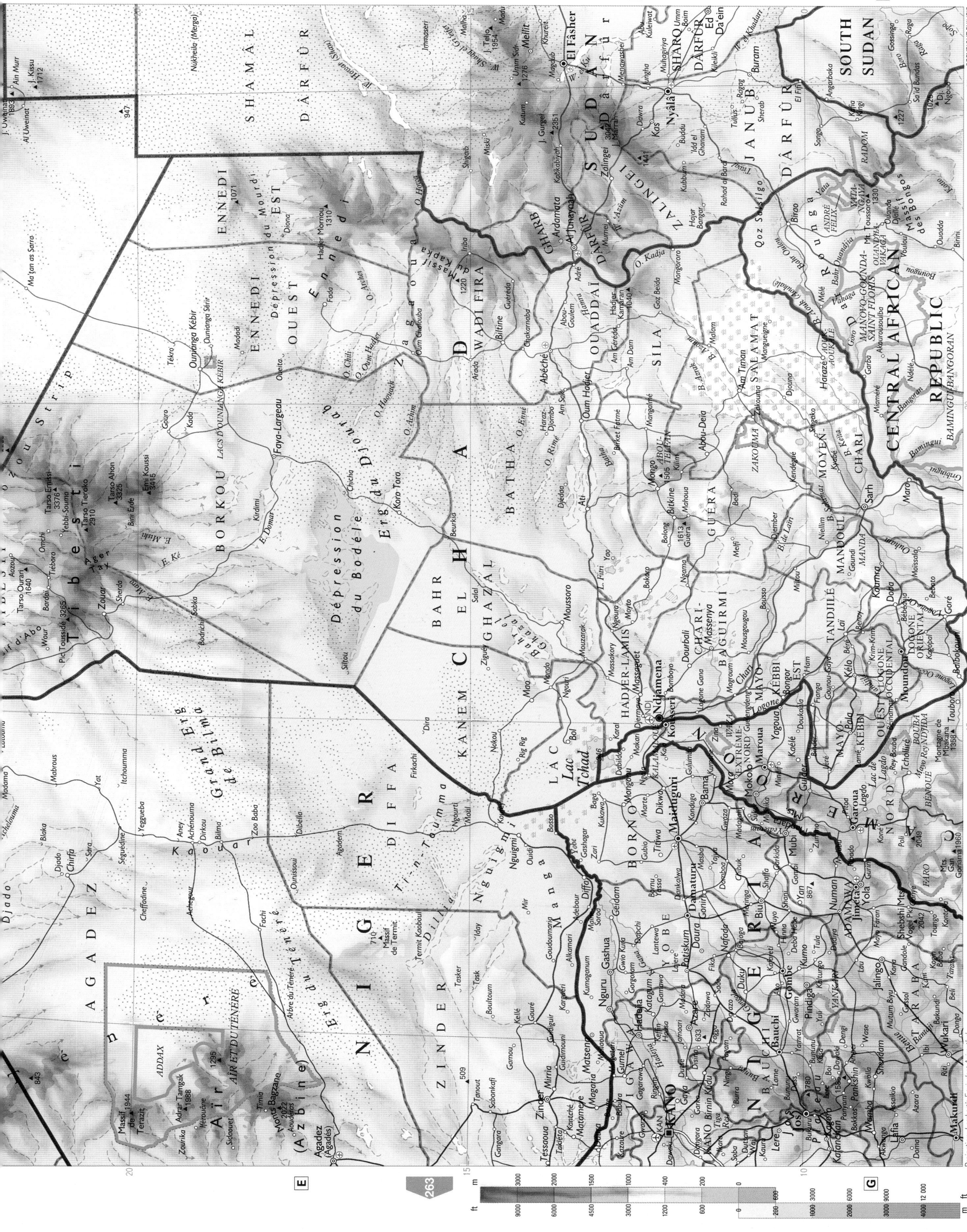

257
263
264
E
F
G
1
2
3
4
5
SUDAN
CHAD
NIGER
NIGERIA
CENTRAL AFRICAN REPUBLIC
SOUTH SUDAN
CAMEROON
Tibesti
Aozou Strip
Borkou
Ennedi
Ennedi Ouest
Ennedi Est
Dépression du Bodélé
Erg du Djourab
Grand Erg de Bilma
Ténéré
Aïr (Azbine)
Agadez
Zinder
Diffa
Kanem
Lac
Lac Tchad
Bahr el Ghazal
Batha
Guéra
Salamat
Ouaddaï
Wadi Fira
Sila
Moyen-Chari
Mandoul
Logone Oriental
Logone Occidental
Tandjilé
Mayo-Kebbi Est
Mayo-Kebbi Ouest
Chari-Baguirmi
Hadjer-Lamis
Borno
Yobe
Jigawa
Kano
Bauchi
Gombe
Adamawa
Taraba
Plateau
Shamâl Dârfûr
Gharb Dârfûr
Janub Dârfûr
Sharq Dârfûr
Zalingei
Ndjamena
Maiduguri
Kano
Nyala
El Fâsher
Abéché
Faya-Largeau
Sarh
Moundou
Bilma
Mongo
Am Timan
Maroua
Garoua
Yola
Jos
Bauchi
Tessaoua
Emi Koussi 3415
Pic Toussidé 3265
Tarso Emissi 3376
Jebel Marrah 3042
Underlined towns give their name to the administrative area in which they stand.
Lava fields
Projection: Lambert's Equivalent Azimuthal
COPYRIGHT PHILIP'S
m
ft
3000
2000
1500
1000
400
200
0
9000
6000
4500
3000
1200
600
200
1000
2000
3000
4000
12 000
9000
6000
3000
600

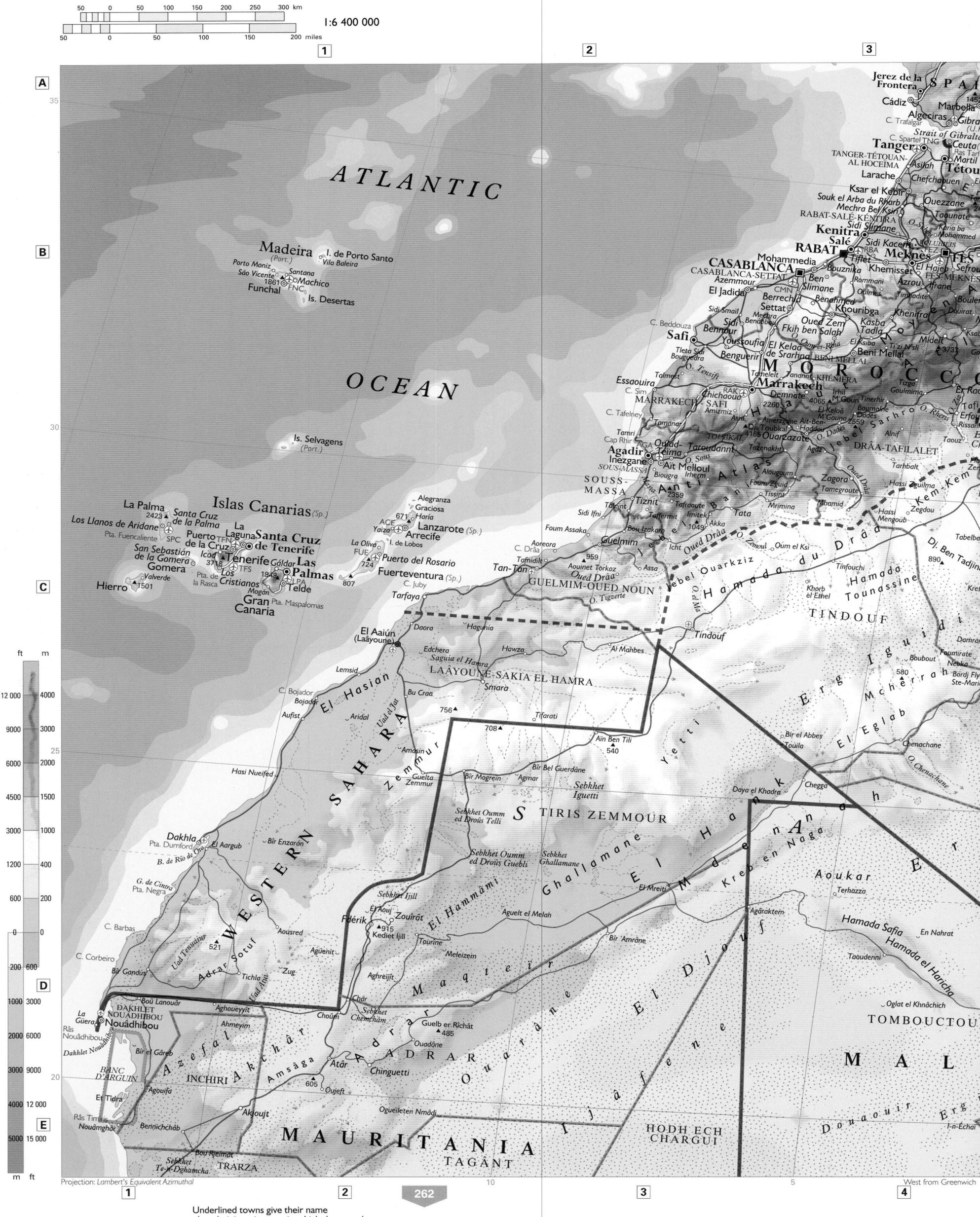

Projection: Lambert's Equivalent Azimuthal

West from Greenwich

Underlined towns give their name
to the administrative area in which they stand

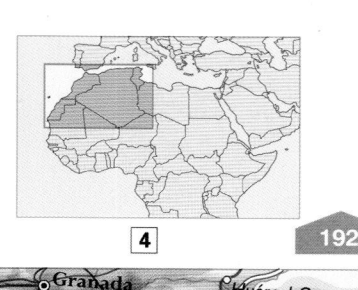

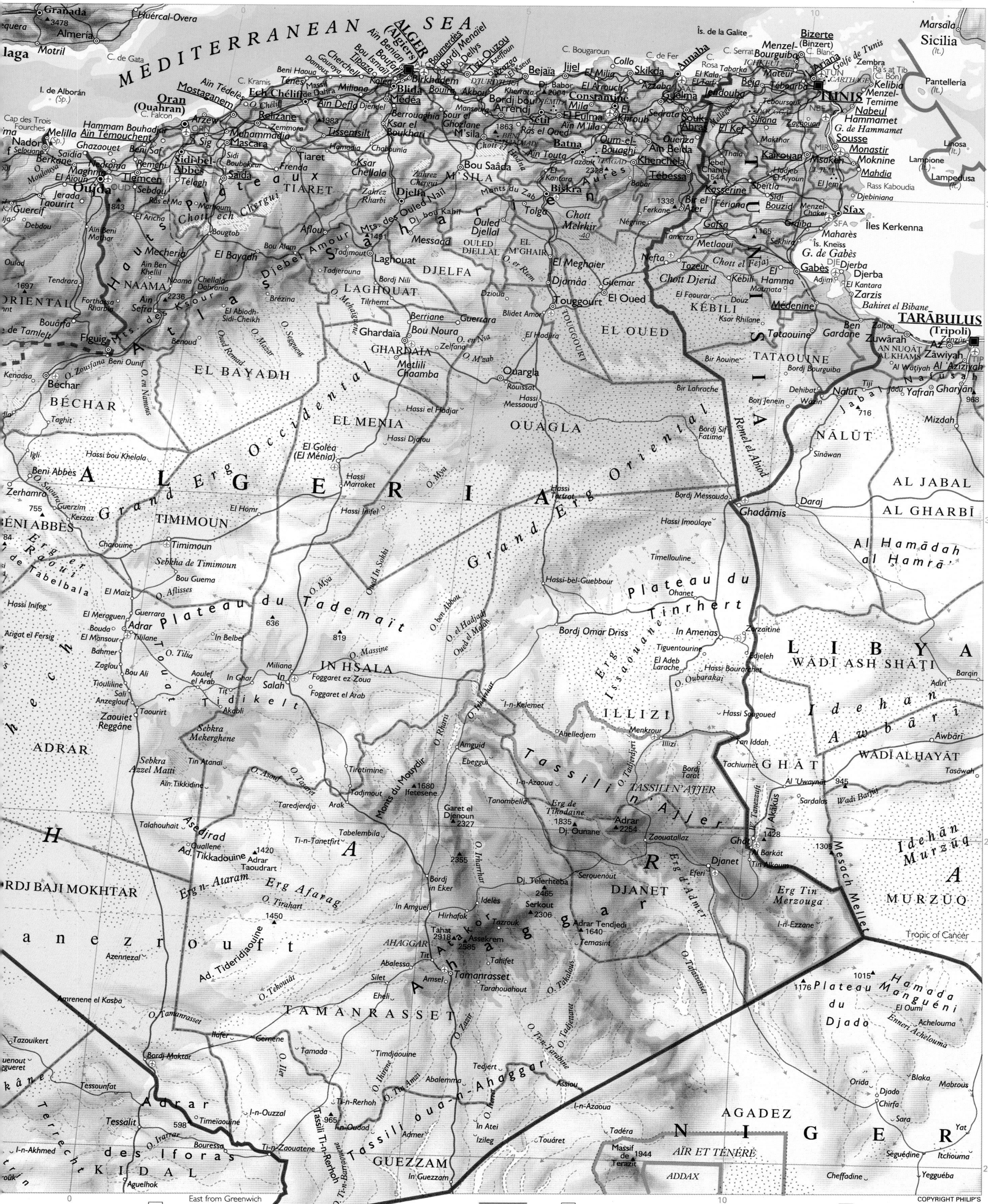

50 0 50 100 150 200 250 300 km

1:6 400 000

50 0 50 100 150 200 miles

Projection : Lambert's Equivalent Azimuthal

Underlined towns give their name to the
administrative area in which they stand.

Administrative division in Côte d'Ivoire:
1 Sassandra-Marahoué

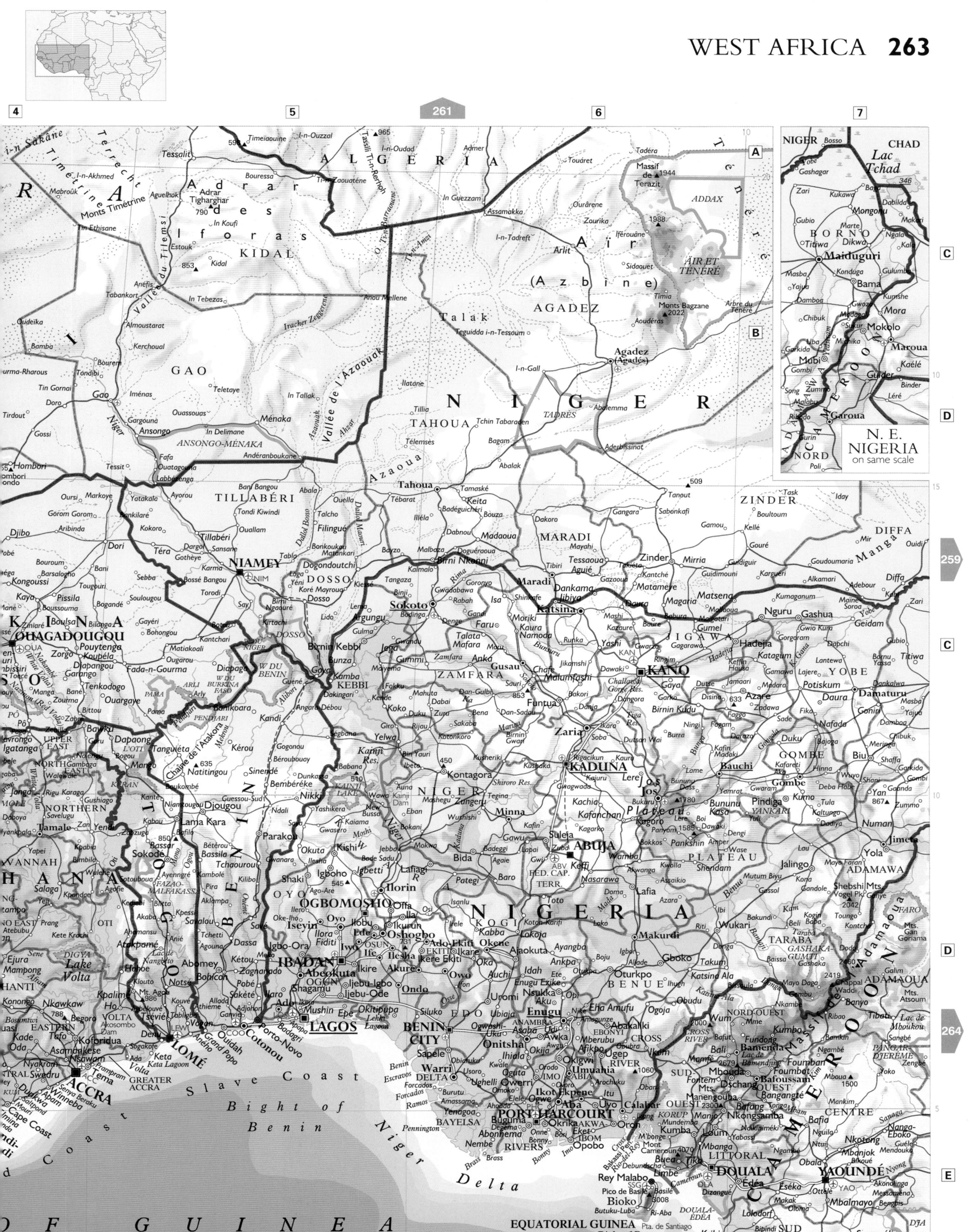

N. E.
NIGERIA
on same scale

East from Greenwich

COPYRIGHT PHILIP'S

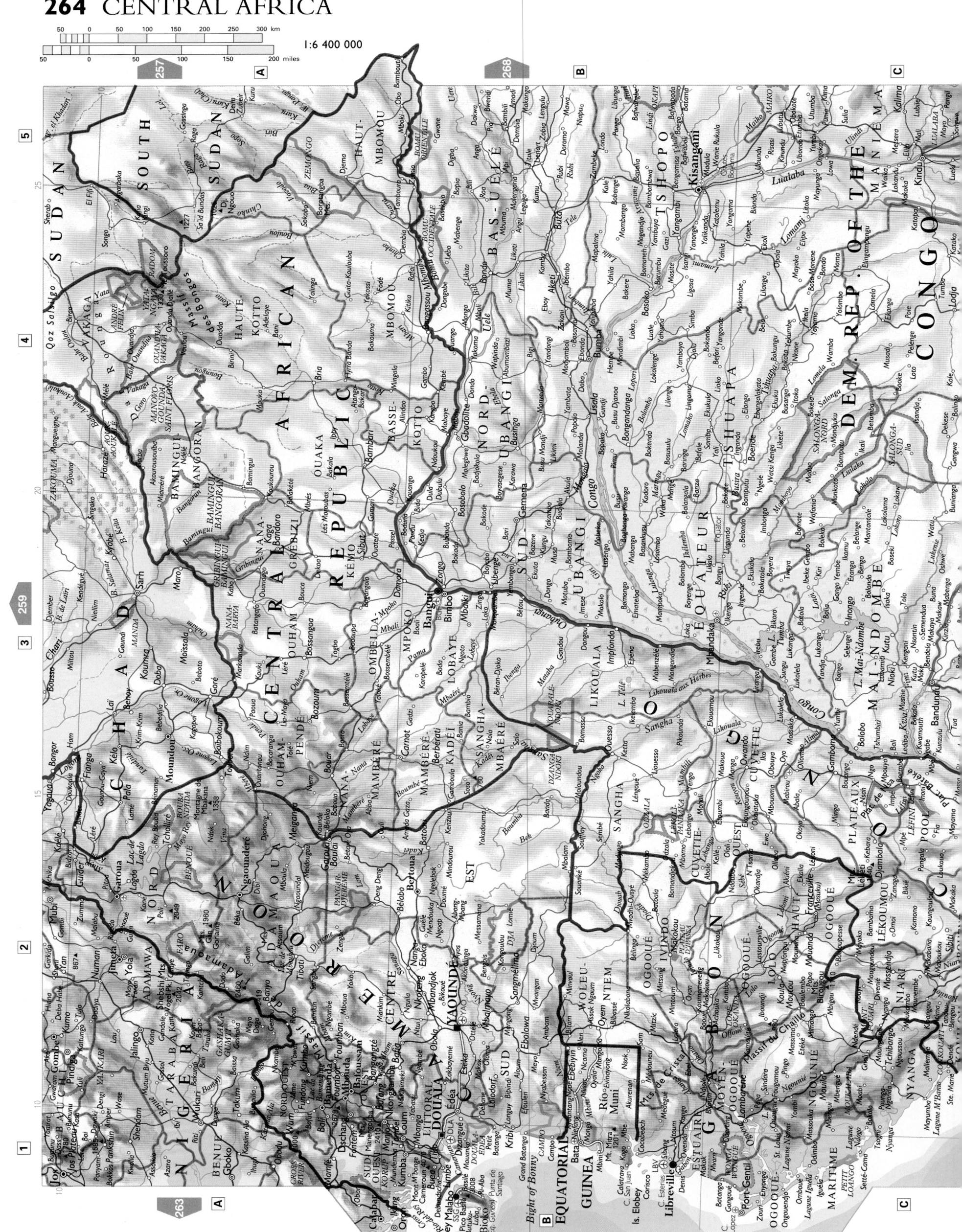

1:6 400 000

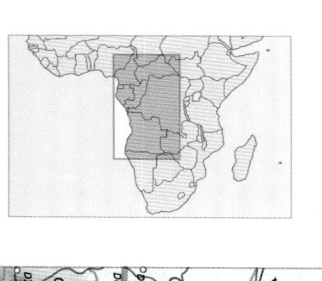

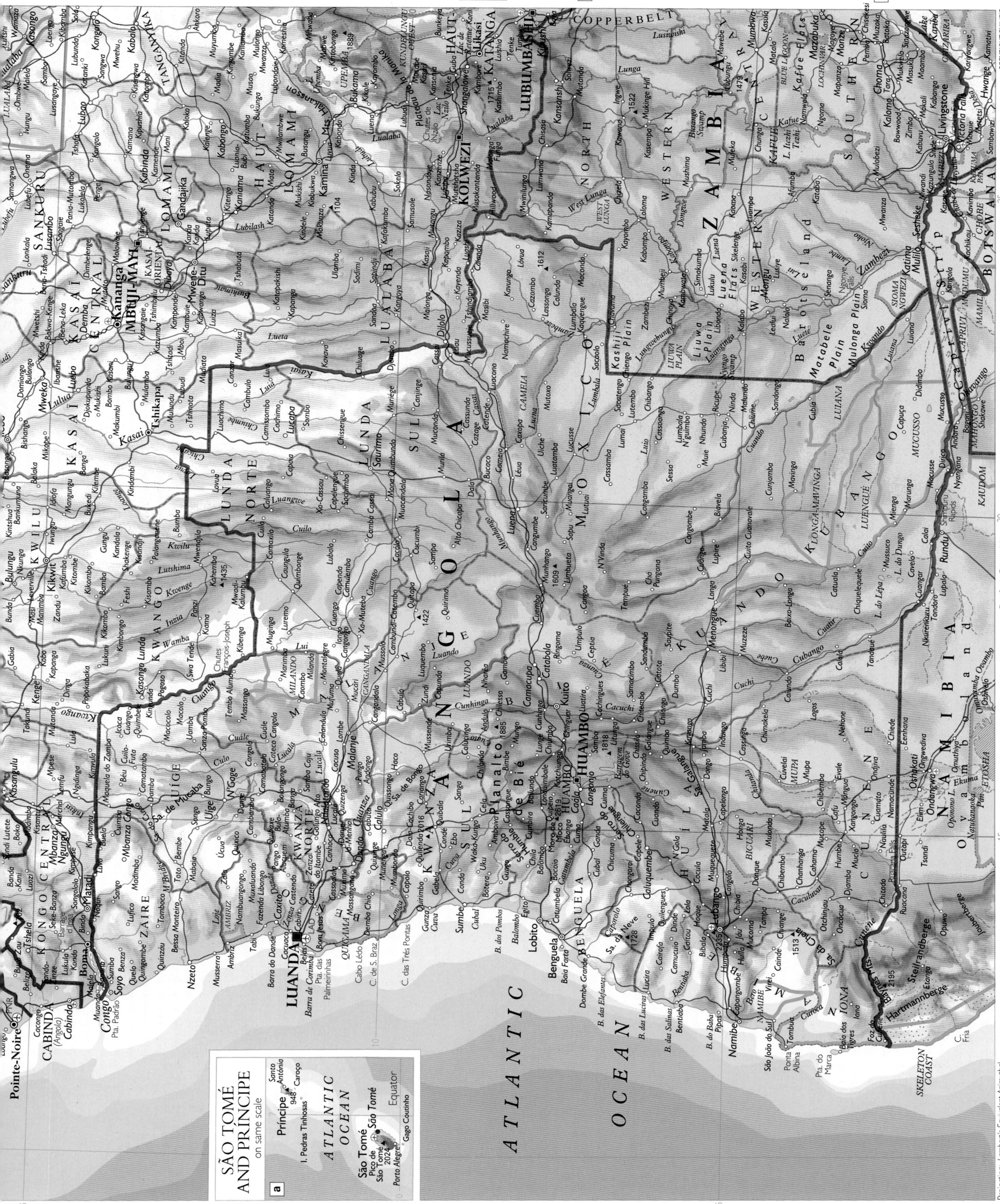

SÃO TOMÉ AND PRÍNCIPE
on same scale

Príncipe 948 Santo António Caroço

I. Pedras Tinhosas

ATLANTIC OCEAN

São Tomé
Pico de São Tomé 2024
São Tomé
Porto Alegre Gago Coutinho

Equator

ATLANTIC OCEAN

ANGOLA

ZAMBIA

NAMIBIA

BOTSWANA

ZAIRE

COPPERBELT

LUBUMBASHI

KOLWEZI

KATANGA

KASAI

SANKURU

KWILU

KWANGO

KWANZA

HUAMBO

BENGUELA

CUANDO

CUNENE

HUILA

LUANDA

Luanda

Livingstone

Victoria Falls

Projection: Lambert's Equivalent Azimuthal

East from Greenwich

COPYRIGHT PHILIP'S

ft m 3000 2000 1500 1000 400 200 0
m 9000 6000 4500 3000 1200 600 200 0 600 1000 3000 6000 9000 12 000 ft

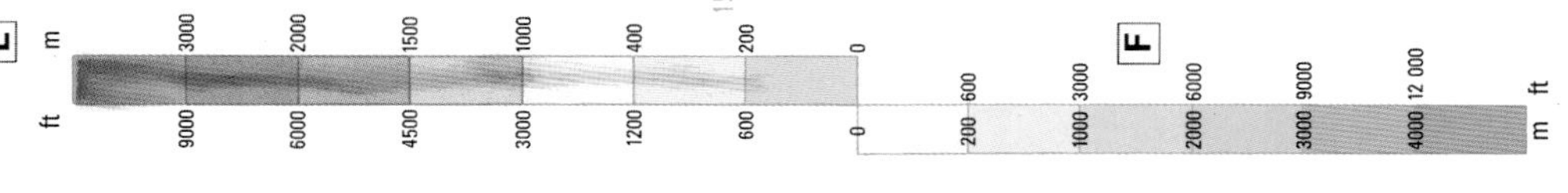

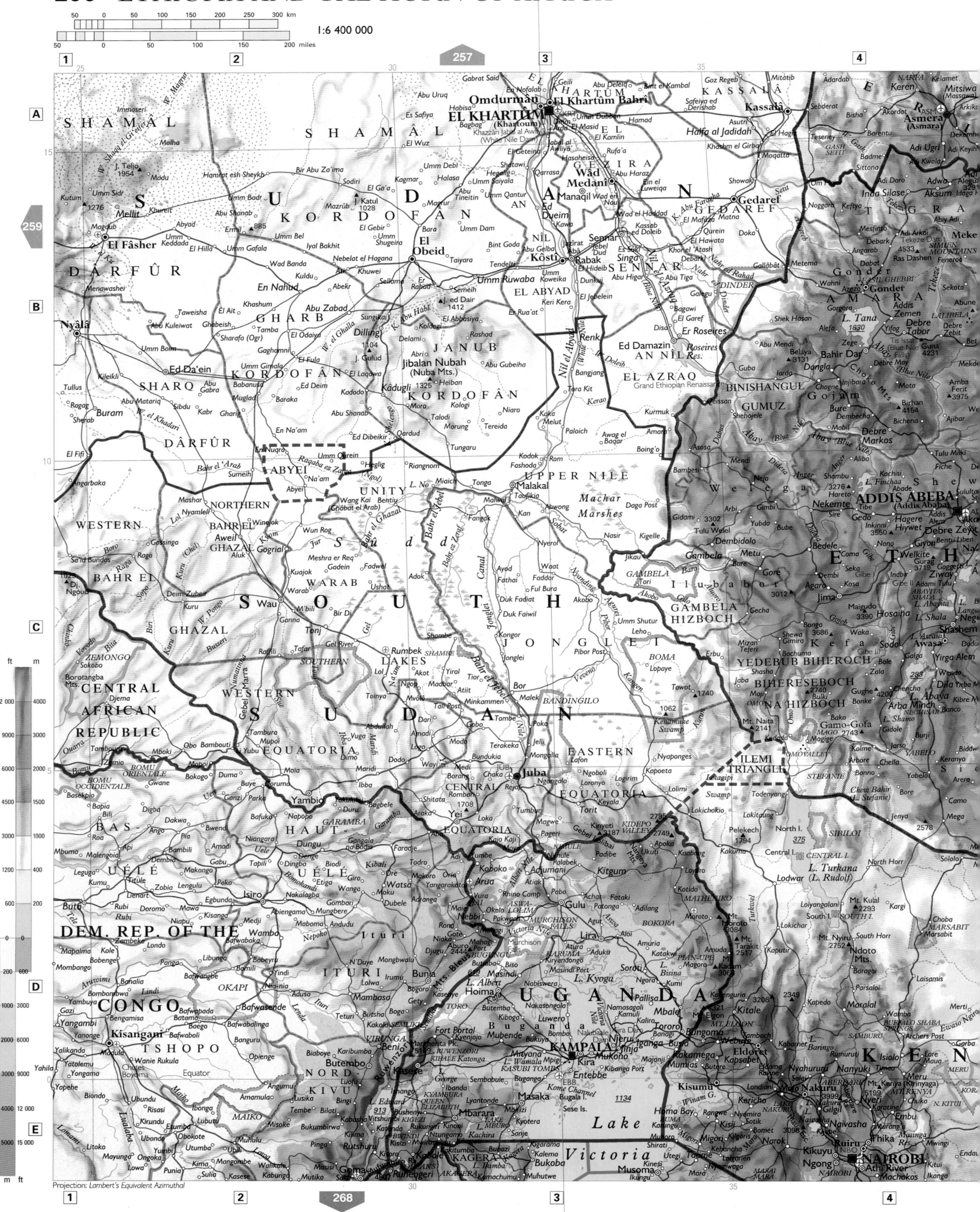

Projection: Lambert's Equivalent Azimuthal

INDIAN

OCEAN

East from Greenwich

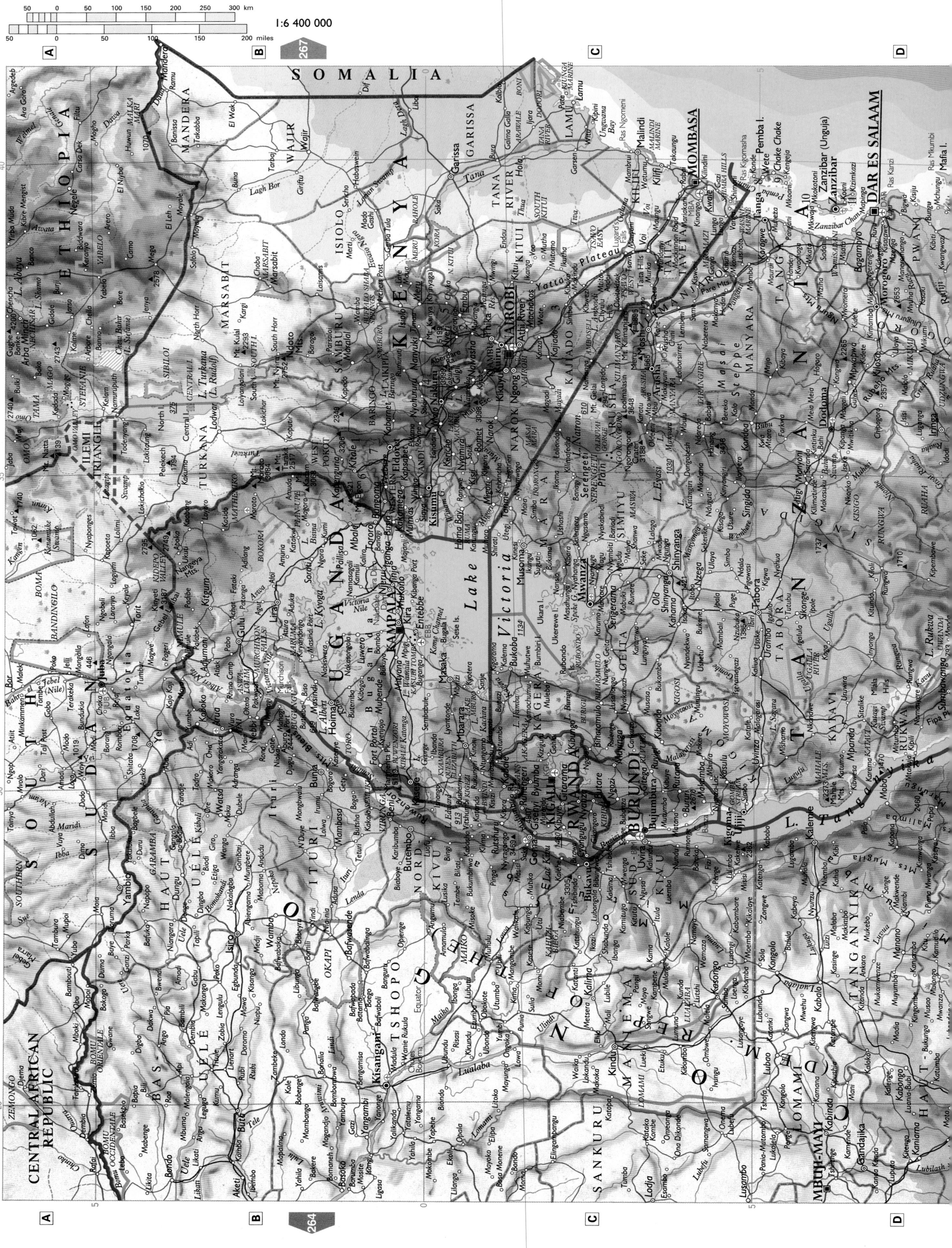

1:6 400 000

50 0 50 100 150 200 250 300 km
50 0 50 100 150 200 miles

SOMALIA

ETHIOPIA

KENYA

SOUTH SUDAN

UGANDA

Lake Victoria

TANZANIA

RWANDA

BURUNDI

DEM. REP. CONGO

CENTRAL AFRICAN REPUBLIC

NAIROBI

KAMPALA

DAR ES SALAAM

MOMBASA

Zanzibar (Unguja)

Pemba I.

Mafia I.

Malindi

Tanga

Arusha

Mwanza

Kisumu

Musoma

Kigali

Bujumbura

Kisangani

L. Tanganyika

L. Turkana (L. Rudolf)

L. Albert

L. Edward

L. Kivu

MARSABIT

TURKANA

ILEMI TRIANGLE

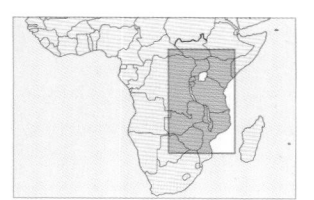

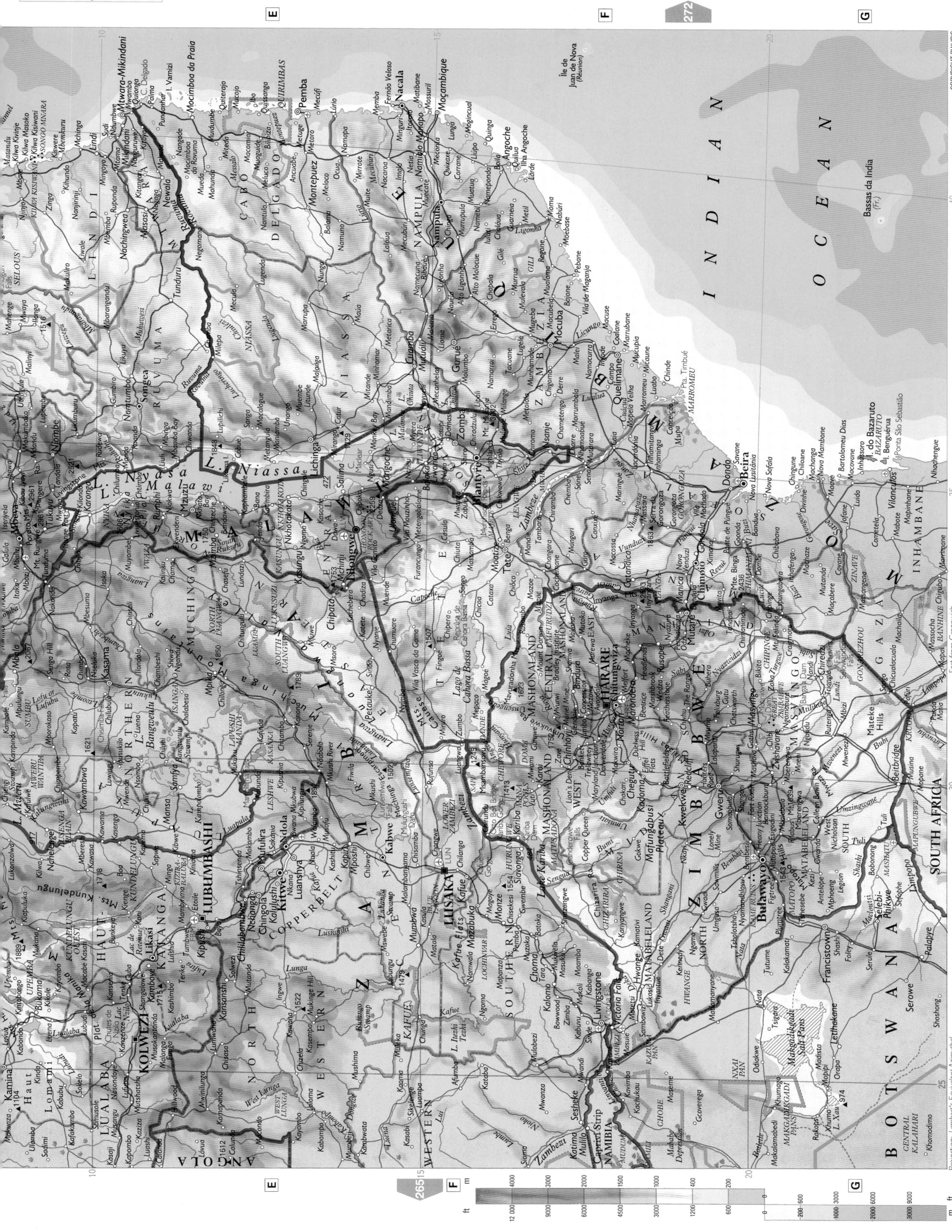

COPYRIGHT PHILIP'S

Underlined towns give their name to the
administrative area in which they stand.

Administrative divisions in Tanzania:
8 North Pemba   10 North Zanzibar
9 South Pemba   11 South Zanzibar

Administrative divisions in Kenya:
1 Elgeyo-Marakwet   3 Makueni   5 Tharaka Nithi   7 Uasin Gishu
2 Kirinyaga   4 Nyandarua   6 Trans-Nzoia

East from Greenwich

Projection: Lambert's Equivalent Azimuthal

ft   m
12 000   4000
9000   3000
6000   2000
4500   1500
3000   1000
1500   600
600   200
0   0
200 · 600
1000 · 3000
2000 · 6000
3000 · 9000
ft   m

1:6 400 000

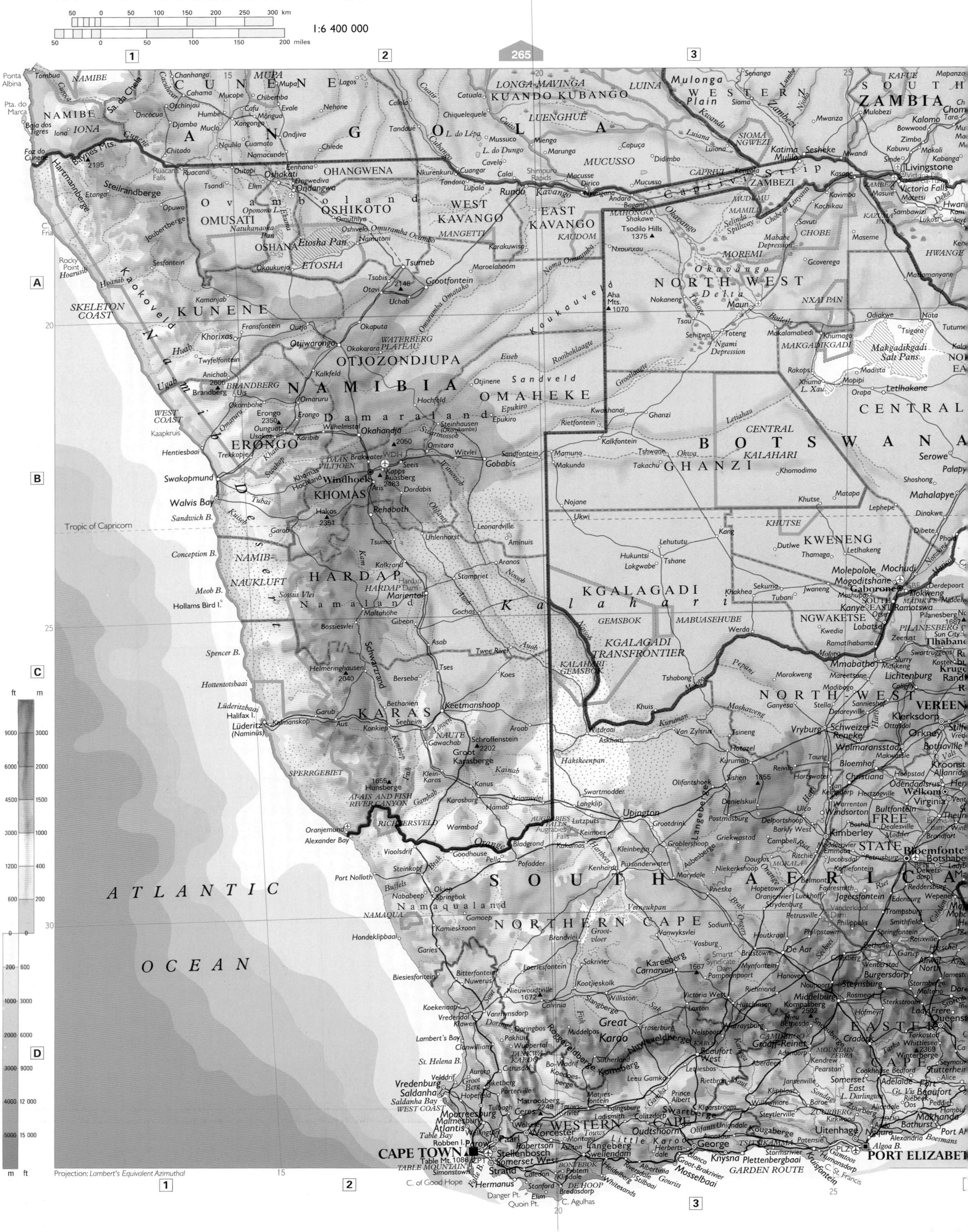

50 0 50 100 150 200 250 300 km

50 0 50 100 150 200 miles

ATLANTIC OCEAN

NAMIBIA

ANGOLA

ZAMBIA

BOTSWANA

SOUTH AFRICA

KUNENE

OTJOZONDJUPA

OMAHEKE

ERONGO

KHOMAS

HARDAP

KARAS

NAMIB

Windhoek

Walvis Bay

Swakopmund

Lüderitz

Keetmanshoop

Mariental

Rehoboth

Gobabis

Grootfontein

Tsumeb

Etosha Pan

ETOSHA

Oshakati

Ondangwa

OVAMBOLAND

OSHIKOTO

OHANGWENA

OMUSATI

OSHANA

CAPRIVI STRIP

EAST KAVANGO

WEST KAVANGO

Katima Mulilo

ZAMBEZI

Livingstone

Victoria Falls

CHOBE

Okavango Delta

NORTH WEST

MOREMI

Maun

Makgadikgadi Salt Pans

GHANZI

Ghanzi

CENTRAL

KGALAGADI

KALAHARI

KALAHARI TRANSFRONTIER

KGALAGADI GEMSBOK

Gaborone

KWENENG

NGWAKETSE

Molepolole

Kanye

Lobatse

NORTH-WEST

Mafikeng

Vryburg

Kuruman

Upington

NORTHERN CAPE

Kimberley

FREE STATE

Bloemfontein

Welkom

Klerksdorp

WESTERN CAPE

EASTERN CAPE

CAPE TOWN

Table Mountain 1086

Stellenbosch

Worcester

George

Oudtshoorn

Knysna

Mossel Bay

PORT ELIZABETH

Uitenhage

Graaff-Reinet

Beaufort West

De Aar

Springbok

Port Nolloth

Alexander Bay

Oranjemund

Namaqualand

NAMAQUA

Tropic of Capricorn

SKELETON COAST

WEST COAST

KAOKOVELD

KUNENE

DAMARALAND

NAMIB-NAUKLUFT

SPERRGEBIET

AI-AIS AND FISH RIVER CANYON

RICHTERSVELD

GARDEN ROUTE

Orange

Okavango

Zambezi

Cunene

C. of Good Hope

C. Agulhas

Ponta Albina

Pta. do Marca

Projection: Lambert's Equivalent Azimuthal

ft m

9000 3000

6000 2000

4500 1500

3000 1000

1200 400

600 200

0 0

200 600

1000 3000

2000 6000

3000 9000

4000 12 000

5000 15 000

m ft

MOZAMBIQUE

CHANNEL

Île de
Júan de Nova
(Fr.)

A

Bassas da India
(Fr.)

B

Île Europa
(Fr.)

Tropic of Capricorn

272

INDIAN

OCEAN

C

D

East from Greenwich

COPYRIGHT PHILIP'S

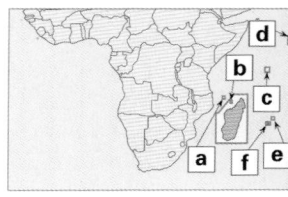

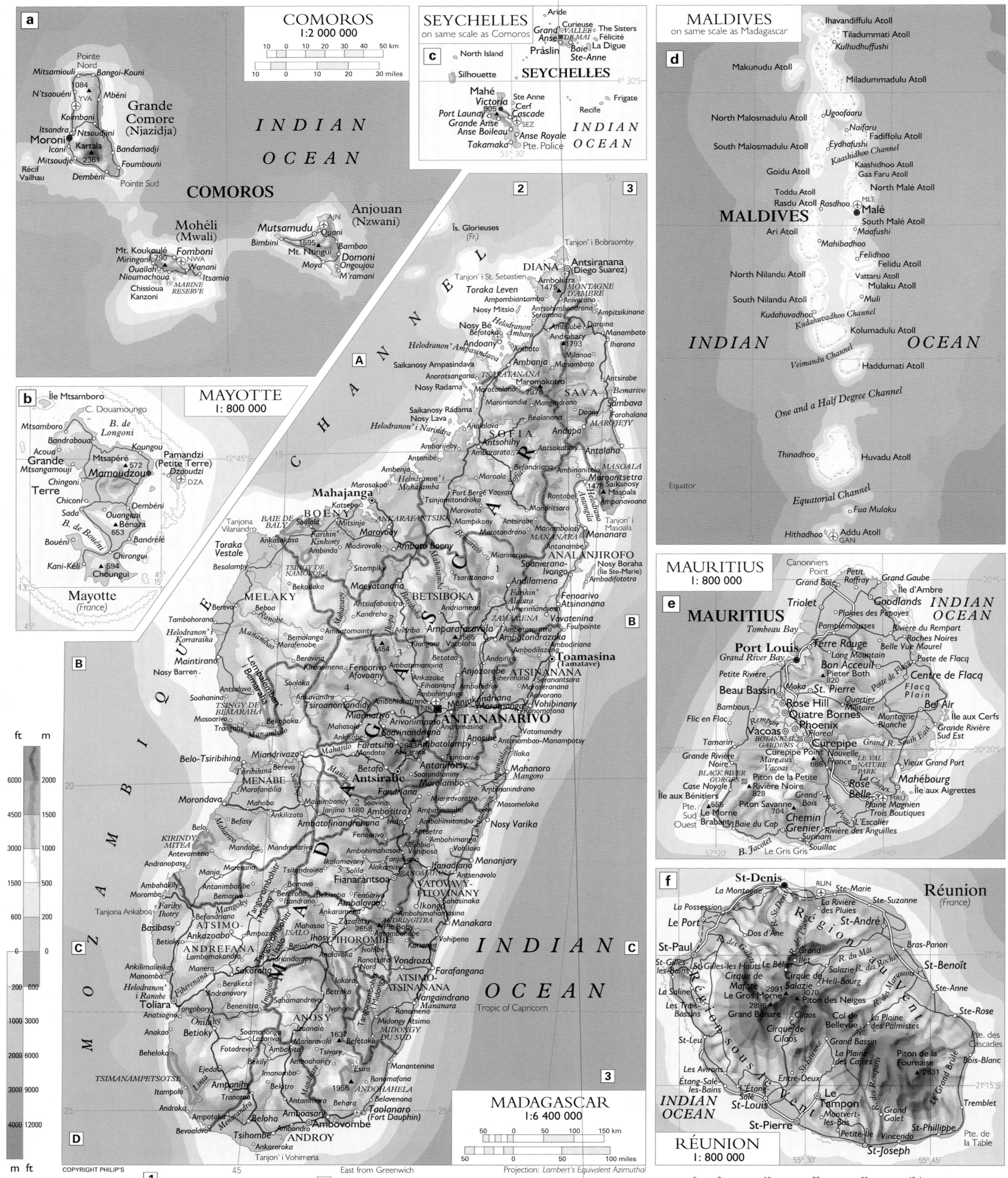

a

COMOROS
1:2 000 000

10   0   10   20   30   40   50 km
10   0   10   20   30 miles

SEYCHELLES
on same scale as Comoros

c

Aride
Grand   Curieuse   The Sisters
Anse   VALLEE
DE MAI
Praslin   La Digue
Ste-Anne

North Island

Silhouette

SEYCHELLES

Mahé
Victoria   Ste Anne
905   Cerf   Cascade
Port Launay   SEZ
Grande Anse   Recife
Anse Boileau   Anse Royale
Takamaka   Pte. Police

INDIAN OCEAN

30°S

55° 30

MALDIVES
on same scale as Madagascar

d

Ihavandiffulu Atoll
Tiladummati Atoll
Kulhudhuffushi

Makunudu Atoll

Miladummadulu Atoll

North Malosmadulu Atoll
Ugoofaaru
Naifaru
Fadiffolu Atoll
South Malosmadulu Atoll
Eydhafushi
Kaashidhoo Channel
Goidu Atoll   Kaashidhoo Atoll
Gaa Faru Atoll
Toddu Atoll   North Malé Atoll
Rasdu Atoll   Rasdhoo   MLE
Malé
MALDIVES   South Malé Atoll
Ari Atoll   Maafushi

North Nilandu Atoll   Mahibadhoo
Felidhoo
Felidu Atoll
South Nilandu Atoll   Vattaru Atoll
Mulaku Atoll
Kudahuvadhoo   Muli
Kudahuvadhoo Channel
Kolumadulu Atoll
Thinadhoo   Veimandu Channel
Haddumati Atoll

INDIAN   OCEAN

One and a Half Degree Channel

Equator
Equatorial Channel

Thinadhoo   Huvadu Atoll
Fua Mulaku

Hithadhoo   Addu Atoll
GAN

INDIAN OCEAN

Pointe Nord
Mitsamiouli   Bangoi-Kouni
N'tsouéni   1084   Mbéni
NWA
Koimbani   YVA
Itsandra   Ntsoudjini   **Grande**
Moroni   Kartala   **Comore**
Iconi   2361   **(Njazidja)**
Mitsoudjé   Bandamadji
Récif   Dembéni   Foumbouni
Vailhau   Pointe Sud

COMOROS

Mohéli
(Mwali)
Mt. Koukoulé   Fomboni
Miringoni 790   NWA
Ouallah   Wanani
Nioumachoua   Itsamia
Chissioua   MARINE
Kanzoni   RESERVE

Mutsamudu   AIN
Bimbini   Quani   Bambao
1595   Domoni
Mt. Ntingui   Ongoujou
Moya   M'ramani

Anjouan
(Nzwani)

Îs. Glorieuses
(Fr.)

b

Île Mtsamboro
C. Douamoungou
Mtsamboro   B. de
Longoni
Acoua
Bandraboua
Koungou   **MAYOTTE**
Grande   Mtsapéré   Pamandzi
Mtsangamouji   572   (Petite Terre)
Terre   **Mamoudzou**   Dzaoudzi
Chingoni   Chiconi   DZA
Sada   Dembéni
Benara
Ouangani   653
Bouéni   Bandrélé
Kani-Kéli   Chirongui
594
Choungui

12° 45'S

45°
15'

Mayotte
(France)

13°

MADAGASCAR

Tanjon' i Bobraomby
DIANA   Antsiranana
Tanjon' i St. Sébastien   Ambohitra   (Diego Suarez)
Toraka Leven   1475   MONTAGNE
Ampombiantambo   D'AMBRE
Nosy Mitsio   Anivorano
Antsohimbondrona   Ampitsikinana
Nosy Bé   Ambilobe   Daraina
Befotaka   Ambato   Antsahabary   Iharana
Andoany   Andrahary   Milanoa
Ambato   Ambanja   1793
Saikanosy Ampasindava   Mahambato
Anorotsangana   Antsirabe
Nosy Radama   Maromokotro   **SAVA**
2876   Bemarivo
Saikanosy Radama   Maromandia   **Sambava**
Nosy Lava   Bealanana   Doany   Farahalana
Helodranon' i Narindra   Analalava   MAROJEJY
Ambarijeby   Antsakabary   Andapa
Antonibé   Ambararata   Antalaha
Ambenjo   **SOFIA**   MASOALA
Marosakoa   Helodranon' i   Befandriana   Ambinanitelo   Maroantsetra
Mahajamba   Maro   Masoala
Katsepo   Tsinjomitondraka   Antsirabe   Ampanavoana
Marovato   Maroala   Tanjon' i
Mahajanga   Mampikony   Marotandrano   Masoala
Sofala   **BOENY**   Antsohihy   Manambolosy
BAIE DE   Madirovalo   Mampikony   Antanambe
BALY   Maevarano   ANKARAFANTSIKA   Mananara
Tanjona   Sitampiky   1   Mananjary
Vilanandro   Maevatanana   Tsaratanana   ANALANJIROFO
Toraka   Bekodoka   Kandreho   Soanierana-
Vestale   MELAKY   Andriamena   Ivongo
Ankasakasa   Fenoarivo   Nosy Boraha
Ambinda   Andriba   Alaotra   (Île Ste-Marie)
Besalampy   TSINGY DE   Antsiafabositra   Imerimandroso   Ambodifototra
Bereva   NAMOROKA   ZAHAMENA   Vavatenina
Beboa   Ambatomainty   Betsiko   Foulpointe
Tambohorana   Ranobe   Betafo   1454   **ATSINANANA**
Helodranon' i   Maintirano   Beravina   Kiangara   Fenoarivo
Korraraika   Bemolanga   Vatolaha   Atsinanana   **Toamasina**
Morafenobe   1565   Ambatondrazaka   (Tamatave)
Nosy Barren   Soalala   Ambodiamontana
Antsalova   Ankavandra   Ankazobe   Ambohitra   Andilamena
Soahanina   TSINGY DE   Tsiroanomandidy   Ambohidratrimo   Vohibinany
BEMARAHA   Miandrivazo   6   Manjakandriana   Moramanga
Masoarivo   Bekopaka   Mahasolo   Arivonimamo   **ANTANANARIVO**
Trangahy   Manambolo   Soavinandriana   Vatomandry
Belo-Tsiribihina   Miarinarivo   Anosibe
Maharivo   Faratsiho   Ambatolampy   Anjozorobe   Antanambao-Manampotsy
Miandrivazo   Mahajilo   Mandoto   Andranomena   Ambatomiady
Belo   **Antsirabe**   Tsinjoarivo   Ilaka
Tsiribihina   Antanifotsy   Mananoro
MENABE   Fandriana   Soanindrariny   Mangoro
Marofandilia   Morolambo   Mahanoro
Mahabo   Miandrarivo   Soavina   Fenoarivo
Morondava   Malaimbandy   1643   Ambositra   Anjiro   Masomeloka
Ambatofinandrahana   Antsenavolo
Maharivo   Ankilizato   Fandriana   Ambohimahasoa   Nosy Varika
KIRINDY   Janjina 1680   Ambositra   Antoetra
MITEA   Soavina   Vohilava
Antevamena   Mandabe   Mandrarivaro
Andranopasy   Manja   Marerano   Vohipeno
Ambakilly   Antanimbaribe   Bemavo   Tsitondroina   Ambohimahasoa
Morombe   Bemahela   Berohangy   Mananjary
Fitampito   Mahasoa   **Fianarantsoa**   Antsenavolo
Befandriana   Ihosy   FENOARIVO   Ikalamavony   Ambalavao
Basibasy   Mangoky   Berenty   IHOROMBE   Manakara
Ankilimalinika   Beroroha   ISALO   Ambalavao   Kianjavato
Manombo   Ilakaka   Vondrozo
Sakaraha   Zazafotsy   ANDRINGITRA   Ikongo
ATSIMO-   Ranohira   Vohitrafeno
ANDREFANA   Ranotsara
Lambomakandro   Nord   Karianga
Manera   Analavoka   Farafangana
Betioky   Ihosy   Vangaindrano
Helodranon' i   Betroka   ATSIMO-
Ranobe   Benenitra   Sahamadio   ATSINANANA   Mananara
Toliara   Berakèta   Beampy   Midongy Atsimo
Tongobory   Andranovory   Vohibato   MIDONGY   Manantenina
Tanjona Ankaboa   Benenitra   DU SUD
Anatsogno   Soamanonga   1637   Befotaka
Betioky   Lazarivo   Manarivolo   Esira
Andranovory   Ampanihy   Tsivory   Ranomafana
Anakao   Bekily   ANDOHAHELA
Behara   1956
Amboasary   Betroka
Beloha   Imanombo   Taolanaro
Bekily   Amboasary   (Fort Dauphin)
Esira
TSIMANAMPETSOTSE   Ampanihy   Ambovombe
Itampolo   Tranomaro   Behara
Androka   Ampotaka   Amboasary   **ANDROY**
Bevoalavo   Ambondro   Ambovombe
Tsihombe   Ankoroka
Tanjon' i Vohimena

INDIAN

OCEAN

Tropic of Capricorn

MOZAMBIQUE   **CHANNEL**

CHANNEL

ft   m
6000   2000
4500   1500
3000   1000
1500   500
600   200
0   0
200   600
1000   3000
2000   6000
3000   9000
4000   12000
m   ft

MAURITIUS
1:800 000

e

Canonniers
Point   Grand Gaube
Grand Baie   Petit   Île d'Ambre
Triolet   Raffray
Goodlands
Plaines des Papayes   *INDIAN*
Pamplemousses   Rivière du Rempart   *OCEAN*
MAURITIUS   Terre Rouge   Roches Noires
Tombeau Bay   Long Mountain   Belle Vue Maurel
Port Louis   Bon Accueil   Poste de Flacq
Grand River Bay   Moka   Pieter Both   820
Petite Rivière   St. Pierre   Centre de Flacq
Beau Bassin   Quartier   Flacq   Bel Air
Militaire   Plain
Bambous   **Rose Hill**   Montagne   Grande Rivière
Flic en Flac   **Quatre Bornes**   Blanche   Sud Est
Phoenix   Île aux Cerfs
Tamarin   Vacoas   Floreal   Mahébourg
Grande Rivière   Curepipe   Grande R. South Est
Noire   Curepipe Point   Nouvelle   Vieux Grand Port
Mare aux   686   France
BLACK RIVER   Vacoas   Rose
GORGES   Piton de la Petite   Belle
Case Noyale   828   Rivière Noire
Île aux Bénitiers   LE VAL   Piton Magnien
Pte.   Le Morne   NATURE PARK   Plaine
Sud   Brabant   Piton Savanne   Magnien   Trois Boutiques
Ouest   704   Baie du Cap   Chemin   Rivière des Anguilles
Grenier   Suriram
B. Jacotet   Le Gris Gris   Souillac

57°20'   20°20'S

Réunion
(France)

f

St-Denis   RUN   Ste-Marie
La Montagne   Ste-Suzanne
La Possession   La Rivière
Le Port   des Pluies   **St-André**
Dos d'Ane   Bras-Panon
St-Paul   Le Brûlé   Salazie
Cirque de   Le Bélier   R. du Mât
St-Gilles-   Mafate   Cirque de   Salazie   **St-Benoît**
les-Hauts   Hell-Bourg   R. des Marsouins
St-Gilles-les-Bains   2991   Salazie   Ste-Anne
La Saline   Le Gros Morne   3070   Piton des Neiges
Les Trois   2896   Col de   La Plaine   Ste-Rose
Bassins   Grand Bénare   Bellevue   des Palmistes
Cirque de   Cilaos   Grand Bassin
St-Leu   Cilaos   Bois-Blanc
Les Avirons   Entre-Deux   Piton de la
Étang-Salé   Fournaise
les-Bains   La Plaine   2631
Étang-   des Cafres   Pte. de
Salé   Le   les Cascades
St-Louis   **Tampon**
St-Pierre   Montvert-   Grand   St-Phillippe
les-Bas   Galet   Vincendo   Pte. de
INDIAN OCEAN   Petite-Île   la Table
St-Joseph

RÉUNION
1:800 000

21°15'

MADAGASCAR
1:6 400 000

50   0   50   100   150 km
50   0   50   100 miles

Administrative divisions in Madagascar:
1 Alaotra-Mangoro   3 Analamanga   5 Haute Matsiatra   7 Vakinankaratra
2 Amoron'i Mania   4 Bongolava   6 Itasy

1:800 000
5   0   5   10   20   30   40 km
5   0   5   10   15   20   25 miles

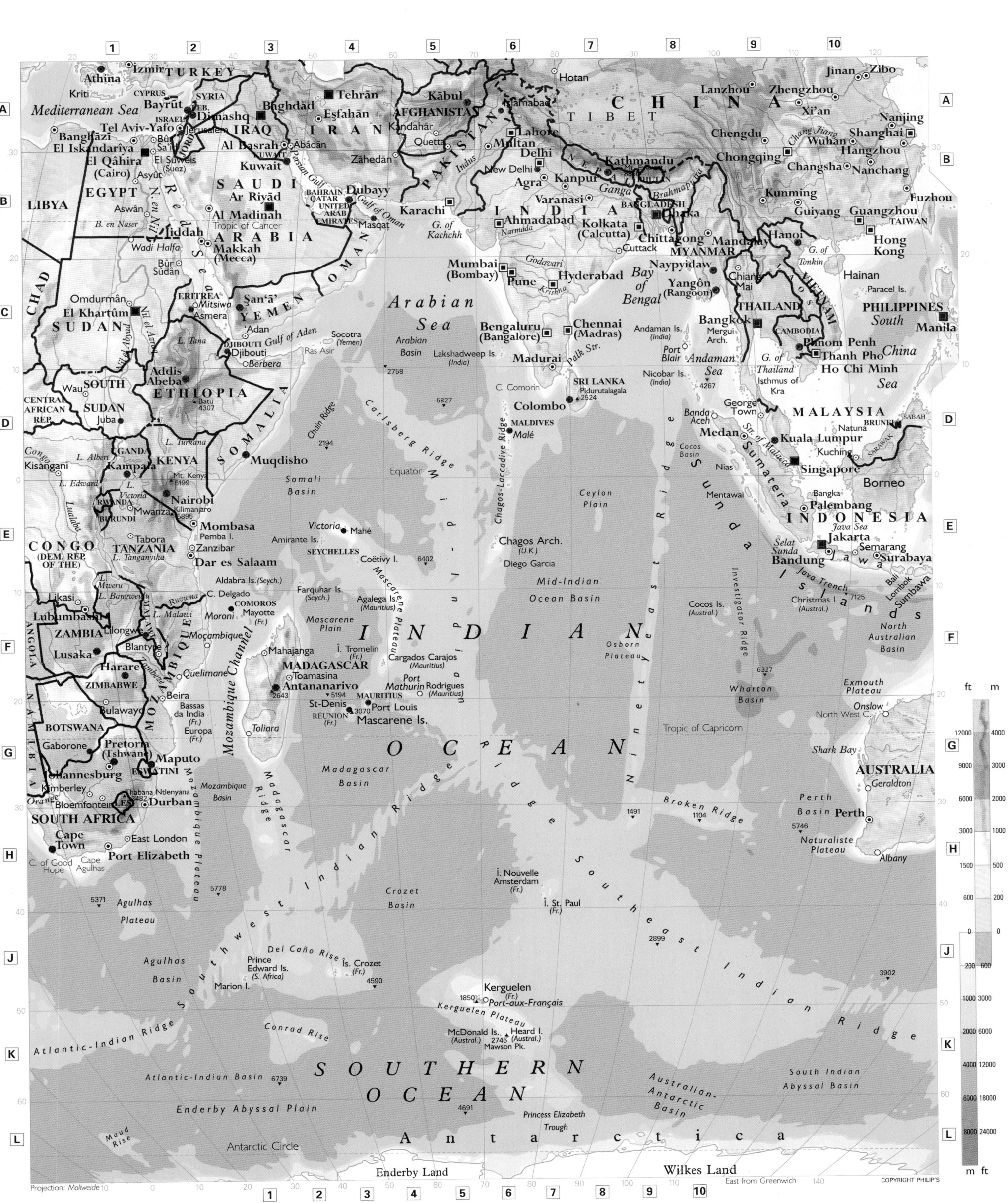

Athina
Kriti
Mediterranean Sea
Izmir TURKEY
CYPRUS SYRIA Baghdad
Bayrūt LEB. Dimashq
ISRAEL Tehrān Kābul Islamabad
Tel Aviv-Yafo Jerusalem IRAQ Esfahān AFGHANISTAN Hotan CHINA
Banghāzī Bûr Sa'īd Al Basrah IRAN Kandahār PAKISTAN Lanzhou Zhengzhou Jinan Zibo
El Iskandarîya KUWAIT Zāhedān Quetta Lahore TIBET Chengdu Xi'an Nanjing
El Qâhira Kuwait Multan Delhi Kathmandu Chongqing Chang Jiang Wuhan Shanghai
(Cairo) SAUDI Abādān New Delhi Kanpur NEPAL Changsha Hangzhou
Asyût Ar Riyād BAHRAIN Dubayy Agra Ganga Guiyang Nanchang
EGYPT QATAR UNITED Karachi INDIA BANGLADESH Kunming Fuzhou
LIBYA Al Madīnah ARAB Masqat Ahmadabad Dhaka Guangzhou Hong
Aswân Tropic of Cancer EMIRATES G. of Narmada Kolkata Chittagong TAIWAN Kong
MAKKAH Kachchh (Calcutta) Mandalay Hainan
Makkah Mumbai Godavari MYANMAR Hanoi Paracel Is.
(Mecca) (Bombay) Pune Hyderabad Bay Naypyidaw G. of
ARABIA San'ā' Krishna of Yangôn Tonkin
Omdurmân ERITREA YEMEN Arabian Bengal (Rangoon) Chiang Hainan
El Khartûm Mitsiwa 'Adan Sea Bengaluru Chennai Andaman Is. Mai PHILIPPINES South
SUDAN Asmera Gulf of Aden Socotra (Bangalore) (Madras) (India) Bangkok THAILAND China
DJIBOUTI (Yemen) Arabian Port Mergui CAMBODIA Manila
Djibouti Ras Asir Basin Lakshadweep Is. Blair Arch. Phnom Penh
Wadi Halfa Berbera Madurai (India) Andaman G. of Thanh Pho China
Bûr Sûdan SOUTH Palk Str. Sea Thailand Ho Chi Minh Sea
Addis Madurai SRI LANKA Nicobar Is. Isthmus of VIETNAM
Wau Abeba Piduratalagala (India) Kra
CENTRAL SUDAN ETHIOPIA C. Comorin Colombo MALDIVES George MALAYSIA SABAH
AFRICAN Juba Batu Málé Town BRUNEI
REP. 4307 Banda Natuna SARAWAK
L. Turkana Medan Aceh Kuala Lumpur
UGANDA Kuching Borneo
Congo SOMALIA Equator Sumatera Singapore
Kisangani L. Albert Muqdisho Nias Bangka
KENYA Ceylon Palembang
L. Edward Somali Plain Mentawai INDONESIA
Kampala Basin Chagos Arch. Java Sea
RWANDA Mt. Kenya (U.K.) Jakarta Semarang
BURUNDI 5199 Victoria Diego Garcia Jawa Surabaya
Nairobi Mahé SEYCHELLES Selat Bandung Jawa
CONGO Mwanza Victoria Amirante Is. Chagos Sunda
Mombasa Mid-Indian
Kilimanjaro Coëtivy I. Ocean Basin
5895 Pemba I. Christmas I.
TANZANIA Zanzibar Cocos Is. (Austral.) North
Tabora (Austral.) Australian
Dar es Salaam Aldabra Is. (Seych.) Mascarene Basin
L. Tanganyika Farquhar Is. Plateau
Ruvuma (Seych.) Agalega Is.
ANGOLA C. Delgado COMOROS (Mauritius)
Likasi L. Malawi Moroni Mayotte
Lubumbashi Moçambique (Fr.) Mascarene Exmouth
ZAMBIA Î. Tromelin Plain Osborn Plateau
L. Bangweulu (Fr.) Cargados Carajos Plateau
Lilongwe Mahajanga (Mauritius)
Lusaka Blantyre Port INDIAN AUSTRALIA
MADAGASCAR Mathurin Rodrigues Onslow
ZIMBABWE Antananarivo (Mauritius) North West C.
Harare Toamasina 2643 5194 MAURITIUS Wharton
MOZAMBIQUE St-Denis Port Louis Basin
Bulawayo Beira RÉUNION 3070 Tropic of Capricorn Shark Bay
BOTSWANA Bassas (Fr.) Mascarene Is. OCEAN Geraldton
da India G
Gaborone (Fr.) Madagascar Broken Ridge
Pretoria Europa Basin Perth
NAMIBIA (Tshwane) (Fr.) Basin Perth
Johannesburg Maputo Mozambique Naturaliste
Kimberley ESWATINI Basin Plateau
Orange Bloemfontein LESOTHO Madagascar Albany
Durban Ridge Southwest Î. Nouvelle
SOUTH AFRICA East London Amsterdam Indian
Cape (Fr.) Ridge Southeast
Town Port Elizabeth Î. St. Paul
C. of Good Cape (Fr.) Indian
Hope Agulhas 5778
Agulhas Crozet Ridge
Plateau Basin
Agulhas Prince Îs. Crozet
Basin Edward Is. (Fr.)
(S. Africa) Del Caño Rise 4590
Marion I.
Atlantic-Indian Ridge Kerguelen
Conrad Rise (Fr.) SOUTHERN
Kerguelen Plateau Port-aux-Français
McDonald Is. Heard I. OCEAN South Indian
(Austral.) (Austral.) Abyssal Basin
Mawson Pk. Australian-
Atlantic-Indian Basin Antarctic
Enderby Abyssal Plain Basin
Princess Elizabeth
Trough
Antarctic Circle A n t a r c t i c a
Projection: Mollweide Enderby Land Wilkes Land East from Greenwich COPYRIGHT PHILIP'S

ft m
12000 4000
9000 3000
6000 2000
3000 1000
1500 500
600 200
0 0
200 600
1000 3000
2000 6000
4000 12000
6000 18000
8000 24000
m ft

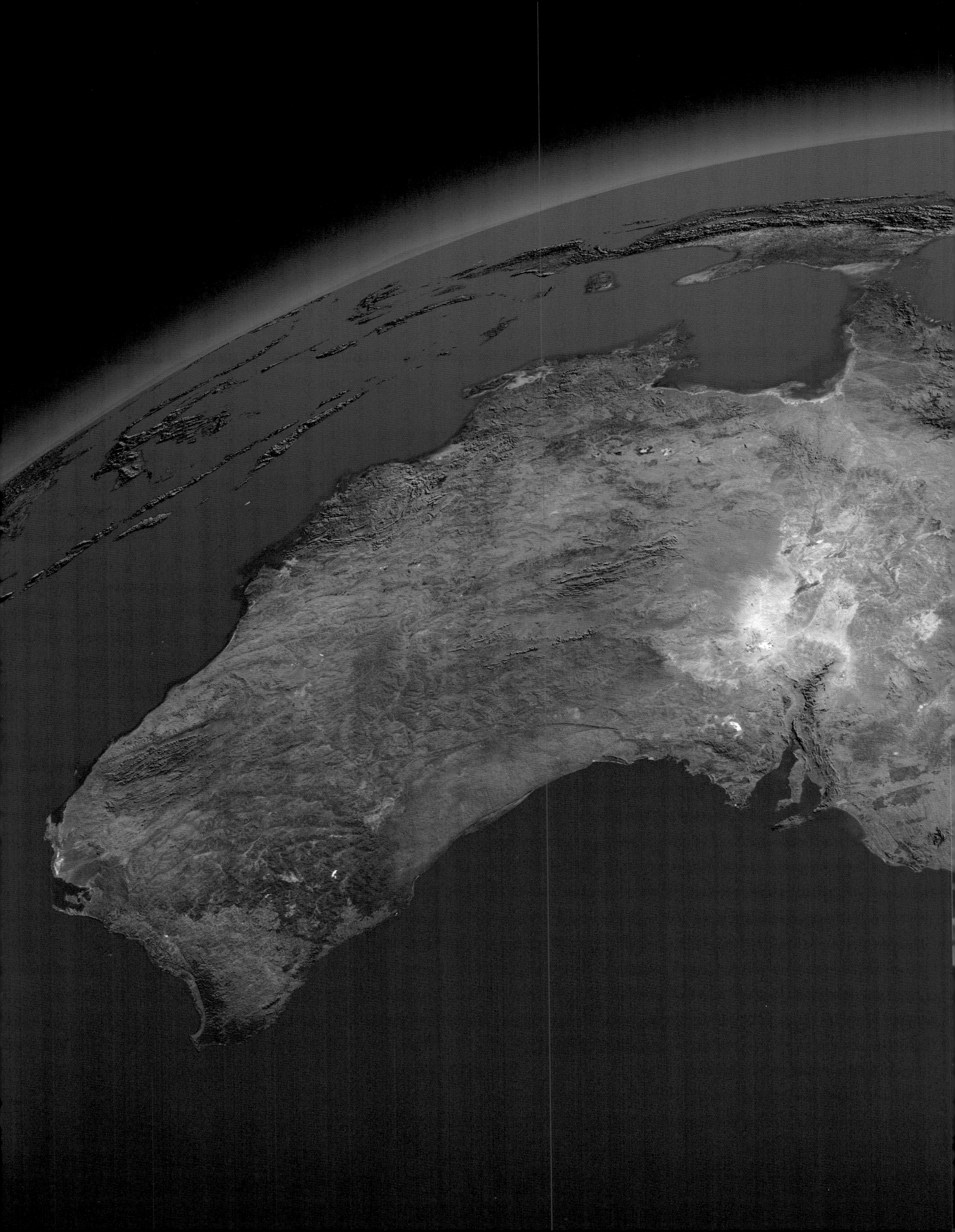

AUSTRALIA AND OCEANIA

1:16 000 000

100 0 100 200 300 400 500 600 700 800 km
100 0 100 200 300 400 500 miles

Projection: Lambert's Equivalent Azimuthal

East from Greenwich

Physical features and labels:

Equator
Maluku (Moluccas)
Sulawesi (Celebes)
Palu
Palopo
Parepare
Kendari
Watampone
Butung
MAKASSAR (Ujung Pandang)
Mamuju
Kep. Sula
Buru
Seram Sea
Seram (Ceram)
Ambon
Banda Sea
Flores Sea
Sumbawa
Raba
Flores
Ende
Timor
Kupang
Savu Sea
Sumba
Roti
Alor
Leti
Babar
Wetar
Dili
TIMOR-LESTE
Timor Sea
North Australian Basin
Ashmore and Cartier Is.
C. Londonderry

Waigeo
Sorong
Misool
Vogelkop Peninsula
Yapen
Biak
Fakfak
Weber
Kep. Kai
Kep. Aru
Basin
Kep. Tanimbar
Pulau Dolak
Arafura Sea
Papua
Pegunungan Maoke
Puncak Jaya
New Guinea
Fly
Gulf of Papua
Jayapura
Wewak
Madang
Mount Hagen
Mt. Wilhelm
Lae
Owen Stanley Range
Port Moresby
Bismarck Sea
Bismarck Archipelago
PAPUA NEW GUINEA
Kavieng
New Ireland
Kokopo
New Britain
New Britain Trench
Solomon Sea
D'Entrecasteaux Islands
Louisiade Archipelago
Coral Sea
Basin

Torres Strait
Badu I. Moa I.
C. York
Prince of Wales I.
Cape York Peninsula
Weipa
Gulf of Carpentaria
C. Croker
Melville I.
Bathurst I.
Coburg Pen.
C. Arnhem
Arnhem Land
Groote Eylandt
Wellesley Is.
Darwin
Katherine
Larrimah
Daly Waters
Tennant Creek

NORTHERN
Tanami Desert
TERRITORY
Great Sandy Desert
Kimberley
Halls Creek
Derby
Broome
Wyndham
Kununurra
L. Argyle
Port Hedland
Dampier
Karratha
N.W. Cape
Pannawonica
Newman
Mt Meharry
Hamersley Range
Paraburdoo
Pilbara
Carnarvon
Gascoyne
Shark Bay
Meekatharra
Murchison

L. Mackay
L. Disappointment
Gibson Desert
AUSTRALIA
WESTERN
MacDonnell Ranges
Mt. Zeil
Alice Springs
Uluru (Ayers Rock)
Mt. Woodroffe
Musgrave Ranges
L. Carnegie
Great Victoria Desert
AUSTRALIA
Lake Barlee
Mount Magnet
Leonora
Kalgoorlie-Boulder
Geraldton
Northam
PERTH
Rockingham
Bunbury
Mandurah
Augusta
Albany
C. Leeuwin
Naturaliste Plateau
INDIAN OCEAN
Norseman
Esperance
Nullarbor Plain

Simpson Desert
Sturt Stony Desert
SOUTH
Cooper Creek
Coober Pedy
Kati Thanda–Lake Eyre
Marree
AUSTRALIA
Lake Torrens
Lake Gairdner
Tarcoola
Penong
Great Australian Bight
Port Augusta
Whyalla
Port Pirie
Eyre Pen.
Port Lincoln
Spencer Gulf
Yorke Pen.
Gulf St. Vincent
ADELAIDE
Kangaroo I.
Encounter B.
Murray Bridge
St. Mary Pk.
Flinders Ranges
Broken Hill

QUEENSLAND
Great Dividing Range
Normanton
Forsayth
Cairns
Bartle Frere
Townsville
Charters Towers
Hughenden
Mount Isa
Cloncurry
Kajabbi
Dajarra
Winton
Longreach
Yaraka
Emerald
Rockhampton
Gladstone
Bundaberg
Maryborough
Gympie
Charleville
Roma
Quilpie
Thargomindah
Cunnamulla
Dirranbandi
Bourke
Cobar
Walgett
Moree
Warrego
Paroo
Darling
NEW SOUTH WALES
Dubbo
Tamworth
Port Macquarie
Taree
Newcastle
Gosford
SYDNEY
Wollongong
Orange
Bathurst
Griffith
Wagga Wagga
Goulburn
Canberra
A.C.T.
Mt. Kosciuszko
Snowy Mts.
Albury-Wodonga
Murray
Murrumbidgee
Hay
Mildura
Swan Hill
Shepparton
Bendigo
Horsham
VICTORIA
Ballarat
MELBOURNE
Geelong
Mount Gambier
Warrnambool
Sale
Wilsons Promontory
C. Howe
Bombala
Bass Strait
King I.
Flinders I.
Furneaux Group
TASMANIA
Burnie
Devonport
Launceston
Mt. Ossa
Hobart
S.E. Cape

Cooktown
Whitsunday Is.
L. Dalrymple
Mackay
Mitchell
Flinders
Grey Range
Barkly Tableland
Diamantina

Queensland Plateau
CORAL SEA ISLANDS TERRITORY
Great Barrier Reef
Coral Sea
Brisbane
Ipswich
Toowoomba
Lismore
Round Mt.

Darling Range
Joseph Bonaparte Gulf
Bonaparte Archipelago
Brisbane

INDIAN OCEAN
South Australian Basin
SOUTHERN OCEAN
Tasman Abyssal Plain
South Tasman Plateau

Elevation scale (ft / m):
6000 / 2000
4500 / 1500
3000 / 1000
1200 / 400
600 / 200
0 / 0
200 / 600
2000 / 6000
4000 / 12 000
6000 / 18 000

Spot heights: 2490, 2452, 2799, 3440, 5300, 2736, 3019, 5123, 2821, 2350, 2963, 3310, 6204, 5632, 1073, 970, 1251, 1126, 867, 1531, 5435, 16, 1168, 1312, 216, 1605, 1585, 2228, 1617, 7260, 3350, 4884, 4072, 3993, 4508, 4121, 1481, 2438, 2027, 3989

Ontong Java Plateau

Bougainville
Balbi
tland Is.
Lavella
1067
Choiseul
New Georgia Is.
Vangunu
Russell Is.
Honiara
Guadalcanal
Santa Isabel
1219
Florida Is.
Makira (San Cristóbal)
Bellona
Rennell
Pocklington Reef

SOLOMON ISLANDS
1432 Malaita
2439
1256
1250

Solomon Rise

South Solomon Trench
7223

Reef Is.
Nendo
9165
Santa Cruz Is.
Vanikoro
Tikopia
Fataka
Duff Is.

Is. Torres
Vanua Lava
Is. Banks
Gaua
Espíritu Santo
1879
Malakula
863
Epi
Shepherd Is.
Port Vila
Efate
Erromango
1084
Tanna
Aneityum
7569

VANUATU (New Hebrides)

Îles D'Entrecasteaux
Îles Chesterfield
Îles Bélep
1628
Îles Loyauté
New Caledonia (Fr.)
La Foa
î. Lifou
î. Maré
Nouméa
Yaté
î. des Pins
î. Matthew
Ceve-i-Ra

Tabiteuea
Onotoa
Tamana
Beru
Nikunau
Arorae

Gilbert Is.

Namumea
Nanumanga
Niutao
Nui
Vaitupu

6195

K I R I B A T I

TUVALU (Ellice Is.)
Funafuti
Fongafale
Nukulaelae
Niulakita

Baker I. (U.S.A.)
Equator
International Date Line

Winslow Reef
McKean
Abariringa
Birnie
Nikumaroro
Carondelet Reef
Orona
Manra

Phoenix Is.
Enderbury
Rawaki

Atafu
Nukunonu
Fakaofo

Tokelau Is. (N.Z.)
International Date Line

Rotuma
Mata-Utu
Uvea
Horn
Alofi

Wallis & Futuna (Fr.)

SAMOA
Savai'i
1858
Apia
'Upolu
Pago Pago
Tutuila

American Samoa (U.S.A.)

Vanua Levu
1031
Taveuni
Viti Levu
1323
Suva
Kadavu

FIJI
Niuafo'ou
Lau Group
Niua Group
Niuatoputapu

West Fiji Basin
South New Hebrides Trench

Vava'u Group
Late
Lau Basin
Ha'apai Group
Nuku'alofa
Tongatapu Group
Eua
Ata

TONGA
Alofi
Niue (N.Z.)

P A C I F I C

5303

Lord Howe Seamount Chain
Caledonia Trough
Norfolk Ridge
Norfolk I. (Austral.)
Norfolk Basin

South Fiji Basin

Lord Howe Rise
Lord Howe I. (Austral.)
734

O C E A N

10 882
Tonga Trench

Tropic of Capricorn

Raoul I.
Kermadec Is. (N.Z.)
Macauley I.
Curtis I.
10 047
Colville Ridge
Kermadec Trench

Southwest

asman Sea

North C.
Kaitaia
Whangarei

AUCKLAND
Hamilton
Bay of Plenty
Tauranga

North Island

Challenger Plateau
New Plymouth
Rotorua
Ruapahu
2797
Gisborne
Napier
Wanganui
Palmerston North
Masterton
Nelson
Cook Strait
Wellington

Pacific

International Date Line

Basin

NEW ZEALAND

5267

South Island
Greymouth
Aoraki Mt. Cook
3724
Southern Alps
Christchurch
Queenstown
Timaru
Invercargill
Stewart I.
Dunedin

Chatham Rise
Chatham I.
Chatham Is. (N.Z.)
Pitt I.

50 0 50 100 150 200 250 300 km

1:6 400 000

50 0 50 100 150 200 miles

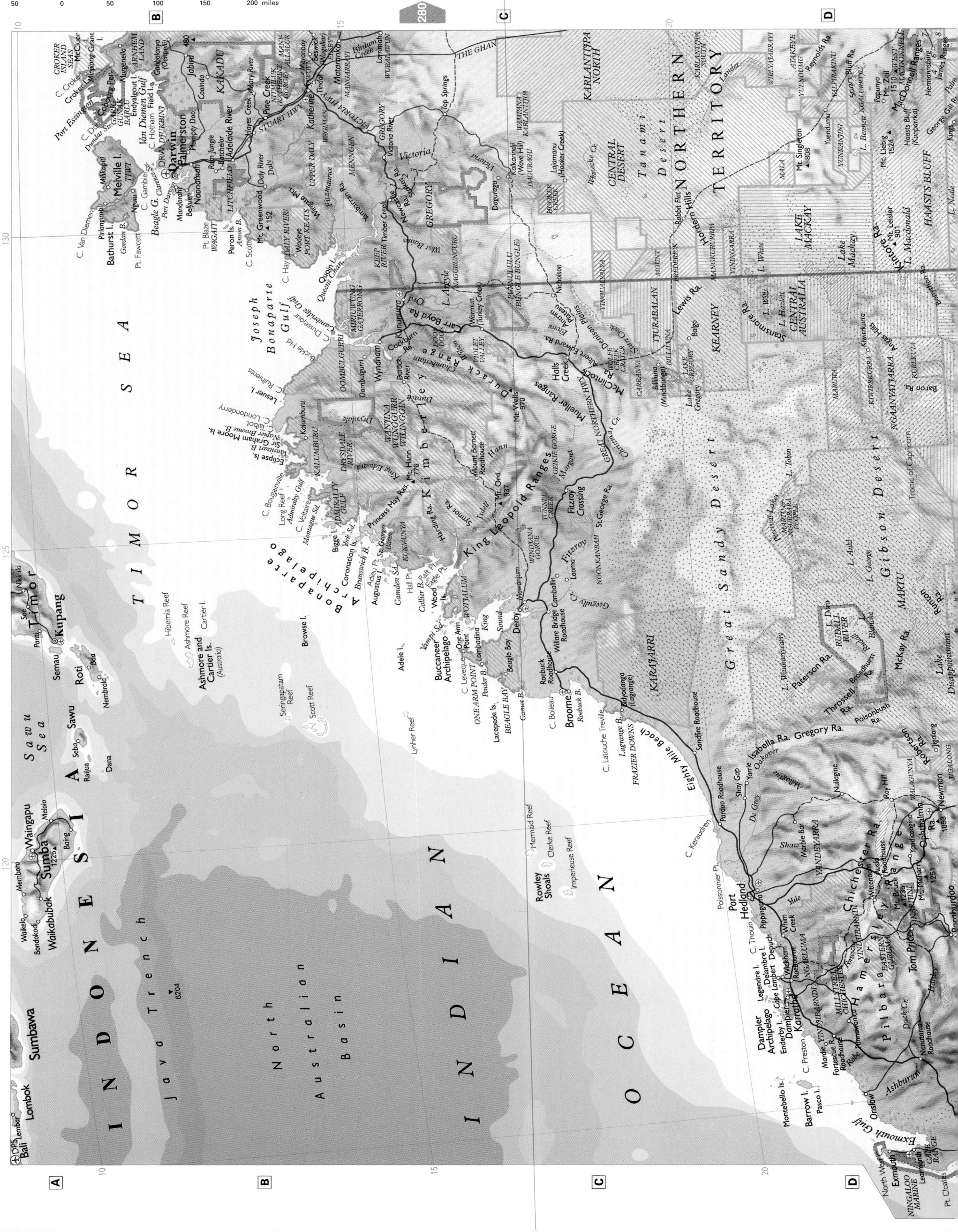

T I M O R   S E A

I N D O N E S I A

Saw u Sea

Java Trench

North Australian Basin

I N D I A N   O C E A N

NORTHERN TERRITORY

Joseph Bonaparte Gulf

Bonaparte Archipelago

KIMBERLEY

King Leopold Ranges

Great Sandy Desert

Gibson Desert

Tanami Desert

CENTRAL DESERT

LAKE MACKAY

Darwin
Palmerston
Katherine
Wyndham
Kununurra
Halls Creek
Derby
Broome
Port Hedland

ARNHEM LAND

KAKADU

Melville I.
Bathurst I.

Sumba
Sumbawa
Lombok
Bali
Kupang
Timor
Roti
Sawu

Fitzroy Crossing

Pilbara
Chichester Range
Hamersley Range

Exmouth Gulf

6204

CAPE RANGE

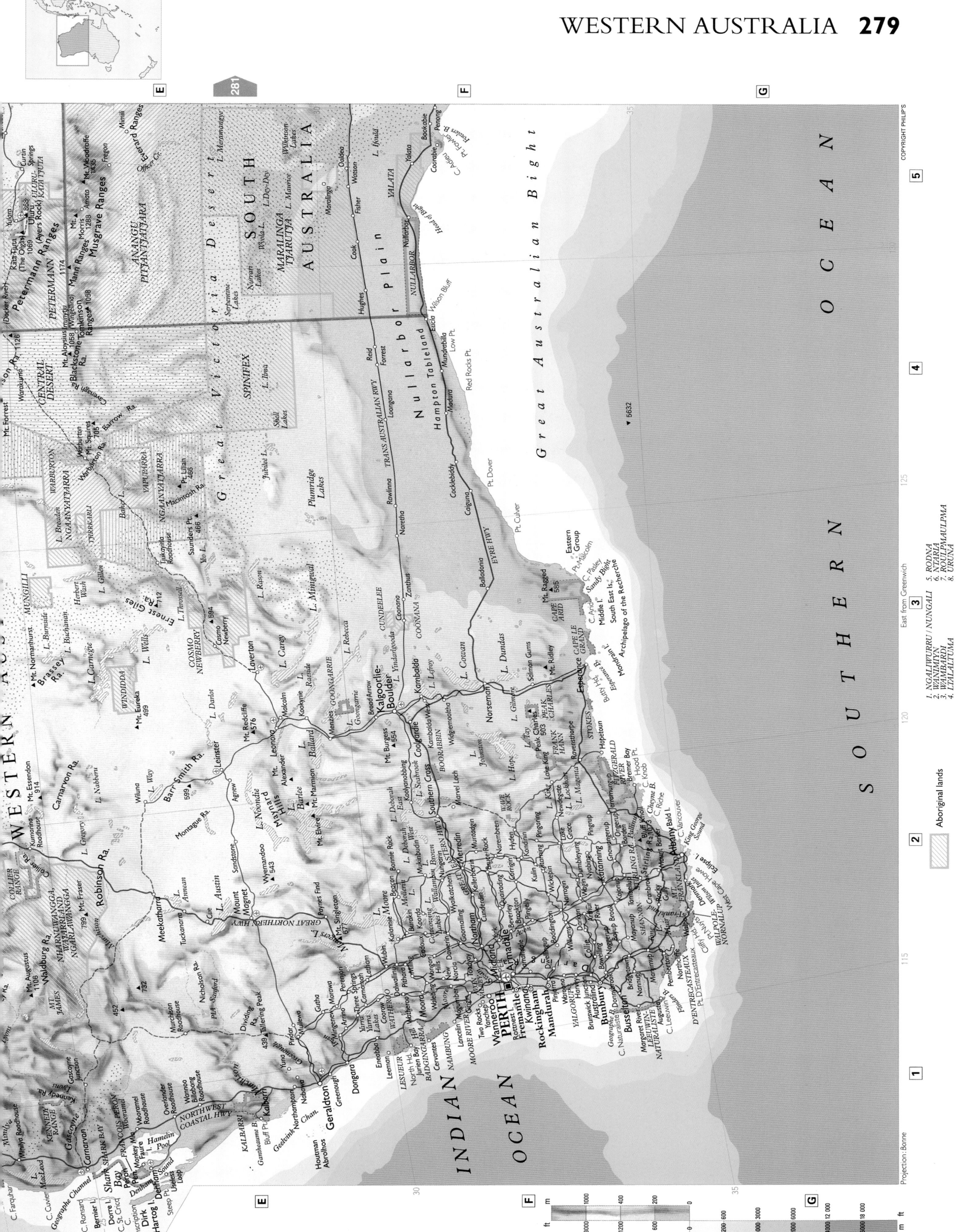

E F G

WESTERN AUSTRALIA

SOUTH AUSTRALIA

Great Victoria Desert

SPINIFEX

Nullarbor Plain

Hampton Tableland

Great Australian Bight

SOUTHERN OCEAN

INDIAN OCEAN

PERTH
Fremantle
Mandurah
Bunbury
Busselton
Geraldton
Kalbarri
Carnarvon

Kalgoorlie-Boulder
Coolgardie
Norseman
Esperance

Albany

Aboriginal lands

1. NGALIWURRU / NUNGALI
2. WANIMYN
3. WAMBARDI
4. LTALALTUMA
5. RODNA
6. NTARIA
7. ROULPMAULPMA
8. URUNA

East from Greenwich

Projection: Bonne

COPYRIGHT PHILIP'S

m
ft
4000 12 000
3000
2000 6000
1000
600 2000
400 1200
200 600
0
0
200
600
1000 3000
2000 6000
4000 12 000
5000 18 000
m ft

1:6 400 000

50 0 50 100 150 200 250 300 km
50 0 50 100 150 200 miles

a

PAPUA NEW GUINEA

Gulf of Papua

CORAL SEA

TORRES STRAIT on same scale as main map

Great Barrier Reef

Torres Strait

QUEENSLAND

Cape York Peninsula

OLD MAPOON

Parama · Daru · Bristow · Darnley · Murray · Mabuiag · Masig · Yam · Sassie · Badu · Moa · Poruma · Turnagain · Gabba · Yorke · Prince of Wales · Thursday I. · Horn I. · Endeavour Str. · Bamaga · INTINOO

b

GLOUCESTER I. · Gloucester Pt. · C. George's Pt. · Bowen

CORAL SEA

Hayman I. · Hook I. · 459 · Whitsunday I. · 390 · Hamilton I. · Lindeman I. · Shaw I. · WHITSUNDAY ISLANDS · Cumberland Islands · Brampton I. · SMITH ISLANDS · Carlisle I. · St. Bees I.

Cumberland Is.

SOUTH CUMBERLAND IS. · CAPE HILLSBOROUGH · Hillsborough Channel · Mackay

Airlie Beach · Cannonvale · Shute Harbour · Proserpine · PROSERPINE · Foxdale · Conway · CONWAY · Whitsunday Pass.

Repulse Bay · C. Conway · REPULSE IS. · Midge Point · Slade Pt.

QUEENSLAND · Mt. McGuire 738 ▲ · Kelsey Creek · EUNGELLA · Broken River · Ra. · Clarke Ra. · Netherdale · Calen · Seaforth · Kuttabul · Farleigh · Kungurri · Mirani · Bucasia

DRYANDER 820 ▲ · Yalboroo · Mt. Dalrymple 1259 ▲

1:2 000 000

WHITSUNDAY ISLANDS

Abington Reef

CORAL SEA

Osprey Reef

Great Barrier Reef

Cape York Peninsula

Gulf of Carpentaria

ARNHEM LAND

NORTHERN TERRITORY

QUEENSLAND

Great Dividing Range

Great Artesian Basin

Cairns · Townsville · Mackay · Rockhampton · Gladstone

Mount Isa · Cloncurry · Winton · Longreach · Barcaldine · Emerald

Alice Springs · MacDonnell Ranges

Simpson Desert

Tropic of Capricorn

Capricorn Channel · Capricorn Coast · Rockhampton Capricorn · Yeppoon · Heron I. · Lady Elliot I.

GREAT BARRIER REEF (CAPRICORN)

Barkly Tableland

Tennant Creek

Channel Country

COPYRIGHT PHILIP'S

TASMAN SEA

QUEENSLAND

NEW SOUTH WALES

SOUTH AUSTRALIA

VICTORIA

TASMANIA

Major cities and towns:

BRISBANE, Gold Coast, Sunshine Coast, Coral Coast, Hervey Bay, Maryborough, Gympie, Noosa Heads, Nambour, Caloundra, Caboolture, Redcliffe, Ipswich, Beenleigh, Southport, Surfers Paradise, Nerang, Tweed Heads, Murwillumbah, Lismore, Ballina, Byron Bay, Grafton, Coffs Harbour, Nambucca Heads, Kempsey, Port Macquarie, Taree, Forster, Tuncurry, Nelson Bay, Newcastle, Raymond Terrace, Maitland, Cessnock, Gosford, Hornsby, SYDNEY, Parramatta, Liverpool, Campbelltown, Wollongong, Shellharbour, Kiama, Nowra, Kiama

Toowoomba, Warwick, Tenterfield, Inverell, Glen Innes, Armidale, Tamworth, Gunnedah, Narrabri, Moree, Goondiwindi, Dubbo, Orange, Bathurst, Lithgow, Katoomba, Mudgee, Wellington, Parkes, Forbes, Cowra, Young, Cootamundra, Wagga Wagga, Albury, Wodonga, Canberra, Queanbeyan, Goulburn, Yass, Cooma, Bega, Batemans Bay, Ulladulla, Narooma, Eden

Broken Hill, Cobar, Bourke, Nyngan, Griffith, Leeton, Narrandera, Hay, Deniliquin, Echuca

ADELAIDE, Elizabeth, Salisbury, Gawler, Port Pirie, Port Augusta, Whyalla, Port Lincoln, Mount Gambier, Naracoorte, Murray Bridge, Victor Harbor, Kingston S.E., Robe

MELBOURNE, Geelong, Ballarat, Bendigo, Shepparton, Wodonga, Wangaratta, Benalla, Seymour, Sale, Bairnsdale, Traralgon, Morwell, Moe, Warragul, Dandenong, Frankston, Mornington, Warrnambool, Portland, Hamilton, Horsham, Ararat, Stawell, Mildura, Swan Hill, Kerang, Maryborough, Castlemaine, Colac

South Australia features: Lake Eyre, Kati Thanda–Lake Eyre (North), Kati Thanda–Lake Eyre (South), Lake Torrens, Lake Gairdner, Lake Frome, Lake Blanche, Lake Callabonna, Flinders Ranges, Gammon Ranges, Gawler Ranges, Eyre Peninsula, Yorke Peninsula, Spencer Gulf, Gulf St Vincent, Kangaroo Island, Simpson Desert, Strzelecki Desert, Sturt Stony Desert, Tirari Desert, Pedirka Desert, Coorong, Coober Pedy, Woomera, Marree, Oodnadatta, William Creek, Innamincka

Coongie L., Cooper Cr., Warburton Cr., Diamantina R.

Murray R., Darling R., Murrumbidgee R., Lachlan R., Macquarie R., Bogan R., Castlereagh R., Namoi R., Gwydir R., Barwon R., Paroo R., Warrego R., Condamine R.

Great Dividing Range, Barrier Range, Grey Range, McGregor Ra., Chesterton Range, Warrego Range, Nandewar Range, Liverpool Range, Warrumbungle Range, Mt Kosciuszko 2228, Snowy Mts., Australian Alps, Blue Mts.

Bass Strait, King Island, Flinders Island, Furneaux Group, Kent Group, Cape Barren Island, Banks Strait

Tasmania: HOBART, Launceston, Devonport, Burnie, Glenorchy, Queenstown, Zeehan, Strahan, Smithton, Stanley, Wynyard, Scottsdale, St Helens, Bicheno, Swansea, Triabunna, Sorell, New Norfolk, Cradle Mt., Mt Ossa 1617, Ben Lomond, Mt Field, Lake St Clair, Great Lake, Tasman Peninsula, Freycinet Pen., Forestier Pen., Bruny I., Maria I., Schouten I., South East C., South West C.

Projection: Bonne

Aboriginal lands

on same scale

m / ft 12 000 6000 4000 3000 2000 1000 600 400 200 0 200 400 600 1200 1500 ft

East from Greenwich 140 145 150

279

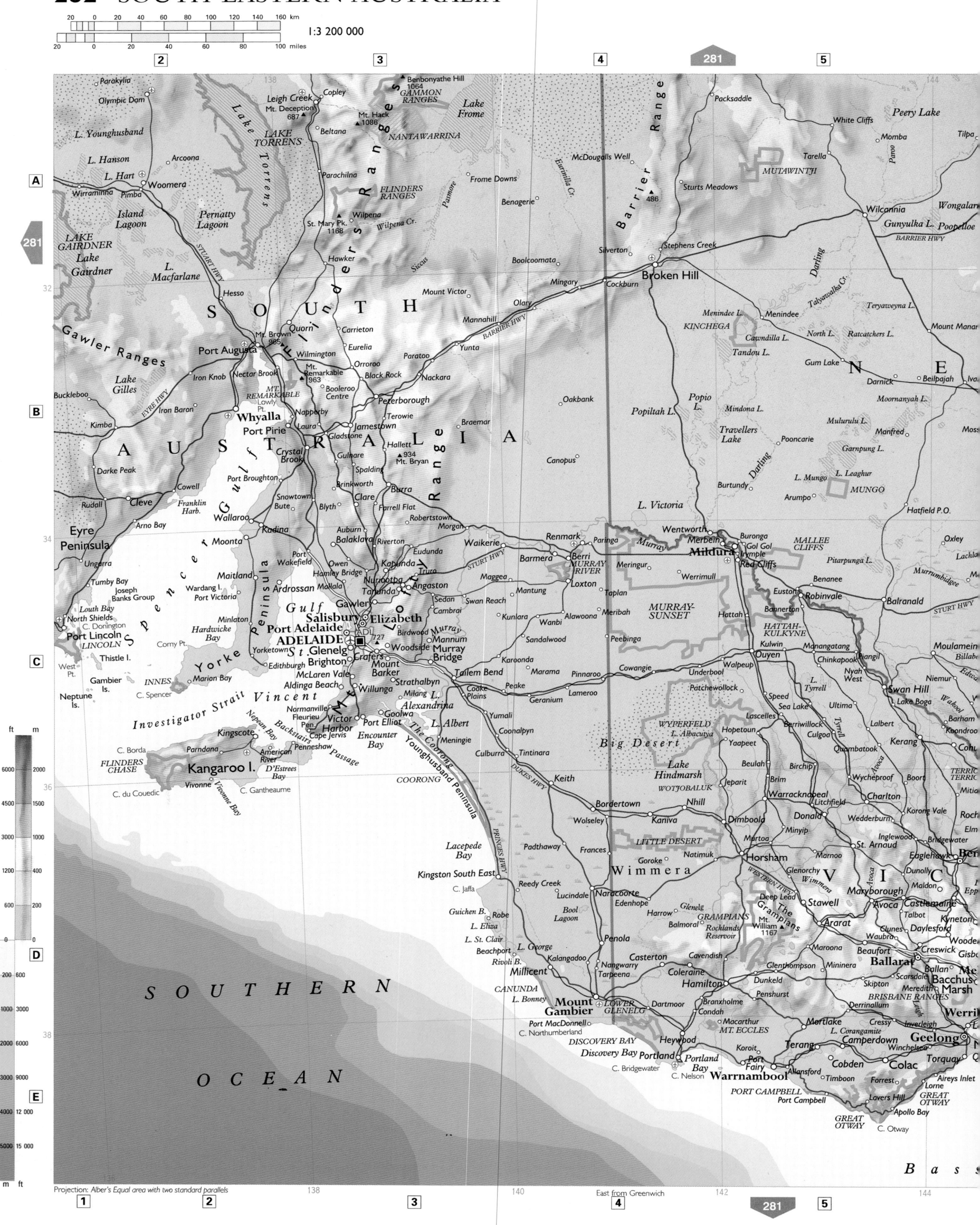

1:3 200 000

20 0 20 40 60 80 100 120 140 160 km
20 0 20 40 60 80 100 miles

Projection: Alber's Equal area with two standard parallels

East from Greenwich

TASMAN

SEA

Aboriginal lands

COPYRIGHT PHILIP'S

East from Greenwich

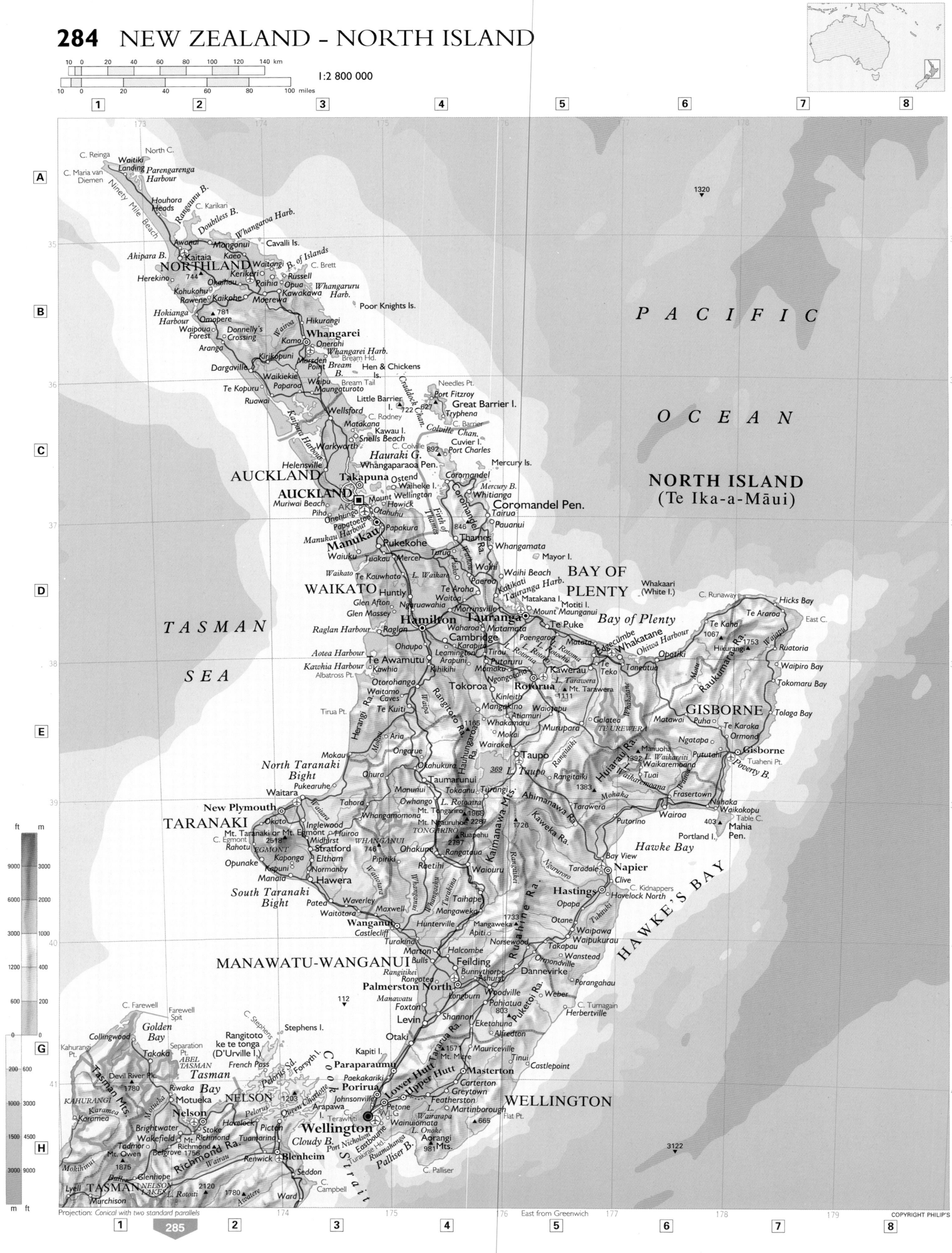

1:2 800 000

10 0 20 40 60 80 100 120 140 km
10 0 20 40 60 80 100 miles

284

NEW ZEALAND – SOUTH ISLAND

T A S M A N   S E A

C. Farewell
Farewell Spit
Golden Bay
Collingwood
Takaka
Separation Pt.
Rangitoto ke te tonga (D'Urville I.)
C. Stephens
Stephens I.
French Pass
Kahurangi Pt.
ABEL TASMAN
Pelorus Sd.
C. Jackson
Forsyth I.
Queen Charlotte Sd.
Devil River Pk.
1780
KAHURANGI
Riwaka
Motueka
Tasman Bay
Arapawa I.
NELSON
Karamea
Mohikinui
Brightwater
Wakefield
Mt. Richmond
1756
Richmond
Stoke
Nelson
Havelock
Pelorus
Picton
Tuamarina
1203
Cloudy B.
Karamea Bight
Karamea
Granity
Millerton
Matiri
Mt. Owen
1875
Glenhope
Richmond Ra.
Renwick
Blenheim
Waimarie
Waimangaroa
Westport
Lyell
Tadmor
Seddon
C. Foulwind
Buller
Gorge
TASMAN
Murchison
St. Arnaud
Wairau
MARLBOROUGH
Ward
Inangahua
L. Rotoiti
2120
1780
Awatere
C. Campbell
Reefton
Mt. Travers
2337
Mt. Franklin
2340
NELSON LAKES
Tapuae-o-Uenuku
2885
Wharanui
PAPAROA
Punakaiki
Paparoa Ra.
Victoria Ra.
Spenser Mts.
Molesworth
Inland Kaikoura Ra.
Ikamatua
Grey
Blackball
Maruia Springs
Seaward Kaikoura Ra.
2608
Manakau
Greymouth
Runanga
Ahaura
Lewis Pass
Hanmer Springs
1747
Kaikoura
Taramakau
L. Brunner
Kumara
L. Kaimata
Mt. Ajax
1834
L. Sumner
1615
Waiau
Kaikoura Pen.
Hokitika
Jacksons
ARTHUR'S PASS
Otira
Mt. Crossley
1980
Culverden
Waiau
Parnassus
Ross
Otira Gorge
Arthur's Pass
926
Hurunui
Domett
L. Kaniere
Waikari
Waipara
Sedgill
Wanganui
Abut Hd.
Harihari
Whataroa
Mt. Murchison
2408
Whitcombe Pass
L. Coleridge
Sheffield
Oxford
Amberley
Sefton
Rangiora
Whataroa
Okarito
Arrowsmith
2781
Lake Coleridge
Springfield
Whitecliffs
Kaiapoi
Belfast
New Brighton
Pegasus Bay
L. Mapourika
Mt. Taylor
2333
Darfield
CHCH
Aorangi
Christchurch
Gillespies Pt.
WESTLAND TAI POUTINI
Franz Josef Glacier
AORAKI MT. COOK
Highbank
Rolleston
Hornby
Sumner
Lyttelton
Fox Glacier
Mt. Tasman 3497
Rakaia
Leeston
Lincoln
919
Little River
Banks Pen.
Bruce B.
Mount Cook
3724
Tasman Gl.
2251
Mount Somers
Methven
Southbridge
L. Ellesmere
Akaroa
Tititira Hd.
Aoraki / Mount Cook
Two Thumbs Ra.
Ashburton
Akaroa Harbour
Jackson
Haast
Okuru
Glenmary
L. Tekapo
Lake Tekapo
Tinwald
Geraldine
Hinds
Ashburton
Jackson Hd.
Jackson B.
Hunter Ra.
2590
L. Pukaki
Fairlie
Winchester
Cascade Pt.
MOUNT ASPIRING
L. Ohau
Lake Pukaki
Temuka
Canterbury Bight
Awarua Pt.
Awarua B.
Olivine Ra.
Mt. Aspiring
3033
Barrier Ra.
Waitaki Plains
1894
Pleasant Point
Timaru
Yates Pt.
Mt. Tutoko
2723
Milford Sd.
L. McKerrow
Young Ra.
L. Wanaka
Benmore Pk.
St. Andrews
Mitre Peak
1683
Milford Sound
Mt. Earnslaw
2819
Hawea
St. Bathan's
2087
Hunter
Bligh Sound
George Sound
Sutherland Falls
Richardson Mts.
Wanaka
1938
Hawea Flat
L. Aviemore
Waitaki
Waihao
Caswell Sound
Harris Mts.
Pisa Ra.
Hakataramea
Kurow
Waimate
Charles Sound
1610
Glenorchy
Cromwell
Duntroon
Waihao
Thompson Sd.
Murchison Mts.
Queenstown
2319
Clyde
Dunstan Mts.
Hawkdun Ra.
Ngapara
Downs
Morven
Glenavy
Secretary I.
Mt. Lyall
1892
L. Wakatipu
Double Cone
Alexandra
St. Bathans
Tokarahi
Maheno
Doubtful Sd.
Jane Pk.
2022
Arrowtown
Roxburgh
Rough Ridge
Naseby
Kakanui Mts.
Pukeuri
Dagg Sd.
Kepler Mts.
Te Anau
Eyre Mts.
Garvie Mts.
Middlemarch
Ranfurly
Oamaru
FIORDLAND
L. Te Anau
Athol
Kingston
1449
Hyde
Hampden
Breaksea Sd.
L. Manapouri
Umbrella Mts.
Waikouaiti Downs
Resolution I.
Heath
Mavora
Waikaia
Miller's Flat
Sutton
Waikouaiti
Dusky Sd.
SOUTHLAND
OTAGO
Edievale
Beaumont
Warrington
Palmerston
Providence
Hunter Mts.
Mossburn
Lumsden
Waikaia
Dunback
Shag Pt.
Chalky
Caroline Pk.
Dipton
Waimea Plain
Dunedin
Otago Harbour
Inlet
463
1794
Monowai
Ohai
Nightcaps
Riversdale
Kelso
Lawrence
Port Chalmers
Otago Pen.
Preservation
L. Hauroko
Birchwood
Tapanui
Waipahi
Clinton
Mosgiel
C. Saunders
Inlet
Coal
Orawia
Otautau
Winton
Gore
Clutha
Milton
Allanton
Puysegur Pt.
Te Waewae
Clifden
Wairio
Waikaka
Balclutha
Taieri
Waihola
B.
Tuatapere
Thornbury
Hedgehope
Stirling
St. Kilda
Pahia Pt.
Makarewa
Edendale
Wyndham
Kaitangata
Riverton
Glenham
Owaka
Nugget Pt.
Orepuki
Wallacetown
Tahakopa
Centre I.
South Invercargill
Invercargill
Catlins
Tokanui
Long Pt.
Bluff
Fortrose
Chaslands Mistake
Toetoes B.
Waipapa Pt.
Foveaux Str.
Mt. Anglem
980
Solander I.
Codfish I.
Ruapuke I.
Mason B.
Halfmoon Bay
Paterson Inlet
Doughboy B.
RAKIURA
Stewart I. (Rakiura)
Port Pegasus
South West C.

SOUTH ISLAND (Te Waipounamu)

Westland Bight

SOUTHERN ALPS (KA TIRITIRI O TE MOANA)

CANTERBURY PLAINS

Mackenzie Plains

4870

P A C I F I C   O C E A N

CHATHAM ISLANDS
on same scale

a

PACIFIC OCEAN

The Sisters
C. Young
Munning Pt.
Western Reef
Te One
Waitangi
Chatham I. (Rekohu)
The Forty Fours
Owenga
C. Fournier

Chatham Islands (Wharekauri)

The Horns
Pitt Strait
Mangere I.
Star Keys
The Pyramid
Pitt I.
Rangatira I.

West from Greenwich

ft m
9000 3000
6000 2000
3000 1000
1200 400
600 200
0 0
200 600
1000 3000
1500 4500
3000 9000
4000 12 000
m ft

Projection: Conical with two standard parallels

East from Greenwich

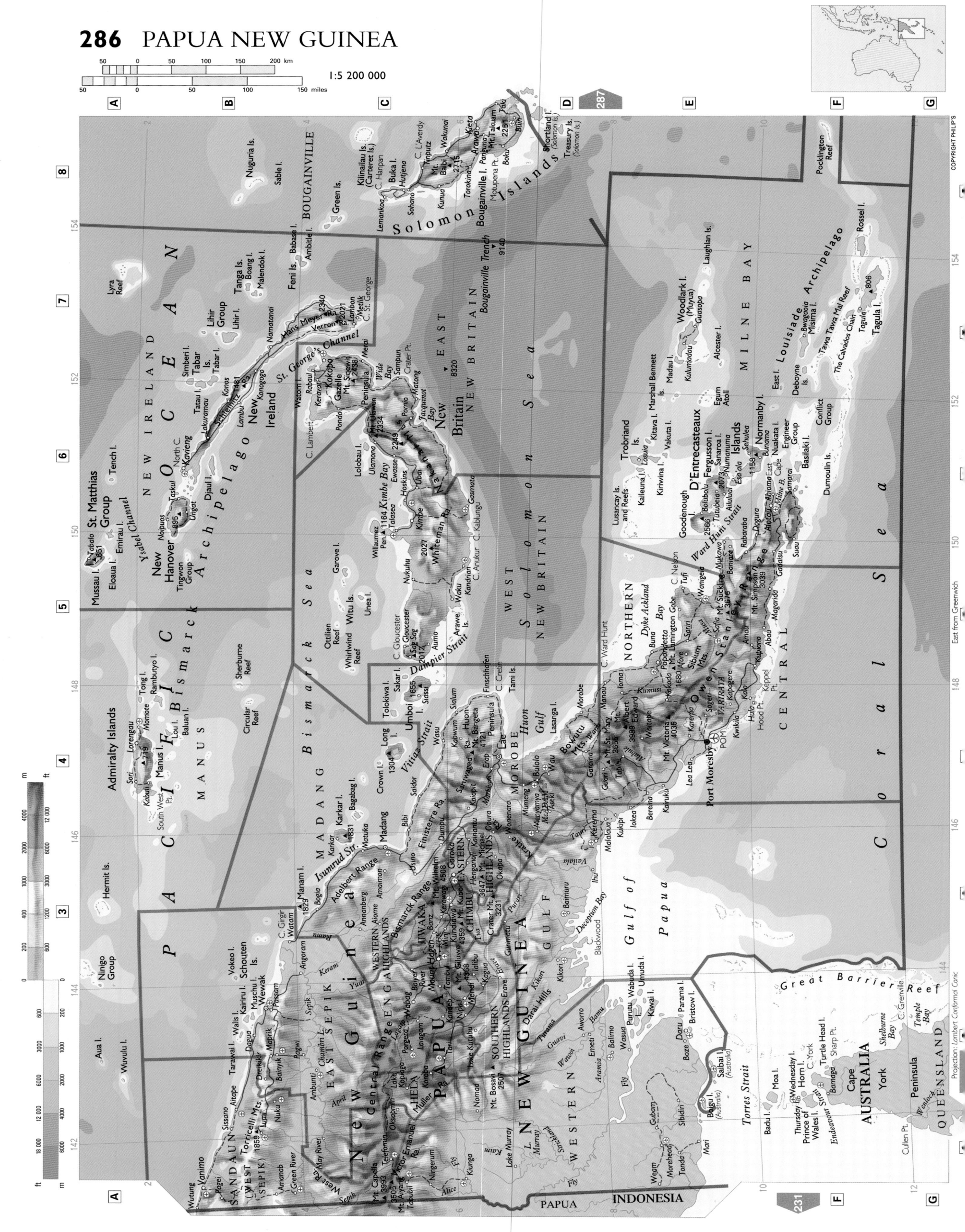

50   0   50   100   150   200 km

1:5 200 000

50   0   50   100   150 miles

COPYRIGHT PHILIP'S

East from Greenwich

Projection: Lambert Conformal Conic

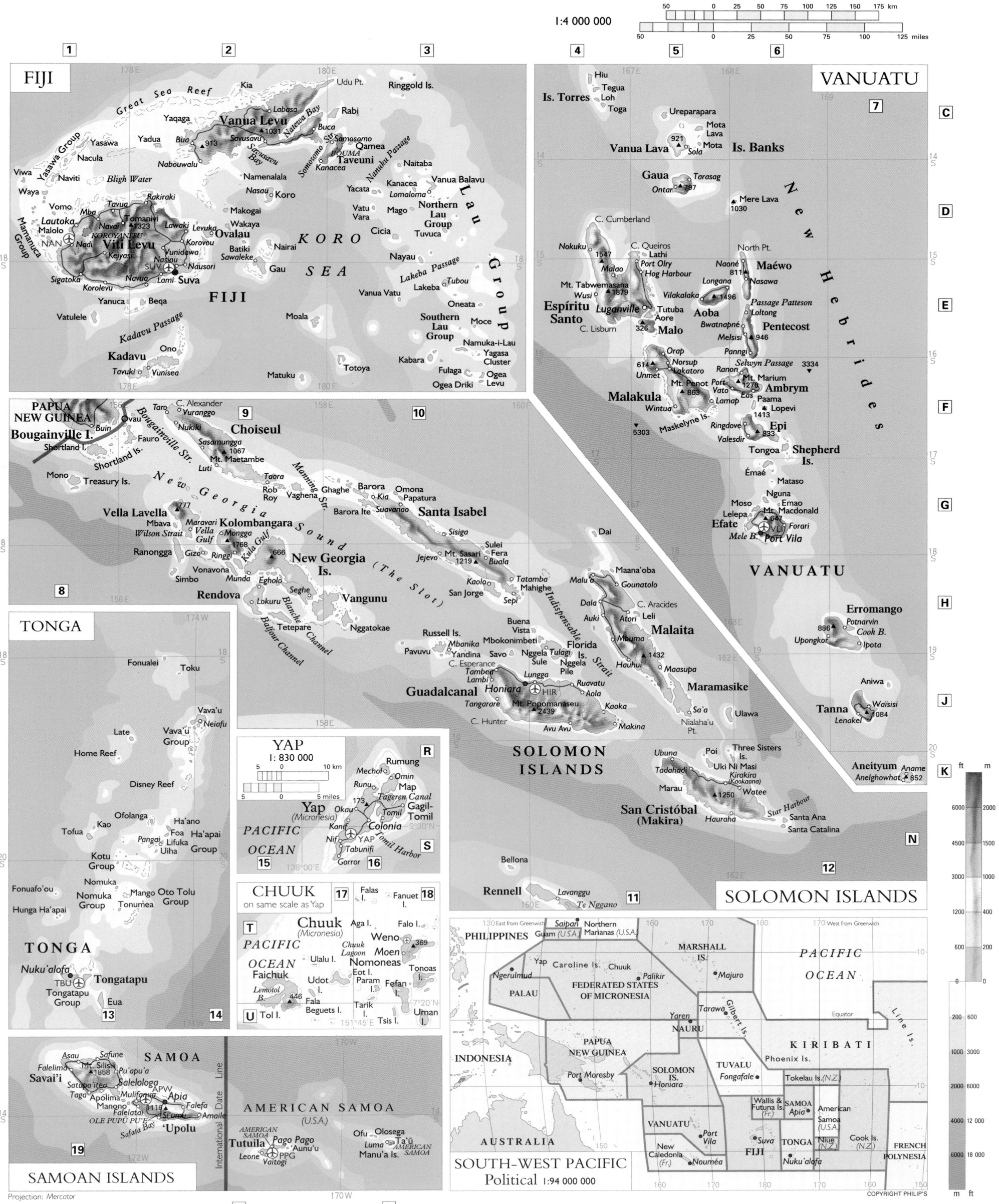

Equatorial Scale 1:43 200 000

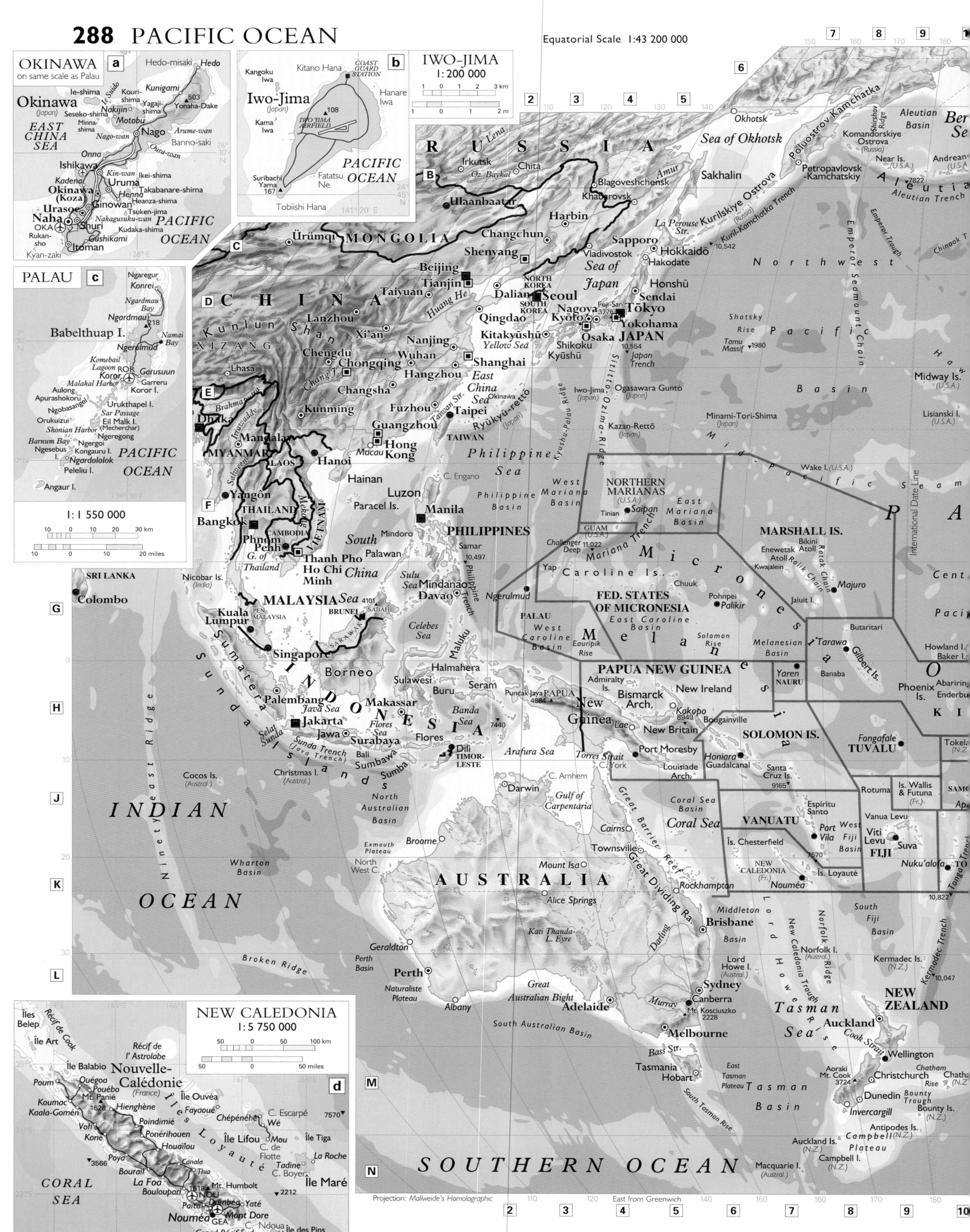

OKINAWA
on same scale as Palau **a**

Okinawa
(Japan)

EAST
CHINA
SEA

Hedo-misaki · Hedo
Kunigami
Ie-shima · Yonaha-Dake 503
Kouri-shima · Nakijin
Seseko-shima · Yagaji-shima
Minna-shima · Motobu
Onna · Arume-wan
Nago-wan · Nago
Ishikawa · Banno-saki
Kadena · Kin-wan · Ikei-shima
Kadena · Henna · Takabanare-shima
Ngobasaruga · Heanza-shima
Okinawa · Kin-wan · Tsuken-jima
(Koza) · Nakagusuku-wan · Kudaka-shima
Ginowan · Nakagusuku-wan
Urasoe
Naha · Shuri
OKA · Gushikami
Rukan-sho · Itoman
Kyan-zaki

PACIFIC
OCEAN

IWO-JIMA **b**
1:200 000

Kangoku
Iwa · Kitano Hana · COAST GUARD STATION
Iwo-Jima · Hanare Iwa
(Japan)
Kama Iwa · IWO JIMA AIRFIELD · 108
Suribachi Yama 167 · Fatatsu Ne
Tobiishi Hana

PACIFIC
OCEAN

PALAU **c**

Ngaregur
Konrei
Ngardmau Bay
Ngardmau 218
Babelthuap I.
Namai Bay
Ngerulmud
Komebail Lagoon · ROR · Garusuun
Koror · Garreru
Malakal Harbor · Koror I.
Aulong · Urukthapel I.
Apurashokoru · Sar Passage
Orukuizui · Eil Malk I. (Mecherchar)
Ngergoi · Ngeregong
Ngesebus · Kongaru I.
Ngesebus · Ngardololok
Peleliu I.
Angaur I.

PACIFIC
OCEAN

1:1 550 000

RUSSIA

Lena
Irkutsk · Oz. Baykal · Chita
Ulaanbaatar

MONGOLIA

Ürümqi

CHINA

Kunlun Shan
XIZANG
Lhasa
Brahmaputra
Irrawaddy
Dhaka
Mandalay
MYANMAR
LAOS
Salween
Yangôn
THAILAND
Bangkok
Mekong
CAMBODIA
Phnom Penh
G. of Thailand
VIETNAM

Lanzhou
Xi'an
Chengdu
Chongqing
Chang J.
Kunming
Changsha
Guangzhou
Macau
Hong Kong

Taiyuan
Beijing
Tianjin
Huang He
NORTH KOREA
Dalian
Qingdao
Nanjing
Wuhan
Hangzhou
Shanghai
Fuzhou
Taipei
TAIWAN
Ryūkyū-retto
(Japan)

SOUTH KOREA
Seoul
Nagoya
Kyōto
Osaka
Shikoku
Kyūshū
Kitakyūshū
Yellow Sea
East China Sea

Sapporo
Hokkaidō
Hakodate
Sea of Japan
Vladivostok
Honshū
Sendai
Tōkyō
Yokohama
JAPAN
Fuji-San 3776
10,554

Okhotsk
Sea of Okhotsk
Sakhalin
Blagoveshchensk
Khabarovsk
Amur
La Perouse Str.
Kurilskiye Ostrova (Russia)
Kuril-Kamchatka Trench
10,542

Poluostrov Kamchatka
Petropavlovsk-Kamchatskiy
7822
Komandorskiye Ostrova (Russia)
Near Is. (U.S.A.)
Aleutian Basin
Andrean
Aleutian Trench

Shatsky Rise
Tamu Massif 1980
Iwo-Jima (Japan)
Ogasawara Gunto (Japan)
Kazan-Rettō (Japan)
Minami-Tori-Shima (Japan)

Midway Is. (U.S.A.)
Lisianski I. (U.S.A.)

Northwest Pacific Basin

Emperor Seamount Chain
Chinook

Mid-Pacific

Wake I. (U.S.A.)
International Date Line

Philippine Sea
West Mariana Basin
NORTHERN MARIANAS (U.S.A.)
Tinian · Saipan
East Mariana Basin
GUAM (U.S.A.)
Challenger Deep 11,022
Mariana Trench
Caroline Is.
Yap
Ngerulmud
PALAU
West Caroline Basin
Eauripik Rise
FED. STATES OF MICRONESIA
East Caroline Basin
Chuuk
Pohnpei · Palikir
Jaluit I.

MARSHALL IS.
Enewetak Atoll
Bikini Atoll
Kwajalein
Ralik Chain
Ratak Chain
Majuro

Butaritari
Tarawa
Banaba
Gilbert Is.
Howland I. (U.S.A.)
Baker I.
Phoenix Is.
Abariringa
Enderbu

PHILIPPINES
Luzon
Paracel Is.
Manila
Mindoro
Samar
Palawan
Sulu Sea
Mindanao
Davao
Philippine Trench

South China Sea

SRI LANKA
Colombo

Nicobar Is. (India)

MALAYSIA
4101
BRUNEI
SABAH
Kuala Lumpur
PEN. MALAYSIA
SARAWAK
Singapore

Sumatera
Sunda Ridge
Palembang
Jakarta
Jawa
Java Sea
Surabaya
Sunda Trench (Java Trench)
Bali
Selat Sunda
Christmas I. (Austral.)
Cocos Is. (Austral.)

Borneo
Celebes Sea
Sulawesi
Makassar
Flores Sea
Flores
Sumba
Sumbawa

Halmahera
Seram
Buru
Maluku
Banda Sea
Dili
TIMOR-LESTE
7440

Puncak Jaya 4884
PAPUA
PAPUA NEW GUINEA
New Guinea
8940
Admiralty Is.
Bismarck Arch.
New Ireland
Kokopo
Lae
New Britain
Bougainville
Arafura Sea
Torres Strait
Port Moresby

Yaren · NAURU
Melanesian Basin
Solomon Rise
SOLOMON IS.
Honiara
Guadalcanal
Santa Cruz Is. 9165

Fongafale
TUVALU
Rotuma
Is. Wallis & Futuna (Fr.)
SAMO

INDIAN
OCEAN

Ninetyeast Ridge

Wharton Basin

Broken Ridge

Darwin
C. Arnhem
Gulf of Carpentaria
North Australian Basin
C. York
Louisiade Arch.

Geraldton
Perth Basin
Naturaliste Plateau
Perth
Albany
North West C.
South Australian Basin
Great Australian Bight
Adelaide
Alice Springs
Mount Isa
AUSTRALIA
Kati Thanda - L. Eyre
Great Dividing Ra.
Cairns
Townsville
Great Barrier Reef
Rockhampton
Brisbane
Darling
Murray
Canberra
Sydney
Mt. Kosciuszko 2228
Melbourne
Bass Str.
Tasmania
Hobart

Coral Sea Basin
Coral Sea
Espíritu Santo
VANUATU
Port Vila
Îs. Chesterield
NEW CALEDONIA (Fr.)
Nouméa
Is. Loyauté
Middleton
Lord Howe I. (Austral.)
Lord Howe Rise
Norfolk I. (Austral.)
New Caledonia Trough
Norfolk Ridge
West Fiji Basin
Vanua Levu
Viti Levu
Suva
FIJI
Nuku'alofa
7570
South Fiji Basin

Tasman Sea
East Tasman Plateau
Tasman Basin
South Tasman Rise
Macquarie I. (Austral.)

NEW ZEALAND
Auckland
Cook Strait
Wellington
Aoraki Mt. Cook 3724
Christchurch
Chatham Rise
Dunedin
Bounty Trough
Invercargill
Bounty Is. (N.Z.)
Antipodes Is. (N.Z.)
Auckland Is. (N.Z.)
Campbell Plateau
Campbell I. (N.Z.)

Kermadec Is. (N.Z.) 10,047
10,822
Tokela (N.Z.)

Micronesia
Melanesia

SOUTHERN OCEAN

NEW CALEDONIA
1:5 750 000 **d**

Îles Belep
Île Art
Île Balabio
Poum
Ouégoa · Pouébo
Quégoa · Hienghène
Koumac
Kaala-Gomén
Voh · 1628
Koné · Mt. Panié
Poindimié
Pouembout
Ponérihouen
Bourail · Houaïlou
3566
Boulouparis
La Foa
Poya
Thio
GEA
NOU
Dumbéa · Yaté
Nouméa · Mont Dore
2212
Île des Pins
Grand Récif Sud

Récif de l'Astrolabe
Récif de Cook
Hienghène
Île Ouvéa
Fayaoué
Île Lifou
Wé
C. Escarpé 7570
Mou
C. de Flotte
Tadine · La Roche
C. Boyer
Île Tiga
Île Maré

Îs. Loyauté

CORAL
SEA

Projection: Mollweide's Homolographic

East from Greenwich

TAHITI (e)

Pte. Aroa B. de Mataiea
Pte. Vénus
Papetoai Mahina
Papeari Popao Arue Papenoo
Mt. Tohiea Papeete Pirae Tiarei
1207 Afareaitu PPT Faaa
Haapiti Punaauia Mt. Aorai Orohena
2241 Faaone
Maraa Paea Mt. Tetufera Lac
Moorea 1798 Vaihiria Hitiaa (France)
Papara Taravao Isthme de
Atimaono Mataiea Afaahiti Taravao Tatutua
Pueu Pte.
Vairao Tautira
PACIFIC Mt. Roonui
1332
OCEAN Teahupoo Presqu'île de Taiarapu

1 : 1 150 000
1 : 1 150 000

FRENCH POLYNESIA (f)

1 : 26 000 000
200 0 200 400 km
200 0 200 400 miles

Hatutu Eiao Îles
Nuku Hiva Ua Huka Marquises
Ua Pu Hiva Oa
6513 Flint I. Tahuata Motané
(Kiribati) Îles 4884

Îles du Roi-Georges Îles du
Tikahau Ahe Manihi Takaroa Désappointement
Îles Sous- Matahiva Rangiroa Tikei Puka Puka
le-Vent Apataki Kauehi Takume
Maupiti Bora Bora Îles du Raraka Raroia Fangatau
Huahine Vent Palliser Fakarava Makemo Tatakoto
Maupihaa Raiatea Ile Raeului Anaa Amanu Puka Ruha
Moorea Tahiti Haraiki Marokau Vahitahi
Papeete Méhétia Ravahere Hao Paraoa Réao
Nengonengo Vairaatea
Îles de la Société Ahunui
Héréhérétué 4616 Vanavana Turéia Groupe
Îles Maria Rurutu Tematagi Mururoa Actéon
Rimatara Tubuaï Tropic of Capricorn Fangataufa Îles Gambier
Îles Tubuaï (Îles Australes) Moraré
Raivavae Récif PACIFIC
Récif Président- OCEAN
Neilson Thiers
Rapa Îlots de Bass Récif Portland

NIUE (g)

1 : 830 000
5 0 10 km
3 0 5 miles

Hikutavake Mutalau
Namukulu Toi
Tuapa Makefu Lakepa Niue
Alofi Liku (N.Z.)
Alofi Fonuakula
Bay Tamakautogá
Halangingie IUE
Pt. Avatele
Tepa Pt. Vaiea Hakupu

PACIFIC OCEAN

RAROTONGA (h)

1 : 415 000
5 km 0
5 miles 0

Rarotonga Avarua Harbour
(N.Z.) RAR Pue
Nikao Avatiu Avarua
Arorangi 509 Te Manga
222 Maungaroa 588 653
Maungatongaiti Te Kou Ngatangiia
329 Matavera Motu Tapu
Taroume Muri Oneroa
Koromiri
Titikaveka Taakoka

PACIFIC OCEAN

Main map labels

ALASKA (U.S.A.)
Arctic Circle
Anchorage
Bristol Bay
Gulf of Alaska
Juneau
CANADA
ROCKY Mts.
Prince of Wales I. (U.S.A.)
Haida Gwaii (Queen Charlotte Is.) (Canada)
Edmonton
Tufts Abyssal Plain
Vancouver Calgary
Vancouver I. Victoria
Seattle
Portland
Snake
Boise
Northeast
Mendocino Fracture Zone C. Mendocino
Sacramento
San Francisco
4418
Salt Lake City
Denver
Pacific 6741
UNITED STATES
Murray Fracture Zone
Colorado
Los Angeles Oklahoma City Memphis Atlanta
Phoenix Dallas
San Diego Mississippi
Guadalupe (Mex.) Ciudad Juárez Houston Jacksonville
Molokai Fracture Zone San Antonio New Orleans
Basin Gulf of Mexico Miami THE BAHAMAS
Tropic of Cancer Florida Str.
Honolulu C. San Lucas 3504
O'ahu Sigsbee La Habana CUBA
4205 Deep Canal de Yucatán
HAWAI'I (U.S.A.) Guadalajara Mérida HAITI
Hawai'i Mexico 5610 7680 JAMAICA Kingston
Clarion Fracture Zone Puebla Acapulco BELIZE
Is. de Revillagigedo (Mex.) GUATEMALA HONDURAS Caribbean Sea
PACIFIC Middle America Trench Guatemala
Î. Clipperton (Fr.) San Salvador NICARAGUA
Clipperton Fracture Zone EL SALVADOR Managua Barranquilla
Guatemala Basin COSTA RICA San José
Galápagos Fracture Zone Colón Panamá
Cocos Ridge I. del Coco (Costa Rica) PANAMA Panama Basin
Equator Medellín
I. de Malpelo (Colombia) Cali
Galápagos (Ecuador) COLOMBIA
Carnegie Ridge Quito ECUADOR
Guayaquil
C. Pariñas

North West Christmas Ridge
Palmyra Is. (U.S.A.)
ston Atoll
Jarvis I. (U.S.A.)
nix Is.
BATI
Teraina
Tabuaeran
Kiritimati
Cooper Ridge
International Date Line
Malden I.
Starbuck I.
Line Islands
Vostok I.
Caroline I. (Millennium I.)
Nuku Hiva
Îs. Marquises
Hiva Oa
Marquesas Fracture Zone
Flint I.
Manihiki
Pukapuka
Manihiki
Plateau
Suwarrow Is.
Îs. de la Société
Bora Bora
Huahine
Raiatea
Tahiti
Papeete
FRENCH POLYNESIA
Îs. Tuamotu
Rangiroa
Penrhyn (Tongareva)
Cook Is. (N.Z.)
Aitutaki
Atiu
Rarotonga
Mangaia
Îs. Tubuaï
Austral Seamount Chain
Mururoa
Îs. Gambier
Oeno I.
Henderson I.
Ducie I.
Pitcairn I. (U.K.)
Rapa
Easter Fracture Zone
Sala-y-Gómez Ridge
Sala-y-Gómez (Chile)
I. de Pascua (Chile)
Easter Fracture Zone
Yupanqui Basin
Mendaña Fracture Zone
Peru Basin
Nazca Ridge
East Pacific Rise
Galápagos Rise
Trujillo
6369
PERU
Lima
Cusco
L. Titicaca
Arequipa Nevado Ancohuma 6550
6866
Peru- La Paz
Arica BOLIVIA
Iquique Chile
Antofagasta PARAGUAY
Chile Basin Asunción
Tropic of Capricorn
8064 San Miguel
Trench de Tucumán
San Félix (Chile) ANDES
San Ambrosio (Chile)
Córdoba Pôrto
Arch. de Juan Fernández (Chile) Aconcagua Alegre
Valparaíso 6962 Rosario
Roggeveen Basin Santiago Buenos URUGUAY
Challenger Fracture Zone Aires Montevideo
Concepción Río de la Plata
ARGENTINA
Menard Fracture Zone Argentine Basin
Nemo Point (furthest point from any land)
Southwest Pacific Basin
Pacific Antarctic Ridge
East Pacific
114 Falkland ATLANTIC
Plateau OCEAN
Punta Arenas 6212
Est. de Magallanes Falkland Is. (U.K.) Georgia Basin
Tierra del Fuego South Georgia (U.K.)
C. de Hornos South Georgia Ridge
Drake Passage
Southeast 4402
Pacific Basin

West from Greenwich

ft m
12 000 4000
9000 3000
6000 2000
3000 1000
1500 500
600 200
0 0
200 600
1000 3000
2000 6000
4000 12 000
6000 18 000
8000 24 000
m ft

NORTH
AMERICA

100 0 200 400 600 800 1000 1200 1400 km
1:28 000 000
100 0 200 400 600 800 1000 miles

B A B

ARCTIC OCEAN

Asia

Chukchi Sea

Lincoln Sea

Greenland

Iceland

Denmark Strait

Mt Forel 3360

Gunnbjørn Field 3693

Petermanns Peak

2119

Wrangel I.
St. Lawrence I.
C. Dezhneva
Bering Strait
Pt. Hope
Icy C.
Pt. Barrow

Columbia
Morris Jesup
2616
Kane Basin
Axel Heiberg I.
Sverdrup Is.
Ellesmere I.
Narres Str.

Nunivak I.
Norton Sound
Prince of Wales
Kotzebue Sound
Brooks Ra.
2761

Parry Is.
Queen Elizabeth Is.
Melville I.
Bathurst
M'Clure Strait
Viscount Melville Sd.
Banks I.
Devon I.
Lancaster Sd.
Bylot I.
Somerset
Mt Clintock Channel
Prince of Wales
Baffin Bay

Diskø I.
Dyer C.
Davis Strait
Cape Farewell

Beaufort Sea

Koyukuk
Yukon
Alaska Range
Denali (Mt McKinley) 6190
Mt St. Elias 5489
Mt Logan 5959
Mackenzie Mts.
2762

Mackenzie Bay
C. Bathurst
Amundsen Gulf
Victoria I.
King William I.
Boothia Pen.
Gulf of Boothia
Melville Pen.
Foxe Basin
Foxe Channel
Southampton I.
Cumberland Sd.
Frobisher B.
C. Chidley

Baffin Island

2447

Labrador Sea

Newfoundland

Unimak I.
Bristol Bay
Bethel L.
Kuskokwim
Alaska Peninsula
Kodiak I.
Cook Inlet
Gulf of Alaska

Canadian
Stewart
Pelly
Liard
Great Bear L.
Back
Thelon
Dubawnt
Chesterfield Inlet
Coats I.
Mansel I.
C. Henrietta Maria
C. Wolstenholme

Ungava Peninsula
Ungava B.
1652
Feuilles
Grande Baleine
L. Caniapiscau
Laurentian Plateau
C. Harrison
Hamilton Inlet

Hudson Bay

Alexander Archipelago
Haida Gwaii (Queen Charlotte Is.)
Mt Logan
Skeena
Stikine
Coast Mountains
Mt Waddington 4019
Queen Charlotte Str.
Str. of Georgia

Rocky
Great Slave L.
L. Athabasca
Athabasca
Reindeer L.
Churchill
Nelson
Seward
Nelson
C. Churchill
Belcher Is.
James Bay
Eastmain
Rupert
Albany
Attawapiskat
Mattagami

Newfoundland
C. Breton I.
Pt. Edward
C. Ray
C. Race

Vancouver I.
Str. of Juan de Fuca
C. Flattery
Mt Robson 3954
Selkirk Mts.
Fraser

Mountains
Peace
Saskatchewan
L. Winnipegosis
L. Manitoba
L. Winnipeg
L. Seul
L. of the Woods
Red L.
L. Nipigon
L. Superior
Niagara Falls
Ottawa
St. Lawrence
Gulf of St. Lawrence
Anticosti I.
Nova Scotia
St. John
B. of Fundy
Sable I.

Great
Mt Rainier 4392
Cascade Range
Columbia Plateau
Columbia
Snake
4202
Missouri
Yellowstone
Frontier
Black Hills
Souris
Red
Des Moines
Illinois
Wabash
Ohio
L. Michigan
L. Huron
L. Erie
L. Ontario
Hudson
Long I.
Mt Washington 1917

Mt Shasta 4317
Sacramento
Sierra Nevada
Mt Whitney 4418
San Joaquin
Death Valley -86
Great Basin
Great Salt Lake
Wasatch Ra.
Green
Mt Elbert 4399
Blanca Peak 4372
Colorado Plateau
Grand Canyon

Plains
Platte
Arkansas
Canadian
Red
Ozark Plateau
Ouachita Mts.
Cumberland Plateau
Mt Mitchell 2037
Tennessee
Allegheny Mts.
Appalachian Mts.
Blue Ridge
Piedmont
Chattahoochee
Savannah
C. Charles
Chesapeake B.
C. Hatteras

Bermuda

C. Blanco
C. Mendocino
Pt. Conception
Channel Is.
3506
San Luis
Baja California
3078

Great
Colorado
Gila
3659
Rio Grande
Pecos
Edwards Plateau
Llano Estacado
Brazos
Alabama
Apalachee B.
C. Canaveral
Florida Strait
The Everglades
L. Okeechobee

ATLANTIC OCEAN
Sargasso
Bahamas
West Indies
Sea

PACIFIC OCEAN

Tropic of Cancer

Guadalupe
I. de Cedros
Pta. Baja
Pta. Falsa
Yaqui
Conchos
Gulf of California
Baja California
Western Sierra Madre
Mexican Plateau
3050
Eastern Sierra Madre
Rio Grande
Mississippi River Delta
Laguna Madre

Gulf of Mexico

Cuba
Hispaniola
8605
3175
Mona Passage
Windward Passage
Greater Antilles
Jamaica
Puerto Rico

Clarion Fracture Zone

C. San Lucas
B. de Banderas
Santiago
C. Corrientes
Balsas
Popocatepetl 5452
5610 Pico de Orizaba
Sa. Madre del Sur
Isthmus of Tehuantepec
Sierra Madre
4093

Revilla Gigedo Is.

C. Rojo
Gulf of Campeche
Yucatán Peninsula
Yucatán Channel
Yucatán Basin
Cayman Is.
Cayman Trench

Caribbean Sea

Colombian Basin

Sierra Nevada de Santa Marta 5775

West Indies

Maracaibo
Cord. de Merida

G. of Tehuantepec
Guatemala Trench
G. of Fonseca
L. Nicaragua
C. Gracias a Dios
Coco
Pta. de Perlas

Central America

Panama Canal
Isthmus of Panama
G. of Darién
G. of Panamá
Pta. Burica
C. Blanco
3819

G. of Venezuela
Magdalena
Andes

ft m
9000 3000
6000 2000
3000 1000
1500 500
600 200
0 0
0 0
200 600
1000 3000
2000 6000
4000 12000
6000 18000
8000 24000
m ft

Projection: Bonne

120 110 West from Greenwich 100 90 80

7 8 9 10 11 12

COPYRIGHT PHILIP'S

1:28 000 000

100 0   200   400   600   800   1000 1200 1400 km

100 0   200   400   600   800   1000 miles

RUSSIA
Asia

St. Lawrence I.

Bering Strait

Bering Sea

ARCTIC
OCEAN

International Date Line

Beaufort Sea

Queen Elizabeth Is.

Ellesmere I.

GREENLAND
(Denmark)

Denmark Strait

ICELAND

Reykjavik

ALASKA
(USA)

Yukon

Porcupine

Anchorage

Fairbanks

Kodiak I.

Gulf of Alaska

Victoria I.

NORTHWEST

Arctic Circle

Great Bear L.

Mackenzie

Back

NUNAVUT

Baffin Bay

Davis Strait

Nuuk

Baffin Island

YUKON

Whitehorse

Juneau

TERRITORIES

Liard

Yellowknife

Great Slave L.

Dubawnt

Hudson Strait

Iqaluit

CANADA

Hudson Bay

BRITISH COLUMBIA

Skeena

Fraser

Peace

ALBERTA

Edmonton

Calgary

Athabasca

Athabasca

SASKATCHEWAN

Saskatchewan

Churchill

Nelson

MANITOBA

L. Winnipeg

ONTARIO

Eastmain

QUÉBEC

St. Lawrence

NEWFOUNDLAND & LABRADOR

St. John's

St-Pierre et Miquelon (Fr.)

PRINCE EDWARD I.

Charlottetown

NOVA SCOTIA

Halifax

Victoria

Vancouver

Regina

Winnipeg

L. Superior

L. Huron

Québec

Fredericton

MAINE

Augusta

N.B.

Montréal

Ottawa

TORONTO

VER.

N.H.

Concord

Boston

Providence

MASS.

Hartford

R.I.

WASHINGTON

Olympia

Seattle

Portland

Salem

Columbia

OREGON

MONTANA

Helena

Missouri

NORTH DAKOTA

Bismarck

SOUTH DAKOTA

MINNESOTA

Minneapolis-St. Paul

WISCONSIN

Madison

MICHIGAN

Lansing

L. Michigan

Milwaukee

CHICAGO

Detroit

L. Erie

Buffalo

NEW YORK

Cleveland

Toledo

PA.

Pittsburgh

Baltimore

NEW YORK

PHILADELPHIA

N.J.

DE.

IDAHO

Boise

Snake

WYOMING

IOWA

NEBRASKA

ILLINOIS

INDIANA

OHIO

Columbus

W.V.

WASHINGTON D.C.

MD.

Richmond

VIRGINIA

Sacramento

Carson City

Salt Lake City

Lincoln

Springfield

Indianapolis

Cincinnati

SAN FRANCISCO

San Jose

NEVADA

UTAH

Denver

Kansas City

Topeka

St. Louis

MISSOURI

KENTUCKY

Nashville

TENNESSEE

Raleigh

NORTH CAROLINA

Bermuda (U.K.)

CALIFORNIA

Las Vegas

COLORADO

KANSAS

Columbia

SOUTH CAROLINA

Charlotte

LOS ANGELES

Santa Fe

Albuquerque

OKLAHOMA

Oklahoma City

ARKANSAS

Little Rock

Memphis

Birmingham

ATLANTA

GEORGIA

Charleston

San Diego

Tijuana

ARIZONA

Phoenix

Tucson

NEW MEXICO

El Paso

Ciudad Juárez

MISSISSIPPI

Jackson

ALABAMA

Montgomery

Jacksonville

ATLANTIC OCEAN

Mexicali

Colorado

DALLAS-FT. WORTH

TEXAS

Austin

HOUSTON

Baton Rouge

New Orleans

LOUISIANA

Tallahassee

FLORIDA

Orlando

Tampa-St. Petersburg

MIAMI

Nassau

THE BAHAMAS

Turks & Caicos Is. (U.K.)

PACIFIC OCEAN

Guadalupe (Mex.)

Hermosillo

San Antonio

Rio Grande

Gulf of Mexico

Florida Str.

Havana

CUBA

Tropic of Cancer

Culiacán

Monterrey

Torreón

MÉXICO

San Luis Potosí

Mérida

Cayman Is. (U.K.)

JAMAICA

Kingston

HAITI

Port-au-Prince

DOMINICAN REP.

Santo Domingo

PUERTO RICO (U.S.A.)

San Juan

León

Querétaro

Guadalajara

Revilla Gigedo Is. (Mex.)

MÉXICO

Toluca

Puebla

Acapulco

Belmopan

BELIZE

Caribbean Sea

Maracaibo

GUATEMALA

Guatemala

HONDURAS

Tegucigalpa

San Salvador

EL SALVADOR

NICARAGUA

Managua

L. Nicaragua

Barranquilla

VENEZUELA

COSTA RICA

San José

PANAMA

Panamá

COLOMBIA

Medellín

South America

Projection: Bonne

West from Greenwich

COPYRIGHT PHILIP'S

7 ■ **MÉXICO** Capital Cities **8** **9** **10** **11** **12**

100 0 100 200 300 400 500 600 km
100 0 100 200 300 400 miles

1:12 000 000

Projection: Bonne

PACIFIC OCEAN

ALASKA
Alaska Range
Mt. McKinley (Denali) 6194
Anchorage
Cook Inlet
Kenai
Seward
Kodiak I.
Gulf of Alaska
Prince William Sd.
Cordova
Valdez
Wrangell Mts.
Mt. St. Elias 5489
Mt. Logan 5959
Elias Mts.
Mt. Fairweather 4663

Alexander Archipelago
Chichagof I.
Baranof I.
Sitka
Admiralty I.
Juneau
Prince of Wales I.
Ketchikan
Wrangell
Petersburg
Cross Sound
Graham I.
Haida Gwaii
(Queen Charlotte Is.)
Moresby I.
Hecate Str.
Dixon Entrance
Prince Rupert

Fort Yukon
Porcupine
Old Crow
Eagle
Fairbanks
Delta Junction
Tanana Tk.
Yukon
Dawson City
Klondike
Mayo
Carmacks
Whitehorse
YUKON
Selwyn Mts.
Faro
Ross River
Teslin
Atlin
Watson Lake
Cassiar Mountains
Dease Lake
Telegraph Creek
Stewart
Terrace
Kitimat
Bella Coola

MACKENZIE Mountains
Inuvik
Tuktoyaktuk
Aklavik
Fort McPherson
Tsiigehtchic
Norman Wells
Tulita
Fort Good Hope
Déline
Great Bear Lake
Fort Simpson
Wrigley
Fort Liard
Fort Nelson
Nahanni
Liard
NORTHWEST TERRITORIES
Yellowknife
Behchoko (Rae)
Fort Providence
Great Slave Lake
Hay River
Fort Resolution
Fort Smith
WOOD BUFFALO NAT. PARK
Lake Athabasca
Fort Chipewyan
Uranium City
Fond-du-Lac
Lutsel K'e

Beaufort Sea
AULAVIK NAT. PARK
Banks Island
Victoria Island
Amundsen Gulf
Prince Albert Pen.
Ulukhaktok (Holman)
Paulatuk
Darnley Bay
TUKTUT NOGAIT NAT. PARK
Wollaston Pen.
Coronation Gulf
Kugluktuk
Echo Bay
Bathurst Inlet
Kitikmeot
Cambridge Bay
Melville Island
Viscount Melville Sound
M'Clure Strait
Prince of Wales I.
Somerset Island
Boothia Peninsula
Gjoa Haven
Taloyoak
King William I.
Queen Maud Gulf
Adelaide Pen.
Baker Lake
Kivalliq
Chesterfield Inlet
Rankin Inlet
Arviat
Churchill

BRITISH COLUMBIA
Rocky Mountains
Columbia Mountains
Vancouver Island
Campbell River
Courtenay
Nanaimo
Port Alberni
VANCOUVER
Victoria
Kamloops
Kelowna
Penticton
Prince George
Quesnel
Williams Lake
Vanderhoof
Smithers
Fort St. John
Dawson Creek
Chetwynd
Grande Prairie
Peace River
High Level
Manning
Slave Lake
High Prairie
Fort McMurray
Fort McKay
Lac la Biche

ALBERTA
EDMONTON
Red Deer
CALGARY
Lethbridge
Medicine Hat
Banff
Jasper
JASPER NAT. PARK
BANFF NAT. PARK
Wetaskiwin
Camrose
Lloydminster
Vegreville
Stettler
Drumheller
High River
Airdrie
Hanna

SASKATCHEWAN
Saskatoon
Regina
Prince Albert
North Battleford
Moose Jaw
Swift Current
Weyburn
Estevan
Yorkton
Melville
PRINCE ALBERT NAT. PARK
Lake Athabasca
Reindeer Lake
La Ronge
Flin Flon
Meadow Lake
Biggar
Kindersley
Rosetown
Humboldt
Tisdale
Nipawin
Watrous
Assiniboia
L. Diefenbaker

MANITOBA
WINNIPEG
Brandon
Portage la Prairie
Thompson
Gillam
Lynn Lake
The Pas
Cedar Lake
L. Winnipegosis
Lake Winnipeg
Churchill
Norway House
Grand Rapids
Dauphin
Neepawa
Selkirk
Morden
Winkler
Virden
Hadgson
Red Lake
L. of the Woods
Kenora
Dryden

UNITED STATES
WASHINGTON
Seattle
Tacoma
Everett
Olympia
Bellingham
Spokane
Yakima
Walla Walla
Pullman
OREGON
PORTLAND
Salem
Eugene
Corvallis
Albany
Springfield
Medford
Roseburg
Coos Bay
Klamath Falls
Bend
Pendleton
La Grande
Baker City
The Dalles

CALIFORNIA
SACRAMENTO
SAN FRANCISCO
Oakland
San Jose
Santa Rosa
Modesto
Stockton
Redding
Eureka
Crescent City
C. Mendocino
Santa Cruz
Ukiah
NEVADA
Carson City
Reno
Elko
Winnemucca
Great Basin
IDAHO
Boise
Nampa
Caldwell
Twin Falls
Idaho Falls
Pocatello
Rexburg
Mountain Home
MONTANA
Helena
Butte
Billings
Bozeman
Great Falls
Missoula
Kalispell
Miles City
Livingston
Anaconda
GLACIER NAT. PARK
Bitterroot Range
WYOMING
Cody
Casper
Cheyenne
Gillette
Rock Springs
Green River
Laramie
Rawlins
Sheridan
YELLOWSTONE NAT. PARK
Gannett Peak 4202
UTAH
SALT LAKE CITY
Ogden
Provo
Orem
Great Salt Lake
Brigham City
Evanston
Montpelier
Logan
NORTH DAKOTA
Bismarck
Fargo
Grand Forks
Minot
Jamestown
Dickinson
Williston
Devils Lake
SOUTH DAKOTA
Pierre
Rapid City
Aberdeen
Huron
Mobridge
Sioux Falls
Mitchell
Yankton
BADLANDS
Black Hills
NEBRASKA
Chadron
Alliance
Scottsbluff
MINNESOTA
MINNEAPOLIS
ST. PAUL
St. Cloud
Duluth
Rochester
Mankato
Bemidji
Hibbing
Virginia
Brainerd
Moorhead
Thief River Falls
IOWA
Sioux City
Mason City
Austin
WISCONSIN
Superior
Rhinelander

West from Greenwich

ft m 15000 5000 12000 4000 9000 3000 6000 2000 3000 1000 1000 300 400 150 0 0
m ft 200 600 1000 3000 2000 6000 4000 12000 6000 18000

150

154

NORTHERN CANADA
continuation northwards on same scale as main map

8 9 10 11 12 13 14 15 16 17 18 19

ARCTIC OCEAN

GREENLAND (KALAALLIT NUNAAT)

Kronprins Frederik Land

QUTTINIRPAAQ NAT. PARK
Lincoln Sea
Alert
Lake Hazen
Barbeau Pk.
Eureka
Greely Fiord
Ellesmere Island
Petermann Gletscher
Kane Basin
Knud Rasmussen Land
Sermersuaq (Humboldt Gletscher)
Qeqertarsuaq (Qaanaaq) (Thule)
Lauge Koch Kyst
Kap York
Melville Bugt

C. Thomas Hubbard
C. Columbia
Nansen Sd.
Meighen I.
Sverdrup Islands
Axel Heiberg Island
Prince of Wales Icefield
Norwegian Bay
Amund Ringnes
Graham
Grise Fiord
Jones Sound
Coburg I.
Grinnell Pen.
Devon Island
Lancaster Sound
SIRMILIK NAT. PARK
Bylot I.
Pond Inlet

Borden Island
Brock I.
Mackenzie King I.
Ellef Ringnes Island
King Christian I.
Prince Patrick Island
Eglinton I.
Emerald I.
Lougheed I.
Cornwall
Cornwallis Island
Resolute
N.W.T.
Queen Elizabeth Islands
NUNAVUT
Parry Islands
Melville Island
Bathurst Island
Byam Martin I.
Viscount Melville Sound
Lowther I.
Stefansson Island
Prince of Wales I.
Somerset Island
Borden Pen.
Nanisivik
Arctic Bay
Parry Channel
Baffin Bay

ARCTIC OCEAN

Baffin Bay
Lancaster Sound
SIRMILIK NAT. PARK
Arctic Bay
Nanisivik
Borden Pen.
Eclipse Sd.
Bylot I.
Pond Inlet
C. Adair
Clyde River
C. Raper
C. Dyer

GREENLAND (Denmark)

Davis Strait

Baffin Bay

Island
Admiralty Inlet
Iglulik
Rowley
Hall Beach
Spicer Is.
Prince Charles I.
Air Force I.
AUYUITTUQ NAT. PARK
Cumberland Peninsula
Pangnirtung
Qikiqtarjuaq
Cumberland Sd.
C. Mercy
Hoare B.
Home B.

Baffin Island (Qikiqtaaluk)

Foxe Basin
Melville Peninsula
Fury and Hecla Str.
Committee B.
Repulse Bay
NUNAVUT
Southampton I.
Coral Harbour
Bell Pen.
Vansittart I.
C. Dorchester
Foxe Channel
Amadjuak
Nettilling L.
Koukdjuak
Iqaluit
Hall Peninsula
Meta Incognita Peninsula
Frobisher Bay
Kimmirut
Resolution I.

Rees Welcome Sd.
Coats I.
Mansel I.
Nottingham I.
Digges Is.
Salluit
Ivujivik
Kangiqsujuaq
Quaqtaq
Akpatok I.
Kangirsuk
C. Chidley
Killiniq I.
Torngat Mts.
TORNGAT MTS. NAT. PARK

Hudson Strait

Cratères du lac Nouveau-Québec
Péninsule d'Ungava
Arnaud
Feuilles
Ungava Bay
Kangiqsualujjuaq
Mt. d'Iberville/Mt. Caubvick
Hebron
Nain

Labrador Sea

ATLANTIC

Puvirnituq
Inukjuak
L. Payne
L. Minto
Mélèzes
Kuujjuaq
Baleine
Hopedale

Hudson Bay
Ottawa Is.
Sleeper Is.
King George Is.
Sanikiluaq
Belcher Is.
C. Henrietta Maria
Kuujjuarapik
La à l'Eau Claire
Bakers Dozen Is.
Nunavik
QUÉBEC
L. Bienville
Grande Baleine
Kanaaupscow
La Grande
Chisasibi
Wemindji
Eastmain
Kawawachikamach
Schefferville
Petitsikapau L.
Esker
Smallwood Rés.
North West River
Happy Valley-Goose Bay
Churchill Falls
Churchill
L. Ashuanipi
Fermont
Labrador
Rigolet
Cartwright
Port Hope Simpson
Belle Isle
St. Anthony
Grey Is.

NEWFOUNDLAND & LABRADOR

James Bay
Twin Is.
Akimiski I.
Charlton
Fort Albany
Attawapiskat
Waskaganish
Rupert
Nottaway
L. Mistassini
L. Albanel
Gagnon
Mts. Otish
Manicouagan
Groulx
Moisie
Havre-St-Pierre
Natashquan
St-Augustin
Str. of Belle Isle
Baie Verte
Long Range Mts.
Deer Lake
Corner Brook
Grand Falls-Windsor
Lewisporte
Gander
Bonavista
Trinity B.
Carbonear
St. John's

ONTARIO
Moosonee
Albany
Peawanuck
Winisk
Attawapiskat
Hearst
Nakina
Geraldton
Kapuskasing
Oba
Cochrane
Abitibi
Val-d'Or
Amos
Rouyn-Noranda
Chibougamau
Dolbeau-Mistassini
Alma
Chicoutimi
Saguenay
Baie-Comeau
Sept-Îles
Port-Cartier
Dét. d'Honguedo
Gaspé
Pén. de la Gaspésie
Matane
Rimouski
Rivière-du-Loup
Gulf of St. Lawrence
Île d'Anticosti
Îs. de la Madeleine
Cabot Strait
Channel-Port aux Basques
ST-PIERRE et MIQUELON (Fr.)
Stephenville
PRINCE EDWARD I.
Summerside
Charlottetown
Cape Breton I.
Glace Bay
Sydney
Port Hawkesbury
Antigonish
Placentia B.
Avalon Pen.
C. Race
Marystown
Sable I. (Nova Scotia)

Thunder Bay
Marathon
Wawa
Chapleau
Timmins
Kirkland Lake
New Liskeard
Rés. Gouin
La Tuque
Shawinigan
Trois-Rivières
Québec
Lévis
St-Georges
Thetford
Mineso
Drummondville
Sherbrooke
NEW BRUNSWICK
Grand Falls
Edmundston
Miramichi
Moncton
Fredericton
Woodstock
Saint John
Bay of Fundy
NOVA SCOTIA
Truro
New Glasgow
Dartmouth
Halifax
Bridgewater
Liverpool
Yarmouth
C. Sable
Digby

Lake Superior
Houghton
Marquette
Sault Ste. Marie
Elliot Lake
Greater Sudbury
Nipissing
North Bay
Pembroke
Mont-Laurier
Outaouais
MAINE
Bangor
Augusta
Lewiston
Portland
NEW HAMPSHIRE
VERMONT
Manchester
Montpelier

MONTRÉAL
OTTAWA
Huntsville
Orillia
Barrie
Owen Sound
Georgian Bay
Manitoulin
TORONTO
Kitchener
Hamilton
Niagara Falls
Peterborough
Belleville
Kingston
Brockville
Cornwall
Plattsburgh
Burlington
Concord
BOSTON
C. Cod
MASS.
Springfield
HARTFORD
CONN.
New Haven
PROVIDENCE
R.I.
NEW YORK
Albany
Syracuse
ROCHESTER
BUFFALO
Jamestown
Binghamton
Scranton
PENNSYLVANIA
Erie
CLEVELAND
Toledo
DETROIT
Windsor
L. Erie
London
Sarnia
Flint
Lansing
Grand Rapids
Saginaw
Lake Huron
Lake Michigan
MILWAUKEE
Madison
Green Bay
Sheboygan
Appleton
WISCONSIN
Escanaba
Menominee
Traverse City
Cadillac
Petoskey
Manistique

ATLANTIC OCEAN

COPYRIGHT PHILIP'S

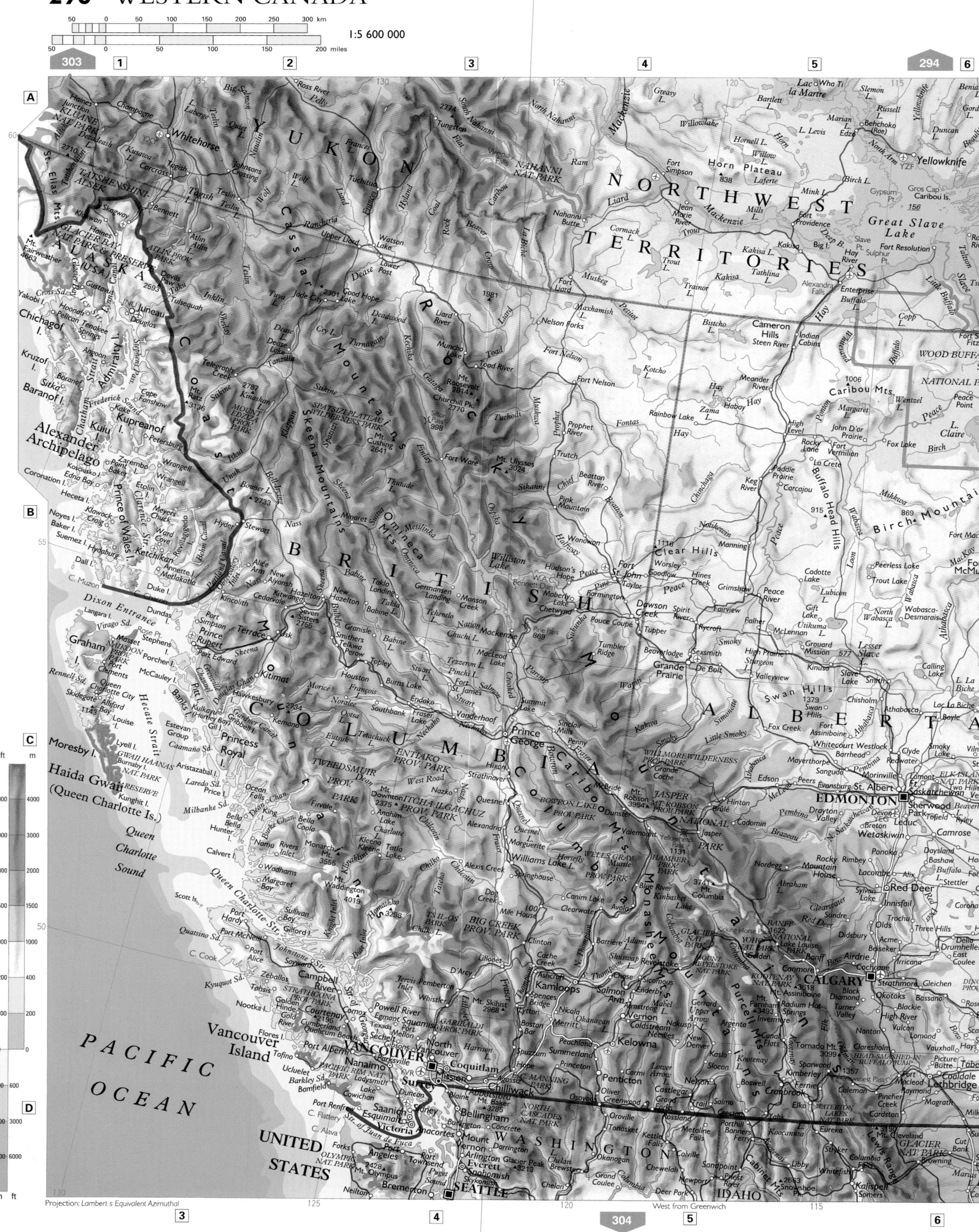

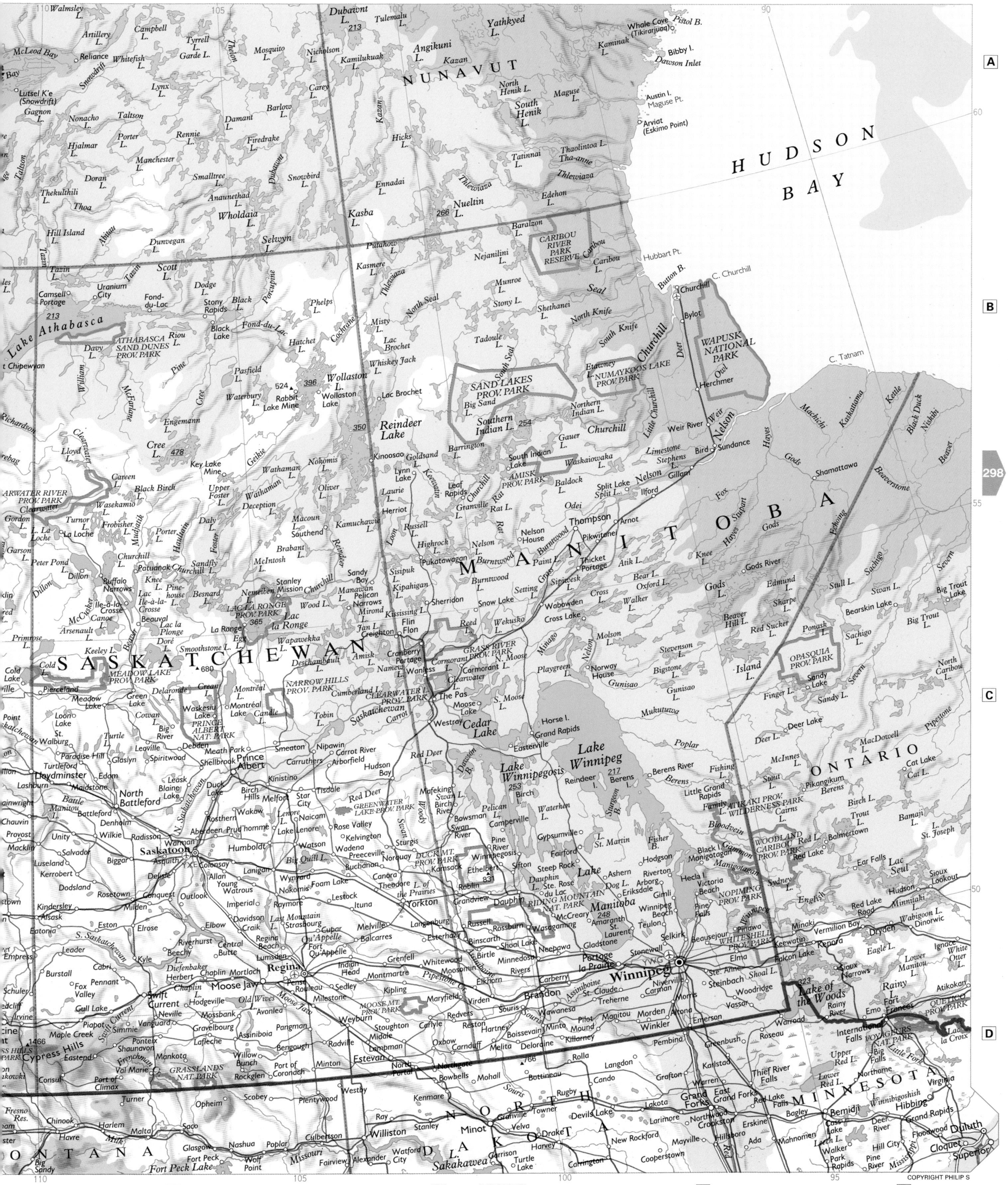

1:5 600 000

50 0 50 100 150 200 250 300 km

50 0 50 100 150 200 miles

297

308

Projection: Lambert's Equivalent Azimuthal

309

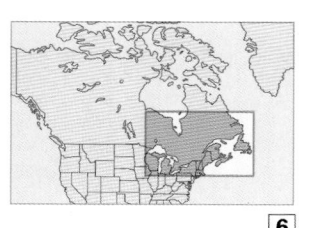

West from Greenwich

COPYRIGHT PHILIP'S

1:12 000 000

100 0 100 200 300 400 500 600 km
100 0 100 200 300 400 miles

11 **12** **13** **14** **16** 294 **17**

Anchorage
3363 miles
5412 km
Washington D.C.
2010 miles
3234 km
2785 miles
4482 km
2438 miles
3923 km
San Francisco
2395 miles
3854 km
Honolulu
Tropic of Cancer

PACIFIC OCEAN

West from Greenwich

BRITISH COLUMBIA
Kelowna
VANCOUVER
Vancouver
Penticton
ALBERTA
Chilliwack
Trail Cranbrook Crowsnest Pass Medicine
Victoria Bellingham Franklin D. Roosevelt L. Milk
Everett Mt. Olympus Columbia Kalispell Shelby
WASHINGTON Spokane Flathead Lake
SEATTLE Wenatchee Coeur d'Alene Great Falls
TACOMA Olympia Mt. Rainier Yakima Pullman Moscow Missoula Helena
PORTLAND Vancouver McMinnville Pendleton Lewiston IDAHO Bozeman Livingston
Salem Mt. Hood The Dalles La Grande Grangeville Butte Anaconda
Corvallis Albany Day Baker Salmon YELLOWSTONE NATIONAL PARK
Eugene Springfield Bend OREGON Ontario Payette Boise Idaho Falls Grand Teton
Coos Bay Roseburg Harney L. Nampa Caldwell Sun Valley Rexburg
C. Blanco Grants Pass High Desert Mountain Home Pocatello
Crescent City Medford Klamath Falls Twin Falls Burley Montpelier
Eureka Mt. Shasta NEVADA UTAH Logan Evanston
Redding Lassen Pk. Winnemucca Elko Brigham City OGDEN SALT LAKE CITY
Red Bluff Honey L. Great Salt Lake Wasatch Uinta Mts.
Chico Pyramid L. Ruby Mts. Sandy Provo Vernal
SACRAMENTO Reno Sparks Carson Sink Orem
Santa Rosa Napa Roseville Carson City Ely Nephi Price Grand Junction
Vallejo Concord Tahoe Walker Lake Hawthorne Richfield Moab
SAN FRANCISCO Oakland Stockton Wheeler Pk. Sevier L.
SAN JOSE Modesto YOSEMITE NAT. PARK Tonopah
Santa Cruz Merced Cedar City ZION NAT. PARK L. Powell
Salinas Fresno St. George Page
Monterey Visalia Hanford Mt. Whitney Death Valley Kingman GRAND CANYON NAT. PARK Colorado Plateau
Tulare SEQUOIA NAT. PARL LAS VEGAS Lake Mead Flagstaff Gallup
Paso Robles Bakersfield Henderson Hoover Dam Humphreys Peak Winslow
San Luis Obispo Mojave Desert Bullhead City Prescott
Santa Maria Barstow L. Havasu City ARIZONA
Pt. Conception Oxnard Santa Clarita San Bernardino Baldy Pk. Globe
Channel Islands LOS ANGELES Glendale Pasadena Riverside PHOENIX Mesa
Long Beach Anaheim Mission Viejo Palm Springs Salton Sea Payson
Oceanside Glendale Casa Grande Tucson
SAN DIEGO Centro Yuma Sonoyta
TIJUANA MEXICALI Sonoran Desert SONORA Nogales Douglas
Agua Prieta

ALASKA on same scale

RUSSIA
Penzhino Anadyr Arctic Circle Vankarem
Koryakskoye Nagorye ARCTIC OCEAN
Tilichiki CHUKCHI SEA Cape Lisburne Barrow Pt. Barrow
Kayacha Chukotskiy Nagorye Point Hope Wainwright
Khatyrka Anadyrskiy Zaliv Mys Dezhneva (East Cape) De Long Mts. North Slope Prudhoe Bay
Mys Navarin Providenya Poluostrov Chukotskiy Bering Strait Kotzebue Brooks Range Endicott Mts. Davidson Mts.
Mys Olyutorski Little Diomede I. Cape Prince of Wales Baird Mts. Schwatka Mts. Philip Smith Mts. British Mts.
St. Lawrence I. (U.S.A.) Teller Seward Peninsula Kobuk Wiseman Yukon Flats Old Crow Fort McPherson
International Date Line Nome Selawik L. Koyukuk Fort Yukon
St. Matthew I. Council Norton Sound Nulato Ray Mts. Circle
BERING SEA Stuart I. Emmonak Kotlik Tanana Nenana Fairbanks Eagle
Hooper Bay Yukon Delta Unalakleet Kaltag Anderson College Eielson
Cape Romanzof Bethel Holy Cross Kuskokwim Mountains U.S.A. Healy Delta Junction Dawson City
Nunivak I. Etolin Str. Aniak Alaska Range Denali (Mt. McKinley) Mt. Hayes Tok
St. Paul I. Kuskokwim Kilbuck Mts. Mt. Foraker Klondike
Pribilof Is. St. George I. Tikchik Lakes Iliamna Lake McGrath Palmer Copper Center Mt. Sanford Beaver Creek
Near Islands Hagemeister I. Dillingham Anchorage Wasilla Mt. Marcus Baker Mt. Wrangell Carmacks
Attu I. Bristol Bay Becharof Lake Homer Kenai Whittier Valdez Cordova Mt. Blackburn Mt. Lucania
Agattu Aleutian Islands Sutwik I. Kodiak I. Chugach Mts. Seward Prince William Sound Mt. St. Elias Mt. Logan
Andreanof Islands Alaska Peninsula Shelikof Strait Afognak I. Montague I. Bering Glacier Malaspina Glacier
Amchitka I. Fox Islands Trinity Is. Kayak I. Gulf of Alaska Yakutat
Rat Islands Unalaska Chirikof I. Middleton I. Cross Sound
Shumagin Is. Kodiak Chichagof I. Alexander Archipelago

Projection: Albers' Equal Area with two standard parallels
West from Greenwich

4 **5** **6** **7** **8** **9** **10** **11** **12**

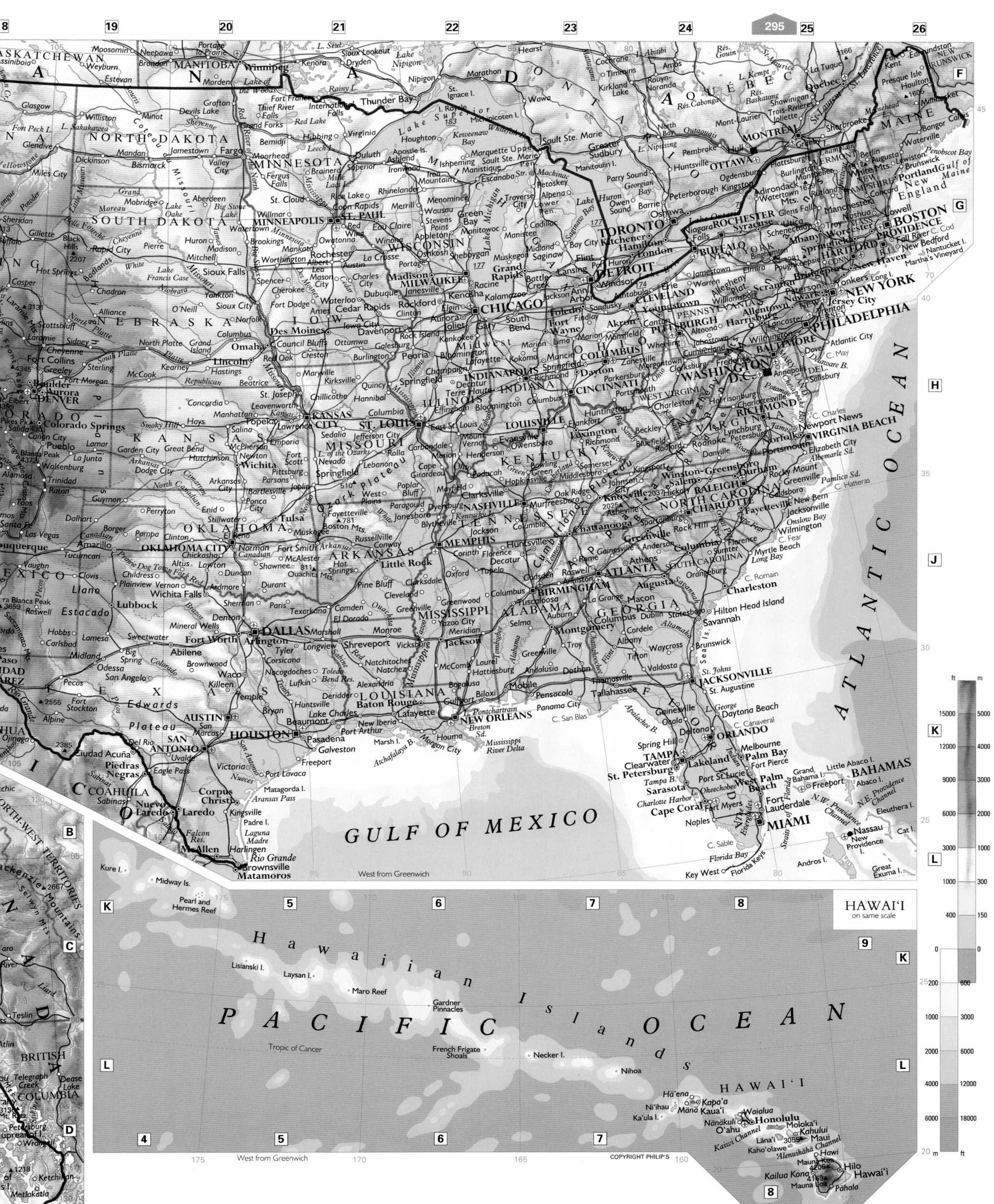

HAWAI'I
on same scale

COPYRIGHT PHILIP'S

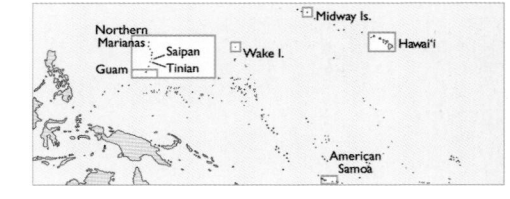

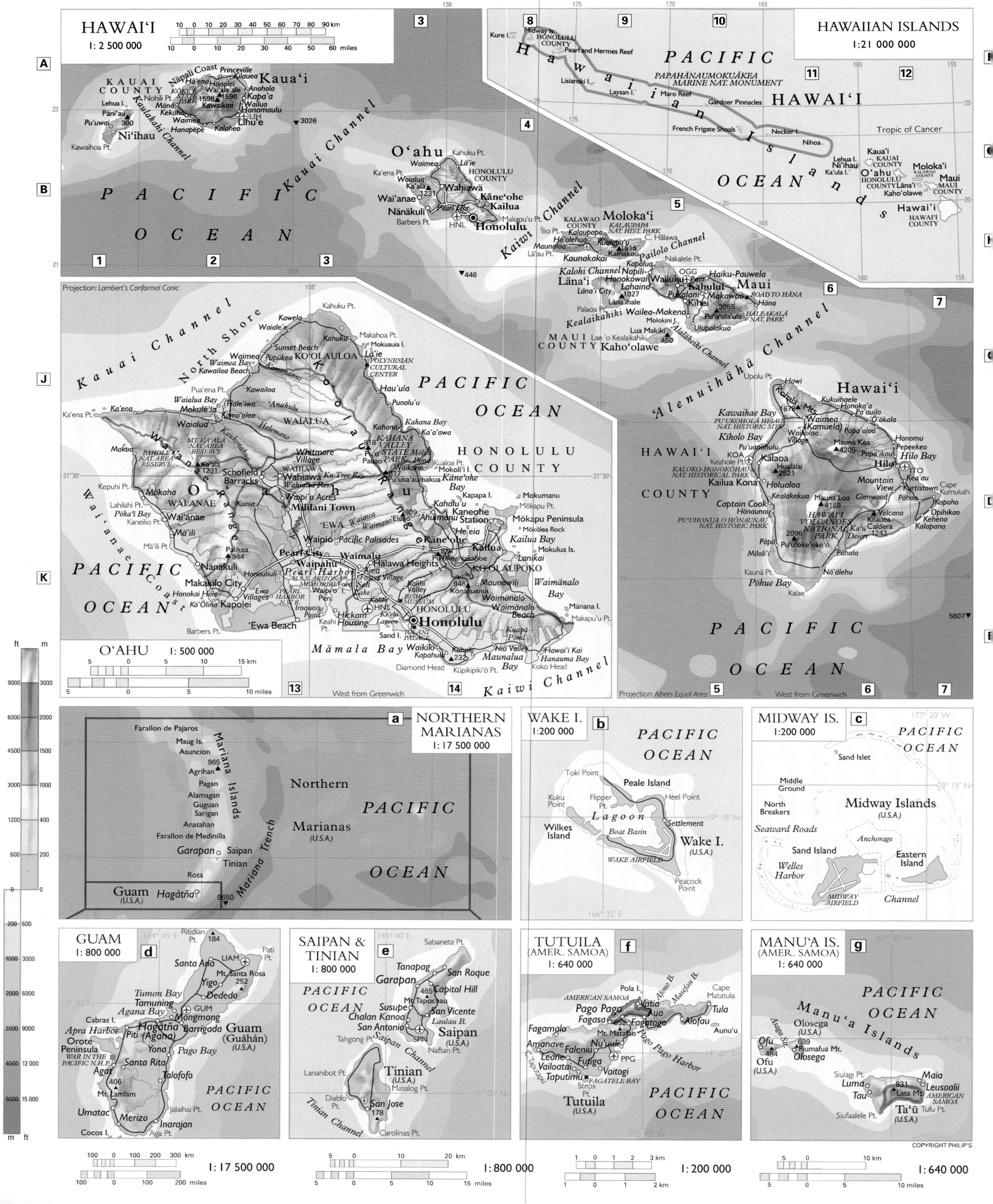

HAWAI‘I
1 : 2 500 000

10 0 10 20 30 40 50 60 70 80 90 km
10 0 10 20 30 40 50 60 miles

KAUAI COUNTY
Nāpali Coast · Princeville
Hā‘ena · Hanalei · Kīlauea
Nohili Pt. · KŌKE‘E · Wai‘ale‘ale 1598 · 1596 · Anahola · Kapa‘a
Lehua I. · Mānā · Kekaha · Waimea · Kawaikini · Wailua
Pāni‘au · Pu‘uwai · Hanapēpē · Kalaheo · Kalāheo · Līhu‘e · LIH
Ni‘ihau · Kawaihoa Pt. · 390
▼3026

Kaua‘i

HAWAIIAN ISLANDS
1 : 21 000 000

PACIFIC

O C E A N

Papahānaumokuākea Marine Nat. Monument
Kure I. · Midway Is. HONOLULU COUNTY · Pearl and Hermes Reef
Lisianski I. · Laysan I. · Maro Reef · Gardner Pinnacles
French Frigate Shoals · Necker I. · Nihoa
Tropic of Cancer

HAWAI‘I

Lehua I. · Kaua‘i · KAUAI COUNTY
Ni‘ihau · Ka‘ula I. · O‘ahu · HONOLULU COUNTY · Moloka‘i
Lāna‘i · MAUI COUNTY · Kaho‘olawe · Maui
Hawai‘i · HAWAI‘I COUNTY

O‘ahu
Kahuku Pt. · Waimea · Lā‘ie
Ka‘ena Pt. · HONOLULU COUNTY
Wai‘anae · Waialua · Wahiawā · Kāne‘ohe · Kailua
1231 · Nānākuli · Pearl Hbr. · Honolulu · Makapu‘u Pt.
Barbers Pt. · HNL

PACIFIC

O C E A N

KALAWAO COUNTY · **Moloka‘i**
‘Īlio Pt. · Kalaupapa · KALAUPAPA NAT. HIST. PARK
Kaunakakai · Kamakou · C. Hālawa · 1515
Maunaloa · Nakalele Pt. · Kapalua · Pailolo Channel
Lā‘au Pt. · Kalohi Channel · Napili · Haiku-Pauwela
Lāna‘i · Honokōwai · Pā‘ia · Ha‘iku-Pauwela · OGG
Lāna‘i City · Lahaina · Wailuku · Kahului · ROAD TO HĀNA
1027 · Lana‘ihale · Pukalani · Makawao · Hāna
Palaoa Pt. · Kīhei · 3055 · HALEAKALĀ NAT. PARK
MAUI Molokini I. · Wailea-Makena · Pu‘u‘ula‘ula · Ulupalakua
COUNTY · Kealaikahiki · Wailea-Makena · Lua Makika
Kaho‘olawe · Lae ‘o Kealaikahiki · 450
Kealaikahiki Channel · Alalākeiki Channel

PACIFIC

O C E A N

Projection: Lambert's Conformal Conic

O‘AHU
Kahuku Pt.
Kawela · Waiale‘e
Sunset Beach · Kahuku
North Shore · Waimea Bay · Makahoa Pt.
Pūpūkea · Mokuauia I.
Waimea · Kawailoa Beach · KO‘OLAULOA · Lā‘ie
Kamananui · Hau‘ula · POLYNESIAN CULTURAL CENTER
Pua‘ena Pt. · ‘Anahulu · Punalu‘u
Hale‘iwa · Kamo‘oloa · KAHANA VALLEY STATE PARK
Waialua Bay · Kahana · Kahana Bay
Mokulē‘ia · Helemano · Pu‘u · Ka‘a‘awa
Ka‘ena Pt. · WAIALUA · 518 · Pauao Pt.
Waialua · Whitmore Village · Kualoa Pt.
Maunawili · MT. KA‘ALA NAT. AREA RESERVE · Ku Tree Res. · Mokoli‘i I.
Makua · PAHOLE NAT. AREA RESERVE · WAHIAWA · Waiāhole · PACIFIC OCEAN
Ka‘ala 1231 · Schofield Barracks · Pu‘u‘aumakua
Kepuhi Pt. · Wahiawā Res. · Kāne‘ohe Bay
Waialua · Kunia · Pacific Palisades · Kapapa I.
Mākaha · O‘ahu · Mililani Town · Mokumanu
Lahilahi Pt. · WAI‘ANAE · ‘Ewa · 809 · Ahuimanu · Mōkapu Pt.
Pōka‘ī Bay · Waipi‘o · Kāne‘ohe · Mōkapu Peninsula
Kaneilio Pt. · Mā‘ili · Kahalu‘u · Mōkōlea Rock
Wai‘anae · 944 · Waimalu · Kailua Bay
Mā‘ili Pt. · Palikea · He‘eia · Lanikai
Nānākuli · Waipahu · Waimānalo · Mokulua Is.
Honouliuli · Pearl City · Waimalu · KO‘OLAUPOKO
Makakilo City · Pearl Harbor · Hālawa Heights · Maunawili
‘Ewa Villages · ‘Aiea · 946 · Waimānalo
Kō ‘Olina Kapolei · PEARL HARBOR NWR · Kalihi Valley · Waimānalo Bay
Iroquois Point · Waipi‘o Pen. · Foster Village · Konahuanui
Honokai Hale · Hickam Housing · Mānana I.
Barbers Pt. · Keahi Pt. · Ke‘ehi Lagoon · HNL · Kāne‘ohe
‘Ewa Beach · Sand I. · Waikīkī · Hawai‘i Kai
Keahi · Kūpikipiki‘ō Pt. · Kuapā Pond
Diamond Head · **Honolulu** · Hanauma Bay
IOLANI PALACE · BISHOP MUSEUM · Koko Head
Māmala Bay · Kahala · Kuli‘ou‘ou · Niu Valley
Maunalua Bay
5807 ▼

PACIFIC

O C E A N

O‘AHU 1 : 500 000
5 0 5 10 15 km
5 0 5 10 miles

West from Greenwich · *West from Greenwich*
Projection: Albers Equal Area

HAWAI‘I
HAWAI‘I COUNTY
Upolu Pt. · Hāwī
Kohala Mts. · Kukuihaele · Honoka‘a · Pa‘auilo
Kawaihae Bay · 6784 · Waimea · Papa‘aloa · ‘O‘ōkala
PU‘UKOHOLA HEIAU NAT. HISTORIC SITE · Kamuela · Honomu
Kīholo Bay · Waikōloa Village · Pepeekeo
KOA · Kalaoa · Mauna Kea ▲4205 · Papa‘ikou · Hilo Bay
HAWAI‘I · Keahole Pt. · Hilo
Kailua Kona · Mauna Kea · ITO
HAWAI‘I · KALOKO-HONOKŌHAU NAT. HISTORICAL PARK
Holualoa · 2521 · Mountain View · Kurtistown
COUNTY · Kealakekua · Mauna Loa ▲4169 · Glenwood · Pāhoa · Cape Kumukahi
Captain Cook · Hōnaunau · Kapoho
Kalihi Valley · PU‘UHONUA O HŌNAUNAU NAT. HISTORICAL PARK
PU‘U OKE‘OKE‘O · HAWAI‘I VOLCANOES NATIONAL PARK · Kīlauea Caldera · ‘Opihikao
2096 · Pāpā · Ka‘ū Desert 1243 · Kehena
Miloli‘i · Pāhala · Kalapana
Kaunā Pt. · Nā‘ālehu
Pōhue Bay
Kalae

PACIFIC

O C E A N

Elevation scale
ft / m
9000 / 3000
6000 / 2000
4500 / 1500
3000 / 1000
1200 / 400
600 / 200
0 / 0
200 / 600
1000 / 3000
2000 / 6000
3000 / 9000
4000 / 12 000
5000 / 15 000
m / ft

NORTHERN MARIANAS
1 : 17 500 000

Farallon de Pajaros
Maug Is. · Asuncion
Agrihan ▲965
Pagan
Alamagan
Guguan
Sarigan
Anatahan · **Northern Marianas (U.S.A.)**
Farallon de Medinilla
Garapan · Saipan
Tinian · **Marianas (U.S.A.)**
Rota
PACIFIC OCEAN
Guam (U.S.A.) · Hagåtña ▲9850
Mariana Islands · Mariana Trench

WAKE I.
1 : 200 000

Toki Point
Kuku Pt. · Peale Island · Heel Point
Flipper Pt.
Wilkes Island · *Lagoon* · Settlement
Boat Basin · Wake I. (U.S.A.)
WAKE AIRFIELD
Peacock Point

PACIFIC OCEAN

MIDWAY IS.
1 : 200 000

Sand Islet
Middle Ground
North Breakers · **Midway Islands (U.S.A.)**
Seaward Roads · Anchorage
Sand Island · Eastern Island
Welles Harbor · *Channel*
MIDWAY AIRFIELD

PACIFIC OCEAN

177° 20' W
28° 15' N

GUAM
1 : 800 000

Ritidian Pt. · 184
Pati Pt.
Santa Ana · UAM · Mt. Santa Rosa 252
Tumon Bay · Yigo
Tamuning · Dededo
Agana Bay · GUM · Mongmong
Cabras I. · Hagåtña (Agana) · Barrigada · **Guam (Guåhån) (U.S.A.)**
Apra Harbor · Piti · Yona · Pago Bay
Orote Peninsula · WAR IN THE PACIFIC N.H.P. · Santa Rita
Agat · 406 · Talofofo
Umatac · Mt. Lamlam
Merizo · Inarajan
Cocos I. · Aga Pt.

PACIFIC OCEAN

144° 45' E
13° 30' N

SAIPAN & TINIAN
1 : 800 000

Sabaneta Pt.
Tanapag · San Roque
Garapan
465 · Mt. Tapochau · Capitol Hill
Chalan Kanoa · San Vicente
Susupe · **Saipan (U.S.A.)**
San Antonio · Laulau B.
Tahgong Pt. · SPN · Naftan Pt.
Lananibot Pt. · *Saipan Channel*
Masalog Pt.
Diablo · **Tinian (U.S.A.)**
San Jose · 178
Tinian Channel · Carolinas Pt.

PACIFIC OCEAN

145° 40' E

TUTUILA
(AMER. SAMOA)
1 : 640 000

Pola I. · Ofisana B.
AMERICAN SAMOA · Aoa · Masefau B.
Pago Pago · Vatia · Cape Matatula
Fagasa · Aua
Fagamalo · Mt. Matafao · Fagaitua · Tula
Amanave · Faleniu · Nu‘uuli · Alofau
Leone · Fagaalu · Aunu‘u
Vailoatai · Fugia · PPG
Taputimu · Vaitogi · Pago Pago Harbor
Steps · FAGATELE BAY
Siufaalele Pt.

Tutuila (U.S.A.)

PACIFIC OCEAN

MANU‘A IS.
(AMER. SAMOA)
1 : 640 000

PACIFIC OCEAN

Olosega (U.S.A.)
639 · Piumafua Mt.
Ofu 484 · Olosega
Ofu (U.S.A.) · *Manu‘a Islands*
931 · Maia
Luma · Lata Mt. · Leusoalii
Tau · AMERICAN SAMOA
Ta‘u (U.S.A.)
Siufaalele Pt. · Tufu Pt.

169° 20' W
14° 20' S

COPYRIGHT PHILIP'S

---

1 : 17 500 000
100 0 100 200 300 km
100 0 100 200 miles

1 : 800 000
5 0 5 10 20 km
5 0 5 10 15 miles

1 : 200 000
1 0 1 2 3 km
1 0 1 2 miles

1 : 640 000
5 0 5 10 km
5 0 5 10 miles

1:8 000 000

Projection: Bipolar oblique conformal

COPYRIGHT PHILIP'S

continuation westwards
on same scale

County boundaries

1 ANCHORAGE
2 BRISTOL BAY
3 HAINES
4 SKAGWAY-HOONAH-
  ANGOON
5 KETCHIKAN
  GATEWAY

1:5 360 000

50 0 50 100 150 200 250 300 km

50 0 50 100 150 200 miles

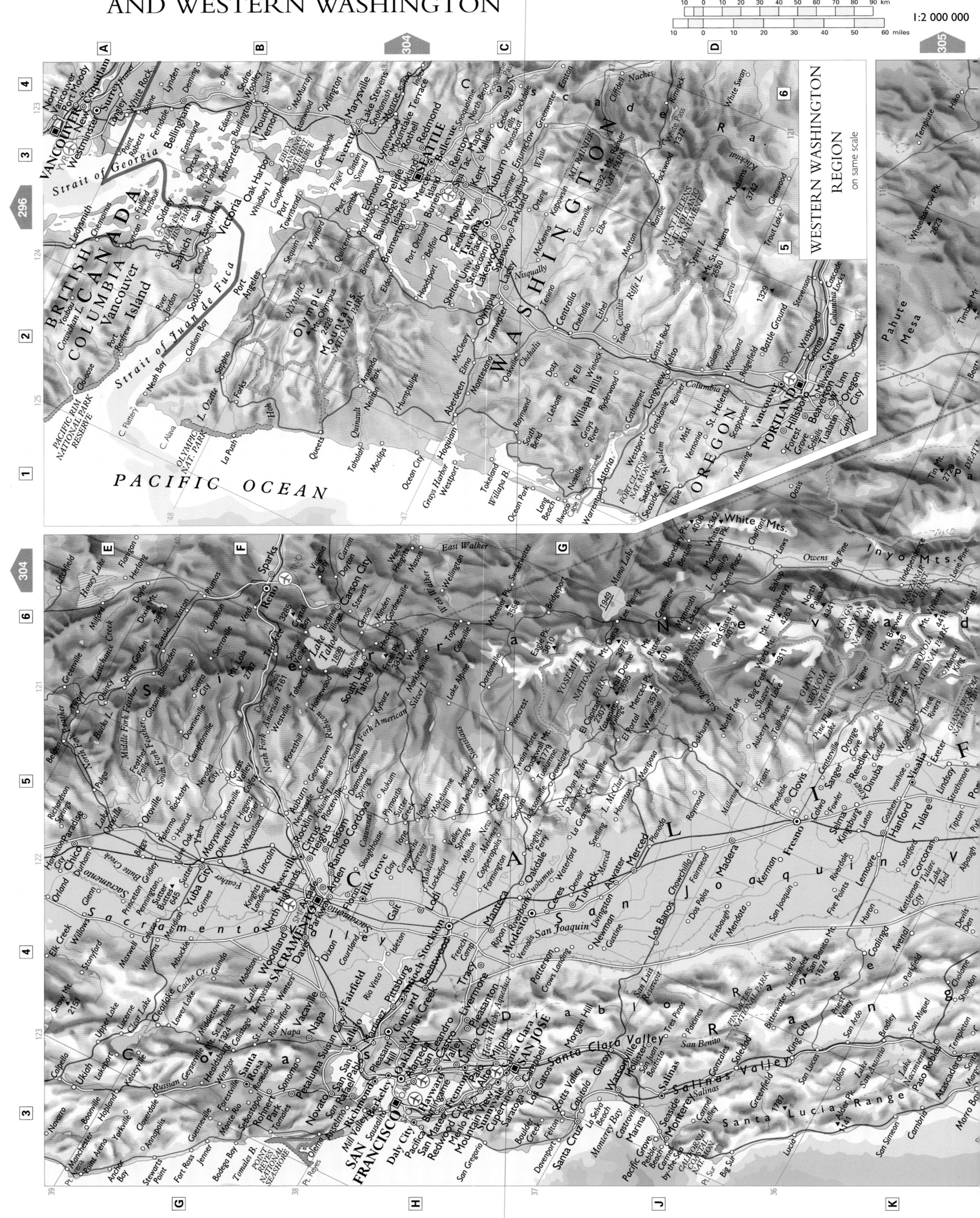

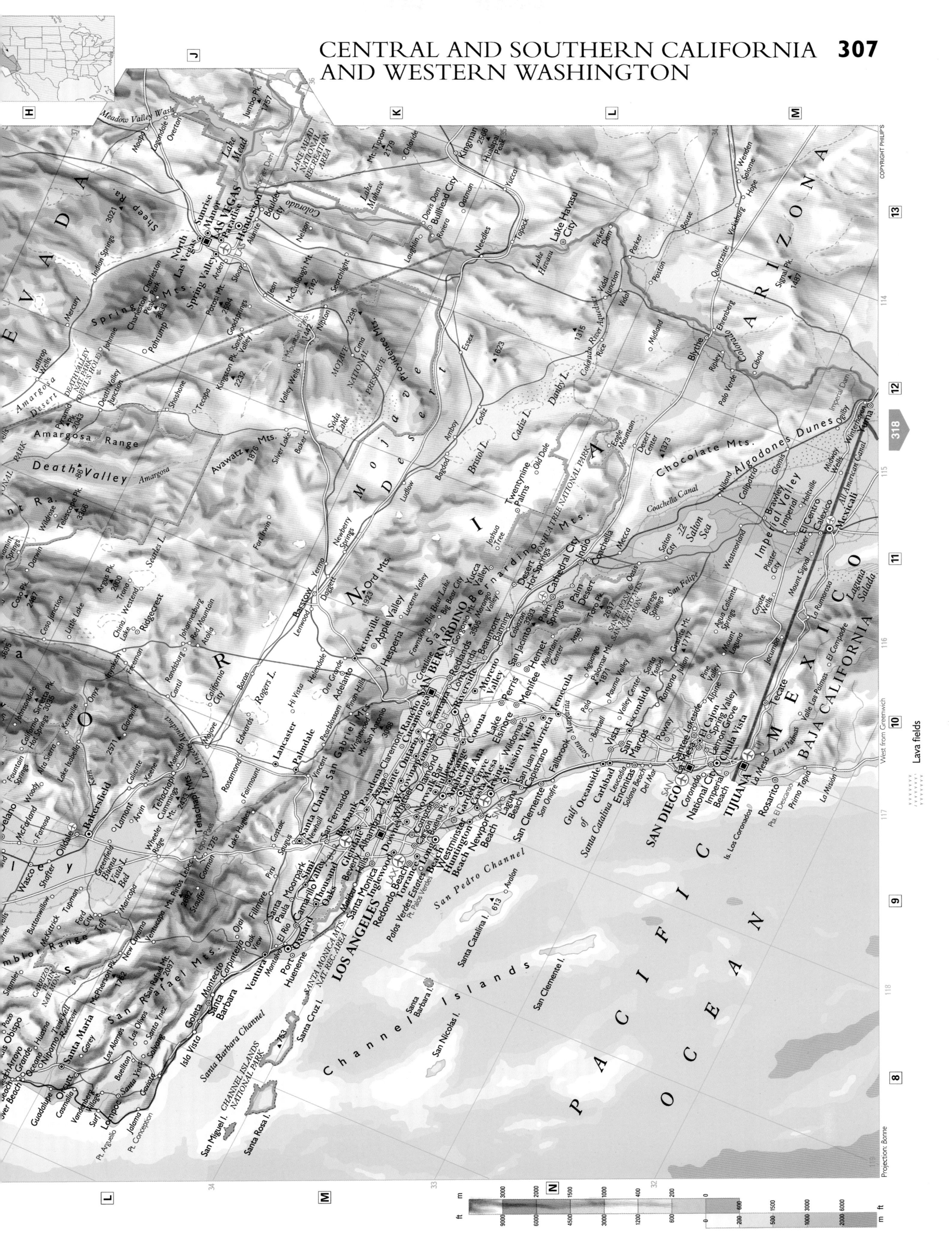

318

Lava fields

West from Greenwich

Projection: Bonne

COPYRIGHT PHILIP'S

1:5 360 000

Projection: Albers' Equal Area with two standard parallels

West from Greenwich

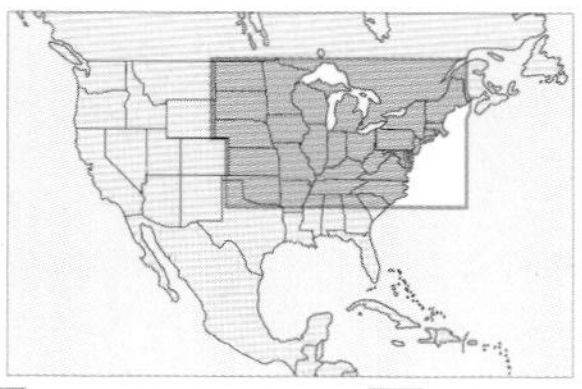

ONTARIO

QUÉBEC

CANADA

MAINE

NEW HAMPSHIRE

VERMONT

NEW YORK

PENNSYLVANIA

OHIO

WEST VIRGINIA

VIRGINIA

MARYLAND

NEW JERSEY

NORTH CAROLINA

SOUTH CAROLINA

GEORGIA

KENTUCKY

NEW BRUNS.

MASS.

CONN.

R.I.

DELAWARE

LAKE SUPERIOR

LAKE HURON

LAKE ERIE

LAKE ONTARIO

Georgian Bay

Gulf of Maine

Chesapeake Bay

Delaware Bay

Albemarle Sd.

Pamlico Sound

ATLANTIC OCEAN

Major cities:
MONTREAL, OTTAWA, TORONTO, BUFFALO, ROCHESTER, DETROIT, CLEVELAND, COLUMBUS, CINCINNATI, PITTSBURGH, PHILADELPHIA, NEW YORK, BOSTON, PROVIDENCE, HARTFORD, BALTIMORE, WASHINGTON D.C., RICHMOND, VIRGINIA BEACH, RALEIGH, CHARLOTTE, ATLANTA, Québec

COPYRIGHT PHILIP'S

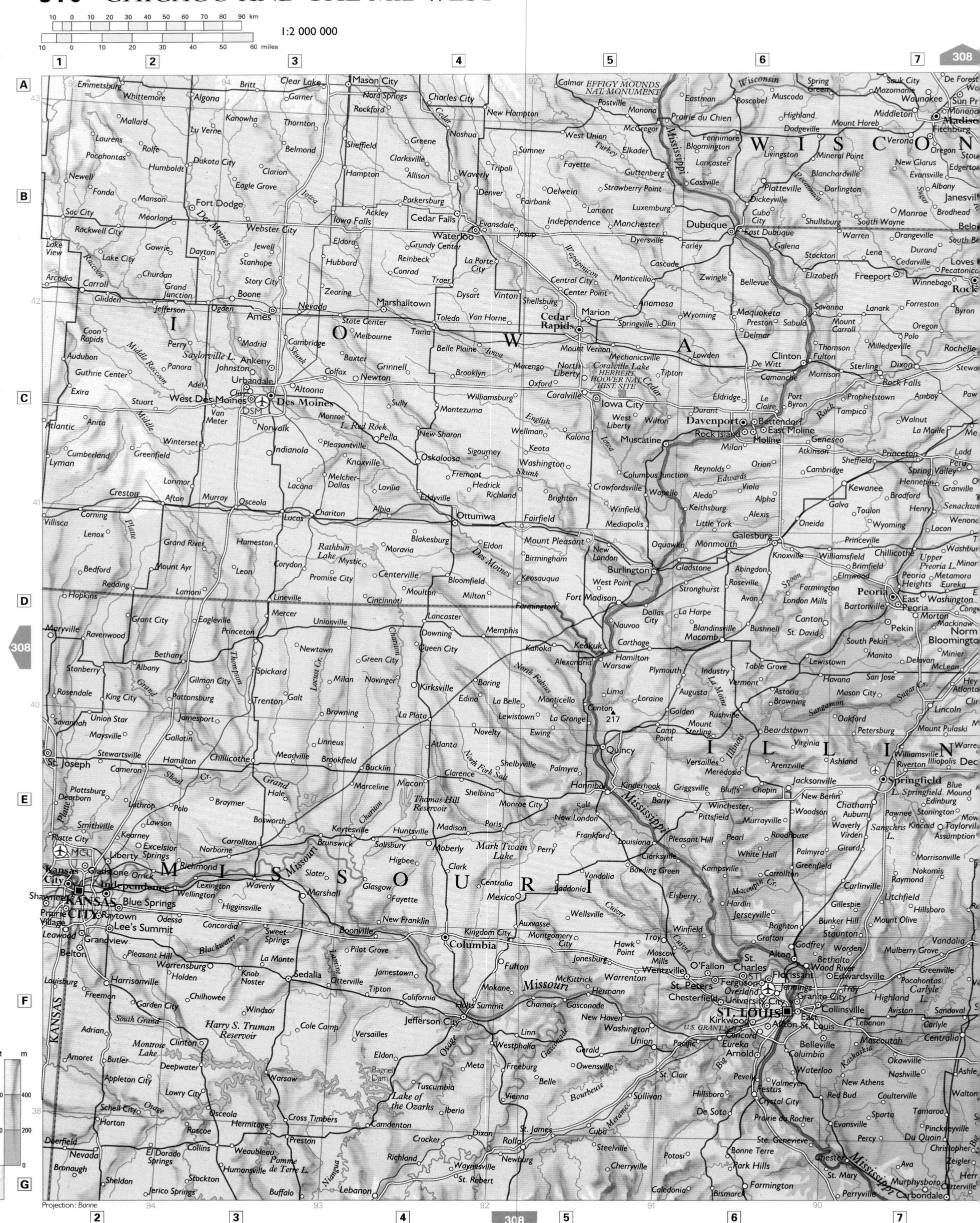

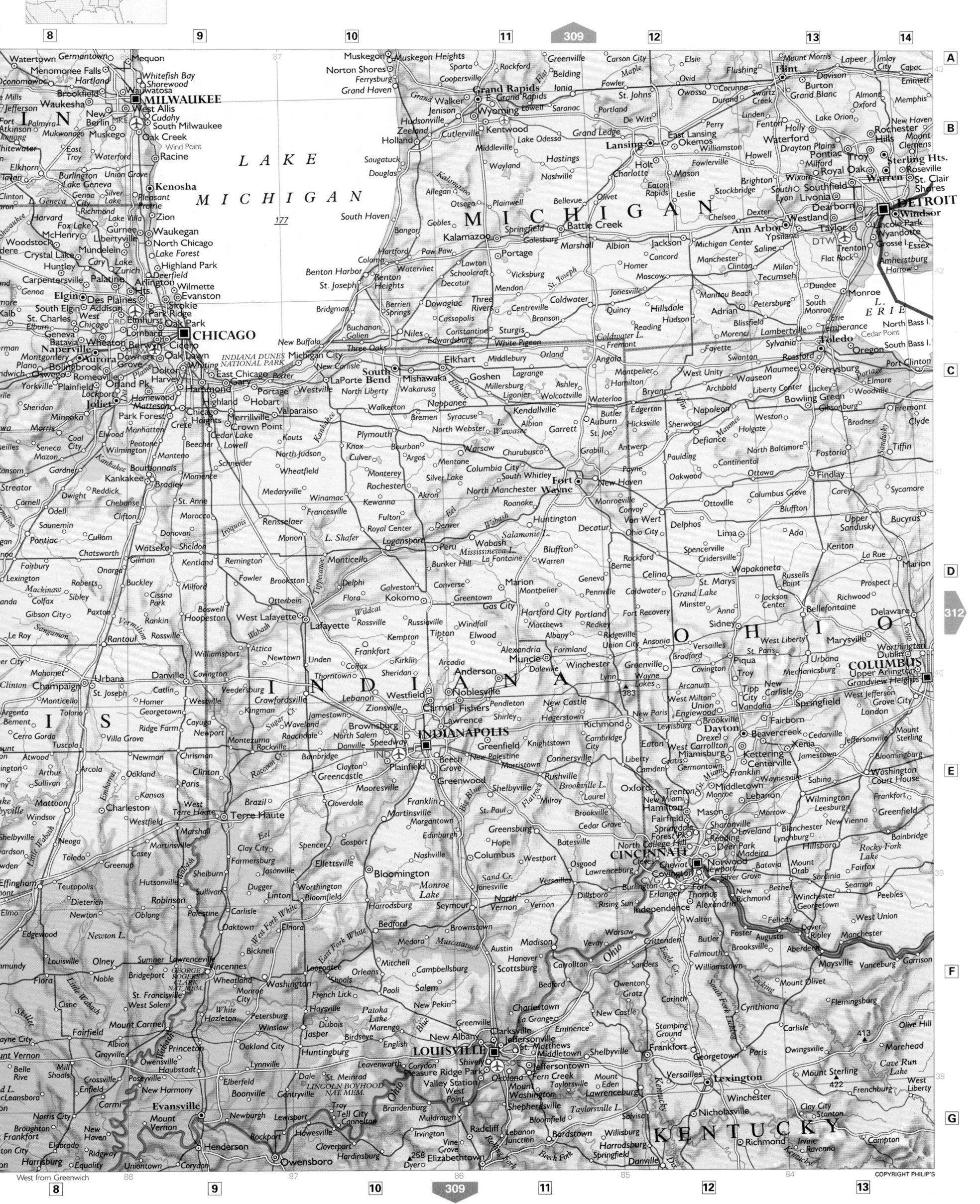

West from Greenwich

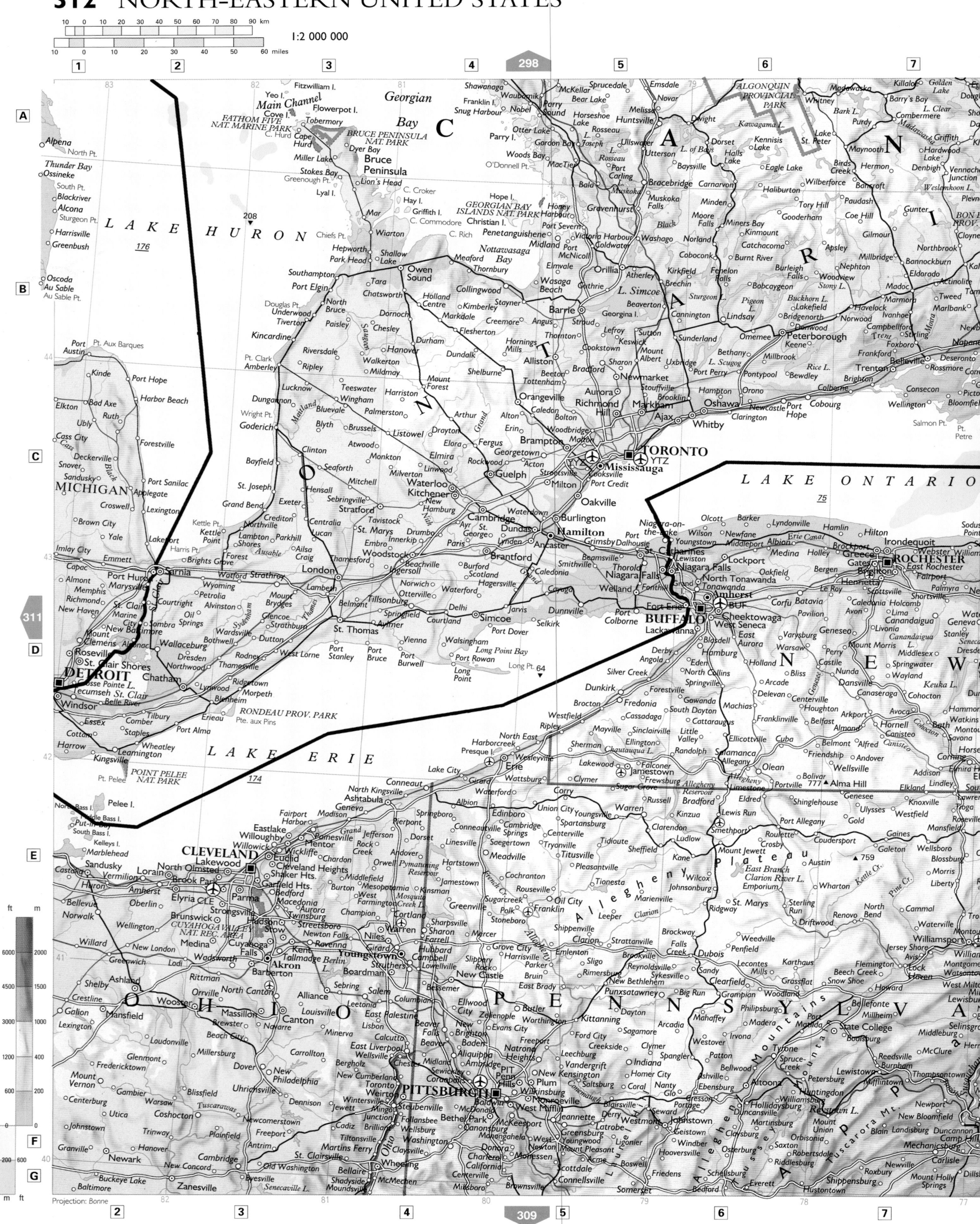

Projection: Bonne

1:2 000 000

298

309

311

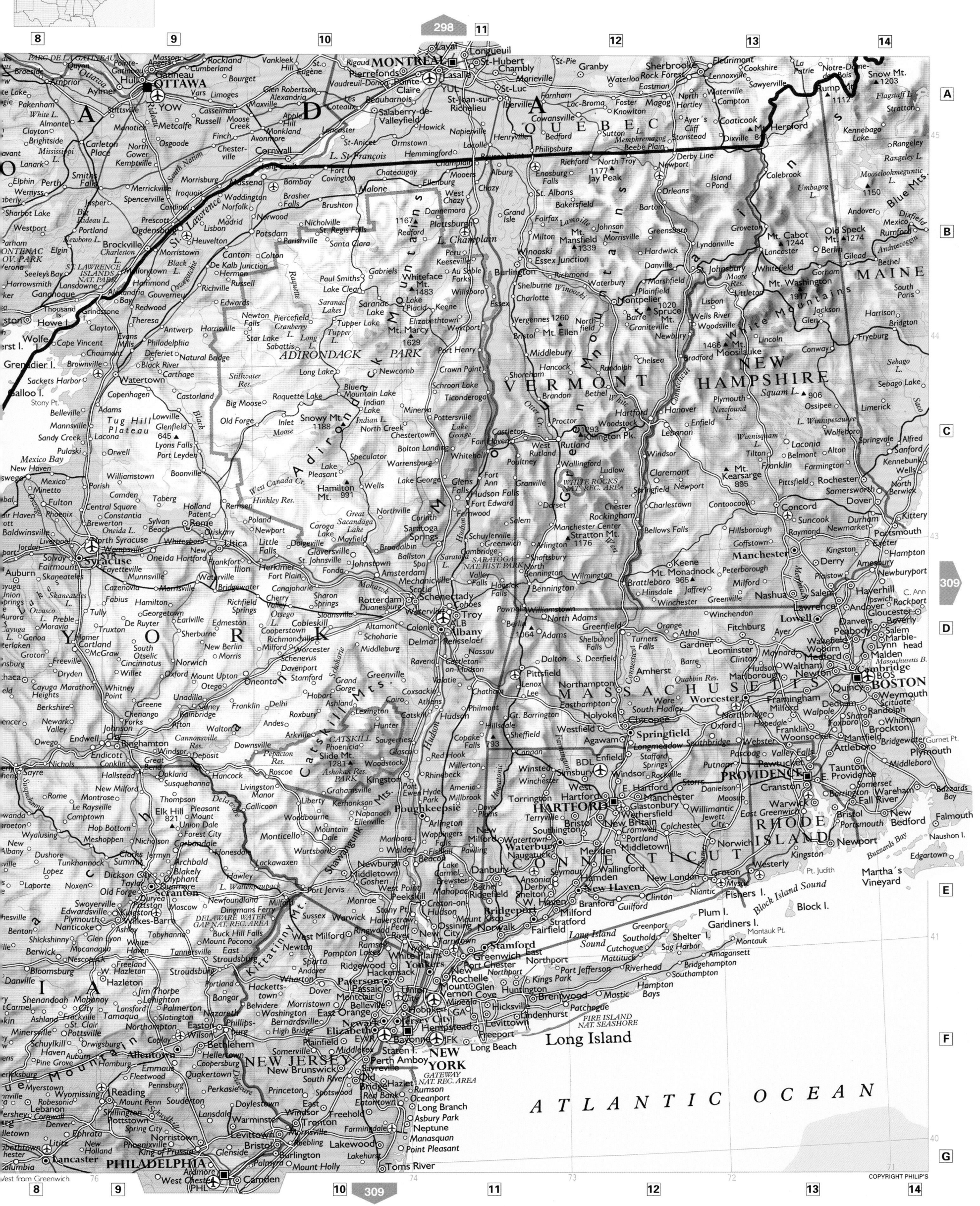

1:5 360 000

Projection: Albers' Equal Area with two standard parallels

West from Greenwich

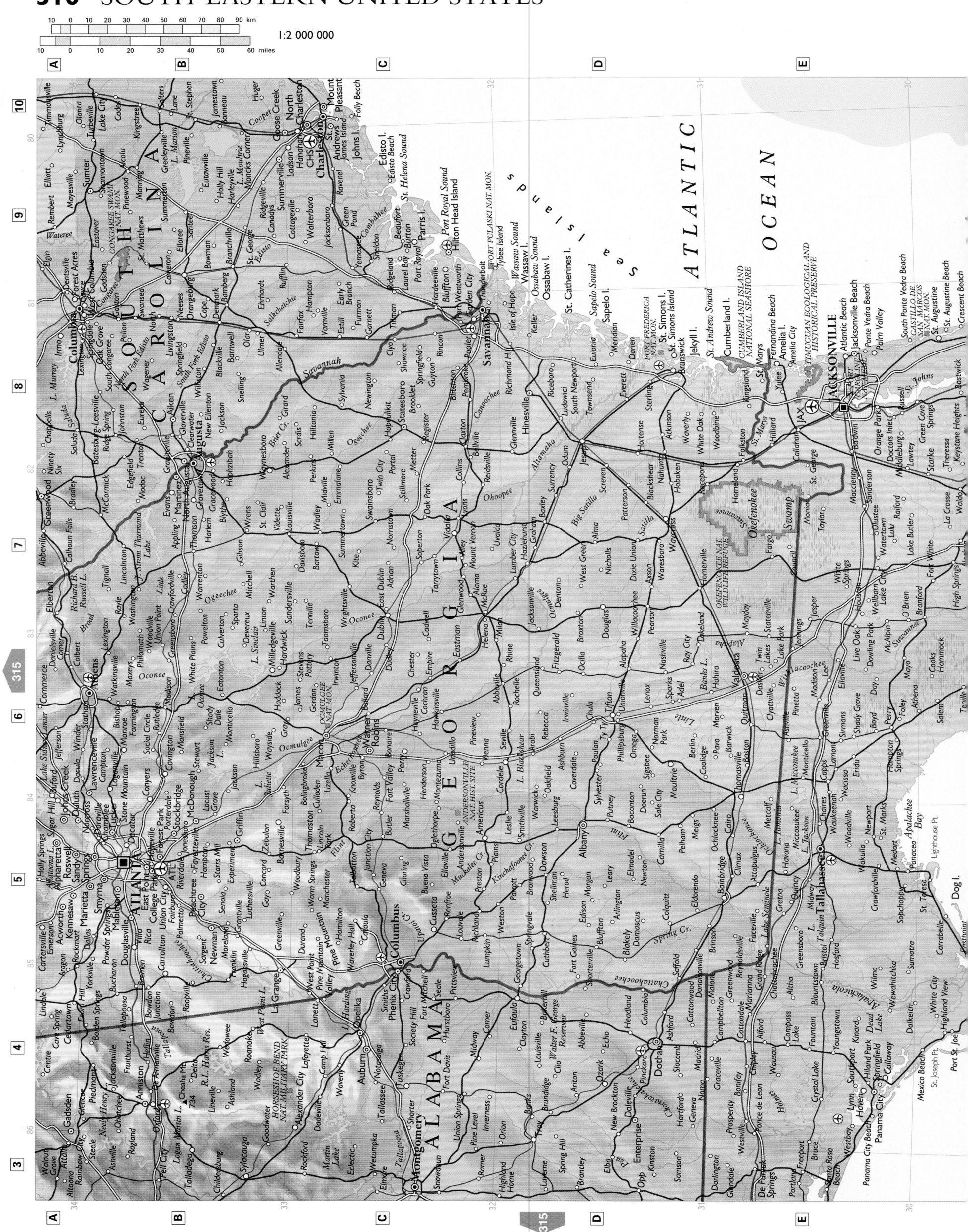

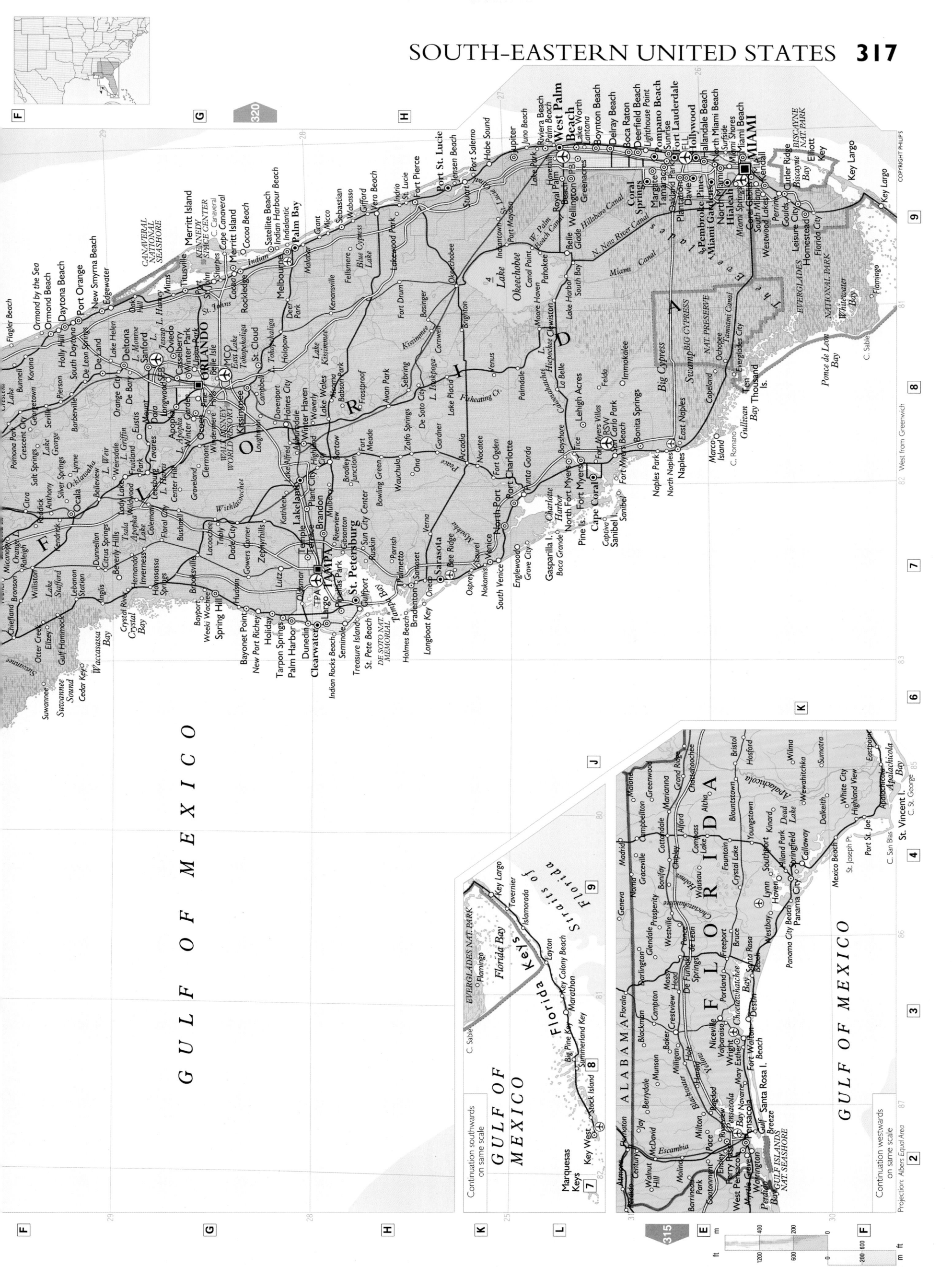

GULF OF MEXICO

GULF OF MEXICO

GULF OF MEXICO

F L O R I D A

A L A B A M A

Continuation southwards
on same scale

Continuation westwards
on same scale

Projection: Albers Equal Area

1:6 400 000

50 0 50 100 150 200 250 300 km
50 0 50 100 150 200 miles

Projection: Bi-polar oblique Conical Orthomorphic

West from Greenwich

State names in Central Mexico

1 DISTRITO FEDERAL 3 GUANAJUATO 5 MÉXICO 7 QUERÉTARO
2 AGUASCALIENTES 4 HIDALGO 6 MORELOS 8 TLAXCALA

United States / New Mexico region

Roswell Llano Estacado Lubbock
Las Cruces Hobbs Midland Odessa Big Spring Sweetwater
El Paso CIUDAD JUÁREZ Carlsbad Van Horn
Deming Lordsburg

Mexico — states and cities

BAJA CALIFORNIA
TIJUANA Tecate Mexicali
Ensenada San Luis Río Colorado
Santo Tomás El Rosario
Pta. Baja Guayaquil
Vicente Guerrero Venustiano Carranza
El Rosario

SONORA
Nogales Tucson Yuma
Puerto Peñasco Caborca Altar
Magdalena de Kino Santa Ana Arizpe
HERMOSILLO Ures Moctezuma
Guaymas Empalme
Ciudad Obregón Navojoa Etchojoa
Huatabampo Yávaros Álamos

CHIHUAHUA
Nuevo Casas Grandes Villa Ahumada
CHIHUAHUA Cuauhtémoc Ciudad Guerrero
Delicias Saucillo Meoqui
Hidalgo del Parral Santa Bárbara
Jiménez Ciudad Camargo

COAHUILA
Piedras Negras Zaragoza Nava Allende Sabinas
Nueva Rosita Melchor Múzquiz Juárez
MONCLOVA Cuatrociénegas Parras
SALTILLO Ramos Arizpe

DURANGO
DURANGO Santiago Papasquiaro Canatlán
Sombrerete El Salto Gómez Palacio
TORREÓN Ciudad Lerdo

SINALOA
Los Mochis Guasave Guamúchil
CULIACÁN Navolato El Dorado
MAZATLÁN Rosario Escuinapa de Hidalgo

NAYARIT
TEPIC Santiago Ixcuintla Tecuala Acaponeta
Compostela

JALISCO
GUADALAJARA ZAPOPAN Tlaquepaque Tonalá
Tequila Ameca Ocotlán La Barca
Puerto Vallarta Autlán de Navarro

ZACATECAS
ZACATECAS Guadalupe Fresnillo Valparaíso
Jerez de García Salinas Villa de Cos

AGUASCALIENTES
AGUASCALIENTES Calvillo Jalpa de Díaz

SAN LUIS POTOSÍ
SAN LUIS POTOSÍ Matehuala Venado Charcas
Cedral Salinas

GUANAJUATO
LEÓN Irapuato Celaya Salamanca
Guanajuato Silao

MICHOACÁN
MORELIA Uruapan Apatzingán Zamora
Zitácuaro Pátzcuaro Lázaro Cárdenas
Ciudad Altamirano Huetamo Coalcomán

COLIMA
COLIMA Manzanillo Tecomán

Islands
Islas Marías
I. María Madre I. Isabela I. Magdalena I. Cleofas

Revillagigedo Archipelago National Park
Is. de Revillagigedo (Mexico)
I. San Benedicto I. Roca Partida I. Socorro I. Clarión (Mexico)

Baja California Sur
BAJA CALIFORNIA SUR
Santa Rosalía Mulegé Loreto
Ciudad Constitución I. Magdalena I. Santa Margarita
LA PAZ Todos Santos
Cabo San Lucas San José del Cabo CABO PULMO

Water bodies
PACIFIC OCEAN
Golfo de California / Gulf of California
Mar de Cortés
B. de Banderas

Tropic of Cancer

Acapulco Trench
Cedros Trench

Elevation scale
ft / m
9000 / 3000
6000 / 2000
4500 / 1500
3000 / 1000
1200 / 400
600 / 200
0 / 0
200 / 600
1000 / 3000
2000 / 6000
4000 / 12 000
m / ft

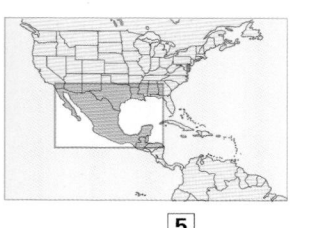

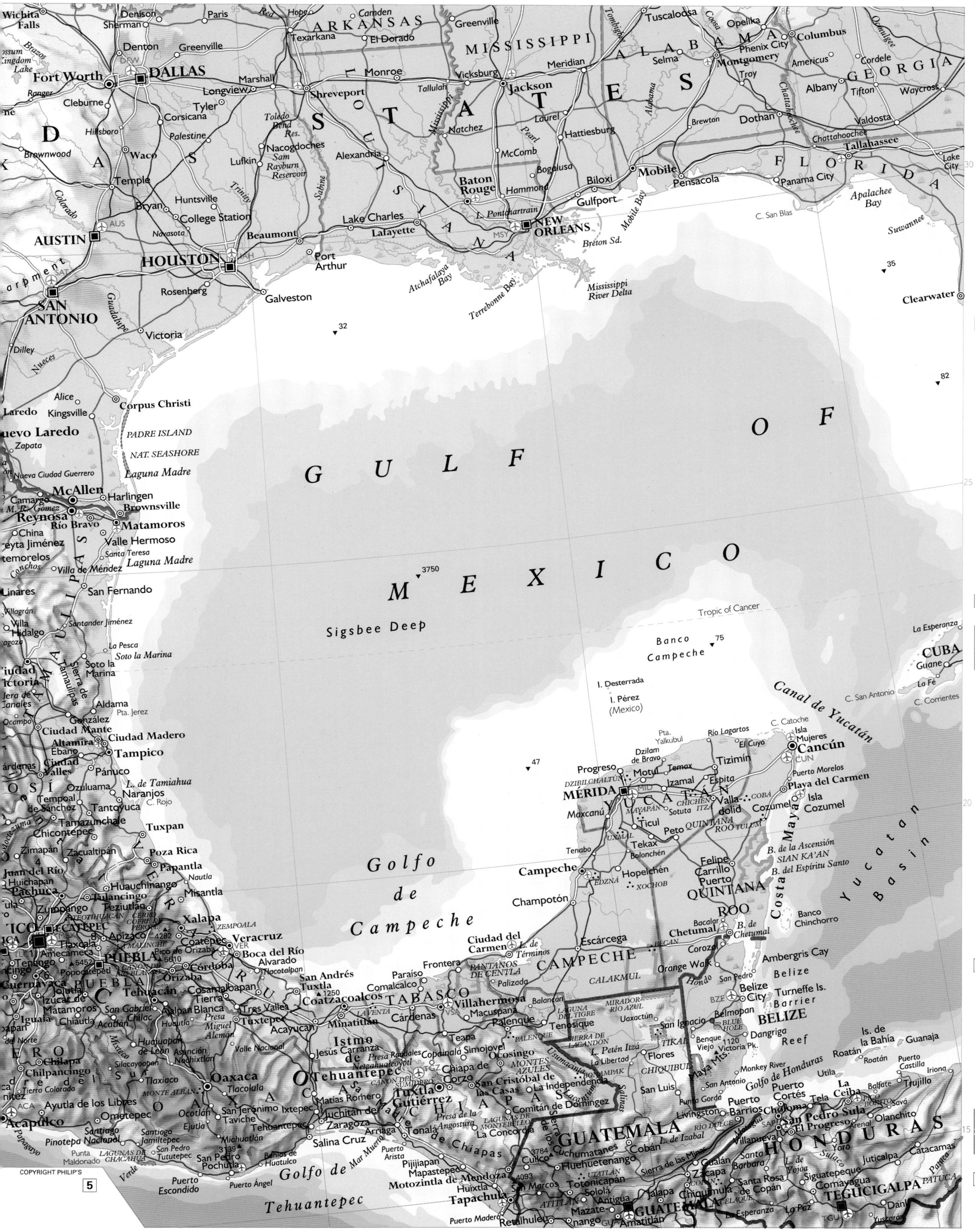

JAMAICA
1:1 600 000
a

PANAMA CANAL
1:800 000
c

■ Place of interest

Projection: Conical with two standard parallels

1:6 400 000

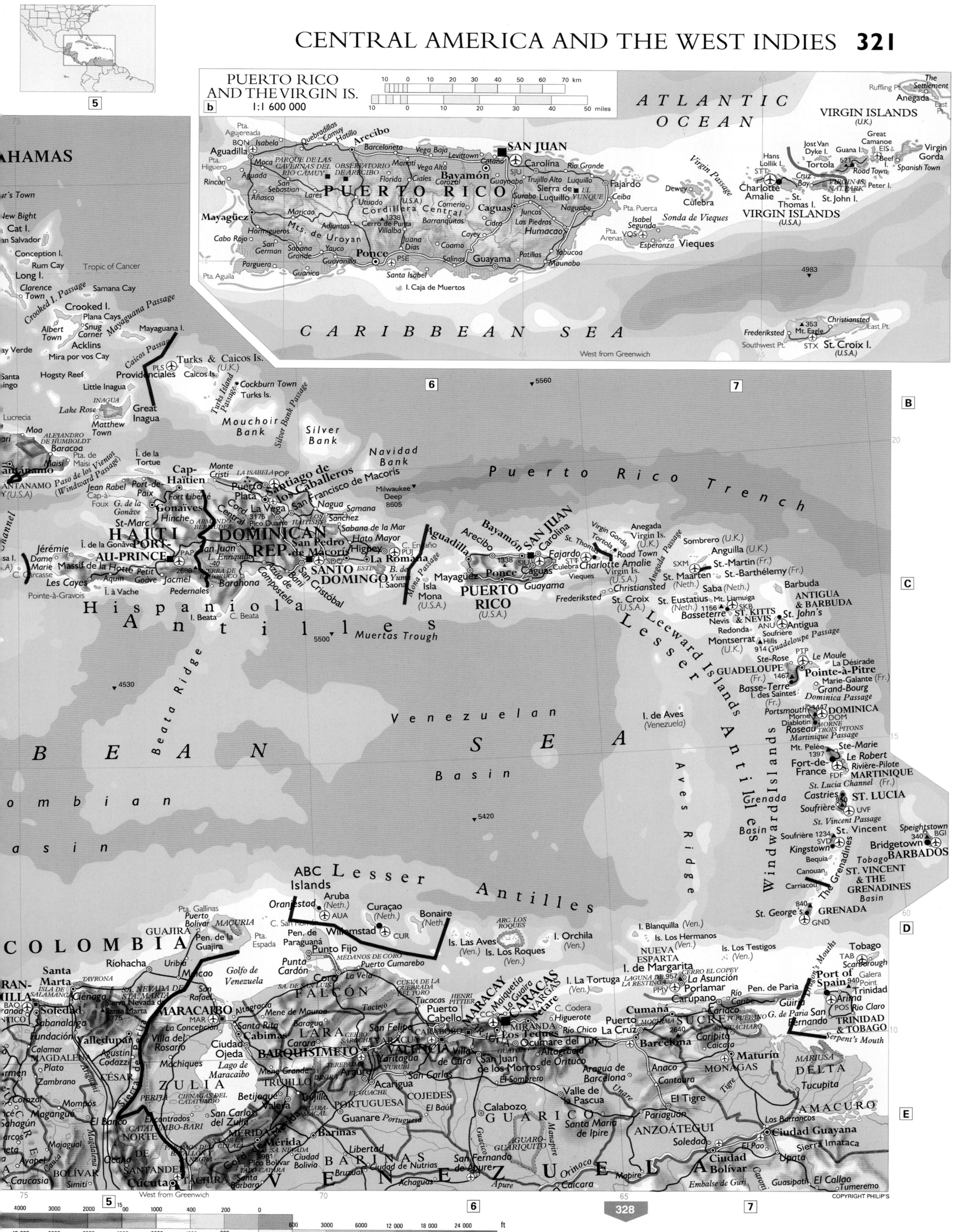

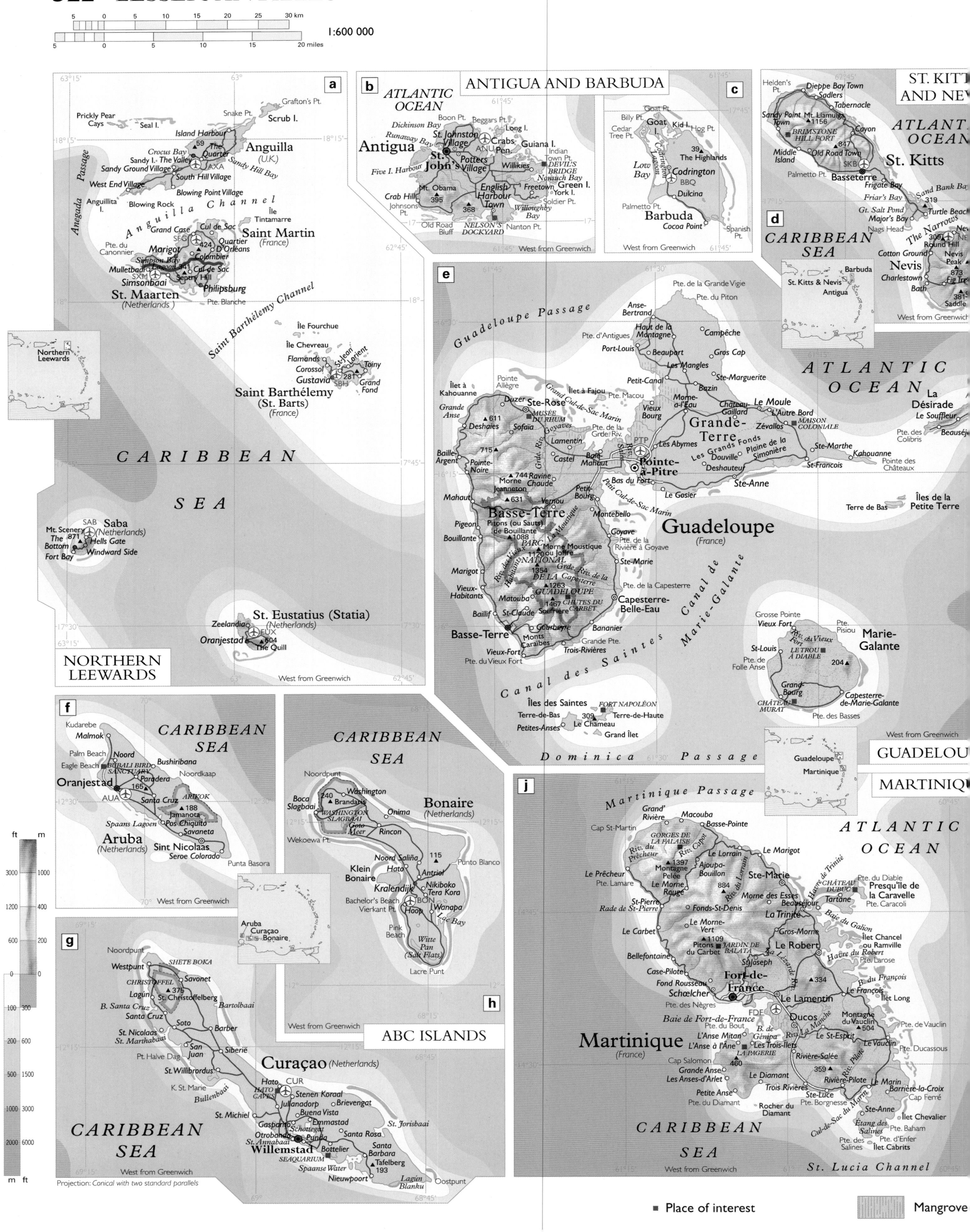

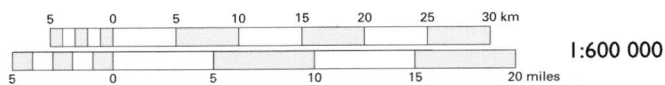

1:600 000

■ Place of interest   Mangrove

Projection: Conical with two standard parallels

Coral reef

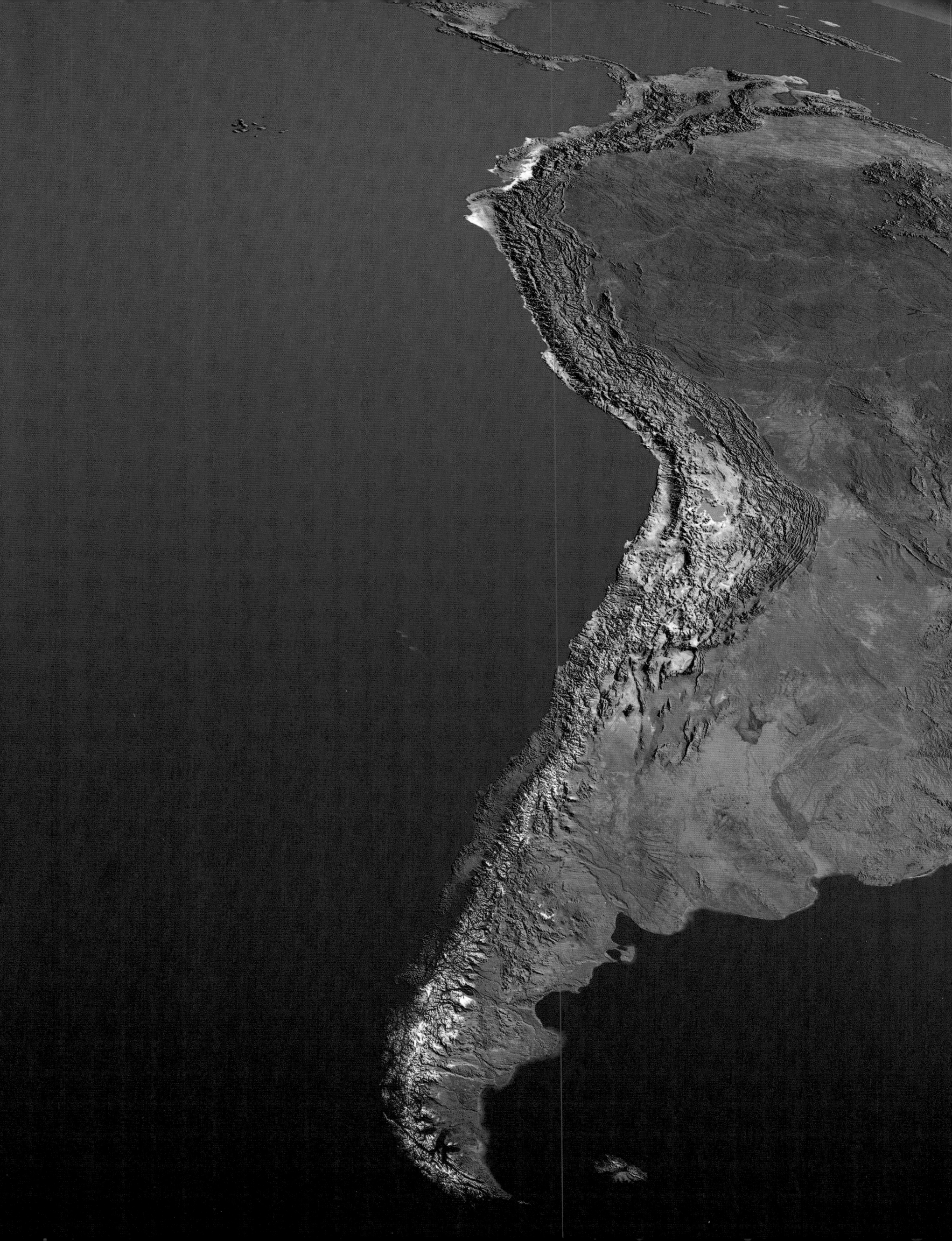

SOUTH
AMERICA

1:28 000 000

| 100 | 0 | 200 | 400 | 600 | 800 | 1000 | 1200 | 1400 km |

| 100 | 0 | 200 | 400 | 600 | 800 | 1000 miles |

1 **2** **3** **4** **5** **6** **7**

Tropic of Cancer

A

Bahamas

Yucatán Channel

Cuba

West Indies

Turks & Caicos Is.

Greater Antilles

Hispaniola

▲3175

8605

Puerto Rico

Leeward Islands

Gulf of Campeche

Yucatán Peninsula

Isthmus of Tehuantepec

G. de Honduras

Jamaica

Guadeloupe

Dominica

Martinique

St. Lucia
St. Vincent

Barbados

ATLANTIC

B

Central America

▲4093

Coco

C. Gracias a Dios

Caribbean Sea

Lesser Antilles

Grenada

Tobago

Trinidad

OCEAN

Guatemala Trench

L. Nicaragua

Guajira Peninsula

G. of Venezuela

Curaçao

▲5775

Paraguaná Peninsula

L. Maracaibo

Margarita

Panama Canal

▲3819

G. of Darién

Isthmus of Panama

Sierra Nevada de Santa Marta

C. de la Aguja

Orinoco

Embalse de Guri

C

I. del Coco

Cordillera Occidental

Cordillera Central

Cordillera Oriental

Cord. de Mérida

Apure

Meta

Llanos

Cuyuni

Angel Falls

▲2810
Mt. Roraima

Guiana Highlands

Devil's I.

C. Orange

Buenaventura B.

I. de Malpelo

Guaviare

Casiquiare

Sierra Pacaraima

Caroní

Essequibo

Serra Tumucumaque

Maroni

Oyapock

I. de Maracá

C. de San Francisco

Caquetá

Vaupés

Pico de Neblina
2994

Negro

Branco

Represa de Balbina

Equator

D 0

Galapagos Is.

▲1707

Cotopaxi
5897

Chimborazo
6267

Putumayo

Japurá

Amazon

Amazon

Amazon

San Marcos B.

Marajó I.

Marajó B.

C. de São Roque

G. of Guayaquil

Napo

Marañón

Ucayali

Juruá

Purus

Madeira

Tapajós

C. Branco

Pta. Pariñas

Andes

Montaña

Amazon Basin

Roosevelt

Aripuanã

Xingu

Tocantins

Itapicuru

Parnaíba

Plat. of Borborema

Pta. Negra

Sechura Desert

Huascarán
6768

Mamoré

Sa. dos Parecis

Guaporé

Arinos

Teles Pires

Araguaia

Tocantins

Represa de Sobradinho

Sertão

Mato Grosso

E

PACIFIC

Chincha Alta

Nevado Coropuna
6425

L. Titicaca
3812

Nevado Ancohuma
6550

Beni

Iténez

Pantanal

Plateau of Mato Grosso

São Francisco

Serra do Espinhaço

Brazilian Highlands

Sa. Geral

Abrolhos Bank

L. de Poopó

Salar de Uyuni

Chaco Boreal

Paraguay

Paranaíba

Serra da Mantiqueira

Doce

B. de Tôdos os Santos

F

OCEAN

Tropic of Capricorn

San Félix

San Ambrosio

Pta. Tetas

8050

Atacama Desert

Cerro Ojos del Salado
▲6893

Monte Pissis
6793

Cerro Bonete
6759

Salinas Grandes

Altiplano (Bolivian Plateau)

Cord. de Calalaste

Gran Chaco

Chaco Austral

Pilcomayo

Bermejo

Dulce

Salado

Rep. de Itaipú

Paraná

Grande

Tietê

Iguaçu Falls
Iguaçu

Serra do Mar

Campos

2890
Pico da Bandeira

C. de São Tomé

I. de São Sebastião

C. Frio

C. Santa Marta Grande

Grand

Cerro Mercedario
6720

Mt. Aconcagua
6962

L. Mar Chiquita

Sa. de Córdoba

Paraná

Entre Ríos

Uruguay

Negro

L. dos Patos

G 30

OCEAN

Arch. de Juan Fernández

Robinson Crusoe

Pta. Lengua da Vaca

Andes

Pampas

Salado

Colorado

Río de la Plata

B. Samborombón

C. San Antonio

L. Mirim

Pta. Lavapié

Negro

Bahía Blanca

ATLANTIC

OCEAN

Chile Rise

Chiloé I.

Límay

Chubut

San Matías G.
▲40

Valdés Peninsula

Argentine Abyssal Plain

Chonos Archipelago

Taitao Peninsula

Mte. San Valentín
4058

L. Buenos Aires

Negro

Chico

G. of San Jorge

C. Tres Puntas

6212
▼

H

Wellington I.

G. of Penas

Madre de Dios I.

Patagonia

L. Argentino

L. Viedma
-105

C. del Carbón

West Falkland

Falkland Is.

▲705

East Falkland

Riesco I.

Santa Inés I.

Magellan's Str.

Tierra del Fuego

Staten I.

South Georgia

Cockburn Chan.

C. Horn

Beagle Chan.

Mt. Paget
2937

90 80 70 60 West from Greenwich 50 40 30

Projection: Lambert's Azimuthal Equal Area

COPYRIGHT PHILIP'S

ft	m
12000	4000
9000	3000
6000	2000
3000	1000
1500	500
600	200
0	0
600	200
3000	1000
6000	2000
12000	4000
18000	6000
24000	8000

1:28 000 000

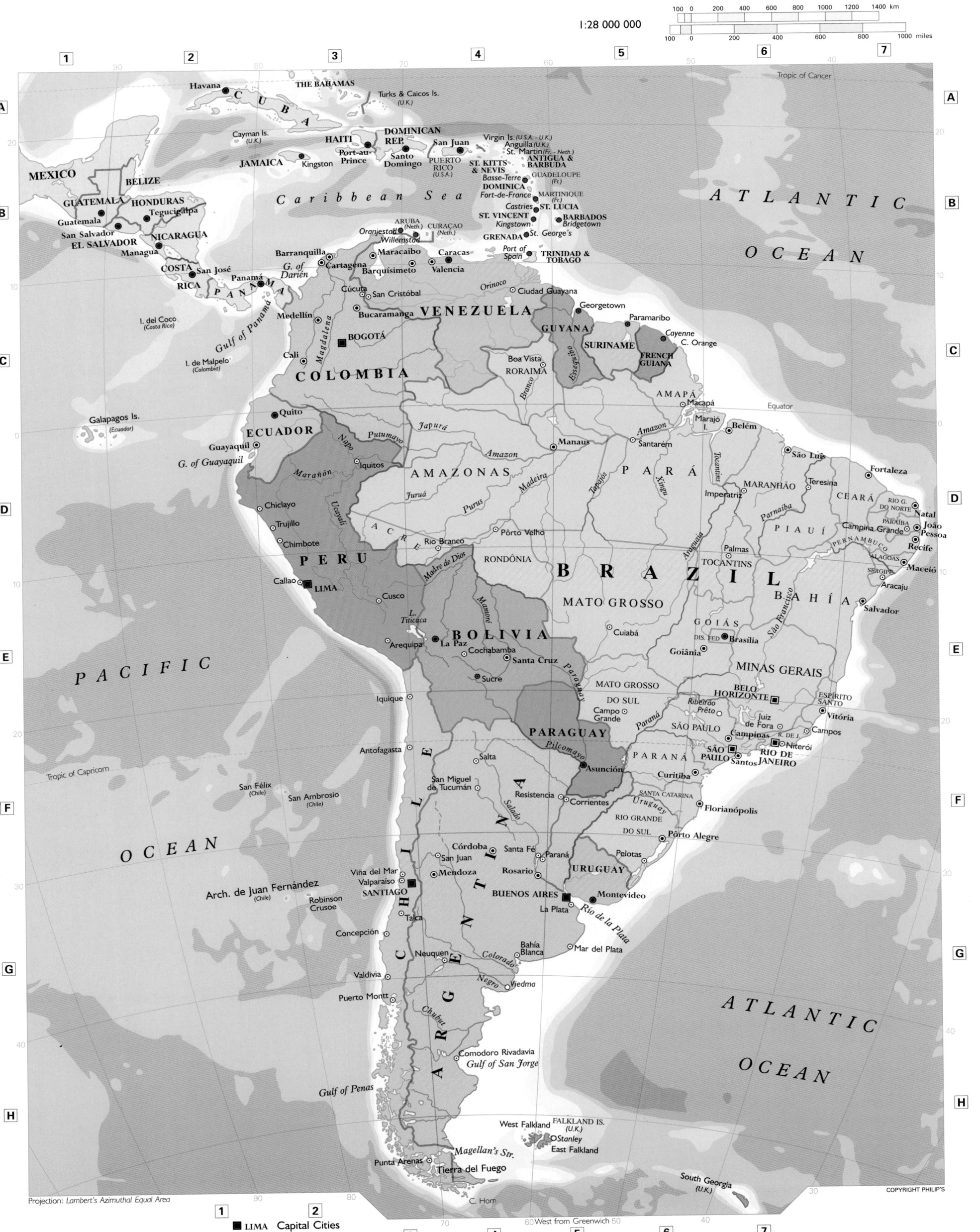

100   0   200   400   600   800   1000 1200 1400 km

100   0   200   400   600   800   1000 miles

A Havana ● CUBA   THE BAHAMAS   Tropic of Cancer
Turks & Caicos Is.
(U.K.)

Cayman Is.
(U.K.)   HAITI   DOMINICAN
REP.   San Juan   Virgin Is. (U.S.A - U.K.)
Port-au-   Santo   Anguilla (U.K.)
JAMAICA ● Kingston   Prince ● Domingo   St. Martin (Fr. - Neth.)
                              PUERTO   ST. KITTS   ANTIGUA &
MEXICO   RICO   & NEVIS ●   BARBUDA
                              (U.S.A.)   Basse-Terre ● GUADELOUPE
BELIZE   DOMINICA   (Fr.)

GUATEMALA   HONDURAS   Fort-de-France ● MARTINIQUE
Guatemala ■ Tegucigalpa   Castries ● ST. LUCIA   (Fr.)
San Salvador ■   ST. VINCENT ●   BARBADOS
EL SALVADOR NICARAGUA   Kingstown ●   Bridgetown
             Managua ●   GRENADA ●
COSTA   Caribbean Sea   St. George's   TRINIDAD &
San José ●   Port of   TOBAGO
RICA   ARUBA CURAÇAO   Spain ●
Panamá ■   (Neth.) (Neth.)
PANAMA   Oranjestad ●
            Willemstad ●

I. del Coco
(Costa Rica)   Barranquilla ●   Maracaibo ● Caracas ● Valencia ●
G. of Darién   Cartagena ●
               Barquísimeto ●
I. de Malpelo Cúcuta ●
(Colombia)   San Cristóbal ●   Ciudad Guayana ●
Gulf of Panamá   Orinoco
               Medellín ● Bucaramanga ● VENEZUELA   Georgetown ●
               Cali ●   Paramaribo ●
                          BOGOTÁ ■   GUYANA   Cayenne ●
Galapagos Is.   COLOMBIA   SURINAME   FRENCH   C. Orange
(Ecuador)   Boa Vista ●   GUIANA
                                         RORAIMA
               Quito ●   AMAPÁ
ECUADOR   Macapá ●   Equator
Guayaquil ●   Putumayo   Amazon   Marajó
G. of Guayaquil Napo   I.   Belém ●
               Iquitos ●   Marañón   Japurá   São Luís ●
               Chiclayo ●   Amazon   Santarém ●
                          AMAZONAS   MARANHÃO   Fortaleza ●
Trujillo ●   Juruá   Purus Madeira Tapajós   Teresina ●
Chimbote ●   ACRE   PARÁ   Imperatriz ●   CEARÁ
               Rio Branco ●   RIO G.   Natal ●
PERU   Pôrto Velho ●   Xingu   Araguaia   PIAUÍ   DO NORTE
Callao ■   RONDÔNIA   Palmas ● PARAÍBA Campina Grande ● João
LIMA   TOCANTINS PERNAMBUCO   Pessoa ●
               Cusco ●   Madre de Dios   B R A Z I L   Recife ●
               L.   ALAGOAS Maceió ●
               Titicaca   Mamoré   MATO GROSSO   GOIÁS   SERGIPE
Arequipa ●   La Paz ●   DIS. FED.   Aracaju ●
               BOLIVIA   Cochabamba ●   Brasília ●
               Sucre ● Santa Cruz ● Cuiabá ●   São Francisco B A H Í A   Salvador ●
Iquique ●   Goiânia ●
               Paraguay   MATO GROSSO   MINAS GERAIS
                          DO SUL   Campo   Ribeirão   ESPÍRITO
Antofagasta ●   Grande ● Prêto ● BELO HORIZONTE ■ SANTO   Vitória ●
Tropic of Capricorn   Juiz de Fora ●
                          PARAGUAY   Paraná   Campos ●
San Félix   SÃO PAULO ■ Campinas   R. DE J.
(Chile)   Salta ●   Pilcomayo   SÃO ● Niterói
San Ambrosio   PAULO Santos RIO DE JANEIRO
(Chile)   San Miguel   Asunción ● PARANÁ
              de Tucumán ●   Curitiba ●
              Resistencia ● Corrientes ● Uruguay SANTA CATARINA
                                                    Florianópolis ●
              A R G E N T I N A   Salado   RIO GRANDE
                                            DO SUL   Pôrto Alegre ●
              Córdoba ● Santa Fé ● Paraná ● Pelotas ●
Arch. de Juan Fernández San Juan ● URUGUAY
(Chile)   Viña del Mar ● Mendoza ● Rosario ●
Robinson   Valparaíso ●   MONTEVIDEO ●
Crusoe   SANTIAGO ■ CHILE BUENOS AIRES ■
              Talca ●   La Plata ● Rio de la Plata
              Concepción ●   Mar del Plata ●
                          Neuquén ● Bahía
                                     Blanca ●
              Valdivia ●   Colorado
                           Negro ● Viedma ●
              Puerto Montt ●
                           Chubut
              PACIFIC
              OCEAN   Comodoro Rivadavia ●
                                     Gulf of San Jorge
                                                          ATLANTIC
                          Gulf of Penas   OCEAN
              Magellan's Str.
              Punta Arenas ●   West Falkland FALKLAND IS.
              Tierra del Fuego   ● Stanley   (U.K.)
              C. Horn   East Falkland   South Georgia
                                                          (U.K.)

Projection: Lambert's Azimuthal Equal Area

West from Greenwich

■ LIMA Capital Cities

1:6 400 000

50 0 50 100 150 200 250 300 km
50 0 50 100 150 200 miles

Projection: Lamberts Equivalent Azimuthal

C A R I B B E A N   S E A

PACIFIC OCEAN

PANAMA

COLOMBIA

VENEZUELA

ECUADOR

PERU

BARRANQUILLA
CARTAGENA
Santa Marta
MARACAIBO
BARQUISIMETO
VALENCIA
CARACAS
MARACAY
MEDELLÍN
BUCARAMANGA
CÚCUTA
BOGOTÁ
CALI
MÉRIDA
Cúcuta
San Cristóbal
Valledupar
Riohacha
Maicao
Coro
Punto Fijo
Willemstad
ARUBA (Neth.)
CURAÇAO (Neth.)
Bonaire (Neth.)
Oranjestad

Popayán
Pasto
Ibarra
QUITO
Ambato
Riobamba
GUAYAQUIL
Cuenca
Loja
Machala
Tumbes

Iquitos
Leticia
Tabatinga

Villavicencio
Yopal
Puerto Carreño
Puerto Ayacucho
San Fernando de Atabapo

FALCÓN
ZULIA
LARA
BARINAS
APURE
GUÁRICO
ANTIOQUIA
CÓRDOBA
CHOCÓ
CAUCA
CASANARE
VICHADA
META
GUAVIARE
GUAINÍA
VAUPÉS
CAQUETÁ
PUTUMAYO
AMAZONAS
NARIÑO
LORETO

Río Magdalena
Río Orinoco
Amazonas
Marañón
Napo
Putumayo
Caquetá

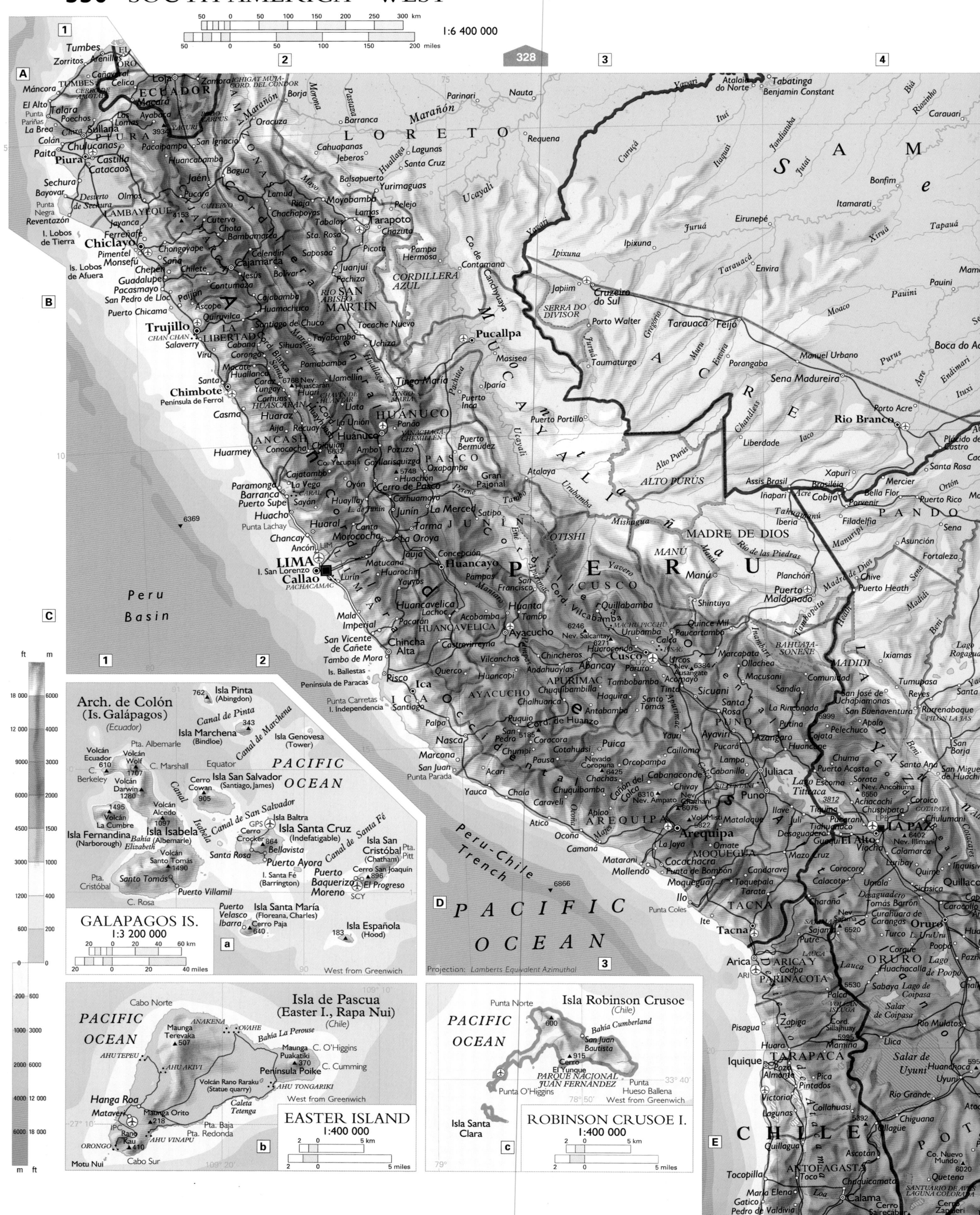

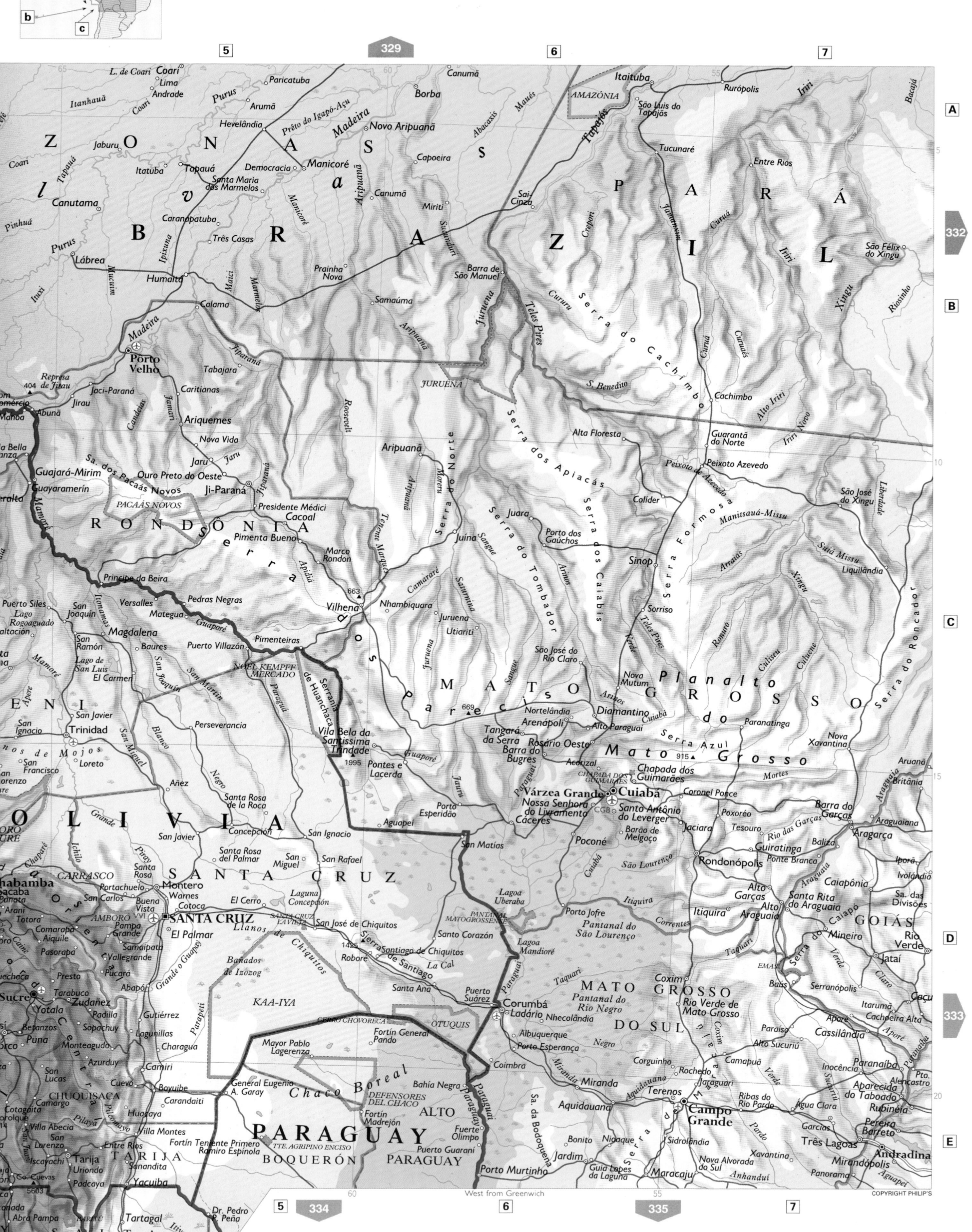

50 0 50 100 150 200 250 300 km

1:6 400 000

50 0 50 100 150 200 miles

A B C

ATLANTIC OCEAN

Equator

Ceará Abyssal Plain

Mouths of the Amazon

Ilha de Marajó

CABO ORANGE

AMAPÁ

Macapá

PARÁ

BELÉM

Baía de Marajó

I. Mexiana

I. Caviana

Salinópolis

Bragança

Vigia

Castanhal

Cametá

Tocantins

Serra dos Carajás

Serra das Gradaús

MARANHÃO

SÃO LUÍS

Caxias

Codó

Imperatriz

Balsas

Carolina

PIAUÍ

Teresina

Parnaíba

Floriano

Picos

Oeiras

Chapada das Mangabeiras

SERRA DA CAPIVARA

Petrolina

Juazeiro

RIO GRANDE DO NORTE

NATAL

Mossoró

Açu

FORTALEZA (Ceará)

CEARÁ

Sobral

Crato

Juazeiro do Norte

PARAÍBA

JOÃO PESSOA (Paraíba)

Campina Grande

PERNAMBUCO

RECIFE (Pernambuco)

Olinda

Caruaru

ALAGOAS

MACEIÓ

São Francisco

Penedo

Propriá

Aracaju

TOCANTINS

Palmas

Araguaína

Araguaia

Represa de Tucuruí

328 A B C 331

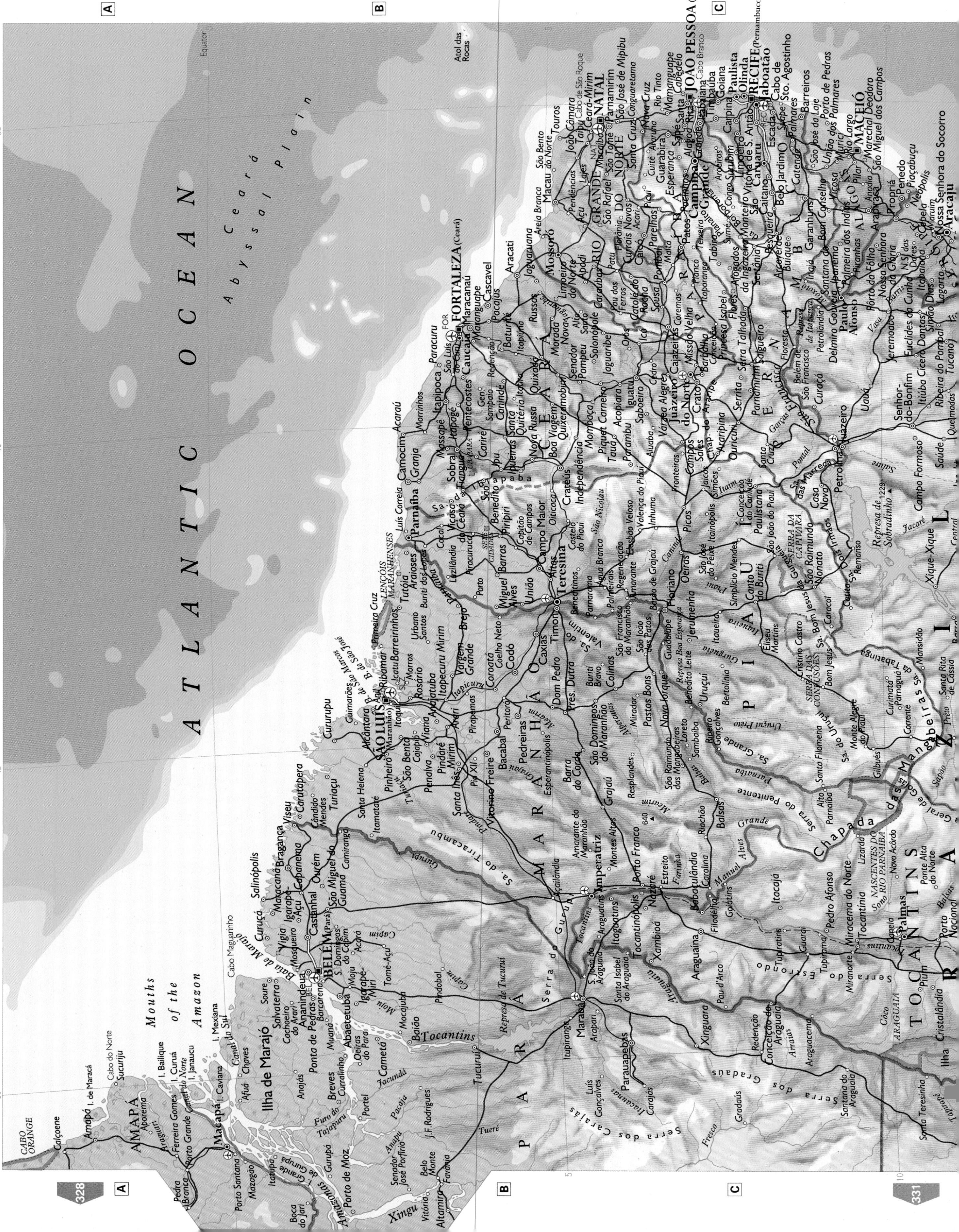

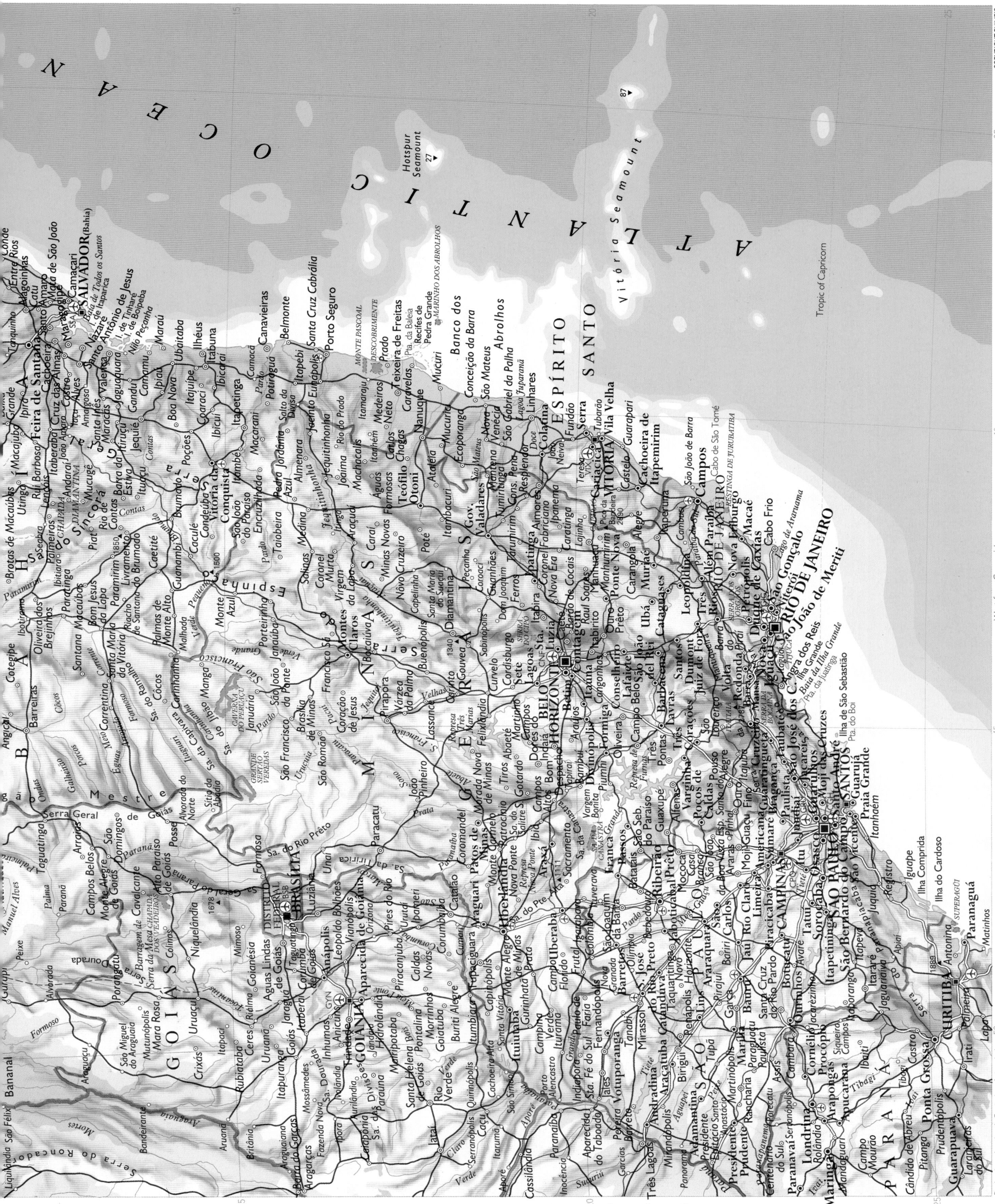

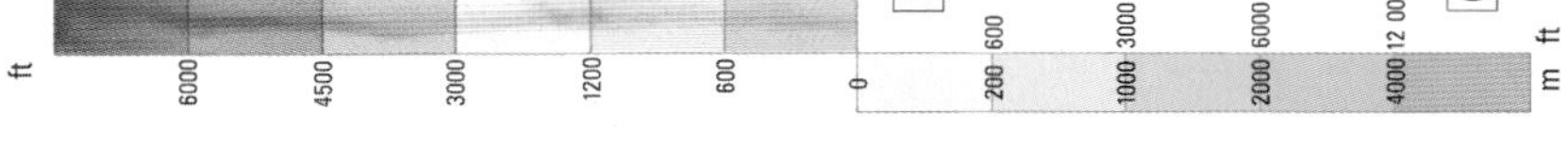

1:6 400 000

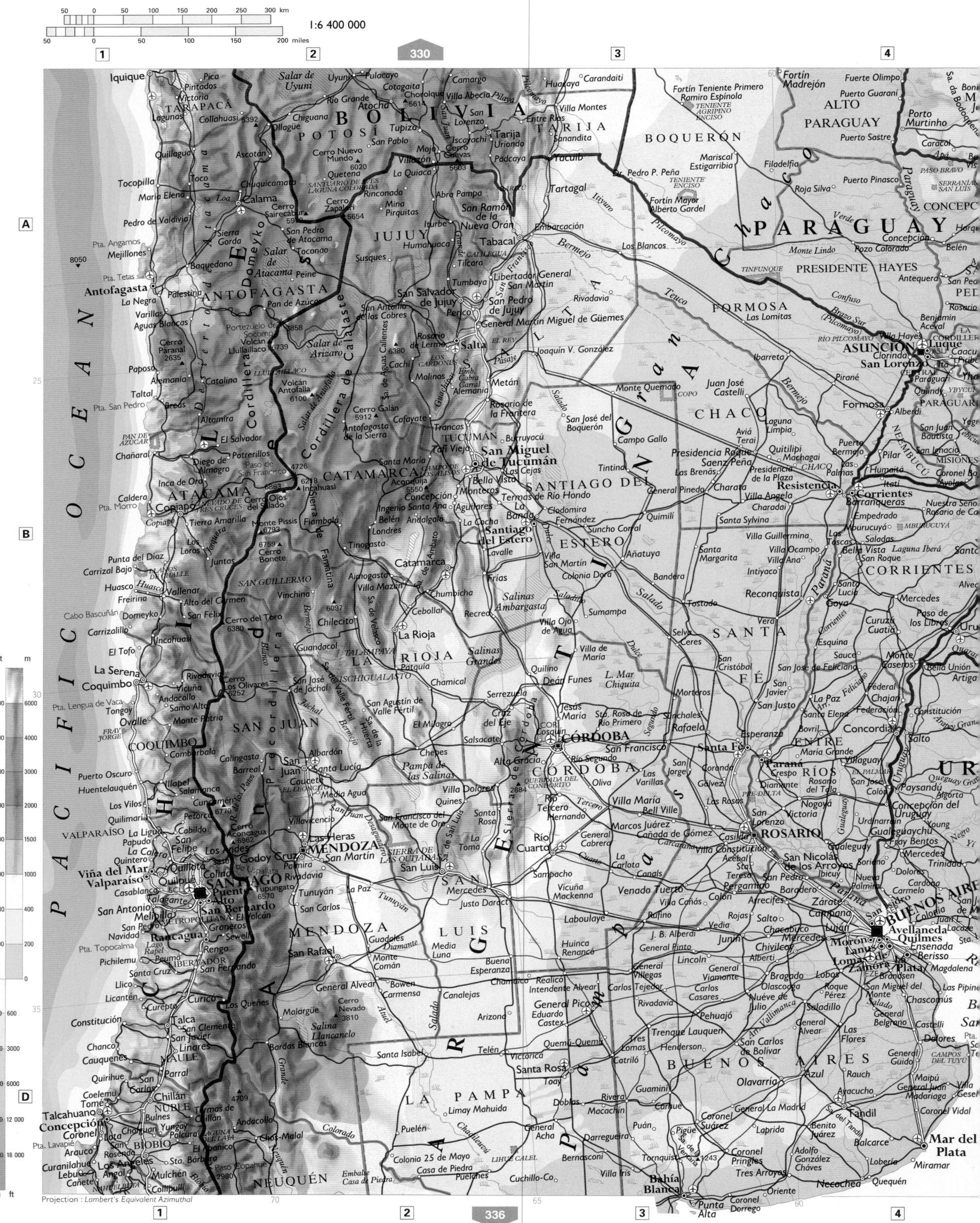

A

B

C

D

A T L A N T I C

O C E A N

BRAZIL

MATO GROSSO DO SUL

SÃO PAULO

PARANÁ

SANTA CATARINA

RIO GRANDE DO SUL

MISIONES

Tropic of Capricorn

BELO HORIZONTE

RIO DE JANEIRO

SÃO PAULO

CURITIBA

FLORIANÓPOLIS

PORTO ALEGRE

MONTEVIDEO

VITÓRIA

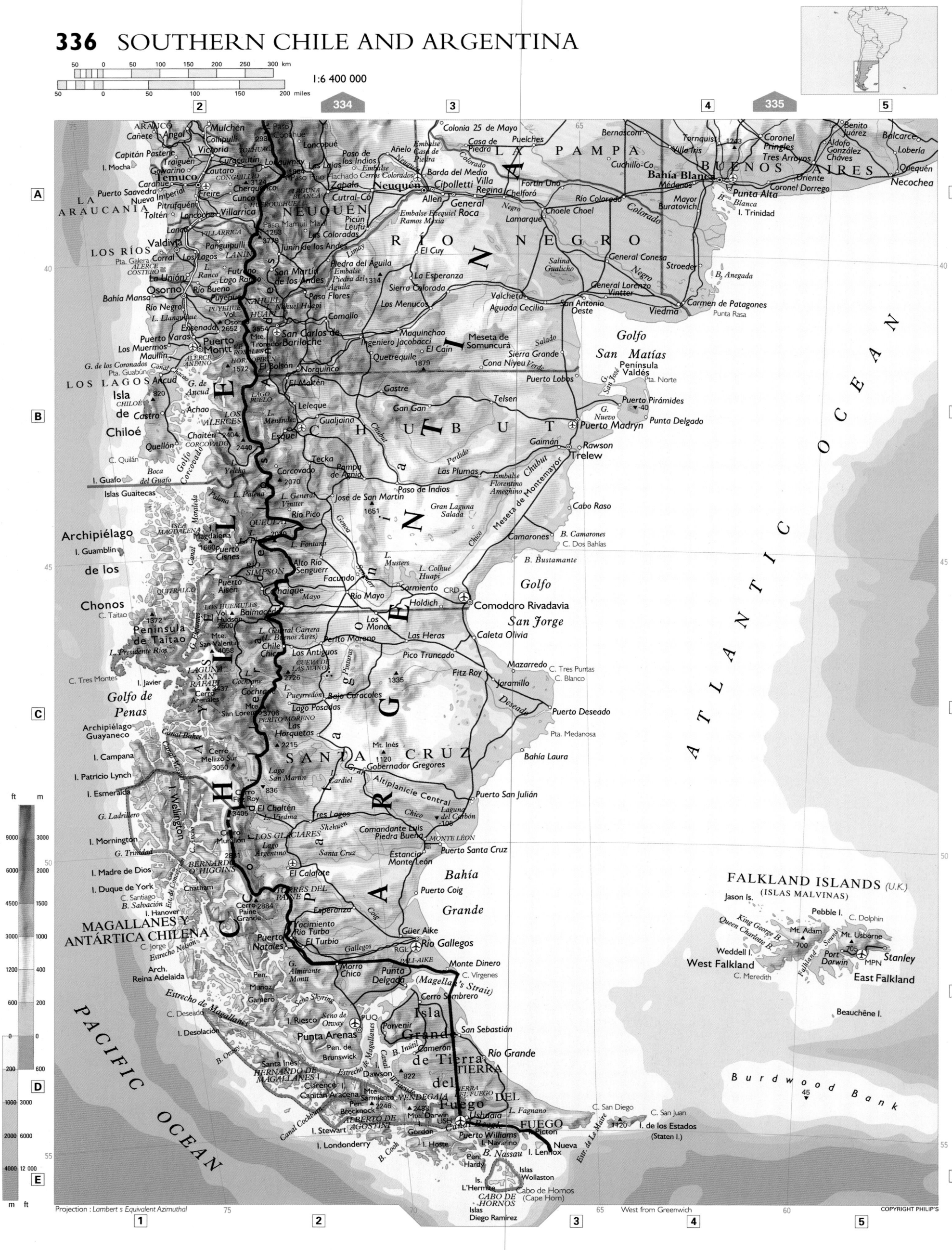

FALKLAND ISLANDS (U.K.)
(ISLAS MALVINAS)

West Falkland
East Falkland
Port Stanley
Stanley

PACIFIC OCEAN

ATLANTIC OCEAN

Projection : Lambert's Equivalent Azimuthal

COPYRIGHT PHILIP'S

GEOGRAPHICAL GLOSSARY

This is a list of the geographical terms from various foreign languages that are found in the place names on the maps and in the index. Each is followed by the language and its English meaning.

Afr. Afrikaans
Alb. Albanian
Amh. Amharic
Ar. Arabic
Belo. Belorussian
Berb. Berber
Bulg. Bulgarian
Burm. Burmese
Cam. Cambodian
Cat. Catalan
Chin. Chinese
Czec. Czech
Dan. Danish
Dut. Dutch
Est. Estonian
Fin. Finnish
Fr. French
Gae. Gaelic
Ger. German
Gr. Greek
Heb. Hebrew
Hin. Hindi
Hung. Hungarian
I.-C. Indo-Chinese
Ice. Icelandic
It. Italian
Indo. Indonesian
Jap. Japanese
Kaz. Kazakh
Kor. Korean
Kyrg. Kyrgyz
Lapp. Lapp (Sami)
Lat. Latvian
Lith. Lithuanian
Malag. Malagasy
Mong. Mongolian
Nor. Norway
Pash. Pashto
Per. Persian
Pol. Polish
Port. Portuguese
Rom. Romanian
Russ. Russian
Sin. Sinhalese
Ser.-Cr. Serbo-Croat
Slov. Slovene
Som. Somali
Span. Spanish
Swe. Swedish
Tib. Tibetan
Turk. Turkish
Ukr. Ukrainian
Viet. Vietnamese

-á *Ice.* river
-å *Dan., Nor., Swe.* stream
-abad *Farsi, Russ.* town
Abyad *Ar.* white mountain
Ada, Adasi *Turk.* island
Addis *Amh.* new
Adrar *Ar., Berb.* mountains
Aiguille *Fr.* peak
Aïn, Aïn (A.) *Ar.* spring
Åkra *Gr.* cape, point
Akrotíri *Gr.* cape, point
Alb *Ger.* mountains
Albufera *Span.* lagoon
-ålen *Nor.* islands
Alpen *Ger.* mountain ranges
Alpes *Fr.* mountains
Alpi *It.* mountains
Alt *Ger.* old
Alta, Alto *Port.* high, upper
Altos *Span.* mountains
-älv, -älven *Swe.* stream, river
Amtskommune (Amt.) *Dan.* first-order administrative division
-ån *Swe.* river
Anse *Fr.* bay
Ao *Thai* bay
Appennino *It.* mountain range
Archipel *Fr.* archipelago
Archipiélago (Arch.) *Span.* archipelago
Arcipélago *It.* archipelago
Arquipélago (Arq.) *Port.* archipelago
Arrecife *Span.* reef
Arroyo (Arr.) *Span.* stream
-ås, -åsen *Nor., Swe.* hill
Ayios *Gr.* island
Ayn *Ar.* well, waterhole

Baai, -baai *Afr., Dut.* bay
Bāb *Ar.* gate, strait
Bäck, -bäcken *Swe.* stream
Back, -backen, *Swe.* hill
Bad, -baden *Ger.* spa
Badia *Cat.* bay
Bādiyah, Bādiyat *Ar.* desert
Bæk *Dan.* stream
Bælt *Dan.* strait
Baharu *Malay* new
Bahía (B.) *Span.* bay
Bahiret *Ar.* lagoon
Bahr *Ar.* sea, lake, river
Bahra Bahrat *Ar.* lake
Baía (B.) *Port.* bay
Baie (B.) *Fr.* bay
Baixa, Baixo *Port.* lower
Baja, Bajo *Span.* lower
Bakke *Nor.* hill
Bala *Farsi* upper
Ballon *Fr.* dome
Baltă *Rom.* marsh, lake
Ban *Lao, Thai* village
-Bana *Jap.* cape
Banc *Fr.* bank
Banco *Span.* bank
Bandao *Chin.* peninsula
Bandar *Ar., Malay* port, harbour
Bandar *Farsi* bay
Banja *Ser.-Cr.* spa, resort
Banjaran *Malay* mountain range
Baraji *Turk.* dam
Barat *Indo., Malay* western
Barrage (Barr.) *Fr.* dam
Barragem (Barr.) *Port.* dam, reservoir
Bas, basse *Fr.* lower
Bassin *Fr.* basin
-batang *Indo.* river
Baţlaq *Farsi* marsh
Batu *Malay* mountain
Bayt *Heb.* house, village
Bazar *Hin.* market, bazaar
-beek *Afr., Dut.* river
Be'er *Heb.* well
Bei *Chin.* north, northern
Beinn, Ben *Gae.* mountain
Beit *Heb.* village
Belaya, Belo, Beloye, Belyy *Russ.* white
Belogorye *Russ.* hills, mountain range
Bender *Som.* harbour
Berg(e), -berg(e) *Afr., Ger.* mountain(s)
-berg, -en, -et *Nor., Swe.* hill, mountain, rock
Besar *Indo., Malay* big
Bet *Heb.* house, village
Bir, Bîr, Bi'r *Ar.* well
Birkat, Birket *Ar.* lake, marsh, well
Bishti *Alb.* cape
-bjerg *Dan.* hill, point
Blaenau *Welsh* upland
-bo *Chin.* lake
Boca *Port., Span.* river mouth, inlet
Bodden *Ger.* bay, inlet
Bogaz, Boğazı *Turk.* channel, strait
Bogd *Mong.* mountain range
Bois *Fr.* woods
Boka *Ser.-Cr.* gulf, inlet
Bolshoi, Bolshaya, Bolshoye (Bol.) *Russ.* great, large
Bordj (Bj.) *Ar.* fort
-borg *Dan., Nor., Swe.* castle, fort
Bory *Pol.* woods
Bosque *Span.* woods
-botn *Nor.* valley floor
Bouche(s) *Fr.* mouth(s)
Braţul *Rom.* distributary stream, branch
-bre, -breen *Nor.* glacier
Bredning *Dan.* bay
Brücke *Ger.* bridge
-brug *Dut.* bridge
-brunn *Swe.* well, spring
Bucht *Ger.* bay
Bugt *Dan.* bay
-bugten *Dan.* bay
Buheirat *Ar.* lake, reservoir
Bukit *Malay* hill
-bukt, -a *Nor.* bay
-bukten *Swe.* bay
-bulag *Mong.* spring
Bulag *Chin.* lake
Bulu *Malay* mountain
Bum *Burm.* mountain
Bûr *Ar.* port
Burg. *Ar.* fort
Burg, -burg *Ger.* castle
Burnu, Burun *Turk.* cape
Butt *Gae.* promontory
Büyük *Turk.* big
-by *Dan., Nor., Swe.* town
-byen *Nor., Swe.* town

Cabeza *Span.* peak, hill
Cabo (C.) *Port., Span.* headland, cape
Cachoeira *Port.* waterfall
Cala Cat. *It.* bay
Camp Port. *Span.* land, field
Câmpia *Rom.* plain
Campo *It., Port., Span.* plain
Campos *Span.* upland
Canal (Can.) *Fr., Port., Span.* canal, channel
Canale (Can.) *It.* channel
Canalul (Can.) *Ser.-Cr.* canal
Cao Nguyen *Thai* plateau, tableland
Cap (C.) *Cat., Fr.* cape
Capo (C) *It.* cape
Carn *Gae.* hill
Carse *Gae.* valley
Catarata *Port., Span.* cataract
Cauce *Span.* intermittent stream
Causse *Fr.* limestone plateau
Cay, Cayi, -cay, -cayi *Turk.* river
Cayo(s) *Span.* rock(s), islet(s)
Cefn *Welsh* hill
Cerro *Span.* hill, peak
Česká, Český, České *Czec.* Czech
Chaco *Span.* jungle
Chaîne(s) *Fr.* mountain range(s)
Chang *Chin.* mountain
Chapa *Span.* hills, upland
Chapada *Port.* hills, upland
Chaung *Burm.* stream, river
Chi *Chin.* small lake
-ch'ŏn *Kor.* river
-chŏsuji *Kor.* reservoir
Chott *Ar.* salt lake, depression
Chu *Tib.* river
Chute *Fr.* waterfall
Città *It.* city
Ciudad *Span.* city
Co *Tib.* lake
Cochilla (Coch.) *Port.* hills
Col *Fr., It.* pass
Colina(s) *Span.* hill(s)
Colle *It.* pass
Colline(s) *Fr.* hill(s)
Conca *It.* plain, basin
Cordillera (Cord.) *Span.* mountain range
Costa *It., Port., Span.* coast
Côte *Fr.* coast, slope, hill
Coteaux *Fr.* hills
Cuchilla *Span.* hills
Cuenca *Span.* river basin
Cu-Lao *Viet.* island

Da *Chin.* big
Da *Viet.* river
Daban *Mong.* pass
Dağ(ı) *Turk.* mountain(s)
Dāgh *Farsi* mountain
Dağları *Turk.* mountain range
-dai, -daichi *Jap.* plateau
-Dake *Jap.* mountain
-dal, -e *Dan., Swe.* valley
-dal, -en *Swe., Nor.* valley, stream
Dalay Mong. large lake
-ðalir, -ðalur *Ice.* valley
-damm, -en *Swe.* lake
Danau *Malay* lake
Dao *Chin., Viet.* island
Dar *Ar.* region
Darya *Russ.* river
Daryācheh *Farsi* marshy lake, lake
Dasht *Farsi* desert, steppe
Daung *Burm.* mountain, hill
Dayr *Ar.* monastery
Debre *Amh.* hill
Deli *Ser.-Cr.* mountain
Deniz, -i *Turk.* sea
Département (Dépt.) *Fr.* first-order administrative division
Dere *Turk.* stream
Desierto (Des.) *Span.* desert
Détroit *Fr.* strait
Dhar *Ar.* region, mountain range
Diep *Dut.* channel
Dijk *Dut.* dyke
Ding *Chin.* mountain
Dingzi *Chin.* hill, mountain
Djebel (Dj.) *Ar.* mountain
-djúp *Ice.* fjord
-djupet *Swe.* channel, sound
-Do *Jap., Kor.* island
Dolina *Russ.* valley
Dolna, Dolni *Bulg.* lower
Dolna, Dolne, Dolny *Russ.* lower
Dolní *Czec.* lower
Dolok (D.) *Malay* mountain
-dong *Kor.* village, town
Dong *Chin.* east, eastern
Donja, Donji *Ser.-Cr.* lower
-dorf *Ger.* village
-dorp *Afr.* village
-drif *Afr.* ford
-dybet *Dan.* marine channel
Dzong *Tib.* town, settlement
Dzüün *Mong.* east, eastern

-egga *Nor.* peak
-eiland, -en (eil.) *Afr., Dut.* island(s)
Eilean *Gae.* island
-elv, -a *Nor.* river
Embalse *Span.* reservoir
'Emeq *Heb.* plain, valley
Ensenada *Span.* bay
Erg *Ar.* sand desert
Estero *Span.* estuary
Estrada *Span.* bay
Estrecho *Span.* strait
Estuaire *Fr.* estuary
Estuario *Span.* estuary
Étang *Fr.* lagoon, lake
-ey, -jar *Ice.* island(s)
-ežeras *Lith.* lake
-ezers *Lat.* lake

Falaise *Fr.* cliff
-fallet *Swe.* waterfall
Farihy *Malag.* lake
Faro *Span.* lighthouse
-feld *Ger.* field
-fell *Ice.* mountain, hill
Feng *Chin.* mountain range
Fiume (F.) *It.* river
-fjäll, -en, -et *Swe.* hill(s), mountain(s), ridge
-fjärden *Swe.* fjord
Fjeld *Dan.* mountain
-fjell, -et *Nor.* mountain range
-fjord, -en *Dan., Nor., Swe.* fjord
-fjörður *Ice.* fjord, bay, inlet
Fleuve (Fl.) *Fr.* river
-flói *Ice.* bay, marshy country
Fluss (F.) *Ger.* river
Foce, Foci *It.* mouth(s)
Folyó (F.) *Hung.* river
-fonn *Nor.* glacier
-fontein *Afr.* fountain, spring
Forêt *Fr.* forest
-fors, -en *Swe.* waterfall, rapids
-foss, -en *Ice., Nor.* waterfall
Forst *Ger.* forest
Foum *Ar.* pass
Fuente *Span.* source
-furt *Ger.* ford
Fylke *Nor.* first-order administrative division

-gang *Chin.* bay, harbour
-gang *Kor.* river
Ganga *Hin., Sin.* river
Gangri *Tib.* mountain
Gaoyuan *Chin.* plateau
-gat *Dan.* sound
-Gata *Jap.* lake
-gau *Ger.* district
-Gawa *Jap.* river
Gebel (G.) *Ar.* mountain
Gebirge (Geb.) *Ger.* hills, mountains
Gezirat, Geziret *Ar.* island
Ghat *Hin.* range of hills
Ghiol *Rom.* lake
Ghubbat *Ar.* bay, inlet
Gjiri *Alb.* bay
Gjol *Alb.* lagoon, lake
Glava (Gl.) *Ser.-Cr.* mountain, peak
Glen *Gae.* valley
Gletscher (Gl.) *Ger.* glacier
Gobi *Mong.* desert
Gol *Mong.* river
Göl *Azeri, Turk.* lake
Golfe (G.) *Fr.* gulf
Golfo (G.) *It., Span.* gulf
Gölü *Turk.* lake
Gomba *Tib.* settlement
Gora, Góra *Bulg., Russ., Ser.-Cr., Pol.* mountain
Gorje *Ser.-Cr.* hills, mountains
Gorno *Russ.* mountainous
-gorod *Russ.* small town
Gory, Góry *Pol., Russ.* mountain
-grad *Bulg. Russ., Ser.-Cr.* town, city
-grada *Russ.* ridge
Gran *It., Span.* big, great
Grand, -e *Fr.* big, great
Groot (Gt.) *Afr., Dut.* big, great
Gross, -e, -en, -er *Ger.* big, great(er)
Grupo *Span.* group
Gruppo *It.* group
Guan *Chin.* pass
Guba (G.) *Russ.* bay
-Guntō *Jap.* island group
Gunong, Gunung (G.) *Indo., Malay* mountain
Gură *Rom.* passage

Hadabat *Ar.* plateau
Hadjer *Ar.* mountain
-hafen *Ger.* harbour, port
Haff *Ger.* bay, lagoon
Hai *Chin.* lake, sea
Haixia *Chin.* channel, strait
Halbinsel *Ger.* peninsula
Halvø *Dan.* peninsula
Halvøya *Nor.* peninsula
Hāmad, Hamada, Hammādah, Hammādat *Ar.* stony desert, plateau
-hamn *Swe., Nor.* harbour, anchorage
Hāmūn *Farsi* marsh, lake
-Hantō *Jap.* peninsula
Har(e) *Heb.* hill(s), mountain(s)
Hassi (Hi.) *Ar.* well
-haug *Nor.* hill
Hav, Havet *Nor., Swe.* sea
-havn *Dan., Nor.* bay, harbour
Havre *Fr.* harbour
Hawd *Ar.* oasis
Hawr *Ar.* lake, marsh
He *Chin.* river
-hegység *Hung.* hills, forest
Heide *Ger.* heath, moor
Helodranon' *Malag.* bay
Higashi *Jap.* east, eastern
-ho *Kor.* lake
-hø *Nor.* peak
Hoch *Ger.* high
Hochland *Afr.* highland
Hoek, -hoek *Afr., Dut.* cape, point
-höfn *Ice.* harbour, port
-hög, -en, -högar, -högarna *Swe.* hill(s), peak, mountain
Höhe *Ger.* height
Hohen *Ger.* high, upper
-hoi *Chin.* bay
-høj, -e *Dan.* hills
-holm, -holme, -holmen *Dan., Nor., Swe.* island
Hon *Viet.* island
Hoog *Dut.* high
Hora *Czec., Ukr.* mountain
-horn *Ger.* peak
Hory *Czec.* mountains, hills
-hot *Mong.* town
-hoved *Dan.* point, headland, peninsula
-hrad *Czec.* town
Hráun *Ice.* lava
-hsi *Chin.* river
-hsia *Chin.* gorge, strait
-hsien *Chin.* district
Hu *Chin.* lake, reservoir
Huk *Dan., Ger.* cape
-huk *Swe.* cape
Huken *Nor.* cape

Idd *Ar.* well
Idehan *Ar., Berb.* sandy plain, dunes
-ike *Jap.* lake
Île(s) (I(s).) *Fr.* island(s)
Ilha(s) (I(s).) *Port.* island(s)
imeni *Russ.* 'in the name of'
Inish *Gae.* island
Insel(n) (I.) *Ger.* island(s)
Irmak *Turk.* river
'Irq *Ar.* dunes
Isla(s) (I(s).) *Span.* island(s)
Iso *Fin.* big, great
Isol, -a, -e (I.) *It.* island(s)
Isthme *Fr.* isthmus
Istmo *Span.* isthmus
-iwa *Jap.* island

Jabal *Ar.* mountain range
Järv *Est.* lake
järvi *Fin.* lake, bay, pond
-jaur, -javre *Lapp.* lake
Jazā'ir *Ar.* islands
Jazīra, jazīrat *Ar.* island
Jazireh *Farsi* island
Jebel *Ar.* mountain
Jezero *Ser.-Cr.* lake
Jezioro *Pol.* lake
Jiang *Chin.* river
Jiao *Chin.* cape
-Jima *Jap.* island
Jøkulen *Nor.* glacier, ice cap
-joki *Fin.* river
-jökull *Ice.* glacier, ice cap
Jūras Līcis *Lat.* bay, gulf

Kaap (K.) *Afr.* cape
-kai *Jap.* bay, channel, sea
-kaikyō *Jap.* strait
-kaise *Lapp.* mountain
kalnas *Lith.* hill
Kamennyy *Russ.* stony
Kampong *Cam.* village
Kampung *Malay* village
-kanaal *Dut.* canal
Kanal *Dan.* channel, gulf
Kanal *Ger., Swe.* canal
-kanal *Ser.-Cr.* channel, canal
Kanava *Fin.* canal
Kang *Kor.* river, bay
Kap (K.) *Dan., Ger.* cape, point
-kapp *Nor.* cape, point
-kaupstaður *Ice.* market town
-kaupunki *Fin.* town
Kavīr *Farsi* salt desert
Kébir *Ar.* great
Kecil *Malay* lesser, little
Kefar *Heb.* village, hamlet
-Ken *Jap.* first-order administrative division
Kep, -i (K.) *Alb.* cape
Kepulauan (Kep.) *Indo., Malay* archipelago
Keski- *Fin.* middle, central
Khalig, Khalīj *Ar.* gulf
-khamba *Tib.* source, spring
Khawr *Ar.* bay, channel, wadi
Khlong *Thai* river
Kho Khot *Thai* isthmus
Khōr *Farsi* bay, estuary
Khrebet *Russ.* mountain range
Kita- *Jap.* north
Klein,-e, -er *Ger.* small
-klint *Dan.* cliff
Klintar *Swe.* hills
-kloof *Afr.* gorge, pass
Knude *Dan.* point
-Ko *Jap.* lake
Ko *Thai* island
-kōchi *Jap.* mountainous region
-kōgen *Jap.* plateau
Kohi *Pash.* mountains
Kol *Kaz., Kyrg.* lake
Kólpos *Gr., Turk.* gulf, bay
Kolymskoye *Russ.* mountain range
Kompong *Malay* landing place
-kop *Afr.* hill
-kopf *Ger.* hill
-köping *Swe.* market town
Körfäzi *Azeri* gulf
Körfezi *Turk.* gulf
Kosa *Russ., Ukr.* spit
-koski *Fin.* rapids
-kraal *Afr.* native village
-kraj *Czec., Pol., Ser.-Cr.* region
Krasnyy *Russ.* red
Kryazh *Russ.* ridge, hills
Kuala *Malay* bay
-kuan *Chin.* pass
Kūh(ha) *Farsi* mountain(s)
Kul *Russ.* lake
-kulle *Swe.* hill
Kum *Russ.* sandy desert
Kumpu *Fin.* hill
Kwe *Burm.* bay, gulf
-kylä *Fin.* village
Kyst, -en *Dan., Nor.* coast
Kyun(zu) *Burm.* island(s)

La *Tib.* pass
-laagte *Afr.* watercourse

Lääni *Fin.* first-order administrative division
Lac (L.) *Fr.* lake
Lacul (L.) *Rom.* lake, lagoon
Lago (L.) *It., Port., Span.* lake, lagoon
Lagoa (L.) *Port.* lagoon
Lagos *Port., Span.* lakes
Laguna (L.) *It., Span.* lagoon, lake
Lagune (L.) *Fr.* lake
-laht *Est.* bay
Lahti *Fin.* bay, gulf, cove
Lakhti *Russ.* bay, gulf
Lam *Thai* river
Lampi *Fin.* lake
Län *Swe.* first-order administrative division
Land *Ger.* first-order administrative division
-land *Dan.* region
-land *Afr., Nor.* land, province
Lande *Fr.* heath
Laut *Indo.* sea
Law *Gae.* hill, mountain
Līcis *Lat.* gulf
Lido *It.* beach, shore
Liedao *Chin.* islands
Lilla *Swe.* small
Lille *Dan., Nor.* small
Liman *Russ.* bay, gulf
Límni (L.) *Gr.* lake
Ling *Chin.* mountain range
-linna *Fin.* fort
Llano *Span.* prairie, plain
Llyn *Welsh* lake
Loch (L.) *Gae.* lake, inlet
Lough (L.) *Gae.* lake, inlet
Lum *Alb.* river
Lund *Dan.* forest
-lund, -en *Swe.* wood(s)
-luoto *Fin.* island

-maa *Est.* island
Madīnat *Ar.* town, city
Madiq *Ar.* strait
Maja *Alb.* mountains
-mäki *Fin.* hill, hillside
Mal *Alb.* mountain
Maloye, Malyy, Malyya *Russ.* little, small
Mala, Mali, Malo *Ser.-Cr.* little, small
Malaya *Belo.* small
Malé *Czec., Slovak* small
Mali *Alb.* mountain
-man *Kor.* bay
Mar *Span.* lagoon, sea
Marais *Fr.* marsh
Mare *It.* sea
Mare *Rom.* great
Marisma *Span.* marsh
-mark *Dan., Nor.* land
Marsâ *Ar.* anchorage, bay, inlet
Masabb *Ar.* river mouth, estuary
Massif *Fr.* upland, mountains
Mato *Port.* forest
Mazar *Farsi* shrine, tomb
Meer, -meer *Afr., Dut., Ger.* lake, sea
-men *Chin.* bay, gorge, channel
Mesto *Ser.-Cr., Czec.* town
Mezzo *It.* middle
Midbar *Heb.* wilderness
Mierzeja *Pol.* spit
Mifraz *Heb.* bay
Mina *Ar.* port
Minami *Jap.* south, southern
-misaki *Jap.* cape, point
Mittel *Ger.* central, middle
-mo *Nor., Swe.* heath, island
-mon *Swe.* heath
Mong *Burm.* town
Mont(s) (Mt(s).) *Fr.* hill(s), mountain(s)
Montagna (Mt.) *It.* mountain
Montagne(s) (Mt(s).) *Fr.* hill(s), mountain(s)
Montaña(s) (Mt(s).) *Span.* mountain(s)
Montanyes *Cat.* mountains
Monte(s) (Mte(s).) *It., Port., Span.* mountain(s)
Monti (Mti.) *It.* mountains
More *Russ.* sea
Mörön *Mong.* river
Moyen *Fr.* central, middle
Muang *Malay* town
Mui *Viet.* cape
Mull *Gae.* promontory
Mund, -mund *Afr.* mouth
Munkhafed *Ar.* depression
Munte (Mte.) *Rom.* mount
Munţi(i) (Mti.) *Rom.* mountain(s)
Muong *Malay* village
Myit *Burm.* river
Myitwanya *Burm.* mouths of river
Mynydd *Welsh* mountain
-myr *Nor., Swe.* swamp
-mýri *Ice.* swamp
Mys (M.) *Russ.* cape

-Nada *Jap.* bay, gulf
-næs *Dan.* point, cape
Nafūd *Ar.* sandy desert
Nagorye *Russ.* hills, mountains
Nagy *Hung.* big
Nahal (N.) *Heb.* river
Nahr (N.) *Ar.* river, stream
Najd *Ar.* plateau, pass
Nakhon *Thai* town
Nam *Kor., Viet.* river
-nam *Kor.* south
Namakzār *Per.* salt flat
Nan *Chin.* south, southern
-nao *Chin.* lake
-näs *Swe.* cape
Neder *Dut.* lower
Nedre *Nor.* lower
Nei *Chin.* inner
Nek *Afr.* pass
-nes *Ice., Nor.* cape
Ness, -ness *Gae.* promontory, cape
Nevada, Nevado *Span.* snow-capped mountain
Nez *Fr.* cape
Nieder *Ger.* lower
-niemi *Fin.* cape, point, peninsula, island
Nieuw, -e *Dut.* new
Nishi *Jap.* west, western
Nisos, Nisoi *Gr.* island(s)
Nizhneye, Nizhniy *Russ.* lower
Nizina *Belo., Pol.* lowland
Nizmennost *Russ.* plain, lowland
Nízní *Czec.* lower
Noord *Dut.* north, northern
Nord *Fr.* north, northern
Norra *Swe.* north, northern
Nørre *Dan.* north, northern
Norte *Port., Span.* north, northern
Nos *Bulg., Russ.* cape, point
Nosy *Malag.* island
Nouveau, Nouvelle *Fr.* new
Nova, Novi *Bulg., Port., Serb.-Cr.* new
Novaya, Novo, Novoye, Novyy *Russ.* new
Nové, Novy *Czec., Slovak* new
Novo *Port.* new
Nowa, Nowe, Nowy *Pol.* new
Nudo *Span.* mountain
Nueva, Nuevo *Span.* new
Nur *Chin.* lake
Nur *Tib.* peak
Nuruu *Mong.* mountain range
Nusa *Indo.* island
Nuur *Mong.* lake
Ny *Dan., Nor., Swe.* new

-ø *Dan., Nor.* island
-ö *Swe.* island,
-öar, -na *Swe.* islands
Ober *Ger., Ukr.* upper
Oblast *Russ.* administrative division
Öbor *Mong.* inner
Occidental *Fr., Span.* western
-odde *Dan., Nor.* point, peninsula, cape
Oeste *Span.* west, western
Oglat *Ar.* well
Oji *Alb.* bay
Ojo *Span.* spring
-Oki *Jap.* bay
-ön *Swe.* island
Ondör *Mong.* upper
Oost(er) *Dut.* east(ern)
Oraşu *Rom.* city
Ord *Gae.* point
Óri *Gr.* mountains
Oriental, -e *Fr., Span.* east, eastern
Órmos *Gr.* bay
Óros *Gr.* mountain(s)
Ort *Ger.* point, cape
Ost *Ger.* east
Øst(er) *Den., Nor.* east(ern)
Öst(ra) *Swe.* east(ern)
Ostriv *Ukr.* island
Ostrov(a) *Russ.* island(s)
Otok(i) *Ser.-Cr.* island(s)
Ouabi, Ouadi (O.) *Ar.* dry watercourse, wadi
Oud, -e *Dut.* old
Oued, -i (O.) *Ar.* watercourse
Ouest *Fr.* west, western
Ouzan *Farsi* river
Ova, -si *Turk.* plains, lowlands
Over- *Dan., Dut.* upper
Över-, Övre *Nor., Swe.* upper
-øy, -a *Nor.* island(s)
Oya *Hin.* point
Oya *Sin.* river
Ozero, Ozera (Oz.) *Russ., Ukr.* lake(s)

-pää *Fin.* hill(s), mountain
Pahta *Lapp.* hill
Pampa(s) *Span.* plain(s)
Pantanal *Port.* marsh
Pantano *Span.* reservoir
Pantao *Chin.* peninsula
Parbat *Urdu* mountain
Pas *Fr.* strait
Paso (P.) *Span.* pass
Passage *Fr.* channel
Passe *Fr.* channel
Passo (P.) *It.* pass
Pasul (P.) *Rom.* pass
Patam *Hin.* small village
Patna, -patnam *Hin.* small village
Pegunungan *Indo., Malay* mountain range
Pei, -pei *Chin.* north
Pélagos *Gr.* sea
Pen *Welsh* hill
Peña *Span.* rock, peak
Pendi *Chin.* basin, depression
Péninsule *Fr.* peninsula
Penisola (Pen.) *It.* peninsula
Pereval (Per.) *Russ.* pass
Pervo-, Pervyy- *Russ.* first
Pertuis *Fr.* channel, strait
Peski *Russ.* sand desert
Petit, -e *Fr.* small
Phanom *Thai* mountain
Phnum *Cam.* mountain
Phou *Lao.* mountain
Phu *Thai, Viet.* mountain
Piano *It.* plain
Pic *Cat., Fr.* peak
Pico(s) *Span.* peak(s)
-piggen *Dan.* peak
Pik *Russ.* peak
Pingyuan *Chin.* plain
Pique *Fr.* peak
Piton *Fr.* peak
Pivostriv *Ukr.* peninsula
Piz, Pizzo *It.* peak
Plage *Fr.* beach
Plaine *Fr.* plain
Planalto *Port.* plateau
Planina (Pl.) *Bulg., Ser.-Cr.* mountain range
Plato *Russ., Bulg.* plateau
Playa *Span.* beach
-po *Chin.* lake, wetland
Pointe (Pte.) *Fr.* point, cape
Pojezierze *Pol.* lakes
Polder *Dut.* reclaimed farmland
-pólis *Gr.* city, town
Poluostrov (Pov.) *Russ.* peninsula
Połwysep *Pol.* peninsula
Pont *Fr.* bridge
Ponta (Pta.) *Port.* point, cape
Ponte *Port.* bridge
Poort *Afr.* passage, gate
-poort *Dut.* port
Porta *Port.* pass
Porţile *Rom.* gate
Portillo *Span.* pass
Porto *It., Port., Span.* port
Potámi, Potamós *Gr.* river
Pradesh *Hin.* state
Praia *Port.* beach, shore
Presa *Span.* reservoir
Presqu'île *Fr.* peninsula
Prokhod *Bulg.* pass
Proliv *Russ.* strait
Promontorio *Span.* promontory
Průsmyk (Pr.) *Czec.* pass
Pueblo *Span.* village
Puerto (Pto.) *Span.* port
Puig *Cat.* peak
Pulau (P.) *Indo., Malay* island
Puna *Span.* desert plateau
Puncak *Indo.* peak
Punta (Pta.) *It., Span.* point, peak
Puy *Fr.* peak

Qal'at *Ar.* fort
Qanat *Ar.* canal
Qasr *Ar.* fort
Qiryat *Heb.* town
Qiuling *Chin.* plateau
Qolleh *Farsi* mountain
-qundao *Chin.* islands

Rach *Viet.* river
Rags *Lat.* cape
Rambla *Cat.* river
Ramlat *Ar.* sandy desert
Rão (R.) *Port.* river
Rann *Hin.* swampy region
Rao *I.-C.* river
Ras *Amh., Ar., Farsi* cape, point
Récif(s) *Fr.* reef(s)
Recife(s) *Port.* reef(s)
Reka *Bulg.* river
Repede *Rom.* rapids
Represa *Port.* reservoir
Reshteh *Farsi* mountain range
-rettō *Jap.* group of islands, chain
Ria *Port., Span.* estuary, bay
Ribeirão (R.) *Port.* river
Ribera (R.) *Span.* river bank
Rijeka *Ser.-Cr.* river
Rio (R.) *Port., Span.* river
Rivier (R.) *Afr., Dut.* river
Riviera *It.* coastal plain, coast
Rivière (R.) *Fr.* river
Roca *Span.* rock
Rocca *It.* rock, peak
Roche *Fr.* rock
Rt *Ser.-Cr.* cape, point
Rubh', Rubha *Gae.* cape, point
-rück *Ger.* ridge
Rūd *Farsi* stream, river
Rudohorie *Slovak* mountains
Rzeka (R.) *Pol.* river

-saar *Est.* island
-saari *Fin.* island
Sabkhat, Sabkhet *Ar.* salt flats
Sadd *Ar.* dam
Sagar,-a *Hin., Urdu* lake
Sahrâ *Ar.* desert
-Saki *Jap.* cape, point
Salar *Span.* salt flat
Salina(s) *Span.* salt marsh(es)
-salmi *Fin.* strait, sound, lake, channel
Saltsjöbad *Swe.* resort
-Sammyaku *Jap.* mountain range
Samut *Thai* gulf
San (S.) *It., Port., Span.* saint
-San *Jap., Kor.* hill, mountain
-Sanchi *Jap.* mountain range
Sankt (St.) *Ger., Russ.* saint
-sanmaek *Kor.* mountain range
-sanmyaku *Jap.* mountain range
Santa (Sta.) *It., Port., Span.* saint
Santo (Sto.) *It. Port., Span.* saint
São (S.) *Port.* saint
Sarīr *Ar.* desert
Sasso *It.* mountain
Satu *Rom.* village
Saurums *Lat.* strait
Sebkha, Sebkhet *Ar.* salt flat
See, -see *Ger.* lake
-şehir *Turk.* town
Selat *Indo., Malay* strait
Selatan *Indo.* southern
-selkä *Fin.* bay, lake, ridge, hills
Selo *Ser.-Cr., Russ.* village
Selva *Port., Span.* forest, wood
Seno *Span.* bay, sound
Serir *Ar.* stony desert
Serra (Sa.) *Cat., Port.* range of hills
Serranía *Span.* mountain ridge
Severo, Severnaya, Severnoye, Severnyy (Sev.) *Russ.* north, northern
Sfântu *Rom.* saint
Shahr, -shahr *Farsi* city, town
Shamo *Chin.* desert
Shan *Chin.* hills, mountains
Shankou *Chin.* pass
Shanmo *Chin.* mountain range
Sharm *Ar.* bay
Shatt *Ar.* river mouth, estuary
-Shima *Jap.* island
Shimāli *Ar.* northern
-Shotō *Jap.* group of islands
-shui *Chin.* river
-shuiku *Chin.* reservoir
Sierra (Sa.) *Span.* mountain range
-sjö, -sjön, -sjø *Swe., Nor.* lake
-sjøen *Dan.* sea
-sjór *Ice.* lake
-sker *Ice.* island
-skär *Swe.* island, rock, cape
-skog, -skogen *Nor., Swe.* wood(s)
-skov *Dan.* forest
Slieve *Gae.* hill, mountain
Sø *Dan., Nor.* lake
Söder, Södra *Swe.* south, southern
Sør *Nor.* south, southern
Solonchak *Russ.* salt lake, marsh
Sønder, Søndra *Dan.* south, southern
Song *Viet.* river
Souk *Ar.* market
-spitze *Ger.* peak, mountain
-spruit *Afr.* stream
Sredna, Sredno *Bulg.* middle, central
Sredne, Sredneye *Russ.* middle, central
Srednja *Ser.-Cr.* middle, central
-stad *Afr., Nor., Swe.* town
-stadt *Ger.* town
-staður *Ice.* town
Stara, Stari *Ser.-Cr.* old
Stará, Staré, Stary *Czec.* old
Staraya, Staroye, Staryy *Russ.* old
Stare, Staro, Stary *Ukr.* old
Stausee *Ger.* reservoir
Stenón *Gr.* strait, pass
Step *Russ.* steppe
Stor, -a *Swe.* big
Store *Dan.* big
-strand *Dan., Ger., Nor., Swe.* beach
-strede *Nor.* straits
Strelka *Russ.* spit
-strete *Nor.* straits
Stretto (Str.) *It.* strait
Strædet (Str.) *Dan.* strait
-ström, -strömmen *Swe.* stream(s)
-stroom *Afr.* large river
Sud *Fr.* south, southern
Süd, -er *Ger.* south, southern
Suid *Afr.* south, southern
-Suidō *Jap.* strait, channel
Sul *Port.* south, southern
Sūn *Burm.* cape
-sund, -et *Swe., Nor.* sound, estuary, inlet
Sungai *Indo., Malay* river
Sur *Span.* south, southern
Sveti *Bulg.* saint
Syd *Dan., Swe.* south, southern
Sýsla *Ice.* first-order administrative division

-tag *Uighur* mountain
Tai -tai *Chin.* tower
-Take *Jap.* mountain
Tal *Mong.* plain, steppe
-tal *Ger.* valley
Tall *Ar.* hills
Tanjona *Malag.* cape, point
Tanjung, Tanjong (Tg.) *Indo., Malay.* cape, point
Tao *Chin.* island
Tasik *Malay* lake
Tassili *Ar.* rocky plateau
Tau *Russ.* mountain range
Taung *Burm.* mountain
Taungdan. *Burm.* mountain range
Taunggya *Burm.* pass
-tekojärvi *Fin.* reservoir
Teluk *Indo., Malay* bay, gulf
Ténéré *Berb.* desert
Tengah *Indo.* middle, central
-thal *Ger.* valley
Thok *Tib.* town
Tien *Chin.* lake, marsh
Tierra *Span.* land, country
Timur *Indo.* eastern
-tind *Nor.* peak
-ting *Chin.* mountain
Tjärn, -en, -et *Swe.* lake
-Tō *Jap.* island
Tong *Kor.* village, town
Tong *Burm., Thai, Kor.* mountain range
Tonlé *Cam.* lake
Top *Dut.* peak
-topp, -en *Nor.* peak
-träsk *Swe.* lake, swamp
Tsangpo *Tib.* large river
Tso *Tib.* lake
Tsu *Jap.* entrance, bay
Tsui *Chin.* cape, point
Tulur *Ar.* hill
-tunturi *Fin.* hill(s), mountain(s), ridge

Uad *Ar.* dry watercourse, wadi
Über *Ger.* upper
-udde, -udden *Swe.* point, cape
Uebi *Som.* river
Ujung *Indo., Malay* cape
Unter- *Ger.* lower
Us *Mong.* water
Ust, Ustye *Russ.* river mouth
Utara *Indo.* north, northern
Uttar *Hin.* north, northern
Uul *Mong., Russ.* mountain range

-vaara *Fin.* hill, mountain ridge, peak
Vaart *Dut.* canal
-våg *Nor.* bay
Val *Fr., Port., Span.* valley
Valea *Rom.* valley
-vall, -en *Swe.* mountain
Valle *It., Span.* valley
Vallée *Fr.* valley
Valli *It.* lake, lagoon
-város *Hung.* town
-varre *Nor.* mountain
Väst, Västra *Swe.* west, western
-vatn *Ice., Nor.* lake
-vatnet *Nor.* lake
-vatten, vattnet *Swe.* lake
-vecchio *It.* old
Vechi *Rom.* old
-ved, -veden *Swe.* hills
Veld, -veld *Afr.* field
Velha, Velho *Port.* old
Velika, Velike, Veliki, Veliko *Ser.-Cr., Slov.* big, large
Velikaya, Velikiy *Russ.* big, large
Velká, Velké, Velký *Czec.* big, large
Verkhne, Verkhniy *Russ.* upper
-vesi *Fin.* water, lake, bay, sound, strait
Vest, Vester, Vestre *Dan., Nor.* west, western
-vidda *Nor.* plateau
Vieille, Vieux *Fr.* old
Vieja, Vejo *Span.* old
Vig *Dan.* bay, inlet, cove, lagoon, lake
-vík *Ice.* bay
-vik, -a, -en *Nor., Swe.* bay, gulf, inlet, lake
Vila *Port.* small town
Villa *Span.* town
Ville *Fr.* town
Vinh *Viet.* bay
Vîrful (Vf.) *Rom.* peak, mountain
-viz *Hung.* river
-víztároló *Hung.* reservoir
-vlei *Afr.* lake, salt pan
-vliet *Dut.* canal
-vloer *Afr.* salt pan
Vodokhranilishche (Vdkhr.) *Russ.* reservoir
Vodoskovyshche (Vdskh.) *Ukr.* reservoir
Volcán (Vol.) *Span.* volcano, mountain
Vorota *Russ.* pass, channel, strait
Vostochno, Vostochnyy *Russ.* east, eastern
-vötn *Ice.* lakes
Vozvyshennost *Russ.* heights, uplands
Vozyera *Belo.* lake
Vrata *Bulg.* gate, pass
Vrchovina *Czec.* mountainous country
Vrch(y) *Czec.* mountain (range)
Vung *Viet.* bay, gulf
-vuori *Fin.* mountain, hill
Vychodné *Slovak* east, eastern
Vysochyna *Ukr.* upland

-waard *Dut.* polder
Wadi (W.) *Ar.* dry watercourse
Wāhāt *Ar.* oasis
Wald *Ger.* forest, mountains
-Wan *Chin., Jap.* bay, harbour
Wāw *Ar.* well
Webi *Amh.* river
Wes *Afr.* west, western
Wielka, Wielki, Wielko *Pol.* big, large
Woestyn *Afr.* desert
Wysoka, Wysoki *Pol.* upper
Wyżyna *Pol.* plateau

Xi *Chin.* river
Xia *Chin.* gorge, strait
Xiao *Chin.* small

Yam *Heb.* sea
-Yama *Jap.* mountain
-yan *Chin.* gorge, island
Yang *Chin.* bay, sea, sound
Yangi *Russ.* new
Yazovir *Bulg.* reservoir
Yeni *Turk.* new
Yli *Fin.* upper
Ynys *Welsh* island
Yoma *Burm.* mountain range
Ytre-, Ytter- *Nor., Swe.* outer
-yuan *Chin.* stream
Yugo- *Ser.-Cr.* south, southern
Yunhe *Chin.* canal
Yuzhni, Yuzhno *Russ.* south, southern

-Zaki *Jap.* point
Zalew *Pol.* lagoon, swamp
Zaliv *Russ.* bay, gulf
-Zan *Jap.* mountain
Zangbo *Tib.* stream, river
Zapadnaya, Zapadno, Zapadnyi (Zap.) *Russ.* west, western
Zatoka *Pol., Ukr.* bay, gulf
-zee *Dut.* lake, sea
Zemlya *Russ.* land, island(s)
Zhang *Chin.* mountain
-zhou *Chin.* island
Zhong *Chin.* middle, central
Zhou *Chin.* island
Zizhiqu *Chin.* autonomous region
Zuid, Zuider *Dut.* south, southern

INDEX TO WORLD MAPS

HOW TO USE THE INDEX

The index contains the names of all the principal places and features shown on the World and City Maps. Each name is followed by an additional entry in italics giving the country or region within which it is located. The alphabetical order of names composed of two or more words is governed primarily by the first word, then by the second, and then by the country or region name that follows. This is an example of the rule:

Mir *Niger*	14°5N 11°59E	**259**	F2
Mīr Kūh *Iran*	26°22N 58°55E	**247**	E8
Mīr Shahdād *Iran*	26°15N 58°29E	**247**	E8
Mira *Italy*	45°26N 12°8E	**199**	C9

Physical features composed of a proper name (Erie) and a description (Lake) are positioned alphabetically by the proper name. The description is positioned after the proper name and is usually abbreviated:

Erie, L. *N. Amer.*	42°15N 81°0W	**312**	D4

Where a description forms part of a settlement or administrative name, however, it is always written in full and put in its true alphabetical position:

Mount Olive *U.S.A.*	39°4N 89°44W	**310**	E7

Names beginning with M' and Mc are indexed as if they were spelled Mac. Names beginning St. are alphabetized under Saint, but Sankt, Sint, Sant', Santa and San are all spelt in full and are alphabetized accordingly. If the same place name occurs two or more times in the index and all are in the same country, each is followed by the name of the administrative subdivision in which it is located.

The geographical co-ordinates which follow each name in the index give the latitude and longitude of each place. The first co-ordinate indicates latitude – the distance north or south of the Equator. The second co-ordinate indicates longitude – the distance east or west of the Greenwich Meridian. Both latitude and longitude are measured in degrees and minutes (there are 60 minutes in a degree). Latitude and longitude references are not given on the Central Area City Maps.

The latitude is followed by N(orth) or S(outh) and the longitude by E(ast) or W(est).

The number in bold type which follows the geographical co-ordinates refers to the number of the map page where that feature or place will be found. This is usually the largest scale at which the place or feature appears.

The letter and figure that are immediately after the page number give the grid square on the map page, within which the feature is situated. The letter represents the latitude and the figure the longitude. A lower-case letter immediately after the page number refers to an inset map on that page.

In some cases the feature itself may fall within the specified square, while the name is outside. This is usually the case only with features that are larger than a grid square.

Rivers are indexed to their mouths or confluences, and carry the symbol ➛ after their names. The following symbols are also used in the index: ■ country, ▨ overseas territory or dependency, ▢ first-order administrative area, ☆ U.S. county, △ national park, ◌ other park (provincial park, nature reserve or game reserve), ◔ Australian aboriginal land, ▲ U.S. Indian reservation, ✈ (LHR) principal airport (and location identifier).

HOW TO PRONOUNCE PLACE NAMES

English-speaking people usually have no difficulty in reading and pronouncing correctly English place names. However, foreign place name pronunciations may present many problems. Such problems can be minimized by following some simple rules. However, these rules cannot be applied to all situations, and there will be many exceptions.

1. In general, stress each syllable equally, unless your experience suggests otherwise.
2. Pronounce the letter 'a' as a broad 'a' as in 'arm'.
3. Pronounce the letter 'e' as a short 'e' as in 'elm'.
4. Pronounce the letter 'i' as a cross between a short 'i' and long 'e', as the two 'i's in 'California'.
5. Pronounce the letter 'o' as an intermediate 'o' as in 'soft'.
6. Pronounce the letter 'u' as an intermediate 'u' as in 'sure'.
7. Pronounce consonants hard, except in the Romance-language areas where 'g's are likely to be pronounced softly like 'j' in 'jam'; 'j' itself may be pronounced as 'y'; and 'x's may be pronounced as 'h'.
8. For names in mainland China, pronounce 'q' like the 'ch' in 'chin', 'x' like the 'sh' in 'she', 'zh' like the 'j' in 'jam', and 'z' as if it were spelled 'dz'. In general, pronounce 'a' as in 'father', 'e' as in 'but', 'i' as in 'keep', 'o' as in 'or', and 'u' as in 'rule'.

Moreover, English has no diacritical marks (accent and pronunciation signs), although some languages do. The following is a brief and general guide to the pronunciation of those most frequently used in the principal Western European languages.

		Pronunciation as in
French	é	day and shows that the 'e' is to be pronounced; e.g. Orléans.
	è	mare
	î	used over any vowel and does not affect pronunciation; shows contraction of the name, usually omission of 's' following a vowel.
	ç	's' before 'a', 'o' and 'u'.
	ë, ï, ü	over 'e', 'i' and 'u' when they are used with another vowel and shows that each is to be pronounced.
German	ä	fate
	ö	fur
	ü	no English equivalent; like French 'tu'.
Italian	à, é	over vowels and indicates stress.
Portuguese	ã, õ	vowels pronounced nasally.
	ç	boss
	á	shows stress.
	ô	shows that a vowel has an 'i' or 'u' sound combined with it.
Spanish	ñ	canyon
	ü	pronounced as 'w' and separately from adjoining vowels.
	á	usually indicates that this is a stressed vowel.

ABBREVIATIONS

A.C.T. – Australian Capital Territory
A.R. – Autonomous Region
Afghan. – Afghanistan
Afr. – Africa
Ala. – Alabama
Alta. – Alberta
Amer. – America(n)
Ant. – Antilles
Arch. – Archipelago
Ariz. – Arizona
Ark. – Arkansas
Atl. Oc. – Atlantic Ocean
B. – Baie, Bahía, Bay, Bucht, Bugt
B.C. – British Columbia
Bangla. – Bangladesh
Barr. – Barrage
Bos.-H. – Bosnia-Herzegovina
C. – Cabo, Cap, Cape, Coast
C.A.R. – Central African Republic
C. Prov. – Cape Province
Calif. – California
Cat. – Catarata
Cent. – Central
Chan. – Channel
Colo. – Colorado
Conn. – Connecticut
Cord. – Cordillera
Cr. – Creek
D.C. – District of Columbia
Del. – Delaware
Dem. – Democratic
Dep. – Dependency
Des. – Desert
Dét. – Détroit
Dist. – District
Dj. – Djebel
Dom. Rep. – Dominican Republic
E. – East

El Salv. – El Salvador
Eq. Guin. – Equatorial Guinea
Est. – Estrecho
Falk. Is. – Falkland Is.
Fd. – Fjord
Fla. – Florida
Fr. – French
G. – Golfe, Golfo, Gulf, Guba, Gebel
Ga. – Georgia
Gt. – Great, Greater
Guinea-Biss. – Guinea-Bissau
H.K. – Hong Kong
H.P. – Himachal Pradesh
Hants. – Hampshire
Harb. – Harbor, Harbour
Hd. – Head
Hts. – Heights
I.(s). – Île, Ilha, Insel, Isla, Island, Isle
Ill. – Illinois
Ind. – Indiana
Ind. Oc. – Indian Ocean
J. – Jabal, Jebel
Jaz. – Jazīrah
Junc. – Junction
K. – Kap, Kapp
Kans. – Kansas
Kep. – Kepulauan
Ky. – Kentucky
L. – Lac, Lacul, Lago, Lagoa, Lake, Limni, Loch, Lough
La. – Louisiana
Ld. – Land
Liech. – Liechtenstein
Lux. – Luxembourg
Mad. P. – Madhya Pradesh
Madag. – Madagascar

Man. – Manitoba
Mass. – Massachusetts
Md. – Maryland
Me. – Maine
Medit. S. – Mediterranean Sea
Mich. – Michigan
Minn. – Minnesota
Miss. – Mississippi
Mo. – Missouri
Mont. – Montana
Mozam. – Mozambique
Mt.(s) – Mont, Montaña, Mountain
Mte. – Monte
Mti. – Monti
N. – Nord, Norte, North, Northern, Nouveau, Nahal, Nahr
N.B. – New Brunswick
N.C. – North Carolina
N. Cal. – New Caledonia
N. Dak. – North Dakota
N.H. – New Hampshire
N.I. – North Island
N.J. – New Jersey
N. Mex. – New Mexico
N.S. – Nova Scotia
N.S.W. – New South Wales
N.W.T. – North West Territory
N.Y. – New York
N.Z. – New Zealand
Nac. – Nacional
Nat. – National
Nebr. – Nebraska
Neths. – Netherlands
Nev. – Nevada
Nfld. & L. – Newfoundland and Labrador
Nic. – Nicaragua
O. – Oued, Ouadi
Occ. – Occidentale

Okla. – Oklahoma
Ont. – Ontario
Or. – Orientale
Oreg. – Oregon
Os. – Ostrov
Oz. – Ozero
P. – Pass, Passo, Pasul, Pulau
P.E.I. – Prince Edward Island
Pa. – Pennsylvania
Pac. Oc. – Pacific Ocean
Papua N.G. – Papua New Guinea
Pass. – Passage
Peg. – Pegunungan
Pen. – Peninsula, Péninsule
Phil. – Philippines
Pk. – Peak
Plat. – Plateau
Prov. – Province, Provincial
Pt. – Point
Pta. – Ponta, Punta
Pte. – Pointe
Qué. – Québec
Queens. – Queensland
R. – Rio, River
R.I. – Rhode Island
Ra. – Range
Raj. – Rajasthan
Recr. – Recreational, Récréatif
Reg. – Region
Rep. – Republic
Res. – Reserve, Reservoir
Rhld-Pfz. – Rheinland-Pfalz
S. – South, Southern, Sur
Si. Arabia – Saudi Arabia
S.C. – South Carolina
S. Dak. – South Dakota
S.I. – South Island
S. Leone – Sierra Leone
Sa. – Serra, Sierra

Sask. – Saskatchewan
Scot. – Scotland
Sd. – Sound
Sev. – Severnaya
Sib. – Siberia
Sprs. – Springs
St. – Saint
Sta. – Santa
Ste. – Sainte
Sto. – Santo
Str. – Strait, Stretto
Switz. – Switzerland
Tas. – Tasmania
Tenn. – Tennessee
Terr. – Territory, Territoire
Tex. – Texas
Tg. – Tanjung
Trin. & Tob. – Trinidad & Tobago
U.A.E. – United Arab Emirates
U.K. – United Kingdom
U.S.A. – United States of America
Univ. – University, Université, Universidad
Ut. P. – Uttar Pradesh
Va. – Virginia
Vdkhr. – Vodokhranilishche
Vdskh. – Vodoskhovyshche
Vf. – Vîrful
Vic. – Victoria
Vol. – Volcano
Vt. – Vermont
W. – Wadi, West
W. Va. – West Virginia
Wall. & F. Is. – Wallis and Futuna Is.
Wash. – Washington
Wis. – Wisconsin
Wlkp. – Wielkopolski
Wyo. – Wyoming
Yorks. – Yorkshire

A

A ‘Âli an Nîl = Upper Nile □ South Sudan 9°30N 33°0E 257 F3
A Baiuca Spain 43°19N 8°29W 194 B2
A Baña = San Vicenzo Spain 42°58N 8°46W 194 C2
A Cañiza Spain 42°13N 8°16W 194 C2
A Carballa Spain 43°13N 8°54W 194 B2
A Carreira Spain 43°21N 8°12W 194 B2
A Coruña Spain 43°20N 8°25W 194 B2
A Coruña □ Spain 43°10N 8°30W 194 B2
A Cruz do Incio Spain 42°39N 7°21W 194 C3
A Estrada Spain 42°43N 8°27W 194 C2
A Feira do Monte Spain 43°12N 7°34W 194 B3
A Fonsagrada Spain 43°8N 7°4W 194 B3
A Guarda Spain 41°56N 8°52W 194 D2
A Gudiña Spain 42°4N 7°8W 194 C3
A Pobre Spain 42°58N 7°3W 194 C3
A Ramallosa Spain 42°45N 8°30W 194 C2
A Rúa Spain 42°24N 7°6W 194 C3
A Serra de Outes Spain 42°52N 8°55W 194 C2
A Shau Vietnam 16°6N 107°22E 236 D6
A.N.R. Robinson Int. ✕ (TAB) Trin. & Tob. 11°9N 60°50W 323 s
A.N.Z. Stadium Sydney, Australia 33°51S 151°5E 139 B1
A.R.M.M. = Bangsamoro □ Phil. 8°0N 123°0E 233 H3
Aabenraa Denmark 55°3N 9°25E 163 J3
Aabybro Denmark 57°10N 9°44E 163 G3
Aachen Germany 50°45N 6°6E 178 E2
Aalām Iraq 33°19N 44°23E 113 B2
Aalborg Denmark 57°2N 9°54E 163 G3
Aalborg Bugt Denmark 56°50N 10°35E 163 H4
Aalen Germany 48°51N 10°6E 179 G6
Aalestrup Denmark 56°42N 9°29E 163 H3
Aalsmeer Neths. 52°16N 4°46E 112 B1
Aalst Belgium 50°56N 4°2E 170 D4
Aalten Neths. 51°56N 6°35E 170 C6
Aalter Belgium 51°5N 3°28E 170 C3
Äänekoski Finland 62°36N 25°44E 160 E21
Aarau Switz. 47°23N 8°4E 179 H4
Aarberg Switz. 47°2N 7°16E 179 H3
Aare → Switz. 47°33N 8°14E 179 H4
Aargau □ Switz. 47°26N 8°10E 179 H4
Aarhus Denmark 56°8N 10°11E 163 H4
Aarlen = Arlon Belgium 49°42N 5°49E 170 E5
Aars Denmark 56°48N 9°30E 163 H3
Aarschot Belgium 50°59N 4°49E 170 D4
Aasiaat Greenland 68°43N 52°56W 154 D5
Ab-i-Istada Afghan. 32°29N 67°55E 240 B3
Ab-i-Panja = Pyandzh → Asia 37°6N 68°20E 240 A2
Aba Sichuan, China 32°59N 101°42E 228 A3
Aba Dem. Rep. of the Congo 3°58N 30°17E 268 B3
Aba Nigeria 5°10N 7°19E 263 D6
Âbâ, Jazîrat Sudan 13°30N 32°31E 257 E3
Abacaxis → Brazil 3°54S 58°47W 329 D6
Abaco The Bahamas 26°25N 77°10W 320 A4
Abadab, J. Sudan 18°54N 35°56E 256 D4
Ābādān Iran 30°22N 48°20E 247 D6
Abade Ethiopia 9°22N 38°3E 257 F4
Ābādeh Iran 31°8N 52°40E 247 D7
Abadín Spain 43°21N 7°29W 194 B3
Abadla Algeria 31°2N 2°45W 261 B4
Abaeté Brazil 19°9S 45°27W 333 E2
Abaeté → Brazil 18°2S 45°12W 333 E2
Abaetetuba Brazil 1°40S 48°50W 332 B2
Abagnar Qi = Xilinhot China 43°52N 116°2E 226 C9
Abah, Tanjung Indonesia 8°46S 115°38E 231 K18
Abai Paraguay 25°58S 55°54W 335 B4
Abakaliki Nigeria 6°22N 8°2E 263 D6
Abakan Russia 53°40N 91°10E 217 B12
Abala Congo 1°17S 15°35E 264 C3
Abala Niger 14°56N 3°22E 263 C5
Abalak Niger 15°22N 6°21E 263 B6
Abalemma Algeria 20°51N 5°59E 261 D6
Abalemma Niger 16°12N 7°50E 263 B6
Abalessa Algeria 22°58N 4°47E 261 D5
Abana Turkey 41°59N 34°1E 212 B6
Abancay Peru 13°35S 72°55W 330 C3
Abang, Gunung Indonesia 8°16S 115°25E 231 J18
Abanga → Gabon 0°20S 10°30E 264 C2
Abano Terme Italy 45°22N 11°46E 199 C8
Abapó Bolivia 18°48S 63°25W 331 D5
Abarán Spain 38°12N 1°23W 197 G3
Abariringa Kiribati 2°50S 171°40W 277 A16
Abarqū Iran 31°10N 53°20E 247 D7
Abasha Georgia 42°11N 42°13E 191 J6
Abashiri Japan 44°0N 144°15E 220 B12
Abashiri-Wan Japan 44°0N 144°30E 220 C12
Abau Papua N. G. 10°11S 148°46E 286 F5
Abaújszántó Hungary 48°16N 21°12E 182 B6
Abava → Latvia 57°6N 21°54E 184 A8
Ābay = Nîl el Azraq → Sudan 15°38N 32°31E 257 D3
Abay Kazakhstan 49°38N 72°53E 217 C8
Abaya, L. Ethiopia 6°30N 37°50E 257 F4
Abaza Russia 52°39N 90°6E 217 B12
Abba C.A.R. 5°20N 15°11E 264 A3
Abbadia di Fiastra ⌂ Italy 43°12N 13°24E 199 E10
Abbadia San Salvatore Italy 42°53N 11°41E 199 F8
‘Abbāsābād Iran 33°34N 58°23E 247 C8
Abbay = Nîl el Azraq → Sudan 15°38N 32°31E 257 D3
Abbaye, Pt. U.S.A. 46°58N 88°8W 308 B9
Abbazia = Opatija Croatia 45°21N 14°17E 199 C11
Abbé, L. Ethiopia 11°8N 41°47E 257 E5
Abbeville Somme, France 50°6N 1°49E 173 B8
Abbeville Ala., U.S.A. 31°34N 85°15W 316 D4
Abbeville Ga., U.S.A. 31°59N 83°18W 316 D6
Abbeville La., U.S.A. 29°58N 92°8W 314 G8
Abbeville S.C., U.S.A. 34°11N 82°23W 316 A7
Abbey Wood U.K. 51°29N 0°7E 125 B4
Abbeyfeale Ireland 52°23N 9°18W 166 D2
Abbeyleix Ireland 52°54N 7°22W 166 D4
Abbiategrasso Italy 45°24N 8°54E 198 C5
Abbot Ice Shelf Antarctica 73°0S 92°0W 151 D16
Abbotsford Canada 49°5N 122°20W 296 D4
Abbottabad Pakistan 34°10N 73°15E 242 B5
Abbou, O. ben → Algeria 28°32N 5°14E 261 C6
ABC Islands W. Indies 12°15N 69°0W 322 g
Abcoude Neths. 52°17N 4°59E 112 B2
Abd al Kūrī Yemen 12°5N 52°20E 249 D6
Ābdānān Iran 32°56N 47°28E 213 F12
Ābdar Iran 30°16N 55°19E 247 D7
Âbdîn Egypt 30°2N 31°14E 117 A2
‘Abdolābād Iran 34°12N 56°30E 247 C8
Abdulino Russia 53°42N 53°40E 216 B4
Abdullah South Sudan 5°30N 29°55E 257 F3
Abdulpur Bangla. 24°15N 88°59E 243 G13
Abéché Chad 13°50N 20°35E 259 F4
Abejar Spain 41°48N 2°47W 196 D2
Abekr Sudan 12°45N 28°50E 257 E2
Abel Tasman △ N.Z. 40°59S 173°3E 285 A8
Abengourou Côte d'Ivoire 6°42N 3°27W 262 D4
Abeno Japan 34°38N 135°31E 133 B2
Abenójar Spain 38°53N 4°21W 195 G6
Åbenrå = Aabenraa Denmark 55°3N 9°25E 163 J3
Abensberg Germany 48°48N 11°51E 179 G7
Abeokuta Nigeria 7°3N 3°19E 263 D5
Aberaeron U.K. 52°15N 4°15W 169 E3
Aberayron = Aberaeron U.K. 52°15N 4°15W 169 E3
Aberchirder U.K. 57°34N 2°37W 167 D6
Abercorn = Mbala Zambia 8°46S 31°24E 269 D3
Abercorn Australia 25°12S 151°5E 281 D5
Abercrombie River △ Australia 34°5S 149°40E 283 C8
Aberdare U.K. 51°43N 3°27W 169 F4
Aberdare △ Kenya 0°22S 36°44E 268 C4
Aberdare Ra. Kenya 0°15S 36°50E 268 C4
Aberdaugleddau = Milford Haven U.K. 51°42N 5°7W 169 F2
Aberdeen N.S.W., Australia 32°9S 150°56E 283 B9
Aberdeen Sask., Canada 52°20N 106°8W 297 C7
Aberdeen Hong Kong, China 22°14N 114°8E 122 B2
Aberdeen Eastern Cape, S. Africa 32°28S 24°2E 270 D3
Aberdeen Aberd. City, U.K. 57°9N 2°5W 167 D6
Aberdeen Idaho, U.S.A. 42°57N 112°50W 304 E7
Aberdeen Md., U.S.A. 39°31N 76°10W 309 F15
Aberdeen Miss., U.S.A. 33°49N 88°33W 315 E10
Aberdeen Ohio, U.S.A. 38°39N 83°46W 311 F13
Aberdeen S. Dak., U.S.A. 45°28N 98°29W 308 C4
Aberdeen Wash., U.S.A. 46°59N 123°50W 306 D3
Aberdeen City □ U.K. 57°10N 2°10W 167 D6
Aberdeen Country Park ⌂ Hong Kong, China 22°16N 114°9E 122 B2
Aberdeen L. Canada 64°30N 99°0W 294 E12
Aberdeenshire □ U.K. 57°17N 2°36W 167 D6
Aberdour U.K. 56°3N 3°18W 121 A2
Aberdour Castle U.K. 56°3N 3°18W 121 A2
Aberdovey = Aberdyfi U.K. 52°33N 4°3W 169 E3
Aberdyfi U.K. 52°33N 4°3W 169 E3
Aberfeldy U.K. 56°37N 3°51W 167 E5
Aberfoyle U.K. 56°11N 4°23W 167 E4
Abergavenny U.K. 51°49N 3°1W 169 F4
Abergele U.K. 53°17N 3°35W 168 D4
Abergwaun = Fishguard U.K. 52°0N 4°58W 169 E3
Aberhonddu = Brecon U.K. 51°57N 3°23W 169 F4
Abermaw = Barmouth U.K. 52°44N 4°4W 168 E3
Abernathy U.S.A. 33°50N 101°51W 314 E4
Aberpennar = Mountain Ash U.K. 51°40N 3°23W 169 F4
Abert, L. U.S.A. 42°38N 120°14W 304 E3
Abertawe = Swansea U.K. 51°37N 3°57W 169 F4
Aberteifi = Cardigan U.K. 52°5N 4°40W 169 E3
Aberystwyth U.K. 52°25N 4°5W 169 E3
Abfanggraben → Germany 48°10N 11°41E 131 A3
Abhā Si. Arabia 18°0N 42°34E 248 C3
Abhar Iran 36°9N 49°13E 213 D13
Abhayapuri India 26°24N 90°38E 241 B3
Abia □ Nigeria 5°30N 7°35E 263 D6
Abiad, Es Sahrâ el Egypt 28°0N 28°0E 256 B2
Abide Turkey 38°55N 29°20E 205 C11
Abidiya Sudan 18°18N 34°3E 256 D3
Abidjan Côte d'Ivoire 5°26N 3°58W 262 D4
Abidjan □ Côte d'Ivoire 5°20N 4°0W 262 D4
Abilene Kans., U.S.A. 38°55N 97°13W 308 F5
Abilene Tex., U.S.A. 32°28N 99°43W 314 E5
Abingdon Ill., U.S.A. 40°48N 90°24W 310 D6
Abingdon Va., U.S.A. 36°43N 81°59W 309 G13
Abingdon, I. = Pinta, I. Ecuador 0°35N 90°44W 330 a
Abingdon-on-Thames U.K. 51°40N 1°17W 169 F6
Abington Reef Australia 18°0S 149°35E 280 B4
Abiod, Remel el Tunisia 31°45N 9°35E 261 B6
Abisko △ Sweden 68°18N 18°44E 160 B18
Abitau → Canada 59°53N 109°3W 297 B7
Abitibi → Canada 51°3N 80°55W 298 B3
Abitibi, L. Canada 48°40N 79°40W 298 C4
Abiy Adi Ethiopia 13°39N 39°3E 257 E4
Abiyata, L. Ethiopia 7°37N 38°36E 266 C4
Abiyata-Shala △ Ethiopia 7°40N 38°37E 257 F4
Abkhaz Republic = Abkhazia □ Georgia 43°12N 41°5E 191 J5
Abkhazia □ Georgia 43°12N 41°5E 191 J5
Ablon-sur-Seine France 48°43N 2°25E 134 B3
Abminga Australia 26°8S 134°51E 281 D1
Abnûb Egypt 27°18N 31°4E 256 B3
Åbo = Turku Finland 60°30N 22°19E 188 B2
Abo, Massif d' Chad 21°41N 16°8E 259 D3
Abohar India 30°10N 74°10E 242 D6
Aboisso Côte d'Ivoire 5°30N 3°5W 262 D4
Abolo Congo 0°8N 14°16E 264 B2
Abomey Benin 7°10N 2°5E 263 D5
Abong-Mbang Cameroon 4°0N 13°8E 264 B2
Abongabong Indonesia 4°15N 96°48E 234 B1
Abonnema Nigeria 4°41N 6°49E 263 E6
Abony Hungary 47°12N 20°3E 182 C5
Abor Hills India 28°25N 94°46E 241 A5
Aborlan Phil. 9°26N 118°33E 233 G2
Aboso Ghana 5°23N 1°57W 262 D4
Abou-Deïa Chad 11°20N 19°20E 259 F3
Abou-Goulem Chad 13°37N 21°38E 259 F4
Abou-Telfan ⌂ Chad 12°2N 18°58E 259 F3
Abovyan Armenia 40°16N 44°37E 191 K7
Aboyne U.K. 57°4N 2°47W 167 D6
Abra □ Phil. 17°35N 120°45E 232 C3
Abra de Ilog Phil. 13°27N 120°44E 232 E3
Abra Pampa Argentina 22°43S 65°42W 334 A2
Abraham L. Canada 52°15N 116°35W 296 C5
Abramtsevo Russia 55°49N 37°49E 129 B3
Abrantes Portugal 39°24N 8°7W 195 F2
Abreojos, Pta. Mexico 26°50N 113°40W 318 B2
Abri Esh Shamâliya, Sudan 20°50N 30°27E 256 C3
Abri Janub Kordofân, Sudan 11°40N 30°21E 257 E3
Abrolhos, Banco dos Brazil 18°0S 38°0W 333 E4
Abrud Romania 46°19N 23°5E 182 D8
Abruzzo □ Italy 42°15N 14°0E 199 F10
Absaroka Range U.S.A. 44°45N 109°50W 304 D9
Abşeron Yarımadası Azerbaijan 40°28N 49°57E 191 K9
Abtenau Austria 47°33N 13°21E 180 D6
Abu India 24°41N 72°50E 242 G5
Abū aḍ Ḍuhūr Syria 35°44N 37°2E 250 C8
Abū al Abyaḍ U.A.E. 24°11N 53°50E 247 E7
Abū al Khaşīb Iraq 30°25N 48°0E 246 D5
Abū ‘Alī Si. Arabia 27°20N 49°27E 247 E6
Abū ‘Alī → Lebanon 34°25N 35°50E 250 D6
Abū ‘Arīsh Si. Arabia 16°53N 42°48E 248 C3
Abu ‘Aweigîla Egypt 30°50N 34°7E 251 H5
Abu Ballas Egypt 24°26N 27°36E 256 C2
Abu Deleiq Sudan 15°57N 33°48E 257 D3
Abu Dhabi = Abū Ẓāby U.A.E. 24°28N 54°22E 247 E7
Abu Dis Sudan 19°12N 33°38E 256 D3
Abu Dis West Bank 31°46N 35°16E 123 B2
Abu Dom Sudan 16°18N 32°25E 257 D3
Abū Du'ān Syria 36°25N 38°15E 213 D8
Abu el Gaīn, W. → Egypt 29°35N 33°30E 251 J4
Abû en Numrus Egypt 29°57N 31°12E 117 B2
Abu Fatma, Ras Sudan 22°25N 36°25E 256 C4
Abu Gabra Sudan 11°2N 26°50E 257 E2
Abu Ga'da, W. → Egypt 29°15N 32°53E 251 J3
Abu Gelba Sudan 13°11N 31°52E 257 E3
Abu Ghosh Israel 31°48N 35°6E 123 B1
Abu Gubeiha Sudan 11°30N 31°15E 257 E3
Abu Habl, Khawr → Sudan 12°37N 31°0E 257 E3
Abū Ḩadrīyah Si. Arabia 27°20N 48°58E 247 E6
Abu Hail U.A.E. 25°17N 55°20E 119 A2
Abu Hamed Sudan 19°32N 33°13E 256 D3
Abu Haraz An Nîl el Azraq, Sudan 18°1N 33°58E 256 D3
Abu Haraz El Gezira, Sudan 14°35N 33°30E 257 E3
Abu Haraz Esh Shamâliya, Sudan 19°8N 32°18E 256 D3
Abu Higar Sudan 12°50N 33°59E 257 E3
Abū Kamāl Syria 34°30N 41°0E 213 E9
Abu Kebîr Egypt 30°43N 31°40E 251 H2
Abu Kuleiwat Sudan 12°20N 26°0E 257 E2
Abū Madd, Ra's Si. Arabia 24°50N 37°7E 246 E3
Abu Matariq Sudan 10°59N 26°9E 257 E2
Abu Mena = Abu Mina Egypt 30°51N 29°40E 256 H6
Abu Mendi Ethiopia 11°48N 35°42E 257 E4
Abu Mina Egypt 30°51N 29°40E 256 H6
Abū Mūsā U.A.E. 25°52N 55°3E 247 E7
Abū Nujaym Libya 30°35N 15°24E 258 B3
Abū Qaşr Si. Arabia 30°21N 38°34E 246 D3
Abu Qireiya Egypt 24°5N 35°28E 256 C4
Abu Qurqâs Egypt 28°1N 30°44E 256 B3
Abū Raşāş, Ra's Oman 20°10N 58°38E 249 B7
Abu Rudeis Egypt 28°54N 33°11E 251 K4
Abu Shagara, Ras Sudan 21°4N 37°19E 256 C4
Abu Shanab Janub Kordofân, Sudan 10°47N 29°32E 266 B2
Abu Shanab Shamâl Kordofân, Sudan 13°58N 27°49E 257 E2
Abu Simbel Egypt 22°18N 31°40E 256 C3
Abu Soma, Râs Egypt 26°51N 33°58E 256 B3
Abū Şukhayr Iraq 31°54N 44°30E 213 G11
Abu Sultân Egypt 30°24N 32°21E 256 H8
Abu Tabari Sudan 17°32N 28°32E 256 D2
Abu Tig Egypt 27°4N 31°15E 256 B3
Abu Tiga Sudan 12°47N 34°12E 257 E3
Abu Tineitin Sudan 14°24N 31°1E 257 E3
Abu Uruq Sudan 15°52N 30°25E 257 D3
Abu Zabad Sudan 12°25N 29°10E 257 E2
Abū Ẓāby U.A.E. 24°28N 54°22E 247 E7
Abū Zeydābād Iran 33°54N 51°45E 247 C6
Abufari Brazil 5°25S 62°59W 331 B5
Abuja Nigeria 9°5N 7°32E 263 D6
Abukuma-Gawa → Japan 38°6N 140°52E 220 E10
Abukuma-Sammyaku Japan 37°30N 140°45E 220 F10
Abulug Phil. 18°27N 121°27E 232 B3
Abumombazi Dem. Rep. of the Congo 3°42N 22°10E 264 B4
Abunã Brazil 9°40S 65°20W 331 B4
Abunã → Brazil 9°41S 65°20W 331 B4
Abune Yosef Ethiopia 12°5N 39°12E 257 E4
Aburatsu Japan 31°34N 131°24E 222 F3
Aburo Dem. Rep. of the Congo 2°4N 30°53E 268 B3
Abut Hd. N.Z. 43°7S 170°15E 285 D5
Abuye Meda Ethiopia 10°30N 39°49E 257 E4
Abuyog Phil. 10°45N 125°0E 233 F5
Abwong South Sudan 9°2N 32°14E 257 F3
Åby Sweden 58°40N 16°10E 163 F10
Aby, Lagune Côte d'Ivoire 5°15N 3°14W 262 D4
Abyad Sudan 13°47N 26°24E 257 E2
Abyān □ Yemen 13°50N 46°0E 248 D4
Abyei Sudan 9°36N 28°26E 257 F2
Abyei ☑ Sudan 9°30N 28°30E 257 F2
Ābyek Iran 36°4N 50°33E 247 B6
Acacías Colombia 3°59N 73°46W 328 C3
Acacias Madrid, Spain 127 c2
Academy Gletscher Greenland 82°2N 34°0W 154 A7
Acadia △ U.S.A. 44°20N 68°13W 309 C19
Açailândia Brazil 4°57S 47°30W 332 B2
Acajutla El Salv. 13°36N 89°50W 320 D2
Acámbaro Mexico 20°2N 100°44W 318 D4
Acandí Colombia 8°32N 77°14W 328 B2
Acanthus Greece 40°27N 23°47E 202 F7
Acaponeta Mexico 22°30N 105°22W 318 C3
Acapulco Mexico 16°51N 99°55W 319 D5
Acapulco Trench Pac. Oc. 12°0N 88°0W 318 D4
Acará Brazil 1°57S 48°11W 332 B2
Acaraí, Serra Brazil 1°50N 57°50W 329 C6
Acarai Mts. = Acaraí, Serra Brazil 1°50N 57°50W 329 C6
Acaraú Brazil 2°53S 40°7W 332 B3
Acari Brazil 6°31S 36°38W 332 C4
Acarí Peru 15°25S 74°36W 330 D3
Acarigua Venezuela 9°33N 69°12W 328 B4
Acassuso Argentina 34°29S 58°30W 117 A2
Acatlán Mexico 18°12N 98°3W 319 D5
Acayucán Mexico 17°57N 94°55W 319 D6
Accademia, Galleria dell' Venice, Italy 142 b2
Accademia, Ponte dell' Venice, Italy 142 b2
Accéglio Italy 44°28N 7°0E 198 D4
Accomac U.S.A. 37°43N 75°40W 309 G16
Accous France 43°0N 0°36W 174 E3
Accra Ghana 5°35N 0°6W 263 D4
Accrington U.K. 53°45N 2°22W 168 D5
Acebal Argentina 33°20S 60°50W 334 C3
Aceh □ Indonesia 4°15N 97°30E 234 B1
Acerra Italy 40°57N 14°22E 201 B7
Aceuchal Spain 38°39N 6°30W 195 G4
Achacachi Bolivia 16°3S 68°43W 330 D4
Achaguas Venezuela 7°46N 68°14W 328 B4
Achaia Greece 38°5N 21°45E 204 C3
Achalpur India 21°22N 77°32E 244 D3
Achao Chile 42°28S 73°30W 336 B2
Acharnes Greece 38°5N 23°44E 204 C5
Achegour Niger 19°10N 11°54E 259 E2
Acheloos → Greece 38°19N 21°7E 204 C3
Achelouma Niger 22°12N 12°50E 259 D2
Achelouma, Enneri → Niger 21°55N 13°35E 259 D2
Acheng China 45°30N 126°58E 227 B14
Achenkirch Austria 47°32N 11°45E 180 D4
Achénouma Niger 19°7N 12°55E 259 E2
Achensee Austria 47°26N 11°45E 180 D4
Achentrias Greece 34°59N 25°13E 205 G7
Acher India 23°10N 72°32E 242 H5
Achères France 48°57N 2°3E 134 A1
Achern Germany 48°37N 8°4E 179 G4
Acheron → N.Z. 42°16S 173°4E 285 C8
Achill Hd. Ireland 53°58N 10°15W 166 C1
Achill I. Ireland 53°58N 10°1W 166 C1
Achim Germany 53°1N 9°3E 178 B5
Achinsk Russia 56°20N 90°20E 215 D10
Achladokambos Greece 37°31N 22°35E 204 D4
Achouka Gabon 0°52S 9°45E 264 C2
Acıgöl Turkey 37°50N 29°50E 205 D11
Acília Italy 41°47N 12°21E 136 C1
Acıpayam Turkey 37°26N 29°22E 205 D11
Acireale Italy 37°37N 15°10E 201 E8
Ackerman U.S.A. 33°19N 89°11W 315 E10
Ackley U.S.A. 42°33N 93°3W 310 B3
Acklins The Bahamas 22°30N 74°0W 321 B5
Aclimação Brazil 23°34S 46°37W 137 B2
Acme Alta., Canada 51°33N 113°30W 296 C6
Acme Pa., U.S.A. 40°8N 79°26W 312 F5
Acobamba Peru 12°52S 74°35W 330 C3
Acomayo Peru 13°55S 71°38W 330 C3
Aconcagua, Cerro Argentina 32°39S 70°0W 334 C2
Aconquija, Mt. Argentina 27°0S 66°0W 334 B2
Acopiara Brazil 6°6S 39°27W 332 C4
Açores, Is. dos Atl. Oc. 38°0N 27°0W 153 d1
Acorizal Brazil 15°12S 56°22W 331 D6
Acornhoek S. Africa 24°37S 31°2E 271 B5
Acoua Mayotte 12°43S 45°4E 272 b
Acquapendente Italy 42°44N 11°52E 199 F8
Acquasanta Terme Italy 42°46N 13°24E 199 F10
Acquasparta Italy 42°41N 12°33E 199 F9
Acquaviva delle Fonti Italy 40°54N 16°50E 201 B9
Ácqui Terme Italy 44°41N 8°28E 198 D5
Acraman, L. Australia 32°2S 135°23E 281 E2
Acre = ‘Akko Israel 32°55N 35°4E 250 F6
Acre □ Brazil 9°1S 71°0W 330 B3
Acre → Brazil 8°45S 67°22W 330 B4
Acri Italy 39°29N 16°23E 201 C9
Acropolis Athens, Greece 112 c2
Acs Hungary 47°42N 18°2E 182 C3
Actæon Mt. = Diana's Peak St. Helena 15°58S 5°42W 153 h
Actéon, Groupe French Polynesia 21°20S 136°30W 289 f
Actinolite Canada 44°32N 77°19W 312 B7
Actium Greece 38°57N 20°45E 207 B2
Acton Ont., Canada 43°38N 80°3W 312 C4
Acton London, U.K. 51°30N 0°16W 125 A2
Açu Brazil 5°34S 36°54W 332 C4
Açúcar, Pão de Brazil 22°56S 43°9W 135 B2
Acul = Vidin Bulgaria 43°59N 22°50E 202 C6
Acworth U.S.A. 34°4N 84°41W 316 A5
Ad Dafinah Si. Arabia 23°18N 41°58E 248 B3
Ad Dafrah U.A.E. 23°30N 54°30E 249 B6
Ad Daghghāran Iraq 32°8N 44°55E 213 G11
Ad Ḑahī Yemen 15°13N 43°4E 248 D3
Ad Dahnā Si. Arabia 24°30N 48°10E 249 A5
Ad Dākhilīyah □ Oman 22°30N 57°30E 249 B7
Ad Ḑāli' Yemen 13°42N 44°44E 248 D4
Ad Ḑāli' □ Yemen 13°42N 44°44E 248 D4
Ad Dammām Si. Arabia 26°20N 50°5E 247 E6
Ad Dāmūr Lebanon 33°43N 35°27E 250 E6
Ad Darb Si. Arabia 18°2N 43°7E 248 C3
Ad Dawādimī Si. Arabia 24°35N 44°15E 246 E5
Ad Dawḩah Qatar 25°15N 51°35E 247 E6
Ad Dawr Iraq 34°27N 43°47E 213 E10
Ad Dhakhīrah Qatar 25°44N 51°33E 247 E6
Ad Ḑiffah Libya 30°30N 24°30E 258 B4
Ad Dilam Si. Arabia 23°55N 47°10E 248 B4
Ad Dir'īyah Si. Arabia 24°44N 46°35E 246 E5
Ad Dīwānīyah Iraq 32°0N 45°0E 213 F11
Ad Dujayl Iraq 33°51N 44°14E 213 F11
Ad Duqm Oman 19°39N 57°42E 249 C7
Ad Duwayd Si. Arabia 30°15N 42°17E 246 D4
Ada Ghana 5°44N 0°40E 263 D5
Ada Serbia 45°49N 20°9E 182 E5
Ada Minn., U.S.A. 47°18N 96°31W 308 B5
Ada Ohio, U.S.A. 40°46N 83°49W 311 D13
Ada Okla., U.S.A. 34°46N 96°41W 314 D6
Ada Beja Portugal 38°47N 9°13W 126 A1
Adad Somalia 9°27N 46°49E 267 C6
Adado, Ras Somalia 11°19N 48°39E 267 B6
Adair, C. Canada 71°30N 71°34W 295 C17
Adaja → Spain 41°32N 4°52W 194 D6
Adak U.S.A. 51°45N 176°45W 303 L3
Adak I. U.S.A. 51°45N 176°45W 303 L3
Ådalsbruk Norway 60°43N 11°19E 164 D8
Adam Oman 22°15N 57°28E 249 B7
Adam, Mt. Falk. Is. 51°34S 60°4W 153 f
Adama = Nazret Ethiopia 8°32N 39°22E 257 F4
Adamantina Brazil 21°42S 51°4W 333 F1
Adamaoua □ Cameroon 6°30N 13°30E 263 D7
Adamaoua, Massif de l' Cameroon 7°20N 12°20E 263 D7
Adamasta Channel Hong Kong, China 22°14N 114°1E 122 B2
Adamawa □ Nigeria 9°20N 12°30E 263 D7
Adamawa Highlands = Adamaoua, Massif de l' Cameroon 7°20N 12°20E 263 D7
Adamello, Mte. Italy 46°9N 10°30E 198 B7
Adamello ⌂ Italy 46°4N 10°28E 198 B7
Adami Tulu Ethiopia 7°53N 38°41E 257 F4
Adaminaby Australia 36°0S 148°45E 283 D8
Adams Mass., U.S.A. 42°38N 73°7W 313 D11
Adams N.Y., U.S.A. 43°49N 76°1W 313 C8
Adams Wis., U.S.A. 43°57N 89°49W 308 D9
Adams, Mt. U.S.A. 46°12N 121°30W 306 D5
Adam's Bridge Sri Lanka 9°15N 79°40E 245 K4
Adams L. Canada 51°10N 119°40W 296 C5
Adams Park U.S.A. 33°43N 84°27W 113 B2
Adam's Peak Sri Lanka 6°48N 80°30E 245 L5
Adamuz Spain 38°2N 4°32W 195 G6
‘Adan Yemen 12°45N 45°0E 248 D4
Adana Turkey 37°0N 35°16E 250 B6
Adana □ Turkey 37°0N 35°30E 250 B6
Adanero Spain 40°56N 4°36W 194 E6
Adang, Ko Thailand 6°33N 99°18E 237 J2
Adapazarı = Sakarya Turkey 40°48N 30°25E 212 B4
Adar Gwagwa, J. Sudan 22°15N 35°20E 256 C4
Adarama Sudan 17°10N 34°52E 257 D3
Adare Ireland 52°34N 8°47W 166 D3
Adare, C. Antarctica 71°0S 171°0E 151 D11
Adarte Eritrea 13°18N 42°8E 257 E5
Adaut Indonesia 8°8S 131°7E 231 F8
Adavale Australia 25°52S 144°32E 281 D3
Adda → Italy 45°8N 9°53E 198 C6
Addatigala India 17°31N 82°3E 244 F6
Addax ⌂ Niger 19°17N 9°22E 259 E1
Addis Ababa = Addis Abeba Ethiopia 9°2N 38°42E 257 F4
Addis Abeba Ethiopia 9°2N 38°42E 257 F4
Addis Alem Ethiopia 9°0N 38°17E 257 F4
Addis Zemen Ethiopia 12°7N 37°47E 257 E4
Addiscombe U.K. 51°22N 0°4W 125 B3
Addison Ill., U.S.A. 41°55N 88°0W 311 C8
Addison N.Y., U.S.A. 42°1N 77°14W 312 D7
Addo S. Africa 33°32S 25°45E 270 D4
Addo △ S. Africa 33°30S 25°50E 270 D4
Addu Atoll Maldives 0°38S 73°10E 272 d
Adebour Niger 13°17N 11°50E 259 F2
Ādeh Iran 37°42N 45°11E 246 B5
Adeje Canary Is. 28°7N 16°43W 153 e1
Adel Ga., U.S.A. 31°8N 83°25W 316 D6
Adel Iowa, U.S.A. 41°37N 94°1W 310 C2
Adel Bagrou Mauritania 15°29N 6°57W 262 B3
Adelaide S. Austral., Australia 34°52S 138°30E 282 C3
Adelaide Eastern Cape, S. Africa 32°42S 26°20E 270 D4
Adelaide I. Antarctica 67°15S 68°30W 151 C17
Adelaide Pen. Canada 68°15N 97°30W 294 D12
Adelaide River Australia 13°15S 131°7E 278 B5
Adelaide Village The Bahamas 25°0N 77°31W 153 b
Adelanto U.S.A. 34°35N 117°22W 307 L9
Adelaye C.A.R. 7°7N 22°49E 264 A4
Adele I. Australia 15°32S 123°9E 278 C3
Adélie, Terre Antarctica 68°0S 140°0E 151 C10
Adelie Land = Adélie, Terre Antarctica 68°0S 140°0E 151 C10
Adelong Australia 35°16S 148°4E 283 C8
Adelphi U.S.A. 39°0N 76°58W 143 A3
Adelsk Belarus 53°24N 23°47E 184 E10
Adelunga Toghi Uzbekistan 42°7N 70°58E 217 D8
Ademuz Spain 40°5N 1°13W 196 E3
Aden = ‘Adan Yemen 12°45N 45°0E 248 D4
Aden, G. of Ind. Oc. 12°30N 47°30E 267 B6
Adendorp S. Africa 32°15S 24°30E 270 D3
Aderbissinat Niger 15°34N 7°54E 263 B6
Aderklaa Austria 48°17N 16°32E 142 A3
Adh Dhayd U.A.E. 25°17N 55°53E 247 E7
Adhoi India 23°26N 70°32E 242 H4
Adi Indonesia 4°15S 133°30E 231 E8
Adi Arkai Ethiopia 13°35N 37°57E 257 E4
Adi Daro Ethiopia 14°20N 38°14E 257 E4
Adi Keyih Eritrea 14°51N 39°22E 257 E4
Adi Kwala Eritrea 14°38N 38°48E 257 E4
Adi Ugri Eritrea 14°58N 38°48E 257 E4
Adieu, C. Australia 32°0S 132°10E 279 F5
Adieu Pt. Australia 15°14S 124°35E 278 C3
Adigala Ethiopia 10°24N 42°15E 257 E5
Adige → Italy 45°9N 12°20E 199 C9
Adigrat Ethiopia 14°20N 39°26E 257 E4
Adıgüzel Barajı Turkey 38°13N 29°14E 205 C11
Adilabad India 19°33N 78°20E 244 E4
Adilcevaz Turkey 38°47N 42°43E 213 C10
Adīrī Libya 27°32N 13°2E 258 C2
Adirondack ⌂ U.S.A. 44°0N 74°20W 313 C10
Adirondack Mts. U.S.A. 44°0N 74°0W 313 C10
Adis Abeba = Addis Abeba Ethiopia 9°2N 38°42E 257 F4
Adıyaman Turkey 37°45N 38°16E 213 D8
Adıyaman □ Turkey 37°30N 38°10E 213 D8
Adjim Tunisia 33°47N 10°50E 258 B2
Adjohon Benin 6°41N 2°32E 263 D5
Adjud Romania 46°7N 27°10E 183 D12
Adjumani Uganda 3°20N 31°50E 268 B3
Adjuntas Puerto Rico 18°10N 66°43W 321 b
Adlavik Is. Canada 55°0N 58°40W 299 B8
Adler Russia 43°28N 39°52E 191 J4
Adler Planetarium Chicago, U.S.A. 41°51N 87°36W 119 B3
Admer Algeria 20°21N 5°27E 261 D6
Admer, Erg d' Algeria 24°0N 9°5E 261 D6
Admiralteyskaya Storona Russia 59°56N 30°20E 137 B2
Admiralty G. Australia 14°20S 125°55E 278 B4
Admiralty Gulf ✪ Australia 14°16S 125°52E 278 B4
Admiralty I. U.S.A. 57°30N 134°30W 296 B2
Admiralty Inlet Canada 72°30N 86°0W 295 C14
Admiralty Is. Papua N. G. 2°0S 147°0E 286 B4
Admiralty Island ⌂ U.S.A. 57°40N 134°10W 303 H14
Adnan Menderes, İzmir ✕ (ADB) Turkey 38°23N 27°6E 205 C9
Ado Nigeria 6°36N 2°56E 263 D5
Ado-Ekiti Nigeria 7°38N 5°12E 263 D6
Adok South Sudan 8°10N 30°20E 257 F3
Adola Ethiopia 11°14N 41°44E 257 E5
Adolfo González Chaves Argentina 38°2S 60°5W 334 D3
Adolfo Ruiz Cortines, Presa Mexico 27°15N 109°6W 318 B3
Adonara Indonesia 8°15S 123°5E 231 F6
Adoni India 15°33N 77°18E 245 G3
Adony Hungary 47°6N 18°52E 182 C3
Adour → France 43°32N 1°32W 174 E2
Adra India 23°30N 86°42E 243 H12
Adra Spain 36°43N 3°3W 195 J7
Adrano Italy 37°40N 14°50E 201 E7
Adrar Algeria 27°51N 0°19W 261 C4
Adrar □ Algeria 27°0N 1°0W 261 C5
Adrar □ Mauritania 20°10N 10°0W 260 D3
Adrar des Iforas Africa 19°40N 1°40E 261 D5
Adré Chad 13°40N 22°20E 259 F4
Ádria Italy 45°3N 12°3E 199 C9
Adrian Ga., U.S.A. 32°33N 82°35W 316 C7
Adrian Mich., U.S.A. 41°54N 84°2W 311 C12
Adrian Mo., U.S.A. 38°24N 94°21W 310 F2
Adrian Tex., U.S.A. 35°16N 102°40W 314 D3
Adrianople = Edirne Turkey 41°40N 26°34E 203 E10
Adriatic Sea Medit. S. 43°0N 16°0E 193 C7
Adua Indonesia 1°45S 129°50E 231 E7
Adung Long Myanmar 28°7N 97°42E 241 A6
Adur India 9°8N 76°40E 245 K3
Adwa Ethiopia 14°15N 38°52E 257 E4
Adygea □ Russia 45°0N 40°0E 191 H5
Adzhar Republic = Ajaria □ Georgia 41°30N 42°0E 191 K6
Adzhibakul = Qazımämmäd Azerbaijan 40°3N 49°0E 191 K9
Adzopé Côte d'Ivoire 6°7N 3°49W 262 D4
Aegae = Aigai Greece 40°28N 22°19E 202 F6
Ægean Sea Medit. S. 38°30N 25°0E 205 C7
Aerhtai Shan Mongolia 46°40N 92°45E 217 C12
Ærø Denmark 54°52N 10°25E 163 K4
Ærøskøbing Denmark 54°53N 10°24E 163 K4
Aetdia-Akarnania = Etoloakarnania Greece 38°45N 21°18E 204 C3
Aetos Greece 37°15N 21°50E 204 D3
Afaahiti Tahiti 17°45S 149°17W 289 e
Afafi, Massif d' Niger 22°11N 15°10E 259 D3
‘Afak Iraq 32°4N 45°15E 213 F11
Afandou Greece 36°18N 28°12E 206 E12
Afar □ Ethiopia 12°0N 41°0E 257 E5
Afarag, Erg Algeria 23°50N 2°47E 261 D5
Afareaitu Moorea 17°33S 149°47W 289 e
Åfarnes Norway 62°40N 7°32E 164 B4
Afdega Ethiopia 6°4N 43°30E 267 C5
Afdem Ethiopia 9°28N 41°0E 267 C5
Áffori Italy 45°31N 9°10E 128 A2
Affton U.S.A. 38°33N 90°20W 310 F6
Afghanistan ■ Asia 33°0N 65°0E 240 B2
Afgooye Somalia 2°7N 44°59E 267 D5
‘Afif Si. Arabia 23°53N 42°56E 248 B3
Afikpo Nigeria 5°53N 7°54E 263 D6
Aflandshage Denmark 55°33N 12°35E 118 B3
Aflisses, O. → Algeria 28°40N 0°50E 261 C5
Aflou Algeria 34°7N 2°3E 261 B5
Afmadow Somalia 0°31N 42°4E 267 D5
Afogados da Ingàzeira Brazil 7°45S 37°39W 332 C4
Afognak I. U.S.A. 58°15N 152°30W 303 G9
Afono B. Amer. Samoa 14°15S 170°38W 302 f
Afore Papua N. G. 9°9S 148°23E 286 E5
Afragóla Italy 40°55N 14°18E 201 B7
Afram → Ghana 7°0N 0°52W 263 D4
Afrera Ethiopia 13°16N 41°5E 257 E5
Africa 10°0N 20°0E 254 E6
‘Afrīn Syria 36°32N 36°50E 250 B7
‘Afrīn → Syria 36°20N 36°35E 250 B7
Afşar → Turkey 37°2N 32°35E 250 A3
Afsarīyeh Iran 35°39N 51°30E 141 B2
Afşin Turkey 38°14N 36°55E 212 C7
Afton Iowa, U.S.A. 41°2N 94°12W 310 C2
Afton N.Y., U.S.A. 42°14N 75°32W 313 D9
Afton Wyo., U.S.A. 42°44N 110°56W 304 E8
Afuá Brazil 0°15S 50°20W 329 D7
‘Afula Israel 32°37N 35°17E 250 F6
Afumba Zambia 15°38S 24°56E 265 F4
Afyon Turkey 38°45N 30°33E 205 C12
Afyon □ Turkey 38°25N 30°30E 205 C12
Afyonkarahisar = Afyon Turkey 38°45N 30°33E 205 C12
Aga Egypt 30°55N 31°10E 256 H7
Aga I. Micronesia 7°29N 151°43E 287 T18
Āgā Jarī Iran 30°42N 49°50E 247 D6
Agadem Niger 16°50N 13°11E 259 E2
Agadés = Agadez Niger 16°58N 7°59E 259 E1
Agadez Niger 16°58N 7°59E 259 E1
Agadir Morocco 30°28N 9°55W 260 B3
Agaete Canary Is. 28°6N 15°43W 153 e1
Agaie Nigeria 9°1N 6°18E 263 D6
Agalas Greece 37°43N 20°47E 207 D2
Agalega Is. Mauritius 11°0S 57°0E 273 F4
Agana = Hagåtña Guam 13°28N 144°45E 302 d
Agana B. Guam 13°29N 144°45E 302 d
Ağapınar Turkey 39°48N 30°47E 205 B12
Agar India 23°40N 76°2E 242 H7
Agar → India 21°0N 82°57E 244 D6
Agâraktem Mali 23°8N 6°22W 260 D3
Agaro Ethiopia 7°50N 36°38E 257 F4
Agartala India 23°50N 91°23E 241 D3
Agaş Romania 46°28N 26°15E 183 D11
Agassiz Canada 49°14N 121°46W 296 D4
Agassiz Icecap Canada 80°15N 76°0W 295 A16
Agat Guam 13°25N 144°40E 302 d
Agats Indonesia 5°33S 138°0E 231 F9
Agatti I. India 10°50N 72°12E 245 J1
Agattu I. U.S.A. 52°25N 173°35E 303 K1
Agawam U.S.A. 42°5N 72°37W 313 D12
Agbélouvé Togo 6°35N 1°14E 263 D5
Agboville Côte d'Ivoire 5°55N 4°15W 262 D4
Agboyi Cr. → Nigeria 6°33N 3°24E 124 A2
Ağcabädi Azerbaijan 40°5N 47°27E 191 K8
Ağdam Azerbaijan 40°0N 46°58E 191 K8
Ağdara Azerbaijan 40°13N 46°49E 191 K8
Ağdaş Azerbaijan 40°44N 47°22E 191 K8
Agde France 43°19N 3°28E 174 E7
Agde, C. d' France 43°16N 3°28E 174 E7
Agdz Morocco 30°47N 6°30W 260 B3
Agdzhabedi = Ağcabädi Azerbaijan 40°5N 47°27E 191 K8
Agen France 44°12N 0°38E 174 D4
Ageo Japan 35°58N 139°36E 223 B11
Ager Tay Chad 20°0N 17°41E 259 E3
Agerbæk Denmark 55°36N 8°48E 163 J2
Agersø Denmark 55°13N 11°12E 163 J5
Ågerup Denmark 55°43N 12°19E 118 A1
Ågesta Sweden 59°12N 18°6E 139 B2
Ageyevo Russia 54°10N 36°27E 188 E9
Aggteleki △ Hungary 48°27N 20°36E 182 B5
Āgh Kand Iran 37°15N 48°4E 213 D13
Aghathonisi Greece 37°28N 27°0E 205 D8
Aghia Anna Greece 38°52N 23°24E 204 C5
Aghia Deka Greece 35°3N 24°58E 207 E5
Aghia Ekaterinis, Akra Greece 39°50N 19°50E 206 B9
Aghia Galini Greece 35°6N 24°41E 207 E5
Aghia Marina Athina, Greece 37°48N 23°51E 112 C3
Aghia Marina Kasos, Greece 35°27N 26°53E 205 F8
Aghia Marina Leros, Greece 37°11N 26°48E 205 D8
Aghia Paraskevi Athina, Greece 38°1N 23°49E 112 A2
Aghia Paraskevi Voreio Aigaio, Greece 39°14N 26°21E 205 B8
Aghia Roumeli Greece 35°14N 23°58E 207 E4
Aghia Varvara Greece 35°8N 25°1E 207 E6
Aghiasos Greece 39°5N 26°23E 205 B8
Aghios Theodori Greece 37°55N 23°9E 204 D5
Aghion Oros = Athos Greece 40°9N 24°22E 203 F8
Aghion Oros □ Greece 40°25N 24°6E 203 F8
Aghios Andreas Greece 37°21N 22°45E 204 D4
Aghios Dimitrios Greece 37°53N 23°44E 112 B2
Aghios Efimia Greece 38°18N 20°36E 207 C2
Aghios Efstratios Greece 39°34N 24°58E 204 B6
Aghios Georgios Greece 37°28N 23°57E 204 D5
Aghios Ioannis, Akra Greece 35°20N 25°40E 207 E6
Aghios Ioannis Rendis Greece 37°57N 23°39E 112 B1
Aghios Isidoros Greece 36°9N 27°51E 206 E11
Aghios Kirikos Greece 37°34N 26°17E 205 D8
Aghios Leon Greece 37°47N 20°43E 207 D2
Aghios Matheos Greece 39°30N 19°47E 206 C9
Aghios Mironas Greece 35°15N 25°1E 207 E6
Aghios Nikolaos Etoloakarnania, Greece 38°52N 20°48E 207 B2
Aghios Nikolaos Kriti, Greece 35°11N 25°41E 207 E6
Aghios Nikolaos Lefkada, Greece 38°36N 20°34E 207 B2
Aghios Petros Greece 38°40N 20°36E 207 B2
Aghios Stephanos Greece 39°46N 19°39E 206 B9
Aghios Thekli Greece 38°15N 20°23E 207 C1
Aghios Thomas Greece 38°58N 20°47E 207 B2
Aghiou Orous, Kolpos Greece 40°6N 24°0E 202 F7
Aghireşu Romania 46°53N 23°15E 183 D8
Aghoueyyît Mauritania 21°10N 15°6W 260 D1
Aghreïjît Mauritania 21°58N 12°11W 260 D2
Agia Greece 39°43N 22°45E 204 B4
Agincourt Canada 43°47N 79°16W 141 A3
Aginskoye Russia 51°6N 114°32E 215 D12
Agjert Mauritania 16°23N 9°17W 262 B3
Ağlasun Turkey 37°39N 30°31E 205 D12
Agly → France 42°46N 3°3E 174 F7
Agmar Mauritania 25°18N 10°50W 260 C2
Agnew Australia 28°1S 120°31E 279 E3
Agnibilékrou Côte d'Ivoire 7°10N 3°11W 262 D4
Agnita Romania 45°59N 24°40E 183 E9
Agnone Italy 41°48N 14°22E 199 G11
Ago Japan 34°20N 136°51E 223 C8
Ago-Are Nigeria 8°30N 3°25E 263 D5
Agofie Ghana 8°27N 0°15E 263 D5
Agogna → Italy 45°4N 8°54E 198 C5
Agoitz = Aoiz Spain 42°46N 1°22W 196 C3
Agön Sweden 61°34N 17°23E 162 C11
Agon-Coutainville France 49°2N 1°34W 172 C5
Agoo Phil. 16°20N 120°22E 232 C3
Agora Athens, Greece 112 c1
Agordo Italy 46°18N 12°2E 199 B9
Agori India 24°33N 82°57E 243 G10
Agouifa Mauritania 19°57N 16°10W 260 E1
Agouna Benin 7°39N 1°47E 263 D5
Agout → France 43°47N 1°41E 174 E5
Agra India 27°17N 77°58E 242 F7
Agra Canal India 28°33N 77°17E 120 B2
Agrakhanskiuy Poluostrov Russia 43°42N 47°36E 191 J8
Agram = Zagreb Croatia 45°50N 15°58E 199 C12
Agramunt Spain 41°48N 1°6E 196 D6
Ágreda Spain 41°51N 1°55W 196 D3
Ağri Turkey 39°44N 43°3E 213 C10
Ağri □ Turkey 39°45N 43°5E 213 C10
Agri → Italy 40°13N 16°44E 201 B9
Ağrı Dağı Turkey 39°50N 44°15E 213 C11
Ağrı Karakose = Ağri Turkey 39°44N 43°3E 213 C10
Agria Greece 39°20N 23°1E 204 B5
Agricola Oriental Mexico 19°23N 99°4W 128 B2
Agrigento Italy 37°19N 13°34E 200 E6
Agrihan N. Marianas 18°46N 145°40E 302 a
Agrinio Greece 38°37N 21°27E 204 C3
Agrópoli Italy 40°21N 14°59E 201 B7
Ağstafa Azerbaijan 41°7N 45°27E 191 K7
Água Branca Brazil 5°50S 42°40W 332 C3
Agua Caliente Mexico 32°29N 116°59W 307 N10
Agua Caliente Springs U.S.A. 32°56N 116°19W 307 N10
Água Clara Brazil 20°25S 52°45W 331 E7
Agua Espraiada → Brazil 23°36S 46°41W 137 B2
Agua Fria ⌂ U.S.A. 34°14N 112°0W 305 J8
Agua Hechicera Mexico 32°28N 116°15W 307 N10
Agua Preta → Brazil 1°41S 63°48W 329 D5
Agua Prieta Mexico 31°18N 109°34W 318 A3
Aguachica Colombia 8°19N 73°38W 328 B3
Aguada Puerto Rico 18°23N 67°11W 321 b
Aguada Cecilio Argentina 40°51S 65°51W 336 B3
Aguadas Colombia 5°40N 75°38W 328 B2
Aguadilla Puerto Rico 18°26N 67°10W 321 C6
Aguadulce Panama 8°15N 80°32W 320 E3
Agualva-Cacem Portugal 38°46N 9°15W 126 A1
Aguanga U.S.A. 33°27N 116°51W 307 M10
Aguanish Canada 50°14N 62°2W 299 B7
Aguanish → Canada 50°13N 62°5W 299 B7
Aguapeí Brazil 16°12S 59°43W 331 D6
Aguapeí → Brazil 21°0S 51°0W 333 F1

E

G

H

Hsiyu *Taiwan* 23°36N 119°30E **225** C1
Hsopket *Myanmar* 23°11N 98°26E **228** F2
Hsüchou = Xuzhou *China* 34°18N 117°10E **227** G9
Hsüeh Shan *China* 24°24N 121°12E **225** B3
Hsüehchia *Taiwan* 23°14N 120°10E **225** C2
Hsühaitsun *Taiwan* 22°12N 120°52E **225** D2
Htawei = Dawei *Myanmar* 14°2N 98°12E **236** E2
Hu Xian *China* 34°8N 108°42E **226** G5
Hua Hin *Thailand* 12°34N 99°58E **236** F2
Hua Lamphong Railway Station *Bangkok, Thailand* **113** c2
Hua Muang *Laos* 20°13N 103°52E **236** B4
Hua Shan *China* 34°28N 110°4E **226** G6
Hua Xian *Henan, China* 35°30N 114°30E **226** G8
Hua Xian *Shaanxi, China* 34°30N 109°48E **226** G5
Hua Yü *Taiwan* 23°24N 119°19E **225** C1
Hua'an *China* 25°1N 117°32E **229** E11
Huab → *Namibia* 20°52S 13°25E **270** A2
Huacaya *Bolivia* 20°45S 63°43W **331** E5
Huachacalla *Bolivia* 18°45S 68°17W **330** D4
Huacheng *China* 24°4N 115°37E **229** E10
Huachinera *Mexico* 30°9N 108°55W **318** A3
Huacho *Peru* 11°10S 77°35W **330** C2
Huachón *Peru* 10°35S 76°0W **330** C2
Huade *China* 41°55N 113°59E **226** D7
Huadian *China* 43°0N 126°40E **227** C14
Huadu *China* 23°22N 113°12E **229** F9
Huahine, Î. *French Polynesia* 16°46S 150°58W **289** f
Huai Hat △ *Thailand* 16°52N 104°17E **236** D5
Huai He → *China* 33°0N 118°30E **229** A12
Huai Kha Khaeng ⌂ *Thailand* 15°20N 98°55E **236** E2
Huai Nam Dang △ *Thailand* 19°30N 98°30E **236** C2
Huai Yot *Thailand* 7°45N 99°37E **237** J2
Huai'an *Hebei, China* 40°30N 114°20E **226** D8
Huai'an *Jiangsu, China* 33°30N 119°10E **227** H10
Huaibei *China* 34°0N 116°48E **226** G9
Huaibin *China* 32°32N 115°27E **229** A10
Huaicho = Puerto Acosta *Bolivia* 15°32S 69°15W **330** D4
Huaide = Gongzhuling *China* 43°30N 124°40E **227** C13
Huaidezhen *China* 43°48N 124°50E **227** C13
Huaihua *China* 27°32N 109°57E **228** D7
Huaiji *China* 23°55N 112°12E **229** F9
Huainan *China* 32°38N 116°58E **229** A11
Huaining *China* 30°24N 116°40E **229** B11
Huairen *China* 39°48N 113°20E **226** E7
Huairou *China* 40°20N 116°35E **226** D9
Huaiyang *China* 33°40N 114°52E **226** H8
Huaiyin *China* 33°30N 119°2E **227** H10
Huaiyuan *Anhui, China* 32°55N 117°10E **229** A11
Huaiyuan *Guangxi Zhuangzu, China* 24°31N 108°22E **228** E7
Huajuapán de León *Mexico* 17°48N 97°46W **319** D5
Hualālai *U.S.A.* 19°42N 155°52W **302** D6
Hualapai Peak *U.S.A.* 35°5N 113°54W **307** K13
Hualian = Hualien *Taiwan* 23°59N 121°36E **225** C3
Hualien *Taiwan* 23°59N 121°36E **225** C3
Hualien □ *Taiwan* 23°45N 121°25E **225** C3
Huallaga → *Peru* 5°15S 75°30W **330** B2
Huallanca *Peru* 8°50S 77°56W **330** B2
Huamachuco *Peru* 7°50S 78°5W **330** B2
Huambo *Angola* 12°42S 15°54E **265** E3
Huambo □ *Angola* 13°0S 16°0E **265** E3
Huan Jiang → *China* 34°28N 109°0E **226** G5
Huan Xian *China* 36°33N 107°7E **226** F4
Huancabamba *Peru* 5°10S 79°15W **330** B2
Huancane *Peru* 15°10S 69°44W **330** D4
Huancapi *Peru* 13°40S 74°0W **330** C3
Huancavelica *Peru* 12°50S 75°5W **330** C2
Huancavelica □ *Peru* 13°0S 75°0W **330** C3
Huancayo *Peru* 12°5S 75°12W **330** C2
Huanchaca *Bolivia* 20°15S 66°40W **330** E4
Huanchaca, Serranía de *Bolivia* 14°30S 60°39W **331** C5
Huang Hai = Yellow Sea *China* 35°0N 123°0E **227** G12
Huang He → *China* 37°55N 118°50E **227** F10
Huang Xian *China* 37°38N 120°30E **227** F11
Huangchuan *China* 32°15N 115°10E **229** A10
Huangdao *China* 36°0N 120°7E **227** G11
Huanggang *China* 30°29N 114°52E **229** B10
Huangguoshu *China* 26°0N 105°40E **228** E5
Huanghua *China* 38°22N 117°20E **227** E9
Huanghuagang *China* 38°20N 117°54E **227** E9
Huanghuagang Mausoleum *China* 23°9N 113°17E **121** B2
Huangling *China* 35°34N 109°15E **226** G5
Huanglong *China* 35°30N 109°59E **226** G5
Huanglong ⌂ *China* 32°44N 103°50E **228** A4
Huanglongtan *China* 32°40N 110°33E **229** A8
Huangmei *China* 30°5N 115°56E **229** B10
Huangpi *China* 30°50N 114°22E **229** B10
Huangping *China* 26°52N 107°54E **228** D6
Huangpu *China* 31°14N 121°30E **138** B2
Huangpu Jiang → *China* 31°11N 121°29E **138** B1
Huangshan *Anhui, China* 30°8N 118°9E **229** B12
Huangshan *Anhui, China* 29°42N 118°25E **229** C12
Huangshi *China* 30°10N 115°3E **229** B10
Huangsongdian *China* 43°45N 127°25E **227** C14
Huangtugang *China* 39°49N 116°15E **114** C1
Huangyan *China* 28°38N 121°19E **229** C13
Huangyangsi *China* 26°33N 111°39E **229** D8
Huaning *China* 24°17N 102°56E **228** E4
Huanjiang *China* 24°50N 108°18E **228** E7
Huanren *China* 41°23N 125°20E **224** B2
Huanren Shuiku *China* 41°17N 125°34E **224** B2
Huanta *Peru* 12°55S 74°20W **330** C3
Huantai *China* 36°58N 117°56E **227** F9
Huánuco *Peru* 9°55S 76°15W **330** B2
Huánuco □ *Peru* 9°55S 76°14W **330** B2
Huanuni *Bolivia* 18°16S 66°51W **330** D4
Huanzo, Cordillera de *Peru* 14°35S 73°20W **330** C3
Huaping *China* 26°46N 101°25E **228** D3
Huara *Chile* 19°59S 69°47W **330** D4
Huaral *Peru* 11°32S 77°13W **330** C2
Huaraz *Peru* 9°30S 77°32W **330** B2
Huari *Peru* 9°14S 77°14W **330** B2
Huarmey *Peru* 10°5S 78°5W **330** C2
Huarochirí *Peru* 12°9S 76°15W **330** C2
Huarocondo *Peru* 13°26S 72°14W **330** C3
Huarong *China* 29°29N 112°30E **229** C9
Huascar *Peru* 11°59S 77°1W **124** A2
Huascarán, Nevado *Peru* 9°7S 77°37W **330** B2
Huasco *Chile* 28°30S 71°15W **334** B1
Huasco → *Chile* 28°27S 71°13W **334** B1
Huasna *U.S.A.* 35°6N 120°24W **307** K6
Huatabampo *Mexico* 26°50N 109°38W **318** B3
Huauchinango *Mexico* 20°12N 98°3W **319** C5
Huautla de Jiménez *Mexico* 18°8N 96°51W **319** D5
Huaxi *China* 26°25N 106°40E **228** D6
Huay Khwang *Thailand* 13°47N 100°33E **113** B2
Huayhuash, Cordillera *Peru* 10°30S 76°45W **330** B2
Huayin *China* 34°35N 110°5E **226** G6
Huaying *China* 30°8N 106°44E **228** B6
Huayllay *Peru* 11°3S 76°21W **330** C2
Huayuan *China* 28°37N 109°29E **228** C7
Huazhou *China* 21°33N 110°33E **228** G7
Hubballi *India* 15°22N 75°15E **245** G2
Hubbard *Iowa, U.S.A.* 42°18N 93°18W **310** B3
Hubbard *Ohio, U.S.A.* 41°9N 80°34W **312** E4
Hubbard *Tex., U.S.A.* 31°51N 96°48W **314** F6
Hubbard, Mt. *N. Amer.* 60°19N 139°4W **303** F13
Hubbard Glacier *Canada* 60°18N 139°22W **294** E4
Hubbart Pt. *Canada* 59°21N 94°41W **297** B10
Hubei □ *China* 31°0N 112°0E **229** B9
Hubli = Hubballi *India* 15°22N 75°15E **245** G2
Huch'ang *N. Korea* 41°25N 127°2E **224** B3
Huchow = Huzhou *China* 30°51N 120°8E **229** B13
Hucknall *U.K.* 53°3N 1°13W **168** D6
Huddersfield *U.K.* 53°39N 1°47W **168** D6
Huddinge *Sweden* 59°14N 18°0E **139** B2
Hude *Germany* 53°7N 8°26E **178** B4
Hudi *Sudan* 17°43N 34°18E **256** D3
Hudiksvall *Sweden* 61°43N 17°10E **162** C11
Hudson *Ont., Canada* 50°6N 92°9W **298** B1
Hudson *Fla., U.S.A.* 28°22N 82°42W **317** G7
Hudson *Mass., U.S.A.* 42°23N 71°34W **313** D13
Hudson *Mich., U.S.A.* 41°51N 84°21W **311** C12
Hudson *N.Y., U.S.A.* 42°15N 73°46W **313** D11
Hudson *Wis., U.S.A.* 44°58N 92°45W **308** C7
Hudson *Wyo., U.S.A.* 42°54N 108°35W **304** E9
Hudson → *U.S.A.* 40°42N 74°2W **313** F10
Hudson, C. *Antarctica* 68°21S 153°45E **151** C10
Hudson, Vol. *Chile* 46°4S 72°55W **336** C2
Hudson Bay *Nunavut, Canada* 60°0N 86°0W **295** F14
Hudson Bay *Sask., Canada* 52°51N 102°23W **297** C8
Hudson Falls *U.S.A.* 43°18N 73°35W **313** C11
Hudson Mts. *Antarctica* 74°32S 99°20W **151** D16
Hudson River Park *New York, U.S.A.* **132** e1
Hudson Str. *Canada* 62°0N 70°0W **295** E18
Hudson's Hope *Canada* 56°0N 121°54W **296** B4
Hudsonville *U.S.A.* 42°52N 85°52W **311** B11
Hue *Vietnam* 16°30N 107°35E **236** D6
Huebra → *Spain* 41°2N 6°48W **194** D4
Huechuraba *Chile* 33°22S 70°39W **137** B1
Huedin *Romania* 46°52N 23°2E **182** D8
Huehuetenango *Guatemala* 15°20N 91°28W **320** C1
Huejúcar *Mexico* 22°21N 103°13W **318** C4
Huélamo *Spain* 40°17N 1°48W **196** E3
Huelgoat *France* 48°22N 3°46W **172** D3
Huelma *Spain* 37°39N 3°28W **195** H7
Huelva *Spain* 37°18N 6°57W **195** H4
Huelva □ *Spain* 37°40N 7°0W **195** H4
Huelva → *Spain* 37°27N 6°0W **195** H5
Hueneme = Port Hueneme *U.S.A.* 34°7N 119°12W **307** L7
Huentelauquén *Chile* 31°38S 71°33W **334** C1
Huércal-Overa *Spain* 37°23N 1°57W **197** H3
Huerquehue △ *Chile* 39°6S 71°42W **336** A2
Huerta, Sa. de la *Argentina* 31°10S 67°30W **334** C2
Huertas, C. de las *Spain* 38°21N 0°24W **197** G4
Huerva → *Spain* 41°39N 0°52W **196** D4
Huesca *Spain* 42°8N 0°25W **196** C4
Huesca □ *Spain* 42°20N 0°1E **196** C5
Huéscar *Spain* 37°44N 2°35W **197** H2
Hueso Ballena, Pta. *Chile* 33°40S 78°46W **330** c
Huetamo *Mexico* 18°35N 100°53W **318** D4
Huete *Spain* 40°10N 2°43W **196** E2
Huevos I. *Trin. & Tob.* 10°42N 61°43W **323** t
Huger *U.S.A.* 33°6N 79°48W **316** B10
Hugh → *Australia* 25°1S 134°1E **280** D1
Hugh Taylor Birch State Recr. Area ⌂ *U.S.A.* 26°8N 80°6W **129** B3
Hughenden *Australia* 20°52S 144°10E **280** C3
Hughes *U.S.A.* 66°3N 154°15W **303** C9
Hughesville *U.S.A.* 41°14N 76°44W **313** E8
Hugli → *India* 21°56N 88°4E **243** J13
Hugo *Colo., U.S.A.* 39°8N 103°28W **304** G12
Hugo *Okla., U.S.A.* 34°1N 95°31W **314** D7
Hugoton *U.S.A.* 37°11N 101°21W **308** G3
Huguang Opera Museum *Beijing, China* **114** c2
Huhehaote = Hohhot *China* 40°52N 111°40E **226** D6
Huhsi *Taiwan* 23°35N 119°39E **225** C1
Hui Xian = Huixian *China* 35°27N 113°12E **226** G7
Hui Xian *China* 33°50N 106°4E **226** H4
Hui'an *China* 25°1N 118°43E **229** E12
Hui'anbu *China* 37°28N 106°38E **226** F4
Huiarau Ra. *N.Z.* 38°45S 176°55E **284** E5
Huichang *China* 25°32N 115°45E **229** E10
Huichapan *Mexico* 20°23N 99°39W **319** C5
Huichon *N. Korea* 40°10N 126°16E **224** B3
Huidong *Guangdong, China* 22°58N 114°43E **229** F10
Huidong *Sichuan, China* 26°34N 102°35E **228** D4
Huifa He → *China* 43°0N 127°50E **227** C14
Huila *Angola* 15°4S 13°32E **265** F2
Huíla □ *Angola* 14°0S 15°0E **265** E2
Huila □ *Colombia* 2°30N 75°45W **328** C2
Huila, Nevado del *Colombia* 3°0N 76°0W **328** C2
Huilai *China* 23°0N 116°18E **229** F11
Huili *China* 26°35N 102°17E **228** D4
Huimin *China* 37°27N 117°28E **227** F9
Huinan *China* 42°40N 126°2E **224** A3
Huinca Renancó *Argentina* 34°51S 64°22W **334** C3
Huining *China* 35°38N 105°0E **226** G3
Huinong *China* 39°5N 106°35E **226** E4
Huiroa *N.Z.* 39°15S 174°30E **284** F3
Huishui *China* 26°7N 106°38E **228** D6
Huisne → *France* 47°59N 0°11E **172** E7
Huiting *China* 34°5N 116°5E **226** G9
Huitong *China* 26°51N 109°45E **228** D7
Huixian *China* 35°27N 113°12E **226** G7
Huixtla *Mexico* 15°9N 92°28W **319** D6
Huize *China* 26°24N 103°15E **228** D4
Huizhou *China* 23°0N 114°23E **229** F10
Huizingen *Belgium* 50°45N 4°17E **116** B1
Hukawng Valley *Myanmar* 26°30N 96°30E **241** B6
Hukeri *India* 16°14N 74°36E **245** F2
Hukou *Jiangxi, China* 29°45N 116°21E **229** C11
Huk'ou *Taiwan* 24°54N 121°2E **225** B3
Hukuntsi *Botswana* 23°58S 21°45E **270** B3
Hula *Papua N. G.* 10°5S 147°43E **286** F4
Ḩulayfā' *Si. Arabia* 25°58N 40°45E **246** E4
Huld = Ulaanjirem *Mongolia* 45°5N 105°30E **226** B3
Hulin *China* 45°48N 132°59E **219** B15
Hulin He → *China* 45°0N 122°10E **227** B12
Hull = Kingston upon Hull *U.K.* 53°45N 0°21W **168** D7
Hull *Canada* 45°26N 75°43W **313** A9
Hull → *U.K.* 53°44N 0°20W **168** D7
Hulst *Neths.* 51°17N 4°2E **170** C4
Hultschin = Hlučín *Czechia* 49°54N 18°11E **181** B11
Hultsfred *Sweden* 57°30N 15°52E **163** G9
Huludao *China* 40°45N 120°50E **227** D11
Hulun = Hailar *China* 49°10N 119°38E **219** B12
Hulun Nur *China* 49°0N 117°30E **219** B12
Hulunbuir = Hailar *China* 49°10N 119°38E **219** B12
Hulyaypole *Ukraine* 47°45N 36°21E **189** J9
Huma, Tanjung *Malaysia* 5°29N 100°16E **237** c
Humacao *Puerto Rico* 18°9N 65°50W **321** b
Humahuaca *Argentina* 23°10S 65°25W **334** A2
Humaitá = Porto Walter *Brazil* 8°15S 72°40W **330** B3
Humaitá *Brazil* 7°35S 63°1W **331** B5
Humaitá *Paraguay* 27°2S 58°31W **334** B4
Humansdorp *S. Africa* 34°2S 24°46E **270** D3
Humansville *U.S.A.* 37°48N 93°35W **310** G3
Humara, J. *Sudan* 16°16N 30°59E **257** D3
Humayun's Tomb *India* 28°35N 77°15E **120** B2
Humbe *Angola* 16°40S 14°55E **265** F2
Humbe, Serra do *Angola* 12°10S 15°25E **265** E2
Humber → *Ont., Canada* 43°47N 79°38W **141** A1
Humber → *England, U.K.* 53°42N 0°27W **168** D7
Humber B. *Canada* 43°37N 79°27W **141** B2
Humber Bay *Canada* 43°38N 79°29W **141** B2
Humber Bay Park *Canada* 43°37N 79°28W **141** B2
Humber College *Canada* 43°35N 79°30W **141** B1
Humber Summit *Canada* 43°45N 79°32W **141** A1
Humber Valley Village *Canada* 43°40N 79°31W **141** A1
Humberlea *Canada* 43°43N 79°31W **141** A1
Humberwood Park *Canada* 43°44N 79°37W **141** A1
Humboldt *Sask., Canada* 52°15N 105°9W **297** C7
Humboldt *Iowa, U.S.A.* 42°44N 94°13W **310** B2
Humboldt *Tenn., U.S.A.* 35°50N 88°55W **315** D10
Humboldt → *U.S.A.* 39°59N 118°36W **304** G4
Humboldt Gletscher = Sermersuaq *Greenland* 79°30N 62°0W **154** B4
Humboldt Mts. *N.Z.* 44°30S 168°15E **285** E3
Humboldt Park *U.S.A.* 41°54N 87°42W **119** B2
Humbolt, Mt. *N. Cal.* 21°53S 166°25E **288** d
Hume *U.S.A.* 36°48N 118°54W **306** J8
Hume, L. *Australia* 36°0S 147°5E **283** D7
Humen *China* 22°50N 113°40E **219** a
Humenné *Slovakia* 48°55N 21°50E **181** C14
Humera *Spain* 40°25N 3°46W **127** B1
Humeston *U.S.A.* 40°52N 93°30W **310** D3
Hummelsta *Sweden* 59°34N 16°58E **162** E10
Hummelvika *Norway* 63°29N 8°19E **164** A5
Hummingbird Centre *Toronto, Canada* **141** b3
Hummock Hill = Whyalla *Australia* 33°2S 137°30E **282** B2
Humpata *Angola* 15°2S 13°24E **265** F2
Humphreys, Mt. *U.S.A.* 37°17N 118°40W **306** H8
Humphreys Peak *U.S.A.* 35°21N 111°41W **305** J8
Humpolec *Czechia* 49°31N 15°20E **180** B8
Humptulips *U.S.A.* 47°14N 123°57W **306** C3
Humula *Australia* 35°30S 147°46E **283** C7
Hūn *Libya* 29°2N 16°0E **258** C3
Hun He → *China* 40°41N 122°8E **224** B1
Hun Jiang → *China* 40°50N 125°38E **227** D13
Húnaflói *Iceland* 65°50N 20°50W **155** B6
Hunan □ *China* 27°30N 112°0E **229** D9
Húnavatnssýsla *Iceland* 65°30N 20°25W **155** B6
Hunaydī *Iraq* 33°18N 44°29E **113** B2
Hunchun *China* 42°52N 130°28E **227** C16
Hundested *Denmark* 55°58N 11°52E **163** J5
Hundewali *Pakistan* 31°55N 72°38E **242** D5
Hundige *Denmark* 55°35N 12°18E **118** B1
Hundige Strand *Denmark* 55°35N 12°20E **118** B2
Hundorp *Norway* 61°33N 9°59E **164** C7
Hundred Islands △ *Phil.* 16°10N 120°2E **232** C3
Hundred Mile House *Canada* 51°38N 121°18W **296** C4
Hundvåg *Norway* 59°0N 5°43E **164** E2
Hunedoara *Romania* 45°40N 22°50E **182** E7
Hunedoara □ *Romania* 45°50N 22°54E **182** E7
Hunei *Taiwan* 22°53N 120°14E **225** D2
Hünfeld *Germany* 50°39N 9°46E **178** E5
Hung Hom *Hong Kong, China* 22°18N 114°11E **122** B3
Hung Yen *Vietnam* 20°39N 106°4E **228** G6
Hunga Ha'apai *Tonga* 20°41S 175°7W **287** G13
Hungary ■ *Europe* 47°20N 19°20E **181** D12
Hungary, Plain of *Europe* 47°0N 20°0E **158** F10
Hungerford *Australia* 28°58S 144°24E **281** D3
Hungnam *N. Korea* 39°49N 127°45E **224** C3
Hungt'ou Hsü = Lan Yü *Taiwan* 22°4N 121°25E **225** D3
Huni Valley *Ghana* 5°33N 1°56W **262** D4
Hunjiang *China* 41°54N 126°26E **224** B3
Hunneberg *Sweden* 58°18N 12°30E **163** F6
Hunnebostrand *Sweden* 58°27N 11°18E **163** F5
Hunsberge *Namibia* 27°45S 17°12E **270** C2
Hunsrück *Germany* 49°56N 7°27E **179** F3
Hunstanton *U.K.* 52°56N 0°29E **168** E8
Hunsur *India* 12°16N 76°16E **245** H3
Hunte → *Germany* 53°14N 8°28E **178** B4
Hunter *N.Z.* 44°36S 171°2E **285** E6
Hunter *N.Y., U.S.A.* 42°13N 74°13W **313** D10
Hunter → *N.S.W., Australia* 32°52S 151°46E **283** B9
Hunter → *N.Z.* 44°21S 169°27E **285** E4
Hunter, C. *Solomon Is.* 9°48S 159°50E **287** M10
Hunter Hills, The *N.Z.* 44°26S 170°46E **285** E5
Hunter I. *Tas., Australia* 40°30S 144°45E **281** G3
Hunter I. *B.C., Canada* 51°55N 128°0W **296** C3
Hunter Mts. *N.Z.* 45°43S 167°25E **285** F2
Hunter Ra. *Australia* 32°45S 150°15E **283** B9
Hunters Hill *Australia* 33°50S 151°9E **139** B1
Hunters Pt. *U.S.A.* 37°43N 122°21W **136** B2
Hunters Road *Zimbabwe* 19°9S 29°49E **269** F2
Hunterville *N.Z.* 39°56S 175°35E **284** F4
Huntingburg *U.S.A.* 38°18N 86°57W **311** F10
Huntingdon *Cambs., U.K.* 52°20N 0°11W **169** E7
Huntingdon *Pa., U.S.A.* 40°30N 78°1W **312** F6
Huntington = Shelton *U.S.A.* 41°19N 73°5W **313** E11
Huntington *Ind., U.S.A.* 40°53N 85°30W **311** D11
Huntington *N.Y., U.S.A.* 40°52N 73°26W **313** F11
Huntington *Oreg., U.S.A.* 44°21N 117°16W **304** D5
Huntington *Utah, U.S.A.* 39°20N 110°58W **304** G8
Huntington *Va., U.S.A.* 38°47N 77°4W **143** C2
Huntington *W. Va., U.S.A.* 38°25N 82°27W **309** F12
Huntington Beach *U.S.A.* 33°40N 118°5W **307** M9
Huntington Park *U.S.A.* 33°58N 118°13W **126** C3
Huntley *Jamaica* 18°4N 77°35W **320** a
Huntley *Ill., U.S.A.* 42°10N 88°26W **311** B8
Huntly *N.Z.* 37°34S 175°11E **284** D4
Huntly *Aberds., U.K.* 57°27N 2°47W **167** D6
Huntsville *Ont., Canada* 45°20N 79°14W **312** A5
Huntsville *Ala., U.S.A.* 34°44N 86°35W **315** D11
Huntsville *Mo., U.S.A.* 39°26N 92°33W **310** E4
Huntsville *Tex., U.S.A.* 30°43N 95°33W **314** F7
Hunyani → *Zimbabwe* 15°57S 30°39E **269** F3
Hunyuan *China* 39°42N 113°42E **226** E7
Hunza → *India* 35°54N 74°20E **243** B6
Huo Shan *China* 36°26N 111°52E **226** F6
Huo Xian = Huozhou *China* 36°36N 111°42E **226** F6
Huocheng *China* 44°0N 80°48E **217** D10
Huolin Gol *China* 45°32N 119°38E **227** B10
Huon G. *Papua N. G.* 7°0S 147°30E **286** D4
Huon Pen. *Papua N. G.* 6°20S 147°30E **286** D4
Huong Khe *Vietnam* 18°13N 105°41E **236** C5
Huonville *Australia* 43°0S 147°5E **281** G4
Huoqiu *China* 32°20N 116°12E **229** A11
Huoshan *China* 31°25N 116°20E **229** B11
Huoshao Dao = Lütao *Taiwan* 22°40N 121°30E **225** D3
Huozhou *China* 36°36N 111°42E **226** F6
Hupeh = Hubei □ *China* 31°0N 112°0E **229** B9
Ḩūr *Iran* 30°50N 57°7E **247** D8
Hurand *Iran* 38°51N 47°22E **213** C12
Ḩuraymila *Si. Arabia* 25°8N 46°8E **246** E5
Hurbanovo *Slovakia* 47°51N 18°11E **181** D11
Hurd, C. *Canada* 45°13N 81°44W **312** A3
Hurdiyo *Somalia* 10°33N 51°6E **267** B7
Hure Qi *China* 42°45N 121°45E **227** C11
Hurezani *Romania* 44°49N 23°40E **183** F8
Hurghada *Egypt* 27°15N 33°50E **256** B3
Hurīya *Iraq* 33°21N 44°19E **113** A1
Hurley *N. Mex., U.S.A.* 32°42N 108°8W **305** K9
Hurley *Wis., U.S.A.* 46°27N 90°11W **308** B8
Huron *Calif., U.S.A.* 36°12N 120°6W **306** J6
Huron *Ohio, U.S.A.* 41°24N 82°33W **312** E2
Huron *S. Dak., U.S.A.* 44°22N 98°13W **308** C4
Huron, L. *U.S.A.* 44°30N 82°40W **312** B2
Huron East *Canada* 43°31N 81°18W **312** C3
Hurricane *U.S.A.* 37°11N 113°17W **305** H7
Hurso *Ethiopia* 9°35N 41°33E **257** F5
Hurst *U.S.A.* 32°49N 97°10W **120** B3
Hurstville *Australia* 33°57S 151°6E **139** B1
Hurtsboro *U.S.A.* 32°15N 85°25W **316** C4
Hurungwe ⌂ *Zimbabwe* 16°7S 29°5E **269** F2
Hurunui → *N.Z.* 42°54S 173°18E **285** C8
Hurup *Denmark* 56°46N 8°25E **163** H2
Húsafell *Iceland* 64°42N 20°53W **155** C6
Husan *West Bank* 31°42N 35°8E **123** B1
Húsavík *Iceland* 66°3N 17°21W **155** A9
Husby *Sweden* 59°24N 17°56E **139** A1
Huşi *Romania* 46°41N 28°7E **183** D13
Huskisson *Australia* 35°2S 150°41E **283** C9
Huskvarna *Sweden* 57°47N 14°15E **163** G8
Huslia *U.S.A.* 65°41N 156°24W **303** D8
Husnes *Norway* 59°52N 5°45E **164** E2
Hustad *Norway* 62°57N 7°6E **164** B4
Hustadvika *Norway* 63°0N 7°0E **164** A3
Hustontown *U.S.A.* 40°3N 78°2W **312** F6
Hustopeče *Czechia* 48°57N 16°43E **181** C9
Husum *København, Denmark* 55°42N 12°27E **118** A2
Husum *Schleswig-Holstein, Germany* 54°28N 9°4E **178** A5
Husum *Sweden* 63°21N 19°12E **162** A13
Huszt = Khust *Ukraine* 48°10N 23°18E **183** B8
Hutanopan *Indonesia* 0°40N 99°42E **234** B1
Hutchins *U.S.A.* 32°38N 96°42W **120** C5
Hutchinson *Kans., U.S.A.* 38°5N 97°56W **308** F5
Hutchinson *Minn., U.S.A.* 44°54N 94°22W **308** C6
Ḩūth *Yemen* 16°14N 43°58E **248** C3
Hutiao Xia *China* 27°13N 100°9E **228** D3
Hutjena *Papua N. G.* 5°23S 154°42E **286** C8
Hutsonville *U.S.A.* 39°7N 87°40W **311** E9
Hutte Sauvage, L. de la *Canada* 56°15N 64°45W **299** A7
Hütteldorf *Austria* 48°12N 16°15E **142** A1
Hüttenberg *Austria* 46°56N 14°33E **180** E7
Hüttener Berge ⌂ *Germany* 54°24N 9°40E **178** A5
Hutton, Mt. *Australia* 25°51S 148°20E **281** D4
Huvadu Atoll *Maldives* 0°30N 73°15E **272** d
Hűvösvölgy *Hungary* 47°32N 19°0E **117** A2
Huwaki *Indonesia* 7°55S 126°30E **231** F7
Huwei *Taiwan* 23°42N 120°26E **225** C2
Huwei Hsi → *Taiwan* 23°37N 120°22E **225** C2
Huwon Secret Garden *S. Korea* 37°34N 126°59E **137** B1
Huwun *Ethiopia* 4°23N 40°6E **257** G5
Huy *Belgium* 50°31N 5°15E **170** D5
Huzhou *China* 30°51N 120°8E **229** B13
Huzurabad *India* 18°12N 79°25E **244** E4
Huzurnagar *India* 16°54N 79°53E **244** F4
Hvalfjörður *Iceland* 64°20N 21°40W **155** C5
Hvalpsund *Denmark* 56°42N 9°11E **163** H3
Hvalstad *Norway* 59°51N 10°27E **133** A1
Hvalstrand *Norway* 59°50N 10°30E **133** A2
Hvammsfjörður *Iceland* 65°4N 22°5W **155** B4
Hvammstangi *Iceland* 65°24N 20°57W **155** B6
Hvammur *Norðurland Vestra, Iceland* 65°53N 19°51W **155** B7
Hvammur *Vesturland, Iceland* 64°50N 21°21W **155** C5
Hvannadalshnúkur *Iceland* 64°1N 16°41W **155** C10
Hvanneyri *Iceland* 64°34N 21°36W **155** C5
Hvar *Croatia* 43°11N 16°28E **199** E13
Hvarski Kanal *Croatia* 43°15N 16°35E **199** E13
Hveragerði *Iceland* 64°0N 21°12W **155** C5
Hvidovre *Denmark* 55°38N 12°27E **118** B2
Hvítá → *Iceland* 64°30N 21°58W **155** C5
Hvítárvatn *Iceland* 64°37N 19°50W **155** C7
Hvittingfoss *Norway* 59°29N 10°0E **164** E7
Hvizdets *Ukraine* 48°35N 25°17E **183** B10
Hvolsvöllur *Iceland* 63°45N 20°14W **155** D6
Hwacheon-Cheosuji *S. Korea* 38°5N 127°50E **224** C3
Hwagok *S. Korea* 37°32N 126°51E **137** B1
Hwainan = Huainan *China* 32°38N 116°58E **229** A11
Hwaiyin = Huaiyin *China* 33°30N 119°2E **227** H10
Hwang Ho = Huang He → *China* 37°55N 118°50E **227** F10
Hwange *Zimbabwe* 18°18S 26°30E **269** F2
Hwange △ *Zimbabwe* 19°0S 26°30E **270** A4
Hwanghaebuk-do □ *N. Korea* 38°30N 126°25E **224** C3
Hwanghaenam-do □ *N. Korea* 38°15N 125°30E **224** C2
Hwangju *N. Korea* 38°40N 125°46E **224** C2
Hwangshih = Huangshi *China* 30°10N 115°3E **229** B10
Hwaseong *S. Korea* 37°12N 126°48E **224** D3
Hwasun *S. Korea* 35°3N 126°59E **224** E3
Hwekum *Myanmar* 26°7N 95°22E **241** B5
Hwlffordd = Haverfordwest *U.K.* 51°48N 4°58W **169** F3
Hyaing *Myanmar* 22°39N 94°44E **241** D5
Hyannis *Mass., U.S.A.* 41°39N 70°17W **309** E18
Hyannis *Nebr., U.S.A.* 42°0N 101°46W **308** E3
Hyargas Nuur *Mongolia* 49°0N 93°0E **217** C12
Hyattsville *U.S.A.* 38°57N 76°57W **143** B3
Hybo *Sweden* 61°49N 16°15E **162** C10
Hydaburg *U.S.A.* 55°15N 132°50W **296** B2
Hyde *N.Z.* 45°18S 170°16E **285** F5
Hyde Park *Sydney, Australia* **139** b2
Hyde Park *Guyana* 6°30N 58°16W **329** B6
Hyde Park *Gauteng, S. Africa* 26°6S 28°2E **123** A2
Hyde Park *London, U.K.* 51°30N 0°10W **125** A2
Hyde Park *Calif., U.S.A.* 33°58N 118°19W **126** C3
Hyde Park *Ill., U.S.A.* 41°47N 87°35W **119** C3
Hyde Park *Mass., U.S.A.* 42°15N 71°7W **116** B2
Hyde Park *N.Y., U.S.A.* 41°47N 73°56W **313** E11
Hyden *Australia* 32°24S 118°53E **279** F2
Hyder *U.S.A.* 55°55N 130°5W **296** B2
Hyderabad *India* 17°22N 78°29E **244** F4
Hyderabad *Pakistan* 25°23N 68°24E **242** G3
Hydra *Greece* 37°20N 23°28E **204** D5
Hyen *Norway* 61°44N 5°56E **164** C2
Hyères *France* 43°8N 6°9E **175** E10
Hyères, Îs. d' *France* 43°0N 6°20E **175** F10
Hyesan *N. Korea* 41°20N 128°10E **224** B4
Hyland → *Canada* 59°52N 128°12W **296** B3
Hylestad *Norway* 59°6N 7°29E **164** E4
Hyllestad *Norway* 61°10N 5°17E **164** C2
Hyltebruk *Sweden* 56°59N 13°15E **163** H7
Hyndman Peak *U.S.A.* 43°45N 114°8W **304** E6
Hynnekleiv *Norway* 58°36N 8°25E **164** F5
Hyōgo □ *Japan* 35°15N 134°50E **222** B6
Hyrra Banda *C.A.R.* 5°58N 22°4E **264** A4
Hyrum *U.S.A.* 41°38N 111°51W **304** F8
Hysham *U.S.A.* 46°18N 107°14W **304** C10
Hythe *U.K.* 51°4N 1°5E **169** F9
Hyūga *Japan* 32°25N 131°35E **222** E3
Hyvinge = Hyvinkää *Finland* 60°38N 24°50E **188** B3
Hyvinkää *Finland* 60°38N 24°50E **188** B3

I

I-n-Akhmed *Mali* 19°49N 0°56W **261** E4
I-n-Azaoua *Illizi, Algeria* 25°42N 6°54E **261** C6
I-n-Azaoua *Tamanrasset, Algeria* 20°46N 7°32E **261** D6
I-n-Échaï *Mali* 20°10N 2°5W **260** D4
I-n-Ezzane *Algeria* 23°29N 11°15E **261** D7
I-n-Gall *Niger* 16°51N 7°1E **263** B6
I-n-Kelemet *Algeria* 26°57N 5°47E **261** C6
I-n-Oudad *Algeria* 20°17N 4°38E **261** D5
I-n-Ouzzal *Algeria* 20°41N 2°34E **261** D5
I-n-Tadreft *Niger* 19°5N 6°38E **263** B6
Iabès, Erg *Algeria* 27°30N 2°2W **261** C4
Iablaniţa *Romania* 44°57N 22°19E **182** F7
Iaco → *Brazil* 9°3S 68°34W **330** B4
Iacobeni *Romania* 47°25N 25°20E **183** C10
Iaçu *Brazil* 12°45S 40°13W **333** D3
Iakora *Madag.* 23°6S 46°40E **272** C2
Ialibu *Papua N. G.* 6°17S 143°59E **286** D2
Ialissos *Greece* 36°24N 28°10E **206** E12
Ialomiţa □ *Romania* 44°30N 27°30E **183** F12
Ialomiţa → *Romania* 44°42N 27°51E **183** F12
Ialoveni *Moldova* 46°56N 28°47E **183** D13
Ialpug → *Moldova* 45°41N 28°35E **183** E13
Iamonia, L. *U.S.A.* 30°38N 84°14W **316** E5
Ianca *Romania* 45°6N 27°29E **183** E12
Iara *Romania* 46°31N 23°35E **183** D8
Iarda *Ethiopia* 11°9N 35°53E **257** E4
Iargara *Moldova* 46°24N 28°23E **183** D13
Iaşi *Romania* 47°10N 27°40E **183** C12
Iaşi □ *Romania* 47°20N 27°0E **183** C12
Iasmos *Greece* 41°8N 25°11E **203** E9
Iauaretê *Colombia* 0°36N 69°12W **328** C4
Ib → *India* 21°34N 83°48E **243** J10
Iba *Phil.* 15°22N 120°0E **232** D2
Ibadan *Nigeria* 7°22N 3°58E **263** D5
Ibagué *Colombia* 4°20N 75°20W **328** C2
Ibaiti *Brazil* 23°50S 50°10W **333** F1
Ibajay *Phil.* 11°49N 122°10E **233** F4
Iballë *Albania* 42°12N 20°2E **202** D4
Ibăneşti *Botoşani, Romania* 48°4N 26°22E **183** B11
Ibăneşti *Mureş, Romania* 46°45N 24°57E **183** D9
Ibanshe *Dem. Rep. of the Congo* 4°58S 21°30E **265** C4
Ibar → *Serbia* 43°43N 20°45E **202** C4
Ibara *Japan* 34°36N 133°28E **222** C5
Ibaraki *Ibaraki, Japan* 36°20N 140°30E **223** A12
Ibaraki *Ōsaka, Japan* 34°49N 135°34E **223** C7
Ibaraki □ *Japan* 36°10N 140°10E **223** A12
Ibarra *Ecuador* 0°21N 78°7W **328** C2
Ibb *Yemen* 14°2N 44°10E **248** D4
Ibb □ *Yemen* 14°2N 44°10E **248** D4
Ibba *South Sudan* 4°49N 29°2E **257** G2
Ibba, Bahr el → *South Sudan* 5°30N 28°55E **257** F2
Ibbenbüren *Germany* 52°16N 7°43E **178** C3
Ibeke Gembo *Dem. Rep. of the Congo* 1°24S 18°51E **264** C3
Ibembo *Dem. Rep. of the Congo* 2°35N 23°35E **264** B4
Ibenga → *Congo* 2°19N 18°9E **264** B3
Ibera, L. *Argentina* 28°30S 57°9W **334** B4
Iberia *Peru* 11°21S 69°35W **330** C4
Iberia *Mo., U.S.A.* 38°5N 92°18W **310** F4
Iberian Peninsula *Europe* 40°0N 5°0W **158** H5
Iberville *Canada* 45°19N 73°17W **313** A11
Iberville, Mt. d' *Canada* 58°50N 63°50W **295** F19
Ibese *Nigeria* 6°33N 3°28E **124** A2
Ibeto *Nigeria* 10°29N 5°8E **263** C6
Ibi *Nigeria* 8°15N 9°44E **263** D6
Ibi *Spain* 38°38N 0°34W **197** G4
Ibiá *Brazil* 19°30S 46°30W **333** E2
Ibiapaba, Sa. da *Brazil* 4°0S 41°30W **332** B3
Ibicaraí *Brazil* 14°51S 39°36W **333** D4
Ibicuí *Brazil* 14°51S 39°59W **333** D4
Ibicuí → *Brazil* 29°25S 56°47W **335** B4
Ibicuy *Argentina* 33°55S 59°10W **334** C4
Ibirapuera *Brazil* 23°36S 46°40W **137** B1
Ibirapuera, Parque do *Brazil* 23°35S 46°38W **137** B2
Ibitiara *Brazil* 12°39S 42°13W **333** D3
Ibiza = Eivissa *Spain* 38°54N 1°26E **206** D1
Ibiza ✕ (IBZ) *Spain* 38°53N 1°22E **197** G6
Íblei, Monti *Italy* 37°15N 14°45E **201** E7
Ibn Hāni', Ra's *Syria* 35°35N 35°43E **250** C6
Ibo *Mozam.* 12°22S 40°40E **269** E5
Ibonma *Indonesia* 3°29S 133°31E **231** E8
Ibotirama *Brazil* 12°13S 43°12W **333** D3
Iboundji *Gabon* 1°0S 11°51E **264** C2
Ibrā' *Oman* 22°41N 58°33E **249** B7
İbradı *Turkey* 37°4N 31°35E **250** A2
Ibrāhīm → *Lebanon* 34°4N 35°38E **250** D6
'Ibrī *Oman* 23°14N 56°30E **249** B7
İbriktepe *Turkey* 41°0N 26°30E **203** E10
Ibshawâi *Egypt* 29°21N 30°40E **256** J7
Ibu *Indonesia* 1°35N 127°33E **231** D7
Ibuki-Sanchi *Japan* 35°25N 136°18E **223** B8
Ibusuki *Japan* 31°12N 130°40E **222** F2
Ica *Peru* 14°0S 75°48W **330** C2
Ica □ *Peru* 14°20S 75°30W **330** C2
Iça → *Brazil* 2°55S 67°58W **330** A4
Icabarú *Venezuela* 4°20N 61°45W **329** C5
Icabarú → *Venezuela* 4°45N 62°15W **329** C5
Icacos *Trin. & Tob.* 10°3N 61°54W **323** t
Icacos Pt. *Trin. & Tob.* 10°3N 61°57W **323** t
Içana *Brazil* 0°21N 67°19W **328** C4
Içana → *Brazil* 0°26N 67°19W **328** C4
Icarai *Brazil* 22°54S 43°6W **135** B2
Icatu *Brazil* 2°46S 44°4W **332** B3
Icaturama = Santa Rosa de Viterbo *Colombia* 5°53N 72°59W **328** B3
İçel = Mersin *Turkey* 36°51N 34°36E **250** B5
Iceland ■ *Europe* 64°45N 19°0W **155** C8
Iceland Basin *Atl. Oc.* 61°0N 19°0W **150** C7
Icelandic Plateau *Arctic* 64°0N 10°0W **150** C7
Içerenköy *Turkey* 40°58N 29°6E **122** C2
İçeriçumra *Turkey* 37°34N 32°39E **212** D5
Ichalkaranji *India* 16°40N 74°33E **244** F2
Ich'ang = Yichang *China* 30°40N 111°20E **229** B8
Ichchapuram *India* 19°10N 84°40E **244** E7
Icheon *S. Korea* 37°17N 127°27E **224** D3
Ichgao *Japan* 35°32N 139°32E **140** B2
Ichhawar *India* 23°1N 77°1E **242** H7
Ichigat Muja-Cordillera del Condor ⌂ *Peru* 4°20S 77°30W **330** A2
Ichigaya *Tokyo, Japan* **140** a3
Ichihara *Japan* 35°28N 140°5E **223** B12
Ichikawa *Japan* 35°43N 139°54E **140** A4
Ichilo → *Bolivia* 15°57S 64°50W **331** D5
Ichinohe *Japan* 40°13N 141°17E **220** D10
Ichinomiya *Gifu, Japan* 35°18N 136°48E **223** B8
Ichinomiya *Kumamoto, Japan* 32°58N 131°5E **222** E3
Ichinoseki *Japan* 38°55N 141°8E **220** E10
Ichkeul △ *Tunisia* 37°5N 9°37E **258** A1
Ichnya *Ukraine* 50°52N 32°24E **189** G7
Icht *Morocco* 29°6N 8°54W **260** C3
Ichu *Taiwan* 23°20N 120°14E **225** C2
Ichun = Yichun *China* 47°44N 128°52E **219** B14
Ickenham *U.K.* 51°33N 0°26W **125** A1
Icó *Brazil* 6°24S 38°51W **332** C4
Icoca *Angola* 6°12S 16°20E **265** D3
Icod *Canary Is.* 28°22N 16°43W **153** e1
Içoguz *Turkmenistan* 40°11N 58°24E **216** D5
Iconi *Comoros Is.* 12°21S 43°51E **272** a
Icy C. *U.S.A.* 70°20N 161°52W **303** A7
Ida Grove *U.S.A.* 42°21N 95°28W **308** D6
Idaan *Somalia* 6°10N 48°55E **267** C6
Idabel *U.S.A.* 33°54N 94°50W **314** E7
Idaga Hamus *Ethiopia* 14°13N 39°48E **257** E4
Idah *Nigeria* 7°5N 6°40E **263** D6
Idaho □ *U.S.A.* 45°0N 115°0W **304** D6
Idaho City *U.S.A.* 43°50N 115°50W **304** E6
Idaho Falls *U.S.A.* 43°30N 112°2W **304** E7
Idalia △ *Australia* 24°49S 144°36E **280** C3
Idanha-a-Nova *Portugal* 39°50N 7°15W **194** F3
Idar-Oberstein *Germany* 49°43N 7°16E **179** F3
Iday *Niger* 14°54N 11°33E **259** F2
'Idd el Ghanam *Sudan* 11°30N 24°19E **259** F4
Iddo *Nigeria* 6°28N 3°22E **124** B2
Idelès *Algeria* 23°50N 5°53E **261** D6
Idensalmi = Iisalmi *Finland* 63°32N 27°10E **160** E22
Idfû *Egypt* 24°55N 32°49E **256** C3
Idi *Indonesia* 5°2N 97°37E **234** A1
Idi, Oros = Psiloritis, Oros *Greece* 35°15N 24°45E **207** E5
Idi Amin Dada, L. = Edward, L. *Africa* 0°25S 29°40E **268** C2
Idi-Oro *Nigeria* 6°31N 3°21E **124** A2
İdil *Turkey* 37°20N 41°53E **213** D9
Idiofa *Dem. Rep. of the Congo* 4°55S 19°42E **265** C3
Idjil = Fdérik *Mauritania* 22°40N 12°45W **260** D2
Idkerberget *Sweden* 60°22N 15°15E **162** D9
Idku *Egypt* 31°18N 30°17E **256** H7
Idku, Bahra el *Egypt* 31°18N 30°18E **256** H7
Idlib *Syria* 35°55N 36°36E **250** C7
Idlib □ *Syria* 35°45N 36°45E **250** C7
Idomeni *Greece* 41°7N 22°31E **202** E6
Idra = Hydra *Greece* 37°20N 23°28E **204** D5
Idre *Sweden* 61°52N 12°42E **162** C6
Idria *U.S.A.* 36°25N 120°41W **306** J6
Idrija *Slovenia* 46°0N 14°5E **199** C11
Idritsa *Russia* 56°17N 28°53E **188** D5
Idutywa = Dutywa *S. Africa* 32°8S 28°18E **271** D4
Ie Shima *Japan* 26°43N 127°48E **288** a
Ie Suido *Japan* 26°42N 127°51E **288** a
Ieper *Belgium* 50°51N 2°53E **170** D2
Ierapetra *Greece* 35°1N 25°44E **207** F6
Ierissos *Greece* 40°22N 23°52E **202** F7
Ierissos Kolpos *Greece* 40°27N 23°57E **202** F7
Iernut *Romania* 46°27N 24°15E **183** D9
Ieshima-Shotō *Japan* 34°40N 134°32E **222** C6
Iesi *Italy* 43°31N 13°14E **199** E10
Iet *Ethiopia* 4°33N 43°1E **267** D5
Ifac, Penyal d' *Spain* 38°38N 0°5E **197** G5
'Ifāl, W. al → *Si. Arabia* 28°7N 35°3E **251** K6
Ifanadiana *Madag.* 21°19S 47°39E **272** C2
Ife *Nigeria* 7°30N 4°31E **263** D5
Iférouâne *Niger* 19°5N 8°24E **259** E1
Ifetesene *Algeria* 25°30N 4°33E **261** C5
Iffley *Australia* 18°53S 141°12E **280** B3
Ifon *Nigeria* 6°58N 5°40E **263** D6
Iforas, Adrar des *Africa* 19°40N 1°40E **261** D5
Ifould, L. *Australia* 30°52S 132°6E **279** F5
Ifrane *Morocco* 33°33N 5°7W **260** B3
Ifugao □ *Phil.* 16°40N 121°10E **232** C3
Iga *Japan* 34°45N 136°10E **223** C8
Igalo *Montenegro* 42°28N 18°30E **202** D2
Iganga *Uganda* 0°37N 33°28E **268** B3
Iganmu *Nigeria* 6°28N 3°22E **124** B2
Igara-Paraná → *Colombia* 2°9S 71°47W **328** D3
Igarapava *Brazil* 20°3S 47°47W **333** F2
Igarapé-Açu *Brazil* 1°4S 47°33W **332** B2
Igarapé-Miri *Brazil* 1°59S 48°58W **332** B2
Igarka *Russia* 67°30N 86°33E **214** C9
Igatpuri *India* 19°40N 73°35E **244** E1
Igbetti *Nigeria* 8°44N 4°8E **263** D5
Igbo-Ora *Nigeria* 7°29N 3°15E **263** D5
Igbobi *Nigeria* 6°31N 3°22E **124** A2
Igboho *Nigeria* 8°53N 3°50E **263** D5
Igbologun *Nigeria* 6°24N 3°19E **124** B1
Igbor *Nigeria* 7°27N 8°34E **263** D6
Iğdır *Turkey* 39°55N 44°2E **213** C11
Igelfors *Sweden* 58°52N 15°41E **163** F9
Iggesund *Sweden* 61°39N 17°10E **162** C11
Ighil Izane = Relizane *Algeria* 35°44N 0°31E **261** A5
Igiugig *U.S.A.* 59°20N 155°55W **303** G9
Iglau = Jihlava *Czechia* 49°28N 15°35E **180** B8
Iglésias *Italy* 39°19N 8°32E **200** C1
Igli *Algeria* 30°25N 2°19W **261** B4
Igloolik = Iglulik *Canada* 69°20N 81°49W **295** D15
Igluligaarjuk = Chesterfield Inlet *Canada* 63°30N 90°45W **294** E13
Iglulik *Canada* 69°20N 81°49W **295** D15
'Igma, G. el *Egypt* 29°10N 34°0E **251** J5
Ignace *Canada* 49°30N 91°40W **298** C1
İğneada *Turkey* 41°52N 27°59E **203** E11
İğneada Burnu *Turkey* 41°53N 28°2E **203** E12
Igny *France* 48°44N 2°13E **134** B2
Igoumenitsa *Greece* 39°32N 20°18E **206** B10
Igrim *Russia* 63°12N 64°30E **214** C7
Iguaçu → *Brazil* 25°36S 54°36W **335** B5
Iguaçu, Cat. del *Brazil* 25°41S 54°26W **335** B5
Iguaçu △ *Brazil* 25°30S 54°0W **335** B5
Iguaçu Falls = Iguaçu, Cat. del *Brazil* 25°41S 54°26W **335** B5
Iguala *Mexico* 18°21N 99°32W **319** D5
Igualada *Spain* 41°37N 1°37E **196** D6
Iguape *Brazil* 24°43S 47°33W **333** F2
Iguaratinga = São Francisco do Maranhão *Brazil* 6°15S 42°52W **332** C3
Iguassu = Iguaçu → *Brazil* 25°36S 54°36W **335** B5
Iguatu *Brazil* 6°20S 39°18W **332** C4
Iguazú △ *Argentina* 25°42S 54°22W **335** B5
Iguéla *Gabon* 2°0S 9°16E **264** C1
Iguéla, Lagune *Gabon* 1°48S 9°16E **264** C2
Iguidi, Erg *Africa* 27°0N 6°0W **260** C3
Iguig *Phil.* 17°45N 121°44E **232** C3
Igumen = Cherven *Belarus* 53°45N 28°28E **177** B15
Iharana *Madag.* 13°25S 50°0E **272** A3
Ihavandiffulu Atoll *Maldives* 7°0N 72°50E **272** d
Ihbulag *Mongolia* 43°11N 107°10E **226** C4
Iheya-Shima *Japan* 27°4N 127°58E **221** L3
Ihiala *Nigeria* 5°51N 6°55E **263** D6
Ihirene, O. → *Algeria* 20°28N 4°37E **261** D5
Ihorombe □ *Madag.* 22°25S 46°10E **272** C2
Ihosy *Madag.* 22°24S 46°8E **272** C2
Ihotry, Farihy *Madag.* 21°56S 43°41E **272** C1
Ihu *Papua N. G.* 7°55S 145°24E **286** D3
Ihugh *Nigeria* 7°2N 9°0E **263** D6
Ii *Finland* 65°19N 25°22E **160** D21
Ii-Shima *Japan* 26°43N 127°47E **221** L3
Iida *Japan* 35°35N 137°50E **223** B9
Iijoki → *Finland* 65°20N 25°20E **160** D21
Iisalmi *Finland* 63°32N 27°10E **160** E22
Iiyama *Japan* 36°51N 138°22E **221** F9
Iizuka *Japan* 33°38N 130°42E **222** D2
IJ, Het → *Neths.* 52°23N 4°54E **112** A2
IJ-meer *Neths.* 52°23N 4°54E **112** A3
Ijâfene *Mauritania* 20°40N 8°0W **260** D3
IJburg *Neths.* 52°22N 5°0E **112** A3
Ijebu-Igbo *Nigeria* 6°56N 4°1E **263** D5
Ijebu-Ode *Nigeria* 6°47N 3°58E **263** D5
Ijesa-Tedo *Nigeria* 6°29N 3°19E **124** B1
Ijevan *Armenia* 40°52N 45°8E **191** K7
Ijill, Sebkhet *Mauritania* 22°47N 12°53W **260** D2
IJmuiden *Neths.* 52°28N 4°35E **170** B4
Ijo älv = Iijoki → *Finland* 65°20N 25°20E **160** D21
Ijora *Nigeria* 6°27N 3°22E **124** B2

INDEX
Nares Str. 405

Mussomeli *Italy* 37°35N 13°45E **200** E6
Mussoorie *India* 30°27N 78°6E **242** D8
Mussuco *Angola* 17°2S 19°3E **265** F3
Mustafakemalpaşa *Turkey* 40°2N 28°24E **203** F12
Mustahil *Ethiopia* 5°16N 44°45E **267** C5
Mustang *Nepal* 29°10N 83°55E **243** E10
Mustansiriya *Iraq* 33°22N 44°24E **113** A2
Musters, L. *Argentina* 45°20S 69°25W **336** C3
Mustique I. *St. Vincent* 12°52N 61°11W **323** n
Musturud *Egypt* 30°8N 31°17E **117** A2
Musudan *N. Korea* 40°50N 129°43E **224** B4
Muswell Hill *U.K.* 51°35N 0°8W **125** A3
Muswellbrook *Australia* 32°16S 150°56E **283** B9
Muszyna *Poland* 49°22N 20°55E **185** J7
Mût *Egypt* 25°28N 28°58E **256** B2
Mut *Turkey* 36°40N 33°28E **250** B4
Mutalau *Cook Is.* 18°56S 169°50W **289** g
Mutanabi *Iraq* 33°19N 44°21E **113** B2
Mutanda *Dem. Rep. of the Congo* 5°17S 16°34E **265** D3
Mutanda *Mozam.* 21°0S 33°34E **271** B5
Mutanda *Zambia* 12°24S 26°13E **269** E2
Mutankiang = Mudanjiang *China* 44°38N 129°30E **227** B15
Mutanshe *Taiwan* 22°9N 120°48E **225** D2
Mutare *Zimbabwe* 18°58S 32°38E **269** F3
Mutawintji △ *Australia* 31°10S 142°30E **281** E3
Mutha *Kenya* 1°48S 38°26E **268** C4
Muthana *Iraq* 33°19N 44°27E **113** B2
Muting *Indonesia* 7°23S 140°20E **231** F10
Mutirikwe Dam *Zimbabwe* 20°15S 31°0E **269** G3
Mutki = Mirtağ *Turkey* 38°23N 41°56E **246** B4
Mutoko *Zimbabwe* 17°24S 32°13E **271** A5
Mutomo *Kenya* 1°51S 38°12E **268** C4
Mutoray *Russia* 60°56N 101°0E **215** C11
Mutoto *Dem. Rep. of the Congo* 5°42S 22°42E **265** D4
Mutoxo *Angola* 12°17S 21°40E **265** E4
Mutsamudu *Comoros Is.* 12°10S 44°25E **272** a
Mutshatsha *Dem. Rep. of the Congo* 10°35S 24°20E **265** E4
Mutsu *Japan* 41°5N 140°55E **220** D10
Mutsu-Wan *Japan* 41°5N 140°55E **220** D10
Muttaburra *Australia* 22°38S 144°29E **280** C3
Muttalip *Turkey* 39°50N 30°32E **205** B12
Mutton I. *Ireland* 52°49N 9°32W **166** D2
Muttra = Mathura *India* 27°30N 77°40E **242** F7
Muttukuru *India* 14°16N 80°6E **245** G5
Mutuáli *Mozam.* 14°55S 37°0E **269** E4
Mutum Biyu *Nigeria* 8°40N 10°50E **263** D7
Mutumba *Burundi* 3°25S 29°21E **268** C2
Mutunópolis *Brazil* 13°40S 49°15W **333** D2
Mutur *Sri Lanka* 8°27N 81°16E **245** K5
Muweilih *Egypt* 30°42N 34°19E **251** H5
Muxaluando *Angola* 8°8S 14°18E **265** D2
Muxia *Spain* 43°3N 9°10W **194** B1
Muxima *Angola* 9°33S 13°58E **265** D2
Muy Muy *Nic.* 12°39N 85°36W **320** D2
Muyinga *Burundi* 3°14S 30°33E **268** C3
Mŭynoq *Uzbekistan* 43°44N 59°10E **216** D5
Muyua = Woodlark I. *Papua N. G.* 9°10S 152°50E **286** E7
Muyunkum, Peski = Moyynqum *Kazakhstan* 44°12N 71°0E **217** D8
Muz Tag *China* 36°25N 87°25E **217** E11
Muzaffarabad *Pakistan* 34°25N 73°30E **243** B5
Muzaffargarh *Pakistan* 30°5N 71°14E **242** D4
Muzaffarnagar *India* 29°26N 77°40E **242** E7
Muzaffarpur *India* 26°7N 85°23E **243** F11
Muzafirpur *Pakistan* 30°58N 69°9E **242** D3
Mużakowski, Park = Muskauer Park *Europe* 51°34N 14°43E **178** D10
Muzeze *Angola* 15°3S 17°43E **265** F3
Muzhi *Russia* 65°25N 64°40E **186** A11
Muzillac *France* 47°35N 2°30W **172** E4
Muzon, C. *U.S.A.* 54°40N 132°42W **303** J14
Muztagh-Ata *China* 38°17N 75°7E **217** E9
Muztor = Toktogul *Kyrgyzstan* 41°50N 72°50E **217** D8
Muzūra *Egypt* 28°53N 30°48E **256** J7
Mvadhi-Ousyé *Gabon* 1°13N 13°12E **264** B2
Mvam *Gabon* 0°13S 9°39E **264** C1
Mvangan *Cameroon* 2°17N 11°43E **264** B2
Mvolo *South Sudan* 6°2N 29°53E **257** F2
Mvuma *Zimbabwe* 19°16S 30°30E **269** F3
Mvurwi *Zimbabwe* 17°0S 30°57E **269** F3
Mwabvi ⌓ *Malawi* 16°42S 35°0E **269** F4
Mwadi-Kalumbu *Dem. Rep. of the Congo* 7°53S 18°43E **265** D3
Mwadui *Tanzania* 3°26S 33°32E **268** C3
Mwali = Mohéli *Comoros Is.* 12°20S 43°40E **272** a
Mwambo *Tanzania* 10°30S 40°22E **269** E5
Mwandi *Zambia* 17°30S 24°51E **269** F1
Mwanza *Katanga, Dem. Rep. of the Congo* 7°55S 26°43E **265** D5
Mwanza *Tanzania* 2°30S 32°58E **268** C3
Mwanza *Zambia* 16°58S 24°28E **265** F4
Mwanza □ *Tanzania* 2°0S 33°0E **268** C3
Mwaya *Tanzania* 9°32S 33°55E **269** D3
Mweelrea *Ireland* 53°39N 9°49W **166** C2
Mweka *Dem. Rep. of the Congo* 4°50S 21°34E **265** C4
Mwendjila *Dem. Rep. of the Congo* 7°12S 18°51E **265** D3
Mwene-Ditu *Dem. Rep. of the Congo* 6°35S 22°27E **265** D4
Mwenezi *Zimbabwe* 21°15S 30°48E **269** G3
Mwenezi ➜ *Mozam.* 22°40S 31°50E **269** G3
Mwenga *Dem. Rep. of the Congo* 3°1S 28°28E **268** C2
Mweru, L. *Zambia* 9°0S 28°40E **269** D2
Mweru Wantipa △ *Zambia* 8°39S 29°25E **269** D2
Mwetshi *Dem. Rep. of the Congo* 4°50S 22°38E **265** C4
Mweza Range *Zimbabwe* 21°0S 30°0E **269** G3
Mwilambwe *Dem. Rep. of the Congo* 8°7S 25°5E **265** D5
Mwimbi *Tanzania* 8°38S 31°39E **269** D3
Mwingi *Kenya* 0°56S 38°4E **268** C4
Mwinilunga *Zambia* 11°43S 24°25E **265** E4
My Son *Vietnam* 15°48N 108°7E **236** E7
My Tho *Vietnam* 10°29N 106°23E **237** G6
Mya, O. ➜ *Algeria* 30°46N 4°54E **261** B5
Myajlar *India* 26°15N 70°20E **242** F4
Myakka ➜ *U.S.A.* 26°56N 82°11W **317** J7
Myall Lakes △ *Australia* 32°25S 152°30E **283** B10
Myanaung *Myanmar* 18°18N 95°22E **241** F5
Myanmar ■ *Asia* 21°0N 96°30E **241** E6
Myaung *Myanmar* 21°50N 95°25E **241** E5
Myaungmya *Myanmar* 16°30N 94°40E **241** G5
Mycenæ = Mykenes *Greece* 37°43N 22°46E **204** D4
Myebon *Myanmar* 20°3N 93°22E **241** E4
Myedna *Belarus* 51°52N 23°42E **185** G10
Myeik = Mergui *Myanmar* 12°26N 98°34E **236** F2
Myeik Kyunzu *Myanmar* 11°30N 97°30E **237** G1
Myerstown *U.S.A.* 40°22N 76°19W **313** F8
Myingyan *Myanmar* 21°30N 95°20E **241** E5
Myitkyina *Myanmar* 25°24N 97°26E **241** C6
Myitson *Myanmar* 23°16N 96°34E **241** D6
Myittha *Myanmar* 21°21N 96°6E **241** E6
Myittha ➜ *Myanmar* 23°12N 94°17E **241** D5
Myjava *Slovakia* 48°41N 17°37E **181** C10
Mykenes *Greece* 37°43N 22°46E **204** D4
Mykhaylivka *Ukraine* 47°12N 35°15E **189** J8
Mykines *Færoe Is.* 62°7N 7°35W **160** E9
Myking *Norway* 60°41N 5°19E **164** D2
Mykolayiv *Ukraine* 46°58N 32°0E **189** J7
Mykolayiv □ *Ukraine* 47°20N 31°50E **189** J6
Mykonos *Greece* 37°30N 25°25E **205** D7
Mylius Erichsen Land *Greenland* 81°30N 27°0W **154** A8
Myllypuro *Finland* 60°13N 25°3E **121** B3
Mymensingh *Bangla.* 24°45N 90°24E **241** C3
Mymensingh □ *Bangla.* 24°50N 90°30E **241** C3
Mynydd Du *U.K.* 51°52N 3°50W **169** F4
Myo-gyi *Myanmar* 21°27N 96°22E **241** E6
Myohaung *Myanmar* 20°35N 93°11E **241** E4
Myohla *Myanmar* 19°16N 95°25E **241** F5
Myotha *Myanmar* 21°41N 95°43E **241** E5
Myothit *Kachin, Myanmar* 24°24N 97°24E **241** C6
Myothit *Magway, Myanmar* 20°12N 95°27E **241** E5
Myrasýsla *Iceland* 64°45N 21°30W **155** C5
Mýrdalsjökull *Iceland* 63°40N 19°6W **155** D7
Myrhorod *Ukraine* 49°58N 33°37E **189** H7
Mýri *Iceland* 65°23N 17°23W **155** B9
Myrina *Greece* 39°53N 25°4E **205** B7
Myrtle Beach *U.S.A.* 33°42N 78°53W **315** E15
Myrtle Creek *U.S.A.* 43°1N 123°17W **304** E2
Myrtle Grove *U.S.A.* 30°23N 87°17W **317** E2
Myrtle Point *U.S.A.* 43°4N 124°8W **304** E1
Myrtleford *Australia* 36°34S 146°44E **283** D7
Myrtoan Sea = Mirtoo Sea *Greece* 37°0N 23°20E **204** D5
Myrtou *Cyprus* 35°18N 33°4E **207** E9
Myrviken *Sweden* 62°58N 14°20E **162** B8
Mysen *Norway* 59°33N 11°20E **164** E8
Mysia *Turkey* 39°50N 27°0E **203** G11
Myślenice *Poland* 49°51N 19°57E **185** J6
Myślibórz *Poland* 52°55N 14°50E **185** F1
Mysłowice *Poland* 50°15N 19°12E **185** H6
Myslowitz = Mysłowice *Poland* 50°15N 19°12E **185** H6
Mysore = Karnataka □ *India* 13°15N 77°0E **245** H3
Mysore = Mysuru *India* 12°17N 76°41E **245** H3
Mystic *Conn., U.S.A.* 41°21N 71°58W **313** E13
Mystic *Iowa, U.S.A.* 40°47N 92°57W **310** D4
Mystic ➜ *U.S.A.* 42°22N 71°3W **116** A2
Mystras *Greece* 37°4N 22°22E **204** D4
Mysuru *India* 12°17N 76°41E **245** H3
Myszków *Poland* 50°45N 19°22E **185** H6
Myszyniec *Poland* 53°23N 21°21E **184** E8
Mytilene = Mitilini *Greece* 39°6N 26°35E **205** B8
Mytishchi *Russia* 55°50N 37°50E **188** E9
Mývatn *Iceland* 65°36N 17°0W **155** B10
M'Zab, Oued ➜ *Algeria* 32°15N 5°0E **261** B6
M'Zab Valley = M'zab, Oued ➜ *Algeria* 32°15N 5°0E **261** B6
Mže ➜ *Czechia* 49°46N 13°24E **180** B6
Mzimba *Malawi* 11°55S 33°39E **269** E3
Mzimkulu ➜ *S. Africa* 30°44S 30°28E **271** D5
Mzimvubu ➜ *S. Africa* 31°38S 29°33E **271** D4
Mzuzu *Malawi* 11°30S 33°55E **269** E3

N

N.S.C.B. Int. ✕ (CCU) *India* 22°38N 88°26E **124** B2
Na Clocha Liatha = Greystones *Ireland* 53°9N 6°5W **166** C5
Na Haeo △ *Thailand* 17°31N 100°58E **236** D3
Na Hearadh = Harris *U.K.* 57°50N 6°55W **167** D2
Na Hearadh, Caolas = Harris, Sd. of *U.K.* 57°44N 7°6W **167** D1
Na-lang *Myanmar* 22°42N 97°33E **241** D6
Na Noi *Thailand* 18°19N 100°43E **236** C3
Na Phao *Laos* 17°35N 105°44E **236** D5
Na Sam *Vietnam* 22°3N 106°37E **228** F6
Na Sceirí = Skerries *Ireland* 53°35N 6°8W **166** C5
Na Thon *Thailand* 9°32N 99°56E **237** b
Naab ➜ *Germany* 49°1N 12°2E **179** F8
Nā'ālehu *U.S.A.* 19°4N 155°35W **302** D6
Na'am *Sudan* 9°42N 28°27E **257** F2
Na'am ➜ *South Sudan* 6°48N 29°57E **257** F2
Naama *Algeria* 33°16N 0°19E **261** B5
Naama □ *Algeria* 33°15N 0°45E **261** B5
Naantali *Finland* 60°29N 22°2E **188** B1
Naas *Ireland* 53°12N 6°40W **166** C5
Nababeep *S. Africa* 29°36S 17°46E **270** C2
Nabadwip = Navadwip *India* 23°34N 88°20E **243** H13
Nabari *Japan* 34°37N 136°5E **223** C8
Nabawa *Australia* 28°30S 114°48E **279** E1
Nabberu, L. *Australia* 25°50S 120°30E **279** E3
Nabburg *Germany* 49°27N 12°11E **179** F8
Naberezhnaya Tower *Russia* 55°45N 37°32E **129** B2
Naberezhnyye Chelny *Russia* 55°42N 52°19E **190** C11
Nabesna *U.S.A.* 62°22N 143°0W **303** E12
Nabeul *Tunisia* 36°30N 10°44E **258** A2
Nabeul □ *Tunisia* 36°30N 10°40E **261** A7
Nabha *India* 30°26N 76°14E **242** D7
Nabī Sālih *Egypt* 28°37N 33°59E **251** K4
Nabid *Iran* 29°40N 57°38E **247** D8
Nabire *Indonesia* 3°15S 135°26E **231** E9
Nabisar *Pakistan* 25°8N 69°40E **242** G3
Nabisipi ➜ *Canada* 50°14N 62°13W **299** B7
Nabiswera *Uganda* 1°27N 32°15E **268** B3
Nablus = Nābulus *West Bank* 32°14N 35°15E **251** F6
Naboomspruit *S. Africa* 24°32S 28°40E **271** B4
Nabou *Burkina Faso* 11°25N 2°50W **262** C4
Nabouwalu *Fiji* 17°0S 178°45E **287** A2
Nabq *Egypt* 28°6N 34°25E **251** K5
Nabq △ *Egypt* 28°6N 34°25E **251** K5
Nabua *Phil.* 13°24N 123°22E **232** E4
Nābulus *West Bank* 32°14N 35°15E **251** F6
Nabunturan *Phil.* 7°35N 125°58E **233** H5
Nacala *Mozam.* 14°32S 40°34E **269** E5
Nacaome *Honduras* 13°31N 87°30W **320** D2
Nacaroa *Mozam.* 14°22S 39°56E **269** E4
Naches *U.S.A.* 46°44N 120°42W **304** C3
Naches ➜ *U.S.A.* 46°38N 120°31W **306** D6
Nachicapau, L. *Canada* 56°40N 68°5W **299** A6
Nachikatsuura *Japan* 33°33N 135°58E **223** D7
Nachingwea *Tanzania* 10°23S 38°49E **269** E4
Nachna *India* 27°34N 71°41E **242** F4
Náchod *Czechia* 50°25N 16°8E **180** A9
Nachuge *India* 10°47N 92°21E **245** J11
Nacimiento, L. *U.S.A.* 35°46N 120°53W **306** K6
Nacka *Sweden* 59°19N 18°10E **139** B3
Nackara *Australia* 32°48S 139°12E **282** B3
Naco *Mexico* 31°19N 109°56W **318** A3
Nacogdoches *U.S.A.* 31°36N 94°39W **314** F7
Nácori Chico *Mexico* 29°40N 108°57W **318** B3
Nacozari de García *Mexico* 30°25N 109°38W **318** A3
Nacula *Fiji* 16°54S 177°27E **287** A1
Nada = Danzhou *China* 19°31N 109°33E **229** a
Nådendal = Naantali *Finland* 60°29N 22°2E **188** B1
Nadezhdinsky = Serov *Russia* 59°29N 60°35E **186** C11
Nadi *Fiji* 17°42S 177°20E **287** A1
Nadi *Sudan* 18°40N 33°41E **256** D3
Nadiad *India* 22°41N 72°56E **242** H5
Nădlac *Romania* 46°10N 20°50E **182** D5
Nador *Morocco* 35°14N 2°58W **261** A4
Nadur *Malta* 35°54N 14°22E **206** F7
Nadur *Gozo, Malta* 36°2N 14°18E **206** E7
Nadūshan *Iran* 32°2N 53°35E **247** C7
Nadvirna *Ukraine* 48°37N 24°30E **183** B9
Nadvoitsy *Russia* 63°52N 34°14E **186** B5
Nadvornaya = Nadvirna *Ukraine* 48°37N 24°30E **183** B9
Nadym *Russia* 65°35N 72°42E **214** C8
Nadym ➜ *Russia* 66°12N 72°0E **214** C8
Nærbø *Norway* 58°40N 5°39E **164** F2
Nærøyfjorden *Norway* 60°55N 6°55E **164** D3
Næsnes *Norway* 59°45N 10°27E **133** B1
Næstved *Denmark* 55°13N 11°44E **163** J5
Nafada *Nigeria* 11°8N 11°20E **263** C7
Nafarroa = Navarra □ *Spain* 42°40N 1°40W **196** C3
Nafpaktos *Greece* 38°24N 21°50E **204** C3
Nafplio *Greece* 37°33N 22°50E **204** D4
Naft-e Safīd *Iran* 31°40N 49°17E **247** D6
Naftan Pt. *N. Marianas* 15°5N 145°45E **302** e
Naftshahr *Iran* 34°0N 45°30E **213** E11
Nafud Desert = An Nafūd *Si. Arabia* 28°15N 41°0E **246** D4
Nafūsah, Jabal *Libya* 32°12N 12°30E **258** B2
Nag Hammâdi *Egypt* 26°2N 32°18E **256** B3
Naga *Japan* 26°34N 127°43E **288** a
Naga *Camarines S., Phil.* 13°38N 123°15E **232** E4
Naga *Cebu, Phil.* 10°13N 123°45E **233** F4
Naga *Zamboanga del S., Phil.* 7°46N 122°45E **233** H4
Naga, Kreb en *Africa* 24°12N 6°0W **260** D3
Naga Hills = Nagaland □ *India* 26°0N 94°30E **241** C5
Naga-Shima *Kagoshima, Japan* 32°10N 130°9E **222** E2
Naga-Shima *Yamaguchi, Japan* 33°49N 132°5E **222** D4
Nagagami *Canada* 50°23N 84°20W **298** B3
Nagahama *Ehime, Japan* 33°36N 132°29E **222** D4
Nagahama *Shiga, Japan* 35°23N 136°16E **223** B8
Nagai *Japan* 38°6N 140°2E **220** E10
Nagai I. *U.S.A.* 55°5N 160°0W **303** J8
Nagaland □ *India* 26°0N 94°30E **241** C5
Nagambie *Australia* 36°47S 145°10E **283** D6
Nagano *Japan* 36°40N 138°10E **223** A10
Nagano □ *Japan* 36°15N 138°0E **223** A10
Nagaoka *Japan* 37°27N 138°51E **221** F9
Nagaon *India* 26°20N 92°50E **241** B4
Nagappattinam *India* 10°46N 79°51E **245** J4
Nagar ➜ *Bangla.* 24°27N 89°12E **241** C2
Nagar Karnul *India* 16°29N 78°20E **245** F4
Nagar Parkar *Pakistan* 24°28N 70°46E **242** G4
Nagara-Gawa ➜ *Japan* 35°40N 136°43E **223** B8
Nagaram *India* 18°21N 80°26E **244** E5
Nagarhole △ *India* 12°0N 76°10E **245** J3
Nagari Hills *India* 13°3N 79°45E **245** H4
Nagarjuna Sagar *India* 16°30N 79°13E **245** F4
Nagasaki *Japan* 32°47N 129°50E **222** E1
Nagasaki □ *Japan* 32°50N 129°40E **222** E1
Nagato *Japan* 34°19N 131°5E **222** C3
Nagatsuta *Japan* 35°32N 139°31E **140** B2
Nagaur *India* 27°15N 73°45E **242** F5
Nagayo *Japan* 32°48N 129°50E **222** E1
Nagbhir *India* 20°34N 79°55E **244** D4
Nagda *India* 23°27N 75°25E **242** H6
Nagercoil *India* 8°12N 77°26E **245** K3
Nagina *India* 29°30N 78°30E **243** E8
Nagīneh *Iran* 34°20N 57°15E **247** C8
Naginimara *India* 26°49N 94°50E **241** B5
Nagir *Pakistan* 36°12N 74°42E **243** A6
Naglarby *Sweden* 60°25N 15°34E **162** D9
Nagles Mts. *Ireland* 52°8N 8°30W **166** D3
Nago-wan *Japan* 26°34N 127°57E **288** a
Nagod *India* 24°34N 80°36E **243** G9
Nagold *Germany* 48°32N 8°43E **179** G4
Nagold ➜ *Germany* 48°52N 8°42E **179** G4
Nagoorin *Australia* 24°17S 151°15E **280** C5
Nagorno-Karabakh □ *Azerbaijan* 39°55N 46°45E **213** C12
Nagornyy *Russia* 55°58N 124°57E **215** D13
Nagoya *Indonesia* 1°15N 104°5E **234** B2
Nagoya *Japan* 35°10N 136°50E **223** B8
Nagoya ✕ (NGO) *Japan* 34°53N 136°45E **223** C8
Nagpartian = Burgos *Phil.* 18°31N 120°39E **232** B3
Nagpur *India* 21°8N 79°10E **244** D4
Nagqu *China* 31°29N 92°3E **218** E7
Nags Head *St. Kitts & Nevis* 17°13N 62°38W **322** d
Nagua *Dom. Rep.* 19°23N 69°50W **321** C6
Naguabo *Puerto Rico* 18°13N 65°44W **321** b
Nagurunguru ⊙ *Australia* 16°45S 129°45E **278** C4
Nagyatád *Hungary* 46°14N 17°22E **182** D2
Nagyecsed *Hungary* 47°53N 22°24E **182** C7
Nagykálló *Hungary* 47°53N 21°51E **182** C6
Nagykanizsa *Hungary* 46°28N 17°0E **182** D2
Nagykőrös *Hungary* 47°5N 19°48E **182** C4
Nagyszombat = Trnava *Slovakia* 48°23N 17°35E **181** C10
Nagytétény *Hungary* 47°23N 18°59E **117** B1
Nagyvárad = Oradea *Romania* 47°2N 21°58E **182** C6
Naha *Japan* 26°13N 127°42E **288** a
Nahabuan *Indonesia* 0°49N 114°45E **235** B4
Nahalin *West Bank* 31°41N 35°7E **123** B1
Nahan *India* 30°33N 77°18E **242** D7
Nahanni △ *Canada* 61°36N 125°41W **296** A4
Nahanni Butte *Canada* 61°2N 123°31W **296** A4
Nahargarh *Mad. P., India* 24°10N 75°14E **242** G6
Nahargarh *Raj., India* 24°55N 76°50E **242** G7
Nahariyya *Israel* 33°1N 35°5E **250** F6
Nahāvand *Iran* 34°10N 48°22E **213** E13
Nahe ➜ *Germany* 49°58N 7°54E **179** F3
Nahirne *Ukraine* 45°26N 28°27E **183** E13
Nahīya, W. ➜ *Egypt* 28°55N 31°0E **256** B3
Nahuel Huapi, L. *Argentina* 41°0S 71°32W **336** B2
Nahuel Huapi △ *Argentina* 41°3S 71°59W **336** B2
Nahuelbuta △ *Chile* 37°44S 72°57W **334** D1
Nahunta *U.S.A.* 31°12N 81°59W **316** D8
Nai Yong *Thailand* 8°14N 98°22E **237** a
Naic *Phil.* 14°19N 120°46E **232** D3
Naicá *Mexico* 27°53N 105°31W **318** B3
Naicam *Canada* 52°30N 104°30W **297** C8
Naifaru *Maldives* 5°26N 73°20E **212** d
Naikoon ⌓ *Canada* 53°55N 131°55W **296** C2
Naikul *India* 21°20N 84°58E **244** D7
Naila *Germany* 50°19N 11°42E **179** E7
Naimisharanya *India* 27°21N 80°30E **243** F9
Naimona'nyi Feng *China* 30°26N 81°18E **243** D9
Nain *Nfld. & L., Canada* 56°34N 61°40W **299** A7
Nā'īn *Iran* 32°54N 53°0E **247** C7
Nain *Jamaica* 17°57N 77°38W **320** a
Naini Tal *India* 29°30N 79°30E **243** E8
Nainpur *India* 22°30N 80°10E **243** H9
Naintré *France* 46°46N 0°29E **172** F7
Nainwa *India* 25°46N 75°51E **242** G6
Naipu *Romania* 44°12N 25°47E **183** F10
Nairai *Fiji* 17°49S 179°15E **287** A2
Nairn *U.K.* 57°35N 3°53W **167** D5
Nairobi *Kenya* 1°17S 36°48E **268** C4
Nairobi △ *Kenya* 1°22S 36°50E **268** C4
Naissaar *Estonia* 59°34N 24°29E **188** C3
Naita, Mt. *Ethiopia* 5°30N 35°18E **257** F4
Naitaba *Fiji* 17°0S 179°16W **287** A3
Naivasha *Kenya* 0°40S 36°30E **268** C4
Naivasha, L. *Kenya* 0°48S 36°20E **268** C4
Najac *France* 44°14N 1°58E **174** D5
Najaf = An Najaf *Iraq* 32°3N 44°15E **213** G11
Najafābād *Iran* 32°40N 51°15E **247** C6
Najafgarh Drain ➜ *India* 28°39N 77°4E **120** B1
Najd *Si. Arabia* 26°30N 42°0E **248** A3
Nájera *Spain* 42°26N 2°48W **196** C2
Najerilla ➜ *Spain* 42°32N 2°48W **196** C2
Najibabad *India* 29°40N 78°20E **242** E8
Najin *N. Korea* 42°12N 130°15E **224** A5
Najmah *Si. Arabia* 26°42N 50°6E **247** E6
Najrān *Si. Arabia* 17°34N 44°18E **248** C4
Najrān □ *Si. Arabia* 18°30N 45°50E **248** C4
Naju *S. Korea* 35°3N 126°43E **224** E3
Naka *Japan* 36°30N 140°35E **223** A12
Naka-Gawa ➜ *Japan* 36°20N 140°36E **223** A12
Nakadōri-Shima *Japan* 32°57N 129°4E **221** H4
Nakagusuku-wan *Japan* 26°14N 127°53E **288** a
Nakahara *Japan* 35°33N 139°37E **140** B2
Nakal = Nakło nad Notecią *Poland* 53°9N 17°38E **185** E4
Nakalagba *Dem. Rep. of the Congo* 2°50N 27°58E **268** B2
Nakalele Pt. *U.S.A.* 21°2N 156°35W **302** B5
Nakama *Japan* 33°56N 130°43E **222** D2
Nakambé = White Volta ➜ *Ghana* 9°10N 1°15W **263** D4
Nakaminato *Japan* 36°21N 140°36E **223** A12
Nakamura = Shimanto *Japan* 32°59N 132°56E **222** E4
Nakanai Mts. *Papua N. G.* 5°40S 151°0E **286** C6
Nakano *Nagano, Japan* 36°45N 138°22E **223** A10
Nakano *Tōkyō, Japan* 35°42N 139°39E **140** A2
Nakano-Shima *Japan* 29°51N 129°52E **221** K4
Nakanojō *Japan* 36°35N 138°51E **223** A10
Nakashibetsu *Japan* 43°33N 144°59E **220** C12
Nakatsu *Japan* 33°34N 131°15E **222** D3
Nakatsugawa *Japan* 35°29N 137°30E **223** B9
Nakfa *Eritrea* 16°40N 38°32E **257** D4
Nakfa △ *Eritrea* 17°28N 38°55E **257** D4
Nakha Yai, Ko *Thailand* 8°3N 98°28E **237** a
Nakhichevan = Naxçıvan *Azerbaijan* 39°12N 45°15E **213** C11
Nakhichevan Rep. = Naxçıvan □ *Azerbaijan* 39°25N 45°26E **213** C11
Nakhl *Egypt* 29°55N 33°43E **251** J4
Nakhl-e Taqī *Iran* 27°28N 52°36E **247** E7
Nakhodka *Russia* 42°53N 132°54E **220** C6
Nakhon Nayok *Thailand* 14°12N 101°13E **236** E3
Nakhon Pathom *Thailand* 13°49N 100°3E **236** F3
Nakhon Phanom *Thailand* 17°23N 104°43E **236** D5
Nakhon Ratchasima *Thailand* 14°59N 102°12E **236** E4
Nakhon Sawan *Thailand* 15°35N 100°10E **236** E3
Nakhon Si Thammarat *Thailand* 8°29N 100°0E **237** H3
Nakhon Thai *Thailand* 17°5N 100°44E **236** D3
Nakhtarana *India* 23°20N 69°15E **242** H3
Nakijin *Japan* 26°40N 127°58E **288** a
Nakina *Canada* 50°10N 86°40W **298** B2
Nakło nad Notecią *Poland* 53°9N 17°38E **185** E4
Naknek *U.S.A.* 58°44N 157°1W **303** G8
Nako *Burkina Faso* 10°40N 3°4W **262** C4
Nakodar *India* 31°8N 75°31E **242** D6
Nakskov *Denmark* 54°50N 11°8E **163** K5
Naktong ➜ *S. Korea* 35°7N 128°57E **224** E4
Nakuru *Kenya* 0°15S 36°4E **268** C4
Nakuru, L. *Kenya* 0°23S 36°5E **268** C4
Nakusp *Canada* 50°20N 117°45W **296** C5
Nal *Pakistan* 27°40N 66°12E **242** F2
Nal ➜ *Pakistan* 25°20N 65°30E **242** G1
Nalázi *Mozam.* 24°3S 33°20E **271** B5
Nalchik *Russia* 43°30N 43°33E **191** J6
Nałęczów *Poland* 51°17N 22°9E **185** G9
Nalerigu *Ghana* 10°35N 0°25W **263** C4
Nalgonda *India* 17°6N 79°15E **244** F4
Nalhati *India* 24°17N 87°52E **243** G12
Naliya *India* 23°16N 68°50E **242** H3
Nallamalai Hills *India* 15°30N 78°50E **245** G4
Nallıhan *Turkey* 40°11N 31°20E **212** B4
Nalolo *Zambia* 15°33S 23°7E **265** F4
Nalón ➜ *Spain* 43°32N 6°4W **194** B4
Nalong *Myanmar* 24°44N 97°28E **241** C6
Nalubaale Dam *Uganda* 0°30N 33°5E **268** B3
Nalumasortoq *Greenland* 60°23N 44°28W **154** E6
Nālūt *Libya* 31°54N 11°0E **258** B2
Nālūt □ *Libya* 31°52N 10°58E **258** B2
Nam Can *Vietnam* 8°46N 104°59E **237** H5
Nam-ch'on *N. Korea* 38°15N 126°26E **224** C3
Nam Co *China* 30°30N 90°45E **218** E7
Nam Dinh *Vietnam* 20°25N 106°5E **228** G6
Nam Du, Quan Dao *Vietnam* 9°41N 104°21E **237** H5
Nam Hka ➜ *Myanmar* 21°34N 95°41E **228** G2
Nam Loi ➜ *Myanmar* 21°3N 98°27E **228** G3
Nam Nao △ *Thailand* 16°44N 101°32E **236** D3
Nam Ngum Res. *Laos* 18°35N 102°34E **236** C4
Nam Phan *Vietnam* 10°30N 106°0E **237** G6
Nam Phong *Thailand* 16°42N 102°52E **236** D4
Nam Theun Res. *Laos* 17°51N 105°3E **236** D5
Nam Tok *Thailand* 14°21N 99°4E **236** E2
Nam Un Res. *Thailand* 17°13N 103°44E **236** D4
Namacunde *Angola* 17°18S 15°50E **265** F3
Namacurra *Mozam.* 17°30S 36°50E **271** A6
Namadgi △ *Australia* 35°42S 149°0E **283** C8
Namai B. *Phil.* 7°31N 134°38E **288** c
Namak, Daryācheh-ye *Iran* 34°30N 52°0E **247** C7
Namak, Kavir-e *Iran* 34°30N 57°30E **247** C8
Namakkal *India* 11°13N 78°13E **245** J4
Namakzār, Daryācheh-ye *Iran* 34°0N 60°30E **240** B1
Namaland *Namibia* 26°0S 17°0E **270** B2
Namanga *Kenya* 2°33S 36°47E **268** C4
Namangan *Uzbekistan* 41°0N 71°40E **217** D8
Namangan □ *Uzbekistan* 41°0N 71°15E **217** D8
Namapa *Mozam.* 13°43S 39°50E **269** E4
Namaqua △ *S. Africa* 30°0S 17°30E **270** D2
Namaqualand *S. Africa* 30°0S 17°25E **270** D2
Namasagali *Uganda* 1°2N 33°0E **268** B3
Namatanai *Papua N. G.* 3°40S 152°29E **286** B7
Namber *Indonesia* 1°2S 134°49E **231** E8
Nambour *Australia* 26°32S 152°58E **281** D5
Nambouwalu = Nabouwalu *Fiji* 17°0S 178°45E **287** A2
Nambuangongo *Angola* 8°1S 14°12E **265** D2
Nambucca Heads *Australia* 30°37S 153°0E **283** A10
Nambung △ *Australia* 30°30S 115°5E **279** F2
Namcha Barwa *China* 29°40N 95°10E **218** F8
Namche Bazar *Nepal* 27°51N 86°47E **243** F12
Namchonjŏm = Nam-ch'on *N. Korea* 38°15N 126°26E **224** C3
Namdapha △ *India* 27°30N 96°50E **241** B6
Namecunda *Mozam.* 14°54S 37°37E **269** E4
Nameh *Indonesia* 2°34N 116°21E **235** B5
Namen = Namur *Belgium* 50°27N 4°52E **170** D4
Nameponda *Mozam.* 15°50S 39°50E **269** F4
Nameri △ *India* 26°55N 92°55E **241** B4
Namerikawa *Japan* 36°46N 137°20E **223** A9
Náměšť nad Oslavou *Czechia* 49°12N 16°10E **181** B9
Námestovo *Slovakia* 49°24N 19°25E **181** B12
Nametil *Mozam.* 15°40S 39°21E **269** F4
Namew L. *Canada* 54°14N 101°56W **297** C8
Namgia *India* 31°48N 78°40E **243** D8
Namhkam *Myanmar* 23°50N 97°41E **228** E1
Namhsan *Myanmar* 22°48N 97°2E **241** D6
Namialo *Mozam.* 14°55S 39°59E **269** E4
Namib Desert *Namibia* 22°30S 15°0E **270** B2
Namib-Naukluft ⌓ *Namibia* 24°40S 15°16E **270** B2
Namibe *Angola* 15°7S 12°11E **265** F2
Namibe □ *Angola* 16°35S 12°30E **265** F2
Namibe ⌓ *Angola* 16°35S 12°20E **265** F2
Namibia ■ *Africa* 22°0S 18°9E **270** B2
Namibia Abyssal Plain *Atl. Oc.* 30°0S 5°30E **152** J12
Namibwoestyn = Namib Desert *Namibia* 22°30S 15°0E **270** B2
Namīn *Iran* 38°25N 48°30E **213** C13
Naminüs = Lubango *Angola* 14°55S 13°30E **265** E2
Naminüs = Lüderitz *Namibia* 26°41S 15°8E **270** C2
Namjeju *S. Korea* 33°14N 126°33E **224** a
Namlan *Myanmar* 22°15N 97°24E **241** D6
Namlea *Indonesia* 3°18S 127°5E **231** E7
Namoi ➜ *Australia* 30°12S 149°30E **283** A9
Namous, O. en ➜ *Algeria* 31°0N 0°15W **261** B4
Nampa *U.S.A.* 43°34N 116°34W **304** E5
Nampala *Mali* 15°20N 5°30W **262** B3
Namp'o *N. Korea* 38°52N 125°10E **224** C2
Namp'o □ *N. Korea* 38°52N 125°25E **224** C2
Nampō-Shotō *Japan* 32°0N 140°0E **221** J10
Nampula *Mozam.* 15°6S 39°15E **269** F4
Namrole *Indonesia* 3°46S 126°46E **231** E7
Namsan Park *S. Korea* 37°32N 126°59E **137** B1
Namse Shankou *China* 30°0N 82°25E **243** E10
Namsen ➜ *Norway* 64°28N 11°37E **160** D14
Namslau = Namysłów *Poland* 51°6N 17°42E **185** G4
Namsos *Norway* 64°29N 11°30E **160** D14
Namtok Chat Trakan △ *Thailand* 17°17N 100°40E **236** D3
Namtok Huay Yang △ *Thailand* 11°35N 99°30E **237** G2
Namtok Mae Surin △ *Thailand* 18°55N 98°2E **236** C2
Namtok Ngao △ *Thailand* 9°58N 98°46E **237** H2
Namtok Phlew △ *Thailand* 12°32N 102°13E **236** F4
Namtok Yong △ *Thailand* 8°15N 98°45E **237** H2
Namtsy *Russia* 62°43N 129°37E **215** C13
Namtu *Myanmar* 23°5N 97°28E **241** D6
Namtumbo *Tanzania* 10°30S 36°4E **269** E4
Namu *Canada* 51°52N 127°50W **296** C3
Namuka-i-Lau *Fiji* 18°53S 178°37W **287** B3
Namukulu *Cook Is.* 18°57S 169°54W **289** g
Namumea *Tuvalu* 5°41S 176°9E **277** B14
Namur *Belgium* 50°27N 4°52E **170** D4
Namur □ *Belgium* 50°17N 5°0E **170** D4
Namurupath *Kenya* 4°34N 35°57E **268** B4
Namutoni *Namibia* 18°49S 16°55E **270** A2
Namwala *Zambia* 15°44S 26°30E **269** F2
Namwon *Jeju-do, S. Korea* 33°16N 126°43E **224** a
Namwon *Jeollabuk-do, S. Korea* 35°23N 127°23E **224** E3
Namyang *N. Korea* 42°57N 129°52E **224** A4
Namyangju *S. Korea* 37°38N 127°12E **224** D3
Namyeong *S. Korea* 37°32N 126°57E **137** B1
Namyit I. *S. China Sea* 10°11N 114°22E **230** C4
Namysłów *Poland* 51°6N 17°42E **185** G4
Nan *Thailand* 18°48N 100°46E **236** C3
Nan ➜ *Thailand* 15°42N 100°9E **236** E3
Nan Ling *China* 25°0N 112°30E **229** E9
Nan Xian *China* 29°20N 112°22E **229** C9
Nana *C.A.R.* 5°0N 15°50E **264** A3
Nana *Romania* 44°17N 26°34E **183** F11
Nana-Barya ⌓ *C.A.R.* 7°40N 17°29E **264** A3
Nana-Grébizi □ *C.A.R.* 7°0N 19°20E **264** A3
Nana Kru *Liberia* 4°55N 8°45W **262** E3
Nana-Mambéré □ *C.A.R.* 5°30N 15°30E **264** A3
Nanaimo *Canada* 49°10N 124°0W **296** D4
Nānākuli *U.S.A.* 21°24N 158°9W **302** K13
Nanam *N. Korea* 41°44N 129°40E **224** B4
Nan'an *China* 24°59N 118°21E **229** E12
Nanango *Australia* 26°40S 152°0E **281** D5
Nan'ao *Guangdong, China* 23°28N 117°5E **229** F11
Nanao *Japan* 37°0N 137°0E **221** F8
Nanao *Taiwan* 24°28N 121°48E **225** B3
Nanbiancun *China* 23°4N 113°10E **121** B1
Nanbu *China* 31°18N 106°3E **228** B6
Nanchang *China* 28°42N 115°55E **229** C10
Nanchang He ➜ *China* 39°58N 116°14E **114** B1
Nancheng *China* 27°33N 116°35E **229** D11
Nanching = Nanjing *China* 32°2N 118°47E **229** A12
Nanchong *China* 30°43N 106°2E **228** B6
Nanchuan *China* 29°9N 107°6E **228** C6
Nanchung = Nanchong *China* 30°43N 106°2E **228** B6
Nancowry *India* 7°59N 93°32E **245** L11
Nancy *France* 48°42N 6°12E **173** D13
Nanda Devi *India* 30°23N 79°59E **243** D8
Nanda Devi △ *India* 30°30N 79°50E **243** D8
Nanda Kot *India* 30°17N 80°5E **243** D9
Nandan = Minamiawaji *Japan* 34°10N 134°42E **222** C6
Nandan *China* 24°58N 107°29E **228** E6
Nandang *China* 23°6N 113°12E **121** B2
Nanded *India* 19°10N 77°20E **244** E3
Nandewar Ra. *Australia* 30°15S 150°35E **281** E5
Nandgaon *India* 20°19N 74°39E **244** D2
Nandi = Nadi *Fiji* 17°42S 177°20E **287** A1
Nandi *Zimbabwe* 20°58S 31°44E **269** G3
Nandi □ *Kenya* 0°10N 35°10E **268** B4
Nandigama *India* 16°47N 80°18E **244** F5
Nandigram *India* 22°1N 87°58E **243** H12
Nandikotkur *India* 15°52N 78°18E **245** G4
Nandura *India* 20°52N 76°25E **244** D3
Nandurbar *India* 21°20N 74°15E **244** D2
Nandyal *India* 15°30N 78°30E **245** G4
Nanfeng *Guangdong, China* 23°45N 111°47E **229** F8
Nanfeng *Jiangxi, China* 27°12N 116°28E **229** D11
Nang Rong *Thailand* 14°38N 102°48E **236** E4
Nanga-Eboko *Cameroon* 4°41N 12°22E **263** E7
Nanga Parbat *Pakistan* 35°10N 74°35E **243** B6
Nangade *Mozam.* 11°5S 39°36E **269** E4
Nangal Dewat *India* 28°33N 77°5E **120** B1
Nangalao I. *Phil.* 11°26N 120°10E **233** F3
Nangamau *Indonesia* 0°6S 111°55E **235** C4
Nangamentebah *Indonesia* 0°33N 112°46E **235** B4
Nangapinoh *Indonesia* 0°20S 111°44E **235** C4
Nangar △ *Australia* 33°23S 148°3E **283** B8
Nangarhār □ *Afghan.* 34°20N 70°0E **240** B3
Nangatayap *Indonesia* 1°32S 110°34E **235** C4
Nangbéto, L. de *Togo* 7°26N 1°25E **263** D5
Nangeya Mts. *Uganda* 3°30N 33°30E **268** B3
Nangis *France* 48°33N 3°1E **173** D10
Nangnim-sanmaek *N. Korea* 40°13N 126°51E **224** B3
Nangong *China* 37°23N 115°22E **226** F8
Nangtud, Mt. *Phil.* 11°17N 122°11E **233** F4
Nanguneri *India* 8°29N 77°40E **245** K3
Nangwarry *Australia* 37°33S 140°48E **282** D4
Nanhua *Yunnan, China* 25°13N 101°21E **228** E3
Nanhua *Taiwan* 23°2N 120°28E **225** C2
Nanhuang *China* 36°58N 121°48E **227** F11
Nanhui *China* 31°5N 121°44E **229** B13
Nanhunan Shan *Taiwan* 24°21N 121°26E **225** B3
Nanisivik *Canada* 73°2N 84°33W **295** C15
Naniwa *Japan* 34°39N 135°29E **133** B1
Nanjangud *India* 12°6N 76°43E **245** H3
Nanji Shan *China* 27°27N 121°4E **229** D13
Nanjian *China* 25°2N 100°25E **228** E3
Nanjiang *China* 32°28N 106°51E **228** A6
Nanjing *Fujian, China* 24°25N 117°20E **229** E11
Nanjing *Jiangsu, China* 32°2N 118°47E **229** A12
Nanjirinji *Tanzania* 9°41S 39°5E **269** D4
Nankana Sahib *Pakistan* 31°27N 73°38E **242** D5
Nankang *Jiangxi, China* 25°40N 114°45E **229** E10
Nankang *Taiwan* 25°3N 121°35E **225** A3
Nanking = Nanjing *China* 32°2N 118°47E **229** A12
Nankoku *Japan* 33°39N 133°44E **222** D5
Nanlang *China* 22°30N 113°32E **219** a
Nanliao *Taiwan* 24°50N 120°55E **225** B2
Nanling *China* 30°55N 118°20E **229** B12
Nannial *India* 19°4N 79°38E **244** E4
Nanning *China* 22°48N 108°20E **228** F7
Nannup *Australia* 33°59S 115°48E **279** F2
Nanole *India* 19°0N 72°55E **130** A2
Nanortalik *Greenland* 60°10N 45°17W **154** E6
Nanpan Jiang ➜ *China* 25°10N 106°5E **228** E6
Nanpara *India* 27°52N 81°33E **243** F9
Nanping *Fujian, China* 26°38N 118°10E **229** D12
Nanping *Henan, China* 29°55N 112°3E **229** C9
Nanpu Bridge *China* 31°12N 121°30E **138** B2
Nanri Dao *China* 25°15N 119°25E **229** E12
Nansang *Myanmar* 20°53N 97°43E **241** E6
Nansei-Shotō = Ryūkyū-Rettō *Japan* 26°0N 126°0E **221** M3
Nansen Basin *Arctic* 84°0N 50°0E **150** A10
Nansen Land *Greenland* 83°0N 43°0W **154** A6
Nansen Sd. *Canada* 81°0N 91°0W **295** A13
Nansha *China* 22°45N 113°34E **219** a
Nansha Port *China* 22°40N 113°40E **219** a
Nanshan *China* 18°19N 109°10E **229** a
Nanshan I. *S. China Sea* 10°45N 115°49E **230** B5
Nanshi *China* 31°12N 121°29E **138** B1
Nansio *Tanzania* 2°3S 33°4E **268** C3
Nant *France* 44°1N 3°18E **174** D7
Nantan *Japan* 35°6N 135°28E **223** B7
Nantawarrinna ⊙ *Australia* 30°49S 138°58E **281** B2
Nanterre *France* 48°53N 2°12E **134** A2
Nantes *France* 47°12N 1°33W **172** E5
Nantiat *France* 46°1N 1°11E **174** B5
Nanticoke *U.S.A.* 41°12N 76°0W **313** E8
Nanton *Canada* 50°21N 113°46W **296** C6
Nanton Pt. *Antigua & B.* 17°0N 61°45W **322** b
Nantong *China* 32°1N 120°52E **229** A13
Nantou *China* 22°32N 113°55E **219** a
Nant'ou *Taiwan* 23°55N 120°41E **225** C2
Nant'ou □ *Taiwan* 23°50N 121°0E **225** C3
Nantua *France* 46°10N 5°35E **173** F12
Nantucket *U.S.A.* 41°17N 70°6W **309** E18
Nantucket I. *U.S.A.* 41°16N 70°5W **309** E18
Nantulo *Mozam.* 12°32S 38°45E **269** E4
Nantung = Nantong *China* 32°1N 120°52E **229** A13
Nantwich *U.K.* 53°4N 2°31W **168** D5
Nanty Glo *U.S.A.* 40°28N 78°50W **312** F6
Nantzu *Taiwan* 22°44N 120°19E **225** D2
Nanuku Passage *Fiji* 16°45S 179°15W **287** A3
Nanumanga *Pac. Oc.* 6°18S 176°20E **277** B14
Nanuque *Brazil* 17°50S 40°21W **333** E3
Nanusa, Kepulauan *Indonesia* 4°45N 127°1E **231** D7
Nanutarra Roadhouse *Australia* 22°32S 115°30E **278** D2
Nanwan *Taiwan* 21°57N 120°46E **225** E2
Nanxi *China* 28°54N 104°59E **228** C5
Nanxiong *China* 25°6N 114°15E **229** E10
Nanyang *China* 33°11N 112°30E **226** H7
Nanyi Hu *China* 31°5N 119°0E **229** B12
Nanyuan *China* 39°47N 116°24E **226** E9
Nanyuki *Kenya* 0°2N 37°4E **268** B4
Nanzhang *China* 31°45N 111°50E **229** B8
Nanzhao *China* 33°30N 112°20E **226** H7
Nanzi = Nantzu *Taiwan* 22°44N 120°19E **225** D2
Nao, C. de la *Spain* 38°44N 0°14E **197** G5
Naococane, L. *Canada* 52°50N 70°45W **299** B5
Naogaon *Bangla.* 24°52N 88°52E **241** C2
Naoné *Vanuatu* 15°0S 168°8E **287** E6
Naoussa *Cyclades, Greece* 37°7N 25°14E **205** D7
Naoussa *Imathia, Greece* 40°42N 22°9E **202** F6
Naozhou Dao *China* 20°55N 110°20E **229** G8
Napa *U.S.A.* 38°18N 122°17W **306** G4
Napa ➜ *U.S.A.* 38°10N 122°19W **306** G4
Napaimiut *U.S.A.* 61°33N 158°42W **303** F8
Napakiak *U.S.A.* 60°42N 161°57W **303** F7
Nāpali Coast *U.S.A.* 22°11N 159°39W **302** A2
Napanee *Canada* 44°15N 77°0W **312** B8
Napanoch *U.S.A.* 41°44N 74°22W **313** E10
Napaskiak *U.S.A.* 60°43N 161°55W **303** F7
Nape *Laos* 18°18N 105°6E **236** C5
Nape Pass = Keo Neua, Deo *Vietnam* 18°23N 105°10E **236** C5
Naperville *U.S.A.* 41°46N 88°9W **311** C8
Napier *N.Z.* 39°30S 176°56E **284** F5
Napier Broome B. *Australia* 14°2S 126°37E **278** B4
Napier Mole *Pakistan* 24°49N 66°58E **123** B1
Napier Pen. *Australia* 12°4S 135°43E **280** A2
Napierville *Canada* 45°11N 73°25W **313** A11
Napili-Honokowai *U.S.A.* 20°58N 156°39W **302** C5
Naples = Nápoli *Italy* 40°50N 14°15E **201** B7
Naples *Fla., U.S.A.* 26°8N 81°48W **317** J8
Naples Park *U.S.A.* 26°17N 81°49W **317** J8
Napo *China* 23°22N 105°50E **228** F5
Napo □ *Ecuador* 0°30S 77°0W **328** D2
Napo ➜ *Peru* 3°20S 72°40W **328** D3
Napoleon *N. Dak., U.S.A.* 46°30N 99°46W **308** B4
Napoleon *Ohio, U.S.A.* 41°23N 84°8W **311** C12
Napoleon's Tomb *St. Helena* 15°56S 5°42W **153** h
Nápoli *Italy* 40°50N 14°15E **201** B7
Nápoli, G. di *Italy* 40°43N 14°10E **201** B7
Nápoli Capodichino ✕ (NAP) *Italy* 40°53N 14°16E **201** B7
Napopo *Dem. Rep. of the Congo* 4°15N 28°0E **268** B2
Nappanee *U.S.A.* 41°27N 86°0W **311** C11
Napperby *Australia* 33°9S 138°7E **282** B3
Naqadeh *Iran* 36°57N 45°23E **213** D11
Naqb, Ra's an *Jordan* 29°48N 35°44E **251** J6
Naqqāsh *Iran* 35°40N 49°6E **247** C6
Når *Sweden* 57°15N 18°35E **163** G10
Nara *Japan* 34°40N 135°49E **223** C7
Nara *Mali* 15°10N 7°20W **262** B3
Nara □ *Japan* 34°30N 136°0E **223** C8
Nara Canal *Pakistan* 24°30N 69°20E **242** G3
Nara Visa *U.S.A.* 35°37N 103°6W **305** J12
Naracoorte *Australia* 36°58S 140°45E **282** D4
Naradhan *Australia* 33°34S 146°17E **283** B7
Naraina *India* 28°36N 77°8E **120** B1
Naraini *India* 25°11N 80°29E **243** G9
Naranjos *Mexico* 21°21N 97°41W **319** C5
Narasannapeta *India* 18°25N 84°3E **244** E7
Narasapur *India* 16°26N 81°40E **245** F5
Narasaraopet *India* 16°14N 80°4E **245** F5
Narathiwat *Thailand* 6°30N 101°48E **237** J3
Narayanapatnam *India* 18°53N 83°10E **244** E6
Narayangadh = Bharatpur *Nepal* 27°34N 84°10E **243** F11
Narayanganj *Bangla.* 23°40N 90°33E **241** D3
Narayanpet *India* 16°45N 77°30E **244** F3
Narbada = Narmada ➜ *India* 21°38N 72°36E **242** J5
Narberth *U.K.* 51°47N 4°44W **169** F3
Narbonne *France* 43°11N 3°0E **174** E7
Narborough, I. = Fernandina, I. *Ecuador* 0°25S 91°30W **330** a
Narbuvoll *Norway* 62°21N 11°27E **164** B8
Narcea ➜ *Spain* 43°33N 6°44W **194** B4
Narcondam I. *India* 13°20N 94°16E **245** H12
Nardīn *Iran* 37°3N 55°59E **247** B7
Nardò *Italy* 40°11N 18°2E **201** B11
Narembeen *Australia* 32°7S 118°24E **279** F2
Nares Abyssal Plain *Atl. Oc.* 22°0N 67°0W **152** D5
Nares Str. *Arctic* 80°0N 70°0W **154** B3

Ogawa Japan 35°44N 139°28E 140 A1
Ogbomosho Nigeria 8°1N 4°11E 263 D5
Ogden Iowa, U.S.A. 42°2N 94°2W 310 B2
Ogden Utah, U.S.A. 41°13N 111°58W 304 F8
Ogden Park U.S.A. 41°46N 87°39W 119 C2
Ogden Slip Chicago, U.S.A. 119 b3
Ogdensburg U.S.A. 44°42N 75°30W 313 B9
Ogea Driki Fiji 19°12S 178°27W 287 B3
Ogea Levu Fiji 19°8S 178°24W 287 B3
Ogeechee → U.S.A. 31°50N 81°3W 316 D8
Ogi Japan 33°20N 130°15E 222 D2
Ogikubo Japan 35°42N 139°37E 140 A2
Ogilby U.S.A. 32°49N 114°50W 307 N12
Ogilvie Transportation Center
Chicago, U.S.A. 41°52N 87°38W 119 B3
Oglat Beraber Algeria 30°15N 3°34W 260 B4
Oglat el Khnâchich Mali 21°51N 3°58W 260 D4
Oglesby U.S.A. 41°18N 89°4W 310 C7
Oglethorpe U.S.A. 32°18N 84°4W 316 C5
Ogliastra □ Italy 39°50N 9°35E 200 C2
Oglio → Italy 45°2N 10°39E 198 C7
Oglio Nord △ Italy 45°22N 9°54E 198 C6
Oglio Sud △ Italy 45°7N 10°24E 198 C7
Ogmore Australia 22°37S 149°35E 280 C4
Ognon → France 47°16N 5°28E 173 E12
Ogogoro Nigeria 6°25N 3°24E 124 B2
Ogoja Nigeria 6°38N 8°39E 263 D6
Ogoki Canada 51°38N 85°58W 298 B2
Ogoki → Canada 51°38N 85°57W 298 B2
Ogoki L. Canada 50°50N 87°10W 298 B2
Ogoki Res. Canada 50°45N 88°15W 298 B2
Ogooué → Gabon 1°0S 9°0E 264 C1
Ogooué-Ivindo □ Gabon 1°0N 13°30E 264 B2
Ogooué-Lolo □ Gabon 1°0S 12°30E 264 C2
Ogooué-Maritime □ Gabon 1°0S 9°0E 264 C1
Ogōri Fukuoka, Japan 33°25N 130°30E 222 D2
Ogōri Yamaguchi, Japan 34°6N 131°24E 222 C3
Ogosta → Bulgaria 43°48N 23°55E 202 C7
Ogou → Togo 7°50N 1°19E 263 D5
Ogoueïleten Nmâdi
Mauritania 19°46N 11°1W 260 E2
Ogowe = Ogooué → Gabon 1°0S 9°0E 264 C1
Ogoyo Nigeria 6°25N 3°29E 124 B2
Ogr = Sharafa Sudan 11°59N 27°7E 257 E2
Ogražden N. Macedonia 41°30N 22°50E 202 E6
Ogre Latvia 56°49N 24°36E 188 D3
Ogrein Sudan 17°55N 34°50E 256 D3
Ogudu Nigeria 6°34N 3°24E 124 A2
Ogulin Croatia 45°16N 15°16E 199 C12
Ogun □ Nigeria 7°0N 3°0E 263 D5
Ogunu Japan 33°11N 131°8E 222 D3
Ögur Iceland 66°2N 22°44W 155 A4
Ogurja Ada Turkmenistan 38°55N 53°2E 247 B7
Oguta Nigeria 5°44N 6°44E 263 D6
Oğuzeli Turkey 36°57N 37°30E 250 B8
Ogwashi-Uku Nigeria 6°15N 6°30E 263 D6
Ogwe Nigeria 5°0N 7°14E 263 E6
Ohai N.Z. 45°55S 168°0E 285 F3
Ohakune N.Z. 39°24S 175°24E 284 F4
Ohanet Algeria 28°44N 8°46E 261 C6
Ohangwena □ Namibia 17°30S 17°0E 270 A2
Ōhara Japan 35°15N 140°23E 223 B12
O'Hare Int., Chicago ✈ (ORD)
U.S.A. 41°59N 87°54W 311 C9
Ohata Japan 41°24N 141°10E 220 D10
Ohatchee U.S.A. 33°47N 86°0W 316 B4
Ohau, L. N.Z. 44°15S 169°53E 285 E4
Ohaupo N.Z. 37°56S 175°20E 284 D4
O'Higgins, C. Chile 27°5S 109°15W 330 b
O'Higgins, Parque Chile 33°27S 70°40W 137 B2
O'Higgins, Pta. Chile 33°41S 79°0W 330 c
Ohio □ U.S.A. 40°15N 82°45W 312 F2
Ohio → U.S.A. 36°59N 89°8W 308 G9
Ohio City U.S.A. 40°46N 84°37W 311 D12
Ohiwa Harbour N.Z. 37°59S 177°10E 284 D6
Ohlau = Oława Poland 50°57N 17°20E 185 H4
Ohře → Czechia 50°30N 14°10E 180 A7
Ohre → Sachsen-Anhalt,
Germany 52°18N 11°46E 178 C7
Ohrid N. Macedonia 41°8N 20°52E 202 E4
Ohridsko Jezero
N. Macedonia 41°8N 20°52E 202 E4
Ohrigstad S. Africa 24°39S 30°36E 271 B5
Öhringen Germany 49°12N 9°31E 179 F5
Ohura N.Z. 38°51S 174°59E 284 E3
Oi Qu → China 28°37N 98°16E 228 C2
Oiapoque Brazil 3°50N 51°50W 329 C7
Oiapoque → S. Amer. 4°8N 51°40W 329 C7
Oikou China 38°35N 117°42E 227 E9
Oil City U.S.A. 41°26N 79°42W 312 E5
Oil Springs Canada 42°47N 82°7W 312 D2
Oildale U.S.A. 35°25N 119°1W 307 K7
Ōimachi Japan 35°35N 139°43E 140 B3
Oinousa = Inousses
Greece 38°33N 26°14E 205 C8
Oise □ France 49°28N 2°30E 173 C9
Oise → France 49°0N 2°4E 173 C9
Oistins Barbados 13°4N 59°33W 323 r
Ōita Japan 33°14N 131°36E 222 D3
Ōita □ Japan 33°15N 131°30E 222 D3
Oiticica Brazil 5°3S 41°5W 332 C3
Ojai U.S.A. 34°27N 119°15W 307 L7
Ojcowski △ Poland 50°15N 19°50E 185 H6
Ojhar India 20°6N 73°56E 244 D1
Ojinaga Mexico 29°34N 104°25W 318 B4
Ojiya Japan 37°18N 138°48E 221 F9
Ojo Caliente Mexico 22°34N 102°15W 318 C4
Ojo de Liebre, L. Mexico 27°45N 114°15W 318 B2
Ojos del Salado, Cerro
Argentina 27°0S 68°40W 334 B2
Ojota Nigeria 6°35N 3°23E 124 A2
Ojus U.S.A. 25°26N 80°9W 129 C3
Oka Nigeria 7°9N 3°38E 263 D5
Oka → Russia 56°20N 43°59E 190 B7
Okaba Indonesia 8°6S 139°42E 231 F9
Okahandja Namibia 22°0S 16°59E 270 B2
Okahukura N.Z. 38°48S 175°14E 284 E4
Okaihau N.Z. 35°19S 173°47E 284 B2
Okakarara Namibia 20°35S 17°27E 270 B2
Okalataka Congo 0°18S 14°54E 264 C2
Okanagan L. Canada 50°0N 119°30W 296 D5
Okandja Gabon 0°35S 13°45E 264 C2
Okano → Gabon 0°5S 10°57E 264 C2
Okanogan U.S.A. 48°22N 119°35W 304 B4
Okanogan → U.S.A. 48°6N 119°44W 304 B4
Okanogan Range
N. Amer. 49°0N 119°55W 296 D5
Okány Hungary 46°52N 21°21E 182 D6
Okapa Papua N. G. 6°38S 145°39E 286 D3
Okapi △
Dem. Rep. of the Congo 2°30N 27°20E 268 B2
Okaputa Namibia 20°5S 17°0E 270 B2
Okara Pakistan 30°50N 73°31E 242 D5
Okarito N.Z. 43°15S 170°9E 285 D5
Okarukambe = Steinhausen
Namibia 21°49S 18°20E 270 B2
Okato N.Z. 39°12S 173°53E 284 F2
Okau Micronesia 9°32N 138°6E 287 R16
Okaukuejo Namibia 19°10S 16°0E 270 A2
Okavango = Cubango →
Africa 18°50S 22°25E 265 F4
Okavango Delta Botswana 18°45S 22°45E 270 A3
Okavango Swamp = Okavango
Delta Botswana 18°45S 22°45E 270 A3
Ōkawa Japan 33°9N 130°21E 222 D2
Okawville U.S.A. 38°26N 89°33W 310 F7
Okaya Japan 36°5N 138°10E 223 A10
Okayama Japan 34°40N 133°54E 222 C5
Okayama □ Japan 35°0N 133°50E 222 C5
Okazaki Japan 34°57N 137°10E 223 C9
Oke-Iho Nigeria 8°1N 3°18E 263 D5
Oke-Ira Nigeria 6°29N 3°22E 124 B2
Okęcie Poland 52°11N 20°56E 143 B1
Okęcie, Warszawa ✈ (WAW)
Poland 52°9N 20°59E 143 B1
Okeechobee U.S.A. 27°15N 80°50W 317 H9
Okeechobee, L. U.S.A. 27°0N 80°50W 317 J9
Okefenokee △ U.S.A. 30°45N 82°18W 316 E7
Okefenokee Swamp
U.S.A. 30°40N 82°20W 316 E7
Okehampton U.K. 50°44N 4°0W 169 G4
Okemos U.S.A. 42°43N 84°26W 311 B12
Okene Nigeria 7°32N 6°11E 263 D6
Okeogbe Nigeria 6°24N 3°23E 124 B2
Oker → Germany 52°32N 10°22E 178 C6
Okha Gujarat, India 22°27N 69°4E 242 H3
Okha Russia 53°40N 143°0E 215 D15
Okhla India 28°33N 77°16E 120 B2
Okhotsk Russia 59°20N 143°10E 215 D15
Okhotsk, Sea of Asia 55°0N 145°0E 215 D15
Okhotskiy Perevoz
Russia 61°52N 135°35E 215 C14
Okhta → Russia 59°56N 30°25E 137 B2
Okhtyrka Ukraine 50°25N 35°0E 189 G8
Oki-no-Shima Japan 32°44N 132°33E 222 E4
Oki-Shotō Japan 36°5N 133°15E 222 A5
Okiep S. Africa 29°39S 17°53E 270 C2
Okigwi Nigeria 5°52N 7°20E 263 D6
Okija Nigeria 5°54N 6°55E 263 D6
Okinawa Japan 26°19N 127°46E 288 a
Okinawa □ Japan 26°40N 128°0E 288 a
Okinawa-Guntō Japan 26°40N 128°0E 221 L4
Okinawa-Jima Japan 26°32N 128°0E 221 L4
Okino-erabu-Shima
Japan 27°21N 128°33E 221 L4
Okitipupa Nigeria 6°31N 4°50E 263 D5
Okkervil → Russia 59°56N 30°30E 137 B2
Oklahoma □ U.S.A. 35°20N 97°30W 314 D6
Oklahoma City U.S.A. 35°30N 97°30W 314 D6
Oklawaha → U.S.A. 29°28N 81°41W 317 F8
Okmulgee U.S.A. 35°37N 95°58W 314 D7
Oknitsa = Ocniţa
Moldova 48°25N 27°30E 183 B12
Oko, W. → Sudan 21°15N 35°56E 256 C4
Okolo Uganda 2°37N 31°8E 268 B3
Okolona Ky., U.S.A. 38°8N 85°41W 311 F11
Okolona Miss., U.S.A. 34°0N 88°45W 315 E10
Okombahe Namibia 21°23S 15°22E 270 B2
Okonek Poland 53°32N 16°51E 184 E3
Okotoks Canada 50°43N 113°58W 296 C6
Okoyo Congo 1°28S 15°0E 264 C3
Okrika Nigeria 4°40N 7°10E 263 E6
Okrzeszyn Poland 52°8N 21°8E 143 C2
Oksapmin Papua N. G. 5°17S 142°15E 286 C2
Øksendalsøra Norway 62°42N 8°27E 164 B5
Oksovskiy Russia 62°33N 39°57E 186 B6
Oksval Norway 59°51N 10°40E 133 A3
Oktwin Myanmar 18°49N 96°26E 241 F6
Oktyabrsk = Qandyaghash
Kazakhstan 49°28N 57°25E 187 E10
Oktyabrsk Russia 53°11N 48°40E 190 D9
Oktyabrskiy = Aktsyabrski
Belarus 52°38N 28°53E 177 B15
Oktyabrskiy Bashkortostan,
Russia 54°28N 53°28E 186 D9
Oktyabrskiy Kamchatka,
Russia 52°39N 156°14E 215 D16
Oktyabrskiy Moskva,
Russia 55°41N 37°35E 129 B2
Oktyabrskiy Rostov, Russia 47°30N 40°4E 191 G5
Oktyabrskoy Revolyutsii, Ostrov
Russia 79°30N 97°0E 215 B10
Oktyabrskoye = Zhovtneve
Ukraine 46°54N 32°3E 189 J7
Ōkubo Tokyo, Japan 140 a2
Ōkuchi Japan 32°4N 130°37E 222 E2
Okulovka Russia 58°25N 33°19E 188 C7
Okuru N.Z. 43°55S 168°55E 285 D3
Okushiri-Tō Japan 42°15N 139°30E 220 C9
Okuta Nigeria 9°14N 3°12E 263 D5
Okwa → Botswana 22°30S 23°0E 270 B3
Ola Russia 59°35N 151°17E 215 D16
Ola Ark., U.S.A. 35°2N 93°13W 314 D8
Ólafsfjörður Iceland 66°4N 18°39W 155 A8
Ólafsvík Iceland 64°53N 23°43W 155 C3
Olaine Latvia 56°48N 23°59E 184 B10
Olancha U.S.A. 36°17N 118°1W 307 J8
Olancha Pk. U.S.A. 36°16N 118°7W 307 J8
Olanchito Honduras 15°30N 86°30W 320 C2
Öland Sweden 56°45N 16°38E 163 H10
Ölands norra udde
Sweden 57°22N 17°5E 163 G11
Ölands södra udde
Sweden 56°12N 16°23E 163 H10
Olanta U.S.A. 33°56N 79°56W 316 B10
Olar U.S.A. 33°11N 81°11W 316 B8
Olargues France 43°34N 2°53E 174 E6
Olari Finland 60°10N 24°44E 121 B1
Olaria Brazil 22°50S 43°16W 135 B1
Olary Australia 32°18S 140°19E 282 B4
Olascoaga Argentina 35°15S 60°39W 334 D3
Olathe U.S.A. 38°53N 94°49W 308 F6
Olavarría Argentina 36°55S 60°20W 334 D3
Oława Poland 50°57N 17°20E 185 H4
Olbernhau Germany 50°40N 13°19E 178 E9
Ólbia Italy 40°55N 9°31E 200 B2
Ólbia, G. di Italy 40°55N 9°39E 200 B2
Olching Germany 48°12N 11°21E 179 G7
Olcott U.S.A. 43°20N 78°42W 312 C6
Old Admiralty
Saint Petersburg, Russia 59°55N 30°20E 137 B1
Old Bahama Chan. = Bahama,
Canal Viejo de
W. Indies 22°10N 77°30W 320 B4
Old Baldy Pk. = San Antonio, Mt.
U.S.A. 34°17N 117°38W 307 L9
Old Bar Australia 31°58S 152°35E 283 A10
Old Bridge U.S.A. 40°25N 74°22W 313 F10
Old Castile = Castilla y Leon □
Spain 42°0N 5°0W 194 D6
Old City Shanghai, China 31°13N 121°29E 138 B1
Old City Delhi, India 120 a3
Old City Jerusalem 123 b3
Old Crow Canada 67°30N 139°55W 294 D4
Old Dale U.S.A. 34°8N 115°47W 307 L11
Old Forge N.Y., U.S.A. 43°43N 74°58W 313 C10
Old Forge Pa., U.S.A. 41°22N 75°45W 313 E9
Old Fort = Purana Qila Delhi, India 120 c3
Old Fort B. The Bahamas 25°3N 77°32W 153 b
Old Fort Pt. Montserrat 16°40N 62°11W 323 p
Old Fort York Canada 43°39N 79°24W 141 B2
Old Harbor Alaska,
U.S.A. 57°12N 153°18W 303 H9
Old Harbor Mass., U.S.A. 42°19N 71°1W 116 B2
Old Harbour Jamaica 17°56N 77°7W 320 a
Old Harbour Bay Jamaica 17°54N 77°6W 320 a
Old Ironsides = U.S.S. Constitution
Boston, U.S.A. 116 a3
Old Mapoon ✪ Australia 11°5S 142°22E 280 A3
Old Panamao Phil. 5°59N 121°13E 233 J3
Old Perlican Canada 48°5N 53°1W 299 C9
Old Road Bluff
Antigua & B. 16°59N 61°50W 322 b
Old Road Town
St. Kitts & Nevis 17°17N 62°47W 322 d
Old Roundhouse Toronto, Canada 141 c2
Old Shinyanga Tanzania 3°33S 33°27E 268 C3
Old Speck Mt. U.S.A. 44°34N 70°57W 313 B14
Old Town = Stare Miasto
Warsaw, Poland 143 a2
Old Town Edinburgh, U.K. 121 b2
Old Town Fla., U.S.A. 29°36N 82°59W 317 F7
Old Town Ill., U.S.A. 41°54N 87°37W 119 B3
Old Town Maine, U.S.A. 44°56N 68°39W 309 C19
Old Town Hall = Altes Rathaus
Munich, Germany 131 b3
Old Town Square Warsaw, Poland 143 a2
Old U.S. Mint New Orleans, U.S.A. 131 a3
Old Washington U.S.A. 40°2N 81°27W 312 F3
Old Wives L. Canada 50°5N 106°0W 297 C7
Oldbury U.K. 51°38N 2°33W 169 F5
Oldcastle Ireland 53°46N 7°10W 166 C4
Oldeani Tanzania 3°22S 35°35E 268 C4
Olden Norway 61°49N 6°49E 164 C3
Oldenburg Niedersachsen,
Germany 53°9N 8°13E 178 B4
Oldenburg Schleswig-Holstein,
Germany 54°17N 10°52E 178 A6
Oldenzaal Neths. 52°19N 6°53E 170 B6
Oldham U.K. 53°33N 2°7W 168 D5
Oldman → Canada 49°57N 111°42W 296 D6
Oldmeldrum U.K. 57°20N 2°19W 167 D6
Olds Canada 51°50N 114°10W 296 C6
Oldsmar U.S.A. 28°2N 82°39W 317 G7
Olduvai Gorge Tanzania 2°57S 35°23E 268 C4
Öldziyt Mongolia 44°40N 109°1E 226 B5
Ole Rømer Land
Greenland 74°10N 24°30W 154 C8
Olean U.S.A. 42°5N 78°26W 312 D6
Oleby Sweden 60°8N 13°2E 162 D7
Olecko Poland 54°2N 22°31E 184 D9
Oléggio Italy 45°36N 8°38E 198 C5
Oleiros = O Real Spain 43°20N 8°19W 194 B2
Oleiros Portugal 39°56N 7°56W 194 F3
Olekma → Russia 60°22N 120°42E 215 C13
Olekminsk Russia 60°25N 120°30E 215 C13
Oleksandrivka Ukraine 48°55N 32°20E 189 H7
Oleksandriya Kirovohrad,
Ukraine 48°42N 33°3E 189 H7
Oleksandriya Rivne,
Ukraine 50°37N 26°19E 177 C14
Olema U.S.A. 38°3N 122°47W 306 G4
Ølen Norway 59°36N 5°48E 164 E2
Olenegorsk Russia 68°9N 33°18E 160 B25
Olenek Russia 68°28N 112°18E 215 C12
Olenek → Russia 73°0N 120°10E 215 B13
Olenino Russia 56°15N 33°30E 188 D7
Olenya = Olenegorsk
Russia 68°9N 33°18E 160 B25
Oléron, Î. d' France 45°55N 1°15W 174 C2
Olesk Ukraine 51°6N 24°11E 185 G11
Oleśnica Poland 51°13N 17°22E 185 G4
Olesno Poland 50°51N 18°26E 185 H5
Oleta River State Rec. Area
U.S.A. 25°55N 80°8W 129 C3
Olevsk Ukraine 51°12N 27°39E 177 C14
Olga, L. Canada 49°47N 77°15W 298 C4
Olgas, The = Kata Tjuta
Australia 25°20S 130°50E 279 E5
Olgino Russia 60°0N 30°10E 137 B1
Ölgiy Mongolia 48°56N 89°57E 217 C11
Ølgod Denmark 55°49N 8°36E 163 J2
Olhão Portugal 37°3N 7°48W 195 H3
Olhopil Ukraine 48°12N 29°30E 183 B14
Olhovatka Russia 54°30N 22°18E 184 D9
Olib Croatia 44°23N 14°44E 199 D11
Oliena Italy 40°16N 9°24E 200 B2
Oliete Spain 41°1N 0°41W 196 D4
Olifants = Elefantes →
Africa 24°10S 32°40E 271 B5
Olifants → Namibia 25°30S 19°30E 270 B2
Olifantshoek S. Africa 27°57S 22°42E 270 C3
Olimbos Greece 35°44N 27°11E 205 F9
Ólimbos, Óros = Olympos Oros
Greece 40°6N 22°23E 202 F6
Olímpia Brazil 20°44S 48°54W 335 A6
Olimpico, Estadio Mexico 19°20N 99°11W 128 C1
Olimpos-Beydagları △
Turkey 36°36N 30°30E 205 E12
Olin U.S.A. 42°0N 91°9W 310 B5
Olinda Brazil 8°1S 34°51W 332 C5
Olite Spain 42°29N 1°40W 196 C3
Oliva Argentina 32°0S 63°38W 334 C3
Oliva Spain 38°58N 0°9W 197 G4
Oliva de la Frontera Spain 38°17N 6°54W 195 G4
Olivais Portugal 38°45N 9°7W 126 A2
Olivar de los Padres
Mexico 19°21N 99°14W 128 B1
Olivar del Conde Mexico 19°22N 99°12W 128 B1
Olivares, Cerro los
Argentina 30°18S 69°55W 334 C2
Olivares de Júcar Spain 39°46N 2°20W 196 F2
Olive Branch U.S.A. 34°57N 89°49W 315 D10
Olive Hill U.S.A. 38°18N 83°13W 311 F13
Olive Park Chicago, U.S.A. 119 b3
Olivehurst U.S.A. 39°6N 121°34W 306 F5
Oliveira Brazil 20°39S 44°50W 333 F3
Oliveira de Azeméis
Portugal 40°49N 8°29W 194 E2
Oliveira do Douro Portugal 41°5N 8°2W 194 D2
Oliveira dos Brejinhos
Brazil 12°19S 42°54W 333 D3
Olivenza Spain 38°41N 7°9W 195 G3
Oliver Canada 49°13N 119°37W 296 D5
Oliver L. Canada 56°56N 103°22W 297 B8
Oliver, Mt. of West Bank 31°46N 35°15E 123 B2
Olivet Loiret, France 47°51N 1°55E 173 E8
Olivet Mich., U.S.A. 42°27N 84°56W 311 B12
Olivia, L. U.S.A. 28°31N 81°31W 133 A1
Olivine Ra. N.Z. 44°15S 168°30E 285 E3
Olivos Argentina 34°30S 58°28W 117 B2
Olkhovka Russia 49°48N 44°32E 190 F7
Olkusz Poland 50°18N 19°33E 185 H6
Ollachea Peru 13°49S 70°29W 330 C3
Ollagüe Chile 21°15S 68°10W 334 A2
Ollombo Congo 1°18S 15°53E 264 C3
Olloua Congo 0°54S 14°34E 264 C2
Olmaliq Uzbekistan 40°50N 69°35E 217 D7
Olmedo Spain 41°20N 4°43W 194 D6
Olmeto France 41°43N 8°55E 175 G12
Olmos Peru 5°59S 79°46W 330 B2
Olmütz = Olomouc
Czechia 49°38N 17°12E 181 B10
Olney Ill., U.S.A. 38°44N 88°5W 311 F8
Olney Tex., U.S.A. 33°22N 98°45W 314 E5
Olofström Sweden 56°17N 14°32E 163 H8
Oloitokitok Kenya 2°56S 37°30E 268 C4
Oloi Congo 0°15S 14°36E 264 C2
Oloma Cameroon 3°29N 11°19E 264 B2
Olomane → Canada 50°14N 60°37W 299 B7
Olomouc Czechia 49°38N 17°12E 181 B10
Olomoucký □ Czechia 49°45N 17°5E 181 B10
Olona → Italy 45°29N 9°6E 128 B1
Olonets Russia 61°0N 32°54E 188 B7
Olongapo Phil. 14°50N 120°18E 232 D3
Olonkinbyen Norway 70°55N 8°43W 154 C10
Olonne-sur-Mer France 46°32N 1°47W 174 B2
Oloron, Gave d' → France 43°33N 1°5W 174 E2
Oloron-Ste-Marie France 43°11N 0°38W 174 E3
Olosega Amer. Samoa 14°10S 169°37W 302 g
Olosenga = Swains I.
Amer. Samoa 11°11S 171°4W 289 J11
Olot Spain 42°11N 2°30E 196 C7
Olovo Bos.-H. 44°8N 18°35E 182 F3
Olovyannaya Russia 50°58N 115°35E 215 D12
Oloy → Russia 66°29N 159°29E 215 C16
Olsberg Germany 51°21N 8°31E 178 D4
Olshammar Sweden 58°45N 14°48E 163 F8
Olshanka Ukraine 48°16N 30°58E 189 H6
Olshany Ukraine 50°3N 35°53E 189 G8
Olsztyn Poland 53°48N 20°29E 184 E7
Olsztynek Poland 53°34N 20°19E 184 E7
Olt □ Romania 44°20N 24°30E 183 F9
Olt → Romania 43°43N 24°51E 183 G9
Oltedal Norway 58°49N 6°2E 164 F3
Olten Switz. 47°21N 7°53E 179 H3
Olteniţa Romania 44°7N 26°42E 183 F11
Olton U.S.A. 34°11N 102°8W 314 D3
Oltu Turkey 40°35N 41°58E 213 B9
Oluan Pi Taiwan 21°53N 120°51E 225 E2
Oluanpi Taiwan 21°54N 120°51E 225 E2
Olula del Rio Spain 37°21N 2°18W 197 H2
Olur Turkey 40°49N 42°8E 213 B10
Olustee U.S.A. 30°12N 82°26W 316 E7
Olutanga Phil. 7°26N 122°54E 233 H4
Olutanga I. Phil. 7°22N 122°52E 233 H4
Olvega Spain 41°47N 2°0W 196 D2
Olvera Spain 36°55N 5°18W 195 J5
Olymbos Cyprus 35°21N 33°45E 207 E9
Olymbos Oros Greece 40°6N 22°23E 202 F6
Olympia Greece 37°39N 21°39E 204 D3
Olympia London, U.K. 125 c1
Olympia Wash., U.S.A. 47°3N 122°53W 306 D4
Olympia, L. U.S.A. 28°34N 81°31W 133 A1
Olympic △ U.S.A. 47°45N 123°43W 306 C3
Olympic Dam Australia 30°30S 136°55E 282 A2
Olympic Green China 39°59N 116°23E 114 B2
Olympic Mts. U.S.A. 47°55N 123°45W 306 C3
Olympic Stadium = Turner Field
Atlanta, U.S.A. 33°44N 84°23W 113 B2
Olympic Stadium Beijing,
China 39°59N 116°23E 114 B2
Olympic Stadium Helsinki,
Finland 60°11N 24°55E 121 B2
Olympique, Stade
Montréal, Canada 45°33N 73°33W 130 A2
Olympus Cyprus 34°56N 32°52E 207 F8
Olympus, Mt. = Olymbos Oros
Greece 40°6N 22°23E 202 F6
Olympus, Mt. = Uludağ
Turkey 40°4N 29°13E 203 F13
Olympus, Mt. U.S.A. 47°48N 123°43W 306 C3
Olyphant U.S.A. 41°27N 75°36W 313 E9
Olyutorskiy, Mys
Russia 59°55N 170°27E 215 D18
Om → Russia 54°59N 73°22E 217 B8
Om Hajer Eritrea 14°20N 36°41E 257 E4
Om Koi Thailand 17°48N 98°22E 236 D2
Ōma Japan 41°45N 141°5E 220 D10
Ōmachi Japan 36°30N 137°50E 223 A9
Omae-Zaki Japan 34°36N 138°14E 223 C10
Ōmagari = Daisen
Japan 39°27N 140°29E 220 E10
Omagh U.K. 54°36N 7°19W 166 B4
Omagh □ U.K. 54°35N 7°15W 166 B4
Omaha U.S.A. 41°17N 95°58W 308 E6
Omaheke □ Namibia 21°30S 19°0E 270 B2
Omak U.S.A. 48°25N 119°31W 304 B4
Omalos Greece 35°19N 23°55E 207 E4
Omalur India 11°44N 78°4E 245 J4
Oman ■ Asia 23°0N 58°0E 249 B7
Oman, G. of Asia 24°30N 58°30E 247 E8
Omapere N.Z. 35°37S 173°25E 284 B2
Omar Combon Somalia 3°10N 45°47E 267 D6
Omaruru Namibia 21°26S 16°0E 270 B2
Omaruru → Namibia 22°7S 14°15E 270 B1
Omate Peru 16°45S 71°0W 330 D3
Ombai, Selat Indonesia 8°30S 124°50E 231 F6
Ombella-Mpoko □ C.A.R. 5°30N 17°30E 264 A3
Omboué Gabon 1°35S 9°15E 264 C1
Ombrone → Italy 42°42N 11°5E 198 F8
Omchi Chad 21°22N 17°53E 259 D3
Omdurmân Sudan 15°40N 32°28E 257 D3
Ōme Japan 35°47N 139°15E 223 B11
Omegna Italy 45°53N 8°24E 198 C5
Omemee Canada 44°18N 78°33W 312 B6
Omeo Australia 37°6S 147°36E 283 D7
Omeonga
Dem. Rep. of the Congo 3°40S 24°22E 264 C4
Ometepe, I. de Nic. 11°32N 85°35W 320 D2
Ometepec Mexico 16°41N 98°25W 319 D5
Ōmi-Shima Ehime, Japan 34°15N 133°0E 222 C5
Ōmi-Shima Yamaguchi,
Japan 34°25N 131°9E 222 C3
Omihachiman Japan 35°7N 136°3E 223 B8
Omin Micronesia 9°36N 138°9E 287 R16
Ominato Japan 41°17N 141°10E 220 D10
Omineca → Canada 56°3N 124°16W 296 B4
Omineca Mts. Canada 56°30N 125°30W 296 B3
Omiš Croatia 43°28N 16°40E 199 E13
Omišalj Croatia 45°13N 14°32E 199 C11
Omitara Namibia 22°16S 18°2E 270 B2
Ōmiya = Saitama Japan 35°54N 139°38E 223 B11
Ommaney, C. U.S.A. 56°10N 134°40W 303 H14
Omme Å → Denmark 55°56N 8°32E 163 J2
Ommen Neths. 52°31N 6°26E 170 B6
Ömnögovĭ □ Mongolia 43°15N 104°0E 226 C3
Omo → Ethiopia 6°25N 36°10E 257 F4
Omo △ Ethiopia 5°54N 35°55E 257 F4
Omo Valley Ethiopia 5°7N 36°0E 257 F4
Omodeo, L. Italy 40°8N 8°56E 200 B1
Omodhos Cyprus 34°51N 32°48E 207 F8
Omoï Congo 2°56S 13°13E 264 C2
Omoko Nigeria 5°19N 6°40E 263 D6
Omolon → Russia 68°42N 158°36E 215 C16
Omono Solomon Is. 7°30S 158°43E 287 L10
Omonoia Square Athens, Greece 112 b1
Omono-Gawa → Japan 39°46N 140°3E 220 E10
Ōmori Japan 35°34N 139°43E 140 B3
Ompha Canada 45°0N 76°50W 313 B8
Omsk Russia 55°0N 73°12E 217 B8
Omsukchan Russia 62°32N 155°48E 215 C16
Ōmu Japan 44°34N 142°58E 220 B11
Omul, Vf. Romania 45°27N 25°29E 183 E10
Omulew → Poland 53°5N 21°33E 185 E8
Ōmura Japan 32°56N 129°57E 222 E1
Ōmura-Wan Japan 32°57N 129°52E 222 E1
Omuramba Omatako →
Namibia 17°45S 20°25E 270 A2
Omuramba Ovambo →
Namibia 18°45S 16°59E 270 A2
Omurtag Bulgaria 43°8N 26°26E 203 C10
Omusati □ Namibia 18°30S 15°0E 270 A1
Ōmuta Japan 33°5N 130°26E 222 D2
Omuthiya Namibia 17°43S 16°13E 270 A2
On-ma-thi Myanmar 22°17N 96°41E 241 D6
Ōna-Take Japan 31°35N 130°39E 222 F2
Oña Spain 42°43N 3°25W 194 C7
Ona Fla., U.S.A. 27°29N 81°55W 317 H8
Ona Dikonde
Dem. Rep. of the Congo 3°51S 24°11E 264 C4
Onaga U.S.A. 39°29N 96°10W 308 F5
Onalaska U.S.A. 43°53N 91°14W 308 D8
Onancock U.S.A. 37°43N 75°45W 309 G16
Onang Indonesia 3°2S 118°49E 231 E5
Onangue, L. Gabon 0°57S 10°4E 264 C1
Onaping L. Canada 47°3N 81°30W 298 C3
Onarga U.S.A. 40°43N 88°1W 310 D8
Oñati Spain 43°3N 2°25W 196 B2
Onavas Mexico 28°31N 109°35W 318 B3
Onawa U.S.A. 42°2N 96°6W 308 D5
Oncócua Angola 16°30S 13°25E 265 F2
Onda Spain 39°55N 0°17W 196 F4
Ondangwa Namibia 17°57S 16°4E 270 A2
Ondarroa Spain 43°19N 2°25W 196 B2
Ondas → Brazil 12°8S 44°55W 333 D3
Ondava → Slovakia 48°27N 21°48E 181 C14
Ondjiva Angola 16°48S 15°50E 265 F3
Ondo Japan 34°11N 132°32E 222 C4
Ondo Nigeria 7°4N 4°47E 263 D5
Ondo □ Nigeria 6°45N 5°0E 263 D6
Öndörhaan Mongolia 47°19N 110°39E 219 B11
Öndverðarnes Iceland 64°52N 24°0W 155 C2
One and a Half Degree Channel
Maldives 1°30N 73°20E 272 d
One Arm Point Australia 16°26S 123°3E 278 C3
One Arm Point ✪
Australia 16°31S 122°53E 278 C3
One Prudential Plaza Chicago, U.S.A. 119 c2
One Tree Australia 34°11S 144°43E 281 E3
One World Trade Center
New York, U.S.A. 40°43N 74°1W 132 e1
Oneata Fiji 18°26S 178°25W 287 B3
Oneco U.S.A. 27°25N 82°31W 317 H7
Onega Russia 64°0N 38°10E 186 B6
Onega → Russia 63°58N 38°2E 186 B6
Onega, G. of = Onezhskaya Guba
Russia 64°24N 36°38E 186 B6
Onega, L. = Onezhskoye Ozero
Russia 61°44N 35°22E 188 B8
Onehunga N.Z. 36°55S 174°48E 284 C3
Oneida Ill., U.S.A. 41°4N 90°13W 310 C6
Oneida N.Y., U.S.A. 43°6N 75°39W 313 C9
Oneida L. U.S.A. 43°12N 75°54W 313 C9
O'Neill U.S.A. 42°27N 98°39W 308 D4
Onekotan, Ostrov
Russia 49°25N 154°45E 215 E16
Onema
Dem. Rep. of the Congo 4°35S 24°30E 265 C4
Oneonta U.S.A. 42°27N 75°4W 313 D9
Onerahi N.Z. 35°45S 174°22E 284 B3
Oneroa Cook Is. 21°55S 159°43W 289 h
Oneşti Romania 46°17N 26°47E 183 D11
Onezhskaya Guba Russia 64°24N 36°38E 186 B6
Onezhskoye Ozero Russia 61°44N 35°22E 188 B8
Ongarue N.Z. 38°42S 175°19E 284 E4
Ongea Levu = Ogea Levu
Fiji 19°8S 178°24W 287 B3
Ongers → S. Africa 31°4S 23°13E 270 D3
Ongerup Australia 33°58S 118°28E 279 F2
Ongi Mongolia 45°27N 103°54E 226 B2
Ongjin N. Korea 37°56N 125°21E 224 D2
Ongkharak Thailand 14°8N 101°1E 236 E3
Ongniud Qi China 43°0N 118°38E 227 C10
Ongoka
Dem. Rep. of the Congo 1°20S 26°0E 268 C2
Ongole India 15°33N 80°2E 245 G5
Ongon = Havirga
Mongolia 45°41N 113°5E 226 B7
Ongouendjo Gabon 1°23S 9°5E 264 C1
Ongoujou Comoros Is. 12°18S 44°30E 272 a
Ongtüstik Qazaqstan □
Kazakhstan 43°0N 68°0E 217 D7
Ongwediva Namibia 17°47S 15°46E 270 A2
Oni Georgia 42°33N 43°26E 191 J6
Onida U.S.A. 44°42N 100°4W 308 C3
Onilahy → Madag. 23°34S 43°45E 272 C1
Onima Bonaire 12°15N 68°19W 322 h
Onisigun Nigeria 6°35N 3°24E 124 A2
Onitsha Nigeria 6°6N 6°42E 263 D6
Onna Japan 26°29N 127°51E 288 a
Onne Nigeria 4°47N 7°9E 263 E6
Ono Fiji 18°55S 178°29E 287 B2
Ono Fukui, Japan 35°59N 136°29E 223 B8
Ono Hyōgo, Japan 34°51N 134°56E 222 C6
Onoda Japan 33°59N 131°11E 222 D3
Onohara Japan 34°5N 133°40E 222 C5
Onoke, L. N.Z. 41°22S 175°8E 284 H4
Onomichi Japan 34°25N 133°12E 222 C5
Onotoa Kiribati 1°52S 175°34E 277 A14
Ons, I. de Spain 42°23N 8°55W 194 C2
Onsala Sweden 57°26N 12°0E 163 G6
Onslow Australia 21°40S 115°12E 278 D2
Onslow B. U.S.A. 34°20N 77°15W 315 D16
Onsŏng N. Korea 42°57N 129°30E 224 A4
Ontake-San Japan 35°53N 137°29E 223 B9
Ontar Vanuatu 14°17S 167°27E 287 D5
Ontario Calif., U.S.A. 34°4N 117°39W 307 L9
Ontario Oreg., U.S.A. 44°2N 116°58W 304 D5
Ontario □ Canada 48°0N 83°0W 298 B2
Ontario, L. N. Amer. 43°20N 78°0W 312 C7
Ontario Science Centre
Canada 43°43N 79°20W 141 A2
Ontinyent Spain 38°50N 0°35W 197 G4
Ontonagon U.S.A. 46°52N 89°19W 308 B9
Ontong Java Plateau
Pac. Oc. 1°0N 157°0E 277 A10
Ontur Spain 38°38N 1°29W 197 G3
Onverwacht Suriname 5°35N 55°11W 329 B6
Onyx U.S.A. 35°41N 118°14W 307 K8
Oodaaq Greenland 83°40N 30°40W 154 A8
Oodnadatta Australia 27°33S 135°30E 281 D2
Oodweyne Somalia 9°25N 45°4E 267 C6
'Ō'ōkala U.S.A. 20°1N 155°17W 302 C6
Ookayama Japan 35°36N 139°40E 140 B3
Ooku = Ōma Japan 41°45N 141°5E 220 D10
Ooldea Australia 30°27S 131°50E 279 F5
Oombulgurri Australia 15°15S 127°45E 278 C4
Oombulgurri ✪ Australia 15°10S 127°50E 278 C4
Oorindi Australia 20°40S 141°1E 280 C3
Oost-Vlaanderen □ Belgium 51°5N 3°50E 170 C3
Oostende Belgium 51°15N 2°54E 170 C2
Oosterhout Neths. 51°39N 4°47E 170 C4
Oosterschelde → Neths. 51°33N 4°0E 170 C4
Oosterwolde Neths. 53°0N 6°17E 170 B6
Oosteschelde △ Neths. 51°40N 3°40E 170 C3
Oostpunt Curaçao 12°2N 68°44W 322 g
Oostvaardersplassen △
Neths. 52°27N 5°22E 170 B5
Oostzaan Tuindorp Neths. 52°25N 4°54E 112 A2
Ootacamund = Udagamandalam
India 11°30N 76°44E 245 J3
Ootha Australia 33°6S 147°29E 283 B7
Ootsa L. Canada 53°50N 126°2W 296 C3
Ooty = Udagamandalam
India 11°30N 76°44E 245 J3
Op Luang △ Thailand 18°12N 98°32E 236 C2
Opa-Locka U.S.A. 25°54N 80°15W 129 C1
Opa-Locka ✈ (OPF)
U.S.A. 25°54N 80°16W 129 C1
Opacz Poland 52°10N 20°53E 143 B1
Opaka Bulgaria 43°28N 26°10E 203 C10
Opala Dem. Rep. of the Congo 0°40S 24°20E 264 C4
Opale, Côte d' France 50°30N 1°30E 172 B8
Opalenica Poland 52°18N 16°24E 185 F3
Opan Bulgaria 42°13N 25°41E 203 D9
Opanake Sri Lanka 6°35N 80°40E 245 L5
Opapa N.Z. 39°47S 176°42E 284 F5
Opasatika Canada 49°30N 82°50W 298 C3
Opasquia △ Canada 53°33N 93°5W 298 B1
Opatija Croatia 45°21N 14°17E 199 C11
Opatów Poland 50°50N 21°27E 185 H8
Opava Czechia 49°57N 17°58E 181 B10
Opelika U.S.A. 32°39N 85°23W 316 C4
Opelousas U.S.A. 30°32N 92°5W 314 F8
Opémisca, L. Canada 49°56N 74°52W 298 C5
Opera House Sydney, Australia 139 a2
Opheim U.S.A. 48°51N 106°24W 304 B10
Ophir U.S.A. 63°10N 156°31W 303 E8
Ophirton S. Africa 26°13S 28°1E 123 B2
Ophthalmia Ra.
Australia 23°15S 119°30E 278 D2
Opi Nigeria 6°36N 7°28E 263 D6
Opihikao U.S.A. 19°26N 154°53W 302 D7
Opinaca → Canada 52°15N 78°2W 298 B4
Opinaca, Rés. Canada 52°39N 76°20W 298 B4
Opinnagau → Canada 54°12N 82°25W 298 B3
Opiscotéo, L. Canada 53°10N 68°10W 299 B6
Opobo Nigeria 4°35N 7°34E 263 E6
Opochka Russia 56°42N 28°45E 188 D5
Opoczno Poland 51°22N 20°18E 185 G7
Opol Phil. 8°31N 124°34E 233 G5
Opole Poland 50°42N 17°58E 185 H4
Opole Lubelskie Poland 51°9N 21°58E 185 G8
Opolskie □ Poland 50°30N 18°0E 185 H5
Opon = Lapu-Lapu Phil. 10°20N 123°55E 233 F4
Oponono L. Namibia 18°8S 15°45E 270 A2
Opornyy = Borankul
Kazakhstan 46°11N 54°25E 216 C4
Oporto = Porto Portugal 41°8N 8°40W 194 D2
Opotiki N.Z. 38°1S 177°19E 284 E6
Opp U.S.A. 31°17N 86°16W 316 D3
Oppdal Norway 62°35N 9°41E 164 B6
Oppegård Norway 59°45N 10°49E 133 B3
Oppeln = Opole Poland 50°42N 17°58E 185 H4
Oppem Belgium 50°56N 4°18E 116 A1
Óppido Mamertina Italy 38°16N 15°59E 201 D8
Oppland □ Norway 61°15N 9°40E 164 C6
Opportunity U.S.A. 47°39N 117°15W 304 C5
Oppsal Norway 59°53N 10°50E 133 A4
Oprişor Romania 44°17N 23°5E 182 F8
Oprtalj Croatia 45°23N 13°50E 199 C10
Opua N.Z. 35°19S 174°9E 284 B3
Opunake N.Z. 39°26S 173°52E 284 F2
Opuwo Namibia 18°3S 13°45E 270 A1
Opuzen Croatia 43°1N 17°34E 199 E14
Oquawka U.S.A. 40°56N 90°57W 310 D6
Or → Kazakhstan 51°11N 58°32E 216 B5
Or, Côte d' France 47°10N 4°50E 173 E11
Ora Cyprus 34°51N 33°12E 207 F9
Ora Israel 31°45N 35°9E 123 B1
Oracabessa Jamaica 18°24N 76°57W 320 a
Oracle U.S.A. 32°37N 110°46W 305 K8
Oracuzar Peru 4°42S 78°6W 328 D2
Oradea Romania 47°2N 21°58E 182 C6
Oradell U.S.A. 40°57N 74°2W 132 A1
Oradell Res. U.S.A. 40°57N 74°1W 132 A1
Öræfajökull Iceland 64°2N 16°39W 155 C10
Orahovac = Rahovec
Kosovo 42°24N 20°40E 202 D4
Orahovica Croatia 45°35N 17°52E 182 E2
Orai India 25°58N 79°30E 243 G8
Oraiokastro Greece 40°44N 22°55E 202 F6
Oraison France 43°55N 5°55E 175 E9
Oral = Zhayyq →
Kazakhstan 47°0N 51°48E 187 E9
Oral Kazakhstan 51°20N 51°20E 190 E10
Oran Algeria 35°45N 0°39W 261 A4
Oran □ Algeria 35°0N 0°45W 261 A4
Orang △ India 26°37N 92°29E 241 B4
Orange N.S.W., Australia 33°15S 149°7E 283 B8
Orange Vaucluse, France 44°8N 4°47E 175 D8
Orange Calif., U.S.A. 33°47N 117°51W 307 M9
Orange Mass., U.S.A. 42°35N 72°19W 313 D12
Orange Tex., U.S.A. 30°6N 93°44W 314 F8
Orange Va., U.S.A. 38°15N 78°7W 309 F14
Orange → S. Africa 28°41S 16°28E 270 C2
Orange, C. Brazil 4°20N 51°30W 329 C7
Orange City U.S.A. 28°57N 81°18W 317 G8
Orange Cove U.S.A. 36°38N 119°19W 306 J7
Orange Free State = Free State □
S. Africa 28°30S 27°0E 270 C4
Orange Grove U.S.A. 27°58N 97°56W 314 H6
Orange Hill Barbados 13°12N 59°36W 323 r
Orange Hill Jamaica 18°16N 77°59W 320 a
Orange Hill St. Vincent 13°19N 61°7W 323 n
Orange L. U.S.A. 29°25N 82°13W 317 F7
Orange Park U.S.A. 30°10N 81°42W 316 E8
Orange River Colony = Free State □
S. Africa 28°30S 27°0E 270 C4
Orange Walk Belize 18°6N 88°33W 319 D7
Orangeburg U.S.A. 33°30N 80°52W 316 B9
Orangeville Ont., Canada 43°55N 80°5W 312 C4
Orangeville Ill., U.S.A. 42°28N 89°39W 310 B7
Orangi Pakistan 24°54N 67°0E 123 A2
Orango Guinea-Biss. 11°5N 16°0W 262 C1
Orani Italy 40°15N 9°11E 200 B2
Orani Phil. 14°49N 120°32E 232 D3
Oranienburg Germany 52°45N 13°14E 178 C9
Oranje = Orange →
S. Africa 28°41S 16°28E 270 C2
Oranjemund Namibia 28°38S 16°29E 270 C2
Oranjerivier S. Africa 29°40S 24°12E 270 C3
Oranjestad Aruba 12°32N 70°2W 322 f
Oranjestad St. Eustatius 17°28N 62°59W 322 a
Orap Vanuatu 15°58S 167°20E 287 E5
Oras Phil. 12°9N 125°28E 232 E5
Orašje Bos.-H. 45°1N 18°42E 182 E3
Orăştie Romania 45°50N 23°10E 183 E8
Orava → Slovakia 49°9N 19°8E 181 B12
Orava, Vodna nádrž
Slovakia 49°25N 19°35E 181 B12
Oraviţa Romania 45°2N 21°43E 182 E6
Orawia N.Z. 46°1S 167°50E 285 G2
Orb → France 43°15N 3°18E 174 E7
Orba → Italy 44°53N 8°37E 198 D5
Ørbæk Denmark 55°17N 10°39E 163 J4
Orbe Switz. 46°43N 6°32E 179 J2
Orbec France 49°1N 0°23E 172 C7
Orbetello Italy 42°27N 11°13E 199 F8
Órbigo → Spain 42°5N 5°42W 194 C5
Orbisonia U.S.A. 40°15N 77°54W 312 F7
Orbost Australia 37°40S 148°29E 283 D8
Örbyhus Sweden 60°15N 17°43E 162 D11
Orcadas Antarctica 60°44S 44°37W 151 C18
Orcas I. U.S.A. 48°42N 122°56W 306 B4
Orce Spain 37°44N 2°28W 197 H2
Orce → Spain 37°44N 2°28W 197 H2
Orchard City U.S.A. 38°50N 107°58W 304 G10
Orchard Homes U.S.A. 46°55N 114°4W 304 C6
Orchard Road Singapore 138 a1
Orchid I. = Lan Yü
Taiwan 22°4N 121°25E 225 D3
Orchies France 50°28N 3°14E 173 B10
Orchila, I. Venezuela 11°48N 66°10W 321 D6
Orchilla, Pta. Canary Is. 27°42N 18°10W 153 e1
Órcia → Italy 42°58N 11°21E 199 F8
Orco → Italy 45°10N 7°52E 198 C4
Orcopampa Peru 15°20S 72°23W 330 D3
Orcutt U.S.A. 34°52N 120°27W 307 L6
Ord U.S.A. 41°36N 98°56W 308 E4
Ord → Australia 15°33S 128°15E 278 C4
Ord, Mt. Australia 17°20S 125°34E 278 C4
Ord Mts. U.S.A. 34°39N 116°45W 307 L10
Ordenes = Ordes Spain 43°5N 8°29W 194 B2
Orderville U.S.A. 37°17N 112°38W 305 H7
Ordes Spain 43°5N 8°29W 194 B2
Ordesa y Monte Perido △
Spain 42°40N 0°10W 196 C4
Ording = Sankt Peter-Ording
Germany 54°20N 8°36E 178 A4
Ordos = Mu Us Shamo
China 39°0N 109°0E 226 E5
Ordos China 39°50N 110°0E 226 E6
Ordrup Denmark 55°45N 12°34E 118 A3
Ordu Turkey 40°55N 37°53E 212 B7
Ordu □ Turkey 41°0N 37°50E 212 B7
Ordubad Azerbaijan 38°54N 46°1E 213 C12
Orduña Álava, Spain 42°58N 2°58W 196 C2
Orduña Granada, Spain 37°20N 3°30W 195 H7
Ordway U.S.A. 38°13N 103°46W 304 G12
Ordzhonikidze = Denisovka
Kazakhstan 52°27N 61°39E 216 B6

KEY TO EUROPEAN MAP PAGES

Large scale maps
(>1:3 900 000)

Medium scale maps
(1:4 000 000 – 1:7 900 000)

Small scale maps
(<1:8 000 000)

Paris p134   City maps

155

ICELAND

Arctic Circle

160

Færoe Is.

165

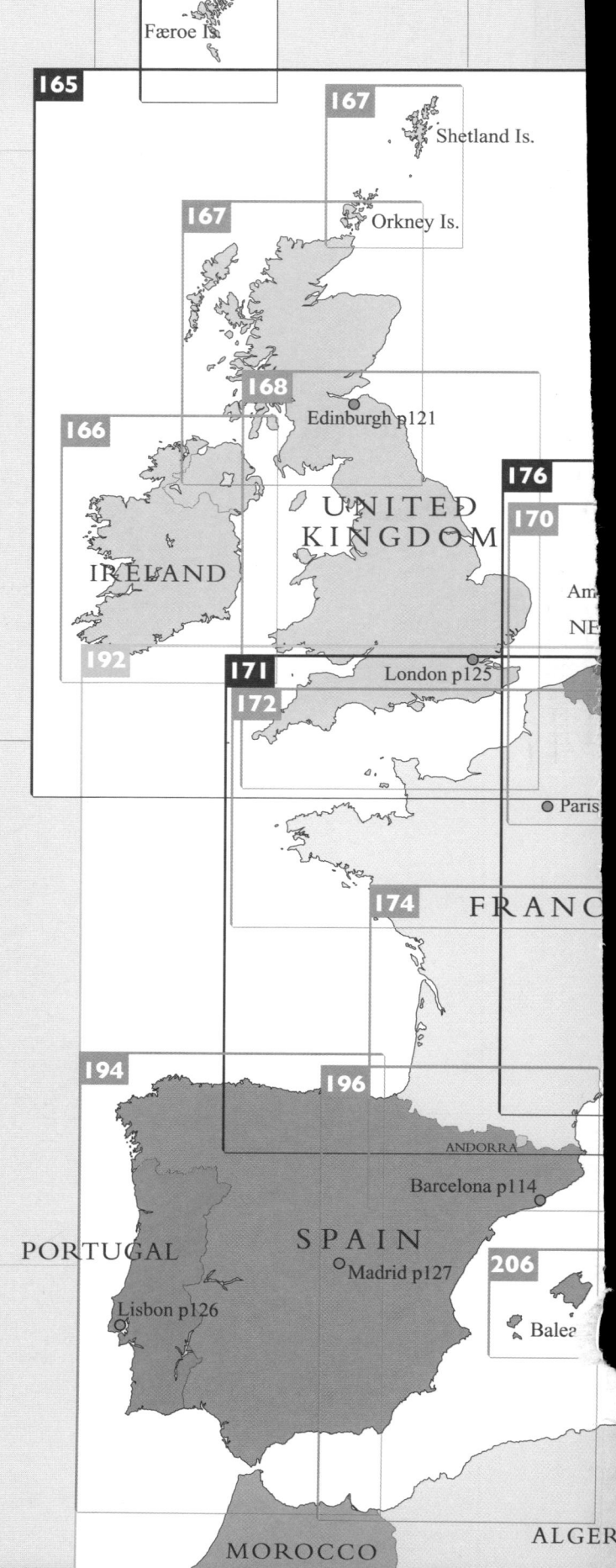

167

Shetland Is.

167

Orkney Is.

168

166

Edinburgh p121

176

170

SCOTLAND

IRELAND

UNITED KINGDOM

Am
NE

192

171

London p125

172

174   FRANC

194

196

ANDORRA

Barcelona p114

PORTUGAL

SPAIN

Madrid p127

206

Bale

Lisbon p126

MOROCCO

ALGER

WORLD COUNTRY INDEX